NUBIA
CORRIDOR TO AFRICA

WILLIAM Y. ADAMS

ALLEN LANE
PRINCETON UNIVERSITY PRESS

TO THE MEMORY OF

GEORGE ANDREW REISNER

GREAT EGYPTOLOGIST
PIONEER SALVAGE ARCHAEOLOGIST
FATHER OF NUBIOLOGY

ALLEN LANE PRINCETON UNIVERSITY PRESS
Penguin Books Ltd   Princeton
536 King's Road   New Jersey
London SW10 0UH   USA

First published 1977
Reprinted with a new Preface 1984

ISBN 0 7139 0579 4 (Allen Lane)
ISBN 0-691-09370-9; LCC Number 76-9394 (Princeton)

Set in Monotype Times Roman
Printed in Great Britain by
Richard Clay (The Chaucer Press) Ltd,
Bungay, Suffolk

CONTENTS

PROLOGUE

PART ONE   TRIBAL BEGINNINGS

CONTENTS

PART THREE   MEDIEVAL CIVILIZATIONS

CONTENTS

EPILOGUE

ACKNOWLEDGEMENTS

Acknowledgements for permission to quote are due to the authors and publishers of the following books:

F. Wendorf, ed., *Prehistory of Nubia*, The Southern Methodist University Press, Dallas, Texas, 1968
Copyright © The Fort Burgwin Research Center, 1968

W. B. Emery, *Egypt in Nubia*, Hutchinson, 1965
Copyright © W. B. Emery, 1965

J. S. Trimingham, *Islam in the Sudan*, Oxford University Press, 1949
Copyright © J. S. Trimingham, 1949

A. Moorehead, *The White Nile*, Harper & Row Publishers, Inc., New York, 1960, and Hamish Hamilton, 1960
Copyright © Alan Moorehead, 1960, 1971

Acknowledgement is also made to N. B. Millet for permission to quote from his doctoral dissertation, *Meroitic Nubia*, submitted to Yale University in 1968.

The publishers wish to thank all those who gave permission for photographs to be used. Individual acknowledgement is made in the List of Plates.

LIST OF PLATES

x

LIST OF PLATES

LIST OF FIGURES

(All maps, plans, and line drawings are designated as Figures and are
numbered sequentially throughout the book)

LIST OF FIGURES

LIST OF FIGURES

LIST OF FIGURES

LIST OF TABLES

PREFACE

The idea for this book dates back to the seven-year period I spent in Nubia (1959–66), directing archaeological salvage operations for UNESCO and the Sudan Antiquities Service. I hope, therefore, that it may be accepted as a contribution from the Nubian Monuments Campaign – a modest return on the investment of time and effort which not only UNESCO but the whole world made in the study and conservation of Nubia's antiquities.

Scores of men and women of every nationality – my colleagues in the Nubian campaign – have contributed to this book. Not that they are responsible for its theoretical approach; many of them will disagree, and have disagreed, wholeheartedly with my ideas, and I hope that the dialogue will continue in the future. These same colleagues have nevertheless done the work and provided the data which make it possible for me to offer my particular assessment of Nubian history. Since much of the recent archaeological work necessitated by the Aswan High Dam has not yet been published, it has only been through personal contacts and through correspondence that I have been able to remain *au courant* and to incorporate in my book the results of the latest work. My heartfelt thanks go, then, to all of those Nubian archaeologists, philologists and historians whom space does not permit me to name individually.

I must, however, pay tribute by name to a small group of scholars with whom I have been particularly closely associated over the years, and whose contribution to my work has been of the highest order. Among these I count Ricardo Caminos, Sergio Donadoni, the late W. B. Emery, Robert A. Fernea, Andreas Kronenberg, Kazimierz Michalowski, J. Martin Plumley, Torgny Säve-Söderbergh, Peter Shinnie, Bruce Trigger, Jean Vercoutter, and André Vila. Evenings spent in their camps, and in their homes in Europe and America, have been high intellectual encounters as well as delightful personal experiences. It was the association of these and other men during part of each season which made the years in Wadi Halfa not only tolerable but memorable.

I owe an incalculable debt of gratitude to the Sudan Antiquities Service and its Directors, Thabit Hassan Thabit and Negm el-Din Mohammed Sherif, for continuing support and encouragement of my work. Year after year they found the resources to keep me going in the field, even in times of serious shortages and of financial and political crises. I have to thank also my other friends within the Antiquities Service, particularly Fritz Hinkel, and the successive assistants whom UNESCO sent me, Jan Verwers, Hans-Åke Nordström, and Tony Mills. It will take much more than a book to repay what I owe to all of them. UNESCO too deserves my thanks not only for paying my salary for seven years, but for politely closing its eyes to archaeological activities which were no part of my official duties. If official sanction for my field work could never be given, tacit acknowledgement was nevertheless indispensable.

It is not necessary for me to cite here the many and invaluable published works upon which I have drawn. Many of them are discussed prominently in the chapters which follow, and all of them are adequately acknowledged in the notes at the back of the book. The notes to each chapter are headed by a paragraph in which I have singled out for special recognition the most important sources on which I have drawn in that chapter. Published sources have of course been supplemented by a great deal of personal observation, and by private communications which are also cited in the notes.

I owe a special debt to the many colleagues who have been kind enough to send me, in advance of publication, manuscript copies of their latest contributions to the study of Nubia and its history. Access to these works – some of them of the first importance – has enabled me to present a much more up-to-date picture than would have been possible on the basis of published sources alone. The numerous titles which are cited as 'in press' in the Notes (pp. 681–772) are testimony to the amount of scholarly co-operation of this sort which I have received.

Above and beyond my thanks for the information they have supplied, I have to express an even deeper gratitude to those colleagues who have read and commented upon my manuscript in the course of its preparation. Foremost among them are Torgny Säve-Söderbergh, Bruce Trigger, and Jean Vercoutter, who read the work in its entirety. Less important only in a quantitative sense have been the contributions of those who have read portions of the manuscript: Fred Wendorf (Chapter 4), Roy Carlson (Chapters 4–5), David O'Connor (Chapters 5–8), H. S. Smith (Chapters 5–9), the late Bryan Haycock (Chapters 10–18), P. L. Shinnie (Chapters 10–16), Fritz Hintze (Chapters 10–11), Sir Laurence Kirwan (Chapters 11–16), N. B. Millet (Chapters 12–16), Yusuf Fadl Hasan (Chapters 16–18), and Robert A. Fernea (Chapters 19–20); I doubt if any book in history has had, in relation to its subject matter, a more distinguished or a more conscientious group of critics in advance of its publication. Their comments and suggestions have enriched the work tremendously, as well as saving me from countless errors of omission and commission; whatever

PREFACE

shortcomings remain are assuredly my fault and not theirs. I have also to thank Glyn Daniel for encouraging me to write the book, though neither he nor I foresaw the magnitude of the task involved.

Additional thanks are due to all those who have generously furnished photographic illustrations for my book: Dows Dunham, Fritz Hintze, Jean Jacquet, Rex Keating, Andreas Kronenberg, Kazimierz Michalowski, N. B. Millet, Hans-Åke Nordström, David O'Connor, J. M. Plumley, Serge Sauneron, Torgny Säve-Söderbergh, P. L. Shinnie, Jean Vercoutter, Jan Verwers, and above all Fritz Hinkel.

My thanks go too to the girls in the office, Teresa Freeman, Marcia Montgomery, and Virginia Slattery, who have patiently and wearily ploughed through two drafts of the manuscript, and to the University of Kentucky for releasing their time and efforts to work on my book.

My wife, Nettie, is an equal partner in this as in every undertaking. All those who know her, or who know camp life in Nubia, will understand the extent of her contribution.

PREFACE (1984)

When I had completed the original manuscript of this book, nearly a decade ago, the great Nubian Archaeological Salvage Campaign had only recently come to an end. I assumed that there would be a lull in the volume of archaeological work, as there was after the previous salvage campaigns in 1907–11 and 1929–34. It is gratifying to report that my forecast was incorrect. Although the northern part of Nubia has been destroyed forever by the filling of the Aswan Reservoir, no fewer than sixteen expeditions, representing ten different countries, have carried on archaeological work in other parts of the Sudan since 1975.[1] In addition the excavations at Qasr Ibrim, the last major site in Egyptian Nubia which has not been destroyed, have continued down to the present day.[2]

Printing costs preclude any revisions of my original text at this time, but the publishers have kindly allowed me a few extra pages to mention some of the most important discoveries and developments since 1975. In the discussion that follows, numbers in parentheses refer to pages in my original text that are affected by the new developments.

Prehistoric periods (Ch. 4). One of the most significant developments of recent years has been the discovery of what appear to be agricultural sites in southern Egypt, dating back as much as 18,000 years. They antedate by several thousand years the supposed origins of wheat and barley cultivation in the 'Fertile Crescent' (pp. 110–11).[3] The evidence for cultivation at these sites is not wholly conclusive, and it has not yet been accepted by all scholars. If substantiated by further research, it will certainly require a

xxi

major revision in our understanding of the later prehistory of the Nile Valley, and indeed of the whole Near East.

Neolithic remains have engaged the attention of no fewer than five expeditions in the Sudan since 1975. There have been major excavations in the riverain sites of Kadero and Kadada, north of Khartoum, and surveys in the deserts to the east, west, and south.[4] These have verified that the Khartoum Neolithic culture was very widespread both east and west of the Nile in the fifth millennium BC (pp. 113–14). The extensive and continuing Polish excavations in the mound site of Kadero have added greatly to our understanding of this cultural phase. It is now established that the Khartoum Neolithic people were heavily dependent for subsistence on domesticated cattle, and to a lesser extent on sheep and goats.[5] They buried their dead within the confines of their settlements, in contracted burials that were frequently accompanied by pottery and other offerings.

East of the Nile, but not along the river itself, the Khartoum Neolithic gave way to a later culture called the Butana tradition, characterized by large village sites, distinctive orange and purple pottery wares, and burials marked by round stone tumuli at the surface. This tradition appears to be contemporaneous with the A Horizon and/or the early C Horizon in Lower Nubia. At the same time a rather different local Neolithic tradition developed along the Nile, as revealed in the French excavations at Kadada. The pottery shows some affinities to the Nubian A Horizon, and is believed to be contemporaneous in date.[6]

The impression now gained is that the Khartoum Neolithic culture, once widespread in the Sudan, gave way in the fourth millennium BC to various localized cultural traditions. One of these, the Abkan, had already been recognized (pp. 114–15). In northern Nubia these late Neolithic cultures gave way in turn to the A Horizon, while in more southerly areas some of them may have persisted as late as Meroitic times.

A Horizon and C Horizon (Chs. 5 and 6). The most important developments with respect to these two cultures are negative. No trace of either has been found in the area to the south of Lake Nubia, and it is therefore evident that these were localized, peripheral Egyptian cultures. Farther south in the Sudan, their place was taken by the more primitive Neolithic cultures described in the last paragraph.

On the basis of evidence previously excavated at Qustul, Bruce Williams has advanced the revolutionary theory that the institutions of pharaonic monarchy originated in the Nubian A Horizon before their appearance in Egypt itself.[7] However, the evidence for this is somewhat tenuous, and it has not yet found wide acceptance.[8]

Kerma Culture (Ch. 8). Apart perhaps from the prehistoric investigations, the most important archaeological work carried out in the Sudan since 1975 has been that pertaining to the Kerma Culture. The site of

Kerma itself has been under investigation by a Swiss mission since 1977. The excavators have uncovered an extensive town-site, with densely clustered mud brick houses and round grain silos comparable to those of the later C Horizon further to the north (pp. 201–2).[9] Another important discovery is a complex of religious buildings adjoining the great tower of the Western *Deffufa*. It now appears that the *Deffufa* itself was originally a temple, and was only later filled solidly with masonry to provide a platform for some more elevated structure (pp. 199–201).[10] Traces of New Kingdom and Napatan occupation have also been uncovered at Kerma.[11]

The non-royal cemeteries at Kerma, excavated by Reisner before 1916, were finally published in 1982 (p. 203).[12] Of much more importance, however, is the work carried out by a French mission in the great Kerma cemetery at Sai Island (p. 213).[13] On the basis of these and other published materials Brigitte Gratien has developed a general chronology for the Kerma Culture, which she divides into Early, Middle, Classic, and Late phases. These are roughly contemporaneous with the Nubian A Horizon, the early C Horizon, and later C Horizon (Second Intermediate Period), and the beginning of Egyptianization (18th Dynasty), respectively.[14] This general sequence and dating appears to be confirmed by the excavations at Kerma.[15]

The full geographical range of the Kerma Culture is still very poorly understood, but Kerma-like potsherds have now been found in the Butana Steppe [16] and in the Gash River Delta, close to the Ethiopian border.[17]

Pharaonic occupations (Chs. 7 and 9). H. S. Smith has published new textual evidence pointing to a continued Egyptian presence in the fortress of Buhen between the Middle and New Kingdoms. The resident officials are believed to have been in the service of the Kerma ruler, as was Sepedher at a later date (pp. 190–91).[18] Farther south, a substantial part of the new Kingdom fortress at Sai Island has now been uncovered (p. 227), but no detailed report is yet available.[19]

Napatan period (Ch. 10). There has been continuing excavation in and around the temples at Jebal Barkal (pp. 271–4), but no very startling results have been reported.[20] Farther north, an extensive Napatan cemetery has been excavated near Abri.[21] The grave types and their furnishings are closely similar to those previously excavated by Griffith at Sanam (pp. 286–8).[22] The Napatan graves in the Abri area are the most northerly yet found; they are the only Napatan remains discovered in a survey of more than 500 sites between Dal and Abri.[23]

Meroitic period (Chs. 11 and 12). Excavations in the town-site of Meroë in 1975 and 1976 uncovered the remains of four small, previously unsuspected temples (pp. 316–17).[24] After a hiatus of several years, the excavations at Meroë are about to resume as this is written. At Kerma [25] and at Abri,[26] two cemeteries of very early Meroitic date have yielded pottery of previously unfamiliar types. A few sherds of the same wares have been found in the Ptolemaic and Roman levels at Qasr Ibrim.[27] This is the first archaeological material which in any way fills the gap between the Napatan and later Meroitic occupations in northern Nubia (p. 345).

Laszlo Török has produced two important studies of Meroitic economic and political organization, based on textual sources.[28] The evidence leads him to challenge my view that northern Nubia was unoccupied in Napatan and early Meroitic times, in spite of the absence of any archaeological remains.[29]

Ptolemaic and Roman occupation (Ch. 12). Excavations at Qasr Ibrim have considerably modified our picture of Ptolemaic and Roman activity in Lower Nubia. It is now apparent that the main fortification walls at Qasr Ibrim were built by the Ptolemies, around or before AD 100 (pp. 336–8), and the place was then occupied by a Ptolemaic garrison until the coming of the Romans in 30 BC. The romans repaired and enlarged the fortifications not once but several times, and it appears that they remained in occupation for more than a century (pp. 338–44). Even after the fortress was returned to Meroitic control, perhaps around AD 100, there is evidence of a Roman colony or garrison on the site until much later.[30]

An important new literary work, surveying the available classical sources on Nubia and the Sudan, is Jehan Desanges, *Recherches sur l'Activité des Méditerranéens aux Confins de l'Afrique*.[31]

Ballana Culture (Ch. 13). The excavations at Qasr Ibrim have yielded a mass of material from the Ballana period which is still under study. On the basis of pottery types it is now possible to subdivide the period as a whole into four sub-phases of about fifty years' duration.[32] This should prove enormously helpful in dating the numerous Ballana graves that were previously excavated (pp. 393–7).

Christian period (Chs. 14–16). Excavations have recently been resumed at Soba, the capital of medieval Alwa (p. 471), but not much has yet been reported.[33] The same is true with respect to the Polish excavations at Old Dongola (p. 464), which have now been in progress intermittently for twenty years.[34] At Kulubnarti, excavation of the Christian cemeteries has yielded important information about medieval demography and pathology.[35]

Father Giovanni Vantini has produced two works of enormous value for the study of the medieval Sudan. *Oriental Sources Concerning Nubia* (Society for Nubian Studies, Heidelberg and Warsaw, 1975) contains translations of what more than 130 Arab authors had to say about Nubia between AD 555 and 1700. *Christianity in the Sudan* (Bologna, 1981) is a more general work, tracing the history both of medieval Christianity and of missionary efforts in the recent past.

Islamic period (Ch. 17). Excavations at Qasr Ibrim have recently produced a wealth of both archaeological and textual evidence from the Islamic period. As this site was occupied by an Ottoman garrison, however, the finds are of limited relevance for our understanding of the more general history of the Sudan. Most of the texts refer either to military or to commercial matters (p. 611).[36]

Ali Osman has produced an interesting history of the post-medieval Kingdom of Kokka, in the Abri-Delgo Reach, which persisted until the Turkish conquest of 1820. He finds some suggestions of continuity with the late medieval Kingdom of Dotawo (pp. 531–6).[37]

Modern period (Ch. 19). Students in the Department of Archaeology at the University of Khartoum have conducted important 'ethnoarchaeological' studies of pottery making and other local handicrafts in the Sudan. The results will greatly aid in the interpretation of materials recovered archaeologically.

Nubian Ceremonial Life, edited by John G. Kennedy (Berkeley, 1978) is an important study of the folk religions of the Nubians, both before and after their relocation (pp. 574–9). *Egyptian Nubians*, by Hussein M. Fahim (Salt Lake City, 1983) is the first extended study of how the Egyptian Nubians are coping with their new surroundings since relocation (pp. 654–8).

Southern Sudan. The years since 1975 have witnessed the first systematic archaeological activity in the southern part of the Sudan. Between 1977 and 1981 a British expedition carried out surveys and text excavations at many localities in Equatoria and Bahr el Ghazal provinces. The expedition found a large number of sites, ranging in time from the early Neolithic to the recent past. The remains were generally similar to prehistoric cultures already known from Uganda and northern Kenya, but they bore no close resemblance to any of the known cultures of the central and northern Sudan.[38]

During the same years, Else Kleppe excavated two mound sites in the Upper Nile province. They are believed to be Shilluk villages dating from the Funj period.[39]

Post script. I am pleased to report that this book was awarded the Melville J. Herskovits Prize of the African Studies Association in 1978. Even more gratifying is the fact that, on the strength of it, I have been proclaimed an ' honorary Nubian ' by an organization called the Society for the Preservation of Nubian Cultural Heritage. For an anthropologist, the approval of the people studied is the ultimate accolade.

PREFACE

1. Preliminary reports of most of these expeditions will be found in *Nyame Akuma*, the Newsletter of African Archaeology published in Calgary (and latterly in Edmonton), Alberta, Canada. Except in special cases these reports will not be cited individually in the present text.

2. Preliminary reports are in *Nyame Akuma* and in *Journal of Egyptian Archaeology*, Vols. 63, 65, 69.

3. See Fred Wendorf and Romuald Schild, *Prehistory of the Eastern Sahara* (New York, 1980), pp. 273–80; Fred Wendorf, Romuald Schild, and Angela E. Close in *Science 82*, Vol. 3, No. 9, pp. 68–73.

4. For the survey in the west see Abbas S. Mohammed-Ali in *Current Anthropology*, Vol. 22 (1981), pp. 176–8. For surveys to the east and south see *Nyame Akuma* op. cit. (n. 1).

5. See especially Lech Krzyzaniak in J. M. Plumley, Ed., *Nubian Studies* (Warminster, 1982), pp. 151–4.

6. See especially Franics Geus, in *Service des Antiquités du Soudan, Section Française de Recherche Archéologique, Rapport Annuel d'Activité*, 1978–1979, pp. 15–16.

7. See *Archaeology*, Vol. 33, No. 5 (1980), pp. 12–21.

8. For discussion see W. Y. Adams, ' Doubts about the " Lost Pharaohs " ', *Journal of Near Eastern Studies* (in press).

9. See Charles Bonnet in *Genava*, Vol. XXVI (1978), pp. 107–34; Vol. XXVIII (1980), pp. 31–72; Vol. XXX (1982), p.p 29–70. Also Charles Bonnet in J. M. Plumley, op. cit. (n. 5), pp. 45–56.

10. See especially Charles Bonnet in *Genava*, Vol. XXX (1982), pp. 44–6.

11. See Charles Bonnet in *Genava*, Vol. XXVI (1978), pp. 116–20; Vol. XXVIII (1980), p. 59; and in *Nyame Akuma* No. 22 (1983), pp. 23–4.

12. Dows Dunham, *Excavations at Kerma*, Part VI (Boston, 1982).

13. See especially Brigette Gratien in *Cahiers de Recherche de l'Institut de Papyrologie et d'Égyptologie de Lille*, No. 3 (1975), pp. 43–66; No. 6 (1981), pp. 132–48.

14. Brigitte Gratien, *Les Cultures Kerma* (Lille, 1978).

15. Charles Bonnet in *Genava*, Vol. XXVIII (1980), pp. 50–58.

16. Anthony Marks et al. in *Nyame Akuma* No. 21 (1982), pp. 39–40.

17. Rodolfo Fattovich and Marcello Piperno in *Nyame Akuma* No. 19 (1981), pp. 29–30

18. H. S. Smith, 'The Fortress of Buhen; the Inscriptions' (*Egypt Exploration Society, Excavation Memoir* 48, 1976), pp. 80–85.

19. See Jean Vercoutter in *Cahiers de Recherche de l'Institut de Papyrologie et d'Égyptologie de Lille*, No. 1 (1973), pp. 7–38; Michel Azim in *Cahiers de Recherche de l'Institut de Papyrologie et d'Égyptologie de Lille*, No. 3 (1975), pp. 91–126.

20. See Sergio Donadoni and Sergio Bostico in Nicholas B. Millet and Allyn L. Kelley, Eds., 'Meroitic Studies' (*Meroitica* 6, 1982), pp. 291–301.

21. André Vila, *La Prospection de la Vallée du Nil au Sud de la Cataracte de Dal*, 12 (1980).

22. Ibid., p. 169.

23. André Vila, *La Prospection de la Vallée du Nil au Sud de la Cataracte de Dal*, 11 (1979), pp. 7–8, 37.

24. See *Nyame Akuma* No. 9 (1976), p. 44.

25. Charles Bonnet in *Genava*, Vol. XXVI (1978), pp. 123–5.
26. Victor Fernandez in *Meroitic Newsletter* No. 20 (1980), pp. 13–22 and pls. I–IV.
27. See W. Y. Adams, 'Ptolemaic and Roman Occupation at Qasr Ibrim', *Cahiers de Recherche de l'Institut de Papyrologie et d'Égyptologie de Lille*, No. 7 (in press).
28. *Economic Offices and Officials in Meroitic Nubia (Études Publiées par les Chaires d'Histoire Ancienne de l'Université Loránd Eötvös de Budapest*, 26 1979); *The Meroitic Economy and its Written Sources: a Survey of Informations and Illusions* (pre-publication MS).
29. *The Meroitic Economy and its Written Sources: a Survey of Informations and Illusions* (pre-publication MS), pp. 63–4.
30. See Adams, op. cit. (n. 27), and id., 'Primis and the "Aethiopian" Frontier', *Journal of the American Research Center in Egypt* (in press).
31. *Collection de l'École Française de Rome*, 38 (1978).
32. See W. Y. Adams, 'From Pottery to History: the Dating of Archaeological Deposits from Ceramic Evidence', paper read at the Working Conference on the Use of Numerical Methods in the Study of Meroitic Culture, Fürstenberg, GDR, October 11, 1983.
33. See *Nyame Akuma* No. 20 (1982), pp. 50–53, and No. 22 (1983), pp. 30–33.
34. For a recent report see Stefan Jakobielski in J. M. Plumley, op. cit. (n. 5), pp. 116–26.
35. See Dennis Van Gerven in *Nyame Akuma* No. 15 (1979), pp. 53–5.
36. See W. Y. Adams and John Alexander in *Journal of Egyptian Archaeology*, Vol. 69 (in press).
37. Ali Osman in J. M. Plumley, op. cit. (n. 5), pp. 185–205.
38. See *Nyame Akuma* No. 14 (1979), pp. 52–6; No. 16 (1980), pp. 37–40; and No. 18 (1981), pp. 48–50.
39. See *Nyame Akuma* No. 15 (1979), pp. 63–7; and No. 21 (1982), pp. 36–8.

ARCHAEOLOGICAL EXPEDITIONS TO NUBIA AND THE SUDAN SINCE 1975

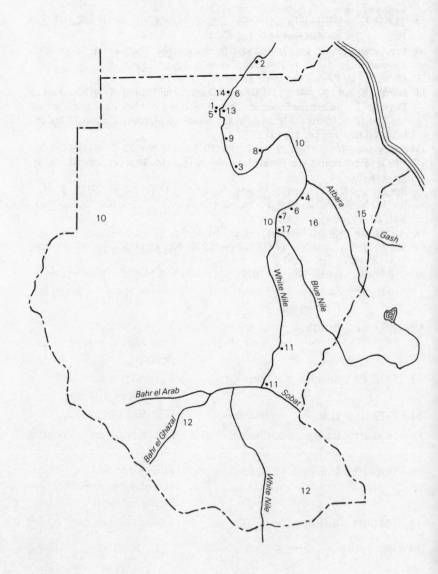

KEY

	Years	Nationality	Area of work	Periods and remains
1	1957–P*	Italian/ French	Seddenga	New Kingdom temple; Meroitic cemetery
2	1963–P*	British/ U.S.	Qasr Ibrim	Pharaonic to Islamic fortress
3	1964–P*	Polish	Old Dongola	Christian town-site and churches
4	1965–P*	Canadian/ Sudanese	Meroë	Meroitic town-site and temples
5	1969–P*	French	Sai Island	Pharaonic to Islamic fortress and cemeteries
6	1969–75	French/ Sudanese	Dai to Abri	Survey; all periods
	1976–P*	French/ Sudanese	Shendi area	Primarily Neolithic sites and Meroitic cemeteries
7	1971–P*	Polish	Kadero	Neolithic settlement and cemetery
8	1973–P*	Italian	Jebel Barkal	Napatan and Meroitic temples
9	1974–P*	Swiss	Kerma	Kerma town-site, temples and cemeteries
10	1975–P*	Sudanese	(Various)	Surveys; all periods
11	1976–82	Sudanese/ Norwegian	Upper Nile Province	Shilluk sites of Funj period
12	1977–81	British	Equatoria and Bahr el Ghazal	Surveys and test excavations; various periods
13	1978–P*	Spanish	Abri area	Kerma, Napatan, and Meroitic cemeteries
14	1979	U.S.	Kulubnarti	Christian cemeteries
15	1980–P*	Italian	Gash R. Delta	Survey; primarily Neolithic sites
16	1980–P*	U.S.	Butana Steppe	Survey and test excavations; primarily Neolithic sites
17	1981–P*	British	Soba	Christian town-site

* Present

INTRODUCTION –

Egypt, at the lower end of the Nile, has the longest recorded history in the world. Inner Africa, at the headwaters of the same river, has almost the shortest. Nubia, the land between, alternates for 5,000 years between history and dark ages. The oldest written record from Nubia may date from the fourth millennium BC; the last dark age ended in 1813.

The intermittent character of Nubia's recorded history reflects, more than anything else, the outside world's fluctuating and uncertain interest in this remote and inhospitable land. For millennia Egypt treated it as a kind of private hunting preserve for human and animal game. If Egyptian historians and scribes deigned to notice it, they spoke of it in the contemptuous terms reserved for 'lesser breeds without the law'. In hieroglyphic texts we seldom encounter the name of Kush (an early name for Nubia) without the epithet 'miserable' or 'abominable'.[1]

The Nubians did themselves somewhat more justice when after 2,000 years they began to write their own history. Nevertheless, their royal proclamations are not much more informative than are those of their Egyptian mentors. They are full of the selfsame vainglorious boasts and fictitious exploits which we associate with the Pharaohs – and they were written in the same exotic characters. There is nothing distinctively Nubian in them save the names of the actors.

It was left for Herodotus (or perhaps his predecessor Hecataeus) to bring a new viewpoint to the study of Nubia and its people. To the wide-eyed Greek, Egypt and Nubia were equally exotic, equally compelling – and equally ancient. If the 'Father of History' was not really the first writer on Nubian history, he was at least the first who took it seriously, and tried to report it objectively.[2]

The remote land of the Upper Nile, with its outlandish fauna and its black-skinned people, captured the romantic imagination of Greeks and Romans as it never did that of the Egyptians. Homer himself wrote that 'they are the remotest nation, the most just of men; the favourites of the gods. The lofty inhabitants of Olympus journey to them, and take part in their feasts; their sacrifices are the most agreeable of all that mortals can offer them.'[3] Even in the heyday of Hellenistic scepticism, all kinds of fantastic legends flourished about the sources of the Nile, as they did in

1

medieval times about the kingdom of Prester John. It was Diodorus the Sicilian, a latter-day Greek historian and contemporary of Lucretius (c. 50 BC), who recorded and bequeathed to posterity the then current tradition that Nubia was the original home of the Egyptians and the fountainhead of civilization itself.[4]

[In the Middle Ages, the opening of trans-Saharan caravan trade gave the Arabs of North Africa a much more realistic and prosaic view of their southern neighbours. Several distinguished Islamic scholars, among them the great Ibn Khaldun,[5] composed histories and geographies of Nubia.] [Few of these were translated into European languages until the nineteenth century, however, and some are untranslated to this day.] Until 150 years ago, European notions about Nubia were still largely derived from the romantic traditions of Herodotus and Diodorus.

[The short-lived Napoleonic occupation of Egypt, 1798–1801, opened the lands of the Nile to European scholarship. Burckhardt,[6] Cailliaud,[7] and Hoskins[8] visited Nubia and wrote detailed and perceptive accounts of its people and culture. The epoch-making journey of Richard Lepsius in 1842–4, resulting in a 12-volume work on Nubian and Egyptian antiquities,[9] put Nubia on the historical map for all time.] Meanwhile the continuing discovery and decipherment of hieroglyphic texts throughout the nineteenth century opened up an entirely new approach to Nubian history.

The picture of the southern land which emerged from Egyptian texts was in many ways diametrically opposed to that which had come down from the classical authors. Nubia, it appeared, was no more than a poor and barbarous frontier province which had been exploited and tyrannized at will by the Egyptians, primarily for the sake of its gold, ivory and slaves. As the field of Egyptology developed, and historians came to rely more and more on hieroglyphic texts and less on classical sources, the ancient Egyptian attitude towards Nubia took root in their minds, until by the end of the century it had entirely supplanted the old notion of Nubia as the well-spring of civilization. In 1907, when Wallis Budge published the first modern history of the region, he wrote:

> Many archaeologists have imagined that we shall find in the Sudan the ruins of purely native buildings and monuments which will enable them to reconstruct a connected history of the country, but none of the surveys and explorations which have been made by ancient and modern travellers has resulted in the finding of any ruins which are not, . . . in fact, the work of foreigners.[10]

It is ironic that the same year which saw the publication of Budge's pessimistic view witnessed also the inauguration of archaeological research in Nubia which was to prove it drastically wrong. This was the great Archaeological Survey of Nubia, the world's first organized salvage campaign, made necessary by the building of the Aswan Dam. Its earliest director was George A. Reisner, who thus began a lifelong involvement which was to make his name pre-eminent among students of Nubian history.

The Archaeological Survey almost at once encountered remains that were not of Egyptian origin; so many of them that by the end of the first season Reisner had identified no fewer than four Nubian cultural stages which had no Egyptian equivalents. Because history provided no names for these cultures (or peoples, as Reisner considered them), he gave them alphabetical designations – 'A', 'B', 'C', and 'X' – by which they are still commonly known sixty years later. If they did not exactly permit Reisner 'to reconstruct a connected history of the country' (in Budge's phrase), they did at least account for most of the dark ages in Nubian history, between episodes of Egyptian colonization or influence.[11]

In his direction of the Archaeological Survey of Nubia, and in his later investigations of the Nubian royal cemeteries, Reisner added immeasurably to the meagre picture of history which Budge had been able to assemble from documentary sources. The culture periods which he defined, and the order of their succession, have remained the standard framework for all studies of Nubian history since his day, much as Manetho's chronology of the pharaonic dynasties has remained the standard framework for studies of ancient Egyptian history.[12] Yet Reisner too could write: '"Wretched Nubia" was at first a part of Egypt. After the First Dynasty it was only an appendage of the greater country, and its history is hardly more than an account of its use or neglect by Egypt.'[13]

Reisner headed the Archaeological Survey of Nubia only during the first of its four seasons, after which C. M. Firth took over. There was a second survey of comparable size and duration between 1929 and 1934, when the original Aswan Dam was enlarged. Several private expeditions also worked in Nubia in the period between the two surveys, and to a lesser extent after the second survey, until the outbreak of the Second World War brought a halt to archaeological operations on the Nile. It was not until the announcement of the Aswan High Dam, in 1959, that they were revived on anything like their pre-war scale.[14]

Monumental and indeed unprecedented as were the first and second surveys of Nubia, their scope was humble when compared with that of the Nubian Salvage Campaign of 1959–69, so successfully publicized by the United Nations Educational, Scientific, and Cultural Organization (UNESCO). Although priority was necessarily given to the conservation of already known monuments, more than forty expeditions, representing most of the industrial nations of the world, engaged in purely archaeological explorations in Egypt and the Sudan. More than a million dollars was spent for survey and excavation alone. Certainly no comparable effort to investigate and recover the past has ever been made anywhere in the world in so short a time. The reports of the latter-day investigations in Nubia are only now beginning to appear, but those already published have doubled the volume of existing literature on Nubian history.

  In one sense it is amazing how little the subsequent work has added to, or subtracted from, Reisner's original formulation. No new cultural periods have been added to those discovered by him, and there has been no revision of their sequence. It is an enduring tribute to Reisner's genius that a scheme which he was able to propose within a few months of his entry into the field should have stood the test of sixty years' subsequent excavation. W. B. Emery's *Egypt in Nubia*,[15] the most recent popular work on Nubian history (and the only one to draw extensively on the results of the recent campaigns), retains almost *in toto* the Reisnerian formula. While much of the descriptive material is new, the theoretical and analytical portions of *Egypt in Nubia* could have been written by Reisner himself.

  It is unfortunately also true that Reisner's work, and most subsequent work, seems to confirm Budge's prediction that archaeologists would be unable to reconstruct a connected history of Nubia. Reisner all his life interpreted Nubian history largely in terms of the comings and goings of different peoples; in effect as a series of disconnected scenes performed by different actors. If there was any thread of continuity in his picture of Nubia, it was an Egyptian and not an indigenous one. This view has been accepted by nearly all of Reisner's successors, and it is implicit in the title of *Egypt in Nubia*.[16]

  The 'episodic' view of Nubian history propounded by Reisner, and endorsed by most of his successors, has probably been influenced by three factors. First of all, 'Nubia' at the beginning of the twentieth century meant for all practical purposes Lower Nubia; there was almost no systematic knowledge of the region beyond the Second Cataract. It must be acknowledged that the northern region does indeed seem to have had a discontinuous history of occupation and cultural development. Even today, after half a century of intensive investigation, there are lacunae in the archaeological record which oblige us to think in terms of periodic abandonment and re-occupation. We are now able to recognize, however, that most of these population movements were no more than migrations back and forth between Lower Nubia and Upper Nubia, and that the peoples who periodically re-occupied the northern district were in most cases the direct descendants of those who had previously quitted it.

  In addition, the general absence of archaeological information in Reisner's time forced scholars to rely overheavily on the textual record of Nubian history, and it too is a discontinuous one. Dark ages alternate with periods of recorded history, and often when the story is resumed we are given a new or a somewhat altered view of Nubia and its people. In these circumstances imagination can easily picture major disruptions, population replacements, or periods of abandonment corresponding to the intervals for which historical information is lacking.

Making due allowance for the two foregoing factors, it is also probable that the theories of Reisner and his contemporaries reflect a certain residual influence of pre-scientific historical thought. In their day it was still popular, as it had been for centuries earlier, to attribute cultural change more or less automatically to the coming of new peoples, as though there were a fixed relationship between peoples and their cultures.[17] Similar explanations were applied at one time or another to the history of Egypt, Sumer, Troy, China, Mexico, and just about every other region which exhibits a succession of historical or archaeological cultures without obvious connecting links. Thus when Reisner encountered the mysterious 'A', 'B', and 'C' grave types at Shellal, they took shape in his mind, *a priori*, as distinct groups of people rather than as successive stages in the cultural development of the same people. His anatomist colleague Elliot Smith, whose objectivity was often overridden by his zeal for particular historical theories, was able to find racial differences as well, in the skeletal remains from the different grave groups identified by Reisner.[18] Here, it seemed, was unmistakable evidence of the comings and goings of discrete peoples. (As will be seen in Chapter 3, the anatomical differences adduced by Elliot Smith have not stood the test of modern re-examination.)

Fifty years of intensive investigation have filled in many of the gaps in the picture which Reisner was able to perceive. Even where lacunae remain, it is now apparent that the cultural similarities between any two successive states in Nubian history far outweigh the differences. With the broadened perspective which is available to us, it is no longer necessary to bring in alien peoples to account for the relatively minor differences between 'A-Group' and 'C-Group' or between Meroitic and 'X-Group'; we can see them as the result of normal on-going processes of cultural evolution and diffusion. Yet the 'episodic' view of history persists – more perhaps as a tribute to Reisner the man than to the evidence which is now available.

In the study of Nubian history today, what is lacking is not so much historical fact as an intelligible and coherent point of view around which to arrange the known facts. To my anthropologist's mind such a point of view is offered by the perspective of cultural evolution. Without seriously challenging the historical evidence, therefore, or even (with one exception) the time-tested Reisnerian chronology of cultural periods, I propose in this volume to tell the old story of Nubia in a new way: as a continuous narrative of the cultural development of a single people, in which the comings and goings of particular actors have been unimportant. Migrations there have undoubtedly been, but they have been for the most part migrations within Nubia: rearrangements of peoples all drawing on a common

5

reservoir of indigenous tradition and experience. Such comings and goings have temporarily disturbed but have never, I believe, permanently altered the on-going process of cultural evolution.

My point of view differs from that of many colleagues and predecessors in other respects as well. Students of Nubian history from Budge and Reisner to Emery have been mostly Egyptologists, whose involvement in Nubia has been more or less a by-product of their primary commitment to Egypt and its civilization. It is almost inevitable that they should view Nubian history chiefly as a reflection (usually a pale reflection) of events and conditions in the northern country, and should dwell upon the similarities rather than the differences between Nubia and Egypt. Their attitude may perhaps be justly compared to the typical English view of the Irish.

By contrast, I have no training in Egyptology and little personal experience in the northern country, whereas I resided for seven years in the Sudan, have revisited it several times since, and have made what I regard as a lifelong commitment to the study of its cultures and history. The result is that I offer a 'Nubiocentric' point of view in place of the 'Egyptocentric' one which I see reflected in most of my colleagues. It is in no sense a more objective outlook; merely a different one. If I am able to paint Nubia in fuller and brighter colours than has usually been done, it is partly (so some of my correspondents have already complained) at the expense of reducing events and personalities in Egypt to the compass of a kind of two-dimensional backdrop. Perhaps someday a wholly impartial appraisal of Egyptian–Nubian relations may be offered by someone equally sympathetic and equally knowledgeable of both peoples (though I am not convinced that such total objectivity is any more possible than in the case of England and Ireland); in the meantime I believe that a 'Nubiocentric' outlook, if not more accurate, is at least more appropriate to the Nubians whose story I propose to tell.

Not being an Egyptologist or philologist, it is also true that I have no competence in the ancient and medieval languages, and this is undoubtedly the greatest shortcoming of my book. Although textual evidence is essential to my story at many points, I have had to draw in every case on translations whose reliability I am unable to judge. On the other hand, as an experienced field archaeologist as well as a student of comparative cultures I believe that I can 'read' things in the archaeological record which are unintelligible to most philologists. At any rate I place greater trust in archaeological evidence than I do in textual evidence in reaching my own historical conclusions, and this too accounts for certain differences between my view of Nubian history and that of my colleagues.

Although my approach to the Nubian data is new in several respects, I have avoided as far as possible the temptation to buttress it with new terminology or taxonomic schemes. It has been necessary for me to re-designate Reisner's A, B, and C 'Groups' as 'Horizons' in order to emphasize my belief that they do not represent separate populations, but otherwise I am content to stick with the alphabetic designations which are now hallowed by tradition. I have superimposed over the old cultural sequence of Reisner a four-fold division into Tribal, Dynastic, Medieval, and Modern periods, but these are descriptive rather than taxonomic terms. However, those less respectful of tradition may prefer the new cultural terminology proposed in Bruce Trigger's *History and Settlement in Lower Nubia*.[19] The correspondence between Trigger's cultural phases, my own, and those originally proposed by Reisner is shown in Table I.

Some Africans and Africanists will perhaps be disappointed in my book. While I have considerable sympathy with the current ideological

TABLE I

COMPARATIVE NOMENCLATURE
OF NUBIAN CULTURAL STAGES

According to different authors

	Adams[1]	*Reisner*[2]	*Trigger*[3]		*Dates*
‡ MEDIEVAL	Modern	*	†		
	Islamic				
	Christian	Coptic	Christian		1500
	X Horizon	X-Group	Ballana	LATE NUBIAN	500 A D
‡ DYNASTIC	Meroitic	↑ Ptol.-Rom. 'Ethiopian'	Meroitic and Ptolemaic-Roman		BC
	Napatan		Napatan		1000
	New Kingdom	New Kingdom	New Kingdom		1500
‡ DYNASTIC	Kerma	§	†		
TRIBAL	C Horizon	C-Group	IV C-Group (New Kng.) III C-Group (2nd Int.) II C-Group (Mid. Kng.) I C-Group (1st Int.)	MIDDLE NUBIAN	2000
	A Horizon	B-Group	III B-Group	EARLY NUBIAN	
		A-Group	II A-Group (Early Dyn.) Ib A-Group (Pre-dyn.) Ia Gerzean		2500
	Neolithic	*	Neolithic		3500

[1] *Sudan Notes and Records*, Vol. XLVIII (1967), p. 5.
[2] cf. Emery, *Egypt in Nubia*, p. 44.
[3] Yale University Publications in Anthropology, No. 69 (1965), p. 46.
* Not included in Reisner's formulation. † Not included in Trigger's formulation.
‡ Transitional stage. § Reisner incorrectly dated Kerma contemporaneous with Middle Kingdom.

ferment on the southern continent, it is not my place or my intention to make propaganda for nationalist or racist movements. Consequently, I have made relatively little of the Nubians' 'Africanness'. Their interest for me has nothing to do with their skin colour or with the continent on which they happen to live; they are in their own right a fascinating people with a fascinating history. If I deplore the earlier tendency of Egyptologists to see the Nubians as nothing more than second-class Egyptians, I am equally resentful of efforts to place them in another historical pigeonhole as 'Africans' or 'blacks'. On the contrary it is my fondest hope that readers of this book may come to share my appreciation of them for their own sake, and not for whatever light others may reflect on them, or they on others.

I have seldom referred to the Nubians as 'black', not out of any racial sensitivity but because they have only intermittently been black. By that I do not mean that their skin colour and facial features have changed significantly in the historic period; I believe in fact that they have remained pretty much the same since the earliest times. But race is largely in the eye of the beholder; it is more a matter of social ascription than of biology, and its defining characteristics have changed from age to age and from place to place. To be technically accurate the Nubians are mostly of a chocolate-brown colour; one could, and can, see them either as 'black' or as 'white' according to the prejudices of one's time and temperament. There have certainly been periods when they have been subject to prejudice and oppression as a result of their dark skin colour, and when to call them 'black' would be sociologically meaningful in today's terms. There have also been times when they were subject to the same attitudes and treatment not because of their skin colour but because they were unlettered barbarians, or because they were Christians surrounded by Moslems. There have been other times when the Nubians have joined with their northern neighbours in oppressing and exploiting the much darker peoples of inner Africa, and when it would be more sociologically meaningful to call them 'white'. Rather than hang any permanent racial label on them, I have attempted to characterize them at each stage of their history according to the prevailing attitudes of the time.

My fellow cultural anthropologists will perhaps take complacent satisfaction in what I have written thus far, feeling that I have at last introduced the comparative and inductive approach of our discipline into a field which has too long been dominated by humanists and particularists. As they read on they will find, however, that in Nubia history has at least as much to teach anthropology as vice versa. Although it is true that, as a good anthropologist, I see Nubian history primarily in terms of cultural evolution, the actual evolutionary stages which I have recognized, and which I believe to be applicable far beyond the borders of Nubia, are more nearly

8

those of the historian than of the anthropologist. I will not further enlarge on this topic here; my final chapter is devoted chiefly to a discussion of the limitations of anthropological theory as applied to Nubian history.

I did not originally set out to write this book for anthropologists, Egyptologists, or any of the other scholarly specialists to whom the foregoing paragraphs are chiefly addressed. My intention was merely to make Nubian history known in an intelligible form to the general public, or at least to that part of it whose interest was kindled by the publicity given Abu Simbel and the High Dam salvage campaign. Yet I found that, in the present state of our knowledge, I could not write a wholly popular book, knowing all the while that my professional colleagues would be looking over my shoulder. For their sake (and sometimes at their insistence) I have introduced passages of discussion, debate, and sometimes downright quibbling which I had no original thought of including; as a result the lay reader may at times see more of the 'dirty linen' of historical scholarship than he wished to. Yet I have tried throughout not to lose sight of him altogether, but rather to arrive at a reasonable compromise between his interests and those of professional scholars. Certainly this is more difficult than any writing task I have previously attempted; whether it has succeeded only time will tell.

My book is not in any sense meant to be the 'last word' on Nubian history; indeed I hope there may never be such a 'last word'. Although the filling of Lake Nasser has put a permanent end to archaeological work in Lower Nubia, except at Qasr Ibrim, much of the material excavated in the 1960s is still under study, and fresh insights are appearing with each new published report. Meanwhile the continuing excavations in Upper Nubia, and at Qasr Ibrim in Lower Nubia, may at any time yield discoveries which will substantially alter the picture I have presented. Indeed, discoveries at Qasr Ibrim in 1972 and 1974[20] have already necessitated important additions to Chapter 13 and Chapter 16 at the galley-proof stage. Finally, even when and if the archaeological facts are all in, their interpretation is sure to remain a matter of controversy for generations to come.

For the sake of the general reader I have avoided the use of technical terms except insofar as they are explained in the text, and when it has been necessary to introduce abstruse discussion I have tried to explain its significance in terms which would permit the layman to follow the arguments. Finally, I have hidden my footnotes (necessary for those colleagues who have not only a right but a duty to demand the sources of my facts and ideas) at the back of the book, where they will not interfere with casual reading.

Despite my objection to the 'episodic' character of earlier histories, my own book is episodic to the extent that each succeeding stage of Nubian history is described in a separate and self-contained chapter. These chapters are so written that they can generally be read independently by those whose interest is confined to specific periods of history.

The wealth of bizarre and exotic names with which this history is encumbered will, I suppose, be attractive to some and repellent to others. Because my overriding concern is to reach and interest a non-professional audience, I have tried whenever possible to use the simplest and most nearly phonetic transcriptions of proper names, even though these will in some cases be objectionable to philological purists.

PROLOGUE

1
THE NUBIAN CORRIDOR

Egypt has always inspired man to monumental endeavours. The Old Kingdom built pyramids; the Middle Kingdom built immense fortresses; the New Kingdom built temples and subterranean tombs; the Greeks built the world's greatest library and the world's tallest lighthouse. Modern man, nominally more utilitarian in his aspirations, proclaims his immortality with mighty dams, submerging at a stroke both nature and the achievements of his own past in a reckless display of technical virtuosity. It is only fitting that in our own time one of the greatest of these twentieth-century monuments should once again be rising in the Valley of the Nile, where it may vie in splendour with the monumental extravagances of yester-year. The Aswan High Dam, built by Russia as a gift to Egypt and a rebuke to America, says to the twentieth century, 'Look on my works, ye Mighty, and despair!'[1]

The High Dam is an engineering masterpiece. Two hundred feet high and more than three miles long, it can impound four trillion cubic feet of water in a lake extending far into the inner reaches of Africa. Beneath that lake has vanished an ancient and storied land, known at the dawn of history as the Land of Kush, to Herodotus and his contemporaries as Aethiopia, and since medieval times as Nubia.

What is, or was, Nubia? The question has often been asked in recent years, for the High Dam, in the very act of destroying Nubia, has made its name known around the world. Yet it is not a name commonly found on maps, for there is no such political or administrative entity. The land known as Nubia lies today partly in Egypt and partly in the Republic of the Sudan, but comprises only a small part of either country.

The reader inquisitive enough to look for Nubia on the map of Africa should begin by locating the mouth of the Nile River, in the extreme northeast corner of the map (Fig. 1). Following the course of the river southwards, or upstream, he will presently pass the border between Egypt and the Sudan. Just beyond it, he may be surprised to discover that the course of the Nile describes a huge 'S' curve – one of the largest meanders in the world. Here, if anywhere, he may find the name 'Nubia' printed on the map. He will in any case note that the line representing the Nile is interrupted at fairly regular intervals by short, transverse lines which are

13

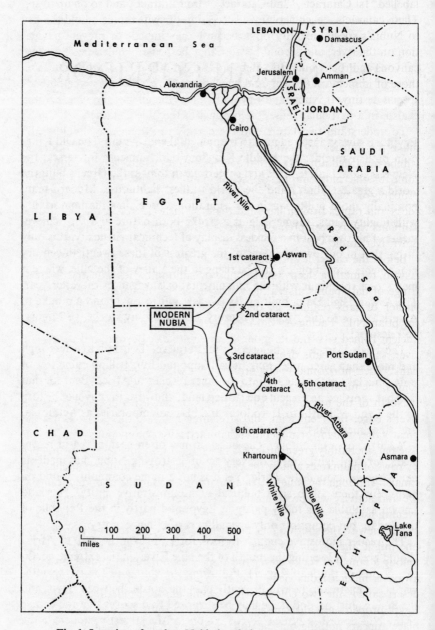

Fig. 1. Location of modern Nubia in relation to surrounding countries

labelled '1st Cataract', '2nd Cataract', '3rd Cataract', and so on up to six. These cataracts – each actually a succession of swift rapids – hold the key to Nubia's special identity: first, because they impede or prevent navigation on the river, and second because they bespeak a landscape of narrow canyons and rocky outcrops. Here are two conditions vastly different from those of immemorial Egypt, and which have done much to shape Nubia's special destiny. If Nubia and Egypt are alike 'the gifts of the Nile', Nubia is also, in a particular sense, the product of the Nile Cataracts.

To understand the nature and the destiny of Nubia one should really make the journey to Aswan, in Upper Egypt. The traveller who does so will be rewarded not only with the majesty of the High Dam, but also with some of the most impressive scenery on the Nile. His attention will probably be claimed initially by the First Cataract, a chaotic tumble of rocks and rapids broken here and there by lush green islands. Occasional sailboats will be seen plying between the islands, but there is no upriver or downriver traffic.

Below the cataract and along the right bank of the Nile lies crowded Aswan, formerly a sleepy village but now humming with industry. A green fringe of date palms marks the water's edge; immediately below them, a cluster of sails reminds us that this is the head of navigation on the Egyptian Nile. Facing Aswan is the large island of Elephantine, with its ancient ruined city and its modern luxury hotels. Beyond and across the river, sandstone cliffs drop directly from the desert plateau to the riverbank. Their horizontal line is broken by a series of distinctly visible rock tombs, the monuments of Aswan's earlier masters.

North of the town, the enclosing cliffs retreat for a distance from the river's edge. Between them, and stretching away to the horizon, lies the great valley which for millennia was practically synonymous with Egypt. The flat, incredibly green surface is marked off into squares and rectangles by rows of palm trees and by the glistening water of a thousand ditches and canals. Although the valley often appears deserted in the noonday stillness, life and activity will proclaim themselves everywhere in the morning and evening hours.

The view to the south offers a startling contrast. Here is no river valley; one might almost say no river. The Nile is lost to view almost at once among a tangle of rocky crests and slopes; even the dam, only a few miles away, is hidden from view. The green of vegetation and the yellow of desert sand – the two colours which dominate the landscape throughout Egypt proper – are alike missing as one looks south from Aswan. In their place appears nothing but the dull, dark grey of naked granite.

No wonder, then, that Aswan marks the age-old frontier of Egypt's peasant civilization. The land beyond the First Cataract offered few attractions either to farming or to commerce, and the ordinary Egyptian

15

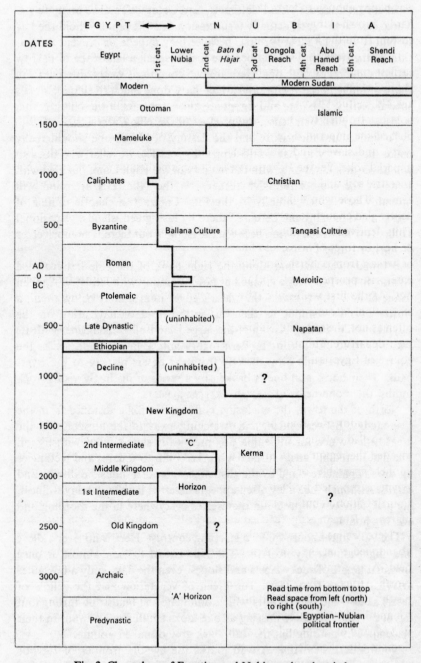

Fig. 2. Chronology of Egyptian and Nubian cultural periods

was happy enough to leave it in the hands of its immemorial occupants: a hardy, brown-skinned race differing alike in appearance, in speech, and in custom from the Egyptians.

It was otherwise, however, with Egypt's ambitious rulers. From the earliest times they had imperial aspirations, and Nubia, the closest inhabited neighbour, was nearly always their first victim. Thus the stable and age-old cultural frontier at Aswan has been anything but stable as a political frontier (cf. Figs. 2 and 3). Generations of warrior-pharaohs pushed the imperial dominions far up the Nile in their search for gold, ivory, and slaves, and Nubians as well as Egyptians suffered under the imperial yoke. Yet the Egyptian peasant remained stubbornly rooted to his ancestral soil, and few colonists entered Nubia in the wake of the victorious armies. Those who did so acted at the pharaoh's bidding, and were evidently glad enough to get back to Egypt at the end of their term of service. Thus deprived of any local support, Egypt's Nubian conquests could only be held by force of arms, and financed by whatever wealth or tribute could be wrung from a harsh land and a recalcitrant populace. Inevitably, this enterprise prospered only so long as the pharaoh's will and his funds held out. At the first weakening of royal authority garrisons, administrators, and colonists came streaming back across the Aswan frontier, while, as often as not, the resentful Nubian populace rose at their heels and hastened their departure. The story was to be repeated at least five times in the long course of Egyptian–Nubian relations (Fig. 2).

WHY NUBIA?

It is a paradox of Nubian history that this barren land has at once attracted and repelled outsiders from the beginning. Egyptians in the pharaonic era invaded the region again and again, yet seldom referred to it without the epithet 'miserable' or 'abominable'.[2] Cambyses, the Persian conqueror of Egypt, is reported by Herodotus to have ascended the Nile as far as the Fourth Cataract, but he nearly lost both his army and his life on the return march. A Roman army reached and sacked Napata in the first century BC, yet Nero declined to annex Nubia to the Roman dominions, and Diocletian abandoned even the northern extremity which Egypt had immemorially held. Arab armies, which elsewhere swept Christianity from the face of North Africa, arrived before Dongola within ten years of Mohammed's death – and there concluded a treaty which left Nubia in Christian hands for another 800 years. Salah-ed-Din (Saladin), conqueror of Richard *Cœur de Lion* and of Egypt and Syria, gave up all thought of adding Nubia to his domain after the briefest of forays. Within the past century Great Britain at the height of her imperial power abandoned the whole of the Sudan to a dervish horde armed chiefly with knives and spears. Fifteen years later she

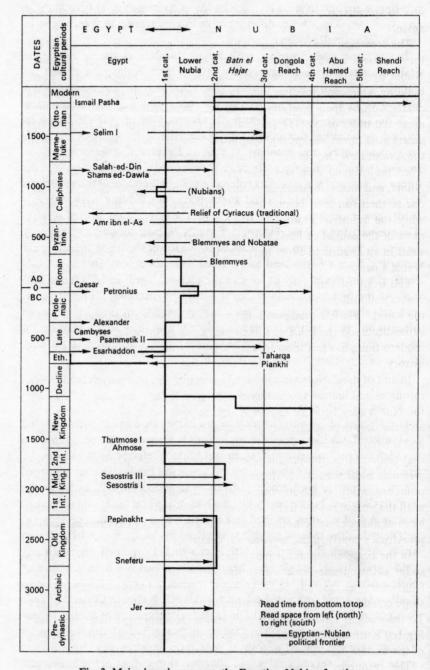

Fig. 3. Major invasions across the Egyptian–Nubian frontier

was to spend two years and an enormous sum of money to win it back again.

The crowning irony of Nubian history has, however, been reserved for the twentieth century. Egypt's rulers, having secured control of Lower Nubia by treaty in 1899, embarked at once on the programme of dam-building which will finally obliterate this region, so long coveted and so dearly won by their forefathers. The old Dodekaschoenos (the northern-most 100 miles of Nubia), for centuries held by Egypt as a route to her desert gold mines, disappeared within a few years after the completion of the Aswan Low Dam in 1907. Most of the rest of Egyptian Nubia followed when the original dam was enlarged in 1929. The destruction of Lower Nubia, and much of Sudanese Nubia as well, will be final when the waters rise to their full level behind the Aswan High Dam in the 1970s. Mean-while the industrial nations of Europe and America, which contributed most of the capital to build the Aswan dams, have raised vast additional sums in an anguished effort to rescue from destruction the monuments of Nubia's past.

The irony of simultaneously spending millions for the destruction of Nubia and millions more to save its antiquities has been noted by much of the world.[3] Yet few thoughtful observers question the legitimacy of either expenditure. At the heart of this paradox lies an essential truth: Nubia in modern times has lost the importance which long gave it a unique place in history.

In and of itself, Nubia has always been a hot, dry and barren land of few resources and limited subsistence potential. Poor as it was and is, however, the Nile Valley between Aswan and Khartoum offered, for millennia on end, the only dependable way across the great desert barrier of the Sahara, and the only contact between the civilized world and Africa. To the extent that the cultures, the products, and, in time, the bloodstreams of black men and white men met and mingled, they met and mingled here. Nubia's unique position as the meeting ground of two worlds was unchallenged until the opening of the trans-Saharan caravan trade in the last millennium BC, and did not finally disappear until the great Age of Exploration opened up Africa's coasts in the seventeenth century.

In the beginning, and for many centuries afterwards, Nubia *was* Africa so far as the outside world was concerned. Along the whole of the Saharan frontier it was the only place where the dwellers on the Mediterranean shore could catch a glimpse of another world beyond the southern horizon. To the ancient Egyptians, and even down to the time of Herodotus and Strabo, Kush and Aethiopia were practically synonymous with the region of the middle Nile. The rest of black Africa was unknown.

The resources for which Egypt and her Mediterranean neighbours coveted Nubia were precisely those resources for which the white man has always coveted Africa. They were partly mineral, partly animal, but above all human resources. The Nubian people were the first victims in a process of exploitation which in later times spread over the whole of the African continent.

At first, the Nubians undoubtedly found the role of black man in a white man's world as detrimental as have all black races everywhere. Their close proximity to the earliest centres of civilization, however, offered advantages which few native races in later times have had. After an initial period of subjugation and total exploitation, they were able to absorb a good deal of the civilization of their neighbours, and in so doing to detach themselves from the wholly primitive world of black Africa. From being Africa itself, Nubia became a transition zone, or rather *the* transition zone, between the civilized world and Africa. The narrow green strip of the middle Nile Valley, from Khartoum to Aswan, was the corridor through which men, things and ideas passed from the one world to the other, and within which they met and mingled. The dwellers in this corridor became in every sense middle men – racially and culturally as well as economically. Their unique position between the black and the white worlds has persisted down to modern times.

Nubia, then, is part culture province, part historical province, and part geographic province – a region in which human destiny has been shaped in particular and distinctive ways by a unique combination of historical advantages and environmental disadvantages. It is, specifically, that part of native Africa which has never been permanently colonized by foreign peoples but has always been influenced by them. Since the dawn of history it has lain upon the frontier of civilization, without ever fully moving across it.

THE BOUNDARIES OF NUBIA

The northern limit of Nubia is, and has always been, as sharply defined as the First Cataract itself.[4] The eastern and western limits are equally clearly marked, for they are nothing more than the limits of cultivation and of habitation, a mile or two on either side of the great river. Beyond that narrow compass lies waterless desert (Pl. Ib) which is either entirely lifeless, or, in the upper reaches of Nubia, is inhabited by nomads who are not historically or culturally Nubians, although (like the Egyptians) they have played their part in Nubian history.

It is only the southern, or upper, limit of Nubia which is difficult to define. If we acknowledge that Nubia is a culture province, whose people are not Egyptian but have been continually influenced by Egyptian culture, then we have to recognize that the extent and persistence of that influence have been different at different times in history. So, in a sense, Nubia has had a shifting southern frontier. The general pattern was one of southward extension from the first introduction of civilization, in the third millennium BC, until the rise of pastoral nomadism in the first millennium AD. During that time Egyptian influence spread southwards from the Second Cataract of the Nile (in the Old and Middle Kingdoms) to the Fourth Cataract (in the New Kingdom) and ultimately at least as far as the confluence of the Blue and White Niles (modern Khartoum) by the beginning of the Christian era. The rise of pastoral nomadism, and particularly the coming of hordes of Arab immigrants, created the first counter-pressure to the further spread of sedentary, civilized life, and in recent times there has been a gradual northwards retreat of the Nubian–Arab frontier, until today it is once again below the Fourth Cataract (Figs. 8, 9).

If I may sum up the definition of Nubia in a few words, it is the land of the Nile cataracts: that part of the Nile Valley, directly south of Egypt, which is occupied by peoples African in origin and speech but strongly influenced by Egyptian and Mediterranean culture. The special ethnic characteristics of the Nubians, and the question of their origin, will be discussed in the next two chapters.

It is necessary to remark before proceeding that the flexible geographic definition of Nubia which I have given here, and which is implicit in my essentially cultural approach to history, does not necessarily correspond to the usage of other writers. For precisely the historical reasons already noted, there is no general agreement as to the boundaries of Nubia either in modern or in ancient times. Because the term is technically a linguistic one, some writers apply it – at all periods of history – only to the area which today is occupied by Nubian speakers, between Aswan in the north and Debba in the south (Fig. 8). It is also true that in many early archaeological reports 'Nubia' tends to stand only for that area in which systematic archaeological work had been carried out; i.e. Lower Nubia. Throughout this work, however, I shall adhere to the broader definition which I have previously given.

GEOGRAPHIC SUBDIVISIONS

Conventional practice divides Nubia into two unequal parts: Lower Nubia, extending from the First to the Second Cataract, and Upper Nubia, above the Second Cataract. This distinction corresponds closely to the modern division between Egypt and the Republic of the Sudan (Fig. 1), but in other respects it is more meaningful historically than it is geographically. While Lower Nubia is in fact a fairly homogeneous topographic zone, the far larger area of Upper Nubia includes within itself a variety of environments, some similar to Lower Nubia and others markedly different. From the standpoint of physiography we must speak not of two Nubias but of five or six.

Geology holds the key to Nubia's topographic diversity. Throughout its lower course the Nile traverses three major surface formations: limestone, sandstone, and a group of hard igneous rocks (the North African 'basement complex') of which granite is the principal component (Fig. 4). The great valley of Egypt proper is carved from limestone; it is enclosed by limestone cliffs, and the bare desert on either side of it is in fact a limestone plateau, drifted over in most places with wind-blown sand.

At Jebel Silsila, a few miles north of Aswan, limestone gives way to the coarse, yellow-brown Nubian sandstone which covers a huge area of the eastern Sahara, extending south as far as the confluence of the Niles and west across Libya. This relatively thin and heavily eroded surface deposit is everywhere underlain by the much harder granite and other formations of the basement complex. In structurally uplifted areas the basement complex appears at the surface, the overlying sediments having been entirely stripped away by erosion, or perhaps surviving in an occasional isolated desert *jebel*.

From Khartoum to Aswan, the Nubian Nile traverses an alternating succession of granite zones and sandstone zones, as shown in Fig. 4. This circumstance is due partly to the irregular distribution of the two formations, but even more to the seemingly quixotic course of the river itself. After flowing continuously northward from its origin in the East African highlands, the Nile at Abu Hamed abruptly turns off to the south-west for 175 miles, before resuming its normal course to the sea. The resulting 'S'-shaped meander nearly doubles the length of the river in the northern Sudan, and has played a considerable part in determining the course of Nubian history. Topographically it means that the Nile, after entering a granite zone near the mouth of the tributary Atbara, returns to a sandstone bed at the Fourth Cataract. Resuming its northwards course at Debba, it enters a second granite zone near the Third Cataract, before emerging once again into sandstone at the Second Cataract.

As in all deserts, the character of the Nubian landscape has been determined almost entirely by erosion. And it is the markedly different erosion patterns of the two formations, sandstone and granite, which have produced the main variations in the Nubian environment. The igneous formations of the basement complex are hard and resistant; here erosion takes place principally along faults and fissures. The surface configuration of the granite zones is one of sharp fingers and ridges of stone, separated by narrow, deep *wadis*. The river-bed is narrow, steep-walled, broken by numerous islands and cataracts, and there are few sizeable tracts of alluvial soil.

By contrast, Nubian sandstone is soft and horizontally bedded; erosion produces a series of more or less level terraces, broken at intervals by isolated, flat-topped remnants of higher formations, and crosscut by broad,

22

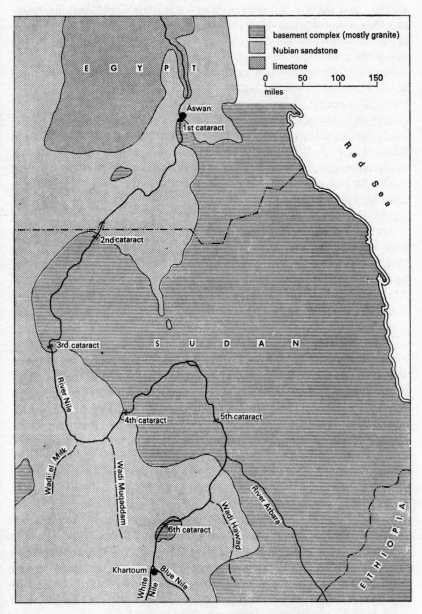

Fig. 4. Surficial geology of Nubia (simplified)

shallow *wadis* (Pl. Ib). In sandstone zones the bed of the Nile is broad and smooth, and there is a nearly continuous alluvial floodplain, although generally not a very broad one, along one or both banks (Pl. Ia). In areas of low relief, abandoned river channels become additional alluvial basins beside the main valley.

In general, the descent gradient of the Nile averages one foot in ten miles in the sandstone zones, as against one foot in half a mile in the granite zones. The abrupt change of gradient where the river crosses from one formation to the other is responsible for most of the major Nile cataracts. The Fourth Cataract marks the passage from granite to sandstone near Kareima; the Third Cataract at Kerma corresponds to the river's re-entry into granite, and the Second Cataract at Wadi Halfa marks its return to a sandstone bed once again. Both the Sixth and the First Cataracts are associated with localized outcrops of granite in predominantly sandstone regions.

The main physiographic subdivisions of Nubia, which we shall now consider individually, are thus marked off in a general way (and with one exception to be noted) by the main or 'numbered' cataracts of the Nile. In upstream order, these subdivisions are Lower Nubia, the *Batn el Hajar*, the Abri-Delgo Reach, the Dongola Reach, the Abu Hamed Reach, and the Shendi Reach (Fig. 5).

LOWER NUBIA

Lower Nubia extends from the First to the Second Cataract, and today lies almost wholly within the borders of Egypt. (Being the part of Nubia closest to the Aswan Dam, it also lies almost wholly under water, so that any descriptive statements about it should properly be phrased in the past tense.) This region is set off from the great valley of Egypt proper by an outcrop of granite which has produced the First Cataract, and which gives to the landscape south of Aswan the forbidding aspect which we have already described. This particular exposure of the basement complex, however, is a very restricted one, extending upstream only as far as the 'Kalabsha Gate', some thirty-five miles south of Aswan. From here to the Second Cataract there is an uninterrupted and generally level expanse of Nubian sandstone, through which the river has cut a broad, shallow trench. Floodplain is not continuous along either bank of the river, but there are extensive alluvial deposits, especially at the mouths of the larger *wadis*, which formerly supported a regular succession of farming hamlets (Pl. Ia). The stream itself is broad, placid, and easily navigated; all kinds of river craft used to ply between Shellal, above the First Cataract, and Wadi Halfa, below the Second. Thus Lower Nubia, geographically closest to Egypt, was also topographically most similar to it. It is no wonder that this region in particular invited Egyptian colonization, or at least Egyptian

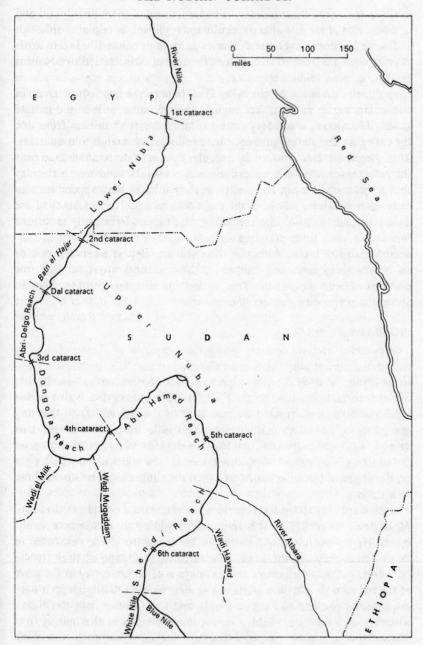

Fig. 5. Physiographic subdivisions of Nubia

exploitation, throughout most of its history, and is thus set apart culturally
and historically (as it is also politically today) from the rest of Nubia.

The valley floor in Lower Nubia is generally enclosed between bluffs
varying in height from 100 to 300 feet. Because of the soft nature of Nubian
sandstone, these seldom approach a vertical angle except where they have
been directly undercut by the Nile. The bluffs to the west of the river, in
particular, are in many places engulfed under immense falling dunes of
golden desert sand, which may extend as far as the riverbank itself. Outside
the valley, an undulating surface of bare yellow sand extends to the horizon
in all directions. It is crosscut by a regular system of dry *wadis* tributary to
the Nile; these are incised successively deeper into the sandstone plateau as
they approach the main river, until at their mouths they appear as side-
canyons branching away from the main Nile trench. The regularity of the
desert surface is also interrupted by flat-topped remnants of higher
formations, sometimes standing as isolated *jebels* and sometimes in connected chains of bluffs. Although these features impart a certain relief to
an otherwise monotonous landscape, they nowhere approach the proportions of true mountains. The highest summits are perhaps 500 feet
above the surrounding desert floor.

THE *BATN EL HAJAR*

The peaceful and moderately prosperous expanse of Lower Nubia is
terminated abruptly by the Second Cataract of the Nile, immediately upstream from Wadi Halfa. The aspect of river and landscape here is even
wilder than that presented by the First Cataract. Over a distance of twelve
miles the Nile is obstructed by hundreds of tiny islands and glistening
granite rocks, and its normally majestic flow is diverted into a labyrinth of
narrow, swift channels and tumbling rapids. Upstream navigation under
sail or steam is an impossibility; boats can only be winched through, at the
greatest hazard, from the banks, and then only at the highest season of the
Nile flood.

Southwards for 100 miles from the Second Cataract stretches the *Batn el
Hajar* ('belly of rock'), most barren and forbidding of all Nubian environments. Here we can hardly differentiate between littoral and desert, for in
many places they are the same. The tortured landscape of bare granite
ridges and gullies which characterizes this part of Nubia begins at the bank
of the river itself; alluvium exists not as a continuous floodplain, but only
in protected pockets and coves. Fields and tiny hamlets hug the banks
wherever such soil is available, but for long stretches neither natural nor
cultivated vegetation is to be seen. The narrow channel and steep riverbanks
make agriculture difficult even where alluvium is present, because of the
extreme differential between high and low Nile levels. At the slack season
the surface of the stream may be fifty feet or more below the neighbouring

fields; in these circumstances irrigation is a practical impossibility without the aid of modern pumps.

Throughout the *Batn el Hajar* the Nile is not only narrow but swift. At Semna during the low-water season the river's entire flow is squeezed through a 'funnel' hardly more than 100 feet wide, and many other places are not much wider. Islands and shoals are innumerable; the course of the Nile is broken by sizeable rapids ten times in 100 miles. Long-distance navigation, particularly against the current (i.e. from Egypt to Nubia) is impossible at the season of low water, and is difficult and hazardous at the best of times. Trade and travel through this region have mostly gone overland, preferring the hazards of the bank to those of the river.

No wonder, then, that the *Batn el Hajar* failed to attract Egyptian colonization, and for centuries served as a shield behind which the cultures of Upper Nubia could develop in their own way. It was more than a thousand years after the first Egyptian penetration of Lower Nubia before any effort was made to exploit the land beyond the Second Cataract, and even then outright political control by the Pharaohs was short-lived. Penetration of the 'granite curtain' did, however, establish a cultural contact between the people of Upper Nubia and those of Egypt which profoundly influenced the course of Nubian history from that time onward.

In later centuries, the unproductive nature of the *Batn el Hajar* in turn became a barrier to the northward expansion of Islamic culture, which was introduced and spread initially by pastoral nomads. It was in the rocky cataract zone, rather than in the more fertile and prosperous region upstream, that the last Christian Nubian farmers apparently held out against the tide of Islam.

Away from the river's edge, the aspect of the *Batn el Hajar* has been described as 'lunar'. Recent explorations may have cast doubt on the appropriateness of this simile, but certainly the region shares with the lunar surface an appearance of lifelessness and of formlessness such as is found in few places on earth. It is neither a sea of sand, like the deserts of Egypt and Lower Nubia, nor a mountainous desert like those of Asia and America. It appears, rather, as a planless jumble of boulders, ridges, rocky fingers, and sharp *wadis*, without any distinctive landmarks. Over vast areas the maximum relief scarcely exceeds two or three hundred feet, and yet level spaces are few indeed.

Aerial photography reveals a striking anomaly in the *Batn el Hajar*. Not only is physiographic relief far less sharply defined to the west of the Nile than it is to the east, but the prevailing colour of the land surface is noticeably lighter. Both circumstances result from the fact that throughout Nubia the wind blows almost continually from the north, while in the *Batn el Hajar* the course of the Nile is from south-west to north-east. The southerly winds, constantly eroding the bare sandstone plateau of Lower Nubia, carry southwards a heavy burden of coarse yellow sand, which has engulfed most of the *wadis* and level areas to the north and west of the river. Isolated granite ridges and knobs project through this yellow sea; often their lee sides are marked by huge trailing dunes, miles in length.

Since the heavy Nubian sand travels by tumbling rather than by flying through the air, the water-barrier of the Nile has acted to arrest its further southward spread in much the same way as a fire-break checks the spread of a fire. Hence not only the east (i.e. south-east) bank of the river, but also all of its islands, are free from the overburden which has engulfed much of the west bank. Their prevailing colour is the dark grey of granite rock, interspersed here and there with residual clay plains.

The modern vehicle track through the *Batn el Hajar* ('road' by courtesy), following the line of a short-lived military railway, keeps to the east bank of the Nile. Before the advent of wheeled traffic, however, overland travellers apparently found easier going on sand than on rock, for the west bank is historically the main caravan route along the Nile. (It is still followed by thousands of camels which are annually driven northwards from the western Sudan to Egypt for slaughter.) It is probably not entirely accidental, therefore, that most of the major archaeological remains both in Lower Nubia and in the *Batn el Hajar* are located on the west bank of the Nile. (Parenthetically, the heavy overburden of sand makes for much better preservation of archaeological remains on the west bank.)

THE ABRI-DELGO REACH

The Dal Cataract, about 100 miles south of Wadi Halfa, may conveniently serve to mark the southern limit of the *Batn el Hajar*. The stretch of Nile Valley between here and the Third (Kerma) Cataract, a distance of 120 miles, presents something of an anomaly. It is the only exception to the general pattern of barren granite zones alternating with more productive sandstone zones. In the Abri-Delgo Reach the basement complex is still exposed at the surface, but it assumes a characteristic physiography quite different from that of the neighbouring *Batn el Hajar*. The tangle of ridges and valleys gives way to tall, isolated buttes separated by wide clay plains. Here as everywhere, the plains to the west of the river are largely buried under yellow sand. The tallest summits, in the Firka region, tower more than 1,000 feet above the surrounding country; this is the only part of the Nile Valley between Khartoum and the sea which has something like a mountainous aspect. Yet the average river gradient between Kerma and Dal is less than anywhere else in Nubia (Fig. 6). Navigation presents no problem for smaller vessels, in spite of some minor rapids.

In much of the Abri-Delgo Reach, as in the Dongola Reach to the south, there are no bluffs to mark the boundary between river valley and desert. Cultivated alluvium gives way to rolling, gravelly slopes or, on the west

28

bank, to dunes, without any sharp rise in elevation. The floodplain, although interrupted here and there by *jebels* at the river's edge, is in many places wide and intensively cultivated, particularly on the east bank where it is free of sand. The northern part of this region, near the administrative centre of Abri, supports a nearly continuous string of well-populated farming villages.

The broad vistas and open river of the Abri-Delgo Reach must have been welcome indeed to those who had passed the rigours of the *Batn el Hajar*. Perhaps for this reason, Nubia's Egyptian conquerors erected more

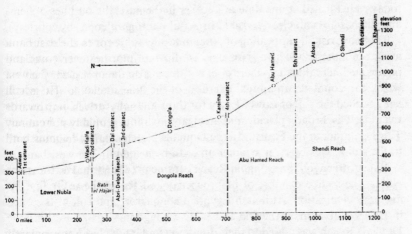

Fig. 6. Schematic profile of the Nile Valley from Khartoum to Aswan
Vertical exaggeration 2,400 times

temples and other monuments between Abri and Kerma than in any comparable area of Upper Nubia. In this and many other respects, the Abri-Delgo Reach clearly forms an extension of the Dongola Reach to the south, and not of the *Batn el Hajar* to the north, in spite of its closer geological affinity with the latter. We may therefore perhaps regard the Dal Cataract, at the northern limit of the Abri-Delgo Reach, as the true frontier of Upper Nubia, leaving the *Batn el Hajar* as a kind of transitional no-man's-land which does not belong properly to either Upper Nubia or Lower Nubia.

THE DONGOLA REACH

The Dongola Reach extends for over 200 miles, from the Third to the Fourth Cataract, and embraces the western half of the great 'S' bend along the middle Nile. Here again Nubian sandstone is the surface formation, but the bluffs and buttes of Lower Nubia are absent. Indeed, the terrain in the Dongola Reach, as in much of the area stretching away to the south, is almost featureless. Where it is not encumbered by dunes, potentially cultivable land extends for a mile or more on either side of the river. There are in addition large overflow basins, like those at Kerma and Letti, representing abandoned beds of the Nile which are still capable of extensive cultivation.

For the most part, the borderline between valley and desert is visible to the eye only as the difference between green and yellow-brown. Desert begins wherever cultivation stops. Where cultivation stops depends, in most cases, less upon absolute topographic limitations than upon the limits of human ambition and ingenuity. Thousands of acres which are desert today were farmed at one time or another in the past; the outlines of fields and ditches are still clearly visible in aerial photographs.

This least visually appealing of Nubian topographic zones is also far and away the most productive. Not only is alluvium more extensive and uninterrupted here than anywhere else, but this is also the only part of Nubia which can count on an annual overflow of the Nile similar to that which has enriched the soil of Lower Egypt for thousands of years. Moreover, the river itself is broad, placid, and navigable without hindrance from the Third Cataract to the Fourth. In the Dongola Reach nearly all commercial traffic still moves by river steamer and sail-boat today.

Not surprisingly, the Dongola Reach became in time the heart of ancient Nubia, the source of most of its prosperity and the cradle of its first indigenous civilization. Although Egyptian conquerors and colonists settled in Lower Nubia under the Old and Middle Kingdoms, it was not until the Dongola Reach was added to their dominion under the New Kingdom that the transplant of civilization really took root south of Aswan. In later centuries it was at Napata, near the upper end of the Dongola Reach, that the great Nubian kings established their own seat of power, and it was from here that they embarked on the wars of conquest which made them for a time Pharaohs of Egypt as well. Here too the great medieval kingdom of Makouria had its capital, in the city which has given the region its name.

Entering the Dongola Reach from the north, we have passed beyond the totally rainless belt of the Sahara. The modern town of Dongola records about one inch of rainfall annually, in the midsummer months (Fig. 7). Although this trifling precipitation has no effect in the open desert, it supports an intermittent growth of vegetation along the broad, shallow *wadis* which meander over its surface. Stunted, thorny acacia trees are joined, after the summer runoff, by considerable stands of grass. From here southwards all travel need no longer hug the banks of the Nile – particularly since the introduction of the camel within the last 2,500 years. From the Dongola Reach, overland trails cross the steppeland to the south-east and south-west, one rejoining the Nile far upstream, the other leading away to the great pasturelands of the western Sudan and beyond. Over these trails

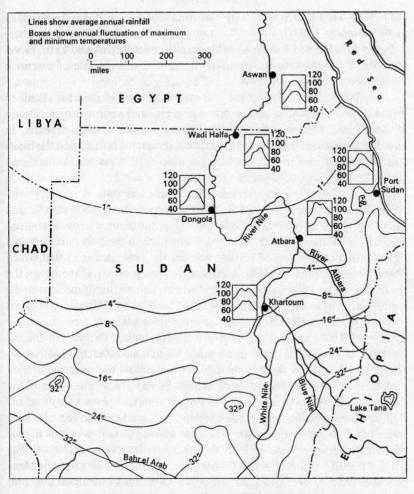

Fig. 7. Climate in Nubia and the Central Sudan

have come not only trading caravans but invading nomads, who have played an intermittent but important role in the history of Upper Nubia, and who still today appear regularly along the banks of the Nile.

THE ABU HAMED REACH

The Fourth Cataract, near Kareima, marks the limit of the fertile Dongola Reach. For the first half of the historic period it also marks, so far as our knowledge goes, the limit of Nubia itself. Beyond is another region of barren granite which, if topographically less rugged than the *Batn el Hajar*, is certainly no more productive. It is today the least populated stretch of the Nile between Khartoum and the sea, and is utilized as much for grazing as for farming.

In the Abu Hamed Reach, as in all granite zones, the course of the Nile is impeded by cataracts, shoals, and innumerable islands. Here, however, the accidents of geography have added a further impediment to navigation. The south-westerly course of the river between Abu Hamed and Debba means that in this region, and in this region alone, the prevailing direction of wind and current are the same. The usual practice of sailing upstream and drifting downstream is not a practical possibility in the Abu Hamed Reach. Downstream travel may be rapid indeed, but upstream navigation without power is usually out of the question.

If the Second Cataract checked the southwards spread of Egyptian power for a thousand years, the Fourth Cataract had a similar effect in the following millennium. Indeed, outright Egyptian control never extended beyond the Dongola Reach, and it was not until around 500 BC that the Egyptianized civilization of Napata was finally transplanted to the fertile Shendi Reach, above the Fifth Cataract. In the centuries of the Meroitic era (c. 300 BC to AD 300), however, the wealth and power of the upstream region ultimately outstripped those of the Dongola Reach itself.

It is a suggestive fact that there are impressive Meroitic monuments in the Shendi Reach and in the Dongola Reach (as well as in the Abri-Delgo Reach), but none at all in the intervening Abu Hamed Reach. In all probability travel between the two regions did not follow the river at all, but took the present-day caravan route across the Bayuda Steppe. If so, then the spread of civilization beyond the Fourth Cataract presumably had to wait upon the development of the overland caravan trade, in the last centuries BC. This may explain why the Abu Hamed Reach does not figure importantly in any phase of Nubian history; it is equally devoid of important remains from the Napatan–Meroitic civilization and from the high period of the medieval kingdoms. Its only conspicuous relics belong to the Medieval age of military feudalism, when this area, with its numerous and inaccessible islands, provided a perfect refuge for predatory warlords.

THE SHENDI REACH

The uppermost portion of what we shall choose to call Nubia extends from about the mouth of Atbara River to the confluence of the Blue and White Niles. The Shendi Reach is similar in most respects to the Dongola Reach, save that the granite rocks of the basement complex are much closer to the surface, and break through in numerous *jebels* and extensive local outcrops. The largest of these, straddling the Nile a few miles north of Khartoum, has produced the Shabaloka Gorge and the Sixth Cataract. Except within the Shabaloka Gorge there is nearly continuous alluvium along both banks of the river, and farming villages are numerous and well populated.

In the Shendi Reach we have entered the true Sudan – a belt of semi-desert grassland and scattered thorn trees extending all the way across Africa south of the Sahara. In this region pastoral nomads are very much a part of the human scene; during part of each year they camp in large numbers along the Nile Valley, just beyond the limits of cultivation.

The Shendi Reach, like the Abu Hamed Reach, has been only imperfectly explored by archaeologists. However, it contains a number of well-known and important monumental sites which have been the subject of sporadic investigation since the beginning of the twentieth century. All of the sites so far known date either from the late Napatan and Meroitic periods (c. 500 BC to AD 300) or from the later Christian period (c. AD 1000–1500), and all of them are located to the east of the Nile. By far the most famous is Meroë, whose name was known to us from the writings of Herodotus and Strabo long before its actual whereabouts was discovered, and which has given its name to the Meroitic culture. There are other ruined Meroitic cities, some of them still unexcavated, not only along the banks of the Nile but in the dry hinterland between the valleys of the Nile and the Atbara – the so-called 'Island of Meroë' (not actually an island but a broad steppeland bounded on three sides by rivers).

So far no archaeological sites are known from the west bank of the Nile, and only a couple of isolated Meroitic cemeteries have been discovered upstream from Khartoum. However, this probably reflects nothing more than the absence of proper archaeological exploration. For the time being we remain ignorant of the ultimate limits to which Egyptianized culture penetrated into Africa; we can only say that systematic archaeological and historical knowledge stops at the confluence of the Niles (modern Khartoum). We may, therefore, take this point as a convenient upper limit for Nubia, without prejudice to the possibility that we may one day hope to include areas still further to the south.

CLIMATE

Nubia enjoys, if that is the proper word, one of the most extreme climates on earth. At Wadi Halfa, on the border between Lower and Upper Nubia, the mean daily temperature from May to September is about 90 degrees; the daily high nearly always exceeds 100 degrees, and may reach above 120 degrees (Fig. 7). Winter, from November to March, is mild, with mean daily temperatures between 60 and 70 degrees, and occasional cold spells when the thermometer drops nearly to freezing.[5]

The effects of summer heat are somewhat mitigated by absence of humidity. The northern half of Nubia, from Aswan to Dongola, is for all practical purposes rainless. Sprinkles of a few minutes' duration occur locally and sporadically in the winter and spring, but a generation may elapse before rain falls a second time on the same spot. Humidity seldom exceeds 20 per cent in the winter, and 15 per cent in the summer.

South of Dongola a somewhat different climatic régime is encountered. Here there is a well defined 'rainy' season of eight to ten weeks, in July and August. The amount of actual precipitation is small, increasing as one goes southwards from about one inch at Dongola to seven inches at Khartoum. However, the frequent leaden skies and high humidity, both day and night, add greatly to the discomfort of the summer season. The sticky, hot spell immediately following the rains is particularly unpleasant.

Wind is another frequent irritant in the Nubian environment. Over the whole of the eastern Sahara the wind blows out of the north the year around, seldom varying in direction more than 45 degrees. Enormous trailing dunes on the lee side of desert outcrops, all pointing virtually due south, testify both to the force and to the constant direction of the winds. A steady wind of 10–15 miles per hour is usual, but gales with gusts up to 50 miles per hour occur at least once a month, and frequently keep up for two or three days at a time. Crossing the bed of the Nile, the high winds pick up a load of fine riverain sand and powdery silt which is duly deposited on everyone and everything along the river's east (lee) bank. Winter winds bring masses of cold air from the desert interior, and can make life surprisingly uncomfortable in the large, bare, and unheated Nubian houses. Summer winds are more welcome, for they generally mark the onset of a cooling trend. For the most part, the extremes of winter weather are much more disliked by Nubians than are those of summer; rain is particularly dreaded because of the damage it does to mud houses and other structures.

Throughout the year, the Nubian weather runs in cycles of one to two weeks' duration. A mild spell in winter, or a hot spell in summer, will become warmer on each successive day until it is abruptly terminated by a blast of wind out of the north. Strong, gusty winds persist for two or three days, then taper off. A day or two of mild, relatively calm weather is followed by a second warming trend as the cycle begins again.

The prevailing winds have been an active and important factor in the Nubian environment throughout history. On the beneficial side, they make possible upstream navigation on the Nile even in the face of a stiff current. All along the great river, except in the reverse bend between Abu Hamed and Debba, the trend of wind and the trend of current are in opposite directions, so that navigation is facilitated in either direction. In the cataract regions a stiff breeze is a necessity for crossing the river; without it the unwieldy craft used in Upper Nubia (*nuggars*) are at the mercy of the current, and are liable to be swept onto shoals and rapids. Hence in these regions all river traffic comes to a halt on the comparatively rare still days.

Detrimental effects of the wind can be seen in the constant encroachment of dunes on agricultural land, particularly on the west (windward) bank of the Nile. Not only fields but houses as well are often swallowed up, for any structure not built in a protected location will immediately begin accumulating a dune along its northern and western side. Eventually the weight of drifted sand against unreinforced mud walls makes houses too dangerous for further occupation. Migration of dunes has resulted in the abandonment of a good many villages, as well as large farming tracts, in the recent past. This process, disastrous to the inhabitants, is of course a boon to the archaeologist, for it means that ancient remains on the west bank of the Nile are often extraordinarily well preserved. Houses are sometimes buried to the rooftops before wind and time can do their work of erosion. In addition, the necessity for frequent repair and rebuilding makes for wonderfully consistent and clear-cut stratification of habitation sites.

Nubia's harsh and exacting climate has undoubtedly been repellent to most outsiders. While it has not protected the region from frequent invasion, it may be partly responsible for the relatively short duration of most foreign occupations, and for the lack of permanent colonization. On the other hand the Nubian climate is not in any absolute sense detrimental to settlement or to productivity, or even very important to them. It is the Nile, rising in highlands 2,000 miles further south, which brings both the water and the soil necessary to life in Nubia. Nothing is demanded of the local environment except a growing season long enough to take advantage of these exotic resources. Neither Nubia nor Egypt contributes a drop of water to the Nile, nor an acre of their own soil to its banks.

If the Nile is the central feature of the Nubian scene, it is by no means an unvarying one. The annual fluctuation in volume between the season of low water and the season of high water is enormous, amounting in fact to an increase of over 1,000 per cent. The normal minimum of about 60 million cubic feet per day is reached at the beginning of May; this rises to nearly 800 million cubic feet per day at the beginning of September.[6]

In Egypt the rise and fall of the Nile, annually replenishing silt over enormous areas of the floodplain, is well known, and in fact served as the basis for one of history's oldest calendars. Nevertheless, the natural régime of the river is erratic in many respects. According to Vercoutter,

. . . if the flood is beneficial to Egypt, it can also be catastrophic. The rise of the Nile is sudden, sharp; left to itself the towering current would uproot everything in its path. And most important of all, the flood is entirely undependable; true, it arrives every year, but hardly three times out of ten does it deliver the amount of water necessary for cultivation – the other seven, it brings too little or too much.[7]

The 'seven fat years and seven lean years' in Joseph's time[8] are the best-known instance of the Nile's capriciousness, but the account of the Jesuit

Father Jeronymo Lobo attests to the same uncertainty in the seventeenth century of our era. Speaking of the gauge at Cairo where the flow of the Nile was annually measured, he wrote:

> On the walls of this tower, from the bottom upward, are made marks, or degrees; and, by ancient custom, as more or fewer of these are covered with water, the magistrates make it to be proclaimed every night in the streets, that the knowledge of how many degrees the Nile hath that day overflowed may be general. This proclamation begins at the end of July, and continues all August, when the rise or fall of the river is particularly observed by the degrees. The abundance of the year is thus guessed at. When the water covers not sixteen degrees, the defect of it suggests fear of a famine; rising towards twenty-five, the higher it ascends the fairer are the hopes of a fruitful season; passing that number, they are assaulted with new fears of death, the quantity of water not allowing them to sow, or house their harvest. These months pass not away without some trouble and anxiety, the weather being every where subject to irregularity, so rain is sometimes too much, sometimes too little, by which the crop is altered.[9]

The Egyptian Nile has been trained and subdued over thousands of years by means of dikes, diversions, and reservoirs; the process is still going on today. The Nubian Nile, equally unpredictable, remained untamed until the twentieth century. Even today the Nubian farmer is beset by many of the same uncertainties which confronted the Egyptian at the dawn of history.

The Nubian Nile does not ordinarily overflow its banks, save in areas such as Letti and Kerma where it may spill over into its own abandoned channels. The sporadic floods which do occur are an unmitigated disaster, sweeping away houses and fields alike. The most recent major flood, in 1946, is said to have destroyed 90 per cent of the houses in the villages around Wadi Halfa.

Although the river can usually be counted on to stay within its banks, the variation in level between high Nile and low Nile is enormous – particularly in granite zones where the channel is narrow and deep. Fields which are within a few feet of the water's edge at the flood season are left literally high and dry, sometimes as much as fifty feet above the river, at the slack season. Irrigation is difficult or even impossible with the simple man- or animal-powered devices traditional in the Nile Valley. It is estimated that the ox-driven waterwheel (*saqia*) can irrigate four or five acres at one time during the high-water season, but no more than one third of that area at the lowest season.[10] The man-powered lever-lift (*shaduf*) is comparatively little used in Nubia, as it is incapable of a sufficient lift to bring water to most parts of the floodplain. Next to the shortage of soil itself, the difficulty of raising irrigation water over the high, steep riverbanks has been the principal factor inhibiting Nubia's economic development throughout history.

Unrestrained by dikes and flood control measures, the Nubian Nile shifts periodically within its narrow bed. In the process, the region's scanty alluvium may be partially redistributed, as floods carry away silt from one bank of the river and deposit it further downstream, perhaps against the opposite bank. New islands are formed from time to time, and old ones disappear as the channels which formerly separated them from the banks dry up. (Many islands are of course separated from the mainland only at the high-water season.) Population shifts inevitably follow. We find the remains of once flourishing villages where today there is no arable land to support them, or we find areas of broad fields and prosperous modern villages with no archaeological remains to match.

Under the circumstances prevailing in much of Nubia, the agricultural subsistence base is necessarily precarious. A drop of a few feet in the level of the Nile may make irrigation impossible over large areas, and may take half or more of the arable land out of production in a given year. A series of low years can only and inevitably result in wholesale depopulation. We shall observe this process more than once in the course of Nubian history, for the rainfall in the East African highlands has been far from constant. The Nubians, economically immune to the rigours of their own climate, have instead been at the mercy of climatic fluctuations thousands of miles to the south.

Annual fluctuation of the Nile level also affects navigation on the river. Of the thirty or more cataracts between Aswan and Khartoum, all but three (the First, Second, and Fourth) can be negotiated, albeit with difficulty, at the high Nile. As the flow of the river drops, however, hundreds of rocks and shoals emerge in the granite regions, and long-distance navigation becomes an impossibility. Boats are numerous both in *Batn el Hajar* and in the Abu Hamed Reach today, but during most of the year they can be used only to cross the river.

We know from numerous inscriptions that an extensive Egyptian waterborne commerce passed through the *Batn el Hajar* during the Middle and New Kingdoms. Unless the average flow of the Nile was substantially higher than it is today (a distinct possibility during the Middle Kingdom, as we shall see), we can be fairly confident that these expeditions must have been confined to the months between July and October.

FLORA

Biologically, the Nubian environment divides itself quite readily into two life-zones: the river littoral and the desert. Vegetation along the riverbank is hardly affected by latitude; it is for all practical purposes the same from Khartoum to Aswan. The desert, however, supports vegetation only where it receives rainfall. North of Dongola it can hardly be called a life-zone at all.[11]

The date palm (*Phoenix dactylifera*) might serve as the trade-mark for the whole of the Nile Valley. From Khartoum to Cairo, there are few places where at least a fringe of these trees cannot be seen bordering the river. Although properly a domestic tree (and the source of Nubia's only cash crop), date palms are so numerous and so little tended that they appear as part of the natural vegetation. They are seen most frequently in rows between cultivated fields and in an irregular fringe along the riverbank, but in places they have also been planted in dense groves.

A native of Nubia and the Sudan, today much less abundant than the date palm, is the little, low-branching *dom* palm (*Hyphaena thebaica*). These trees grow individually or in small, scattered clumps along the desert margin; they are seldom found close to water. The hard, white nut of the *dom* was once the principal material used in making buttons, but today it has no commercial value. However, the trunk of the *dom*, which is considerably harder than that of the date palm, furnishes roof timbers for Nubian houses.

Most of the other trees found in Nubia are members of the ubiquitous acacia family, of which at least half a dozen species occur. These thorny, rather sparse-leafed trees are scattered in groves and open stands along the floodplain where the ground has not been cleared for cultivation. Their principal value is as browse for goats and camels. The wood of the most common acacia, called *sunt* (*A. arabica*), is the main source of timber for boats and for house doors and windows.

Tamarisk (*Tamarix articulata*) forms dense, tangled thickets along the steeply sloping riverbanks and in nearby dune areas. Carpets of new tamarisk shoots spring up each year below the high-water level as the Nile recedes, only to be swept away at the next flood season. Several other trees and shrubs grow sporadically in Nubia, but none of them contributes significantly to the environment either economically or aesthetically.

Apart from trees, most of the vegetation seen along the banks of the Nile comprises cultivated plants of one sort or another. These will be described in later pages (Chapter 2). Uncultivated portions of the floodplain are often entirely bare, or support only a few low-growing shrubs. However, tough, spiky halfa grass (*Cynodon dactylon*) grows thickly along the steep-cut banks of river channels, and wherever else it can find moisture. The young shoots provide important forage for domestic animals, but the mature plant is spiny and inedible.

In the cataract regions of Nubia, a fringe of papyrus reed (*Cyperus papyrus*) can be seen at the water's edge during the low Nile. This plant was once abundant along the whole length of the river, but it has now disappeared from Egypt and most of Lower Nubia as a result of intensive cultivation of the foreshores.

The vegetation of the Nubian Desert, when present, consists mostly of various acacia trees, tough, wiry grasses, and low-growing shrubs. The amount of vegetation which the desert supports is governed entirely by rainfall, and increases gradually but continuously from north to south along with the rainfall itself. The sandstone plateau adjoining Lower Nubia is entirely devoid of permanent vegetation, but local rainstorms will produce a short-lived crop of grass almost anywhere. South of Wadi Halfa, scattered acacia trees as well as stands of grass are found in some of the larger *wadis* of the *Batn el Hajar*, which collect runoff from a very large area. In the Dongola Reach, as well as in the Shendi Reach, a fairly regular scattering of acacias as well as good seasonal stands of grass can be found in nearly all of the desert *wadis*, and by the time Khartoum is reached they have become a continuous cover over the steppeland east and west of the river. It is only here that nomads find a secure livelihood; they have been an important element in the population for many centuries.

ANIMAL LIFE

Nubian rock drawings from the Neolithic and even from the early historic periods depict a variety of large game animals, including elephant, rhinoceros, hippopotamus, giraffe, and probably buffalo. Intensive human occupation has since displaced all of these creatures. Of the many members of the antelope family which once roamed the lower Nile Valley, the only survivor today is the little Thomson's gazelle (*Gazella thomsonii*). Solitary individuals of this species may be encountered in the desert *wadis* up to thirty miles from the Nile; they come down at night to feed and drink along the riverbank. Jackals, foxes, and, reputedly, hyenas, lead a similar furtive existence between the desert and the sown. Apart from these scavengers, the only other wild mammalia in Nubia are the ground-dwelling rodents which everywhere accompany human habitation. Domestic animals, an important part of the scene since early times, will be discussed in the next chapter.

Bird life is seasonally abundant in Nubia, for many migrating species follow the Nile Valley. Most characteristic of the larger birds are wild geese, which are very often seen in pairs, skimming along just above the water's surface. Cranes and egrets are also common along the riverbanks. Kites are the most numerous of Nubia's scavengers; they usually hover on the fringes of human settlements. The most striking of smaller birds is the colourfully marked hoopoe, which stalks among the fields, continuously bobbing its head. Crows and sparrows infest the cultivated areas and do extensive damage to grain crops.

More than forty species of fish are known from the Nile, and nearly all are edible. The Nile perch (*Lates niloticus*) is particularly and justly esteemed for its flavour. Archaeology reveals that fishing was once an

39

important Nubian subsistence activity, but it is comparatively little practised today. Other denizens of the Nile are large aquatic lizards (*waran*)
and crocodiles, although the latter are becoming scarce north of the Third
Cataract. Farther south, they are still commercially hunted for their
skins.

Terrestrial reptiles are much less common in Nubia than in more humid
regions to the south. There are two poisonous snakes, the cobra (*Naja* sp.)
and the horned viper (*Cerastes cornutus*), and several non-poisonous ones,
but they are not often seen. Lizards are similarly scarce except for the
house-dwelling spotted gecko, which appears on the walls of every Nubian
home during the *nimitti* season (see below).

House flies swarm around every settlement and animal pen, although not
in the extreme numbers sometimes found in Egypt. The tsetse fly is happily
absent, and mosquitoes are not a problem. Their place is taken, however,
by another pest particular to Nubia, the *nimitti* (*Simulium* sp.). It is a
minute, gnat-like flying creature which swarms along the riverbank in
dense, humming clouds during the spring months of each year. The black
or Dongola *nimitti* (*S. damnosum*), found chiefly between the Fourth and
Third Cataracts, has an irritating bite, making it necessary to protect
exposed areas of skin. At the height of the *nimitti* season, dwellers in the
Dongola Reach who must go out of doors wear a sock-like veil of gauze
over the head and neck. Some Dongolawis make the most of the unpleasant necessity by using the brightest of coloured materials for their
'*nimitti* veils' as a further means of personal adornment, albeit one which
entirely hides the facial features.

Green or Halfa *nimittis* (*S. griseicollis*), found chiefly in the *Batn el
Hajar* and Lower Nubia, swarm even more thickly than their black cousins.
Unlike Dongola *nimittis*, they are as much at home indoors as out, and
they are a plague in every Nubian house during the spring months.
Although they do not bite or sting, their proximity causes a severe asth-
matic reaction in many persons. Some Wadi Halfa residents used to camp
out in the desert, miles from the river, for several weeks each year in order
to avoid the worst effects of *nimitti*.[12]

One other unpleasant resident of Nubia is the scorpion. It is found
chiefly in settled areas, and often makes its home in roof thatch. Infestation
by scorpions and other vermin is a reason often given for the temporary or
permanent abandonment of houses. Happily none of the several species
found in Nubia has a deadly sting, and scorpion stings, unlike snake bites,
are not a cause for grave concern among the region's populace.

More harmful than any form of life so far mentioned is bilharzia, the
minute blood fluke (*Schistosoma* sp.) that causes schistosomiasis, or
bilharziasis. 'Snail fever', as the disease is popularly called, has been a
spreading curse throughout the tropics, and is probably nowhere more

prevalent than in the Nile Valley. The larvae which cause this debilitating malady are nurtured in aquatic snails, then swim free in stagnant water until they find an opportunity to invade the human bloodstream, where they begin attacking the liver and other organs. A gradual weakening and organic decay begins, and may continue for twenty years or more.

It has been estimated that as much as 50 per cent of Egypt's peasant population suffers from schistosomiasis. The figure for Nubia is probably not so high, due to the swiftness of the river and the absence of irrigation canals, but the disease is undoubtedly prevalent. Malaria, tuberculosis, and trachoma are other maladies common in Nubia today.

NATURAL RESOURCES

Nubia's slender agricultural production could never do more than feed her own population. The resources for which the region was perennially coveted, and repeatedly invaded, were not necessities but luxuries: gold, ivory and slaves. Although none of these commodities necessarily originated within the borders of Nubia, all had to pass through it on their way to Egypt. The traffic in natural resources brought little but misery to Nubia's people for many centuries, but in due time they turned middlemen and were able to derive a considerable profit from it.

Curiously enough, the commodity which apparently first attracted foreigners to Nubia was copper. The oldest known Egyptian settlement south of Aswan, at Buhen (near the Second Cataract), seems to have been devoted to the smelting of copper ore, which was then probably shipped downriver by boat. The actual source of the ore has never been discovered. It may have been soon exhausted, for the smelting operation lasted only a couple of centuries.[13] There may also have been some copper production at the Wadi Allaqi,[14] in Lower Nubia, but for most of its history Nubia was an importer and not an exporter of copper and bronze.

Gold, although scarce, is the only metal to be found in most of Nubia. Pockets of ore occur here and there throughout the whole vast region where the igneous basement complex is exposed, both in Egypt and in the Sudan. The desert upland from the Nile Valley to the Red Sea is dotted with scores of abandoned mines and prospect holes,[15] for the pharaohs had an insatiable appetite for gold.

The most numerous and most productive of Egypt's mines were those along the Wadi Allaqi and its tributaries, between Lower Nubia and the Red Sea. They lay in the desert far to the east of the inhabited river valley, and were in a sense not part of Nubia, but their situation had an important bearing on Nubian history. First of all, they obliged Egypt to control the Nile Valley as far upstream as the mouth of the Wadi Allaqi, seventy miles south of Aswan, in order to keep open the main caravan route to the mines.

Second, they may have placed a considerable demand on Nubia as a source of labour for the mines, although this is not definitely attested by historical records.

A number of much less productive gold workings were scattered along the Nile Valley itself, chiefly in the *Batn el Hajar*. Literary sources have less to say about them than about the desert mines, but they are well attested archaeologically. A particularly productive cluster of mines was located at Duweishat, south of Semna; mining activity here has continued sporadically down to modern times.[16]

Other important inorganic products of Nubia in ancient times were fine-grained igneous stones. The pink granite of Aswan, although too hard and heavy to serve as ordinary building material, was highly prized for monolithic constructions such as columns, obelisks, and stelae. As the use of granite was practically confined to royal monuments, the demand was necessarily limited and was easily met by the quarries in the immediate vicinity of Aswan. Somewhat more remote were the quarries in the desert west of Toshka (Lower Nubia) from which came the diorite favoured for royal statues in the Old and Middle Kingdoms.[17]

During the heyday of Egyptian and Nubian civilization there was also extensive quarrying of sandstone in many parts of Nubia for the building of local temples, but this was never significant as an export industry.

Wild animals were once abundant along the whole of the Nile Valley, and supplied a variety of human wants and needs. As intensive cultivation spread over the lower valley, however, the indigenous animal life gradually disappeared, and Egypt came more and more to rely upon Nubia for animal products no longer available within her own borders. Among these were ostrich eggs and feathers, various kinds of skins, live animals for the amusement of the pharaonic court, and, above all, ivory.

We know comparatively little about the organization of Egypt's ivory trade, although it is continually mentioned in texts relating to Kush. Egyptian military expeditions apparently took the opportunity to collect ivory whenever they penetrated into Upper Nubia; whether they obtained it from the natives or from the original source is uncertain. If there was any ivory trade in the intervals between raids, it must necessarily have depended to some extent on Nubian suppliers. Elephants ranged at least as far north as the Fifth Cataract 2,000 years ago; it was apparently the Meroitic inhabitants of Upper Nubia who first tamed the African elephant as a beast of war. Today elephants are found only in the equatorial regions of the Sudan, far to the south of Nubia.

The disappearance of wild game from Egypt was repeated, although perhaps at a slower rate, in Nubia. From being a primary supplier of animal products, Nubia became simply an entrepôt through which they passed on their way northward. However, the trade continued to be important to the extent that it could be taxed, or at times plundered, by the dwellers along the Middle Nile.

What was true of the animal game was equally true of the human game. Nubia was above all else a source of slaves to pharaonic Egypt. The numbers of captives must have been enormous, even if they are much exaggerated in some of the conquest stelae. Slave-trading was certainly a primary objective of the numerous Egyptian military expeditions against Nubia, and it is noteworthy that these operations kept up, under one pretext or another, long after the region was nominally pacified and annexed to Egypt itself. In later times the Nubians in their turn became slave-raiders as well as slave-traders, the principal victims being the more primitive tribes further up the Nile.

The traffic in slaves through Nubia continued to be important long after the sun set on pharaonic Egypt. It was the principal subject of a trade treaty between Egypt and Nubia, enacted in AD 652, which remained in force throughout the Middle Ages.[18] It was also the main consideration which impelled Egypt's re-conquest of the Sudan at the beginning of the nineteenth century, the subsequent intervention of Great Britain, and finally the Mahdist rebellion which engulfed the country at the end of the century.

2
THE PEOPLE OF THE CORRIDOR

Who are the Nubians? We cannot speak of them simply as the inhabitants of the Nile corridor, for this land has seldom been the exclusive domain of any one people. Foreign conquerors, alien merchants and adventurers, and friendly as well as hostile nomads have always rubbed shoulders with the indigenous peasant population of Nubia, and have contributed no little to its cultural as well as to its racial history. It is, however, the settled riverain farmers, descended in all probability from Nubia's earliest inhabitants, with whom we shall be particularly concerned throughout this book, and whom we shall designate as Nubians.

We can differentiate the modern Nubians from some of their neighbours on racial grounds, from others on cultural grounds, and from all of them on linguistic grounds. For much of the past, however, linguistic evidence is lacking, and racial evidence is ambiguous. Historically, we shall be obliged to use the term 'Nubian' in a cultural sense, to refer to the settled farming peoples of the Nile Valley above Aswan[1] whose cultures, though not originally derived from Egypt, were strongly influenced by their Egyptian neighbours. We cannot always be certain about the racial, ethnic, or linguistic character of these peoples; they may have varied to some extent from region to region and from age to age. It is, however, primarily through their cultural debris (i.e. through archaeology) that we know them, and here we see evidence of a general continuity of development throughout Nubian history, regardless of the comings and goings of particular peoples. It is with this continuing thread of cultural development, rather than with the accidents of history *per se*, that we shall be primarily concerned.

Today, however, 'Nubian' is less meaningful as a cultural term than formerly, for the expansion of agriculture and the general adoption of Islam have gradually obliterated the cultural differences between the Nubians and other farming peoples of the Sudan. The term is therefore used today, both in Egypt and in the Sudan, in a more restricted sense, to designate a specific and self-acknowledged ethnic minority which occupies the Nile Valley between the First and Fourth Cataracts. These people are

44

racially distinct from the majority of Egyptians, though not from other Sudanese peoples, by virtue of their fairly high proportion of Negro blood. What chiefly sets the modern Nubians apart from their southern neighbours is their language, which belongs to an old African family (Eastern Sudanic) antedating the introduction of Islam and of Arabic. To the south, the dwellers on the Nile above the Fourth Cataract are racially indistinguishable from the Nubians, and were formerly also speakers of Nubian languages, but today they speak only Arabic. These people are no longer considered, and do not consider themselves, as Nubians.

In short, 'Nubian' today is primarily a linguistic term, designating an island of surviving African speech surrounded on all sides by Arabic (Figs. 8, 9). It is important to recognize, though, that the people whom we call, and who call themselves, Nubians today are not the only descendants of the Nubians of yesterday, and that their present-day habitat comprises no more than half of the Nubia of old. However, it is the self-proclaiming Nubians of today whose culture most fully preserves whatever survives from the pre-Islamic past, and who acknowledge a certain sense of identity with the earlier inhabitants of the region.[2] It is primarily these people who will concern us, as representing the end-product of the processes of history considered in this book. Their present-day culture has still much to tell us about the Nubia of the past, and we shall be obliged to turn to ethnographic evidence again and again in attempting to reconstruct the cultures of earlier times.

Today's Nubians number perhaps 200,000 individuals, of whom about one quarter live in Egypt and the remainder in the Sudan. Before the building of the Aswan dams they formed a nearly continuous population bloc along the Nile Valley between Aswan in the north and Debba, at the bottom of the great reverse bend of the river, in the south. There were, however, enclaves of non-Nubian settlers within the Nubian 'heartland'. There were also, long before the dams made emigration a necessity, scattered colonies of Nubians living beyond the borders of their homeland, both in Egypt and in the Sudan.

PHYSICAL CHARACTERISTICS

The visitor to Cairo or Alexandria will encounter considerable numbers of Nubians, as waiters, servants, and taxi drivers. Comparing their facial features and their café-au-lait complexions with those of the light-skinned Egyptian population, he will probably think of them first of all as Negroes. The visitor to Khartoum, capital of the Sudan, will also meet many Nubians, not only as waiters and cab drivers, but at every level of society and government up to and including cabinet ministers. Observing their dress and manners, and comparing them with the much darker southern and western Sudanese who form the bulk of Khartoum's labouring population, he will almost certainly think of them primarily as Arabs.

Both characterizations of the Nubian – as Negro and as Arab – are in some sense correct. The Nubian has a much higher proportion of African blood than the Egyptian, amounting perhaps to 50 per cent of his total genetic make-up. The Nubians are at the same time the most thoroughly Islamized of all the Sudan's peoples, even while they cling to a mother-tongue which is purely African. In dress and manner they follow the time-honoured conventions of the Arab world (cf. Pl. IIIa).

Racially, the Nubians of today are little different from many other peoples of the northern Sudan. They exhibit an old, stable blend of African Negro and Mediterranean Caucasian elements, in which the two strains are about equally represented. The most common skin pigmentation is a light to medium brown – about the same as that of North American Indians or Polynesians, but without the bronze tone. Individuals vary considerably in colouring, however, for there has been constant intermarriage on the one hand with black slaves from the south, and on the other with Egyptians and occasional European peoples who garrisoned the frontiers of the Ottoman Empire.

Aside from pigmentation, African ancestry is most prominently proclaimed in the hair form of the Nubians, which is almost always frizzy or kinky. Everted lips are common but by no means universal. Many Nubians have the sharp, aquiline features characteristic of the pure Arab. Facial scarification, practised by many of the peoples of the Sudan, is only occasionally seen among the Nubians except in the case of the southern-most (Dongolawi) group. Scarification is confined to the cheeks, and most often takes the form of three parallel, vertical scars on each cheek. Other patterns are three short horizontal scars, or scars in the shape of the letters H or T.

The majority of individuals are of medium stature and build. Nubians are on the average perhaps an inch taller than Egyptians; they are notably shorter than the Nilotic giants of the southern Sudan. Corpulence is prized, up to a point, as a mark of beauty in women and as a sign of affluence in men, so that one encounters a great many stout individuals, especially among those in later life. On the whole, however, younger Nubians tend to be wiry and well-knit. The excessive thinness characteristic of the southern Sudanese population is rarely seen.[3]

CULTURAL CHARACTERISTICS

Culturally, the Nubians of today have absorbed most of the Islamic traditions of their northern neighbours while retaining certain indigenous characteristics as well. Although proud to a degree of their distinct ethnic identity, all Nubians also consider themselves Arabs, and most can trace their descent from the Prophet or from one of the early Caliphs, as a good Moslem should. Arabic is the second language of most of the male population, and the only written language. Probably 50 per cent of Nubian men can read and write at least a few words – a higher rate of literacy than is found in any other ethnic group in the Sudan. Command of Arabic among Nubian women is much less common, and literacy is almost non-existent.

Like most African peoples, the Nubians are in fact fairly recent converts to Islam. Unlike their neighbours, however, they are not converts from paganism, for they were Christian throughout the Middle Ages, and before that adhered to a succession of state cults of Egyptian origin. Consequently one does not encounter in Nubian culture the genuinely primitive survivals which are so conspicuous in the western Sudan or in Nigeria. There are instead Medieval Christian and even ancient Egyptian survivals.

The Nubian of today is nevertheless culturally as much an Arab as is the Egyptian *fellah*. Indeed, in some respects he is more so, for his culture has been even less modified by Western influence. Here is perhaps the outstanding cultural difference between Egypt and Nubia today. The northern land is gradually but inexorably being transformed into a modern, partially industrialized nation, while the Sudan clings, to some extent deliberately, to the traditions of medieval Islam. The Nubian man, unlike the Egyptian, will nearly always be found wearing the traditional Arab gown (*gellabiyah*) and turban (Pl. IIIa) in preference to Western dress, and will keep his womenfolk fairly rigorously secluded. Nubian women do not actually take the veil, but they always wear out of doors a loose black outer garment (*tob*) over the head and shoulders, and this is at least perfunctorily drawn across the mouth when a stranger approaches. Nubians are also conspicuously more attentive to their daily prayers than are their Egyptian neighbours, and make, at least publicly, a sincere effort to keep the *Ramadan* fast.

LANGUAGE

The only characteristic of modern Nubians which remains wholly and unmistakably African is their native speech. The Nubian dialects belong to the Sudanic family of languages, which were once widely and continuously distributed over much of north-east Africa. Nubian forms a distinct subgroup within the Sudanic family, having no close relatives except for some isolated languages of the western Sudan. Much more distantly related are the languages of the Shilluk, Nuer, Dinka, Masai, and other pagan tribes of the southern Sudan and adjoining countries. The fact that the Nubian languages have no close relatives elsewhere (with the exceptions just noted) complicates the problem of tracing the origins of the Nubian people, as we shall see in later pages.[4]

The Nubians of the Nile Valley are divided into three speech groups: the *Kanuz* (sing. *Kenzi*) in the north, the *Mahas* in the centre, and the *Danagla* (sing. *Dongolawi*) in the south. Curiously enough, the northern and southern of these dialects are mutually intelligible and are said to comprise a single language (*Dongola-Kanuz*), while the intervening Mahasi dialect is markedly distinct. Mahasi Nubians are obliged to converse with members of the other two groups in Arabic, as they are also with non-Nubian peoples. Arabic is also the one written language today, although in the Middle Ages an older form of the Mahasi dialect (Old Nubian) was written.

The Nubian languages as a whole provide their speakers with a sense of special identity, but dialect differences are apparently not recognized in the same way. Individual Nubians are apt to identify themselves by region – as Dongolawis or Aswanis – rather than by dialect, as Mahasi or Kenzi.

LIFE IN NUBIA

For 2,000 miles, from Khartoum to the sea, the Nile Valley is pre-eminently a land of mud villages and small fields. To a degree Egyptian *fellaheen*, Nubians, and Sudanese Arabs alike share the immemorial, earth-bound life of the peasant farmer. Within that rigid frame, however, there are differences in the pattern of human life and activity; differences resulting partly from environmental variation and partly from historical and cultural background. Life in Nubia today still exhibits distinctive features not found in Egypt or in the central Sudan.

Perhaps the most visibly distinct feature of Nubian culture is the Nubian house. It is large and spacious to a degree unmatched in Egypt, or else-where in the Sudan. The typical modern dwelling, except in the far north, is built of *jalus* (adobe or mud laid up in horizontal courses about one foot thick), and consists of several large rooms surrounding an open courtyard. One room, close to the front of the house, will always be specially decorated and furnished for the reception of guests. Another room, usually near the back of the house, will have both its floor and ceiling raised two or three feet above those in the rest of the house, and will be unwalled on the wind-ward (north) side. This room, designed to catch the breeze, serves as a veranda for relaxation and conversation during the hot season. Other rooms serve as required for cooking, sleeping, storage of grain and belongings, and as goat pens.[5] The usual residents of any house are a married couple and their offspring, although parents and unmarried brothers or sisters of the husband may also live in. If a man has two wives (comparatively rare in Nubia today), each has a separate house.

A distinctive and much-remarked feature of the modern Nubian house is its highly ornamented façade surrounding the main entrance, which opens directly into the courtyard. In Mahasi and Dongolawi houses the flat mud surface of the façade is carved into elaborate geometric patterns in low relief; these are often whitewashed as well (Pl. IIb). China saucers set into the designs add a further decorative note. Additional saucers, alone or in groups, may be set into the wall above each door in the house. In the north, the houses of the Kenzi Nubians usually have polychrome painted rather than carved decoration, which may cover the whole front wall of the house.[6]

Ceilings may be of split palm ribs (*gerid*) overlaid with mud, or they may simply be lightweight grass or woven mats, laid upon logs of acacia or palm. In the north, the Kenzi Nubians still prefer the vaulted brick ceiling of ancient and medieval times. Floors are universally of hard packed mud. Most houses are built initially with numerous rectangular window openings, but these are often simply blocked with mud, except for a slit at the top, since wooden shutters are expensive and must usually be purchased from itinerant carpenters. However, at least the 'reception' or guest room in most houses will be fitted with hinged shutters, which are often brightly painted. Doors are usually heavy and crudely made, often from three hand-wrought planks fastened together with home-made nails. They are not hinged, but pivot on a vertical beam which is lashed to the wall at the top, and rests in a hollowed-out pivot stone at the bottom. The closing mechanism is a heavy sliding wooden bolt. Front doors are fitted with ingenious home-made wooden locks, often bearing carved decoration.[7]

The only common item of furniture in Nubian houses is the *angareeb*, a native bed made of woven rope or split palm ribs stretched on a wooden frame, with a leg at each corner. There may be several of these in each room, for they serve as much for tables and chairs as they do for beds. Also occasionally seen are small tripod tables locally made from sheet iron. Most houses have broad, built-in mud benches (*mastabas*) along some of the walls, both within rooms and in the central courtyard. Clothing and personal belongings are stored in trunks or chests.

The large Nubian house of today contrasts sharply with the much smaller and more crowded dwellings of Egypt and of the central Sudan.[8] It is, however, a fairly recent development, having been introduced into Nubia from the south or west in modern times.[9] It has apparently spread northwards from the Shaiqiya to the Dongolawi and Mahasi[10] Nubians, but has not been adopted by the Kenzi in the north. Their compact, barrel-vaulted houses of mud brick (rather than *jalus*) preserve the architectural traditions of Medieval Nubia.

Also seen in every village are lightweight rectangular shelters known as *rakubas* (literally, 'portable'), made of several straw mats lashed to a framework of vertical and horizontal poles. Rakubas come in a variety of sizes and shapes, depending on the number of mats and poles available and their intended purpose. They serve as temporary summer shelters near the fields, and sometimes as animal shelters.

Like all Middle Eastern and North African peoples, the Nubian is by preference a village dweller. His villages, like his houses, lack the compactness and density characteristic of Egypt (cf. Pl. IIa). A Nubian village may vary in size from two or three to several hundred houses, depending primarily on the amount of farm land locally available. Even in the most densely settled areas, however, houses are rarely built directly contiguous to one another, and structures of more than one storey are unknown. In poor regions such as the *Batn el Hajar*, houses may be widely scattered in very small clusters, and sometimes even wholly isolated, while in more prosperous areas they form a continuous, straggling line along both sides of the river. In these areas it is often difficult to tell where one village ends and another begins. Houses usually stand immediately behind the fields, on the margin between desert and floodplain. Wherever possible they occupy elevated ground, to be out of the way of floods.[11]

In a typical Nubian village the buildings are nearly all alike, and all are private dwellings. Shopkeepers, if there are any, do business in one or more rooms within their ordinary houses. Only the largest villages have specialized shops, tea houses, and small mosques.

Needless to say, modern conveniences and public utilities do not exist in Nubia, save in a handful of administrative centres. The round of life and activity corresponds closely to the daylight hours; what light is required after dark is provided mainly by kerosene lanterns. Charcoal is the primary fuel for cooking and for heat, though kerosene stoves are also used. The airy Nubian houses are well designed to keep out the worst of the summer heat, but can be uncomfortably cold in winter. Since there are no fireplaces and little wood, the only defence against cold is to bundle up in warm clothing, and perhaps to huddle over a small heap of coals. Nubians are apt to accept the blistering heat of midsummer with good-humoured resignation, but complain vociferously of winter cold spells. The Nile is, of course, the universal source of water; carrying water (mostly in five-gallon gasoline tins, which are balanced on the head) is a primary obligation of Nubian girls.

Where houses are present, fields and date groves are never far away. A few favoured areas of Nubia, such as the Dongola Reach, present vistas of broad, waving fields worthy of the great valley of Egypt itself. Much more characteristic are small, irregular patches of cultivation along the riverbank, separated by broad expanses of dunes or by rocky headlands. Each cultivated area comprises a maze of tiny rectangular plots arranged along a network of small ditches (Pl. Ia), all of which are fed from one or more ox-driven waterwheels (*saqias*). Several families may contribute to the building and operation of a *saqia*; each has specifically defined water rights depending upon its contribution of materials and labour. This highly formalized pattern of mutuality has probably been an integrating force in Nubian society since the introduction of the *saqia* 2,000 years ago.

Holdings in irrigated land tend to be small and, through inheritance, have become highly fragmented as well. A single individual may own fields in several different localities, and an energetic farmer may cultivate additional fields leased from his neighbours. Very often, however, the lessees are non-Nubians, and sometimes even non-Sudanese, the Nubians preferring the role of landlord to that of tenant. Because of fragmented holdings families often maintain houses in several different villages and move about frequently.

For a description of modern Nubian farming, I can do no better than quote Bruce Trigger's distinguished *History and Settlement in Lower Nubia*.[12]

There are three sorts of arable land in the Nile Valley: *seluka* land, *saqia* and *shaduf* land, and basin land. A basin is a depression, usually lying between the natural levees of the river and the desert, into which the flood waters are directed [at the high Nile] and from which they can be drained off after the ground has been thoroughly soaked. In Egypt large basins are usually divided into small sections, and the water is passed on from higher to lower ones after being allowed to stand for a predetermined length of time. The basins between Khartoum and Kerma are smaller and simpler than the Egyptian ones; each has a feeder canal, one or more drains, and a few internal divisions. Basins allow for the efficient use of water but require organization and cooperation among large numbers of farmers.

The saqia lands are fields, often above the high-water mark, which are irrigated by an ox-driven waterwheel called a *saqia*. Some of these fields are natural; others have been laboriously built up with silt carried down from natural deposits high on the sides of the valley. The saqia, which was introduced into Egypt in Hellenistic times, is built of wood and consists of a large cogged wheel mounted horizontally on a vertical shaft over a supply of water. A horizontal beam projects from the upper part of the shaft to which one or two draft animals are yoked. This wheel drives a large vertical one to which a series of jars or gasoline tins is attached on an endless rope. When the oxen push the beam, each pot is filled in turn and carried to the top of the wheel where it is emptied into a trough built of stones and earth, which carries the water to the fields. These saqias may be worked by relays of oxen and some are in action twenty hours a day. The oxen are usually tended by a young boy.

Saqia land can support heavy crops and is usually intensively cultivated. To conserve and direct the water supply, the fields are divided into small soaking beds separated from one another by small dirt walls. Saqia land can yield up to 350 bushels of wheat an acre.[13] The total holding watered by a saqia is usually no more than 10 feddans (a feddan is slightly less than one acre), of which about one-third is worked at any one time. The area that can be irrigated varies according to the height to which the water must be lifted. At high Nile with a lift of 2 meters, a saqia may water 4 or 5 feddans; during the winter, when the lift may be up to 8 meters, it may water only 2·5 feddans and, during the early summer when the river is low and evaporation high, 1 to 1·5 feddans. If the plain is low and broad, saqias located far back from the river may draw water from a well. Along fertile stretches of the river, saqias may be found at intervals of every 300 yards.

As a lifting device the saqia is inefficient, since a good part of the water being raised is lost, and nearly half the crop must go to feed the oxen which run the machine, unless natural fodder is available. When the soil is not inundated it becomes either salty or sand-covered so that it must frequently be dressed with new earth dug from terraces which are beyond the reach of lift irrigation. This soil is called *sebakh*. The saqia's main advantage is that it can be made entirely from local materials. Minor repairs can be made by the owner, and experts for construction and major repairs are easy to find. Being a self-contained unit it is ideally suited for use on small individual land-holdings.

The *shaduf* is first recorded in Egypt in the New Kingdom. It is nothing more than a counterpoised lever with a bucket at one end – easy to construct and worked by hand. It can lift water up to 3 meters, but the higher the lift, the fewer the strokes that can be made per minute. With a lift of 2 meters a shaduf can water about half a feddan. They are usually used to water vegetable patches during the flood season.[14]

Seluka land is found on the fertile portion of the floodplain. It consists of the banks and islands of the river which receive a sufficient wetting during the annual Nile flood to produce a crop without receiving further moisture. . . The amount and configuration of [seluka] land in any one area varies from year to year as banks or islands are scoured away and new soil is deposited. Seluka cultivation, while confined to a single growing season, requires a minimal effort and produces a wide range of crops at little expense. [It takes its name from the fact that the crops grown here must be individually planted with a digging stick, or seluka, rather than broadcast-sown as in the case of saqia land. Fodder crops are an important product of seluka land.] In places where arable land is scarce, families will cultivate small patches of seluka land that are a good distance from their homes.

The winter growing season (*shitwi*) extends from November until March and is the time when cooler conditions encourage wheat and barley. Burckhardt says that immediately after the inundation the farmers planted millet [locally called *dura*], the stalks of which provided fodder for their cattle for the rest of the year. Then barley, beans, tobacco, lentils, peas, and water-melons were planted. Wheat was said to be rather rare. Summer (*seifi*) crops were less abundant and consisted mainly of millet (*Sorghum vulgare*), and other crops were reduced for fear that the river might begin to flood prematurely and destroy the crop before it could be harvested. Perennial crops like lucerne and fruit trees had to be kept alive during this season. Dates, mangoes, and citrus trees also required watering until their roots reached the water table. During the flood season (*damira*) from August

52

to November only the saqia fields were producing food. Millet, beans, and maize were the main crops.[15]

No description of Nubian agriculture would be complete without some mention of date cultivation. In the words of Hassan Dafalla, the former District Commissioner for Wadi Halfa:

Whenever one thinks of Nubia, the main feature that strikes the mind is 'Date Trees'. The Nubians find in their date trees a compensation from heaven for the scarcity of their land. They consider them as their most cherished possession and an invaluable gift of nature. They are the social backbone of their local economy and the only reliable source of cash return. In fact, they are the only sign of wealth. They are the subject of boast among the existing generations and the prized investment for the future children. Every village, every household and nearly every individual have their own palm-tree or share of a tree. The whole river bank is lined with forests of date palms and in some places . . . the palms are so thick that the eye cannot penetrate the broad wall of their trunks and see what lies behind.[16]

Perhaps no tree in the history of horticulture has so deeply penetrated into the social and economic life as the date tree in Nubia. It affects so many sides of the lives of the inhabitants, and its traces are observed everywhere. Its uses are varied and considerable and nothing is wasted. Date trees are sold for cash return and they realize good prices. They can be mortgaged, and the mere existence of a tree is economic insurance. Families draw their day-to-day requirements from the village traders on credit and as long as there are date trees, they are sure to get their money back either in the form of dates or cash. Date trees are also paid as gifts on marriage occasions. Out of their leaves . . . the Nubians weave ropes, and manufacture mat trays, baskets, and rugs. Out of them they make crude sponges for bathing purposes and for cleaning their utensils. They are also fed to animals and used as fuel.[17]

In spite of the foregoing encomium, it must be observed that Nubian date trees are often so haphazardly pruned and so little attended that they reach only a fraction of their bearing potential. This may in part reflect the expense and difficulty of marketing the crop in the more remote parts of the country.[18]

An important difference between the Nubian and the Egyptian peasant is reflected in the Nubian's far greater dependence on animal husbandry. Again quoting Trigger:[19]

Cattle, sheep, and goats are herded, and animal husbandry is today only slightly less important than agriculture. The Nubians use both milk and butter. Although cattle are not [ordinarily] used to plow the fields, they are needed to run the saqias. Many people own donkeys, which are the common means of transportation, but few own camels. Chickens and pigeons are common, and dogs, though despised, are kept to guard the houses. Horses and pigs are virtually nonexistent. In 1962 the hamlet of Duki Duwur with a population of approximately 200 had 29 cattle, 100 sheep, 60 each of goats and donkeys, and several hundred chickens. In early times the animals were able to graze on the grass or stubble of the floodplain during most of the year.

The 1963 livestock census of Sudanese Nubia (i.e. that portion which was destined to be flooded by the Aswan Dam) listed 2,831 cattle, 19,335 sheep, 34,146 goats, 86 horses, 3,415 donkeys, 608 camels, 34,583 chickens, 27,520 pigeons, and 1,564 ducks in an area which had just over 50,000 human inhabitants.[20]

Historically, the importance of the pastoral element in Nubian life cannot be overstated. It was the earliest basis for sedentary life, and has continued to provide both a supplement and an alternative to farming in all later times. Poor as it is, therefore, the Nubian economic base is nevertheless more flexible and more diversified than is that of the *fellah*, and it has probably saved him at times both from serfdom and from starvation. While the Egyptian has endured ages of tyranny for want of any means of escape, the Nubian could and at times did abandon the pursuit of agriculture and revert to a pastoral way of life when natural resources or political stability failed. Interludes of this kind, involving a temporary dissolution of sedentary life, probably account for some of the mysterious lacunae in the Nubian archaeological record.

The absence of pigs in modern Nubia is of course a reflection of the overwhelmingly Moslem predilection of the population. The absence of horses is more surprising, for in medieval times the Nubians were famous horsemen, and their animals were prized even by the Arabs. Nevertheless, the universal means of local transport today are the donkey, for travel along the banks, and the sailboat for crossing the river.

Since there is a road of sorts only along one bank of the Nile, families living on the opposite bank are obliged to have, or have access to, sailboats in order to obtain the various goods which now arrive in Nubia by road. In Lower Nubia, as in Egypt proper, the prevailing form of boat was a trim craft with retractable centreboard, of European design. Beyond the Second Cataract was and is the domain of the age-old *nuggar*, a clumsy and broad-beamed but eminently serviceable craft which is locally made from acacia timber. The majority of *nuggars* are small and are used only for crossing the river, but some vessels are up to fifty feet in length, and carry commercial cargoes between Khartoum and the Shendi Reach.[21]

The form of long-range transport varies from one part of Nubia to another. In the placid waters of Lower Nubia nearly everything formerly moved by boat, and boats also carry most of the cargoes and many passengers through the Dongola Reach, although there is a road along the west bank of the Nile as well. In the Abri-Delgo Reach and the *Batn el Hajar*, the only through transport is by a very rough and sometimes impassable road which in places hugs the riverbank and in other places follows a winding course through the desert several miles east of the Nile. Over this uncertain lifeline pass heavily loaded lorries carrying the Nubian date crop to market in Wadi Halfa, and bringing back those manufactured goods (hardware, cloth, processed foods, etc.) upon which the region depends. Until quite recently, camel caravans also carried a part of this trade. In the Shendi and Abu Hamed reaches, a railway follows the river-bank and carries most of the through traffic.

Although the majority of Nubia's people are necessarily peasant farmers, the region provides a living of sorts for a few specialized artisans as well. Among them are house-builders, house-decorators, carpenters, boat-wrights, *saqia* builders, and metalsmiths. Since the demand in any given area is apt to be limited, the majority of artisans are obliged to practise their trades either on a part-time basis or as itinerants.

Somewhat more numerous than artisans, and considerably more respected in the Nubian social scheme, are shopkeepers. Nearly every village of any size boasts at least one small shop, which may be no more than a single room in the owner's house with a minuscule stock of cloth, matches, hardware, tea and sugar. The shopkeeper is often a farmer as well, and the total value of his inventory seldom exceeds a few hundred dollars. Other types of entrepreneurs occasionally found in Nubia are operators of tea- and coffee-houses, truck drivers and owners, commercial boatmen, and merchant-financiers who sometimes underwrite boatmen, truckers, and shopkeepers. Banks are almost non-existent, but money-lending is widely and profitably undertaken by many wealthy individuals. Savings are invested in property and goods.

Although Nubia is pre-eminently a land of villages, the requirements of commerce and of centralized government have led at various times in history to the growth of towns and even what in ancient times might have been termed cities. Meroë in classical times and Old Dongola in the Middle Ages probably numbered several thousand inhabitants, although both have since crumbled into ruin. The 'urban' centres of modern times – Derr and Aniba in Egyptian Nubia, Wadi Halfa and New Dongola [22] in the Sudan – are of fairly recent development, and are associated with the colonial and national régimes of the nineteenth and twentieth centuries. These places boasted not only government offices and facilities but such private enter-prises as hotels and restaurants, gasoline stations and repair shops, mercan-tile warehouses, and *suqs* (market streets) lined with all kinds of small retail enterprises. In the present as in much of the past, however, the 'urban' centres have been essentially foreign enclaves within Nubia; their most important officials and many of their other residents have been non-Nubians (see below).

Until the second decade of the twentieth century the Nile Valley continued, as in earlier times, to provide the Sudan's principal link with the outside world. Travellers as well as cargoes went by rail from Cairo to Shellal, a few miles south of Aswan at the head of the First Cataract. From here they transferred to river steamers for the journey to Wadi Halfa, below the Second Cataract. From Wadi Halfa they went once again by rail to Khartoum, over the desert line originally built for Kitchener's campaign of reconquest in 1898.

Inevitably Wadi Halfa and Aswan, as the major entrepôts in the Nile trade, far outstripped in their development the other communities in and near Nubia. Before its inundation in 1964, Wadi Halfa and its outlying villages had a population of about 20,000 individuals,[23] including a large number of artisans, shopkeepers, merchants, and civil servants. Smuggling as well as legitimate enterprise was a prime source of income for this lively community, for the rigid currency and import restrictions in Nasser's Egypt created a fertile field for illicit trade. In the Wadi Halfa *suq* one could acquire all manner of electrical appliances, wrist watches, and other goods never intended for a local clientele.

NON-NUBIAN PEOPLES

As we mentioned earlier, Nubia has rarely if ever been the exclusive domain of the Nubians. Foreign rulers and merchants, pastoral nomads, and immigrant settlers have always been and are today a part of the Nubian scene. Individual immigrants and even large groups have nearly always, sooner or later, been absorbed into the native population, but they have sometimes persisted for as much as a century or two as unassimilated minorities.[24]

Perhaps the most frequent alien visitors and sometime settlers in Nubia have been the pastoral nomads of the Red Sea Hills. Because the deserts immediately bordering the Nile are too barren, except in the extreme south, to afford any amount of subsistence to men or animals, neither Egypt nor Nubia has experienced either the close symbiosis or the perennial conflict between the desert and the sown which has been characteristic of other parts of the Middle East. Nevertheless the higher elevations near the Red Sea coast, from fifty to two hundred miles east of the Nile, have long supported a nomadic population. Throughout history these people have appeared intermittently in the Nile Valley, sometimes as raiders and sometimes as settlers. After AD 1200 the large-scale migration of bedouin Arabs to Egypt and the Sudan caused a rapid spread of pastoralism across the central Sudan as well, profoundly affecting the older riverain civilizations.

Two main nomadic peoples have played a part in Nubian history: the Beja and the Arabs. The former, immortalized by Kipling as 'Fuzzy-Wuzzies', are the age-old inhabitants of the Red Sea Hills (cf. Fig. 8); their Hamitic (or Kushitic) language links them with other pre-Arabic peoples

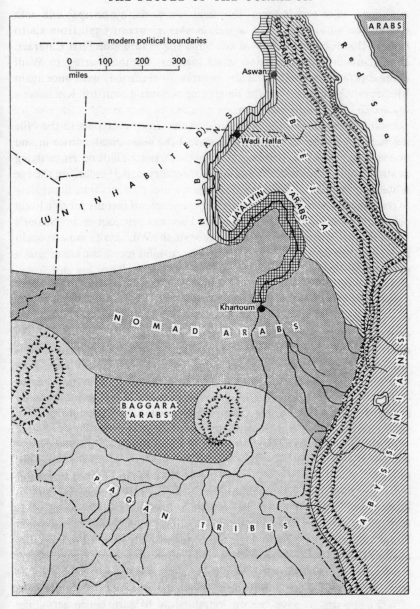

Fig. 8. Major population groups of Nubia and surrounding regions

over most of North Africa. The Beja can probably be recognized as descendants of the *Medjay*,[25] a people who appear in Egyptian texts as early as the VI Dynasty (*c.* 2400 BC).[26] It was partly as a protection against their depredations that the Middle Kingdom Pharaohs built a chain of enormous fortresses on the border between Lower and Upper Nubia. The Medjay are mentioned in a variety of texts from dynastic Egypt, nearly always in connection with wars or raids. If they could comprise an occasional nuisance to the rulers of faraway Egypt, their menace to the defenceless farmers of Nubia must have been substantial. However, we find in later times that Nubians and Beja sometimes made common cause in attacking the southern frontier outposts of Egypt, particularly in the unsettled late Roman and medieval eras.

Despite their warlike reputation the Beja peoples remained primitive and pagan until well into the Christian era. For the most part they wandered about in family-size groups, tending very small herds and constantly seeking grass. According to Trimingham, 'They exhibit the characteristics of a patriarchal society of which the unit is the family. They are not found making any great organized communal movements like the Arab tribes . . .'[27] They might at times disturb the peace in Nubia, but their numbers and their simple technological level were not such as to pose a permanent threat to the security of the valley dwellers. There seems on the contrary to have been a *modus vivendi* between nomads and farmers which was only intermittently disturbed. Some groups of Beja may have been subject to, and paid tribute to, the Nubian empires of Napata and Meroë, and groups of Beja periodically settled among the Nubians and adopted their sedentary life. Over the centuries this contact probably contributed substantially to the bloodstream if not to the culture of the valley dwellers.[28]

Particularly closely associated with Nubia has been the Ababda tribe, whose original habitat was that portion of the Red Sea Hills lying immediately to the east of Lower Nubia (Fig. 9). In the recent past villages of sedentary Ababda were to be found at various places in Egyptian Nubia, more or less scattered among the villages of the Nubians. The immigrants had almost completely accepted the agricultural way of life of their neighbours, but had not yet lost their older speech or their sense of separate identity.[29] Other Ababda groups who clung to a nomadic life were seasonal residents of Nubia, pasturing their flocks along the fringes of the Nile for part of each year, both in Egypt and in the Sudan.[30]

What appears to have been a longstanding balance between Nubian farmers and Beja pastoralists was drastically upset in the Middle Ages, when Arab nomads began pouring into the Sudan (cf. Ch. 17). Many of these people had long ago migrated from Arabia and Syria to Upper Egypt, from whence they were expelled by the harshly anti-bedouin policy of the Mamelukes. Moving southward through the Red Sea Hills, they at first

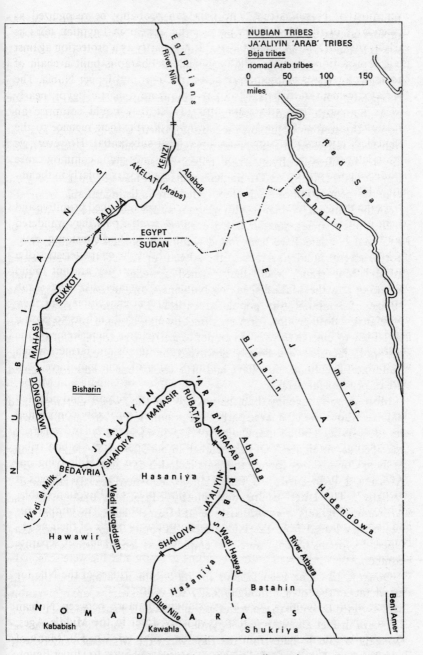

Fig. 9. Tribes of Nubia and surrounding regions

infiltrated and intermarried with the Beja tribes, who in the process were rapidly converted to Islam. From here the tide of migration turned westwards to the Nile, and beyond to Kordofan and Darfur (cf. Fig. 81, p. 555). Arabs and Arabized Beja in time became politically dominant in the old Nubian kingdom of Makouria (Dongola), resulting in the conversion of its ruling family from Christianity to Islam in the fourteenth century. The tide of Arab migration resulted eventually in the even more complete Arabization of the southern Nubians (above the Fourth Cataract), who lost not only their religion but their Nubian language as well. These people today are the so-called Ja'aliyin 'Arab' tribes, the southern neighbours of the true Nubians (Fig. 8). As Trimingham remarks, 'These tribes have only the minutest proportion of Arab blood. They are indistinguishable ethnically from the Danagla [Nubians], with whom it would be better to class them.'[31]

In modern times, unassimilated enclaves both of true Arabs and of Arabized Nubians have been found within the borders of Nubia. In the north, several hundred Arabs of the Akelat (or Aliqat) tribe were settled around Maharraqa, where they formed a wedge between the Kenzispeaking and the Mahasi-speaking Nubians.[32] In the *Batn el Hajar*, the village of Ambikol was populated entirely by Shaiqiya 'Arabs' (ex-Nubians).[33] Both groups, formerly camel-owning nomads, originally came to Nubia to engage in caravan trade. Since the development of modern transport facilities has largely destroyed or at least undermined their traditional livelihood, they have had little choice but to adopt the settled life of peasant farmers.

More important today than the nomads are the foreign merchants and officials who make up a large part of the population in Nubia's few towns. In 1960, Wadi Halfa's population of 11,056 included 3,119 individuals classified as 'foreigners'. Of this number all but 90 were Egyptians – many of them Copts. Other foreign residents included 58 East Africans, 3 North Africans, 1 West African, 1 Ethiopian, 10 Lebanese and Syrians, and 7 Indians.[34] The latter groups were mostly engaged in trade, while the African immigrants were primarily tenant farmers cultivating small plots which they leased from the Nubians. In Egyptian Nubia, a good many Upper Egyptians (*Saidis*) were also employed as tenant farmers or sharecroppers.[35]

Dongola has long been famous for its 'white *suq*', meaning that the merchants of the town, although mostly Sudanese citizens, are remarkably light-skinned by comparison with the residents of the surrounding district. They are in fact almost purely Egyptian in origin, and their presence at Dongola is said to date from the time when the Mameluke rulers were expelled from Egypt and fled to Nubia at the beginning of the nineteenth century.

Another minority which is only gradually disappearing comprises the descendants of former slaves. Before it was outlawed at the beginning of the present century a good many Nubians owned slaves on a small scale. Nearly all of them were of southern Sudanese origin. Their descendants today live mainly in and near the larger towns, where they work as labourers or tenant farmers; few if any of them own land. Although they are now all Moslems and speakers of Arabic, they continue to be set apart by their very dark pigmentation and by their known slave ancestry. They are not considered desirable marriage partners by the Nubians, and are only very slowly being absorbed into the dominant population. A recent and very perceptive study of a northern Sudanese village has disclosed that the descendants of slaves not only continue to suffer social disabilities, but are by no means fully emancipated from their obligations towards their former masters.[36]

EMIGRATION

If numbers of foreigners have come at times to settle in Nubia, there has also been throughout the historic period a considerable emigration of the native population, or at least of its able-bodied males. In ancient times Nubians served in the armies of the pharaohs, and also as domestic servants in the courts of Egypt. Some of them were undoubtedly slaves, but others seem to have migrated voluntarily to the northern country in search of a more secure livelihood or a fuller life than was offered by the meagre resources of Nubia. All evidence suggests that the pattern of Nubian labour migration (which was apparently established as early as the Egyptian VI Dynasty[37]) has continued uninterrupted until modern times. The Fatimid Caliphs of medieval Egypt relied heavily on Nubian troops to support their rule, while in the fifteenth century, and again in the seventeenth century, Nubians were said to dominate the guilds of construction workers, watchmen, and slave-dealers in Cairo.[38] No definite information is available from earlier times, but it seems probable that many of the Nubian emigrés then as now left their families at home to tend the ancestral flocks and fields, returning to Nubia for occasional visits and perhaps to retire there in their old age.

The beginnings of industrialization and the growth of cities in the nineteenth century provided many new opportunities for Nubian migrant labour, and the exodus rose to a flood after the building of the first Aswan dams destroyed many of the indigenous resources of Egyptian Nubia. In 1964 Fernea estimated that there were twice as many Egyptian Nubians living outside their homeland as within it.[39] Even though the productive resources of Sudanese Nubia were not affected by the earlier Aswan dams, the pattern of labour migration was well established here also: the 1960 census of the area surrounding Wadi Halfa listed 27,422 residents and

14,431 absentees.[40] Nubia in the twentieth century had become in large part a land of women, children, and old men, the able-bodied males having gone abroad in search of employment. In the urban centres of Egypt and the Sudan Nubians had acquired (and still retain) a virtual monopoly of many service occupations, including especially those of cook, waiter, house servant, and watchman. The emigrés returned every year or two for brief visits to their families, and in between times often remitted money and gifts from abroad.

Whether in Cairo or in Khartoum, the Nubian emigrant labourer retains his sense of ethnic identity and of obligation to his own people. Although their residences may be widely scattered throughout the city, Nubians abroad join in 'village associations' which keep alive their ties with one another and with the home community. Some of these organizations were studied by Andreas and Waltraud Kronenberg in 1963, and are described by them as follows:[41]

Nubians working abroad unite in associations having a common interest in their place of origin. These associations are a means of transferring the social ties which operate in the *balad* [village] to the place of wage-earning and provide immigrants in search of labor with the necessary social security. They also contribute to the economic and social stability of the *balad* and have a tendency to speed up progress and economic development in the home community through the collection of money for co-operative projects such as mills, hospitals, schools, and pump-schemes. Thus modern development increases to a certain degree the importance of locality ties, and, although less obviously, the importance of survivals as distinctive features in each locality. The feeling of being an individual group sharing the same customs increases in foreign surroundings, and so does the cohesion of people from the same locality.

Although *balad* divisions are the basis of Nubian associations in the places of wage-earning, there is an interrelationship between the ecological situation in the *balad*, the density of its population, and the associations: if there are not enough people from one *balad*, men from two or more *balads* will unite into one association. Ard el Hagar is a very large geographical area with a small population. The *balads* north of Wadi Halfa are relatively densely populated and occupy a relatively small area. Therefore nearly every *balad* north of Halfa has an association of its own in the places of wage-earning, whereas Ard el Hagar has just one association in Khartoum, but it is so organized that there is closer collaboration among members from neighboring *balads* than among those from more distant ones.

The readjustment of the boundaries of a *balad* has its repercussions in the associations abroad. When Aksha split away from Serra West the men from Aksha working in Alexandria and Cairo left the Serra West association and founded one of their own, and both associations entered into competition, each trying to contribute more money to its *balad* than the other. The Serra West association speeded up the collection of money for a pump-scheme in order to prove that they did not depend on the contributions of the men from Aksha.

Before the split, 300 Sudanese Pounds was collected in three years, while after the split 500 Sudanese Pounds was collected in only two months and a further 300 Sudanese Pounds in another three months. This was enough to buy a mill as well as a pump.

In addition to the temporary emigration of wage labourers, there has been some permanent resettlement of Nubian families, and sometimes even whole villages, even before the destruction of their homeland made this a necessity for many. Several villages in the vicinity of modern Khartoum are partly or wholly descended from Nubian immigrants. Unlike individual migrants, the resettled villagers have freely intermarried with local peoples and have lost their Nubian language and all other sense of special identity.[42]

On the other hand, many Nubians have stubbornly clung to their rocky ancestral land even after the loss of their fields has ended any chance of wresting a living from it. When the Aswan Low Dam was built, most of the villages of Egyptian Nubia chose to 'stay put', rebuilding at higher levels along the rocky shores of the newly filled lake. The absence of any trees or growing vegetation gave them a singularly desolate appearance, and for three generations they were supported largely from the absentee earnings of their male inhabitants. More recently a considerable number of Sudanese Nubians have refused to accept the new land offered them in the central Sudan, preferring to take their chances along the shores of the now filling Lake Nasser. Others who accepted resettlement allotments at 'New Halfa' (see Ch. 19) have leased their lands to local residents and have returned to their old haunts.

The building of the High Dam has, however, left the majority of Lower Nubians with no choice but to seek new homes. Those resident in Egypt have in fact been given no option of remaining in their ancestral land; the whole district between Aswan and the Sudanese border has been closed to settlement. The Egyptian Government has offered its Nubian citizens new lands and new homes at Kom Ombo, a short distance north of Aswan. Sudanese Nubians from the condemned area have been resettled much further from home, along the upper Atbara River not far from the border between Sudan and Ethiopia. Here the Government has provided extensive new landholdings and a whole series of newly founded villages, each bearing the name of one of the inundated villages of Old Nubia: New Halfa, New Faras, New Serra, and so on. It is too early yet to measure the full impact of this transplantation upon Nubian society and culture, but some discussion of it will be found in Chapter 19.

THE CHARACTER OF NUBIAN SOCIETY

The foregoing discussion illustrates five characteristics of modern Nubian society which are also important for an understanding of Nubian history. First, it is an open or peasant society rather than a closed or tribal one. Although Nubians have a strong sense of ethnic distinctness, they do not attempt to maintain it by means of geographical boundaries, nor do they exclude foreigners from their midst. Outsiders, alien in speech and appearance and sometimes even in religion, have been able to settle among them both as individuals and as unassimilated cultural minorities. As a result, at least in the more recent past Nubian culture has been much more receptive to external influence and to cultural change than have the closed, tribal societies of the southern Sudanese peoples.

Second, Nubian society is not notably class-structured along occupational lines, but it is still to some extent caste-structured along ethnic lines. At the top is a small élite of Egyptian (and very occasionally Syrian or Lebanese) merchants and civil servants; at the bottom are the descendants of former slaves, mostly of southern Sudanese origin.

Third, the Nubian economy involves a combination of subsistence farming, animal husbandry, and commercial date production. This multiple subsistence base, in spite of its poverty, has given to the Nubian a certain adaptability and flexibility in the face of both natural disaster and human oppression, enabling him to survive and often to prosper in an unpromising environment.

Fourth, the Nubian society and economy have long been partly integrated with, and dependent upon, those of neighbouring peoples. This is true both in regard to the Egyptians and to the desert nomads.

Lastly, the shadow of Egypt has seldom been absent from the land. If nomads sometimes came to raid, Egyptians came to rule. When they intermarried with the Nubians it was not, as in the case of the nomads, to be absorbed into the local populace, but to increase their control of it. The overwhelming concentration of capital and trade in the hands of Egyptian merchants in Wadi Halfa and Dongola in 1960 only reflects a condition which has been prevalent in Nubia since the beginning of history.

3

HISTORY AND ARCHAEOLOGY IN NUBIA

We know that Nubia has been at least intermittently occupied since the Stone Age, but we cannot be sure that it has always been occupied by the same people. Neither the racial nor the linguistic nor the cultural characteristics which we can observe in the modern population can be traced back continuously through history. Evidence of the Nubian speech is lacking before the Middle Ages, and racial evidence, as reconstructed primarily from skeletal remains, is ambiguous at best. Nubian culture seems to show a fairly continuous development from beginning to end, but there are enough interruptions in the story so that the inference of a single population is by no means beyond dispute.

The interpretation of Nubian history which was developed at the beginning of this century, and which still underlies most modern theory, holds that the area has been inhabited by a succession of peoples whose comings and goings are largely responsible for the culture changes in Nubian history. As I suggested in the Introduction, this view is understandable in terms of the limited knowledge (nearly all of it pertaining to Lower Nubia) which existed in the first decade of the twentieth century, but it is no longer tenable in the light of modern evidence. In the broader perspective of Nubia which is now available to us, we can visualize a continuous process of cultural development, in which the identity of particular actors is unimportant. We must, however, consider briefly how and why the earlier theory of history developed, and where it went astray in interpreting the evidence available.

Our picture of Nubian history today is drawn from two sources: historical documents and archaeological remains. The peculiar, intermittent nature of Nubia's recorded history, with its alternation of documented periods and dark ages, has made this land pre-eminently the meeting ground of the philologist and the 'dirt' archaeologist. Each has been obliged to study at least in some degree the results as well as the methods of the other; together they have pieced together a picture of development which neither could have hoped to achieve alone.

Archaeology is, however, entirely the child of the twentieth century in

65

Nubia. Before that time whatever was known of the history of the southern land was known from textual records – most of them compiled by non-Nubians, in alien languages, and often at distant second-hand. It was from such material that the first attempt at a comprehensive history of Nubia was compiled at the beginning of the twentieth century.

HISTORICAL SOURCES

Wallis Budge's *The Egyptian Sudan*,[1] written to commemorate the country's recovery from the Dervishes, must serve as the point of departure for any discussion of the textual sources on Nubian history. Because it was written just before the inauguration of systematic archaeology, and is therefore put together entirely from literary sources, Budge's narrative accurately reflects both the extent and the limitations of historical material on Nubia. Those accustomed to think of 'darkest Africa' may be surprised at the knowledge which even the ancients possessed; those expecting to find a connected history cannot help but be struck by the enormous lacunae in the record.

Budge did a remarkably thorough and conscientious job of pulling together the scattered and fragmentary sources on Nubia which exist in half a dozen languages. *The Egyptian Sudan* is still, sixty years later, the basic corpus of textual material on Nubian history. The sources fall chronologically and philologically into six groups:

1. Egyptian hieroglyphic texts, from the II to the XX Dynasty.
2. Nubian hieroglyphic texts of the Napatan period.
3. Historical and geographical works by classical authors.
4. Medieval ecclesiastical histories.
5. Medieval Arab histories and geographies.
6. Works by European travellers in the early modern period.

Except in the second and sixth groups the number of primary sources is of course small. Most of the classical and medieval works were written at very distant second-hand, and their authors sometimes allowed their imaginations to supply what they lacked in first-hand information.

EGYPTIAN TEXTS

Kush and other ancient Egyptian names for Nubia appear in a substantial number of hieroglyphic and hieratic texts, but in a great many of them they are the subject of little more than passing reference. For the whole 3,000 years of Pharaonic–Nubian relations there are scarcely half a hundred texts which are wholly or even primarily concerned with Nubian affairs.[2] All of them are of course intended to celebrate the exploits of Egypt or of Egyptians rather than to convey any objective description of the southern land, and their chief value is for the reconstruction of political and economic history. For other aspects of Nubian life we are obliged to read between the lines – always a dubious practice, and doubly so when the lines themselves are far from clear.

The oldest known historical record pertaining to Nubia belongs almost to the dawn of history itself. It is a pictorial representation found on a rocky outcrop near the Second Cataract, apparently commemorating a military success of the First Dynasty Pharaoh Jer (or Zer) over a local foe.[3] Other inscriptions, found in Egypt, make brief mention of military expeditions to Nubia in the II and III Dynasties, and from a slightly later period there are prospectors' and quarrymen's graffiti from various places in the Nubian deserts. From the VI Dynasty come two long biographical texts recounting both military and trading operations in the Sudan. They are far more detailed than anything preceding, and provide our first insight into cultural conditions in the southern lands.

There is almost no literary record of Egyptian–Nubian relations during the First Intermediate period (Dynasties VII–X).[4] The XI Dynasty apparently waged intermittent war in the south, setting the stage for the conquest and occupation of Lower Nubia by the first Pharaohs of the XII Dynasty. Accounts of their campaigns, and proclamations of Egyptian sovereignty, are the principal documents on Nubia in the Middle Kingdom. After the XIII Dynasty the record is again silent for a considerable time, until the story of conquest and exploitation is repeated almost verbatim under the New Kingdom.

The New Kingdom texts (Dynasties XVIII–XX) are a dreary record of military operations against a seemingly defenceless population. No fewer than eight kings claim to have conquered or reconquered parts of Nubia, although the archaeological record points to a more or less continuous Egyptian occupation.[5] Some of these expeditions can only have been slave-raids, thinly disguised under the pretext of restoring civic order. The last textual record of Egyptian rule in Nubia records the receipt of tribute in the reign of Rameses IX. After his time there was another silence of centuries, until the Nubians themselves took up the story.

Additional information about the earliest Nubians may be obtained from the pictorial evidence of Egyptian temple and tomb reliefs. They often show captives and servants from the southern lands, easily recognizable by their features and, in the case of paintings, by their pigmentation. From them we can learn something about the appearance and dress of the people, and of the roles they could occupy in the Egyptian social system.

NUBIAN HIEROGLYPHIC TEXTS

Nubians, or at least Nubian kings, finally got a chance to record their own version of history after their conquest of Egypt in the eighth century BC. As rulers of the northern land they fell heir to the elaborate publicity apparatus which the pharaoh always commanded, and they were not slow to use it. If their royal proclamations and annals are hardly different in style and substance from those of earlier and later pharaohs, they at least display, for the first time in history, a pro-Nubian point of view. They were nevertheless written down by Egyptian scribes in the Egyptian language and characters, and must have been addressed in considerable part to an Egyptian audience. Many of them are not 'Nubian' documents at all, but the annals of Nubian rulers and would-be rulers of Egypt. They tell us no more about life in the Nubian homeland than do the purely Egyptian texts of other times.

From the standpoint of political history, on the other hand, the texts of the Napatan period (the era of Nubian rule in Egypt and the centuries immediately following) have at least as much interest as have the annals of earlier reigns. Outstanding among them are the stelae of Piankhi, who conquered Egypt, and of Taharqa, who lost it. From the two centuries following Taharqa there are three more royal inscriptions of considerable length, all recounting military operations within the Sudan. Although the Napatan kings retained the traditional pharaonic title 'Lord of the Two Lands' (i.e. Upper and Lower Egypt), there is no evidence that they made any practical effort to assert it after the time of Taharqa. The stele of Nastasen, now dated about 336 BC, is the last historically coherent text of Nubian origin. Later inscriptions provide us with little more than the names of rulers, and even these cannot be arranged in an obvious succession.

It is in one sense fortunate that the Napatan kings chose the Egyptian language and characters for their royal annals, for it means that we can read them without difficulty. On the other hand we are deprived of any clue to the native Nubian speech, and therefore to the ethnic identity and affinities of the population. In later times a purely indigenous written language (Meroitic) was in fact developed, but it is so far unintelligible to modern scholars. It does not appear to be closely related to Nubian or any other present-day language. It was employed in a few monumental inscriptions, but more often for short votive and possibly commercial texts.

CLASSICAL AUTHORS

Greek adventurers and settlers were numerous in Egypt long before Alexander. As mercenaries in the Egyptian army, some of them accompanied the Pharaoh Psammetik II on an expedition to Nubia in the sixth century BC. The graffiti which they left in the temple of Abu Simbel, and in one or two other places,[6] are our first evidence of entry into Nubia by any European.

The visit of Herodotus in the fifth century BC marks a turning point in the recording of Nubian as well as of Egyptian history. The 'Father of History' never journeyed in person beyond Aswan, but from travellers and merchants he put together a surprisingly accurate (for him) geographical description of the lands further up the Nile.[7] Even today our knowledge of the Meroitic kingdom rests in part on the evidence of Herodotus, although he never saw it. His is the oldest surviving work on Nubian history or geography which makes any pretence at either comprehensiveness or objectivity, although it may have been preceded by the lost account of Hecataeus.

Not surprisingly, in view of the paucity of source material, most of the classical accounts of Nubia are stronger on geography and ethnology than they are on history. Many of their authors copied generously from Herodotus; only a few added further significant detail. Among the latter were Strabo[8] (whose geographical description of Nubia is largely copied from a lost work of Eratosthenes), Diodorus Siculus,[9] and Pliny.[10] In addition to their descriptions of the land and people, these writers are our principal sources on Ptolemaic–Nubian and Roman–Nubian relations. Near the end of the classical period, three writers have given us an incidental picture of the chaotic conditions prevailing in Nubia after the disintegration of the Meroitic state. The enigmatic and at times conflicting accounts of Priscus,[11] Olympiodorus,[12] and Procopius[13] are valuable sources on political history, but they have also contributed more than their share to the fog surrounding the Nubian 'X-Group' question, which will be extensively discussed in later pages (Ch. 13).

One document stands unique among the 'classical' records of Nubia. It is the sixth-century victory proclamation of a certain Nubian King Silko, inscribed in primitive and ungrammatical Greek on the stones of the temple of Kalabsha.[14] Despite its limited scope and imprecise language, it is the last deliberate historical text of Nubian authorship down to modern times.

ECCLESIASTICAL HISTORIES

Two early church historians, John of Ephesus[15] and John of Biclarum,[16] and two later ones, Eutychius[17] and Michael the Syrian,[18] wrote about the conversion of Nubia to Christianity in the sixth century. Their accounts differ at a number of important points, reflecting partisanship for one or another of the contending Orthodox sects of the time. Like the late classical texts, they have given rise to controversies which are still with us. Such light as they shed is largely confined to the first century of Nubian Christianity, for after the Arab conquest of Egypt the outside world lost sight of Christendom on the Nile until the end of the Middle Ages.

MEDIEVAL ARAB SCHOLARS

The greatest of Arab historians, ancient or modern, was Ibn Khaldun (late fourteenth century). His account[19] is not, however, the best medieval source on Nubian history or geography. That honour belongs to his contemporary, the geographer Maqrizi, whose major work is unfortunately still awaiting translation into English. Maqrizi's *al-Khitat* is not only an important original source; it also preserves a long passage from a first-hand visitor, Ibn Selim el Aswani, whose tenth-century account of Nubia is otherwise lost.[20] Other important works combining history and geography are those of Mas'udi[21] and al-Umari.[22] They provide a chronicle of Nubian relations with the Islamic Caliphate, and later with the schismatic dynasties in Egypt. A purely geographical work is the thirteenth-century *Churches and Monasteries of Egypt and some Neighbouring Lands*, attributed to a certain Abu Salih, 'The Armenian'.[23]

Darkness descends on Nubia, so far as Arabic sources are concerned, with the Ottoman conquest of 1520. However, it seems probable that the manuscript sources for the late medieval period are far from exhausted. The Ottoman archives, the annals of Portuguese and Genoese exploration, commercial accounts and the journals of forgotten travellers might all shed further light on a period which remains up to now one of the darkest in Nubia's history.[24]

EARLY MODERN TRAVELLERS

In the same year that Nubia disappeared behind the 'Ottoman curtain', the neighbouring land of Ethiopia was introduced to European consciousness through the first of several Portuguese missions. At this time, therefore, such feeble light as we have on Nubia comes from the south rather than from the north. The accounts of the Jesuit fathers[25] have little to say about events on the Nile, but they are almost all we have for their century.

At the beginning of the eighteenth century two intrepid travellers, the Frenchman Poncet[26] and the German Krump,[27] ascended the Nile from Cairo, the first as far as Ethiopia and the second as far as Sennar. Near the end of the century James Bruce[28] descended via the same route. All of them hurried through what they considered to be the inhospitable land of the Upper Nile, and they have left us only hasty sketches of scenes along the way. It was the great scholar-travellers who followed in the wake of Mohammed Ali's conquest who really ushered in the modern era in Nubian history. Foremost among them were Burckhardt,[29] Waddington and Hanbury,[30] Cailliaud,[31] Linant de Bellefonds,[32] and, a generation later, Hoskins[33] and Lepsius.[34] Their voluminous and profusely illustrated accounts are the starting point for a continuous history of Nubia which extends down to our own times.

ARCHAEOLOGICAL SOURCES

The handful of excavations which were carried out in Nubia prior to 1907 were either clearing operations designed to reveal hieroglyphic inscriptions, architectural stabilizations, or out-and-out treasure hunts.[35] For all practical purposes systematic archaeology began with George A. Reisner and the First Archaeological Survey of Nubia, made necessary by the enlargement of the original Aswan Dam (built 1898–1902; first enlarged 1908–10). At that time the challenge of salvage archaeology (i.e. the systematic and non-selective excavation of all sites which are threatened with destruction) was unprecedented. Reisner was obliged to develop his methodology as he went along; some of his procedures, such as the use of standard forms for data recording, have since found worldwide acceptance.[36]

THE FIRST ARCHAEOLOGICAL SURVEY

The First Archaeological Survey was in the field for four seasons, from 1907 to 1911, and explored ninety-five miles of the Nile Valley between Shellal and Wadi es-Sebua (Fig. 10). The survey was directed in the first season by G. A. Reisner and in the three subsequent seasons by C. M. Firth. By its own reckoning it excavated 151 cemeteries and over 8,000 individual graves. Only about half a dozen sites other than cemeteries were investigated, and only one of them with any thoroughness. A tabulation of the work of the survey by seasons is given in Table II. These results, and more particularly those of the first field season, are the data base upon which Reisner's and all subsequent reconstructions of Nubian history are built.

Two characteristics stand out in the work of the First Archaeological Survey: first, it was devoted to mortuary remains almost to the exclusion of other archaeological evidence, and second, a disproportionately heavy emphasis was placed upon investigation of the earlier phases of Nubian history. Both circumstances were to some extent deliberate. Reisner and Firth never doubted that literary evidence would furnish the main picture of the later historical phases, and their choice of sites for investigation was based on the sound principle of concentrating on the least-known periods. Moreover, it was still taken for granted in 1907 that the first principle of all archaeology – even salvage archaeology – was the recovery of transportable (and exhibitable) objects. The excavation and recording of living sites was very much an incidental and subsidiary operation. (There was, however, a concurrent architectural and epigraphic survey of the temples of Lower Nubia; see below.) Firth once or twice expressed regret that the pressure of time did not permit his field parties to examine some of the ruined cities which they noted along the way,[37] but he never seriously con-

TABLE II

SUMMARY OF EXCAVATIONS BY THE ARCHAEOLOGICAL SURVEY OF NUBIA, 1907–11

Season	1907–8		1908–9		1909–10		1910–11		TOTALS	
Period	*Graves*	*Sites*	*Graves*	*Sites*	*Graves*	*Sites*	*Graves*	*Sites*	*Graves*	*Sites*
Christian	2044	25	42	9	83	1	48	4	2217	39
X-Group	124	11	51	6			243	11	418	28
Ptolemaic–Roman	629	18	1	9	381	1	78	11	1089	39
New Kingdom	99	13	113	13	138	7	444	20	794	53
C-Group	401	11	385	11	474	6	355	16	1615	44
B-Group	347	9	66	9	1	1	1	2	415	21
A-Group	518	18	377	15	564	8	232	13	1691	54
TOTALS	4162	*60	1035	*36	1641	*19	1401	*42	8239	*151

* These are totals of individual, separately numbered sites investigated in each season. They do not equal the sum of the sites listed in the columns directly above. (Since many sites contained graves of more than one period, they are listed more than once in the table.)

sidered that the detailed investigation of these cities might be given priority over the continued excavation of graves and cemeteries whose typology was by then well known. The same scale of priorities was to be adopted by later archaeologists, and has profoundly influenced our approach to Nubian history down to the present day. As a result, we often seem to know more about how the early Nubians died than about how they lived.

The treatment of Christian antiquities offers an interesting sidelight on the work of the First Archaeological Survey. In the opening weeks of the initial campaign Reisner's crew excavated all 1,625 graves in a Christian cemetery near Shellal – a far larger number of graves than was subsequently investigated in any cemetery of any period.[38] They were of course devoid of any offerings, since the placing of objects in the tomb was not a feature of Christian mortuary practice. After this frustrating experience the survey never again opened any appreciable number of Christian graves, and by the last seasons their presence was not even being systematically recorded.

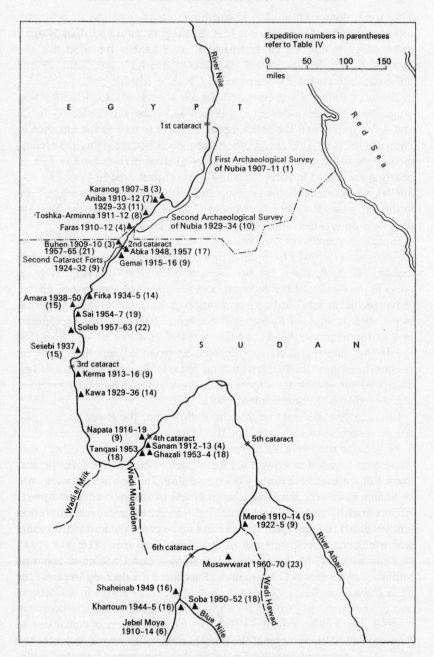

Fig. 10. Excavations in Nubia, 1907–60

73

They were, along with Moslem remains, relegated to a period too poor and too recent to be of any interest. It is precisely because Christian Nubian archaeology is not 'burial archaeology' that neither the First nor the Second Archaeological Survey contributed anything significant to our understanding of this 900-year phase of Nubian history.

The outstanding achievement of the First Archaeological Survey was unquestionably the discovery and definition of the unrecorded A, B, C, and X 'Groups', and the arrangement of these as well as the historically known cultures of Nubia in an ordered sequence. In a sense this was accomplished almost at the outset. Remains of all four periods (and in fact of nearly every period in Nubian history) were encountered in Cemetery 7 at Shellal, whose excavation was completed within the first ten weeks of the initial campaign.[39] Cemetery 7 might thus be described as the ultimate data base upon which all modern histories of Nubia rest.

Preliminary reports of the work of the survey were published in the form of small *Bulletins*, which appeared quite promptly during and after each season. The A, B, and C 'groups' were already identified (as grave types only) in the earliest of the *Bulletins*, and the complete sequence of phases (now specifically identified with population groups) was formally proposed in the opening pages of *Bulletin 3*, published in 1909.[40] A year later, in the first of the definitive *Reports of the Archaeological Survey of Nubia* (for the 1907-8 campaign), Reisner devoted an extended definition and discussion to each of the Nubian cultural phases.[41] It was repeated and updated by Firth in each of the three later *Reports*, but the essentials remained unchanged from Reisner's initial effort.

It has to be added that neither the *Bulletins* nor the *Reports* are in any sense comprehensive accounts of the work of the First Archaeological Survey. Some sites were never described in print, and in many other cases we remain ignorant of how much was done or was not done. In the first decade of the twentieth century documentation and publication were only beginning to be recognized as essential parts of the archaeologist's task.

Concurrently with the Archaeological Survey, but independently of it, architectural and epigraphic studies were made of the numerous Pharaonic and Ptolemaic-Roman temples in the threatened area. This work was carried out by A. M. Blackman, H. Gauthier, and C. Roeder, and was published in a series of volumes under the collective title *Temples Immergés de la Nubie*.[42]

OTHER PIONEER EXPEDITIONS

Five more expeditions entered the Nubian field within a year or two of the First Archaeological Survey. Those of the University of Pennsylvania, Oxford University, and the Vienna Academy of Sciences worked in Lower Nubia, upstream from the area threatened by the Low Dam. Far to the south, the Meroë Expedition began uncovering the fabled royal city of that name, and the Wellcome Excavations explored prehistoric remains in the *Gezira* between the Blue and White Niles.[43] Except for the Vienna expedition, all of these digs supplemented the work of the Archaeological Survey in two important respects. First, they gave far more attention to architectural remains, both domestic and monumental, than did the survey. Second, they were all concerned to a very considerable extent with remains of the Meroitic period, which happen to be unrepresented in the extreme north of Nubia and hence did not figure in the work of Reisner and Firth. The Oxford and Pennsylvania expeditions also made the first significant contributions to the study of Christian Nubian archaeology, again on the basis of architectural rather than funerary remains. During the same years the architect Somers Clarke was making a survey of Christian remains between Khartoum and Cairo; his *Christian Antiquities in the Nile Valley*[44] is the pioneer work in this field.

In 1913 Reisner returned to Nubia after an absence of several years as Director of the Harvard–Boston Expedition. This expedition, jointly sponsored by Harvard University and the Boston Museum of Fine Arts, had secured an excavation licence which amounted to a virtual monopoly of the important archaeological remains in the northern Sudan. During the next eighteen years investigations were carried on in nearly all of the monumental sites dating from the dynastic periods in Nubian history (Pharaonic, Napatan, and Meroitic). The work of the expedition falls under three headings:

1. Excavation of the great Egyptian trading emporium and the Nubian royal cemetery at Kerma. This was accomplished between 1913 and 1916 and was published in the *Harvard African Studies*.[45] Our knowledge of the distinctive Kerma Culture (cf. Ch. 8) still rests almost exclusively on these reports.

2. Excavation of several of the enormous fortresses in the Second Cataract region, originally built during the Middle Kingdom and enlarged under the New Kingdom. This work was carried on intermittently over several years, under different directors. The results have only very recently appeared, in the two volumes entitled *Second Cataract Forts*.[46]

3. Excavation of the Napatan and Meroitic royal cemeteries, and certain associated temples, near Kareima and at Meroë. This was undoubtedly Reisner's *chef d'œuvre* in the Sudan. From it he reconstructed the royal succession of the Napatan and Meroitic dynasties which is still the basic chronological framework for discussions of this phase of Nubian history. Again, the major substantive results were not published until long after Reisner's death, in a series of superbly illustrated volumes prepared by Dows Dunham and collectively titled *Royal Cemeteries of Kush*.[47]

75

Excavations in the Sudan were only a subsidiary part of the work of the Harvard–Boston Expedition. From its organization in 1905 until Reisner's death nearly forty years later, the expedition was engaged first and foremost in the excavation of the Old Kingdom cemetery at Giza, in the shadow of the Great Pyramids. Operations in the Sudan were carried on concurrently as best they could be. Often the work in Nubia was done late in the season, after the close of the digs in Egypt. The Nubian excavations were nevertheless the largest body of coordinated archaeological work ever carried out in Upper Nubia, and their results will always form the backbone for studies of Napatan–Meroitic history.[48]

THE SECOND ARCHAEOLOGICAL SURVEY

A second enlargement of the original Aswan Dam extended the impounded waters of the Nile as far upstream as the Sudanese frontier, and made necessary the Second Archaeological Survey of Nubia between 1929 and 1934 (Fig. 10). This operation, directed by W. B. Emery and L. P. Kirwan, was similar to its predecessor both in its methods and in its results. Again the emphasis was heavily on mortuary remains; 76 cemeteries and about 2,400 individual graves were investigated. An overall tabulation of the results of the Second Archaeological Survey is given below:

TABLE III

SUMMARY OF EXCAVATIONS BY THE SECOND ARCHAEOLOGICAL SURVEY OF NUBIA, 1929–34

Period	Number graves	Number sites
Christian	17	9
X-Group	178	20
Meroitic*	585	29
New Kingdom	405	18
C-Group	975	28
B-Group	4	1
A-Group	218	15
TOTALS	2,382	76†

* These take the place of Ptolemaic–Roman graves excavated by the First Archaeological Survey. The Roman–Meroitic frontier corresponded fairly closely to the point where the first survey ended and the second survey began (Wadi es-Sebua).
† This is the actual total of sites numbered and investigated by the survey, not the total of the column above, since multi-phase sites are listed in more than one category.

In addition to its work on cemeteries, the Second Archaeological Survey did a thorough excavation of the Middle and New Kingdom fortress of

Kubban and of C-Group and Meroitic town sites in the Wadi el-Arab. The really outstanding (and wholly unexpected) achievement of the survey was however the discovery and exploration of the great 'X-Group' royal tombs at Ballana and Qustul. The published report on these two sites[49] alone bulks considerably larger than the report on the other 74 sites investigated by the expedition.[50] Incidentally, these well-organized and well-illustrated reports represented the chief methodological advance of the Second Archaeological Survey in comparison with its predecessor.

Also part of the 1929–34 salvage campaign were the work of G. A. Steindorff at Aniba, and the survey of Christian remains by Ugo Monneret de Villard. Steindorff made the most complete investigation yet undertaken of A-Group and C-Group remains.[51] Monneret de Villard undertook an exhaustive survey, both literary and archaeological, of material pertaining to Christian Nubia, resulting in the four-volume *La Nubia Medioevale*.[52] He was able from documentary sources to put together a reasonably connected history of the Christian period, but his promised synthesis of the archaeological material was never achieved. Although its analytical and interpretive sections are rudimentary, *La Nubia Medioevale* nevertheless remains the basic corpus for any study of medieval Nubian archaeology.

LATER EXPEDITIONS

The inundation of Lower Nubia, combined with a worldwide economic depression, brought a predictable reduction in archaeological activity in the 1930s. The Harvard–Boston excavations were suspended in 1932, although the Expedition was not formally liquidated until some years later. However, F. Ll. Griffith revived the Oxford excavations in 1929, and they were continued after his death by L. P. Kirwan. Towards the end of the decade the venerable Egypt Exploration Society, long in the forefront of field work in Egypt, also made its first entry into the Nubian field with a series of excavations in the Abri-Delgo region. This work was necessarily suspended during the Second World War, but was resumed between 1947 and 1950.

There was little other foreign activity in Nubia during the early post-war years. In part the vacuum was filled by local expeditions from Gordon Memorial College (later Khartoum University) and the Sudan Antiquities Service. Beginning in 1950 the Antiquities Service inaugurated a series of regular annual excavations which set the stage for the later active part which the Service was to play in the High Dam Salvage Campaign. Meanwhile interest abroad gradually revived. A French expedition began work near Wadi Halfa in 1953, and in 1957 no fewer than three foreign groups, from Great Britain, Germany, and Italy, began large-scale excavations in the Sudan.[53] Two years later, announcement of the Aswan High Dam launched the third massive salvage campaign in Nubia within sixty years.

TABLE IV

CHRONOLOGY OF EXPEDITIONS TO NUBIA, 1907–58

(See also Fig. 10)

No.	Institution and country	Director	Years	Areas worked*	Principal work or remains investigated	Publications†
1	Archaeological Survey of Nubia (Egypt)	Reisner, Firth	1907–11	Shellal–Wadi Sebua (LN)	Survey-excavations	ASN
2	Egyptian Antiquities Service	Blackman et al.	1907–11	Shellal–Wadi Sebua (LN)	Epigraphy of temples	TIN
3	University of Pennsylvania, E.B. Coxe Expedition (U.S.A.)	MacIver, Woolley	1907–8	Amada–Aniba (LN)	C-Group town; Meroitic and X-Group remains	EBC
			1908–9	Faras area (LN)	Christian churches	EBC
			1909–10	Buhen (LN)	Pharaonic fortress	EBC
4	Oxford University Excavations (U.K.)	Griffith	1910–12	Faras area (LN)	Pharaonic temples; Meroitic to Christian sites	LAAA
			1912–13	Sanam (DR)	Napatan temple and cemetery	LAAA
5	Liverpool University (U.K.)	Garstang	1910–14	Meroë (SR)	Napatan and Meroitic city and temples	LAAA, Meroë
6	Wellcome Excavations (U.K.)	Wellcome	1910–14	Jebel Moya (CS)	Villages and cemeteries of uncertain age	WES
7	Siegelin Expedition (Germany)	Steindorff	1910–12	Aniba (LN)	Pharaonic fortress; C-Group cemeteries	
8	Vienna Academy of Sciences (Austria)	Junker	1911–12	Toshka–Arminna (LN)	Cemeteries of all periods	AWW

No.	Institution	Director	Dates	Site	Description	Ref.
9	Harvard–Boston Expedition (U.S.A.)	Reisner	1913–16	Kerma (DR)	Pharaonic colony; Kerma cemeteries	HAS
			1915–16	Gemai (BH)	Cemeteries of various periods	HAS RCK, BT
			1916–19	Napata (DR)	Napatan and Meroitic tombs and temples	
			1922–5	Meroë (SR)	Meroitic cemeteries	RCK
			1924–32	Batn el Hajar (BH)	Pharaonic fortresses	SCF
10	Egyptian Antiquities Service	Emery, Kirwan	1929–34	Wadi Sebua–Adindan (LN)	Survey-excavations	MAN
11	,, ,,	Steindorff	1929–33	Aniba (LN)	A-Group, C-Group and Pharaonic cemeteries	MAN
12	,, ,,	M. de Villard	1929–34	All Nubia	Inventory of Christian remains	MAN
13	Oriental Institute of Chicago (U.S.A.)	Sandford, Arkell	1929–31	All Nubia	Paleolithic remains	OIP
14	Oxford University Excavations (U.K.)	Griffith, Kirwan	1929–36	Kawa (DR)	Pharaonic and Napatan temples	Kawa
		Kirwan	1934–5	Firka (AD)	X-Group tombs	Firka
15	Egypt Exploration Society (U.K.)	Blackman	1937	Sesebi (AD)	Pharaonic town and temple	JEA
		Fairman, Shinnie	1938–9 1947–50	Amara (AD)	Pharaonic temple	JEA
16	Sudan Antiquities Service	Arkell	1944–5	Khartoum (CS)	Mesolithic remains	EK
			1949	Shaheinab (CS)	Neolithic remains	Shah
17	Khartoum University (Sudan)	Myers	1948, 1957	Abka (BH)	Neolithic remains	Kush

TABLE IV (Cntd)

No.	Institution and country	Director	Years	Areas worked*	Principal work or remains investigated	Publications†
18	Sudan Antiquities Service	Shinnie	1950–52 1953 1953–4	Soba (CS) Tanqasi (DR) Ghazali (DR)	Christian town and church X-Group tombs Christian monastery and church	SASOP Kush SASOP
19	French Archaeological Mission	Vercoutter	1953–4 1954–7	Kor (LN) Sai Is. (AD)‡	Pharaonic town Pharaonic fort; cemeteries of all periods	Kush Kush
20	Sudan Antiquities Service	Thabit	1955	Debeira (LN)	Pharaonic tomb	Kush
21	Egypt Exploration Society (U.K.)	Emery	1957–65	Buhen (LN)§	Pharaonic fortress	Kush JEA
22	University of Pisa (Italy)	Schiff–Giorgini	1957–63 1964	Soleb (AD) Seddenga (AD)¶	Pharaonic temple Pharaonic temple; Napatan and Meroitic cemetery	SS Kush
23	Humboldt University (D.D.R.)	Hintze	1957–8 1960–70	Butana (CS) Musawwarat (SR)	Reconnaissance survey Meroitic city	Kush Kush
24	Sudan Antiquities Service	Vercoutter	1958–60	Wad ben Naqa (SR)	Meroitic palace and temple	Syrie

* Abbreviations for regions of Nubia as follows: AD, Abri-Delgo Reach; AH, Abu Hamed Reach, BH, *Batn el Hajar*; CS, Central Sudan; DR, Dongola Reach; LN, Lower Nubia; SR, Shendi Reach. See Chapter 1.

† For explanation of abbreviations and full references see Notes, pp. 681–772. ‡ Work at Sai Island was resumed in 1969.

§ This expedition became part of the Nubian Salvage Campaign. See Table V, Expedition no. B-10. ¶ Excavations still in progress.

THE HIGH DAM CAMPAIGN

The first two Archaeological Surveys of Nubia were carried out respectively by the Egyptian Survey Department and the Service des Antiquités, in each case with a credit from the Ministry of Finance. The demands created by the High Dam, however, were far beyond the resources of either the Egyptian or the Sudanese Governments. It was in these circumstances that the United Nations Educational, Scientific, and Cultural Organization (UNESCO) decided on an appeal to the conscience of the world, to contribute scientific, intellectual, and financial resources toward the conservation of Nubia's threatened monuments. If the results of this endeavour have not in the end quite lived up to the glowing promise which the UNESCO publicists held out, they still add up to an unprecedented record of achievement in both excavation and conservation.

The requirements of the High Dam Campaign were different in several respects from those of the earlier salvage programmes. Because the old Aswan Reservoir was emptied during part of each year, the submerged temples and other monuments of Lower Nubia could still be seen during the summer months, and it was not considered necessary to re-locate them. The High Dam on the other hand will create a permanent lake, and anything covered by its waters is presumably lost forever. It was therefore necessary to plan for the dismantling, transportation, and reconstruction on higher ground of some thirty-five major temples and a host of lesser monuments. The saving of the incomparable Abu Simbel was of course the most dramatic and infinitely the most expensive of these undertakings, but the work of conserving thirty or so other temples probably cost, in the aggregate, as much or more.

The High Dam Campaign was thus, unlike its predecessors, primarily a conservation programme, and its biggest challenge was to the engineers rather than to the archaeologists. Even so the amount of archaeological activity was prodigious. In response to UNESCO's appeal there was a virtual 'gold rush' of archaeologists to the banks of the Nile, and more than forty expeditions staked out claims up and down the river. (In the first rush of excitement there were even rival claims and boundary disputes.) The inventory of full-fledged expeditions (Table V) by no means exhausts the list of contributions to the Nubian archaeological campaign, for several nations and institutions also sent technical missions to assist the work of UNESCO and of the Egyptian and Sudanese Governments. All in all the sum of archaeology accomplished in Nubia since 1959 not only exceeds that from all previous periods; it is probably also greater than would have been achieved in the next two or three centuries without the stimulus of the High Dam.

It is impossible here to do more than enumerate the various expeditions which have worked in Egyptian and Sudanese Nubia in the last dozen years (Table V). Their published reports are only now beginning to appear, and it will be years before we can measure their full contribution to the study of Nubian history. In view of the considerable data base provided by earlier work, however, it is not surprising that the recent archaeological campaign has not yielded, and could not yield, results of the same magnitude as did its predecessors. The law of diminishing returns operates as much in archaeology as in any other field of endeavour. The High Dam Campaign has supplied a few of the still missing pieces of the Nubian picture, but its principal accomplishment has been to throw more light upon every part of it. The most substantial additions have understandably been made in those periods at the beginning and the end of Nubian history (the prehistoric and the medieval) which were largely ignored by the earlier surveys.

Although UNESCO generated the publicity and collected most of the money for the Nubian Salvage Campaign, the actual organization and management of this complex enterprise was left to the two governments involved. Rather different strategies were developed in the two cases. The Egyptian Government divided up the whole of Lower Nubia into geographical parcels of about equal size, and allowed expeditions to pick and choose among them on a first-come first-served basis. An expedition was of course responsible for the investigation of everything important within its chosen territory. The lure of subsequent concessions in the rich necropoli of Lower Egypt insured that even the least promising parcels of Nubia were not wanting for applicants. In view of the extensive work already done by the earlier surveys, and the destruction of sites by the previous inundations, the need in most of Egyptian Nubia was for detailed investigation of a few selected sites rather than for further general exploration.

The situation in Sudanese Nubia differed from that in Egypt in two respects. First, there had been no previous surveys to provide a data base comparable in any way to that in Egypt. Second, the Sudan Antiquities Service could not offer to participants in the Nubian Campaign the prospect of later rich pickings in other parts of the country. The Antiquities Service therefore decided to allow foreign concessionaires to confine themselves to sites of their own choosing, and, concurrently, to organize from its own resources a survey similar to the earlier surveys in Egyptian Nubia. The purposes of the survey were, first, to find and define remains worthy of excavation by foreign expeditions, and second, to supplement the work of the foreign expeditions by excavating anything not claimed by them.

The Survey of Sudanese Nubia, organized at the beginning of 1960 with assistance from UNESCO, ultimately explored the full length of the Nile

TABLE V

ARCHAEOLOGICAL EXPEDITIONS TO NUBIA, 1959–69

In order from North to South

[See Fig. 11]

A. *Egyptian Nubia*

No.	Area explored	Institution and country	Principal work or remains investigated
A-1	Dabod	Polish Centre for Mediterranean Arch.	Pharaonic temple
A-2	Dehmit	Egyptian Museum of Turin (Italy)	Pharaonic remains
A-3	Kertassi–Taifi	Czechoslovak Inst. of Egyptology	Roman fort; Pharaonic site
A-4	Khor Dehmit–Beit el Wali	Swiss Institute–Oriental Institute of Chicago (U.S.A.)	X-Group cemeteries
A-5	Beit el Wali	Oriental Institute of Chicago (U.S.A.)	Pharaonic temple
A-6	Sabagura	University of Milan (Italy)	Christian fortified town
A-7	Kubban–Maharraqa	University of Milan (Italy)	Pharaonic remains; Christian towns
A-8	Dakka–Wadi Allaqi	Leningrad Academy of Science (U.S.S.R.)	A-Group and C-Group remains
A-9	Seyala	University of Vienna (Austria)	Survey-excavations
A-10	Sheima–Wadi es-Sebua	French Institute–Swiss Institute	C-Group village; Pharaonic remains; Churches
A-11	Wadi es-Sebua	Egyptian Antiquities Service	Pharaonic temple
A-12	Amada	German Institute	C-Group and Pharaonic remains
A-13	Korosko–Qasr Ibrim	Egyptian Museum of Turin (Italy)	Survey-excavations
A-14	Tomas	University of Strasbourg (France)	C-Group and Pharaonic cemeteries; Meroitic village

TABLE V (Cntd)

A. *Egyptian Nubia*

No. Area explored	*Institution and country*	*Principal work or remains investigated*
A-15 Afyeh	Archaeological Survey of India	A-Group and C-Group remains
A-16 Skeikh Daud	Spanish Nat. Comm. for Nubia	Christian fortress
A-17 Aniba	University of Cairo (U.A.R.)	Cemeteries of all periods
A-18 Qasr Ibrim	Egypt Exploration Society (U.K.)	Meroitic to medieval fortress and cemeteries
A-19 Masmas	Spanish Nat. Comm. for Nubia	Meroitic cemetery
A-20 Toshka–Arminna	Pennsylvania–Yale Expedition (U.S.A.)	Cemeteries of various periods; Meroitic to Christian town
A-21 Tamit	University of Rome (Italy)	Christian town and churches
A-22 Abdullah Nirqi	University of Leiden (Netherlands)	Meroitic and Christian towns and church
A-23 Gebel Adda	University of Alexandria (U.A.R.)	Survey-excavations
A-24 Gebel Adda	American Research Center in Egypt	Meroitic to medieval town and cemeteries
A-25 Qustul	Oriental Institute of Chicago (U.S.A.)	Survey-excavations
A-26 Ballana	Egyptian Antiquities Service	X-Group tombs
A-27 Qasr el-Wizz	Oriental Institute of Chicago (U.S.A.)	Christian monastery
A-28 (Whole area)	Combined Prehistoric Expedition (U.S.A.)	Prehistoric remains
A-29 (Whole area)	Egypt Exploration Society (U.K.)	Reconnaissance survey

N.B. Surveys north of Aswan by the Yale Prehistoric Expedition and the National Museum of Canada are not included in this list.

TABLE V (Cntd)

B. *Sudanese Nubia* No. Area explored	*Institution and country*	*Principal work or remains investigated*
B-1 Faras West– Gemai West	Sudan Antiquities Service	Survey-excavations, all periods
B-2 Faras East– Gemai East	Scandinavian Joint Expedition	Survey-excavations, all periods
B-3 Faras West	Polish Centre for Mediterranean Arch.	Christian churches and palace
B-4 Aksha	Franco-Argentine Expedition	Pharaonic temple; Christian town
B-5 Serra East	Oriental Institute of Chicago (U.S.A.)	Pharaonic fort; Christian town and churches
B-6 Serra West	Scandinavian Joint Expedition	Pharaonic tomb
B-7 Debeira West	University of Ghana	Christian town and churches
B-8 Argin	Spanish Nat. Comm. for Nubia	Cemeteries of all periods
B-9 Dabarosa West	University of Colorado Museum (U.S.A.)	Prehistoric remains; X-Group and Christian towns
B-10 Buhen	Egypt Exploration Society (U.K.)	Pharaonic fortress
B-11 Meinarti	Sudan Antiquities Service	Meroitic to Christian town and church
B-12 Dorginarti	Oriental Institute of Chicago (U.S.A.)	Pharaonic fortress
B-13 Qasr Iko	Spanish Nat. Comm. for Nubia	Christian churches
B-14 Mirgissa	French Archaeological Mission	Pharaonic fortress, town and cemeteries
B-15 Dabenarti	University of California (U.S.A.)	Pharaonic fortress
B-16 Abkanarti	Spanish Nat. Comm. for Nubia	Christian fortified town
B-17 Kasanarti	Sudan Antiquities Service	Christian town

TABLE V (Cntd)

No.	Area explored	Institution and country	Principal work or remains investigated
B-18	Gemai–Dal	Sudan Antiquities Service (UNESCO)	Survey-excavations, all periods
B-19	Gemai–Murshid	Finnish Nubia Expedition	Survey-excavations
B-20	Murshid–Dal West Bank	University of Colorado (U.S.A.)	Prehistoric sites
B-21	Askut	University of California (U.S.A.)	Pharaonic fortress; Christian town
B-22	Semna–Kumma	Brown University (U.S.A.)	Pharaonic temples
B-23	Semna South	Oriental Institute of Chicago (U.S.A.)	Pharaonic fortress; Meroitic cemetery
B-24	Melik en-Nasir	German Institute (D.F.R.)	Christian remains
B-25	Sonqi West	University of Rome (Italy)	Christian church
B-26	Akasha–Ukma	University of Geneva (Switzerland)	Survey-excavations; Christian churches
B-27	Kulubnarti	University of Kentucky (U.S.A.)	Christian villages
B-28	Kulb	German Institute (D.F.R.)	Christian fortified town
B-29	(Whole area)	Combined Prehistoric Expedition (U.S.A.)	Prehistoric remains
B-30	(Whole area)	German Academy of Science (D.D.R.)	Rock pictures and inscriptions

Valley between the Egyptian border and the head of the proposed reservoir (about 100 miles), discovered over 1,000 sites, and carried out some excavation in more than one third of them.[54] In the wake of the survey party, or in a few cases before it, some 18 concessions were eventually taken up by foreign expeditions (Fig. 11). Although their territory covered less than a quarter of the total threatened area of Sudanese Nubia, they included most of the monumental sites and many of the largest cemeteries. There were in addition surveys other than that of the Antiquities Service. A Scandinavian group made an exhaustive exploration of one section of

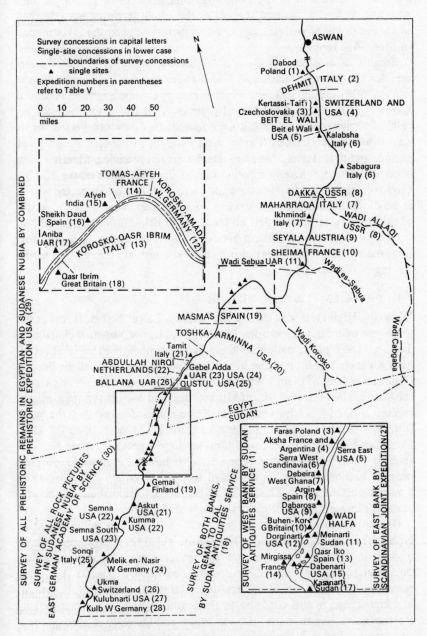

Fig. 11. Excavation concessions in Nubia, 1960–70

Inserts show enlargements of the Aniba and Wadi Halfa areas.

Sudanese Nubia and at the same time excavated all of the major sites within it. Other, specialized surveys of the whole territory were devoted to the recording of rock inscriptions and pictures and to the investigation of Stone-Age remains.

Because of its unique position of 'residual responsibility' it was necessary for the Survey of Sudanese Nubia to remain in close touch with the work of other expeditions, and where necessary to supplement it. A central archive was maintained for several years in Wadi Halfa, in which the results of each expedition's work were recorded as they progressed. In its own work the Antiquities Service survey sought to concentrate on those periods and those types of remains which were not receiving attention from other expeditions, thereby assuring that at the conclusion of the Nubian Campaign the various parts would add up to some sort of connected whole. It was initially through this strategy of supplementation that the writer of this book became an expert on the study of habitation remains, and on the Christian phase of Nubian history. (The Wadi Halfa archive – now removed to Khartoum – has also made a substantial contribution to the writing of this book.)

THE PRESENT AND THE FUTURE

While the High Dam was closing the book on Lower Nubia, it was at the same time opening a new chapter in the study of Upper Nubian archaeology. Through their participation in the salvage campaign many archaeologists got their first look at the intriguing lands to the south of the Second Cataract; several of them have now taken up concessions in other parts of the Sudan. The Meroitic cities of Musawwarat and Meroë, the old medieval capital of Dongola, the temples of Soleb and Seddenga and the great fortress of Sai have all been under excavation in the years since the High Dam Campaign, and other expeditions are in prospect for Upper Nubia.[55] Interest in this long-neglected region can only increase as its archaeological promise becomes better known – and with the alternative of working in Lower Nubia removed. The reader of this book should therefore be prepared for important additions to the story at any time.

On the whole archaeologists can look back on their achievement in Nubia with considerable pride. The record which they have been able to uncover in three quarters of a century is in many ways far more complete than that which was offered by documented history in 1900. Yet there remain enormous lacunae. Systematic exploration, and therefore systematic knowledge, is still confined to those areas which were destroyed by the successive Aswan dams – Lower Nubia and the *Batn el Hajar*. Extensive and detailed as is the evidence of occupation in these regions, it is by no means complete. Whole chapters – the so-called 'B-Group', the Napatan period, and even the later medieval period – seem to be missing.

We may epitomize the history of excavation in Nubia with the observation that here as elsewhere in the world field investigation has gone through three phases, which may conveniently be designated as 'random', 'selective', and 'comprehensive'. The random phase is characterized by haphazard and completely unscientific looting in search of *objets d'art* or treasure trove. This has been the unhappy fate of ancient monuments in all of the more accessible parts of the world; in Nubia such activities have been mercifully few. Until the twentieth century the region was too remote and too unsettled to attract any but the hardiest of dilettantes.

The beginnings of scientific archaeology are heralded by the increasingly systematic and careful excavation of a few selected sites, usually by large and well-equipped expeditions headed by professional scholars (though not necessarily by trained excavators). The sites which are singled out for attention in the 'selective' phase of excavation are nearly always the great artistic and imperial monuments – above all the royal temples, palaces and tombs. Such remains preserve of course only the culture of a tiny élite. Their excavation contributes immeasurably to the study of art history and of dynastic history, but at the same time furnishes an incomplete and one-sided picture of the cultural development of a whole people.

'Comprehensive' archaeology begins when attention turns from the great monumental remains to smaller and less dramatic sites, and a region-wide effort is made to sample sites of every type and of every historic period. From such small pieces a large picture is gradually constructed of the cultures and cultural histories of whole peoples.

In many parts of the world the comprehensive stage of archaeological investigation has not yet arrived. In a few, it has come about following the exhaustion of the monumental sites, on the *faute de mieux* principle. In the great majority of cases where comprehensive archaeology has developed, however, it has been forced upon the archaeologist by the requirements of salvage. Excavators of the future will perhaps recognize the emergence of salvage archaeology in the decades following the Second World War as one of the most revolutionary developments in the history of their discipline. Within the present generation this newly comprehensive approach to excavation – made necessary by the great outburst of building activity in the post-war years – has led to quantum increases, and sometimes to drastic revisions, in our knowledge of cultural history in many parts of the world. The investigation of some of the enormous areas destroyed by dams and reservoirs has forced us to think of culture and history, sometimes for the first time, in region-wide terms instead of in the more conventional and more parochial terms of site, city, or dynasty.[56]

The reader will recognize that the majority of excavations carried out in Nubia before 1960 belong to the second or selective phase of archaeological development. This is true in particular of the great Harvard–Boston

Expedition, whose work in many ways forms the backbone of Upper Nubian archaeology down to the present day. Although the expedition held an excavation concession covering the entire northern Sudan, and was active in the field nearly every year from 1913 to 1932, its attentions were almost entirely confined to the great fortresses, temples, and tombs of Upper Nubia. So to a large extent were the excavations of half a dozen other major expeditions which entered the field during the first half of the twentieth century.

If excavation in Nubia has been largely of the selective kind, however, it must also be recognized that this same region is in one sense the cradle of comprehensive archaeology. As already noted, the First Archaeological Survey (1907–11) was the world's premier salvage campaign, and set the standard for many which followed. Reisner's discovery and detailed cultural description of the A, C, and X 'Groups', worked out within a few months of the beginning of the campaign, stands as an enduring example of how much comprehensive investigation can add to the incomplete picture which emerges from the study exclusively of monumental remains.

In spite of the auspicious results obtained by the First Archaeological Survey, there was comparatively little follow-up. Once the salvage operation was completed archaeologists (including Reisner himself) reverted to their predilection for monumental sites, and for the next half century the only comprehensive excavation programme carried out in Nubia was that made necessary by the enlargement of the Aswan Dam (the Second Archaeological Survey, 1929–34). The threat of the High Dam has of course resulted in a great deal more systematic work since 1960, as has already been noted. It is worth emphasizing, nevertheless, that up to today no comprehensive survey and excavation has been carried out in any part of Nubia save in those areas which have been inundated by the successive Aswan dams, and which are now closed to all further investigation. This point is of fundamental importance in understanding some of the lacunae in the history which follows.

In effect, Nubian archaeology has reached the comprehensive stage only in Lower Nubia and the *Batn el Hajar*. Throughout the whole vast region south of the Dal Cataract – the ancient heartland of Nubian civilizations – we have not progressed beyond the selective stage.[57] We can, therefore, offer a reasonably complete and well-balanced picture of development only for those cultures and cultural periods which happen to be well represented in the northern part of Nubia. Our treatment of the cultures of Upper Nubia – some of the most important in the country's history – must often be sketchy and conjectural. This will be particularly apparent to readers of Chapters 10 and 11, dealing with a historical interval when Lower Nubia seems to have been largely depopulated.

90

THE RACIAL QUESTION

In addition to textual and archaeological evidence, the skeletal remains of the ancient Nubians have contributed importantly to many of the earlier efforts to reconstruct Nubian history. When the First Archaeological Survey of Nubia was organized, Sir Grafton Elliot Smith, a distinguished anatomist then living in Cairo, agreed to undertake the analysis and description of the skeletal remains to be uncovered. He accompanied the first expedition in the field, and made measurements and observations on the bones *in situ*. Those which were well enough preserved (primarily skulls) were then removed and sent to Cairo for more extensive study. The number of crania thus collected never amounted to more than fifteen or twenty per cent of those exhumed, for most of the Lower Nubian burials were in a bad state of preservation.

Elliot Smith, like Reisner, was obliged to leave the survey after the first season, but his work and his methods were carried on by Douglas Derry, initially under Smith's supervision, in the following campaigns. Their anatomical analyses were published alongside the purely archaeological results in all of the early *Bulletins* of the Archaeological Survey, and more fully in the *Report* for 1907–8.[58] The pattern set by Smith and Derry was also followed a generation later by Ahmed Batrawi in his study of anatomical remains from the Second Archaeological Survey.

Elliot Smith and Derry had no difficulty in recognizing significant racial differences among the skeletons from the various Nubian grave types. The people of the 'A-Group' they believed to be identical with the pre-dynastic Egyptians, while in the 'B-Group' they perceived a much stronger Negro strain. This element was still believed to be present, although much diluted, in the 'C-Group' – a circumstance which led both Elliot Smith and Reisner to postulate a second migration of northerners into the Sudan at this time. The same racial amalgam was seen in the subsequent Nubian populations down to the 'X-Group', when there was a second heavy Negro infusion. It was these anatomical differences – seemingly evidence of racial migrations – which led Reisner to identify the Nubian grave types with distinct population groups, and which thus underlay the whole 'multi-layer' interpretation of Nubian history.

The anatomical work of Smith and Derry can be criticized on a number of grounds. Even with the best intentions and under the best conditions, the methods available to them at the beginning of the twentieth century were primitive and highly subjective. Heavy emphasis was placed on a small number of characteristics, such as the much abused cephalic index, and many of them were morphological features which could not be verified by measurement. Perhaps more serious than methodological naïveté

91

was the implicit racism of the early comparative anatomy. It was in many respects a pseudo-science, intent on differentiating the living varieties of man as though they were distinct species of animals or plants. Its strategy was to recognize and define the consistent differences between the intuitively recognized races, ignoring the similarities – and without considering the question of whether the 'races' themselves had any validity as type-concepts. This was a far cry from today's scientific study of population dynamics.

Given the methods and the assumptions prevailing in 1907, even the best of comparative anatomists could find in their material confirmation for whatever historical theories they wished to believe. This unquestionably happened in the case of Smith, Derry, and Reisner. It must be acknowledged too that the racist point of view which was shared by nearly all the early students of Nubian history condemns the age more than the men. Elliot Smith was perhaps the most outspoken of them, asserting in one of his reports that '... the smallest infusion of Negro-blood immediately manifests itself in a dulling of initiative and a "drag" on the further development of the arts of civilization,'[59] but the same belief can be found expressed in one way or another in the writings of most of his contemporaries. It was, after all, not until a generation later that notions of racial superiority and inferiority came seriously to be questioned.[60]

Physical anthropology made significant strides in the generation separating the first and second Archaeological Surveys of Nubia. Ahmed Batrawi, in studying the skeletal material from the Emery–Kirwan surveys, had the advantage both of a more refined methodology and of a much less biased mind than had his predecessors. His studies failed for the most part to verify their conclusions, particularly in regard to the racial question. So dominant was the influence of Elliot Smith, however, that Batrawi was reluctant to challenge his historical theories even while he disputed their empirical foundation. His own published conclusions were prefaced by a somewhat hesitant expression of concurrence in the theories of his predecessors,[61] which seems to be largely contradicted in the later paragraphs of his work.

Batrawi was more forthright a decade later, after taking a second look not only at his own work but at that of the First Archaeological Survey as well. In an article published in the *Journal of the Royal Anthropological Institute* (1946),[62] he expressly repudiated the multi-racial hypothesis and recognized the indigenous Nubian population (i.e. exclusive of Egyptian colonists) as a single and remarkably stable genetic pool from beginning to end. He also recognized that 'failure to distinguish clearly between the achievements of populations and their inherent biological characteristics has caused much confusion in anthropological writings. The literature dealing with the racial history of Egypt [and Nubia] provides an outstanding example of the danger of assessing biological relationships from cultural evidence.'[63] This long-overdue admonition, appearing in a journal little consulted by historians, went almost entirely unheeded. As a result the multi-racial theory is still very much with us, for example in the pages of Emery's recent *Egypt in Nubia*. Supported by a web of historical fantasy which has been woven around it, the theory survives long after the demolition of its empirical underpinnings.

Batrawi's revised view of Nubian racial history received further confirmation from the comparative studies of Jebel Moya skeletal material undertaken by Mukherjee, Rao and Trevor. Using a complex set of statistical indices, they calculated degrees of relationship among some twenty African population groups, including 'pure' Negroes as well as Nubians, Ethiopians, and Egyptians. In their formulation the seven Nubian groups (i.e. all of those originally studied by Smith and Derry, and later by Batrawi) emerge as a distinct and closely homogeneous genetic cluster, widely separated from all but two of the remaining thirteen groups with whom they were compared (Fig. 12).[64] Like Batrawi, they concluded that the Nubian groups represent a single and little-varying genetic pool. Still more recently, a study of dental characteristics (lately recognized as particularly sensitive genetic indicators) has failed to disclose any significant differences between the Meroitic X-Group, and Christian populations.[65]

The most recent publication on Nubian anatomical remains is Vagn Nielsen's analysis of the skeletal material, from several different historic periods, unearthed by the Scandinavian Joint Expedition to Sudanese Nubia between 1961 and 1964.[66] From his studies the author finds limited confirmation for many of the earlier theories of Elliot Smith and Derry; that is, he finds minor but consistent differences in the population at each successive stage of Nubian history. His characterization of these differences in racial terms is, however, almost at the farthest remove from Smith and Derry:

As to the question of negroid influence in Nubia generally, it must be stated from these examinations that the C-Group population were characterized by very little, or no negroid characteristics. The Pharaonic series was without negroid characteristics. Not until the Meroitic series a beginning negroid admixture is found, but only in the X-Group one can talk of more characteristic general negroid traits, even though the group in no way can be described as negroes.[67]

It is clear that in Vagn Nielsen's mind 'Negro' represents some kind of a 'pure' type – something which of course has never existed in Nubia in the historic period. The author is, at all events, properly cautious about attributing minor genetic differences to wholesale migrations or population replacements; he is inclined to see them as the result of normal evolution and the gradual, steady infusion of new blood (sometimes from the south, sometimes from the north) into the Nubian population.[68] Another recent

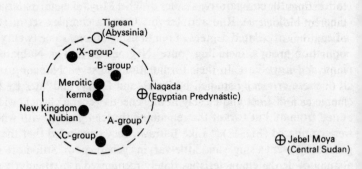

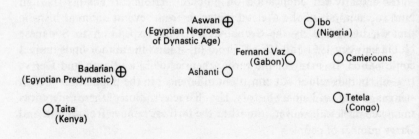

● ancient Nubian groups

⊕ other ancient populations

○ modern peoples

Degree of general affinity is indicated by distance. Note that all Nubian
groups fall within the dotted circle — much closer to each other than to
any non-Nubian peoples except the Predynastic Egyptians of Naqada
and the modern Tigreans of Abyssinia.

Fig. 12. Racial affinities between the ancient Nubian peoples
and other ancient and modern peoples of Africa

94

study has shown, too, that there may have been as much diversity within the Nubian population at certain periods of history as there was between one period and the next.[69]

Three generations of anatomical studies have left us just about where we began: knowing that Nubia has always had an African or part-African population different from that of Egypt, and knowing also that this leaves us no wiser about the political, social, or cultural history of the country. For the time being we can do no better than to heed Batrawi's admonition to 'distinguish clearly between the achievements of populations and their inherent biological characteristics'.[70] We should also note that the absence of anatomical confirmation does not at all rule out the possibility of migrations in Nubian history, nor does the now apparent racial homogeneity imply linguistic or cultural homogeneity. The only legitimate conclusion is that to learn about language and society we must look to the evidence of language and society, and not to that of biology.

LINGUISTIC HISTORY

Language is the prime source of self-identification for most of mankind. Among primitive peoples there is a close correspondence between dialect groups and kin networks; in more complex societies national states are often similarly defined by language. Thus our efforts to discover the origins and social affinities of early peoples often begin with an attempt to find out what language they spoke.

Direct evidence of language is of course lacking for the whole prehistoric period. It is the invention of writing which gives us our first clue to speech. In the early civilizations, however, the relationship between written language and spoken language was not necessarily a close one, and for many centuries a small number of writing systems had to make do for a large number of peoples. Those who had developed no writing of their own borrowed the written language of their neighbours. This phenomenon is particularly apparent in Nubia, where no fewer than six written languages were used at different times in history. Of the five which we can decipher – hieroglyphics, Greek, Coptic, Old Nubian, and Arabic – only one corresponds to an indigenous spoken language. An undeciphered sixth language, Meroitic, is believed to be indigenous because of its lack of relationship to any known language, but this of course remains hypothetical.

We will never know what languages were spoken during the pre-literate, Tribal phase of Nubian history. However, the close cultural homogeneity of the A and C Horizons, together with the low population density, carries a considerable probability that a single language was in use throughout the area where these cultural remains are found. Dynastic civilization, however, extended the frontiers of Nubia much farther afield, and almost

certainly brought into the fold diverse linguistic groups. From New Kingdom times onwards we should probably picture at least a variety of dialects, if not completely independent languages, along different parts of the
Nile.

The linguistic situation in modern Nubia is probably typical of much of
the past. Speakers of the three native dialects, as well as non-Nubian colonists among them, employ a common written language which is equally
foreign to all of them. Two important lessons may be drawn here. First,
the use of a single written language throughout the area does not necessarily imply a single spoken language. Second, the written language may
not be the mother-tongue of any of the groups employing it.

The relationship of modern Nubian to the earlier languages of the region
has always caused difficulty. The apparent lack of resemblance to the undeciphered Meroitic language, coupled with evidence of racial difference
as adduced by Elliot Smith, led to a widespread supposition that the
present-day language came to Nubia with the Negro invaders of the
'X-Group', who displaced or absorbed their Meroitic predecessors. The
anatomical basis for this theory has since been shown to be spurious; in
addition, we have really no way of knowing what language was spoken
by the Meroitic inhabitants of Lower Nubia. The written language which
they occasionally used may well be that of a ruling tribe far to the south
(i.e. at Meroë), and quite different from their everyday speech.[71] If linguistic evidence is ever to help unravel the social history of Nubia, we must
not only decipher the Meroitic language but also discover who spoke it.
In the meantime the evidence of language leaves us not much wiser,
historically, than does that of race.

THE PROBLEM OF SYNTHESIS

Winston Churchill, with customary perceptiveness, spoke of 'the spade of
the archaeologist, correcting and enlarging the historian's study'.[72] The
phrase seems particularly appropriate to Nubia when we compare the
picture of history offered by Wallis Budge in 1907 with that which Reisner,
aided by his archaeological discoveries, could present even a couple of
years later. Yet there is a difference between 'correcting' and 'enlarging'
the historian's study, and this too is manifest in the Nubian case. Historians of Nubia from Budge to Emery have relied on archaeology primarily
to enlarge, rather than to correct, their historical view. Because they have
been trained for the most part as philologists and historians, they have
accorded to archaeological evidence a supplementary role rather than the
complementary role which it deserves.

Descriptions of A-Group, C-Group, and the other undocumented
phases of Nubian history necessarily rest on archaeological discoveries.

At the same time many descriptions of the Pharaonic, Meroitic, and Christian phases hardly acknowledge the existence of an archaeological record. It is the reluctance to fall back on archaeology, except in the complete default of textual records, which gives to many studies of Nubian history not only an episodic but a disjointed quality. We seem at one moment to be studying political and social history and at the next moment to be studying cultural history, as we veer back and forth between the textual and the artifactual record.

To some extent this discrepancy is inherent in the evidence. Archaeology and recorded history not only give us views of very different aspects of life, they also provide us with different measures of identity and of relationships. Archaeology can only furnish us with the concrete and imperishable products of culture, and what we can read from them about the customs and beliefs of their makers. Within this limited scope we apply criteria of identity and relationship of our own devising – based primarily on our ability to recognize distinctive patterns. We thus accord overwhelming importance, as measures of identity, to pottery styles and to burial practices, without considering whether they were of any conscious importance to the people who created them. To the extent that we can reconstruct history, by comparing the remains of one period with those of another, we are of course reconstructing only the development of culture, not of man.

With the coming of written texts we begin to see history through the eyes of its participants, or at least of its observers. The perspective of culture *per se* may be no broader than that which archaeology affords us; indeed it is often narrower. Many areas of culture, and particularly the material and technological areas, remained unrecorded and therefore 'prehistoric' long after the invention of writing. The first writers of history were interested not in broad generalities but in particular people and particular events. Even when they spoke of 'peoples' rather than 'people', they spoke in ethnic, not cultural, terms. The communities which were important to them were communities of language, law, and social tradition, not communities of material culture and trade such as we are obliged to treat of in archaeology. To the extent that they go beyond the mere recording of events, textual records give us social and ethnic history, while archaeology gives us cultural history.[73]

Archaeology and textual history obviously can and should complement one another. Together they can furnish a more complete picture of life at any time in history than can either source by itself. They cannot, however, be used in alternation, as has been done in Nubia, to produce a coherent and continuous story of either social or cultural development. Sooner or later one has to make a choice whether to let the textual record or the archaeological record carry the main burden of the story, and therefore whether to write a social or a cultural history.

Wallis Budge had no such choice in 1907. Lacking the cultural record as it has since been revealed to us through archaeology, his *Egyptian Sudan* was necessarily a social and ethnic history, albeit a very incomplete one. However, so little additional textual material has come to light since his time, except in regard to the Christian period, that we are hardly better prepared to write a social history today. Moreover, it seems unlikely that many of the lacunae will ever be filled. The continuing use of Reisner's alphabetic designations is eloquent testimony to our lack of solid ethnic and social information for many periods in Nubian history. His theories of ethnic discontinuity will probably also be with us for all time, for archaeology alone will neither verify nor disprove them.

If we are still unable to call many Nubian peoples by their proper names, we have nevertheless made continuing progress in the study of their cultural development through archaeology. The story of Nubiology in the twentieth century is *par excellence* the story of the three great dams, and the archaeological salvage programmes they have engendered. Through them we have not only our sole evidence of the undocumented stages of Nubian history, but also a mass of comparable and largely unrecorded detail in regard to the cultures of the historically known stages. In other words, we still have texts only for selected periods in Nubian history, but we now have archaeology for nearly all periods. What we can now do, therefore, is to elevate archaeology to its proper place, and let it tell a continuous story of cultural development from prehistoric times to the present.

PART ONE
TRIBAL BEGINNINGS

·4·

THE STONE AGES

We have already observed that Herodotus and most of his contemporaries looked upon 'Aethiopia' as the fountainhead of all civilization. Once the fables of antiquity gave way to the scientific investigation of prehistory, however, scholarly opinion swung to a strongly opposite view. It suited the nineteenth-century notion of European supremacy to believe that the 'Dark Continent' had always been in the rearguard of the evolutionary process. The spectacular discoveries of Early Man in East and South Africa are now beginning to correct this ethnocentric point of view, and a new interest in African prehistory has arisen as a result. It begins to look as if the ancients were not entirely wrong after all.

In keeping with the general lack of interest in African prehistory, the first archaeological surveys of Nubia paid scant attention to Stone-Age remains. Reisner and Firth actually believed that migrating Egyptians in the fourth millennium BC (progenitors of their 'A-Group') were the region's earliest inhabitants. Not until a generation later did the first prehistoric reconnaissance, by Sandford and Arkell, reveal the presence of genuinely Stone-Age cultures.[1] The remains discovered were nevertheless few and unimportant, and seemed to confirm the general impression of cultural marginality.

Prehistoric archaeology has made important advances in both method and theory since the Second World War. In particular, the rapprochement between prehistorians and Pleistocene geologists has led to a much more perceptive view of evolution in relation to environment. These developments, coupled with the growing recognition of Africa as one of the earliest arenas of human development, assured that Stone-Age remains would receive much more respectful attention during the recent Nubian Salvage Campaign than in any of its predecessors. The largest single expedition in the field between 1961 and 1966 was devoted wholly to the study of prehistory, and four other groups also did important work in this field.[2] If their endeavours have not completely dispelled the earlier impression of Nubian backwardness in prehistoric times, they have at least brought to light a long sequence of indigenous cultures antedating, and probably ancestral to, those discovered by Reisner.

Nevertheless, the investigation of Nubian prehistory remains today in its early infancy.[3] Systematic exploration has been largely confined to the immediate vicinity of Wadi Halfa: of more than a dozen Stone-Age industries which have been identified here, only three or four are known to be represented in other areas.[4] Even within the limited compass of the Wadi Halfa area the results obtained by different expeditions are not entirely in agreement, and a fully standardized descriptive and classificatory terminology has not yet been developed. As usual in the early stages of theoretical development, imagination has sometimes taken the place of solid distributional evidence as a basis for aetiological theories which are more distinguished for ingenuity than they are for probability. To account for the presence of particular stone-working traditions along the Nile, we are offered theories of long-range migration strikingly reminiscent of those devised by Reisner sixty years ago, when the study of the Nubian historic periods was similarly in its infancy. Once again, these reconstructions of social history from cultural (i.e. artifactual) evidence involve assumptions of fixed relationship between society and culture whose probability cannot be demonstrated (cf. Introduction). It is precisely to emphasize the lack of known behavioural correlates that we usually refer to the remains of Stone-Age man as 'industries' or 'assemblages' rather than as cultures.

For the time being the most authoritative work on Nubian prehistory is the two-volume *Prehistory of Nubia*,[5] reporting in detail the results of the Combined Prehistoric Expedition. The authors have identified some fourteen or fifteen Stone-Age industries, ranging in time from the Lower Paleolithic to the immediate threshold of recorded history, and have postulated a series of chronological and historical relationships among them as well as with cultural assemblages further afield (see Fig. 13). If only by right of priority this work must serve as the point of departure for future studies of Nubian prehistory, as Reisner's initial formulation of the alphabetic 'groups' has served as the point of departure for studies of the later Nubian periods. It is also certain that, as further knowledge develops, there will be important additions and revisions to this pioneer effort at classification of the Nubian Stone-Age cultures.

If there is not yet full agreement in regard to the prehistoric cultures of Nubia and their relationships, there is also uncertainty as to the nature of the environment in which they developed. The geological record indicates substantial fluctuations of climate in North Africa, as in the rest of the world, throughout the Pleistocene era (i.e. during the last two million years or so). In Europe and North America those fluctuations were expressed in the alternation of ice ages and warm periods; in Africa there was an alternation of wet periods ('pluvials') and dry periods. However, there is no general agreement as to the relative duration of wet and dry periods. Some geologists believe that the desert conditions of today have been typical of the Sahara during most of its history, so that the potential for human settlement, except during the brief 'pluvial' periods, was pretty well confined to the valleys of a few exotic streams like the Nile.[6] Others, however, envision much longer intervals when North Africa was a land of rolling savanna or woodland – an invitation rather than a barrier to the settlement of man.[7] There is also disagreement in regard to the drainage of the ancient Sahara. Some scholars regard the Nile, as we now know it, as a relatively young river, dating back no more than thirty-five or forty thousand years,[8] while others claim a much greater antiquity for it.[9] Obviously, our understanding of the earliest human inhabitants of Nubia will remain somewhat clouded until we have a clearer picture of the habitat into which they moved.

It would be presumptuous for me to attempt a detailed synthesis of the prehistory of Nubia at a time when the experts themselves are not yet wholly agreed on it. I had in fact intended to ignore this formative stage of cultural development altogether, and to begin my narrative with the earliest Nubian cultures of the Neolithic period; that is, at the threshold of sedentary life. However, the still older cultural developments which preceded and led up to the adoption of agriculture and of settled life are now at least sufficiently recognizable for it to seem worthwhile to hazard a few words of general comment on them.

INDUSTRIES OF THE LOWER AND MIDDLE PALEOLITHIC

The prehistoric surveys in Nubia have failed to disclose any trace of those primordial ape-men whose remains have lately assumed such importance in East and South Africa. For the time being it appears that the Saharan region was not part of that African arena in which the earliest ancestors of the human race may have developed. By the time early man appeared in North-east Africa, perhaps 70,000 years ago, he had long outgrown the experimental stages of tool-making and was producing and using a highly distinctive complex of stone implements. These implements, which can be found today over much of Europe, Africa, and Western Asia, are known collectively as the Acheulean industry.

If Nubia today is a special environment, the product of river and desert, then we cannot speak of the first inhabitants of our area as Nubians, for it is not certain that either desert or river as we now know them existed in their time. Acheulean stone tools have been picked up all over the Sahara, suggesting that their makers lived in one of those relatively moist intervals when the desert blossomed into savanna and woodland, offering an attractive habitat to Stone-Age hunters and gatherers.[10]

What sort of men roamed this 'pre-Nubian' landscape we do not know, for their skeletal remains have not come to light. If they were similar to the makers of Acheulean tools elsewhere, they were probably of the genus *Homo erectus*: true men, but not yet of the modern species *sapiens*. Their stone tools are mostly large bifacial chopping implements, including the distinctive Acheulean 'hand-axe'. The unspecialized nature of these tools gives little indication of their intended use. Again by analogy with other and better-known areas, it can probably be assumed that the Acheuleans of North Africa lived by hunting medium-size game, supplemented by the gathering of wild plants. Such a mode of subsistence would necessarily have dictated a migratory life, probably in small bands. The homes of the Acheuleans can hardly have been more than temporary camps without any kind of structures. However, most of the known Acheulean tools from Nubia have been found not in campsites but in the stone quarries where they were made.

Acheulean remains are found all along the lower course of the Nile, from Khartoum to the Delta, and isolated hand-axes have been found in every part of North Africa.[11] This was evidently a very widespread and undifferentiated stone technology shared by a large part of mankind, from the Cape of Good Hope to the British Isles, and as far east as the Ganges Valley. For the time being we can recognize only minor differences between the Acheulean industries of North-east Africa and those of other areas, and we are probably safe in assuming a general similarity of life and subsistence over much of the inhabited world.

In the Middle Paleolithic, perhaps 50,000 years ago, the Acheulean of Nubia gave way to a series of industries which are distinguished by a much greater abundance and variety of tools made from stone flakes, and by the gradual disappearance of hand-axes. These industries seem, like their predecessor, to be the remains of relatively unspecialized hunting–gathering peoples, but whether they were the direct descendants of the Acheuleans or whether they were newcomers to the region cannot be determined. Some of the Nubian Middle Paleolithic industries are recognizably akin to the well-known Mousterian of Europe, North Africa, and Western Asia, while others show affinities with contemporary Stone-Age cultures of the Central African forests (Sangoan and Lupemban). The apparent co-existence of different industries at the same time seems to point to a sharing of the Nubian environment, during part of the Middle Paleolithic period, by peoples of different origin. In due time, however, their varying techniques of tool-making seem to have fused into a common and distinctively Nubian tradition.[12]

THE LATER PALEOLITHIC

Over much of the world the Late Paleolithic era marks the appearance both of men (*Homo sapiens*) and of cultures recognizably akin to those of historic times. In Nubia, this stage witnessed also the emergence of an environment like that of today. The Sahara became (not necessarily for the first time) a waterless desert, within which the Nile Valley emerged as the principal oasis and the principal trans-Saharan corridor.

The number and diversity of Late Paleolithic industries which have been identified in Nubia contrasts strikingly with the seeming cultural uniformity of earlier times. Wendorf and his colleagues have recognized ten different lithic assemblages from the 25,000-year interval between the beginning of the Late Paleolithic and the final end of the Stone Age (Fig. 13).[13] They do not seem to represent a uniform sequence of development; on the contrary, some of the later Paleolithic industries have affinities to the south, some to the north, and some to the west. On the basis of these indications Wendorf postulates a series of prehistoric migrations into Nubia, followed by the co-existence over long periods of time of distinct population groups within the same environment.[14]

The desert conditions prevailing in Late Paleolithic times lend a certain plausibility to the suggestion that peoples from various neighbouring regions might have been driven to seek refuge along the Nile, or at least to include it in their hunting territory during unfavourable seasons. Nevertheless we do not yet know for certain that different lithic industries are indicative of different groups of people. The same people might perhaps produce different tools, to do different jobs, at localities only a few miles distant from one another.[15] Conversely, different and even unrelated peoples might produce identical tools when faced with the same environmental resources; particularly if they had had a chance to observe and to learn from one another. The stylistic component in chipped stone implements is not so great that we can assume, *a priori*, that different peoples will express their individuality in different styles, as we habitually do in the case of pottery and other more advanced manufactures.[16] Hence it is relatively easy for us to recognize relationships between groups of tools (especially with the aid of statistical analysis), but we are never certain what were the historical processes which account for the resemblances. They might be evidence of the diffusion of ideas, or of things, or the migration of individuals or of whole tribes, or they might be cases of accidental parallelism.

Setting aside the largely technical differences between the Nubian cultures of the Late Paleolithic, they have certain broad similarities which point to a common and increasingly specialized adaptation to the Nile

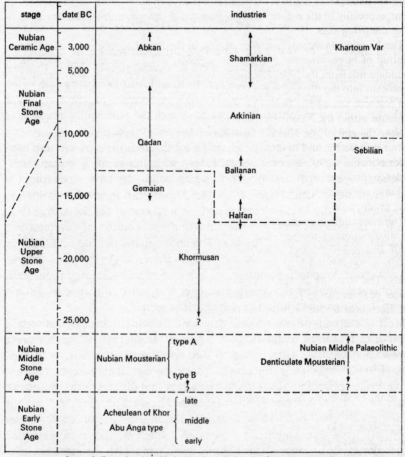

stage	date BC	industries

Arrows indicate duration of industries through time. Read time from bottom to top.

Fig. 13. Chronological development of Nubian prehistoric industries

environment. This adaptation is termed by Wendorf the 'Nilotic adjustment', and is characterized by him in the following terms:

The Nubian Nilotic culture area begins to emerge shortly after the first evidence that the modern regime of the Nile had been established. The most important factor in the development of the Nubian Nilotic culture area was the adjustment to the micro-environment of the Nile Valley . . . Once this adjustment was made the result was a general stability of population. Some movements occurred up and down the Nile, but rarely beyond it.

The adjustments to the Nilotic environment are evident in many aspects of the archaeological materials . . . The shift from ferrocrete sandstone and Precambrian rocks to Nile chert and agate pebbles in the manufacture of tools is an excellent example. It is also reflected in a change in the utilization of the environment, especially in the reduction in the number of quarries and workshops away from the living sites.

The Nilotic adjustment is expressed also in the mixed economy based on the hunting of large savanna and aquatic animals, and on the utilization of the abundant fish from the Nile. The fishing is particularly important, and it remains significant into the historic period. The absence of evidence for the utilization of this resource among the Sebilian is a strong indication that the Sebilian did not originate within the Nilotic micro-environment.

Near the end of the Nubian Final Stone Age, techniques were developed to permit the effective use of the wild grain which grew along the Nile, and thus to make possible the exploitation of a new and rich source of food. There is no evidence, however, that the utilization of grain, which occurred very early in Nubia in comparison with the rest of the Near East, led to a local development of food production.

These economic patterns are reflected in the character of the communities and the distribution of the settlements. From the beginning the communities are small and compact, and probably rarely exceeded twenty individuals. Most appear to be of the size of a small extended family with several distinct households. The structure of these Nilotic groups is further indicated by the tight cluster of from two to four hearth areas which comprise the typical occupation site. Each hearth area probably was utilized by a single household.

Most of the occupations appear to be brief; only the Halfan sites yielded evidence of prolonged continuous use. Many of the sites, however, were repeatedly utilized, presumably because that locality had some particular advantage, at least seasonally.

The population appears to have remained numerically stable until near the end of the Final Stone Age . . . With the Qadan there is a marked increase in the number of sites, even though the size of the communities does not significantly change. It is not known if this apparent increase in population is a result of more effective hunting and fishing techniques, or if the development of the new food resources from ground grain is responsible. Whatever led to the population increase, however, there is evidence that the inhabitants of the Nubian Nile Valley were increasingly competitive with each other, as expressed in the high frequency of violent deaths found among the skeletons in the graveyard at Jebel Sahaba.

It is clearly evident that the prehistoric cultural events which transpired in Nubia have served to set this area apart both from North Africa and East Africa. The distinctive aspects of the Nubian industries are evident in the earliest phases of the Nilotic adjustment, and they persist throughout.[17]

Here, then, we have the beginnings of a uniquely Nubian cultural history.

As Wendorf has noted, the Late Paleolithic Sebilian industry seems to represent a partial exception to the general pattern of Nilotic adjustment. Sebilian remains are rather widely distributed both in Nubia and Upper Egypt; in fact this is one of the few Paleolithic industries of Nubia which was well known before the beginning of the most recent salvage campaign. The lithic technology is essentially Middle Paleolithic, and for that reason the culture was assigned an early date by its first discoverers.[18] This now appears to be in error; Sebilian sites discovered by the Combined Prehistoric Expedition were dated to the tenth millennium B C.[19] At such a late date the culture represents a distinct and surprising anomaly. Not only the tools but the material employed (ferrocrete sandstone in preference to chert and agate) differ from those of contemporary Upper Paleolithic industries, as does the economy with its absence of any suggestion of fishing or aquatic hunting. If the proposed dating is substantiated, Wendorf's suggestion of an intrusion by primitive hunters seems highly plausible. They may have stood in relation to their more technically advanced neighbours much as do the modern-day pygmies to the Bantu tribes of Central Africa.

As a way of life, the Late Paleolithic undoubtedly reached its climax in the highly specialized sub-Arctic hunting cultures of Europe, with their fine chipped tools, abundant bone and ivory, and magnificent graphic art. These developments are only dimly reflected south of the Mediterranean littoral. Most of Africa and Asia evolved much more gradually in the direction of cultural specialization, retaining the use of many Middle Paleolithic techniques until the end of the Stone Age. The stimulus of developments farther north was certainly felt, however, and a number of tool types characteristic of the European Late Paleolithic (here usually termed Upper Paleolithic) are also found in the Nubian industries of this time.

Technically, the end of the Paleolithic is signalled by the appearance over much of the world of composite, microlithic implements. These were essentially objects of wood or bone, tipped or edged with sharp flints. Some were undoubtedly arrows; others were knives, sickles, and perhaps scrapers. In Europe and the Near East this new approach to tool-making coincided with the abandonment of big-game hunting and the beginnings of specialized, semi-sedentary life based on fishing, marsh hunting, and the extensive gathering of wild grain – an adjustment which set the stage for the ensuing Neolithic revolution. Because they are associated with a distinct ecological change which is transitional between the Paleolithic and Neolithic ways of life, the microlithic industries of Europe and the Near East have usually been assigned to an intermediate stage of development termed the Mesolithic.

Microlithic technology in due time spread from Europe and the Near East to Africa, if it did not actually originate there. Microliths (the tiny flints which served as cutting edges and points) are the most abundant feature of all of the latest prehistoric industries of Nubia. Here, however, (with one important exception to be noted later) they do not appear to be connected with any significant ecological change. The Nilotic hunting–

fishing adjustment remained characteristic of Nubia until the end of the prehistoric times. Probably for this reason, Wendorf gives to the Nubian microlithic industries the collective designation 'Nubian Final Stone Age'[20] (sometimes also 'Epipaleolithic') rather than 'Mesolithic'.

We can observe in the Late Paleolithic the beginnings of that ecological conservatism which characterizes Africa, including Egypt, through all later history. Perhaps because the large herd-animals which elsewhere disappeared at the end of the Pleistocene survived in abundance on the southern continent, man was slow to adapt his subsistence patterns to the newly developing Neolithic way of life even while accepting many of its technological innovations. The story of African civilization was and is very largely one of technical and social innovations grafted to a relatively primitive subsistence base.

STONE-AGE CEMETERIES

While evidence of human activity in Nubia goes back over 100,000 years, it is not until the end of the Stone Age that we find the first remains of man himself. The migratory and uncertain nature of early prehistoric life militated against any consistent burial ritual, and certainly against the development of large cemeteries. It was probably the development of semi-sedentary life, near the end of the Stone Age, which made possible the continued use of certain localities for the disposal of the dead. Three such cemeteries came to light in the course of the recent salvage campaign. Although none of them can be dated precisely, the absence of pottery offerings (a nearly universal feature of Neolithic burials) makes it virtually certain that they antedate the development of the ceramic art.

The three known Stone-Age cemeteries contained respectively 58, 39, and 19 skeletons.[21] All of them had been buried in shallow oval pits in a flexed position, with knees drawn up more or less at right angles to the body and hands arranged close to the face. The majority of individuals rested on the left side, but this was not universal. There was no consistent orientation in one direction or another. Two of the cemeteries included multiple interments: two, three, or even four individuals buried at the same time in the same grave. It is noteworthy that the same burial customs remained characteristic of Nubia until the coming of Dynastic civilization.

No objects were found in the Stone-Age graves which could be interpreted as mortuary offerings. However, the largest cemetery, at Jebel Sahaba (near Wadi Halfa), was remarkable for the presence of 116 chipped stone artifacts within the earth filling of the graves. The presence of some of these may have been fortuitous, but a few were found actually embedded in the bones of the deceased. These, together with the evidence of traumatic injury on many of the bones, point to the probability that many and perhaps most of the individuals buried at Jebel Sahaba were victims of prehistoric strife. If so, a new dimension is added to our picture of Nubian society at this time.[22]

Physically, these earliest known Nubians did not closely resemble the population of historic times. They were tall and robust, with angular features and prominent chins. They apparently belonged to that Cro-Magnon race of *Homo sapiens* which was widely distributed over Europe and North Africa at the end of the Stone Age. Their closest resemblance is to other African populations of Mesolithic and Neolithic age whose remains have been found in Morocco and Algeria.[23] Possibly these southerners had the same dark pigmentation as today's Africans, for this is generally regarded as a common adaptation of tropical peoples.

THE TRANSITION TO SEDENTARY LIFE

Nineteenth-century prehistorians distinguished the Neolithic or New Stone Age from the Paleolithic or Old Stone Age by the presence of ground stone tools and of pottery. Later scholars have recognized that the real significance of these innovations lies not in their technology but in their use, in many cases, for the preparation and storage of agricultural products. In short, it was in Neolithic times, perhaps 10,000 years ago, that man finally gave over his reliance on natural bounty and began producing his own food. Somehow and in some place – perhaps in several places almost simultaneously – he learned to propagate both plants and animals for his own use, thereby achieving a command of his destiny undreamed of by his forefathers. Within a few millennia – almost within centuries – human society was transformed beyond recognition, and civilization itself was only a step further removed. Gordon Childe, one of the most far-seeing of twentieth-century cultural historians, gave to this transformation the name 'agricultural revolution' or 'food-producing revolution'.[24]

The twin activities of farming and of animal husbandry seem to have developed very nearly at the same time; there is still some uncertainty among scholars as to which actually came first.[25] Once developed, the two usually went hand in hand; nearly all early Neolithic farmers also kept a few domestic animals. In time, however, the keeping of livestock spread beyond the fertile regions where agriculture was possible; here nomadic or semi-nomadic pastoralism developed as a specialized offshoot of the 'food-producing revolution'.

The Neolithic transformation was most immediate and most dramatic in South-western Asia, and particularly in its upland regions. Stoutly built villages numbering more than a thousand inhabitants, producing and exchanging all kinds of luxury goods, sprang up where only bands of migrant hunters had roamed just a few centuries earlier. For this and other reasons, scholarly opinion has long inclined to view the Near Eastern highlands as the original home of the agricultural revolution.[26] The prevailing desert conditions of the Sahara seem initially to have prevented its spread to the African continent, where hunting and gathering economies persisted long after the establishment of sedentary village life in the Near East. Beginning perhaps in the sixth millennium BC, however, there was an unexpected respite: a period of substantially increased rainfall which saw the appearance of typically Mediterranean flora over regions which had been lifeless for millennia. Desiccation soon set in again, but the return of desert conditions was hardly complete until the beginning of historic times. It was apparently during this 'Neolithic wet phase' that the food-producing way of life was permanently established in Africa. In the course of centuries it spread gradually over the whole continent, until only the primitive Bushmen of the South African deserts survived to exemplify the pre-agricultural way of life.[27]

The Neolithic influences which appeared in Africa during the 'wet phase' seem to have been of two distinct sorts, both of which are important in the history of Nubia. One comprised the establishment of a primarily agricultural economy on the Lower Nile, as exemplified by the Delta Neolithic (Fayyum and Merimde) cultures of Lower Egypt and the Badarian of Upper Egypt. The other was the seemingly concurrent spread of pastoralism over vast stretches of the newly inhabitable Sahara.[28] These two ways of life met and partially coalesced in the Nile corridor, and their interplay forms a large part of the history of Nubia in later times.

The Asiatic origin of the Egyptian farming economy seems beyond dispute.[29] The antecedents of African pastoralism are much less certain. The cattle whose remains we find in early African Neolithic sites are not recognizably Asiatic strains; they might represent a case of indigenous domestication of local species.[30] Alternatively, pastoral life might have reached East Africa from the Arabian peninsula by way of the Strait of Bab-el-Mandeb, or it might have spread southward from Sinai along the Red Sea highlands, as did bedouin nomadism in the Middle Ages.

Further complicating the problem of sedentary origins in North-east Africa is the first appearance of pottery (a sure indication of sedentary life) in advance of either agriculture or animal husbandry. The use of pottery vessels is one of the most widespread features of Neolithic life, but in South-west Asia it followed a few centuries after the initial domestication of plants and animals. The oldest Neolithic sites in the Near East (and perhaps also in the Balkans) are therefore lacking ceramic remains and belong to the short-lived 'Pre-pottery' or 'Pre-ceramic Neolithic'.

In Nubia this sequence of development seems to have been reversed. The so-called Khartoum Mesolithic culture, discovered some years ago in the Central Sudan, exhibits a typical microlithic stone industry along with surprisingly well-developed pottery, but no evidence of either plant or animal domestication.[31] Here, as so often, Africa seems to have been more receptive to purely technological innovations than to the ecological advances which brought them into being. However, the foreign origin of the Khartoum Mesolithic pottery industry is not certain, for it has no known antecedents either at home or abroad. It may represent one more instance of the independent invention of pottery – possibly stimulated by an awareness of similar manufactures elsewhere.[32] For the time being the absence of radiocarbon dates makes any sort of historical correlation for the Khartoum Mesolithic difficult.

The Khartoum Mesolithic culture suggests a highly specialized adaptation to the prevailing moist conditions. The people apparently lived in large semi-permanent camps, though without constructed dwellings, along the banks of streams and ponds. A large part of their livelihood was derived from fishing and from hunting reed-rats and other small game characteristic of a marsh environment. A habitat closely similar to that of the marshy Southern Sudan of today is suggested by this mode of existence. The abundance of natural food is attested by the ability of the Khartoum Mesolithic people to lead a sedentary life (and therefore to make and use pottery) without either agriculture or animal husbandry. No cemeteries of this period have been found, but at the discovery site of 'Early Khartoum' a number of individuals had been buried within the settlement – another practice characteristic of settled peoples of the early Neolithic.[33] The method of interment, in a flexed position in shallow oval pits, is indistinguishable from that of both earlier and later Nubian peoples.

Remains of the Khartoum Mesolithic have been found over a considerable range east and west of the Nile. The associated stone industry has a much wider distribution, and is closely similar to microlithic industries both in north-west Africa and in Kenya.[34] Even the mysterious and seemingly autochthonous Khartoum Mesolithic pottery has analogues farther west in the Sahara, although they may represent a later diffusion of the idea.[35]

In most respects, the Khartoum Mesolithic has a distinctly African rather than a Near Eastern flavour. As Desmond Clark has observed, 'The Sahara at this time must have been a meeting ground for peoples from North and Central Africa. These peoples were more or less sedentary hunters and fishermen who concentrated on the permanent lakes, pans and watercourses that existed at that time and lived in midden settlements of the nature of Early Khartoum, Taferjit, and Tamaya Mellet.'[36] It is worth adding that the skeletal remains found at all three of the above named localities show unmistakable African characteristics. Culturally, and perhaps also genetically, these peoples were the direct ancestors of today's Nubians.[37]

THE NUBIAN NEOLITHIC

In the Central Sudan the Khartoum Mesolithic was succeeded, perhaps around 3500 BC,[38] by a derivative industry called the Khartoum Neolithic (sometimes also called the Shaheinab Culture after its discovery site[39]). A direct continuity between the earlier and later cultures is suggested by their closely similar pottery and lithic industries. Both groups made unpainted brown pottery which was elaborately decorated with punched and incised designs, often involving combinations of dotted and continuous lines. A. J. Arkell has suggested that these were executed with a catfish spine.[40]

The most significant innovation to be seen in the Khartoum Neolithic is the presence of a small domestic goat, possibly though not certainly of Near Eastern derivation. In other words, food production of a sort was finally developed on the Upper Nile at this time, almost coeval with the rise of civilization itself in Egypt and Mesopotamia. Even now, however, the economy of the Nubians was hardly transformed: the Khartoum Neolithic industry bespeaks a continued heavy reliance on fishing and marsh hunting, with goat herding perhaps only an incidental supplement in the beginning. In most respects the culture still exemplifies the Nilotic adjustment in its ultimate stage of specialization. There are similarities indicative of contact with the Neolithic peasant cultures of Egypt (Fayyum and Badarian), but the character of the southern culture remains markedly distinct and essentially African.[41] Evidence of agriculture is still lacking.

The long-established hunting and fishing economy evidently continued to provide a more than ample livelihood, at least along the Upper Nile. The cultural remains from Shaheinab and other sites in the Central Sudan give a remarkable impression of affluence and luxury. Beads and other ornaments of amazon stone, carnelian, bone and shell; ground-stone mace heads, adzes, and celts; and pottery are all found in profusion.[42] Although desiccation of the Sahara may have been once again in process, there was not yet a complete return of desert conditions, for Khartoum Neolithic remains have been found at considerable distances from the present Nile in areas which are now quite lifeless.[43]

Remains typologically similar to the Khartoum Mesolithic and Khartoum Neolithic are also found in the northern part of Nubia, at least as far as the Second Cataract. They do not show a close affinity to the Nubian Final Stone-Age industries of this area, and are therefore believed to represent an intrusion from elsewhere.[44] Nearly a dozen sites of Khartoum Neolithic type (called 'Khartoum Variant' by Wendorf and his associates) were excavated in the Wadi Halfa area during the last salvage campaign.[45]

Although the Neolithic sites in the north show some similarity to those

113

near Khartoum, there is not the same suggestion of prosperity and abundance as is characteristic of the southern remains. The numerous ornaments as well as the wood-working tools (adzes and celts) found at Shaheinab have not been found in Lower Nubia. Desert conditions were perhaps more advanced in the north, as they are today, and the game resources diminished accordingly. Unfortunately the economic activities of the Khartoum Neolithic people in Lower Nubia are not clearly indicated by the remains so far discovered. Neither the bones of wild nor domesticated animals, nor definite evidence of fishing, have yet come to light. For the sites far removed from the banks of the river, however, it is difficult to imagine any subsistence activity other than pastoral herding or small-game hunting.

All of the known Khartoum Neolithic sites in Lower Nubia are small and impermanent camps. A fragment of plastered mud floor was found at one place,[46] and rude hearths at another,[47] but there is nothing to suggest the building of permanent structures. Again, the absence of cemeteries points to a shifting pattern of settlement. All in all, the Neolithic remains from Lower Nubia suggest a ruder and more exacting life than that enjoyed by the inhabitants of Shaheinab.

There is evidence in the Wadi Halfa area of a second Neolithic culture, termed the Abkan by Wendorf and his associates.[48] The associated lithic industry, unlike that of the 'Khartoum Variant', seems to be of local origin and derived from the Qadan industry in the Final Stone Age.[49] Abkan pottery on the other hand shows generalized similarities with that of Neolithic Egypt. The vessels are mostly very thin-walled, plain hemispherical bowls, occasionally with a red slip. Although indented decoration sometimes appears, there is nothing comparable to the complex designs characteristic of the Khartoum Neolithic. Nevertheless, the occasional finding of Abkan pottery in Khartoum sites and vice versa suggests the contemporaneity of the two industries.

In contrast to the Khartoum Neolithic remains, all known sites of the Abkan culture are located close to the present Nile, and they show evidence of a heavy dependence on fishing. According to Joel Shiner:

Abkan economy, according to our evidence, would have been heavily based on fishing. Some hunting and gathering must have played a part, though direct evidence is scanty. Grinding stones occur, though they are not numerous. . . If there were significant differences in seasonal activity, those activities were carried out from a single somewhat permanent location. Six of the eight Abkan sites are situated within a few meters of possible sites for fish traps.[50]

So far Abkan Neolithic sites are known only from the Second Cataract area and the *Batn el Hajar*.[51] Apart from consistent differences in ceramic and lithic technology, there is little to differentiate them from the sites of the Khartoum Neolithic. Both were essentially camps without any evidence of permanent structures or even of carefully prepared hearths or living floors in most instances. However, some Abkan dwelling areas in the cataract area took advantage of the protection offered by natural outcrops and boulders. The extent and depth of occupation deposit in these places suggests a larger population and a more settled way of life than do the Khartoum Neolithic remains in the same area.

In the coexistence of two industries, one confined to the riverbanks and the other more widely dispersed, it is tempting to see the genesis of that agricultural–pastoral dichotomy which is so characteristic of the later Near East. Such a hypothesis might even account for the seeming poverty of the Khartoum Neolithic remains in the north, assuming that the Khartoum people were late arrivals after the Abkans had pre-empted the best parts of the valley. Nevertheless there are formidable objections to any such interpretation. The Abkans appear to have been primarily fishermen rather than farmers, and we know that at least in the south fishing was also an important source of livelihood to the Khartoum people. Even the contemporaneity of the two traditions is not beyond dispute, since actual dates are lacking. They could conceivably represent successive developments, the Abkan being almost certainly the later. At all events the dichotomy is no longer apparent in the succeeding A Horizon, and both Abkan and Khartoum Neolithic traditions seem to be blended in this earliest Nubian culture of the historic period (cf. Ch. 5).

PREHISTORIC ART

No description of prehistoric life in North Africa would be complete without some mention of the rock engravings which are its characteristic artistic expression. Representations of animals, and less frequently of men and their products, are found carved (or occasionally painted) on rock outcrops all over the Sahara and beyond. The variety of styles and motifs attests to a long artistic history.

The dating of epigraphic remains always presents difficulties, for they are seldom associated with occupational debris. However, the prehistoric origin of much of the Saharan rock art seems beyond dispute. Many of the drawings are found in places which have not been inhabitable since the Neolithic wet phase, and the fauna depicted have long been extinct in the northern part of Africa. The largest and best executed of the drawings appear on a number of grounds to be the earliest. Their artistic resemblance to the great Magdalenian cave paintings of France and Spain is so striking as to suggest a historical connection by way of the Strait of Gibraltar.[52] In later times the epigraphic art seems to have undergone a gradual stylistic deterioration, perhaps corresponding to the decline and disappearance of heavy game itself. However, the practice of rock engraving and painting survived well down into historic times, and is still practised today by Bushmen hunters in the southern deserts of Africa.

Rock engravings are abundant along the whole length of the Nile Valley, at least from Khartoum to the Delta. Nearly a thousand groups of pictures were recorded by a single expedition in the Second Cataract and *Batn el Hajar* areas.[53] They apparently date from all periods from the prehistoric to the fairly recent past. The prehistoric drawings show the typical savanna game animals found today in Central and South Africa (and presumably found also in Nubia at the time they were drawn), while cattle are the favourite theme of most later periods. There are also a number of motifs, such as a large boat with mast and steering oar, of unmistakable Egyptian derivation. Similar boat drawings are found all over the Sahara, and are thought to be associated with specific mortuary beliefs.[54]

Although the earliest Nubian rock pictures are certainly prehistoric, they do not belong to the initial, monumental phase of Saharan rock art. Nothing comparable to the dynamic, Magdalenian-type drawings of the Central and Western Sahara has yet been found in the Nile Valley. The animals are always represented in miniature, and the attitudes are stiff and formalized.

One of the largest and best-known finds of Nubian prehistoric art was at Abka, closely associated with occupational remains of the Qadan and Abkan industries of the Final Stone Age and the Neolithic.[55] Hundreds of individual drawings were engraved on a group of granite boulders scattered over several acres, some in dense clusters and others isolated (Pl. IVa). The largest single aggregation included more than fifty animals as well as innumerable other designs. Although some groups of two or three figures were clearly executed at the same time, there was no real effort at scene composition, and the proximity of many figures was evidently fortuitous. There was some superimposition of later over earlier drawings, but no suggestion of the deliberately created 'palimpsests' characteristic both of the Western Sahara and of Magdalenian cave art.[56]

Identifiable fauna among the Abka rock pictures include giraffe, oryx, gazelle, hartebeeste, wild ass, elephant, hippopotamus, rhinoceros, ostrich, and hare. Curiously, in view of the presumed subsistence activity of the people who lived at Abka, there are no representations of fish, although one semi-abstract design might be a fish trap.[57] There are also hunters with bows and arrows and with dogs, and various other human figures. The best of the figures are executed with considerable care, but without any suggestion of life or motion. There are in addition a large number of purely abstract designs. The height of individual drawings rarely exceeds ten or twelve inches.

The occupations at Abka are dated between 7000 and 4000 B C.[58] Since the drawings here seem to be of the earliest type found in Nubia, this probably also fixes the date for the introduction of rock art into the Nile Valley.

INTERPRETATIVE SUMMARY

The history of Nubia in the Stone Ages is characterized by the gradual development of an oasis-type environment, and by the increasingly special-ized adaptation of the indigenous population to the resources of that environment. So successful was this 'Nilotic adjustment' that it was long unaffected either by climatic change or by the development of more advanced lifeways in neighbouring regions. The gathering of cereal grains, which in the Near East portended a cultural and social revolution, in Nubia was never more than an unimportant dietary supplement. Neither the later introduction of domestic animals nor the possibly autonomous development of pottery had any important, transforming influence on Nubian society. The Neolithic wet phase made possible the spread of the Near Eastern farming life into Egypt, but on the Upper Nile its primary effect was to enrich the already well-established hunting–fishing–gathering economy. In the end, sedentary life seems to have come about not through the development of food production but through the extraordinary pro-ductivity of hunting and fishing during the Neolithic wet phase. It was not until the end of the Stone Age, when Egypt and Sumer were already at the threshold of civilization, that farming life was finally established in Nubia. That story properly belongs to the A Horizon of the historic period.

5

THE SHADOW OF CIVILIZATION

THE NUBIAN A HORIZON

In the fourth millennium BC the influence of developing civilization in the Near East finally made itself felt in Africa. Along the Lower Nile there was an enlargement of society, a quickening of the pace of life, and a refinement of the arts which set the stage for the emergence of the pharaonic state near the end of the millennium. With the concurrent appearance of hieroglyphic writing, we are abruptly in the historic period. At once our picture of life and society in Egypt is far broader and more complete than in any previous period.

The dawn of history in Egypt sheds at best a feeble and uncertain light on the land to the south, which remained Neolithic and illiterate for centuries to come. From the annals of Egyptian kings and officials we catch fleeting and sometimes enigmatic glimpses of Nubia, but for solid evidence of culture and its development we must continue to rely almost exclusively on archaeology. Not until dynastic civilization itself came to Nubia, 1,500 years later, can we form any kind of picture of everyday life in the southern land from textual evidence.

The period of emerging civilization in Egypt is generally contemporary with the A Horizon in Nubia. This is Reisner's old 'A-Group' – the first of the unrecorded cultures which he discovered sixty years ago at Shellal, and which he identified as the earliest occupation of Nubia. Noting the resemblance of 'A-Group' pottery to that of the Predynastic Egyptians, as well as the seeming absence of older remains in Nubia, Reisner quite understandably conceived of a southward migration of Egyptian settlers into a previously uninhabited land.[1] His history of Nubia, and many which have followed it, therefore begins with the 'A-Group' occupation.

The existence of the 'A-Group' as a distinct cultural complex has been thoroughly validated by archaeological work since Reisner's time. On the other hand we can also recognize today that many of Reisner's ideas in regard to the origins and relationships of the 'A-Group' were incorrect. The weight of modern evidence indicates that both culture and society

118

were unmistakably Nubian, and related to those of earlier and later times in the same area. In the beginning, a connection with the Neolithic Abkan tradition, and perhaps also with other Neolithic cultures of Lower Nubia, now seems evident.[2] At the end, the supposed distinction between 'A-Group' and 'B-Group' appears to be entirely spurious. There are substantial links even with the 'C-Group', which is usually thought of as much later in time. It seems best therefore to avoid the social implications of the word 'group' and to speak instead of a widespread cultural horizon, encompassing both 'A-Group' and 'B-Group': the A Horizon, for want of a better name.

In defence of Reisner's original hypothesis, the influence of Egypt in the Nubian A Horizon can hardly be exaggerated. The main cultural innovations as well as the great historical events of this period are nearly all traceable directly or indirectly to the Egyptians. It is the ever-present shadow of civilization in the north which distinguishes the Nubia of this time from all earlier periods. In the beginning, however, it was the spread of ideas and things, not the movement of peoples, which set in motion the developments of the A Horizon. The Egyptians themselves came later, and with different results. The colonial adventures of Egypt in Nubia (to borrow Emery's title)[3] will be the subject of later chapters (cf. esp. Chs. 7 and 9).

Apart from a wealth of imported ideas and objects, four indigenous characteristics serve to distinguish the culture of the A Horizon from its Neolithic predecessors: the definite cultivation of cereal grains, the beginnings of domestic architecture, the making of a distinctive black and red pottery, and the practice of interring material offerings with the dead. The first two of these characteristics have only lately been verified. It was on the basis of graves, and above all of the pottery found in them, that Reisner long ago defined the 'A-Group' and reconstructed its social history.

Sites of the A Horizon have been found in abundance throughout Lower Nubia (Fig. 14).[4] How much further south this first Egyptian-influenced culture of Nubia extended remains, for the time being, undetermined. A few A Horizon sites were found in the recently completed survey of the *Batn el Hajar*,[5] but a much more southerly find, comprising a few graves, has recently been reported from Seddenga in the Abri-Delgo Reach.[6] The culture of the A Horizon thus appears to have been considerably more widely distributed than was any previous Neolithic industry of Lower Nubia; we should therefore perhaps regard it as a synthesis of a number of different local traditions, all responding to a common influence from the north. It must however be emphasized that for the time being systematic knowledge of the A Horizon is virtually confined to Lower Nubia.

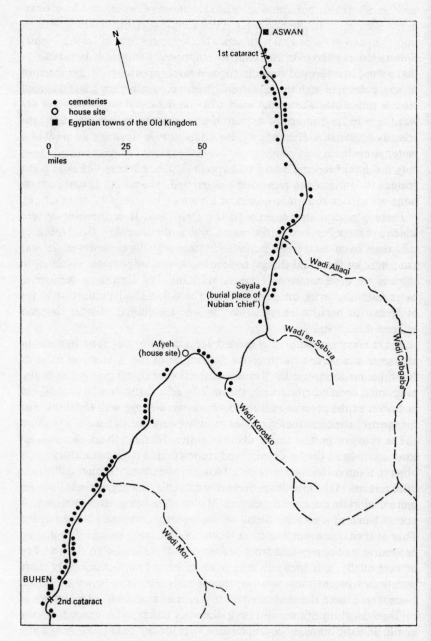

Fig. 14. Distribution of known sites of the A Horizon

POTTERY AND HISTORY

Pottery looms so large in our definition of the later Nubian cultural phases that a word must be said about its general role in archaeology. The amount of space devoted to the discussion of pottery vessels in archaeological reports might lead the casual reader to conclude that their manufacture was the primary concern of prehistoric peoples. Few archaeologists consciously believe this, although in their attempts to reconstruct history from material evidence they sometimes forget that what is important to them may not have been important to its makers. There are nevertheless good reasons for our interest in the ceramic art, quite apart from any considerations of functional importance.

There is general agreement that the arts – those expressions of culture which are most free from the dictates of necessity – are the most sensitive indicators of cultural tradition *per se*. This is above all true of the verbal arts; it is by their language, literature, and mythology that we identify cultures and civilizations in our own time. Unhappily these expressions are not preserved for us from the prehistoric cultures of antiquity. We are obliged to fall back, therefore, on the one art which is extensively developed in Neolithic societies and which is also universally and abundantly preserved: that of the shaping and decoration of pottery vessels. It is not in any sense a pure art, yet even in the rudest wares there are choices of form, colour, and surface treatment which must be based on aesthetic preference, or in other words on tradition. In default of more conventional and overt expressions of cultural identity, therefore, pottery styles become for the archaeologist the 'signatures' of prehistoric peoples.

The value of pottery as an index of cultural identity has been demonstrated through a century's experience in the field. In any given site we can observe that ceramics are not only far more abundant than are other cultural remains; they are also more uniform, more consistent, and above all more distinctive than are the designs of houses, implements, and the other imperishable products which largely make up the archaeological record. They also change more consistently, both in time and in space. The same decorative traditions will usually be shared by all of the members of a society or community, but they are seldom shared in their entirety with other societies or communities, nor do they persist over long periods of time. Even where there is a common general influence, the caprices of fashion (or the availability of materials) will make themselves felt in local variations and in periodic innovations. As a result, prehistoric 'cultures' can be quite accurately and consistently differentiated by their pottery even when they are alike in all other respects.

The importance of pottery is of course taxonomic rather than functional

– a point which archaeologists sometimes overlook. Its utility to us as a classificatory device is no indication of its importance to its makers, which may have been slight. The heart and core of a cultural system is not necessarily made up of those aspects which most distinguish it from other cultural systems. Pottery styles in fact provide a convenient and indeed an indispensable basis for the differentiation of archaeological remains in time and space, while telling us comparatively little about the lives and aspirations of their makers.

Because scientific description must begin with definition, there is always a temptation to let it end there. When this happens the distinctive becomes, automatically, the significant. In the field of archaeology, pottery becomes the tail wagging the twin dogs of culture and society – a tendency which we shall observe over and over again in the study of Nubian history. Differences and similarities in the ceramic art which are important chiefly for the chronological ordering of sites have served instead as a basis for the reconstruction of human history – often at the expense of more functionally significant cultural evidence. Had Reisner, for example, been preoccupied with cultural expressions other than pottery he would certainly have observed that the similarities between his 'A', 'B', and 'C' groups outweigh the differences by something like ten to one, and he would probably not have viewed them as distinct populations. Again, had his attention not been focused on certain specific similarities in the pottery, he might not have identified the Nubian 'A-Group' with the predynastic Egyptians.[7] In both cases he argued from pottery to people, not only ignoring other aspects of culture but forgetting, as many archaeologists do, that arts and ideas once created have a life and a history of their own, independent of their makers. 'Ideas have wings,' as Sir Mortimer Wheeler has observed;[8] they can girdle the earth in a matter of years while their originators remain firmly rooted at home.

The Nubians of the A Horizon made pottery vessels of several different kinds, some of which are clearly derivative from the Abkan Neolithic tradition.[9] The diagnostic or 'signature' vessels of this period are however bowls and jars having a polished, red exterior and a shiny, black interior and rim. This effect seems to have been produced by first rubbing the surface of the unfired vessel with powdered hematite (red ochre), and then, at the conclusion of firing, by placing it rim-downwards in a bed of leaves or straw while still red hot.[10] The result was a smudging or blackening of the rim and interior. The principle may have been discovered in the beginning by accident, but it was soon deliberately applied for aesthetic effect.

Black-topped pottery seems to have been made at one time or another by many Neolithic peoples both in North Africa and in South Asia. In the Nile Valley, its first users (and perhaps its original inventors) were the predynastic Badarians of Upper Egypt, though the ware became even more

122

popular in the succeeding Amratian (Naqada I) period.[11] The idea was carried southwards either by Nubian travellers or Egyptian settlers, and soon caught the fancy of the peoples above Aswan. The earliest Nubian sites with black-topped pottery are all in the extreme north, suggesting that the idea was at first slow to catch on, although Reisner attributed it rather to the gradual southwards migration of the Egyptians themselves.[12] There are however rather consistent differences from the beginning between the black-topped pottery of Nubia and that of Egypt, which point to the diffusion of an idea rather than the migration of a people.[13] By the later A Horizon it had reached at least as far southward as the Abri-Delgo region, and had been taken up by all of the indigenous peoples between there and Aswan.

Once established in Nubia, the black-topped pottery tradition persisted long after its demise in Egypt. Vessels of this type were still made on a small scale in the last Predynastic period which followed the Amratian in Egypt, but the art was completely dead by the beginning of historic times. In Nubia it remained in vogue for another 1,500 years, until supplanted by the wheel-made wares of the Egyptian New Kingdom. This phenomenon of 'marginal survival' we shall observe again and again in Nubian history, and above all with reference to pottery designs.

EVERYDAY LIFE IN THE A HORIZON

Most of the cultural differences between the A Horizon and its Neolithic predecessors are, like the pottery, of more chronological than functional significance. As in contemporary Egypt the major innovations were in the realms of wealth and luxury rather than in the circumstances of everyday life. Subsistence, housing, and the domestic arts were little changed, while in the development of society and economy we can perceive only the continuation of that gradual process of 'settling down' which characterizes Nubia throughout the prehistoric period. The Neolithic 'revolution' which transformed Near Eastern society in a matter of centuries was here a drawn-out evolutionary process which was still far from complete in the A Horizon.

Sites of the A Horizon are absolutely more numerous than are those of earlier periods, suggesting an increase in population. Still, the largest settlement probably numbered fewer than one hundred individuals, and Trigger estimates the maximum population for the whole of Lower Nubia at 8,000.[14] The cemeteries and abundant pottery point to a more settled life than was possible in earlier Neolithic times, but there were still no large communities. The dwelling places of the A Horizon were mostly seasonal or temporary camps, though some of them might have been intermittently re-occupied for generations. Their physical amenities were hardly superior to those of Neolithic or even Mesolithic times. Trigger describes a midden site from the early A Horizon in the following terms:[15]

There were no traces of walls anywhere on the site, but sixteen hearths were found scattered in no particular order over an area about 100 feet square. Even in the last century, however, many families in Upper Nubia lived in houses made of mats fastened onto poles. Several [Egyptian] jars were found at the site, which shows that they were used in daily life as well as for burials. In the camp litter were slate palettes, rubbing stones, and stone axheads as well as a heavy copper ax. Fishbones, ostrich eggs, and unidentified animal bones were also found. The fish bones suggest that the river must have been an important source of food at this time, as it probably had been during the Mesolithic period. About a hundred yards to the southwest, Reisner found a small cemetery which he believed was associated with the camp. There were only seventeen bodies in this cemetery.

If this site is at all typical, the Nubian community of [the early A Horizon] must have been quite small, consisting of no more than a half dozen nuclear families. The site appears to be a temporary camp rather than a permanently inhabited site. This particular one appears to have been abandoned unexpectedly, otherwise it is unlikely that so much valuable material would have been left behind. Despite the appearance of unsettled, virtually nomadic, conditions in this and later living sites, there is other evidence suggesting considerably more stability. In particular there are secondary burials in a large number of graves which appear to have been made some time after the original burial. This seems to indicate that a band or family was able to use the same cemetery over a long period of time. Perhaps each of these groups tended to keep to a limited section of the river, a way of life more in keeping with at least a partial dependence on agriculture than nomadic wandering. Since the habitations were very flimsy the settlements could be moved fairly often. During most of the year the camps were probably located along the edge of the river, and it was only during the flood period that their inhabitants retreated to the edge of the flood plain.

Of the forty or more living sites of the A Horizon which have now been investigated, only three exhibit unmistakable remains of structures.[16] The largest and best-preserved of these sites, near Afyeh, was excavated by an Indian expedition in 1962. It is described as follows by Trigger:[17]

At A. 5, near Afyeh, the 1961 survey discovered a site at least 150 by 80 meters, which, like some from Predynastic Egypt, stretched across a desert bluff between two wadis. Traces of rough stone walls were found throughout the site, which formed houses containing up to six rooms . . . The British uncovered the remains of a two-room house at the north end of the site. Both rooms were rectangular and had outside doors facing north. The inner and outer faces of the walls were built of dry masonry; the space between was filled with sand and mud. The external corners were thicker than the rest of the wall and slightly rounded. Both rooms had mud floors.

The stone houses of the A Horizon are the earliest examples of architecture in Nubia, but at best they can have been little more than huts. The abundance of post-holes suggests that poles still played an important part in their construction. The stone walls perhaps began as a masonry shell added to a house of grass or reeds. To judge by the extreme scarcity of structural remains, grass or reeds alone must have sufficed for the vast majority of the houses.[18]

The indigenous domestic arts of the A Horizon show similarly little advancement over those of earlier times. Pottery, grindstones, cutting tools, and all kinds of household goods are naturally more abundant, in view of the more settled life of the A Horizon, but those which were locally made are not, for the most part, noticeably superior to the products of Neolithic times. An exception must however be made in the case of certain painted pottery vessels, which may have been produced by Nubia's first specialists (see 'Cultural development in the A Horizon', below). These vessels, like the objects of Egyptian manufacture which appear in graves of the A Horizon, are sufficiently rare as to be regarded as luxuries rather than as everyday possessions. Agriculture was certainly practised on a much more systematic basis in the A Horizon than in earlier times, but again the difference was quantitative rather than qualitative. Farming was as yet unaided by such technological advances as animal power and the plough.

The subsistence activities of the A Horizon are very poorly attested, partly because archaeologists in Nubia have only recently developed an appreciation for cultural ecology. Even the practice of agriculture, although long inferred, was not definitely established until the excavations at Afyeh in 1962. Here at last were found the carbonized grains of wheat, barley, lentils, and peas – the typical crop complex of the Near Eastern Neolithic.[19] It must certainly have been the cultivation of these crops which required the Nubians of the A Horizon to lead a more sedentary life than had their ancestors. Still, the continued impermanence of settlements indicates that agriculture was far from providing a complete subsistence base. Fishing certainly remained important, and perhaps hunting as well.

The role of animal husbandry in the A Horizon remains a moot question – the largest missing piece in our puzzle, so far as this particular period in history is concerned. Domestic goats were already kept by the Neolithic dwellers at Shaheinab,[20] although their presence in Lower Nubia has yet to be firmly established. The rearing of livestock was a central concern of Nubians in the C Horizon, which followed the A Horizon. Logically, then, the A Horizon should be the connecting link between these two developments, and the formative period for those pastoral traditions which are so conspicuous in the C Horizon. Such a hypothesis receives a measure of support from the fact that leather garments are common in graves of the A

Horizon,[21] and that both cattle and sheep are mentioned as booty from Nubia in an Egyptian text of the IV Dynasty.[22]

A suggestion that cattle breeding was the primary subsistence activity of the A Horizon has recently been advanced by the Russian archaeologist Boris Piotrovsky, on the basis of excavations at Khor Daud in Lower Nubia. According to him,

> ... the excavated settlement was the place to which the breeders brought the milk to be processed, and ... dairy produce was then ferried over the opposite bank of the Nile where the chief settlements and fields were situated. The fact that the breeders were often obliged to make use of boats is illustrated by rock carvings of cattle being ferried across the river, and also by the presence in tombs, together with statuettes of horned cattle, of the clay model of a boat. The early dynastic settlement at Khor Daud represents a new type of archaic Egyptian settlement based on cattle-breeding. This settlement, like the whole cattle-breeding zone in general, has not attracted attention, and yet the role of cattle breeding in the process of class formation and Egypt's economy ... was considerable.[23]

In another place, the author acknowledges that 'there were no bones of animals to be found among the food remains',[24] although barley and two kinds of wheat were present. Moreover, the tombs and the rock pictures alluded to belong not to Khor Daud but to other sites, and probably to other time horizons. The whole discourse on the role of cattle in the A Horizon (which continues for several pages) is in fact a classic specimen of Marxian dialectic, based not on empirical evidence but on a supposed analogy with early Mesopotamia. Such an analogy is valid only by appeal to that rigid theory of evolutionary parallelism which is one of the sacred tenets of Marxist ideology. It has long been discredited by scholars who are willing to make some allowance for the variations of geography and the accidents of history. In a land which, in 3200 B C, was already approaching its modern condition of aridity,[25] the suggestion of commercial dairying operations at Khor Daud shows a gross disregard for ecological reality. It seems to be an instance of the triumph of ideology over common sense.

Up to now, the practice of animal husbandry in the A Horizon has very little empirical confirmation; only a few bones of domestic livestock have yet been identified in sites of this period.[26] Although we can logically infer their presence, we cannot be certain how much they contributed to the Nubian diet in the early historic period. On the other hand the finding of several hundred gazelle bones in a camp-site in the *Batn el Hajar*, dated around 3000 B C, shows that at least in this unproductive locality the hunting of wild game remained economically important. In the same site there were only five bone fragments which might be those of cattle, and no specimens of sheep or goat.[27]

Contrasting the art and mortuary customs of the A Horizon with those of the C Horizon, we can at least be certain that cattle, if present, had not the same ideological importance which they assumed in later times. The problems of the origin and significance of cattle domestication and of cattle worship will be discussed further in the next chapter.

THE MORTUARY COMPLEX

All in all, the habitation sites of the A Horizon barely hint at an enrichment of life in comparison with earlier times. When we turn to the cemeteries, however, a vastly different picture confronts us. Although the grave pits and the position of interment are unchanged since the Final Stone Age, there is now an abundance of mortuary offerings, many of them of foreign manufacture. Directly and indirectly, the graves of the A Horizon reveal three distinct innovations: a growing concern for the afterlife, the accumulation of substantial wealth in the form of luxury goods, and, most important of all, the establishment of commercial relations with the developing civilization of Egypt. Imported goods and an imported ideology: here are represented, for the first time, the transforming characteristics of the historic period in Nubia.

Cemeteries of the A Horizon have been a focus of special interest for archaeologists since their first discovery, and few graves of this period have been knowingly left unexcavated. Consequently we can speak with far more confidence about mortuary practices than we can about the circumstances of everyday life at this time in history. 'A-Group' graves have yielded a wealth of material goods, many of which have never been found in the poor and denuded habitation sites, so that we are unable to say what part they played in this world.

Well over one hundred cemeteries of the A Horizon have now been investigated.[28] The largest of them remains the 'discovery site' (Cemetery 7) at Shellal, which contained 66 graves of the 'A-Group' and over a hundred attributed to the 'B-Group'.[29] However, as we shall see, most of the latter have no clearly distinguishing features. The largest number of definitely identifiable graves in any one cemetery of the A Horizon is 117,[30] while the usual number is between 30 and 80. We have already noted that the cemeteries often show a pattern of intermittent use over long periods of time; many of them in fact remained in use during the C Horizon.

The burial customs of the A Horizon are described as follows by W. B. Emery:[31]

In burying their dead, the A-Group people used two types of graves: one was a simple oval pit, nearly round, cut to an average depth of 0·80 metre and the other, less common, was a sort of lateral niche grave formed by an oval pit with a sunk chamber on one side, cut to an average depth of 1·30 metres [cf. Fig. 15].

The bodies were laid in a contracted position on the right side with the head usually to the west. Surrounding the body were objects of daily use such as pottery vessels, alabaster grinding stones, palettes of alabaster and sandstone, wooden boomerangs, copper borers. Simple jewelry adorned the body, such as shell bracelets and bead necklaces of carnelian, blue-glazed steatite and shell. The pottery in general was rather fine both in design and manufacture, and it shows a considerable variety of form and ware. The most common types were

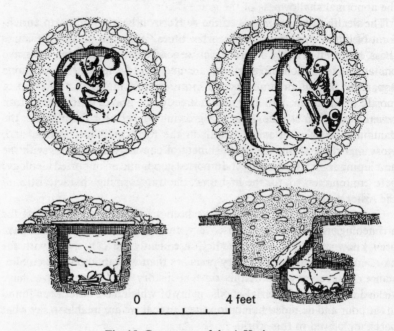

Fig. 15. Grave types of the A Horizon

large pink ware jars to contain liquid, large red ware bulbous jars with a pointed base for storing food, and deep bowls and cups of thin polished red ware, black polished inside with re-painted decoration outside, usually in imitation of basketwork; vessels of this type were probably used for eating purposes.

The vast majority of A Horizon graves are unaccompanied by any structures or marking at the surface of the ground, and it was long believed that the Nubians of this period had not yet adopted the practice of building tumuli or grave superstructures. A recent find from Egyptian Nubia, however, requires some modification of this view. H. S. Smith, the discoverer, reports that 'in Cemetery 268 at Tunqala West, which being away from any *wadi* and at a relatively high level had not been affected by denudation like most A-Group cemeteries, there were found (i) tumuli built of courses of dry undressed stone over the mouth of the grave, of approximately circular shape; (ii) an offering place constructed of upright stones placed at right angles to the tumulus containing offering pottery; (iii) what were in all probability uninscribed grave stelae.'[32] All of these occurrences anticipate the common mortuary practices of the C Horizon, and further reinforce the suggestion of continuity between the two periods. The general absence of grave superstructures in the A Horizon may therefore be due to their destruction by sheet erosion, a process which is also suggested by the abnormal shallowness of the grave shafts.

The wealth of luxury goods buried with the Nubians of the A Horizon is, for a Neolithic people, astonishing. Even the poorest of graves (excluding those of the 'B-Group' whose status we shall have to consider presently) contain a few such objects, and most notably jewelry, which was apparently seldom inherited by the living. Common items of adornment, mostly of Egyptian manufacture, were beads of faience (frit or limestone covered with a blue-green glaze), shell, and various kinds of stone, pendants and amulets of faience and stone, ivory combs, and bracelets of ivory and shell. Other Egyptian-made grave goods included copper tools and surprising quantities of wheel-made pottery.

In contrast to the 'A-Group' graves, the graves of Reisner's 'B-Group' are either devoid of offerings or contain only a few simple goods, mostly of local manufacture. Reisner believed that these belonged to a later era and a different people, but they are in fact indistinguishable from 'A-Group' graves except in their poverty. There is reason to believe, therefore, that 'A-Group' and 'B-Group' may in reality comprise the upper and lower social classes in the same population, the difference between them being socio-economic rather than chronological. If this is so, it says a good deal about the extent to which economic differentiation, and perhaps even social differentiation, had already advanced at the dawn of the historic era.

At the other extreme from the 'B-Group' graves are a number of particularly wealthy burials, such as one excavated by Firth near Seyala, and described as follows by Trigger:[33]

Some idea of the possessions of a Nubian chief can be gained from Cemetery 137 just south of Seyala, which Firth considered to be the burial place of such a man and his family. The graves, although large, were of a form common to all graves in Nubia at this time. They consisted of rectangular pits with rounded corners dug in the alluvium and roofed with sandstone slabs often of considerable dimensions. Each grave had been used for several burials, which appear to have been made at different times. The artifacts found in one of the graves included several stone vessels, a large number of heavy copper axes, bar ingots and chisels, a dipper made of banded slate, two immense double-bird-shaped palettes, a lion's head of rose quartz covered with green glaze, a mica mirror, and two maces with gold-plated handles. A series of animals, portrayed in low relief on the handle of the smaller mace, was executed in the same style as animals found on slate palettes from the reign of King Narmer. Helene Kantor[34] has dated this cemetery to the early part of the [Egyptian] First Dynasty . . .

The implications of the term 'chief' require some qualification. The rather primitive technology and society which is revealed by the material remains of the early Nubians makes it unlikely that they had achieved anything like a hereditary monarchy as we now understand the term. Probably, like most primitive peoples, they continued to be governed very largely through the institutions of kinship. If any individual or lineage wielded more formal authority, it was probably authority of the highly restricted (and frequently elective) sort which we are apt to find among Neolithic farmers or herdsmen, and which is exemplified today by the 'rain chiefs' of the Upper Nilotic tribes.[35]

It is also possible, however, that the individual buried at Seyala was not a political leader at all. He might have been nothing more than an unusually successful middleman in the growing Nubian–Egyptian trade – one of those 'culture brokers' who regularly appear, and who rapidly acquire authority, when alien cultures come into contact. Or, he might have been a commander of mercenary troops in the service of the Egyptians (a profession followed by many later Nubians), and derived his wealth as a reward from his masters. This possibility is suggested by the maces found in the Seyala grave, which are traditional Egyptian insignia of military command. At all events we can be fairly certain that a substantial part of the wealth and of the power of our early Nubian 'chief' followed him to the grave. It is another 1,500 years before we can perceive the trappings of genuine hereditary monarchy in Lower Nubia.

CULTURAL DEVELOPMENT IN THE A HORIZON

The presence of Egyptian trade goods in the A Horizon affords a basis for the dating of archaeological sites which is lacking in all earlier periods. For the first time we can study growth and change within the same cultural horizon, and not merely between one horizon and the next. Reisner and Firth from the beginning distinguished between Predynastic and Early Dynastic phases of the 'A-Group', using the terms applicable to contemporary Egypt. Trigger has gone a step further and divided his 'Early Nubian' period into four phases, the last being Reisner's old 'B-Group', which we shall discuss presently.[36]

The problem of dating and chronology remains nevertheless a vexed one – unhappily more so than most Nubiologists realize. Very few of our chronological schemes for the earlier periods of Nubian history rest upon such usually reliable evidence as stratigraphy and radiocarbon dates.

Even where a series of living surfaces is present (as in some camp sites of the A Horizon), the few and fragmentary remains found on them cannot usually be differentiated. [The great bulk of our cultural material comes from cemeteries, which are not stratified in any intelligible way. Graves are customarily dated not by their relation to one another but by the objects found in them.]

[Nubian graves of the early historic periods are dated mostly by objects made in Egypt. These in turn are dated not by any absolute measure of age, but by a series of ingenious calculations which were undertaken more than three generations ago by the great Egyptologist Flinders Petrie.[37] These 'Sequence Dates' have stood the test of time remarkably well, but the data base upon which they were built was a small one, and they are certainly not infallible guides even to relative chronology.[38] The stretches of imagination which are necessary to make them fit the Nubian archaeological data suggest that at the very least they ought to be carefully re-examined.]

Even under the best of circumstances, the dating of graves from their contents must be approached with caution. This is particularly true in the case of imported luxuries, which may be conserved by the living for long periods of time before being interred with the dead. The presence of a given type of object in a given type of grave therefore does not prove their contemporaneity, although the probability increases with the number of such associations. On the other hand, the fact that a given type of object is never found in a given type of grave is no proof at all that they are not contemporaneous. It may reflect an interruption in the supply of goods, changing economic circumstances, or simply an altered notion of what will and will not be needed in the next world.

[The differences between the 'Predynastic' and the 'Early Dynastic' graves of the A Horizon, such as they are, seem well established. They are to be seen mainly in the much greater quantity and sophistication of Egyptian manufactured goods in the later period, reflecting the great flowering of craftsmanship at the dawn of pharaonic civilization.] The Nubians themselves, in addition, developed a new form of pottery which represents one of the highest achievements of their ceramic art. The vessels are mostly large bowls, sometimes broad and shallow and sometimes deep, with a pointed bottom. The walls are exceptionally hard and thin, and the surfaces highly polished. The most characteristic and distinctive feature of this ware is the use of geometric designs in red on an orange background, both colours being produced by the use of hematite in different concentrations (Pl. IV b). It is this feature which has given to the decorated pottery of the later A Horizon the name 'variegated hematitic ware'.[39] It is not common, and was perhaps the product of a small group of specialists.[40] Black-topped pottery continued to be made in more or less the same forms as before. Many of the red-on-orange vessels also had black interiors.

It is in the later stages of the A Horizon (or perhaps we should say the lack of them) that established chronological theory seems clearly at fault. No Egyptian articles datable to a reign later than the Second Dynasty have been found in Nubian 'A-Group' graves, and it has therefore been conventional practice to mark the end of the 'A-Group' concurrent with the end of the Second Dynasty, or at about 2800 BC. This leaves an interval of six centuries – roughly comparable to that between Plantagenet times and our own – before the next definitely attested occupation of Nubia in the C Horizon. It was to fill this awkward gap that Reisner originally proposed the 'B-Group'.

THE IMAGINARY 'B-GROUP'

The 'B-Group', like its alphabetic cousins, was first recognized in a group of graves in Cemetery 7 at Shellal. It is the only one of Reisner's 'groups' which has not found confirmation in later archaeological work. While Reisner and Firth in the First Archaeological Survey assigned 21 sites and 415 graves to the 'B-Group',[41] Emery and Kirwan a generation later found only three sites and a handful of graves which they attributed to this period. No other expedition, then or subsequently, has found unmistakable 'B-Group' material. Because there should be something to fill the large gap between the A and C Horizons, most archaeologists have nevertheless continued to accept it in principle while failing to recognize it in fact. As early as 1919, however, Junker[42] had suggested that the 'B-Group' people were only the poor relations of the 'A-Group', and this idea has found considerable support during the recent Nubian campaign.[43] As a *coup de grâce* to the original hypothesis, H. S. Smith has reviewed in detail the evidence of Reisner and Firth and has discovered that more than a quarter of their 'B-Group' graves were devoid of all remains, while at least thirty contained animal rather than human interments.[44] Of the remaining graves containing offerings of one sort or another, he shows convincingly that some belong to the A Horizon and some to the C Horizon, while the largest number are simply indeterminable by virtue of excessive plundering or the absence of distinctive objects. No single positive criterion of 'B-Group' emerges.

Firth's method of grave classification is thus described by Smith:

His principles seem to have been these: – in C-Group cemeteries, he termed 'B-Group' any grave which appeared to him on the basis of stratigraphy or grave type to be earlier than the C-Group, providing it contained no distinctive grave goods: in Late Predynastic and A-Group cemeteries he attributed to the 'B-Group' any grave which he considered showed signs of decadence.[45]

Smith's article on the 'B-Group' should be required reading for archaeologists. It is a masterly demonstration of how a dubious type-concept gradually fastens itself upon the imagination when it proves to be a useful classificatory pigeonhole. This is precisely what the 'B-Group' did for Reisner and Firth: at one and the same time it filled the awkward gap between 'A-Group' and 'C-Group', and provided a handy label for unclassifiable graves. The concept of the 'B-Group' as representing a separate chronological phase was, of course, reinforced by the evidence of racial distinctness adduced by Elliot Smith; evidence which we now recognize as spurious (cf. 'The racial question', Ch. 3).

It should not be supposed that none of Reisner's 'B-Group' graves belong to the time interval to which he assigned them. We have good reasons (among them Egyptian texts) for believing that Nubia was not abandoned altogether between 2800 and 2200 BC, and also for believing that this was a time of considerable impoverishment as a result of the increasingly hostile and exploitative attitude of Egypt. In the northern kingdom itself there is a marked decline of wealth in the graves of the ordinary people once the pharaohs had consolidated their power in the Third Dynasty.[46] If the 'B-Group' are only the poorer members of the 'A-Group', they may nevertheless have become increasingly numerous in the population as trade withered and slave-raiding increased.[47] In this as in so many areas, therefore, Reisner's theories were not without foundation. His fault was in differentiating qualitatively what was only a quantitative difference.

It is the supposedly long hiatus between 'A-Group' and 'C-Group' which ultimately underlies the 'B-Group' fallacy; had there been no such lacuna there would have been no need for a *populus ex machina* to fill it. A close look at the evidence, however, suggests that the time gap itself may be partly imaginary. The theory that the Nubian A Horizon persisted no later than the Egyptian Second Dynasty is open to question on two grounds. First, the pottery types and other archaeological criteria for the early Egyptian dynasties are not that accurately defined and dated even on their native soil. More importantly, as we have already noted, negative evidence is never a basis for positive dating. It is very conspicuous that Nubia in the early historic period was participating in a general, Egypt-wide trade network, and that after the Second Dynasty this was no longer true. It is also well established that at many later periods Nubia participated only in a local trade network centred on Aswan, which often supplied goods quite different from those circulating in the rest of Egypt, and probably designed specifically for the Nubian trade. Very often they perpetuated the earlier traditions of Egypt in deference to the conservatism of the southerners, just as Maria Theresa silver dollars are still manufactured by European powers for circulation in Ethiopia and East Africa.

Reisner himself recognized the possibility I have been discussing. In the first *Report of the Archaeological Survey of Nubia* he wrote:

When the facts are considered, it is at once clear that the cemeteries which I propose to date to the Early Dynastic period have, for the greater part, the characteristics of the Predynastic period or the early First Dynasty; and it is clear that many of the graves belong to that date. But it is equally clear from the occurrence of the pottery forms E.D. V, the burial types and positions, the amulets and beads, the stone vessels, that *these graves may be in part much later* [italics his]. The continuance of the black-topped pottery through all cemeteries down to the New Empire, the continued use of stone mace-heads and axes subsequent to these graves, the manifest inertia in its primitiveness of the Nubian culture down to the Hyksos period – all these considerations make it probable that the pottery and many other objects of the Late Predynastic period in Nubia continued in use long after the rapid development in Egypt had made them things of the past. One other point strengthens this conclusion – the great number of graves of this period when compared with the graves representing other periods, such as the New Empire. In this case it seems to me necessary to allow for these graves a period equal to that of any of the other great periods, probably from the latest Predynastic to the end of the Third Dynasty.[48]

A further objection to conventional chronological theories is posed by the cultural and social continuities between the A and C Horizons, which make an interval of 600 years between them unlikely. No one, comparing the two cultural complexes *in toto*, could reasonably doubt that they represent two stages in a continuum of development. The differences between them are of a much lower order than, for example, those between the Early and Classic Christian periods in medieval Nubia. Only an over-emphasis on pottery (which itself shows many continuities) has led to the suggestion of an ethnic difference between the A and C peoples.

Even more suggestive than cultural continuities is the regularity with which the C people sought out and re-occupied both the camps and the cemeteries of their predecessors.[49] There was no practical necessity for this; suitable campsites and burial places are numerous along the flanks of the Nile Valley. The re-occupation is intelligible only as the result of persisting traditions of residence or ownership, which would certainly not have survived a lapse of centuries. The mere effort to discover the earlier sites after a long interval of time would have been considerable, in view of the general absence of structural remains.

In sum, we can agree with established theory to the extent of envisioning a stable and prosperous Nubian population in the time of the Egyptian First and Second Dynasties (the 'A-Group'), a rapid impoverishment (accompanied perhaps by a substantial decline in the population, through emigration or enslavement) corresponding to the time of the Old Kingdom (the 'B-Group'), and an abrupt return of prosperity at the end of the Sixth Dynasty (the 'C-Group'). We cannot, however, regard these changes as breaks in the continuity of Nubian cultural history, nor can we attribute them to racial migrations. They may have been brought about by the encroachment and then withdrawal of the Egyptians (see esp. Ch. 7), but it now seems unlikely that they reflect any change in the fundamental character of the Nubian population.]

[Notwithstanding the foregoing arguments, it must be emphasized that the cultural and chronological gap between the A and C Horizons – the gap which is left when we eliminate the 'B-Group' as a distinct chronological stage – cannot be entirely filled on the basis of existing evidence. Nothing Nubian can be securely dated to the Third, Fourth, or Fifth Dynasty,[50] and the actual connecting links between 'A-Group' and 'C-Group' pottery have yet to be discovered.[51] We have therefore to entertain the possibility that Lower Nubia was largely abandoned by its native population – perhaps as the result of Egyptian encroachment – in the time of the Old Kingdom, that the cultural transition between the A and C Horizons took place somewhere in Upper Nubia, and that there was a re-immigration from the south at the time when the Egyptians withdrew from Lower Nubia.[52] Alternatively, it might be suggested that environmental deterioration and Egyptian pressure had forced the Nubians to revert temporarily to a pastoral and nomadic existence which has left few archaeological traces.[53] This seems to have happened once or twice in later Nubian history; most recently at the end of the Middle Ages (Ch. 17). It is to be hoped that answers to these questions will be forthcoming when systematic archaeological exploration begins in Upper Nubia.]

THE SHADOW OF EGYPT

Our concern has thus far been with the cultural and social developments of the A Horizon, both of which can be traced in considerable part to local antecedents. Because we are now in the historic period, however, we have some record of actual events and personalities in addition to the archaeological evidence of culture and society. We can therefore look upon this time as a chapter in Nubian history as well as a horizon of cultural development. If we adopt the historian's point of view we will find our perspective on Nubia considerably altered, and a good deal closer to that of Reisner.

[What distinguishes the Nubian A Horizon and all later periods from the Neolithic and all earlier periods is the ever-present shadow of Egypt and her civilization. This transforming influence is apparent even before the beginning of the historic period. We can also observe, however, that Egyptian influence was not exerted in the same way or to the same degree throughout the time of the A Horizon. It began as a source of wealth and prosperity unheard of in earlier times; it ended as a menace and finally a blight.

[A number of Egyptian hieroglyphic texts make reference to Nubia in

135

the time of the A Horizon. Even before the invention of writing, however, the Egyptian presence in the south is attested by the considerable volume of Egyptian-made goods in Nubian sites of the later Predynastic period. This mute testimony is, as usual, more informative in regard to everyday relations between the two peoples than is the textual record, and we shall examine it first here.

Even the earliest of 'A-Group' graves (those designated as 'Early Predynastic' by Reisner and Firth) contain substantial quantities of Egyptian-made pottery. It is however the much greater access of this imported wealth which chiefly distinguishes the 'Early Dynastic' from the 'Predynastic' phase of the A Horizon. Emphasis has naturally been placed upon the copper tools, the carved stone vessels, and the luxurious ivory ornaments as the most striking examples of Egyptian influence in the A Horizon. Distinctive as are these Egyptian luxury goods, their economic importance can perhaps be exaggerated. The whole volume of copper, ivory, and carved stone found in 'A-Group' sites would scarcely make a full cargo for one of the larger Egyptian sailboats of the period. In terms of bulk, it is wheel-made pottery which makes up over 95 per cent of Egyptian exports to Nubia during the A Horizon. These prosaic vessels, rather than luxury goods, provide the real measure of Egyptian–Nubian commerce at the dawn of history.

Very few of the Egyptian pots found in sites of the A Horizon are of luxury wares. The pottery made by the Nubians themselves – particularly after the development of 'variegated hematitic ware' – was superior in aesthetic quality and was certainly ample in quantity. There is in fact no reason to suppose that the Nubians of the A Horizon had any need to import pottery vessels for their own sake. Much more probably the foreign vessels served, as a great deal of Egyptian pottery has always served, as shipping containers for liquid and bulk cargoes. This is borne out by the large size of the imported vessels and by the predominance of the more durable, but least decorative, Egyptian wares.

The quantity and variety of imported pottery in the A Horizon suggests that Egyptian traders must have been frequent visitors to Nubia over a long period of time. Perhaps the first of these entrepreneurs were itinerant boat-captains and caravaneers from Aswan, for we have no evidence of royal interest in the Nubian trade during the earliest Egyptian dynasties (cf. Ch. 7). It seems unlikely that many traders ventured beyond the Second Cataract, or that they attempted to set up permanent trading emporia within Nubia. Probably they were content to deal with local suppliers along their route – among whom we can perhaps recognize the Nubian 'chief' buried at Seyala. One would logically suppose that the trade in bulk commodities moved primarily along the Nile, as has trade in all later periods, but Säve-Söderbergh has pointed out the curious fact that the Egyptians in the Old Kingdom seem to have preferred don-key caravans for the transport of all but the heaviest commodities.[54] Perhaps the First Cataract acted at this time as a deterrent to riverain trade, for it was towards the close of the Old Kingdom that the Pharaoh Mernere ordered a channel to be cleared through it.[55]

What were the commodities exchanged in the Nubian trade? They are not likely to have been the food products which were common to both countries: cereals, cheese, and beer. Fortunately we have a commercial text from the Sixth Dynasty which mentions the export of ointment, honey, clothing, and oil 'for the gratification of the Nubians'.[56] All of these are recurring themes in Egyptian–Nubian trade in later times, but most important among them were cosmetics and oil, with which African peoples have long been accustomed to anoint their bodies.

What the Nubians gave in exchange is less certain. The 'gold of Kush' had not yet been discovered, and when it was the Egyptians took immediate steps to monopolize its production and supply in their own hands (Ch. 9). Ivory and slaves, the other traditional exports of Nubia, might already have figured to some extent in the commerce of the A Horizon, although it seems unlikely that the small and scattered population of Lower Nubia was capable either of organizing a large-scale trade in tropical products or of supplying any substantial number of slaves. It is also possible, as Bruce Trigger has suggested, that the early Nubians were not engaged in trade at all, but were receiving Egyptian goods as a reward for military services per-formed in the northern country. The impoverishment which is evident after the Second Dynasty would thus represent the time when the pharaoh turned from voluntary recruitment to the forcible enslavement of Nubian troops.[57] It must be observed in regard to this theory that the widespread and sur-prisingly equitable distribution of Egyptian goods in 'A-Group' graves is more suggestive of the results of peaceful trade than of mercenary soldier-ing.[58]

The volume of Egyptian–Nubian commerce probably reached its peak in the First Dynasty, which seems to mark the apogee of Nubian prosperity in the A Horizon. We have already noted that there are no datable goods of Egyptian manufacture after the Second Dynasty, and that Reisner be-lieved there had been an almost total cessation of trade in the time of his 'B-Group'. There are reasons for regarding this as an overstatement, but a considerable decline in the quantity and quality of Egyptian exports to Nubia is certainly evident in the later A Horizon. If anything, it was second-hand goods and the products of provincial factories which the later Egyptians were shipping to the south, as modern industrial nations have been wont to dump obsolete and surplus products on the African and Latin-American markets.

Impoverishment under the Egyptian Old Kingdom was not confined to

Nubia. The peasantry of the northern country suffered almost equal deprivation, if grave goods are any measure of accumulated wealth. The reason in both cases appears to have been the same: the concentration of wealth and commerce in the hands of the pharaoh.[59] In Egypt this was achieved by ruinous taxation; in Nubia by the elimination of native enterprise. For the story of this side of Egyptian–Nubian relations we must turn to the hieroglyphic texts of Archaic Egypt and the Old Kingdom.

THE TEXTUAL RECORD

The earliest known text from Nubia already portends the shape of things to come. On an outcrop near the Second Cataract (Jebel Sheikh Suleiman) was carved the name of King Jer of the First Dynasty[60] and a short text which is partly pictorial and partly hieroglyphic.[61] 'This representation shows a Nubian chief bound to the prow of an Egyptian ship. A bound figure on the left bears the curved bow which is the traditional hieroglyph for Lower Nubia and corpses lie in the water under the boat. The scene apparently commemorates the conquest of two villages or regions identified by a bird and an unknown sign respectively [Fig. 16].'[62]

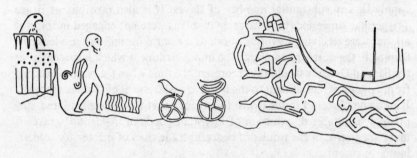

Fig. 16. Inscription of King Jer from Jebel Sheikh Suleiman

As the record of a particular event, the exploit of King Jer does not amount to much. There was hardly a permanent building from one end of Nubia to the other, and the entire Lower Nubian population would probably not have filled a large lecture hall today.[63] The Egyptians perhaps routed the inhabitants from a couple of grass villages and killed a few stragglers – something which has happened so often in history that it hardly deserves recording. The claim of subjugation would in any case be meaningless without the effort and expense of establishing a garrison, which no pharaoh undertook for generations to come. Nevertheless, as a portent of the historic role of Egypt in Nubia the inscription of King Jer has symbolic importance.

[The next two textual references to Nubia are also military in character. In a fragmentary victory stele, King Kha-sekhem of the Second Dynasty is shown triumphing over a foe whose hieroglyph probably identifies him as a Nubian. The stele was found in Egypt, and the action, if it ever took place, could of course have occurred either on Egyptian or on Nubian soil.[64] The seemingly unwarlike character of the early Nubians makes an invasion of Egypt unlikely.

[Much more definite is the inscription of King Sneferu of the Fourth Dynasty, contained in the famous Palermo Stone.[65] According to the text his armies 'hacked up' the Nubians and brought home 7,000 prisoners and 200,000 head of cattle. Here we have nothing other than the record of a highly successful slave-raid, perhaps in the guise of a military reprisal.] Even if the numbers are grossly exaggerated, as they often are in Egyptian boasts, no purely military objective could have justified operations on such a scale. The effect upon Nubia must have been shattering. Such an expedition and others like it could very well have put an end to the partially settled life of the A Horizon, by forcing the Nubians either to retreat out of range of Egyptian rapacity or else to adopt a more elusive and nomadic mode of existence. Either recourse would have resulted in the seeming gap in the archaeological record between the A and C Horizons. It is worth noting, however, that if the proportion of captured animals to humans claimed by Sneferu (about 30 to 1) is anywhere near correct, then pastoral nomadism must already have been developed in Nubia in Sneferu's time. No sedentary people could raise livestock on such a scale in the Nile Valley.

[In the time of Sneferu there already existed at least one Egyptian settlement on Nubian soil. This was the 'Old Kingdom Town' at Buhen,[66] just below the Second Cataract and close to the scene of King Jer's 'exploit' of 400 years earlier] The same locality was to be a focus of Egyptian activity for centuries to come. There is some evidence, in the form of extraordinarily large mud bricks, that Egyptians may have built here as early as the Second Dynasty, but this is not certain.[67] In the late Fourth and early Fifth Dynasties there was definitely a settlement of considerable size, surrounded by a stone wall and ditch. These measures were common in many ancient communities, including predynastic villages in Egypt, and are not necessarily evidence that enemies were in the vicinity. Some nondescript vessels of black-topped and other hand-made wares ('B-Group' pottery, according to Emery)[68] were found in the site, suggesting that the community included at least a few Nubian camp followers. However, for reasons previously discussed it is impossible to estimate the native population of Lower Nubia at this time.

[The Egyptians at Buhen during the Fourth and Fifth Dynasties were employed chiefly in smelting and refining copper ore, from a so far undiscovered source. This enterprise will be described more fully in a later chapter (Ch. 7). At about the same time other Egyptians were extracting diorite, for use in the royal statues, from the desert west of Lower Nubia.[69] The finding of a number of Fourth and Fifth Dynasty inscriptions near Toshka West, on the banks of the Nile, suggests that this was the point of departure for the diorite caravans, although no remains of a trans-shipment depot were found.[70] The mineral operations both at Buhen and in the desert seem to have come to an end before the Sixth Dynasty.

From the very end of the Old Kingdom comes a long text recounting the exploits of an Egyptian trader in Nubia. It is the funerary biography of Harkhuf, an important official in the reigns of Mernere and Pepi II, and is the first Egyptian text on Nubia which is essentially commercial rather than military in character.[71] Harkhuf claims to have led four separate trading expeditions into the southern countries, and furnishes a great deal of information about their people and products. However, his narrative clearly relates to a different time, and possibly also to different peoples, from those we have been discussing in this chapter. It belongs properly to the story of the C Horizon.

In one sense, all of the Egyptian hieroglyphic texts seem to be describing a different Nubia from that which is known to us archaeologically. Part of this is attributable to the well-known Egyptian capacity for hyperbole, part to the ignorance of the first explorers in a little-known land, and part perhaps to the universal propensity to embellish a good story. The tales which the first Egyptians brought back from Nubia, and which probably inspired many a later expedition, are suspiciously reminiscent of the fables spread by the first *conquistadores* in the New World. We know now how little underlay the embroidery of some of these yarns.

INTERPRETATIVE SUMMARY

The A Horizon represents that stage of cultural development at which the Nubians began the fateful transition from tribesmen to peasants. Although their subsistence, their technology, and their material circumstances were little altered from Neolithic times, they were drawn into a system of commercial relations with Egypt through which their cultural autonomy of earlier times was partially lost, and was never fully recovered. Their political institutions remained independent during this period, but through economic interdependence the stage was already set for the colonialism of later times.

The influence of Egypt, at first beneficial and enlightening, grew increasingly oppressive (as it did also for the Egyptian *fellah*) as the pharaoh consolidated his power and enlarged his ambitions. Until the end of the Second Dynasty he was generally busy within his own borders, and trade with the south flourished as the Nubians supplied either tropical goods or mercenary soldiers to their northern neighbours. Under the Old Kingdom the pharaoh gathered the sources of supply and the mechanisms of distribution into his own hands, and Nubian prosperity was at an end. As so often in international commerce, trading gave way to raiding and then to subjugation. The story was to be repeated in the Middle Kingdom and again in the New Kingdom. Like most of mankind, the Egyptians were rarely content to pay for what they could as easily seize by force of arms. The balance of power might force them to treat on commercial terms with the empires of the Levant, but with the unresisting southerners they stooped to trade mostly when their military organization was in disarray. Thus it came about that the periods of Nubia's greatest prosperity were usually those of Egypt's greatest weakness.

6

THE PASTORAL IDEAL

THE NUBIAN C HORIZON

The last centuries of the third millennium BC witnessed two significant and possibly related developments: the decline and temporary dissolution of the unified Egyptian monarchy, and the abrupt return of population and prosperity to Lower Nubia. The latter event was signalled by the appearance of the 'C-Group', or, as I prefer to call it, the C Horizon, a distinctive and remarkably stable cultural adjustment which was to persist for nearly a thousand years. Reisner, the original discoverer of the 'C-Group', looked on it as a kind of renaissance, following the supposed poverty and cultural retrogression of the 'B-Group'. For once, however, he did not attribute the new development to foreign influence. In the first *Report of the Archaeological Survey of Nubia* he wrote: 'It is as if the old Nubian Culture of the [A Horizon] had been quickened into an activity of its own by a period of prosperity, and had produced that which may certainly be called the Nubian culture *par excellence*.'[1] Put in slightly different terms, the long process of cultural development in the Tribal period reached its climax in the C Horizon: the most uniquely Nubian of all cultures. This view seems entirely consistent with the archaeological evidence as we know it today.

While most scholars have agreed with Reisner in regard to the distinctively 'Nubian' character of the C Horizon, many have nevertheless disputed its indigenous origin. They have pointed to the undoubted cultural innovations of the 'C-Group', in such matters as pottery and grave types, and above all to the seemingly abrupt introduction of a pastoral economy by the newcomers. In the skeletal remains, too, there seemed to be evidence of a new, Caucasian element in the 'C-Group' population.[2] The combination of supposed racial and cultural innovations led, as usual, to an identification of the 'C-Group' as a newly immigrant people. Because most of their cultural characteristics were not Egyptian, while their genetic characteristics were supposedly non-African, only east and west were left as possible source areas for the newcomers. Several scholars have attempted to trace a connection with Libya, where there is evidence of a cattle complex in the early historic period.[3] Others, however, have been content simply to speak of 'the mysterious C People'.[4]

There can be no doubt that the C Horizon first appears quite abruptly in Lower Nubia, following a period of several centuries when the region was culturally impoverished and perhaps largely depopulated. Nevertheless the 'mystery' of its origin does not appear, from the standpoint of the cultural historian, to be very great. We have already noted (Ch. 3) that the supposed racial difference between the 'A-Group' and the 'C-Group' has been invalidated by later research. Properly considered, the cultural differences between the two 'peoples' are also relatively minor, and are of an evolutionary rather than of a revolutionary sort. Notwithstanding their minor divergences the graves and the pottery of the A and C Horizons are remarkably like each other; so much so that a close cultural connection between them can hardly be questioned. Given the fact that there may be a lapse of several centuries between our latest known remains of the A Horizon and our earliest remains of the C Horizon, the wonder is not that they are different but that they are so little different. Finally, the pastoralism of the C Horizon – supposedly the main cultural innovation of this period – is almost certainly more image than reality, as we shall observe presently. Insofar as there was any cultural transformation associated with the introduction of cattle to Nubia, it was a transformation in the ideological rather than in the material sphere.

In sum, it is unthinkable to the cultural historian that the 'mysterious C People' are anyone but the descendants of the A People and their Stone-Age predecessors. Immigrants they certainly were in Lower Nubia, but immigrants in all probability only from some neighbouring region where the actual process of cultural transition from the A to the C Horizon took place. As obvious as this now appears on deductive grounds, however, it is necessary to emphasize that empirical confirmation is still lacking. The transitional pottery and grave types which should link the earlier and later stages of Nubia's Tribal phase remain to be discovered – presumably when systematic exploration is undertaken in Upper Nubia.[5]

CHRONOLOGY AND HISTORY

The archaeological 'diagnostics' of the Nubian C Horizon are polished black pottery with incised geometric designs, and graves with round stone superstructures. It was originally believed that these traits were first introduced into Lower Nubia in the time of the Egyptian First Intermediate Period, or around 2250 BC.[6] As in the A Horizon the dating was based wholly on Egyptian trade goods found in the Nubian graves, and is far from conclusive. There are a number of reasons today for believing that the first appearance of the new Nubian culture was contemporary with the Egyptian VI Dynasty, or somewhat earlier than was originally supposed. Egyptian seals of the VI Dynasty have been found in considerable numbers in 'C-Group' graves, and 'C-Group' pottery is said to occur in association with late Old Kingdom pottery in Egypt.[7]

Perhaps more convincing than archaeological finds is the evidence of Egyptian biographical texts bearing upon this pivotal point in Nubian history. Towards the end of the Old Kingdom two important officials, Uni and Harkhuf, travelled far into the interior of Nubia; precisely how far we shall probably never know.[8] In their biographical accounts they give us a picture of prosperous and well-populated lands which is much more consistent with the archaeological remains of the C Horizon than with what little we know of the later A Horizon. It seems that they everywhere met with a thriving native society and economy, which they were obliged to treat with more respect than had any earlier Egyptian adventurer.[9] Both Uni and Harkhuf had to secure the collaboration of local 'chiefs' in their commercial enterprises – a conspicuous innovation in Egyptian–Nubian relations. It was during the same VI Dynasty that the Egyptian governor of Aswan assumed special importance and powers as 'Keeper of the Door to the South';[10] a further indication of the growing prosperity and importance of Nubia. Here, then, is documentary evidence of that 'quickening into activity by a period of prosperity' which Reisner associated with the beginning of the C Horizon.[11]

Although the origin of the C Horizon can no longer be attributed to foreign immigration, some external factor must nevertheless have contributed both to the revitalization of Nubian culture and to the re-occupation of Lower Nubia. That factor was in all probability the decline of Egyptian imperialism. We noted in the last chapter that the fortunes of Nubia have often risen and fallen in inverse proportion to those of her northern neighbour. It was when their own political and military establishment was in disarray that the Egyptians were obliged to treat on something like equal terms with the southerners, and to pay honestly for commodities which at other times they happily seized as plunder.

The IV Dynasty (the earlier phase of the Old Kingdom, which witnessed the building of the great pyramids) marked one of the peaks of totalitarianism in Egyptian history. If the evidence of graves is to be believed, both Nubians and Egyptians suffered as a result of the excessive concentration of wealth in a few hands at this time.[12] In the later dynasties of the Old Kingdom, however, there is evidence of a gradual weakening of the pharaonic authority. The militant thrust of imperial expansion had spent itself, and a more peaceful if less vigorous state emerged. So far as Nubia is concerned, nothing is more indicative of this change than the contrast between the IV Dynasty inscription of Sneferu, with its boast of 7,000 men and 200,000 animals enslaved, and the VI Dynasty inscription of Harkhuf with its record of careful and scrupulous negotiations with Nubian 'chiefs'. It was in the VI Dynasty, too, that the Egyptians abandoned their only permanent colonies in Nubia, at Buhen and the diorite quarries.[13] Only a short time later the central authority of the state disintegrated altogether, and for a time rival pharaohs held sway in different parts of the country. Here, in the decline of Egyptian imperialism, must surely be found one key to the revival of Nubian prosperity.

Once established, the culture of the C Horizon persisted in Lower Nubia for something like 800 years. During that time, as at all times in the historic period, the shadow of Egypt was never entirely absent from the southern land. Yet it is surprisingly difficult to form a clear picture of Egyptian–Nubian relations in the C Horizon, for the archaeological and the textual evidence does not give a consistent picture. The cultural remains of the Nubians themselves point only to a continuation of that gradual process of sedentarization and Egyptianization which is already apparent throughout the A Horizon. Had we no evidence but the graves and villages of the 'C-Group', we should hardly conceive of anything but a peaceful and unbroken contact between Nubians and Egyptians, during which the former came more and more to imitate the latter in their manners and customs.

The Egyptian evidence, both textual and archaeological, gives not only a vastly different picture of Egyptian–Nubian relations but a violently fluctuating one. We see trade at times thriving and at times largely neglected; intervals of peace terminated by Egyptian depredations, and even a 200-year episode of military occupation under the Middle Kingdom. At other times we find Nubians serving as respected officers in the service of the pharaoh, both at home and abroad. None of this, however, has left any trace in the archaeological record of the Nubians themselves. There are no sudden increases or decreases in the volume of trade goods in the 'C-Group' graves, to mark the fluctuations of Egyptian policy, and there are no recognizable lacunae in the record of occupation at villages or cemeteries which might point to the temporary disruption of Nubian society.

In the material remains of the C Horizon it is possible to recognize, on typological grounds, three or four developmental stages, but the changes in each case are of a gradual and evolutionary sort.[14] One might suppose that Egyptian cultural influence would reach its peak at the time (about the middle of the C Horizon) when Lower Nubia was under direct Egyptian control, but this is by no means the case. Rather, each succeeding stage of the C Horizon shows a higher degree of Egyptianization than does the preceding. It is because of this discrepancy, which is still not fully understood, that it seems best to let the Nubian archaeological remains tell their own story of cultural development in the present chapter, while reserving for the next chapter a history of concurrent Egyptian activities in Nubia.

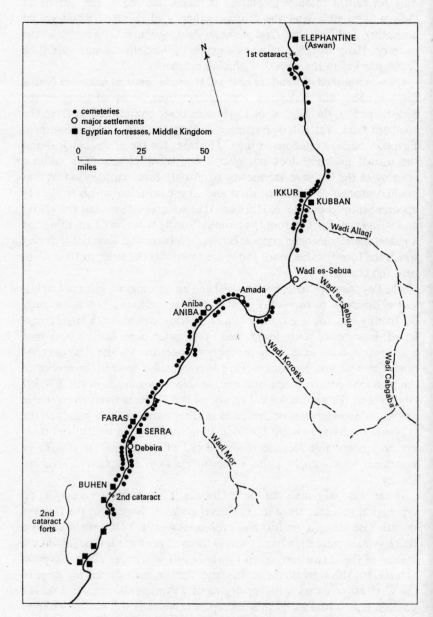

Fig. 17. Distribution of known sites of the C Horizon

The fertile Nile floodplain in lower Nubia

The lifeless Nubian desert

IIa (*above*). Modern Nubian village in the Delgo area

IIb (*below*). Decorated Nubian house façade

IIIa (*above*). A group of modern Nubians

IIIb (*below*). Archaeological excavations in progress, Wad ben Naqa

IVa. Neolithic rock pictures, Abka

IVb. Painted pottery of the A Horizon

a. Fortified village of the C Horizon, Wadi Sebua

b. Typical C-Group and Kerma pottery

VI (*opposite*). Semna Cataract from the air. The ruined fortresses of Semna and Kumma can be seen immediately to each side of the cataract

VIIa. Fortifications at Buhen: the inner girdle wall

VIIb. The slipway for boats at Mirgissa

VIIIa (*above*). The Lower (Western) *Deffufa* at Kerma

VIIIb (*below*). The brick skeleton of Tumulus K. 111 and the Upper (Eastern) *Deffufa*, Kerma

THE MATERIAL CULTURE OF THE C HORIZON

As we shall observe presently, the most important transformations of the C Horizon may have occurred in the social and ideological spheres. Material changes, though they are the basis for archaeological recognition of this period, are more conspicuous quantitatively than qualitatively. Once again, the dwelling sites show little functional improvement over those of earlier times. There is a gradual increase in the size and perhaps in the permanence of settlements, but a fully developed village life comparable to that of the Near East is not recognizable until late in the C Horizon. Trigger offers the following generalized description of the dwelling sites of this period:

All of them were open villages or campsites. Most yielded traces of stone walls, which suggest that the population as a whole was beginning to live in more or less permanent villages by this time. At Aniba, Alexander Langsdorff dug a stratified village site. In the lowest level he found three tent circles, each 4 to 5 meters in diameter. In each of them there had been a center pole and a fireplace that was somewhat off center, and around the perimeter of the tent there was a series of smaller posts. The entrances to the various tents faced in no one direction. Langsdorff found traces of the skins which had roofed the tents. Although only a small part of the site was dug to this level, it appears that each tent stood separately from the rest. The level immediately above this one consisted of semi-subterranean houses, the lower parts of which consisted of large upright slabs of stone cemented together and covered with mud and smaller pieces of stone. Instead of a center post, a complex structure of beams supported the roof. The entrance-way was in the form of a small separate room which cut off a direct view of the interior. The village was made up of both one-roomed circular houses and structures that were agglomerations of several circular or curvilinear rooms. The one-roomed houses were carefully built, but there is no evidence to suggest that they were any sort of ritual structure . . . One of the circular houses was 6 meters in diameter and had inside it three hearths, which were arranged in a row. The agglomerated houses were up to 17 meters long and consisted of seven or eight rooms and courtyards. Elsewhere in Nubia similar houses have been found. Within them there were special areas for silos and tethering posts for animals. The villages do not appear to have been large and, although there is a marked tendency for each house to be located at some distance from the others, the houses were distributed in no particular order.[15]

The Aniba site included a third, uppermost level with small rectangular rooms of mud brick. Although the dating of all three levels is uncertain, there is an obvious developmental sequence, beginning with tents, progressing to semi-subterranean huts, and ending with Egyptian-style rectangular houses at the surface. A similar developmental chronology,

147

although not within a single site, was encountered by the Scandinavian Joint Expedition in Sudanese Nubia. It is described by Säve-Söderbergh:

Three C-Group houses were excavated . . . One . . . was very damaged, but seemed to be of the ordinary type with walls of standing slabs and the rounded form of rooms. This is the type found, e.g. at Aniba and Amada.

Another house . . . was comparatively well preserved, especially the part of it which was built in the more traditional C-Group technique with standing slabs. It is an oblong room with rounded corners and is of special interest as the upper parts of the walls are intact, showing the construction above the standing slabs at the base. Next to this room are brick constructions – a rectangular room with straight walls and a store in the form of a cupola, a type well known from Egyptian pictures of grain stores and similar buildings [cf. Fig. 18]. In these rooms the bricks are used in the same way as the standing slabs, and are not laid horizontally, as if the builder was not yet familiar with the proper way to use bricks.

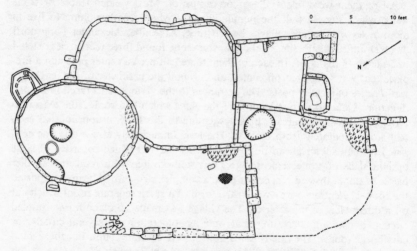

Fig. 18. House of the C Horizon, Debeira

The third C-Group house . . . excavated by the expedition was built exactly like an Egyptian house to judge by what is left. The rooms are square and have ordinary mudbrick walls on foundations of stone. Had it not been for the C-Group ceramic the house could well have been taken for an Egyptian building.[16]

The last of these three houses clearly belongs to a late and highly Egyptianized phase of the C Horizon. The brick additions to the second and largest house may also belong to a late period. Mud (unfired) brick is a fairly consistent feature of the later tombs of the C Horizon (see below). Although it had long been the common building material in Egypt, it was at first used in a very haphazard and unsystematic way by the Nubians, more or less like another form of stone. Not until the Egyptian colonization of the New Kingdom did brick construction become fully and systematically developed. Thereafter, it remained the standard Nubian building medium down to the end of the Middle Ages.

The first suggestions of 'urbanization', or at least of defensive nucleation, are manifested by two walled villages of the later C Horizon, both in the far north of Nubia. At Wadi es-Sebua, about one hundred houses are densely clustered within a stout perimeter wall of dry-laid stone masonry (Fig. 19; Pl. Va). The construction and plan of the houses is closely similar

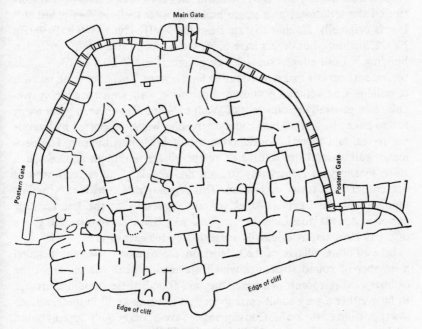

Fig. 19. Fortified village of the C Horizon, Wadi es-Sebua
(*Scale and orientation not given*)

to that of the second level at Aniba; there are both one-room round buildings and agglomerations of several rooms of irregular shape. Most of the surviving walls are upright stone slabs, but charred remains of the wooden superstructures were also found. The perimeter wall, of large, irregularly piled stone blocks, is about one metre thick at the base and stands to a height of two metres in places. It describes a half-circle around the western side of the village; the eastern side is protected by a precipice which falls directly to the Nile. The perimeter wall is pierced by three gateways, of which the largest, at the west side, is further protected by spur walls and a 'guardhouse'. There are also thirty-two archers' loopholes at fairly regular intervals along the length of the wall. The inspiration for these measures undoubtedly came from the great Egyptian fortresses which were built within Nubia in the middle of the C Horizon (see Ch. 7), although the workmanship at Wadi es-Sebua was unquestionably local. The site is dated by the excavators to a period immediately following the abandonment of the Egyptian fortresses, or around 1800 B C.[17]

Similar in many respects to the village at Wadi es-Sebua, but evidencing further architectural development, is the walled settlement at Amada excavated more than sixty years ago by the Eckley B. Coxe Expedition (Fig. 20). So densely clustered are the houses at Amada that the excavators treated the settlement as a single building: a 'castle', as they called it.[18] It was originally thought to date from the XVIII Dynasty (i.e. Egyptian New Kingdom), but others have proposed a much earlier date for its first building.[19] Both suggestions may be correct, for the plan of the Amada settlement suggests that it had a rather long history. There are some remains of buildings, as well as a portion of a perimeter wall, which are highly irregular and generally reminiscent of Wadi es-Sebua. However, a great many rooms have much straighter and more regular walls, supported by interior buttresses, and there is considerable use of brick partitioning. The perimeter wall around the south half of the village, although still of rough stone masonry, is remarkably straight and regular, and is reinforced at one corner by a tower or bastion. This regularity of construction points unmistakably to Egyptian tutelage, and suggests that the last building period at Amada does indeed belong to a very late and Egyptianized phase of the C Horizon, as originally suggested by the excavators.

Like all other villages of the C Horizon, the Amada settlement included a number of round structures which are readily distinguished from the ordinary living rooms. Wherever they are found, these buildings are apt to have either a very small entrance, or no opening at all in the surviving lower portion of the walls. Consequently, Säve-Söderbergh's interpretation of them as granaries seems highly plausible.[20] However, Trigger notes that some of the circular rooms at Aniba contained hearths, and thus must have been designed for human occupancy.[21]

The domestic arts of the C Horizon are little different from those of earlier times. Black-topped pottery was still made in abundance, although some new forms were preferred. The ceramic innovation which has become the 'signature' of this period consists of shiny black vessels whose outer surfaces are covered with fine, incised geometric designs. After firing the designs were rubbed with chalk or talc, so that they give the appearance of very fine painted white lines on a black background, rather than of incised designs (Pl. Vb). Once introduced, this tradition too had a very long vogue. Black pottery with incised and white-filled designs was still being made in Meroitic times. Although the wares of the C Horizon, like those of the A Horizon, reached a high level of aesthetic excellence, they

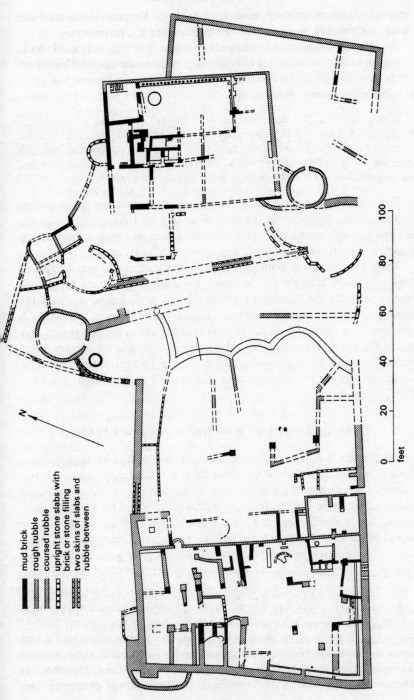

Fig. 20. Fortified village of the late C Horizon, Amada

mud brick
rough rubble
coursed rubble
upright stone slabs with
brick or stone filling
two skins of slabs and
rubble between

feet

N

were still made entirely by hand – probably by women – long after the potter's wheel had been adopted in neighbouring Egypt.

Evidence of clothing and ornament is provided by the burials of the C Horizon, and to some extent also by the crude human figures which were sometimes incised as decoration on 'C-Group' pots.[22] Trigger has given the following general description:

> Most clothing at this time was made of leather. Men usually wore a kilt, sandals, and a cap. Cloth is normally found only as a wrapping for copper mirrors. Most jewelry was homemade of shell, bone, or stone, although the shell occasionally came from as far away as the Red Sea. Faience trade beads are not uncommon, but metal and especially metal weapons are rare.[23]

The fact that woven cloth is found only as a covering for imported copper objects suggests that it was itself an import. Evidently the weaver's art had not yet been adopted by the Nubians, who, like many other African peoples down to modern times, were content to dress in skins.

There seem to have been considerable fluctuations in the volume of Egyptian trade during the C Horizon, although it was never completely interrupted. On the whole, the graves of this period contain about the same quantity and variety of imported goods as do those of the earlier A Horizon. The types and shapes of imported pottery in the two periods are much the same. However, the substitution of bronze for copper made possible a much more sophisticated metallurgy, and this is reflected in the occasional presence of such items as mirrors and daggers in the graves of the C Horizon.

SUBSISTENCE: IMAGE AND REALITY

As we saw in Chapter 5, it is not certain that the Nubians in the A Horizon derived any part of their subsistence from the keeping of cattle. A few centuries later, however, cattle were not only reared in considerable numbers but were a main focus of cultural interest. This seeming innovation has received more attention from historians than has any other aspect of the C Horizon, and has led to a widespread belief that the 'newcomers' were a pastoral people. Emery has voiced the general view in this regard:

> To what extent the C-Group devoted themselves to agriculture is not known with any degree of certainty, for no implements for tilling the soil have been found in these graves. But they were certainly cattle owners on a large scale: rough clay models of cattle, sheep and goats are frequently found in their settlements and with their burials; these animals are often drawn as decorations on their pottery and are shown in rock drawings which almost certainly belong to them. Nubia today has not the pasturage for cattle rearing and we can only con-

clude that climatic conditions were very different when the C-Group people reared their herds of livestock on the banks of the Nile 4,000 years ago.[24]

The image of the ancient Nubians which is presented by Emery and others is strikingly reminiscent of a modern anthropologist's description of the Nuer, a tribe of the Upper Nile:

. . . At heart they are herdsmen, and the only labor in which they delight is care of cattle. They not only depend on cattle for many of life's necessities but they have the herdsman's outlook on the world. Cattle are their dearest possession and they gladly risk their lives to defend their herds or to pillage those of their neighbors. Most of their social activities concern cattle and *cherchez la vache* is the best advice that can be given to those who desire to understand Nuer behavior.[25]

That the Nubians of the C Horizon set great store by the ownership of cattle, and perhaps rated them the highest form of wealth, can hardly be doubted. Their graphic art for nearly a thousand years was largely confined to representations of cows, bulls, and herding activities, which they drew on just about any available surface: rock outcrops, grave stelae, pottery vessels (Fig. 21), and the walls of abandoned houses. They also

Fig. 21. Graffiti on 'C-Group' pots

buried clay models of cattle, and sometimes the skulls of slaughtered animals, in their cemeteries. Yet it seems unsafe to conclude from this evidence that cattle-keeping was the basis of the Nubian subsistence economy. Cattle may serve as wealth and as a focus of social and ritual activity without making any significant contribution to the diet, as in fact they do among many Central African peoples today. Elsewhere and at other times horses and camels have been similarly prized, without constituting an important food resource.

153

The impression of pastoralism, which is gained primarily from the art of the C Horizon, is not supported by more direct archaeological evidence. The village sites, the abundant pottery, and the extensive cemeteries all point to a life more sedentary and urbanized than in any earlier time; a life which is hardly consistent with extensive dependence on animal husbandry. If, on the other hand, our interpretation of the round houses as granaries is correct (see above), then we can hardly doubt that agriculture in the C Horizon was producing substantial surpluses, and that it was the main basis of Nubian subsistence. Further evidence in this direction is provided by the walled settlements at Wadi es-Sebua and Amada, within which there were granaries but no recognizable animal pens.

Climatic evidence casts further doubt on the hypothesis of widespread pastoralism in the C Horizon. Long before this time the Neolithic wet phase (cf. Ch. 4) had come to an end, and the prevailing conditions over the Sahara were essentially those of today.[26] The only possible subsistence for men and animals was along the banks of the Nile, where today two to four acres are required to support a single cow. Finally, a comprehensive analysis of animal bone recovered from a site in the *Batn el Hajar*, dated around 1600 BC, has revealed only 6 per cent cattle bones, 40 per cent bones of goats and sheep, and 54 per cent bones of gazelle.[27] It seems that in this region hunting was still more important than all forms of animal husbandry.

Apparently, then, the Nubians of the C Horizon should be compared not to the Nuer but to their neighbours the Shilluk – a people who (like many others in East Africa) count their wealth in cattle but derive most of their livelihood from agriculture.[28] If this interpretation is correct, then we shall look in vain for the vast herds envisioned by Emery and Arkell.[29] The statement that 'they were cattle owners on a large scale'[30] should probably be amended to read 'they aspired to be cattle owners on a large scale'. For most of them it was an ideal which could never be realized. The Nubians of the C Horizon may nevertheless have been the first African people to develop that elaborate complex of social and ritual activities centred around the rearing of cattle, which is so conspicuous in East and Central Africa today.

THE MORTUARY COMPLEX

Preoccupation with the afterlife, already apparent in the graves of the A Horizon, becomes increasingly manifest during the Nubian C Horizon. Here, as in so many other aspects of culture, we can recognize a continuation of earlier traditions and at the same time the growing ideological influence of Egypt. In their subterranean features there is comparatively

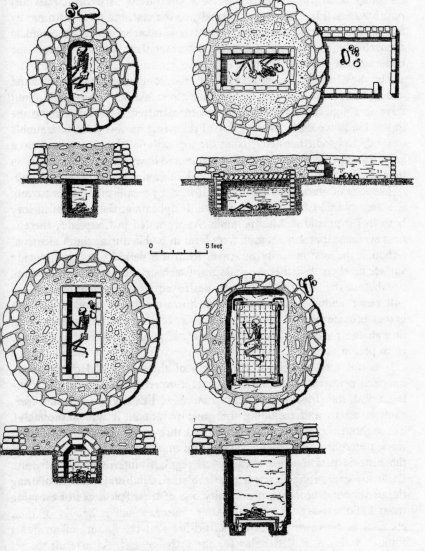

0   5 feet

Fig. 22. Development of grave types in the C Horizon
Earliest type at upper left, latest type at lower right

little difference between the graves of the A and C Horizons. They are plain vertical shafts, oval or rectangular with rounded corners, in which the body is laid on its right side in a contracted or partly contracted position (Fig. 22). The head is normally to the east, but there is no rigidly fixed rule of orientation. Pottery vessels and other offerings are placed in no particular order within the grave, wherever there is room between the body and the sides of the shaft.

The most distinctive features of the 'C-Group' grave are to be found above the ground. A ring of dry-laid stone masonry, generally about three feet high and five to fifteen feet in diameter, was built around the top of the grave shaft. The interior of the structure was filled with rubble or sand, and sometimes covered at the top with flat slabs, so as to form a solid tumulus. Since the burials of this period have almost invariably been plundered, however, the interior fill of the tumulus is rarely found intact.

The idea of marking graves at the surface, by means of stelae or tumuli, is a very old and very widespread one. It appears at the dawn of history both in Egypt and in Mesopotamia. As we noted in Chapter 5, there is now evidence that some tumuli were built in Nubia during the A Horizon, although the vast majority of graves from this period have no surviving surface markers. Whether the building of such structures was not common, or whether the majority have been destroyed by subsequent erosion, we will never know. In the C Horizon, however, the practice of marking graves became general throughout Nubia. It has remained so ever since, though the particular fashion of grave marking has varied enormously from period to period.

It is not certain whether the tumuli of the A and C Horizons were intended primarily as memorials, or as a deterrent to plundering. If the latter was the principal consideration, then, like every other such precaution up to and including the great pyramids, it was unsuccessful. Throughout the Nile Valley (and indeed throughout most of the ancient world) there is hardly such a thing as an unplundered tomb from any of the historic periods when wealth was regularly interred with the dead. Evidently grave-robbing was a great proletarian industry, perhaps offering the earthbound peasants of antiquity one of their few hopes of escaping from lifelong poverty and toil. After centuries and millennia of their clandestine burrowing, it is not surprising that the finding of an intact tomb is today a red-letter day for the archaeologist. As a result we get only occasional and accidental glimpses of the full mortuary cult of the ancient civilizations; for the most part we have to content ourselves with the broken pots, trinkets, and other odds and ends which our predecessors overlooked or disdained.

The graves of the C Horizon, including their tumuli, show clearer evidence of chronological change than does any other aspect of culture (cf. Fig. 22). The earliest graves were, as might be supposed, most like those of the A Horizon. The shaft was most commonly round, and the superstructure relatively small although well built. In later times the tumuli became increasingly large but were less carefully constructed. Pots and other mortuary offerings were sometimes placed against the base of the tumulus instead of, or in addition to, inside the grave. The external offerings may be evidence of commemorative feasts or ceremonies held at later dates, as was common in the Egyptian mortuary cult. In the latter days of the C Horizon rectangular rooms of mud brick were built against the east sides of some tomb superstructures, for the placement of offerings.[31]

Grave shafts gradually evolved from a round to a rectangular shape. By the middle of the C Horizon they were sometimes lined with upright slabs or with mud brick, which must have been covered over with wood or additional slabs. The idea was evidently to preserve the body within an air chamber, as had long been the practice in Egypt and elsewhere. This method of interment reached its fullest development at the close of the C Horizon, when the body was laid within a rectangular brick chamber covered over with a brick vault. The crown of the vault normally projected above the surface of the ground, but was encased within the fill of the tumulus.

Sacrificial animals were often buried within the later cemeteries of the C Horizon. Skeletons of sheep, goats, gazelles and dogs are found sometimes within the same grave shafts as the human interments, and sometimes in separate, shallow pits of their own. Cattle burials are also present, though they are less numerous than sheep and goats, and are represented only by the skulls. Whereas one or two sheep or goat skeletons are found in many graves, cattle skulls are usually found in clusters of six or more, in association with the largest and richest graves.[32] Evidently in the mortuary complex, as in life, cattle represented wealth while the lesser animals represented sustenance. Some cemeteries of the later C Horizon include upright stone stelae with incised drawings of cattle.[33] These may represent an attempt by the Nubians to 'have their cake and eat it too'; that is, to make a symbolic offering of cattle to the dead without actually depriving the living.

THE CHARACTER OF NUBIAN SOCIETY

In the earliest cemeteries of the C Horizon the graves show comparatively little variability in size and wealth, suggesting that Nubian society at this time was still essentially democratic and egalitarian. With the passage of time an increasing variability can be observed in the graves, probably reflective of growing disparities in wealth and power. This tendency is particularly marked in the Second Intermediate Period, following the withdrawal of direct Egyptian rule from Lower Nubia (see Ch. 7).[34] At no time, however, is there evidence of clearcut social stratification such as is observable in the cemeteries of pharaonic Egypt. The differences between the richest and the poorest Nubian graves are quantitative rather than qualitative, and there is no consistent physical separation between the two. Our picture, therefore, must be of a society characterized by increasing discrepancies of wealth and power, but in which these discrepancies did not become formalized in hereditary social distinctions.

Social disparities are even less conspicuous in the habitation remains of the C Horizon. Emery has attempted to account for this circumstance as follows:

> The homes of the richer citizens would probably be situated in the fertile land areas near the banks of the Nile and in consequence would be obliterated without trace because of the intensive cultivation of such valuable land. And so only the humble settlements of the poorer class situated on the desert edge have survived and these only give an impression of a people living under very primitive conditions; whereas the character of many of the graves indicates that such was by no means the case.[35]

It seems probable, however, that the builders of elaborate houses – had there been any such – would have taken special pains to locate them on high or protected ground, out of the reach of Nubia's periodic floods. A much more plausible explanation for the habitation remains is to suppose that all of the early Nubians, like most other tribal peoples, shared a more or less common material standard of living, and that disparities of wealth and power were reflected in social status and in such luxuries as funerary monuments rather than in the circumstances of day-to-day living. We need not travel very far to the south of Nubia to find peoples of whom this is still true.

Nowhere in the archaeological record of Lower Nubia are we confronted with the recognizable trappings of monarchy: neither palaces nor royal tombs nor conventional royal insignia. Yet Egyptian texts from the VI Dynasty onward are full of references to Nubian rulers. Uni secured the assistance of the Chief of Wawat in building wooden barges.[36] On one of his expeditions to the southern lands Harkhuf found the 'King' of Yam at war with the 'King' of Themeh;[37] on another occasion he was provided with an escort by the 'King' of Yam while travelling through the lands of a rival monarch.[38] The Pharaoh Mernere on a state visit to Aswan received the homage of the rulers of Medjay, Irtet, and Wawat.[39] Nearly a dozen localities are mentioned in connection with 'chiefs' in one context or another. Most of them were apparently in Lower Nubia, although their specific locations cannot always be established.[40]

Apart from the evidence of the texts there are other, deductive reasons for believing that Nubian society in the C Horizon was coming under increasingly formalized political control. For one thing, the population appears to have been larger than in any earlier time, and to have increased throughout the period of the C Horizon. At its end, Trigger estimates the population of Lower Nubia at about 17,000 or nearly one third of the modern figure.[41] The proliferation of place names in Egyptian texts carries too a suggestion of ethnic or local diversity, and with it the possibility of strife. It is out of such circumstances that the institution of kingship has often arisen. Yet the evidence of archaeology makes it plain that we cannot think of 'kings' in Nubia in the same sense as we do in contemporary Egypt, and in fact the hieroglyphic character by which the Egyptians designated the Nubian rulers was not the same as that which they applied to their own pharaohs. In the south, as in tribal societies generally, political power was probably still restricted by considerations of kinship and ritual, and it was certainly restricted geographically – perhaps even to individual villages. In the terminology of modern political theory, the Nubian rulers of the C Horizon were village headmen or chiefs, not kings.[42]

In the absence of more specific data from the past, we should probably take as our model for ancient Nubia the society and polity of certain modern tribes on the Upper Nile: peoples whose material circumstances are not greatly different from those of the early Nubians, and who share their specific preoccupation with cattle. Among these peoples the principal instrument of government is the 'segmentary lineage system', through which all residents of a village are linked together by a network of kinship obligations.[43] This 'web of kinship'[44] extends beyond the village, however; the residents of neighbouring villages, and in fact all members of the tribe, can claim a measure of kinship by virtue of their supposed descent from a common ancestor. Political leadership is exercised largely, and sometimes entirely, by the acknowledged heads of families and lineages, who when necessary sit together as a governing council. If any more centralized authority exists, it is apt to be vested in a 'rain chief' whose functions are as much ritual as political.[45] Evans-Pritchard has given us a succinct description of such a system among the modern Shilluk:

The hamlets of the Shilluk . . . are almost continuous, like beads on a string along the west bank of the Nile . . . They are predominantly agricultural and sedentary, for their long river frontage gives them adequate water and grazing in the dry season for the comparatively few cattle . . . they possess.

The hamlets . . . built from 100 yards to a mile or so apart on high ground parallel to the river, vary in size from one to fifty homesteads . . . Each hamlet is occupied by members of an extended family, or small lineage, with their wives, and the homesteads of this group are arranged in rough horseshoe shape around a common cattle byre, which shelters the animals in the rains and is used as a club at all seasons . . . The headman of a hamlet, who is also the head of a line-age in the settlement of which it forms part, represents the hamlet on the council of the settlement and receives in consequence a robe of honor from the king or from the chief of the settlement.[46]

It is noteworthy that the Shilluk did until recently have a tribal 'king', but he did not live in conspicuous state, nor were his bones interred in a great royal tomb. His funeral was in fact 'more a clan than a national affair'.[47] By analogy, we cannot entirely rule out the possibility of central-ized monarchy in the C Horizon, merely because it has left no trace in the archaeological record.

Among primitive peoples, strong chieftainship has usually gone hand in hand with a high development of warfare. Scholarly opinion has however been sharply divided in regard to the warlike propensity of the early Nubians. Emery has characterized them as 'a non-aggressive race of seden-tary cattle owners', and pointed to the suggestive absence of weapons in the graves of the C Horizon.[48] Yet others have observed that Nubians at this time were valued as mercenary troops in Egypt,[49] and that there are abundant suggestions of local strife in the biographical texts of Harkhuf.[50] It might be added that there is virtually no such thing as a 'non-aggressive race of cattle owners' on the African continent today; all of the cattle-owning tribes are involved in a continual round of inter-village and inter-tribal cattle-raiding. At least that much warlike propensity we should probably attribute to the ancient Nubians as well.

Far more dramatic evidence of Nubian military prowess has been seen in the great chain of fortresses which Egypt's rulers were moved to build in Nubia during the XII Dynasty, corresponding more or less to the middle period of the C Horizon. If these enormous buildings were meant to subdue and intimidate the Lower Nubians, as some writers have suggested,[51] then the latter must indeed have been a formidable and well organized foe. Yet nothing in their archaeological remains really justifies such a view. The Egyptian occupation of the XII Dynasty was preceded by a series of armed incursions into Nubia,[52] but these appear more as plundering expeditions than as genuine military operations against organized resistance. Once the Egyptian garrisons were established in Lower Nubia, their presence so little disturbed the tenor of native life that we cannot be certain which 'C-Group' graves and settlements belong to the 200-year interval of Egyptian occupation and which to earlier and later times.[53] These con-siderations, together with the nature and location of the fortresses them-selves, suggest to me that their building was prompted by a more distant and more formidable enemy – a question which will be taken up at length in the next chapter. So far as the Lower Nubians are concerned, they seem to have lived for two centuries under nominal subjection to the Egypt-ians without otherwise having much to do with them.

INTERPRETATIVE SUMMARY

Nubian society in the C Horizon resumed the gradual processes of growth and sedentarization which, though interrupted in the later A Horizon, had been at work since the end of the Stone Age. No revolutionary cultural advance marked the beginning of the new period, or any later phase of its 800-year duration. There was an abrupt return of prosperity and, it seems, a wholesale reoccupation of Lower Nubia, but the material innovations which distinguish the early C Horizon from the A Horizon are few and unimportant. There were innovations of greater importance later on in the period, such as the introduction of mud brick and the building of the first nucleated villages and fortifications. By the end of the C Horizon, the Nubians had finally achieved the sort of settled village life which had developed in the Near East thousands of years earlier.

Subsistence during the C Horizon was evidently based on cereal agriculture, augmented to some extent by animal husbandry and by hunting and fishing. By the latter part of the period farmers were producing surpluses large enough to warrant the consolidation and fortification of settlements as a precaution against attack, either by their fellow Nubians or by foreign enemies. Domestic cattle were accumulated in considerable numbers and became a primary symbol of wealth, although their contribution to the subsistence economy was probably not large. They were however very probably a main focus of religious and social activity, and as such represent an important ideological innovation of the C Horizon.

Increasing prosperity made possible considerable accumulations of individual wealth, and with them a growing disparity between rich and poor. However, a fluid society and an uncertain economy prevented occupational specialization and the permanent monopoly of wealth and power in a few hands. Throughout the C Horizon we find no clear evidence of class differentiation or of the emergence of an aristocracy. Clan and village leaders were sometimes powerful enough to win Egyptian recognition, but there is nothing to suggest that their authority was more than local, and it was probably tempered by traditional obligations of kinship and ritual. The threat or actuality of Egyptian intervention may have combined with primitive economic and social conditions to prevent the emergence of a centralized monarchy in Lower Nubia at any time during the C Horizon.

Egyptian colonial enterprise, at first confined to Lower Nubia, soon found a more fertile field of exploitation further to the south (see Chs. 7 and 8). Thereafter Egypt's chief concern with the northern region was simply to keep open her trade routes to Upper Nubia and the deserts. The people of the C Horizon assumed only a minor importance in the Egyptian colonial scheme, although they probably furnished some taxes and forced labour during the period of Egyptian military occupation, and they were at all times a market for some of the cheaper manufactured goods of the northern country. They were also occasional victims of plundering expeditions, particularly under the militant pharaohs of the XI and early XII Dynasties.

While the material culture of the Nubians became increasingly Egyptianized during the C Horizon, their social and political institutions lagged far behind. Until the day when they became outright subjects of the pharaoh, the outlook of the Lower Nubians remained essentially democratic and tribal.

7

THE RISING TIDE OF
IMPERIALISM

EGYPT IN NUBIA, 3200–1800 BC

'Miserable Kush', the oft-repeated epithet of Egyptian conquest texts, expresses succinctly the disdain which civilized peoples have often felt towards their barbarian neighbours. Something of the same attitude is conveyed in the nineteenth-century term 'Darkest Africa'. African darkness, as the Victorians conceived it, was more than a matter of skin colour; it was a darkness of the mind as well. Implicit therein was the justification for Europe's 'civilizing mission' – in part genuine, in part an excuse for colonial exploitation. Repeated and gratuitous allusion to Nubian backwardness evidently provided the ancient Egyptians too with a sense of moral justification for the exploitation of their African neighbours.

At first glance the Egyptians' belief in their superiority seems warranted by their material accomplishments. While the pharaoh was surrounded by every kind of luxury, and his subjects raised some of history's most enduring monuments on his behalf, the conditions of life in Nubia had changed little since the Stone Ages. Nevertheless the attitude of the Egyptians smacks to some extent of the exaggerated haughtiness of the *nouveauriche*, for their own rise from savagery to civilization had been recent and rapid. The earlier Neolithic cultures of the Lower Nile – Badarian, Fayyum, and Merimde – were hardly more advanced than were those of Nubia and other parts of Africa. The Egyptians may have farmed rather more systematically than did the Nubians, but they were equally ignorant of the bustling village life and the growing commerce of the contemporary Near East. It was only towards the close of prehistoric times, in the Amratian and Gerzean (or Naqada I and II) periods, that there was a certain quickening of life along the Lower Nile. Settlements became larger and more permanent, mud-brick architecture was introduced, pottery-making and weaving were developed artistically as well as technically, and copper tools came into use even while stone chipping and carving reached their peaks of artistic excellence. Egypt at last began to outstrip the rest of Africa and to achieve that pre-eminence in the material sphere which was never to be relinquished.[1]

In Egypt, far more than in Nubia, growing wealth and population led to the growth and consolidation of political power. Petty chieftains became regional warlords, who vied for control over larger and larger territories. Gradually, perhaps over several generations, the dynasts of Thinis in Upper Egypt overcame their rivals and extended their hegemony from Aswan to the sea. In that achievement were born the pharaonic state and the court civilization of Egypt. It was, perhaps, a natural and inevitable development in view of the close cultural (and presumably linguistic) homogeneity which seems to have been characteristic of Egypt since the earliest times.[2]

That Egyptian civilization was influenced by the example of Mesopotamia seems indisputable. Yet even in its heyday life on the Nile was something far removed from the cosmopolitan hurly-burly of the Near East. Egypt for more than a thousand years remained a land of country estates, without great cities and their complex social and commercial life.[3] Over this bucolic scene there presided a kind of tribal superchief and his personal household. If the proudest of French monarchs could boast that 'l'état, c'est moi', the pharaoh could almost assert that 'la civilisation, c'est moi'. There is hardly an achievement of Egyptian civilization in any field of endeavour which does not bear the stamp of the ruler: soldiers, scholars, artisans, and statesmen were alike his personal retainers. Even the abundant and magnificent products of Egyptian craftsmanship went, for the most part, not to the marketplace but to adorn the tombs of kings and nobility.

In the beginning the towering edifice of pharaonic pomp did not rest on a complex infrastructure. The whole panoply of court civilization was sustained not by commerce and industry but by a rigidly managed agrarian economy, of which the pharaoh and the nobility were the chief beneficiaries. According to 'official sources' (i.e. the biographical texts of kings and nobles) the peasantry also benefited from their incorporation into a manorial system: they became eligible for grain from the royal storehouses in times of famine, and for work on the royal monuments and other state enterprises during the agricultural slack season. The provision of economic security has been a traditional self-justification of totalitarian régimes, however, and we are at liberty to question if the Egyptian *fellaheen* really appreciated the benefits which they derived from serfdom. At all events their day-to-day standard of living does not seem to have been improved by their subjection to pharaonic authority: the ordinary tombs of the Old Kingdom were almost devoid of offerings, even while the royal and noble tombs were reaching a pinnacle of splendour.[4]

For the man in the field, then, the difference between Stone-Age barbarism and civilization was more shadow than substance – the shadow of a sometimes paternal but more often oppressive and extravagant court. It fell in different ways on Egyptians and on Nubians. For the *fellah* it brought economic security of a sort, but at the price of an unending burden of conscription and taxation. For the Nubian it offered widened trade opportunities, but with them the intermittent disasters of plunder and enslavement. Centuries of subjugation to the pharaoh transformed the two peoples into the internal and the external proletariat of the Egyptian empire, to use Arnold Toynbee's striking phrase.[5]

THE PATTERN OF EGYPTIAN IMPERIALISM

Once the pharaonic rule was firmly established, Egypt's foreign policy was of a piece with her other totalitarian institutions. While needed raw materials were occasionally obtained through peaceful commerce, more often the pharaoh's armies marched forth and seized what they wanted from neighbouring lands. Except for the wily peoples of the Levant, foreign nations seldom profited for long from traffic with ancient Egypt.

Egyptian imperialism – economic and political – was a continuing factor in Nubian history for more than 2,000 years, from the foundation of the pharaonic state until its final centuries of decline. During that time the extent and character of Egyptian influence fluctuated considerably, reflecting the relative strength or weakness of the pharaoh as well as his vacillating interest in various kinds of luxury goods. The three main phases of imperial power – the Old, Middle, and New Kingdoms – each witnessed a different stage of colonial development in Nubia. To a striking degree these stages parallel the colonial expansion of the Western powers between the fifteenth and nineteenth centuries.

The Egyptian Old Kingdom was an age of exploration, characterized at first by sporadic and uncoordinated raiding and trading expeditions into the southern lands. With minor exceptions (to be noted below) no effort was made to extend Egyptian political control or to establish permanent relations with the Nubian peoples, except perhaps for some frontier chiefs in the immediate vicinity of Aswan.[6]

The Middle Kingdom was a period of armed trade monopoly, operating through one or more established trading posts in the interior. Its main concern was not the subjugation of territory or of the native population, and production (except in the case of minerals) was left in Nubian hands. Animal and forest products, which were perhaps still more important than minerals at this period, were obtained through subsidization of native suppliers, meaning in all probability local rulers. There was no significant movement of Egyptian settlers into the southern lands. However, an enormous military effort was devoted to the protection of the trade routes to the south, and the assurance of a complete Egyptian monopoly of the trade along them. This type of economic imperialism is strongly reminiscent both of the French fur trade in Canada and of the earlier stages of the Portuguese and Dutch seaborne empires in the Orient, with their 'factory' ports on the coasts of Africa, India, and the Indies.

Finally, the New Kingdom saw the extension of imperialism from the economic to the political sphere. Outright Egyptian control was extended over the Nubian territory and people, displacing or subordinating the native rulers with whom the Egyptians had formerly been content to deal. Control of raw material production, and probably also of agriculture, passed directly into Egyptian hands, and the Nubians in their turn became *fellaheen.* Here, then, was full-scale colonialism and the establishment of a 'plantation' economy, comparable to the later stages of European colonialism in many parts of the world.

The traditional African products for which the southern continent has been exploited since time immemorial were gold, ivory, and slaves. The first two of these, however, only serve to head a long list of mineral and animal products which have figured prominently in the African trade. We can better understand the pattern of Egyptian colonial expansion in the second millennium B C, as well as that of the European powers in the recent past, if we consider the resources of Africa under three more general headings: animal resources, human resources, and mineral resources. These have traditionally been obtained in rather different ways, the first by trading, the second by raiding, and the third by colonization. Fluctuating demand for the different types of commodities therefore played some part in the changing character of Egyptian–Nubian relations. We shall consider them briefly here in the chronological order of their development.

ANIMAL PRODUCTS

Animal products were probably the earliest commodities which moved from Nubia to Egypt. As we saw in Chapter 5, the graves of the early Nubian A Horizon already give evidence of a flourishing trade with Egypt even before the unification of the pharaonic state. In these early and uncomplicated days there was certainly no organized gold production, and it is unlikely that the society and economy of predynastic Egypt had much place for Nubian slaves. We are left to assume, therefore, that wild products which had lately disappeared from the Lower Nile Valley were the principal objects of Egypt's early commerce with the south. Among African products mentioned by Gardiner as possibly figuring in this trade were ivory, ebony, incense, aromatic oil, and leopard skins.[7] In later days many other kinds of skins, ostrich eggs and feathers, and hippopotamus ivory were also exported from or via Nubia.

The earliest Nubian trade, antedating a strong Egyptian state, was most probably developed by private entrepreneurs. As Reisner has written:

'The local market went on – that cumbersome process by which goods passed up and down the river by exchanges between traders who ranged only from one local market to the next and back again. Market to market exchanges can be inferred even from predynastic times and go on today between the Nubian villages. Some present-day traders even range from Aswan to Halfa, stopping at all the villages.'[8]

A good deal of private trade in animal and forest products may have been carried on at all times in Nubian history, and particularly during those periods (such as the First and Second Intermediate Periods) when the central government was too weak to exercise a monopoly. However, the great southern trading expeditions of which we have record, from the later Old Kingdom onward, were all organized by or on behalf of the pharaoh. With the increasing concentration of wealth in a few hands, the king and his courtiers probably represented the only real market for the more expensive luxury goods from the south. Thus the Nubian trade, like most of Egypt's foreign commerce, became largely if not entirely a royal enterprise.

SLAVES

The First Dynasty inscription of King Jer – the oldest document in Nubian history – probably marks incidentally the beginning of the slave trade.[9] Whether or not it was the prospect of human captives which attracted this shadowy monarch into the southern lands, they were a part of the spoil of his campaign, for his inscription at Jebel Sheikh Suleiman shows at least two bound captives alongside the more numerous slain. Captives in increasing numbers figure in most of the subsequent military texts dealing with Nubia down to the time of the New Kingdom. Evidently they were a major impetus for Egyptian military operations in the south. Such operations are recorded from the First, Second, Fourth, Sixth, Eleventh, Twelfth, Thirteenth, Eighteenth, Nineteenth, and Twentieth Dynasties,[10] or in other words whenever the power of the pharaoh was at its strongest. Whatever the ostensible purpose of these expeditions, every one of them probably yielded as a by-product a considerable harvest of prisoners.

Some Nubian slaves were undoubtedly obtained through commerce (that is, enslaved by the Nubians themselves and traded by them to the Egyptians), but the greater number appear to have been captured directly by the pharaoh's armies. We can therefore assume that the slave trade was largely a royal enterprise, if not a monopoly. What its economic and social importance may have been is difficult to estimate. The number of captives claimed in some of the more extravagant conquest texts is surely exaggerated; for example, Sneferu's purported 7,000 prisoners in the Fourth Dynasty is nearly equal to the total estimated population of Lower Nubia at that time.[11] It is also true that slave labour was never a significant feature of the Egyptian economy. On the other hand possession of a large number of Nubian domestic slaves may have been an important status symbol for the Egyptian nobility, as it was in later times for Oriental monarchs and nobles generally. More than anything else, however, Nubian slaves were probably needed to bolster the ranks of the Egyptian army itself.[12] The same consideration was to lead to the enslavement of Nubia by Egypt as recently as the nineteenth century (cf. Ch. 18).

MINERAL RESOURCES

The later Egyptian pharaohs developed an insatiable appetite for gold, and it became the most important and most coveted of all products from the southern lands. The 'Gold of Wawat' (probably Lower Nubia) and 'Gold of Kush' (Upper Nubia) figure repeatedly in the annals of the New Kingdom.[13] However, there is no indication that this industry was extensively developed before the New Kingdom. We now know that gold mining in Nubia was preceded by copper mining and by diorite quarrying, both of which began as early as the Old Kingdom.

All of the mineral operations in Nubia, whether mining or quarrying, appear to have been Egyptian state enterprises organized and supervised by Egyptian officials, although Nubians may have provided the unskilled labour force. The inscriptions found at the diorite quarries and in many mining districts leave no doubt that the supervisory officials were directly responsible to the pharaoh.[14] Here then was an enterprise involving a certain amount of outright colonization: a cadre of supervisors, skilled prospectors and quarrymen, and presumably a military force sufficient to protect them from potentially hostile natives.

To sum up, three different types of extractive industry were developed in ancient Nubia under Egyptian stimulus, and each was exploited in a somewhat different way. Wild animal and forest products were obtained through a genuine two-way trade which was presumably mutually beneficial. It was probably this commerce which provided most of the Egyptian goods which came into Nubian hands. Slaves, on the other hand, were seized by periodic raiding expeditions which brought to the Nubians nothing but suffering and destitution. Mineral resources, finally, were obtained through direct Egyptian enterprise operating on Nubian soil, and again brought little benefit to the native populace.

Throughout the pharaonic period, the picture of Egyptian–Nubian relations which emerges from the hieroglyphic texts is one of almost unrelieved oppression. The pharaohs often asserted the justness of their rule in their own land,[15] but none ever boasted of bringing justice to the Nubians. Yet it is necessary to recognize that the royal and official annals do not tell the whole story. In common with most imperialists the Egyptians glorified the conqueror and disdained the merchant; it was their exploits on the battlefield, not in the marketplace, which they celebrated and probably exaggerated.

When we consider the contents of the Nubian graves of the A and C Horizons, another side of the picture is revealed to us. Except (perhaps) in the later A Horizon, the abundance of Egyptian-made goods in these graves is astonishing. A rapid tally of 1,484 'C-Group' graves investigated by the First and Second Archaeological Surveys of Nubia (see Ch. 3) reveals that nearly half of them had contained one or more objects of foreign origin. Beads, bracelets, and other ornaments were the most common, occurring in 528 out of 1,484 graves, or more than one third of the total. One out of every five graves also contained one or more Egyptian-made pottery vessels. Ground slate palettes, alabaster vessels, and various objects of copper and bronze were less common, but still conspicuous. Considering that the great majority of 'C-Group' graves had been heavily plundered, and that in many cases the investigators cleared only the superstructure and not the grave shaft, it seems that the original proportion of Egyptian-made goods may have been higher still. These goods assuredly did not come to the Nubians as gifts, nor is it likely that they were often received as compensation for labour. Much more probably, they are indicative of a continuing flow of peaceful, two-way trade between Egypt and Nubia throughout most of the pharaonic period, in spite of the fluctuations of political policy and economic fortune.

In the two previous chapters we have dealt with various aspects of Egyptian trading and raiding, and their effects on the Nubian society and economy. In this chapter it remains to consider the evidence of outright Egyptian colonization in Nubia during the A and C Horizons – activities which are not reflected to any extent either in the hieroglyphic record or in the archaeological remains of the contemporary Nubians. Our knowledge of them comes from another and unrelated group of archaeological remains, left by the Egyptians who came to live and work in Nubia.

MINERAL INDUSTRIES OF THE OLD KINGDOM

Diorite, a hard black-to-grey crystalline rock, was the favoured material for statues and stelae in the early Egyptian dynasties. It was obtained from several sources, one of which was located in the Nubian desert about forty miles west of Abu Simbel. According to Kees:

What the ancient prospector could accomplish is demonstrated in the modern rediscovery of the place from which in Dynasty IV came the diorite used for the statues of Chephren in his mortuary temple and probably also the paving blocks in the mortuary temple of Cheops. The labor corps euphemistically called this place 'Place of snaring of Cheops,' as if it were a fertile oasis. It lies in the desolate Libyan desert ... northwest of Abu Simbel and not very far from the

169

caravan route which led from Aswan by way of the Oasis of Dunkul to Nakhle and the [western Sudan]. The place was marked by cairns. Stelae found there bearing the names of Cheops and Djedefre prove that it was already being exploited at a time when tradition is silent at [Aswan]. Nearby lay an amethyst mine. The transport route that can still be distinguished reached the Nile in the neighbourhood of Toshka, a little to the north of Abu Simbel [Fig. 23]. From here by river to Giza was a distance of more than 750 miles.[16]

No trace was found of permanent Egyptian settlement either at the quarries or on the riverbank at Toshka, although fragments of a mud jar-sealing and of a stone stele, both of Old Kingdom date, have been found at the latter place.[17] Given the intermittent nature of the demand for diorite, it seems probable enough that quarrying activity was carried on only occasionally and for relatively brief periods, by expeditions specially sent out for the purpose.

Prior to the most recent archaeological campaign it was generally assumed that Egyptian activity in Nubia during the Old Kingdom had been limited to intermittent forays, whether for trading, raiding, or quarrying. We now know, however, that at least one Egyptian colony was planted on Nubian soil during the Fourth and Fifth Dynasties. At Buhen, on the west bank of the Nile a few miles downstream from the Second Cataract, were found the remains of a sizeable town-site which had been surrounded by a massive though crude stone wall. The buildings were symmetrical, rectangular constructions of stone and mudbrick, recognizably Egyptian in character and quite unlike anything attempted by the Nubians until centuries later. Some were apparently residences, while others were unmistakably workshops (Fig. 24). Although extremely denuded, like the contemporaneous remains of the Nubian A Horizon, the Buhen town could be dated to the Old Kingdom both by the pottery found in it and by mud jar-stoppers bearing the royal cartouches of several pharaohs of the Fourth and Fifth Dynasties. Excavations below the main level of occupation revealed traces of even older buildings, possibly dating back as far as the Second Dynasty.[18]

While the presence of an Egyptian colony at Buhen in the Old Kingdom was in itself a surprise, the purpose for which it was established is even more astonishing. To quote from the excavator's report:

Rough stone mortars set in the floors of cubicle type rooms, for use in the pounding of the ore, together with the remains of pottery crucibles and ingot moulds, showed that we were clearing an area of the town which was obviously a metal-working factory. Charcoal and copper slag together with the droppings of pure copper from the crucibles confirmed this . . .
. . . Under 1 m. of drift sand we uncovered a well-built stone structure with walls standing 1·15 m. high. On each side of it, at a still lower level, we discovered three well-preserved furnaces in which the copper ore had been smelted.[19]

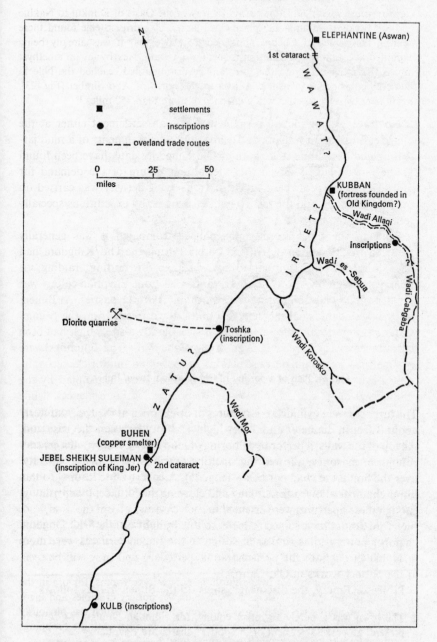

Fig. 23. Lower Nubia showing Egyptian activities in the Old Kingdom

171

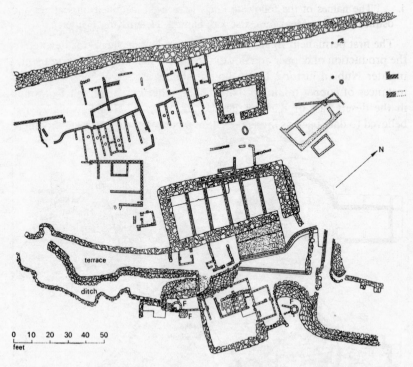

Fig. 24. Plan of a portion of Old Kingdom town, Buhen

The furnaces were cylindrical structures of brick, open at the top, and were about 3 feet in diameter and 3 feet high. Halfway between the base and the top of the walls, a perforated flooring of mud bricks, resting on a central column of masonry, allowed the smelting crucibles to be placed directly over the fire in the chamber below (Fig. 25). A covered flue leading to the lower chamber allowed for stoking and cleaning the furnace. (Surprisingly enough these apertures were oriented in each case away from the wind, and therefore cannot have served to increase the draught on the fire.) Double-chamber pottery kilns similar in design to the Buhen furnaces were used in Nubia throughout the post-pharaonic periods,[20] and may still be seen at the pottery works in Old Cairo.

Professor Emery, the discoverer, sums up the Buhen find as follows:

1. The town was a purely Egyptian colony, for although Nubian B-Group is present, at least 95 per cent of the pottery sherds are Egyptian.[21]
2. Copper working was one of its industries, and so we may conclude that deposits of this metal are to be found somewhere in the northern Sudan.
3. A well-organized despatch service was maintained with Egypt throughout the IVth and Vth Dynasties, to judge from the mass of papyrus jar sealings.

4. . . . The names of the following kings have been identified on sealings and ostraca: Khafra, Menkaura, Userkaf, Sahura, Neferirkara, Neuserra.[22]

The first permanent Egyptian settlement in Nubia, then, was devoted to the production of copper and not to the gold which figured so prominently in later Nubian history. Up to now it stands as one of the two known instances of copper mining in Nubia. The other is represented by a mine in the desert east of Kubban, in the far north of Nubia, which is not believed to date back as far as the Old Kingdom.[23] In the present day there

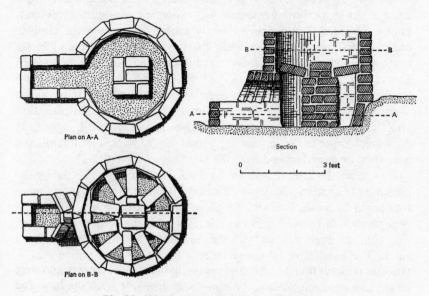

Plan on A-A

Section

0   3 feet

Plan on B-B

Fig. 25. Old Kingdom copper furnace at Buhen

are no known copper deposits in the northern Sudan, and the source of the ores smelted at Buhen remains a mystery. Presumably they were brought from some point in the western desert, perhaps at a considerable distance from the Nile, to the nearest point on the riverbank where fuel and water were available for smelting.

The location of the Buhen settlement is itself something of a puzzle. It is situated within a few miles of the Second Cataract, which marks the effective head of navigation in Lower Nubia, but the rocky and unprotected shore at Buhen does not offer a particularly favourable anchorage for large vessels. A better landing is available a few miles further south, at the immediate foot of the cataract, and this would seem a more logical place for the loading and off-loading of overland cargoes from the south. Buhen might have been the terminus of a desert road over which the copper ore was brought to the Nile from its inland source, but it is notable that the site remained important long after the cessation of the copper industry. The same locality in the Middle Kingdom was the site of one of the largest fortresses ever built by Egyptians in Nubia, and substantial temples were added to it during the New Kingdom, and later still by the Nubian Pharaoh Taharqa. Buhen, then, was a place of importance to the Egyptians throughout the history of their colonial ventures in Nubia, for reasons which are probably now forever lost. Perhaps its later importance was symbolic, commemorating the site of the earliest Egyptian settlement on Nubian soil.

The initial discoveries of copper and diorite in Nubia can only have come about as a result of extensive and systematic prospecting. Mineral-hunters in the Old Kingdom evidently ranged far beyond the familiar confines of Lower Nubia, for their inscriptions have been found as far south as Kulb in the *Batn el Hajar*[24] and in the Wadi Allaqi in the Eastern Desert (Fig. 23).[25] The authors of the Kulb inscriptions are identified as a 'scribe of prospectors' and two 'overseers of prospectors'; those in the Wadi Allaqi are called 'chiefs of caravans'. The titles make it plain that all of this exploration was state enterprise. The inscriptions suggest, as does much other evidence, that Egyptians ranged freely and unmolested over large areas of Nubia during the first 'age of exploration'.

How much the lives of Nubians in the A Horizon were affected by the presence of Egyptian colonies in their midst is difficult to say. According to traditional theory the later Old Kingdom was a time of poverty and partial depopulation in Lower Nubia (see Ch. 5), so that the number of Nubians who came in direct contact with the foreign settlements may have been small. The handful of 'B-group' sherds (i.e. the poorer varieties of A Horizon pottery) found at Buhen suggest that only a few native labourers or servants were employed in the camp, and there was no congregation of hangers-on outside the walls. Presumably Nubian labourers would have been employed in the more menial tasks of extracting and transporting the ore, but again the numbers required may not have been large. The defensive wall surrounding the Buhen settlement suggests on the other hand that the neighbouring region was not entirely deserted.

On the whole, it seems unlikely that the Egyptian mineral operations at Toshka and Buhen had much influence on contemporary Nubian life. Considering their limited scale, it is most improbable that they had anything to do with the concurrent depopulation of Lower Nubia. If any activity of the Egyptians was responsible for that development, it is much more likely to have been the slave-raiding of Kha-sekhem and Sneferu (cf. Ch. 5).

No names of VI Dynasty pharaohs have been found either at the Buhen settlement or at the diorite quarries in the western desert.[26] This was a time of conspicuous weakening of the pharaonic authority, and perhaps the royal purse could no longer afford such costly enterprises on foreign soil. At all events Egypt's first venture as a colonial power came to an end considerably earlier than did the unified Egyptian state itself. The VI Dynasty texts of Uni and Harkhuf, as we mentioned in Chapter 5, are the records of trade between sovereign powers and not of conquest and colonization.

THE FORTRESSES OF THE MIDDLE KINGDOM

For a period of two hundred years at the close of the second millennium BC Egypt had no effective central government. The extravagance of the Old Kingdom monarchs had apparently combined with a series of natural disasters[27] to exhaust the power and wealth of the state, resulting in the breakaway of local princes in various parts of the country. Four short-lived 'dynasties' (Dynasties VII–X) held sway in different parts of Egypt during the First Intermediate Period, which intervened between the Old and Middle Kingdoms. From the standpoint of the literary record this is one of the darkest ages in Egyptian history; it has left few monuments in Egypt, and none at all in Nubia. Evidently the local dynasts were too busy contending with one another to have time for colonial adventures in the south.

Egypt's weakness may well have contributed to the revival of Nubian prosperity at the beginning of the C Horizon. Some idea of the altered relationship between the Egyptians and their neighbours is conveyed by a hieroglyphic text of the First Intermediate Period, lamenting that 'foreigners have everywhere become *people*'.[28] Nubians were not only serving as mercenaries in the Egyptian army (as they had also in the later Old Kingdom), but were settling permanently and achieving positions of some prominence in the northern country, as is shown by their funerary inscriptions found near Gebelein in Upper Egypt.[29] The considerable volume of Egyptian-made goods in the earliest 'C-Group' graves may represent the rewards of military service in the north; at all events, it testifies to the rapid return of Nubian prosperity.

In the latter part of the First Intermediate Period the main centres of power in Egypt were in the Fayyum Basin, where the IX and X Dynasty 'pharaohs' ruled, and at Thebes (modern Luxor) in Upper Egypt. A century of intermittent warfare ended with the triumph of the southern dynasts and the re-establishment of unified rule under the Theban XI Dynasty. For most of the next 1,000 years Egypt was to be governed from Thebes. The XI and XII Dynasties, known collectively as the Middle Kingdom, represent the second climax of imperial power in Egyptian history, sometimes referred to as Egypt's feudal age.[30]

The pharaohs of the XI Dynasty were apparently occupied chiefly in restoring order in their own country. There are suggestions of military campaigns as far south as the Second Cataract during the later reigns of the dynasty, but their scope and duration seem to have been small.[31] It was, at all events, under the more secure and more militaristic XII Dynasty that the full tide of Egyptian imperialism in Nubia set in again. Major campaigns undertaken during the first two reigns of the XII Dynasty are commemorated in a number of hieroglyphic inscriptions. The texts leave no doubt as to the nature and intent of the Egyptian operations: 'we came to overthrow Wawat'; 'I have brought . . . all countries which are in Nubia beneath thy feet, Good God'; 'their life is finished'; 'fire in their tents'; 'their grain has been cast into the Nile' are some typical phrases found in them, along with the ubiquitous representations of bound captives.[32]

The conquest texts of the XII Dynasty are little different in substance from those commemorating the slave raids of Kha-sekhem and Sneferu in the Old Kingdom. Their aftermath, however, was without precedent in the history of Egyptian–Nubian relations. Not content with the spoil of the southern lands, the pharaohs proceeded to fortify the Nile in the northern *Batn el Hajar* with a chain of the mightiest fortifications ever erected in the ancient world (Fig. 26; Pl. VIIa). Four thousand years after their building, and three thousand years after their final abandonment, the mud walls of these gargantuan relics still rose, in places, over forty feet above the desert sand. With Abu Simbel, they rank among the foremost monuments to Egyptian enterprise in Nubia or anywhere else. But whereas Abu Simbel has been saved, to UNESCO's and the world's credit, the fortresses have disappeared without a trace beneath the Nile waters.

The most impressive and most concentrated group of Middle Kingdom forts, the so-called Second Cataract Forts, numbered ten major installations.[33] They were ranged along the Nile over a distance of forty miles, from Buhen in the north to Semna in the south. All but one of the fortresses were on the west bank of the river or on islands accessible from the west bank. Only at Semna was there an installation on the east bank, directly opposite a larger fort on the west. (For the geographical distribution of the Second Cataract Forts see Fig. 27.)

The Second Cataract Forts were apparently built over a period of about a hundred years, in the reigns of Senusret I, Senusret II, and Senusret III.[34] They were evidently conceived as forming a single complex, and may have been under a unified command.[35] Similarities of plan suggest that several of the forts were designed by the same architect and were built almost simultaneously (Fig. 28).[36]

A papyrus found in the Ramesseum at Thebes in 1896 gives the names of seventeen Egyptian fortresses from the later Middle Kingdom.[37] Of these the first eight are evidently the Second Cataract Forts, and seven of them have been specifically identified by name. The truculent names which

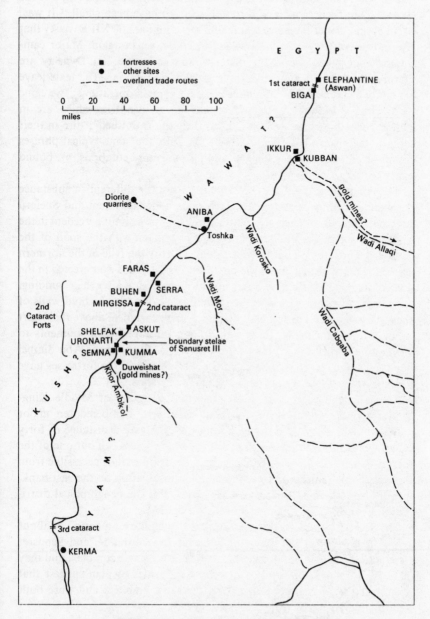

Fig. 26. Egyptian colonization in the Middle Kingdom

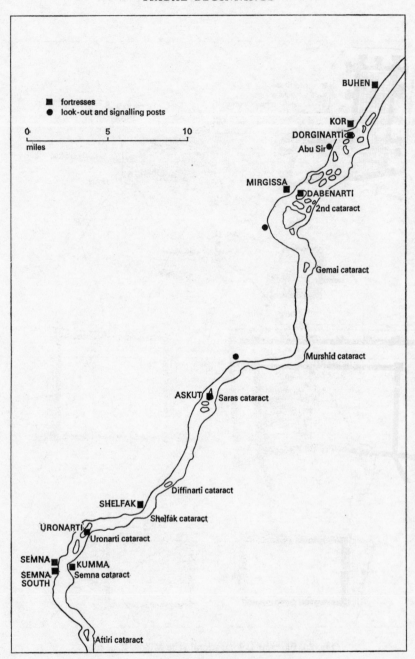

Fig. 27. The Second Cataract Forts

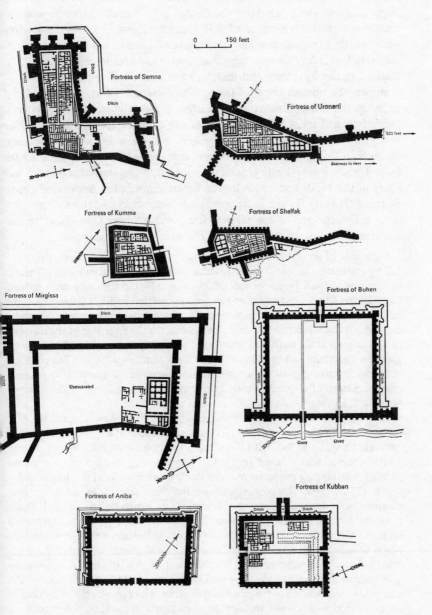

Fig. 28. Ground plans of Second Cataract Forts

some of them bore – 'Repelling the Seti',[38] 'Warding off the Bows', 'Repelling the Inu', 'Curbing the Countries', 'Repelling the Medjay' – clearly reflect the self-image of XII Dynasty Egypt.[39] It is noteworthy, however, that the two northerly fortresses of Iken and Buhen were given ordinary local place-names, suggesting that these were localities previously familiar to the Egyptians and therefore not in need of re-naming.

Buhen, the northernmost of the Second Cataract Forts, served in later times as the administrative headquarters for the whole group.[40] It was located several miles below the foot of the cataract, and less than half a mile from the long-deserted town which had been Egypt's first colony on Nubian soil. Excavations at Buhen were carried out in the early 1900s by a University of Pennsylvania Expedition,[41] and then for nearly ten years in the 1950s and 1960s by the Egypt Exploration Society of Great Britain.[42] It is by far the most completely excavated and (up to now) the most fully reported of the fortress sites, and may serve to illustrate the features of the group as a whole. In the words of the excavator:

It consists of an elaborate series of fortifications built on a rectangular plan, 172 by 160 meters [c. 560 × 525 ft], which enclosed a town containing domestic habitations, barrack buildings, workshops, a temple, and the Governor's palace. Excavation of this great structure has been completed and has revealed a carefully laid out example of rectangular town planning with paved arterial roads, each with its own independent drainage system. On the river side of the fortress, two great gates in the walls lead directly to the stone quays from which ships were loaded with tribute and products of trade from conquered Nubia. The contents of tombs discovered outside the town, and the condition of houses within it, give ample evidence of a rich and even luxurious standard of living in this outpost of colonial Egypt.

The elaborate defense system which enclosed this small town consisted of a massive brick wall, 4·8 meters [11 ft] thick and 11 meters [36 ft] high, relieved at intervals on its outer face with the usual projecting rectangular towers. At the foot of the wall was a paved rampart with a firestep, protected by a loopholed parapet overhanging the scarp of a dry ditch about 9 meters [30 ft] wide and 7 meters [23 ft] deep. The counterscarp on the other side of the ditch was surmounted by a narrow covered way of brickwork, beyond which was a glacis rising from the natural ground level. Projecting into the ditch from the scarp were round bastions with a system of triple loopholes with single embrasures, through which archers could direct a cross-fire which would completely cover the ditch [see Pl. VIIa]. The most strongly fortified part of the structure was the great gate built in the center of the west wall facing the desert from which came the long trade roads leading to the mines and quarries. The gate was closed by double doors, beyond which was a wooden drawbridge which could be pulled back on rollers. The gate and bridge were flanked by two spur walls which extended over the dry ditch, forming a narrow corridor through which an attacking force would have to battle its way exposed to a rain of missiles from the battlements on three sides. Even when the storming party had broken through the gate, their difficulties would not be at an end, for they would find themselves in an enclosed square with exits giving access to the town only through narrow roads immediately under the inner sides of the walls of the fortification, thus coming under fire once again from the defenders.[43]

Buhen staggers the imagination not only by its size but by the complexity of its defences. Bastions, loopholes, fosse, drawbridge, glacis – virtually all of the classic elements of medieval fortification are present in this structure which was built 3,000 years earlier in the Nubian desert. To a greater or lesser degree, the same features are incorporated in most of the other Middle Kingdom fortresses.[44]

Ten miles to the south of Buhen, the even larger fortress of Mirgissa[45] guarded the upper end of the Second Cataract.[46] Facing it across the main channel of the Nile was the island fortress of Dabenarti, apparently never finished or occupied.[47] Further south again were the isolated strongholds of Askut[48] and Shelfak,[49] both built on rocky summits high above the river. Finally, the southern end of the chain was marked by a cluster of four separate forts (Semna, Kumma,[50] Semna South,[51] and Uronarti[52]) surrounding the Semna Cataract – the most constricted passage along the entire course of the Nile (Pl. VI). It was at this easily controlled point, apparently, that the Egyptians chose to establish the limit of their sovereignty in the Middle Kingdom.

At least five additional fortresses were located to the north of the Second Cataract group, within Lower Nubia (Fig. 26).[53] They too apparently date initially from the reign of Senusret I. They did not form a tight cluster like the Second Cataract Forts, but were widely scattered; most of them seem to have been situated close to the main areas of native settlement. All of the northern forts had a regular rectangular plan, and the outer defences were similar in design to those at Buhen. The interior arrangements, except at Kubban,[54] were too denuded to be worked out in any detail.

Most of the Egyptian fortresses had undergone extensive renovation both in the Middle and New Kingdoms, so that the interior features found by the excavators did not necessarily reflect the original plan. The two fortresses which showed least evidence of alteration were Shelfak and Uronarti. At Buhen, although the buildings had a particularly long and complex history, the excavator was at special pains to work out the original plan and to distinguish it from later modifications.[55] It appears from these investigations that all of the Middle Kingdom fortresses were originally divided into 'quarters' consisting of store rooms, workshops, living quarters and barracks, and officers' quarters. Each fortress was thus a self-contained community. The greatest regularity and symmetry was apparently incorporated in the original design of the forts: streets and drains were perfectly straight and uniformly spaced, and rooms were uniform in size and design. In later years, as is so often the case, increasing departures were made from the original 'ideal plan' in the interests of comfort and convenience.

Recent excavations at the fortress of Mirgissa have revealed, among many other details, the armoury in which weapons were made and stored. Here were found stone 'lasts' upon which hide shields were stretched and formed, a number of finished wooden cross-handles for the shields, and quantities of raw wood and hides for the making of additional shields. More than seventy-five spears and javelins had been carefully stacked around the walls of the room; the wooden shafts had long since disintegrated, but the points were intact. They were made, even at this late date in the Bronze Age, not of metal but of chipped flint. The excellent quality of the stone work recalls the best flint chipping of Pre-dynastic Egypt. A neighbouring room yielded a very large number of crescent-shaped stone arrowheads.[56] Evidently it was not considered necessary at this time to supply the colonial garrisons with the latest in weapons.

We know comparatively little about the military organization of the frontier garrisons. Emery believes that their composition in Middle Kingdom times was almost purely Egyptian,[57] and on that basis has given us a picture which is based largely on our knowledge of army organization in Egypt:

> While the private soldier was simply called a 'member of the army,' there was a variety of titles of rank for the officer corps, such as 'General,' 'Commander of the Shock Troops,' 'Commander of the Recruits,' or 'Instructor of Retainers.' There was also the 'Army Scribe' who functioned in the quartermaster's department and the 'Master of the Secrets of the King in the Army' – which surely indicates the existence of an Intelligence Corps attached to the command of the major units.
>
> The army of the Middle Kingdom consisted entirely of infantry variously composed of archers, slingers, spearmen and axemen, who wore little in the nature of defensive body armor as we know it. The soldier wore a loincloth and sometimes webbing bands over the shoulders and across the chest, which would give some protection from sword cuts, but he depended mostly for bodily defense on bull-hide shields which appear to have varied in size according to whether the owner belonged to heavy or light infantry.[58]

Others believe that the Nubian garrisons from the beginning included considerable numbers of native conscripts, and that the military equipment and organization were not necessarily the same as those in contemporary Egypt.[59] The size of the garrisons at the largest forts has been variously estimated from 300[60] to 3,000;[61] under normal conditions of occupation the lower figure seems considerably the more realistic.[62] The group of Second Cataract Forts, from Buhen to Semna, was certainly under a unified command in the time of the New Kingdom,[63] but this is less clearly attested for the Middle Kingdom. There was, however, a system of visual communication between the major fortresses in the group. From Uronarti, the command headquarters of the most southerly cluster,[64] it was possible to see upstream to Semna and Kumma and downstream to Shelfak. Below Shelfak, where the distance between fortresses was greater, lookout and signalling posts were established on some of the high bluffs west of the river. Five such stations were discovered by the archaeological surveys of the 1960s.[65] In each place were rude stone huts containing purely Egyptian pottery, evidently the temporary residences of the sentries. One lookout post south of Mirgissa also bore traces of a round platform of brick, perhaps intended for the building of signal fires.

The best-preserved of the lookout posts was perched atop the Rock of Abu Sir, a locality famed in recent times for its splendid panoramic vista over the whole length of the Second Cataract. Fires built here could be seen at Buhen in the north and at Mirgissa in the south. A very large number of huts and several inscriptions were found just below the summit o rock, over 200 feet directly above the riverbank. Beneath them, the base of the cliff was lined with more than 300 additional inscriptions commemorating the passage of merchants, boatmen and officials in the Middle Kingdom.[66]

POLITICAL SIGNIFICANCE OF THE FORTRESSES

Emery writes that 'the discovery of the complex and elaborate fortifications at Buhen shows that the Egyptian conquerors of the Twelfth Dynasty were holding their newly won territory against a well-organized enemy whose military prowess was by no means negligible.'[67] In fact, the names of the fortresses indicate several potential enemies: the Seti, the 'Bowmen', the Inu, the 'Countries', and the Medjay. Some of these were evidently not riverain peoples, and none of them is necessarily to be identified with the Nubians of the C Horizon. As we have already seen (Ch. 6), the Lower Nubians do not at any time seem to have posed much of a threat either to the security or to the foreign interests of Egypt.

Nothing in the surviving record of Egyptian–Nubian relations seems fully adequate to account for the Second Cataract Forts. They were not intended simply to overawe and hold in subjection the people of Lower Nubia,[68] for the greater number of them were built in the most remote and inhospitable part of the region, far from the centres of population in the C Horizon. In any case subjugation is not achieved through the elaboration of defensive measures, which are in the last analysis a sign of weakness rather than of strength. They may inspire respect, but not fear. In more recent times Aden was held for more than a century, and Gibraltar for more than two, in defiance of hostile neighbours, but both of them notably failed to intimidate the surrounding regions. In ancient Nubia, occasional predatory sallies from Aswan probably accomplished far more towards the subjugation of the native population than did all of the massive Middle Kingdom fortifications.

Neither can the Second Cataract Forts be considered simply as the outermost defences of Egypt. It is true that the XII Dynasty pharaohs laid claim to Lower Nubia, but their purpose in so doing was certainly not to protect either Egypt or Nubia itself against attack from the south. The fortresses are not properly territorial defences at all, for they hug the bank of the Nile and could easily have been outflanked by any determined invader. Nowhere, however, is there evidence of any attempt by the Egyptians to patrol or to protect their desert flanks.[69]

The Second Cataract Forts are functionally intelligible only in relation to the Nile, and more specifically to the Nile cataracts. All of them are situated at or close to the largest of the *Batn el Hajar* rapids: places where riverain cargoes would have to be transferred from larger to smaller vessels, or perhaps off-loaded onto donkeys for overland portage, while the vessels themselves were laboriously dragged through or around the rapids. From these circumstances it seems logical to infer that the fortresses were designed chiefly to provide assistance to riverain commerce, and at the same time to protect it at those points where it was most vulnerable to attack from the bank.[70] They are, in short, the Gibraltars, the Adens, and the Suezes of the Nile trade. The garrisons might have been recruited for military service, but their most important day-to-day activity was probably that of stevedoring.

It is noteworthy that both at Mirgissa[71] and at Buhen[72] there were well-developed port and warehouse facilities, situated respectively at the head and at the foot of the main chain of rapids forming the Second Cataract. These facilities were located in each case at a considerable distance from the main fortified enclosures, and were not themselves heavily fortified, yet they seem to have been major centres of Egyptian activity during the Middle Kingdom. Presumably the great enclosures merely provided shelter and occasional protection for the work-forces, while their main daily activity was carried on at the docks.

A recent discovery at Mirgissa even more dramatically underscores the primary function of the Second Cataract Forts. Immediately downstream from Mirgissa lies the Kabuka Rapid, the most formidable of the more than 200 rapids making up the Second Cataract, and a place where several boats have been lost within the last century. Here, on the sandy desert flat west of the river, the French Archaeological Mission at Mirgissa found the remains of a mud-lined slipway two yards wide and a mile and a half long, over which boats had been dragged around the worst of the rapids (Pl. VIIb). The mud was evidently kept wet while dragging operations were in progress, for bare footprints as well as the marks of boat keels were clearly visible along the track. It is now believed that this was a common method used by the Egyptians for the transport of large statues and building blocks, although its use as a means of portaging boats has not previously been recorded.[73]

Further insight into the nature of Egypt's interest in the Second Cataract region is provided by the 'boundary' stele which was erected at Semna in the name of Senusret III. In translation it reads:

Southern boundary, made in the year 8, under the majesty of the King of Upper and Lower Egypt, Khakaura Senusret III who is given life forever and ever; in order to prevent that any Negro should cross it, by water or by land, with a ship, or any herds of the Negroes; except a Negro who shall come to do trading in Iken [Mirgissa], or with a commission. Every good thing shall be done with them, but without allowing a ship of the Negroes to pass by Heh,[74] going downstream, forever.[75]

The message here is perfectly clear. There is no rattling of the sword; the king's concern is purely economic.[76] The border is simply closed in perpetuity to all commerce in foreign bottoms, unless it be destined for trans-shipment immediately downstream at Mirgissa. Here, beyond doubt, is the hoary ancestor of all those decrees of commercial monopoly which have played so large a part in colonial history down to modern times. It serves once more to underscore the dictum of John Stuart Mill that distribution is a political, not an economic, process.[77]

The Second Cataract Forts were, then, at once the defences and the customs posts of the Nile trade. Their function was not to keep the Nubians under control, but rather to keep the Nile under Egyptian control. They had their counterpart millennia later in the castles along the Rhine and Danube, and later still in the 'castles' which reappeared in Nubia in the late Middle Ages. (Senusret would have been startled beyond measure had he known that 3,000 years later the kings of Nubia would themselves garrison the *Batn el Hajar* against Egyptian commerce, and would proclaim their commercial monopoly in words strikingly reminiscent of his own; see Ch. 15.) That the frontier forts also enabled the Egyptians to keep an eye on the movements of the native population is attested by a series of despatches from the Semna garrison which were found at Thebes;[78] there is no reason to suppose, however, that this was the principal purpose of the forts or that it offers any explanation for their awesome size.

If we have correctly identified the most important function of the Second Cataract Forts, then several important corollaries follow. First, there must already have existed in the Twelfth Dynasty a very substantial volume of trade between Egypt and the lands to the south of Semna, since the Egyptians were at such pains to control and protect it. Second, some desert or Upper Nubian people must have developed the habit of preying on the riverain 'caravans' – another probable indication of their volume and wealth. Third, the Egyptian 'boundary' at Semna, and the effort to enforce a monopoly of trade only below that point, indicate that the upstream origins of the Nile trade were not under direct Egyptian control. Finally, the absence of Egyptian forts at the cataracts above Semna (admittedly not as dangerous as those further downstream) suggests the possibility that the Nile above Semna was effectively controlled by another power. If so, this was a genuine international trade.

What was the nature and source of this flourishing commerce, which played so large a part in shaping Egypt's foreign policy during the Middle Kingdom? As Trigger has observed, 'Since the region between Kerma and Semna is dangerous and there were marauding tribes in the Eastern Desert, it is unlikely that this river traffic consisted of occasional individuals bringing produce north to trade with the Egyptians. More likely it consisted of regular flotillas which were despatched by the king of Kush, who was probably the successor of the ruler of Yam with whom Harkhuf had traded.'[79]

As far back as the late Old Kingdom, we noted that the pharaoh's interest had already turned from the unproductive lands along his immediate frontier to the greener pastures further upriver. The principal objective of each of the four major expeditions of Harkhuf was not the familiar regions of Irtet and Wawat but the more remote and more affluent land of Yam. It is doubtful that this profitable contact was maintained during the turbulent years of the First Intermediate Period, but its restoration seems to have been the principal goal of the Middle Kingdom Pharaohs who conquered and garrisoned Lower Nubia.

The name of Yam is never heard after the Old Kingdom, and its exact location will probably never be known. It may or may not have lain to the south of the Second Cataract.[80] On the other hand the main source of Egypt's foreign commerce in the Middle Kingdom can almost certainly be identified with the site of Kerma, not far from the Third Cataract. Here in later times was the seat of the most autocratic chief who ever ruled in pre-pharaonic Nubia, and here also are the remains of an Egyptian trade emporium.[81] Kerma, then, is the probable missing piece in our puzzle: the key to Egypt's colonial policy in the Middle Kingdom. The place of Kerma in Nubian history will be discussed at length in the next chapter.

The subjugation of Lower Nubia under the XII Dynasty was, then, in all probability coincidental to the securing of the cataracts and the southern trade route. It was one of those numerous instances of military occupation designed not so much for the exploitation of the conquered territory as to provide a buffer against more warlike peoples beyond: perhaps, in this case, either the Upper Nubians or desert nomads.[82] As we have already seen, the Egyptian yoke seems to have rested rather lightly on the necks of the Nubian villagers who lived within the occupied territory, if their archaeological remains are any gauge.[83] Nevertheless, some of the fortresses which were built to the north of Buhen, and which are not obviously associated with rapids or natural hazards, can only have been intended for the subjugation and administration of the native populace. This is particularly true of the fortress of Aniba, situated in the middle of a broad and fertile plain which is thickly dotted with 'C-Group' remains.[84] Kubban, another fort situated at the mouth of the Wadi Allaqi, was more probably intended originally as a supply and control point for traffic along the desert road which led to some of Egypt's richest mines and quarries (see below), but it may have served as a local administrative centre as well.[85] The Lower Nubian fortresses of Faras[86] and of Serra[87] are more difficult to account for; they are distant alike from cataracts, from overland trade routes, and from known centres of Nubian population.[88] We do not know, and probably will never know, what considerations prompted the Egyptian occupation and fortification of these places.

While we can, on various grounds, explain the locations of all but a few of the Middle Kingdom forts, nothing which has thus far been said seems adequate to explain their colossal size and complexity. Nowhere on the Nubian scene are we aware of 'men to match these mountains'. It is notable that in later times, when Egypt was genuinely threatened by far stronger enemies both in the north and in the south, the defensive measures which she adopted were not even remotely comparable to the Middle Kingdom fortresses.

Any attempt to account for the fortresses on pragmatic military grounds alone[89] seems as futile as an attempt to account for the pyramids in terms of a need to dispose of the dead. Both are examples of the material hypertrophy which is characteristic of Egyptian civilization. Once the decision to build them was taken, the rest followed from force of habit. In the long run the size of the fortresses might be less a reflection of the pharaoh's will than of his inability to curb his architect's ambition – an experience not unfamiliar to royal patrons.

The rigid canon of their design, as well as their history of continual aggrandizement, make it plain that the fortresses must be regarded primarily as monuments. The formal symmetry of bastions and embrasures bears comparison to the exterior decoration of a temple or cathedral, rather than to any known military challenge of the times. The fortresses are the chosen form of self-expression for the militarist civilization of Egypt's Middle Kingdom, as the pyramids are for the Old Kingdom and Karnak is for the New Kingdom. That they were built in Nubia and not in Egypt was an accident of circumstance which did not affect their primarily symbolic function. They 'showed the flag' to the Nubians, but also, and perhaps even more importantly, to the pharaoh himself, and to posterity. (We may note parenthetically that both Rameses II in the New Kingdom and Gamal Abdel Nasser in modern times have followed the Middle Kingdom example in erecting some of their proudest monuments south of Aswan.)

The full significance of the fortresses can only be understood in relation to their times. The Middle Kingdom was not an age of creative flowering to the same extent as were the Old Kingdom and the New Kingdom; it was an interval of uneasy stability following two centuries of anarchy. The tenor of the times was sober, cautious, and authoritarian, and its watchwords were Law and Order.[90] The great fortresses were the physical embodiment of those ideals.

MINES AND QUARRIES IN THE MIDDLE KINGDOM

Although it was not the main focus of Egypt's attention in the Middle Kingdom, Lower Nubia was not wholly without productive resources. Presumably a certain volume of tax or tribute could be wrung from the native inhabitants, and they could perhaps be conscripted for work in the Egyptian mines and quarries. The diorite mines west of Toshka seem to have been reopened at the beginning of the XII Dynasty and to have been worked intermittently until the end of the Middle Kingdom.[91] Amethysts were also mined in the same general region.[92] An inscription from the time of Amenemhat II records that a work party heading for the desert quarries consisted of 20 'chamber officials', 50 lapidaries, 200 stone-cutters, 1,006 workmen, 1,000 pack-asses, and an unspecified number of guardsmen.[93]

Copper smelting at Buhen was not resumed in the Middle Kingdom, but a mine at Abu Seyal, in the desert east of Kubban fortress, is believed to date from this time. An inscription from the reign of Senusret I records that a certain official named Horus was ordered by the king to collect 'copper from the land of Nubia'.[94] A large heap of slag found at Kubban itself[95] is believed to represent ore from the Abu Seyal mine; however, the remains of furnaces and slag heaps show that a good deal of smelting was done directly at the mine.[96]

Nubian gold production was developed primarily under the New Kingdom, but there are at least a few suggestions that it originated earlier. Among the hundreds of miners' and prospectors' inscriptions found in the Nubian gold-mining districts (cf. Ch. 9), only three can be attributed, somewhat hesitantly, to the Middle Kingdom.[97] However, a Middle Kingdom stele from Edfu states that its owner 'brought back gold and maidservants from southern Kush'.[98] Perhaps more convincing than this direct evidence of gold-mining activity is the indirect evidence represented by the great fortress of Kubban, which was almost certainly built primarily to control traffic along the Wadi Allaqi – the desert watercourse which led to Nubia's richest goldfield.[99] A very small balance-scale of the type traditionally used in Egypt to weigh gold was also found in the Semna fortress, apparently in a Middle Kingdom context.[100] Its presence might suggest that the Egyptians at Semna were buying gold in small quantities from native suppliers, who perhaps obtained it from the outcrops at Duweishat, a few miles upstream. This was another major centre of gold production in the New Kingdom,[101] but here too activity is not clearly attested in earlier times. At all events, it seems clear that the volume of mineral production could hardly have provided the main justification for Egypt's occupation of Lower Nubia during the Middle Kingdom.

'OVERTHROW' OF THE FORTS

Unified rule in Egypt came to an end in the XIII Dynasty; during the Second Intermediate Period (Dynasties XIII–XVII) the country was once again divided among warring factions. The shadowy XIII and XIV Dynasties together lasted just over a century. In the meantime intruders from Asia (the Hyksos) entered the Delta region and set up a kingdom of their own. They reigned as the pharaohs of the XV and XVI Dynasties. Quasi-independent Egyptian rule was maintained at Thebes in the south, but the Theban dynast was obliged to pay tribute to his stronger neighbour and to allow Hyksos trade to pass through his territory.

While Egypt was thus divided, the power and wealth of Nubia increased apace. By 1700 BC there were three major powers on the Nile in place of the former one, prompting the Theban ruler to complain: 'a chieftain is in Avaris [in the Delta] and another in Kush: I sit united with an Asiatic and a Nubian, each man in possession of his slice of this Egypt.'[102] An uneasy balance of power was maintained by an alliance between the Nubian and Hyksos kings, which recalls the historic alliance of France and Scotland against England. Economic as well as political relations were maintained between Kerma and the Hyksos;[103] evidently control of the profitable Nubian trade had passed from the hands of the Theban pharaohs into those of their northern rivals.

What happened to the Egyptian colonial venture in Lower Nubia during these chaotic times? Apparently it did not come to an immediate end, for garrisons were maintained at several of the fortresses at least during the earlier reigns of the XIII Dynasty. A watch was still kept on the movements of the Nubians, as is shown by the 'Semna despatches' dating apparently from the early XIII Dynasty.[104] By the time that Hyksos rule was firmly established in the north, however, it seems certain that Egyptian political control in Nubia had come to an end.[105]

As a result of his discoveries at Buhen, W. B. Emery has popularized the idea that the Middle Kingdom forts were 'overthrown' and 'destroyed by fire'.[106] This conclusion rests not on any contemporary texts but on archaeological evidence of burning and destruction. As I have written elsewhere, however, archaeological evidence of warfare is likely to be ambiguous. Most sites in the course of time have been ravaged by one destructive force or another, and after the passage of centuries or millennia it is seldom possible to distinguish the handiwork of man from the handiwork of nature.[107]

At Buhen there was undoubted evidence of burning between the Middle and New Kingdom occupation levels, most conspicuously in the vicinity of the western gate and the 'Commandant's palace', but to see this as evidence of armed conflict requires considerable imagination. The signs of fire in the 'Commandant's palace' are mostly at floor level, and are unlikely to have resulted simply from the burning of the roof, which was presumably the only flammable part of the structure. It looks much more as though a fire had been deliberately built within the structure, which could hardly have been done while hostilities were in progress. It may have been an act of symbolic destruction, carried out either by the retreating Egyptians or by the Nubians after they took possession of the abandoned fortress.

One thing seems certain: no attack against the fortresses could have succeeded in the face of an organized and systematic defence. Whether or not a token force was overcome or driven out by Nubian attackers, I think it can safely be assumed that the bulk of the garrisons had already been withdrawn. It is inconceivable that the Theban pharaoh, beset as he was in the north, could have spared any number of men and supplies for the continued occupation of Nubia. It also seems at least possible that the evacuation proceeded peacefully, and that the fires at Buhen and Semna[108] were set by the retreating Egyptians themselves. Destruction of immovable supplies and installations prior to evacuation is, after all, standard military procedure.[109]

The conditions encountered at Buhen and Mirgissa point to a considerable hiatus between the Middle Kingdom and New Kingdom occupations. There had been some deterioration of the ramparts, and also a large accumulation of sand within, by the time the buildings were renovated in the XVIII Dynasty. Yet the forts were not completely abandoned during the Second Intermediate Period. The presence of Nubian squatters at Dorginarti fortress is attested by their carvings of bulls on door lintels and jambs;[110] squatter occupation is also suggested at Askut.[111] Much more suggestive, though enigmatic, is a group of hieroglyphic stelae found at Buhen, which seem to indicate that at some time during the Second Intermediate Period the one-time Egyptian stronghold was governed by an Egyptian family on behalf of the ruler of Nubia (meaning presumably

Kerma).[112] The stele of Sepedher, the longest of the group, reads in part: 'I was a valiant commandant of Buhen, and never did any commandant do what I did: I built the temple of Horus, Lord of Buhen, to the satisfaction of the ruler of Cush.'[113] Another stele gives the Nubian king a name, making it plain that it is indeed a native ruler and not the pharaoh who is designated by the term 'ruler of Cush'.[114]

While the King of Kerma thus apparently replaced the pharaoh as master of Lower Nubia during the latter part of the Second Intermediate Period, Egyptian influence was not thereby brought to an end. The volume of trade goods in the late graves of the C Horizon is greater than at any previous time, and Egyptian influence is now manifest also in the appearance of mud-brick architecture and in the increasing Egyptianization of burial customs (cf. Ch. 6). Effective interchange between Egypt and Nubia evidently did not depend, after all, upon Egyptian control of the cataracts: it flourished even more conspicuously under Nubian control.

INTERPRETATIVE SUMMARY

Egypt's colonial interest in Nubia dates back almost to the foundation of the pharaonic state. During the early centuries, however, there does not seem to have been a fully articulated political or economic policy towards the southern countries. Various exploitative activities were begun during the Archaic period and the Old Kingdom, but they were mostly of a sporadic and uncoordinated nature. Slaves and plunder were taken by occasional military forays, and there was intermittent prospecting and quarrying in the Nubian deserts. Only at Buhen was a permanent Egyptian colony planted on Nubian soil, apparently for the smelting of copper ore obtained somewhere in the desert hinterland. There is nothing to suggest, however, that the Buhen colony was an administrative centre, or in fact that any systematic effort was made to extend the pharaoh's authority over the Lower Nubian population. Apparently the natives were too few and too weak in Old Kingdom times to offer either a threat or an opportunity to the Egyptians.

By the later Old Kingdom, the pharaoh had already become aware of richer lands to the south of Lower Nubia, and from that time onward Egyptian policy centred upon the development of commerce with the southern lands. Major expeditions during the last reigns of the VI Dynasty brought back all kinds of exotic products from the Land of Yam, probably in Upper Nubia.

Commerce with the far south was probably interrupted during the turbulent years of the First Intermediate Period, but it was resumed at the outset of the Middle Kingdom. By the time of the XII Dynasty trade with the Upper Nile had reached such proportions that it was subject to depredation by Upper Nubian or desert peoples. In order to secure the southern trade route, and also to assure an Egyptian monopoly of trade, the XII Dynasty pharaohs fortified the most vulnerable points in the Second Cataract region with a series of enormous military posts, which served at the same time as frontier customs stations. They were meant to show the flag in the southern lands, but were also, in a larger sense, the major architectural monuments of a militaristic age.

Concurrently with the building of the fortresses, the pharaoh assumed outright political control over Lower Nubia. This was a holding operation designed primarily to protect Egyptian commercial interests, and had little visible effect on the lives of the riverain farmers of the C Horizon. However, quarrying and copper mining were resumed on a small scale, and native levies were undoubtedly employed.

The unity of the Egyptian state was again destroyed during the XIII Dynasty, and the local ruler at Thebes was too weak and too preoccupied at home to maintain his hold on Nubia. The last of the southern garrisons were withdrawn or chased out by the native populace, and the fortresses fell into a state of partial disrepair. Nevertheless trade continued to flourish, apparently under the protection of the Nubian king at Kerma, long after the departure of the Egyptian garrisons.

PART TWO
DYNASTIES AND EMPIRES

8

TRANSITION TO EMPIRE

THE NUBIAN KINGDOM OF KERMA

In the days of the Moorish caravan trade, the wealth and power of West African kingdoms were legendary. Yet when European trading vessels began calling at West African ports in the Age of Exploration, they found the coastal districts poor and culturally backward, and their rulers no more than petty chieftains. The mighty kingdoms, they learned, lay in the steppe and savanna lands far in the interior. Thereafter the guiding policy of the colonial powers was to establish relations with, and ultimately control over, the great inland domains.

The experience of Egypt in ancient Nubia was similar. The pharaoh was at first conscious only of the impoverished lands immediately beyond his borders, whose people and resources hardly justified the effort of colonization. Later he became aware that much richer lands lay beyond. Increasingly he turned his attention to Upper Nubia and its rulers; relations with them became the key to Egyptian policy, and ultimately domination, in the south.

Who were the southern people, whose wealth and power so far outstripped their Lower Nubian neighbours? For the time being we can give only a very incomplete answer. Upper Nubia has not yet been systematically explored, and archaeological work has been confined to a handful of monumental sites and cemeteries. None of these can be dated with certainty to a time earlier than the Second Intermediate Period. We therefore know nothing definite about the origins of the Upper Nubian people, and little enough about their culture even in its heyday.

For a thousand years, our evidence for the existence of a thriving culture and society in Upper Nubia is inferential. From the late Old Kingdom we have Harkhuf's account of the Land of Yam, whose location is unspecified but which can hardly have been elsewhere than in Upper Nubia. From the Middle Kingdom we have the indirect but nevertheless suggestive evidence of large-scale trade with the south as attested by the Second Cataract Forts. But it is not until a still later date, perhaps following the initial abandonment of the forts, that we can recognize archaeologically a culture which might correspond both to Yam and to the conjectural Upper Nubian kingdom with which XII Dynasty Egypt traded. This culture is known to us chiefly from one spectacular site, Kerma, from which it has taken its name.[1]

As we shall observe presently, the dates both for the beginning and for the end of the Kerma Culture are undetermined. However, there seems to be little doubt that its climax of development occurred during the period of Hyksos domination in Egypt; that is, in the latter part of the Second Intermediate Period. The Kerma people were, then, contemporary with the later C Horizon. It is hardly surprising to discover that the two cultures have much in common, pointing in all probability to a common ancestry.

CHARACTERISTICS OF THE KERMA CULTURE

No habitation sites of the Kerma people have yet been identified; for the time being our knowledge of the purely indigenous aspects of their culture comes entirely from cemeteries. Once again, we are obliged to recognize and distinguish the Kerma Culture primarily by its pottery and its burial customs (cf. Ch. 5).

The Kerma people, like the Lower Nubians, made pottery of several kinds. Their larger and coarser utility vessels are almost indistinguishable from those of the C Horizon. They also made black polished bowls with incised, white-filled decoration, again paralleling the Lower Nubian tradition. At Kerma, however, such pottery constituted only a small percentage of the ceramic complex. The most abundant and most distinctive of luxury wares was a black-topped red ware, conforming to the general Nubian tradition but achieving, in the hands of the Kerma people, a refinement never approached in the pottery of the A and C Horizons. So finely made is Kerma ware that Reisner, its discoverer, mistakenly believed that it had been made on the wheel (and therefore that it was really the product of Egyptian craftsmen, since the potter's wheel was then unknown to the Nubians).[2]

The best of the Kerma black-topped pottery has extremely thin walls and sharp rims, recalling those of the 'variegated hematitic' ware of the A Horizon (Ch. 5). The vessels have a glossy, jet black interior and rim, the black band usually extending downwards for about an inch over the vessel exterior. The lower exterior is a deep red. In most cases the black upper body and the red lower body are separated by a narrow, irregular strip of a whitish metallic colour. This feature is not found in any of the other black-topped wares of Nubia, and its origin and purpose have been the subject of much discussion.[3]

The most typical vessel form in Kerma black-topped ware is a round-bottomed, wide-mouthed beaker (Fig. 29), which has no parallel in the pottery industries of Lower Nubia. These vessels are found 'nested' together in clusters in nearly every Kerma grave, sometimes numbering dozens in a single grave. So common are they that the black-topped ware as a whole is sometimes designated as 'Kerma Beaker Ware'. However, it occurs in various other shapes such as hemispherical bowls and a distinctive form of spouted pot (Fig. 29).

The mortuary practices of Kerma have much in common with those of the C Horizon. The grave pit proper is a rather shallow square or rectangular excavation with rounded corners (Fig. 29). The dead were laid on the right side, in a contracted position, facing north. Mortuary offerings are

Fig. 29. Typical Kerma grave and mortuary offerings

abundant within the tombs. Usually toilet articles and other personal belongings are arranged close to the body, while pottery vessels containing food and drink line the chamber walls. Sacrificial rams are very often included with the burial. After filling, the grave was covered by a round tumulus of earth marked at the edge by a ring of stones. In many cases a row of ox skulls was ranged around the southern edge of the tumulus.

While the above practices belong to a common and probably Nubia-wide tradition, five characteristics distinguish the Kerma burials from those of Lower Nubian peoples:

BED BURIAL

In nearly every Kerma grave which has not been plundered beyond recognition, the main burial is found reclining on a native bed (*angareeb*) of the type still used in Nubia (see Ch. 2). This custom is encountered only very rarely in graves of the C Horizon.[4] It has, however, a long subsequent history in Nubia, as will be seen in later chapters.

KERMA POTTERY

Trade vessels of the distinctive Kerma black-topped pottery are occasionally found in non-Kerma graves in Lower Nubia and even in Egypt, but they are a near-universal feature of genuine Kerma graves, and usually occur in large clusters.

DOMED TUMULI

The round tumulus, or grave mound, is a common feature of Upper and Lower Nubian burials. As we saw in Chapter 6, however, the typical 'C-Group' tumulus is cylindrical in shape, being built up within a vertical retaining wall of masonry. The Kerma tumulus is dome-shaped, sloping downwards from a low crown to the level of the ground in all directions. The ring of stones delimiting the tumulus is only a few inches high; it is primarily decorative and perhaps to protect the edges of the mound from erosion. In many Kerma graves the encircling ring of stones is dark in colour, while the surface of the mound within the ring is covered with white or yellow pebbles. Kerma tumuli are even more variable in size than are those of the C Horizon; the largest of them are far larger than anything found in Lower Nubia.

RAM SACRIFICES

Sacrificial animals – mainly sheep and goats – are found occasionally in the graves, and even more often in independent sacrificial pits, within the cemeteries of the C Horizon. They are a consistent feature of Kerma burial, occurring always within the grave chamber itself. Usually they lie directly in front of the bed on which the corpse rests; in one or two instances they were placed on the foot of the bed itself. As many as six sacrificial animals have been found in the same grave.

More distinctive than any of the foregoing are:

HUMAN SACRIFICES

A surprisingly large number of Kerma graves – at least of those dating from the heyday of the kingdom – contain the bodies of one or more sacrificial victims who were buried at the same time as the 'owner' of the grave. They were found even in the small and unimposing cemetery at Mirgissa, to be discussed later, but much more consistently and abundantly at Kerma itself. Many relatively small and humble graves contained one or two sacrificed retainers, while the largest of the royal tombs may have had four hundred. From the positions of the bodies, Reisner concluded that they had been buried alive and had died from suffocation.[5]

The formal differences between the C Horizon and the Kerma culture are, as will be seen, of a relatively minor sort. The two are at the very least 'cultural cousins', and may very well have diverged from a common ancestry in the A Horizon.[6] The most significant differences between them, however, are seen not so much in form as in the relative scale and intensity of their development. In order to appreciate this difference it is necessary to consider the great archaeological site of Kerma, which has no counterpart in Lower Nubia.

THE SITE OF KERMA

Modern Kerma is a straggling village of several thousand inhabitants situated on the east bank of the Nile at the extreme northern end of the Dongola Reach – the most fertile region in Upper Nubia (see Ch. 1). Not only is the floodplain here exceptionally broad, but the area available for cultivation is tremendously increased by the presence of a former channel of the Nile, the so-called Kerma Basin, which is annually flooded at the high Nile. This is one of the few places in the Sudan where natural basin irrigation, of the type characteristic of ancient Egypt, can be practised. Here, within sight of the modern village, would appear to have been the earliest seat of autocratic power in ancient Nubia.

The archaeological site of Kerma was excavated between 1913 and 1916 by George A. Reisner, and was the first major enterprise undertaken by the Harvard–Boston Expedition in the Sudan. It has been more fully reported than any of Reisner's subsequent Nubian excavations.[7] Even so, large areas of the site have never been explored, and a considerable part of the excavated material is still unpublished.

The site of Kerma as investigated by Reisner comprised two major areas. About a mile and a half from the riverbank, and not far behind the line of modern houses, was a great, decayed mass of mud brick locally known as the Western or Lower *Deffufa* (a Nubian term for any upstanding brick ruin). Two miles farther east, across an open clay plain (now mostly under cultivation), was a large necropolis and also the remains of a second brick building, the Upper *Deffufa*.

The Western *Deffufa*, which first claimed Reisner's attention, is one of the most extraordinary structures in Nubia, and the only one of its kind in existence. As originally constructed it was a solid rectangular mass of mud brick more than 150 feet long and 75 feet wide, and probably stood to a height considerably greater than the 60 feet which are still preserved (Pl. VIIIa). Within this solid mass there were no interior apartments; only the remains of a narrow, winding stairway which had evidently led to the top of the structure (Fig. 30). The stairway within the building began at a height several feet above the ground; it was continued downwards to ground level by a projection westwards from the main mass of the building. At the first landing the stairway was widened to form a sort of guardroom – the only space within the solid mass of brickwork which could be described as a room.

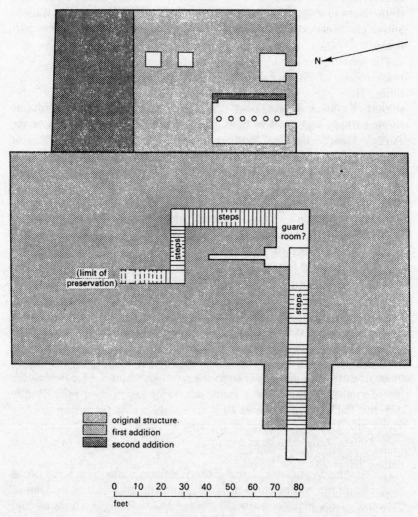

N

steps

steps

guard room?

(limit of preservation)

steps

original structure
first addition
second addition

0 10 20 30 40 50 60 70 80
feet

Fig. 30. Plan of the Lower (Western) *Deffufa*, Kerma

After the original building of the Lower *Deffufa*, two additions were made which added a kind of salient to its eastern face. Both, like the original building, were nearly solid brick, and both probably rose to the full height of the original structure so as to enlarge the platform at the top. However, the earlier and larger of the two additions contained two small rooms, entered through doorways at ground level, and also two vertical shafts which had no lateral openings (Fig. 30).

The character of the *Deffufa* brickwork is unmistakably Egyptian. It shares with the Middle Kingdom Forts the regular use of timber bonding: large, rough-hewn beams set horizontally in the brickwork at right angles to the faces of the wall.[8] The *Deffufa* is certainly not a fortress, however, and in fact bears no resemblance to any other known building of Egyptian design.

The western face of the *Deffufa* was adjoined by an irregular cluster of brick rooms which appeared to have been rebuilt and enlarged several times. Here again the extreme straightness and evenness of the walls suggests Egyptian work. The abundant refuse found within these western rooms furnishes the one real clue as to the date and function of the Lower *Deffufa*. Most conspicuous were fragments of 565 mud seal-impressions of Egyptian type, which had been affixed to pots, baskets, and some sort of wooden container. There were also fragmentary remains of many objects of Egyptian manufacture, such as alabaster ointment jars (twenty-five of them bearing the name of the Old Kingdom Pharaoh Pepi I), other and larger stone vessels, faience and pottery vessels, beads and stone crystals for making beads, and pieces of bronze. Except for the ointment jars these objects were mostly of Middle Kingdom or later types, according to Reisner.[9]

Also represented in the refuse from the Western *Deffufa* were various kinds of raw materials:

While the seal-impressions stand in a way for the administrative activities of the Egyptian occupation, the raw materials and the unfinished products stand for the manufacturing activities. The raw materials found consisted of several lumps of *keriak* used for polishing pottery, lumps of red color used for the red wash on pottery, one large and several small lumps of copper oxide used for coloring faiences and other glazes, lumps of resin, a block of mica for mica ornaments, several large deposits of rock crystals and carnelian pebbles of the same materials as those found in the stone beads, and fragments of ostrich eggshell from which small disc-beads were made. Many pebbles stained with green glaze were also found, which had been used as setters in glazing faiences. Polishing pebbles for pottery and bivalve shells for dressing pottery forms occurred in small numbers. Quantities of unfinished or misfired black-topped beakers, some misfired faience vessels, and many partly finished beads, several apparently cracked in glazing, were also recorded. The sum of the evidence is that the manufacture of pottery, faience, glazed quartzite, beads, and mica ornaments at the Lower Deffufa was

carried on during the period of the . . . cemetery at the Upper Deffufa and produced the same types of objects as those found in that cemetery.

. . . Many points are not determined by the evidences at our disposal. Nevertheless, the main point stands out that the Deffufa was the center of a considerable business, whether storage or otherwise, in more or less valuable commodities. But there were undoubtedly other activities concerned – the trade for
the products of the more southern lands, and the receipt and despatch of goods
from and to Egypt.[10]

Here surely is one of the depots or 'factories' from which emanated that
great Nile trade, which Egypt was at such pains to protect on its downstream passage.

That the Lower *Deffufa* was designed and constructed under Egyptian
supervision seems evident from the nature of the brickwork. It would be a
mistake, however, to assume that the origin of the Upper Nubian trade was
in Egyptian hands. The permanent Egyptian colony at Kerma may have
been quite small, since no unmistakable Egyptian graves have been found
here, whereas they are prominent at all of the Second Cataract Forts. The
resident Egyptians at the *Deffufa* were probably for the most part clerks,
who recorded the arrival and departure of cargoes and perhaps supervised
the work of a group of local craftsmen making Egyptian-style beads and
faiences for the local market. As the evidence from the eastern cemetery
shows (see below), they lived and worked under the patronage of a local
ruler who was the real controlling force in the Nile trade.[11]

All of the foregoing interpretation is based on the finds within the western
rooms of the Lower *Deffufa*. It does nothing to explain the great, solid
mass of brickwork which towers above them. This has customarily been
regarded as some sort of defensive arrangement, and the complex as a
whole has been called a fortified trading post.[12] Yet the great *Deffufa* makes
no sense as a fortification; it defends nothing but itself, and it contains
nothing. While the resident merchants and officials might possibly take
refuge from attack on its upper platform, a building more vulnerable to
siege would be difficult to imagine. Its one exit could be barred by a mere
handful of armed men, and the occupants would be reduced by thirst in a
matter of days.

Up to a thickness of ten or twelve feet, the size of brick walls may indeed
be an indication of their defensive nature. Beyond that point, however,
nothing is gained by additional mass. Thickness of walls, relative to the
area enclosed, can be consistently related to only one functional requirement: height. Given this consideration, it seems apparent to me that the
Kerma *Deffufa* was designed as an enormous watchtower, rising perhaps to
two or three times the height to which it is now preserved.

The purpose of such a structure is not difficult to visualize. If, as has been
suggested, the upbound cargoes arrived only at infrequent intervals, and in

large convoys,[13] it would undoubtedly be to the advantage of the king and his officers to have first news of the coming of the boats, so as to have loading parties ready for them and to forestall competition from private entrepreneurs. Since there are no mountains in the vicinity of Kerma, an elevated position could only be constructed artificially.[14] Admittedly this does not account for the additions to the eastern face of the *Deffufa* – a mystery which may never be resolved.

THE ROYAL CEMETERY

The great eastern cemetery at Kerma covers an area perhaps a mile long and half a mile wide. In all probability it contains several thousand graves, although large parts of it have not been surveyed to this day. The number of graves excavated by Reisner in his three seasons of work is not specified in any of his reports, but it can only have been a fraction of the total. Of those excavated, 388 have been individually reported;[15] many others, particularly in the northern part of the cemetery, remain unreported.

The essential features of mortuary practice at Kerma were virtually the same in every grave excavated, and conform to the general plan which we have already described. The grave furniture too was remarkably consistent in form if not in quantity. Enormous variability, however, was found in the overall size and complexity of the Kerma graves. It was primarily on this basis that Reisner divided them into four groups: great tumuli, minor tumuli, subsidiary graves, and independent graves.

THE GREAT TUMULI

The great tumuli numbered only eight examples, which were ranged more or less in a line at the southern edge of the cemetery. These structures are without parallel among the funerary monuments of Nubia. The largest of them is nearly 300 feet in diameter, and its interior chambers are far more extensive than are those of any Egyptian pyramid.[16] To complete the picture of barbarian magnificence it may be added that the number of human sacrifices in Tumulus X at Kerma – 322 by actual count, and perhaps as many as 400 before plundering[17] – is larger than in any other known tomb of any civilization.

The internal conditions encountered in the great tumuli are thus described by Reisner:

The chief burial lay on the south side of the grave, usually on a bed, on the right side, with the legs slightly bent at the knees, the right hand under the cheek and the left hand on or near the right elbow. The body was apparently clothed in linen, with the usual weapons and personal adornments. On the bed was placed, as a rule, a wooden headrest, an ostrich-feather fan, and a pair of rawhide sandals. At or on the foot of the bed were also placed certain toilet articles and bronze implements. Near the bed and around the walls of the pit were arranged a large number of pottery vessels.

The chief burial and the grave furniture occupied only a small part of the floor area of the grave. The rest was taken up by other human bodies, ranging from one to twelve or more in number, and the bodies of one to six rams. The positions of these human bodies did not follow strictly any one rule; the majority were on the right side; of these again a majority lay with the head east; but almost every possible position occurred. The extent of the contraction varied quite as much – from the half extended position of the chief body to the tightest possible doubling up. Some even were on the back and some on the stomach. The hands were usually over the face or at the throat, sometimes twisted together, sometimes clutching the hair. In only a few cases was a person seen who lay in the attitude of the chief person, but in a number of cases a modification of that attitude was seen.

The chief body appears always to have been covered with a hide, usually an ox-hide, and in some cases at least the hide covered the sacrifices as well. It will be recalled by Egyptologists that in the letter of Amenemhat III to Sinuhe, the king, after promising Sinuhe a princely Egyptian burial, goes on to say: 'Let not thy death take place in a foreign land, let not the Bedouin make thy funeral procession, let thyself not be placed in the hide of a ram.'[18]

The three largest of the great tumuli, designated as III, IV, and X, had special peculiarities of their own. In each of these cases the mass of the tumulus was given a certain rigidity by a 'core-structure' of enormously long, straight, brick walls whose only purpose was apparently to provide a kind of skeleton for the mound (cf. Pl. VIIIb). A long, unbroken corridor ran across the entire width of each mound, while the remaining walls of the core-structure emanated from it at right angles. The main burial chamber opened directly onto the south side of the corridor near the centre of the tumulus (Fig. 31). Sacrificial burials were found primarily within the transverse corridors, which were therefore designated by Reisner as sacrificial corridors.

SUBSIDIARY BURIALS

Subsidiary burials are a feature of all but two of the great tumuli, and also of a few of the minor tumuli. They are burials without grave-mounds of their own, but intruded through the surface of the existing tumuli at some time after their completion. The nature and distribution of these graves show that they were not simply random intrusions by disrespectful posterity, for they were carefully placed in such a way as to avoid disturbing the main burial chamber or damaging the core walls. In Tumulus III, the grave chambers for all of the subsidiary burials were made by running short cross-walls between the already existing walls of the core-structure so as to form small brick chambers (Fig. 31). Reisner has suggested that the very large size of many Kerma tumuli was intended deliberately to leave

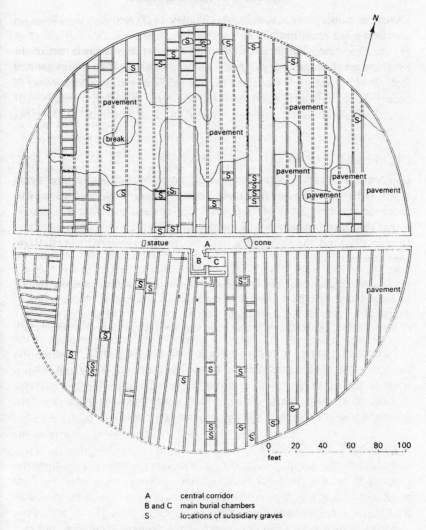

A   central corridor
B and C   main burial chambers
S   locations of subsidiary graves

Fig. 31. Plan of the internal brickwork skeleton in Tumulus III, Kerma

room for such burials. The largest number of them encountered in any one tumulus was 102.[19] Although lacking superstructures of their own, the subsidiary burials are often remarkably rich in their own right, and many are accompanied by human sacrifices.

THE MINOR TUMULI

The minor tumuli are smaller versions of the great tumuli, without sacrificial corridors or masonry core-structures. In nearly every case there is only a single rectangular or square burial chamber excavated into the alluvium, containing the main burial, the grave goods, and sacrificial burials when present. The tumuli in these cases are still far larger than is necessary to cover the grave proper, varying in diameter from about 75 to more than 150 feet. However, only a few of them include subsidiary graves. Minor tumuli occurred sporadically in many parts of the Kerma cemetery, but were most conspicuously clustered at the south end, in close proximity to the great tumuli.

INDEPENDENT GRAVES

Independent graves was the designation given by Reisner to interments which either lacked superstructures or had tumuli only large enough to cover the grave pit. Some of the poorest (and earliest?) of these had an oval rather than a rectangular pit, like graves of the A Horizon (Ch. 5). Even in very small graves the standard Kerma mortuary equipment was regularly encountered:

> . . . a rectangular open pit, a bed-burial under the hide, accompanied by one or more human sacrifices clothed in cloth tunics and leather skirts, a ram, a dagger of the peculiar Kerma form, a headrest, a fan, a pair of sandals, a number of black-topped beakers, bowls, and pots, and a number of jars of other wares.[20]

Independent graves were found in every part of the Kerma cemetery. At the south end they were scattered around and among the larger tumuli, while at the north they were apparently the only form of grave present. Reisner noted that animal sacrifices were most abundant in the northern graves, where they largely replaced human sacrifices.

MORTUARY BUILDINGS

In addition to its tumuli great and small the Kerma cemetery contained the remains of two massive brick buildings reminiscent in some respects of the great Lower *Deffufa*. One of them, which still stands to a considerable height, is in fact known as the Eastern or Upper *Deffufa*. The second of the cemetery buildings was found in much more denuded condition, but was closely similar in plan to the first. Both consist of two long chambers connected by a narrow passage between them and a second passage to the outside. A row of columns down the centre of each room apparently supported a ceiling of transverse beams (Fig. 32). Both structures had massive brick walls, exceeding 30 feet in thickness. One of them – presumably the earlier[21] – had grown by accretion from a smaller nucleus, while the second had been built from the beginning in its final form. The seemingly earlier building also included a narrow inside stairway leading to an upper storey or to the roof. The inner rooms of both buildings bore the remains of painted decoration in red, black, and yellow. The paintings are

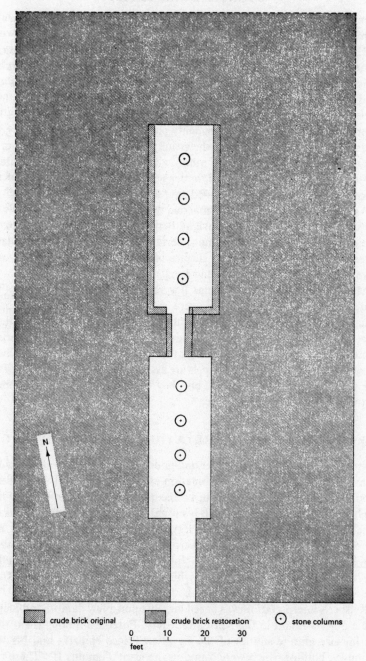

crude brick original   crude brick restoration   ⊙ stone columns

0   10   20   30
feet

Fig. 32. Plan of the Upper (Eastern) *Deffufa*, Kerma

unmistakably Egyptian in style and theme, showing familiar scenes of human and animal activity.

The two great buildings are situated near the southern end of the Kerma cemetery, in each case just to the north of one of the largest of the tumuli. Reisner not unnaturally concluded that they were mortuary chapels associated with the great tumuli, each one having perhaps served over a long period of time and in conjunction with several successive tombs. The interior chambers had been thoroughly plundered in antiquity, but a great mass of broken objects found in the vicinity might have been cleared out by the robbers. A large number of mud sealings, similar in type and date to those found at the Lower *Deffufa*, suggested to Reisner that one of the cemetery buildings had been sealed shut and re-opened many times.[22]

As in the Lower *Deffufa*, the massive walls of the mortuary chapels (?) are suggestive of extraordinary height. Perhaps their summits were lookout stations for the cemetery watchmen. Certainly keeping watch over so large a cemetery, with its undulating surface of large and small tumuli, would have been a difficult job at ground level.

Much smaller mortuary chapels (?) were found associated with six of the minor tumuli at Kerma. These were small, square chambers of brick situated just off the edge of the tumulus, more or less along its southern side. Presumably they were for the deposit of commemorative offerings subsequent to the closing of the grave, although all of them had been ransacked in antiquity. Such chapels are associated with many tombs of the late C Horizon in Lower Nubia, but they were apparently an uncommon feature of Kerma burial practice.

PROBLEMS OF INTERPRETATION AND CHRONOLOGY

Reisner's interpretation of the Kerma finds exemplifies the best and worst of his intuitive genius. By a combination of carefully detailed analysis and prodigious flights of imagination, he reconstructed both the identity and the history of the Kerma site with his usual confident assurance. It was, he concluded, a colony of Nubianized Egyptians in the Middle Kingdom, and the seat of the earliest Egyptian Viceroys of Kush.[23] From this it followed that Egyptian hegemony in Upper Nubia had already been established in the Middle Kingdom, an inference which cannot otherwise be drawn from the textual or archaeological record.

Reisner's interpretation was based largely upon a few datable and identifiable objects found in the Kerma cemetery. Foremost among them were the life-size granite statues of the Egyptian Prince Hepzefa and his wife Sennuwy, both of which were found in the great Tumulus III. These two individuals were already well known from finds at Assiut, in Middle Egypt, and could be dated to the reign of Senusret I at the beginning of the XII

Dynasty. The finding of the two statues led Reisner to conclude that Tumulus III was the burial place of Hepzefa himself, and that (in view of the size and splendour of his tomb) he was none other than the Viceroy of Kush. It followed, therefore, that the neighbouring great tumuli were those of his successors in the viceregal office.

Other Egyptologists were quick to challenge Reisner's view.[24] They pointed out that the tomb of Hepzefa (admittedly unfinished) was already known from Assiut, that burial on foreign soil was abhorrent to Egyptian officials, that alien burial rites were doubly abhorrent, and that in any case Tumulus III contained material datable to later reigns than that of Senusret I. It was suggested that the inscribed statues,[25] as well as a good deal of other Egyptian-made material found at Kerma, were the discarded status symbols of a bygone age in Egypt, which enterprising merchants had unloaded on the gullible and status-conscious Nubian kings.

The half century since Reisner's excavations has done little to clear up the mysteries of Kerma.[26] Until systematic archaeology is inaugurated in Upper Nubia, much will remain as obscure as it has been since 1916. Because of the critical importance of Kerma to any interpretation of later Nubian history, however, it seems desirable here to reconsider some of the problems raised by the Kerma site and culture.

SCOPE AND SIGNIFICANCE OF THE EGYPTIAN PRESENCE

That there were Egyptians at Kerma seems beyond dispute. Yet it is almost equally certain that Reisner overestimated their numbers and their role. This was due in part to his interpretation of the imported statues, which we have just considered, but also to his mistaken belief that Kerma black-topped pottery was made on the wheel, and therefore was the work of Egyptian craftsmen.[27] It would indeed have required a large colony of potters to furnish the quantity of beakers found in the Kerma cemetery. However, my own investigations have established to my satisfaction that the vessels were made by hand, and therefore almost certainly by native potters.

Most scholars today would agree with Junker and Säve-Söderbergh[28] that the burials at Kerma could not possibly be those of Egyptians. What, then, is left as evidence of the Egyptian presence? We can cite with varying degrees of confidence the architecture of the *Deffufas*, the brickwork within the largest of the tumuli,[29] the paintings in the mortuary chapels, the manufactures and commerce carried on at the trading post, and some of the distinctive grave goods found in the cemetery. The latter evidence must however be regarded with a certain degree of caution. It seems worthwhile to quote Trigger in this regard:

Although heavily influenced by Egyptian techniques of manufacture and design, much of the material that was produced at Kerma reflects a local cultural tradition. For example, the design and carpentry of the beds which were found are typically Egyptian, but many of them have footboards that are inlaid in a style that is not. Likewise, the mica figures that were made to be sewn on leather caps are not Egyptian. The copper daggers, of which 130 were found, are a distinct local variant of the standard Egyptian variety, and the metal work copies the shapes of the local pottery. Although much of this material has been interpreted as the output of Egyptian craftsmen accommodating themselves to local tastes, it is also possible that local craftsmen acquired Egyptian techniques of manufacture which they then applied to their own cultural idiom.[30]

None of the foregoing necessarily points to a large Egyptian population. It is only at the managerial level that we clearly recognize the Egyptian touch: in the design of the great brick structures, and in the supervision of craft production and commerce. A small Egyptian élite, supervising native commerce and industry on behalf of a Nubian king, would best account for the archaeological facts at Kerma as we now know them.[31]

IDENTITY OF THE SITE

In the Kerma cemetery, not far from the Upper *Deffufa*, Reisner found the fragments of a hieroglyphic stele which he described and translated as follows:

Above was a winged sun-disc with uraeus on each side. There followed eight lines of hieroglyphic inscription dated on the first day of the first month of the third season (month Pachon) of the 33rd year of Amenemhat III: 'Year 33, first month of the third season, day 1 under the majesty of the King of Upper and Lower Egypt, Nemaatra, the son of Ra, Amenemhat, living forever. List of bricks which came down to the *snb-t* which is in Inebuw-Amenemhat [Walls of Amenemhat] . . . by the act of the hereditary prince, the sole friend, whom his Lord sent because of his value in increasing his boundaries and because of the excellence of his planning, the Chancellor Intef, son of Semib, when he was with a company from Elephantine – 31,305 (or 35,300).'[32]

Reisner immediately identified 'Walls of Amenemhat' (a place-name otherwise unknown in Egyptian annals) with the settlement at Kerma. Pointing out that 35,000 bricks would not go very far towards building any of the known structures there, he further reasoned that Intef could only have instituted repairs to a previously existing building – presumably the nearby Upper *Deffufa*. From this it followed that the great structure had already been built prior to the reign of Amenemhat III. It was also inferable that a town named after the Egyptian king (a name which contrasts markedly with those of the Second Cataract Forts) was an Egyptian town.

Viewed realistically, the interpretation of the Intef stele presents all kinds of difficulties. Nobody knows what a *snb-t* was, since the word occurs in no other text. Whatever it was, why should Intef have commemorated, in a form usually reserved for heroic exploits, the receipt of a shipment of bricks sufficient only for a modest construction? Why should bricks be shipped at all, when they can be made on the spot anywhere in the Nile Valley? The only justification for transporting such a cheap and unremunerative commodity would be in cases where construction was required far from available sources of water or clay – conditions which do not prevail at Kerma.

While many mysteries connected with the Intef stele may never be resolved, the same *caveat* surely applies to this find as to the various inscribed statues and statuettes from Kerma. A stele of one's own was, after all, one of the prime status symbols of antiquity, and an illiterate Nubian king might well have been content to impress his equally illiterate subjects with a second-hand model. If the Intef stele was brought from somewhere else, however, then neither the identity of 'Walls of Amenemhat' nor the Middle Kingdom date is necessarily applicable to Kerma.[33]

INTERPRETATION OF THE CEMETERY

If we acknowledge, as most scholars now do, that the burial customs at Kerma are those of Nubians and not of Egyptians, we can nevertheless hardly avoid the conclusion that they represent a group of extraordinarily wealthy and powerful individuals or families. We are probably safe in identifying them as the first royal tombs in Nubian history. Although the order of their development is uncertain,[34] the greatest of the tumuli can hardly represent anything but a succession; the coexistence of two or more such powerful individuals in the same time and place is unthinkable.

While we are clearly in the presence of a highly, even excessively, centralized authority, we cannot yet recognize the existence of a class-stratified society. The differences between the grandest and the meanest tombs are primarily quantitative rather than qualitative; moreover the tombs are all more or less jumbled together in the same cemetery. We can draw no sharp line between the great and the lesser tumuli, many of which may also be the tombs of kings in humbler days. The subsidiary burials represent, presumably, important members of the king's household who were permitted to outlive him but who wished to renew their association with him in the afterworld.

The contrast between the subsidiary interments and the sacrificial burials suggests that while the former may have been important royal retainers, the latter were more probably slaves. If so, slave-holding must have been developed on a large scale during the heyday of the Kerma kingdom. It may well have been stimulated by the example of the pharaohs, as the excessive slave-holding of West African kings in the eighteenth century was a byproduct of their dealings with European slave traders. The apparent presence of large numbers of slaves is one of several indications that the people of Kerma were a far more warlike race than were their cousins in Lower Nubia.

PROBLEMS OF CHRONOLOGY

An initial problem concerns the temporal relationship of the two parts of the Kerma site. We have as a common bond between them, however, the brickwork of the Upper and Lower *Deffufas*, the numerous mud sealings (mostly of Hyksos date) found in both places, and the various manufactures carried on at the trading post which were paralleled by goods found in the cemetery graves. It seems logical in any case to assume, as Reisner did, that the great brick buildings and tumuli are representative of a single climax of wealth and power.

The absolute dating of the Kerma heyday is a much more difficult problem. Reisner's original belief in a Middle Kingdom date was based almost entirely on the statues of Hepzefa and Sennuwy, the stele of Intef, and a few other inscribed objects of Egyptian manufacture. If we recognize, however, that material of later date was found in the same tumuli, and that all of the inscriptional material found at Kerma may represent second-hand goods brought in at a later date, then no solid basis is left for a Middle Kingdom dating. There remains only the inferential evidence of the Second Cataract Forts, pointing to the existence of some sort of power centre farther to the south, and the specific resemblances of the *Deffufa* brickwork to that of the fortresses.

Far more trustworthy than inscribed stones are the numerous mud-seal impressions found both in the Lower *Deffufa* and in the Kerma cemetery. The great majority of these are assignable to the Hyksos period. This was recognized by Reisner himself, but he got over the difficulty in part by assuming that the type of seal normally identified with the Second Inter-mediate Period must in fact have been developed earlier.[35] His conclusion has not, however, been verified by subsequent work in Egypt. Taking the seals together with other lines of evidence, both at Kerma and elsewhere, the most likely dating for the Kerma heyday would seem to be concurrent with the climax of Hyksos power in Lower Egypt, in the sixteenth century B C.[36]

The great tombs may of course represent only a short chapter in a much longer history. Depending on the population of the Kerma settlement, the thousands of graves in the eastern cemetery could represent an occupation of many centuries, or they could all belong to a much shorter period. A certain degree of cultural change is manifest between the graves in the southern and northern parts of the cemetery; it is signalized in part by the paucity of sacrificial burials in the north. Reisner's assumption was that the cemetery had grown from south to north, and that the change repre-sented a progressive Nubianization and impoverishment.[37] However, the possibility of development in the other direction cannot be ruled out. In the light of our general knowledge of Egyptian–Nubian relations, a long period of development leading up to the Kerma climax seems more probable than does a long period of degeneration following it (cf. Ch. 9). We have to acknowledge, however, that the time span represented by the Kerma cemetery and by the Kerma culture may not be long. The culture as we now know it shows far less developmental change from beginning to end than does the C Horizon of Lower Nubia (Ch. 6).

KERMA SITES IN THE NORTH

For a long time after its excavation the Kerma site remained the only significant exemplar of the Kerma culture. More recently, however, a few other sites have been found within what is presumed to be 'Kerma territory'. Still others have been found much further to the north, under special circumstances which add an extra dimension to the Kerma problem.

If the Kerma climax is accepted as contemporary with the late C Horizon, then there must somewhere be a cultural frontier or transition zone between them. The logical place to look for such a frontier would be at Semna, since it was the frontier chosen by the Middle Kingdom rulers of Lower Nubia.[38] This supposition, though not fully confirmed, receives considerable support from the recently concluded archaeological survey in the *Batn el Hajar*. Cemeteries of the C Horizon have been found only as far south as Saras, ten miles to the north of Semna.[39] In the area immediately south of Semna a number of Kerma cemeteries have been found.[40] Kerma cemeteries have also been found to the north of Semna, but only under special conditions which will be described presently.

Kerma territory, then, presumably extended from somewhere above Kerma in the south to Semna in the north. In all probability it was the original Land of Kush, as the term first appears in texts of the Middle Kingdom.[41] Within this territory two important cemeteries have been investigated in addition to the 'discovery site'. The necropolis at Sai Island (an important local seat of power during most of later Nubian history) is enormous; perhaps as large as the Kerma cemetery itself. Here too are some very large tumuli, though none approaches the dimensions of the largest of the royal tombs in the south. The necropolis at Sai was partially excavated between 1970 and 1972; the graves and their contents were found to be identical in every respect to the minor tumuli at Kerma except for the apparent absence of sacrificial burials.[42]

A Kerma cemetery of several hundred graves at Ukma, in the *Batn el Hajar*, has been excavated in its entirety. The work has just been completed, and no published report is yet available. While most of the finds evidently conform to the expected Kerma pattern,[43] the excavator believes that several of the graves represent a divergent cultural tradition: an alien group

213

perhaps living in a symbiotic relationship with the dominant Kerma population.[44]

To the north of Semna, Kerma cemeteries or isolated graves have been reported at Saras,[45] Abka,[46] Mirgissa,[47] Abu Sir,[48] Buhen,[49] Aniba,[50] and Kubban.[51] Of these the cemetery at Mirgissa, which contained twenty-two graves, has been fully excavated. The graves were situated close to the walls of the great fortress, but in a somewhat secluded *wadi* well away from the main Egyptian cemeteries. All of the graves were relatively small, but in other respects exhibited the typical Kerma mortuary complex. There were at least four instances of human sacrifice.[52]

At the foot of the rock of Abu Sir, halfway between Mirgissa and Buhen, a tiny cluster of seven Kerma-like graves was found. Here, however, there were departures from the normal burial practice. The bodies were laid either on the right or on the left side, without consistent orientation, and there were no traces of beds. The tumuli, if they ever existed, had been destroyed by erosion.[53]

The known Kerma burials north of Semna have one peculiarity in common. The great majority of them are associated with the great Egyptian fortresses, or, in the case of Abu Sir, with a lookout post maintained in conjunction with the fortresses (Ch. 7). The conclusion seems inescapable that at some point in their history the forts were manned in part by Kerma troops, who came or were brought far from their homeland for that purpose.

What were the time and circumstances of Kerma occupation in the forts? All of the known finds point unmistakably to a time late in the Second Intermediate period – presumably concurrent with the heyday of Kerma itself. This would theoretically fall between the major Egyptian occupations of the fortresses. It appears unlikely, however, that Kermans were the sole occupants of these great structures. Twenty-two men could hardly man the ramparts at Mirgissa, and the Kerma contingents at the other forts appear to have been smaller still. There may also be Egyptian graves at Mirgissa and elsewhere datable to the same period as the Kerma cemeteries.

The available evidence suggests that, during the Hyksos period, the fortresses of Lower Nubia were being manned by small cadres of Egyptian officials supported by a few native troops. Yet we know that the mandate of the Egyptian dynast at Thebes did not extend beyond Aswan, and the garrisons in Nubia were therefore not his. The only reasonable conclusion is that both officers and men were in the service of the King of Kerma. This seems to be attested too by the stele of Sepedher (cf. Ch. 7): 'I was a valiant commandant of Buhen, and ... I built the temple of Horus, Lord of Buhen, to the satisfaction of the ruler of Cush.'[54] It would seem, in short, that at the height of their power the rulers of Kerma replaced the pharaoh himself as overlords of Lower Nubia and its trade.[55] It was no doubt this state of affairs which provoked the would-be pharaoh at Thebes to utter his celebrated complaint, 'I sit united with an Asiatic and a Nubian, each man in possession of his slice of this Egypt.'[56]

THE 'PAN-GRAVE CULTURE'

One more group of archaeological remains, contemporary with the Kerma period, requires mention in this chapter. These are the 'pan-graves' (so called because the grave pit retains the shallow oval form characteristic of earlier times in Nubia) which occur sporadically both in Lower Nubia and in Egypt. Although they exhibit many generalized Nubian characteristics, and sometimes occur in the midst of 'C-Group' cemeteries, the pan-graves are distinguishable on a number of grounds from the typical graves of the later C Horizon, and seem to represent a foreign intrusion alike in Egypt[57] and in Lower Nubia.[58] They were once thought to show closer affinities with Kerma, and on that basis it was suggested that they were in fact the burials of mercenary soldiers from the Upper Nubian kingdom who had served in the northern countries.[59] More detailed analysis has suggested however that the pan-graves are distinct alike from 'C-Group' and from Kerma burials, and they are now believed to represent still a third Nubian population group,[60] which Säve-Söderbergh identifies with the formidable Medjay of Egyptian texts.[61] These, it appears, were not riverain peoples but nomads of the eastern desert, who perhaps sold their services as mercenaries both to the King of Kerma and to the pharaoh. It is now believed that all of the known pan-graves date from the Hyksos period,[62] when the power of Kerma was also at its height.

INTERPRETATIVE SUMMARY

While the culture of the C Horizon was developing slowly and peacefully in Lower Nubia, a much more vigorous and warlike culture emerged in the better-favoured lands to the south. The material aspects of the Kerma culture and of the C Horizon are generally similar, and probably sprang from a common origin, but the wealth and power of Kerma far outstripped those of the Lower Nubians. Kerma in its heyday became an absolute monarchy of awesome proportions, while the social institutions of the C Horizon never progressed beyond a segmentary lineage system which probably lacked any central authority. The contrast between them may be likened to that between the highly autocratic Baganda and the much more democratic Nuer in modern times: they are culturally related peoples, but exhibiting very different levels of political development.

That the Upper Nubians had already moved ahead of their neighbours by the end of the Old Kingdom seems evident from the Egyptian accounts of the Land of Yam. By the Middle Kingdom the value of Egyptian trade with Upper Nubia was sufficient to inspire the pharaoh to a major effort for its protection and control, as attested by the Second Cataract Forts. Yet it is not until a still later date that we can recognize archaeologically the source of all this interest and activity in Upper Nubia. The great royal tombs and architectural monuments of Kerma apparently belong to the Second Intermediate Period, when the power of the Nubians grew in proportion to the weakness and division within Egypt.

The wealth if not the power of Kerma evidently depended on an economic symbiosis with Egypt, and in particular with Lower Egypt. It was trade with the Delta which kept the Nubian king and nobles supplied with imported luxuries, and which induced them to keep open the trade route to the north by the establishment of small garrisons in the former Egyptian forts of Lower Nubia. In the interest of maintaining and expanding this trade, the Nubian kings probably undertook extensive military and commercial ventures in the lands still further to the south.

A small, élite corps of Egyptian officials oversaw the manufactures and the export trade of Kerma on behalf of the native ruler. They were, however, commercial rather than military or political figures. The Kerma kingdom was independent, self-governing, and capable not only of defending its own territory but, in the absence of Egyptian authority, of maintaining a loose hegemony over Lower Nubia as well. The picture of Kerma in the second millennium BC presents many parallels with the eighteenth-century kingdom of Dahomey, whose wealth and power depended on firearms supplied by the European powers in exchange for slaves, which were delivered to their resident 'factors' in the great slave-port of Whydah.[63]

Kerma represents a transitional step between the Tribal and Dynastic stages of Nubian cultural development. Its material and to some extent even its social institutions are those of the Tribal period, and are little different in substance from the Lower Nubian A and C Horizons. Yet its autocratic, presumably divine king and its state-organized trade represent a first, long step down the road towards empire. Had the culture been left to develop unmolested, stratified society, peasant economy, bureaucratic government, and the other 'blessings' of imperial civilization must inevitably have followed in time.

As it turned out, the indigenous development of an imperial system in the Sudan was forestalled by the Egyptians (Ch. 9). Thrusting aside the native rulers, they established their own hegemony from the First to the Fourth Cataract. The full complex of civilization thus arrived in Nubia not as the outcome of local cultural developments, but as a transplant from Egypt. It was many centuries later before a genuinely Nubian empire was achieved, but when it came, it owed much to the legacy of Kerma.

9
THE VICEROYALTY OF KUSH
NUBIA UNDER THE EGYPTIAN NEW KINGDOM

The episode of Hyksos rule in Egypt has been characterized by John Wilson as 'the Great Humiliation'.[1] The humiliation must have been particularly keen for the erstwhile 'pharaohs' who continued to maintain a precarious independence at Thebes, while the formerly Egyptian lands to the north and south of them passed under the control of foreigners. For several generations the Theban dynasts had to bear with their ignominy, at times paying tribute to the Hyksos and allowing free passage to their commerce with Kerma. All the while they were biding their time and awaiting their chance to turn the tables. Kamose, the last ruler of the Theban XVII Dynasty, clearly sounded the theme of *revanche*: 'No man rests, being wasted through servitude of the Asiatics. I will grapple with him and rip open his belly, for my desire is to deliver Egypt and to smite the Asiatics.'[2]

The gradual expulsion of the Hyksos, begun by Kamose, reached its triumphant conclusion under his successor Ahmose, the founder of the illustrious XVIII Dynasty and of Egypt's greatest empire. After a long siege the intruders were dislodged from their capital in the Delta and driven back into the Asiatic lands from which their ancestors had perhaps originally come. The momentum of pursuit carried the Egyptian armies across Sinai and into Palestine, where in a series of stubborn actions the Hyksos were forced out of one stronghold after another, and their power was finally crushed.[3] At the conclusion of the campaign Ahmose found himself master not only of Egypt but of substantial territories in Palestine and Syria. From that time onwards it was Egypt's fortune, and ultimately her undoing, to be a power in Asia as well as in Africa.

Ahmose had no sooner returned in triumph from his Asiatic campaigns than he turned his attention to Nubia, the erstwhile ally of the Hyksos (cf. Ch. 8). A lightning campaign in the twenty-second year of his reign was sufficient to recover the former Egyptian territory of Lower Nubia, apparently meeting with little resistance from local or Kerma-backed forces. The fortress of Buhen was reoccupied, a temple was begun there, and a permanent Egyptian governor was appointed. In the next reign he was to become the first Viceroy of Kush.[4]

The warrior-pharaohs who succeeded Ahmose – Amenhotep I and the

217

first three Thutmoses – consciously strove to extend the frontiers of empire both in Asia and in Africa. Their armies penetrated Nubia far beyond the limits of previous exploration, ultimately establishing Egyptian dominion as far upstream as the Fourth Cataract and perhaps even beyond. 'Boundary' steles of Thutmose I and Thutmose III have been found beyond Abu Hamed, not far from the Fifth Cataract, where the great desert road from Korosko rejoins the Nile (Fig. 33).[5] Like the earlier inscription of Senusret at Semna (Ch. 7), these were probably meant to proclaim an Egyptian monopoly, in this case of overland trade along the great desert road.

The last major campaign of conquest and annexation was undertaken in the reign of Thutmose II. Slave-raids, disguised as punitive expeditions, are occasionally reported until the end of the New Kingdom, but they had little to do with political events during the later reigns.[6] For all practical purposes Nubia was Egyptian territory, and its people were Egyptian subjects. Having acquired this vast and lucrative domain – equal in size to Egypt itself, and far exceeding in size the imperial domains in Asia – the Pharaoh set out to govern and exploit it, and ultimately to Egyptianize it. In the end these efforts succeeded beyond expectation, and the effect was to be felt in Egypt for centuries to come.

CONQUERORS AND BUILDERS

The New Kingdom pharaohs were among history's greatest builders. Their adventures in Asia brought them into direct contact with the other great civilizations of antiquity, and opened Egypt's first real window on the outside world. Traditional provincialism gave way to a new and more cosmopolitan outlook. The result, as usual, was an enormous stimulation of the monumental arts. The colossal temples of the New Kingdom were probably meant to impress not only Egyptians, but the whole civilized world. The number of these monumental structures, both in Egypt and in Nubia, far exceeds the total of surviving monuments from all other ages.

The earliest pharaohs of the XVIII Dynasty were too preoccupied in the military field to undertake major construction programmes. In Nubia they were content at first to reoccupy and repair the existing fortresses. This work was apparently already begun in the reign of Ahmose, and was carried out on a considerably larger scale under the first two Thutmoses. The high priority given to the renovation of the forts might have been justified on the ground that a firm hold was needed on the newly reconquered territory, but it was probably also a symbolic act designed to re-establish Egyptian prestige, since the fortresses had been and remained the principal symbols of Egyptian rule in Nubia. The repairs in many cases can only be interpreted as face-lifting; for example, the 'skin walls' which were added to the already massive fortifications at Buhen and Mirgissa can

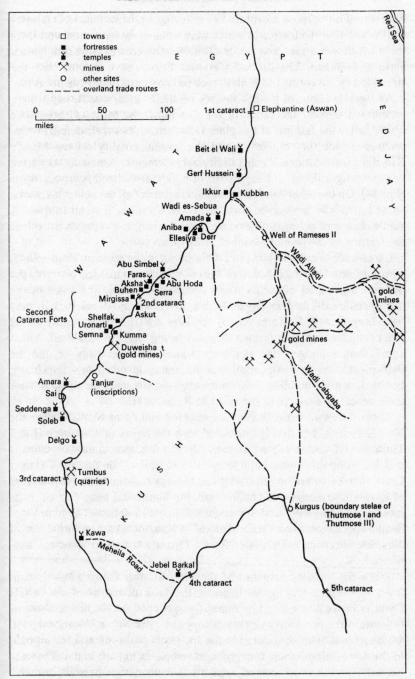

Fig. 33. Egyptian colonization in the New Kingdom

have served no purpose except that of restoring a pristine façade. It is noteworthy too that the fortresses which were extensively renovated were only those which were to serve as major administrative centres: Kubban, Aniba, Serra and Buhen. The Second Cataract Forts above Buhen, once the strategic keys to control in Nubia, received comparatively little attention.

As Egyptian control pushed farther up the Nile, new settlements were established beyond the range of the existing forts. Most of these were walled, after the fashion of the older installations, but their defences conspicuously lack the complexity and the 'monumentality' of the Middle Kingdom fortifications. Their interior arrangements, insofar as they have been investigated, are not suggestive of highly disciplined garrison towns (Fig. 34). On the other hand, a prominent feature of all the new settlements, as well as of the reoccupied forts of Lower Nubia, is a stone temple.[7] A subtle change of policy is observable here: the temple has begun to replace the fortress as the primary symbol of Egyptian rule.

Large-scale temple-building in Nubia began in the reign of Thutmose II, who completed the pacification of the country. From his time onwards the building and repair of fortifications declined markedly, and some of the last towns established in Upper Nubia, at Kawa and Jebel Barkal, may have been unwalled. Moreover, by the later XVIII Dynasty many of the older settlements had outgrown their defending walls. At Kubban, Aniba and Buhen, a hodgepodge of private houses stretched away beyond the battlements. While fortification was becoming less and less important, however, temple-building was undertaken on an increasingly grandiose scale, reaching a climax in the reign of Rameses II.

There were two main 'waves' of temple-building in Nubia during the New Kingdom. The first is associated with the reigns of Thutmose II and Thutmose III, and to a lesser extent with their five immediate successors. It was the Thutmoses who built temples in several of the Second Cataract Forts, thereby combining the older and the newer monumental expressions of Egyptian sovereignty. Though small, the Thutmosid temples are for the most part solidly built and are elegantly simple in design. The temples of Semna and Kumma (now reconstructed in Khartoum) are among the most complete surviving examples of XVIII Dynasty temple architecture anywhere.[8]

While the building activities of the early Thutmoses were largely confined to the old fortress settlements, the later pharaohs of the XVIII Dynasty broke new ground by establishing temples and walled settlements together in the previously virgin territory of Upper Nubia. Amenhotep III, whose reign is often considered as the apogee of pharaonic splendour, built in the Abri-Delgo Reach a magnificent temple to himself and a second to his wife. In the same general area his successor, the 'heretic-pharaoh', Akhenaton, built temple-towns at Sesebi and at Kawa (Fig. 33). Tutan-

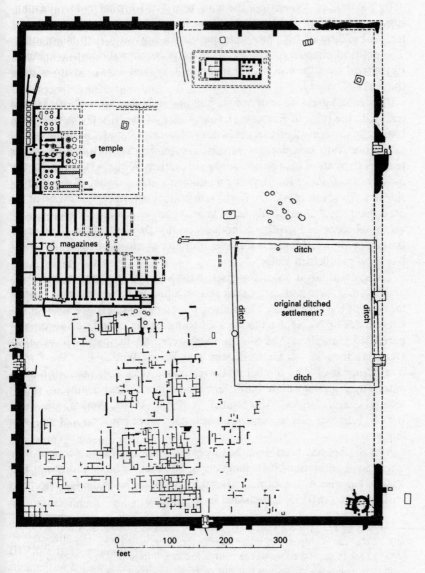

temple

magazines

ditch

ditch

ditch

original ditched settlement?

ditch

0   100   200   300
feet

Fig. 34. Plan of New Kingdom walled town, Sesebi (Delgo)

221

khamen, one of the last kings of the XVIII Dynasty, built minor temples within the existing settlements at Faras and at Kawa.

By the time of Akhenaton, the main thrust of Egyptian colonial expansion was clearly spent. No new towns were founded after his reign, and the temple-building of his immediate successors was on a very minor scale. The political chaos wrought by his attempt to alter the state religion of Egypt weakened the country for half a century, and led to the downfall of the XVIII Dynasty.

The second great wave of temple-building in Nubia virtually begins and ends with the reign of Rameses II, fourth king of the XIX Dynasty and the last really towering figure in the history of ancient Egypt. In Egypt as well as Nubia, this vainglorious monarch commissioned more and larger temples than all of his predecessors put together. While Abu Simbel is the most conspicuous of his surviving monuments, it is only one of ten Rameside temples south of Aswan. In the reliefs at Abu Simbel and several of his other temples, Rameses is depicted kneeling in obeisance to a god – a conventional scene in Egyptian temple decoration, except that in these cases the god being worshipped is Rameses himself! As an act of hubris this must have few parallels in history.[9]

The great innovation of Rameses' reign was the rock-cut temple. This architectural form had been developed on a limited scale before, at least as far back as the time of the Thutmoses, but all of the really grandiose rock-cut temples of Nubia are the work of Rameses II. In addition to the unparalleled example at Abu Simbel, there were rock temples of Rameses at Derr, Wadi es-Sebua, Gerf Hussein, and Beit el Wali. All of these were located north of Abu Simbel in Lower Nubia (Fig. 33), where the comparatively high sandstone bluffs lent themselves to this distinctive architectural canon. Beyond Abu Simbel, at Faras, Aksha, Amara, and Jebel Barkal, Rameses had to content himself with more conventional masonry temples.

Abu Simbel has been described as everything from a masterpiece to a 'gigantic abomination'.[10] Its uniqueness, however, is beyond dispute. The ecstatic surprise of the explorer Burckhardt, when he stumbled upon the buried colossi in 1813, is recorded in his journal:

Having, as I supposed, seen all of the antiquities of Ebsambal, I was about to ascend the sandy side of the mountain by the same way I had descended; when having luckily turned more to the southward, I fell in with what is yet visible of four immense colossal statues cut out of rock; . . . they stand in a deep recess, excavated in the mountain, but it is greatly to be regretted, that they are now almost entirely buried beneath the sands, which are blown down here in torrents. The entire head, and part of the breast and arms of one of the statues are yet above the surface; of the one next to it scarcely any part is visible, the head being broken off, and the body covered with sand to above the shoulders; of the other two the bonnets only appear. It is difficult to determine whether these statues are in a sitting or standing posture; their backs adhere to a portion of rock, which projects from the main body, and which may represent a part of a chair, or may be merely a column for support. The head which is above the surface has a most expressive, youthful countenance, approaching nearer to the Grecian model of beauty, than that of any ancient Egyptian figure I have seen; indeed, were it not for a thin, oblong beard, it might well pass for a head of Pallas.[11]

The removal of hundreds of tons of sand, since Burckhardt's visit, has made possible the more detailed description of the temple given by Emery:

The main features of the exterior of the temple are the four gigantic statues of the king which have been carved out of the living rock of the hillside [Pl. IXa]. The seated figures, two on each side of the entrance, are more than 65 feet in height, and they represent Rameses wearing the Double Crown of Egypt. On either side of, and between the legs of, each statue are figures of Queen Nefertari and some of the royal children, themselves represented in statues of great size but dwarfed by the side of the colossi. Each of the four groups stands on a high pedestal on which are carved the cartouches of Rameses and groups of Asiatic and Negro captives; while the box-like thrones on which the colossi are seated are decorated with conventional groups representing the union of the Two Lands. The façade which forms the background to the colossi is carved in pylon form with a cornice decorated with a row of baboons, their arms upraised in the worship of the rising sun. Over the entrance to the interior of the temple is a statue of the falcon-headed sun god Re-Harmachis. . .

The entrance to the temple leads directly into the great hall, the main features of which are two rows of four square pillars against whose fronts are colossal standing figures of the King, who is represented again wearing the Double Crown and holding the crook and flail sceptres [Pl. IXb]. The pillars and walls of the great hall, which measure 30 feet in height, are covered with scenes and inscriptions relating to religious ceremonies and to the King's military exploits in his struggle with the Hittites in Syria, and with the Kushites in the Sudan. The ceiling is decorated with a conventional design of cartouches and vultures with outstretched wings.

In the north and west walls of the hall, doors lead into a series of rooms which were probably used as vestries and stores for the priesthood [cf. Fig. 35]. The reliefs on their walls are devoted entirely to religious subjects.

The central door in the west wall gives access to a smaller hall, the roof of which is supported by four square pillars, and here again the wall reliefs are entirely religious in character. Beyond this hall is the anteroom of the sanctuary, which has three doors in the west wall, two on either side leading to small uninscribed rooms and the central one on the direct axis of the temple, leading into the sanctuary. In the west wall of the sanctuary is a row of four seated statues carved in the living rock. These are the principal deities of the temple: Ptah, Amen, Rameses himself and Re-Harmachis. In front of them, in the centre of the room, is a small uninscribed altar, and it was here that the sacrifice would have been made and the offerings placed, when the light of the rising sun illuminated the sanctuary at dawn.[12]

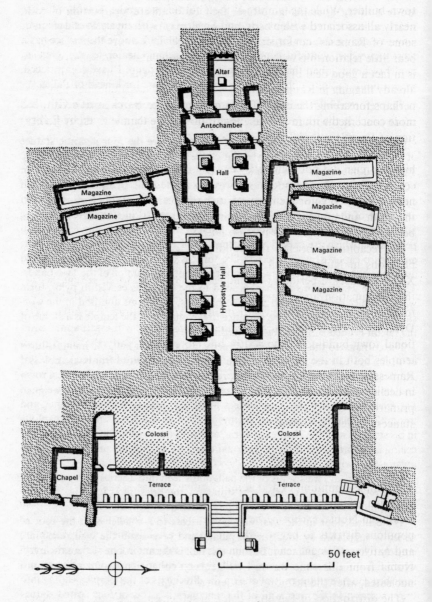

Fig. 35. Interior plan of rock-cut temple, Abu Simbel

Unlike his predecessors, Rameses was purely a temple-builder, not a town-builder. While the temples of the Thutmoses and the Amenhoteps are nearly all associated with existing settlements or with newly founded ones, some of Rameses' constructions, particularly in Lower Nubia, seem to bear little relationship to existing centres of population and activity. There is in fact a good deal of evidence that the colonial enterprise in Nubia was already flagging in Rameses' day (see below). The megalomaniac pharaoh, perhaps foreseeing the end of the imperial age, seems to have been much more concerned with immortalizing his own name than with the revitalization of Egypt's colonial régime.

Rameses II was the Louis XIV of Egyptian history. The extravagances of his long reign did not completely exhaust the Egyptian state, but le déluge could perhaps already be foreseen by his successors. They were left with neither the energy nor the resources to carry on his building programme in the south, and none of them tried. After Rameses II it was nearly 500 years before another temple was built in Nubia.

To recapitulate briefly, the building activities of the New Kingdom pharaohs in Nubia exhibit three main phases. The early reigns of the XVIII Dynasty, a period of reconquest and consolidation, are marked by the reoccupation and enlargement of the existing forts and by the first foundation of new, fortified settlements in Upper Nubia. The later XVIII Dynasty, a period of stabilization and colonization, witnessed some additional town-building in the south, but more importantly the building of temples both in the older settlements and in the newly founded ones. The Ramesside period, when the Nubian population and economy were already in decline, was characterized by a second wave of temple-building designed primarily to glorify the pharaoh, and having little relation to the circumstances of everyday life in Nubia.

THE 'URBAN' CENTRES

The temple-communities and administrative centres of the New Kingdom provided a kind of social and political nucleus which had previously been lacking in Nubia, except perhaps at Kerma. They were mostly situated in populous districts to begin with; after their establishment both Egyptian and native settlement tended to cluster around them. The demography of Nubia from this time onward, if never precisely 'urban', was at least nucleated, after the fashion of settlement in the Near East.[13]

The distribution of Egyptian colonial settlement and industry in Nubia was far from uniform. The northern part of Lower Nubia was comparatively poor in resources and offered few inducements to colonization per se. Its control, however, was essential for the exploitation of the most important Egyptian gold mines, which were reached by way of Lower

Nubia and the Wadi Allaqi. The fortress of Kubban, situated at the mouth of the *wadi*, was the pivotal point in this operation. During the New Kingdom it became the centre of a sizeable community, which included also the fertile plain of Dakka across the river. With this exception, however, there are few remains of New Kingdom activity in northern Nubia except for the rock temples of Rameses at Beit el Wali, Gerf Hussein, and Wadi es-Sebua.[14]

By contrast to the region immediately to the north, the southern half of Lower Nubia was exceptionally fertile and populous; it was a centre of power and wealth at many times in Nubian history (cf. Ch. 1). More than one third of the surviving monuments and two thirds of the known graves from the New Kingdom occupation of Nubia are concentrated within the seventy-five-mile stretch of the Nile Valley between Aniba and the Second Cataract. The administrative capital of the whole region was evidently the fortress of Aniba, which may at times have been the residence of the Viceroys of Kush.[15] Other, perhaps local administrative centres were located at Serra and Buhen, near the Second Cataract. In both places, as at Aniba, the Middle Kingdom fortress walls were restored and enlarged.

Important temples were built at Amada and at Ellesiya, not far from Aniba, and two temples were situated within the fortress walls at Buhen. However, the most important religious centre in Lower Nubia was not at any of the main administrative settlements but at Faras, thirty miles north of the Second Cataract. There had been a small military installation here during the Middle Kingdom, but it was not restored after the reconquest, and the place apparently had little political or military importance under the New Kingdom. Nevertheless, at least five temples were built at Faras and in the immediate vicinity by various rulers of the XVIII and XIX Dynasties. There seems to be a functional contrast between these establishments, situated in open country presumably for the propagation of the Egyptian state cults among the Nubians, and the temples within the fortress walls, which may have been part and parcel of the administrative machinery. The importance of Faras was evidently due almost entirely to indigenous tradition, and it remained a major religious centre long after the Egyptians themselves had departed from Nubia (cf. Ch. 12 and Ch. 15).

As Egyptian dominion was extended southwards beyond the *Batn el Hajar*, the cataract region lost most of its strategic importance. Egyptian activities there during the New Kingdom were relatively insignificant. The forts were reoccupied after a fashion, presumably for the assistance of boats passing through the cataracts, but only at Semna is there evidence of major repairs. However, temples were built in three of the four Semna forts (Semna, Kumma, and Uronarti) under the Thutmoses, and the number of New Kingdom burials at Semna West bespeaks a considerable population.[16]

Upstream from Semna, Egyptian presence is attested by the gold workings at Duweishat, to be described below, and by rock inscriptions at various points. The extraordinary concentration of inscriptions on the island of Tanjur suggests that an outpost was maintained here for the assistance of boats in passing a nearby cataract, although its remains have not been discovered.[17] Upstream from Tanjur no Egyptian monuments of any kind are encountered until the fertile Abri-Delgo region is reached.

The broad fields and placid water of the Abri-Delgo Reach must have been a welcome sight to the Egyptians after passing the rigours of the *Batn el Hajar*, for the majority of them went no farther. The main Egyptian colonial enterprise in Upper Nubia was concentrated in the region between Abri and Delgo, just upstream from the last of the *Batn el Hajar* cataracts. Although this area has not yet been systematically explored, its known Egyptian monuments include four major temples and three walled settlements (Fig. 33).

The first colonies in the Abri-Delgo Reach were apparently planted in the time of the Thutmoses or even earlier; the fortress at Sai Island may have been begun in the reign of Ahmose.[18] The curious ditched enclosures (apparently without walls) which underlay the later settlements at Soleb and Sesebi must also belong to the early reigns of the XVIII Dynasty.[19] These pioneer colonies were never completed in the form originally planned; they were overbuilt and replaced by rectangular, walled towns in the time of the Amenhoteps.

The main colonial establishments in the Abri-Delgo Reach, in addition to Sai, were Amara, Soleb–Seddenga, and Sesebi (Delgo). The foundation date of Amara is uncertain, but probably belongs to the middle or latter part of the XVIII Dynasty.[20] The magnificent temple of Soleb (Pl. Xa) and the nearby, much-destroyed temple of Seddenga were both built by Amenhotep III.[21] The town and temple of Sesebi were founded by his successor Akhenaton (Amenhotep IV).[22] The main colonization of the Abri-Delgo Reach therefore clearly belongs to the middle period of the XVIII Dynasty.

Amara, Sai and Sesebi were all walled towns, nearly square in outline (Fig. 34).[23] At Soleb too there was a massive wall, or rather a succession of walls, surrounding the temple, but this appears to be the traditional Egyptian *temenos* wall enclosing the sacred precincts rather than the defences of a settlement.[24] Although Soleb and Seddenga are both named as major settlements in New Kingdom texts, the town-sites and their fortifications have never been located.[25] At Amara and at Delgo, however, there was an integrated complex of town and temple. Neither of these sites has been investigated with any thoroughness, but the buildings encountered in the partial excavation of Amara were extremely complex, and had undergone innumerable modifications down to the end of the XX Dynasty.[26] The Amara temple was built by Rameses II, though possibly it replaced an earlier building. The town was clearly an important administrative centre in the later New Kingdom, and may have been the seat of the Deputy Viceroy for Upper Nubia.[27]

The Dongola Reach, although it has been the heartland of most later Nubian civilizations, seems to have attracted little colonization during the New Kingdom. The main surviving Egyptian monuments are at Napata, at the extreme upstream end of the region, and at Kawa, near the downstream end. These two settlements are the only Egyptian colonies in Upper Nubia which were located on the east bank of the Nile. They are very close to the present termini of the Meheila Road, a desert caravan route which by-passes the reverse bend of the Nile in the Dongola Reach (Fig. 33). The emergence of Napata and Kawa as major urban centres, contrasting with the absence of any known settlements along the river valley between them, strongly suggests that the Meheila Road was already in use in New Kingdom times. Its advantage over the river route, besides directness, is in avoiding the contrary winds of the upper Dongola Reach (cf. Ch. 1).

The area of Napata, just below the Fourth Cataract, emerged as the great political and religious centre of Nubia under the empire of Kush (Ch. 10), but its foundation goes back to the period of New Kingdom colonization. Stelae and re-used building blocks of Thutmose III and Thutmose IV suggest that there was already a temple and town here in the XVIII Dynasty,[28] while the great Amon Temple, which later became the 'Karnak' of the Napatan Empire (Fig. 39 and Pl. XIa), was certainly founded by Rameses II.[29] These buildings were erected immediately beneath the cliffs of Jebel Barkal, a towering desert butte which was perhaps already sacred to the local population (Pl. Xb). However, large temples of Rameses do not necessarily betoken important settlements, as we have already observed; until more excavation is undertaken at Jebel Barkal we will be unable to estimate the importance of Napata during the New Kingdom.

The settlement at Kawa, opposite modern Dongola, bore the name Gem-Aten. This identifies it almost certainly with the 'heretic-pharaoh', Akhenaton, who attempted to supplant the long-established state cult of Amon with that of his own personal deity, Aten. If Akhenaton ever built a temple at Kawa, it was entirely destroyed by his successors, as were his temples at Thebes and Tell el-Amarna. The little pharaonic temple which survives at Kawa today was built in the reign of Tutankhamen, near the end of the XVIII Dynasty. There was also a sizeable town, most of which remains unexcavated.[30] Kawa, like Napata, had a long subsequent history, and was an important centre throughout the Napatan and Meroitic periods. A short distance further downstream, on the Island of Argo, re-used temple blocks have recently come to light which suggest that here too was an important settlement in the XVIII Dynasty.[31]

Conspicuously missing from the list of New Kingdom 'urban' centres in Nubia is Kerma. Although the historical record is silent as to its fate, the Nubian kingdom evidently went under in the first rush of the reconquest, and we never hear of it again. The Egyptian conquerors felt no need to identify themselves as its successors, since they let the monuments and tombs of Kerma fall into ruin, and the place has remained a backwater until modern times.

POLITICAL AND ECONOMIC ORGANIZATION

Thuwre, the Commandant of Buhen appointed by Ahmose, was given the title 'King's Son of Kush' in the reign of Amenhotep I. He was the first or second[32] of a line of twenty-five or more officials who bore that title, and who governed both Nubia and the southernmost district of Egypt as deputies of the pharaoh.[33] They are usually designated as Viceroys of Kush, although strictly speaking their mandate included both Kush (Upper Nubia) and Wawat (Lower Nubia) as well as the region from Aswan to El Kab in Egypt. In time, through the operation of Toynbee's 'law of peripheral domination',[34] they became the most powerful officers in Egypt itself, as we shall see later.

The viceregal régime in Nubia is thus described by A. J. Arkell:

The Viceroy was responsible for the punctual payment of the tribute of Nubia (both from Wawat and Kush). He was usually chosen from the royal entourage, to ensure his fidelity, and he was directly responsible to the king. He seems to have brought the tribute personally and to have handed it over with ceremony to the vizier or treasurer.

The staff of the Viceroy included a Commander of the Bowmen of Kush, and two deputies, one for Wawat and the other for Kush, and . . . it is thought that during the Nineteenth Dynasty the Deputy of Kush resided at Amara. Most of the Viceroy's officials were no doubt Egyptians, but they included some Egyptian-ized Nubians . . . No doubt loyal native chiefs were left in charge of their tribal areas, and chiefs of Ma'am (modern Aniba) and Wawat are depicted leading their people to bring tribute to Tutankhamen. Such chiefs were no doubt held respon-sible for the tribute of their people, although attempts at independence such as some chiefs made early in the Eighteenth Dynasty were naturally crushed with severity.

The children of Nubian chiefs were taken to Egypt, originally as hostages, but they were given both Egyptian education and rank; thus a chief of Ma'am in a rock inscription at Toshka calls himself sandal-bearer[35] and page of the king. Pages were children who were brought up with the young princes, and they kept the title in later life. There is no doubt that Egyptian policy towards Nubia aimed at a peaceful symbiosis of Egyptians and natives.[36]

Assimilation, rather than symbiosis, would seem more accurately to describe the goal of Egyptian policy in Nubia. The sending of Nubian princes to be educated in Egypt foreshadows a policy followed by many 'assimilationist' rulers in later times. Like the substitution of temples for fortress walls as the main symbolic expression of Egyptian power, it betokens an important change in Egypt's attitude toward the Nubians. The pharaoh no longer seeks to maintain his rule by a show of force, but to legitimize it by ideological indoctrination – by the propagation of the state cult and the dissemination of the national culture. The crude paraphernalia of physical captivity are discarded in favour of the subtler and more effective trammels of the mind. The successful, though no doubt unexpected, effects of this policy can be seen in the emergence of the classic 'successor state' at Napata five hundred years later.

The extent to which native dignitaries were absorbed into the Egyptian governing class is uncertain, and poses problems which we shall consider at greater length later. Heka-Nefer, one of the local chiefs from Aniba previously referred to,[37] was certainly a Nubian, for he is both pictured and named in the tomb of the Viceroy Huy at Thebes.[38] His own tomb, which is purely Egyptian in style and copied after that of Huy, has recently been discovered at Toshka.[39] Two brothers whose funerary monuments identify them as 'Princes of Tekhet' (Serra) are also believed to have been Nubians. Once again, their elaborate chamber tombs are purely Egyptian in style and decoration, and their identification as Nubians is based upon patronyms which are not recognizable as Egyptian names.[40] On the other hand the official Pennut, who governed at Aniba in the XX Dynasty and was buried near by, appears to have been an Egyptian.[41]

Under the imperial régime the Nubian economy was transformed from a subsistence to a manorial basis. The change is thus characterized by Trigger:[42]

During the New Kingdom the economic life of Lower Nubia was much more complex than it had ever been before. It was also more closely integrated with that of Egypt. Although hunting and pastoralism must have remained important, especially in the poorer localities, a portion of the catch or herd was probably now required by the government or temple as tribute. At the same time the pattern of landholding which had prevailed in [the C Horizon], probably based largely on community ownership, was replaced by an Egyptian one. Most, if not all, farmers now worked on lands that were owned by the crown, the local princes, government administrators, or by the temples which were built throughout the region. The shift in the patterns of land ownership seems to have been accompanied by a shift away from pastoralism and in the direction of more intensive agriculture. The plantation scene in the tomb of Djehuty-Hotep suggests that the Nubians may already have been producing and exporting dates . . .[43] Beekeepers and wine growers are mentioned for the region farther south, and there were probably such specialists in Lower Nubia also.[44] Basin agriculture which was important in Egypt was impossible in Nubia because of the terrain, but the shaduf was likely introduced at this time,[45] and simple hand watering may have been used to increase the amount of arable land. This no doubt helped to compensate for the lowering of the flood level since the Middle Kingdom. Grain was probably also sent from Egypt to feed or pay those who were employed by the government.

The profits which the temples derived from their estates and the dues which some of them were able to levy on goods passing on the river[46] were used to support not only officials, priests, and their servants but also specialists such as traders, miners, shipbuilders, and craftsmen.[47] By the end of the Eighteenth Dynasty some manufactured goods begin to appear as part of the tribute which was sent to Egypt. Among the tribute in the tomb of Huy we find shields, stools, beds, and armchairs.[48]

Slaves and prisoners of war were sent to Lower Nubia to provide the labor force in such large state projects as the building of temples. Libyan captives were employed at Wadi Sebua in the forty-fourth year of the reign of Rameses II.[49] The kings of Egypt also made permanent donations of slaves to temples. A decree from the early Nineteenth Dynasty records that the king supplied the workshops of a temple in Buhen with male and female slaves which His Majesty had captured.[50]

With the establishment of a 'plantation economy' and the large-scale alienation of native landholdings, the historic sequence of colonial development was complete. The bulk of the Nubians were now *fellaheen*, and perhaps shared the unhappy lot of their fellow peasants in Egypt and other parts of the world. The landlords whom they served were for the most part absentees – Egyptian nobles or temple officials. Those Nubians like Djehuty-Hotep and Heka-Nefer who managed to find a place in the new landlord class were thoroughly Egyptianized in manner, and their class identification with the Egyptian nobility no doubt far outweighed their ethnic identification with their fellow Nubians. Class stratification began to replace ethnic division as the main cleavage in Nubian society.

Agrarian development was only one aspect of Egyptian colonialism in Nubia. A certain amount of slave-raiding continued until the end of the XX Dynasty,[51] and the Nubians themselves provided additional slaves – perhaps seized from their still more southerly neighbours – among their annual tribute to the Viceroy.[52] Some idea of the quantity and variety of the Nubian tribute can be gained from the *Annals of Thutmose III*, towards the middle of the XVIII Dynasty:[53]

Tribute of Wawat

Year 31. 92 cattle, 1 harvest.

Year 33. 20 slaves, 104 cattle, 1 harvest.

Year 34. 254 *deben** of gold, 10 slaves, and an unknown number of cattle.

Year 35. 34 slaves, 94 cattle, 1 harvest.

Year 38. 2844 *deben* of gold, 16 slaves, 77 cattle.

Year 39. 89 cattle, ivory and ebony.

231

Year 41. 3144 *deben* and 3 *kidet* of gold, 114 cattle, and an unknown quantity of ivory.

Year 42. 2374 *deben* and 1 *kidet* of gold, 1 harvest.

Tribute of Kush

Year 34. 300 *deben* of gold, 60 Negro slaves, 275 cattle, ivory and ebony.

Year 35. 70 *deben* and 1 *kidet* of gold; an unknown quantity of slaves, cattle, ivory and ebony, and 1 harvest.

Year 38. 100 *deben* and 6 *kidet* of gold, 36 Negro slaves, 306 cattle, ivory and ebony, 1 harvest.

Year 39. 144 *deben* and 3 *kidet* of gold, 101 Negro slaves, and an unknown quantity of cattle.

Year 41. 94 *deben* and 2 *kidet* of gold, 21 Negro slaves, and an unknown quantity of cattle.

*1 *deben* = approximately 20 pounds of gold. A *kidet* was a ring of gold weighing about 5 pounds.

THE GOLD INDUSTRY

As the European wars of Philip II were financed by the silver of Mexico, so the power of Egypt in Asia was maintained by Nubian gold. During most of the XVIII Dynasty the hand of the pharaoh was strong enough to maintain a firm grip on Palestine and Syria, though the cost of military occupation was undoubtedly high. The weakening of the state under Akhenaton furnished ready pretexts for local rebellion and foreign intrigue, and by the end of the XVIII Dynasty most of the Egyptian conquests in Asia had slipped away. The rise of Hittite power in Anatolia and of the 'Sea Peoples' (Cretans, Phoenicians, and others) in the eastern Mediterranean threatened Egyptian hegemony everywhere, foreshadowing the 'clash of empires' which occupied so large a part of the last millennium B C.

Seti I restored the Egyptian frontiers in Syria at the beginning of the XIX Dynasty. Threatened with a fresh Hittite incursion, Rameses II mounted a massive and enormously expensive Asiatic campaign which, while it ended in a stand-off with the Hittites, managed to preserve the *status quo* for a while longer. The Hittites in their own turn were destroyed by the Sea Peoples, and the Egyptians had to contend with a whole series of new enemies both in Asia and at home. The successors of Rameses fought a long series of rearguard actions, but by the end of the XX Dynasty their empire was gone for good. Thereafter Egyptian influence was maintained in Palestine through subsidy and intrigue rather than through the imperial mandate.

As long as the pharaoh's gold went primarily to adorn the royal monuments, its production was not a matter of high national priority. When it was spent in ever-larger quantities to support the imperial ambitions in

Asia, however, the development of new gold sources became a critical concern of the state. Egyptian prospectors ranged far and wide over the eastern desert, seemingly leaving no ridge and valley unexplored between the Nile and the Red Sea. More than eighty-five ancient mines are known from the barren wastelands of the north-eastern Sudan alone.[54]

Although gold was accumulated in quantities by every pharaoh from the First Dynasty onwards, the source of Egypt's gold before the New Kingdom is very imperfectly known. There are, as we saw in Chapter 7, some indications of Nubian gold production in the Middle Kingdom, but the quantities do not appear to have been large. The main gold mines of the Middle Kingdom were probably those in the Desert of Coptos, between Upper Egypt and the Red Sea.

The 'Gold of Coptos' still figures in the treasury receipts of the New Kingdom, but it is greatly overshadowed by the 'Gold of Wawat' (Lower Nubia) and the 'Gold of Kush' (Upper Nubia). The *Annals of Thutmose III*, quoted earlier, reveal an aggregate of 8,682 *deben* (1,710 pounds) of Gold of Wawat and 595 *deben* (120 pounds) of Gold of Kush received in the thirty-fourth, thirty-eighth, and forty-first years of his reign.[55] At today's price, the King's Nubian tribute would be worth over three million dollars.

The enormous quantity of Gold of Wawat recorded in the *Annals of Thutmose* can only mean that this figure includes the output of the innumerable mines in the Wadi Allaqi and the Wadi Cabgaba, which was brought to the Nile at Kubban in Lower Nubia.[56] These mines, which number more than a hundred, were scattered over the eastern desert at distances up to 150 miles from the banks of the Nile. As the records of Thutmose show, they were far and away the most valuable of Egypt's mineral properties in the New Kingdom, and their efficient exploitation became one of the most critical necessities of the empire. In later times the same mines provided economic support for the Nubian empires of Napata and Meroë, and for a time they were also the key to Roman policy both in Egypt and in Nubia.

The anchor-point of the Lower Nubian gold industry was the fortress of Kubban, at the mouth of the Wadi Allaqi. Men and supplies were brought here by river from Aswan, and from here they began the long and dangerous overland trek to the goldfields. Slaves probably made up the bulk of the labour force.[57] The conditions of life were obviously hard, for a stele of Rameses II records that 'if a few of the caravaneers of the gold washing went thither, it was only half of them that arrived there, for they died of thirst on the road, together with the asses which they drove before them. There was not found for them their necessary supply of drink, in ascending and descending, from the water of the skins. Hence no gold was brought from this country, for lack of water.'[58]

233

In order to alleviate these conditions Rameses had a well sunk in the Wadi Allaqi. As the stele makes plain, his concern was not so much for the welfare of the labourers as to be able to exploit the mines more profitably. That the effort was successful may perhaps be inferred from the fact that the bulk of the inscriptions found by a recent Russian expedition in the Wadi Allaqi belong to the XIX and XX Dynasties. The Russians have also discovered what appears to be the actual site of Rameses' well, about forty miles inland from the Nile.[59]

A record of a mining expedition found in the Wadi Hammamat, in the Desert of Coptos, records that a party of 8,368 persons of various ranks and professions went forth to the mines in the reign of Rameses IV (later XX Dynasty). The text makes particular note of the fact that 900 of the party perished in the course of the expedition. A large number of the private inscriptions found in the Wadi Allaqi also carry valedictory and funeral texts.[60]

According to Lucas, whose *Ancient Egyptian Materials and Industries* is an invaluable source book on ancient technology:

The Egyptian method of extracting gold from the veins in quartz rock is described by Agatharchides, a Greek writer of the second century BC, who visited the mines and wrote a detailed account of what he had seen. Although the original work has been lost, the description of the gold mines has fortunately been preserved by Diodorus, who quotes it in full. The rock was first cracked and broken by means of fire and then attacked by hammers and picks. The broken rock was then carried outside the mine, where it was crushed in large stone mortars to the size of peas and afterwards ground to fine powder in hand mills, the powder being washed with water on a sloping surface in order to separate the metal, which probably finally was fused into small ingots. Many of the old stone grinding mills, and remains of the stone tables for treating the pulverized ore to extract the gold, are still to be seen at the ancient mines.[61]

In reference to the Nubian mines, Vercoutter adds that 'only a few mines have permanent installations, huts, washing tables, furnaces, remains of melting pots and slag heaps. Usually the ancient gold mines show only a heap of broken stones and disused mills for crushing the ore. There are few traces of settlements, no washing tables, no furnaces, nor even wells . . . Probably most of the final extraction of the gold from the crushed ore and the smelting was performed on the river banks.'[62]

The Gold of Kush came primarily from the district of Duweishat, close to the Nile and a few miles upstream from Semna. The site has recently been investigated systematically by the Sudan Antiquities Service archaeological survey, but no report is yet available.[63] A large number of galleries and prospect holes were found, but a far larger number may have been obliterated by later activity, for gold mining has been carried on intermittently at Duweishat until modern times. The Egyptian miners evidently lived in rude stone huts which are thickly scattered throughout the area. The situation of Duweishat, close to the river, seems to invite permanent settlement and perhaps the building of a residence for the mining supervisor, but no such building was found. It seems probable that mining at Duweishat, as in the eastern desert, was an intermittent activity carried on when the treasury was in particular need of replenishment, rather than a year-round industry.

WHAT BECAME OF THE NUBIANS?

Discussion in this chapter has thus far been concerned chiefly with Egyptian activities in newly reconquered Kush. I have avoided dealing squarely with the vexing question of what became of the native populace when their country was overrun for a second time, and they became subjects of the pharaoh. Unfortunately, we do not really know what became of the great majority of them; neither history nor archaeology supplies a satisfactory answer.

In Lower Nubia, we can recognize the persistence of a distinct 'C-Group' population at least until the middle of the XVIII Dynasty, coexisting with Egyptians and perhaps also with Egyptianized Nubians. The Nubian 'castle' at Amada, described in Chapter 6, was still in use in the reign of Thutmose III.[64] Many of the richest graves of the C Horizon also belong to the early XVIII Dynasty, while Säve-Söderbergh reports a group of 'hybrid' graves from Debeira which may represent a still later phase of indigenous cultural development:

The tombs consist of rectangular shafts chiselled in the hard, stony silt, and the superstructures, which are often destroyed by plunderers, were of the ordinary type of rough stone rings, sometimes with indications of an offering niche on the east side. The shafts were covered with flat slabs, and vertical slabs were placed against the walls of the shafts. The burial customs are thus typical of the C-Group, but no C-Group pottery was found, and only New Kingdom ceramic occurred. Among the stones of one of the best preserved superstructures several fragments of a faience vessel, imitating the form and decoration of a Mycenaean stirrup vase, were found. A rather similar stirrup vase was found in Soleb in a tomb dated to the reign of Thutmose III (scarabs). But . . . our specimen must be of a much later date.[65]

If the suggested dating is correct, these are the last unmistakably native graves in Lower Nubia for a thousand years. By the late XVIII Dynasty the ascendancy of Egyptian burial rites and burial furniture was complete, and a distinct Nubian population can no longer be identified either by graves or by pottery.

We have already noted, in Chapter 6, that the cultural influence of Egypt is increasingly manifest in the later C Horizon, both in the houses and in the graves of the Nubians. It would seem logical to assume that the process of acculturation was further accelerated by the Egyptian annexation of Nubia, and that the transformation was virtually complete by the later XVIII Dynasty. This view has generally prevailed among Egyptologists for the last thirty years. They regard the hundreds of 'New Kingdom' graves in Lower Nubia as belonging, with a few exceptions, to Egyptianized Nubians who are no longer culturally distinguishable from their colonial overlords.[66]

There is much to support the theory of 'C-Group acculturation'. It accounts satisfactorily for the disappearance of recognizably Nubian graves, if not for the seeming abruptness of their disappearance. There is also the suggestive fact that a number of New Kingdom cemeteries are adjoined by C Horizon cemeteries,[67] and seem to be continuations of them, although the tendency towards continued use of the same necropoli is apparent at all phases of Nubian history. The skeletal remains from the Lower Nubian graves excavated by the First and Second Archaeological Surveys suggested too that there were no racial differences between the 'C-Group' and 'New Kingdom' populations.[68] Finally, there are the examples of the undoubtedly Egyptianized Nubian 'Princes', Heka-Nefer, Djehuty-Hotep, and Amenemhat, already alluded to.

In spite of these positive indications, there are still difficulties in the way of a full acceptance of the 'acculturation theory'.[69] The most formidable of them is a question of chronology. If we suppose that the 'New Kingdom' graves in Nubia are those of Egyptianized Nubians, then the number of such graves should increase as the number of 'C-Group' graves declines. In fact, however, the reverse is true. Over three quarters of the datable New Kingdom graves in Nubia belong to the XVII and early XVIII Dynasties – to the same period when we can still recognize a culturally distinct Nubian population. In the later XVIII Dynasty the Nubian graves disappear, but there is a marked decline in the number of Egyptian (or Egyptianized) graves as well.[70]

The contemporaneity of late 'C-Group' graves with the majority of 'New Kingdom' graves obliges us to visualize two coexisting Nubian populations: one fully Egyptianized and the other clinging to tribal ways. Such a division is by no means improbable; it might represent the difference between dispossessed Nubians who were obliged to join the ranks of the peasantry and more conservative groups who retained their tribal lands and herds. Similar divisions between tribal and detribalized elements can be observed in many African and American Indian societies of the recent past. In ancient Nubia, however, the extraordinary wealth which we often find interred with the New Kingdom burials is hardly suggestive of a recently detribalized peasantry.

In colonial societies, detribalization usually results in a loss both of status and of material wealth, even while new technologies often bring an increase in the day-to-day standards of nutrition and health. As the status symbols of the old society lose their value, while those of the new, stratified societies are beyond reach, the rewards of productive activity go more and more to the satisfaction of immediate needs and wants and less to the accumulation of tangible goods. Peasants, unlike tribesmen, have few luxury possessions. As alienation of landholdings progresses, moreover, even their standard of daily living is apt to sink to a marginal level, under the weight of debt and servitude. One incidental result of this process is that peasant populations tend to 'disappear' archaeologically. Whether they can no longer afford funerals and mortuary offerings or whether they no longer care about them, their graves can seldom be recognized. Where are the *fellaheen* of the great imperial ages in Egypt and Mesopotamia? Certainly not in the rich cemeteries which have claimed the archaeologist's attention up to now.

In Nubia, as in Egypt, the recognizable New Kingdom graves do not appear to be those of *fellaheen*. While few of them exhibit the extreme wealth found in a few of the largest graves of the A and C Horizons, the average volume of mortuary goods in the New Kingdom is nevertheless higher than in any preceding period. The New Kingdom mortuary customs of Nubia are thus described by Emery:

No longer do we find the body laid out on its side in a semi-contracted position; instead, following Egyptian custom, the deceased was laid fully extended on his back, and in richer interments was placed within plain wooden coffins. The graves were of three types: a plain rectangular pit [Fig. 36], a rock-cut pit with a subterranean end chamber for the burial, and a rectangular pit with a lateral niche cut on one of the long sides. In most of the graves, the grouping of the burial equipment appears to follow a certain system, so that in the New Kingdom period we find pottery and other objects arranged as follows:

Red ware dish	*At the head*
Large red ware drop pot	
Small red ware drop pot	
Toilet objects, such as bronze mirrors and wooden combs	
Painted buff ware unguent pot	*Near the left arm*
Red ware dish	
Alabaster kohl pot and stick	
Red ware dish	*At the feet*
Large red ware drop pot	
Small red ware drop pot	
Poor class *ushabtis* of pottery, clay, faience	*Between the knees*

237

Jewelry consisted of ear-rings of bronze, carnelian and jasper, finger rings of gold and bronze, scarabs and amulets of carnelian, steatite, glass, jasper and faience, and bead necklaces of faience, gold, carnelian, glass, and shell. Weapons, such as bronze spear-heads, arrow-heads, axe-heads and daggers, are sometimes found with the dead, but these are a rarity, particularly in Lower Nubia. Except in the limited rock-cut tombs of more prosperous citizens, such objects are usually of poor quality and the general impression given from the evidence of burial installations other than those in the vicinity of the military stations is that Nubia after the conquest was populated by a poor subject race largely dependent on poor-class imports from Egypt, with little or no cultural background of its own.[71]

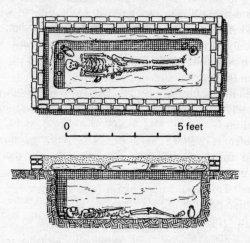

Fig. 36. Typical grave of the New Kingdom

The Nubian graves of the New Kingdom can only be characterized as 'poor' by comparison with the abnormally high standard of living which was maintained by the Egyptian nobility; they are well-to-do by ordinary Nubian standards, and they are rich by the standards of almost any 'subject race'. Moreover, and contrary to Emery's suggestion, some of the rural cemeteries of Lower Nubia exhibit an even higher standard of wealth than do the cemeteries close under the walls of Aniba, Buhen and Mirgissa.[72] It is noteworthy both in the rural cemeteries and in those attached to the major administrative centres that the mortuary offerings are entirely factory-goods imported from Egypt rather than local manufactures. They can only have been obtained by barter or as compensation for services, in either case bespeaking a specialized and differentiated economy. Was the manorial economy of New Kingdom Nubia really capable of providing manufactured goods on such a scale to the native populace? If so, they enjoyed a standard of living far higher than that of their fellow peasants in Egypt.

238

The totally Egyptian character of the mortuary offerings in New King-dom graves casts further doubt on the 'C-Group acculturation' hypothesis. While abrupt changes of mortuary ritual seem to be the common rule, both in Nubia and elsewhere,[73] there is usually some carry-over from one period to the next in the objects which are interred with the dead. In Nubia, how-ever, the goods buried in even the latest graves of the C Horizon (excepting only the small 'hybrid' group mentioned earlier)[74] are more than 75 per cent of Nubian origin, while those buried in graves of Egyptian type are more than 99 per cent of Egyptian origin. There seems to be insufficient middle ground to support a theory of transition. We know that the manu-facture of hand-made pottery by Nubian women persisted until a much later date, and it reappears regularly in the graves of the post-pharaonic periods. The only way to account for its exclusion from the New Kingdom graves is to suppose that the Egyptian mortuary canon was so rigid that it precluded even the introduction of non-Egyptian goods as grave furniture. Such an explanation cannot of course be ruled out, for mortuary practices were more closely bound up with the central ideology of Egypt than in any other civilization.

A final problem is that of cultural persistence. We know that the pottery traditions and the burial practices of pre-pharaonic Nubia were not exterminated under Egyptian domination, for they reappeared at Napata centuries later.[75] This would argue against the complete Egyptianization of the whole Nubian population. However, the main centre of persistence was undoubtedly in Upper Nubia, from which we have so far very little in-formation about the New Kingdom colonization and its cultural effects.

If the New Kingdom graves in Lower Nubia are not those of Egyptian-ized Nubians, then they can only be those of Egyptian colonists. While this must certainly be true in individual cases, it is as difficult to ascribe all of the XVIII and XIX Dynasty graves of Nubia to Egyptian colonists as it is to ascribe them to Egyptianized Nubians. The number of such graves, particularly in some of the rural districts, far exceeds the colonial popula-tion which we should have expected to find in those places. One cemetery at Debeira, several miles from the nearest 'urban' centre, numbered more than 600 graves from the New Kingdom.[76] It is nevertheless true that the bulk of New Kingdom graves are concentrated in the general vicinity of the major administrative and religious centres, where we know Egyptians were resident.

Anatomical evidence might have been expected to settle once and for all the question of whether the New Kingdom inhabitants of Lower Nubia were Egyptians or Egyptianized Nubians. Up to now, however, this is not the case. While earlier studies suggested that there was no racial difference between the New Kingdom and earlier population groups,[77] and therefore favoured the 'acculturation hypothesis', more recent and precise examination has revealed that there are indeed consistent differences between the 'C-Group' and New Kingdom skeletons.[78] However, the significance of these differences has yet to be determined. In addition, the lack of adequate comparative material from Egypt proper makes it impossible to say whether the New Kingdom inhabitants of Nubia were racially closer to the Egyptians or to the earlier inhabitants of the same region.[79]

After reviewing the various possible implications of the anatomical evidence, the anthropologist Vagn Nielsen has concluded that the hypothesis of Egyptian immigration '. . . seems to be the most obvious one from the point of view of a physical anthropologist'.[80] If this is so, then of course the question of what became of the Nubians remains unanswered. We are obliged to assume either that they were killed off, that they were driven or moved out, or that they sank to the status of dispossessed *fellaheen* who have left behind no recognizable archaeological remains.

In the last analysis there may be some truth in all of these theories. A few Nubians were undoubtedly casualties of the reconquest, although the number actually killed was probably small in proportion to those who were enslaved and sent to Egypt or to the gold mines. Many were left, however, and for a time they were evidently able to continue their tribal way of life. From the beginning, discontented or progressive individuals and families may have left the ranks of the Nubians and attached themselves to the growing Egyptian colonies. The burden of taxation probably reduced others to peonage.

As the numbers and power of the Egyptians grew, and as tribal landholdings were absorbed into manorial estates, most Nubians must have seen the handwriting on the wall. Individual by individual and group by group, they faced the choice whether to stay and be absorbed into the colonial peasant economy or whether to flee before the advance of civilization with what they could salvage of their herds and chattels. The same choice has been forced on tribal peoples over and over again in the outward march of civilization. Usually it has split their societies apart, some preferring to stay and some to migrate. Probably it was the same with the Nubians.

For the time being, the abrupt disappearance of the last vestiges of 'C-Group' culture in the middle of the XVIII Dynasty can best be explained by supposing that the more conservative elements in the Nubian population, who had thus far held out against subjugation and acculturation, betook themselves to safer regions in Upper Nubia, where the Egyptian grip was not so strong.[81] It is here, at any rate, that we can perceive their cultural legacy in the empire of Napata long after its disappearance from Lower Nubia.

WHAT BECAME OF THE EGYPTIANS?

The unparalleled building programme undertaken by Rameses II might suggest that his reign marks the zenith of Egyptian power and wealth in Nubia. In one sense this is true, for the gold industry undoubtedly reached its highest development during his or the immediately subsequent reigns. Yet there is much to suggest that the agrarian economy of the riverain lands was already in a serious decline in Rameses' time, and within a century after his death it collapsed altogether.

Evidence bearing upon the decline of Nubia in the later New Kingdom is of two sorts: demographic and ecological. Demographically, there is a marked and continuing decline in the number of graves, both Egyptian and native, after the middle of the XVIII Dynasty. At the conclusion of the First Archaeological Survey of Nubia, C. M. Firth reported that not more than a dozen graves from the XIX and later dynasties had been identified in the entire four years of field work. In describing the Nubia of Rameses II he wrote:

The great group of buildings associated with the name of Rameses II are very difficult to reconcile with the almost complete absence of cemeteries from this period. Such huge shrines as Gerf Hussein, Wadi es-Sebua, and Abu Simbel, could not have been built by the local population, or if they were, the people which produced them has left, so far as is known, no traces of its existence. It is difficult to avoid the conclusion that Nubia had become a sort of no man's land ruled by the gods and peopled by the ghosts of the dead.[82]

Firth certainly understated the number of later New Kingdom graves in Lower Nubia, yet the contrast between the number of known graves from the XVIII Dynasty and from all subsequent reigns is striking by anyone's estimate. Even within the XVIII Dynasty graves from the earlier reigns seem to outnumber those from later times in a proportion of about 2 to 1.[83] Such population as remained in Nubia in the later New Kingdom was heavily concentrated in a few favoured localities where there were probably large manorial estates. Elsewhere, rural settlement had virtually ceased to exist.

While such centres as Aniba, Buhen, and Amara remained important into the XX Dynasty, they were all abandoned before its end. No more Egyptian towns or monuments were ever built in Nubia; the next great building enterprises were undertaken by the Nubians themselves, more than 200 years after the Egyptian departure. In Lower Nubia the hiatus was much longer still. For all practical purposes the land between the First and Second Cataracts lay deserted for the best part of a thousand years. Even the great Napatan emperors who conquered Egypt and defied Assyria never succeeded in recolonizing the deserted northern province.

The almost total depopulation of Lower Nubia in the last millennium BC remains, up to now, one of the most provoking enigmas in Nubian history.[84] The long decline of the Egyptian state after the reign of Rameses II might possibly account for the withdrawal of Egyptian colonists, but hardly for the concurrent disappearance of the native populace, or for their failure to reoccupy the northern district for nearly a thousand years. For the time being the most reasonable explanation would still seem to be that which was put forward by Firth fifty years ago: that a decline in the average level of the Nile had rendered Lower Nubia unfit for irrigation.[85] We know from a famous series of inscriptions at Semna that flood levels in the Middle Kingdom were often substantially higher than they are today;[86] we can also infer from various evidence that flood levels were considerably lower in the New Kingdom.[87] If from these two datum points we can extrapolate a continuing drop in the average flow of the river, then it is indeed possible, as Firth suggested, that by the XX Dynasty the average water level was too low to permit effective irrigation in regions where the riverbanks are exceptionally high, as is generally the case in Lower Nubia and the *Batn el Hajar*. Indirect support for this hypothesis is afforded by the fact that the major reoccupation of Lower Nubia, probably in the first century AD, seems to have been concurrent with the introduction of the ox-driven waterwheel – a device which for the first time made it possible to raise irrigation water more than the twenty or twenty-five feet which are possible with the man-powered *shaduf* (see Ch. 12). Yet it must be acknowledged that geological evidence has so far failed to confirm that the average level of the Nile was abnormally low in the last millennium BC.[88]

Although the date and circumstances of final abandonment are thus obscure, it is apparent that by 1100 BC both the Egyptians and the Nubians were gone from Lower Nubia and the *Batn el Hajar*. It can be presumed that the Egyptians retreated primarily to the north and the Nubians to the south, so that a kind of buffer zone was opened up between them for the first time in a thousand years. Yet their interaction did not cease; in many respects it was intensified during the centuries when Lower Nubia lay as a no-man's-land between them.

The retreat from Lower Nubia had political and cultural repercussions both in Egypt and in Upper Nubia. In Egypt the line of 'King's Sons of Kush' continued unbroken until the end of the XX Dynasty, but the viceroys now resided at Thebes itself.[89] The later viceroys wielded enormous power both through their control of the gold production, which was of course unaffected by the collapse of the agrarian economy, and because they commanded a large body of Nubian levies who were probably the only effective military force in Upper Egypt. Not surprisingly they became the main support of the pharaonic throne, and then assumed the throne itself.[90] Toynbee's principle, that whoever controls the frontier marches against the barbarian holds the keys of empire, had once again proved true.[91]

In Upper Nubia the consequences of Egyptian withdrawal and the immigration of Lower Nubians are more conjectural. It is not certain that the Egyptian political grip was immediately broken when Lower Nubia was abandoned. Reisner and others[92] have suggested that the emigrés to Upper Nubia included Egyptians as well as Egyptianized Nubians, and that through them nominal Egyptian sovereignty was maintained at Jebel Barkal. Their main instrumentality would appear to have been the great Temple of Amon, originally built by Rameses II.[93] They may indeed have been in communication with the priesthood of Amon at Thebes, but it is also probable that the link was religious rather than political in nature, just as the Egyptian Coptic Church provided the *Abuna* of Ethiopia until modern times. It was at all events sufficient to keep Egyptian influence alive and to provide an ideological foundation for the Nubian empire of Napata 300 years later. The rather obscure circumstances surrounding the origins of that empire will be discussed in the following chapter.

INTERPRETATIVE SUMMARY

Egypt's pharaohs in the XVIII Dynasty expelled their Hyksos rivals from the Delta, possessed themselves of a considerable territory in Asia, and then turned their energies to the reconquest of Nubia. Within a matter of fifty years the whole region was overrun, the native dynasty at Kerma disappeared without a trace, and Egypt was master of the Nile as far upstream as the Fourth Cataract. A viceroy was appointed for the newly recovered territories, and he and his successors governed Nubia as an Egyptian province for the next 500 years.

At first, the new administration followed the lead of the previous Egyptian occupation of Nubia. The initial act of the conquering pharaohs was to restore and enlarge the great fortresses which had symbolized Egyptian rule in the Middle Kingdom. In this case, however, merchants and administrators accompanied the garrisons, and a genuine colonial enterprise was begun. New fortified towns were established in the Abri-Delgo Reach and the Dongola Reach, far beyond the previous limits of Egyptian sovereignty.

As time went on and Egyptian rule in Nubia grew more secure, the military grip was gradually relaxed. Towns were allowed to grow up outside the fortress walls, and some of the latest settlements in Upper Nubia may have been unwalled. At the same time a significant change took place in Egyptian policy towards the conquered region and its people. The pharaohs turned from fortress-building to temple-building, seeking to legitimize their rule not by intimidation but by the propagation of the state ideology. The effort met with considerable success, hastening the Egyptian-ization of the native population. By the end of the XVIII Dynasty no un-assimilated tribal elements were left in Lower Nubia.

Under the viceregal administration a plantation economy was developed in the more favoured areas of Nubia. The estates were largely in foreign hands, and some of them were controlled by royal or temple trusts, but in a few cases Nubian dignitaries were included in the new landlord class. Their completely Egyptianized tombs and cultural mannerisms herald an important transformation in Nubian society: class stratification between noble and serf begins to replace ethnic division between Nubian and Egyptian as the primary social cleavage.

What happened to the rank and file of the Nubian populace under Egyptian domination is far from clear. Some were apparently seized as slaves, some were dispossessed and driven out, and a fair number took their places in the growing landless peasantry and in Egyptian industries. Those who deserted their tribal fields and herds probably adapted them-selves as fully as they could to the ways of their masters. Others hung back and clung to traditional ways of life as long as they could. Some of these conservatives may ultimately have migrated into the more loosely con-trolled region of Upper Nubia rather than face cultural extinction in the Egyptianized north.

The level of the Nile probably fell during the New Kingdom, and by the XIX Dynasty effective irrigation was possible only in a few favoured places in Nubia. There was steady emigration from Lower Nubia until in the XX Dynasty only a handful of settlers remained, and even they were gone in the XXI Dynasty. Egyptian colonialism was at an end, but its after-effects were felt for a thousand years. Egyptianized Nubians, perhaps aided by Egyptian emigrés, kept the pharaonic traditions alive in Upper Nubia, laying the ideological foundations for the 'successor state' of Napata.

Although the first glimmerings of a monarchical state can be discerned in the Kingdom of Kerma, the Viceroyalty of Kush marks the real begin-ning of Dynastic civilization – the second major stage of Nubia's cultural development. The social and political revolution which was begun by the Egyptians during their New Kingdom colonization was carried on by the Nubians themselves, and in their hands the pharaonic tradition survived even after its extinction in Egypt. The transformation of society is already recognizable in the disappearance of a tribal population by the middle of the XVIII Dynasty, and by the appearance of Nubians in the ranks of the élite. From this time onwards Nubian civilization was organized around a stratified society, a peasant economy, and an imperial ideology.

A declining Nile and a crumbling empire forced the Egyptians out of Nubia in the XX Dynasty, but the Nubians were not immediately able to exploit their new strength or Egypt's weakness. It took some time for the lesson of the pharaohs to sink in. When it did, however, an Egyptianized, politically aroused Nubia, with its enormous resources in gold, was to emerge as a major force on the Nile. For two thousand years the shadow of Egypt had lain upon Nubia; at the end of the New Kingdom the shadow of Nubia was beginning to be visible in Egypt.

10

THE HEROIC AGE

THE NUBIAN EMPIRE OF NAPATA

'Now behold, thou trustest upon the staff of this broken reed, even upon Egypt, whereon, if a man lean, it will go into his hand and pierce it; so is Pharaoh, king of Egypt, unto all that trust on him.'[1] These words, addressed to the King of Judah by the envoys of Assyria, aptly suggest the estate to which Egypt's imperial fortunes had fallen in the eighth century B C. The passage, despite its mocking tone, is dear to the hearts of historians of Nubia, for it recalls the one brief appearance of Kush upon the stage of world history. The King of Egypt whose strength was likened to that of a broken reed[2] was in fact a Nubian; for a hundred years (751–635 B C) he and his house ruled over the Two Lands as pharaohs of the XXV or 'Ethiopian' dynasty. The considerably longer period of their ascendancy in Nubia is usually referred to as the Napatan period, after the region (immediately below the Fourth Cataract) in which the Nubian monarchy first arose.

The extraordinary turn of events which brought a Nubian to the pharaonic throne might perhaps have been foreseen at the close of the XX Dynasty, when southern gold and southern troops already held the keys to power in Upper Egypt (cf. Ch. 9). Yet it was not until many generations after the collapse of the Egyptian empire that a full-fledged successor state emerged in Nubia. In the meantime Egypt was once again divided among warring principalities. The main arena of contention was now the Delta region, which for some centuries had been subject to invasion and depredation by alien peoples both from the sea and from Libya in the west. For a time the Libyans, centred upon the Delta city of Bubastis, gained supremacy over their neighbours and established themselves as pharaohs of the XXII Dynasty.

While Lower Egypt was thus in turmoil, Thebes, once the proud centre of pharaonic power, relapsed into a relatively quiet backwater. The priesthood of Amon, whose oligarchic power had grown throughout the New Kingdom, had now formally assumed the reins of government in Upper Egypt and perhaps in Nubia as well; at any rate the offices of King, Viceroy of Kush, and Chief Priest of Amon seem to have been absorbed into one.[3] The Theban priest-kings maintained a measure of independence throughout the period of the XXI–XXIII Dynasties, although they were occasionally obliged to pay tribute to one or another of the more powerful dynasts in the north.

Who really exercised power in Nubia during the long years of Egypt's decline it is almost impossible to say. A certain Piankhi, son of the Theban priest-king Herihor, was named as 'King's Son of Kush' in the latter part of his father's reign (c. 1060 BC), but he was the last Egyptian to bear that illustrious title.[4] The extinction of a separate viceregal office does not necessarily signify the end of Egyptian rule,[5] yet it is clear that in the time of Viceroy Piankhi Lower Nubia was already depopulated, and continued Egyptian presence in Upper Nubia is not clearly attested either by textual or by archaeological evidence.[6] The one persisting Egyptian influence, apparently, was the state cult of Amon at Napata, near the Fourth Cataract. Originally planted at Jebel Barkal in New Kingdom times, it was to persist for well over a thousand years and to provide the central ideology of the independent Kingdom of Kush.

Not until the end of the ninth century BC,[7] some 200 years after the vice-royalty of Piankhi, can we perceive clearly the re-emergence of secular authority in Nubia. As in the days of Kerma, its presence is first signified not by textual records but by the appearance of what are unmistakably royal tombs in the cemetery of El Kurru, some ten miles down-stream from Jebel Barkal. Once again, and for the first time in many centuries, Nubia was ruled by a Nubian.

The rise of the independent Nubian monarchy at Napata can only be described as meteoric. No more than six or seven generations elapsed between its unpretentious and somewhat obscure beginnings and the time when a Nubian prince occupied the historic throne of the pharaohs. The rapid ascendancy of Kush is undoubted testimony to the weak and divided state of Egypt, but even more to the power vacuum which was created by the decline of Egyptian influence in Nubia. In the end it was a classic example of a barbarian people turning the tables on its former overlords and oppressors. Such incidents have disturbed the declining years of many civilizations; they are thus explained in general terms by Arnold Toynbee:

When a growing civilization breaks down through the deterioration of an actively creative into an odiously dominant minority, one of the effects of this sinister change in the broken down society's leadership is the estrangement of its former proselytes in the once-primitive societies round about, which the civiliza-tion in its growth stage was influencing in divers degrees by the effects of its cultural radiation. The ex-proselytes' attitude changes from an admiration expressing itself in [cultural imitation] to a hostility breaking out into warfare . . . between the disintegrating civilization and its alienated external proletariat.[8]

The common outcome of such conflicts has been the establishment of short-lived barbarian successor states upon the ruins of the older civiliza-tions. Toynbee has given to these ephemeral empires the somewhat ironic designation 'heroic ages'.[9] They are of course heroic only in the eyes of the barbarian conquerors, for whom they constitute a measure of revenge after centuries of cultural and political domination. For the fallen 'master races' who now find themselves subject to their long-despised vassals, they may represent a particularly bitter humiliation.

The brief interval of Nubian rule in Egypt clearly exemplifies one of Toynbee's 'heroic ages'.[10] Yet the term is also appropriate in another, non-Toynbeean sense. As rulers of Egypt the Nubian kings fell heir to the scribal publicity apparatus which was always at the pharaoh's command, and it enabled them to leave to posterity the sort of personal testaments which have always been dear to conquerors and despots. This opportunity was denied to most of the Nubian rulers in the largely illiterate ages which preceded and followed the Napatan period. Thus, the only figures who stand out individually and by name against the vast, impersonal backdrop of Nubian history are two rulers of the XXV Dynasty: Piankhi the conqueror and Taharqa the builder. They are the only legitimate 'heroes' whom the historian of Nubia can acknowledge. If, as is possible, there were greater and wiser rulers in other ages, their names and their accomplishments are lost in the anonymity of the archaeological record.

The commemorative stele of Piankhi, recounting in detail the campaigns of this first great Nubian conqueror, is one of the masterpieces of ancient literature.[11] Almost equally informative in their way are numerous shorter inscriptions of Taharqa. These personal documents are however by no means the only annals of Nubian rule in Egypt. Once the princes of Kush had stepped onto the world stage, their activities engaged the attention of chroniclers in many lands. Numerous traditions of the XXV Dynasty are preserved in the annals of Assyrian kings, in the Hebrew chronicles found in 2 Kings and Isaiah, and in the later histories of Herodotus and Manetho.[12] Taharqa, the next-to-last 'Ethiopian' pharaoh, is the only Nubian to be mentioned by name in the Bible.[13]

Altogether, the various historical texts of the XXV Dynasty impart to our picture of Nubian history a kind of human foreground which has heretofore been lacking. At the same time we must acknowledge that much of the cultural background which has so largely concerned us in earlier chapters is missing. The texts of the XXV Dynasty are not, after all, the annals of Nubia but of Nubian rule in Egypt. Within the southern land itself, we know as little about social and cultural conditions in the Napatan period as at any time since the beginning of history. This condition will hopefully be temporary; for the present it is due to the almost total absence of Napatan archaeological remains in Lower Nubia, and to the lack of systematic archaeological work in the more southerly regions which were the Napatan homeland.

For the time being, our archaeological knowledge of the Napatan period comes chiefly from the two royal cemeteries of El Kurru and Nuri – both excavated in their entirety by Reisner half a century ago – and from a few of the larger temples, also investigated mostly by Reisner. In short, we have as cultural evidence from Napata only the royal monuments, without (as at Kerma) the testimony of ordinary houses and humble graves to balance the picture. Such a record, like the textual evidence, is more conducive to a study of dynastic than of cultural history, and it is not surprising that the main historical work which resulted from Reisner's numerous excavations was an elaborate reconstruction of the Nubian royal succession.[14] Like all Reisner's theoretical work it is a monument to ingenuity, combining a painstaking sifting of the empirical evidence with sweeping interpolations. Inevitably much of it remains conjectural, and it has given rise to controversies which are far from settled at the present time.[15] These we can largely ignore for the moment, partly because there is substantial agreement in regard to the earlier phases of the chronology and partly because the proper ordering of the Napatan and Meroitic kings is not in any case a matter of great concern to the cultural historian. It is nevertheless true, in view of the available source material, that our story of Nubia in the Napatan period must be more a personal and dynastic history, and less a cultural history, than has been true in earlier chapters.

TERMINOLOGY AND CHRONOLOGY

The episode of Nubian rule in Egypt was only a brief chapter in a longer story. On its home ground, the successor state which arose at Napata in the ninth century BC proved unexpectedly hardy. It persisted without significant interruption for a thousand years, not only surviving a number of foreign invasions but achieving a notable renaissance in its late centuries. In the further confines of Upper Nubia, the traditions of pharaonic Egypt remained alive in Nubian hands even after they had vanished from Egypt itself.

With the termination of direct Egyptian rule in Nubia, it was inevitable that purely indigenous and non-Egyptian cultural traditions should increasingly reassert themselves. Until the end of the Dynastic era, however, the monarchical institutions – the central framework of Nubian government – never consciously diverged from the pattern which had been set by the pharaohs. In its own eyes the independent kingdom of Nubia which arose from the ashes of Egyptian rule was a continuation – the only legitimate continuation – of the immemorial pharaonic state of Egypt, founded on the worship of the Theban state deity. As late as the third century AD Nubian rulers still called themselves by the pharaoh's traditional titles, 'Lord of the Two Lands' (i.e. Upper and Lower Egypt), 'Beloved of Amon', and so on, though none of them had set foot in Egypt for nearly a thousand years. They might also, on occasion, style themselves 'rulers of Kush',[16] but this was a purely secular designation identifying the territory actually under their control; it did not provide the ideological basis of their rule. Theirs was always, in principle, a Government of Egypt (including its legitimate Nubian dependency) in exile, rather than a purely indigenous Government of Nubia. It was a political fiction comparable to the Holy Roman Empire and to today's Nationalist China.

Because it never developed a conscious style or an official name of its own, there has been some uncertainty as to what the pseudo-pharaonic state of Nubia should be called. Most scholars until fifty years ago referred to it as the Kingdom of Ethiopia,[17] retaining the name used by classical writers. However, the latter-day adoption of this name by another kingdom far to the east of Nubia raises the possibility of confusion, and makes it desirable to find another name for the ancient Nubian monarchy. 'Kingdom of Kush' has been preferred by many recent writers,[18] and will be employed henceforth in the present work.

By whatever name it is called, the Kingdom of Kush represents a period of remarkable political and social stability. Whether one or a succession of dynasties was involved will perhaps never be known, but the unbroken continuity of the monarchy seems beyond dispute. Its 1,200-year span includes all but the earliest and the latest centuries of Nubia's Dynastic Age (Table VI), and incidentally far exceeds the duration of any of Egypt's unified kingdoms.

In spite of political and social continuities, there were two quite distinct peaks of cultural development under the Kingdom of Kush, separated by a 'dark age' of several centuries. As a result it is common practice to divide the history of the kingdom into two phases, called Napatan and Meroitic after their respective geographical centres. During the period of Nubian sovereignty in Egypt, and for at least a century afterwards, the 'capital' of Kush was unquestionably at Napata, just downstream from the Fourth Cataract. Thereafter, and increasingly in later centuries, the centre of power shifted towards the south, where an important settlement had grown up at Meroë, above the mouth of the Atbara River (Fig. 37). Both the circumstances and the reasons for this transition are far from clear, and the date when the 'capital' was formally transferred has been the subject of much debate.[19] However, it is apparent that after the fourth century BC the main foci of royal authority – palaces, temples, and royal tombs – were situated in the southern region.

If the only differences between Napatan and Meroitic Nubia involved the location of the royal monuments, the distinction between them would hardly be worth making. The geographical shift was, however, only an incidental development which provides us with convenient labels for two rather distinct phases of cultural development.

From the beginning of the XXV Dynasty onwards, the culture of Napata

TABLE VI

CHRONOLOGY OF NAPATAN AND MEROITIC RULERS

(After Shinnie, *Meroe*, pp. 58–61. The dates and sequence of reigns follow Hintze, *Studien zur Meroitischen Chronologie und zu den Opfertafeln aus den Pyramiden von Meroe*, pp. 23–4, 33.)

Ruler	Approx. dates	Place of burial
Kashta	806–751 BC	Napata (El Kurru)
Piankhi	751–716	,, ,,
Shabaka	716–701	,, ,,
Shabataka	701–690	,, ,,
Taharqa	690–664	Napata (Nuri)
Tenutamon	664–653	Napata (El Kurru)
Atlanersa	653–643 BC	Napata (Nuri)
Senkamanisken	643–623	,, ,,
Anlamani	623–593	,, ,,
Aspalta	593–568	,, ,,
Amtalqa	568–555	,, ,,
Malenaqen	555–542	,, ,,
Analmaye	542–538	,, ,,
Amani-nataki-lebte	538–519	,, ,,
Karkamani	519–510	,, ,,
Amaniastabarqa	510–487	,, ,,
Siaspiqa	487–468	,, ,,
Nasakhma	468–463	,, ,,
Malewiebamani	463–435	,, ,,
Talakhamani	435–431	,, ,,
Aman-nete-yerike	431–405	,, ,,
Baskakeren	405–404	,, ,,
Harsiotef	404–369	,, ,,
(unknown king?)	369–350	Napata (El Kurru)
Akhratan	350–335	Napata (Nuri)
Nastasen	335–310	,, ,,
Amanibakhi?	310–295	Napata (Nuri?)
Arkakamani	295–275 BC	Meroë (South Cem.)
Amanislo	275–260	,, ,,
Queen Bartare	260–250	,, ,,
Amani . . . tekha?	250–235 BC	Meroë (North Cem.)
Arnekhamani	235–218	,, ,,
Arkamani (Ergamenes?)	218–200	,, ,,
Tabirqa?	200–185	,, ,,
. . . iwal?	185–170	,, ,,
Queen Shanakdakhete	170–160	,, ,,
(unknown king)	160–145	,, ,,

Ruler	Approx. dates	Place of burial
Naqrisan?	145–120 BC	Meroë (North Cem.)
Tanyidamani?	120–100	„ „
. . . khale?	100–80	„ „
. . . amani?	80–65	„ „
Amanikhabale?	65–41	„ „
Queen Amanishakhete	41–12	„ „
Natakamani and Queen Amanitere	12 BC– 12 AD	„ „
Sherkarer	12–17 AD	„ „
Pisakar?	17–35	„ „
Amanitaraqide	35–45	„ „
Amanitenmemide	45–62	„ „
Queen Amanikhatashan	62–85	„ „
Tarekeniwal	85–103	„ „
Amanikhalika?	103–108	„ „
Aritenyesbekhe?	108–132	„ „
Aqrakamani?	132–137	„ „
Adeqetali?	137–146	„ „
Takideamani	146–165	„ „
. . . reqerem?	165–184	„ „
(unknown ruler)	184–194	„ „
Teritedakhatey?	194–209	„ „
Aryesbekhe	209–228	„ „
Teritnide	228–246	„ „
Aretnide	246	„ „
Teqerideamani	246–266	„ „
Tamelerdeamani?	266–283	„ „
Yesbekheamani?	283–300	„ „
Lakhideamani?	300–308	„ „
Maleqerabar?	308–320	„ „

(or what little we know of it) was almost wholly imitative of pharaonic Egypt, albeit in a somewhat diluted and provincial form. The known monuments and other archaeological remains of the Napatan period are for the most part so little different from those of the last phase of Egyptian colonial occupation that it is not easy to distinguish the two on internal grounds. Thus John Wilson aptly remarks of Piankhi, the first Nubian ruler in Egypt, that 'his culture was a provincial imitation of earlier Egypt, fanatical in its retention of religious form'.[20] The great achievements of Piankhi and his immediate successors were in the political rather than in the cultural sphere,[21] and they were all attained within a period of less than a century. After the Nubian withdrawal from Egypt there followed several

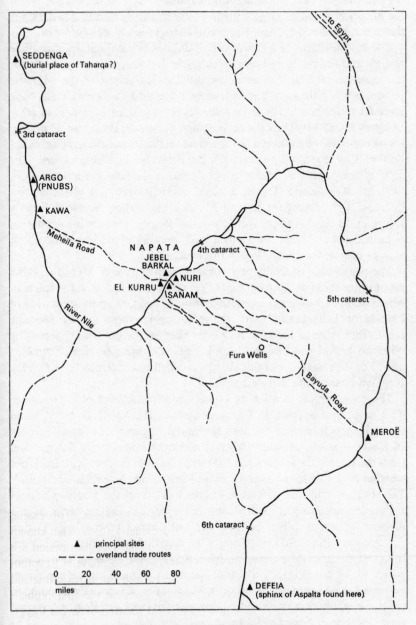

Fig. 37. Upper Nubia in Napatan times

centuries of political stagnation and cultural retrogression, during which the historical record is largely silent. It was evidently during this dark age that the shift of power from Napata to Meroë took place.

The establishment of a new 'capital' did not bring about an immediate revitalization of the Kingdom of Kush. The darkness which enshrouds the last centuries at Napata covers as well the beginnings of the Meroitic period. It was ultimately, and indirectly, dispelled by an event which took place far to the north: the arrival of Alexander and his Macedonian army in Egypt in 332 BC. The Graeco-Egyptian Ptolemaic Dynasty founded by his successors brought about the last great revitalization of Egypt's civilization, and its repercussions were felt unmistakably in Nubia as well. The cultural renaissance at Meroë which began in the last century BC[22] was, like that of Ptolemaic Egypt, a blend of Hellenistic and pharaonic influences. If the dominant style of Meroitic civilization remained stolidly Egyptian, its newfound prosperity resulted largely from the incorporation of both Egypt and Nubia into a worldwide network of maritime trade. This was, of course, the special legacy of Greece.

The prosperous economy and cosmopolitan culture of Meroitic Nubia far outshine those of Napatan times. Yet none of the few Meroitic rulers of whom we have individual knowledge seem to measure up to the stature of Piankhi or Taharqa. In short, the major achievements of the Meroitic renaissance were in the cultural rather than in the political sphere. The Napatan period was Nubia's 'heroic age'; the Meroitic was its 'golden age'. For the remainder of this chapter we shall be concerned only with the Napatan phase – the 'heroic age'.

The geographical location of Napata requires a word of explanation. This name first appears in Egyptian texts of the XVIII Dynasty,[23] and thereafter was in regular use until the final disappearance of the Kingdom of Kush. It refers unquestionably to a district immediately downstream from the Fourth Cataract of the Nile (the region of modern Kareima), but whether or not there was ever a specific town named Napata is uncertain.[24] The royal monuments which are known to us from the Fourth Cataract region are not concentrated at any one spot, but are scattered over a distance of about fifteen miles along both banks of the Nile. Within this area are the royal cemeteries of El Kurru, Jebel Barkal, and Nuri, the great complex of temples at Jebel Barkal, and the lesser temple and palace at Sanam (Fig. 38). Because the name Napata can be associated in one sense or another with all of these localities, it is usually assumed to cover the whole district extending downstream from the Fourth Cataract for a distance of fifteen miles or so.

The long and almost impassable barrier to navigation represented by the Fourth Cataract provided a natural frontier for Egypt's Nubian empire, and the settlement which grew up immediately below the cataract under the

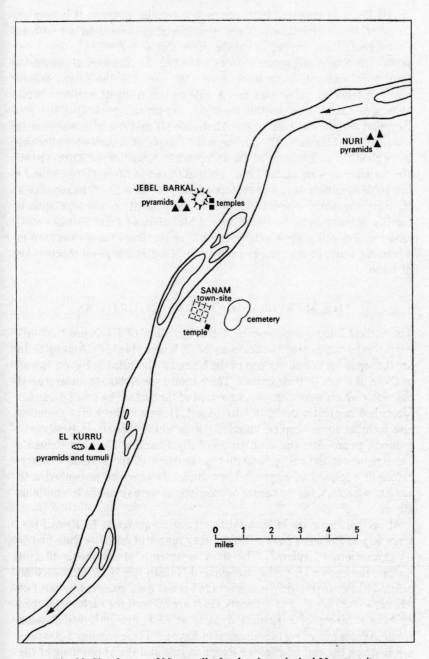

Fig. 38. Sketch map of Napata district showing principal Napatan sites

XVIII Dynasty may well have begun as a frontier outpost. It is notable, however, that no fortifications and no important town-site have ever been found here; from the beginning the place seems to have been more important as a religious centre than as a political or commercial centre. Its focal point was not the cataract or even the river, but the Sacred Mountain[25] of Jebel Barkal which stood a mile or two from its northern bank. It was in the shadow of this towering, flat-topped butte that the first Egyptian temple was built under Thutmose III or IV, and it was here in later days that Rameses II built the great Temple of Amon which became in its time the cult centre for the independent Kingdom of Kush. Other, smaller temples were added both in Napatan and in Meroitic times, and a few royal pyramids were located immediately to the west of the mountain. If, then, the name Napata deserves to be applied to any one specific locality, it must surely be to the Sacred Mountain of Jebel Barkal and its environs. For our purposes, however, it is convenient to apply the term in a broader sense, to the area embracing all of the earlier royal monuments of Kush.

THE MYSTERY OF NAPATAN ORIGINS

The earliest known monuments of the Kingdom of Kush are thirty-six royal tombs comprising the cemetery of El Kurru (Fig. 38). Among them are the sepulchres of all but one of the Nubians who ruled in Egypt, as well as those of many of their queens. These tombs are elaborate underground chambers which were apparently covered at the surface by small pyramids (described in greater detail in later pages). However, the Kurru cemetery also includes some simpler, tumulus graves which appear, on typological grounds, to antedate the main group of royal burials. These, in Reisner's view, represent the early, formative generations of the Nubian dynasty, before its conquest of Egypt.[26] They cannot however be associated with any known rulers, for no names or inscriptions were found in the tumulus graves.

Altogether there are at least thirteen tumulus graves at El Kurru, but, according to Reisner's interpretation, they represent no more than five or six generations of rulers.[27] The sixth or seventh generation is that of Kashta, the known king who inaugurated Nubian rule in Egypt sometime before 750 BC. If this view is correct (and it has been accepted by most of Reisner's successors), and if twenty years are allowed for each reign, then we have evidence of a Kushite dynasty at El Kurru only for about a hundred years preceding the conquest of Egypt.[28] There remains a 200-year gap between the end of effective Egyptian rule and the appearance of the first recognizable king of Kush.

The antecedents of the Nubian dynasty have naturally been the subject of much speculation.[29] Reisner at first believed that the kings of Kush were of Libyan origin, and that their claim to rule both in Egypt and in Nubia was based upon kinship to the Libyan pharaohs of the XXII Dynasty.[30] This theory hung upon the slenderest of archaeological and philological evidence, and it has been rejected by nearly all recent scholars.[31] There is in any case no indication that the Nubian pharaohs ever based their claim to rule in Egypt on dynastic grounds.

Another theory holds that the kings of Kush arose from the ranks of the priests of Amon at Jebel Barkal.[32] These, it is suggested, were probably for the most part Egyptians – many of them emigrants from now-deserted Lower Nubia.[33] The fact that the first great Nubian king, Piankhi, took the same name as the last known viceroy, who was himself the son of a Theban priest-king, has been cited in support of this view.[34] Yet the special peculiarities of the earliest tombs at El Kurru are neither Libyan nor Egyptian, but unmistakably Nubian. They include the use of a round tumulus and the interment of the corpse on a bed – both practices associated in particular with the great Nubian kingdom of Kerma. While these traits can hardly point to a revival of the Kerma dynasty after a lapse of seven hundred years, they are at least a sufficient warrant for the native origins of the Nubian kings.[35] It has been pointed out, too, that in the royal monuments at Thebes the Nubian pharaohs are depicted with unmistakably African features and details of dress.[36]

If the kings of Kush were not literally descended from the priesthood of Amon, however, there can be no doubt that their legitimacy and their power rested ultimately on the sanction of the priests. It was perhaps as temporal patrons of the great Amon cult – the 'established religion' of both Nubia and Upper Egypt since the New Kingdom – that they first rose to power at Napata, and it was certainly in that guise that they first appeared on the scene in Egypt. Almost certainly, it is no accident that the Nubian dynasty originated in the shadow of Jebel Barkal, which had been established as the centre of Amon-worship in Nubia early in the New Kingdom.

The cult of Amon forms the main thread of ideological continuity throughout Nubia's Dynastic Age. This rather vaguely defined deity, originally no more than a local tutelary at Thebes, had emerged as high god in Egypt in the days of Theban political supremacy (Middle and New Kingdoms).[37] The focal point of Amon-worship was the great temple precinct at Karnak, which generation after generation of pharaohs embellished with monuments to the state god until it achieved a colossal hypertrophy unequalled by any other religious monument.

Amon-worship was transplanted to Nubia under the New Kingdom, and there as in Egypt became the state cult. The selection of Jebel Barkal as its main centre was probably dictated by the fact that the great mountain was already sacred in local tradition. It was here that Rameses II built the enormous temple which was intended to be the Nubian counterpart of Karnak – the symbolic focus of power and authority in the southern lands. The design succeeded beyond the dreams of the Egyptians who conceived it: so important did the temple of Jebel Barkal remain throughout the history of Kush that its destruction was the main objective of a Roman punitive expedition a thousand years later.

We have already observed how the priesthood of Amon assumed the reins of government in Upper Egypt following the dissolution of a unified monarchy in the XXI Dynasty. Perhaps the same pattern was repeated in Nubia. In practice this would have meant little more than the continued functioning of an acephalous bureaucracy after the removal of its nominal head. The 'government' which the priests provided both in Egypt and in Nubia probably consisted chiefly in the continued administration of the temple estates, which by now were the backbone of the manorial economy in both regions. The ascendancy of the priests of Amon may thus have resulted less from their own ambitions than from the decay of all other forms of authority. Their situation may perhaps be compared to that of the Popes in post-imperial Rome.

Given the disturbed conditions in Lower Egypt and the growing menace of Assyria, the priestly oligarchs at Karnak may well have regretted the disappearance of an independent secular power upon which they could rely for protection. We may surmise that the theocratic government suffered from the traditional disability of oligarchies: it could manage the economic and political affairs of the state well enough, but could not provide effectively for defence. In troubled times it was obliged to cast around for a military deliverer, and if necessary to hand over a considerable share of power to him. Such has been the historic origin of tyrannies, in the Greek sense of the term.

In Nubia there was of course no serious external threat to the hegemony of Amon. Once the Egyptian garrisons were withdrawn, however, the continued maintenance of control by a small Egyptian or Egyptianized élite, without any local base of support, must have been a difficult and uncertain business. It was probably considerations of this sort which led the priests at Jebel Barkal to seek the alliance and protection of locally influential chiefs – the ancestors of Piankhi and Taharqa. Such appears the most probable explanation for the origin of the Kushite monarchy, though the precise details will almost surely never be known.

Once the dichotomy of priesthood and secular power had been established, the two naturally and inevitably reinforced each other. The Kushite monarchs relied on the priests of Amon to sanction and legitimize their rule, and also to provide their administrative bureaucracy. In exchange they assumed the functions if not the title of defenders of the faith, and they heaped upon the temples the fruits of their foreign conquests. The persistence of this relationship is attested by the fact that Nubian rulers until the end of their kingdom took the name of Amon (-amani-) as one element of their throne names. The historian Diodorus Siculus records too that until the third century B C the priests of Amon had the right to depose and kill any Nubian king who displeased them, and to designate his successor.[38]

THE ROYAL SUCCESSION

The precise genealogical relationships between the various rulers of Kush are known only in a few cases. The kinship terms found in the royal inscriptions are, like the characters in which they are written, Egyptian, and the Egyptian system of recording kinship was notoriously imprecise.[39] Many terms are evidently used fictively in some contexts and literally in others, so that it is often not clear whether the term 'sister-wife', for example, should be taken as evidence of sibling-marriage or only as a hyperbolic expression for 'beloved wife'.[40]

The Kushite monarchy from the beginning was evidently hereditary. Royal descent was a necessary but not a sufficient condition to rule; personal merit was required as well. Like most relatively primitive peoples the early Nubians could not afford the uncertainties associated with a child-monarch or an imbecile-monarch, for too much of their fate depended upon the personal character and judgement of their leader. As a result there was not and could not be an absolutely fixed rule of royal succession.

The preferred order of succession in Kush seems to have been for the crown to descend in turn to each of the surviving brothers of a deceased king, and then, after the death of the last brother, to revert to the eldest son of the original brother, and from him in succession to his brothers. This rule, unlike the generational succession in European monarchies, would usually assure that the crown went to the eldest, and therefore presumably the most experienced, claimant. However, there seem to have been many exceptions to it in practice. A number of intervening brothers were apparently passed over when Taharqa was named as successor to Shabataka (see below), perhaps because he had shown exceptional ability at an early age.[41] To some extent the office may have been elective among the eligible brothers and sons, the choice being made either by the claimants themselves or (more probably) by the priesthood of Amon. However, the privilege which the priests enjoyed of deposing the king and appointing his successor, reported by Diodorus Siculus, was probably only a temporary state of affairs resulting from weakness or internal division in the royal family. There were certainly times when the balance of power tipped the other way, and the king could command the priests even in religious matters.[42]

On some occasions the succession seems to have passed not to the son of any previous king but to the son of one of the king's sisters. This has been taken as evidence that ancient Nubia, like much of pre-Islamic Africa, adhered to a matrilineal rule of descent.[43] However, the evidence on this point is not certain, and there are enough instances of patrilineal succession in the royal family of Kush to cast doubt on it. If brother-sister marriage was as frequent as some of the royal texts would suggest, the question is an academic one: the offspring of such marriages could of course equally claim royal descent on either side.

While Nubian society was by no means matriarchal, there can be no doubt that queens enjoyed an unusually high place both as consorts and as dowagers. They figure prominently in many royal inscriptions and reliefs, and it is evident that they often acted as counsellors, and sometimes as regents, for their sons.[44] The XXV Dynasty pharaoh, Taharqa, records in one of his inscriptions that he summoned his mother all the way from Napata to be present at his coronation in Egypt.[45] The wealth and prominence of queens' tombs in the Nubian royal cemeteries are further testimony to their high status.

It must have been the prestige and behind-the-scenes power enjoyed by the Nubian queens which gave rise to the Roman tradition that Kush was governed by a hereditary line of female rulers, all named Candace.[46] The name seems in fact to be a corruption of a Meroitic title (*kdke*) which was borne by all the royal consorts or queen-mothers of Kush; it does not specify a queen-regnant.[47] There were indeed at least five queens regnant during the later centuries of the Kushite dynasty, but no two of them reigned in succession, and it is not certain that they bore the title *kdke*. The circumstances which brought them to the throne, in preference to male claimants (if any), are not known.[48]

THE CONQUEST OF EGYPT

Kashta, the first Nubian king whom we can recognize by name,[49] belongs to the sixth generation of the Kushite Dynasty according to Reisner's speculative chronology. His name occurs only in one or two very brief inscriptions, and we know few details of his reign.[50] At some point in his career, however, he seems to have made his way northwards as far as Thebes, where he was confirmed in power by the priests of Amon, and where he obliged the High Priestess to adopt his daughter as her successor-designate.[51] In thus formalizing the alliance between the monarchy and the Amon cult he was following the practice of a number of earlier pharaohs.[52] There is no suggestion of military activity connected with Kashta's visit; apparently he journeyed in peace and was acclaimed at Thebes, as he was at Jebel Barkal, as the appointed patron of Amon and defender of the faith. To the Egyptian priests, threatened as they were from the north and long accustomed to rely on Nubian troops for their protection, the rise of a new and effective Nubian commander may well have appeared as a deliverance. They hastened to recognize him and to claim his protection. The ensuing spectacle of an ancient civilization delivered into the hands of a barbarian upstart by its own spiritual guardians must have been enjoyed by the Nubians present; it was to be re-enacted with only minor variations at the coronation of Charlemagne 1,500 years later.[53] Although he did not claim the pharaoh's full titles,[54] Kashta's assumption of power at Thebes set the stage for the brief, meteoric appearance of Kush as a world power.[55]

Kashta died about 751 BC, and was succeeded by his son Piankhi.[56] The new king seems to have passed the first twenty years of his reign at Napata, giving little thought to the northern territory for which his father had assumed responsibility. In due time, however, word reached him that Thebes was threatened by an army under Tefnakht, one of the Delta dynasts who aimed to restore pharaonic rule over the whole of Egypt. The military officials at Thebes implored Piankhi to protect the domains of Amon against the intruder. It is at this point that the story is taken up by the great Piankhi Stele (found at Jebel Barkal in 1862, and now in the Cairo Museum; see Pl. XII).[57]

Piankhi ordered the forces in Egypt to resist as best they could, and shortly afterwards dispatched a more fully equipped expedition to repel the invader. This was successful in its immediate objective, but did not pursue and destroy the retreating forces of Tefnakht. Piankhi was not satisfied with the news of these half-way measures, and determined to take the field in person. He first proceeded to Thebes, where he celebrated with great pomp the annual festival of Opet in the Temple of Karnak. This astute act of statecraft publicly proclaimed his sacred mission in Egypt as the patron and protector of the Amon cult. That done, he turned northwards in pursuit of the erstwhile enemies of Thebes. His first action was against the Middle Egyptian city of Hermopolis, which had already been under siege for several months.

Namlot, its king, finding that gifts, even when his own royal crown was cast down among them, availed nothing with Piankhi, sent out his queen to plead with the women of the Nubian that they might intercede with him on Namlot's behalf. This device was successful, and, assured at last of his life, Namlot surrendered and turned over the city and all his wealth to Piankhi, who immediately took possession of the place. After an inspection of Namlot's palace and treasury, Piankhi entered the stables . . . 'His majesty proceeded to the stables of his horses,' so say his annals, 'and the quarters of the foals. When he saw that they had suffered hunger, he said: "I swear as Re loves me . . . it is more grievous in my heart that my horses have suffered hunger than any evil deed that thou hast done in the prosecution of thy desire." '[58]

After the fall of Hermopolis, Piankhi's remaining objectives were soon accomplished.

Piankhi moved against the Delta, taking Memphis by assault, in which he made use of his fleet as well as his army. On this many of the princes of the Delta submitted, and he then went to Heliopolis and received the surrender of Osorkon IV [nominally the last Pharaoh of the XXIII Dynasty] as well. Tefnakht then took refuge in an inaccessible island in one of the western mouths of the Nile and persuaded Piankhi to accept his surrender. Regarding the conquest of Egypt as now complete, Piankhi returned home to Napata, erected the stela, and reconstructed the great temple of Amon-Re there . . .[59]

Here the official text ends. Piankhi reigned quietly for at least a decade longer, but his days as a campaigner were over, and he never returned to Egypt. It was nevertheless he who, having defeated the erstwhile pharaoh, Osorkon IV, first assumed the full titles of the monarch of Egypt. He is generally regarded as the founder of the XXV Dynasty, although Manetho gives that honour to his successor.

Although he assumed the titles of the pharaoh, Piankhi was neither a conqueror nor a despot of the ordinary sort. His intervention in Egypt was prompted by direct and repeated pleas from the north, and his chief interest from beginning to end seems to have been to relieve the threat to Thebes, and thus protect the domains of Amon. The vigorous pursuit of that policy led him to subdue every rival prince in Egypt, but having obtained their nominal submission he was content to return homeward and leave Egypt to its own devices. Not surprisingly, his enemies rewarded his humane and lenient treatment by repudiating their oaths and resuming their dynastic ambitions the moment his back was turned. Piankhi was undoubtedly soon apprised of this, but as long as the threat to Thebes was not resumed he was content to let matters rest. Until the end of his life he made no move to restore his authority in the north of Egypt.

Of Piankhi's great testament, Breasted has written that:

. . . this remarkable literary monument is the clearest and most rational account of a military expedition which has survived from ancient Egypt. It displays literary skill and an appreciation of dramatic situations which is notable, while the vivacious touches found here and there quite relieve it of the arid tone usual in such hieroglyphic documents. The imagination endues the personages appearing here more easily with life than those of any other similar historical narrative of Egypt; and the humane Piankhi especially, the lover of horses, remains a *man* far removed from the conventional companion and equal of the gods who inevitably occupies the exalted throne of the Pharaohs in all other such records.[60]

Wilson further observes that:

The story of Piankhi's conquest of Egypt is an extraordinarily interesting human document, particularly in the contrast between this backwater puritan and the effete and sophisticated Egyptians. His chivalry in battle, his austere avoidance of captured princesses, his delight in horses, his scrupulous perform-ance of religious ritual, and his refusal to deal with conquered princes who were ceremonially unclean – 'they were uncircumcised and eaters of fish' – are told in elegant Egyptian with solemn gusto.[61]

The simple and rather austere character which Piankhi exhibited in Egypt may have been a bit of supremely adroit role-playing, designed to reinforce his image as Deliverer. Lacking any claim to dynastic legitimacy, he, like many a subsequent usurper, may well have found it expedient to wrap himself in a cloak of personal righteousness.[62] His character, like his career, exhibits uncanny parallels to that which Moslem tradition attributes to the usurper and redeemer Salahed-Din (Saladin), who came to power in Egypt 2,000 years later.[63] At home, however, neither the tomb of Piankhi nor those of his several queens proclaim him as a particularly humble or abstemious man.

Piankhi's two immediate successors, Shabaka and Shabataka, are some-what shadowy figures, neither of whom left an important personal testa-ment. Shabaka was apparently a younger brother of Piankhi and Shabataka a son of Piankhi, in accordance with the preferred order of succession. Between them they reigned from perhaps 711 to 689 BC.[64]

Shabaka and Shabataka evidently regarded themselves as pharaohs in the true sense of the word; that is, first and foremost as rulers of Egypt. They established the royal seat at Thebes, and pursued a much more for-ward and less circumspect policy in the north than had Piankhi. Shabaka resumed the campaign against his rivals in the Delta and soon restored Nubian rule over the whole of Egypt; in addition, his imperial ambitions led him to intrigue with the petty rulers of Palestine and Syria against the Empire of Assyria. These imprudent efforts only provoked the scornful Assyrian response quoted at the beginning of this chapter. Their immediate upshot was the devastation of Judah, and, forty years later, the Assyrian cataclysm which overwhelmed the Nubian dynasty in Egypt.

As in so many later ages, Palestine was the chief bone of contention between the Near Eastern powers. Long an Egyptian sphere of influence, the unhappy Hebrew and Philistine kingdoms had fallen under the Assyrian yoke in the ninth century BC. They were rebellious provinces, however, calling forth repeated Assyrian reprisals and punitive expeditions. Twice during the reign of Piankhi there were campaigns against Judah which carried to the very borders of Egypt; each time the Assyrian armies turned back rather than plunge into the Delta swamps which had so long protected the approaches to the Nile. In spite of, or possibly because of, these narrow escapes Shabaka sought by intrigue and subsidy to provoke rebellion in the Levantine states and to set them up as a buffer against the Assyrian threat.

Remembering the ancient supremacy of Egypt, failing to understand the state of decadent impotence into which she had fallen, and anxious to shake off the Assyrian yoke, they lent a ready ear to the emissaries of Shabaka. Only in Judah did the prophet-statesman Isaiah foresee the futility of depending upon Egypt and the final catastrophe which should overtake her at the hands of Assyria.[65]

The machinations of Shabaka finally convinced the Assyrian Emperor Sennacherib that the Egyptian nuisance must be disposed of. In 701 BC he led a considerable army west, intending to crush Egypt and put an end once and for all to the chronic rebellions in Palestine and Syria. According to the Hebrew chronicle Shabaka did not take the field against Sennacherib in person, but entrusted command of the Egyptian army to his twenty-year-old nephew Taharqa,[66] who was later to reign as the fourth 'Ethiopian' pharaoh. The Nubian commander hastened to Palestine, intending to meet the foe before he reached the gates of Egypt. There is some uncertainty as to what happened next, but evidently no decisive engagement ever took place; the Assyrian army was providentially decimated by an outbreak of plague. Once again fortune had spared the Kushite régime in Egypt.

Shabaka evidently finished his reign in peace; fragments of a clay tablet bearing his royal seal and that of an Assyrian king may indicate that some sort of truce was concluded between the two rulers.[67] The brief reign of Shabataka seems also to have been uneventful, although it has left few records either in Egypt or in Nubia. For twenty years the Assyrian emperor was busy upon other frontiers, and was probably glad enough to have peace in the west. Shabataka nevertheless found it necessary to maintain personal rule in Egypt, although, like all his predecessors, he was buried at El Kurru.

Taharqa, the younger brother of Shabataka and son of Piankhi, came to the throne some time around 689 BC. He appears to have been a man of considerable ability, even if he was one of the most unsuccessful military commanders in history. It was his misfortune to reap the harvest of his predecessors' foolhardy ambitions in Asia, and he came to the throne when the forces of Assyria were gathering for a final showdown with Egypt. The latter years of his reign were filled with a continuing series of abortive campaigns and rearguard actions against the advancing Assyrian host under Esarhaddon, the son and successor of Sennacherib. The Egyptian and Nubian forces were routed in nearly every one of these engagements, and at the end only Thebes and Upper Egypt were left in the Nubian grasp. Taharqa thus ended his reign where his father Piankhi had begun.

In spite of the military reverses which overshadowed his reign, Taharqa was the first and only member of the Nubian dynasty who turned seriously from the task of conquest to that of consolidation. Like other rulers of Egypt, he attempted to reinforce his rule and that of his successors by a great programme of commemorative temple-building. He thus stands out as the one great builder of the Kushite dynasty. The surviving monuments of Taharqa, both in Egypt and in Nubia, outnumber those of all the other XXV Dynasty pharaohs combined.

Taharqa's building activities are thus enumerated by Emery:

In the temple of Karnak he embellished the Great Court with a processional way flanked by huge columns of superb proportions, one of which survives, and it would appear that he was partly if not wholly responsible for the unfinished pylons which flank the main entrance of the temple. Apart from these major works, Taharqa erected other buildings of lesser importance in the Karnak complex as well as at Medinet Habu on the west side of the Nile, and from inscribed material we may conclude that he built both at Tanis and at Edfu. His building operations in his homeland were perhaps even more extensive, and at Napata he restored and embellished the great temple of Amon, and built a small rock-cut temple in the sacred mountain behind it. On the river side of the mountain, the face is so formed that it gives the appearance of an artificial façade consisting of four colossal figures, and it has been suggested that these are the remains of a rock-cut temple of the style of Abu Simbel and of even greater size. But many authorities doubt the existence of these rock-cut statues, and believe that they are merely chance formations of the natural rock.[68]

Taharqa is also responsible for the temple of Kawa, which became, with Jebel Barkal, one of the great religious centres of the Kushite régime. The most astonishing monuments of his reign, however, are those from Lower Nubia and the *Batn el Hajar*. He evidently built small temples at Semna,[69] at Buhen,[70] and at Qasr Ibrim,[71] and inscribed blocks bearing his name have been found elsewhere in Lower Nubia as well.[72] It is difficult to account for these monuments in a region which was to all intents and purposes deserted, though it was of course regularly traversed by emissaries and merchants going back and forth between the king's Nubian and Egyptian dominions. The great Second Cataract Forts and their XVIII Dynasty temples had certainly long been in ruins in Taharqa's time, yet their symbolic value as expressions of the pharaonic authority apparently remained such that Taharqa chose to erect his own monuments on the same sites. They are almost the only datable indications of human activity in the Second Cataract region during the last millennium BC.

Taharqa has left three important commemorative stelae in the temple of Kawa, detailing various events in his career.[73] Another, of which only fragments are preserved, was set up at Tanis on the occasion of his accession to power in Egypt. In it Taharqa tells how he sent for his mother, whom he had not seen since he left Napata many years earlier, so that she might see him crowned 'even as Isis saw her son Horus on the throne of his father'.[74] This inscription has generally been taken to indicate that Taharqa governed primarily from Tanis. Other records of his reign include a number of temple dedication texts and the long and detailed commemorative stele of his faithful deputy Mentuemhat at Thebes,[75] as well as the Assyrian and Hebrew annals relating to his military encounters with Esarhaddon.

Like most of his predecessors Taharqa retired to Napata in his last years, having appointed his nephew and successor Tenutamon to look after what remained of the Nubian holdings at Thebes. He did not, however, erect his funerary monument at El Kurru. Following the example of some of Egypt's earliest pharaohs,[76] he seems to have prepared two different tombs in different parts of his empire: one apparently to serve as a cenotaph and the other as his actual place of interment. The localities selected by Taharqa were at Nuri, across the river from Jebel Barkal and about twenty-five kilometres upstream from El Kurru, and Seddenga in the Abri-Delgo Reach. In succeeding generations Nuri was to replace El Kurru as the royal cemetery, and all but one or two of the remaining Napatan kings were buried there.

Although Taharqa's is the first of the forty or so royal pyramids at Nuri, it is not certain that the king was ever buried under it. The burial chamber (which like all those at Nuri had been thoroughly plundered) was found quite empty,[77] and recent discoveries suggest that Taharqa's last resting place may have been his much less pretentious tomb at Seddenga.[78] (The chronology and development of the Nubian royal cemeteries will be discussed at more length later.)

Taharqa died still in possession of the Upper Egyptian territories which his father and grandfather had ruled; fortune was kind enough to postpone the final débâcle of the XXV Dynasty until after his death. The blow fell early in the reign of his successor Tenutamon, and once again it was brought on by the ambition and imprudence of the pharaoh himself. Soon after his arrival on the throne Tenutamon made one last attempt to reunite Egypt under his rule. He descended with an army to Memphis, which he besieged and possibly captured. The Assyrians after their defeat of Taharqa had left no army of occupation in Lower Egypt, with the result that Tenutamon and his relatively weak force were once again able to compel the temporary submission of the Delta cities. The Assyrian reprisal, however, was swift and devastating, as related in the annals of Assurbanipal:

On my second campaign, I directed my way to [Egypt] and [Nubia]. Tenutamon heard of my campaign and that I trod the soil of Egypt. He abandoned Memphis and fled to Thebes to save his life. The kings, viceroys, and burgraves whom I had set in Memphis came to me and kissed my feet. After Tenutamon I pursued my way and came to Thebes, the place of his strength. He fled to Kipkip [Napata?]. Thebes in its entirety I conquered with the help of Ashur and Ishtar. Silver, gold, precious stones, all the possessions of his palace, many-colored clothing, linen, great horses, men and women attendants, two high obelisks of shining orichalcum, 2,500 talents in weight, the doorposts of the temple door I took from their bases and removed to Assyria. Heavy booty, beyond counting,

I took away from Thebes. Against Egypt and Nubia I let my weapons rage and showed my might.[79]

The sack of Thebes ended that city's days of glory for good. It was still remembered fifty years later when the prophet Nahum foretold the destruction which would fall upon Assyria in her turn:

Art thou better than populous [Thebes] that was situate among the rivers, that had the waters round about it, whose rampart was the sea and her wall was from the sea? Ethiopia and Egypt were her strength, and it was infinite . . . Yet was she carried away . . . into captivity; her young children were dashed in pieces at the top of all the streets, and they cast lots for her honorable men, and all her great men were bound in chains.[80]

After this disaster Tenutamon passed the remainder of his brief reign at Napata; neither he nor any of his successors ever set foot in Egypt again. Tenutamon did not follow the example of Taharqa in erecting his pyramid at Nuri. He preferred the ancestral cemetery at El Kurru, and was the last Nubian king to be buried there.[81] He was also the last Nubian who could legitimately claim the title Pharaoh, though his successors continued to do so for sixty-five more reigns. The passing of Tenutamon marks the end of the XXV Dynasty, and of Nubia's Heroic Age.

The achievements of the 'Ethiopian' pharaohs during the three generations of their rule in Egypt had not been inconsiderable. They restored the northern country to unity, however temporarily, for the first time in more than three hundred years. Their building activities in and around Thebes, though modest by New Kingdom standards, were nevertheless more extensive than those of any ruler since Rameses IV.[82] Although they were the offspring of once despised barbarians, their aim was nothing less than the restoration of Egyptian culture and religion to their original 'purity', and in this they were not wholly unsuccessful. The archaizing tendencies which are first apparent in the monuments and literature of the XXV Dynasty were to persist through succeeding generations until the final downfall of the pharaonic state.

THE LATER NAPATAN KINGS

When the kings of Kush departed from Egypt, they departed also from the world stage. The Hebrew and Assyrian chroniclers took no further interest in them, the scribes of Egypt were no longer theirs to command, and they had few press-agents at home. In any case they probably found little enough to boast of – particularly while the memory of past glories remained green. In consequence, the historic record ceases almost at once with the collapse of Nubia's imperial fortunes, and darkness falls again upon the southern dynasty.

After Taharqa, twenty more generations of kings were buried at Nuri. We know the names of all but one of them, for they were written upon their tombs or on some of the objects found within them. Only five of the twenty, however, have left any other record of themselves. Their inscriptions are mostly campaign annals, owing much in style and even in content to the great testaments of Piankhi and Taharqa. The enemies are no longer the mighty Assyrians and Egyptians, but obscure tribal peoples of uncertain origin. The execution of the texts shows a declining familiarity with a language which was no longer spoken; in the end the phraseology and even the events of earlier times were being mechanically repeated by half-comprehending scribes.[83]

The first Napatan king of the twilight period to leave a record was Anlamani, apparently a great-grandson of Taharqa who ruled about fifty years after him (c. 623–593 BC).[84] Anlamani's inscription commemorates a visit to the temple of Kawa, where he celebrated the festival of Amon, and also a military expedition against the desert Beja. It sounds two themes familiar from earlier times: the queen-mother is brought to Kawa to witness her son on the throne, and the sisters of the king are installed as sistrum-players in each of the great Amon temples of the realm.[85]

Aspalta, the brother and successor of Anlamani,[86] left two stelae in the temple at Jebel Barkal. In his accession stele he tells how he was elected by Amon himself from among the eligible princes – meaning presumably by the priesthood of Amon. Paradoxically, in his other inscription Aspalta tells of calling together the priests to hear and ratify his own choice of Mediken, the widow of Anlamani,[87] as high priestess.[88] Evidently the delicate balance between monarchy and priesthood had tipped first one way and then the other.

Attributable to the reign of Aspalta, though understandably omitted from his annals, is the Egyptian invasion of Nubia in the reign of the XXVI Dynasty pharaoh, Psammetik II. The campaign is recorded in Herodotus[89] and in two inscriptions of Psammetik himself, but the geographical details are scanty. The expedition certainly traversed Lower Nubia, for the Greek and Carian mercenaries who now made up the bulk of the Egyptian forces left their graffiti on the statues at Abu Simbel and at the Second Cataract.[90] It now seems possible (as Herodotus reported) that the campaign carried upriver as far as Napata itself. Broken statues of Aspalta and several of his predecessors, found in the temple of Jebel Barkal, are interpreted as evidence of the depredations of Psammetik.[91] However, the invasion had no lasting effect on the course of Nubian history or on Egyptian–Nubian relations. The centres of power in Egypt were now entirely in the north; those in Nubia were in the south; a broad no-man's-land yawned between the two, and after the destruction of Thebes they had few interests in common. Both were now second-rate powers, preoccupied with local affairs.

Aspalta is the first Nubian king whose name has been found in the ruins of Meroë, though evidence that he actually resided at the southern city is far from conclusive.[92] He might of course have taken temporary refuge there during the invasion of Psammetik. However, it is clear from his inscriptions that he was involved in a behind-the-scenes power struggle with the priests at Jebel Barkal,[93] and we can therefore hardly doubt that the Nubian 'capital' was still at Napata in Aspalta's time. The oft-repeated suggestion that the depredations of Psammetik were directly responsible for the removal of the 'capital' to Meroë[94] has little to recommend it, as we shall observe presently.

After Aspalta there is a gap of perhaps 150 years in the historical record; the remaining royal inscriptions all belong to the last reigns of the Napatan era. In the temple of Kawa there are four inscriptions of Aman-nete-yerike, the twenty-first ruler of the Kushite dynasty (and sixteenth successor of Taharqa) according to Reisner's chronology.[95] One of the inscriptions contains a great deal of historical interest, although it is somewhat ungrammatical and linguistically 'barbarized'. Shinnie tells us:

The great inscription of Aman-nete-yerike is of fundamental importance for the history of the period, since it contains the first mention of Meroë, and tells us that the king resided there. Inscribed when he was forty-one years old,[96] it first describes a campaign against the *Rehrehs*, who seem to have been occupying the north end of the Island of Meroë. After defeating them, he went to Napata to be accepted as king by the priesthood of Amon, and took part in a ceremony in the Barkal temple where he was recognized in the traditional way by the god. From Napata, he sailed downstream to an unidentified place called *Krtn*, probably on the right bank, where he fought the *Meded*, a people described as 'desert-dwellers;' later he went on a seventeen-day journey from Napata to Kawa and to Pnubs [Argo?], where he gave land to a temple. He then returned to Kawa, where he cleared the approach to Taharqa's temple and ordered repairs to be carried out to a number of buildings. The other inscriptions of this king are extremely obscure in meaning, and add nothing to history . . .[97]

The two remaining royal inscriptions, those of Harsiotef (twenty-third generation) and Nastasen (twenty-sixth generation) were both inscribed in the temple at Jebel Barkal.[98] They are closely patterned after the inscription of Aman-nete-yerike, and repeat many of the same details. The stele of Nastasen also contains a good deal of original information, including a description of the desert route by which he travelled from Meroë to Napata for his coronation.[99] The importance of this route for our interpretation of the history of Kush will be discussed in the following chapter.

Aman-nete-yerike and his successors all claim to have campaigned against the *Meded* (probably Beja) and the *Rehreh* – peoples who would seem to have been persistent and perhaps traditional enemies of the Kushite state. From the descriptions they sound like typical bedouin nomads. In addition, Nastasen fought against a foreign invader who came from the north with a fleet.

The name of Nastasen's mysterious northern enemy reads something like *Kmbswdn*, and it was long identified with that of the Persian emperor Cambyses. He conquered Egypt in 525 BC and, according to Herodotus, sent an expeditionary force into Nubia which perished miserably in the desert.[100] This expedition – once dismissed as another of Herodotus' romantic fantasies – seemed to find historical confirmation in the stele of Nastasen. Yet the dates are impossible to reconcile, for according to Reisner's chronology Nastasen reigned two hundred years after the time of Cambyses. The northern enemy must therefore have been someone else – perhaps a certain Khabbash who is mentioned as a rebel in Upper Egypt or Lower Nubia around 335 BC.[101]

There seems little doubt that Aman-nete-yerike, Harsiotef and Nastasen all resided chiefly at Meroë. However, upon their accession each of them made the journey northwards to be acclaimed at Jebel Barkal, and each was buried across the river from the Sacred Mountain, in the great cemetery begun by Taharqa. To that extent we are still justified in speaking of them as Napatan kings even if the preferred royal residence was now in the south. Only when the great southern city has been excavated far more systematically than has been attempted up to now will we be able to say when Meroë replaced Napata as the spiritual centre of the Kushite empire.

The prolonged and continuing dispute over the location of the Nubian 'capital'[102] is virtually meaningless unless we specify (as few writers have) what is meant by 'capital'. Many early empires were multi-centred, if only because the ruler and his household could and did move about freely. Even after the development of more sedentary rule there were often several royal residences in different parts of the empire. Only with the emergence of a powerfully entrenched and relatively immobile central bureaucracy does it become meaningful to talk of a geographical 'capital' in the modern sense.

The ancient state of Kush clearly rested upon two interacting power structures: the monarchy and the priesthood of Amon. Each had potentially more than one locus of power. The late Napatan monarchs whose inscriptions imply that they resided at Meroë surely had residences at Napata as well, whether or not they chose to occupy them for any great lengths of time. The priests also had at least two main loci, and possibly three. Kawa might perhaps be dismissed as a provincial centre, but the great temples of Amon at Jebel Barkal and at Meroë were almost equally important in the history of Kush. Barkal was clearly most important at the beginning of the Kushite dynasty, and Meroë at the end, but there was a long period of coexistence during which it is impossible to say which was dominant. Very possibly the late Napatan kings had to receive the election of the god in both places, as Kashta and Piankhi had to receive it at Napata and at Thebes. We may therefore legitimately speak of a 'capital' at Napata until the time of Nastasen without prejudice to the possibility that there was a 'capital' at Meroë as well.[103] Since Nastasen was (according to Reisner's scheme) the last king who chose to be buried in the north, however, we may conveniently select his reign as marking the close of the Napatan era.

TEMPLES AND TOWNS

Jebel Barkal, the sacred mountain of the Nubians, rises like a giant altar above the Nile floodplain. The top is a level expanse of stone and gravel several acres in extent; to the north it dips downwards rather gradually to the bare desert surface. The face which Jebel Barkal presents towards the Nile, however, is a nearly vertical cliff over 300 feet high (Pl. Xb). It was in the shadow of this great precipice that Rameses II erected the temple which was to remain for many centuries the spiritual centre of Nubia.

The Temple of Amon as excavated by Reisner in 1916[104] comprised the usual succession of rectangular, colonnaded halls and courts extending along what was probably intended to be an east–west axis,[105] with the sanctuary at the west end (cf. Pl. XIa). The total length of the building in its final form was nearly 500 feet – larger than any contemporary Egyptian temple except Karnak.[106] The original nucleus built by the Egyptians was considerably smaller; there were substantial additions both in Napatan and in Meroitic times (Fig. 39). As at Karnak, so much alteration and rebuilding was undertaken in the course of the centuries that it was not always easy for Reisner to be sure which structures were the work of which rulers.[107] The style and decoration, as in all Nubian temples, remained essentially Egyptian from beginning to end.

At Jebel Barkal as at Karnak, the great Temple of Amon was only the central feature of a much larger religious complex. In the immediate vicinity (and probably within the same precinct wall, though it was never found) were at least six other temples and probably a number of secular buildings as well (Fig. 40). Two of the lesser temples, dating from the XXV Dynasty, were built directly against the face of the cliff, the sanctuaries being rock-cut chambers within the sacred mountain itself. Two other temples of Napatan origin had been restored and enlarged in the Meroitic period, and one small temple was wholly Meroitic. Most of the subsidiary temples consisted of either two or three chambers, and none was of a size remotely comparable to that of the great Amon Temple.[108]

The Barkal temples were found in an extremely bad state of preservation, for the whole region has been subject to excessive sheet erosion. The buildings themselves, like most of those in the southern land, had been built of inferior Nubian sandstone – the only material available for hundreds of

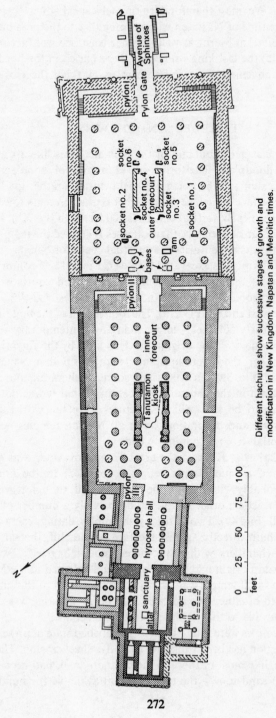

Different hachures show successive stages of growth and modification in New Kingdom, Napatan and Meroitic times.

Fig. 39. Great Temple of Amon at Jebel Barkal.

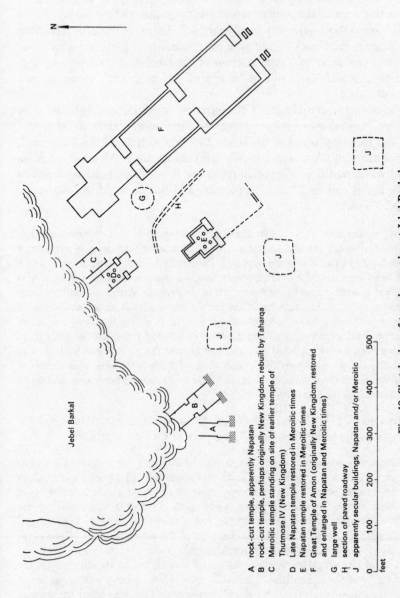

N

Jebel Barkal

A rock-cut temple, apparently Napatan
B rock-cut temple, perhaps originally New Kingdom, rebuilt by Taharqa
C Meroitic temple standing on site of earlier temple of
  Thutmose IV (New Kingdom)
D Late Napatan temple restored in Meroitic times
E Napatan temple restored in Meroitic times
F Great Temple of Amon (originally New Kingdom, restored
  and enlarged in Napatan and Meroitic times)
G large well
H section of paved roadway
J apparently secular buildings, Napatan and/or Meroitic

0   100   200   300   400   500
feet

Fig. 40. Sketch plan of temple complex at Jebel Barkal

miles. (In most of the smaller temples the exterior wall was faced with mud brick as a partial protection against erosion.) Because of their denuded condition none of the temples was excavated in full, and the areas between and around them were only briefly sampled. There are traces of a number of ordinary mud-brick buildings in the immediate vicinity, but whether or not one can speak of a regular town-site at Jebel Barkal remains a moot question. Hopefully it will be 'answered with a shovel' in the not too distant future.

Across the river and a short distance downstream from Jebel Barkal, at Sanam, was another very important Napatan centre. Here stood one of Taharqa's many temples, dedicated to 'Amon, Bull of the Bow-land', which is to say, Amon in a purely local manifestation,[109] since the Bow-land was a traditional Egyptian name for Nubia. This building seems to have had a curious history, as recounted in the words of the excavator, F. Ll. Griffith:

Our excavations showed that the temple at Sanam was of considerable size, with a fore-court surrounded by a colonnade entered through a pylon gate; a second pylon opened into the hypostyle hall beyond which were a *pronaos* and a sanctuary surrounded by various chambers. All this was built by Taharqa, who also put a small chapel in the north half of the *pronaos*. Aspalta, a century later, added another in the south half. The temple was evidently soon occupied to a large extent by manufacturers of *ushabti* [mortuary votive figurines] and other figurines and ornaments in glazed ware, molds for these and a few figures having been found scattered through and around the greater part of it. It was probably for these artisans that rough walls of crude brick were built almost at random within the temple, blocking the bays; the side entrances north and south were carefully blocked with stone . . .[110]

In spite of erosion and plundering, there were unmistakable signs of a very large town-site at Sanam. The report of Griffith continues:

The temple stood on the south-east edge of the town ruins. Along the south-west edge (i.e. down-river) of the town and about half a kilometer to the south of the temple, began a large cemetery most of which we cleared, finding over 1,500 cave-graves, brick-lined graves, and burials in the sand. The contents were of the Ethiopian period, probably beginning about the time of Piankhi and continuing long after Taharqa's reign; only at the west end a few of the cave-graves gave evidence of re-use in the Meroitic period.

A third site which we worked was about a kilometer to the north from the cemetery and the same distance from the river. Here an extraordinary series of columned chambers was disclosed which appear to have been royal storehouses of the Ethiopian dynasty. Burnt and denuded by wind, the walls were reduced to a maximum height of eighteen inches. Opposite the west end were considerable remains of brickwork and traces of stone columns which probably belonged to the royal Palace and linked this 'Treasury' to the town.[111]

Our excavations, so far as they went, showed that the remains represented one long narrow range of building, 256 meters long and about 45 meters broad running from east to west, apparently isolated entirely in the desert except at its west end. At this end perhaps only a roadway separated it from an important brick building with some stone columns, perhaps a royal palace . . . The Treasury appeared to consist of a double series of seventeen equal chambers ranged on either side of a spinal wall. We cleared entirely the southern series, and also two or three chambers at the east end of the northern half . . .[112]

What were the nature and purpose of the building? We began by calling the place 'The Palace' because of the large proportion of objects with royal cartouches which were found there. But as the plan developed we recognized that it was no palace in itself though perhaps connected with the palace, and we renamed it 'The Treasury'. In one of the southern chambers was found a tiny fragment of the treasure carried off by Piankhi from Hermopolis, and part of the floor in No. 15 was covered with tusks of raw ivory injured by fire. But there are considerable difficulties in the way of this or any other interpretation of the ruins. One would have expected a royal magazine or treasury to have been enclosed by a thick outer wall with guardrooms, etc., of which some considerable traces would have been preserved.[113]

Imagination has suggested to several writers that Sanam may have been the principal town-site of Napata, as well as the royal residence.[114] Although, as Griffith explains, a palace was not actually identified, his reasons for believing that one was not far away appear sound. The dedication of the Sanam temple to a Nubian manifestation of Amon, rather than to his universal manifestation, may also suggest that this was in a sense a house-shrine of the royal family, not controlled by the entrenched priesthood at Jebel Barkal. The physical separation of the sacred and secular powers, on opposite sides of the river, reminds us of the Vatican and the Quirinale; it may have been necessary to prevent the generation of sparks from the too-close proximity of the two powers. There is certainly a suggestion of such conflict in the stelae of Aspalta, in one of which the king's name has been vindictively erased by the priests.[115]

After the abandonment of Lower Nubia and the loss of Egypt, the main northern metropolis of Kush was Kawa, near the downstream end of the Dongola Reach (Fig. 37). As we saw in Chapter 9, this settlement dates from the XVIII Dynasty, and the earliest surviving temple is attributable to Tutankhamen. It was restored and enlarged by later Egyptian pharaohs as well as in the early Napatan period, and Shabaka seems to have built a second structure alongside it. The principal temple at Kawa is, however, another of Taharqa's monuments. It is almost identical in size and plan to that at Sanam, but is much better preserved (Fig. 41).[116] As at Sanam, there seems to have been a good deal of commercial activity in the forecourt, as evidenced by flimsy walls built between the great columns. A sizeable town immediately surrounded the temple, and both temple and town were

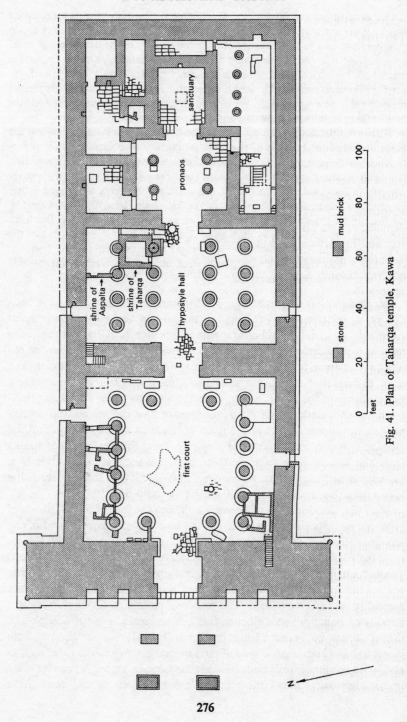

Fig. 41. Plan of Taharqa temple, Kawa

sanctuary

pronaos

shrine of Aspalta →
shrine of Taharqa →

hypostyle hall

first court

mud brick

stone

feet 0 20 40 60 80 100

enclosed within a stout *temenos* wall which is probably also the work of Taharqa.[117] As in all Upper Nubian sites, the town-site remains largely un-excavated.

The excavation of Kawa provided a treasure trove of Nubian royal in-scriptions second only to Jebel Barkal.[118] Evidently it was a local centre of considerable importance so that many kings found it desirable to pay state visits and to make endowments to the temple. Kawa retained its importance well down into the Meroitic period, and perhaps until the end of the Kushite kingdom.

Another important Napatan settlement must have been on the large island of Argo, a short distance downstream from Kawa (Fig. 37). This is usually identified with the *Pnubs* mentioned in several of the royal in-scriptions, although the identification is not absolutely certain.[119] The very denuded temple which has recently come to light here is so similar both in size and in plan to those at Sanam and Kawa as to suggest another of Taharqa's monuments. However, all of the datable material so far re-covered belongs to the Meroitic period; the result, perhaps, of later restoration.[120]

Seddenga, in the Abri-Delgo Reach, must have been an important locality in Napatan times if it was really selected by Taharqa as his final resting place, as is now suggested (see 'The royal cemeteries', below). We have already mentioned (Ch. 9) the XVIII Dynasty temple built here by Amenhotep III, and there are numerous Meroitic remains in the vicinity as well. Yet the only suggestion of Napatan occupation so far identified at Seddenga is the tomb attributed to Taharqa himself.[121]

The great southern metropolis of Kush was undoubtedly the city of Meroë. In later Napatan times it may already have eclipsed the northern settlements in size and importance. Yet it too remains for the time being largely unexcavated. This should soon be rectified by investigations which are now in progress; so far they have revealed chiefly that the depth of occupation deposit at Meroë exceeds thirty feet, and that the foundation of the town probably dates back to the seventh century B C.[122] A century after its founding Meroë was already important enough for the rulers Amtalqa and Malenaqen to build a small palace (or temple?) there,[123] and from the time of Aman-nete-yerike at least one of the royal residences was at Meroë.[124] For the moment we can hardly say more, and further dis-cussion of the southern city and its history will be deferred until the following chapter.

How far Napatan dominion extended southwards beyond Meroë will also remain moot until systematic exploration is undertaken in the central Sudan. A number of objects of Napatan date have been found in sites as far south as modern Khartoum,[125] but actual settlements have not yet been discovered. Whatever the limits of Kushite political hegemony, however, it is quite possible that the cultural influence of Napata extended considerably further – perhaps southwards up the Blue Nile, and westwards into Kordofan.[126]

THE ROYAL CEMETERIES

The most numerous monuments of Kushite civilization, and by far the most distinctive, are its royal tombs. In this as in several other respects, the development of Dynastic Nubia seems to parallel that of Egypt 2,000 years earlier. It was in the Old Kingdom, before the rise of an entrenched priesthood, that the king and his personal household were for all practical purposes the state, and the royal tomb was the principal state monument. There may even be some significance in the fact that the form of funerary monument selected by Piankhi and all his successors until the end of the dynasty was the pyramid – the supreme expression of the cult of the divine king in Egypt, but long out of fashion when Piankhi came to the throne.

The known royal cemeteries of Kush are five: El Kurru, Nuri, and Jebel Barkal in the Napata region, and two cemeteries just east of the town of Meroë. The first two of these belong clearly to the Napatan period, and the last two to the Meroitic. The status of the tombs at Jebel Barkal is in considerable doubt, as we shall discuss in the next chapter.

The five royal cemeteries were excavated almost in their entirety by the Harvard–Boston Expedition.[127] Altogether they included nearly 400 individual tombs, including those of at least seventy-two rulers and a much larger number of royal wives and dependents. The four main cemeteries (that is, excluding Jebel Barkal) were believed by Reisner to represent an unbroken sequence of development, beginning with El Kurru, then Nuri, then the south cemetery at Meroë, and finally the north Meroë cemetery. Nominally, the earliest royal tomb in each cemetery was supposed to be the immediate successor to the last tomb in the preceding cemetery.

Above ground, the basic feature of every Nubian royal tomb from the time of Piankhi onwards was the pyramid. The Kushite royal pyramid is a far smaller affair than that of Old Kingdom Egypt, the largest known example (that of Taharqa at Nuri) measuring only about 95 feet along the base, as compared with 750 feet for the Pyramid of Cheops at Giza. The Nubian pyramid is also considerably taller in proportion to its base than is its Egyptian counterpart, giving it a conspicuously pointed appearance (Pl. XIIIb). The average slope angle is between 60 degrees and 70 degrees,[128] in contrast to the 50 degree slope of most Old Kingdom pyramids. These characteristics are also found in certain Egyptian noble tombs of the New Kingdom;[129] it was presumably they, rather than the great funerary monuments of the Old Kingdom, which served as the immediate models for the Kushite royal tombs. The earlier Nubian pyramids were built of solid stone

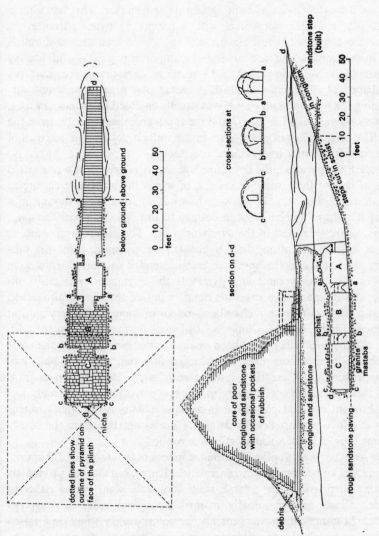

Fig. 42. Plan and cross-section of a typical Napatan royal tomb (Pyramid VII at Nuri)

below ground | above ground

0 10 20 30 40 50
feet

dotted lines show
outline of pyramid on
face of the plinth

niche

cross-sections at

section on d–d

core of poor
conglom and sandstone
with occasional pockets
of rubbish

conglom and sandstone

rough sandstone paving

debris

schist

granite
mastaba

steps cut in schist

in conglom

sandstone step
(built)

0 10 20 30 40 50
feet

masonry – usually of rather small blocks – but those of late Meroitic times were only a heap of loose rubble with a facing of dressed stone.[130]

There was no interior chamber within the pyramids, but almost every one had a mortuary chapel built against its eastern face. This was a plain rectangular chamber, sometimes with a sculptured pylon entrance. At Meroë the largest and most elaborate chapels were decorated with reliefs and inscriptions which are among the important artistic and literary remains of the Meroitic period.[131] There are no comparable remains from the chapels at El Kurru and Nuri. A rectangular area immediately surrounding the pyramid and chapel was usually enclosed by a masonry wall, and was entered, like the chapel and the tomb chamber beneath, from the east. The original height of these enclosure walls is not known, since all of them were found in a badly ruined condition.

Beneath the pyramid, the royal tomb generally consisted of a connected series of two or three small chambers, of which the innermost contained the burial (cf. Fig. 42). These were hewn from solid rock, though in a few of the Kurru tombs it was necessary to provide them with masonry because of the weakness of the overlying strata. The main burial chamber was, at least by intention, directly beneath the pyramid, while the subsidiary chambers and the approach ramp extended eastwards from it. In some of the crudely built late pyramids the alignment is notably off-centre, and in one or two cases the builders missed their mark altogether. Access to the underground chambers, except in some of the very earliest and latest tombs, was by a long flight of steps descending from the east. After the royal interment had been made, the doorway between the steps and the easternmost chamber was blocked with masonry or rubble, and the approach ramp was then re-filled with earth. However, in no case were these arrangements found intact; every Kushite royal tomb had been broken into and plundered in antiquity. As a result, the archaeologist is left to reconstruct the details of burial practice from the scanty remains overlooked or disdained by the robbers.

The royal corpse was placed within the innermost subterranean chamber. The practice of bed burial was general at El Kurru, but did not survive the move to Nuri. All of the later Kushite monarchs were buried either in wooden coffins, or, occasionally, in stone sarcophagi, after the Egyptian manner. Mummification was general. The coffin usually stood on a raised platform or bench of stone which was left standing when the chamber was hewn out. Because of the extreme disturbance of the burial chambers it is almost impossible to say anything meaningful about the original distribution of mortuary offerings, except that they were numerous and rich. Objects of Egyptian manufacture make up the bulk of offerings in the tombs of the Napatan period.

During most periods the tombs of the queens were of the same general style as those of the kings, but considerably smaller and less elaborately embellished. They are not usually ranged alongside the menfolk; at El Kurru[132] and at Nuri the queens occupied separate portions of the cemeteries, and at Meroë they occupied a separate cemetery altogether. Some burials of queens (or concubines?) seem to have lacked super-structures.

Not surprisingly, in the course of a thousand years there were numerous changes in the details of style and construction of the Nubian royal tombs. On the basis of these Reisner worked out a very complex typology and developmental sequence which is the main backbone of his chronology of the Kushite monarchy.[133] Since most of the later rulers left no historical records, they were assigned to a place in the succession on the basis of the typological characteristics and location of their tombs. The complete scheme is too complex to reproduce here; it is based upon observed varia-tion in no fewer than ten characteristics of the royal tomb (superstructure, enclosure, chapel, access to the burial place, entrance doorways, door blocking, number and construction of burial chambers, vaulting of burial chambers, niches in burial chambers, and method of burial), as well as upon offerings found in the tomb.[134]

The pyramid chronology, like much of Reisner's theoretical work, is more impressive for induction than for deduction. The typological categories as such appear eminently sound, but the logic by which they are arranged in a chronological sequence is not always clear. The whole scheme hangs, of course, upon the *a priori* assumption that all of the known Kushite royal tombs (except those at Jebel Barkal) represent one and only one sequence of development, with no breaks and no overlaps. The four main cemeteries thus each represent a chronological segment of the same dynasty, each beginning where the last ends. While this theory is supported to a considerable extent by the typological evidence, it is by no means empirically demonstrated. It remains one of the historian's de-ductive assumptions.[135] However, the chronological picture is reason-ably clear for the Napatan cemeteries with which we shall be concerned here.

Since the Kushite royal tomb consists essentially of a series of under-ground chambers covered by a heavy superstructure, the main requisites for a royal cemetery were a reasonably level area with a stratum of good, hard rock immediately beneath the surface. These conditions are met at many places in the Napata region, both to the north and to the south of the Nile floodplain. The locations actually selected, at El Kurru, Nuri, and Jebel Barkal, were certainly determined in part by considerations of geo-logical structure, but other factors must have played a part as well. El Kurru, the earliest of the cemeteries, is situated at a considerable distance downstream from Jebel Barkal; since there are no other known remains in the vicinity, we remain ignorant as to why this particular locality was chosen as the resting place of the earliest kings of Kush.

The cemeteries of El Kurru and Nuri appear to be exclusively royal cemeteries; that is, they contain only the tombs of kings and their consorts. El Kurru is the final resting place of five of the six Nubian kings of Egypt, of sixteen of their queens, and of five generations of their unnamed ancestors. The development of the cemetery is thus described by Arkell:

At Kurru the main cemetery with the tombs of the first four kings is a sand-stone plateau between two wadis, beyond which on either side are the tombs of the queens of those kings. The best site was occupied by a small . . . grave of tumulus type, and the next fifteen places in point of desirability were filled with a succession of tombs of increasing size and excellence of construction; and then came the four royal tombs in the four worst sites in the cemetery, obviously the latest burials in a cemetery which had been in continuous use since about 860 BC . . . There is a gradual development in tomb form – first, the simple pit grave under a tumulus with the corpse buried on the right side with the knees slightly bent, head north, face west; then an improved tumulus with a casing of sandstone masonry, a mud brick chapel, and a horseshoe-shaped enclosing wall; then a roughly square masonry mastaba[136] over a pit tomb with masonry chapel, the whole surrounded by a rectangular enclosing wall; and then a later type of mastaba under which the burial pits were oriented east–west, the orienta-tion of all the later royal tombs. Next in point of time came the graves of six queens of Piankhi, in which the burial pits were roofed with corbel-vaults of masonry. The tomb of King Piankhi himself was situated in front of a row of mastabas, lower down the slope towards the river; and in it, in order that the vault could be built before the funeral, a small stairway was cut into the rock and opened into the eastern end of the pit through a rock-cut doorway. This was the first of a long series of royal stairway tombs. It is impossible to say, since the material has been robbed in antiquity, whether the superstructure was a mastaba or a pyramid, but it is generally assumed to have been a pyramid, as in the suc-ceeding tombs.[137]

After Piankhi, all of the superstructures at El Kurru are relatively small (c. 30 feet square), smooth-faced pyramids without embellishment except for a plain masonry chapel at the east side. The underground portion consists of two chambers in the tombs of the kings and one chamber in those of the queens. Some of the burial chambers are completely decorated with painted mortuary scenes and texts after the fashion of rock-cut tombs in Egypt.[138]

A unique feature of the Kurru cemetery is a group of twenty-four horse burials, in an area a short distance away from the main tombs. 'The graves were in four rows, two rows with four horses in each, and two with eight. The graves were side by side and equally spaced, each horse buried stand-ing with its head to the south. The second and third rows were attributed from amulets . . . to Shabaka and Shabataka, and the first row therefore is almost certainly to be attributed to Piankhi and the last to Tenutamon. The graves had all been plundered, but remains of trappings, including plume-carriers, silver headbands, beads and amulets were found, indicating that they must be the teams of horses from the royal chariots.'[139] This pre-occupation with horses, already manifest in the Piankhi Stele, is a theme which recurs periodically in Nubian history until the end of the Middle Ages.

The Nuri cemetery occupies a setting not greatly different from that of El Kurru: a sandy desert plateau just beyond the limit of the Nile flood-plain. It is, however, one of the very few monuments of ancient Kush which is located on the 'west' bank of the Nile.[140] The suggestion that Taharqa built his pyramid here because El Kurru was 'full' may contain some truth,[141] but it obviously fails to account for the choice of localities, since many other places would have served as well. In fact, Taharqa was almost certainly imitating the practice of imperial Egypt; the great royal cemeteries both in Upper and in Lower Egypt are on the margin of the western desert, opposite the great temples of Karnak and Memphis. Nuri stands opposite Jebel Barkal in just such a fashion.

The cemetery of Nuri is about twice the size of that of El Kurru and contains, according to Reisner's interpretation, the tombs of nineteen kings and fifty-three queens.[142] The great pyramid of Taharqa, the largest royal monument of Kush (95 feet on a side), stands near the centre of the necropolis, while the pyramids of later kings are ranged in two lines to the south-east of it (Fig. 43). Closely packed on the opposite side of Taharqa's tomb (or cenotaph) are the much smaller pyramids of the queens (Fig. 43). The characteristic form of the pyramids at Nuri is 'stepped'; that is, the sides rise in a succession of short, narrow steps instead of having a con-tinuously sloping facing as at El Kurru. The Nuri tombs therefore resemble the present-day appearance of the Giza pyramids (Pl. XIb). Most of the kings' tombs have three subterranean chambers.

The much-destroyed pyramid at Seddenga which is attributed to Taharqa presents both an anomaly and a mystery. First discovered in 1963, it is described as follows by the excavators:

This tomb consisted of a pyramid (9·80 m. [32 ft] square at the base) built in black stones, filled with gravel and painted red. The pyramid, the remains of which stand to a height of 1·70 m. [5 ft] was surrounded on three sides by a girdle wall of black stones. On the eastern side the wall bordered a courtyard, entry to which had been by way of a sandstone pylon. We found many vestiges of this pylon, in the stairway leading down to the burial chamber and also in the court-yard; some of the blocks were decorated and showed a royal figure wearing a red crown, a vertical band of text and the lower parts of two cartouches of Taharqa. The tomb, which had been very carefully cut into the rock, consisted of an ante-room (2·30 × 2·35 m. [7 ft 6 ins. × 7 ft 8 ins.]) with a corbel-vaulted roof,

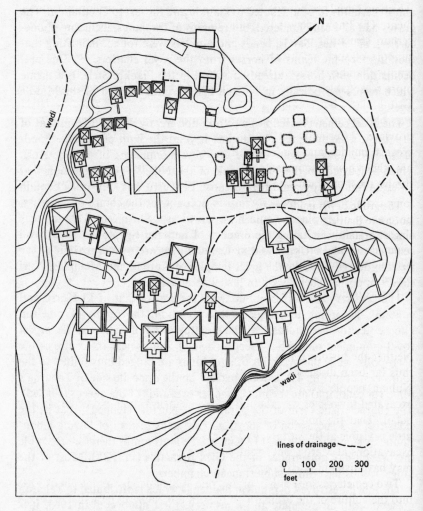

Fig. 43. Plan of Napatan royal cemetery, Nuri

and, to the west of it, a vaulted burial chamber (2·25 × 3·25 m. [7 ft 6 ins. × 10 ft 8 ins.]). The ante-room was coated with red ochre. In the center of the burial chamber there was a coffin-bench cut in the floor and paved with black slabs. The floor of the tomb was covered with a layer of earth strewn with debris, amongst which we found numerous fragments of gold leaf and scattered bones.

All the fragments of bones collected in the two rooms were consolidated and identified individually. Study has shown that they are the complete elements of a single skeleton.[143]

On the basis of this find the excavators have suggested that Seddenga is the true burial place of Taharqa, while the great pyramid at Nuri (beneath

which no burial was found) is merely a cenotaph or commemorative monument. The known cenotaph of the Pharaoh Seti I at Abydos, which has
certain structural resemblances to the pyramid of Taharqa, is cited in
support of such an interpretation.[144] In view of the fact that there are
empty chambers beneath the pyramid at Nuri, however, it seems much
more reasonable to believe that Taharqa had fully intended it as his final
resting place, but perhaps due to some mischance or fall from power he
was obliged to settle for a relatively unpretentious tomb in a remote
province.[145] Certainly the tomb at Seddenga is out of character for Nubia's
greatest builder, and contrasts strikingly with his pyramid at Nuri and all
his other known monuments. Moreover it is one of a very small group of
tombs, most of which are of Meroitic date. To quote the excavators again:

> The group of pyramids situated near the tomb of Taharqa comprises probably
> not more than eight tombs, placed east–west. Two of them were topped by a
> single pyramid with an enclosure wall ... The other six tombs had coupled-
> pyramids, in mud bricks, each pyramid built in two different periods; the first
> pyramid was situated above the burial place and the second, a smaller one, was
> placed to the east of the first one and covering the entrance to the stairway.
> The six tombs would appear to date from Meroitic times.[146]

THE HUMBLER FOLK

Neither the historical records nor the archaeological remains which have
thus far been discussed tell us much of anything about how the mass of
Nubian people lived under the Kushite monarchy. In the absence of
excavated town-sites we cannot describe a single Napatan dwelling in any
detail. That the houses were primarily of brick is inferrable from what
little is visible at the surface, and seems to be confirmed by the recent trial
excavations at Meroë, but for all we know some of the southern Nubians
may have lived in grass houses.[147]

Two cemeteries, one at Meroë and one at Sanam, give an insight of sorts
into the culture of the ordinary Nubian in the Napatan period. The South
Cemetery at Meroë, although it became the burial place of the first Meroitic
kings, had been in use as an ordinary cemetery since a much earlier date.[148]
Of its 204 known burials, therefore, all but a few are 'non-royal', and most
antedate the Meroitic period as we define it here (i.e. the time when the
royal cemeteries were established in the south). The earliest burials in the
South Cemetery belong to the time of Piankhi and Shabataka, and they
show the same preference for bed burial characteristic of the tombs at El
Kurru. The main conclusions which Reisner drew from the excavation of
the non-royal tombs are summarized by Shinnie:

> The earliest graves of the South and West Cemeteries, those in use before
> the time of Aspalta, are of special interest since here ... two traditions can be

seen existing contemporaneously. Two quite different types of burial were found. The first, or native type, consisted of a rectangular grave in which the non-mummified body was laid, usually on its left side, on a wooden bed as in the early burials at Kurru. These burials contained rich grave goods of a type known from the Kurru and earlier Nuri cemeteries. The content of the other burials is much poorer; they are narrower and contain mummified bodies placed in wooden coffins and frequently covered with a bead net of a type well known from contemporary burials in Egypt. The presence of contemporary burials of two such distinctive kinds is remarkable and it has been suggested that there were two separate communities living at Meroë at this time; that the bed burials are those of the local . . . aristocracy whilst the coffin burials of Egyptian type are those of a colony of Egyptian artisans and scribes.[149]

It has to be added by way of caution that the relative dating of the non-royal burials at Meroë is even more fraught with uncertainty than is that of the pyramids. All of them had been plundered, few contained inscribed or otherwise closely datable objects, and the growth patterns exhibited by the cemeteries as a whole were far from obvious. As a result Reisner's chronological interpretations were often largely intuitive. Not all scholars have agreed with his ordering of the sequence of graves or with his theory of two contemporary burial rites, preferring to believe that the difference between the 'native' and the 'Egyptian' graves is primarily a chronological one.

Reisner described the South Cemetery at Meroë as 'an old family cemetery which became a royal cemetery when the heads of the family became rulers of the kingdom'.[150] If this view is correct, then the 'non-royal' burials in the South Cemetery must nevertheless be those of a small governing élite, perhaps very different in life-style from the average man in the field.

A less ambiguous and more comprehensive picture of Napatan burial rites is furnished by the cemetery of Sanam, where the Griffith expedition uncovered more than 1,500 graves. The site occupied a silt bank rather than a rock shelf, and for that reason had suffered far more surface erosion than had the royal cemeteries excavated by Reisner. This may explain why no traces of enclosures or superstructures were found. Even underground, however, the graves at Sanam were relatively unpretentious.

In all the cemetery there was no sign of expensive construction, nor even of excavated chambers on a large scale. The funerary deposits were indeed plentiful in some cases and included an appreciable weight of precious metal and small objects of fine workmanship; but here again there was nothing suggestive of magnificence. One might hazard the conjecture that the leading courtiers and great princes of the land of Kush were buried elsewhere than at Sanam.[151]

Three types of graves were identified at Sanam:

1. Chamber graves with a stairway entrance, either dug as caves in the silt or walled and vaulted with brick. The burials found in these graves were

all mummified and placed in coffins or cartonnage, and they were accompanied by wheel-made pottery and other objects of Egyptian manufacture.

2. Extended burials in simple rectangular pits. They were laid on the back with the head to the west. Grave goods were not numerous, but the pottery when present was restricted to wheel-made vessels of Egyptian type.

3. Contracted burials in broad rectangular or oval pits. The body lay on either the right or left side with the hands towards the face and heels drawn up tightly to the thighs; the head was generally but by no means always to the west. These graves contained large Egyptian-made jars of a type not found in the other graves, but also included numbers of local hand-made vessels in the general tradition of the C Horizon and Kerma.

In spite of their typological distinctness, Griffith was able to demonstrate fairly conclusively that the extended and contracted burials were contemporaneous, for there were instances where each type had been intruded upon an earlier grave of the other type, and two double graves contained simultaneous burials of both types. 'In No. 221 an extended skeleton without antiquities lay head riverwards in the south half, and in the north half a contracted skeleton (on its right side, with skull in the opposite direction) accompanied by beads and characteristic ... hand-made pottery. Presumably they were man and wife.'[152]

These circumstances led Griffith to the same conclusion as Reisner:

It would seem as if they must characterize two classes of the population or two creeds rather than two periods. The Egyptianizing element would have favored the extended position, while the less cultivated and more aboriginal and conservative element, even if prosperous, preferred the primitive crouched or contracted position for the dead. According to this view the woman in 221 held to the aboriginal custom with proper conservatism while her husband followed the more fashionable style.

The contracted burials are particularly numerous at the south end of the cemetery ... Here they are almost entirely without admixture of extended burials ... while in all other parts they were very thinly scattered among vast numbers of extended burials. Several of the contracted burials in their special quarter are well furnished with jars and cups though without a single ornament. This may suggest that the people whom they represent took a very materialistic view of their requirements after death, caring only that there should be plenty of beer.[153]

Griffith's use of the term 'classes' is significant, for he evidently saw the difference between the two types of burials primarily in socio-economic terms rather than in purely ethnic terms as did Reisner. On the one side are Egyptians and 'Egyptianizing' Nubians; on the other are conservative Nubians. This is very much in keeping with the state of affairs which we have already envisioned for Lower Nubia under the New Kingdom (Ch. 9).

It is notable that at Sanam the relative statuses of the two groups seem to be the reverse of those at Meroë: the mummy-graves are the richest and the contracted burials the poorest. Somewhat surprising is Griffith's failure to identify any bed burials at Sanam; however, this may reflect the very poor preservation of organic remains in this often-flooded cemetery.

While the distinction between 'native' and 'Egyptianized' graves at Sanam and at Meroë may reflect either social or cultural factors, or a combination of the two, it is also just possible that a sex difference has gone unrecognized here. At Sanam, the distribution of contracted burials *vis-à-vis* extended burials almost exactly parallels the distribution of queens as opposed to kings in the royal cemeteries: that is, concentrated heavily in one area, but also thinly scattered among the male burials. This thesis receives some additional support from the two cases of double burial already mentioned, and it is of course very much in keeping with the cultural conservatism usually exhibited by women.

Griffith considered that the chamber tombs with mummies – the most elaborate burials at Sanam – were on the whole earlier than the simple interments, either extended or contracted.[154] If this is true it is a matter of considerable importance for chronological theories, for it suggests a temporary ascendancy of Egyptian burial rites followed by a return to more traditional practice – a reversal of the expected evolutionary sequence. If the mummy-graves are those of actual Egyptians, of course, their gradual disappearance might be explained by the emigration of artisans and scribes following the Nubian loss of Egypt, or by the gradual nativization of the Egyptian element in Nubia. Such a process is suggested also by the infrequency of inscriptions (the work of Egyptian scribes) from the later Napatan period, and by the reappearance of native hand-made pottery in the late Napatan royal tombs. However, the chronological evidence in regard to the Sanam graves is not conclusive. The one condition which this cemetery clearly demonstrates is the survival of a large, non-Egyptianized element in the Nubian population until the end of Napatan times. As we saw in Chapter 9, this is one of the factors which supports a belief that not all of Nubia was 'acculturated' under the New Kingdom.

NAPATAN SOCIETY AND ECONOMY

At first glance the social development of Nubia under the Napatan monarchs is likely to remind us of that in Egypt under the Old Kingdom, 2,000 years earlier. We get the impression of a two-class society comprising a vast peasantry and a tiny hereditary élite – essentially a barbarian chieftainship which has taken on a few of the status symbols of more complex civilization. This is the picture envisioned by Haycock when he writes that:

The social status of the earliest . . . Napatans buried in the tumuli of El Kurru had been comparatively small . . . but the kings had been the principal beneficiaries of the union of the . . . Sudan and the conquest of Egypt, and had gained a quite new status as pharaohs who built great stone pyramids and fine temples, and had commemorative texts in the mystic hieroglyphic. This broad division between rulers and ruled persisted throughout the Napatan and Early Meroitic periods, and it is not until about the reign of Amanishakhete (late 1st century BC–early 1st AD) that one first has much evidence of the emergence of a powerful class of provincial nobles . . .[155]

There may nevertheless have been important divisions in the category of the 'ruled'. If the unexcavated town remains at Kawa, Sanam, and Meroë really date back to the early years of the Kushite monarchy, then we must make room somewhere in our picture for a considerable urban middle class of artisans and small merchants; in fact, for a three-class society. How large a part was played by the middle class we shall never know until the town-sites are actually dug; in the meantime we can only fall back on the indirect and somewhat ambiguous evidence of the cemeteries.

For the time being, the graves at Sanam give us the clearest picture that we possess of Nubian society in the Napatan period. They point unmistakably to the coexistence of Egyptianized and non-Egyptianized elements in the native population. This is the same condition which we envisioned in Lower Nubia under the New Kingdom (Ch. 9), but there is an important difference. In the colonial period those Nubians who had not succumbed to Egyptian ways were still maintaining a more or less independent tribal existence on their own lands and resources – a situation comparable to that of many American Indian groups in the early twentieth century. The 'primitive' graves at Sanam do not suggest the same degree of social and cultural independence in relation to the dominant group. The difference is no longer that between a tribal people and a settled one; if it reflects any social division at all it is that between a conservative *fellaheen* and a progressive, urbanized middle class. (However, we cannot discount the possibility that it is only a difference in burial rites accorded the two sexes.) It is unfortunate that Griffith did not publish a complete register of the graves at Sanam which would allow us to calculate the relative numbers of the two groups.

What percentage of the Napatan middle class was made up of Egyptians is another of the questions for which neither history nor archaeology furnishes a satisfactory answer. The northerners had largely dominated the bureaucracy and trades under the colonial régime, although educated Nubians could find a place among them, as we saw in Chapter 9. Their numbers and their influence must have remained strong in the immediate post-colonial period, like that of the European technicians and teachers in modern African countries. Still, the situation of petty officials and entrepreneurs must have been precarious once the garrisons were withdrawn, and a good many of the Egyptians in Nubia probably gave up and went home.

In Napatan times, the Egyptian hand is unmistakable in the design and execution of the early royal monuments, for which almost certainly no Nubian of that time possessed the necessary expertise. It may also be presumed, in view of the close liaison between Jebel Barkal and Karnak, that some of the priests of Amon were Egyptians, at least until the downfall of the Nubian régime in Egypt. For the rest, the lower bureaucracy and the trades might long since have passed into Nubian hands, although their touch is nowhere evident in the products found in the early royal tombs.

The Napatan cemeteries might be expected to furnish a clue to the ethnic make-up of the middle class. As in Lower Nubia under the New Kingdom, however, the question arises: are the 'Egyptian' graves at Meroë and Sanam really those of Egyptians, or are they Egyptianized Nubians? As we saw, Reisner interpreted the evidence at Meroë in one way, and Griffith at Sanam in the other.

Reisner's picture of Napatan society, as it emerges from a number of his studies,[156] is essentially that of a persisting colonial society; that is, of an ethnically stratified society comprising a native proletariat and an Egyptian middle class. The only change since 'independence' would appear to be in the membership of the upper class, in which a native aristocracy has been substituted for the Egyptian *raj*. In the recent past, ethnically stratified societies of this kind have sometimes developed when a particularly backward colony has been rushed into political independence, or when an old but backward monarchy has undertaken a 'crash' modernization programme. In either case the native population is unable to supply the technicians and officials who make up the middle class, and it becomes necessary to recruit them entirely from abroad. This might have been the case in ancient Nubia, but it is not typical of the development of post-colonial societies.

Griffith's analysis of the Sanam graves implies the existence of a Nubian *fellaheen* and of a middle class made up of Nubians and Egyptians together – he himself made no effort to distinguish the two on ethnic grounds.[157] According to this picture the ethnically stratified society of colonial times has been partially transformed into a class-stratified society through the continual admission of Nubians to the middle class, and their assumption of the status symbols of the middle class. A similar condition prevails in most of the post-colonial societies of today, and it is, *a priori*, a more probable description of ancient Nubia than is that of Reisner. For the time being it is impossible to say more.

A better insight into the structure of society could be obtained if we knew more about the economy of Nubia in Napatan times. Again, we are

baffled by the lack of surviving texts as well as by the paucity of archaeological remains. Dunham has written that:

> The economic basis of power lay in the control of the trade along the river
> highway to Egypt, the traffic in gold from the mines in the Eastern Desert, the
> trade in cattle, hides, slaves, ostrich feathers, ebony, and the many other pro-
> ducts from the south which Egypt imported from the Sudan. In the Napatan
> district itself agriculture, while adequate for local needs, could hardly have
> formed the basis for an extensive and profitable export trade, for the region lies
> north of the rain belt, and land cultivable by irrigation from the Nile was
> limited.[158]

This is a probable assumption in view of the earlier and later history of
Kush, but the existence of an extensive foreign trade in Napatan times
remains so far unsupported by the scanty textual remains from late
dynastic Egypt, even if it seems to be implied by Herodotus.[159]

Indirectly, we can perhaps infer something about economic development
from the nature and distribution of the Napatan towns. Communities of
the size of Kawa and Sanam (so far as we can judge them from their unexcavated remains) can hardly have been supported by any other enterprise than that of trade; they were certainly not manufacturing centres of
any consequence. Moreover, the absence of important settlements between
these two places points to the continued use of the Meheila Road, rather
than the Nile Valley, as the principal route between the Third and the
Fourth Cataract (cf. Fig. 37). As we pointed out in Chapter 9, the advantage of the desert road, in addition to its directness, is in avoiding the
contrary winds in the reverse bend of the Nile between Napata and Debba.
If the towns at either end of the Meheila Road became the main urban
centres of the Napatan period, and if no important settlements grew up
between them, it is a logical inference that trade along the overland route
played an important part in their development. As we shall observe in the
next chapter, the further extension of overland trade was an even more
important factor in the development of Meroë and other cities in the
central Sudan.

Nubian control of at least some of the desert gold mines is attested by the
quantities of gold found in many of the royal tombs; it can hardly have
come from any other source. Again the evidence is wholly inferential, for
there are no inscriptions of the Kushite period at the mines. If they
remained in Nubian hands, however, this alone would be a sufficient explanation for the wealth of the Kushite monarchy. Thus the flourishing
international trade envisioned by Dunham[160] cannot be inferred simply
from the abundance and ostentation of the royal monuments; it will have
to be demonstrated more directly through the excavation of the Napatan
town-sites.

While the worldly wealth of the Nubian rulers is clearly manifest, that of the Amon-priests who shared power with them does not seem to have been on the same scale. The concentration of wealth suggests that 'the things that were Caesar's' were rendered pretty exclusively unto Caesar, and that whatever ostentation the temples enjoyed was largely through the royal largesse.[161] After Taharqa, repairs and additions to them were few and far between. The autonomous power exercised by the priests *vis-à-vis* the monarchy makes it clear that they had their own sources of income, but whether from agricultural estates or from the control of trade is uncertain. At Sanam they seem to have derived outside income from the production and sale of *ushabtis* – our earliest evidence of a manufacturing industry in Nubia.

INTERPRETATIVE SUMMARY

The collapse of Egypt's colonial empire left a power vacuum both in Nubia and in Upper Egypt. At Karnak and at Jebel Barkal the priests of Amon carried on some of the functions of government, but in time they found it necessary to ally themselves with local strongmen for support and protection. In the vicinity of Jebel Barkal their choice fell upon – or was preempted by – a Nubian family of whose origins we know nothing. From the evidence of their graves they did not belong to the Egyptianized element in the population, and we may perhaps assume that they were typical of the unschooled but militarily able commanders whom unsettled times have often raised to high place. At Jebel Barkal they became the patrons and protectors of the great cult of Amon, and from this alliance of native rulers and Egyptian or Egyptianized priesthood there arose the Kushite monarchy and the semi-theocratic state which were to dominate Nubia's dynastic age.

The power exercised by the earliest Kushite rulers probably stemmed directly from their ability to muster and command the Nubian troops upon whom both Nubia and Upper Egypt had long relied for protection. It was this factor which led to their acceptance as temporal rulers by the priests of Amon not only at Jebel Barkal, but at Karnak as well. By the sixth or seventh generation of their rule, their domains included Upper Egypt as well as Nubia.

As rulers of Upper Egypt the Nubian kings could not avoid involvement in the dynastic struggles of the northern country. In the time of Piankhi, the greatest Kushite ruler, Thebes was threatened with an invasion from the Delta, and the king was obliged to launch a major expedition for its relief. This was overwhelmingly successful and led, perhaps unexpectedly, to the submission of all of the rival dynasts in Egypt. Egypt and Nubia were temporarily reunited under a Nubian monarch, and Piankhi assumed the immemorial titles of the pharaoh.

Piankhi retired with his honours to Nubia, but the imperial ambitions of his successor provoked the hostility of Assyria, the rising power in western Asia. The later Nubian pharaohs became involved in a long struggle with Assyria for the control of Lower Egypt and Palestine. Essentially it was a tug-of-war between Nubian intrigue and Assyrian military power; each time an Assyrian army appeared the Delta princes submitted, and each time it withdrew, the Nubians were somehow able to re-establish control. In the end, however, might triumphed over cunning, and the Nubian régime was brought to an end after less than a century of rule in the north. Their brief tenure as Lords of the Two Lands had nevertheless given to the Nubian kings the experience and the outlook which enabled them to retain power in their own country for another thousand years. First at Napata and then at Meroë they continued to maintain the semblance of a pharaonic court, and they never relinquished the pharaoh's titles.

The Kingdom of Kush furnishes a classic example of a successor state: a barbarian people assuming the mantle and the burdens of empire from the hands of their former overlords. As with most barbarian empires the 'heroic age' was brief, but the parochial, pseudo-pharaonic state which succeeded it in Upper Nubia survived for a thousand years. Its ethnic make-up was non-Egyptian, and probably increasingly so with the passage of centuries, but its ideology and its cultural aspirations never significantly deviated from those of the northern country. Politically and ideologically, the balance which had been struck between Nubian strongmen and Egyptian priests in the immediate post-colonial period remained in force until the end of the kingdom.

In the early centuries of Kush, both the temporal and the spiritual centres of power were in the Napata district, close to the Fourth Cataract. We do not have a clear picture of social and economic conditions at this time, but the archaeological and textual evidence does not point to a complex, urbanized society or to extensive commerce. We seem to see rather a primitive, largely agrarian state with a small middle class, whose rulers derived their excessive wealth primarily from a monopoly of gold production. It is this condition which chiefly sets the earlier, Napatan phase of Kushite civilization apart from the later, Meroitic phase which will be considered in the following chapter.

11

THE SOUTHWARD COURSE
OF EMPIRE

THE MEROITIC CIVILIZATION OF THE STEPPELANDS

The name of Meroë, the mysterious city deep in Africa, was known to the classical world through a number of historical traditions and legends. Herodotus, relying on information supplied by travellers in Upper Egypt, described it in the fifth century BC:

> After . . . forty days' journey on land one takes another boat and in twelve days reaches a big city named Meroë, said to be the capital city of the Ethiopians. The inhabitants worship Zeus and Dionysus alone of the gods, holding them in great honour. There is an oracle of Zeus there, and they make war according to its pronouncements, taking from it both the occasion and the object of their various expeditions. . .[1]

Elsewhere he describes the 'Table of the Sun' which was allegedly the main object of Cambyses' expedition against Nubia (cf. Ch. 10):

> The Table of the Sun is said to be a meadow, situated in the outskirts of the city, where a plentiful supply of boiled meat of all kinds is kept; it is the duty of the magistrates to put the meat there at night, and during the day anyone who wishes may come and eat it. Local legend has it that the meat appears spontaneously and is the gift of the earth.[2]

Meroë was still flourishing 400 years after Herodotus, for it is mentioned by various authors of the Roman period, of whom the most important are Diodorus Siculus,[3] Strabo,[4] and Pliny.[5] None of them visited the city in person, but the relative accuracy of their information – as well as the frequent mention of Meroë by other contemporary writers[6] – is testimony to the regular intercourse which existed between imperial Rome and its southernmost neighbour.[7] If we consider also the classical influences in Meroitic culture, and the truly extraordinary quantities of foreign-made goods which are found in Meroitic archaeological sites, we can begin to appreciate the special and distinctive character of the Meroitic age. Nubia as never before and rarely since was a part of the ancient world *oikoumêne*.[8]

The monumental expressions of Meroitic civilization – the temples, the tombs, the great mural reliefs – are virtually the same as those of Napatan times. Yet the underlying social and economic basis appears significantly different. Meroitic civilization is no more the simple and direct culmination of Napatan civilization than is Ptolemaic Egypt the climax of the pharaonic ages. Each represents a major cultural renaissance after centuries of stagnation and decline. The revitalizing force in each case was the same: contact with, and partial integration into, the classical world. Pharaonic Egypt and Napatan Kush were parochial civilizations; Ptolemaic Egypt and Meroitic Kush were provincial expressions of a world civilization.[9]

The Meroitic renaissance probably reached its peak in the first century AD – long after the decline of Napata and the southward shift of the main centres of power and wealth in Kush. In the next two centuries the southern kingdom in turn suffered a rapid decline. The great upheavals and population movements which finally engulfed the Roman Empire were beginning to stir in Africa as well as in Asia, affecting the vassal states along the Empire's frontiers long before they overwhelmed its centre. Meroë may have been one of the early victims of that process. The great city seems to have been largely abandoned by the fourth century AD, and its name was soon forgotten. No memory of it survived in local tradition, and the 'City of the Ethiopians' was lost to the world's knowledge until the revival of classical learning made it known once again through the pages of Herodotus and Strabo. Even then it was often dismissed as fable: not until the end of the eighteenth century was the legend of Meroë invested with any substance. In 1772 the quixotic explorer James Bruce came upon the 'heaps of broken pedestals and pieces of obelisks' near the modern village of Bagrawiya, and wrote in his journal that 'it is impossible to avoid risking a guess that this is the ancient city of Meroë'.[10] The subsequent discovery of the remains at Napata, while verifying beyond question the existence of an ancient Nubian civilization, left some doubt as to which of its two main centres was the 'capital' known to Herodotus. The matter was not finally settled until 1910, when excavations by the University of Liverpool Expedition encountered the name Meroë in numerous inscriptions in the southern city.[11]

Since its original discovery by Bruce, the 'City of the Ethiopians' has had a chequered archaeological history. In the 1830s an unscrupulous doctor named Ferlini systematically ransacked the royal pyramids and even, by his own account, knocked the tops off several of them.[12] Reputable investigation had to wait until nearly a century later, and even then its beginnings were not auspicious. The excavations of Budge in 1903 were hardly more scientific than those of Ferlini,[13] while the five-year campaign of the University of Liverpool (1910–14), directed by John Garstang, produced little for posterity but a series of brief interim reports which appeared at the end of each season.[14] No definitive reports were ever issued, and the original field notes and collections are long since dispersed and largely inaccessible. As Shinnie somewhat charitably observes, 'The excavations were carried out in the wholesale way traditional in those days in the Nile Valley, and it is very difficult to extract from the annual reports of the excavation a proper description of those parts of the site which were excavated.'[15] The rather limited trial excavations undertaken by Shinnie himself between 1965 and 1971[16] remain up to now the only properly scientific investigations ever carried out in this most important of Nubian town-sites. The ordinary cemeteries of Meroë were also excavated in large part by the Liverpool Expedition, and have been reported only in cursory fashion. The three so-called royal cemeteries have fared somewhat better, after their initial plundering by Ferlini, for they were largely spared by the Liverpool group. All of them were excavated with customary thoroughness by the Harvard–Boston Expedition in the 1920s, and the results have recently been published in a series of monumental volumes issued by Dows Dunham, who has devoted half a lifetime to the publication of Reisner's unfinished work.[17]

It is fortunate for the archaeologist that the Meroitic was an urban age, and has left us many town remains besides those of its capital city. In the south, the important city of Musawwarat es-Sufra has been the scene of several years' recent investigations by a German expedition.[18] In the north, Meroitic remains (unlike those of the Napatan period) are abundant in Lower Nubia and the *Batn el Hajar*, and have therefore received the same systematic attention as have other archaeological sites in the region of the Aswan reservoirs. Several Meroitic villages and innumerable cemeteries have been excavated in whole or in part.[19] Thanks to this fact as well as to the inherent richness of its remains, the culture of Meroitic times is far better known than is that of any earlier period in Nubian history.

The documentary record of Meroitic times remains, however, as spotty as ever. Our external sources are no longer arrogant and boastful Egyptians, but inquiring and sometimes admiring Greeks and Romans. They furnish a good deal of objective description which the Egyptians never deigned to record, but what they gain in objectivity they lose in originality, for none of the classical authors ever saw Nubia at first hand.

The classical authors were not always as critical as they should have been and much of what was recorded was merely hearsay. They are in conflict on many points and it is significant to find one of them – Diodorus Siculus – advising the reader not to trust their accounts of Ethiopia too implicitly because most of them seemed to him either too credulous, or else purveyors of fantasies invented as a diversion.[20]

There exists also an 'internal record' of the Meroitic period, for some

Fig. 44. Example of Meroitic writing: the 'Great Stele' of Amanirenas and
Akinidad from Meroë

time in the second century BC the Nubians began, for the first time in
history, to write their own language. For their earliest inscriptions they
borrowed the Egyptian hieroglyphic characters of earlier times, but these
were soon simplified and streamlined into a cursive, purely alphabetic
script of twenty-three characters (Fig. 44).[21] The phonetic values of most
of the characters are known,[22] yet the language expressed in this long-
forgotten alphabet continues to baffle scholars despite fifty years' intensive

study. It may belong, as does modern Nubian, to the general Sudanic family of African languages, but it shows no close affinity to any known speech of today.[23] Thus, as Shinnie remarks:

> Meroitic has, with Etruscan, the distinction of being one of the two ancient languages the phonetic values of whose signs can be read with reasonable certainty, but the meaning of whose words cannot be understood. This is a great barrier to a complete understanding of Meroitic history and culture, and until this language has been successfully read and the inscriptions translated, much of the story of Meroë will remain unknown.[24]

If, then, our picture of Napatan times was long on history and short on cultural description, our picture of Meroitic times must be rather the reverse.

THE ORIGINS OF MEROË

The great city which has rightly given its name to the Meroitic age appears from the surface to be the largest community of ancient Nubia. It stands upon an undulating terrace of gravel and silt immediately overlooking the east bank of the Nile and its floodplain, which is here very narrow. The ruins confront the eye as innumerable mounds of earth thickly strewn with broken brick and fallen building stone, as well as great heaps of iron slag. Only here and there can the buildings excavated at the beginning of the century be made out; all of them are in very denuded condition. The town-site is thickly dotted over with acacia trees, for it lies within the rainfall belt. Eastwards from the town a bare and eroded gravel terrace rises gradually towards a line of low, flat-topped desert hills two or three miles distant. Here, at the foot of the hills, are the famous pyramids of Meroë; between them and the town are the 'non-royal' cemeteries and a few additional buildings, some excavated and others not (cf. Fig. 45). A short distance south of the ruins is the broad, dry bed of the Wadi Hawad, an ephemeral stream which carries much of the seasonal runoff from the great Butana Steppe.

The locale of Meroë was reported by Diodorus and several of his contemporaries to be an island,[25] and the name 'Island of Meroë' has survived to modern times. It has been and continues to be a source of misunderstanding, for the city stands high and dry upon the east bank of the Nile, and not upon an island in its midst. The 'island' referred to is the Butana Steppe, an area more than 120 miles wide which lies between the Nile and its eastern tributary, the Atbara River (Fig. 46).[26] (In similarly metaphoric fashion, modern Sudanese apply the Arabic word for island, *Gezira*, to a vast tract lying between the Blue and White Niles above their confluence at Khartoum.)

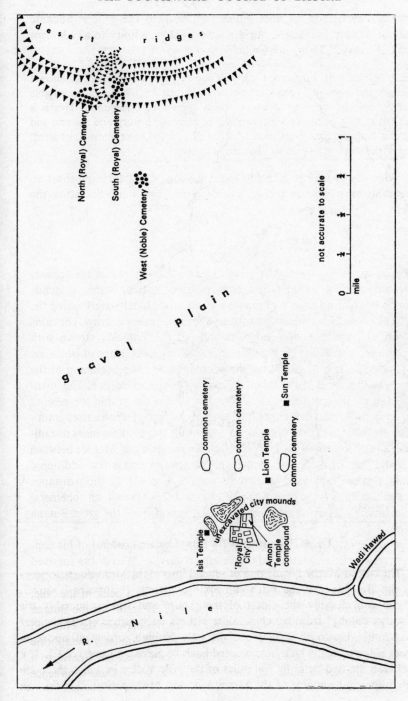

Fig. 45. Sketch map of Meroë and vicinity

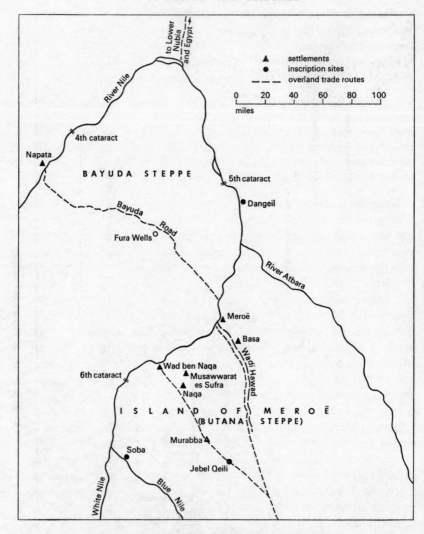

Fig. 46. Principal Meroitic sites of the steppelands

The city of Meroë is only one of several important Meroitic settlements in the area between the Fifth and Sixth cataracts. It appears, however, to be considerably the oldest of the group, and was presumably the 'mother-colony' from which Kushite settlers later spread out to the east and south. Up to now, Meroë is the only Nubian settlement upstream from Napata itself which can be dated back to Napatan times (cf. Ch. 10). Between the two cities lie 300 miles of the Nile Valley in which there are few important remains of the Meroitic or any other period. It is thus an intriguing question why advancing civilization should at this point have jumped over so large an intervening tract, to establish itself far upstream from its previous limit of penetration at the Fourth Cataract.

Many writers have stressed the environmental advantages of the 'Island of Meroë'. Dunham, for example, has written that

... Meroë lay further south, within the area of annual summer rains. While less advantageously placed than Napata for control of trade with Egypt, it was more favorable for cattle raising and was closer to the sources of wealth from the central and southern Sudan. But more important than these factors was the extensive iron smelting industry, of which the great slag heaps in the immediate vicinity of Meroë still give evidence.[27]

Napata and Meroë – the northern and southern districts in which Kushite civilization originally flourished – are in reality separated by no more than one and a half degrees of latitude (Figs. 46, 47), and the climatic difference between them is correspondingly slight. It is also true that the area of Nile floodplain available for cultivation at Napata is at least as great as that at Meroë. If the southern district enjoys any environmental advantage, it is not so much because of increased local rainfall or soil resources as because the Butana Steppe, the hinterland of Meroë, is traversed by a number of large watercourses whose headwaters lie considerably farther south in the rainfall belt, so that they seasonally carry a substantial runoff. Within these *wadis*, in the season immediately following the rains, sizeable catch-crops of millet can be and are today grown by semi-nomadic peoples who also graze large herds of cattle over the Butana grasslands. Strabo tells us that such peoples formed a large proportion of the subjects of ancient Meroë,[28] and we can also observe that ruined Meroitic cities are dotted over the western portion of the Butana Steppe, at distances up to sixty miles from the banks of the Nile.[29] Thus, Ali[30] and Shinnie[31] have argued that the basis of Meroitic settlement and prosperity in the southern region was the exploitation not of the Nile Valley but of the Butana hinterland, in a mixed economic system based as much on pastoralism as on agriculture (cf. Pl. XIIIa).

The conspicuous slag heaps of Meroë have been much remarked, and caused the great philologist A. H. Sayce to describe the place as 'the Birmingham of ancient Africa'.[32] Without excavation, however, it is impossible to estimate the size and importance of the Meroitic iron industry, or to date its origin. Enormous quantities of slag might have accumulated in the production of a relatively small amount of usable metal; they might also have accumulated over a very long period of time.[33] It is necessary to point out too that the locality of Meroë enjoys no special advantage for a smelting industry; low-grade ores are found throughout the sandstone regions of the northern Sudan, and the timber necessary for smelting can

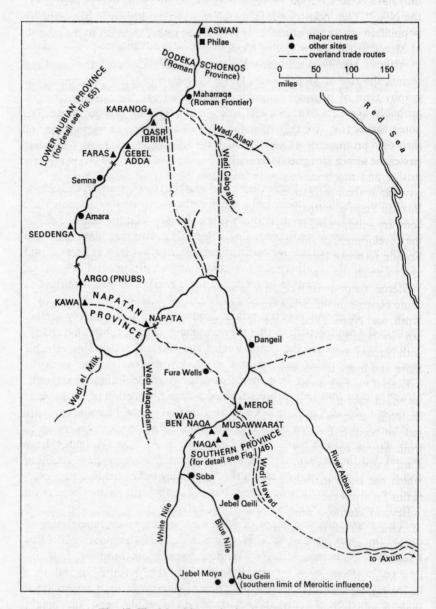

Fig. 47. The Meroitic empire in the third century A D

only have come from the acacia groves which are found everywhere along the Nile.[34] The industry could therefore have developed in any existing population centre; most probably it followed rather than led to the growth of Meroë as the major city of Kush.

Without wholly discounting the natural advantages of the southern region, the rise of Meroë seems better explained in terms of human geography than of physical geography. Like nearly all the world's cities, it probably owed its existence less to natural resources than to trade. We noted earlier (Ch. 10) that Napata and Kawa may have achieved some of their own prominence as the termini of the Meheila desert road, which bypasses the upper Dongola Reach and its adverse winds. Meroë represents a further and much more significant extension of this overland trade. The city lies at the upstream end of a great desert road which cuts across the Bayuda Steppe, by-passing both the Fifth and Fourth Cataracts and the contrary winds of the Abu Hamed Reach (Fig. 46). Almost certainly, it was the development of this overland route which enabled commerce and civilization to break through the longstanding barrier of the Fourth Cataract and to reach the central Sudan.

Meroë, then, owed its existence at first to the Bayuda Road. The desert route became the lifeline connecting the northern and southern districts of Kush, and Napata and Meroë were its termini. Once established, the southern city became also the main staging point for overland trade not only with Napata, but ultimately with Egypt as well. Napata and Kawa declined more and more to the status of entrepôts.

Even if we had no direct evidence of the existence of the Bayuda Road, we could infer it from the almost total absence of Meroitic remains along the Nile between Meroë and Napata. We have in addition, however, the stele of Nastasen, describing his progress across the desert when he came from Meroë to Napata for his coronation (cf. Ch. 10). At the wells of Fura, halfway across the Bayuda Steppe, there are the ruins of a stone fort which has been attributed to the Meroitic period,[35] though its origin remains far from certain.[36]

Beyond Meroë, a number of trade routes extended far into the interior of Africa. From this point southwards the Nile was navigable without interruption virtually to the farthest reaches of the Sudan, the Sixth Cataract at Shabaloka presenting only a very minor obstacle. The presence of a Meroitic village site at Abu Geili (Fig. 47) suggests that riverain commerce carried far up the Blue Nile and possibly also the White Nile, above their confluence at modern Khartoum. South-eastwards from Meroë across the Butana Steppe ran the historic trade route to the highlands of Abyssinia – the road travelled by the army which may finally have destroyed the Nubian city (cf. Ch. 13). Still another route led eastwards by way of the Sinkat Pass to the ancient Red Sea port of Suakin. It was probably the convergence of these trade routes which in time brought Meroë to the position of political and economic supremacy within the Kushite empire, just as in the late Middle Ages it was the convergence of the same roads which led to the rise of Shendi, twenty-five miles south of Meroë, as the great entrepôt of Sudan caravan trade.[37]

If Meroë owed its beginnings to the Bayuda Road, its final ascendency – and the eclipse of Napata – were due in all probability to the development of still another overland trade route. This was the famed Korosko Road to Egypt. Leaving the river at Abu Hamed and rejoining it far downstream in Lower Nubia, it by-passed the entire great bend of the Nile and its innumerable hazards to navigation (Fig. 47). The route was certainly known as far back as New Kingdom times, for it was in large part the same road which led to the Wadi Cabgaba goldfields.[38] The 'boundary stelae' erected by Thutmose I and Thutmose III at Kurgus, near its southern terminus, probably testify to the existence of the Korosko Road in the early XVIII Dynasty (cf. Ch. 9). It was apparently not until Meroitic times, however, that the desert road became the main link between the Central Sudan and the Mediterranean world.

The early history of trans-Saharan caravan trading is obscure. Although greatly facilitated by the introduction of the camel (probably in the last century BC),[39] its beginnings certainly go back several centuries earlier.[40] The Egyptians had employed donkey caravans to bring goods from Nubia as far back as the Old Kingdom (Ch. 7), but they were at heart a riverain people who preferred to use boats when they could. Carthaginian merchants brought gold and carbuncles from southern Libya, apparently employing donkeys, oxen, and even horses for transport.[41] In Africa as in Asia, however, it seems to have been the indigenous desert dwellers who first developed caravan trading on a large scale, thus turning from simple nomadism to mercantile entrepreneurship. In the last millennium BC their activities largely redrew the economic and political map of the Near East. The great desert 'seas' became increasingly navigable, and new colonies, new civilizations, and finally new empires grew up along their 'shores'. Sabaea in South Arabia, Meroë in the Sudan, and Carthage in North Africa were early beneficiaries of the caravan trade; it found its climactic expression a thousand years later in the great empire and civilization of Islam.

The advent of the caravans ended the age-old dependence of trans-Saharan commerce upon the Nile. While the river route remained important for centuries to come, it no longer monopolized the traffic in the products of tropical Africa. From that moment we can trace the decline in Nubia's economic fortunes which has continued into modern times.

While we know little about the first development of caravan trade over the Korosko Road, it had evidently become the main economic link between the Sudan and Egypt by the last century BC.[42] Its development was a boon to Meroë, for it shortened the distance to Egypt by more than half as well as avoiding the worst navigational hazards of the Middle Nile. As the hub of a network of inland trade routes, the southern city retained its importance as a staging area for the caravan trade. Napata and Kawa, on the other hand, were now largely by-passed. What economic importance they retained was probably chiefly connected with the export of dates, which do not grow well in the rainfall belt farther south. The Korosko Road, then, was in all probability the largest single factor contributing to the supremacy of Meroë and the eclipse of Napata. As a result we can look upon the later phase of the Kushite empire as an important turning point in African history: it is at the same time the last of the great Nilotic empires and the first of the 'empires of the steppes' which arose in the wake of the caravan trade.

The selection of Meroë as the favoured residence of the later Napatan kings may be cited as one additional factor contributing to the rise of the southern city and the decline of Napata. A number of writers have interpreted the 'transfer of the capital' (cf. Ch. 10) as evidence that Meroë had already supplanted Napata as the economic centre of Kush,[43] but this is not necessarily the case. It might be evidence only of the monarchy's desire to escape from the entrenched influence of the priesthood of Amon at Jebel Barkal. History abounds in parallel cases, beginning with the attempt by Akhenaton a thousand years earlier to escape from the selfsame priesthood, by removing the pharaonic court from Thebes to Tell el-Amarna. The royal courts of China, Persia, and the Islamic Empire were notoriously peripatetic for the same reason, and even some of the mighty Caesars found it expedient to reside far from Rome, to be free from the dictates of the Senate and the Praetorian Guard. The localities favoured by these monarchs were frequently unimportant prior to their selection as royal residences.

We saw in Chapter 10 that the 'constitution' of the Kushite state rested upon a delicate balance of power between the monarchy and the priesthood, with all its latent potential for rivalry and intrigue. We know of at least two occasions, in the reigns of Aspalta and of Arkamani, when the power struggle broke out into open conflict. This persisting tension within the state may well have been the factor which first induced the Napatan kings to reside across the river from the main religious centre at Jebel Barkal (cf. Ch. 10), and later to remove themselves altogether from its proximity by establishing their principal residence at Meroë. The result was a kind of geographical compromise between church and state, which persisted during the centuries when Napata remained the religious 'capital' while Meroë was the secular 'capital'. Since the control of wealth was largely in the hands of the monarchy, however, the removal of the royal court can only have benefited Meroë at the expense of Napata.

So long as the ruins of Meroë remain largely unexcavated it will be fruitless to speculate further about the date and the reasons for the city's rise. Whatever survives from its early history lies buried beneath the accumulated debris of later centuries, and very little of it has been brought to light. From chance finds in the town and from the indirect evidence of its cemeteries we can be reasonably sure that the settlement goes back to the time of Piankhi,[44] that it was a place of sufficient importance to merit a royal inscription in the time of Aspalta,[45] and that it was the preferred residence of some of the last Napatan kings. We cannot, however, identify it as the spiritual centre of Kush until it became also the locus of the royal cemeteries. For this reason the reign of Arkakamani, the first ruler to be buried at Meroë, has been selected in this work to mark the beginning of the Meroitic era.

MONARCHS AND MONUMENTS

According to the chronology of Reisner, forty generations of kings and queens ruled at Meroë and were buried in its royal cemeteries.[46] Our knowledge of all but a handful of them begins and ends with their tombs. Their dates, their achievements, and even in many cases their names are unknown to us; were it not for their pyramids we could not even be sure that ancient Kush was always a monarchy. From this it should be apparent that Reisner's great historical scheme is not so much a dynastic chronology as it is a developmental study of the royal tombs, from which the existence of a succession of rulers is inferred. It is impossible even today to discuss the Meroitic monarchy in any other context than that of its funerary monuments.

The royal cemeteries of Meroë are situated in the desert two to three miles east of the city. Unlike the other Kushite royal monuments they are not conspicuously visible from the riverbank, for the pyramids blend into the background of higher desert hills which rise just behind them. Approached more closely, however, the largest and best preserved of the pyramids take shape as an impressive, serried rank along the crest of a rocky desert ridge, rising perhaps 100 feet above the surrounding gravel plain (Pl. XIIIb). From the summit of the ridge, other and smaller pyramids are seen scattered rather irregularly along its eastern flank. This group of tombs comprises the so-called North Cemetery of Meroë. Looking southwards across a broad, sandy *wadi*, the much more destroyed pyramids of the South Cemetery can be seen at the top of another stony ridge, about 250 yards distant. The West Cemetery, which is not conspicuous from its surface remains, lies between the two pyramid groups and the remains of the town (Fig. 45).

The physical separation of the North, South, and West Cemeteries has some social and historical significance, as we shall note in a moment. The three nevertheless represent a continuum of historical development, and can be treated for all practical purposes as a single burial complex. As a group, they present the largest collection of pyramids anywhere in existence.

The South Cemetery at Meroë is considerably older than the northern; it was the burial place at least of the upper-class families of the town from the days of Piankhi.[47] By the time the rulers of Kush chose it for their burial place, however, most of the suitable building sites had been exhausted, and as a result only three kings and six royal consorts found room for their pyramids there. This group of tombs is thus unique among the royal cemeteries of Kush in that it comprises only a few genuinely royal monuments surrounded by a much larger number of humbler tombs – nearly two hundred in all. Reisner described it as 'an old family cemetery which became a royal cemetery when the heads of the family became rulers of the kingdom'.[48]

After the third royal interment in the South Cemetery, it was necessary to choose a new burial site about 250 yards further north. In this North Cemetery all or nearly all of the remaining Meroitic rulers were buried until the end of the dynasty. Unlike its neighbour, the North Cemetery is the most exclusively royal of all the Kushite cemeteries; all but six of its forty-four tombs are believed to be those of actual reigning monarchs or crown princes.[49] Retainers, lesser nobility, and even the queens consort were relegated to the West Cemetery, situated in the gravel plain below the royal pyramids. The West Cemetery therefore contains no tombs of reigning monarchs; it is nevertheless classed among the royal cemeteries of Kush because it was the burial place of lesser members of the royal family and other nobility. The common people of Meroë were buried in a series of cemeteries immediately beyond the outskirts of the city, which have been excavated but never published.[50]

The pyramids at Meroë continue the evolutionary development begun at El Kurru and Nuri (Ch. 10).[51] The tombs in the South Cemetery, while not identical to those at Nuri, are reasonably close to them in size and design. In both places the superstructure is stair-stepped, and rests upon a conspicuously projecting foundation course. The same characteristics are found in what are presumed to be the first four tombs in the North Cemetery. Beginning in the fifth generation, however, a structural innovation appears. The faces of the pyramid are still stair-stepped, but the corners are now dressed off to a smooth and continuous slope (Pl. XIVa). The corner-dressed pyramids, as I will call them, represent the most distinctive achievement of the Kushite royal tomb. There are ten of these structures at Meroë and eight at Jebel Barkal (to be discussed presently). In addition to their embellished corners they have unusually large and elaborately decorated chapels adjoining the east face of the pyramid, and most have three underground chambers. Their typical arrangement and decoration is described by Reisner:

> The first room of the three was a small ante-chamber on the walls of which were inscribed the paragraphs of the 125th Chapter of the Book of the Dead [cf. Pl. XIVb]; the second room was very wide across the axis of the pyramid and bore the 'Negative Confession,' also from the Book of the Dead; the third room, a long one, contained the actual burial. The greater part of the offerings were in the third room but they also overflowed into the other two. This three-room type continued in use as the traditional form of the king's tomb for five centuries (600–100 BC).[52]

It will be noted that the three-room royal tomb reproduces, in miniature, the layout of the typical Kushite temple (cf. Figs. 40, 41). The outer offering chamber of the tomb corresponds to the forecourt of the temple; the transversely extended second chamber takes the place of the great pylon gate, and the inner, burial chamber represents the sanctuary. In the largest of the burial chambers pillars of rock were left, either standing free or adjoining the side walls, to help support the roof. In a few tombs there are painted scenes in Egyptian style in addition to the hieroglyphic inscriptions.[53]

Subsequent changes in the architecture of the royal tombs were nearly all of a degenerative nature.[54] After about ten generations the pyramid with dressed corners was abandoned; there was a return at first to the simpler form of stepped pyramid, and then to the still older smooth-faced pyramid which had characterized the early Kushite royal tombs at El Kurru (Ch. 10). The later pyramids, however, had only a facing of dressed stone over a poorly constructed inner core of rubble, and the last three or four were built of brick. From the time of the corner-dressed pyramids onwards there was also a continual reduction in the size of both superstructures and burial chambers. Some of the last of the royal pyramids measured no more than twenty-three feet on a side – 'miserable little red-brick copies of the fine earlier pyramids of masonry', as Arkell describes them.[55] The burial chambers were hardly more than rough-hewn caves, without decoration.

The objects found in the Meroitic royal tombs convey only a hint of their original wealth, for every one of the chambers had been thoroughly plundered. Even so, the abundance and variety of goods left behind by the robbers is astonishing. In the later tombs we can also observe another kind of offering, which harks back to the mortuary practices of a much earlier time. 'In almost all these tombs evidences were found of *sati*-burial, that is, the burial of the hareem and of servants with the king in order that their spirits might serve him in the other world.'[56] Sacrificial burials were found also in some of the largest 'private' tombs in the West Cemetery. In most cases plunderers had so disturbed the remains that it was impossible to ascertain the original burial position or even the number of the sacrificed retainers. The largest number of *sati* burials which could be identified in any one tomb was six [57] – a relatively modest figure in comparison with the wholesale human sacrifices of both earlier and later times (Ch. 8 and Ch. 13). Sacrificial burials of dogs, camels and horses were considerably more common than were human interments; their remains were found chiefly on the stairways leading down to the burial chambers.[58]

Reisner believed that the royal cemeteries were established at Meroë when the pyramid-field at Nuri was 'full', the earliest of the southern tombs being the direct successor of the last tomb at Nuri.[59] This theory left unexplained the little cluster of pyramids which stands in rather forlorn isolation in the desert west of Jebel Barkal. They are unquestionably later in date than any of the other tombs in the Napata district; their closest typological affinities are not to Nuri or El Kurru but to some of the pyramids at Meroë. There seems little doubt, in fact, that the cemetery at Jebel Barkal is in part contemporary with those in the south, which makes it difficult to explain in terms of a single, uninterrupted royal succession. A further complication arises from the fact that the Barkal pyramids are themselves divided into two distinct clusters of rather different type.[60] One group comprises corner-dressed pyramids comparable to the best of those at Meroë; the other is made up of plain, stepped pyramids.

Superstructures of the size and type found at Jebel Barkal are associated only with the tombs of reigning monarchs at Meroë, and it therefore seems reasonable to assume that the Barkal pyramids are also those of kings and queens. Nevertheless only one royal name, that of Queen Nawidemak,[61] has been found in any of the twenty-three Barkal pyramids. The others, like many of the later pyramids at Meroë, cannot be definitely associated with any known ruler.

The anomalies of the Barkal cemetery have been explained in several ways. Reisner envisioned two short-lived rival dynasties which had been set up at Napata, one immediately following the emigration of the main ruling family to Meroë and the other 150 years later.[62] This was, typically, the theory which offered the most logical explanation for the typology of the Barkal pyramids, rather than that which best fitted the external evidence. Contemporary texts, in fact, make it certain that there were rulers at Meroë whose fiat was acknowledged both at Napata and at Kawa during the times when the supposed rival dynasties held sway.[63] As a result Macadam has rejected Reisner's 'First Meroitic Kingdom of Napata', preferring to view the plain pyramids at Jebel Barkal as part of the mainstream of Kushite cemetery development, intermediate in time between Nuri and the South Cemetery at Meroë.[64] Dunham has taken just the opposite tack, accepting the first rival dynasty at Napata but rejecting the second. The corner-dressed pyramids at Barkal are viewed by him as the tombs of legitimate rulers at Meroë who for one reason or another preferred burial in the hallowed ground of their earlier ancestors.[65] Hintze, whose *Studien zur Meroitischen Chronologie*[66] is the most recent important work on the subject, has come out in favour of Reisner's original scheme, but has since been forced to modify a good part of his own chronology in the light of his discoveries at Musawwarat es-Sufra.[67] As Gadallah remarks, 'it appears that Meroitic chronology will remain for a long time subject to changes and modifications whenever new evidence appears'.[68] The continuing debate can only serve to illustrate how much we have still to learn about even the most essential features of the Kushite monarchy.[69]

While the correct succession of the Meroitic kings need not greatly trouble the cultural historian, the question of unity or division within the state is of course important to our understanding of the social and political tenor of the times. So long as we have no more reliable guide than the typology and presumed sequence of the pyramids we can never hope to answer it; we can only observe that the history of other regions furnishes many parallels to the situation originally envisioned by Reisner. Very few multi-centred empires have persisted for as long as did Kush without coming unstuck at least once or twice, and the tendency of many was to come unstuck at the same places again and again. Egypt, Mesopotamia, and China all present examples of repeated disintegration and reunification.

Unlike the empires just named, ancient Kush was not put together by the forcible unification of ethnically and socially distinct regions. In the beginning it was a compact socio-political unit administered from a single centre at Napata. It nevertheless became a multi-centred empire after the establishment of extensive colonies in the Meroë region, and more particularly after the migration thither of the royal court, leaving the priesthood of Amon still entrenched in its ancient seat at Napata. That this geographical separation of the spiritual and temporal powers was fraught with danger of political schism appears self-evident. In a sense the monarchy had abdicated the historic role as patron and protector of the Amon-cult which had brought it to power five hundred years earlier (cf. Ch. 10). We should therefore have no difficulty in envisioning, as did Reisner, that someone arose or was created to fill the vacated seat of royal power at Napata.

While the coexistence of two royal powers thus seems a logical possibility, the relationship between them poses a more difficult problem. A number of alternative explanations suggest themselves. On one hand, we can easily imagine the priests of Amon setting up a puppet dynasty in retaliation for the emigration of the legitimate rulers. The proximity of its tombs to the sacred precinct of Amon might be significant in this regard; at the very least it suggests that the individuals buried at Jebel Barkal enjoyed the special favour and support of the priesthood. At the same time we have to acknowledge the absence of any suggestion of strife within the Meroitic state, while the architectural similarity of the pyramids at Jebel Barkal and at Meroë seems to indicate close communication between the two groups of rulers. If contemporaneous dynasties did indeed rule at Meroë and at Napata, then, it seems that they did so by mutual consent.

What might have been the terms of their agreement? Was there a temporary division of the empire, similar to that which was made in the Roman Empire when it became too unwieldy to govern from a single centre? Or, as seems more probable, were the Napatan monarchs vassals of the Meroites, under the kind of feudal arrangement which was already familiar in Egypt and the Near East? Or, finally, were the Napatans simply viceroys or satraps of the southern monarchy? Whatever the explanation, there is much besides the Barkal pyramids to suggest that Napata remained a political power centre long after the emigration of the main ruling family to Meroë. Both Strabo[70] and Dio Cassius[71] regarded it as the Nubian capital in 23 BC, when it was attacked and pillaged by a Roman army. Millet believes that in the second and third centuries AD the whole of northern Nubia, from the Fourth Cataract to the Egyptian frontier, was a semi-autonomous region governed by a line of hereditary viceroys at Napata.[72]

ROYAL INSCRIPTIONS

Only about a dozen Meroitic kings have left any account of themselves other than their tombs. One of the earliest and best known of them is Arkamani, who is probably to be recognized as the Ergamenes of Diodorus Siculus.[73] He is important historically as the first Nubian king who established formal relations with the Ptolemaic rulers of Egypt – a circumstance which will be discussed more fully in the next chapter.[74] His dates have been the subject of a good deal of dispute, but most writers place him in the latter half of the third century BC.[75] According to Diodorus he had a smattering of Greek learning; how he came by it is not specified. The same author relates that Arkamani slew the priests of Amon at Jebel Barkal and put an end to their historic power of life and death over the Kushite monarch. The pyramid of Arkamani is probably the third of those built in the North Cemetery at Meroë; its chapel is remarkable for containing one of the last intelligible texts in Egyptian hieroglyphics inscribed on any Meroitic funerary monument.[76] Subsequent inscriptions are in Meroitic hieroglyphics or Meroitic cursive, or, not infrequently, in meaningless imitations of Egyptian hieroglyphics.

Several rulers of the second and first centuries BC left dedicatory or commemorative inscriptions in the temples of Meroë and Napata. All of them are in the Meroitic cursive script, and their subject matter can be made out only vaguely if at all. The longest and best known of the group is the 'Great Stele' of Queen Amanirenas and her son and co-regent Akinidad, found in one of the temples at Meroë. It seems to be in part an account of military operations, one of which may have been against the Roman army of Petronius which attacked Napata in 23 BC (see Ch. 12).[77]

The great builders of the Meroitic era were King Natakamani and Queen Amanitere, whose joint reign probably coincides more or less with the lifetime of Christ. They were apparently co-rulers for life, and their names never appear in royal inscriptions except in conjunction with one another. From their various dedication stelae it appears that they undertook major restorations in the Great Temples of Amon both at Napata and at Meroë and in several other temples, as well as building at least two wholly new temples in the southern city of Naqa. They are associated in their inscriptions with three different crown princes; apparently the first two died in infancy. A third son, Sherkarer, lived to succeed them. His only known monument is a victory stele carved on a rock at Jebel Qeili, far out in the grassland of the Butana Steppe (for the location see Fig. 46).[78] It shows the king receiving the blessing of the sun god and triumphing over unnamed enemies, and is remarkable for its conjunction of Egyptian, Hellenistic, and perhaps oriental artistic influence (Fig. 48).[79] It is the most southerly Meroitic royal monument yet known, and also the last royal inscription of any consequence in the history of Kush. The kingdom as a whole was neither impoverished nor culturally backward during the first and second centuries AD, but its rulers must have been undistinguished, for almost no record survives of them. Of the twenty or more kings who followed Sherkarer, fewer than half can be named (cf. Table VI).

It should not be supposed that the textual history of Kush ends with the royal inscriptions. As of now the bulk of our documentary material from the Meroitic period comes not from the region of the capital but from the far northern frontier of the empire, in the immediate vicinity of Aswan. Here a large number of scribes – Greek and Egyptian as well as Nubian – were employed in the service of various Meroitic officials, and they have left a veritable library of graffiti on the walls of the Lower Nubian temples. Fortunately for the historian many of these are in Greek and Egyptian demotic rather than in Meroitic, and can be read without much difficulty.[80] However, they have little to say about the kingdom far away in the south; their concern is for people and events closer at hand. Discussion of

Fig. 48. Victory relief of King Sherkarer, Jebel Qeili

them is therefore best reserved until we consider the whole important question of Meroitic reoccupation in Lower Nubia, in Chapter 12.

THE CITIES OF THE STEPPELANDS

The ruins of Meroë may cover an area up to a mile square, though their full extent has never been determined. We have no idea of the layout of the town as a whole; the Liverpool Expedition concentrated on a few of the monumental buildings and did not sample the intervening areas. Red (burned) brick was certainly used extensively as a building material, for fragments of it litter the unexcavated mounds of the city. However, we can

313

hardly doubt that, as in all periods of Nubian history, the bulk of the humbler buildings were of mud (unburned) brick.

Of the excavated parts of the site, which can be described after a fashion from the brief published reports,[81] the largest and most interesting is the so-called Royal City. This was a walled precinct more or less rectangular in shape, some 300 yards long and about half as wide. Within the walls was a veritable labyrinth of buildings, most of them monumental in size and ornamentation, which were presumed by Garstang to be the main installations of the royal family (Fig. 49). Except for the enclosure wall itself there was very little building in stone; most of the buildings were of mud

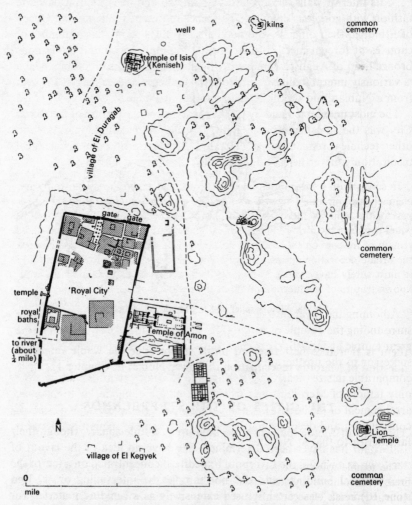

Fig. 49. Plan of the 'Royal City' and adjacent portions of the ruins of Meroë

brick, though many had an exterior facing of burned brick. (The use of this material as an exterior veneer is explained by the location of Meroë within the rainfall belt. Burned brick was almost never employed in sites further north because its resistance to erosion was unneeded.) The buildings in the Royal City had been repaired and rebuilt innumerable times, bespeaking a very long and complex history of occupation.

Near the centre of the royal enclosure were two very large square buildings, nearly identical in size, which were believed to be palaces. Other buildings were interpreted as magazines, audience chambers, and domestic quarters for the palace staff. There was also a little prostyle temple: '... its interior walls are covered with stucco and decorated in barbaric fashion with gorgeous colours. The scenes represent the King and Queen of Ethiopia, their officials, and maybe, their allies, as well as a number of captives of foreign race.' [82] In front of this temple was found the famous bronze head of Augustus, frequently illustrated in books on Nubia, which is variously interpreted as a gift from the emperor and as part of the loot from a Nubian raid on the Roman temples at Philae. [83]

The most unexpected and by far the most distinctive feature of the Royal City was the so-called Roman Bath. It lacks the heating apparatus and other technical refinements of Roman baths in Europe, but its classical inspiration is nevertheless unmistakable.

It consists of a large brick-lined tank with an elaborate system of water channels leading into it from a well nearby. A ledge running round the upper part of the tank was decorated with plaster figures and medallions, as well as water spouts in the form of lion heads. All these features were painted, and traces remain of frescoes on the stump of an upper wall. Both the general design and the ornate decoration strongly suggest that this was a place of recreation, and it must surely have been a swimming bath, a provincial variant of the well-known feature of Mediterranean life of the period. [84]

Adjoining the royal enclosure on its eastern side was a smaller enclosure surrounding the Temple of Amon (Fig. 49) – the southern equivalent of the great temple at Jebel Barkal. That it was intended as a rival and perhaps a successor to the northern temple is suggested by the fact that it is nearly comparable in size (nearly 500 ft long) and to some extent in plan; it is the only temple of Meroitic times which retains the elongate, multiple-court arrangement of the largest Egyptian and Napatan temples. In all aspects of construction and decoration, however, the Temple of Amon at Meroë is far inferior to that at Napata.

The temple was constructed largely of brick, the facing bricks alone being fired, with columns, pylons, and doorways faced with dressed blocks of sandstone. It consists of an outer hall of peristyle type showing signs of at least two periods of building. In the middle of the hall was a small stone shrine with the names of Netekamani and Amanitare on the walls, and to the west of it a stone dais, or pulpit, with steps and engraved scenes of bound and kneeling prisoners. Beyond this court was a series of smaller ones leading to the sanctuary in which was an altar decorated with religious scenes. The so-called Hall of Columns is an unusual feature and its purpose is not clear. The pillars were painted with blue and other colors on white stucco, and at the west end is a raised dais approached by a short flight of steps.[85]

There is unfortunately no clue as to when the Temple of Amon was originally built. Its restoration by Natakamani and Amanitere suggests that it was at least several decades old in their time, about the beginning of our era. In the immediate vicinity of the Amon Temple, the University of Calgary Expedition in 1976 found traces of four additional temples the presence of which had been previously unsuspected.

The Liverpool Expedition excavated four other temples and shrines at Meroë: the so-called Isis, Lion, and Sun Temples and the Shrine of Apis. All of them are situated at or beyond the outskirts of the main settled area. They are small, stone buildings of one or two rooms, typical of later Meroitic temples and in no way comparable to the great Amon Temple. (The characteristics of the Meroitic temple will be discussed more fully in later pages.) The most interesting of the lesser temples is the 'Sun Temple', whose plan is shown in Fig. 50. As Shinnie describes it:

> The temple was surrounded by a *temenos* wall of red brick with stone-faced doorways as in the Amon Temple. Inside this enclosure a ramp led to a platform with a colonnade enclosing the sanctuary. The outside wall of this platform was decorated with a series of reliefs, now very much disintegrated. The sanctuary was approached by a flight of stone steps, and its floors and walls were covered with blue glazed tiles. That there had also been reliefs on the walls of the corridor surrounding the sanctuary is shown by a surviving portion depicting a royal figure and three cartouches which give the name of Akinidad . . .[86]

Because of its location in a 'meadow' outside the city, and the finding in it of a stone block inscribed with a solar disc, this building has been somewhat imaginatively identified as the 'Table of the Sun' of which Herodotus wrote (see above).

The famous slag heaps of Meroë are a series of very large mounds strewn over with discarded matrix and other refuse from smelting operations. They have been the subject of a great deal of discussion and the basis for much historical speculation. Dunham has identified the iron industry as the foundation of Meroitic prosperity,[87] and other writers have confidently spoken of Meroë as the centre from which iron-working spread to all the peoples of tropical Africa.[88] A. H. Sayce set the tone for much of the later historical speculation when he wrote in one of the early reports on Meroë that

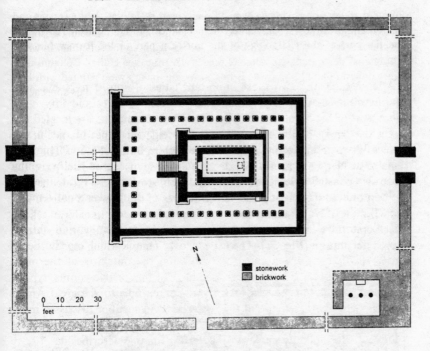

Fig. 50. Plan of Sun Temple, Meroë

... Mountains of iron-slag enclose the city mounds on their northern and eastern sides, and excavation has brought to light the furnaces in which the iron was smelted and fashioned into tools and weapons. Meroë, in fact, must have been the Birmingham of ancient Africa; the smoke of its iron-smelting furnaces must have been continually going up to heaven, and the whole of northern Africa might have been supplied by it with implements of iron. Where the Egyptians used copper or bronze, the Ethiopians used iron. There was no copper or bronze age, apparently, in the Sudan; its inhabitants passed from the age of stone into that of iron.[89]

In spite of this confident assertion we remain almost totally ignorant of the nature and significance of iron-working at Meroë or anywhere else in the Sudan.[90] After the excavation of several thousand Meroitic graves, however, we can be reasonably certain that iron tools were far from abundant during this period; they were in fact much less common than bronze tools.[91] In an article appropriately titled 'The Myth of Meroë and the African Iron Age', Bruce Trigger has recently concluded that

... While iron objects appear in the Sudan early in the twenty-fifth dynasty, an iron-working industry does not appear to have been established there before the fourth century BC,[92] and throughout the Meroitic period most of the iron

317

objects that were produced were small ones, used mainly as light weapons and for household purposes. Only after the decline of Meroë did iron become an essential part of the technology of the northern part of the former Meroitic empire . . .[93]

After Meroë, the two most important cities of southern Nubia were Musawwarat es-Sufra and Naqa, situated between forty and fifty miles south-west of the royal capital (Fig. 46). These settlements are located not along the banks of the Nile but twelve to eighteen miles inland, in the valleys of two great *wadis* which drain the western Butana Steppe. The town remains at Naqa are nearly as extensive as those of Meroë itself, and the place also boasted at least seven temples, all in stone.[94] As a group they are the best built and the best preserved structures of the Meroitic period. The Lion Temple of Natakamani and Amanitere is famous for its exterior reliefs, which epitomize the somewhat hypertrophied Meroitic–Egyptian style of carved decoration (Fig. 51). The little 'kiosk' temple which stands just in

Fig. 51. Meroitic temple reliefs, Lion Temple, Naqa
The scene shows King Natakamani and Queen Amanitere worshipping the lion-god Apedemak (shown with three heads)

front of it exhibits a remarkable combination of Egyptian and Graeco–Roman architectural influences (Pl. XVa).[95] It is unlike any other temple in Upper Nubia, but bears a considerable resemblance to the 'Kiosk of Trajan' on the island of Philae, close to Aswan. The numerous temples at Naqa mark this as one of the most important religious centres in ancient Nubia as well as a town of the first magnitude. Two large cemeteries are also located near by. All of these remains are unexcavated at the present writing.

Ten miles to the north of Naqa lies Musawwarat es-Sufra, in many ways the most extraordinary site in all Nubia. Here there seem to be no town remains and no cemeteries; only a cluster of monumental, stone buildings.[96] The largest and most conspicuous by far is the Great Enclosure – a labyrinthine cluster of open plazas, corridors and chambers which has no parallel in Nubian or Egyptian architecture (Fig. 52). Recent excavations here by the Berlin Academy of Sciences[97] have done much to clarify the plan of the enclosure, but have shed no light on its origin or purpose. The acres of bare, beautifully smooth sandstone walls are entirely devoid of reliefs or inscriptions, though they have been an irresistible temptation to graffito-writers from ancient to modern times. Shinnie describes the site as follows:

The 'Great Enclosure' consists of a number of buildings and walled enclosures surrounding a temple built on a platform, rather similar in lay-out to the Sun

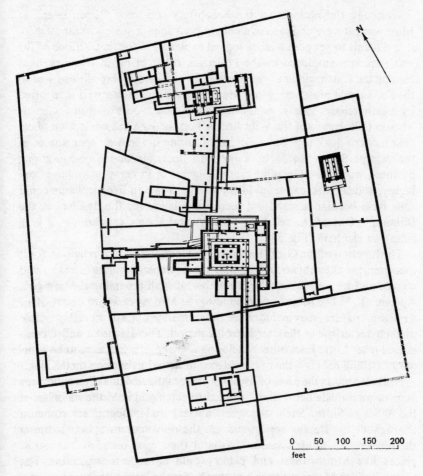

Fig. 52. Plan of the Great Enclosure, Musawwarat es-Sufra

319

Temple at Meroe. On stylistic grounds, this central temple appears to belong to the first century AD or a little earlier,[98] but there are no inscriptions other than secondary graffiti, which are plentiful. This temple is surrounded by a colonnade, some of whose columns have interesting reliefs. Outside the colonnaded temple is a series of corridors and ramps which connect the various parts of the complex, and which are not known from any other Meroitic site. The number of representations of elephants in the sculptures suggests that this animal played an important part at Musawwarat es-Sufra; the large enclosures may have been designed to herd them in, the ramps being for their convenience since they could more easily negotiate them than they could steps. It may be that here was a center for the training of elephants for military and ceremonial purposes. The remarkable wall terminating in the figure of an elephant is unique and is further evidence of the importance of this animal.[99]

Although the notion that the beautifully constructed open courts at Musawwarat were designed as elephant pens sounds somehow far-fetched, it is difficult to propose a more logical explanation for them. Some of the war elephants employed by the Ptolemaic rulers of Egypt – and perhaps also by the Carthaginians – were certainly obtained by expeditions sent to the Sudan, and presumably into Meroitic territory. Ptolemy III is reported by Agatharchides to have established an 'elephant-port' named Ptolemais Theron ('Ptolemais of the Wild Beasts') on the Red Sea coast somewhere near modern Suakin.[100] Since elephant-hunting in the wide-open spaces of the central Sudan would have been an uncertain and time-consuming business, we can well imagine that the agents of Ptolemy might have been happy to deal with native middlemen. The traffic in live elephants could thus have become a small but lucrative sideline for the dwellers of the Butana.[101] One of the reliefs at Musawwarat shows, incidentally, a king riding an elephant (Fig. 53).

The function of the Great Enclosure was certainly in part religious, for it incorporated at least two and possibly three temples amid its corridors and courts, and its walls bear a large number of graffiti naming the lion god, Apedemak.[102] The other known buildings at Musawwarat are nearly all of a religious nature; they include three more small temples of the rather simple plan characteristic of the later Meroitic period. There is also a walled compound (the 'Little Enclosure') enclosing a group of what seem to be ordinary dwelling rooms – the only evidence of actual habitation on the site.

Notable among the ruins of Musawwarat are the remains of an enormous *hafir* or man-made depression intended to catch and hold the runoff from the Wadi es-Sufra. Such structures, ancient and modern, are common throughout the Butana region and are the only sources of water during the nine-month rainless season. Without them year-round habitation at places like Musawwarat and Naqa would have been impossible. The Great *Hafir* at Musawwarat is however by far the largest of those known –

large enough perhaps to provide water for a herd of elephants. It is over 1,000 feet across and 20 feet deep, the sides being built up above ground level with material excavated from the bottom, and then partially reinforced and faced with stone. The shape is more or less round, with an intake channel leading away to the east.[103] A second, smaller *hafir* is located close to the Great Enclosure.

Musawwarat and Naqa, though by far the largest, are not the only Meroitic settlements in the dry Butana Steppe. More than a dozen other

Fig. 53. Relief showing a Meroitic king riding an elephant, Musawwarat

sites have been found, at distances up to sixty miles from the banks of the Nile.[104] Many are, like Musawwarat, associated with ruined *hafirs*. At Basa, a group of carved stone lions was ranged around the perimeter of the reservoir, as if guarding the precious water supply.[105] There are ruined temples in at least four of the Butana sites in addition to those at Musawwarat and Naqa. These colonies, made possible by considerable feats of hydraulic engineering, are the only permanent settlements which the Butana Steppe has ever supported; they offer a unique sidelight on the vigour and prosperity of Nubian civilization in the last centuries BC and the first century AD.

It has been suggested that the Butana sites were administrative and religious centres for the pastoral segment of the Meroitic population,[106] but this is not supported by the evidence of their distribution. The known remains are all in the western part of the Butana, whereas the best grasslands lie farther to the east. Ancient *hafirs* abound in both areas, and cannot be regarded as distinctive of Meroitic settlement.[107] It is notable that all of the 'inland' Meroitic sites lie along three great *wadis* which carry a large part of the Butana runoff. Probably, then, they reflect a temporary extension of agriculture into the hinterlands, perhaps during a period when the seasonal rainfall was a bit higher than it is today. It is worth recalling that the alluvial resources of the Nile itself are not particularly abundant in the vicinity of Meroë.

Forty miles upstream from Meroë, on the east bank of the Nile, are the ruins of Wad ben Naqa. This place is sometimes identified as the 'river-port' for the city of Naqa, since it lies at the mouth of a *wadi* coming down from the inland city.[108] Recent excavations here uncovered an enormous square building, nearly 200 feet on a side, strongly resembling the palaces at Meroë and also identified by the excavators as a royal residence (Fig. 54).[109] It was built entirely of brick; the exterior walls were faced with

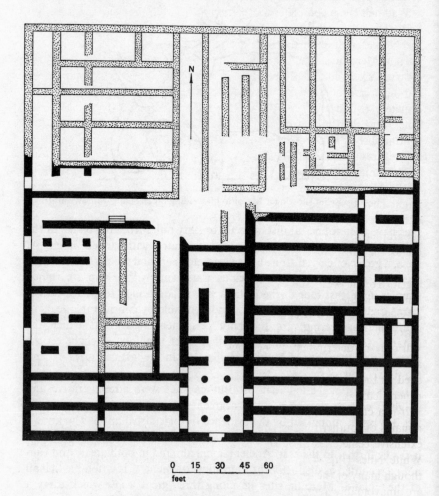

0   15   30   45   60
feet

Fig. 54. Plan of Meroitic palace, Wad ben Naqa

burned brick and plastered over with white stucco. The building had at least two storeys, although only the lower floor was preserved. The long, narrow plan of the interior rooms suggests that they were covered by brick vaults – a method of roofing characteristic of Meroitic public buildings.

If Vercoutter's designation of the palace is correct, we must recognize Wad ben Naqa as another sometime residence of the Kushite royal family, probably in the first century BC and the first century AD.[110] Other buildings on the site include two small temples and an enormous round structure of brick, like a huge silo, whose purpose is entirely unknown. There is also evidence of a considerable town, but it has not been excavated.

Wad ben Naqa completes our list of known Meroitic cities in the central Sudan. Smaller communities, however, were widely scattered up and down the Nile as well as in the Butana Steppe. There may have been an important Meroitic settlement at Soba, not far from modern Khartoum, for a carved stone lion of Meroitic origin was found there some years ago.[111] Far upstream at Sennar, on the Blue Nile, are the remains both of a cemetery (Makwar)[112] and a sizeable village (Abu Geili)[113] of Meroitic times, and there is no reason to suppose that settlement did not extend continuously along the river between this point and the main population centres in the Island of Meroë.[114]

The ruins at Sennar are up to now the southernmost known remains of the Meroitic period. How much farther the kingdom or its influence might have extended to the south and to the west has been the subject of a great deal of speculation. As Vercoutter has pointed out, there are no geographical barriers to prevent the spread of agricultural civilization as far as the great Sudd marshes of the southern Sudan.[115] However, the whole region to the south of Sennar remains *terra incognita* to the archaeologist. To the west, the evidence which has been adduced for Meroitic influence in the steppelands of Kordofan and Darfur (western Sudan)[116] is of such a speculative nature that it probably should not be taken too seriously.[117] The ultimate limits of Kushite cultural expansion into Africa will only be determined by systematic exploration. For the time being we are compelled to accept Sennar as the Meroitic high-water mark, and indeed as the southernmost point to which any purely Nubian civilization penetrated.

It is a curious fact, so far unexplained, that all of the known Meroitic remains of southern Nubia are located to the east of the Nile.[118] Even the extensive cemeteries of Jebel Moya, in the region between the Blue and White Niles (Fig. 47), are not unmistakably Meroitic in character, although many of the graves contain objects of Meroitic manufacture.[119] We are unavoidably reminded of Ptolemy's statement (c. AD 150) that the west bank of the Nile was occupied by another people, the Nubae, who were not subject to Meroë.[120] As unlikely as this proposition seems, it cannot be wholly disregarded in the light of archaeological evidence now available.

To the north of Meroë, a few Meroitic sites have been found in the Nile Valley as far downstream as Berber, seventy-five miles below the capital city. None of them has yet been systematically investigated.[121] Between Berber and Napata are no known remains of either the Napatan or the Meroitic period. As we noted earlier, Napata itself had probably become a cultural and economic backwater by Meroitic times; Haycock speaks of it even in the early seventh century BC as ' . . . a town full of aged buildings crumbling into ruin, which the kings did not care to visit often because they were importuned by the priests . . . to pay for urgent repairs'.[122] Yet this was not the end of its story, for the Barkal temples were extensively repaired by Natakamani and Amanitere, and at least one new temple and two or three other buildings were added to the Barkal complex in Meroitic times.[123] Parts of the townsite and cemetery at Sanam are also of Meroitic date.[124] Kawa, too, was a place of considerable importance in the later Meroitic period, and was the site of still another 'palace', though it is hardly comparable to those at Meroë and Wad ben Naqa. In the few areas of the town which were investigated, remains of Meroitic houses overlay those of the Napatan period.[125] The stratigraphic evidence here, as well as at Sanam and Jebel Barkal, points to a marked revival of building activity around the beginning of the Christian era, after several centuries of virtual stagnation. As a result there are clearly distinguishable Napatan and Meroitic occupation levels in most of the sites which belong to both periods, with very little to connect them except for the continued use and repair of the older temples. The stratigraphic evidence clearly points to two quite distinct florescences of the Kushite civilization.[126]

Downstream from Kawa, the effects of the Meroitic Renaissance are apparent also at Argo Island (? Pnubs) and in the Abri-Delgo Reach. At Argo, the temple of Taharqa (cf. Ch. 10) was extensively rebuilt, and its exterior was adorned with two colossal standing figures (Pl. XVb).[127] These activities are naturally attributed to Natakamani, known from other contexts as the great builder and re-builder of Meroitic times.[128] *Atiye* (Seddenga), recently suggested as the burial place of Taharqa himself, is mentioned in several texts as an important locality of the Meroitic period.[129] This is so far attested archaeologically only by a cemetery and a small group of brick pyramids surrounding the tomb attributed to Taharqa.[130] A few miles downstream, however, there was a fairly impressive Meroitic temple at Amara East. It was, fortunately, visited and sketched by several travellers in the nineteenth century, for nearly all trace of it has disappeared in modern times.[131]

Texts of the Meroitic period mention no settlements between Seddenga and Faras,[132] and only a very few sites were found in this region by the High Dam surveys.[133] Evidently the barren and unproductive *Batn el Hajar* was the region last and least affected by the Meroitic Renaissance; much of it probably remained as deserted as it had been since the days of Egyptian rule. By contrast, the area from the Second Cataract northward to the Wadi Allaqi is almost continuously dotted with Meroitic remains.[134] These northern settlements cannot, however, be viewed simply as the frontier outposts of a southern kingdom expanding gradually northwards. They represent in many ways a distinct and detached Meroitic province with a history, an economy, and even a culture of its own,[135] which we shall discuss in Chapter 12.

Many aspects of Meroitic everyday life have not been touched on in the foregoing survey. However, our knowledge on this subject has come so largely as a result of the excavation of Meroitic sites in Lower Nubia that it seems best to defer a consideration of the humbler aspects of Meroitic culture, and an interpretative summary of the period as a whole, until the following chapter. Before we turn our attention to the north, however, a few further characteristics of Meroitic life and society in the steppelands remain to be considered.

MEROITIC RELIGION

Like so many other aspects of life in Upper Nubia, the religion of Meroë must be largely inferred from its monumental remains. Shinnie has aptly summarized the state of our current knowledge:

Until we can read the language, the sources for an appreciation of Meroitic religion are restricted to the temple reliefs and what little the classical writers tell us. The information given by these writers is not very helpful, since they showed little understanding of how the beliefs of others could differ from those they themselves held, and frequently attempt . . . to identify local gods with their own. [cf. the passage from Herodotus quoted at the beginning of this chapter.]

A study of the many deities depicted in the monuments reveals that the Meroitic people derived most of their religious ideas from Egypt, and the majority of their gods and their iconography always remained closely similar to those of the Pharaohs. But they did have gods of their own which had no Egyptian counterparts, and one at least of these, Apedemak, became the most important god of the Island of Meroë.

The earlier Meroitic kings certainly regarded allegiance to Amon as a main element in their tenure of the throne and we know from the inscriptions . . . the veneration in which he was held. The inscriptions are not only in the Egyptian language, but, in the religious ideas which they reveal, show complete conformity with Egyptian thought. It may be that this official religion, derived as it was from the religious observances of the earlier Egyptian occupation, was restricted to the royal family, their court, and the temple priesthoods.[136]

The Meroitic kings were not remarkable for their temple-building activities, except for the one great outburst of building and re-building in the reign of Natakamani and Amanitére. For the rest, the royal funerary monuments far outnumber and outshine all other religious memorials, while among civic buildings the palaces at Meroë and Wad ben Naqa are conspicuously larger than are the temples. The typical Meroitic temple is in fact a relatively modest affair, comprising a single rectangular chamber entered through a massive pylon-gate. The Lion Temple at Naqa (Pl. XVa) is the best surviving example today. Essentially the same plan is reproduced on a smaller scale by the mortuary chapels adjoining the royal pyramids. Some of the large temples had four or six interior columns supporting the flat, timbered roof. In a few cases the sanctuary was screened from the body of the temple by an interior partition, and in a few others there was a walled forecourt in front of the main pylon-gate. Two notable exceptions to the usual plan are the Sun Temple at Meroë and the temple within the Great Enclosure at Musawwarat, both of which had an interior colonnade surrounding a free-standing walled sanctuary in the middle of the building. This style of architecture is described as 'peripteral'; it is believed to represent one of a number of Asiatic influences in the culture of Meroë (see below).[137]

The most interesting features of the surviving Meroitic temples, as well as of the pyramid-chapels, are their carved wall reliefs, best exemplified once again by the Lion Temple at Naqa (Fig. 51). The stylistic canon and the scenes portrayed are unmistakably Egyptian in origin, but there are distinctive local touches. The massive proportioning of the human figure is characteristic of later Meroitic decoration; Dunham aptly characterizes one relief of a queen as showing ' . . . a truly mountainous royal lady . . . positively weighed down by her ornaments as she sits in state on her lion throne'.[138] Other innovative touches are representations of the lion god with three heads and with the body of a snake, and various other composite, mythical beasts among the reliefs at Musawwarat.[139]

Among the religious monuments of Kush the temples of Amon are undoubtedly pre-eminent both in size and in number. The names of the Meroitic kings, with their continued repetition of the 'amani' element, would certainly indicate also that the worship of this Theban deity remained central to the state ideology until the end of the kingdom. It is worth noting, however, that all of the Amon temples except possibly that at Meroë seem to have been built in Napatan times. Amon figures among the reliefs in the purely Meroitic temples, but he is no more prominent than are a number of other deities. This might suggest that organized religion in the Meroitic period was less exclusively a royal affair than in Napatan times, and had to serve the needs of other elements in the population besides the ruling house.

Second in importance to Amon, at least in the Meroë region, was the lion god, Apedemak, who has no Egyptian equivalent. As we have already noted, there were lion temples at Meroë, at Musawwarat, at Naqa, and probably at Basa. The worship of Apedemak seems to have been particularly important at Musawwarat, where he is mentioned in numerous graffiti as well as in long, formal prayers inscribed in good Egyptian hieroglyphs on the walls of his recently excavated temple.[140] The terms in which the god is addressed are significant: 'Thou art greeted, Apedemak, lord of Naqa; great god, lord of Musawwarat es-Sufra; splendid god, at the head of Nubia. Lion of the south, strong of arm.'[141] There is a suggestion here that the lion god was a local tutelary of the Meroitic south (where lions were fairly common until the last century), and it is noteworthy that we seldom hear of him in Lower Nubia. The prominent place accorded the temples of Apedemak in the southern cities would thus represent an important concession to local religious tradition.[142]

The sun god represented in the great victory stele at Jebel Qeili (Fig. 48), and to whom the Sun Temple at Meroë may have been dedicated, remains something of an enigma. Like Apedemak he is not recognizably an Egyptian deity, but he figures much less prominently in the surviving Meroitic religious texts than does the lion god. His worship at Meroë may be evidence of the spread of the Persian Mithraic cult, which was becoming popular in many parts of the Roman Empire at about the same time.[143] It is another of the oriental influences which many scholars profess to recognize in the culture of the Meroitic south.

Isis, the Egyptian manifestation of the age-old Mother Goddess, appears frequently in Meroitic temple reliefs, and there were temples dedicated especially to her at Meroë and at Wad ben Naqa. These probably represent the southward spread of religious influence from Ptolemaic Egypt, where the fertility goddess emerged as the most popular deity in the country under Greek rule. Her worship was for all practical purposes the state cult both of the Ptolemaic and of the Meroitic provinces of Lower Nubia, as we shall observe in the next chapter. She does not seem to have achieved quite the same prominence in the Meroitic south, where older religious traditions lingered longer and died harder. Isis was, however, important in connection with the mortuary ritual of the Meroites, as she was also in Egypt. To quote Shinnie once again:

Some confirmation of Herodotus' view concerning the cult of Isis and Osiris for funerary purposes can be seen in the very large number of funerary offering tables with invocations to these gods. Since Osiris was the traditional god of the dead and Isis his wife, here once more Egyptian ideas can be seen to dominate. Many of these offering tables show the goddess Nephthys and the god Anubis, both concerned with the cult of the dead in Egypt, pouring libations. Although the form of these offering tables and the inscriptions are Meroitic, the theological ideas embodied are Egyptian.[144]

It seems hardly necessary to add that mortuary ritual must have played an important and perhaps even dominant role in the religious life of Meroë, as it did throughout the history of ancient Egypt and Kush. This is the one area of religious observance which we can be sure, from the evidence of the cemeteries, was common to all levels of Meroitic society, and not just to the court and the nobility. The lavishly furnished royal tombs have already been described in earlier pages. The richest of the 'private' tombs in the West Cemetery at Meroë, though smaller in size than the royal tombs, are hardly less opulent. They too are equipped with small pyramids or mastabas, encircling walls, mortuary chapels, and sometimes multiple underground chambers. By contrast, the burial chambers of the ordinary citizens are often of a very simple nature. Yet the abundance of goods found even in the humblest provincial cemeteries from one end of Nubia to the other bears witness to the fact that elaborate mortuary ritual was no monopoly of the upper class. (A more detailed consideration of Meroitic burial practices, which are known to us chiefly from cemeteries in Lower Nubia, will be found in the next chapter.)

THE SOCIETY AND CULTURE OF THE MEROITIC SOUTH

The excavated monuments and the unexcavated town-sites permit us to make only a few summary generalizations about social and cultural conditions in the Meroitic steppelands. To begin with, we can observe that settlement was more urbanized than in any previous period. The process of urbanization was of course not new; town life in Nubia had begun under the Egyptian New Kingdom, and in Napatan times Sanam and Kawa were both important urban centres. Yet the town remains of the Meroitic period are far more numerous and more extensive than are those of earlier times. Even the humblest villages exhibit a surprisingly congested plan, indicating that social nucleation among the peoples of the Nile had reached that degree of development which had long been characteristic of the Near East (see 'Town and village life' in the next chapter).

A number of corollary inferences can be drawn from the urbanized character of Meroitic society. One is the growth of a sizeable middle class, whose power and wealth perhaps increased at the expense of the monarchy. This is attested also by the number of wealthy 'private' tombs in the West Cemetery at Meroë and at Seddenga and elsewhere. As Haycock has remarked,

328

... the later royal sequence of [Meroë] North is the main source of evidence
for the argument ... that there are no rich tombs after the early first century AD.
Yet it should be pointed out that ... despite steady decline in the size of the
tombs and their construction, some were still well equipped with objects ...
These tombs date roughly between the second half of the first century AD and
the end of the third. Private tombs, probably of the second to third century, ...
were often very lavish indeed, and contained large numbers of objects influenced
by Graeco-Roman traditions. Possibly what was happening was not a process
of general impoverishment, but simply that complete royal autocracy was giving
way before the growth of a rich and powerful nobility; thus the economic gap
between rulers and ruled may have become smaller than at any time since the
establishment of the Napatan dynasty.[145]

The social transformation here envisioned is probably symptomatic
in turn of an economic transformation. As we saw in earlier chapters,
the prosperity of Kush always depended to a large extent upon export
trade, and the spread of Kushite civilization to the steppelands was
probably due in large measure to the extension of overland trade routes.
Yet for centuries the means of distribution were monopolized by the ruling
family and a small governing élite, who reaped nearly all the benefits of
Nubia's foreign commerce. This picture was radically altered in Meroitic
times. The volume of goods moving southwards along the Nile and over
the desert caravan routes was conspicuously larger than in any previous
period, and it was reaching a far wider consumer market. Even the little
provincial cemetery at Sennar, at the farthest limit of the Meroitic empire,
abounded in bronze, glass, and other luxury goods which were largely of
foreign manufacture.[146] Such extensive enterprise was surely no royal
monopoly; it can only signify the activity of a host of private entrepreneurs. In sum, material prosperity in the Meroitic period was far more
broadly based than in earlier times, and an active middle class must have
grown up along with an active mercantile economy. Here more than anywhere else we recognize the Greek touch transforming the ancient civilization of the Nile.[147]

Because we know, up to now, so little about village life in the Meroitic
south, it is difficult to generalize about the agrarian economy of the region.
The remains which are known to us in such places as Abu Geili are certainly those of sedentary agriculturalists rather than of pastoralists. Even
in the Butana Steppe, the urban character of most of the known settlements
makes it probable that they were supported by the development of agriculture in the nearby wadis rather than by animal husbandry in the
surrounding grasslands. Strabo's description of Nubia mentions the cultivation of millet,[148] which in later times has become the principal staple grain
of the Sudan (cf. Ch. 2). His account furnishes our first evidence of millet
cultivation south of Egypt; it may very well have been the introduction of

this heat- and drought-resistant cereal which made possible the extension of agriculture from the Nile floodplain into the steppelands.

We have good reason to believe that farming in New Kingdom and Napatan times was organized at least partly on a manorial basis, the land-holders being in many cases the great temple establishments (Chs. 9–10).[149] Whether the more numerous but much smaller temples of the Meroitic period were similarly endowed with manorial estates is uncertain, but seems at least a reasonable supposition. It is unlikely that they were supported entirely by royal largesse, and they do not seem to have engaged to any great extent in trade. At the same time, the relatively small population of Nubia, and the great expanse of potentially arable land in the south, make it certain that a large part of the population – perhaps a substantial majority – were small free-holders, as in all periods of Nubian history.

Strabo also states, as do several later classical writers, that a great many of the subjects of Meroë were poor nomadic pastoralists.[150] This description could not possibly refer to the sedentary, urbanized population whose remains are known to us archaeologically. It can only mean that the Mero-itic kingdom exerted some degree of control over the desert pastoralists during that part of the year when their annual migrations brought them to the edge of the settled region. Very possibly a kind of symbiosis existed between farmers and nomads, as has so often been true in the history of the Middle East. Even today the settled farmers of the Shendi region are able to graze considerable numbers of cattle over the Butana grasslands by em-ploying their nomad neighbours as herdsmen.[151] Yet the pastoralists of today remain poor and backward, and it seems unlikely that their ancestors in ancient times made much of a contribution to the social or economic life of the Kushite empire.[152] Both Strabo[153] and Pliny[154] were particularly impressed with their poverty.

If pastoral nomads contributed little to the civilization of Kush, however, we have nevertheless to recognize that the 'cattle cult' still flourished with considerable vigour among the sedentary farmers. While it is by no means as dramatically manifest as in the C Horizon (Ch. 6), representations of cattle and cattle-herding were popular decorative motifs on pottery and bronze vessels, as well as in the royal tomb reliefs.[155] Cows are usually shown with udders of exaggerated size, and one bronze bowl depicts a milking scene.[156] The quantities of cattle bones recovered in the recent excavations at Meroë show that meat as well as milk was important in the Meroitic diet.[157] Animal husbandry therefore played some part in the life of the Meroitic farmer, whether directly through his own enterprise or indirectly through his contacts with the Butana nomads.

Finally, and connected also with the socio-economic transformation of Nubia, we can observe the emergence of powerful provincial officials both in the old Napatan province and in Lower Nubia. The polity of

Meroitic times became much more decentralized than in any previous period since the establishment of dynastic rule. This was perhaps inevitable in view of the fragmentation of the kingdom into three geographically separate districts, but it surely reflects also the increasing wealth and power of the independent bourgeoisie. The provincial officials in the north may have begun as bureaucratic appointees from the royal household, but as the power and authority of the monarchy declined they seem to have ended as semi-autonomous, hereditary governors.[158] We can thus observe in the later Meroitic period the beginnings of Nubia's first genuinely feudal society. Its development was to be much more pronounced in the post-Meroitic era (Ch. 13).

The transformations which set apart the social, political, and economic life of Meroë from the Nubia of earlier times can nearly all be traced directly or indirectly to the influence of classical civilization. The same is true in other areas of culture as well. Architecture, mural decoration, and the domestic arts are still basically Egyptian, but with Hellenistic overtones; in each case they mirror fairly closely the contemporary developments in Egypt under Ptolemaic and Roman rule. At Meroë, however, we have also to recognize a small group of extraneous influences which do not appear to be of European origin. These are the so-called oriental influences which many scholars have recognized in the Meroitic culture.

Meroitic elements which have been attributed to an eastern origin include the sun god, and particularly the form of his representation at Jebel Qeili; the peripteral temples perhaps also associated with the sun god; the cult of the elephant (if such it was) at Musawwarat; the three-headed and snake-bodied representations of Apedemak at Naqa;[159] the introduction of *hafirs* and of cotton cultivation into the Nile Valley;[160] and the form of certain tripod bronze vessels which are common in Meroitic graves.[161] So strong indeed is this hint of Indian artistic elements in some of the art of Meroë, that it has led Vercoutter to say that he considers Meroitic art to be 'tout aussi indianisant qu'égyptisant'.[162]

In fact, the cumulative effect of the oriental influences at Meroë is trivial indeed when compared to the Egyptian and even the Graeco-Roman influences, and the foreign origin of some of the elements has been denied altogether.[163] What is more to the point, they are 'bits and pieces' which do not add up to an integrated complex, and certainly do not point back to a common place of origin. The different elements might have entered Nubia at different times and over various routes, including from Egypt. India and Persia had after all been a part of the world *oikoumêne* since the conquest of Alexander, and many oriental ideas were afloat in the late classical world. War elephants were ridden by European Greeks and Romans no less than by Carthaginians and Ptolemies, and Mithra was worshipped in far-away Britain and Germany as well as in sunnier climes.

Maritime trade was flourishing in the western Indian Ocean, and many oriental goods found their way to the Mediterranean countries, as well as perhaps more directly to Abyssinia and Nubia, by way of the Red Sea. On the whole the oriental influences to be seen at Meroë are probably no more numerous nor more significant than those to be seen at Rome itself; they are only more conspicuous in the isolated desert cities where they are not surrounded by a welter of conflicting styles and influences.

12
RENAISSANCE IN THE NORTH
PTOLEMAIC, ROMAN, AND MEROITIC
RESETTLEMENT IN LOWER NUBIA

While the political and economic centres of Kush were shifting southwards from the Napata region to the steppelands of Meroë, important political developments of another sort were taking place far away in the north. After the expulsion of her Nubian rulers (Ch. 10), Egypt for several centuries had been the prey of one foreign conqueror after another. Episodes of Assyrian and Persian rule were interspersed with brief restorations of Egyptian independence, until in 332 BC the conquest of Alexander the Great put a final end to the ancient pharaonic succession. A measure of stability and of political autonomy was nevertheless restored after the death of Alexander, when his successor, the Macedonian general Ptolemy, repudiated his foreign allegiances and set up an independent dynasty at Alexandria. For nearly three hundred years thereafter the Ptolemies presided over the decayed remnants of Egypt's civilization, until Cleopatra, the last of the line, took her life in 30 BC. With her died the last semblance of Egyptian independence. The ancient land of the Nile became a Roman province, to be governed for the next six hundred years by alien prefects appointed from Rome or from Constantinople.

The civilization of Ptolemaic Egypt presents a curious hybrid of Hellenistic and pharaonic influences, in which the latter are predominate. As Toynbee has remarked, it is the only instance in which the traditions of an older civilization seem to have triumphed over those of Hellas, rather than vice versa.[1] The Ptolemies not only adopted the pharaoh's grandiloquent titles, but in most other respects they continued the traditions and the style of living of the older Egyptian monarchy. As a result, the change of rulers probably meant little to the *fellaheen* masses. Greek influence nevertheless made itself felt in other areas of Egyptian life, and particularly in finance and commerce. The Ptolemaic period witnessed a major economic revival, resulting both from the expansion of agricultural production[2] and from the development of maritime trade through newly founded ports at Alexandria and on the Red Sea Coast. Through these ports Egypt was linked economically as well as politically and ideologically to the Graeco-Roman *oikoumêne*. The numerous building activities of the

Ptolemies and their Roman successors in Upper Egypt and Lower Nubia are, if nothing else, testimony to the economic vitality of the age.[3]

Concurrently with their programme of economic and political revitalization the Ptolemies sought to reassert Egypt's historic claim to Lower Nubia. The region at this time was still, so far as we know, largely deserted, and it is unlikely that its annexation had anything to do with the more general Ptolemaic programme of agricultural expansion. More probably Egypt's new southern policy was motivated by a desire to establish a direct control over the supply lines from Meroë and the Red Sea coast, over which came not only the familiar tropical products of earlier times but also the war-elephants which were employed in the numerous Ptolemaic military campaigns in Asia.[4] One recent writer has gone so far as to suggest that elephant-hunting may have been the principal motivation for Ptolemaic expansion in the south, which apparently began under the second ruler of the dynasty.[5] By the time of Ptolemy VI (181–145 BC), however, the desert gold mines had also been reactivated, and it appears that gold mining was at least as important a factor in Egypt's southern policy as was elephant-hunting. (The description of Egyptian gold mining quoted in Chapter 9 was in fact written by a Greek visitor to the desert mines during Ptolemaic times.[6])

As usual, Egypt's interest centred primarily in the region between Aswan and the Wadi Allaqi – the principal route to the desert mines. Military and supply posts were established at a number of points along the Nile, and Egyptian sovereignty was proclaimed in the traditional way by the building of temples at Pselchis (modern Dakka) and Dabod, respectively near the upper and lower limits of the reoccupied territory. The distance from Aswan to the Wadi Allaqi was, according to the Graeco-Egyptian system of measurement, twelve *schoenoi* (about seventy-five miles), and the reoccupied district, whose ancient name had probably been forgotten during the centuries of its abandonment, came in time to be known as the Dodekaschoenos – the land of the twelve *schoenoi*. Under that name it gradually developed as the southernmost province of Graeco-Roman Egypt, and so remained until Diocletian abandoned it to the desert nomads 500 years later.

Arkamani ('Ergamenes'[7]), who by all accounts was one of the more energetic Meroitic kings, evidently looked upon Lower Nubia as his own sphere of influence. Apprised of the Ptolemaic activities in the Dodekaschoenos, he felt compelled to make a counter-proclamation of authority. It took the form of a small entrance hall which he added to the temple of Ptolemy IV at Pselchis, inscribed with his own royal cartouches. At about the same time he built a wholly new temple at Philae – to which Ptolemy in his turn added an entrance hall! (Adkeramon, another Meroitic king whose place in the succession has not been determined, also seems to have

334

built a small temple near Philae, to which Ptolemy VII made subsequent additions.[8]) These curious 'hybrid' buildings have been interpreted as evidence both of competition and of collaboration between the Nubian and Egyptian monarchies;[9] the significant point in either case is that both felt it necessary to proclaim their interest in a region which for several centuries had been of concern to neither. It would also appear that each acknowledged the rights of the other, since they allowed one another's temples and inscriptions to stand unmolested. (However, during a subsequent period of hostility Ptolemy V erased some of the cartouches of Arkamani at Philae.[10]) The principle of condominium seems already implicit in the hybrid temples of Pselchis and Philae; it was to be much more explicitly developed under the Roman governors of Egypt. Such an arrangement suggests that the primary interest of both parties was strategic rather than economic.

At first glance, the interest of Arkamani in the Dodekaschoenos is much more difficult to understand than is that of Ptolemy. According to geographical tradition the region immediately south of Aswan was part of Nubia (originally Wawat) rather than of Egypt, but it had been subject to Egyptian control during most of its history. In Arkamani's time no ruler of Kush had set foot in the north, or had laid active claim to it, for several centuries,[11] and even the original Nubian inhabitants had deserted the region in the last millennium BC. There is no archaeological evidence to suggest that anyone at all was living along the Nile between Aswan and the Wadi Allaqi when Ptolemy IV erected his temples there (c. 220 BC). Control of Lower Nubia was, however, necessary to secure the northern end of the trade routes over which most traffic moved between Egypt and Meroë, and this must be the explanation for Arkamani's interest as well as for that of Ptolemy. Under the circumstances the building activities of the Nubian become intelligible as expressing an affirmation of right rather than a claim of sovereignty; he was concerned for the maintenance of a kind of 'free port' status in Lower Nubia.

Having run up the flag, and seen that it was respected, Arkamani and his successors were content to leave the practical administration of the Dodekaschoenos to the Ptolemies. There was no Meroitic effort to colonize or garrison the northern region, and in the centuries that followed it developed culturally and economically as a Graeco-Roman province, despite the fiction of Meroitic co-sovereignty. Under Ptolemy VI (181–145 BC) Egyptian rule was actually extended as far south as the Second Cataract; there is evidence that Ptolemaic garrisons were maintained for a time both at Buhen[12] and Mirgissa,[13] and perhaps also at Gebel Adda and Qasr Ibrim,[14] which later became the most important Meroitic settlements in Lower Nubia. The Egyptian dominions to the south of the Dodekaschoenos are referred to in an inscription from the reign of Ptolemy VI as the Triakontaschoenos – the land of the thirty *schoenoi*.[15]

The reign of Ptolemy VI evidently represents the highwater-mark of Ptolemaic expansion into Nubia.[16] After the death of this monarch the Graeco-Egyptian ruling house was plunged into an almost ceaseless round of dynastic strife, which continued until the final extinction of the dynasty a century later. During this time the garrisons were evidently withdrawn from the Triakontaschoenos; at least there is no more evidence of Ptolemaic activity to the south of the Wadi Allaqi. By the first century BC small Meroitic garrisons were very probably in possession of the fortress sites of Gebel Adda and Qasr Ibrim, and perhaps also of Buhen.[17] The Ptolemies maintained their control over the Dodekaschoenos, though they undertook no further building activity there.[18]

It seems apparent that throughout the Ptolemaic era the interest which was manifested in Nubia both by the Egyptian rulers and by their Meroitic counterparts was largely strategic; neither power made any effort to re-occupy the region in force. Once a *modus vivendi* had been established, it was not necessary for either of them to maintain extensive forces in the buffer zone between them. Thus, the only significant archaeological remains left by either Ptolemies or early Meroites in Lower Nubia are the temples at Pselchis, Dabod and Philae, and possibly the earliest foundations of the fortresses at Gebel Adda and Qasr Ibrim. For the rest, both parties were content to maintain a few small garrisons for the protection of trade. The full-scale resettlement of Lower Nubia, both within and beyond the Dodekaschoenos, had to await the coming of Roman rule.

PHILAE AND THE CULT OF ISIS

Since the time of the Old Kingdom, the main settlement and administrative centre on the Egyptian–Nubian frontier had been that on Elephantine Island, below the First Cataract and directly opposite the site of modern Aswan.[19] It was the traditional 'Door to the South' – the trans-shipment point for cargoes to and from Nubia and the residence of the Egyptian official charged with defending the frontier (cf. Ch. 7). Under Ptolemaic rule Elephantine retained its economic importance, but it was largely supplanted in the political sphere by a new centre some six miles further south. This was on the island of Philae, just above the head of the cataract.

The importance of Philae apparently derived from the fact that the island was sacred to the goddess Isis – the Egyptian version of the immemorial Earth Mother. She had been a part of the Egyptian pantheon since the earliest times, but fertility ritual was never highly developed in pharaonic Egypt, and Isis was greatly overshadowed by her brother and consort Osiris, who became the central figure of mortuary ritual. This relationship was altered under the Greeks, who found in Isis a figure recognizably akin to the Olympian goddesses, and who made her by far the most popular

336

deity in Ptolemaic Egypt.[20] In Roman times her cult was to spread far beyond the Nile, to a large part of the western world.

Very little is known of the early history of Philae. Like its patron goddess, the island was apparently unimportant in pharaonic times, although there may have been a temple of the XVIII Dynasty there. The oldest building which survives today is a small temple begun by Nectanebo I, one of the last purely Egyptian pharaohs (378–360 BC). The half dozen other temples, as well as a score of other buildings on the island, all date from the Ptolemaic and Roman periods. Under these latter-day rulers the little island (it is no more than 500 yards long and 150 yards wide) came to support a veritable city, surrounding and dominated by the great Temple of Isis (Pl. XVIa). The place is variously referred to in contemporary texts as the 'Holy Island', the 'interior of Heaven', and the 'City of Isis'.[21]

As the spiritual power of Isis grew, so also did the temporal power of her earthly ministers. This is particularly apparent in the Dodekaschoenos, the region which immediately surrounded the main centre of Isis-worship. Even in the time of Arkamani, the whole region seems to have been regarded as a kind of estate of Isis, much as the Thebaid was once regarded as the estate of Amon, administered by his earthly representatives at Karnak. As Millet explains it, 'In a text in the hall of Ergamenes, the king formally offers to the goddess the twelve *irtw* of land (Gr. *schoenoi*) on each side of the river from Aswan to Takompso, an act commemorated in many later temple scenes at Philae, and claims that in so doing he is confirming the act of former kings.'[22]

Here can be found the symbolic key to Nubian and Egyptian condominium in the Dodekaschoenos. In theory it was the private estate of Isis, and the Nubian and Egyptian monarchs were her co-sponsors. As Millet puts it, '... they were, officially at least, felt as co-dedicators of the temples of Nubia ... and as both receiving the divine benefits of the "breath of life" from the gods of Nubia in return.'[23] In practice it was a semi-autonomous buffer zone – a feudal principality administered by the priesthood of Isis as nominal vassals both of Egypt and of Nubia. In their inscriptions, the civil and even the military officials of Lower Nubia often designated themselves as 'Agents of Isis'[24] rather than as servants of this or that Egyptian or Meroitic ruler.

The temporal power of the Isis priests never extended beyond Hiera Sykaminos (modern Maharraqa), at the southern limit of the Dodekaschoenos. Their spiritual influence, however, went much further. Far away in the south there were Isis temples at Meroë and Wad ben Naqa (Ch. 11), though they were considerably less important than the great Amon temples through which the authority of the state was principally expressed. When Meroitic settlers returned to the north, however, they seem to have fallen completely under the ideological sway of Philae; by far the most important deity who was worshipped both in the Roman and in the Meroitic provinces of Lower Nubia was Isis.

In the Isis cult of Roman and Meroitic Nubia we have to recognize the beginnings of one of history's most important ideological transformations. Within the microcosm of the Nile lands, the worship of Isis became the first truly international and supra-national religion, no longer claimed as the proprietary cult of any one temporal ruler but sanctioned by, and conferring its blessings upon, several. Philae became a holy city and a place of pilgrimage alike for all classes and all nationalities: Greeks, Romans, Egyptians, Meroites, and desert nomads.[25] No wonder, then, that the temporal influence of the priestly oligarchs of Isis came to resemble that of the Vatican in later times. They were able to maintain their position and their cult, for the benefit of its private votaries, long after it had been formally disestablished in surrounding Egypt.[26] In all these respects, the worship of the age-old fertility goddess of Egypt anticipated the role which was to be played by Christianity and Islam on the larger stage of the Middle Ages.

THE ROMAN PROVINCE

Except for disturbances in the reigns of Ptolemy V and Ptolemy VI,[27] the 'gentleman's agreement' which Arkamani and Ptolemy IV had negotiated in the Dodekaschoenos remained in force throughout the Ptolemaic era. The later Ptolemies were continually occupied with dynastic struggles at home and with the threat of Roman encroachment, and they paid scant attention to their southern provinces. Yet no Meroitic ruler was moved to exploit their weakness by asserting his own authority in the north. There was, on the other hand, a certain amount of Meroitic settlement in the empty region of the Triakontaschoenos, from which Egyptian power was apparently withdrawn after the death of Ptolemy VI. Some sort of Meroitic administrative and military centre seems to have been established at Qasr Ibrim, a place which was later to become the Meroitic capital in Lower Nubia (see Fig. 55). We know of its existence in the first century BC chiefly from textual references, for the archaeological remains which have thus far come to light at Qasr Ibrim date almost entirely from later times.[28]

Throughout the Ptolemaic era the principle of condominium in the Dodekaschoenos was never formally articulated. It was a *de facto* settlement which was possible only so long as neither Egypt nor Nubia maintained a strong force in the buffer zone. So informal and so delicate an arrangement was bound to be upset when the mailed fist of Rome was substituted for the Oriental guile of the Ptolemies. With characteristic Roman directness the first prefect of Egypt, Cornelius Gallus, lost no time in marching southwards to Aswan with a considerable force, intent on

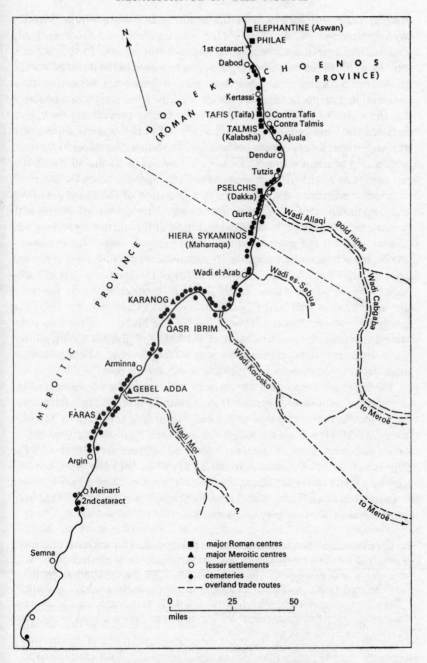

Fig. 55. Lower Nubia in Meroitic and Roman times

making a *de jure* settlement of the southern frontier question. Meeting with the envoys of Meroë at Philae, he negotiated, or more probably dictated, an agreement whereby the imperial frontier was fixed at Aswan, but the whole of the Meroitic kingdom was admitted to the status of Roman protectorate (*in tutelam*). Since there was no important Meroitic official resident in the north, a governor or viceroy (*tyrannus*) was appointed for the whole of the Triakontaschoenos, meaning presumably the region between the First and Second Cataracts.[29] All of this was in keeping with the eastern policy of Augustus, who sought to bolster the imperial frontiers with a ring of client states.[30] The Meroitic envoys, unacquainted with Roman ways and with Roman diplomatic language, probably looked upon their agreement with the prefect as an affirmation of the *status quo*. Even the appointment of a *tyrannus* for Lower Nubia was in accord with precedent, since the practical administration of the northern province had always been left in Egyptian hands.[31] Before long, however, the unsuspecting Nubians began to discover the true significance of *in tutelam*; in Roman eyes they had been demoted from the status of co-regents to that of tributaries, and were treated accordingly. There is some evidence that, following the agreement at Philae, the Dodekaschoenos was administered simply as part of the southernmost nome of Egypt.[32] The Nubians in the area complained bitterly of their treatment at the hands of Egyptian officials, but for several years the presence of a strong Roman force at Aswan prevented them from registering their discontent in stronger terms.

The Meroites found their opportunity in 23 BC when a large part of the frontier garrison was withdrawn from Aswan to take part in what proved to be an abortive campaign in Arabia. According to Strabo a Meroitic army of 30,000 men descended on the southern Egyptian city, sacked it, and tore down the imperial statues which had been erected at Philae.[33] (The fine bronze head of Augustus found at Meroë in 1911 has often been regarded as part of the loot from this raid.[34]) What happened next has been recounted in considerable detail both by Strabo[35] and by Pliny;[36] the brief paraphrase of Kirwan may be quoted here:

The Roman reaction to these events was swift, and as far as relations between Rome and Meroë were concerned, decisive for almost three hundred years. With one legion and auxiliaries, a force of almost 11,000 men, Petronius [who had just replaced Gallus as Prefect of Egypt] drove the Sudanese back to Pselchis (Dakka) which evidently they had occupied. Then negotiations began. The Sudanese, when Petronius demanded the return of prisoners and booty, complained once again about the nomarch . . .

As the Sudanese procrastinated and negotiations broke down, Petronius attacked again. Moving by land and by river he captured Pselchis (Dakka), then Primis (Qasr Ibrim), a naturally strong fortress . . . on a rocky eminence overlooking the Nile and desert routes [Pl. XVIb]. He then marched on Napata, sacked the city and returned with prisoners and plunder to Alexandria. On his way back, as evidence of Rome's determination to tolerate no further Sudanese adventures, Petronius left a garrison of four hundred men with supplies for two years in the rock fortress at Ibrim. But as these two years drew to a close, calculating no doubt that the garrison could not hold out for long, the Meroites attacked once more. Petronius however came to the rescue and this time delegates of the Queen of Meroë were compelled to travel all the way to distant Samos, off the coast of Turkey, to sue for peace in the august and awe-inspiring surroundings of the Imperial Court. On condition that the Sudanese kept the peace, tribute was remitted. But the Romans were far from confident about the security of southern Egypt. The Roman frontier was therefore extended to Hiera Sykaminos (Maharraqa), an extension strategically sound for it not only gave defense in depth to Egypt but gave the Romans access to the gold mines in the Wadi Allaqi and gave them also control of the strategically important desert routes . . .[37]

The expedition of Petronius may have been no more than a reflex gesture of retribution, understood as such by both sides. *Lex talionis* required the desecration of a site comparable in importance to Philae, which explains why Petronius was obliged to go all the way to Napata, and also why he was not obliged to continue on to Meroë.[38] Having suitably avenged the honour of Rome, he made haste to retire northwards without pausing to negotiate or to impose terms on his enemies. There is no reason to suppose that his depredations had any more lasting effect upon the economic and political fortunes of the Meroitic kingdom than had the depredations of the Nubians on the later fortunes of Philae. To interpret this relatively insignificant punitive gesture as a crippling blow to Meroitic power, as some writers have,[39] is to ignore the fact that the greatest achievements of the Meroitic era lay still in the future. In fact, the invasion of Petronius was more probably an important revitalizing influence, for the great outburst of building activity under Natakamani and Amanitere followed immediately after (Ch. 11).

In their campaign against the Romans, the Meroites apparently lost all the battles but won the war, in the sense that their larger objective was attained: the pre-Roman *status quo* was restored in the north. Within the Dodekaschoenos, the principle of condominium seems to have been reaffirmed;[40] beyond it, there was no further effort to assert the Roman authority or to exact tribute. *Pax Romana* ruled over the lands of the Nile, both within and beyond the imperial frontiers.

Only one later Roman ruler displayed any interest in the region to the south of Hiera Sykaminos. In the reign of Nero, an exploring expedition was sent up the Nile not only to Meroë, but deep into the heart of the African continent.

Both Pliny and Seneca have told the story of Nero's remarkable expedition,

341

and Seneca . . . interviewed the explorers on their return to Rome. The expedition was sent out by Nero in the autumn of the year 61 and consisted of a party of Praetorian soldiers under the command of a tribune and two centurions. Travelling, like Petronius, first up the Nile and then across the eastern desert, they reached Meroë nearly a thousand miles from the frontier. They saw parakeets, and monkeys, and the tracks of rhinoceros and elephant in the neighbourhood. They noted that here the grass was of a 'greener and fresher colour' (probably after the rains). They observed too the small, thin trees of the incipient African forest. At Meroë the expedition was provided with a military escort and recommendations to the neighbouring southern tribes beyond the Meroitic kingdom, and they continued their journey up the White Nile until, as they told Seneca on their return to Rome, they 'came to immense marshes' where 'the plants were so entangled with the waters' that they were impenetrable except, perhaps, to a one-man canoe. This has long been recognized as a description of the *Sudd*, the vast area of floating islands of vegetation south of Malakal, which more than once has blocked the flow of the Nile. The journey, by any standards, was a sturdy feat of exploration, and from it the expedition brought back a map and much geographical and zoological information. It marked the southernmost known limit of Roman penetration into Africa.[41]

The purpose of Nero's expedition has never been entirely clear. Seneca[42] states that its mission was to discover the source of the Nile, Pliny[43] that it was a military reconnaissance preparatory to a campaign against Meroë. Both assertions may in fact be correct.[44] In support of Pliny's explanation we may note that it was common Roman practice to annex the client states along the eastern frontier after a generation or two of 'protectorate' status,[45] and Nero may well have been contemplating such a step in Nubia. He was evidently dissuaded by the unfavourable report of the explorers, which ended all further Roman ambitions in the south.

At the same time that they eschewed any interest in the lands of the Upper Nile, the Romans set about colonizing and developing the Dodekaschoenos with characteristic thoroughness and efficiency. The Antonine Itinerary of the second century AD mentions no fewer than ten major settlements between Syene (Aswan) and Hiera Sykaminos, at the lower and upper limits of Roman Nubia.[46] These were located primarily on the west bank of the Nile, with only a few unimportant bridgeheads on the east bank opposite the largest settlements.[47] As in all periods of history, the west bank offered a measure of safety from the nomads of the Red Sea hills, who had no means of crossing the river.

The five most important settlements in Roman Nubia (Fig. 55) were Philae, Tafis (modern Taifa), Talmis (Kalabsha), Pselchis (Dakka), and Hiera Sykaminos (Maharraqa). Each was the site of a Roman or Ptolemaic temple as well as of a sizeable garrison. It is perhaps symbolic of the political and cultural status of the Dodekaschoenos that the temples both at Kalabsha and at the small community of Ajuala were dedicated by Augustus to the Nubian god Mandulis – a deity who was particularly revered by the desert nomads.[48]

The military officials in the Dodekaschoenos were Romans or Romanized Egyptians. However, Millet believes that a considerable part of the civil populace, including some of its high officials, were Nubians.

It would seem that the old territory of the Dodekaschoenos was administered in the name of the two states together, with Rome certainly in control of the roads and military matters, and civil matters being perhaps in the hands of Meroitic officialdom, which also held control of much of the religious and fiscal affairs of the province by the assumption by the *strategos* of the title . . . 'agent of Isis.' The Meroitic *strategos* may have been nominated by agreement between the two powers, or perhaps by the Roman authorities alone, choosing their candidate from the mixed Egyptian–Meroitic population in the Dodekaschoenos.[49]

This hypothesis is in better accord with textual than with archaeological evidence.[50] The ordinary graves and the houses which have been excavated in the Dodekaschoenos are those of Roman Egypt rather than of the neighbouring Meroitic province of Nubia. Trigger observes that:

The common tomb type in the Dodekaschoenos was a pit and end chamber, and was built to hold more than one burial. The tombs were frequently cut in rock or in hard banks of alluvium. Many bodies were embalmed in resin, or at least wrapped in a mummiform fashion and placed in wooden or cartonnage coffins. Pottery and metal grave goods are rare and offering tables are absent. In the Meroitic region the grave styles were different, bodies were not mummified, grave goods of all types were more common, and *ba*-statues and offering tables were set up outside the grave.[51]

In regard to the houses:

Although no living sites have actually been excavated[52] we are fortunate that Weigall[53] has described a number of buildings at Taifa which appear to be houses of the Roman period. The outer walls, like the fort at Kertassi, were built of large stone blocks. They were rectangular, generally 16 to 18 metres [50–60 ft] long, and must have originally been about 5 metres [16 ft] high. Their interiors were divided into rooms, but the plans for the most part were not discernible. Some of them had doorways that were ornamented with winged discs and rows of *uraei*.[54]

Although some recognizably Meroitic pottery and other objects have been found in the Dodekaschoenos, their scarcity in proportion to Egyptian-made objects marks them unmistakably as trade goods.[55] If, then, the population of the Dodekaschoenos was made up partly or largely of Nubians, they can be considered so only in a racial and perhaps in an ethnic sense. Culturally and even linguistically[56] they had adapted themselves to the customs of their northern overlords. The cultural frontier between

Meroitic Nubia and Roman Egypt lay not at Aswan but at Maharraqa, the boundary of the Dodekaschoenos.

Roman military camps were a prominent feature of the landscape in the Dodekaschoenos. Four of them have been identified archaeologically: two opposite Philae, one at Kertassi, and one at Dakka (Pselchis).[57] According to Trigger's description:

> The desolate region around Shellal, where formerly there had only been a fort and a few small villages, was now adorned with large temples and had a sizable population. On the east bank, opposite the island of Philae, Reisner was able to trace the outlines of two Roman camps which probably had been built to guard the temples on the island. The earlier and smaller camp was square, had a gateway in the middle of each side, and was surrounded by a V-shaped trench in typical Roman style. The larger and later camp was irregular in outline and enclosed the higher ground on the west of the plain. Fragments of what appear to be towers were found in the southeast and northeast corners of the fort. There was a gate in the middle of the east wall of the camp and another near the south tower. A considerable amount of mud brick had fallen from the outer walls into the trench that surrounded the fort. The coins, pottery, and stamped amphorae that were found in this debris indicate that the fort had fallen into ruin late in the Roman period. Inside the walls the excavators found two executioner's trenches containing a total of 102 bodies, evidence of the unhappy end of some insurrection against Roman authority or an unsuccessful raid from the Eastern Desert.[58]

The population of the Dodekaschoenos in Roman times probably exceeded that in any other period of history.[59] This was in part the result of deliberate imperial policy. As in so many other frontier districts, the Roman colonizing effort in Nubia has to be seen in strategic rather than in narrowly economic terms. Large garrisons were necessary to guard the supply line to the gold mines; a large industry was necessary to supply the garrisons.

> Since most of Roman Nubia had a very low agricultural potential even with the saqia, trade must have accounted for a good deal of its prosperity. The Roman garrisons, both cavalry and camel corps, were fed with food brought in from Egypt . . . For a time at least the gold and emerald mines of the Eastern Desert were exploited, until they fell under the control of the desert tribes. Quarrying, mainly for temples, provided a livelihood for workmen at such places as Kertassi where *ex votos* from the reigns of Antoninus Pius, Marcus Aurelius, Caracalla, and Gordian have been found.[60]

As we shall observe presently, the food supplies for the Dodekaschoenos probably came not only from Egypt, but from the neighbouring Meroitic territory to the south as well. Mutual trade between industrialized Roman Nubia and agrarian Meroitic Nubia may in fact be the main explanation for the prosperity enjoyed by both regions.

THE MEROITIC PROVINCE

At the time when Roman garrisons were taking possession of the Dodeka-schoenos, the southern half of Lower Nubia, from Maharraqa to the Second Cataract, remained nearly as deserted as it had been throughout the previous millennium. Three centuries later, the same region had emerged as one of the most important provinces of the Meroitic empire, equalling in population and perhaps surpassing in wealth the older provinces in the south.[61] This sudden renaissance in the long-abandoned north of Nubia was the most important single achievement of the Meroitic era, yet many circumstances connected with it are obscure even today. Royal monuments and inscriptions are surprisingly scarce in Lower Nubia,[62] and no one bothered to record the day-to-day process of resettlement by ordinary folk. The archaeological remains, though rich and abundant, exhibit so little stratigraphy or evidence of chronological development that it is almost impossible to place them in any kind of chronological scheme.[63]

On the basis of textual evidence, the bulk of Meroitic resettlement in Lower Nubia appears to date from the second and third centuries AD.[64] However at least one settlement, at Qasr Ibrim, must antedate the Roman era, since it was captured and briefly garrisoned by Petronius in 23 BC (see 'The Roman province', above). Recent excavation has in fact shown that Qasr Ibrim dates back to New Kingdom times, and was also the site of one of Taharqa's temples (see below).[65] Whether or not there was continued occupation from Napatan to Meroitic times is not yet certain, but at all events the Meroites must have been in possession of Qasr Ibrim in 23 BC, when they were driven out by Petronius. Since there was still no appreciable population in the surrounding district at this time,[66] the Meroitic occupation at Ibrim must have been largely a strategic affair, perhaps intended to counterbalance the growing Ptolemaic and Roman presence in the Dodekaschoenos.

One or two other Meroitic settlements in the north may date from as early a time as does Qasr Ibrim. Pliny's account of the campaign of Petronius mentions four towns taken by him between Qasr Ibrim and Napata, but some or all of them may have been in Upper Nubia.[67] If any other settlements existed below the Second Cataract, they were probably in the places which later emerged as the main urban centres of the Meroitic north: Faras, Gebel Adda, and Karanog (see below). The majority of Meroitic sites in Lower Nubia are however at least a century later in date,[68] and there is nothing to indicate that their foundation had anything to do with strategic policy. In fact, the absence of royal installations suggests that the main thrust of Meroitic resettlement in the north went on without encouragement or even acknowledgement from the rulers at Meroë. It was, rather, the accidental by-product of a technical innovation whose effects were probably quite unforeseen: the introduction of the *saqia* or 'Persian' waterwheel.

The *saqia* is a simple, animal-driven mechanism for raising irrigation water (Fig. 56). A large wooden wheel, set horizontally to the ground, is turned by a continuously walking ox. By the meshing of teeth along its edge, the horizontal wheel turns a second, vertical, geared wheel which is attached to one end of an axle. At the other end of the same axle is a third, larger wheel around which are passed two long loops of rope, with a series of pottery buckets lashed between them. As the wheel turns, the buckets (*qadus*) descend one after the other into a well, where they fill with water and then begin their upward journey, all in one continuous movement. As they pass the apogee of the upper wheel and begin their downward descent, their fluid content is spilled into a trough and from there carried away into irrigation channels. The device is primitive and inefficient enough by modern standards, and yet as an advance over the age-old *shaduf* (lever-lift) of Egypt and Nubia it is nothing short of revolutionary. The substitution of animal for human motivation alone permits a fivefold increase in power input. Still more important, the endless bucket chain of the *saqia* can bring up water from a well of any depth without appreciable loss of efficiency, whereas three *shadufs* working in tandem permit a maximum lift of no more than thirty feet (cf. Ch. 2).

For the farmers of Egypt, the *saqia* was a distinct convenience; in Nubia its effects were revolutionary. No longer was irrigation confined to fields lying not more than thirty feet above the river's surface, and in consequence a large part of the Nubian floodplain became cultivable for the first time since the early New Kingdom. If the result was not quite a land-rush, it was at least a very rapid and very thorough reoccupation of the long-abandoned territory between the First and Second Cataracts.[69] Within a few centuries the population of Lower Nubia rose from near zero to something like 60,000;[70] larger than at any other period before modern times.[71]

As with so many technological inventions, no one recorded the time or place of the *saqia*'s origin. It is thought to have been invented somewhere in the Greek orient – perhaps in Mesopotamia – from whence it was introduced into the Nile Valley in the second century BC.[72] Its southward spread up the river must have been slow, for we have no direct evidence of *saqias* in Nubia until the early centuries of our era.[73] Once again the exact date of their introduction is missing, but we can perhaps infer it from the fact that the great majority of Meroitic sites in Lower Nubia date from the second, third, and fourth centuries AD,[74] and these sites are never without the remains of distinctive, knobbed pottery vessels (*qadus*) which were and still are made only for use with the *saqia*.[75] If our reading of this evidence is correct, it would appear that the main thrust of Meroitic resettlement

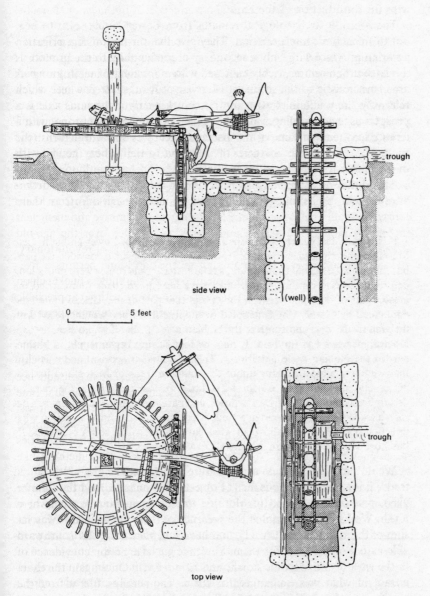

trough

side view

0   5 feet

(well)

trough

top view

Fig. 56. Diagram of *saqia* in operation

in the north, beginning in the second century AD, was directly connected with the introduction of the *saqia*.

The Meroitic archaeological remains from Lower Nubia seem to bear out this economic interpretation. They give the impression of a primarily agrarian province with only a secondary dependence on trade. In place of the large urban centres, richly endowed with monumental buildings, which are characteristic of the southern Meroitic provinces, we find only a few relatively small administrative centres, but a nearly continuous string of prosperous farming villages along the Nile.[76] This important economic difference may explain some of the discrepant features of Meroitic culture in the north, such as the northerners' devotion to the fertility goddess Isis in preference to Amon and Apedemak.

The high level of material prosperity enjoyed by the Meroitic north is attested both by its village remains and by its cemeteries. Yet, as Millet remarks:

It is a great deal easier to describe the relative wealth of Lower Nubia in Late Meroitic times than to account for it; certainly trade played a considerable part, but this is only a partial explanation, as the eastern trade routes were in use long before the second century, and it must have been these roads that carried the greater part of the trade between Egypt and that part of the African hinterland dominated by Meroë. One is tempted to suppose that trade was increased with the area to the west and south of the Nubian Nile . . . but if so, no clear archaeological evidence has survived. It may be that slaving began to play a greater part in the Nubian trade pattern . . . This of course is speculation; it is clear that we know almost nothing about the southern trade of Meroë and its provinces and dependencies, except what little we can infer from the classical descriptions of typically African luxuries, and parallels in more recent times. That such a trade existed is beyond question; what form it took, how far and in what direction it reached, and above all what part Lower Nubia south of the Dodekaschoenos played in it, are matters we can only guess at.[77]

We do not need to guess at the nature and volume of the south-bound trade; it is attested by thousands of objects of Roman or Egyptian bronze, glass, and ceramic found in Meroitic graves throughout the empire of Kush. We have already noted the presence of these goods in the Meroitic sites of the steppelands (Ch. 11), and have said something about the probable nature of the trade for them. Yet trade goods are even more abundant in the sites of the Meroitic north, and here we remain almost entirely ignorant of what was exchanged for them. The supply of exotic tropical products might easily account for the prosperity of the south, but Lower Nubia at the beginning of the Christian era was no longer an important source of such goods. It seems unlikely, too, that overland trade was highly developed between Lower Nubia and the western Sudan, or we should have more evidence of commercial centres and of royal interest in that region.

On the contrary, everything points to the development of trade largely in the hands of small private entrepreneurs.[78] Under the circumstances it is perhaps safest to accept the suggestion, put forward long ago by Griffith, that the prosperity of Lower Nubia rested not upon long-distance trade in luxury goods but simply on the supply of foodstuffs to the overpopulated Roman settlements in the Dodekaschoenos.[79] At all events we know that there was a flourishing market at Hiera Sykaminos, on the border between Roman and Meroitic Nubia.[80]

Within the Meroitic province of Lower Nubia we can recognize only three or four 'metropolitan' centres. Near the middle of the province were the great fortress of Qasr Ibrim (Primis to the Romans, *Pedeme* in Meroitic texts) and the town of Karanog, located a few miles from the fortress on the opposite side of the Nile (Fig. 55). Farther to the south, the fortified settlements of Gebel Adda and Faras (*Pakhoras* in ancient texts) stood at a slightly greater distance from one another. All four of these towns were at one time or another important administrative centres. Their recent destruction has been one of the greatest misfortunes of the Nubian archaeological campaign, for none of the four was investigated as thoroughly or as systematically as its importance warranted. The fault in most cases was not that of the excavators; all of the sites except Karanog had remained important throughout the later stages of history, and their Meroitic structures were so overburdened with later remains that their complete investigation was beyond the resources of any expedition.[81] As a result we remain ignorant of much that we might have hoped to learn about the official aspects of Meroitic settlement in Lower Nubia, and we are left to infer a great deal from little-understood textual evidence.

Qasr Ibrim, Gebel Adda, and Faras were all walled settlements. Though differing considerably in size and in the details of their fortification, the original military function of all three is apparent. Ibrim and Adda stood on high promontories overlooking the east bank of the Nile, and were surrounded by massive girdle walls of brick and stone (Pl. XVIb). Portions of the stone masonry were of much finer quality than is usually found in Meroitic construction;[82] it was apparently this feature which suggested to Monneret de Villard that the two sites were of Ptolemaic origin.[83] However, Millet has been able to show that the stone girdle wall at Gebel Adda was of very late date, and was preceded by an earlier, bastioned fortification of mud brick.[84] At Qasr Ibrim too we now know that the main fortification walls are of post-Ptolemaic date, though the site itself is much older. At Faras the fortified enclosure stood on much lower ground immediately beside the Nile. It was surrounded by a stout, bastioned wall over thirty feet high, of which the lower thirteen feet were of stone and the remainder of mud brick.[85] All of the fortified cities had monumental stone gateways on their landward sides, as well as one or more postern gates.

The Meroitic fortification walls of Lower Nubia were, before their inundation, considerably more imposing and better preserved than anything which was found within them. Griffith assumed that the enclosed area at Faras had been filled up with public and private buildings,[86] but few of these came to light in the course of more recent excavations at Faras by a Polish expedition, although fragments of what had probably been Meroitic temple blocks were found here and there on the site. The few Meroitic houses which were discovered were very irregular structures which had themselves been built from the fallen blocks of older, pharaonic temples.[87]

At Gebel Adda, a large part of the area within the original mud-brick fortification seems to have been entirely devoid of buildings.[88] For much of its history the place was apparently nothing more than a local military post. At a late date, however, it was chosen for development as a major administrative and religious centre. The original brick fortifications were buried and overbuilt with a larger and more impressive wall of dressed stone, and a temple was begun within. In the words of the excavator:

> The fourth building period at Adda was without doubt the result of a decision to change the nature of the settlement; an enormous platform of rubble and debris encased in well-made masonry walls was erected over the northeast corner of the recently repaired fortification system, in such a way as to completely cover it from view. On the great podium thus created, and occupying the whole northern third of it, was erected a temple of well-built sandstone masonry, now preserved only for the lower three courses or so. It is uncertain whether the temple was entirely of stone or whether it followed a familiar Meroitic style . . . and was of mud brick on a base of stone. Bases and drums for columns of almost a metre in diameter were quarried in the sandstone out-croppings south of the citadel, but were never put in place in the outer court of the temple, perhaps because the brick-rubbish and debris forming much of the podium's foundation proved to be insufficiently solid. Doors and openwork window frames were of stone. The sanctuary, a narrow room surrounded by a corridor, was provided with a painted sandstone bark-stand of the usual type; the face of the stand was decorated with the traditional representation of a kneeling king with arms raised to support the sacred boat, but no royal name could be identified on the fragments that survived. Scraps of gold leaf on plastered wood may represent all that is left of the bark itself. Other objects found in the remains point to a modest luxury suitable to the prosperity of the times. At least two large official stelae were set up within the temple area, and the battered head of a sandstone statue of a Meroitic king shows that at least one ruler interested himself in the temple's adornment. No royal name was found anywhere in the temple . . .
>
> At the same time as the building of the platform and its temple . . . was the rebuilding of the single large house identified by the excavators inside the walls . . . Some at least of the new house was built with several stone foundation courses, like the 'palace' at Karanog and so many of the Faras buildings, and decoration in painted plaster – only a few fragments showing a well-drawn procession of cows were found – added to at least one of the new rooms. The

impression gained by the excavators from the small portion of the building which could be cleared was that the rebuilding was on a fairly grand scale and that two storeys were probably involved.[89]

Similar in many respects to Gebel Adda, but even larger in size, was the fortified citadel of Qasr Ibrim. It stood on a lofty headland so high above the river valley that it is even yet above the level of Lake Nasser, and is the sole remaining site of any consequence in Lower Nubia. Excavations at Qasr Ibrim are, happily, still in progress, and are only now beginning to reveal many features of the early history of the site. Discoveries in 1972 revealed for the first time that there was a New Kingdom stone temple at Ibrim, which was partially rebuilt in mud brick in the time of Taharqa and was further repaired in Meroitic times.[90] Another temple of stone was begun at the north end of the site in the late Meroitic period, but it may never have been finished; at all events its walls are entirely devoid of decoration or inscriptions.[91]

A distinctive feature of Qasr Ibrim is a projecting balcony (the so-called Podium) with a finely dressed stone balustrade, which juts out from the west side of the citadel. It is notably unlike anything else on the site and looks in general like Roman workmanship; it is in fact closely similar to balconies at Kalabsha and other Roman sites in the Dodekaschoenos and Upper Egypt.[92] The Podium might therefore be a relic of the brief period of Roman occupation under Petronius, from 23 to 21 BC. Discoveries in 1976 suggest that the Podium may be part of a larger complex of Roman construction.

The massive stone fortification walls of the Qasr Ibrim citadel are clearly later in date than the Podium, and in fact in large part post-Meroitic. As at Gebel Adda, however, there are traces of an older wall which is surely of Meroitic date.

Within the fortification walls the excavations at Qasr Ibrim have penetrated to the Meroitic levels only in a few places; for the most part they are buried beneath from 15 to 25 feet of later deposits. We now have conclusive evidence that the brick temple of Taharqa was repaired in Meroitic times, apparently after a lapse of time during which it suffered extensive damage. There are other, apparently secular Meroitic houses in the vicinity of the temple, but their extent and most details of their construction remain to be ascertained. It is noteworthy that the Meroitic levels at Qasr Ibrim have yielded pottery types markedly distinct from, and almost certainly older than, the typical Meroitic pottery found in most Lower Nubian sites (see 'Arts and industries', below). The wares are mostly undecorated and are much more in keeping with the traditions of pharaonic than of Hellenic times; in this respect they resemble the typical wares found at Meroë and Musawwarat (cf. Ch. 11). This evidence raises (as does a good deal of textual evidence) the distinct possibility that

Qasr Ibrim was occupied at a very early date in the Meroitic period, preceding the main wave of reoccupation in Lower Nubia. We cannot totally rule out the possibility of continued occupation throughout the entire period from Napatan to Meroitic times, when nearly all of the surrounding district was depopulated. If any garrisons at all were maintained in the north during the hiatus period, Qasr Ibrim would have been one of the obvious places.

Karanog represents a different type of settlement from the three just discussed. Its rather scattered cluster of houses was defended not by a girdle wall but by a massive, three-storey castle of mud brick which dominated the surrounding buildings and countryside (Pl. XVIIa). This structure is unique among Nubian buildings of the pre-Christian period. It cannot be dated with absolute certainty to Meroitic times, for nothing distinctive was found within it. The adjoining town-site, although founded in the Meroitic period, continued to be occupied until several centuries later.[93] However, the smooth, whitewashed walls and round, brick vaults of the Karanog castle are much more in character with the best Meroitic houses (see 'Town and village life', below) than they are with any later structures.

If our attempts to describe and interpret the Meroitic cities of Lower Nubia are somewhat meagre, allowance must be made for the fact that these places, except Karanog, became also the great administrative and religious centres of Medieval Nubia. Within the fortification walls there was a great deal of systematic dismantling and overbuilding of the earlier remains, not only because the stone was wanted for churches but because the obliteration of older symbols of religious authority was part of the Christian ideological programme (see Ch. 14). As a result, our picture of the Meroitic occupation at Faras, Gebel Adda, and Qasr Ibrim might have remained quite incomplete even had these cities been fully excavated.

Making all allowances for subsequent destruction, however, the absence of royal monuments and inscriptions in the Meroitic north is striking. The fortress and the palace, rather than the temple and the tomb, seem to be the main symbolic expressions of authority in Lower Nubia. They proclaim the majesty of the state in general, rather than that of the ruling family in particular, since they are unadorned by royal inscriptions. Throughout the whole of Meroitic Lower Nubia, the only rulers' names which have thus far come to light are associated with a small carved lion[94] and with a fragmentary stele,[95] both found at Qasr Ibrim. On the other hand the temple structures themselves, both at Ibrim and at Gebel Adda,[96] seem to have borne no royal inscriptions, in marked contrast to the lavishly inscribed temples of the Meroitic south (cf. Ch. 11). It is necessary to recall too that both of the northern temples seem to have been built at a very late date, and may in fact have been left unfinished.[97] The general absence of religious monuments in Lower Nubia would be incomprehensible were it not for the fact that we can recognize in Philae the great religious centre not only of Roman Nubia, but of the Meroitic province as well. However much the cult of Isis may have been fostered and encouraged by the Meroitic rulers, however, it remained an international religion which could not serve to express and reinforce the authority of the Kushite dynasty in the same way as did the proprietary cults of Amon and Apedemak in the south.

All things considered, it is difficult to avoid the impression that the rulers at Meroë were not much interested in their northern province. Its reoccupation seems to have been in large part a spontaneous movement unconnected with and unencouraged by royal policy. Once resettled, the Meroitic north developed into a largely agrarian district which, though it enjoyed considerable local prosperity, was capable of producing little revenue for the crown. The purely Meroitic portion of Lower Nubia continued to be by-passed by the main long-distance trade routes upon which the prosperity of the south depended, for their northern terminus was within the Dodekaschoenos. As a result, the monarchy may have had more interest in maintaining its position and influence in the Roman province than in exercising its authority in the area south of Maharraqa. Such Meroitic inscriptions as we find in the north are the records of embassies to Philae[98] and to Rome rather than of royal visits or endowments to the Meroitic cities. As Millet observes, '. . . one is forced to conclude that the provincials lived their lives with a minimum of royal interference or interest.'[99]

It is evident that such government as existed in the Meroitic north rested on quite different principles from those which were traditional in the provinces of Napata and Meroë. Neither royal princes nor priestly bureaucracy were resident in Lower Nubia; their place was taken by local officials with distinctive titles which are unknown to us from other areas.[100] Our knowledge of them comes chiefly from their funerary stelae – written in the Meroitic language – and a few commemorative graffiti. Millet has recently made an imaginative effort to sort out this fragmentary and enigmatic evidence, and from it to arrive at some kind of picture of the provincial administration in Lower Nubia.[101] Although his approach remains speculative and in places largely intuitive, it is worth quoting here as representing one possible explanation for the political and cultural discrepancies between the Meroitic north and the Meroitic south.

Millet believes that the earliest administrative centre in the northern province was at Faras, but that it later gave way to Qasr Ibrim.[102] The latter can be identified both archaeologically and textually as the most important Meroitic community in the north during most of its history. At a very late date, however, a separate administrative sub-centre was developed at Gebel Adda.[103] The selection of this site in preference to neighbouring

Faras may have been due to its more impressive physical setting, which is closely reminiscent of Qasr Ibrim.

Millet identifies three main classes of Meroitic officials in the north, whose titles he translates as 'General of the River' (*pelmes*), 'Prince of Akin' (*peste*), and 'Royal Crown-Prince' (*pqr*). It appears that the latter two titles were hereditary in the same family, and that *pqr* was the more important of the two. According to Millet's analysis:

> It would seem that the princely family handed down the offices of *pqr* . . . and *peste* . . . as well as other honors associated with them, in descent by the female line, so that a prince on dying left his offices not to his sons, but to the sons of one of his sisters, and that each brother held the offices in turn, probably by seniority. It is also probable that the system extended itself to the sons of all the sisters in turn, so that first cousins and even possibly second cousins became involved.

Enough of these princes and their kin claim relationship[104] to *pqr*'s . . . to make it fairly certain that they belonged normally to the same family, and that the offices passed down the brotherhood group in close association, and it seems also clear . . . that the office of 'crown-prince' was the more important of the two. Despite the presence of this title . . . there is never a single mention of a king or of a . . . 'queen-mother' as relatives . . . I am driven to the conclusion that the connection of the princely family of Akin to the royal family was remote in the extreme, that the royal-style titles of *pqr*, *peste*, and *qere-sm* were purely traditional, and that we are in fact dealing with a hereditary provincial vice-royalty free from royal appointment, which made use of princely titles either because they did in fact trace their ultimate origin back to a royal ancestor or because it had once been the tradition for the governors of Nubia to be young princes learning the duties of rule in the provinces. The governors of Nubia in Pharaonic times had been styled 'king's sons of Kush,' although they were not so in fact . . .

The usual order of preference in the inscriptions of persons who claim kin to both *pqr*'s and *peste*'s . . . would seem clearly to indicate that the *pqr* . . . was the more important of the two . . . Now we know . . . of some six or seven *peste*'s who were buried in our area, either at Faras or at Karanog. But no tomb or tomb-monument for a crown-prince has ever been found in Lower Nubia, nor do we know of any woman who was a *pqr*'s wife having been buried there. It must be concluded that the burial place and the residence of the *pqr*'s lay elsewhere, and that that place was probably the family's real seat. Men who were commemorated on their tombstones as *peste* only were those who had died before they had inherited the crown-princedom, the real summit of the family's '*cursus honorum*' . . . As to where the crown-princes' seat lay, the only likely choice is, I think, Napata itself.[105]

If we accept this interpretation, we have to visualize a semi-autonomous feudal principality comprising both the Napatan and the Lower Nubian provinces of the Meroitic empire. The local rulers claimed some sort of relationship to the royal family at Meroë, but it was apparently a remote one. The main seat of power of the self-styled crown-princes (*pqr*) was at Napata, while the north was governed by lesser members of the family (*peste*) as their deputies. It is necessary to reiterate however that Millet's reconstruction of the Meroitic scheme in Lower Nubia is highly conjectural; for this and other reasons it is partly rejected both by Haycock[106] and by Trigger.[107] The latter correctly observes that 'Reading texts in a language we don't understand is a hazardous business at best'.[108] Moreover, a few of the mortuary texts from Lower Nubia would seem to suggest that political connections between the northern province and Meroë were closer than Millet believes. One of the *peste*'s of Faras ultimately became High Priest of Amon at Meroë,[109] and two of the individuals buried at Arminna may also have been priests of Apedemak – a deity of whom we have otherwise very little evidence in Lower Nubia.[110] Family connections with Meroë and even with the Meroitic ruling house are claimed in a number of other funerary inscriptions from Arminna and elsewhere.[111]

The relationship of the 'generals of the river' (*pelmes*) to the *pqr* and the *peste* is not at all clearly attested. This office appears to have been hereditary in the male line only.[112] Millet believes that it originated not in the Meroitic province of Lower Nubia but in the Dodekaschoenos, where it evolved from the older Graeco–Roman title of *strategos*.

> That the family had strong ties with the Dodekaschoenos ... region is clear from the titles of Amanitewawi and his brother in the Philae graffiti, his family's close connection with the Philae temple estates ('agents of Isis'), and from the fact that the one General of the River whose tomb we can locate, and his wife ... were buried in the Madiq area ... just south of the frontier of the Dodekaschoenos itself. Presumably their residence was in that general area also, perhaps in the Meroitic town whose ruins occupy a large area at Wadi el-Arab [see 'Town and village life', below]. The other place where members of this family are known to have been buried is Gebel Adda, at almost the furthest possible remove from the Dodekaschoenos.
>
> It would seem, then, that Adda was another seat of the family of the generals, but whether the generals themselves resided there cannot be proven ... In any case, the presence in strength of the Wayekiye family at Adda shows that they did not remain purely a family of the Dodekaschoenos, but were also settled in the more truly Meroitic south.[113]

The implication is that the generals derived their power originally from the Dodekaschoenos, but later extended their influence also into the Meroitic province of Lower Nubia, where they established an independent seat. If this interpretation is correct, we have to recognize a kind of condominium principle in Meroitic Lower Nubia as well as in the Roman province. In theory the *peste* and the *pqr* derived their authority from the south as 'royal crown-princes', the *pelmes* derived his from the north as 'agent of Isis'.[114] These overlapping power structures presented an obvious danger of rivalry and conflict, but it seems to have been averted in typical medieval fashion by a network of intermarriages between the two princely families.[115]

Whatever the details of its administrative organization may have been, there can be no doubt that Lower Nubia from Maharraqa to the Second Cataract was at least nominally subject to the Meroitic king in the south, and that its ruling family was of Meroitic origin and spoke the Meroitic language. The same cannot be said with equal confidence of the subject population. The cultural and social differences between the Meroitic north and the rest of the kingdom are sufficient to raise the possibility that some or most of the northerners belonged to a different ethnic group, subject to Meroë but not sharing all of its cultural traditions. On the one hand many village sites of Lower Nubia show a continuity of occupation from Meroitic to modern times;[116] on the other hand we are unable to recognize in the modern Nubian language a descendant of the ancient Meroitic language. We are therefore obliged to consider the possibility that the pioneer settlers who reoccupied Lower Nubia in the first and second centuries AD came not from the immediate districts of Napata and Meroë but from some outlying, Nubian-speaking province, perhaps to the west of the Nile, which was peripheral to the Meroitic domain.[117] This question will be considered in more detail in the next chapter.

TOWN AND VILLAGE LIFE

Except for the great administrative centres discussed earlier, the Meroitic settlements both in Lower Nubia and in the south were unwalled[118] and relatively planless. The somewhat imaginative picture of Karanog which Woolley painted sixty years ago would serve to describe many another Meroitic settlement as well:

> The town was one of narrow and irregular streets, if streets they could be called, that turned and twisted between houses two and three storeys high which, though oriented regularly, were dotted here and there at random, having no uniform frontage, but set back or projecting forward according as the area occupied was greater or smaller than that of its neighbor. One house, built over the ruins of an older structure, might stand on a roughly levelled plot several feet higher than that next door; the solid walls of some three-storeyed building whose courtyard blocked with storehouses and low-vaulted magazines betokened the wealth of its owner, stood cheek by jowl with the straggling hovel of a poor man . . .[119]

Woolley's description points up two common characteristics of the Meroitic town: its planless congestion, and the surprising diversity of its architecture. As the author perceptively notes, even the everyday dwellings are extraordinarily variable in size and quality, and in fact convey a strong impression of class differentiation.[120] The same conditions can be observed in most of the larger Meroitic communities of Lower Nubia, among them Wadi el-Arab,[121] Arminna,[122] ash-Shaukan,[123] Argin,[124] and Meinarti.[125] At each of these places a few stoutly built 'de luxe' houses were surrounded by an irregular cluster of much less pretentious dwellings.[126]

The 'de luxe' houses of Meroitic times were extremely well and sturdily built, and so consistent in plan as to suggest that they were the work of professional house builders rather than of local villagers – as are the best houses in Nubia today.[127] They were nearly square in outline, with walls nearly thirty inches thick, and were entered by a single door at the south or south-east side (cf. Pl. XVII b). Within, the great majority of houses were divided into two parallel vaulted chambers of nearly equal size, and in many of the larger houses these were further subdivided by cross-partitions (cf. Fig. 57). The stoutness of the walls, the preserved remains of stairways,

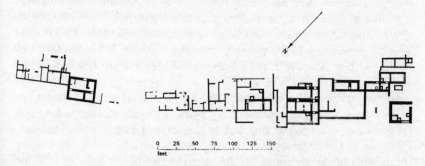

Fig. 57. Plan of a portion of Meroitic town, Wadi el-Arab

and the occasional finding of ground-floor rooms without lateral entrances all make it evident that the largest of the Meroitic houses had two and perhaps even three storeys, as Woolley suggests in the description of Karanog quoted above. Light and air were admitted to the long, vaulted chambers through pairs of narrow, slit-like windows situated just below ceiling level in the end walls – a system of ventilation which has been retained in all later Nubian vaulted houses. Interior walls and ceilings were very smoothly plastered and in nearly every case were white- or yellow-washed. In these characteristics, as well as in the regularity of their construction, the Meroitic 'de luxe' houses exceeded in quality the dwellings of any later period before modern times.[128]

Ordinary Meroitic houses were much less regular in plan and construction than were the 'de luxe' houses. The walls were consistently about fifteen inches thick and were seldom notably straight. A peculiarity of their construction is the general use of 'header' (crosswise) bricks only, without the alternating courses of 'stretcher' (lengthwise) bricks which are

357

usual in brick masonry.[129] These rather thin and irregular walls can only have supported a light roofing of poles and thatch. There are few traces of smooth interior plaster or of whitewash. Most rooms had a storage jar set into the floor in at least one corner, and a fireplace in another. The latter were made in many cases from the necks or bodies of large storage jars which were let into the floor. A common feature of nearly all Meroitic houses, large and small, is the complex stratification of their floors. Apparently ash and refuse accumulated at a very rapid rate, and were never cleared out; instead, new and higher floor levels were periodically established, and new storage pots and fireplaces were installed. As a result the excavator often finds the pots and fireplace structures 'stacked' one above the other as he excavates these dwellings.[130]

A consistent feature of Meroitic ordinary houses is their dense, contiguous clustering. While the 'de luxe' houses always stood slightly apart from one another, and are clearly recognizable as individual family dwellings, the humbler structures often crowded together in clusters of up to fifty rooms, within which it is difficult to recognize individual family units. This characteristic is found not only throughout Lower Nubia, but far away in the south at Abu Geili, the southernmost Meroitic settlement which is so far known to us (cf. Ch. 11).[131]

In one Meroitic village, at Gaminarti Island, the main house cluster can be seen to comprise several recurring pairs of rooms, each including one long and one short room, and each having its own entrance from the outside (Fig. 58).[132] In most cases storage vessels were found in the smaller room while the larger room had fireplaces in two of the four corners, for cooking and heat. Presumably, each pair of rooms was the apartment of an individual family. However, this kind of pairing of rooms has not been observed consistently at other Meroitic village-sites.

As might be expected, the smallest Meroitic villages, like those on the islands of Gaminarti[133] and Meili[134] in the Second Cataract, were made up entirely of the commoner sort of houses, and boasted no 'de luxe' dwellings. Elsewhere the 'de luxe' houses appear in many cases to have been built at a late date, and partly overlying the remains of earlier houses of the humbler type.[135] This probably signifies nothing more than the growing wealth of the Nubian villages, whose most enterprising families could in time afford the luxury of elaborate houses built by itinerant (perhaps Egyptian) specialists. Something very similar can be observed in the Nubian villages of the recent past, in contrast to those of the nineteenth century which contained no conspicuously large houses. The villagers of Meroitic times were perhaps inspired by the example of the more developed Roman–Egyptian communities in the Dodekaschoenos, from whence their professional builders may have come. However, we cannot entirely rule out another interpretation of the 'de luxe' houses: they may signify

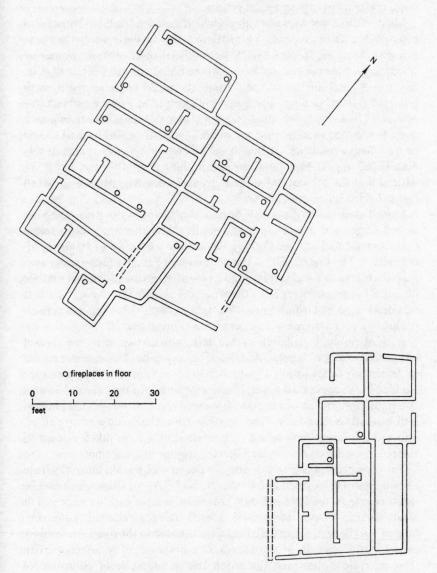

O fireplaces in floor

0   10   20   30

feet

Fig. 58. Plan of Meroitic houses, Gaminarti Island, Second Cataract

359

that the Nubian villages at some point became subject to a new landlord class, under a developing feudal system.

Most of the larger Meroitic villages which included 'de luxe' houses also boasted one or more public installations. Among these we can perhaps recognize temples, 'palaces' or at least official residences, magazines or warehouses, wine presses, and baths. At the island village of Meinarti (Fig. 59), the original nucleus of the community seems to have been a small group of public buildings which was built before any of the surrounding houses.[136] In a slightly elevated position was a monumental building with stone foundations and interior colonnades – perhaps either a small temple or an official residence. It had been so completely and systematically demolished in post-Meroitic times that nothing remained except its foundations and the ornamental stone steps and stone-flagged landing which had provided its original access.

Immediately beside the temple or palace at Meinarti stood a rectangular walled compound whose north and south sides were lined with vaulted chambers of equal size (see Fig. 59). Beneath each floor were two low, vaulted cellars. The finding within the compound of three bronze scales suggests that this was a marketplace and a row of shops maintained as a public facility.[137] A much larger but otherwise very similar installation at Faras was designated by Griffith as the 'Western Palace',[138] but was much more probably also a warehouse and perhaps a caravanserai.[139]

A third public installation at Meinarti, situated close to the market compound, was a wine press. A series of three dug-out basins was arranged in descending series within a long, narrow room (Fig. 59).[140] Grapes were trodden in the uppermost basin; from its sloping floor the juice ran down a gutter and through an ornamental, lion-head spout, from which it plunged into a small settling basin. The overflow from this middle basin ran off into a third, larger tank where fermentation may have taken place, and where amphorae or skins were filled for storage and transport.

The wine press at Meinarti is one of a dozen such installations which are known from various parts of Lower Nubia.[141] All of them which can be dated belong to the later Meroitic era. However, only at Meinarti and at Wadi el-Arab[142] were the presses housed indoors and within the confines of a settlement; elsewhere they were situated in the open, presumably close to the vineyards. Most of them were hewn out of native rock. With these exceptions, however, the dozen known examples of Nubian wine presses are so similar in the details of their design and construction as to suggest that they were contemporaneous in age, and perhaps the work of a single designer. The basins vary only slightly in size from one group to the next, and in every known case they were lined with reddish-tinted cement. In every case, also, the outlet from the pressing tank to the settling tank was carved in the form of a lion's head (Pl. XVIIIa).[143]

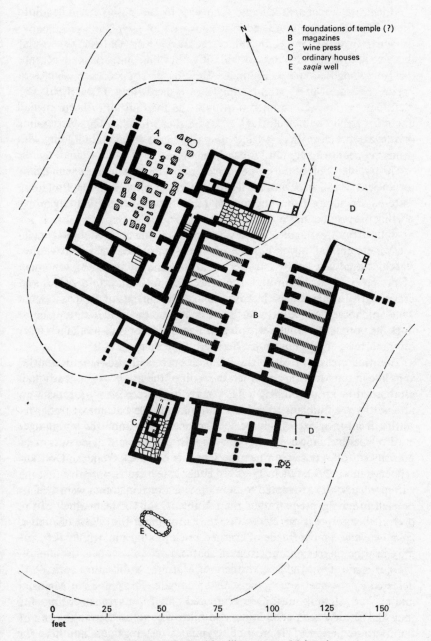

A   foundations of temple (?)
B   magazines
C   wine press
D   ordinary houses
E   *saqia* well

0   25   50   75   100   125   150
feet

Fig. 59. Plan of Meroitic village centre, Meinarti

Viticulture was not a complete novelty to the Nubians of Meroitic times. Wine had been produced in various parts of Egypt, and presumably traded from there into Nubia, since the days of the Old Kingdom, and there were attempts at vine cultivation within the southern lands during the New Kingdom and again under Taharqa.[144] These experiments were apparently short-lived and ultimately unsuccessful. Throughout the pharaonic period, the costs of transport and the difficulties of local production were probably sufficient to insure that wine-drinking remained a privilege of the élite. The mass of Nubians, like the *fellaheen* of Egypt, were primarily beer-drinkers until much later times.

The popular 'cult of the grape' came to Egypt and Nubia, as to much of the ancient world, as part of the legacy of Greek civilization. The Ptolemies fostered viticulture from one end of Egypt to the other, and began exporting the product not only to Nubia but to various Mediterranean lands as well.[145] In Greek hands, however, the development of a popular taste for wine went far beyond the mere mass-production of the beverage. Bacchic ritual was subtly encouraged and ultimately diffused over much of the civilized world through such media as folk-tales, folk ritual, and graphic art. In Meroitic Nubia, thousands of fragments of Egyptian-made wine amphorae bear witness to the ultimate success of this enterprise, as does the popularity of vine-wreath and Bacchic decorative motifs not only on imported pottery, but on native Meroitic pottery as well.

The wine presses of Meinarti, Wadi el-Arab, and elsewhere date from very late in the Meroitic era, when the 'cult of the grape' was already well established in Lower Nubia.[146] They may therefore possibly represent an attempt by the Nubians to redress an unfavourable balance of trade, resulting from their excessively heavy dependence on imported vintages. It is also possible, however, that the supply of imported wine was temporarily cut off – possibly when the Romans withdrew from the Dodekaschoenos in AD 297 (see Ch. 13).[147] In either case it seems probable that the entrepreneurs who attempted to develop viticulture in Nubia were Greeks or Hellenized Egyptians rather than Nubians, for the technology of the presses themselves is distinctly foreign. Throughout the whole of Nubia, *opus signinum* cement (made of crushed brick in a lime matrix)[148] is found only in wine presses and in 'Roman' baths.

Once again, the would-be vintners of Meroitic Nubia were apparently defeated by the heat and dryness of the climate. The presses at Meinarti and at Wadi el-Arab must have been used only for a very short time, for they had already been abandoned and filled with refuse before the end of the Meroitic period.[149] Thereafter Egyptian wines regained, and held for many centuries, their monopoly of the Nubian market. Even after the Moslem conquest of Egypt, the annual supply of 1,300 *kanyr* of wine to Christian Nubia was guaranteed by treaty.[150]

An astonishing discovery at Seyala, near the northern limit of Meroitic Nubia, bears further witness to the flourishing of the vine cult at the close of the Meroitic era. In an area not much more than 160 feet square, an Austrian expedition found no fewer than nineteen tavern-compounds, of which they excavated ten.[151] The sites are thus summarized by a reviewer:

With one partial exception, each of the ten compounds that was excavated conformed to a single plan. The interior walls were lined with a broad mastaba, made of stones and mud-plaster. Near at hand were small tables, again constructed of stone. In one corner of the compound was a 'pantry,' often surrounded with exceptionally thick stone walls and in one instance provided with a bolted door. In the center of the compound was a stone block with circular holes in it, which Kromer believes was used to hold one to three water vessels. Also nearby were traces of a hearth. A small oven was built near one of the walls.

Within and around the houses a considerable amount of pottery was found. Most of it consisted of fragments of amphorae, pitchers and jug-like vases, 'beakers', cups, pottery bells and oil-lamps. Numerous amphorae appear to have been stored in the 'pantries' and cups were found around some of the better preserved tables.

In the light of this evidence, Kromer concluded that his complex was a group of taverns, which also served as guest houses or places to spend the night. The taverns appear to have been located behind the small town or village that used Cemetery 138; of this town all trace has disappeared. Much of the wine consumed in the taverns probably was made in the wine press . . . discovered not far from the site.[152]

The excavator suggested a Roman date and origin for the Seyala taverns.[153] However, the pottery and other objects found in them place these sites unmistakably in the 'twilight zone' between the Meroitic and X Horizons – considerably later in time than the Roman abandonment of the Dodekaschoenos.[154] Moreover the very crude and irregular architecture of the buildings at Seyala is certainly not Roman, but is typical of many Nubian buildings of the X Horizon. A very similar structure at Abd el Qadir, which is certainly also a tavern, dates from the end of the X Horizon and the beginning of the succeeding Christian period.[155] Given this later dating, it is unlikely that the wine which was consumed in the Seyala taverns was produced at the nearby wine press unless it remained in use considerably longer than did those at Wadi el-Arab and Meinarti.

One of the most elaborate of all Nubian taverns was built at Qasr Ibrim in the last years of the Meroitic era.[156] The building stood at the intersection of two of the main streets of the town (cf. Ch. 13), and was notable for the quality of its stonework. The lower walls were of carefully dressed pink sandstone, and were adorned with carvings presumably intended to proclaim the function of the building: bunches of grapes and a representation of an amphora in a stand.[157] The upper walls (destroyed during a later rebuilding) had evidently been of whitewashed brick, and were pierced at intervals by windows with ornamental carved grilles.[158] The building was identified originally as a palace because of its unusually fine stonework and decoration,[159] but the finding in 1972 of masses of broken amphorae and drinking cups left no doubt as to its true function.[160]

One more public installation in Meroitic Nubia deserves mention. At Faras, not far from the so-called 'Western Palace', were found the remains of what seems to have been a tiny bath.[161] Two small sunken basins, one rectangular and the other oval in shape, were connected through their side walls by means of a ceramic pipe. From the bottom of the oval basin, which was situated slightly lower than its neighbour, a drainpipe ran off to a stone-lined water channel near by. Both basins measured about thirty inches by sixty inches – not much larger than a modern bathtub. Since the upper parts of the structures had been destroyed by erosion, the original depth could not be determined, and no trace of an intake mechanism was found. However, a number of lengths of ceramic pipe were discovered lying on the floor of a nearby Meroitic house. The function of these structures as baths is conjectural, but it is difficult to suggest any other use for them. They differ sufficiently in size and design from all of the known wine presses of Nubia to make it unlikely that they were intended for that purpose. They are, however, the only known example of a bathing installation in Nubia except for the baths at Meroë itself (Ch. 11).[162] Like the baths at Meroë, as well as the wine presses of Lower Nubia, the Faras basins were lined with reddish-tinted *opus signinum* cement. Sherds found in and around them, as well as in two nearby houses, date them to the Meroitic age.

In sum, the town- and village-sites of the Meroitic north seem to give a picture of everyday life rather different from that which we associate with the steppelands. In the south, despite the flourishing of private commerce, the ancient symbols and traditions of pharaonic civilization were still strong, and the temple and the tomb were their outstanding public expressions. In the north, the secularizing influence of classical civilization was much more immediately felt, and the foci of public life in many communities were apparently the bath, the tavern, and the market.

The Meroitic towns and villages of Lower Nubia represent one of the urban climaxes in Nubian social history. While none of them was, so far as we know, as large as some of the settlements of later times, their remains indicate a degree of social differentiation and economic specialization which has hardly been duplicated before the twentieth century. We should perhaps also include ethnic diversity in this picture: the vintners at Meinarti and Wadi el-Arab were very probably Greeks, and the merchant class may have been partly or even largely Egyptian, as it is in fact in the larger towns of modern Nubia. As Monneret de Villard pictured it, '. . . Egyptian merchants frequently traversed Meroitic Nubia, or were even settled in it; enterprising and courageous entrepreneurs who ventured wherever trade offered, like the modern Levantines.'[163] Even relatively small provincial towns like Meinarti and Arminna had their markets and their wine presses; only the tiniest and most remote hamlets, like those at Gaminarti and Meili Island, exhibited the sort of social and economic homogeneity which we associate with Nubian settlements of earlier as well as many later times.

ARTS AND INDUSTRIES

A substantial part of the material wealth enjoyed by the Meroitic Nubians consisted of foreign-made goods imported from Egypt and even farther abroad. These categories included, so far as we know, nearly their entire stock of bronze, glass, and faience objects, and even a considerable part of their pottery. However, we can also recognize at least three important local industries in Meroitic Nubia: iron-working, pottery-making, and weaving.

As we saw in Chapter 11, the most direct and dramatic evidence of Meroitic iron-working consists of the great slag heaps at Meroë and a few other urban centres in the southern provinces. On the other hand, the iron objects found in Meroitic house-sites and graves do not testify to that highly developed industry, and mainstay of the Meroitic economy, which some writers have visualized.[164] As Trigger has noted, the objects are nearly all small and consist principally of arrow heads, spear heads, and various ornamental goods.

In the cemeteries at Meroë, the utilitarian objects that are made from iron include knives, tweezers, chisels, shears, wire, and nails, the latter having been used to hold together wooden objects. There are also iron locks for chests, although these, along with many other fancy objects, may have been imports. Ornamental goods include rings, anklets, and clappers for bronze bells. The weapons that appear in graves are tanged spearheads and arrowheads.'[165]

The variety of iron goods found in the Meroitic cemeteries of Lower Nubia is somewhat larger, perhaps due to the prevalence of imports from the neighbouring Roman territories.

Anklets, bracelets, finger rings and ear-rings, kohl sticks, and grooming aids appear frequently, as well as spearheads and arrowheads, the latter weapons being identical in shape to those from Meroë. There seem to be more utilitarian items in the graves at Faras and Karanog than in the ones at Meroë. These items include cutters, tweezers, knives, nails, needles, scissors, and fittings as well as sawblades, chisels, axes, adzes, tongs, and mattocks, although these objects still occur very infrequently, especially the heavier ones.[166]

To quote further from Trigger's perceptive essay on Meroitic iron-working:

. . . very little that is definite is known about the social and political aspects of iron-working in Meroitic culture. Such evidence as there is may be suggestive, but it is not conclusive. Slag heaps have been reported at a number of important Meroitic sites such as Kawa, Napata, and Argo Island:[167] these are presumed to result from iron-working, although this claim has not been verified.[168] At each site the slag heaps occur in connection with a Meroitic temple. No trace of any forge or smelter has been reported, to my knowledge, from any of the smaller sites in Lower Nubia. At least some of the objects found in Lower Nubia appear to be of Egyptian origin, and it appears likely that many of the objects that have been found in the smaller settlements were either imported from the north or manufactured in the larger Meroitic settlements.[169]

The one Meroitic iron furnace which has been definitely identified, at Meroë itself, appears to have been of the cylindrical shaft type familiar to much of the classical world.[170] A forced draught was introduced into the smelting chamber by means of pottery *tuyères* (short, thick-walled sections of pipe with tapered ends), which were found plentifully about the site.[171]

Although no one has suggested that pottery-making played an important part in the Meroitic economy, ceramic vessels rather than iron goods are in fact the most abundant and most widely known manufactures of ancient Nubia. The great cemeteries, particularly in the north, have yielded tens of thousands of ornate and brightly coloured vessels, all testifying to the high development of the ceramic art (for examples see Fig. 60). Because the conservative potters of Nubia clung to exuberant decorative traditions which had gone out of fashion in the Mediterranean world, their products stand out in an age which is otherwise dominated by plain red wares (*terra sigillata*) made in imitation of bronze vessels. As a result, Meroitic pottery is one product of ancient Nubia which has an honoured place in museum collections throughout the world, although it is not infrequently identified as 'provincial Roman'.[172]

In spite of the abundance of Meroitic decorated pottery we remain almost as ignorant of the historical and technical details connected with its development as in the case of the iron industry. The Meroitic sites of the steppelands (as well as the Napatan sites which preceded them) contain for the most part only the plainest and coarsest of wheel-made wares, which seem to continue the heavily utilitarian pottery traditions of pharaonic Egypt.[173] Insofar as fancy decorated wares are found at places like Musawwarat[174] and Meroë, they occur only in the latest and uppermost levels, and in such small quantities as to suggest that they were not locally made. Yet the Meroitic sites of Lower Nubia are accompanied from the moment of their first founding (probably in the second or third century AD in most cases) by great quantities of decorated pottery, but very few utility wares of the type found in the south. There is, in short, an almost total ceramic

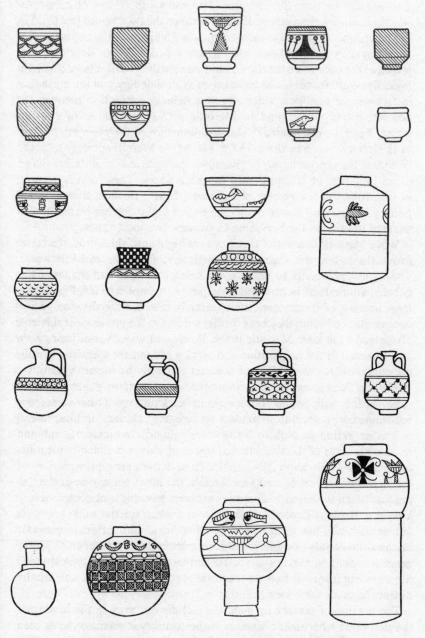

Fig. 60. Meroitic fancy pottery vessels from Lower Nubia

discontinuity between the Meroitic north and south:[175] one of many possible indications of an ethnic division between the two regions (see Ch. 13).

The decorated pottery industry of Lower Nubia gives the appearance of having sprung up full-blown, without any experimental or developmental stages, at the time when the region was first resettled. Its development might logically be attributed to the influence of Ptolemaic Egypt in the north, but in fact we are unable to trace any very definite connection between the decorative traditions found in Meroitic pottery and those of contemporary Egypt or elsewhere.[176] The predominance of Egyptian motifs such as the lotus flower and the *ankh* (cf. Fig. 61) in Meroitic pottery seems to be part of the general legacy of pharaonic influence in Nubia, rather than a direct imitation of contemporary Egyptian wares. These motifs are not, in fact, found in the pottery of Ptolemaic Egypt. If, then, the decorated pottery industry of Lower Nubia developed under foreign inspiration, it adapted itself from the beginning to conservative local tastes.

While Meroitic decorative traditions are highly individualistic, the vessel forms themselves are recognizably derivative from the classical world. They run very heavily to liquid containers of all sizes and shapes: cups, goblets, all kinds of bottles and jugs, jars, and amphorae (cf. Fig. 60). A large number of these vessels were certainly intended for the storage and consumption of wine; they bear further witness to the influence of the 'cult of the grape' in later Meroitic times. Bowls and wider vessel forms such as are needed in the preparation and serving of food are surprisingly rare; it seems probable that this need was met primarily by bronze vessels.[177]

The slip (background colour) in most Meroitic pottery is cream or light yellow-ochre, with painted decoration in black and red. Other vessels are red-slipped, with decoration in black and white.[178] Designs, unlike those in any other period in Nubian history, are primarily representational, and include all kinds of flora and fauna, scenes of human activity, and caricatured human faces. Especially popular floral designs are representations of the lotus flower, trefoil, and vine wreath, the latter being one of the few designs which is shared in common between Meroitic and contemporary Egyptian pottery. Crocodiles, frogs, and snakes are the most common faunal elements, but birds, cattle, giraffes, lions, and various apparently mythical beasts also occur. There is in addition a fair number of purely geometric designs, most of which are formal and rigid.[179] A typical vessel has anything from one to five concentric bands of decoration, each usually distinct from all the others.

The making of pottery by hand did not die out even in the heyday of the decorated wheel-made wares. On the contrary it seems to have been very little affected by the existence of a 'rival' industry. For a short time there were some rather feeble attempts at painted decoration, and at imitation of the more elaborate forms made on the wheel, but in general the

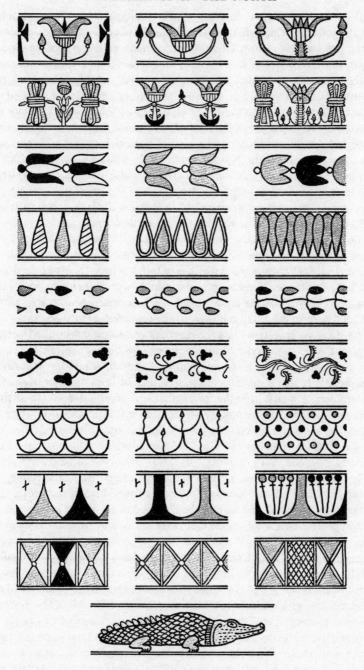

Fig. 61. Examples of Meroitic decorated pottery motifs, Lower Nubia

hand-made wares perpetuated the simple traditions which had character-ized them since prehistoric times – and they have continued to do so down to the present day. From later Meroitic times until the Middle Ages – a span of 1,200 years or more – the Nubian hand-made and wheel-made pottery industries persisted side by side without notably influencing one another. Then, incredible as it seems, the potter's wheel disappeared, so that only the more primitive industry which originated in Neolithic times has survived down to the present. The explanation for this surprising anomaly seems to lie in the fact that the making of pottery by hand was, and still is, a domestic craft of the Nubian womenfolk, while the mass-production of wheel-made wares was the exclusive province of male specialists.[180] Although at times they supplied a large part of the utilitarian market, the wheel-made vessels were nevertheless in the last analysis a luxury which could be and was dispensed with in impoverished times.

The abundance of fancy wheel-made pottery is perhaps the most elo-quent testimony we have of the high level of prosperity in Meroitic Lower Nubia. There is hardly a grave which is without at least three or four decor-ated pots. Moreover, the enormous accumulation of sherds at places like Gaminarti shows that the fancy vessels were not cherished luxuries of the rich, but were in everyday use even in the humblest of villages.[181]

The sheer volume as well as the diversity of Meroitic decorated pottery suggests that it was produced at a number of different centres. However, only one potter's kiln, in Lower Nubia, has been somewhat tentatively identified.[182] It was a cylindrical construction of brick masonry four feet in diameter, of which only the lowest courses were preserved. In slightly later, post-Meroitic times pottery was fired in cylindrical kilns of approxi-mately the same size which were divided into an upper firing chamber and a lower furnace chamber (cf. Ch. 13). The Meroitic kiln may have been similarly designed, but not enough of it was preserved to be certain.

The Meroitic decorated pottery industry centred almost certainly on Lower Nubia. While the identical wares are found also in the south, they are far less numerous, and seem to be confined to the major urban centres. Even at Meroë itself wheel-made sherds are scarce and are found only in the topmost layer of deposit.[183] Only an insignificant number of wheel-made vessels and sherds were found in the far southern village of Abu Geili[184] and the nearby cemetery of Makwar (Sennar),[185] though the bronze vessels from the latter site are of late types which in the north are regularly found in association with typical Meroitic decorated pottery. All of the evidence conspires to suggest that the wheel-made pottery industry of Lower Nubia was a relatively late development, coming perhaps at a time when the south was already undergoing political and economic eclipse, and that such fancy vessels as found their way into the southern provinces went mostly into the hands of a wealthy élite in the major urban centres.

IXb. Interior of Rameses temple
at Abu Simbel

Xa (*above*). Temple of Amenhotep III at Soleb

Xb (*below*). Jebel Barkal with Amon temple in foreground

XIa. Temple of Amon at Napata seen from the top of Jebel Barkal

XIb. The Napatan pyramids of Nuri

XII (*opposite*). The Great Stele of Piankhi

XIIIa. The Butana Steppe or 'Island of Meroë' with ruins of Musawwarat in foreground

XIIIb. The north group of pyramids at Meroë

XIVa. Pyramids with decorated corners, Meroë

XIVb (*left*). Decorated tomb chamber, Meroë

XVa. 'Kiosk' and Lion Temple, Naqa

XVb. Fallen Meroitic colossus, Argo Island

XVIa. The ruined outer court of the Temple of Isis at Philae

XVIb. The fortified citadel at Qasr Ibrim

Although they were abundantly provided with pottery of their own manu-facture – hand-made utility jars as well as luxury wares – the Meroites of Lower Nubia also obtained a surprising number of vessels in trade from Egypt. Most of them apparently were made at or near Aswan. They can be readily recognized not only by their bright, hard, pinkish clay (never found in Nubian-made vessels), but by their forms and very simple decora-tion, which are quite unlike those of Meroitic pottery and are wholly sub-servient to Roman canons.[186] The largest number of these vessels are the amphorae in which Egyptian wine was imported, but there are also various kinds of cups, goblets, bowls and lamps, nearly all of which are imitative of contemporary bronze vessel forms. In the immediate post-Meroitic period, when the native pottery industry once again temporarily disap-peared, the imported vessels from Aswan and elsewhere for a short time captured the bulk of the Nubian pottery market.

Weaving was certainly another domestic industry of the Meroitic period. Much of the evidence for it is indirect; it consists of large numbers of perforated, mud loom-weights which have been found in Meroitic house-sites. Since the other parts of the loom were presumably made of wood, they have not survived, but the numerous weights (over fifty were found in one room at Meili Island[187]) indicate that the Meroites were using the warp-weighted loom, on which weaving is done from the top downwards. This device was not the typical Egyptian loom of antiquity, but was pro-bably a Greek introduction into the Nile Valley.[188] At Meili Island a number of pointed bone shuttles were found in the same room with the loom weights. The presence of these objects in a simple village dwelling suggests that Meroitic weaving was not industrialized, but, like the making of hand-made pottery, was carried on at home by the womenfolk.

Thanks to recent discoveries at Qasr Ibrim, we are beginning to learn a good deal about the textiles which were produced at Nubian looms. They were mostly of cotton, with abundant use of embroidered and macramé decoration. Most garments were white, with blue or green embroidery. Cotton garments have been found also in the cemeteries at Karanog[189] and Meroë.[190] Since Pliny speaks of cotton in the Sudan in the first century AD,[191] and it did not become common in Egypt until much later,[192] there is good reason to believe that the cotton fabrics of Meroitic Nubia were locally produced. Arkell cites cotton cultivation as one of the 'Indian' influences in Meroitic culture (cf. Ch. 12).[193] Some fairly elaborate decorated fabrics of linen were also found at Karanog;[194] these are very probably of Egyptian origin.[195]

Two other crafts whose development in Meroitic Nubia can reasonably be assumed are those of basket-weaving and leather-working. Baskets have been made at all times in Nubian history, and a few insignificant examples of them are known from Meroitic graves in the north.[196] Nubia, with its large pastoral population, has also been at all times a major producer of hides, and the people of pre-pharaonic times habitually dressed in leather garments. The only leather goods which have been found with any regularity in Meroitic graves are sandals,[197] but a few fragments of decorated leather inlaid with ivory were found at Karanog.[198]

Other important possessions of the Meroitic Nubians were objects of bronze, glass, faience, wood, and ivory. All of these goods are much more common in Lower Nubia than in the south, and there is reason to believe that they were largely if not entirely imported from Egypt or farther abroad.[199] The best-known and most lavish examples are the luxury goods found in the great cemeteries of Karanog[200] and Faras,[201] but imported objects of one kind or another are found in nearly every Meroitic site in Nubia.

Bronze was used for various kinds of ornaments, for small toilet articles such as tweezers, scissors, and kohl sticks, but above all for bowls and other vessels. The abundance of these, and the scarcity of comparable forms in pottery, suggests that solid foods were prepared and served primarily in bronze vessels. In addition to these prosaic containers, there were various kinds of ornamental ewers, censers, dippers, cups, and lamps, mostly in well-known classical forms. The quantity of bronze which was in use in Meroitic times is attested by the fact that at Meinarti the refuse fill of the disused wine press contained several hundred 'sherds' of bronze – more than were found in all other levels of the site combined.[202]

The great majority of bronze vessels are in typical Roman or Hellenistic forms, but a few are similar in shape to Meroitic pottery vessels, and even have similar (though stamped rather than painted) decoration.[203] If not actually produced by Nubians, they must have been designed specifically to please Nubian rather than Egyptian tastes. Distinctively Nubian also are the massive anklets, usually with chisel-stamped decoration, which are occasionally found on female burials.[204] Some of these are of iron,[205] but the majority are bronze. Their size and weight must have seriously impeded the wearer; perhaps their social function was equivalent to that of foot-binding among the Chinese.[206]

While some of the bronze found in Nubia may have been locally produced, it was believed until recently that all of the glass vessels were of foreign origin.[207] As the excavators of Karanog noted, 'The vessels are without exception of a foreign type, of the stereotyped patterns that prevailed uniformly throughout the Roman Empire; so little are they peculiar to one region, so devoid of individuality, that any one of the glass vessels found at Karanog might equally have been found anywhere between the Rhine and the Mediterranean.'[208] The most common vessel forms are unguentaria – small bottles with flattened bodies, more or less triangular in section, with tubular necks and widely flared rims. Also found are various larger bottles, flasks, and beakers, all of well-known Roman types. However, a large collection of glass from the recently excavated Meroitic cemetery at Seddenga[209] includes also a few vessels which, like some of the bronzes, were certainly made for a Meroitic or provincial Egyptian market; among them is a jar which unmistakably duplicates a Meroitic hand-made pottery form.[210] Here again the possibility of local manufacture cannot be ruled out, though no glass-making apparatus has yet been found in a Nubian site.[211]

The most common of all imported goods in Meroitic Nubia were beads, of which the great majority were of glass. They are found by the thousands and tens of thousands in every Meroitic cemetery. To quote again the excavators of Karanog:

Beads were very fashionable amongst the Nubian women. They were worn . . . around the neck, the upper arms, the wrists and the ankles, and two necklaces were worn together as often as one single one. These were buried with the bodies, and fortunately the tomb-robbers in their search for precious metals could afford to leave alone altogether or to throw on one side the strings of glass or stone beads that had no intrinsic value. Consequently the number of beads found during the excavation of the cemetery was very great . . .

Surprising for their number, the beads were far more astonishing for their variety and excellent technique. Some were of stone, white quartz, carnelian or agate, steatite and breccia; the great majority were of glass. Some of the latter were of transparent white glass, some opaque in every shade of red, blue and yellow; there were marbled beads, millefiori beads, mosaic beads, inlay beads, and gilded and silvered glass beads.

For the most part the beads are made from glass rods cut and rolled. For the variegated beads this rod is itself a complex one formed of a number of slighter rods of different colors arranged in a bundle and lightly fused together. When such a rod is cut into flat sections each face shows the pattern that runs through the length of the rod; the method employed is that of certain sugar-sticks of our youth.[212]

The prevalence of glass beads, and the almost total absence of coins, in a time when a market economy was certainly flourishing suggests the possibility that beads may have been one of the principal media of exchange.

Faience (blue-green glazed frit) was another imported substance used extensively for beads and pendants, among which we can recognize a considerable number of scarabs.[213] There were also a few small bowls of faience. These vessels and ornaments are indicative of the continuing pharaonic influence in Nubian culture; however, they were much less popular in Meroitic than in earlier times, and they presently disappeared altogether.

Among the most spectacular imported goods which are sometimes found in Nubian graves are elaborately fitted wooden chests inlaid with ivory.

Round, lathe-turned wooden boxes and kohl tubes (deep cylindrical containers in which eye-shadow was kept) were also decorated with ivory inlays. Again, the decoration suggests that they were sometimes designed explicitly for the Nubian market, and were perhaps locally made, although the wood was in some cases cedar of Lebanon.[214]

MORTUARY CUSTOMS

Mortuary ritual provides an important unifying theme throughout the civilization and the empire of Kush. From Maharraqa in the north to Sennar in the south, the grave types, the grave goods, and the mortuary practices were more nearly consistent than was any other aspect of Nubian culture in the Meroitic period.

Cemeteries comprise more than three quarters of all known Meroitic sites.[215] As always in the historic period, the graves are densely clustered together and at times are intruded upon one another. In Lower Nubia the great majority of Meroitic cemeteries are located west of the Nile, perhaps in keeping with the ancient Egyptian mortuary tradition. Thus the enormous necropolis of Karanog, which probably contained between three and four thousand burials,[216] may have served the inhabitants of Qasr Ibrim[217] as well as those of the neighbouring settlements on the west bank. At Gebel Adda, on the other hand, the Meroitic cemeteries were definitely on the east bank and close to the town.[218] In the southern provinces, as we noted in Chapter 11, both the settlements and the burial places were on the east bank, and there are few traces of Meroitic occupation west of the Nile.

The great majority of Meroitic graves were probably unmarked at the surface. However, nearly every cemetery exhibits at least a few brick superstructures, mostly in association with the largest and richest tombs. They consist in most cases of a shell of brick or occasionally stone masonry from six to twenty feet square, with inward-sloping sides enclosing a rubble fill. They have usually been designated as mastabas, but it seems certain that at least in some cases the superstructures were actually miniature pyramids, whose tops have been destroyed by erosion and plundering.[219] The pyramids at Gebel Adda seem to have been covered with white plaster;[220] other Meroitic pyramids at Seddenga were plastered in red.[221] Many but not all tomb superstructures had a small vaulted chamber projecting from the east side, comparable to the mortuary chapels adjoining the royal pyramids. Presumably they served as repositories for postfunerary offerings. Additional offerings were sometimes placed within the fill of the superstructure at the time of its construction.[222]

Meroitic graves show considerable variability in their underground arrangements,[223] but conform to two basic types which may be designated as chamber tombs and niche graves. The largest number of chamber tombs are rectangular caves, six to ten feet long and about half as wide, excavated directly out of hard-packed alluvium. Access is by means of a narrow, sloping ramp (*dromos*), usually from the east side. These details, like those of the superstructures, reproduce in miniature the arrangement of the later royal tombs at Napata and Meroë (Ch. 11). After interment the entrance to the tomb chamber was blocked with brick and the dromos then refilled, leaving the body and offerings in a sealed air-chamber. Some of the larger chamber tombs were family vaults which were reopened from time to time to receive additional burials; as many as eleven bodies were found in the largest tombs at Karanog.[224]

A less common variant of the cave-tomb was the brick vault-tomb. A small, vaulted, brick chamber, of about the same size as the typical dug-out burial chamber, was built in the bottom of a deep rectangular pit, and then was filled over with earth. Subsequent access, as in the cave-tombs, was by means of a dromos and a small doorway in the east end of the vault. Presumably these tombs were built in preference to cave tombs whenever the natural ground was insufficiently compacted to support a dug-out chamber.

Niche graves comprise the second important class of Meroitic burial chambers. They are narrow vertical shafts, more or less of the same proportions as modern graves, at the bottom of which an offset is dug either along one side ('side-niche graves') or at one end ('foot-niche graves') to receive the body and offerings (Fig. 62). After burial the niche was closed over with bricks and the shaft refilled, leaving the body in a kind of natural coffin or air space not much larger than itself.

Meroitic burial chambers show more variability than do the graves of any other period and the significance of the different types is not fully understood even yet. Griffith interpreted the four major grave types at Faras as representing a developmental sequence,[225] but this is not borne out by the objects found in them, which are all more or less of the same types.[226] In fact, the different varieties of Meroitic graves are found in nearly all cemeteries of the period, and it is worth recalling that all of them were found also in the Napatan cemetery of Sanam (Ch. 10).[227] The most likely explanation for the main difference, that between the chamber tombs and the niche graves, is that they represent the upper and lower strata of the same society.[228] The physical relationship of the two types of graves is much like that of the 'de luxe' and ordinary houses in the Meroitic towns: the chamber tombs are heavily clustered in a few areas, while the niche graves are more or less randomly scattered between and around them. Evidently, therefore, the 'social distance' between the two groups was not great.

The difference between the vaulted chamber tombs and the dug-out chamber tombs seems best explained on structural grounds, as we noted earlier. Since the earliest tombs would presumably pre-empt the most suitable ground, however, it seems reasonable to assume that constructed chambers became increasingly necessary, and therefore common, in the later periods. There remains for the time being no satisfactory explanation for the occasional presence of a western dromos in preference to an eastern one, or for the difference between side-niche and foot-niche graves. These differences may indeed be chronological, the side-niche and the western dromos representing late and aberrant developments.

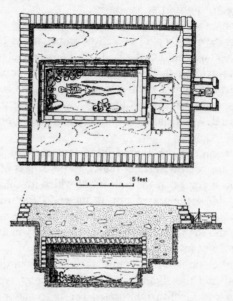

Fig. 62. Meroitic vaulted chamber tomb and superstructure

Nearly all Meroitic tombs are oriented east–west with reference to the Nile (that is, taking the local direction of the river's flow as equivalent to north, as Nubian builders have done at all times in history). Within, the body was extended on its back, head usually to the west, according to the immemorial Egyptian practice. There was no mummification or cartonnage, but in a very few cases the corpse was provided with a pottery or wooden coffin.[229] Equally often, the body was laid on a woven mat or on a low wooden *angareeb* similar to those in use today[230] – the age-old Nubian custom of bed-burial reasserting itself once again. The dead were often and perhaps usually wrapped in a woven or leather shroud, though only tiny scraps of these have survived in most cases.[231] Women and children were regularly decked out in beads and other jewelry.

Grave furniture other than the clothing and jewelry of the deceased was placed wherever room allowed within the burial chamber, but was generally most concentrated near the head.[232] The minimum furniture for any grave seems to have been a pottery jar, presumably containing beer or wine, and a cup which was often inverted over the mouth of the jar.[233] However, the majority of graves contained a good deal more than this; even in their highly plundered condition most Meroitic burials have yielded at least half a dozen objects. Sometimes the number of cups and jars alone runs to more than a dozen.[234] Nearly all of the other material goods which have been discussed in previous pages – objects of iron, bronze, pottery, glass, faience, wood, ivory and precious metals – have also come from Meroitic graves, and testify to the consistent abundance and variety of mortuary offerings. Except for one or two forms of utilitarian pottery,[235] nearly every object which was in everyday use in Meroitic times might be expected to accompany its owner to the afterworld.

The three most distinctive expressions of Meroitic funerary practice were carved stone objects which were placed not within the grave but outside it. These were painted or inscribed stelae, so-called offering tables, and *ba* statuettes. They were not in general use, but seem to have been restricted to the richest tombs; some Meroitic cemeteries have yielded no examples of any of them. Because of the extremely plundered condition of the cemeteries, very few stelae or statuettes have ever been found *in situ*; pieces of them are usually picked up in the surface refuse which has been turned over by robbers again and again. The frequency with which pieces of stelae and statuettes are found in the fill of later graves also suggests that a good deal of plundering was going on while the cemeteries were still in use.[236]

Meroitic stelae are not much different in form or function from tombstones today, save that the inscriptions are ordinarily longer and more explicit, though not necessarily more accurate. The stone slabs are generally rather thin, with straight sides and a straight or rounded top. Some bear painted or rudely incised portraits of the dead, executed in highly stylized fashion, but most are adorned only with several lines of text in Meroitic cursive characters.[237] One stele at Karanog was found in a position which suggested that it had been set up originally within the offering chamber adjoining the east side of a tomb superstructure;[238] however, many other stelae are too tall to have been so placed. They might have stood upright in the ground, or been attached to the facing of the mastaba or pyramid.

'Offering tables' were designed to receive libations and food offered on behalf of the dead after his interment. They are flat, rectangular or square trays of sandstone, most often measuring about ten inches by fourteen inches, with a raised edge surrounding a recessed centre. Usually a gutter runs out at one side, to carry off the liquid which was poured into the centre. The raised border may be adorned with one to three lines of cursive text running all the way around; the inscriptions, like those on the funerary stelae, commemorate the names and titles of the deceased. The recessed centres of the trays carry a variety of carved designs, the most common of which shows two spouted amphorae pouring out their contents, and several round loaves of bread. Another popular design shows the mortuary deities Nephthys and Anubis making offerings on an altar which stands between them.[239] A few offering tables were found *in situ* at Karanog; they were set into the tops of low, crudely built brick altars which stood immediately to the east of some of the larger tomb superstructures.[240]

The most intriguing of all Meroitic mortuary paraphernalia is the *ba* statuette. It is a carving in sandstone, usually about two feet high, depicting a stiffly erect human figure with the folded wings of a bird stretching out and downwards behind it. Most of the surviving examples bear traces of brightly coloured paint.[241] Although the carving is usually crude, the facial features and expressions are rendered in classical rather than in traditional Egyptian style.[242]

These carvings are believed to commemorate the *ba* of the deceased:

. . . the spiritual part of a person, which, after his death, preserves his individuality and is able to wander at its pleasure. In the religious papyri the *ba* is represented as a bird with a human head, which could remain with the dead person in the funerary chamber, but often preferred to go out into the open, and revisit the places beloved by the deceased . . .[243]

At Karanog, as at Shablul, it is evident that the richer tombs were generally furnished each with a single statue, which had been displaced and often flung to some distance from its original position by robbers in ancient days. The type of representation is unknown in Egypt and seems to have been independently developed by the Nubians to satisfy the requirements of a creed which resembled the Egyptian in some respects but was undoubtedly distinct and peculiar in others. The Egyptian sculptor, his thoughts concentrated on the bodily person, wished so exactly to counterfeit the form and lineaments of the deceased that the soul when returning from the grave might mistake the image for the actual self. But the aim of the Nubian was different from the outset; he intended his statues to reproduce not the physical double but the soul . . .[244]

No *ba* statuette has ever been found *in situ,* and it is impossible to say where these highly distinctive sculptures were situated with respect to the tomb superstructure. Most of them are too tall to have stood within the offering chambers which adjoined the mastabas or pyramids. Woolley and MacIver thought that they might have stood on top of the vaulted offering chamber, but this is no more than speculation.[245] *Ba* statuettes, unlike stelae and offering tables, have only been found in the Meroitic north;[246] the destruction of a large part of this region makes it unlikely that we shall ever learn any more about them than we now know.

INTERPRETATIVE SUMMARY

The Meroitic period was the Golden Age of Dynastic civilization in Nubia. Protected by the enfolding deserts, no longer overshadowed by the 'colossus of the north', the fragile transplant of civilization which had been established in the south in colonial days reached its fullest flowering centuries after the parent shoot in Egypt had withered and decayed. Yet the Meroitic florescence was something more than simply the remote, marginal survival of an outmoded civilization. It was, rather, a significant cultural and political renaissance after several centuries of stagnation and decline in Nubia itself. If its ideology was faithful to the ancient traditions of Egypt, its prosperity derived in large measure from the extension of Hellenistic commercial enterprise, while its political stability was in some degree a by-product of *Pax Romana*.

One of the outstanding achievements of Meroitic times was a territorial expansion greater than that of any other indigenous civilization in Nubian history. Caravan trade made possible the development of overland routes deep into the African interior, by-passing the longstanding barrier of the Fourth Cataract and ending the age-old dependence of trans-Saharan trade upon the Nile. The result was a rapid colonization of the steppelands above the Fifth Cataract, which in time supplanted the older Napatan province as the main centre of power and wealth in the Sudan. Meroitic influence ultimately extended as far south as Sennar on the Blue Nile – the farthest point reached by any Nubian civilization before modern times. Meanwhile the development of a direct, overland trade route between Meroë and Egypt, by-passing much of the intervening Nile Valley, led to the economic and political decline of the formerly dominant Napata region.

A late development of Meroitic times was the reoccupation of Lower Nubia and the *Batn el Hajar*. This seems to have been a mass popular movement, unencouraged by official policy, which was made possible by the introduction of the ox-driven waterwheel. The long-abandoned northern region became once again a flourishing agricultural province, supported not so much by long-distance trade in tropical products as by local commerce with the neighbouring Roman colonies in the Dodekaschoenos. In the last century or two of the Meroitic era the population and wealth of the north increased dramatically while those of the southern provinces declined, so that in the end the Nubian 'centre of gravity' shifted back once again to the north, where it was to remain throughout the Medieval era.

In nearly all of its ideological bases, the civilization of Meroë remained faithful to the ancient traditions which had been handed down from Napatan and earlier times. Until the extinction of the Kushite dynasty, perhaps in the fourth century AD, the rulers continued to style themselves by the titles which had been devised three thousand years earlier by Egypt's first pharaohs.[247] The royal tomb was modelled upon that of the Egyptian Old Kingdom, and the worship of Amon, the Theban deity of Middle and New Kingdom times, remained the cornerstone of the state cult. Art, architecture, and popular religion alike hewed close to the canons laid down in the days of the pharaohs.

While the formal expressions of Nubian civilization remained subservient to the past, the economy and society of the southern lands were being subtly transformed by new and invigorating influences. Caravan trade made possible the extension of settlement and civilization into the steppe-lands beyond the Nile in the same period when the Alexandrian conquest was bringing Egypt into alignment with the far-flung network of Hellenistic maritime trade. The result was a flourishing of commerce and an in-pouring of manufactured goods – utilities as well as luxuries – never before seen in the lands of the Nile. So abundant and varied a trade could not remain indefinitely a royal monopoly; before long a large part of it was evidently in the hands of private merchants. Their enterprise reached and developed a popular market which had never been of concern to the crown, so that in the end Meroitic material prosperity was much more broadly based than in any earlier period.

Stimulated by royal as well as private commercial enterprise, Nubian society became urbanized as never before. Large cities, endowed in many cases with monumental palaces and temples, appeared in the steppelands where only nomads had wandered a short time earlier. The older cities of Napata and Kawa, although no longer on the main overland trade routes, were partly rebuilt and revitalized in the Meroitic period, and new communities without number were established in Lower Nubia. Even the small villages of Meroitic times exhibit a degree of urbanization and of commercial enterprise which was unmatched in earlier periods.

Hand in hand with urbanization and economic expansion went the rise of an urban bourgeoisie. No longer was Nubian society sharply divided, as in Napatan and New Kingdom times, between rulers and ruled. In the Meroitic period we have to recognize also, and for the first time in Nubian history, a well-entrenched middle class, whose wealth and influence increased even as those of the monarchy declined. Their substantial houses and rich tombs are to be found not only in the great urban centres, but even in many of the provincial towns of Lower Nubia.

Inevitably, the rise of a wealthy middle class led to political decentralization and a decline in the absolute power of the monarchy. This development may never have progressed very far in the Meroitic south, which seems always to have been a kind of royal fief. In Lower Nubia, however, there is unmistakable evidence in late Meroitic times of a semi-autonomous feudal polity, foreshadowing the eventual break-up of the empire of Kush.

Pharaonic traditions persisted longest and died hardest in the conservative southern provinces which had led in the development of Kushite civilization. From the time of its resettlement, Lower Nubia was much more immediately influenced by the secularizing tendencies of the classical world which lay just beyond its borders. Royal authority and state religion are far from conspicuous in the Meroitic remains from Lower Nubia; the region seems to have been governed by local officials who were not closely involved with the state ideology of the south and its visible symbols. Public life centred upon markets, taverns, and palaces more than upon temples and tombs.

If the Meroitic north had any state religion, it was the cult of Isis at Philae. This was not, however, a proprietary cult of the ruling family and the imperial bureaucracy; it was a supra-national religion whose sanction was claimed alike by Meroitic kings, Roman prefects, and Bedouin chiefs. In this emerging separation between church and state, as in the nascent feudalism of Meroitic Nubia, we can recognize the beginnings of two of the most profoundly important themes of Medieval civilization, which were soon to transform not only Nubia but most of the Western world.

13
EPILOGUE TO EMPIRE
THE NUBIAN X HORIZON

In the fourth century of the Christian era, the Nubian empire founded by Kashta and Piankhi was more than a thousand years old. Born in the declining years of pharaonic civilization, it had long outlived not only the Egyptian civilization which gave it birth, but the Assyrian, Persian and Macedonian powers which had been its successors in the north. Even the Roman Empire had entered its mature phase, and was on the threshold of its ideological rebirth under Christianity, when the last of the Kushite 'Pharaohs' was crowned 'Lord of Upper and Lower Egypt', some time after AD 300.[1]

While the records of Napatan and early Meroitic times tell of intermittent strife both within and beyond the frontiers of Kush, there is hardly a mention of military activity subsequent to the brief invasion of Petronius in 23 BC (Ch. 12). So far as we are able to tell, the Meroites lived for two centuries or more in a state of profound peace with their neighbours, at least in the north. Yet it is clear that their own days of power and vigour were long past. There were no important building activities after Natakamani and Amanitere, at the beginning of the Christian era, and the tombs of the last rulers at Meroë are hardly to be distinguished in size or ostentation from those of their wealthier subjects. In the end, the continued survival of the ancient monarchy seems to have been guaranteed less by its own economic and political vitality than by those of faraway Rome.

On the Nile, no less than on the Rhine and the Danube, *Pax Romana* was first and foremost a state of mind – a willingness on the part of peoples both within and beyond the imperial frontiers to accept Roman economic and political domination as the price of Roman-inspired prosperity. This mantle of protection spread over Meroë and the other client states of Rome as well as over the Empire itself, but it was more a psychological than a military advantage. When imperial prosperity declined, and the barbarians began venting their discontent against their ancient overlords, they learned that the empires of Kush and of Rome no longer possessed the military strength which had been their founding and their integrating principle. The imperial frontiers were soon penetrated; once within, the roads to Meroë and to Rome were wide open. In the face of the barbarian onslaught, vast tracts of empire disappeared almost overnight.

The story of the decline and dissolution of the western Roman Empire has been chronicled in elaborate detail. The circumstances attending the final downfall of Kush are largely unrecorded, but in broad outline the two stories must have been much the same. In the late years of both empires we can observe a decline in prosperity resulting from the disruption of overseas trade, a top-heavy bureaucracy necessitating the division of the empire into semi-autonomous parts, and, perhaps most important of all, the declining force of state ideology as it was challenged and finally superseded by popular, universal cults which even the emperor was obliged, in the end, to acknowledge. Which of these developments had the greatest effect in provoking the barbarian inroads it is difficult to say, but only a short time after them we find the outlanders in possession of the ancient seats of empire (cf. Fig. 63).

The last dated inscription of any Meroitic king is a graffito in the temple at Philae, recording the dispatch of an envoy to Rome by the Meroitic ruler Teqerideamani in AD 260.[2] There are, however, at least four pyramids in the North Cemetery at Meroë which are believed to be later in date than that of Teqerideamani, and consequently the Kushite dynasty is generally believed to have persisted into the fourth century. Hintze estimates the date of its final disappearance at AD 320,[3] and Dunham at AD 339,[4] but these are hardly more than guesses. We have neither internal nor external evidence bearing upon the last half century of the Kushite empire, and we can only reconstruct from inference the story of its final decline and fall.

THE MEROITIC DECLINE AND FALL

Beginning in the second century AD we can recognize an accelerating process of economic and political decline in the Meroitic steppelands, which only recently had been in the forefront of Kushite cultural development. Three factors seem to have contributed to the decline of the Meroitic south. One was the rapid impoverishment of Egypt – the traditional market for most of Nubia's exports – under the harshly exploitative Roman régime.[5] Another was the increasing mobility and military power of the desert nomads, menacing the long and exposed caravan route between Meroë and Egypt. As Trigger has astutely noted, the introduction of the camel seems to have wrought a social and political transformation among the nomad peoples comparable to that which followed the introduction of the horse among American Indians.[6] From being simple pastoralists, narrowly confined within a highly specialized ecological niche, they became far-ranging predators and desert entrepreneurs, under powerful but loosely

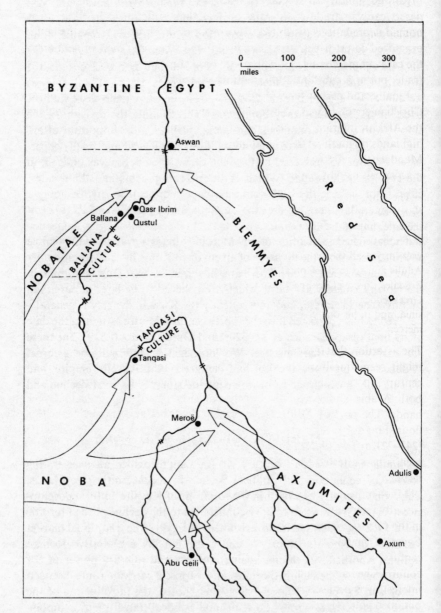

Fig. 63. Migrations and invasions of the late Meroitic and post-Meroitic periods

organized military aristocracies. Once this transformation was achieved, desert caravan trade could exist only at their sufferance. In some areas nomad depredations disrupted the caravan trade altogether, but the better organized desert tribes were more far-sighted; they sold their protection to the caravan merchants at a high price. The end result was a continuation of trade, but at a substantial diminution of profit.

Finally, and perhaps most important of all, Kush at the beginning of the Christian era no longer possessed a monopoly of civilization and of trade in the African interior. A rival civilization, nurtured originally in the fertile highlands of south-west Arabia, had spread its influence across the Bab-el-Mandeb (the narrow strait at the mouth of the Red Sea) to the neighbouring plateau of Abyssinia.

The Abyssinian kingdom is first mentioned in the *Periplus of the Erythraean Sea*, a description of the coasts of the Red Sea and the Indian Ocean written in the latter half of the first century AD. The author describes the port of Adulis and states that eight days' journey inland lay the metropolis of the Axumites, whither was carried all the ivory from beyond the Nile and whence it was exported to Adulis and so to the Roman Empire. The king of all these regions, he adds, is Zoscales, 'a covetous and grasping man but otherwise noble and imbued with Greek education.' Zoscales must . . . rank as the first historical king of Abyssinia, and in his day civilization was already following in the footsteps of commerce.[7]

The assertion that Zoscales possessed a Greek education at this early date might seem questionable, but it is necessary to recall that by the first century AD the control of Red Sea trade, upon which the prosperity of both Arabia and Abyssinia largely depended, had long been in Greek hands. The port of Adulis (near present-day Massawa) might have been flourishing for several centuries already, for an inscription of Ptolemy III (247–221 BC) was later found there.[8] The extent of Greek interest in this area is best attested by the writing of the Periplus (i.e. navigator's guide) itself.[9]

Much more detailed information about the earliest kingdom of Abyssinia (usually referred to as the Axumite kingdom, after its capital) is contained in the *Christian Topography* of Cosmas Indicopleustes.[10] He was a Graeco-Egyptian merchant who wrote down, around the middle of the sixth century, a description of the history, topography, and antiquities of the countries he had visited, among them the kingdom of Axum.[11] Particularly interesting is his account of the 'silent trade' through which the Axumites obtained gold nuggets from their primitive lowland neighbours.[12] Cosmas also mentions that emeralds were obtained from the neighbouring Blemmyes (Beja), and were then traded to India at an enormous profit.[13] These fragmentary traditions do not provide a very full picture of Axumite commerce, but they are enough to indicate that the Abyssinians were ranging far beyond their native highlands, and presumably into the ancient Meroitic sphere of influence, in search of commodities for trade.

Notwithstanding the considerable obstacles to travel in the Abyssinian highlands, the proximity of Axum to the salt-water port of Adulis gave it an enormous competitive advantage over Meroë, with its long and exposed overland supply-line to Egypt. The Axumites were evidently not backward in exploiting this favourable situation. During the same period when they were developing their own export commerce, they may also have incited some of the neighbouring Beja tribes to attack the caravan trade of Meroë.[14] Given the increasing rivalry of the two African powers for the trade resources upon which the prosperity of both depended, an armed clash between them was sooner or later inevitable.

Among the most important traditions recorded by Cosmas Indicopleustes are those relating to the reign of the Axumite king Aezanas, whom we know from other records to have been the first Christian king of Abyssinia, and the founder of what has ever since been his country's state religion. We have, in addition to the work of Cosmas, a number of records of his reign in the form of commemorative stelae of his own authorship, some in Greek, some in Old Ethiopic (Ge'ez), and some in the Sabaean language of south Arabia. In them he claims dominion over large areas not only in central Africa, but in Arabia as well.[15] The latter claim may possibly represent a political fiction much like the Meroitic claim to Upper and Lower Egypt, for Axum was a successor state to Sabaea (the biblical Sheba) just as Meroë was to Egypt. It is worth recalling that the late monarch of Ethiopia (Abyssinia) still based his claim to rule upon descent from the Queen of Sheba – a legitimizing principle older than that claimed by any other government in the world except possibly that of imperial Japan.

One of the stelae of Aezanas is of extraordinary interest to the student of Nubian history, for it records a campaign in which the king led his army into the heart of ancient Kush and apparently to Meroë itself. The relevant passages have been rendered as follows by Budge:

By the might of the Lord of all, I made war upon Noba, for the peoples had rebelled and had made a boast of it. And they were in the habit of attacking the peoples of Mangurto, and Khasa, and Barya, and the blacks, and of making war upon the Red peoples. And as I sent warnings to them, and they would not harken to me, and they refused to cease from their evil deeds, and then betook themselves to flight, I made war upon them. And I rose in the might of the Lord of the Land, and I fought with them on the [Atbara], at the ford of the Kemalke. Thereupon they took flight, and would not make a stand. And I followed after the fugitives for twenty and three days, killing some and making prisoners others, and capturing spoil wherever I tarried. Prisoners and spoil my people who had marched into the country brought back to me. Meanwhile I burnt their towns, both those built of bricks and those built of reeds, and my soldiers carried off its food, and its copper, and its iron, and its brass, and they destroyed the statues of their [temples], and the treasuries of food, and the cotton trees, and cast them into the River [Nile]. And I came to Kasu and I fought a battle and made prisoners of its people at the junction of the rivers [Nile] and [Atbara]. The names of the cities built of bricks were Alwa and Daro. The towns built of bricks which the Noba had taken were Tabito and Fertoti. And I planted a throne in that country at the place where the Rivers [Nile] and [Atbara] join . . .[16]

The date of Aezanas' campaign is not absolutely certain; it is conventionally placed around AD 350.[17] It was apparently one of the king's last military operations, and was undertaken some time after his conversion to Christianity, for the stele which describes it is one of the few inscriptions of Aezanas which begins and ends with Christian invocations.[18]

The inscription is remarkable both for its content and for its omissions. It suggests that the main enemies of Axum in the west were not the Kushites (whom we can probably recognize under the name 'Kasu' in the middle of the text) but the Noba – a people who were earlier described by Strabo[19] and by Ptolemy[20] as dwelling west of the Nile. It would appear that by the time Aezanas arrived with his army, these long-time neighbours and former subjects[21] of Meroë had already moved across the river and possessed themselves of a large part of the traditional domain of Kush, including some of its brick-built cities and temples. While the meaning of the text is not absolutely clear, it seems to suggest that the normal dwellings of the Noba (as of most peoples in the central Sudan today) were of grass, while the brick cities of Tabito and Fertoti which they inhabited had been seized from the Meroites.[22]

It is not certain whether 'Kasu' (Kush) in the latter part of the text refers specifically to the city of Meroë, to the general territory ('island') of Meroë, or to the Meroitic people, but it is significant in any case that no mention is made of the ancient monarchy of Kush. It seems clear, at least inferentially, that by the time of Aezanas the dynasty had already succumbed, either to the inroads of the Noba or to an earlier Axumite invasion.[23] As Kirwan observes:

. . . the evidence is fragmentary, but the impression is that intermittently from the first century AD at least Axum had been a threat to Meroë and the Butana was not infrequently the scene of battles between the two powers. As Hintze has suggested,[24] the incised pictures of King Sherkarer . . . at Jebel Qeili [cf. Ch. 11] may possibly . . . commemorate a Meroitic victory over Axum or the repulse of an Axumite advance. Then there are two other Axumite inscriptions concerned with the Island of Meroë, both probably antedating the Aezanas inscription. One is the very fragmentary Greek inscription on black basalt found by Sayce at Meroë . . . commemorating an Axumite capture of the city. The other is the Greek inscription seen and in part copied at Adulis by the sixth century topographer Cosmas Indicopleustes. This may be the work of King Aphilas, and Glaser and others considered . . . that it dated from the second half of the third century . . . After a long list of territories and peoples conquered to the north, east, and south of Axum, the king in the Cosmas inscription (his name is missing) continues, 'For this success I now offer my thanks to the mighty God Ares who begat me and by whose aid I reduced all the nations bordering on my own country, on the east as far as the land of Incense and on the west as far as the lands of Ethiopia and Sasu.' Sasu here must surely be a mistranscription for Kasu.[25]

The final downfall of the ancient Kushite monarchy is, then, veiled in almost complete darkness. Although its decline was undoubtedly hastened by economic competition and perhaps military pressure from Axum, it may in the end have succumbed to the inroads of more immediately neighbouring barbarians from across the Nile. Aezanas proclaimed himself king of Kasu (along with seven other kingdoms), but it seems to have been the Noba rather than the Abyssinian highlanders who took physical possession of the traditional Kushite territory. Significantly, neither people attempted to build a successor state on the ruins of Meroë and its institutions. In the royal protocols of Aezanas there is no mention of Amon, of 'the Two Lands', or of any of the ancient political and religious traditions upon which the rule of Kush had been based since the days of the pharaohs.

Axumite dominion on the Nile was ephemeral at best, and it did not outlive Aezanas. The later Abyssinian rulers turned their attention eastward, attempting to build an empire in southern Arabia. The subsequent Persian and Arabian conquests of the peninsula destroyed not only their empire, but the Red Sea trade upon which its existence depended. Abyssinia relapsed into a dark age which lasted nearly a thousand years.[26] Nubia too entered a dark age, for Meroitic writing disappeared with the Meroitic civilization.[27] We have, as a result, no historical record of events on the Upper Nile between the campaign of Aezanas and the appearance of a Christian monarchy at Alwa two centuries later (Ch. 14). Presumably the subjects of Alwa were, in part, descended from the ancient Meroites, but the kingdom was in no sense a Meroitic successor state. A complete ideological gulf separates the final disappearance of 'pharaonic' civilization from the beginnings of medieval Christianity.

The final decline of Kushite civilization in Lower Nubia is only slightly better documented than in the south. Here too economic decline seems to have been accompanied by external pressure, and to have ended in political collapse. The contributing factors were somewhat different in the two cases, but the final result was the same.

Lower Nubia was too remote from Abyssinia to be menaced by Axumite military power, and it was not sufficiently dependent on long-range trade to be affected by competition from the highland kingdom. These factors probably explain why the Meroitic north endured and prospered for a considerable time after the decline of the southern provinces. From the second century onwards, however, both Lower Nubia and Upper Egypt were increasingly subject to depredation by the desert nomads – the ferocious Blemmyes whom Pliny described as a 'headless race whose eyes and ears do grow beneath their shoulders'.[28] They appear frequently in classical texts of the third and fourth centuries as the perpetrators of raids upon the settled communities around Aswan and Philae, and on two occasions they seem to have participated in abortive Egyptian rebellions against Roman authority.[29] It is clear from a number of sources that the Blemmyes of classical tradition are to be identified with the Beja tribes of today,[30] as well as in all probability with Medjay or Medju, who are often named as desert raiders in the hieroglyphic texts of the Middle Kingdom (Ch. 7). Throughout the historic period the principal habitat of these people has been the Red Sea Hills, which probably explains why their influence has been most strongly felt in the northernmost part of Nubia and adjacent Upper Egypt – regions which are separated only by a narrow strip of desert from the grass and scrub lands of the Beja habitat.

The transformation wrought upon Beja society and culture by the acquisition of camels has already been remarked. By the end of the third century the nomads were not only in possession of the desert gold and emerald mines,[31] but, according to the historian Procopius, were plundering even the garrisoned settlements of the Roman Dodekaschoenos.[32] Under the circumstances the Emperor Diocletian not unnaturally concluded that the further occupation of Lower Nubia was not justified by the meagre revenue which the province yielded. In AD 297 he withdrew the Roman garrisons and established the imperial frontier at Philae, leaving the Dodekaschoenos at the mercy of the nomads.

Withdrawal of the Roman garrisons did not immediately bring an end to civilization in the Dodekaschoenos, for much of the settled population evidently stayed on, and there are many suggestions of continued Roman cultural and economic influence in the fourth century.[33] The Meroitic province which lay to the south of Maharraqa was even less immediately affected by the Roman withdrawal, for it was less vulnerable to nomad attack than was the Roman province. There are many Meroitic inscriptions from the fourth century which suggest that the flourishing civilization of the north (described in the last chapter) persisted for a considerable time after the Roman retreat, and even after the downfall and disappearance of the Kushite monarchy in the south.[34] Nevertheless, the Roman departure from the Dodekaschoenos probably brought an immediate decline in the economic fortunes of the neighbouring Meroitic province. As we noted in Chapter 12, the supply of food to the Roman garrisons may in itself have been an important industry in Meroitic Nubia. More importantly, however, the Roman withdrawal left the vital trade link between Meroitic Nubia and Roman Egypt squarely in the hands of the Blemmyes. From that moment on, the final collapse of Meroitic prosperity was only a matter of time.

The end of Meroitic prosperity spelled also, to all intents and purposes, the end of Meroitic civilization. The circumstances of its final disappearance in Lower Nubia are, however, no more clearly attested than they are in the steppelands to the south. In the north we cannot even recognize a *coup de grâce*, such as might have been dealt by the Axumite invasion or by the Noba incursions at Meroë. In the absence of contemporary texts, we get the impression that Kushite civilization simply ran down and stopped. By the fifth century monumental architecture, mural art, state religion, writing, and most of the higher arts of civilization were gone; after 1,500 years the land of Kush was plunged once again into a dark age, from which it was not to emerge until the introduction of Christianity two centuries later. For the events of the intervening period we can only rely upon the fragmentary and often contradictory evidence of late classical texts, and upon archaeology.

THE DARK AGE AND THE 'X-GROUP'

Archaeologically, the post-Meroitic dark age in Lower Nubia is filled by the cultural remains which Reisner designated sixty years ago as the 'X-Group'. Like the other alphabetic groups described in Chapters 5–6, remains of the 'X-Group' were first discovered in Cemetery 7 at Shellal, a few miles south of Aswan.[35] As usual, the recognition and description of this new cultural complex were based exclusively upon its mortuary remains; not until more than a generation later was any significant excavation carried out in habitation sites of the post-Meroitic period.

As always, Reisner interpreted the unfamiliar 'X-Group' grave type as evidence of the coming of a new people (cf. Ch. 3). It was, he reported, '. . . a new and distinctly non-Egyptian type of grave . . . entirely different from the preceding Ptolemaic–Roman types. This type of grave . . . was marked by the contraction and the orientation of the body and by the pottery as being unique. The contents of these graves present a non-Egyptian culture, the racial antecedents of which are not clear.'[36] As always, too, the cultural theories of Reisner found instant confirmation in the anatomical evidence of the 'X-Group' skeletons, as adduced by Elliot Smith: 'The X-Group people were strongly negroid aliens who had suddenly made their way north into Nubia, bringing with them a mode of burial and a type of pottery which Dr Reisner has declared to be distinctly non-Egyptian . . . The feature which immediately caught the eye in these skulls was the strikingly negroid facial aspect . . .'[37]

The two statements just quoted illustrate to perfection the confusion of racial and cultural evidence which has always beclouded the 'X-Group' problem. Reisner speaks of a culture as having 'racial antecedents'; Elliot Smith suggests that the non-Egyptian character of the 'X-Group' skulls is somehow confirmed by the non-Egyptian character of their pottery and mode of burial. In fact, we now know that insofar as there were racial and cultural innovations in the post-Meroitic period, they came from opposite directions and were largely unconnected.

It must be added that the theories of Reisner and of Elliot Smith were not wholly mistaken in the context of their time and place. The First Archaeological Survey of Nubia (cf. Ch. 3) was confined to the far north of Nubia, where there had been no Meroitic occupation; thus the 'X-Group' people and culture were initially contrasted not with any Nubian group but with their Ptolemaic and Roman–Egyptian predecessors in the Dode-kaschoenos. In this area there is every reason to assume that the newcomers did indeed represent a racial and cultural intrusion, following the with-drawal of the Roman garrisons (cf. 'The problem of the historical texts', below). Yet when it was later discovered that the main centres of 'X-Group' population and activity were not in the Dodekaschoenos but in the old Meroitic province of Lower Nubia, it was somehow assumed that they represented a racial and cultural intrusion in this area as well. It seemed, in sum, that a new group of southern barbarians had taken possession of the whole of Lower Nubia, displacing Romans and Meroites alike.

Modern anthropological research has not confirmed the theory of 'X-Group' racial distinctness *vis-à-vis* the preceding Meroitic population in Lower Nubia.[38] Although several recent students have observed – as did Elliot Smith – a stronger 'negroid'[39] admixture in the 'X-Group',[40] the differences between the two populations are no longer seen to be large. Batrawi has clearly expressed the modern consensus in writing that 'The Meroitic and X-Group series . . . may be considered to represent variants of the same population. The . . . X-Group series, however, includes those aliens, probably slaves, whose presence caused the series as a whole to exhibit the greatest variability among Nubian populations.'[41]

The notion of cultural discontinuity between the 'X-Group' and their predecessors, legitimate enough as regards the Dodekaschoenos, was also thought to hold for the Meroitic province. After excavating the great Meroitic and post-Meroitic cemetery at Faras, Griffith reported that '. . . there is no real transition to the X-Group, which comes in abruptly'.[42] As knowledge of the Meroitic and 'X-Group' cultures increased, however, the continuities between them became more and more apparent. As early as 1925 Junker could observe that 'There is no striking difference between the X-Group and the Meroitic culture. The grave forms are almost the same in both, the difference being mainly in the preference for individual types. Numerous pottery types were found in both and iron spears, arrowheads and tools are common to both periods. Thus both represent in Nubia a single culture which either directly or indirectly develops into that of the Christian period.'[43] It should be added that some of the most important cultural differences – particularly in the pottery – are certainly due not to southern influence but to the increasing cultural dominance of Byzantine Egypt.[44] Finally, the excavation of a number of stratified settlements in the recent past has demonstrated that there was no break in occupation between the Meroitic and post-Meroitic periods.[45] In Lower Nubia at least, we are no longer justified in thinking of Meroitic and 'X-Group' as anything but successive chapters in the history of the same culture.

Given the present state of our knowledge, the continued use of the noncommittal and misleading 'X-Group' designation seems unjustified. The name 'Ballana Culture', proposed several years ago by Trigger, is manifestly preferable.[46] Like 'Kerma Culture', it identifies a particular stage of Nubian cultural development with its principal monumental expression (see 'The royal tombs', below), and provides a name which is instantly recognizable to anyone already familiar with Nubian history. It also enables us to differentiate between the culture of Lower Nubia and the related but in some ways distinct post-Meroitic culture of the steppelands, which is designated by Trigger as the Tanqasi Culture.[47] For the remainder of this chapter, therefore, I shall use the term Ballana Culture to designate what Reisner called the 'X-Group', while referring to the post-Meroitic period in a broader sense (and including both the Ballana and Tanqasi Cultures) as the X Horizon.

If the archaeological remains of the Meroitic and Ballana phases point unmistakably to cultural and social continuity, there nevertheless remain important differences between them which must be explained. In the cultural sphere we have to account for the disappearance of many of the higher arts which had long been characteristic of Kushite civilization, and at the same time for the revival of burial rites which seem to hark all the way back to pre-pharaonic Kerma (Ch. 8). In the political sphere we have to recognize the appearance of a new, independent monarchy in Lower Nubia which nevertheless represents the last, barbarized manifestation of the pharaonic tradition. To further complicate the picture we have a fairly considerable number of late classical texts which make no mention of Meroë or Meroites, but allude repeatedly to two seemingly new peoples, the Blemmyes and the Nobatae. Finally, we have possible evidence of linguistic discontinuity between the Meroitic and post-Meroitic periods which cannot be ignored. As the reader will discover, it is almost impossible even today to sort out this tangle of seemingly contradictory evidence. The only hope of doing so lies in considering independently the light which history, archaeology, and linguistics throw upon the cultural development of post-Meroitic Nubia.

Studies of post-Meroitic history[48] have generally taken as their point of departure the fragmentary and often enigmatic historical accounts of such writers as Procopius,[49] Olympiodorus,[50] and Priscus.[51] This approach would seem to suggest that the classical authors are our best guides to the events of the post-Meroitic period, and that the archaeological record must somehow be reconciled with them. In fact, just the reverse is true. In the present analysis I will therefore begin on the solid ground of archaeology, and will defer until later a consideration of how it reflects upon the classical texts and their reliability (cf. 'The problem of the historical texts', below).

THE ARCHAEOLOGY OF THE BALLANA CULTURE

Remains of the Ballana Culture have been found from Shellal in the north to Sesebi, in the Abri-Delgo Reach, in the south (Figs. 63, 64).[52] The northern limit is for all practical purposes the immemorial Egyptian–Nubian frontier; that is, the First Cataract. The southern limit is, as usual, not clearly defined; it reflects nothing more than the current limit of exploration. However, it is probable that we shall ultimately find the southern limit of Ballana influence either in the Abri-Delgo Reach or in the lower end of the Dongola Reach, for the upper Dongola Reach seems to belong to the contemporary but distinct Tanqasi culture which will be described later.

The extent and importance of the Ballana Culture, particularly in Lower Nubia, is attested only by its mortuary remains. Of slightly more than 150 Ballana sites which are now known, more than four fifths are cemeteries.[53] The scarcity of habitation sites is probably due to several factors: haphazard survey, the insubstantial character of the Ballana buildings, and the fact that many of them were overbuilt with Christian structures which themselves were not systematically examined. Only in the *Batn el Hajar* do we find something like a proper proportion of habitation and mortuary sites;[54] it is not indicative of heavy occupation, but only of accidental factors which have resulted in better site preservation in this area.

Ballana sites – both villages and cemeteries – are notably smaller and more dispersed than are those of the Meroitic period. While most Meroitic cemeteries contain at least thirty graves, many burial grounds of the Ballana period have less than a dozen. The largest number of Ballana graves which have been excavated at any one site is 495, at the cemetery of Argin near Wadi Halfa.[55] However, it appears probable that some cemeteries which are partly or largely unexcavated may be many times larger.[56] Very few of the larger Ballana cemeteries are 'pure' sites; most of them include also graves of the Meroitic or of the Christian period, or both. In the area immediately surrounding the Second Cataract, for example, there were thirteen cemeteries of the Ballana period which also contained Meroitic

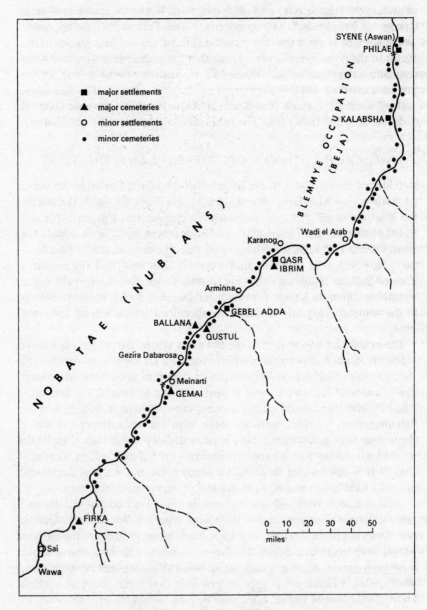

Fig. 64. Lower Nubia in Ballana times

graves, twenty-five cemeteries which contained also Christian graves, and seventeen cemeteries which contained only Ballana graves.[57] This circumstance points both to the relatively brief duration of the Ballana period and to the small size of the population in most settlements.

By far the heaviest concentration of Ballana graves was found in the area just north of the Second Cataract; that is, in the area surrounding what seems to have been the political centre of Ballana times, at or near the modern village of the same name.[58] There is a second concentration farther north, in the vicinity of the old administrative centre of Qasr Ibrim, which evidently retained a position of high importance in post-Meroitic times.[59] Beyond Maharraqa, in the former territory of the Dodekaschoenos, Ballana sites are conspicuously smaller and fewer than in the region farther south. The total number of Ballana graves discovered by the First Archaeological Survey between Shellal and Wadi es-Sebua was only 418 – less than the number of graves from any other historic period.[60]

In the south, we know nothing about the distribution of Ballana graves beyond the limit of systematic exploration at the Dal Cataract. We can observe, however, that Ballana sites are much more numerous in the *Batn el Hajar* than are Meroitic sites.[61] Evidently the re-population of this inhospitable region took place primarily in the post-Meroitic period, rather than a century or two earlier as did the re-population of Lower Nubia. There was even an important administrative centre, or at least the residence of a very wealthy family, at Firka, near the upper end of the *Batn el Hajar*.[62] Some fifteen miles farther upstream, the large but unexcavated necropolis of Sai Island is the southernmost definitely known site of the Ballana Culture.[63] There are random finds of Ballana pottery from places farther south, but their loci have not been clearly established.[64]

Ballana graves differ from those of the Meroitic period chiefly in the form of their superstructures. Instead of a brick pyramid or mastaba, the standard surface marking for graves throughout post-Meroitic Nubia was a low, dome-shaped earth tumulus, strikingly reminiscent of the Kerma tumulus of 2,000 years earlier (cf. Ch. 8). There is some evidence that this form of tomb superstructure had already been adopted by the common people at Meroë well before the final downfall of the Kushite dynasty,[65] the pyramid remaining in use only among the ruling class. In Lower Nubia, however, the earth tumulus is distinctive of the post-Meroitic period; it is never found in association with Meroitic pottery, *ba* statuettes, or stelae.[66]

The typical Ballana tumulus was from 12 to 40 feet in diameter, and might rise to a maximum height of 15 feet. As we shall observe later, the tumuli of kings and nobles could reach far larger proportions. In the ordinary tombs there was no adjoining offering chamber or surface decoration of the earth mound. As in the Meroitic period, many graves seem to have lacked any kind of superstructure; in some places there are whole cemeteries without any tumuli.[67]

In their subterranean arrangements, the Ballana graves show the same variety of chamber types as do Meroitic graves. Although cave graves are rare, the basic two-fold division between vaulted chamber-tombs and niche graves, and the further division of the latter into end-niche and side-niche types, persists throughout the Ballana period (cf. Fig. 65). However, the relative proportions of the two main types are reversed: simple niche graves are much more common than are vaulted tombs in the post-Meroitic

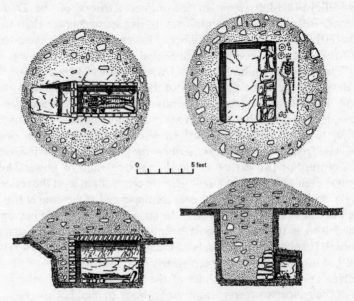

Fig. 65. Grave types of the Ballana Culture

period. A further innovation may be seen in the re-introduction of the contracted burial posture, and of the southward orientation of the body in place of the traditional westward orientation of Meroitic times. The great majority of contracted burials are found in niche-graves; they may represent nothing more than a natural adaptation to this rather constricted type of grave chamber. The bodies in chamber-tombs are most often extended on the back, as in Meroitic times. The practice of wrapping the dead in a shroud remained usual throughout the Ballana period.

The funerary offerings in Ballana graves are of the same general types as are found in Meroitic graves, but are considerably reduced in number and variety. Quantities of cheap, locally made pottery are the most common grave furnishings. Other objects, except beads, are rare, and imported goods exceptionally so. Weapons of one kind and another are found in a good many cases; they include iron spear and arrow heads, leather quivers of a striking and elaborate design,[68] leather bowguards, and archers' stone rings.

The great majority of Ballana cemeteries contain only relatively modest tombs of the kind just described. Larger and more pretentious tombs are conspicuous at only a few places: Qasr Ibrim,[69] Ballana and Qustul,[70] Gemai,[71] and Firka[72] (Fig. 64). Here were enormous earthen mounds, the largest of which rival in size the great tumuli of Kerma (Ch. 8). These royal and noble tombs, which will be described in more detail later, are the only monumental structures which the Ballana period ever produced.

The absence of monumental architecture is one of the most distinctive and surprising features of the Ballana period. Not only was there no further building in stone, but the older temples and/or palaces which had been built at Gebel Adda and at Meinarti in late Meroitic times were deliberately destroyed.[73] This seems to have been a matter of policy rather than an accident of war, for the social and cultural development of the two villages was undisturbed in other respects (see 'Ideology and religion in the post-Meroitic period', below).

What little we know of everyday life in Ballana times comes chiefly from the remains of a few towns and villages which were founded in Meroitic times but continued to be occupied later. Among them were Karanog, Qasr Ibrim, Wadi el-Arab, Arminna West, Gebel Adda, and Meinarti.[74] At none of these places was there any significant break in the continuity of social and cultural development between Meroitic and post-Meroitic times. The clearest and most complete picture of everyday life comes perhaps from Meinarti, a village situated on an island in the Nile just below the Second Cataract (Fig. 64). It was occupied without interruption from Meroitic times to the end of the Middle Ages (c. AD 200–1400); three of its eighteen stratigraphic levels were attributable to the Ballana period.

As we saw in Chapter 12, the original Meroitic settlement at Meinarti consisted of a nucleus of public buildings (temple or palace, market compound, and wine press), a couple of substantial 'de luxe' houses, and a cluster of flimsier houses surrounding them. Before the end of the Meroitic period, the wine press was already disused and filled with trash. Not much later, the village was badly damaged by a flood, which destroyed one side of the market compound and many of the outlying farmhouses. This must have coincided very closely with the end of the Meroitic period, since no more Meroitic pottery is found after the flood. The story of subsequent development in the village is best told by a brief resumé of the stratigraphic levels which overlay the Meroitic remains, and were associated with typical Ballana pottery:

Level 16 . . . was the first of three 'X-Group' levels, and was marked by extensive rebuilding. The restorations and the new buildings were not as massive as their predecessors, but they were still substantially built, and there was no radical departure from the earlier plan. The badly damaged eastern side of the market compound was repaired, and a new ['de luxe'] house was built to the south of it, partly over the buried remains of the Meroitic [wine press]. However, the Meroitic temple (?) was deliberately destroyed by fire and razed, and the whole adjoining part of the mound was left unoccupied. As before, the ordinary farm-houses were presumably located on the neighbouring flats, where, because of their vulnerability to floods, they were eventually destroyed almost without a trace.

Level 15b [cf. Fig. 66]. As will readily be seen, the plan of the village at this period marks a radical departure from earlier times. The older, heavy-walled buildings were quite abruptly surrounded and virtually engulfed by a tight cluster of jerry-built, thin-walled houses which took up nearly every available space on the mound [Pl. XIXa]. Superficially, the alterations . . . might suggest the arrival of a new and less cultured population – a group of squatters moving into a deserted village. However, the unbroken sequence of pottery development and the continued occupation of the older houses do not support such an interpretation. A much more probable explanation is that a rising Nile had finally forced the Meinarti farmers to abandon their homes on the periodically inundated floodplain and to crowd in upon the higher ground which was gradually accumulating around the central buildings. This development foreshadows the long battle against recurring floods which was to occupy the villagers during the first half of the Christian period.

Level 15b is the earliest level at Meinarti which is represented by well preserved domestic, as opposed to public, buildings. The houses themselves are probably little different from those of earlier levels, and the overall plan remains suggestive of the town of Wadi el-Arab,[75] with its mass of rather irregular, thin-walled houses surrounding the more widely scattered heavy-walled buildings. At Meinarti the original nucleus of the old Meroitic [market compound] still remained in use, although it was so much patched and overbuilt as to be hardly recognizable. The ['de luxe'] house of Level 16 also remained in use, and a new building nearly identical in plan, but with heavier walls, was built alongside it. [This] was apparently the last substantial, vaulted structure to be built at Meinarti for a century or more. During the later X-Group periods a progressive architectural deterioration is visible, the houses becoming more and more irregular and insubstantial. As the ['de luxe'] houses and the [market compound] fell into disrepair they were first filled with rubbish and then overbuilt with thin-walled, flat-roofed structures.

Level 15a. Wind-blown sand had accumulated deeply around the lower slopes of the mound, particularly on the west side, causing buckling and collapse of some of the walls. The quantities of whole pottery which were found buried in the sand at this level suggest that there may have been a temporary and unexpected abandonment of part of the village. When it was reoccupied there was considerable replacement and re-arrangement of interior partitions, but no important new building and no essential change in the plan of the village. The

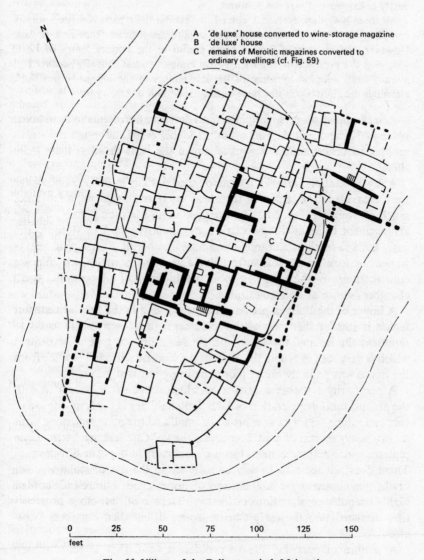

A   'de luxe' house converted to wine-storage magazine
B   'de luxe' house
C   remains of Meroitic magazines converted to
    ordinary dwellings (cf. Fig. 59)

0   25   50   75   100   125   150
feet

Fig. 66. Village of the Ballana period, Meinarti

399

newer and sturdier of the two 'de luxe' houses remained in use, but the older had partly collapsed and was not restored.

All three X-Group levels at Meinarti . . . exhibit the typical X-Group pottery complex, and there is no well-marked evolutionary trend from first to last. However, the number of incised cross graffiti in the pottery lamps of Level 15a, plus the presence of imported votive lamps, suggest that Christianity had already been adopted by some of the inhabitants of the village at this time, although the church was not built until at least half a century later.[76]

A very similar process of architectural deterioration seems to have taken place at Karanog, at Arminna, and at Gebel Adda, although the stratigraphic sequences were not worked out in the same detail at these three sites.

A few habitation sites which were founded initially in Ballana times have been excavated. The largest of them was at Gezira Dabarosa, a few miles north of Meinarti (Fig. 64). The site yielded no Meroitic pottery, but the arrangement of its buildings is strikingly similar to the late Meroitic and early Ballana levels at Karanog, Arminna, and Meinarti. A typical heavy-walled 'de luxe' house was surrounded and virtually engulfed by flimsier constructions, in which the two-room combination of a large and a small chamber is once again recognizable.[77]

A house of the Ballana period which was found in the Second Cataract region is smaller than any of the settlements just described. It seems to represent the isolated residence of a single family – a type of settlement which is very rare in Nubia throughout the historic period.[78] Not far from the house was a family burial plot containing just two graves.[79]

A peculiarity of house construction which seems to be associated with the architectural degeneration of later Ballana times is the frequent use of very rude stone masonry, comprised of small and irregular sandstone slabs set in a heavy mortar of mud. Sometimes the slabs are laid in a herringbone pattern, with alternate courses leaning diagonally in opposite directions.[80] There does not seem to be any consistency in the use of stone *vis-à-vis* brick; some houses were built entirely of stone, some of brick and some of highly irregular combinations of the two. The use of rude stone construction persisted into the early Christian period, but died out soon thereafter.

A picture of everyday life very different from that in the ordinary villages has recently emerged from the excavations at Qasr Ibrim. Although only a small part of the site has yet been excavated to the lowest levels, enough has been uncovered to disclose the presence of a regular, planned city of stoutly built houses arranged in contiguous blocks along nearly straight streets. The village plan itself may be a legacy of the Meroitic period, as are the surrounding fortification walls (cf. Ch. 12), but the houses which have thus far been excavated are identified by their pottery and other contents as belonging to the Ballana and not to an earlier period.[81] They are nearly square in plan and are composed of from four to eight rooms on the ground floor; many houses apparently had an upper floor as well. The walls are of stout stone construction, smoothly plastered and whitewashed, and some bear traces of painted decoration in blue, yellow and red. Most doorways are fitted with monolithic jambs and sills of carefully dressed sandstone. A feature of the Qasr Ibrim houses which is rare in Nubian architecture is the presence of foundations extending to a depth of six to eight feet below the levels of the floors. Many houses are also equipped with carefully constructed sub-floor storage crypts closed with wooden hatch-covers. These features, taken together with the general absence of furniture and living arrangements, suggest that the massive Qasr Ibrim houses may have been designed more as magazines for the safeguarding of grain stores and goods than for everyday living. The elevated situation of the fortress would have made it an inconvenient place to live and work on a regular basis, but at the same time afforded ideal protection both from human predators and from the Nile's moisture and the attendant problem of white ants. The continuing importance of Qasr Ibrim down through history may in fact have been due in considerable measure to its role as a storage centre and a goods depot.[82] Nevertheless, the finding of enormous quantities of occupation debris [83] within the Ballana houses indicates that a good deal of day-to-day living went on at Qasr Ibrim, at least in some seasons.

It seems reasonable to infer that houses similar to those at Qasr Ibrim may have existed in at least one or two other settlements in Lower Nubia. The presence of very large 'X-Group' cemeteries in the neighbourhood of Faras and of Gebel Adda suggests that these places too may have been 'urban' centres in the Ballana period, as they were both in earlier and in later times. However, failure to excavate systematically below the Christian occupation levels has deprived us of any knowledge of the living arrangements at Faras and Gebel Adda in pre-Christian times.[84]

One of the few Nubian manufactures which seems to have flourished widely in the Ballana period was that of pottery-making. It shows, however, an almost complete break with the traditions of Meroitic times, and the final disappearance of any vestige of ancient Egyptian influence. The lack of correspondence between Meroitic and 'X-Group' pottery was one of the factors long regarded as evidence for an 'X-Group invasion' (see 'The dark age and the "X-Group"', above).

Roman influence, already apparent in some of the last Meroitic pottery, became totally predominant in the Ballana period. Nearly all Nubian vessels were made in imitation of contemporary Egyptian forms, which were themselves inspired by the widely popular *terra sigillata* of the late Roman Empire. They are mostly plain red goblets, bowls, and jars, either without decoration or with the simplest of 'splash' and 'blob' designs in which we can probably recognize the final degeneration of the Hellenistic vine-wreath motif (Pl. XIXc).[85]

Ballana pottery is so closely similar to that of Byzantine Egypt, and so different from its Meroitic predecessor, that it might reasonably have been regarded as an import from the north. However, we have been fortunate enough to locate at least one of the factories where it was made, at Debeira East, a short distance north of Wadi Halfa. Here was a cluster of half a dozen cylindrical kilns of brick, each divided into a lower furnace chamber and an upper chamber, open at the top, in which pots were fired. Perforations in the floor carried hot air from the lower to the upper chamber (Fig. 67). The kilns were located out of doors and close to the riverbank; they were surrounded by prepared working floors where wheel-forming, drying, and painting were presumably carried out. Surrounding the site were thick beds of ash and thousands of sherds and 'wasters', all dating from the late Ballana period and the early Christian period.[86]

Given the lack of underlying Meroitic structures at Debeira, and the lack of correspondence between the Meroitic and post-Meroitic ceramic traditions, it seems reasonable to suppose that the Debeira factory and industry were founded by immigrant potters from Byzantine Egypt after the collapse of the older Meroitic industry. The hand-made utility vessels produced by Nubian women on the other hand show no discontinuity between Meroitic and post-Meroitic times. On the contrary, it is impossible to distinguish many vessels of the Meroitic period from those of the early Ballana period. Only towards the end of the Ballana period was there a series of very gradual changes in the hand-made pottery complex.[87]

Pottery vessels seem to have been the only luxury goods which were enjoyed in any quantity by the Ballana people. They are found in enormous numbers not only in the graves, but even abandoned on the floors of houses. Evidently the mass-production methods employed at Debeira resulted in a very inexpensive, and therefore expendable, product.

Iron was certainly another industry of the Ballana period, although it is by no means abundant either in houses or in graves. 'For the first time in Lower Nubia numerous heavy objects made of iron began to appear. At Qustul and Ballana knives, swords, and spears are common, and iron is also used to make horse-bits, chairs, frying pans, and cooking tripods. Royal tombs as well as less important ones yielded numerous axes, hoes, saws, tongs, hammers, chisels, adzes, metal cutters, pincers, and other tools. Many of these had socketed attachments, unlike the tools of the Meroitic culture.'[88] Some of the more elaborate iron goods found in the royal tombs were presumably imported, although the origin of the distinctive Ballana horse-bits remains a mystery to this day.[89]

Another industry of Ballana times which is attested by a few chance finds

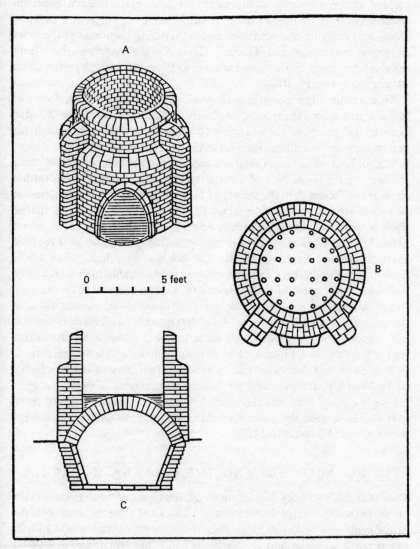

Fig. 67. Double-chamber pottery kiln of the type used in Ballana and Christian times

A: *perspective view*; B: *vertical plan*; C: *cross-section*

is that of basket-making. A grave in a cemetery near the Second Cataract yielded two remarkably well-preserved coiled baskets. Even more interesting was the finding, at the edge of the same cemetery, of a cache of thirty-four carrying-baskets which had presumably been used in the work of grave excavation and filling.[90] Evidently the techniques of earth removal in ancient Nubia were the same as those employed by the archaeologist today (see Pl. IIIb).

Most of the other manufactured goods which are sometimes found in Ballana graves are the same as, or closely similar to, those of the Meroitic period, and many of them appear to have been imported. Except for beads, they are much less common than in earlier times.

Throughout most of Nubia, archaeological remains of the Ballana culture give the impression of a decentralized agrarian society, poorer but more self-sufficient than the society of Meroitic times. Although differences of wealth are perceptible from family to family and from village to village, there is no conspicuously differentiated middle class. Once again, however, Qasr Ibrim represents a partial exception to this generalization. From the material remains found in the Ballana houses and refuse deposits it is evident that the dwellers at Ibrim enjoyed a remarkably high standard of living and were plentifully supplied with luxuries such as have not been found in ordinary village sites or graves. Among these, various kinds of decorative woodwork and wooden implements are particularly abundant – so much so as to suggest that there may have been a woodworking industry on the site. Innumerable spindles, shuttles and loom-weights, as well as plain and decorated cotton fabrics, attest also to the continuing presence of a textile industry, while unfired specimens of pottery suggest the strong possibility that there was a pottery kiln near by. Qasr Ibrim may well have been the great manufacturing centre as well as the storage depot of post-Meroitic Nubia.[91]

THE ROYAL TOMBS AND THE BALLANA MONARCHY

Insofar as there was any élite in post-Meroitic times, we have evidence of it chiefly in the form of tombs substantially larger and richer than those of the ordinary citizens. Such tombs have been found in four places: at Qasr Ibrim in the north, at Firka and Kosha in the south, at Gemai, and at Ballana and Qustul, which stood opposite each other about thirty-five miles north of the Second Cataract (Fig. 64).[92] The tombs at Qasr Ibrim and at Firka are impressive in their size and wealth, but they are vastly overshadowed by the barbaric opulence of the Ballana and Qustul sepulchres. These represent the climactic achievement of the Ballana period, and its only truly monumental constructions. They stand out without peer among the remains of their time just as do the great tumuli of Kerma 2,000 years earlier. They are in fact the only symbolic representations of state authority which we are able to recognize in the post-Meroitic era.

The twin cemeteries of Ballana and Qustul stood directly opposite each other, on the west and east banks of the Nile, in the midst of one of the richest agricultural districts in Lower Nubia. Although their largest tumuli were second in size only to those at Kerma, they had none of the dramatic visibility of the earlier Kushite royal tombs. The low, domed mounds of earth were so encumbered with drifted sand and so overgrown with scrub that in modern times they were often mistaken for natural formations. This circumstance had, in fact, helped to preserve the Ballana and Qustul tombs from the continual ransacking which the pyramid tombs at Napata and Meroë had suffered. In addition, the irregular layout of the interior chambers had, in a few cases, successfully baffled the robbers of antiquity; whole roomfuls of treasure were left undisturbed for the archaeologist. In consequence the tombs of this barbaric and illiterate period produced, paradoxically, the richest archaeological finds ever made in Nubia. Like the accidentally preserved tomb of Tutankhamen in Egypt, they give us a clue – almost the only clue we possess – to the even greater wealth which probably accompanied the tombs of earlier and more prosperous times.

The discovery and excavation of the Ballana–Qustul tombs was the outstanding achievement of the Second Archaeological Survey of Nubia.[93] The circumstances of discovery have been eloquently described by W. B. Emery:

Following our usual practice of exploration we picked our way in extended formation among the dunes and scrub of this rather unattractive country looking for an indication of ancient remains. I myself was exploring the area nearest the river and wandering about in the area just south of the village, and I soon came within sight of a confused jumble of small hills partly covered in scrub. As I approached nearer to them they took on a more circular and regular form, but it was not until I had climbed to the top of one of them, in order to get a better view of the surrounding desert, that I appreciated the regularity of their shape and considered the possibility of their being man-made tumuli [cf. Pl. XIXb].

In this age, when the archaeologist is assisted by air photography, the artificial character of the Ballana mounds would have at once been apparent; but viewing them, as we did, from a very broken and uneven ground-level, this was by no means obvious. In fact a geological expedition which had preceded us two years before had pronounced the mounds to be natural deposits of river silt, blown and weathered to their circular formations. On an archaeological expedition such as ours we were not in a position to bring with us a lot of reference books, and we had hitherto depended, with generally satisfactory results, on Weigall's published account of his preliminary exploration of Lower Nubia which he made on behalf of the Antiquities Service in 1906 . . . We examined his valuable book, but were left even more puzzled by his statement that 'To the archaeologist, the country here is uninteresting, and the writer found no traces of any ancient sites, except where a few Roman and medieval fragments of pottery indicated the existence of villages of that time.'[94]

Excavation soon revealed the true nature of the Ballana and Qustul mounds:

. . . By the end of November we had completed a large V-shaped cut in the mound and on its east side were down to ground level. The head of a ramp sloping downwards toward the west was soon revealed and we commenced the gradual descent toward the entrance of the tomb. The first objects which came to light were two iron axe-heads, so perfectly preserved that they still retained the dark blue color of iron which has just left the smith's anvil . . . Our next find, at the head of the ramp, was a heavy metal object that at the time of its discovery completely puzzled us, and although we laughed at the suggestion we could think of no modern article it resembled more than police handcuffs! Polishing soon revealed that it was made of solid silver, but its true character was not recognized until we had found similar objects later in the course of our work. It was in reality a horse-bit which would have proved a brutal curb to the most fractious animal . . . At the time we had no idea of the purpose of this strange contraption, but the discovery the next day of the skeleton of a horse from which the bit must have come showed us what it was. I cannot say which astonished us more: the revelation of the true purpose of this curious object or the horse itself, and it was not until we had descended further down the ramp and un-covered more skeletons of horses, donkeys, and camels that we realized the significance of this jumble of animal remains. The owner of the tomb took his camels with him for service in the afterlife as in life they would be kept waiting or stabled outside his residence. Soon we reached a small courtyard at the bottom of the ramp in front of the doorway of the tomb. Here we found the remains of what were obviously the favorite horses of the owner, for some of them had silver-mounted wooden saddles and silver trappings consisting of chains of flat or slightly convex disks from which were suspended drop pendants and disks. With the remains of the horses we found the skeletons of the grooms who were to attend to them in the next world. The animals had all been pole-axed, but we found no signs of violence on the human remains, and we can only conclude that they were drugged or poisoned before the entrance of the tomb was filled in.[95]

The initial discovery of the Ballana and Qustul tombs was made in November 1931. During the three seasons that followed, the discoverers went on to investigate some 180 tombs at the two sites, of which perhaps forty might be considered 'royal' on the basis of their size and richness. The character of these largest tombs was nearly uniform, both at Ballana and at Qustul, and has been thus described by Emery:

An inclined passage was cut in the hard alluvium leading down to a large pit, and a series of brick rooms were constructed in this pit, with a small open court into which the inclined passage opened. In some cases each of the brick rooms have been built in separate pits, and are connected by short passages tunneled into the alluvium. The roofing of each room was barrel-vaulted, and in the larger tombs the doors had stone lintels.

It is evident that the owners of these tombs held to the Ancient Egyptian belief of the material survival after death of both animate and inanimate objects, for they buried with their dead wine and food, furniture, cooking utensils, jewels, weapons and the tools and materials to make them, but in place of the Ushabtis [servant-figurines] of the Egyptians they sacrificed their slaves and animals.

One room was usually reserved for the wine jars and drinking cups, and another was devoted to bronze and silver cooking utensils, lamps, jewels, weapons, and tools. In Tomb 80 at Ballana, for example, we found spears and axes together with metal-working tools and iron ingots. In the larger tombs a separate chamber was reserved for the burial of the queen, who was undoubtedly sacrificed, with her attendant slaves. But in the smaller tombs the sacrificed queen was placed beside her consort.

The king was placed in the chamber nearest the main entrance to the tomb, and it is evident that his installation was the last act before the final closing. His body was placed on a canopied wooden bier below which were placed bronze and silver vessels for his immediate use. He was dressed in his royal regalia, and weapons for his protection were left leaning against the foot of the bier, and at its head lay the sacrificed bodies of a male slave and an ox. An iron folding chair was frequently placed by the side of the bier.

The entrance to the tomb was then blocked with bricks and stone, and the owner's horses, camels, donkeys, and dogs, together with their grooms and possibly soldiers, were then sacrificed in the courtyard and the ramp. The animals were buried wearing their harnesses and saddles; the dogs in some cases had collars and leashes. The sacrificed humans met their deaths either by the cutting of the throat or by strangulation, and the animals were pole-axed.

Finally the pit and ramp were filled and a great earthen mound was raised over the tomb; in many cases offerings such as weapons, jewelry, vases, games, etc., were buried in the mound. And at Ballana most of the mounds were covered with a layer of large schist pebbles.[96]

The brief description just quoted conveys only a hint of the enormous wealth and variety of offerings found in the tombs, particularly at Ballana (cf. Pl. XIXd). The definitive report of the excavators describes jewelry, weapons, horse equipment, silver vessels, caskets, a great number and variety of bronze vessels, tools, toilet articles, games, bronze tables, tripods and folding chairs, lamps and incense burners, leather work, stone vessels, glass, weighing instruments, textiles, and pottery.[97] Except for the pottery, most of these objects appear to have been imports from Byzantine Egypt. The bronze lamps and bowls, the inlaid chests of wood and ivory, and many other objects closely resemble the offerings found in the late Meroitic tombs at Karanog and Faras, described in the last chapter. Presumably they came from the same sources. However, as might be expected, the imported items of the Ballana period show a good deal more Christian influence than do those of earlier times. Pagan, Hellenistic motifs still predominate, but the cross often appears side by side with them. This combination of pagan and Christian motifs makes it possible to date many of the imported objects found in the Ballana and Qustul tombs to the fifth and sixth centuries AD.[98]

Despite the predominance of Hellenistic and Byzantine influence, a few of the items found at Ballana and Qustul still conform to the artistic and ideological traditions of Meroitic and pharaonic times. Foremost among them are the silver crowns found at or near the heads of ten of the Ballana burials. They are broad circlets of beaten silver, richly encrusted with gems and adorned with all kinds of royal and divine insignia from bygone ages. Among the divine motifs are representations of Horus, Isis, a ram's head which probably symbolizes Amon or (less probably) the old Nubian god Khnum, the *uraeus* serpent with and without wings, and the sacred *uatchet* eye which often appeared as a decorative motif in pharaonic and Meroitic times. Two crowns are also embossed with human figures wearing the plumed *atef* crown which was one of the traditional symbols of pharaonic authority.[99]

The three most elaborate crowns from Ballana are all closely similar in design. They are broad circlets, from the upper rim of which projects a silver ram's head in full relief. The animal is itself crowned by a majestic, jewelled crest of *atef* plumes which rises high above the rim of the crown (Pl. XIXf). The special interest of these particular crowns lies in their very close resemblance to the royal diadems which are shown in Meroitic temple and tomb reliefs at Meroë and Naqa.[100] Owing to the thorough plundering of the Kushite royal tombs, no actual crowns of the Napatan and Meroitic periods have ever been found, but the temple and tomb reliefs are presumed to give a reasonably accurate representation of them. The Ballana crowns thus furnish the only visible link of ideological continuity between the monarchies of Meroitic and post-Meroitic times.

Although Emery considered that '. . . the X-Group tumulus is the direct descendant of the Meroitic pyramid, with the entrance stairway concealed under the superstructure . . .,'[101] the resemblances between the royal burials of Kush and of Ballana are nearly all general rather than specific. Certainly the two dynasties shared a common view of the afterlife and of their place in it, but the specific preparations which they made for it differed in a number of important respects. The domed earth tumulus, which is the standard superstructure for all burials of the Ballana period, is much more nearly comparable to the tumulus of Kerma times than to anything which was built in the intervening 2,000 years.[102] It may be noted, too, that the largest tumulus at Ballana, measuring 253 feet in diameter and 40 feet high,[103] is far larger than any of the Kushite pyramids, but closely approaches the proportions of the largest tumulus at Kerma.[104] Even more remarkable is the practice of covering the earth mounds at Ballana with white pebbles,[105] a custom which was also widespread in Kerma times. (It has not, however, been observed at Qustul or in any other cemetery of the Ballana period.)

Below ground, the royal tombs of Ballana and Qustul resembled the earlier Kushite tombs to the extent that they were comprised of a series of connected chambers approached by means of a long, sloping ramp from the east. On the other hand the actual arrangement of the chambers at Ballana and Qustul was notably variable and irregular; in only one case did it conform to the simple linear plan (apparently reproducing in miniature the features of the Kushite temple) which was characteristic of the tombs at Napata and Meroë. The most common arrangement comprised a burial chamber opening directly at the foot of the entrance shaft, an offering chamber through its farther end, and a second offering chamber opening through its north wall (see Fig. 68). However, there were many deviations from this plan, and in fact no two of the Ballana and Qustul tombs were identical in design.[106] It seems probable that the irregularity of their plan represents a deliberate attempt to foil would-be plunderers; as we noted earlier, it was partially successful in a few cases. An unexpected peculiarity of the Ballana–Qustul tombs is the placement of the main burial in the outermost chamber, instead of in the inner chamber as in all earlier royal tombs.

Two further practices which can be observed in the Ballana tombs, and which provide a link with the past, are those of bed burial and of human sacrifice. Both occurred to some extent in the Meroitic period, but both, like so much else in Ballana mortuary ritual, hark back more specifically to the Kerma culture of pre-pharaonic times. A good many of the royal dead at Ballana appear to have been laid out on *angareeb* beds of modern type,[107] and most of them were accompanied by at least two or three sacrificed retainers. The largest number of human sacrifices which could be definitely identified in any one tomb was seventeen[108] – a figure far lower than the 300 or so found in some of the Kerma tombs, but still significantly larger than the number of sacrifices found in any tomb of the intervening period.

It is clear that the antecedents of Ballana mortuary practice, and particularly of royal mortuary practice, are not to be found entirely in the preceding Meroitic period.[109] While there are some obvious continuities, many aspects of the post-Meroitic burial complex seem to represent a deliberate break with tradition, and a revival of much older, pre-pharaonic practices. In this category we may note the substitution of round, earth tumuli for stone or brick pyramids, the abandonment of the linear, temple-form arrangement of the subterranean chambers, and the nearly total disappearance of glyptic decoration and inscriptions. These might signify nothing more than the disappearance of stonemasons, lapicides, and scribes in impoverished times; in the light of other evidence, however, it seems

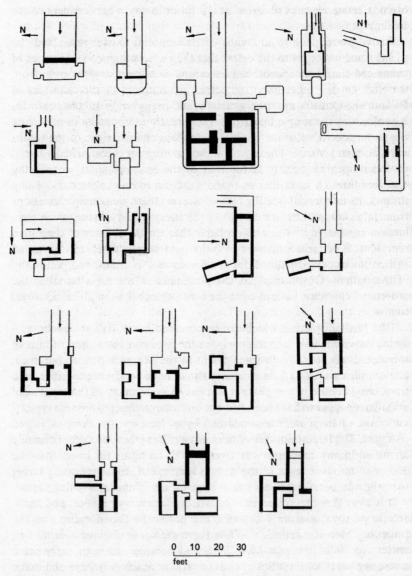

Arrows within chambers indicate direction of entry. Note widely varying plans and orientations.

Fig. 68. Plans of subterranean burial chambers, royal tombs of Ballana and Qustul

probable that something more than mere cultural degeneration was involved. Certain features of Ballana civilization seem to mark a deliberate repudiation of long-established tradition, the significance of which will be considered later ('Ideology and religion in the post-Meroitic period', below).

That some of the tombs at Ballana and Qustul were those of kings and queens can hardly be doubted. In them we recognize many of the immemorial status symbols of royalty: enormous tumuli, numerous human and animal sacrifices, immense wealth of offerings, and diadems adorned with royal and divine insignia. Yet it is also true that our knowledge of the Ballana monarchs, as of many Nubian dynasties before them, begins and ends with their tombs. With one notable exception (to be considered later) they left no other record of themselves, and their lives and achievements went unnoticed by their literate neighbours. Thus we cannot name with certainty a single Ballana ruler, and we know nothing of their origins, of their relationship to one another, of the territory they governed, or of the duration of their dynasty. The political antecedents of their rule are as mysterious as are the cultural antecedents of their tombs. In Trigger's words, 'Ballana and Qustul stand in an historical vacuum.'[110]

The original excavators of Ballana and Qustul believed that the two cemeteries represented a sequential development, the tombs at Qustul being older than those at Ballana.[111] More recently Trigger has suggested that the two sites may have been in use simultaneously, as the burial offerings are much the same in both places.[112] If this is correct, we are confronted with a further mystery: why did some of the rulers choose burial on the east bank of the Nile, and some on the west? We cannot even be positive that the two cemeteries are not those of rival dynasties which held sway on opposite sides of the river, although this seems unlikely in view of the close typological similarity of the tombs.

An additional complication arises from the fact that the cemeteries of Ballana and Qustul were not reserved for the exclusive use of the ruling family or families. The great tumuli were surrounded by numbers of much smaller graves, most of which appear to have been in no way different from the ordinary graves which can be found in any cemetery of the same period. (Here again the burial traditions of Ballana and Qustul are more closely parallel to those of Kerma than to the intervening Kushite periods.) The cemetery at Ballana contained 122 graves and that at Qustul sixty-one graves; in each place there were about twenty conspicuously large and rich tombs which might conceivably have been royal. Ten individuals, in seven tombs, were found wearing crowns, but these were of course fortuitously preserved. A much larger number of crowns may have been stolen by robbers. On the other hand, as Trigger has pointed out, neither very large and rich tombs nor silver crowns are necessarily indicative of reigning monarchs; some of the crowned individuals are in fact quite obviously queens consort, and others may be crown princes.[113] Since we have no certain way of distinguishing the tombs of reigning monarchs from those of subordinate members of the royal family, we cannot know the actual number of rulers buried at Ballana and Qustul or the duration of their dynasty.

The inclusive dates most often assigned to the Ballana culture are from AD 400 to 600.[114] To a large extent these are simply *termini post quem* and *ante quem* – the interval between the probable final disappearance of Meroitic rule and the probable general adoption of Christianity. They may be reasonably valid for the duration of the Ballana Culture as a whole, but we should not necessarily assume that the Ballana dynasty, as a political entity, was co-extensive with the Ballana Culture either in time or in space. Trigger has pointed out that some of the later 'X-Group' pottery types which are plentifully represented in the ordinary houses and cemeteries of Lower Nubia are not found in any of the royal tombs; in consequence, he believes that the time span represented by the two royal cemeteries may have been quite short.[115] If so, there may have been still later Nubian kings of the pre-Christian period, whose tombs have never been found.

Although we know where the Ballana kings were buried, we have still no idea where they lived. There are no important habitation remains in the immediate neighbourhood of the royal tombs, but neither Faras nor Gebel Adda is very far away, and both have been suggested as possible 'capitals' of the Ballana kingdom.[116] If they were we shall probably never know it, for both sites have disappeared beneath the Nile waters with their pre-Christian remains largely unexamined.[117] There is however a remote chance that the Ballana palace – or one of them – may yet come to light at Qasr Ibrim, despite its rather considerable distance from the royal cemeteries. The great fortress was unquestionably a place of the foremost importance, and its excavated remains bespeak a more nearly 'regal' life-style than do those of any other known settlement of the post-Meroitic era.[118]

The territorial limits of Ballana sovereignty are likewise uncertain. It has often been assumed that they are more or less indicated by the distribution of 'X-Group' pottery,[119] but there is no valid basis for such an assumption. Trade networks in historic times have consistently ignored political frontiers, and we have noted plentiful examples in the previous history of Nubia itself. Although their evidence is indirect, the historical texts of the post-Meroitic period suggest that in fact the limits of Ballana sovereignty fluctuated according to the power and fortunes of individual rulers. In the far north of Nubia, effective control was not established until a very troublesome enemy had been subjugated (see 'The problem of the historical texts', below).

It must be reiterated that the Ballana and Qustul tombs are the only remains from post-Meroitic Nubia which convey a suggestion of monarchical authority. At Qasr Ibrim, Gemai and Firka, however, there were clusters of tombs which in size, complexity, and wealth of offerings seem to be intermediate between the royal tombs and those of ordinary citizens.[120] Almost certainly they represent powerful local nobilities. The clustering of their tombs over several generations suggests that their power was hereditary, and therefore at least partially independent of that of the king. Whether they were vassals of the Ballana king, or whether they ruled over small independent principalities, we shall probably never know. A letter found at Qasr Ibrim in 1976 suggests the probability that, at least for a time, there were two or more kinglets ruling simultaneously in different parts of the Nile Valley (see 'The problem of the historical texts', below). As Trigger has observed, 'The ruins of how many dynasties that struggled for power at this time lie buried beneath the waters of Lake Nasser?'[121]

IDEOLOGY AND RELIGION IN THE POST-MEROITIC ERA

In the Dynastic ages, not only in Nubia but throughout the ancient world, church and state were one and the same; by the same token political ideology was inseparable from official religion. The complex religious establishments of antiquity served as much to keep order between man and man as between man and the gods. When political factionalism arose, it resolved itself into a struggle for control of the religious establishment. New dynasties arose when rebellious factions within the state captured the symbols of divinity; successor states arose when external barbarians captured them. As a successor state to pharaonic Egypt, the Empire of Kush for a thousand years presented a classic model of ancient imperial polity. A divine king was supported politically by a priestly oligarchy, and ideologically by a complex of dramatic symbols – architectural, artistic, mythological, and ritual.

Emery and Kirwan, the co-discoverers of the Ballana tombs, have laid great stress upon the ritual symbolism of the Ballana crowns as indicative of ideological continuity between the Meroitic and post-Meroitic monarchies.[122] There can be little doubt that these nameless kings of the post-Meroitic dark age did indeed base their claim to rule upon the same divine mandate as did their Meroitic and Napatan predecessors; to that extent the Ballana kingdom must be recognized as a successor state (not necessarily the only successor state) to Kush. Yet it is also true that the ideological continuities between the Meroitic and Ballana periods are almost confined to the royal crowns and certain other aspects of royal mortuary practice. Viewed in larger perspective, the ideological discontinuities between the two periods are much more numerous and more conspicuous than are the continuities.

Under the Kushite Empire, the royal tomb was only one of many symbolic expressions of political authority. Temples, palaces, glyptic art, stelae, historical traditions and legends, and complex ritual also expressed and reinforced the majesty of the state, no less than of the state gods. Not one of these expressions can be identified in the archaeological remains of the Ballana Culture. The absence of any kind of monumental architecture is one of the most conspicuous and astonishing features of post-Meroitic Nubia; its disappearance necessarily meant also the end of monumental decoration. The only constructions in cut stone which can be certainly identified with the Ballana period are the doorways to some of the royal burial chambers.[123] The lintel in at least one of these was adorned with winged *uraeus* figures in relief,[124] but the representation and carving are so typically Meroitic as to suggest that the block had been removed from an older temple.

The only recognizable representations of divinities from the Ballana period come also from the royal tombs. Outstanding among them are the Horus, Isis, and (probably) Amon figures which appear on the royal crowns; these deities were undoubtedly among the tutelaries of the ruling family.[125] A few other traditional Egyptian deities or royal figures appear as decorative motifs on some of the caskets, saddles, and inlaid chests found in the royal tombs,[126] but their importance was probably more decorative than ideological. The same must surely be true of the pagan Graeco-Roman deities whose figures adorn many of the imported bronze and silver vessels found in the tombs.[127] Like the Achaemenian rulers of Persia in earlier times, the Ballana kings appear to have cultivated a taste for Grecian art, but there is no evidence that they ever venerated the Grecian gods.

The art of writing may not have died out altogether at the end of the Meroitic period. Fragments of Meroitic papyri have been found in post-Meroitic refuse deposits at Qasr Ibrim,[128] and Griffith has pointed out that two letters in the Old Nubian alphabet (which came into use in the eighth century) seem to be derived from Meroitic antecedents.[129] Yet evidence of writing is scanty during the Ballana period. Neither stelae nor ostraka are found in the house sites and graves, and only a single monumental inscription can be definitely attested for the entire period between the end of Meroitic rule and the introduction of Christianity to Nubia. It was written on the wall of the much older temple of Kalabsha, apparently in the late fifth or early sixth century,[130] and recounts the military exploits of a certain King Silko.[131] The text is in very barbarized Greek and is thought to be the work of a Christian scribe, for its only reference to deities is in the phrase 'God gave me the victory'.[132] More will be said of this and other textual records of the Ballana period in later pages (see 'The problem of the historical texts'). The military proclamation of Silko shows that writing could still advance the interests of the state in the post-

Meroitic period, but in a nearly illiterate age its importance must necessarily have been small. The Ballana kings were evidently no longer served by their own scribal establishment; Silko was obliged to borrow the system of writing then current in Egypt.

The disappearance of many of the higher arts of civilization in post-Meroitic Nubia could be, and sometimes has been, attributed to simple poverty and cultural degeneration.[133] The decline in world trade following the break-up of the Roman Empire certainly had its effect on the fortunes of Nubia; it is reflected in the relative scarcity of imported goods among the ordinary people, in the seeming de-urbanization of society, and in the disappearance of a conspicuous middle class. Yet the kings buried at Ballana and Qustul were clearly not poor men. If the royal treasury could no longer afford monumental constructions in cut stone, it is still true that the great earth tumuli of Ballana and Qustul, with their multiple underground chambers, represent a far greater outlay of labour and expense than do the last, brick pyramids at Meroë. The change in form of the royal tomb superstructure can only be explained on the assumption that, as Trigger has suggested, the pyramid had ceased to be a meaningful symbol.[134]

Many aspects of Ballana culture and society, like the substitution of mound tumuli for pyramids, suggest not so much cultural degeneration as the deliberate rejection of Meroitic tradition. In this light must surely be seen the total absence of temples and palaces. The kings who built the Ballana tombs unquestionably commanded the wealth and the expertise necessary to build relatively modest public structures of the kind which had adorned the late Meroitic settlements of Lower Nubia. Not only did they not do so, but they seem deliberately to have destroyed the temples or palaces which stood at Gebel Adda,[135] at Meinarti,[136] and perhaps at Buhen,[137] and the old Napatan and Meroitic temple at Qasr Ibrim was abandoned and partly filled with refuse.[138] Even in the arrangement of their underground tomb chambers the Ballana kings seem consciously to have avoided the Meroitic temple-form, which was always reproduced in the earlier Kushite royal tombs (cf. Ch. 11). Finally, it can hardly be doubted that the Ballana kings could have maintained a scribal and artistic establishment at the royal expense had it suited their purposes; their failure to do so must be interpreted as a reflection of indifference or hostility rather than of incapacity.

In sum, it would appear that the rulers of Ballana times retained the kingly traditions of ancient Kush while abandoning or suppressing everything associated with priestly traditions. The complex and differentiated power structure of Kushite times, which (as we saw in Chapter 10) was sometimes a source of conflict within the state, seems to have been dismantled in favour of a return to personal rule. Once again the whole ideology of the state came to focus upon the person of the divine king, and its chief and perhaps only symbolic expression was his tomb. After 2,000 years the dynastic civilization of Kush had returned to its point of origin; it had reverted from an empire to an autocratic chieftainship.

The many and explicit parallels between the Kerma and Ballana cultures, respectively at the beginning and at the end of Nubia's dynastic age, may reflect something more than historical accident. The close correspondence not only in form but also in size between the largest royal tombs at Ballana and those at Kerma, and even more particularly the covering of the tumulus with a layer of white pebbles, suggests the deliberate revival of an older symbol of royal authority, just as the first Napatan rulers 1,200 years earlier revived the long-outdated pyramid form for their own royal tombs (cf. Ch. 10).

It is possible that the mound grave, with its covering of stones or pebbles, had survived since Kerma times in the western Sudan, and that its reintroduction to the Nile Valley in the post-Meroitic period was due to the influence of immigrants (see especially 'Post-Meroitic history in the south', below). However, it is worth recalling that archaizing movements have characterized the last stages of many civilizations.[139] When the accumulated weight of tradition becomes too heavy and cumbersome for the management of everyday affairs, it becomes necessary to simplify, either by repudiating the new or by repudiating the old. Thus ideologies, political as well as religious, are continually beset on the one hand by puritan, nativistic, and archaizing movements, and on the other hand by modernization movements. Very often the first precedes and clears the way for the second. As we shall observe in the next chapter, this was the sequence of developments in Nubia – as it was throughout much of the ancient world – in the first millennium AD. The retractile Ballana civilization, which appears at first glance like a step back towards the Tribal age, in fact prepared the way for both Christianity and Islam. The specific factors which brought this peculiar, transitional ideology into being in the post-Meroitic age will be discussed more fully later (see 'The problem of the historical texts').

Private religion in Nubia seems to have been little affected by the ideological changes of the post-Meroitic period. As always, mortuary ritual remained a main focus of religious activity. The changes in burial practice which took place in Ballana times were not of a major order, and they affected chiefly the above-ground and external features of the tomb. The adoption of an earth tumulus in place of a brick pyramid may have been in emulation of a practice already established in the south in late Meroitic times,[140] or it may have been inspired more directly by the example of the royal tombs. The disappearance of offering tables, of *ba* statuettes, and of funerary stelae were all, of course, connected with the disappearance of priestcraft. Below ground, on the other hand, the arrangement of burial chambers, of bodies, and of offerings remained much the same as in earlier times.

Another aspect of popular religion which carried over from Meroitic to Ballana times was the cult of Isis at Philae (cf. Ch. 12). Its continuing importance is attested by numerous historical texts from Egypt, some of which will be discussed later in another context. From these sources we learn that the Isis cult was maintained, for the benefit of its Nubian votaries, long after the official Christianization of Egypt (including Philae itself). The edict of Theodosius I (AD 390), which decreed the closing of all pagan temples throughout the Empire, was not enforced at Philae,[141] and later attempts to suppress the cult of Isis seem to have provoked armed clashes between Nubians and Egyptians. Finally, in AD 453, a treaty was signed which recognized the traditional religious rights of the Nubians at Philae. According to the historian Priscus, '. . . they would according to custom have free crossing to the temple of Isis. The Egyptians would have charge of the river boat for taking the statue of the goddess, because the barbarians at a certain period take the statue to their own land and, having used it for the purpose of an oracle, bring it back to the island. It seemed suitable to Maximinus [the Roman general in Egypt] to ratify the treaty in the temple of Philae.'[142] This agreement remained in force for nearly a hundred years, until the pagan temples were closed for good in the time of Justinian.[143]

Various symbols believed to be associated with Isis-worship have been found in the royal tombs and in other graves of the Ballana period.[144] Also suggestive are female pottery dolls, generally about five inches high, which have been found in many Ballana house-sites, though none has yet been found in a grave. The rigid standardization of the figure, with its elaborate head-dress, upraised arms, medallion on the forehead, and pendant medallion on the breast, suggests some sort of canonical representation, although it is not immediately recognizable as any known deity.[145] It must be admitted that the discreetly clothed and nearly shapeless figure does not resemble the traditional representation of Isis; she might in fact be some household deity such as Vesta. Some of the figures are made of hard, bright-pink clay which marks them unmistakably as products of Aswan (see Ch. 12); others seem to be Nubian made. It is a curious fact, however, that none of the figures has yet been found in an Egyptian site; all of the known specimens whose attribution is certain come from Nubia. Since they were presumably pagan fetishes, it seems reasonable to suppose that those made in Egypt were made explicitly for the Nubian trade.

As might be expected, increasing Christian influence is apparent in the late Ballana period. Votive lamps bearing saints' names and Christian insignia were being imported and used in Nubian houses, imitations of them were being made locally, and graffiti in the form of a cross were being incised on other pottery vessels.[146] None of this necessarily means that any

417

Nubian in the Ballana period actively professed the new faith; it means only that the cross and other Christian symbols which were now part of the state cult in Egypt were acquiring a certain charisma among the Nubians as well. As Kirwan has well observed:

No water-tight compartments . . . divided the religions of antiquity, and in Egypt pagan beliefs and practices, including . . . the practice of mummification among Christians, are found mixed together in a strange and bewildering amalgam. Discoveries made in Tomb 2 at Ballana may illustrate similar hybrid beliefs or superstitions among the primitive Nubians. In one of the burial chambers a gold cross, a scarab and four rolled-up strips of metal were lying close together. The gold strip proved to be an Agage, a love charm in corrupt Greek, invoking Isis. The remaining strips were of lead and probably also inscribed, but they could not be unrolled. Charms of this kind, on gold if beneficial, on lead if evil, were worn in a small bag strung from the neck. Probably all four objects had once been in such a bag, providing ample insurance for the living and the dead.[147]

Among the ideological currents which were abroad in post-Meroitic Nubia, some mention must be made of the cult of the grape. Whether or not Bacchic ritual was highly developed is uncertain, but archaeological remains leave no doubt as to the heavy consumption of wine in Ballana times. Taverns and/or wine cellars were prominent features of such settlements as Seyala, Qasr Ibrim, and Meinarti (cf. Ch. 12),[148] and the quantities of broken amphorae and goblets which accumulated within and around these buildings are astonishing. It might be added that the refuse deposits not only in the taverns but throughout the Ballana occupation levels at Qasr Ibrim and Meinarti are nothing short of prodigious: debris from this one 200-year interval accounted for nearly one third of the total deposits at Meinarti,[149] and for as much as half of the deposits at Qasr Ibrim.[150] In both sites the houses of the Ballana period were filled literally from floor to ceiling with all kinds of occupation debris: dung, straw, food remains, broken and discarded implements and vessels, and even substantial numbers of whole pottery vessels which seem to have been uncaringly cast aside. These conditions do not reflect simply the conversion of the buildings from domiciles to refuse dumps, for they were periodically re-floored and reoccupied on top of the accumulated rubbish. In many cases it was necessary to raise the height of the walls because of the depth of accumulated material within. While a causal relationship cannot of course be demonstrated, it is tempting to see a connection between the slovenly living habits and the heavy drinking of post-Meroitic times, and perhaps to link both to the decay of more inspiring ideologies.

Very little Meroitic or ancient influence survived in the secular arts of the Ballana period. The pottery, as has already been noted, was wholly subservient to Roman and Byzantine canons, the elaborate decorative tradition of Meroitic times having disappeared without a trace. The kings themselves, despite the archaic simplicity of their tumuli, displayed a marked pre-dilection for Graeco-Roman art in their selection of objects to be buried with them. This ideological syncretism, looking at once backwards and forwards, is everywhere characteristic of the unsettled age between the end of ancient civilization and the new beginnings which are represented by Christianity and Islam. The situation in Nubia at this pivotal point in history has been thus epitomized by Kirwan:

> Worshipping the ancient Meroitic gods and still practising the savage ritual sacrifices of their forbears, the Nubian kings . . . flaunting their jewelled and silver crowns, set up a state on the Byzantine model, using Greek as their written language, importing *objets d'art* from the workshops of Alexandria and Antioch, and later, with the introduction of Christianity, aping almost to the point of mimicry the elaborate ceremonial of the Byzantine court.[151]

THE PROBLEM OF THE HISTORICAL TEXTS

A bare dozen historical documents refer to Nubia and Nubians in the post-Meroitic era.[152] They are, with one or two exceptions, the work of Egyptians, Greeks, and Romans; most of them make only passing and sometimes enigmatic reference to events in the southern lands. As a group, the texts are fraught with contradictions and ambiguities, and it is imposs-ible to reconcile them entirely with one another or with the archaeological record. An extended commentary on the post-Meroitic historical records would be out of place in the present pages; I will be content here to sum-marize their content in the briefest terms, and to indicate a possible solution to some, though not all, of the problems which they raise.

The writers of late classical times make no mention of Meroë or of Kush; they speak instead of two Lower Nubian peoples, the Blemmyes and the Nobatae, of whom we have not previously heard. Nearly all modern scholars agree in identifying the Blemmyes with the Beja tribes of today and with the Medju or Medjay of antiquity (cf. Ch. 7) – nomads of the Red Sea Hills who reappear at intervals throughout Nubian history.[153] The origins of the Nobatae are more problematical, and various writers have derived them from Upper Nubia,[154] from the western Sudan,[155] and from Libya or even north-west Africa.[156] According to the sixth-century historian Procopius[157] (who wrote long after the event), they came to Lower Nubia at the invitation of the Emperor Diocletian, who hoped that they would form a buffer between Roman Egypt and the warlike Blemmyes.[158]

Understandably enough, students of post-Meroitic history have con-cerned themselves chiefly with efforts to identify the Ballana Culture and monarchy either with the Blemmyes or with the Nobatae. Both groups have their adherents,[159] yet it must be admitted that attribution of the Ballana Culture exclusively to any one people raises more problems than it solves. A certain air of unreality surrounds the whole Blemmye–Nobatae controversy, for it largely ignores the question of what happened to the flourishing Meroitic population which had been in the same area only a short time previously. One might almost think that the two peoples had made their appearance and fought out their battles on an empty stage,[160] though we know from the archaeological record that this was far from true. We may, then, epitomize the riddle of post-Meroitic Nubia by observing that historians tell us of two peoples, the Blemmyes and the Nobatae, where archaeology discloses only one culture, the Ballana; moreover, both history and archaeology leave us in ignorance of the fate of the earlier Meroitic population and culture.

For the time being, the most probable (or rather the least improbable) solution to the problem is to identify the Ballana Culture and monarchy primarily with the Nobatae, and at the same time to recognize that these are probably the erstwhile Meroitic inhabitants of Lower Nubia at a later stage of development, and under a new name. In this way we are no longer obliged to believe in a large-scale 'Nobatian migration' in the post-Meroitic period[161] – an event for which archaeology provides no real confirmation – and we have a ready-made explanation for the cultural continuities between the Meroitic and Ballana periods. We can also recognize that only a century or two earlier a mass migration to Lower Nubia did indeed occur: the 'land-rush' of later Meroitic times which followed the introduction of *saqia* irrigation (cf. Ch. 12). In this earlier migration, if anywhere, is the logical place to look for the advent of the Nobatae, and incidentally for the introduction of Nubian speech into the territory where it is presently found.[162] The newcomers might have come from somewhere in the western Sudan, where there are still surviving 'islands' of Nubian speech,[163] or they might have come from one of the upstream riverain districts, where there is also evidence of the presence of Nubian speakers in very early times.[164] In either case they brought with them to Lower Nubia the language which was to develop into today's Nubian dialects (cf. Ch. 3). Arrived in the north, they became subject to the Meroitic-speaking governing élite which was already occupying the region for strategic purposes. Thus until the end of the Kushite empire Meroitic remained the language of government and of ritual, and the only written language, though it may not have been understood by the Nobatian-speaking masses.

Why, if they arrived in Lower Nubia in Meroitic times, do we never hear of the Nobatae as such before the fifth century?[165] The answer must be that Nobatae is an ethnic and linguistic term which had, in the beginning, no political relevance. Since the immigrants became, after their arrival on the

Nile, subjects of the empire of Kush and of the province of Akin,[166] it is under those names if at all that we hear of them in Meroitic times. It was only after the break-up of the Kushite empire, when the Lower Nubians emerged as an independent political power, that the historian was obliged to give them a name of their own. The name which he has recorded was presumably that by which they had always called themselves. A little later it was to become formalized in the name of the first Christian kingdom, Nobatia.

To carry the Nobatian argument a step further, I suspect that in their original habitat these people were primitive nomads. Arrived on the Nile, they submitted, perhaps reluctantly, to the authority of Kush as represented by officials and garrisons already established in Lower Nubia. Like nomads everywhere, they readily adopted the domestic arts and the utilitarian traditions of the valley dwellers, to the extent that their houses and graves are indistinguishable from those of the Meroitic proletariat in any part of the empire. Like nomads also, however, they may have looked with suspicion or outright hostility on the more complex and esoteric aspects of Kushite civilization. For its part the Meroitic state showed little interest in the ideological indoctrination of its new subjects, and was content to express its authority in the north primarily in secular terms (cf. Ch. 12). Thus, when the Kushite empire disintegrated, the Lower Nubians made no effort to keep alive its literary, artistic, or ideological traditions. They dispensed largely or entirely with Meroitic writing, glyptic art, monumental architecture, state ritual, and everything which was perhaps associated in their minds with an effete and oppressive priesthood.

Of the elements which had once comprised the Kushite 'Great Tradition',[167] only the institution of divine monarchy and some of its symbolic insignia were retained. Even in their royal tombs, however, the Ballana rulers repudiated some of the age-old traditions of Kush. In this way the Nobatians were indeed responsible for the ultimate disappearance of a great many of the higher arts of civilization, though not in the overt and cataclysmic way which has sometimes been attributed to them.[168] Theirs was simply a barbarian successor state of exceptionally primitive character.[169]

Who were the Ballana monarchs? While the bulk of the Lower Nubian population in Ballana times was almost certainly descended from the population of Meroitic times, the possibility that the rulers themselves represent a fresh wave of migration from the south or south-west cannot be entirely ruled out. In view of what we have just said about ideological repudiation, we can hardly suppose that they were descended from the old ruling élite of Meroitic times. They might have arisen from the ranks of the already-settled Nobatian population in the north, but in such case we should have expected to find more ideological and cultural continuity between the Meroitic and post-Meroitic periods than is actually the case. On the whole, the notion that the Ballana rulers represent a newly arrived barbarian élite (who perhaps delivered the *coup de grâce* to the *ancien régime* in the north) seems best to account both for the rapid changes in mortuary ritual which they introduced and for the strongly 'negroid' character which has always been attributed to them.[170] To that extent we can perhaps continue to acknowledge some justice in the old 'X-Group invasion' hypothesis.

The role of the Blemmyes remains to be considered. These indigenes of the Red Sea Hills, newly possessed of camels and of the military capability which went with them, seem to have established a considerable foothold in the Dodekaschoenos even under Roman rule. In the end it was their depredations, and the inability of the Romans to contain them, which resulted in the abandonment of the outlying province and the withdrawal of the imperial frontier to Aswan under Diocletian. The Blemmyes were left in sole possession of the northernmost district of Nubia where groups of them evidently settled down and adopted a farming way of life not essentially different from that of their Nobatian neighbours. Thus the archaeological remains of the Ballana culture must probably be attributed to both groups rather than to either of them exclusively. The Nobatae, encouraged by Rome, made war on the Blemmyes from time to time, but for more than a century they were unable to dislodge them from their strongholds in the north. In the meantime groups of Nobatae and Blemmyes sometimes made common cause against newly Christian Egypt; their hostility was apparently provoked by attempts to suppress the cult of Isis and to re-dédicate the Philae temples as churches. When, in AD 453, the continued right of the Nubian peoples to worship as pagans at Philae was guaranteed, their attacks ceased for more than fifty years.

The two Nubian peoples continued to make war upon each other until, perhaps in the sixth century, a certain Nobatian King Silko achieved a final triumph over his adversaries. This event is documented in the one inscription of post-Meroitic times which is of undoubted Nubian origin. It is written in very ungrammatical Greek on the walls of the temple of Kalabsha, and reads as follows:

I, Silko, King of the Nobatae and of all the Ethiopians, went to Talmis and Taphis once. Twice I fought with the Blemmyes and God gave me the victory. After the third time, once and for all, I conquered them again and made myself master of their cities. I established myself there with my troops for the first time. And they made supplication to me and I made peace with them. And they swore to me by their gods and I trusted to their oath that they were honourable men. Then I went back into my own Upper Country. When I became King I did not follow after other kings but [went] ahead of them.

As for those who strive with me, I do not permit them to sit in their own country unless they esteem me and do homage to me. For in the Lower Country I am a lion and in the Upper Country a bear.

I warred with the Blemmyes from Prim [Qasr Ibrim] to Telelis [Shellal?] once and for all, and the others south of the Nobatae. I ravaged their lands since they contended with me.

The lords of the other nations who war with me, I do not allow them to sit in the shade but outside in the sun, and they cannot take a drink of water in their own houses; as for those who resist me, I carry off their women and their children.[171]

The campaigns of Silko are also the subject of a remarkable letter unearthed at Qasr Ibrim in 1976. It was written in barbarized Greek, either by a king of the Nobatae to a king of the Blemmyes or (more probably) vice versa. In it the writer complains at some length about the depredations of Silko, and invokes the assistance of his fellow monarch in combatting the upstart. Here is unmistakable evidence of the co-existence of a Blemmyan and a Nobatian ruler in the Nile Valley, and also of an alliance, at least temporarily, between them.

The language is Greek; the magniloquent style is unmistakably that of the ancient rulers of Egypt and of Kush. Silko's inscription is thus, like so much in contemporary Nubian culture, a transition-marker, looking at once backwards and forwards. It was probably the last such unashamedly self-aggrandizing proclamation ever dictated by a western monarch.

Silko's inscription is accompanied by a representation of the king

. . . mounted on a gaily caparisoned horse, hung with phalerae round the neck and along the flanks. In his left hand he holds a lance, with which he has transfixed his enemy, who is shown prostrate in the dust. In the meanwhile a Winged Victory, floating above his head, crowns him not with the Roman laurel-wreath but with a very curious head-dress made up of Egyptian emblems; the horns of the Ram-god Khnum, the corn-sheaf of Isis, the feathers of Ma'at, and the royal Uraei. The king is dressed in the fashion of the later Roman emperors with a short tunic of mail, reaching to the knees, and a paludamentum flying out from the shoulders.[172]

It is hardly necessary to add that Silko's crown, as represented at Kalabsha, closely resembles some of those actually found in the Ballana tombs.[173]

The phrase 'God gave me the victory' has sometimes been interpreted to mean that Silko was a Christian, but this is more probably an interpolation of the Christian (or Jewish) scribe he employed.[174] The royal head-dress, with its array of pharaonic emblems, suggests rather that the king still adhered to some of the ancient religious traditions of Kush. Not much later, however, one of his successors was converted to Christianity, and the pagan and barbaric dynasty of Ballana came to an end. 'With them,' says

Emery, 'pass the last lingering religious beliefs and traditions of pharaonic Egypt.'[175]

POST-MEROITIC HISTORY IN THE SOUTH

The post-Meroitic history of Upper Nubia, to the very limited extent that we can perceive it, seems to repeat in even more extreme form the story of cultural impoverishment and ideological simplification which we have observed in the north. Our only historical document for the period between the downfall of Kush and the introduction of Christianity is the stele of Aezanas, discussed at the beginning of this chapter ('The Meroitic decline and fall'). This inscription suggests that when the Axumite king arrived on the Nile, around AD 350, he found the formerly Meroitic steppelands already in the possession of the Noba. These were presumably the Nubae whom Eratosthenes and other writers had described at an earlier date as living west of the Nile.[176] The name suggests that they were relatives of the Nobatae; probably the two peoples sprang from a common origin in the west. In their new habitat, as successors to the Meroites, the Noba showed even less aptitude for the higher arts of civilization than did their northern cousins. Apparently, as the inscription of Aezanas suggests, their houses were of grass, and they soon allowed the temple-cities of Musawwarat, Naqa, and Meroë to fall into ruin. Their only known archaeological remains are mound graves, generally similar to those of the Ballana culture in the north, which are dotted all along the Nile Valley and across the steppelands from Sennar in the south to Tanqasi in the north (Fig. 63).[177] Of these tumuli Chittick observes:

> Mound graves are to be found over very extensive areas of the central and northern Sudan, but they are nowhere so plentiful as on the east bank of the Nile in the Khartoum region, and northwards at least as far as El Metemma. They mostly lie, in groups of varying size, just away from the cultivated land, on the first rise of the gravel desert. Great and small (some are barely perceptible hummocks) their total number must run into many thousands. The surface of the mounds is usually of gravel, presenting much the same appearance as the land round about; but where stone is available close by they are often covered with small boulders. Chronologically, they are usually assigned to that period, of which so little is known, immediately following the disappearance of the Meroitic kingdom. The graves would thus be contemporary with the 'X-group' culture further north; they have been guessed to have been made by the 'Noba' referred to by Aezanas of Axum as being in possession of the area when his forces passed through.[178]

The mound tumuli of Upper Nubia appear much the same from the Napata district to Sennar, and this has led to the assumption that they represent a single cultural horizon. It is usually designated as the Tanqasi

Culture,[179] after one of the most conspicuous of the mound-grave groups (see below). It must be admitted, however, that very few of these interesting structures have ever been excavated, and the assumption of cultural uniformity throughout Upper Nubia is based largely on the similarity of the tumuli. There is, in addition, the suggestive fact that the distribution of the Upper Nubian mound graves corresponds in a general way with the known distribution of Alwa Ware – the distinctive hand-made pottery which has been found in some of the Tanqasi graves. Alwa pottery is therefore sometimes regarded as an additional diagnostic of the Tanqasi culture.[180]

The earliest known examples of mound graves in Upper Nubia are those found in the common (i.e. non-royal) cemeteries of Meroë, excavated by Garstang in the early years of the twentieth century.[181] So incompletely have these excavations been reported that it is impossible to form an accurate impression of the tombs and their contents, and there has been considerable debate over the proper chronological order of the different grave groups.[182] It appears, however, that some of them contained typically Meroitic painted pottery, while others contained only hand-made Alwa Ware; from this it is inferred that the Meroë cemeteries span the interval between Meroitic and post-Meroitic times. The introduction of Alwa Ware, which first appears in the so-called Middle Necropolis, is interpreted by Kirwan as indicating the arrival of the Noba.[183] Since neither the chamber types nor the burial positions have been reported in any detail, however, it is impossible to know whether the appearance of Alwa Ware was concurrent with other changes in burial practice.

Apart from the graves at Meroë, the only excavated mound graves in Upper Nubia which have been fully reported[184] are two very large tumuli at Tanqasi, in the Napata region. The site is thus described by Shinnie:

There are some 170 mounds of various sizes in the main field, and 30–40 more in a group a short distance to the southeast. The mounds are almost all constructed of alluvial soil; the outside appears originally to have been covered with a layer of gravel. Many of them also had a rough revetment of stones round the edge. The mounds can be divided, chiefly according to size, into three main categories:

(a) Very high mounds (height 6–10 metres [20–32 ft]). There are six of these . . . They all appear originally to have been conical, though some have become misshapen. Many have secondary graves, covered with cairns, and apparently later in date, on their flanks. These high mounds were presumably the tombs of the more important chiefs.

(b) Medium-size mounds (height 2–4 metres [6–12 ft]). One of this category is constructed of red-brick rubble. Many of them have a small depression in the center, perhaps due to robbing . . . or possibly to the collapse of a tomb chamber. In some cases the depression is of such large dimensions

425

that it may have been a constructional feature. There is no clear-cut line on grounds of size between this category and the next. •

(c) Low and very low mounds. Some of the low mounds have flat tops, presenting a profile like an inverted plate. They frequently have a large diameter in proportion to their height. Many of the very low mounds amount to hardly-perceptible rises in the ground, marked by a circular patch of gravel. They never have depressions in the center.[185]

Interestingly enough, the cemetery at Tanqasi is located directly across the Nile from the ancient Kushite cemetery of El Kurru (Ch. 10). This location, plus the exceptional size of some of the Tanqasi mounds, led the excavators to hope that they might encounter latter-day royal tombs similar to those at Ballana. This hope was, however, entirely disappointed. The substructure beneath one of the largest mounds proved to be a large square pit, in the bottom of which were sunk four ordinary rectangular graves. Three of these had apparently never been used; the burial in the fourth was so thoroughly plundered that little remained of it. A second very large tumulus had escaped plundering, but its substructure was nothing more than an ordinary side-niche grave of the type common both in the Meroitic and in the Ballana Cultures. It contained a contracted burial, apparently female, accompanied by four Alwa Ware pots, a number of beads, and two silver rings.[186] In quantity and variety this grave furniture compares unfavourably with a great many of the most ordinary burials in Lower Nubia.

If the Tanqasi tombs are those of kings or chiefs, as suggested by the size of the tumuli, then the post-Meroitic rulers of Upper Nubia must have been poor indeed. However, there is a group of even larger mound graves near Shendi, which has not yet been investigated. The largest tumuli here are 100 to 130 feet in diameter, and are similar in construction to those at Tanqasi. The five largest of them are situated within elliptical-shaped enclosures surrounded by low, rough-stone walls – a feature which has so far been observed nowhere else. The enclosure in each case has a north–south orientation, with the tumulus situated at the southern end.[187]

Neither the Tanqasi nor the Shendi tombs necessarily tell the full story of political developments in the post-Meroitic period. When a Christian monarchy arose in the central Sudan towards the end of the sixth century, its capital (and apparently its only urban centre) was not at any of the places previously discussed but at Soba, not far from the junction of the Blue and White Niles (Fig. 69). Here, perhaps, we should look for the power centre of the immediately preceding period as well. For the time being the Soba region remains largely unexplored.

It seems evident that the burial practices of the Tanqasi Culture, like those of the Meroitic and Ballana Cultures, were not entirely uniform. One of the two mounds excavated at Tanqasi contained a contracted burial,

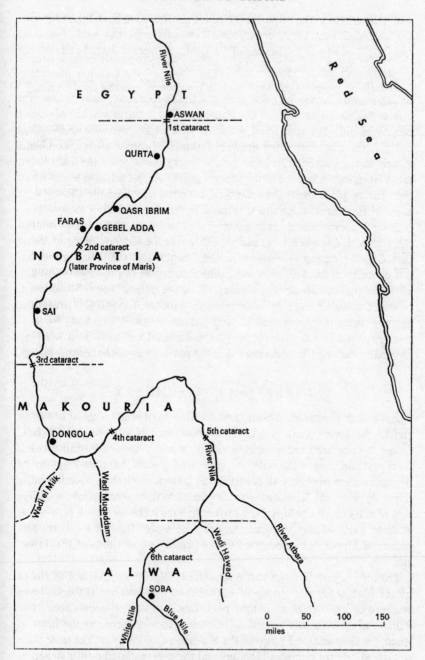

Fig. 69. The three kingdoms of Christian Nubia

while the graves in the other seem (from their shape) to have been prepared for extended burials. A contracted Tanqasi burial has been found at Ushara;[188] at Meroë the burials of Tanqasi type were extended and laid out on beds, after the age-old Kushite practice.[189]

The non-distinctive character of Tanqasi grave goods makes precise dating almost impossible. Some of the beads found at Tanqasi are of a type considered diagnostic of the Ballana period in the north, but of course they date only the individual grave in which they were found.[190] Alwa pottery, the one distinctive product found in Tanqasi graves, conforms closely to the immemorial hand-made pottery tradition of the Sudan, but apart from its occurrence in the mound graves almost nothing is known of the time or place of its manufacture. It shows considerable affinity with some of the wares which are still made in the central Sudan today.[191]

Since Meroitic wheel-made pottery does not seem to be found in conjunction with Alwa Ware, we can probably take the very end of the Meroitic period as a *terminus post quem* for the Tanqasi Culture. With somewhat less confidence, but still with a considerable degree of probability, we can attribute this culture to the coming of the primitive Noba. We cannot, however, establish any kind of terminal date for the Tanqasi Culture on the basis of present knowledge. Mound graves, Alwa Ware, and, for that matter, pagan burial customs may have survived far down into what we nominally call the Christian period in the remoteness of the central Sudan.

INTERPRETATIVE SUMMARY

The erstwhile pharaonic dynasty and civilization of Kush came at last to an end in the fourth century AD. The circumstances attending their final disappearance are obscure, but declining world trade, barbarian inroads from east and west of the Nile, and pressure from the Axumite kingdom of Abyssinia were probably all contributing factors. With the extinction of its ruling dynasty, the Kushite empire seems to have broken up into a collection of petty chieftainships. Noba tribesmen from the west took possession of large parts of the Meroitic steppelands; under them the culture and society of Upper Nubia reverted to the primitive conditions of the Tribal age.

The only suggestion of a successor state to Meroë is found at Ballana in Lower Nubia. Here, a group of barbaric and opulent royal tombs gives evidence of a powerful monarchy persisting over several generations. The Ballana kings evidently regarded themselves in some sense as the heirs of Kush, for they adopted some of the Kushite royal insignia. Yet their state lacked entirely the complex ideology and the differentiated power structure of Napatan and Meroitic times. It was an absolute monarchy more typical of the early Dynastic age.

The origins of the Ballana monarchy are unknown. The rulers may have been newly immigrant barbarians from the south or south-west, who established their rule over their fellow Nobatians already settled in Lower Nubia. In the beginning the area of their hegemony may have been small, for the northernmost districts of Nubia fell under the control of Blemmye tribesmen from the eastern desert at the close of the Meroitic period. A century or more of intermittent hostilities ended in the final defeat and subjugation of the Blemmyes, and the Ballana kingdom, later known as Nobatia, became the sole political power in Lower Nubia. At the time of its conversion to Christianity, in the middle of the sixth century, its frontiers extended from Philae to the Abri-Delgo Reach.

The culture of Lower Nubia, within and perhaps also beyond the dominions of the Ballana kings, was an amalgam of Meroitic survivals and Byzantine Egyptian influences. However, the simple Nobatian tribesmen dispensed with writing, art, monumental architecture, and other sophisticated arts of Kush and of Byzantium. Their population, too, was smaller and more dispersed than in earlier times, and their graves give evidence of a general decline in prosperity. The urban centres of Meroitic times seem to have undergone a partial recession, and the urbanized middle class virtually disappeared. The only social division we can observe in the Ballana period is the ancient one between rulers and ruled.

Bereft of the higher arts of Kushite civilization, while retaining (and in some cases reviving) the more barbarous ones, the culture of Ballana presents uncanny parallels to that of Kerma 2,000 years earlier. Both are transitional cultures, marking respectively the beginning and the end of Nubia's Dynastic age. It would therefore appear almost as if Dynastic civilization in the Sudan had come full circle, and ended where it had begun.[192] Yet Nubia was not, in the sixth century AD, on the verge of a return to a Tribal age. Rather, the simplified and archaized culture of Ballana times prepared the way for a new ideological beginning, and for Nubia's Medieval age.

PART THREE
MEDIEVAL CIVILIZATIONS

14
A NEW BEGINNING
THE CHRISTIANIZATION OF NUBIA

The Near East, cradle of the earliest civilizations, gave birth also to the great religious ideologies of the Middle Ages. Yet the circumstances of creation were profoundly different – even antithetical – in the two cases. The revealed faiths of Christianity and Islam arose not as successors to the outworn creeds of Egypt and the Levant, but in reaction against them. Kroeber's words, written specifically to describe the rise of Islam, are relevant to the early spread of Christianity as well:

. . . Islam arose in the very region of that first hearth of all higher civilization – in the Near Eastern area of the Neolithic Revolution, of the first farming and towns and kings and letters. But it arose at a time when constructive cultural impulses had long since moved out from that hearth, had begun to move beyond Greece and Persia even; yet at a time when the Near East still lay covered with a detritus of forcibly imposed and presumably uncongenial Hellenic and Iranian civiliza-tion – a detritus that had long since become heavier and deader with each generation. There was apparently no longer any hope . . . for a really creative new great civilization . . . to spring up in this Nearer East, among the palimp-sested, tired, worn societies of Egypt, Syria, or Mesopotamia. For that to happen would have been, so to speak, to burn over again the ashes of the past. But there was a chance for a reduced, retractile civilization . . . to throw off the foreign cultural yoke and to establish its own free society – without art, without much intellectual curiosity or profundity, without many of the aspirations customary in civilizations – but fervid over its new autonomy . . .[1]

For three thousand years dynasty had followed dynasty and empire had followed empire, each accepting – or seizing – the divine mandate from its predecessor; each striving to build and enlarge upon the heritage of the past, until at last the sources of tradition by which men lived and died were lost in the remoteness of antiquity. The 'constitutions' which specified the relations between men and their gods were preserved in ancient texts of half-forgotten meaning and wholly forgotten origin; even kings and emperors were dependent upon priestly scholars and antiquarians who could discover and interpret the sources of their power.

As the ancient civilizations drew to a close, their uneasy spiritual leaders became more and more concerned with efforts to recover the lost past. In

Egypt, the last independent pharaohs of the Saite period consciously aped the literary and artistic styles of the Old Kingdom. In Mesopotamia, the last Chaldean emperor ordered the excavation of a long-forgotten temple of his predecessors, hoping to recover some knowledge of their ways. In Palestine, a succession of prophets from Isaiah to Joel urged a return to the stern, simple ways of long-ago pastoral times. These archaizing movements were all, in one way or another, attempts at religious revitalization, yet in the end they suffered the inevitable fate of nativistic revivals. The symbols of the past, even when they could be recovered, had lost their meaning amid the complexities of the classical age.

Everywhere in the classical world, but above all in the Near East, the decay of ancient ideologies left a symbolic and a spiritual vacuum which Hellenistic secularism could not fill. The result was a flowering of esoteric salvationist cults, throughout the Roman Empire and beyond its borders. They offered a revolutionary simplification of doctrine and ritual, yet nearly all of them centred upon the worship of some familiar deity of earlier times: Isis or Mithra or one of the Olympian pantheon.

Christianity was from the beginning a more radical doctrine. Alone among the cult religions of antiquity, it offered a complete break with the past. A new and previously unknown (except to the Jews) god, untouched by the corruption and decadence of the Olympians, had spoken. His message was delivered not through the priestly establishment but through a personal spokesman from among the proletariat, and it was couched in everyday language of indisputable meaning. For those who could accept the message, three thousand years of accumulated tradition became irrelevant. They were washed away, symbolically, in the simple ritual of baptism.

The dead hand of the past must have weighed most heavily upon the urban proletarians of the Roman Empire, for it was among them that Christianity gained its earliest adherents. Peasants, traditionally indifferent to the higher ideological currents, continued to find satisfaction in pagan folk rituals for centuries to come.[2] The privileged classes were understandably hostile in the beginning to a subversive doctrine which seemed to attack established tradition at every point, yet within a short time they too became conscious of the liberating possibilities of the new creed. If Christianity offered the poor a chance to escape from the encumbrance of the past, it offered the rich and powerful a chance to re-consolidate their power and position on a new and more universal basis. Within three centuries of its founding the new creed was accepted and tolerated throughout the Roman Empire; within four centuries it was the state cult of the Empire itself. Among the revolutionary movements of history, only Islam has enjoyed a comparable success in so short a time.

It might be argued that Christianity, once established as the state cult of

Rome and Byzantium, was no longer a revolutionary movement, but this is true only in a narrowly political sense. If the new creed was no longer politically subversive, its revolutionary power in the ideological sphere was, if anything, enhanced by the backing of the Roman state. The destruction wrought upon long-venerated religious monuments and creeds as a matter of deliberate Byzantine policy far exceeded any depredations committed by revolutionary mobs. Viewing the ruins of the earlier Near Eastern civilizations, one is struck again and again by the extent of destruction and defacement inflicted by the early Christians and Moslems upon monuments which had survived, sometimes for thousands of years, down to their times. Unlike any of their predecessors, the new, evangelical faiths had no need to appropriate or to preserve the ideological symbols of the past. Architectural, iconographic, and literary canons alike were discarded.

Once it became the official creed of Rome and Byzantium, the spread of Christianity to their emulative 'external proletariats' was inevitable. Nubia under the Ballana monarchy was already permeated by Christian folk-beliefs, and was developing a taste for Byzantine art, as we saw in Chapter 13. When the new faith was formally introduced by missionaries in the middle of the sixth century, it seems to have been rapidly accepted by rulers and subjects alike from Aswan to the junction of the Niles. Although both the motives and the success of the early evangelists may be attributed partly to political considerations (see below), in a larger sense the rapid spread of Christianity south of Aswan probably reflects the Nubians' desire to rejoin the civilized world.

The advent of Christianity wrought an ideological transformation in Nubia unparalleled since the introduction of civilization itself. Its impact was all the greater because, as Crowfoot observes, 'Nubia was one of the few countries of the Old World which adopted Christianity without having passed under the discipline of Roman law.'[3] In the Mediterranean world the old religions had been undermined by Graeco–Roman secularism before Christianity toppled them, but on the farther fringes of civilization no classical 'Age of Reason' intervened between the ancient and the medieval Ages of Faith. Christianity came to Nubia neither as a reaction against classical secularism nor as the imposed creed of a newly militant empire, but as a needed replacement for the obsolete traditions of the pharaohs. Thus in the whole sweep of Nubian history we can discern no sharper break in the continuity of tradition than that which separates the Dynastic from the Medieval age.

The transforming influence of Christianity is apparent in many aspects of medieval Nubian civilization. Most immediately and conspicuously the royal tomb, for 2,500 years the climactic expression of human and divine authority, ceased overnight to be a meaningful symbol. While we have tombs enough to account for every Nubian king from Kashta to Silko, we have not found the burial place of a single ruler of the Christian and Moslem periods. The result is a curious historical paradox: we know of Nubian monarchs in the pre-Christian periods chiefly through their funerary monuments, and often have no other record of their existence, while in the medieval period our only knowledge of kings comes from documentary sources, and we can find no archaeological evidence for them.

The king whose glory was celebrated in the art, architecture, and literature of the Middle Ages was a heavenly rather than an earthly one. As we know from the parallel example of Western Europe, such a development does not necessarily signify any lessening of the authority of the temporal ruler. It does, however, indicate that he was no longer a god, though his rule might still be divinely sanctioned. Jesus Christ was explicitly designated, by his two names, as the last individual in whom man and god were united; after him the separation of the human and divine realms was final and total. It was this separation which made possible the ideological differentiation of church and state which was the crowning achievement of the Middle Ages.

The separation of church and state had a liberating effect upon both. Government and Law ceased to be the exclusive prerogative of the gods; henceforth men were free to experiment with political and legal forms without awaiting divine revelation or risking divine displeasure. The lawgivers of antiquity gave way to the lawmakers of the Middle Ages. They continued to invoke heaven's blessing, but they no longer claimed personal divinity or direct revelation. As a result there grew up a body of man-made secular law side by side with the canon law of earlier times. It had its origins in the secular constitutions of the Greeks, and perhaps even in the *dat* law of Darius the Great,[4] but its full development had to await the formal divorce of government and religion. Once that happened, the codification of secular law and the development of an independent secular judiciary became one of the ruling preoccupations of medieval civilization.

In medieval Nubia government continued to function largely without the aid of written instruments, as it has in all times. As a result the legalistic outlook which is so characteristic of the medieval West, and even in the world of Islam, is less clearly perceptable in the lands of the Nile. Yet the emergence of a concept of man-made law can be seen in the contrast between two documents which have come down to us, one from the end of the classical era and the other from the early Middle Ages. These are the treaty of Philae enacted in AD 453 (described in Chapter 13), and the treaty called the *Baqt* which was proclaimed at Dongola just two hundred years later.

Both the treaty of Philae and the treaty of Dongola were intended to govern the relations between the Nubians and their Egyptian neighbours. It is notable, however, that at Philae the Nubians were willing in the beginning to make an agreement only for the lifetime of the Roman general who dictated its terms.[5] In this they were guided by the fundamental legal principle of antiquity, that the making of immutable law was the exclusive province of the gods. Treaties and edicts had no sanctity of their own; they derived whatever sanctity they possessed from their proclaimers. Hence the only permanent laws were those which had been handed down directly by the immortal gods; the validity of all other edicts expired with their authors. Yet at Dongola two hundred years later the Nubians enacted a treaty which not only outlived its framers by five centuries, but largely determined the course of medieval Nubian foreign relations. (It will be discussed in much greater detail below; see 'Christian Nubia and the Islamic world'.) The signatories of the *Baqt* claimed the usual divine mandate, but they did not claim personal divinity or direct revelation. The Rule of Man had been accepted, at least in principle, on the Nile.

A relatively minor event of the ninth century which had large historical consequences provides further evidence of the influence of secular law upon the Nubian mentality. Some Nubians in the vicinity of Aswan had sold their lands to Egyptian Moslem purchasers, in defiance both of the *Baqt* agreement and of the medieval legal principle which held that all land belonged to the Crown and could only be transferred by the king's writ. In Nubia this principle was expressed in a legal fiction that all the king's subjects were his slaves. Nevertheless the ninth-century Nubian king did not simply dispossess the buyers and punish the sellers of the lands near Aswan; instead he appealed to the Abbasid Caliph for assistance in recovering his property. The Caliph referred the matter to an Islamic judge, who ruled that according to the principles of Islamic law the Nubians could not be legally regarded as slaves of their king, and therefore that the sale was valid. So far as we know, this decision was not challenged by the Nubian ruler or his successors.[6]

The actions of the Nubian king are more suggestive of political weakness than they are of any transcendent respect for the law. What is interesting and revealing, however, is that acceptance of the Islamic judge's decision in this specific case obliged the king to accept also the legal precedent which it established. Henceforward Lower Nubia was open to settlement by Moslems – a condition which had been specifically precluded under the *Baqt* treaty – and it became necessary to confer a special political status upon the northern district. This development will be considered much more fully in Chapter 15; it is cited here for the light it throws upon the medieval Nubian mentality.

If the separation of church and state liberated government from the restrictions of orthodoxy, it also liberated religion from the taint of subservience to worldly and self-seeking rulers. Thus as the church and the state grew apart, the church and the community of worshippers grew closer together. This too is manifest in the archaeological remains of medieval Nubia. Whereas the temples of the Dynastic age were sometimes located far from centres of population, and in any case were accessible only to an élite few, churches were located in or beside every village of consequence. It is conspicuous, too, that churches were enlarged, or new buildings were undertaken, not for the glorification of kings or bishops but for the accommodation of growing congregations. As a result the total number of surviving Nubian churches (more than 120 from Lower Nubia and the *Batn el Hajar* alone)[7] is more than double the number of religious structures from all earlier times combined.

The transcendental nature of Christian belief wrought one additional transformation in Nubian life. For three thousand years and more no self-respecting man or woman had gone to the afterworld unaccompanied by the best of his or her earthly possessions. With the coming of Christianity that belief and practice disappeared overnight, although it was to be revived on a small scale in the burial of bishops and other church notables. In general, however, burials of the Christian and Moslem periods are remarkable for their simplicity and lack of offerings. Ostentation is displayed, if anywhere, in the building of tomb superstructures, but the largest and most elaborate of them are modest in comparison to the pyramids and tumuli of earlier ages. If the adoption of Christian beliefs did nothing else, therefore, it put an end to the clandestine industry of grave robbing, which for centuries had functioned as a kind of rough-and-ready redistribution system in Nubia (cf. Ch. 6).

It should not be supposed that the adoption of a radically new ideology had important repercussions in everyday life. In the material sphere, the evidence of cultural continuity between the Ballana and Christian periods is stronger that at any other transition point in Nubian history. Towns and villages continued their orderly (or sometimes disorderly) course of development, though in nearly every case a church sooner or later made its appearance alongside the ordinary houses. Economic and social life seem to have been unaffected by the new creed, and even the arts did not immediately feel its impact. Nevertheless, by the high Middle Ages every symbolic expression of Nubian culture reveals a preoccupation with values and symbols radically different from those which had characterized the civilization of the Dynastic Age.

THE CONVERSION OF THE NUBIANS

Egypt was one of the earliest seedbeds of Christianity. According to legend the Egyptian church was founded by the Apostle Mark, who preached at Alexandria in the latter part of the first century. While there is no concrete evidence to support this tradition, Christian communities were certainly flourishing in the second century not only at Alexandria but in the surrounding countryside.[8] Egypt was in fact one of the few Roman provinces in which the new faith took root among peasants almost as soon as it did among city-dwellers.[9] Alexandria itself was to produce an extraordinary number of early theologians and doctors of the church, among them Clement, Origen, St Athanasius, and St Cyril.

Despite its early triumphs, the Egyptian church from the beginning was troubled by heretical and schismatic movements. Most of them developed nominally over abstruse theological questions, but at bottom they were often rooted in a deep-seated anti-Hellenic feeling which was shared by most of the native Egyptian population.[10] The problem was exacerbated after Christianity became the state cult of Byzantium, for then nationalist feeling in Egypt tended continually to associate itself with schismatic religious movements. 'Hence it was natural,' says Bell, 'that when Constantinople . . . was heretical, as under the Arian Emperor Constantius, Egypt should be Catholic; when Constantinople was Catholic, Egypt should be heretical.'[11]

Anti-Byzantine feeling in the eastern provinces of the Empire came to a head in the Chalcedonian controversy of the fifth century. This was nominally a theological debate over whether Jesus had separate human and divine natures or whether his human and divine attributes were blended in a single nature. In practice, it resolved itself into a factional struggle between Hellenic and anti-Hellenic elements within the church. Greek clerics, at Constantinople and throughout the eastern provinces, generally supported the Dyophysite or Melkite doctrine, which attributed two separate natures to Jesus. Ranged against them were the native clergies of Syria, Armenia, and Egypt, who adhered to the Monophysite or Jacobite doctrine, holding that Jesus had only a single nature.

The Council of Chalcedon in AD 451 ruled that 'Christ is consubstantial with his father as regards his Godhead, and consubstantial with us as regards his Manhood', and that he was 'made known to us in two natures'.[12] The issue was therefore officially resolved in favour of the Dyophysites, and Monophysitism joined the already long list of proscribed doctrines. However, the Chalcedonian decrees were never accepted by the majority of native Christians in the eastern provinces. As Shore observes, 'The persistence of the [Monophysite] heresy can be explained only as an expression of political dissatisfaction and of nationalistic sentiments on the part of the provinces, fanned in Egypt by the memory of the loss of precedence by the Alexandrine See to the See of Constantinople . . . Monophysitism was at the beginning no more than an excuse, founded on theological ambiguity, to justify a pre-existent schism.'[13] For two centuries after Chalcedon there was active and sometimes violent competition for the control of church offices and church properties in Egypt and Syria, as there was in northern Europe during the wars of the Reformation. Neither Monophysites nor Dyophysites were able finally to gain the upper hand, and in the end their struggles and their mutual hostility left the eastern provinces an easy prey to the Islamic conquest of the seventh century.

In sixth-century Egypt, according to H. I. Bell:

... the Catholic or Melkite party, dependent upon the support of the Imperial government and therefore obnoxious to the majority of the people, enjoyed but little prestige and commanded a scanty following. The Monophysites or Jacobites, supported by the ignorant monks, who were hostile to Hellenic culture in all forms, were quite incapable of making any important contribution to the thought of the age. Thus Egypt, whose capital, Alexandria, had been in the second and third centuries the seat of the famous Catechetical School and even in the fourth had produced in Athanasius a major figure of ecclesiastical history, became a provincial backwater.[14]

It was against this background of factional strife, and perhaps even largely because of it, that the evangelization of Nubia was undertaken in the sixth century. The effort was inaugurated by the great Byzantine Emperor Justinian as part of a general policy of spreading the Gospel beyond the imperial frontiers. 'The reign of Justinian is marked not only by an elaborate effort to bring many of the pagan peoples on the borders of the empire within the body of the Church – a movement tantamount, in effect, to extending the boundaries of the Christian Empire – but also by an energetic attempt to stamp out the last vestiges of the old religions.'[15]

Justinian's first move in Egypt was to order the final closing of the Temple of Isis at Philae, and the removal of its pagan statues to Constantinople.[16] A short time later the temple was re-dedicated as the Church of St Stephen.[17] As we saw in Chapter 13, a similar attempt a century earlier had provoked the Nubians to armed intervention, ending in the Treaty of Philae in which the right of the southerners to worship as pagans at the Temple of Isis was guaranteed. How far Christian sentiment had progressed among the Nubians during the ensuing century may be judged from the fact that the final closing of the Isis Temple, some time around AD 540, seems to have been accepted without protest.[18]

The closing of the temple at Philae was followed, if not even slightly preceded, by more direct and positive evangelical activity among the Nubians. The surviving accounts of early missions to Nubia, preserved in a number of ecclesiastical histories, are neither entirely clear nor entirely consistent as to the course of events, but they all agree in stating or implying that the conversion of the southern peoples – rulers as well as subjects – was complete by the end of the sixth century. We might be inclined to dismiss these claims as pious exaggerations were it not for the archaeological evidence of the Nubian cemeteries, in which we can discern a rapid and almost total disappearance of pagan burial practices in the later sixth century.

The best-known and most detailed report of early missionary activity in Nubia is that of the contemporary Bishop, John of Ephesus.[19] According to his account the incentive to convert the Nubians came not from Justinian but from his flamboyant and influential wife Theodora. Bishop John's account, as paraphrased by Gadallah, asserts that:

Julian, an able priest (who had been a companion of Theodosius, the Coptic Patriarch of Alexandria, while in exile in Constantinople), was full of an intense desire to convert the Nobadae, the inhabitants of Nobatia. He transmitted his desire to the Empress Theodora, the greatest champion of the Monophysite sect in the reign of Justinian. Theodora received the proposal with ardent zeal and asked Justinian to send Julian as a missionary to Nobatia; but the Emperor, who maintained the decrees of Chalcedon, would not countenance a Monophysite as the agent of conversion; and so a rival (Melkite) mission was sent off in Justinian's name. Nevertheless, Theodora frustrated this mission's work by insisting with threats that the Byzantine governor of Thebaid (Upper Egypt) should detain the Melkite mission until Julian had reached his destination. Julian arrived in Nubia c. AD 543 and was enthusiastically welcomed by the Nobadae who confessed the God of the Christian, saying, 'that He is the one true God and there is no other beside Him.' The statement shows that there was a ready response; and its wording may well reflect the grudge between the Monophysites and the Chalcedonians (Dyophysites) concerning the nature of Christ. Julian taught them Christianity and warned them against the Chalcedonians so that when the imperial counter-mission arrived in Nobatia it did not achieve any success.

Julian returned to Constantinople after two years of earnest work and was succeeded by Theodore, Bishop of Philae, who maintained and consolidated Julian's work. Theodore returned to Philae c. 551 and the work was carried on by Longinus, another able man who was made Bishop of Nubia.

Due to the opposition of the Melkites Longinus had considerable difficulties in getting away from Constantinople and it was only by disguising himself that he was able to slip out and reach his field c. 569. Longinus did fine missionary work in Nobatia – he indoctrinated the Nubians afresh in the faith and practices of the Coptic Church, ordained clergy and built them a church. After six years with the Nobadae, and to their deep distress and tribulation, Longinus left for Egypt to share in the election of the Monophysite patriarch.

But Longinus returned to Nobatia in AD 578 at the request of the king of Alwa, who aspired to have his country evangelized as had been Nobatia with which Alwa was in friendly relations. But when the Melkite Patriarch heard that Longinus was about to preach Monophysitism in this new sphere he deposed him and sent two Melkite bishops to the king of Alwa to inform him about Longinus' deposition and to warn the king that unlike the Melkite bishops, Longinus was unable to baptize or ordain. But as before in Nobatia, the Melkites were frustrated in their attempt through the insistence of the king of Alwa that Longinus only, who had baptized the Nobadae, should baptize the people of Alwa. In AD 580 Longinus set out for Alwa, and because Makouria was unfriendly he had to take a roundabout route through the land of the Blemmyes in which he suffered many hardships. In an interesting letter from the king of Nobatia to the king of Alwa we read: 'But because of the wicked devices of him who dwells between us [i.e., the king of the intervening land of Makouria], I sent my saintly father to the king of the Blemmyes, that he might conduct him thither by routes further inland; but the Makuritae heard also of this, and set people on the lookout in all the passes of his kingdom, both in the mountains and in the plain . . .'

Longinus was accorded a great welcome in Alwa 'and after a few days' instruction both the king himself was baptized and all his nobles; and subsequently in process of time, his people also. There he also met certain Abyssinians following the heresy of Halicarnassus (which claims that Christ's body was incorruptible) and corrected their belief.'[20]

The account of John of Ephesus is full of suggestive details in regard to the topography and climate of Nubia, which lend an air of authenticity to the story as a whole. It provides, also, our first reliable political information about Nubia since the time of the Kushite empire. There were, it appears, three separate and independent kingdoms between Aswan and the junction of the Niles: Nobatia in the north, Makouria in the middle, and Alodia or Alwa in the south. In Nobatia we can recognize almost certainly the great kingdom of Lower Nubia which was discussed at length in Chapter 13. Alwa, far to the south, was evidently the kingdom of the Noba which was established following the collapse of Meroitic power in the steppelands; it is mentioned first (though as a town rather than a kingdom) in the Stele of Aezanas (Ch. 13). Makouria is however a name previously unknown to us, though a Nubian people called the Makkourae are mentioned at a much earlier date by Ptolemy.[21] The kingdom in the time of John of Ephesus must have been centred in the Dongola Reach, and its early rulers might therefore conceivably have been the individuals buried under the great tumuli at Tanqasi, though the poverty of the burials themselves hardly suggests royal status (cf. Ch. 13). It is at least equally likely that the remains of pre-Christian Makouria lie buried beneath the sprawling town-site of Old Dongola, which was to emerge as the political centre of medieval Nubia, and which will be discussed in greater detail later.

It is noteworthy that John of Ephesus says nothing about evangelical efforts in Makouria, a kingdom which was evidently hostile both to Nobatia and to Alwa. The missing information is supplied by another contemporary historian, the Melkite John of Biclarum, who asserts that Makouria was converted to the Dyophysite faith in AD 569 or 570.[22] He, on the other hand, is silent as regards both Nobatia and Alwa. It seems likely enough that we are confronted here with the biased reporting of two ardent propagandists, one Monophysite and the other Melkite, each celebrating the triumphs of his own sect while ignoring those of its rival. Thus, by their eloquent silences, the histories of John of Ephesus and of John of Biclarum seem actually to confirm one another. By combining their information we obtain the following approximate sequence of events:

(1) The conversion of Nobatia to Monophysite Christianity was effected by the missionary Julian some time around AD 543. Shortly afterwards, a rival Dyophysite mission was unsuccessful.

(2) The kingdom of Makouria, which was evidently hostile to Nobatia, was converted to Melkite Christianity around AD 570.

(3) At about the same time, and perhaps inspired by Makouria, there was an unsuccessful attempt to convert the southern kingdom of Alwa to the Melkite persuasion.

(4) Around AD 580, Alwa was successfully converted to Monophysitism by the missionary Longinus.[23]

The two ecclesiastical historians may have ignored or distorted many details, but they leave no doubt that there was a significant outburst of missionary activity in Nubia in the middle of the sixth century, in which both Monophysites and Dyophysites were active. It is not difficult to recognize, too, that the motives which prompted this evangelical effort were as much political as religious. As had happened more than once before, rival factions in Egypt sought to strengthen themselves against each other by enlisting the support of the Nubians. The result was an almost unseemly haste and competition to bring the blessings of the Gospel to the southern kingdoms.[24]

That the motives of the Nubian kings in accepting the Christian faith were also partly political may be inferred from the fact that rival and apparently hostile Nubian rulers seem to have opted for rival sectarian affiliations. They too perhaps saw an opportunity to strengthen themselves against their neighbours by alliance on the one hand with the dominant hierarchy of Egypt, and on the other with the Byzantine Emperor. Whatever their sectarian preferences, however, all of the Nubian rulers of the post-Meroitic era must have felt keenly the need for a new ideological foundation. The obsolete royal symbols of Kush, to which the kings of Lower Nubia still clung (cf. Ch. 13), were increasingly meaningless to the mass of their subjects, while the popular cult of Isis seems to have provided no particular support or sanction for the monarchy as such. The adoption of Christianity not only offered an ideological rapprochement between rulers and subjects, but imparted to both a new legitimacy and respectability in the eyes of their foreign neighbours. For the first time in more than two centuries, Nubia was brought back into the ideological mainstream of the times.

The specific details of the conversion process are, of course, unrecorded. Kirwan has suggested that the spread of Christianity in Nubia was gradual and that it was effected by '. . . the wandering preacher with gifts of oratory and of "story-telling" such as the oriental loves . . . Indeed, it is probable that the theology thus taught was not of the purest kind, and, no doubt, it received more than a touch of local colour to make it acceptable to the audience.'[25] On the other hand the ecclesiastical historians, John of Ephesus and John of Biclarum, would seem to imply that the early missionaries were as much ambassadors as evangelists, and that they began their missionary efforts at the top, with the Nubian kings. At least inferentially, their labours were crowned with success from the moment the monarchs were baptized; sooner or later the conversion of the lower orders was certain to follow.

Both logic and archaeology seem to be on the side of the church historians. While Lower Nubia was certainly permeated with Christian folk-beliefs long before its official conversion, it seems unlikely that the subjects of so absolute a monarchy as that of Ballana would have openly embraced a faith which condemned many of the practices associated with the Ballana monarchy. The evidence of the Nubian cemeteries, too, suggests that the changeover from paganism to Christianity at the end of the sixth century was extremely rapid and thorough, and therefore probably came about as a result of official decree. While most of the Ballana cemeteries of Nubia continued in use into Christian times, the pagan and Christian graves in them are not significantly interspersed. In most cases a sharp and continuous line can be drawn between the two groups of graves, which would of course correspond to the limit of the cemetery at the moment when the new faith was adopted.[26]

The very first church building in Nubia seems to have been established at Qasr Ibrim, which was certainly a major administrative centre if not actually a royal residence. It was made by restoring and remodelling a part of the old brick temple built a thousand years earlier by Taharqa (cf. Ch. 10). The actual date of consecration is not recorded, but archaeology demonstrates that it was at a time when typical Ballana pottery types, rather than specifically Christian types, were still in use.

Whatever the political circumstances may have been, the eventual spread of Christianity to Nubia was inevitable from the moment when it became the state cult of Egypt. Throughout history the northern country has set the standard of civilization for Nubia, and no ideology which has ever developed there, from the cult of the pharaoh to the cult of Nasser, has failed in the end to prevail in Nubia as well. By the end of the sixth century the ideological pull of Christianity, associated for more than two centuries not only with the sophistication of Egypt but with the still greater glories of Rome and Byzantium, must have been strong indeed upon the peoples beyond the imperial frontier. The final adoption of the new faith by their kings was therefore probably a blessing and a relief to the mass of the Nubians, who already had strong leanings towards Christianity.[27] Such at least is suggested by the rapid and total disappearance of the last vestiges of pagan civilization in sixth-century Nubia.

THE CHARACTER OF NUBIAN CHRISTIANITY

The religious heterodoxy which resulted from the conversion of Nobatia and Makouria to rival Christian doctrines cannot have persisted for very long, for sometime in the seventh century Nobatia was conquered or absorbed by its southern neighbour (see below). Thereafter until the end of the Middle Ages there was, at least in theory, only one northern Nubian kingdom, extending from Aswan to the vicinity of Meroë. The result should have been a triumph of Melkite Christianity throughout the newly united kingdom – a development which is in fact suggested by two later historians, Eutychius and Maqrizi. Both of them assert that the Nubian church was 'originally' Dyophysite, and that its conversion to the Monophysite persuasion came about at a later date, after the Monophysite Coptic Church had emerged as the dominant Christian sect in Egypt under Islamic rule.[28] There is, nevertheless, much evidence to suggest that the combined church of Nobatia and Makouria was Monophysite from the beginning, in spite of the earlier Melkite affiliation of the Makourians.[29]

The question of the doctrinal and political affiliation of the early Nubian church is a vexed one, and has been debated by scholars for more than a generation. Various evidence – architectural,[30] artistic,[31] and literary[32] as well as historical – has been cited in favour of both a Dyophysite and a Monophysite affiliation. The most recent investigations have shown, however, that none of this evidence is conclusive.[33] The dispute between the two sects was at bottom more a political than a doctrinal one, and it now appears that no hard-and-fast liturgical differences separated them. The same buildings, the same iconography and the same literary formulae evidently could serve the purposes of both parties. Consequently ambitious or opportunistic princes and prelates could readily change sides according to the shifting of the political winds. In this regard it is worth noting that the original adherence of Makouria to the Dyophysite doctrine was probably inspired chiefly by hostility towards Monophysite Nobatia, and therefore became irrelevant as a political stance once the northern kingdom had been eliminated. By this time, moreover, the Monophysites were clearly gaining the upper hand in Egypt, and the Byzantine grip was weakening. It would therefore have been not only possible but logical for victorious Makouria to adopt, as a matter of political expediency, the faith of defeated Nobatia at the time when the two kingdoms were united. More will be said on this subject when we discuss the subsequent organization of church and state in medieval Nubia (Ch. 15).

Whatever its early character may have been, the Nubian church was essentially Monophysite and Coptic after the seventh century. This development became inevitable when the Monophysites emerged triumphant in Egypt under Islamic rule. Far from resisting the Arab invaders of the seventh century, the native Christians of Egypt and the Near East in many cases welcomed them as liberators from the Byzantine yoke. The Byzantine provinces which fell most immediately to the armies of Islam were, in fact, precisely those which had been weakened and divided by sectarian conflict, and in which the mass of the population was Monophysite and anti-Byzantine. In reward for their loyalty the native Christians of Egypt and the Near East were supported and encouraged under the early caliphates, while the pro-Byzantine Melkite sect was intermittently persecuted and suppressed.[34] Monophysitism thus achieved under Islam the supremacy within the Christian community which had been denied it under Byzantium; it was achieved, however, at the expense of minority status within the Islamic Empire. As a result the autonomous Monophysite churches which developed in Egypt, Syria and Armenia following the Moslem conquests were of necessity parochial and inward-looking, lacking the universal outlook of Western Christianity.

In Egypt the Coptic Church, headed by the Monophysite Patriarch of Alexandria, had gained almost complete supremacy within the Christian community by the eighth century. It was essentially a national church, narrowly Egyptian in outlook and employing the Coptic language, lineally descended from the speech of the pharaohs, in its liturgy. Even before the final rift with Constantinople it had already developed its own distinctive architectural and artistic canons, in which influences from pharaonic days blended with those of Greece and Byzantium.[35]

It was with this parochial and fundamentally Egyptian church that the Nubian Christians were affiliated after the early Middle Ages, if not from the beginning.[36] Although Nubia escaped the political fate of Egypt, and for nearly a thousand years resisted incorporation into the Islamic empires, the Moslem conquests of Egypt and the Near East left the African kingdoms cut off from the rest of Christendom. Once the political and ideological influence of Constantinople was removed, it was inevitable that the native churches both of Nubia and of Abyssinia should fall within the orbit of Monophysite Alexandria. Thus at least from the eighth century onwards the Nubians acknowledged the Coptic Patriarch as their spiritual leader, and their bishops were appointed from Alexandria. Many of the clergy and monks in the southern countries were probably of Egyptian origin, and

Nubia served periodically as a refuge for Copts fleeing from persecution in Egypt.[37] The art, architecture, and literature of medieval Nubia all betray the dominant influence of Coptic Egypt, although, as will be noted later, the Nubian church retained to the end certain distinctive features of its own.

It remains to add that even the Islamic conquest did not finally lay to rest the Chalcedonian controversy. While the orthodox and royally approved bishops who resided at Faras were, with perhaps a few exceptions, Monophysites, there seems to have existed, at least on paper, a rival Melkite see at Taifa. Whether or not it was ever occupied is unclear.[38] Even at Faras, however, there are suggestions of Melkite influence as late as the eleventh century.[39] 'Père Vantini has called our attention to the fact that the Caliph el-Hakim (d. 1021), who was the son of a Greek Melkite concubine, favoured the Melkites and allowed them to go to Syria and Nubia, whereas the Copts were forbidden to leave Egypt. Michael the Syrian, a twelfth-century Monophysite writer, tells us that the patriarchs and bishops of the Chalcedonian Greeks troubled and misled Syria, Palestine, and Egypt and even, when they had an opportunity, the Nubians and the Abyssinians.'[40] As in earlier centuries, the evidence of Melkite influence in eleventh-century Nubia is not incontrovertible, but it seems at least certain that the Nubian church was not wholly free from factional disputes.[41]

For most, if not all, of its history then, Christian Nubia was affiliated not with the universal church of the West but with the captive and (according to the Chalcedonian decree) outlawed national church of Egypt. This condition left the Nubians bereft of political support abroad, and almost assured their eventual subjugation to Islam. Throughout the Middle Ages the Christians of Europe exhibited no interest in their African brethren, and the Nubians and Abyssinians for century after century resisted the encroachment of Islam without assistance from the West. When at last the Nubian church was on the point of collapse, in the fifteenth century, its appeals for help went unanswered not only at Rome, but even in neighbouring and presumably sympathetic Egypt and Abyssinia.[42] The Abyssinian church was more fortunate, for a growing commercial interest in the Indian Ocean brought the Portuguese to East Africa in time to stave off the Islamic onslaught, and to preserve the independence of this last free outpost of Monophysite Christianity.

LITERARY RECORDS

Although the mass of Nubian people has been illiterate at all times, knowledge of writing was probably more widespread in the Middle Ages than at any time before or since. The native language (Old Nubian) was written during most of the Christian period, and Greek and Coptic were also employed to some extent in written texts. Arabic was used in correspondence with Moslem traders and residents in Lower Nubia. Fragments of parchment manuscripts are commonplace finds in Nubian churches and monasteries, as are long, painted, mural inscriptions. Tombstones often carry elaborate funerary formulae. A less formal literature is represented by scratched graffiti upon the walls of churches and houses, and by countless inscribed potsherds (ostraka).

If literacy in medieval Nubia was more widespread than in earlier times, however, its functional role does not seem to have been correspondingly enlarged. The surviving texts, both formal and informal, are mostly of a religious character; they tell us little either of everyday life or of secular history. Throughout the Middle Ages it would appear that commerce and government functioned largely without the benefit of writing. Even state propaganda did not find written expression, as it had under the Kushite empire and even in the reign of Silko (Ch. 13). The ideological separation of church and state in medieval Nubia is nowhere more clearly attested than in the fact that the Christian Nubian kings, despite their substantial power, erected no literary monuments that we know of. The literary art evidently remained largely in the hands of the religious establishment, and it was no longer used for the glorification of a temporal power.

To the foregoing generalization, as to many other generalizations, Qasr Ibrim seems to represent an exception. The great citadel, already a major entrepôt in pre-Christian times (cf. Ch. 13), assumed even greater commercial and political importance in the Middle Ages. It was the centre of a thriving commerce and was also the residence of the Nubian official (the 'Eparch'[43]) specifically charged with the conduct of relations with Moslem Egypt. The excavations at Qasr Ibrim have yielded enormous quantities of manuscript material – more in fact than have come from all other Nubian sites combined – on parchment, papyrus, paper, and leather. Along with the usual number and variety of religious texts, the Qasr Ibrim material also seems to contain a large number of commercial and legal documents. Those which are of purely local concern are in Old Nubian, while texts relating to transactions with Egypt or with Egyptians are in Arabic.[44] Most of the textual finds from Qasr Ibrim have yet to be translated or analysed; eventually they should add very substantially to our picture of everyday life and commerce, at least in this one urban centre. The texts do not however appear to have much specifically historical content. As usual, our knowledge of historical events and personalities in medieval Nubia comes very largely from external sources.

Fragmentary though it is, the historical record of medieval Nubia is more complete, and much more informative, than in any earlier period.

This circumstance is due chiefly to the intellectual curiosity and the broad-minded outlook which for a time characterized the scholarly community of Islam. The Arab conquest of Egypt, following less than a century after the Christianization of Nubia, left the African kingdoms politically independent but economically and culturally oriented towards the world of Islam. Thenceforward Nubia's only close relations were with Moslem countries, and our knowledge of personalities and events in the medieval period has therefore come chiefly from the reports of Arab historians and geographers. They were, happily, both better informed and less prejudiced than most of the annalists of earlier times. Themselves the heirs of an 'upstart' desert civilization, they were less inclined than their predecessors either to look down upon the Africans as social inferiors or to glorify them as happy savages. In their dispassionate and matter-of-fact accounts the Nubians take on, almost for the first time in history, the character of ordinary and unremarkable fellow humans.

The awakening of an interest in medieval Nubia on the part of Western scholars has been extraordinarily recent. In his pioneer work on Sudanese history, written at the beginning of this century, Budge devoted no more than twenty pages to the eight or nine centuries of Christian ascendancy.[45] The abundant and well-preserved archaeological remains of Christian Nubia were left uninvestigated by the First Archaeological Survey, once it was discovered that the Christian graves were devoid of mortuary offerings.[46] It was believed, apparently, that the churches and town-sites had nothing new to tell; their designation as 'Coptic' said everything of interest about them.[47] Even the great Reisner seems to have taken no interest in the archaeological remains of Christian Nubia, though he was the pioneer investigator in every other historical period from the A Horizon to the X Horizon.

The title of pioneer in Christian Nubian studies belongs to Reisner's contemporary F. Ll. Griffith. Early in the twentieth century he investigated a number of churches and other Christian remains in the vicinity of Faras,[48] and at about the same time he inaugurated also the linguistic study of medieval Nubian texts.[49] Although his field methods were notably slipshod, Griffith deserves substantial credit for awakening interest in an unjustly neglected field. The organizing genius of Christian Nubian studies was however a scholar in the following generation, Ugo Monneret de Villard. Largely at his own urging, he was commissioned at the time of the Second Archaeological Survey (1929–34) to make an exhaustive survey of Christian remains not only in the immediately threatened area, but throughout the length of Nubia from Aswan to Khartoum. This arrangement allowed the regular survey, under Emery and Kirwan, to devote itself entirely to remains of the earlier periods. It is notable (and characteristic), however, that Monneret de Villard was provided with virtually no excavation funds, and the exhaustive *Inventario dei Monumenti*[50] which resulted from his labours was based almost entirely upon surface observations.[51] To a very large extent, the systematic excavation of Christian remains had to await the salvage campaign of the 1960s.

Monneret de Villard followed up his field investigations with an equally exhaustive survey of literary source materials, Arabic, Coptic, and classical. From innumerable fragmentary references he put together, as far as possible, both a history and a political description of medieval Nubia. His *Storia della Nubia Cristiana*[52] remains, thirty years later, the only such attempt which has been undertaken, and has served as a point of departure for all subsequent studies. The excavations of recent years have in fact added very little to Monneret's historical picture,[53] for the author's exploration of documentary sources was painstakingly thorough. Archaeology has contributed enormously to cultural and social knowledge of medieval Nubia since the days of Monneret de Villard, but it has told us little new about the region's history. The account which follows is therefore drawn very largely from the pages of Monneret or from sources discovered by him.

CHRISTIAN NUBIA AND THE ISLAMIC WORLD

Nubia had no sooner acceded to the faith of Egypt, as described in earlier pages, than the northern country was overrun and subjugated by invaders of a new faith. The beginning of the Byzantine downfall in Egypt was marked by a Sassanian (Persian) invasion and occupation of the country between AD 616 and 629. According to some sources the Persian armies advanced to the frontiers of Nubia, or even beyond,[54] though there is no archaeological evidence of their presence. Hardly more than a decade after their expulsion came the Arab onslaught which brought a final end to Byzantine rule, and for all practical purposes to classical civilization, on the Nile. The conquest of Egypt was begun in the year 639, only seven years after the death of Mohammed. Little resistance was met except at Alexandria, and the Arab cause was considerably abetted by a large section of the Coptic population. After the surrender of Alexandria in 641 Egypt was for practical purposes in Arab hands, as it has been ever since.[55]

The Arab general Amr ibn el-As had no sooner completed the subjugation of Egypt than he turned his attention to the south. A cavalry force of 20,000 men was dispatched into Nubia, but after penetrating as far as Dongola, between the Third and Fourth Cataracts, it met with a resistance such as no other Arab army encountered in the first century of Islamic expansion. The first Battle of Dongola was disastrous for the invaders, who were compelled to make terms and withdraw. It is noteworthy that the Arab chroniclers of this event were particularly impressed with the devastating effectiveness of the Nubian archers;[56] Nubia had been celebrated for its bowmen as far back as the Middle Kingdom.

A second and more concerted attack upon Nubia was mounted in AD 651–2. Again the invaders advanced to Dongola, where another fierce encounter took place. According to an Arab poet, 'My eyes ne'er saw another fight like Dongola, with rushing horses loaded down with coats of mail.'[57] Catapults were launched against the walls of the Nubian city, and its principal church was damaged or destroyed.

The second Battle of Dongola was evidently inconclusive militarily, and it ended in a negotiated truce. The treaty which was drawn up, called by Arab historians the *Baqt* (apparently from Greek *Pakton*) has been variously interpreted as an imposed tribute and as a commercial treaty between sovereign powers.[58] The terms, according to the geographer Maqrizi, were:

Covenant from the Amir Abd Allah ibn Sa'd ibn Abi Sarh to the king of the Nubians and to all the people of his kingdom; a covenant binding upon great and small among the Nubians from the frontier of the land of Aswan to the border of the land of Alwa. Abd Allah ibn Sa'd ibn Abi Sarh has established it for them as a guarantee and a truce to be effective among them and the Moslems of Upper Egypt who live adjacent to them, as well as other Moslems and client peoples [*dhimmis*; i.e. Christians and Jews]. Verily, you are communities of Nubia enjoying the guarantee of Allah and that of His Messenger Mohammed, the Prophet; with the condition that we shall not wage war against you, nor declare war against you, nor raid you, as long as you abide by the stipulations which are in effect between us and you. [Namely] that you may enter our territories, passing through but not taking up residence in them, and we may enter yours through but not taking up residence in them. You are to look after the safety of any Moslem or ally [of the Moslems] who lodges in your territories or travels in them, until he departs from you.

You are to return every slave of the Moslems who runs off to you, sending him back to the land of Islam. You are to return any Moslem engaged in hostilities against the other Moslems, who seeks refuge with you. You are to send him forth from your territories to the land of Islam, neither inclining to [help] him nor preventing him from [returning].

You are to look after the mosque which the Moslems have built in the courtyard of your capital, and you are not to prevent anyone from worshipping in it, or interfere with any Moslem who goes to it and remains in its sanctuary until he departs from it. And you are to sweep it, keep it lighted, and honour it.

Each year you are to deliver 360 slaves which you will pay to the Imam of the Moslems from the finest slaves of your country, in whom there is no defect. [They are to be] both male and female. Among them [is to be] no decrepit old man or woman or any child who has not reached puberty. You are to deliver them to the Wali of Aswan.

It shall not be incumbent upon any Moslem to defend [you] against any enemy who attacks you or to prevent him on your behalf from doing so, from the frontier of the land of Alwa to the land of Aswan.

If you do harbour a slave belonging to a Moslem, or kill a Moslem or ally, or if you expose to destruction the mosque which the Moslems have built in the courtyard of your capital, or you withhold any of the 360 slaves, this truce and guarantee which we and you have equally set down will be void, 'so that God will judge between us' – 'and He is the Best of Judges.' [59]

Incumbent upon us hereby is observance of the pact of God and His agreement and His good faith, and the good faith of His Messenger Mohammed. And incumbent upon you toward us is the utmost observance of the good faith of the Messiah and that of the Disciples and of any of the people of your religion and community whom you reverence. God be the witness of that between us. [60]

Under the terms of the *Baqt*, Nubia seems to have been granted something like the status of a client kingdom of the Islamic Empire, much as Nobatia was once looked upon as a client kingdom (*foederatus*) of Rome. [61] Whether the arrangement represents a victory for the Nubians or for the Arabs has been much disputed. On the one hand the political and religious integrity of Nubia was guaranteed in perpetuity; on the other hand the Nubians were saddled with a heavy annual indemnity of 360 slaves, to say nothing of the indignity of sweeping and lighting the mosque at Dongola. Other accounts of the treaty, however, speak of an exchange of goods of equal value which the Nubians were to receive when they delivered their slaves to Aswan.

Aly Kheleyfa Homeyd ibn Hesham el Baheyry relates, that the stipulated conditions of peace with the Nubians consisted of three hundred and sixty head of slaves to the Shade of the Moslems, and forty to the governor of Egypt, and that they should receive in return one thousand ardebs of wheat, and their delegates three hundred ardebs of it; the same quantity of barley was to be given, and further, one thousand kanyr of wine to the king, and three hundred kanyr of wine to the delegates, together with two mares of the best kind, fit for princes. Further, of the different stuffs of linen and cloth one hundred pieces, [62] and of the kind called Kobaty four pieces to the king and three to the envoys, of the kind called Baktery eight pieces, and of the Malam five pieces, and moreover a fine Djebbe to the king. Of the shirts called Aly Baktar, ten pieces, and of the first quality of shirts likewise ten, every one of which is equal to three of the common sort. [63]

The *Baqt* treaty, guaranteeing as it did the sovereignty of a non-Moslem nation, was without precedent in the early history of Islam. Alone among the world's peoples, the Nubians were excluded alike from the *Dar-el-Islam* (house of the faithful) and from the *Dar el-Harb* (figuratively, house of the enemy), the two categories into which the rest of the world was divided. [64] Because of its anomalous nature, the meaning of the treaty was debated even by contemporary Arab jurists. According to Forand, '. . . although it is called a *sulh* by some, it did not fall within that category as it is generally understood. The term *sulh* ordinarily implied that the Moslems had occupied a country and were in a position of mastery . . . None of these conditions prevailed at the time; indeed, Nubia was never brought under the control of Moslems during the early centuries of Islam. The treaty was a very special case; it was not a treaty or covenant in the usual sense. It was regarded rather as a "truce" . . . or as an instrument of "neutralization" or "reconciliation." '[65]

Whatever its legal status may have been, the logic behind the *Baqt* seems clear enough. The treaty itself proclaims that the Arabs' chief interest in Nubia was as a source of slaves. Since neither Moslems nor Christians living under their patronage (*dhimmis*) could legally be enslaved, there was obvious advantage in maintaining an independent but politically neutralized Nubia outside the domain of Islam. Some later Arab jurists were to argue that the treaty did indeed confer upon the Nubians the status of *dhimmis*, and therefore that the taking of slaves from them was immoral, but the issue was resolved by the supposition that the Nubians themselves had captured the slaves from their pagan neighbours.[66]

The *Baqt* treaty not only remained in force but largely determined the course of Moslem–Nubian relations for six hundred years. To begin with Nubia was left in peace throughout the centuries when the armies of Islam were overrunning North Africa, Spain, the ever-diminishing Byzantine Empire, and Central Asia. Aswan was in fact the only fixed frontier which the Islamic Empire ever formally recognized. At the same time, the institutionalization of economic relations under the terms of the treaty insured a continuing Egyptian interest in the southern land. Difficulties which arose between Christian Nubia and its Islamic neighbours were chiefly the result of the Nubians' inability or refusal to meet the terms of the *Baqt*; consequently the treaty figures prominently in medieval diplomatic history.

It is noteworthy that the Arab records of the Nubian campaigns make no mention of the northern kingdom of Nobatia. The invaders marched directly south to Dongola,[67] a city of which we have no previous knowledge, but which was evidently by that time the capital of the kingdom of Makouria. The treaty which they negotiated there was binding upon 'the king of the Nubians and all the people of his kingdom . . . from the frontier of the land of Aswan to the border of the land of Alwa'.[68] The Makourian king was therefore presumed to be sovereign over all of the northern Nubians.

The silence of Arab historians in regard to Nobatia would seem unmistakably to suggest that the northern kingdom had ceased to exist as an independent political entity by the middle of the seventh century.[69] On the other hand Monneret de Villard[70] and others[71] have argued that the subjugation of Nobatia by Makouria took place at a later date, under the reign of the Makourian king Mercurios, called by Coptic historians the 'New Constantine'. He is at all events the first Makourian king whose name is mentioned in dedicatory inscriptions from Lower Nubia, dated AD 707 and 710.[72] Thenceforward all authorities agree that there was only a single northern Nubian kingdom, extending from Aswan at least as far south as the Fifth Cataract, with its royal residence and principal city at Dongola (Fig. 69).[73]

The united kingdom of Nobatia and Makouria does not seem to have had a distinctive toponym; it is sometimes called by the name of its dominant province, Makouria, and sometimes by that of its capital, Dongola. Its northern region continued to be separately designated by many writers by the older name of Nobatia, or, in later times, as the Province of Maris.[74] As we shall observe later (Ch. 15), the northern area retained both an ethnic identity and a political status of its own under the hegemony of Makouria.

There is a legend that in AD 745, a hundred years after the *Baqt*, a Nubian army of 100,000 men invaded Egypt and forced the Arab governor to release the Patriarch of Alexandria, whom he had imprisoned.[75] The story is probably a specimen of Christian Egyptian propaganda, and is not supported by reliable evidence,[76] but it does suggest that the Coptic patriarchs may have looked to Nubia for political support, much as the Byzantine Church was forced to turn to the Tsar of Russia following the Turkish conquest of Constantinople. Whether real or imagined, the threat of Nubian intervention probably gave the Egyptian Christians a certain political leverage in their otherwise powerless situation under the Islamic régime.[77]

In AD 758 the newly installed Abbasid Governor of Egypt wrote to the king in Dongola complaining of the Nubians' failure to fulfil some of their obligations under the *Baqt*. Along with other grievances the Egyptian complained of depredations committed in the Aswan district by the Blemmyes (Beja); evidently the Nubians were held accountable, under the treaty, for the good behaviour of their desert neighbours as well. The existence of the governor's letter was unsuspected until in 1972 the letter itself came to light at Qasr Ibrim. It had evidently been forwarded by the king in Dongola to the Eparch at Qasr Ibrim, as the official most directly concerned. It was eventually placed in a storage crypt together with other documents in Coptic, one of which may be a draft of the Eparch's reply. Although the Coptic documents are in fragmentary and incomplete condition, the governor's letter is almost perfectly preserved; it is by far the largest surviving specimen of Arabic writing from so early a date. It is inscribed on a sheet of papyrus three feet wide and over eight feet long, and comprises sixty-nine lines of clear and beautifully executed text. Only the protocols (unhappily including the king's name) are missing.[78]

A NEW BEGINNING

One of the most significant events in Nubian diplomatic history occurred in the early ninth century. Again, opinion is divided as to whether the outcome represents a triumph or a humiliation for the Nubians. During a period of religious disturbance and anti-Coptic persecution in Egypt, the king of Makouria had understandably ceased to render the annual tribute required by the *Baqt*. When the situation was brought to the attention of the Caliph al-Mutasim in Baghdad, he sent a letter demanding not only a resumption of the tribute but the repayment of fourteen years' arrears, which would have amounted to more than 5,000 slaves. Since the Nubian king was unable to meet so heavy a demand, he sent his son, later King George I, to Baghdad to negotiate in person with the Caliph. He was, so far as we know, the first Nubian prince to appear at a foreign court since Tenutamon, the successor of Taharqa (Ch. 10).

The Nubian embassy to Baghdad is, like the Dongola campaigns and the *Baqt* treaty, well known in Arabic literature, and is recounted in a number of different versions.[79] However, 'all the historians who mention the journey say that it was crowned with success. It resulted in a bilateral treaty of non-aggression and non-intervention, guaranteeing security of the Moslem frontiers (Upper Egypt) and the reduction of the *Baqt*.'[80] Among the specific concessions which Prince George seems to have obtained were the release of certain Nubian prisoners, the resumption of an Egyptian payment of commodities in exchange for the Nubian slaves, and a stipulation that the exchange should be made every three years instead of every year.[81] The Caliph, moreover, 'gave him abundant gifts, and sent him back again to his own country with honours'.[82] There is a possibility, however, that George journeyed a second time to Baghdad under less happy circumstances, as a military prisoner following a defeat by the Egyptians. The source of this information is ambiguous; it may be only a zealously Islamic and anti-Nubian version of the first visit.[83]

The centuries following the Nubian embassy to Baghdad witnessed the climax of Christian Nubian political power, but were a time of weakness and turmoil within Egypt. As a result the truce which had been established under the *Baqt* and reaffirmed at Baghdad seems to have been violated much more often by the Nubians than by the Egyptians. After the overthrow of Abbasid power in 868, Egypt was plunged into a long period of political turmoil. The short-lived Tulunid and Ikhshidid Dynasties were seldom able to govern effectively in the provinces, particularly in Upper Egypt. The majority of Upper Egyptians were probably still Coptic at this time, and therefore perhaps more sympathetically inclined towards Christian Nubia than towards the corrupt and oppressive Moslem governments in their own country. In any event the weakness of the central government gave both the riverain Nubians and the Beja an opportunity to resume the sporadic raiding of Upper Egypt and the oases which had

455

been their practice in pre-Christian times (Ch. 13). After one such foray, in 962, a large part of Upper Egypt seems to have been rendered tributary to the kingdom of Makouria for a period of several years.[84]

In AD 969, when the Fatimid Caliphate assumed power in Egypt, the *Baqt* was again in arrears. This time it was the Egyptians' turn to make diplomatic overtures. Gohar, the newly appointed Fatimid governor in Cairo, sent an envoy with a letter to the Nubian king, politely requesting that he either embrace the Islamic faith or resume the payment of the tribute. 'Upon his arrival at the royal court in Dongola, the king received the Moslem ambassador with great politeness. Then the king assembled all the bishops and scholars of his kingdom to meet with the Moslem embassy. After a free discussion, the king read to the assembly an invitation to Gohar to accept the Christian faith. The courageous witness of the Nubian Christians must have impressed the Moslems considerably, for Gohar abstained from any . . . military interventions in Nubia.'[85] We do not know, from this account, whether the *Baqt* was resumed or not; it is not mentioned again in Arabic annals for three hundred years. Relations between the Nubian kingdoms and Fatimid Egypt were, in any case, generally serene.

The overthrow of Fatimid rule in 1171 by Salah ed-Din ibn Ayyub, famous in Western annals as Saladin, was the signal for renewed hostilities in the south. A Nubian army captured and pillaged Aswan and was advancing to the north, either in search of plunder or in support of the Fatimid cause, when word was received that Salah ed-Din was preparing to counterattack. The Nubians then retreated into their own country, where they were overtaken by the pursuing Egyptians, and an indecisive engagement took place.

In the following year Salah ed-Din took more concerted action against Nubia. His interest in the southern land, according to one report, was motivated by the consideration that he might have to fall back upon it as a base of operations if he was forced out of Egypt, either by the Crusaders or by his Moslem enemies.[86] Accordingly he sent his brother, Shams ed-Dawla, at the head of an expeditionary force which seized and occupied the citadel of Qasr Ibrim in Lower Nubia – the same strong-point which had been seized by the Roman Petronius a thousand years earlier (Ch. 12). The contemporary account of Abu Salih relates that the invaders took the impossible total of 700,000 prisoners, all of whom were sold into slavery, and that they killed 700 pigs. The main church at Qasr Ibrim was converted temporarily into a mosque, and the bishop was imprisoned and tortured. However, an expedition to Dongola convinced Shams ed-Dawla that the country was too unproductive to serve as a political or military base, and Salah ed-Din gave up any further ambitions in that direction. The occupying force was withdrawn from Qasr Ibrim, and peace reigned in Nubia for another hundred years.[87]

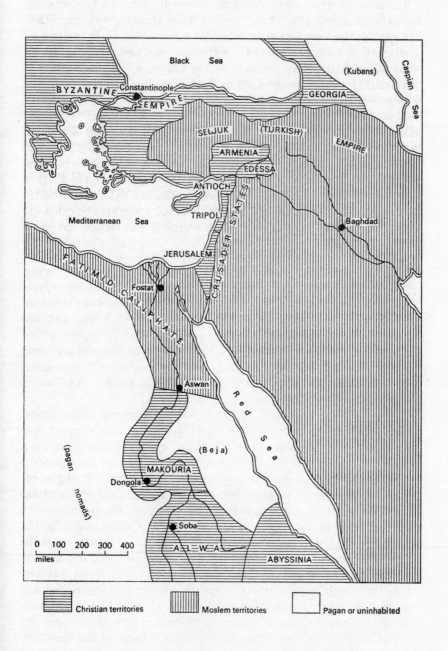

Fig. 70. The Near East at the time of the First Crusade

457

The conflicts which were ultimately to seal the fate of Christianity in Nubia began shortly after 1260, when the Bahri Mamelukes seized control of Egypt. By this time the northern Nubian kingdom was beset by dynastic troubles of its own, and it was the Egyptians' turn once again to fish in troubled political waters. In addition the Christian Nubians were now threatened along their desert flank by Arab nomads who had poured into the Red Sea Hills during the previous century, and who had subsequently infiltrated the Dongola kingdom itself. The militaristic and aggressive Mamelukes pursued a much more active southern policy than did any of their predecessors, and their continual intervention in Nubian affairs after the thirteenth century tipped the balance of power in favour of the growing Islamic element in the population. However, that story belongs to another age, and will be recounted in a later chapter (Ch. 16). Before we consider the decline and fall of Nubian Christianity we must pause for an extended look at the 'second golden age' which is represented by the civilization of the medieval period.

15
THE
CROWN AND THE CROSS
THE CIVILIZATION OF CHRISTIAN NUBIA

In the last chapter our concern was for Nubia's place in the larger world of the Middle Ages – a world which for six centuries was overshadowed by the confrontation between Christianity and Islam. We must now shift our focus to the narrower compass of events and conditions within the borders of Nubia. Here, as before, the historical record is meagre, but in this case archaeology comes enormously to our aid. The tantalizingly brief descriptions of Nubia which have been left us by medieval writers (see below) are supplemented by a rich and varied material record, which in the last decade has finally begun to receive the attention it deserves. As a result our knowledge of everyday life in the medieval period is fuller than for any earlier or later time.

More than a quarter of the known archaeological sites in Nubia date from the Christian period.[1] They include over a hundred churches, great urban centres such as Qasr Ibrim, Faras, and Old Dongola, scores of smaller towns and villages, fortresses, monasteries, industrial sites, and, of course, cemeteries. By virtue of their younger age most of these remains are better preserved than are those of the earlier civilizations; some Nubian churches and many houses have been found virtually intact. The systematic investigation of Christian antiquities, begun in earnest in 1960, has already emerged as the outstanding achievement of the third and final Aswan salvage campaign, compensating for the most conspicuous deficiency of the two earlier campaigns. Excavation is continuing in the area upstream from the Aswan Reservoir, as well as at Qasr Ibrim, and the study of medieval Nubian history and archaeology gives every promise of blossoming into a new and permanent field of scholarly endeavour.[2] Its development has undoubtedly been stimulated by the most exciting archaeological find of our generation: that of the great mural paintings at Faras (see 'Religon and the church', below, and Pls. XXIa–c).

For a long time the sheer quantity and variety of Christian archaeological remains probably served as a deterrent to systematic investigation. There was, in addition, the perennial problem of dating and chronology.

As always in Nubia, only a handful of buildings from the Christian period could be dated by direct evidence;[3] the great majority could only be consigned to the period of eight or nine centuries between the introduction of Christianity and its final disappearance. In the past decade, however, typological studies of pottery,[4] architecture,[5] and painting[6] have revealed developmental sequences which promise to unravel the chronological tangle. Most sites can now be dated within one or two centuries on the basis of their architectural and ceramic remains, and the Christian period as a whole can be subdivided into Early, Classic, Late, and Terminal phases.[7] Thus viewed in developmental perspective, the art and architecture of the medieval period no longer present such a confusion of styles and practices as once seemed to be the case.

As always, the material remains of medieval Nubia are most informative in regard to the circumstances of day-to-day living. In addition, the surviving durable goods give us a rough measure of trade and its fluctuations. The layout of towns and villages, which is much more clearly perceivable in the Middle Ages than in earlier times, tells us a good deal about social conditions and social changes.[8] In the ideological sphere we get also a penetrating insight into the religious life of the times, for the culture of medieval Nubia was rich in religious symbolism, almost to the exclusion of other forms of symbolism. For this very reason the record is, however, uninformative in regard to secular political history; here we must continue to rely on the fragmentary and often unsatisfactory textual evidence which has come down to us.

CONTEMPORARY ACCOUNTS OF MEDIEVAL NUBIA

Although our picture of Nubian life in the Middle Ages must be based largely on archaeological evidence, we can also draw upon the accounts of three contemporary observers: al-Umari, Ibn Selim el-Aswani, and Abu Salih 'The Armenian'. None of these has, however, come down to us in its original and complete form. The adventures of al-Umari and the geographical description written by Ibn Selim are known to us from excerpts in the fifteenth-century geography of Maqrizi,[9] while Abu Salih's 'Churches and Monasteries of Egypt and Some Neighbouring Countries' survives in an incomplete and very slipshod copy of the fourteenth century.[10] Even in this truncated form, however, the authors (and countless later scholars who evidently copied from them) provide our only first-hand glimpse of conditions in medieval Nubia, and the historical value of their reports is incalculable.

Al-Umari was an Arab freebooter very much in the tradition of the American 'filibusters' who terrorized the Central American republics a hundred years ago. At the head of what amounted to a private army he invaded Nubia in the latter part of the ninth century, with the object of seizing control of its storied gold mines. Whether the mines were actually in production at this time, or whether al-Umari was excited by fables of their earlier wealth, is not certain. At all events he established himself in the hills above Abu Hamed, near the Fifth Cataract, and for several years maintained virtually an independent state, partly by force of arms and partly by continual intrigues both with Dongola and with Alwa. After a colourful and thoroughly treacherous career he was finally dislodged by the Makourian King, and was eventually assassinated. The story of his adventures, as retold by Maqrizi, is short on descriptive detail, but it adds a touch of colour and human drama to an otherwise remote and little-known era.[11]

Also preserved in an excerpt by Maqrizi is a description of Nubia written at the end of the tenth century by Ibn Selim el-Aswani. He was the Egyptian official who around the year 970 undertook a diplomatic mission from the Fatimid Governor in Cairo to the court of Makouria, as related in Chapter 14. Despite the failure of his diplomatic efforts Ibn Selim seems to have been a broad-minded and sympathetic observer; his description (as related by Maqrizi) reveals a considerable appreciation for the attractions of Nubia and the virtues of its people. Of the Dongola district he writes:

Nowhere on the Nile have I seen such wide banks. I estimated that the river flows from east to west for a five days' journey [this would describe the great reverse bend above Dongola – see Fig. 5]. Islands break it up between which flow streams through a fertile land where are villages adjoining one another with good buildings and pigeon houses, cattle and flocks, which supply most of the provisions of their towns. Of its birds are the Naqit, the Nubi, the parrot and other lovely birds. Most of the palaces of their Chief are in this province. I was once . . . with him as we passed through narrow canals in the shade of the trees growing on both banks. It is said that the crocodiles never harm people there and I have seen people swimming across many of these streams. Then comes Safad Baqal, a district of narrow banks, resembling the first part of their country, except that in it are lovely islands and at a distance of less than two days' journey about thirty villages with beautiful buildings, churches, monasteries and many palm trees, vines, gardens, fields and large pastures in which graze handsome and well-bred camels. Their Chief visits here frequently, because on the south it borders on their capital city of Dongola.[12]

Ibn Selim is one of the few authors who provide any information about the southern Nubian kingdom of Alwa. However, he implies rather than states that he visited the southern kingdom in person, and his text lacks the ring of authenticity which is so evident in his description of Makouria. He describes the king of Alwa as richer than the king of Makouria,

461

commanding more horses and more soldiers. Soba, the capital of the southern kingdom, was graced by many fine buildings, churches adorned with gold and beautified with gardens, and had a suburb set apart for the Moslems.[13] These rather fanciful claims are not borne out by the unimposing (though largely unexcavated) archaeological remains of Soba;[14] they suggest that the author's information may have been derived from exaggerated travellers' accounts which were told him during his stay at Dongola.

Our last authority on Christian Nubia in its heyday is Abu Salih. Except for the one surviving copy of his work nothing whatever is known about the author; passages in his text suggest that he was a member of the Armenian community in Egypt.[15] Only eight of his 112 folio pages are devoted to Nubia,[16] and it is not certain that he visited the region in person. Much of his information, however, corroborates Ibn Selim. Abu Salih was evidently an ardent Christian propagandist, and he describes both Dongola and Soba as wondrous places, full of beautiful and wealthy churches. His most valuable, and perhaps his most reliable, information is of a political nature, and will be discussed in the next section.

THE ORGANIZATION OF THE MEDIEVAL STATES

The monumental remains of Nubia's earlier civilizations usually allow us to deduce something about concurrent political conditions, even when they tell us nothing else. On the other hand archaeology contributes almost nothing to our understanding of political organization in the Middle Ages. So wholly religious and other-worldly is the symbolism of this period that, had we nothing else to guide us, we would probably conclude that Nubia had been in the grip of a theocratic oligarchy – as in one sense it undoubtedly was. However, the coexistence of a secular monarchy is amply attested by documentary sources if not by the archaeological record.[17] What little we know in detail about the organization of the medieval states comes chiefly from the same alien but sympathetic observers from whom we derive our knowledge of contemporary history (cf. Ch. 14).

At the time of its conversion to Christianity Nubia was, as we saw earlier, divided into the three independent kingdoms of Nobatia, Makouria, and Alwa. A short time later, under circumstances which are not recorded, the two northern kingdoms merged into a kind of confederation in which Makouria was politically dominant. The united realm belonged nominally to the Makourian king, whose chief residence was at Old Dongola. His domain extended at least from Aswan to the vicinity of Abu Hamed, and possibly considerably farther to the south (Fig. 69).

The ideological and legal basis of the Nubian monarchy seems to have been little different from that of other medieval states. The temporal power of the king was, in theory, absolute, and his subjects were regarded as his slaves. He was the sole landowner of the kingdom, conferring and revoking tenures at his pleasure. Whether the royal power was limited in practice by any sort of governing council is uncertain; no formally constituted body of the kind is attested in contemporary documents.[18] However, the conclave of 'bishops and scholars' which was called together to discuss the embassy of Ibn Selim (see Ch. 14) would appear to have functioned at least informally as an executive council.

According to Abu Salih the king had religious as well as secular powers; he could enter the sanctuary area of the church and celebrate the liturgy like any priest. However, this privilege was withdrawn if he had shed human blood.[19] It is apparent in other respects that the king's power in the religious sphere was far from absolute, for he could not (unlike Catholic kings in Western Europe) appoint the bishops in his realm. They were nominated by the Patriarch of Alexandria, who was regarded as the king's superior in religious matters.

Arabic writers refer to the principal Nubian monarch as the 'King of Makouria and Nubia', or sometimes as the 'Great King'. These are evidently descriptive terms, and do not appear in the official royal protocols. A few sources also speak of the Nubian king as bearing the hereditary title *Kamil* or *Kabil*, but this too is unrecorded in native documents. Those Nubian texts which make any reference to the monarchy are conspicuously lacking in the magniloquent protocols of earlier times; they employ simply the Greek title *Basileos* ('king') or its Nubian equivalent, *Ourou*.[20]

According to Monneret de Villard the royal insignia consisted of throne, parasol, and crown.[21] Of these we know of the throne and the parasol only from somewhat dubious historical accounts. On the other hand some of the Nubian church paintings recently found at Faras portray actual rulers in their royal garb.[22] The kings are shown wrapped in richly embroidered gowns and crowned with wide bands of gold encrusted with gems (Pl. XXIa). The style of both robes and crowns is unmistakably Byzantine – so much so as to suggest that the artists may have been inspired more by contemporary canons of mural decoration than by actual models.[23]

It seems clear from a number of records that in early Medieval Nubia the royal succession passed from father to son in the usual Christian fashion.[24] After the eleventh century, however, we can perceive a curious reversion to a much older practice. 'It is said to be the custom among the Nubians, when a king dies and leaves a son, and also a nephew, the son of his sister, that the latter reigns after his uncle, instead of the son; but if there is no sister's son, then the king's own son succeeds.'[25] According to Ibn Khaldun, who records the same custom, it was the rule of matrilineal inheritance which led to the wholesale Islamization of Nubia after Christian women began marrying Moslem immigrants (see Ch. 17).[26]

Old Dongola was certainly the most important if not the only royal residence throughout the Middle Ages. It was a sizeable town spread along the top of a low bluff immediately above the Nile, on its eastern shore. Although there is no evidence of settlement here before the Christian period, the situation of Old Dongola was exceptionally favourable from the standpoint of agriculture, for it was immediately upstream from the Letti Basin, one of the few areas in Nubia where natural basin irrigation can be practised. Whether this factor influenced the selection of Dongola as the royal residence is not known. The ruins of the city, which cover an area of several hundred acres, are only beginning to receive the attention of archaeologists; in time they may add much to our knowledge of secular organization in Medieval Nubia.[27] One large decorated building, long identified as a church, is now believed by the excavators to have been a royal residence, though this is not yet confirmed by positive evidence.[28] The building was re-dedicated as a mosque in the fourteenth century, according to an inscribed tablet which may still be seen in one of the rooms.[29]

Aside from Dongola itself, no important urban centres are known from the province of Makouria, though there were several of them in the northern district of Nobatia (Fig. 71). Nevertheless, Abu Salih reported that 'the number of kings in Nubia is thirteen, and all these rule the land under the supremacy of . . . the Great King.'[30] These would presumably be vassal kings who held sway locally over various parts of the Nile Valley. The existence of one such vassal monarchy has recently been attested by finds at Qasr Ibrim.

After its union with Makouria the formerly independent region of Nobatia still retained an identity and a political status of its own. In later Arabic documents it is usually referred to as the Province of Maris, from a Coptic word for 'south'.[31] It was governed, from the eighth century on, by a special royal deputy bearing the Greek title of eparch.[32] He is frequently referred to by Arabic writers under the title 'Lord of the Mountain' (Sahib ej-Jebel), although a recent find at Qasr Ibrim suggests that his name could also be rendered as 'Lord of the Horses'.[33]

The eparch seems to have been essentially a viceroy for Lower Nubia. His status may therefore be compared to that of the Meroitic peste, who apparently ruled over the same region as deputy for the pqr (cf. Ch. 12). The eparch could evidently perform a number of the traditional royal functions, such as the founding of churches and the celebration of the mass. (He is depicted in a very late wall painting from Abd el Qadir holding a model of the church in his hands.[34]) In addition, the eparch seems to have been specifically charged with the conduct of relations with Moslem Egypt; indeed, this function may explain the emergence and subsequent importance of a separate eparchal office. According to Ibn Selim, he ' . . .

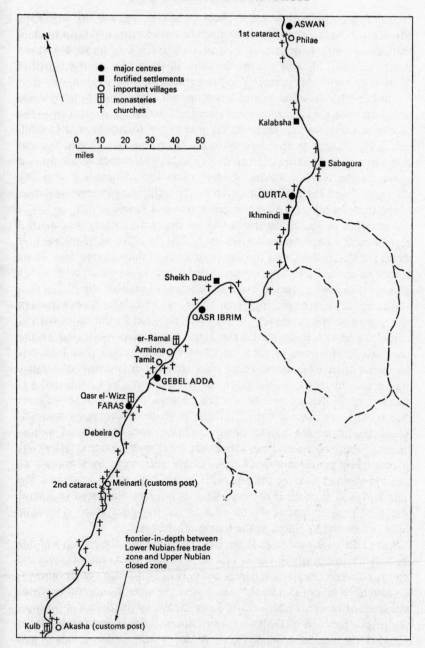

Fig. 71. Lower Nubia in Classic Christian times

is one of their principal governors, because he is so near the territory of the Moslems. Whenever any Moslem travels to this country, and has a stock of merchandise either for sale, or as a present to the king or governor, the latter receives it all, and returns the value in slaves; for no one, whether Moslem or not, is ever permitted to present himself in person to the king.'[35]

Further evidence of the eparch's commercial dealings has recently come to light among the correspondence found at Qasr Ibrim. According to the excavator there are '. . . seven letters sent to the Eparch from a Fatimid palace official who owned ships in the port of Aidhab on the Red Sea and also had a trading business centred at Qus. It appears that he acted as an agent for the Nubian Rulers, sending them various goods and selling slaves on their behalf, etc. The letters . . . contain many interesting details of the trade being carried on between Egypt and Nubia . . .'[36]

According to Ibn Selim the eparch in the tenth century was a royal appointee, but later Arabic writers imply that the office was hereditary. It seems too that in the Late Christian period one of the main responsibilities of the eparch was the defence of the northern frontier; he was in other words charged with the conduct of external relations of another sort.[37]

Among the church paintings from Faras and Abd el Qadir are a number of representations of eparchs.[38] They are depicted in the same stylized attitudes and rich attire as are the kings and bishops portrayed on the same walls. However, in their portraits we can recognize at least one distinctive eparchal insignia: a headpiece with one or two pairs of projecting horns, and sometimes surmounted by a crescent. The origins and significance of this device have been much discussed;[39] Michalowski believes that it was borrowed by the Nubians from the Sassanian Persians.[40] According to him the horned crown could be worn by kings as well as eparchs,[41] but it is much better attested in the case of the latter. (However, in post-Christian times horned crowns have been worn by a number of kings in various parts of the Sudan.[42]) In addition to his headpiece the eparch at Abd el Qadir is depicted wearing a robe emblazoned in several places with the Byzantine double-eagle[43] – a very unexpected symbol of authority to find in Nubia in the fourteenth century.

Recent discoveries at Qasr Ibrim have disclosed that the eparch was not the only civil authority in Lower Nubia. A number of documents from the later twelfth century give the names not only of eparchs and other officials, but also of 'Kings of Dotawo'.[44] These were presumably among the vassal monarchs of Dongola whose existence is implied by Ibn Selim (see above). The precise location of Dotawo is not known, but it is presumed to have included the region around Gebel Adda, whose medieval name was (apparently) Do or Daw.[45] The existence of this kingdom in the fourteenth and fifteenth centuries has been known from earlier finds,[46] but it has always been looked upon as a splinter state which emerged after the disintegration of Makouria (cf. Ch. 16). It is now apparent however that there was a monarchy of Dotawo long before the final decline of Dongola.

It is difficult to know, from the scanty available evidence, what was the relationship between eparchs and vassal kings. In the documents which mention both, the name of the king seems to be given precedence, but this is perhaps only conventional protocol and does not accurately reflect their respective powers. The eparch was of course the direct deputy of the 'great king' at Dongola; as such he might have been responsible for overseeing a number of vassal kingdoms. Significantly, it is the eparch and not the king who bears the title 'of Nobatia', thus seeming to perpetuate the authority of the formerly independent northern monarchy. In the absence of more direct evidence it seems reasonable to assume that the eparch was a general overseer, but was more specifically responsible for the conduct of external relations, while the vassal kings conducted the everyday business of government in their respective principalities.

Both the kings at Dongola and the eparchs in the north were served by various palace functionaries whose titles have come down to us as *domestikos*, *protodomestikos*, *meizon*, *protomeizoteros* and *primikerius*. All of these are Greek titles, familiar from the Byzantine age in Egypt and North Africa.[47] Unfortunately the fragmentary Nubian documents in which they are mentioned give us no clue as to their functions, and we cannot necessarily assume that they were the same as in Egypt or Byzantium.[48] Like most 'external proletarians' the Nubians have been highly prone to adopt the symbols of power, verbal as well as visual, even when they have not understood them, and the fancied resemblance between the Nubian court and the Byzantine court was perhaps more apparent than real.[49] Nevertheless the persistence of Greek titles, the use of Greek as a liturgical language, and the double-eagle device appearing on the eparch's robe (as depicted at Abd el Qadir) all testify to the charisma which still attached to Byzantine institutions long after the collapse of Byzantine power in the Near East.

The 'capital' of Nobatia or Maris is stated by most Arabic writers to have been at Faras. This was certainly the most important episcopal see of Lower Nubia, as is abundantly testified by archaeological evidence (see below). Faras has also been suggested as the residence of the civil governor,[50] but the volume of correspondence to and from the eparch which has been found at Qasr Ibrim makes it much more probable that this was his principal residence.[51] In other texts, however, the eparch is variously associated with Talmis,[52] Gebel Adda,[53] the Island of Michael (Meinarti?),[54] and an unidentified place called Bausaka (Fig. 71).[55] Since the functions of the eparch were (unlike those of the king) primarily practical rather than symbolic, it seems possible that the office was a mobile one, not firmly rooted in any one place. After the thirteenth century, when Faras suffered a drastic decline, there seems to be no doubt that the main seat of both eparchs and bishops was at Qasr Ibrim.[56]

The *Baqt* treaty made no political or economic distinction between different parts of Nubia; it forbade Moslem settlement from Aswan to the frontiers of Alwa (see Chapter 14). In the time of Ibn Selim, however, Lower Nubia seems to have been open to settlement by Moslems. Although the background of this development is far from clear, it probably resulted from the legal ruling, discussed in Chapter 14, which held that the Lower Nubians were not slaves of their king and were therefore free to dispose of their lands to whomever they chose.[57] This seems to have opened the door to Moslem settlement between the First and Second Cataracts, as attested not only by the account of Ibn Selim but by a number of Arabic tombstones which have come to light in various parts of Lower Nubia. All of them which can be dated fall in the interval between AD 832 and 1137.[58]

There is nothing in the archaeological record to suggest the existence of separate Moslem communities in Lower Nubia. Most of the settlers in Ibn Selim's time were probably merchants and artisans who took up residence within the larger Christian towns. Apparently some mosques were established, though none has ever been identified archaeologically.[59] Ibn Selim reports that in Lower Nubia trade was carried on freely between the Nubians and the Moslems, and money was in circulation. On the other hand the region beyond the Second Cataract remained closed both to Arab settlement and to Arab commerce:

On the first cataract of Nubia [i.e. the Second Cataract of the Nile] lies the city called Takoaa, on a level ground, where the boats of the Nubians ascending from the Qasr usually stop. The boats dare not pass this village, and no Moslem, nor any other person, dare ascend the river further up, without permission from the Lord of the Mountain. From hence to the Upper Maqs are six days' journey. Cataracts continue the whole way up. These are the worst parts of Nubia which I have seen . . . The river is constantly interrupted by rapid falls and projecting mountains . . . The district belongs to the territory of Maris, and is governed by the Lord of the Mountain. The garrison in the Upper Maqs is so rigorously governed by an officer named by the Great Chief of Nubia, that when the Great Chief himself passes that way, the governor stands by his side . . .

No money or dinars are here current; they are only used in traffic with the Moslems below the cataracts; above them they are unacquainted with buying or selling. Their trade is limited to mutual exchanges of cattle, slaves, camels, iron and grain. No one passes onward without the king's permission; disobedience to the order is punished with death. On account of this system of prohibition, no intelligence is ever communicated of their movements . . .[60]

It would appear from the description of Ibn Selim that Upper Maqs was somewhere near the southern end of the *Batn el Hajar*. Abu Salih adds the further information that it was located close to a hot spring,[61] which makes

468

possible a tentative identification with the modern village of Akasha, near which is the only known hot spring in Nubia.[62] Ibn Selim speaks of the place as a garrison point, while Abu Salih describes it more specifically as a customs post: 'No one is allowed to pass by the inhabitants of this place without being searched, even if he be a king, and if anyone pushes on and refuses to be searched, he is put to death.'[63]

The existence of customs stations both at Takoaa and at Upper Maqs, respectively at the lower and upper limits of the *Batn el Hajar*, suggests that this inhospitable region served as a kind of frontier-in-depth between the free zone of Lower Nubia and the remainder of the Dongola kingdom (cf. Fig. 71). We are inevitably reminded that it was garrisoned for the same purpose three thousand years earlier, though the political interest was then on the other side. The policy of the medieval Nubian king, that 'no Moslem, nor any other person, dare ascend the river farther up without permission from the Lord of the Mountain'[64] makes a startling and ironic contrast to the Semna Proclamation of Senusret III: '. . . to prevent that any Nubian should cross . . . by water or by land . . . except a Nubian who shall come to do trading in Iken, or with a commission' (cf. Ch. 7).[65]

The picture of Nubian–Moslem relations which emerges from the pages of Ibn Selim and Abu Salih is a familiar one of political and economic accommodation. Either by design or through political impotence, the Nubian king was obliged to maintain a buffer zone in Lower Nubia within which free intercourse between Nubians and Moslems was permitted. The supervision of this traffic was evidently the chief responsibility of the eparch. At the same time, and in compensation for the open frontier policy, stringent and repressive measures were taken to prevent the penetration of Islamic influence into the southern portions of the Christian kingdom.[66]

It is important to notice that the political distinction between the buffer zone of Lower Nubia and the remainder of the Dongola kingdom does not correspond to the geographical distinction between Maris (or Nobatia) and Makouria which is made by most Arab writers. According to Ibn Selim, whose geographical information was often accurate and explicit, the boundary between Maris and Makouria lay somewhere to the south of Sai Island and in the vicinity of a great cataract, which can only have been the Third Cataract (Fig. 69).[67] The author was evidently describing an ethnic and linguistic boundary rather than a political one, however; he speaks of the inhabitants of Maris and of Makouria as different peoples speaking different languages,[68] but does not mention any customs post or military installation at the frontier between them. It is noteworthy too that the modern dialect boundary between Mahasi-speaking and Dongolawi-speaking Nubians is very close to the frontier identified by Ibn Selim.[69] From this and many other examples, it seems clear that the toponyms employed by medieval Arabic scholars had ethnic and linguistic rather than political significance.[70] Throughout the Middle Ages political frontiers fluctuated according to the fortunes of individual rulers; only cultural boundaries had permanence.

The southern Nubian kingdom of Alwa may represent a partial exception to the foregoing generalization. Although Mas'udi speaks of its king as tributary to Makouria,[71] all other writers agree that Alwa was an independent state, as is clearly implied in the *Baqt* treaty (Ch. 14). Apart from the fact of its existence, however, we are told nothing reliable about it. The surviving descriptions of Ibn Selim[72] and Abu Salih[73] are not wholly credible; they evidently contain a mixture of fact and fantasy. They seem to belong to that genre of fabulous literature which so often grows up around remote and little-known kingdoms in the absence of reliable knowledge.

According to Ibn Selim it was further from Dongola to the frontier of Alwa than it was from Dongola to Aswan (i.e. over 500 miles).[74] This cannot possibly have been the case, for it would place the frontier of Alwa far to the south of the confluence of the Niles, where we know that its capital city was located. On the basis of other information, however, Kirwan considers that the northern boundary of Alwa was somewhere near the ruins of Meroë (Fig. 69),[75] while Arkell places it much further to the north.[76] It seems probable that there was in reality no fixed political frontier between Makouria and Alwa; the rocky and unproductive region between the Fourth and Fifth Cataracts would make a natural and effective buffer zone, and its few inhabitants probably did not answer consistently to either king. (It was precisely here that al-Umari was able to set up his renegade state in the ninth century, as related earlier.) The explicit frontier of Alwa to which Ibn Selim referred was probably another dialect boundary.[77]

According to the report of Ibn Selim, 'the Chief of Alwa is a greater person than the Chief of Makouria, he has a stronger army, and his country is more extensive and more fertile.'[78] If this was literally true, the kingdom must have occupied most of what today is the central Sudan. However, archaeological remains suggestive of a Christian occupation have so far been found only in a very limited area from the confluence of the Niles northwards. Christian sites are occasionally reported from as far south as Sennar on the Blue Nile, and even from the Western Sudan,[79] but none of them has been properly verified. (In this part of the country there is an unfortunate tendency to classify as 'Christian', or even as a 'church', any red-brick ruin of any age.) The number of such remains is not in any case sufficient to indicate a very large settled population. If Alwa was indeed possessed of vast territories to the south and west of its capital, they must have been inhabited chiefly by nomadic (and perhaps non-Christian) subject peoples.[80]

Although the evidence is wholly inferential, it seems possible to conclude that Alwa was primarily a slave-trading state, as was its successor the Funj Kingdom in the late Middle Ages (Ch. 18). The proximity of the vast pagan territories of the Upper Nile and Kordofan provided far greater opportunities for slave raiding than were enjoyed by Makouria, encompassed as it was largely by uninhabited deserts. The description of Ibn Selim suggests too that large numbers of Moslem merchants were resident in the capital city of Alwa;[81] presumably their interest was at least partly in the immemorial traffic in ivory and slaves. Finally, the peculiarly cordial relationship which seems to have existed after 1250 between the southern Christian kings[82] and the Mameluke sultans of Egypt (cf. Ch. 16) can only have been motivated by a strong commercial interest, again most probably in slaves.

Within the whole territory attributed to the kingdom of Alwa, the only archaeological remains of any significance which have yet come to light are those of its capital city, Soba.[83] It was situated on the east bank of the Blue Nile, about thirteen miles upstream from its confluence with the White Nile (i.e. from the modern site of Khartoum). Soba was obviously a place of considerable size, for its ruins extend over nearly a square mile and include about a hundred individual mounds.[84] Nevertheless there is nothing to suggest the opulence described by Ibn Selim. The surface of the site is thickly strewn with fragments of red brick, but excavations carried out in the two largest Soba mounds in 1950–52 disclosed only structures of mud brick, none of them of a monumental character.[85] Of the four hundred churches of Abu Salih's description,[86] only one has yet come to light, and very little remains of it. Whatever else we may hope to learn about the southern kingdom and its capital must await further and more systematic archaeological exploration.

RELIGION AND THE CHURCH

Archaeology affords us a rich and detailed picture of the aesthetic and expressive aspects of medieval Nubian religion (see 'Religious art and literature', below), but it has no more to tell us about the administrative organization of the church than it has about the organization of the state. In this area we are still obliged to rely on somewhat scanty and unsatisfactory documentary evidence.

According to an eighth-century Egyptian writer the Nubian church was headed by a Metropolitan, appointed by the Patriarch of Alexandria, who had the responsibility of ordaining bishops and priests throughout the southern countries.[87] The title 'Metropolitan' is associated with the names of five of the Bishops of Faras, and from this it has sometimes been assumed that the Faras bishops were in fact the primates of the Nubian church.[88] It is noticeable, however, that the title claimed by these prelates was 'Metropolitan Bishop of Faras', not 'Metropolitan Bishop of Nubia', and the addition of the one extra word to their customary title may be only a matter of stylistic preference, not signifying any special hierarchical status.

At least inferentially there is a good deal to suggest that the Nubian church was never organized on an autocephalous or national basis, like the Church of Abyssinia. There is no specific claim of primacy in the funerary stelae of any of the bishops, and we can recognize no ecclesiastical title comparable to that of the Abyssinian Abuna.[89] Indeed, the absence of any mention of religious superiors is a striking feature of the bishops' stelae, particularly since some of them mention contemporary kings or eparchs.[90] We might be inclined to infer from this that the Nubian bishops had been appointed by the Crown, after the European practice, but all our literary sources insist that they were nominated by the Patriarch of Alexandria.[91]

From the evidence available it seems safest to conclude that the Nubian bishops were appointed individually by the Patriarch, and were answerable separately to him rather than to one of their own number. This would in any case be in keeping with the traditionally centralized character of the Egyptian Coptic church.[92] There was, therefore, no such thing as a Nubian church in an organic sense; the Nubians were simply members of the Jacobite (Coptic) church of Egypt, not formally distinguished from their co-religionists in the northern country. Almost from the beginning, however, the Nubian Christians developed artistic and literary traditions of their own, so that we can speak of a Nubian church in a liturgical sense if not in an ecclesiastical one.

According to one account there were thirteen episcopal sees in Nubia: seven in the Kingdom of Makouria and six in the Kingdom of Alwa. The list of them has come down to us in a seventeenth-century history of the Church of Alexandria, the origin of which is obscure.[93] The work was composed long after the final disappearance of Christianity in Nubia, and must therefore have been compiled from much older sources. Of the seven episcopates which are listed for the northern Nubian kingdom, those at Qurta, Qasr Ibrim, Faras, Sai, and Dongola have been substantiated by archaeological or textual finds.[94] The existence of the other two northern sees, and of all those in the Kingdom of Alwa, remains unconfirmed.

Presumably the Bishops of Faras and of Dongola enjoyed a certain preference in the worldly sphere by virtue of their residence close to the seats of temporal power.[95] At least, we can infer this from the magnificent proportions of their cathedrals (see below). For the time being we know far more of the Faras bishops and their activities than we do of any of the other prelates, thanks to the extraordinary discoveries and the diligent labours of the Polish Archaeological Mission at Faras between 1961 and

1964.[96] Attacking an enormous artificial mound which rose in the midst of the modern village of Faras, and which was generally believed to be a stratified *tell*, the Poles found instead the ancient episcopal cathedral and palace, both largely intact. They had been buried nearly to the rooftops in sand during the thirteenth century, when the Christian civilization of Nubia was still in full flower. Preserved upon the walls of the Faras Cathedral were 169 coloured paintings, many of them perfectly preserved and representing the finest collection of mural art from Christian Africa. Among them were the portraits of fourteen bishops, as well as the portraits of kings and eparchs already cited. Alongside the paintings were hundreds of inscriptions and graffiti including a list of twenty-seven bishops who had occupied the See of Faras. Funerary stelae of some of the bishops were set into the walls of the cathedral, and several of their number were buried in tombs alongside the building. A spacious two-storey building which adjoined the cathedral on its north side is believed to have been the episcopal palace.[97]

The pictorial representations of bishops at Faras cannot be taken as accurate portraits, for like the kings and eparchs they are shown in stylized attitudes and dress. However, they probably furnish a reasonably accurate picture of the episcopal garb. All of the bishops are shown richly attired in an inner gown and an outer chasuble, with an ornamental sash of office hanging from the shoulders (Pl. XXIb). It is curious that neither a pectoral cross nor a bishop's staff appears in any of the portraits, for both articles have been found in the episcopal tombs at Faras and Qasr Ibrim.[98] Unlike the kings and eparchs, the Bishops of Faras are shown either bare-headed or covered only by a fine white shawl. Each of them carries an ornately decorated holy book in his left hand, and makes the sign of blessing with his right.[99]

The lesser clergy of Nubia are not represented pictorially at Faras or elsewhere. From the evidence of tombstones it appears that they bore the Greek title *presbyteros*. There are also many textual references to deacons (*diakonos*), and a few to archdeacons, 'epideacons', and 'hypodeacons'. The monastic orders consisted of monks and archimandrites.[100]

If the *Ecclesiastical History* of John of Ephesus can be believed, the first Nubian church was built by the missionary Longinus around AD 570 (see Ch. 14).[101] Presumably it was a makeshift affair which has not survived. It is interesting to note, however, that we have in Lower Nubia the remains of two buildings which look very much like ordinary houses adapted for ecclesiastical use by the addition of a few architectural modifications.[102] Neither can be precisely dated, but they belong undoubtedly to the first century or two of the Christian period.

Very soon after the formal introduction of Christianity, trained ecclesiastical architects made their appearance in Nubia. Some of the largest and most ornate churches in the country were in fact built in the first two centuries after Nubia's conversion. The earliest of them may have been the episcopal cathedral at Qasr Ibrim, which remained throughout the Middle Ages the finest example of ecclesiastical architecture south of Aswan.[103] Unlike any of the other churches in the country it was built of carefully dressed stone, and its design exhibits few of the peculiarities which soon came to distinguish Nubian church architecture.[104]

Like most churches of the Christian orient, the Nubian church derived its basic architectural form from the Graeco–Roman basilica rather than from earlier religious structures. It was a relatively long rectangular building, oriented east and west, and divided by internal colonnades into a central nave and two flanking aisles of about equal width. The altar and sanctuary were situated in the east end of the nave, which terminated in a half-circular wall (apse). In Nubian churches the apse was always encased within a rectangular masonry shell (Fig. 72), so that its form was not apparent from the outside of the building. The sanctuary area (called the *haikal* in Coptic churches) was set off from the body of the church by a 'triumphal arch' resting on stone columns, which symbolized the Gate of Heaven. On either side of the sanctuary proper, at the eastern ends of the two side aisles, were small enclosed rooms which served as vestries and for various other functions reserved to the priesthood. All of these arrangements were in accordance with the decree of the fourth-century *Apostolic Constitutions*: 'Let the building be long with its head to the east, with its vestries on both sides of the east end, and so it will be like a ship. In the middle let the bishop's throne be placed, and on each side of him let the presbytery sit down; and let the deacon stand near at hand, with closely girt garments; for they are like the mariners and masters of the ship.'[105]

The earliest Nubian churches were indistinguishable from those of Egypt, and were probably built by Egyptian architects. Many were of roughly dressed stone or of a combination of stone and mud brick (cf. Pl. XXb). The larger churches often had flat, timbered roofs resting upon monolithic columns, while smaller buildings had brick vaults. The latter method of roofing, which became universal after the tenth century, necessitated the use of stout masonry piers in place of columns, for the asymmetrical vault employed in Nubia (the so-called skewed vault) requires a very substantial base.[106]

By the eighth century the Nubian church had acquired a number of distinctive architectural characteristics which were to remain in vogue for several centuries. The most unusual of them was a narrow passage at the eastern end of the building, running behind the apse and connecting the two corner rooms (Fig. 72). Although this feature may have been present from the beginning at Qasr Ibrim, it is not otherwise found in Nubia before the eighth century. Very few examples are known from other

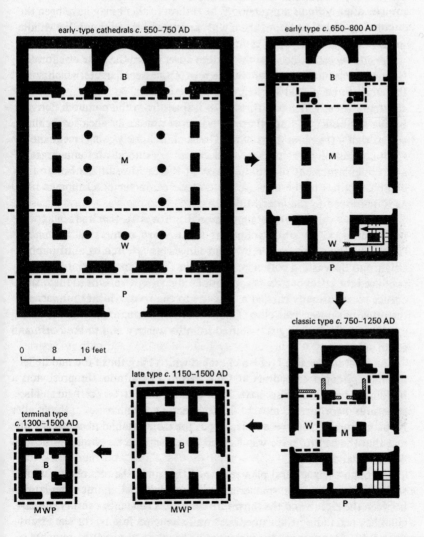

early-type cathedrals *c.* 550–750 AD

early type *c.* 650–800 AD

classic type *c.* 750–1250 AD

late type *c.* 1150–1500 AD

terminal type
c. 1300–1500 AD

0   8   16 feet

MWP   MWP   P

Heavy arrows indicate sequence of chronological development.
B   *Bema* (sanctuary area), accessible to clergy only
M   area of church accessible to men
W   area of church accessible to women
P   area of church accessible to penitents

Fig. 72. Plans of Nubian churches showing architectural development through time

475

parts of the world, and the origins and significance of the eastern passage remain something of a mystery.[107]

Another development of the eighth and later centuries was the enlargement of the sanctuary area to include a considerable part of the nave. This was made necessary because the eastern apse, where the altar was formerly situated, was now occupied by tiers of choir seats, and the altar had therefore to be placed farther west in the church. At the same time the sanctuary area, which was formerly set apart from the congregation only by the symbolic 'triumphal arch', was now physically enclosed behind a screen wall – the *ikonostasis* of the Greek church, or *higab* as it is called in Coptic. This physical separation between priesthood and congregation, and the enlargement of the sanctuary at the expense of the body of the church, testifies to the increasingly esoteric character of Orthodox ritual as it developed in the later Middle Ages.

The area available for congregational use was further reduced by the partitioning off of small rooms at the western corners of the church (Fig. 72). They were apparently introduced as an architectural counterbalance to the eastern corner rooms; in the floor plan of the building they produced the effect of a cross superimposed on a square. One of the western corner rooms usually carried a stairway to the roof, while the function of the other has never been clear. Once the cross-in-square plan was adopted, entrance to the building was shifted from its western end to the north and south sides.

The most impressive Nubian churches which have thus far come to light are the episcopal cathedrals at Qasr Ibrim, Faras, and Dongola, and a building which may also have been a cathedral at Gebel Adda. These structures incorporated most of the architectural peculiarities of the smaller Nubian churches, but were conspicuous for their size and above all for the fact that the central nave was flanked on either side by two aisles instead of the usual one.

Although their general plan remained the same, the churches of Nubia seem to have become smaller and less pretentious in each generation between the eighth and the thirteenth century. The average size of the early churches (excluding the cathedrals) was about 65 feet by 32 feet; by the thirteenth century these dimensions had shrunk to about 48 feet by 30 feet. Heights were correspondingly reduced, and, in the older churches, the original timbered roofs were gradually replaced by vaults. This made it necessary to pull down the monolithic stone columns which were a feature of many early churches and to replace them with masonry piers. The discarded columns are sometimes found outside the church, or, in one case, buried under the floor.

The passage of years brought the same inexorable burden of drifted sand to the churches as it did to the houses of Nubia. Unlike the houses, however, the churches could not be cheaply repaired or rebuilt. Instead, various architectural defences were introduced. Walls were reinforced and buttressed, and wooden members were replaced by stone or brick. As the level of accumulated sand crept upwards it became necessary also to block up the original windows, particularly in the north and west walls, and to cut through new ones at a higher level. Continued access was made possible by the construction of sand-retaining walls surrounding the doorways. In time the north (i.e. windward-side) doorways of many churches were blocked up and disused, while the south doorways were reached by descending ramps or stairways which had to be lengthened in each generation. In their last years the churches at Abdullah Nirqi[108] and at Meinarti[109] were for all practical purposes underground buildings reached by stairways which descended from a level as high as their original roofs. The thrust exerted against exterior walls by tons of accumulated sand was of course enormously dangerous, and led ultimately to the abandonment of many churches long before the end of the Christian period. To this factor the archaeologist of today owes his thanks for the miraculous preservation of the wall paintings in such churches as Abdullah Nirqi, Faras, and Sonqi (see 'Religious art and literature').

In the thirteenth century, when many of the older Nubian churches were surrendering to the encroaching sand, a new and radically simplified form of church was introduced. It was apparently inspired by the little 'cupola-churches' of Greece and Anatolia. The late Nubian churches were nearly square in plan, measuring hardly more than 30 feet on a side, and were crowned by a tall central cupola.[110] They retained the basic threefold division of the earlier churches, but dispensed with nearly all such architectural niceties as the eastern passage, the apse, the segregated sanctuary, and sometimes even one or both of the western corner rooms.

The lack of an *ikonostasis* or *higab*, hiding the sanctuary from the view of the congregation, might argue for the return of a more exoteric and popular rite in the late Nubian church. However, if we may judge from parallel instances in Greece, it seems more probable that the opposite was true. The entire church building had now become the sanctuary, accessible only to the clergy and a few privileged members of the laity. The public portion of the service was probably celebrated outdoors, and the lesson was read from the church doorway, as it is today in the churches of Abyssinia. The widening gulf between clergy and laity which seems to be apparent throughout the history of the Nubian church probably contributed to the weakening and final disappearance of Nubian Christianity in the late Middle Ages (cf. Ch. 16).

After the seventh century the architectural development of the Nubian church shows very little influence from Egypt. Both the cross-in-square plan of the Classic Christian period and the cupola church of the late period seem to have come direct from the Near East, and are not found in Egypt. On the other hand certain distinctive features of Egyptian Coptic architecture were never introduced in Nubia. Despite their doctrinal affiliation with Alexandria the Nubians were evidently in communication with other Christian communities as well, and were able to absorb influences directly from them. This circumstance is apparent also in their religious art (see below). There are numerous records of Nubian pilgrims in the Holy Land, and it may have been through this avenue of communication that artistic influences found their way from Syria and Palestine to the Upper Nile.[111]

Like the temples that preceded them, some of the early Nubian churches seem to have been built with more regard for a prominent physical setting than for the proximity of settlements. In later years, however, there was always a close physical relationship between the church and the community. The great cathedrals of Faras and Qasr Ibrim and a few other churches were located in the centres of their towns, but the usual setting for the church was at the outskirts of a settlement. This was necessary if the building was to be surrounded by a cemetery, as was true in the majority of cases. Churches and houses were often built in close proximity, but the church was never in actual contact with secular buildings. It might however be adjoined by satellite chapels, a clerical residence, or a monastic establishment.

While every Nubian settlement of any consequence had at least one church, the larger towns and even some relatively insignificant villages had as many as five or six.[112] The number of churches per community does not seem to be closely correlated with the size of the population; more probably it reflects the presence of ethnic or familial divisions within the community. The proliferation of churches is particularly conspicuous in the late Christian period, when scattered communities were drawing together for protection but apparently wished to maintain their independent congregational identities. It is also true that the number of churches, both overall and in relation to the size of the population, is far greater in Lower Nubia than elsewhere (cf. Fig. 71), suggesting (as do several other indications) that the power and wealth of the church were developed chiefly in the north, on the borders of Egypt.

The testimony of such authors as Ibn Selim[113] and Abu Salih[114] would suggest that monasteries were a conspicuous feature of the medieval Nubian scene. Perhaps for this reason, and because the monastic movement was highly developed in Coptic Egypt, there has been a tendency to identify as a monastery almost any nucleated village site of the Christian period. Yet definite archaeological evidence of monasteries is extremely scanty.[115] Only three monastic establishments can be recognized with virtual certainty: at er-Ramal[116] and Qasr el-Wizz[117] in Lower Nubia, and at Wadi

Ghazali near the Fourth Cataract.[118] In each instance a central church is enclosed within a compact cluster of adjoining buildings, and the whole is surrounded by a girdle wall. At Qasr el-Wizz, the most fully investigated of the Nubian monasteries, it is possible to recognize a cluster of monks' cells, a central refectory and kitchen, and workshops (Fig. 73).[119]

In the vicinity of Akasha, in the *Batn el Hajar* (Fig. 71), are the remains of a number of other walled compounds which might represent small monastic communities. Detailed reports on these sites are not yet available,[120] but it is clear from their tightly integrated construction and exterior walling that they are not ordinary farming villages (see 'Towns, villages and houses,' below), nor do their arrangements and locations suggest a military

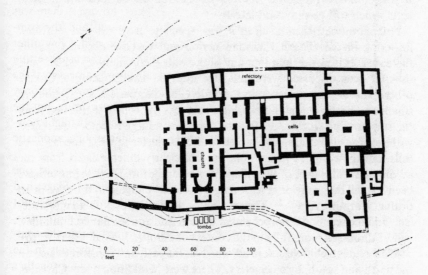

Fig. 73. Plan of Nubian monastery, Qasr el-Wizz

function. In at least two of the sites near Akasha there was a church within the walls,[121] though in other cases no trace of a church can be found. If these rather enigmatic settlements were indeed monasteries, the concentration of half a dozen of them within a space of a few miles would suggest that Akasha was an especially holy place, perhaps because of its hot spring. The sites date chiefly from the Classic Christian period (ninth to twelfth centuries), as do the better-attested monasteries of Qasr el-Wizz and Ghazali.

None of the Nubian monasteries is in any way comparable in size or ostentation to the great monastic establishments of Egypt.[122] It is noteworthy too that the monastic churches at er-Ramal, Wizz, and Ghazali are of distinctly Nubian rather than Egyptian design. Yet the literary texts and even the tombstones which have come from these places are very largely in Coptic,[123] a language which was not very often employed by the native Nubian population (see 'Religious art and literature').[124] We are therefore left in some doubt as to whether the monks of Nubia were recruited from the local population or whether they were primarily refugees from Egypt. In any case their number does not seem to have been large, and they probably did not play as significant a part in the economic and religious life of the country as did the monasteries of Egypt and Europe. In addition to organized monastic communities there probably were solitary anchorites living in caves and ruins here and there; the dwelling place of one such individual has been recognized archaeologically.[125] It is decorated with an extraordinary collection of religious and magical texts which will be discussed later.

Nubian monasticism, such as it was, seems to have reached its fullest flowering in the Classic Christian period and to have declined rapidly thereafter. It is not certain that any of the walled communities which have thus far been discussed were inhabited after the twelfth century. On the other hand we can perceive, in the Late Christian period, suggestions of smaller monastic communities which were less rigorously segregated from the surrounding world. At Meinarti there was a large refectory decorated with religious paintings, and surrounded by a cluster of what appear to be cells, but the complex as a whole was not clearly differentiated from the adjoining secular part of the village.[126] At Tamit, too, there seems to have been a small monastic or at least religious colony clinging to the edge of an ordinary farming village.[127] The reasons for the decline of Nubian monasticism, and the seeming rapprochement of monastic and secular communities, will be discussed more fully in the context of Nubia's Feudal Age (Ch. 16).

Most Nubian churches were adjoined on the east, and sometimes also on the north and south, by a cemetery. There were in addition many Christian cemeteries (including most of those remaining in use from earlier times) which were not associated with a church. About half the known mortuary sites in Sudanese Nubia date wholly or partially from the Christian period.[128]

In their underground arrangements the majority of Christian graves are simple in the extreme. The grave pit is no more than a narrow vertical slot in which the body is laid on its back, head to the west, without any covering except perhaps for a crude 'lean-to' of bricks over the face. The corpse is wrapped in a shroud, and sometimes a few small articles of personal jewelry are left upon it, but there are no mortuary offerings as such. The only exceptions to this generalization seem to be represented by the burials of ecclesiastical dignitaries, who were sometimes buried in elaborate garb, accompanied by their insignia of office and by a jar or jars presumably containing holy water.[129] The placement of these vessels suggests a continuation of the traditional mortuary practice of Meroitic and Ballana times. A burial recently uncovered near Kulubnarti (presumably also that of a church official) is interred on a fully preserved *angareeb* bed[130] – a startling survival or revival of the age-old Nubian custom which was once thought to have disappeared at the beginning of the Christian period.[131]

In addition to single burials the vaulted family tomb, familiar from earlier times, retained a limited popularity in the Christian period. In these chambers the bodies were sometimes laid like cordwood, up to the number of fifteen or twenty, always with the heads to the west. Each time the vault was re-sealed a votive lamp was left burning just inside the doorway, which was at the west end.

The most common Christian grave covering was a rectangular pavement made of bricks set on edge. At its western end there was usually a 'box' formed by two upright bricks with a third brick across the top within which a votive lamp was placed. Presumably it was burned whenever a mass was said for the dead. However, many of the poorer Christian graves, and particularly those in the smaller and more remote cemeteries, had only a rough covering of stone slabs. At the opposite extreme were fairly elaborate tomb superstructures of brick which were built in the cemeteries adjoining some of the more important churches. These took a wide variety of forms: a rectangular mastaba surmounted by a cross in raised relief, or a cruciform mastaba, or a small square chamber capped by a dome. Many of them were covered by white or coloured plaster, and some had a carved tombstone set into the western face. The dimensions of the superstructures were generally limited more or less to those of the underlying grave, and none of them remotely approached in size or shape the tumuli of pre-Christian times (Ch. 13).[132]

Tombstones from the Christian period are relatively numerous, and their texts furnish an important corpus of medieval Nubian literature (see below). Nevertheless, surprisingly few of them have been found *in situ*. Most Christian graves seem to have been neglected after a relatively brief period, and there was a tendency for later dwellers in the neighbourhood to prise out the convenient slabs and put them to other uses. More tombstones have probably been found as door sockets and paving slabs than as grave markers. In some cemeteries it has been found also that the tomb superstructures were systematically levelled after a certain time, and the space reoccupied by new, intrusive burials.[133] All in all, the evidence suggests that mortuary ritual played a lesser part in the religion of the Middle Ages than at any time since the beginning of the historic period.

RELIGIOUS ART AND LITERATURE

Decoration in the early Nubian churches seems to have been confined to the use of sculptured capitals, lintels, and cornices, both of stone and of wood.[134] Very few of these have survived intact, for after the eighth century such features were generally discarded. The specimens which have come down to us are fairly typical of early Christian church decoration; they are wrought into elaborate floral patterns of Hellenistic origin, with only an occasional decorative cross or bird of peace to signify the influence of Christianity.[135]

The sculptured capitals and lintels of the early Nubian churches were probably painted as well, but there is no suggestion of mural decoration as such. At the beginning of the eighth century, however, a new and purely Christian artistic canon made its appearance in the form of brightly coloured wall paintings inspired by the frescoes and mosaics of Byzantium. They soon became, and remained throughout the Middle Ages, the highest artistic expression of Christian Nubian civilization. After their appearance carved decoration rapidly declined in popularity, as it did throughout the Christian East at about the same time.

The high development of church painting in medieval Nubia is attested by scraps of brightly coloured plaster and by occasional remnants of designs which can be found in scores of abandoned churches throughout the country. Yet until a decade ago only a few rather forlorn examples of painting were known to have survived in anything like recognizable form.[136] Even these were sadly damaged, for they had been exposed not only to the ravages of the elements but to defacement by vandals, inspired either by fear of the evil eye or by the Moslem injunction against images. Then came the discovery of the Faras cathedral, abandoned and sanded up during the heyday of Nubian Christianity, with its painted decoration largely intact.[137] Shortly afterwards discoveries of the same sort, though in much smaller churches, were made at Abdullah Nirqi[138] and at Sonqi.[139] Together the paintings from these three churches comprise a treasure-house of medieval art without parallel in Christian Africa. The discovery of the Faras paintings, in particular, must be ranked as the outstanding archaeological find of this generation.

If the discovery of the Faras paintings (popularly though incorrectly called frescoes) was the most fortuitous discovery of the Nubian Monuments Campaign, their preservation and removal from the walls of the cathedral was its greatest technical triumph. Although the building itself is now submerged under Lake Nasser, no less than 169 paintings were successfully removed from its walls, and are now divided between the National Museum in Warsaw and the Sudan Museum of Archaeology in Khartoum.[140] Like most Nubian churches the Faras cathedral had been period-ically redecorated, resulting in an accumulation of paintings one on top of another. The skill of the Polish conservators enabled them to remove the successive layers of paintings individually, thereby revealing a whole developmental history of Nubian church art (cf. Pl. XXIc).

It is impossible to do justice in words to the Faras paintings. Fortunately some of the best of them are now reproduced in colour in a number of popular books.[141] To be fully appreciated, however, the paintings should have been seen in their original setting, as splashes of brilliant colour within a generally monotonous landscape of yellow-brown sand. (Some-thing of this impression is conveyed by the painting shown in the coloured frontispiece in Michalowski's *Faras, die Kathedrale aus dem Wüstensand.*[142] Among the most spectacular of the Faras murals, it is eight feet high and ten feet long and depicts the three Hebrew youths in the fiery furnace, pro-tected by the Archangel Michael.[143] The ornately robed figures are done chiefly in blue and gold against a background of leaping red flames.)

Two other important scenes are represented at Faras: a very elaborate and detailed nativity (in which, for the first time in any known document, the attendant shepherds are identified by personal names[144]) and a cruci-fixion scene. Most of the remaining paintings are idealized portraits, including figures of the Madonna, the Archangels, various apostles and martyrs, and the Nubian kings, eparchs and bishops to whom reference has already been made (Pls. XXIa–b). The figures are accompanied in most cases by painted inscriptions which identify them by name.

The discoveries at Faras, Abdullah Nirqi, and Sonqi have enabled us to reconstruct the painted designs in a great many other churches, of which only small fragments now remain. All of them correspond closely in style and iconography, although the paintings in the smaller churches seldom match the quality and elaborateness of those at Faras. As a result, we can now speak in general terms of a Nubian school of medieval church art.

Unlike the Byzantine church, the Nubian church does not seem to have had a rigidly prescribed programme of mural decoration.[145] However, the same or similar figures occur in the same place in a large number of churches. The apse is generally occupied by a central figure of the Madonna and Child flanked on either side by the apostles,[146] while the half-dome which crowns the apse (a feature found only in the earlier churches) is dominated by the colossal head and shoulders of the Christ *pantocrator* (i.e. at the Last Judgement).[147] There is very often a nativity scene in the north aisle,[148] a standing figure of the Archangel Michael at the head of the south aisle,[149] and a head of Christ with the symbols of the four evangelists along the south wall.[150] Cavalier saints are another popular motif; among them we can recognize the familiar figure of St George spearing the dragon.[151]

At least four periods of stylistic development are represented in the surviving paintings at Faras. They are designated by Michalowski as the Violet Style (early eighth to mid ninth century), the White Style (mid ninth to early tenth century), the Red-yellow Style (tenth century), and the Multi-coloured Style (eleventh and twelfth centuries).[152] These designations reflect changing colour preferences, but there are also important changes in style and iconography. The two earlier styles are characterized by rather muted colours and a sparing use of decorative detail. The figures, according to Weitzmann, are characterized by '. . . straight outlines which tend to flatten the figures while at the same time their somewhat thickset proportions suggest the massive structure of their bodies, underlined by their large, almost clumsy feet and their heavy, square heads. Their faces are designed with thick and almost geometric lines and with enormously large eyes with a blank gaze.'[153] The later periods are characterized by brilliant colours and lavishly ornate detail in the treatment of robes, wings and other features. The facial features are considerably more humanized and animated than in the earlier styles.

As nearly as we can tell, the same sequence of stylistic development is characteristic of all the Nubian churches, though the Multi-coloured Style seems to be fully developed only at Faras. Elsewhere the Red-yellow Style continued in vogue until the end of the Christian period. Some of the very late churches, like that at Abd el Qadir, exhibit a highly simplified and somewhat degenerate style which is not represented at Faras and may have developed after the abandonment of the Faras cathedral.[154]

The dominance of Coptic influence in the Nubian paintings is obvious. It is also noticeable that most of the inscriptions which accompany them are in the Coptic language, suggesting the probability that the painters were Egyptian artisans brought in for the purpose of decorating the Nubian churches. Presumably they worked from a copy-book, since there is a close and detailed (though never exact) similarity between the paintings in churches throughout the country. Even so, the mural art of Nubia is not simply a faithful imitation of the contemporary Christian art of Egypt; it betrays also influences from Palestine, Syria, and Byzantium.[155] A purely local and realistic touch is added by the portrayal of native rulers and bishops with dark features,[156] in contrast to the white faces of the Holy Family, saints, archangels, and nearly all the other figures depicted. In art, as in architecture, it seems that the Nubians were capable of assimilating and combining influences from a variety of sources, and also of adding touches of their own.

The problem of writing in medieval Nubia is an exceedingly complex one.[157] At the time when Christianity was introduced there was, as we saw, no established written language. Meroitic was for all practical purposes extinct, and Greek, although employed in proclamations by one or two pre-Christian kings, was probably not understood by any native Nubian.

The language of the early Egyptian church was Greek, and it became the liturgical language of Nubia as well after the introduction of Christianity. When the Egyptian church shifted from Greek to Coptic following its final rupture with Byzantium, however, the Nubian church does not seem to have followed suit. Greek remained in use, although in increasingly barbarized and ungrammatical form, throughout the Middle Ages. Greek invocatory texts are known from as late as the thirteenth or fourteenth century,[158] and the majority of Nubian tombstones are also inscribed in Greek. After the seventh century, however, there are additional texts and inscriptions both in Coptic and in Old Nubian – the native language of Nubia written in the Coptic alphabet.[159]

Jakobielski has pointed out that the medieval texts from Nubia clearly fall into two groups, one comprising the Greek and Old Nubian texts and the other comprising the Coptic texts.[160] Greek and Old Nubian often appear one above the other in the same inscription, and the grammatical errors which are usual in the Greek passages often show the influence of the Nubian language.[161] On the other hand, written Coptic is rarely found in conjunction with the other languages, and the texts are generally free from grammatical errors. From this Jakobielski concludes that the documents both in Greek and in Old Nubian were the work of native Nubians, while the Coptic texts were written by Egyptians settled in the country. The reluctance of the Nubians to join their Egyptian brethren in the switch from Greek to Coptic may be explained by the fact that Greek had acquired a special prestige in Nubia not merely as a liturgical language, but also as the court language of Nobatia and Makouria (cf. Ch. 14). Thus the educated Nubian of the Middle Ages probably employed Old Nubian in everyday discourse and Greek in official correspondence and inscriptions, just as modern Nubian and Arabic are respectively employed today. At the same time it would appear that the Egyptian clerics in Nubia insisted, with typical parochialism, on the use of their own Coptic tongue. It is noteworthy in this respect that the foundation of the great Faras Cathedral in A D 707 is commemorated in two parallel stelae, one in Coptic and the other in Greek.[162] Presumably this represents a compromise between the Greek-speaking court and the Coptic clergy which seems always to have been predominant at Faras.

The linguistic confusion in medieval Nubia has sometimes been regarded as evidence of a continuing struggle between Monophysites and Melkites (cf. Ch. 14),[163] but this is not justified by the evidence. All three languages evidently had official status and could presumably be employed in the liturgy, as could Arabic after the fourteenth century. In places where Egyptians were in positions of authority, as in the monasteries and perhaps at Faras, Coptic was probably given preference for the most important inscriptions,[164] but elsewhere Greek and Old Nubian were much more widely employed. However, Coptic tombstones are found occasionally in many parts of Nubia; perhaps they are testimony to the number or influence of Egyptian clerics among the Nubian clergy.

Only five Nubian books have survived from the Christian period,[165] although loose pages and smaller fragments are often found. However, the literature of the Middle Ages is preserved after a fashion in many other forms. Jakobielski has published an inventory of textual remains found at Faras, which gives an idea of the extent and variety of medieval religious literature:

Inscriptions incised in stone: Foundation texts and documents of an official nature, 6; Grave stelae, 17; Texts of commemorative character, 7; Graffiti on blocks or architectural elements, 12; Monograms, 8.

Inscriptions on plaster of buildings written in ink or scratched: Legends to mural paintings, 61; Inscriptions commemorating founders of paintings (dedications), 13; Parts of prayers not followed by signatures of visitors, 40; Religious and magic texts: Group of Coptic inscriptions of AD 738 written on the walls of the Anchorite's Grotto by the monk Theophilos; Lists of names of the clergy, 6; Signatures of persons visiting the building – graffiti including names preceded or not by a short invocation, 81; Single names without titles – for the most part names of saints, 64; Parts of lists of movable feasts or calendar concordance, 2; Single dates – month, day or numbers, 9; School inscriptions, the alphabet, list of vowels, samples of writing, 6; Monograms, 30; Fragments of unidentified graffiti, 92; Single letters, 44.

Inscriptions on pottery: Ostraka, 10; Graffiti on vessels, names or monograms, 50; Inscriptions on seals, 2; Inscriptions in white paint on bricks containing names of saints, made for reasons unknown to us, 5.

Scraps of manuscripts on parchment: One leaf of Theotokia in Greek with Old Nubian intercalations; a shred of a leaf of a Greek liturgical manuscript; small shreds of about 50 leaves of Coptic manuscript (preserved lower left edge of a book, with non-identified contents).[166]

In addition to the finds at Faras, the corpus of medieval Nubian textual remains has been enormously enriched in the past decade by the finding of an Old Nubian parchment codex at Serra (apparently matching one published many years ago by Griffith[167]), a Coptic prayer book or breviary from Qasr el-Wizz,[168] and an extraordinary collection of religious, legal and administrative documents from Qasr Ibrim.[169] These new finds have not yet been analysed or published in detail.

The surviving examples of medieval Nubian literature are overwhelmingly religious in character. The longer texts include canonical writings (principally the Gospels), lives and sayings of the saints, prayers, and a variety of ritual formulae, most of which are well known from the world of early Christianity.[170] Like a great deal of medieval literature they seem to range freely between worldly and other-worldly concerns, and between lofty moral precepts and primitive ritual fetishism. However, it is difficult to identify anything specifically Nubian amid this literary hodge-podge.

Perhaps the clearest idea of the content and quality of medieval Nubian literature is conveyed by the inscriptions in the 'Anchorite's Grotto' near Faras. Here in the eighth century a solitary monk took up residence in the outer chamber of a New Kingdom rock-tomb; over the years he proceeded to adorn its walls with a series of inscriptions which provide a unique insight into one man's view of the meaning of Christianity. Griffith, who copied the inscriptions sixty years ago, has given the following description of the Anchorite's Grotto:

The most interesting memorial which the hermit has left us is the series of Coptic texts which he painted upon the whitewashed walls in square compartments like the pages of a book greatly magnified. The first on the north wall is the Nicene Creed; the rest so far as they survive relate edifying anecdotes and sayings of the saints, such as were current in large collections in Greek, Syriac, and Coptic; but they do not appear to agree with those of any known gathering. Only 4, 5, and 6 can be recognized in a Syriac collection, and there too they are in a very different form. This series was continued on the south wall. No. 24 in the middle of this wall is a prayer for the anchorite himself, 'Theophilus, this least of monks, who wrote these writings on my dwelling,' dated in the year AD 739. On this prayer there follows a series of potent amuletic texts like those in a book in the Leyden collection. They consist of the beginnings of the four gospels written in circles, reaching to the end of the wall; and, occupying the irregular corner and the beginning of the west wall to the left of the door, the letter of Christ to King Abgarus of Edessa, the list of the forty martyrs of Sebaste, the much-blundered Latin palindrome *sator arepo tenet opera rotas* (here entitled 'the names of the nails of Christ'), the names of the seven sleepers of Ephesus, etc., followed by a plain and an ornate cross.[171]

The mortuary texts which are inscribed on Christian Nubian tombstones represent a special class of medieval literature. They are usually a dozen or more lines in length, and include a considerable variety of formulae. Most common are variants of a well-known Byzantine text, the *Euchologion Mega* ('great eulogy').[172] A fairly typical specimen from Debeira has been thus translated by Crum:

Jesus Christ, Light of Life. Through the providence of God, the governor of all, He that said unto Adam, the first man, 'Earth thou art, to earth again shalt thou return'; even thus did the deceased Peter the Deacon go to rest – the spiritual son of Abba George, Bishop of Qurta – on the seventh day of the month of Epef in the year 745.[173] And may God the good and benevolent give rest unto his soul in the heavenly kingdom, and place him in the bosom of Abraham and

Isaac and Jacob, in the paradise of joy, whence weeping and grief and sighing do fly away; and may he cause the good Archangel Michael to watch over his bones; and cause him to hear that blessed voice which shall say, 'Come, ye blessed of my father, and inherit the kingdom which has been prepared for you since the foundation of the world.' For thou art the rest and the resurrection of thy servant, Peter the Deacon, and unto thee we send up praise, unto the Father and to the Son and to the Holy Ghost, now and forever and unto the ages of ages. Amen.[174]

TOWNS, VILLAGES AND HOUSES

At least in the north, Nubian society in the Middle Ages was probably more densely urbanized than in any earlier period. Settlements like Qasr Ibrim, Gebel Adda, and Faras may have numbered several thousand inhabitants, and there were many villages whose inhabitants numbered in the hundreds. In Upper Nubia, the capital cities of Dongola and Soba may have been larger still, but in these districts there is little evidence of urban settlement away from the capitals themselves.

As usual, the great urban centres are the least systematically investigated and least understood expressions of medieval Nubian civilization. Excavations on a large scale have not yet been undertaken at Dongola, Soba and Qasr Ibrim[175] while Faras and Gebel Adda have been consigned to the flood with the bulk of their remains uninvestigated. Superficially, all of these settlements convey much the same impression as do medieval European communities: a planless jumble of rather unpretentious houses clustered around one or more monumental buildings. Presumably the northern cities were the nuclei for the flourishing trade described by Ibn Selim,[176] but we have not recognized special market or workshop areas among their remains.

Although smaller in size, the ordinary villages of Lower Nubia were often as densely urbanized as were the major cities. They differed chiefly in lacking, except in a few cases, any recognizable nucleus of public buildings or a market square. Examples of such villages which were investigated in the course of the recent salvage campaign were those at Arminna,[177] Tamit,[178] Debeira West,[179] Meinarti,[180] and Kasanarti.[181] Each of these places appears to have been primarily a farming community numbering between 200 and 400 inhabitants. There was no central plan or nucleus to any of the villages; the houses were tightly clustered into irregular 'blocks' separated by narrow, winding alleys. The architectural features did not remain constant for any length of time, for new rooms or houses were periodically added to the existing aggregations, while older ones were subdivided, converted from human to animal use, or abandoned to drifting sand. As a result it is not always easy to tell where one dwelling unit ends and another begins.

All of the above-named communities included at least one church, which was located at the edge of the settlement. Meinarti may also have been the locus of a small monastic colony, though, as noted earlier, this was not sharply distinct from the secular portion of the village. In addition to their ecclesiastical establishments many villages seemingly included one or two secular buildings which served some public function. At Arminna there was a group of rooms opening onto a central courtyard, which might represent shops;[182] at Meinarti there may have been a public tavern in the Early Christian period.[183] In the latter village there was also, at least for a time, a public latrine in a central location.[184]

The village of Meinarti, unlike the other sites thus far mentioned, was inhabited throughout the entire medieval period, and its twelve strati-graphic levels[185] comprise a kind of microcosm in which we can follow the changing social and economic fortunes of the Christian Nubians from beginning to end.[186] The town was actually founded in late Meroitic times, on a flat alluvial island just below the Second Cataract. Its earlier history has been described to some extent in Chapters 12 and 13.

At the time when Christianity was introduced into Nubia, Meinarti village comprised an irregular jumble of small houses without any public buildings. Soon afterwards a small church, and also what appears to have been a public tavern, were added to the east side of the community, but there was no other change in the plan of village or houses. Early in the Christian period, however, the level of the Nile floods rose considerably,[187] and the houses at Meinarti were extensively and repeatedly damaged by high water. The inhabitants sought for a time to protect themselves by reinforcing and sometimes doubling the thickness of their rather flimsy house walls; then they seem to have given up the struggle, and for a century or two built only the most insubstantial of houses. The church was kept in repair, but the tavern was never rebuilt after its destruction by a parti-cularly severe flood.

In the Classic Christian period, perhaps at the end of the tenth century, there was a major 'urban renewal' at Meinarti which witnessed the rebuild-ing of the entire village within a matter of a few years. The new houses were not substantially built, and were tightly clustered together as before (Fig. 74), but individually they were more spacious than any earlier Nubian dwellings except the 'de luxe' houses of the Meroitic élite (cf. Ch. 12). The village church was also rebuilt once again. That the Nubians would under-take so extensive a building programme suggests that they had reason to believe that the era of high floods was over, and indeed the village was never again seriously damaged by flood waters.

In the early Christian period it is difficult to recognize any distinctive Nubian house plan, either at Meinarti or in other settlements. In the newly rebuilt Meinarti village of the Classic period, however, we can discern a

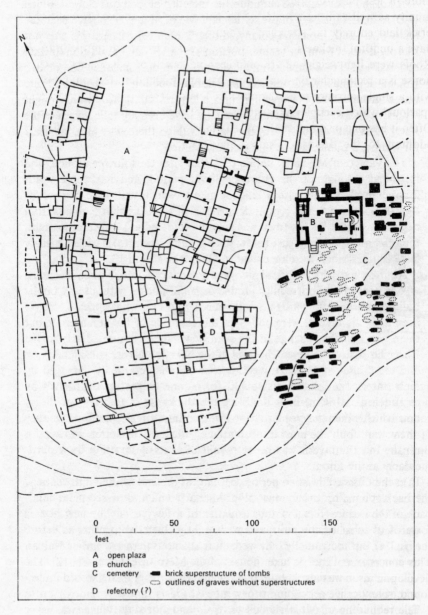

A   open plaza
B   church
C   cemetery   ■ brick superstructure of tombs
               ⊂⊃ outlines of graves without superstructures
D   refectory (?)

Fig. 74. Village of the Classic Christian period, Meinarti

more or less uniform house plan which is reproduced all over the community as well as in other sites of the same era. The houses are built of brick laid entirely in 'stretcher' (lengthwise) courses, so that the walls have a uniform thickness of eight inches, equal to the width of one brick. Roofs were lightweight affairs of poles and brush or grass mats. Each house is a rectangular or square unit, averaging about 16 feet on a side, with a single entrance from the outside. The doorway opens into a large 'parlour' which occupies as much as half of the total area of the house. Often it has one or more small square windows set high up in the wall, in addition to the doorway. Raised mud benches (mastabas) are built

Fig. 75. Artist's reconstruction of medieval Nubian village, Tamit

against one or more of the long walls, to serve as sitting places in the daytime and beds at night. Behind the front parlour are one or two smaller rooms which were used primarily for storage and food preparation; many of them were found to contain a large, mud silo for the storage of grain. Both the front and back rooms usually had cheap pottery jars buried in the floors at the corners, in which charcoal fires could be built for warmth.

In each house a narrow passage led from the front room along the side of the back rooms, then turned a right angle and ended in a latrine at the back of the house. Here a ceramic toilet fixture was set atop a raised platform of wooden beams. A 'cleanout hole' through the exterior wall at the back of the house allowed the periodic removal of accumulated sewage. This concern for 'interior plumbing' represents one of the most striking developments in medieval Nubian house architecture; it is not consistently found at any other period in history before modern times.

The rebuilding of Meinarti village in Classic Christian times was followed by a long period of stability during which the principal architectural modifications were in the nature of defences against accumulating sand. Buttresses and sand-retaining walls were built here and there. In many houses when the pressure of the drifts against outside walls was sufficiently great, it was offset by raising the level of interior floors by a foot or two. This in turn usually necessitated raising the roof level by the addition of a few more courses of brick at the tops of the walls. One building at Meinarti had actually been heightened three times in this fashion, so that its walls, when cleared to the original foundations, were in effect two storeys high.

By the middle of the twelfth century most of the villagers at Meinarti seem to have given up the struggle against the encroaching dunes. Their houses were abandoned and within a relatively short time were sanded up to the level of the roofs, which in many cases were found intact by the archaeologist. Where the people went during this interval is a moot question, but shortly after the sanding-up process was complete they (or else some new group) reoccupied the site, and new houses were built on top of the ever-rising village mound. Often they followed the alignment of the older buildings, using the tops of the buried walls as footing.

The houses which were built at Meinarti from the twelfth century on are of a type which is familiar throughout Nubia in the Late Christian period. In size and floor plan they are similar to the Classic Christian houses, with the same combination of large front rooms, smaller back room or rooms, right-angle passage, and latrine. However, the flimsy construction of the Classic period is replaced by much stouter walls, usually two feet and sometimes up to three feet thick. The light wooden roofs of earlier times gave way to brick vaults, and exterior windows were dispensed with. The inner storage room in some houses no longer had any ground-level entrance; it could be entered only through an overhead hatchway in the roof.

It is a curious fact that the stout Late Christian houses at Meinarti, unlike those of earlier times, were never built in actual physical contact. In one case, two houses were built side by side and so close together that the space between their walls was too narrow to admit a man, yet the principle of actual contiguity seems to have been avoided. At another village, Kasanarti, the Late Christian houses were physically contiguous, but no two of them shared a common wall.[188] In this respect they resemble the buildings in a modern city block – each structurally self-contained but physically contiguous with its neighbours on either side. By contrast, contiguous houses in the Classic and earlier periods at Meinarti had always shared one or more walls in common. While it is very difficult to interpret the significance of this change, there is at least a suggestion that the strong sense of community which seems evident in the Classic Christian period was giving way to more individualistic attitudes.

Stoutly built houses like those at Meinarti and Kasanarti appeared all over northern Nubia in the Late Christian period. Although they were, incidentally, better equipped to withstand sand encroachment than were their predecessors, it is apparent that defensive considerations of another sort were involved in their design. With the passage of time they became increasingly fortified and difficult of access, and were sometimes equipped with elaborately concealed crypts or rooms. These buildings are among the many evidences of a growing preoccupation with defence, which found its fullest expression in Nubia's Feudal Age. Consequently a full consideration of the Late Christian houses and their development is best reserved until the following chapter.

The Classic Christian house type and village plan found at Meinarti were reproduced with only minor variations at Debeira West,[189] Arminna West,[190] and elsewhere. These densely compacted settlements were not, however, the only type of Nubian village in the Classic period. For some reason there was at the same time a great efflux of population into the rocky and inhospitable district of the Second Cataract and the *Batn el Hajar*. Many islands which were, so far as we can tell, previously uninhabited are dotted over with huts and houses built in the eleventh and twelfth centuries. The structures are for the most part crude and irregular by comparison with the spacious houses of Meinarti, and they are built almost entirely from rough-hewn local stone. Sometimes they are tightly clustered, but more often they are irregularly scattered over the crests and slopes of the cataract islands. In many places the number of such houses seems out of all proportion to the local resources, yet the remains of decorated pottery and other luxury goods found within them do not suggest a conspicuously low standard of living.[191]

The reasons for a sudden immigration into the cataract region in a time of peace and prosperity are not at all apparent. Perhaps there was a population explosion in Nubia which made the subjugation of new lands imperative, yet we do not find a conspicuous enlargement or multiplication of settlements in the more favoured parts of the country. I once suggested that the cataract sites were intended primarily as refuges from floodwater in a time of abnormally high Niles, and that they were not designed for permanent habitation.[192] This hypothesis receives some support from the fact that the Nile levels as recorded at Cairo were exceptionally high throughout the twelfth century;[193] however, it must also be noted that the hut colonies are found principally in island localities rather than on the equally protected heights east and west of the river. Military defence would obviously suggest itself as an explanation, and yet this is not consistent with the contemporary development of villages such as Meinarti and Arminna. In Late Christian times, when defence became an obvious concern of the Christian Nubians, most of the island hut colonies were in fact abandoned. The history of these colonies was therefore comparatively brief, and the reason for their development remains one of Nubia's many unresolved mysteries.

Walled settlements were uncommon in the earlier medieval period in

Nubia. Although the great administrative centres of Qasr Ibrim, Gebel Adda, and Faras were fortified in Meroitic times, these settlements in the Christian period outgrew their enclosing walls in much the same way as did the burgs of medieval Europe. At Qasr Ibrim and Gebel Adda a jumble of houses spilled far down the slopes below the citadel walls. Prosperous villages like Arminna, Debeira and Meinarti were never defended; in most of Nubia it was only the monasteries which were surrounded by walls, intended more as a spiritual than as a physical defence against the lay world. Not until the Feudal Age did the walling of secular communities become a common feature.

There were, nevertheless, a few walled settlements in Nubia even in the early Christian period, whose plan and construction differ markedly from those of the ordinary medieval village. The most conspicuous of these are in the far north, at Kalabsha,[194] Sabagura,[195] Sheikh Daud,[196] and Ikhmindi.[197] In each of these places a fairly large square or rectangular area was enclosed within a massive stone wall, reinforced by exterior bastions and corner towers (Fig. 76). Entrance was by means of one or two fortified gateways. Within, the orderly and uniform arrangement of the buildings is clearly indicative of central planning, and contrasts sharply with the helter-skelter plan of the typical Nubian village. At

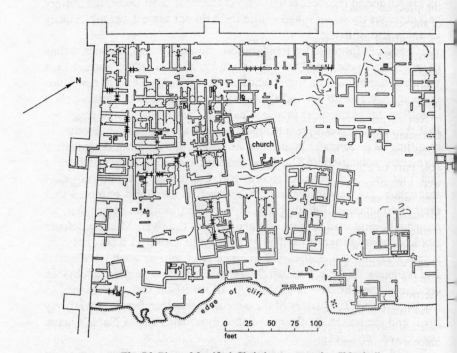

Fig. 76. Plan of fortified Christian community, Ikhmindi

494

Ikhmindi[198] and Sheikh Daud[199] a church occupies a central position within the complex.[200]

The walled settlements of Lower Nubia all seem to have been founded at or shortly after the beginning of the Christian period. The excavators have suggested that the architectural style of the fortifications was of Syrian or Palestinian origin, and that its introduction to Nubia coincided with the introduction of Christianity itself.[201] At Ikhmindi, a dedicatory inscription indicates that the enclosure was built 'for the protection of men and beasts'.[202] This, and the fact that the fortified settlements of northern Nubia are all situated near the termini of the desert caravan routes (e.g. the Wadi Allaqi), suggests that they may have been built as caravanserais.[203] No similar installations have been found in other parts of Nubia.

THE SECULAR ARTS

From the A Horizon to the X Horizon, our knowledge of Nubia's material arts has come chiefly from the contents of graves. In them we can find intact examples of most of the things which were in everyday use, from humble kitchen implements to furniture to the most expensive luxuries. In the sixth century, however, the adoption of Christianity put an end to the practice of interring material offerings with the dead. Our knowledge of the secular arts of the Middle Ages, such as it is, comes from forgotten or discarded objects found on house floors, and above all in refuse middens. These goods are generally in fragmentary condition, and they seldom include valued possessions. Metal objects of all kinds are particularly scarce, for fragments of bronze and iron could nearly always be put to some practical use, and hence were not discarded.

Not surprisingly, in view of the character of its material remains, the Christian period in Nubia was long regarded as a backward and impoverished one.[204] If we have quite a different view today, it is due in considerable part to a few lucky finds of houses which for some reason or other were abandoned with a large part of their material inventory *in situ*, and then were never reoccupied. Several finds of this kind were made at Meinarti, which remains up to now our prime source of information about medieval Nubian material culture.[205] In addition, the systematic sifting and recording of objects from refuse middens has provided us with a rough quantitative measure of material wealth. As a result we now recognize the Classic Christian period as an era of prosperity second only to the Meroitic.

As usual, a large part of the medieval Nubian material inventory consisted of Egyptian-made products. Bronze, glass, glazed pottery, and luxury objects of ivory and ebony continued to come entirely from the north, and even utility goods of pottery and iron were imported in large quantities, at least into Lower Nubia. At times these imports make up as much as 50 per cent of the total material inventory of northern Nubian sites. However the familiar native industries of pottery-making, weaving, and ironmongery also flourished during most of the Christian period, and their products are abundantly represented in our archaeological collections.

Nubian pottery in the Early Christian period continued to imitate the fashions prevalent in Byzantine Egypt.[206] The goblets and bottles which had been popular in Ballana times gave way increasingly to footed bowls and open-mouth jars, but there was a continuing preference for plain, red vessels in the general tradition of Roman *terra sigillata*. Around the ninth century, however, the Nubian pottery industry suddenly blossomed forth with a whole series of new shapes and designs. Plain, red vessels nearly disappeared; in their place appeared all kinds of bowls, vases and jars with highly intricate, painted decoration combining geometric, floral, and animal motifs (Fig. 77). The Classic Christian artistic canon shows much more resemblance to that of Meroitic times than it does to anything in the intervening five centuries.

The inspiration for the Classic Christian artistic innovations is not to be found in contemporary Egyptian pottery, which by this time was wholly under Islamic influence. It seems to have come rather from the mural decoration of the churches, which was just then coming into flower (see 'Religious art and literature', above). The elaborate *guilloche* borders and the lavish use of geometric embellishment which are common both to pottery decoration and to church painting probably drew their ultimate inspiration from Coptic and Byzantine miniature paintings and manuscript illumination.[207] In fact, the extreme fineness and preciseness of execution in Classic Christian pottery designs suggests that the decorators may have been trained as manuscript illuminators.

Although they are surpassed both technically and artistically by Meroitic pottery, the Classic Christian wares nevertheless represent one of the highest artistic achievements of the ancient Nubians. Their abundance and variety suggest that they may have been produced at several different centres. One of the most important factories, located at Faras, was discovered in the early years of the twentieth century,[208] and was more fully excavated in 1960.[209] It is, so far as I know, the most fully investigated example of a pottery factory anywhere in the ancient world.

The Faras Pottery appears to have been originally a monastic establishment which was founded quite early in the Christian period. Pottery was at first produced on a small scale, perhaps to supply the immediate needs of the monks, within one or two rooms set aside for the purpose. Then, after the site was extensively damaged by a flood or rainstorm, it seems to have been restored to use exclusively as a factory. The small indoor kilns of the earlier period were replaced by very large, double-

Fig. 77. Christian Nubian pottery designs: Early Christian designs at left; Classic Christian in centre; Late Christian at right (except zoomorphic figures in bottom row, which are Classic Christian)

chambered cylindrical affairs of the kind already familiar in other parts of the country in Ballana times (cf. Fig. 67). Mixing basins and other pottery-making apparatus were installed in the former monastery rooms; in the course of time the walls became covered with mud splashes and muddy handprints. At the peak of their production the Faras Potteries included at least four great outdoor kilns, each about seven feet in diameter, and several smaller kilns within doors.

The first products which were made at Faras were plain, red vessels of the typical Early Christian forms. When the place was converted to a factory pure and simple, however, it seems to have specialized initially in the production of amphorae. Not long afterwards the manufacture of the fancy Classic Christian decorated wares was begun, and the Faras Potteries remained for perhaps a century one of the chief centres of their production. Fine, beautifully decorated vases and bowls were found throughout the building in all states of manufacture, and the refuse within one of the kilns included the remains of more than 200 vessels which had evidently been destroyed when the floor of the kiln collapsed during the firing operation.

Production at Faras ceased in the tenth or eleventh century. The abandonment of the factory was abrupt and unpremeditated, as is attested by the partially finished vessels left all over the site, many of them fully decorated and ready for the kiln. What precipitated this event we shall never know; it may have been the collapse of the last workable kiln on the site. With the cessation of production at Faras the Nubian pottery industry went into eclipse for a century or more; the vessels which continued to be made at other factories were not particularly numerous, and they lacked the naturalistic decoration and fine finish of the best Faras products. For a time they were actually outsold, at least in Lower Nubia, by cheap imported wares from Aswan.

In the Late Christian period the local pottery industry blossomed once again, and regained much of its fine quality and decorative elegance. The main innovation of the later period was a closer control of firing temperatures and atmospheres which allowed the production of vessels in various shades of orange and yellow, in addition to the red and white wares which had been popular earlier. Painted decoration once again became elaborate, but representational designs were not revived. A Late Christian pottery design is usually a rather simple geometric frieze embellished in every conceivable way with tangent loops, spurs, spots, and other frills (Fig. 77). The high degree of standardization exhibited by the Late Christian wares suggests that they were all produced at a single factory, but its location has not yet been discovered.

Imported pottery played only a small part in the material inventory of the Early and Classic Christian Nubians. Egyptian imitations of *terra sigillata*, which had first made their appearance in the Meroitic period, continued to be imported in small quantities until the middle of the eighth century. Then, perhaps concurrently with the upsurge of local production, the importation of Egyptian pottery almost ceased during the earlier part of the Classic period. After the cessation of production at Faras the northern wares came back strongly for a century or so, only to decline again with the revival of the Nubian pottery industry in Late Christian times.

The ninth and tenth centuries witnessed a new departure in the ceramic field: the first flowering of the Islamic glazed-ware industries. In time, their products were to rank among the finest artistic achievements of Islamic civilization.[210] Although the most celebrated of the glazed wares were made in Mesopotamia and Persia, there was also an important centre of glazed ware production at Fostat, the forerunner of modern Cairo.[211]

Glazed pottery from Fostat began appearing in Nubia in the tenth century,[212] and it is never absent from sites of the later Christian period. The bright-coloured sherds of blue, green, yellow and brown stand out sharply amid the predominantly red and white Nubian wares. The earliest glazed vessels were either monochrome or were decorated with simple painted designs which always have a blurred and 'runny' appearance – a condition which is unavoidable when a lead glaze is used. The substitution of alkaline glaze after the eleventh century made possible much more precise painted decoration, and in the imported pottery of the Late Christian period we find various fine floral and geometric designs. However, some of the most distinctive and artistically appealing of the Fostat wares are monochrome vessels having a fine, incised arabesque design beneath the glaze.

Despite the popularity of glazed pottery in the later Middle Ages, its manufacture seems never to have been undertaken either in Upper Egypt or in Nubia. So far as we are able to tell, all of the glazed vessels which we find in Late Christian Nubian sites came from Fostat or from even farther abroad. It is not surprising that the number of such vessels was never large; they were probably among the most highly prized of luxury goods in medieval Nubia.

Hand in hand with the development of glazed pottery went the revival of glass manufacture in the Islamic Near East.[213] Glass vessels of Roman types had been fairly common in Meroitic Lower Nubia, but had nearly disappeared in the Ballana and Early Christian periods. They began reappearing in quantities at about the same time as did glazed pottery. Among the most common vessels were small cosmetic flasks, but there were also various tumblers, goblets, and bottles. Decorative techniques which can be recognized include marvering (rolled-in glass threads of contrasting colour), painting, cut decoration, and all kinds of appliqué techniques. Not surprisingly, our glass collections from Christian Nubia consist chiefly of small sherds, from which it is not often possible to recognize original vessel forms or decorative designs. About 3,000 glass sherds were found in the upper (i.e. later Christian) occupation levels at Meinarti village. The great majority of the vessels are believed to have been made at Fostat, which was equally important as a manufacturing centre for glass and for glazed pottery.[214]

Metal objects are not commonly found in Christian Nubian sites, for reasons already noted. Bronze was evidently used to some extent for small bowls and for various kinds of small implements and ornaments; the most common bronze objects found in medieval Nubian sites are slender, decorated rods which were used for the application of *kohl* (eye shadow). Their abundance is probably due to the accident that their needle-like shape made them easy to lose or overlook. The bronze goods found in Nubian sites are all of well-known Egyptian types, and were almost certainly manufactured abroad. Iron, which was presumably worked locally, was used for agricultural tools and knives and occasionally for ornaments such as pectoral crosses.

Scraps of woven cloth are found in abundance in Christian Nubian sites, and most Christian burials are wrapped in a linen shroud. Most and perhaps all of the linens used by the Nubians may have been of Egyptian manufacture; we know from the account of Ibn Selim (quoted earlier) that linen goods were among the principal items received in exchange for slaves under the *Baqt* treaty.[215] However, at Meinarti and elsewhere have also been found the remains of a great many woven robes of wool. These garments have no known counterparts in Egypt, and were probably of local manufacture. Most of them exhibit plain patterns of broad and narrow stripes in various bright colours; one or two have more elaborate chequered designs.[216] None of the pieces exhibits any sign of tailoring or sewing; they were apparently plain rectangular robes or blankets. Curiously enough, there is little evidence of the continued weaving of cotton in Christian times (cf. Ch. 12).

The other domestic manufactures of Christian Nubia are those which are familiar to us from all ages: leather sandals and thongs, all kinds of basketry and matting, wooden bowls, grinding apparatus of stone, and occasional ornaments of fine stone and shell. The production of palm fibre mats and sandals seems to have been a specialized industry at the Late Christian sites of Attiri and Kulubnarti, where enormous quantities of matting were found in the occupation refuse.[217]

MEDIEVAL NUBIAN SOCIETY AND ECONOMY

Despite the richness of its archaeological remains, we are still ignorant of some of the most basic features of medieval Nubian civilization. As Trigger has aptly observed:

... it is easy to overestimate how much we know about the cultural history of the region and to underestimate the loss of historical data that has resulted from the building of the High Dam. The reasons for this are clear and mostly understandable. Few archaeologists who worked in Lower Nubia arrived there with specific objectives in mind; their aim was to salvage as much archaeological material as possible before the region was flooded. By the time their research had led them to formulate more detailed problems of Nubian culture history, field-work was no longer possible. Because of this, much of the archaeological work done in Lower Nubia has been repetitive rather than problem-oriented and the amount of material that has been collected greatly exceeds its significance.[218]

The lacunae in our knowledge become apparent when we try to fit the many and detailed pieces of information we possess into an overall picture of medieval Nubian society. On the one hand, Ibn Selim and other Arab writers speak of the Nubians as being legally the slaves of their king.[219] This may have been a very real burden to them, or it may have been no more than a characteristic medieval legal fiction, embodying the principle of 'eminent domain' in the person of the king. The absence of traditional symbols of authority – royal tombs, monuments and inscriptions – leaves us in doubt as to how heavily the yoke of the state actually pressed upon the Nubian populace. At the same time the disappearance of mortuary offerings deprives us of what was heretofore one of our most consistent and reliable measures of social and economic differentiation. We are left to judge the social and economic condition of the medieval Nubians chiefly on the basis of their houses and the refuse found in and around them. Here we can observe a surprising uniformity among the dwellings in any one community, but considerable variation from village to village, as though prosperity were more a communal than an individual or familial affair.

In general the archaeological remains of medieval Nubia convey the impression of a prosperous and at the same time surprisingly free and egalitarian society, seemingly combining the best features of pre-civilized and civilized times. It may be, however, that the archaeological record is deceptive in this regard. Differences in rank and power need not be reflected in material ostentation, particularly in an age notable for its other-worldly preoccupations. The development of manufacturing and trade argue for the existence of a 'burgher' class, at least in Lower Nubia, even if we have no very direct archaeological evidence of it.

Insofar as we can perceive, in the early medieval scene, a social rank

501

intermediate between the monarchy and the unchanging peasantry, it seems to be represented by the clergy. Here we have an obvious parallel with western Europe, where the economic and political influence of the church was strong indeed at the beginning of the Middle Ages. This was not simply a matter of ideological supremacy; it reflects the fact that after the break-up of classical society the church was often left as the only organized body with sufficient wealth and power to engage in many kinds of corporate enterprise which had once been in governmental or private hands. Yet the situation in Nubia was not wholly analogous, and we cannot accept *a priori* the suggestion that the Nubian clergy also occupied the traditional roles of the middle class. What, in fact, were the role and influence of the Nubian church in secular affairs? Was the gathering of local taxes delegated primarily to the clergy? Were they involved, administratively or financially, in the organization of production and trade? Unfortunately neither archaeology nor history provides us with direct answers. The best we can do is consider what we do know about the medieval Nubian economy, and what part the church could potentially have played in it.

It is clear both from historical and from archaeological evidence that small-scale farming continued to provide the basis of subsistence in medieval Nubia.[220] There is nothing to suggest that the crops or the methods were different from those of earlier times, although the growth of population and the expansion of settlements indicate that a great deal of new land was brought under cultivation in the Christian period. This was particularly true in the cataract regions, which may have absorbed a considerable part of the population overflow from Lower Nubia. Here massive retaining walls of stone were needed to protect the meagre alluvial resources from being carried away by periodic floods; the whole of the *Batn el Hajar* is criss-crossed by such walls, apparently built originally in the Christian period.[221] The Nubian farmers kept cattle and sheep in small numbers as before, and pig bones also appear in quantities for the first time in sites of the medieval period.[222]

Presumably each of the Nubian monasteries was endowed with landed estates sufficient for its support. Aside from these, however, we have no clearcut evidence either of feudal tenure or of manorial enterprise in the earlier medieval period. The pattern of settlements and fields suggests rather that most of the land was in small familial holdings devoted to subsistence crops, as it is today. To the extent that the state and the church benefited from agriculture, therefore, it must have been chiefly through the levying of taxes on land (and perhaps also on animals and irrigation devices) rather than through direct enterprise. Unfortunately we know nothing about systems of taxation in medieval Nubia. All land belonged in theory to the king, but whether the church regularly imposed tithes in addition to the royal levy, or whether the exclusive right of taxation on particular lands was granted to ecclesiastical establishments (as it was in Europe and also in neighbouring Abyssinia[223]) we are unable to say. We can only observe that the prosperity exhibited by the earlier Nubian churches must have had some basis in the local economy, and speculate that perhaps the clergy served as tax collectors both for themselves and for the king, or received royal endowments in other forms.

As we noted earlier, there is nothing to suggest that the Nubian monasteries were centres of manufacturing and commercial enterprise in any way comparable to some of the Egyptian and European monasteries. Each monastery was, however, presumably engaged in the production of various kinds of manufactured goods needed by the members themselves, and there is evidence that the products at least in some cases were exported beyond the walls. We recall that the pottery factory at Faras began in what appears to have been a monastery; although after a time the buildings ceased to have any religious function, there is no reason why the enterprise should not have remained under ecclesiastical control. Perhaps the profits accrued to one of the many Faras churches, or to the nearby monastery of Qasr el-Wizz.[224] This continuing affiliation might explain the close parallels between Classic Christian pottery decoration and church decoration.

Arab writers make occasional mention of vineyards, especially in the southern part of Lower Nubia. We noted also that the Faras potters specialized for a time in the production of commercial amphorae, which can only have been for wine. We have no other information about medieval Nubian wine production, but viticulture is an enterprise requiring a considerable amount of communal effort, and for that reason has been regularly associated with monasteries both in Egypt and in Europe.[225] There is thus some *a priori* probability that the vineyards of Nubia were also under monastic control, particularly since they were concentrated in the area where monasteries are best attested.

Except in the cases of decorated pottery and, inferentially, of wine, we have very little evidence of specialized manufacturing or internal trade in medieval Nubia. Basketry, matting and handmade pottery seem hardly to have been involved in commerce, at least until the Late Christian period. For the most part they were produced for home consumption by the women in every part of the country. Ironmongery, leatherwork, carpentry, and the making of pots for use on the *saqia* were presumably more specialized occupations, but there must have been practitioners of these trades in all of the more important population centres. This is specifically attested in the case of *saqia* pots; remains of kilns which produced nothing else have been found in many places.[226] There is no reason to suppose that such enterprises were organized or controlled either by the church or by the state, though taxes were presumably levied upon them by one or both agencies.

It is apparent both from archaeological evidence and from the provisions of the *Baqt* treaty that international trade was an important factor in the medieval Nubian economy, as it was in all of the prosperous periods of Nubian history. However, both the volume and the variety of imported goods fluctuated considerably from century to century. The chief Nubian demand in the Early Christian period, as in Ballana times, seems to have been for wine.[227] Because of the scarcity of imported goods other than wine amphorae, sites of the early Middle Ages are apt to give an impression of poverty which is perhaps not wholly justified; it would be more accurate to say that the Nubians at this time preferred consumable to non-consumable luxuries.

After the eighth century there was a drastic reduction in the volume of wine importation, perhaps because the Caliph al-Mutasim specifically forbade the inclusion of wine in the *Baqt* exchange.[228] (It was at about the same time that the large-scale production of amphorae began at Faras, which suggests the possibility that the Nubians took up viticulture to compensate for the loss of their foreign supplies.[229]) Foreign trade seems to have remained at a low ebb during the earlier part of the Classic Christian period, during which time indigenous Nubian manufactures were in full flower. Then, concurrently with the cessation of pottery manufacture at Faras, imported pottery and glass began flooding into Nubia. Between A D 1050 and 1150 cheap, mass-produced vessels made at Aswan were as common in Lower Nubian sites as were local products. It is an interesting fact that these wares have been found more abundantly in Nubia than in Egypt, suggesting the possibility that they were made primarily for the Nubian market. After the twelfth century their numbers declined somewhat, but the place of the decorated vessels was partly taken by glazed wares from Lower Egypt. Imported cooking pots from Aswan remained popular until the end of the Christian period.[230] Less common but still conspicuous in the archaeological remains of Christian Nubia are luxury goods of bronze, ivory, and ebony, all apparently of Egyptian manufacture. Also prominently mentioned in historical accounts, and sometimes found archaeologically, are all kinds of Islamic woven goods.

So far as we can determine, the church took no hand in Nubia's international trade. The accounts of Ibn Selim and other writers leave no doubt that the import trade in Lower Nubia was chiefly in the hands of Moslem entrepreneurs, who, after the ninth century, were allowed to travel and to settle freely in the northern part of the country. (Presumably it was these individuals who have left us the Arabic tombstones described in an earlier section,[231] as well as a great many of the Arabic commercial documents that have been found at Qasr Ibrim.[232]) Under their aegis Lower Nubia developed a monetary economy, perhaps for the first time in its history. On the other hand trade beyond the Second Cataract remained exclusively a royal monopoly and, according to Ibn Selim, was still conducted entirely by barter. This may partially explain why imported goods are so much rarer south of the Second Cataract than they are in Lower Nubia.

The principal commodity which Nubia exchanged for Egyptian wine, pottery, and luxury goods was slaves. How and by whom the slave trade was organized, and what part it played in the medieval Nubian economy, are among the most important unanswered questions in later Nubian history. The annual *Baqt* quota of 400 slaves was evidently made up chiefly of captives of war, for in the ninth century the Nubians complained that their inability to obtain enough prisoners was obliging them to deliver their own children into slavery.[233] It would be interesting indeed to know who were the victims of medieval Nubian slave-raiding. The Christian kingdom of Alwa lay between Dongola and the traditional slaving-ground of the southern Sudan, so that it is unlikely that the Makourians were able to turn in that direction as a source of slaves. More probably slaves were obtained either from the Beja tribes of the Red Sea Hills or from the Negro peoples of Kordofan and Darfur, west of the Nile. In any case the scale of military operations must have been considerable, and this suggests (as do the terms of the *Baqt* treaty) that slave-dealing was not only a state enterprise, but perhaps the economic mainstay of the medieval Nubian crown. However, we are also told that there was a certain amount of private slave-dealing, at least in Lower Nubia.[234]

In the purely economic sphere, the *Baqt* treaty probably had more influence on the course of Nubian history than had the introduction of Christianity. If the Nubians were not already experienced slave-raiders, the necessity of delivering an annual quota of 400 souls soon turned them in that direction. As a result, their exclusive dependence on their riverain environment came to an end. As the centuries passed they were forced to mount larger and larger efforts, and to look farther and farther afield, for a commodity needed not merely for the sake of luxury trade, but to secure their continued independence from Islamic domination. By the end of the Middle Ages, Nubians were recognized as the principal middle-men in the Nile slave trade, and great numbers of able-bodied men probably turned from farming to slave-raiding as a lucrative source of live-lihood. In the fifteenth century there were already Nubian slave-dealers in Cairo,[235] and the great outburst of slaving which followed the Egyptian conquest of the Sudan in 1821 was largely organized and directed by Dongolawi Nubians.[236] Nubia ceased, under these circumstances, to be a distinct economic province; its later history can only be understood in terms of a growing interdependence with the rest of the Sudan.[237]

Any summary of the social and economic characteristics of medieval

Nubian civilization must begin, as so often in the past, by distinguishing between Lower Nubia and Upper Nubia. In the north we seem to perceive a relatively free society and economy, comprised of Government (represented by the eparch as well as vassal kings), private entrepreneurs (mostly Moslems) and Nubian peasants. The church probably performed some of the functions of local government, and also engaged on a small scale in manufacturing and trade. In Upper Nubia, on the other hand, we can so far perceive only the age-old division between rulers and ruled, with the government monopolizing international trade and probably deriving its principal revenues therefrom. What part the church played in the Upper Nubian scheme remains to be determined; it is sufficient for now to notice that the churches of Upper Nubia were not nearly so numerous or so wealthy as were those in the north.

INTERPRETATIVE SUMMARY

The opening of the Middle Ages witnessed, in rapid succession, two events of profound significance for Nubian history. The first was the introduction of Christianity in the latter part of the sixth century; the second was the fall of Egypt and neighbouring countries to the armies of Islam less than a hundred years later. Nubia thus embraced the faith of the civilized West just in time to be cut off from the rest of Christendom by the Islamic onslaught, and throughout the Middle Ages was obliged to maintain a sometimes perilous neutrality during the long confrontation between East and West.

The advent of Christianity wrought an ideological transformation in Nubia unparalleled since the coming of civilization itself. Within a matter of generations and even years the traditions of the pharaohs, which for 2,500 years had stood as the touchstones of civilization, were discarded in favour of new symbolic orientations. Royal tombs and temples, vainglorious proclamations, glyptic art, mortuary furniture, and the belief in the divinity of kings all disappeared as if overnight, and were replaced by new canons of faith, of art, and of literature.

The Christianity of medieval Nubia was not the Catholic faith of Western Europe but the parochial and inward-looking Christianity of the Egyptian Coptic Church. It was considered heretical by both Rome and Constantinople, and after the seventh century the church in Egypt was compelled in addition to accept the status of a minority religion within the Empire of Islam. In spite of these restrictions Christianity proved a fertile source of literary and artistic inspiration; throughout the Middle Ages nearly all of the symbolic expressions of Nubian civilization derived from its Christian faith. So dominant is the heavenly king in the medieval Nubian ideology that it is hard to find much information about earthly kings and their doings.

The social and economic life of Nubia seems to have developed smoothly and without serious interruption during the earlier part of the Christian period. The monarchy which had been established in Lower Nubia in the Ballana period persisted for a time after the introduction of Christianity, and was then absorbed into a larger state which had its capital at Dongola. The political centre of gravity thus shifted back to Upper Nubia, but the northern region remained in the forefront of economic and cultural development until the end of the Middle Ages.

The Christian kingdom of Makouria, with its capital at Dongola, persisted at least until the fourteenth century. Its frontiers extended from Aswan in the north to and perhaps beyond the Fifth Cataract in the south. Beyond it, in the steppelands of the central Sudan, was another kingdom, Alwa, about which we know very little. Lower Nubia remained under the control of Makouria until the end of the Middle Ages, but after the ninth century it was given a special status as a kind of free-trade zone between Christian Nubia and Moslem Egypt. Here foreign merchants were allowed to travel and settle, goods were freely exchanged, and money was in circulation. As a result the Lower Nubians seem to have enjoyed a considerably higher standard of living than did their southern neighbours. Town life was more highly developed in the north, churches were more numerous and richer, and medieval art and literature also seem to have reached their peak of development in Lower Nubia. In the meantime Upper Nubia was more directly and perhaps more oppressively governed by its king, and trade remained a royal monopoly. In sum, Lower Nubia seems to have witnessed something like a revival of the urban civilization of late Meroitic times, while Upper Nubia was characterized, as in so many earlier ages, by a court civilization.

The Islamic conquest of Egypt in 640–42 was followed almost immediately by an invasion of Nubia. However, the Moslems were unable to gain a foothold in the south, and after a couple of indecisive actions a truce, the *Baqt*, was concluded which remained in force for 600 years. Under its terms the Nubians were to deliver to Egypt an annual quota of slaves, and were to receive in exchange various Egyptian manufactured goods.

The *Baqt* treaty had an enormous influence on subsequent Nubian history. For 600 years it freed Nubia from the threat of Islamic conquest, and thus made possible the prosperous and largely peaceful civilization of the Classic Christian period. At the same time it institutionalized trade relations with the Islamic world, and probably contributed to the prosperity of both Egypt and Nubia. In the end, however, it encouraged and perhaps forced the Nubians to turn more and more from their traditional agricultural and economic pursuits to slave-raiding, and thus opened a new era in Nubian history which will be more fully discussed in later chapters.

16

THE FEUDAL AGE

THE DECLINE AND FALL OF THE CHRISTIAN
MONARCHIES

The heyday of medieval civilization, as described in the last chapters, represents one of the most brightly lighted pages in Nubian history. Ibn Selim, Abu Salih, and other observers have left us a picture of prosperous and well-ordered kingdoms, living generally on good terms with one another and with their Moslem neighbours. Then, abruptly, a shadow falls over the scene. For a hundred years after Abu Salih the historical record is silent; when the story is resumed, late in the thirteenth century, it is a sadly altered Nubia which meets our eye. The kingdom of Alwa has all but dropped from view, while Makouria is clearly tottering towards its fall. The later Arabic sources provide a melancholy record of almost continual dynastic intrigues and factional warfare, culminating in 1323 with the accession of a Moslem prince to the historic throne of Dongola. Within a matter of decades the northern Nubian kingdom, which had preserved its integrity since pre-Christian times, disintegrated into a collection of warring principalities. Ibn Khaldun, the greatest historian of the Middle Ages, seemingly wrote a fitting epitaph for the civilization of Christian Nubia early in the fourteenth century:

Their kingdom was torn in pieces and the Juheina Arabs took possession of their country. No kingly government or policy was possible by reason of the ruination which prevented any union between the princes and split them into factions at this time. Not a trace of kingly authority remained in the country, and the people are now become bedouins, following the rains about as they do in Arabia.[1]

Various causes have been sought for the decline and ultimate disappearance of the Nubian kingdoms. Ibn Khaldun laid the blame squarely upon the bedouins, a people whom he despised as hereditary enemies of civilization and learning.[2] Other writers have pointed to the increasing militancy of Egypt under Mameluke rule, or to the depredations committed by Arabized Nubians within the northern province of Maris, or to the combined action of these various agents of Islam. Nearly all writers are agreed, however, that the fate of the Nubian kingdoms was sealed once they were surrounded and infiltrated by Moslem peoples; since the time of Ibn Khaldun the shadow which darkens the later history of Nubia has generally been recognized as the shadow of Islam.

The evidence now available, including a great deal which has come to light in the last ten years, suggests that this traditional view of Nubia's post-Christian history is not entirely accurate. Historical texts shed only a feeble and intermittent light on the last centuries of the Christian period, and we may never know precisely when and why the Nubians abandoned the faith which they had stoutly defended for more than seven hundred years. It seems apparent, however, that the influence of a rival faith was only one of a number of disruptive forces which were at work in late medieval Nubia. It is also apparent that the Christian religion persisted long after the fall of the Christian monarchy, at least in the north, while evidence of the widespread practice of Islam is not found until a still later date. Certainly there was never a political showdown between the two faiths, and the traditional view of a cause-and-effect relationship between the coming of Islam and the disappearance of Christianity is a considerable oversimplification. It seems better, in fact, to consider the two processes independently. In this chapter we shall be concerned with the events and processes leading to the final extinction of Nubian Christianity; in the next we shall consider the spread of Islam in the post-Christian period.

Contemporary documents leave no doubt that the medieval Nubian kingdoms were in a state of disarray long before they were seriously threatened from abroad, and that the causes of their decline were only partly external. The monarchies were, by the thirteenth century, more than six hundred years old, and they were obviously beginning to show signs of political senility. The Nubian church, too, had become increasingly aloof from everyday affairs and had lost much of its popular appeal, as we saw in Chapter 15. Meanwhile its support from abroad was weakened by the persecutions launched against the church in Egypt under the Mameluke régime. Finally, we have to recognize the growing volume of trans-Saharan caravan trade in West Africa, which probably cut further into Nubia's ever-diminishing share of the trade in gold, ivory and slaves.

At the same time that traditional sources of power and authority were decaying we can perceive in late medieval Nubia the growing influence of a new ideology which was neither Christian nor Islamic. This was the spirit of military feudalism which, by the twelfth century, had already wrought a major transformation upon the societies of Europe and the Near East. Although frequently making common cause with religion, the feudal order was at bottom a secular one; the authority of the military aristocracies rested not upon holy scripture but upon a complex structure of legal and contractual obligations. Their concern, moreover, was for security and order in this world, not for salvation in the next. As that concern came to be shared by a large part of the medieval world, the church- and mosque-centred societies of earlier times gave place to the castle-centred societies of the high Middle Ages.

Although the evidence is largely inferential, it seems certain that an ideological transformation of this kind took place in the society of late medieval Nubia. Probably its inspiration came originally from the Crusades – the crucible in which were forged and perfected the military technologies and the militaristic ideology of the Middle Ages.[3] From here their influence spread, in time, over most of the civilized world. The Nubians took no direct part in the holy wars, and we cannot even be certain where their sympathies lay, but we can hardly doubt that they were keen observers of the conflict and were much influenced by it.

The specific event which triggered the growth of a feudal order in Nubia may have been the invasion of Shams ed-Dawla in 1172 – itself a by-product of the Crusades (cf. Ch. 14). It was the first concerted military operation against the Nubians in more than five centuries, and seems to have awakened in them a concern for their collective security which is not at all evident in the earlier Christian period. At just about this time we can observe the first appearance of the stoutly built, defensively oriented Late Christian houses (Ch. 15), and thereafter an increasing development and elaboration of military architecture at the expense of ecclesiastical architecture. At the end of the Middle Ages the castle had supplanted both the church and the mosque as a symbol of authority to an extent unparalleled in any European or Near Eastern country.

We have, then, to lay aside the traditional designations 'Christian' and 'Islamic' and to name Nubia's late medieval period as a feudal age. It began well before the final disappearance of Nubian Christianity, and continued long afterwards. Only gradually, in the vacuum left by the dissolution of an organized church, did the traditions of Islam come to form the basis of the Nubians' world view. In the meantime the leitmotiv of their civilization was provided neither by Christianity nor by Islam, but by the secular and militaristic spirit of the feudal age. Because the clearest indication of this development is to be found in the archaeological remains of late medieval Nubia, we shall consider their evidence first.

THE EVIDENCE OF ARCHAEOLOGY

We know less about the archaeology of the feudal age than of any earlier period since the Napatan. In none of the Nubian salvage campaigns was any provision made for the investigation of 'Islamic' remains, and many potentially informative sites were by-passed as a result. In great multiphase sites like Qasr Ibrim and Gebel Adda, and in some of the pharaonic fortresses which were reoccupied in the Middle Ages, the main attention of archaeologists was understandably given to the remains of the earlier periods, and those of the Middle Ages were rather summarily dealt with. There is, in any case, a conspicuous paucity of late medieval sites in Lower Nubia, a fact which we will discuss further in a moment.

The picture is somewhat brighter in the *Batn el Hajar*, where late sites are both numerous and well preserved. Most of our knowledge of architectural developments in the feudal age comes in fact from this area, and particularly from a group of sites which were excavated in the last years of the High Dam salvage campaign. South of Dal we have, as usual, almost no specific archaeological information. Although the feudal age found its climactic expression in the castles of the Dongola Reach, all of them are still awaiting the attention of the archaeologist. The generalizations which are made in these pages can therefore be applied with confidence only to Lower Nubia and the *Batn el Hajar*.

The Late Christian period quite obviously witnessed one of the major demographic shifts in Nubian history. In Lower Nubia town-sites are larger but at the same time far less numerous than at any time since the reoccupation of the region a thousand years earlier. Of the widely scattered settlements of the Classic Christian period, only a handful show signs of occupation after the twelfth century. Much of the Lower Nubian population perhaps left the district altogether; those who remained clustered together in a few protected localities. As a result it may be said that Lower Nubian society reached its peak of urbanization under the uncertain conditions of the feudal age.

An Arabic manuscript of the thirteenth century lists no more than seven major settlements between the First and Second Cataracts: Amada, Daw (? Gebel Adda), Qasr Ibrim, Adindan, Faras, Serra (?), and Meinarti (Fig. 78).[4] Of these, Faras, the one-time provincial capital, was in a sadly reduced condition, its cathedral filled with sand and its episcopal functions apparently removed to Qasr Ibrim.[5] Meinarti remained as before a fairly small island settlement at the foot of the Second Cataract, although now invested with important administrative functions. Serra was a new community, huddled within the long-abandoned walls of the Middle Kingdom fortress.[6] It boasted no fewer than four churches, all of the tiny Late Christian type, suggesting that a group of previously scattered settlements had drawn together for protection but had chosen to retain their separate congregational identities. The hilltop fortresses of Qasr Ibrim and Gebel Adda remained the principal centres of power and authority, as they had been intermittently since Meroitic times. Both of them are mentioned repeatedly in the political and military annals of the feudal age. In these places, as at Serra, it would appear that a large civil populace came to cluster for protection within and beneath the older fortification walls.

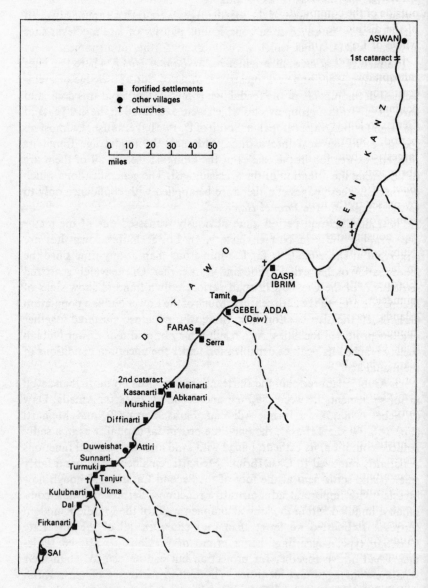

Fig. 78. Lower Nubia and the *Batn el Hajar* in the feudal age

Gebel Adda at the end of the Christian period counted at least seven churches,[7] and Qasr Ibrim four.[8] It is noteworthy, on the other hand, that outside of the communities just named no more than half a dozen churches of the distinctive Late Christian type (cf. Ch. 15) are to be found in the whole of Lower Nubia.[9]

In the *Batn el Hajar* a quite different picture confronts us. This rocky and inhospitable region, which had never before supported more than a scattering of tiny hamlets, is dotted over with remains of Late Christian communities both large and small. The preliminary reconnaissance from Gemai to Dal (Fig. 11) recorded more than 150 sites of the Late Christian period, comprising about 65 per cent of all the sites encountered.[10] The largest of them do not approach in size the great urban centres of Qasr Ibrim and Gebel Adda, but they far surpass anything previously seen in the *Batn el Hajar*. There can be little doubt that this poor and isolated region, by-passed by the main caravan routes of the Middle Ages, served as a major refuge for population fleeing from the political disturbances in the north.

A conspicuous feature of the Late Christian settlements both in Lower Nubia and in the *Batn el Hajar* is their defensive character. Many of them in fact bear a striking resemblance to the hill towns of late medieval Europe: settlements crowding up the sides and over the tops of rocky pinnacles. The topography of the *Batn el Hajar*, with its numerous rocky islands, was particularly well suited for the development of such communities, and more than a dozen of them could be seen between Gemai and Dal. One of the most spectacular was Diffinarti, an island village near Saras whose houses clung to every available ledge and boulder on the sides of a near-vertical pinnacle (Pl. XXIIa). The summit was crowned by a tiny church.[11] In the north, a similar appearance was presented by the hill forts of Gebel Adda and Qasr Ibrim (Pl. XVIb).

As we noted in Chapter 15, the only walled communities of the earlier Christian period were monasteries and perhaps a few caravanserais in the north. In the late period girdle walls were sometimes built around secular communities as well, but their use was never systematically adopted. At Serra, and perhaps on a smaller scale in some of the Second Cataract forts, the late Christians availed themselves of the still-standing girdle walls of pharaonic days, to which they made only minor repairs. At Gebel Adda and Qasr Ibrim the Meroitic fortifications were kept in repair, though much of the civil populace was obliged to huddle outside them. In the *Batn el Hajar*, however, a number of Late Christian communities surrounded themselves with stout fortification walls. Unlike the pharaonic and Meroitic fortifications, those of the medieval period were usually very irregular in shape, reflecting the broken nature of the terrain and also suggesting that the walls were often built later than the settlements they surrounded. One of the best-preserved examples of such a community was on the island of Sunnarti, where a dozen or more houses were enclosed within a massive dry-stone wall.[12] The enclosure, which was roughly triangular in shape, had projecting salients at the corners and was penetrated by a fortified double gateway (Fig. 79). Above and beyond the factor of isolation, however, it appears that most Nubians relied for protection not so much on collective defences as upon the fortified nature of their individual houses. This too probably says something about the character of late medieval society, to which we will return later.

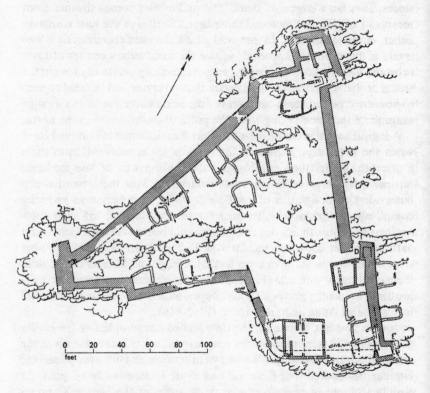

Fig. 79. Plan of Late Christian walled community, Sunnarti

We have already noted, in Chapter 15, the first appearance of the Late Nubian house type, apparently in the latter part of the twelfth century. In its earliest form it was little different from the Classic Christian house save for its much stouter construction and its structural independence of the surrounding buildings. Its basic components were a large room at the front, entered by a single door from the outside, one or more smaller rooms behind the front room, and a narrow, L-shaped passage leading behind the smaller rooms to a latrine at the back of the house.

514

Although this simplest form of Late Christian 'unit house' remained popular until the close of the Christian period, larger and more elaborate versions also made their appearance in the thirteenth and fourteenth centuries. Some houses were built with no lateral entrance to their inner rooms, which could only be reached by means of a hatchway from the roof. We have to assume in these cases that the inner rooms served no practical function in day-to-day activities, but were intended chiefly for the safe storage of the family's most valued possessions, including perhaps its grain stores. They were 'keeps' in embryonic form. The presence of such rooms meant, of course, that some other access to the roof was also necessary, either within or outside the house. Presumably retractable ladders were used for this purpose. Since the Late Christian houses were crowned with substantial brick vaults, capable of supporting any amount of weight, it seems probable that in time a good deal of everyday living activity came to be carried out on the roofs. This is suggested at all events by the parallel example of the Pueblos of North America.

A logical next step was the addition of an upper storey. We do not know when the two-storey unit house first made its appearance, but by the fourteenth century such buildings were to be found in most of the larger settlements of northern Nubia. Probably they were built in the south as well, but evidence from here is thus far lacking. The best preserved and most completely studied group of two-storey unit houses is to be found in the southern part of the *Batn el Hajar*, in the island communities of Kulubnarti and Dal.[13] In each of these places a few rather widely scattered two-storey buildings tower over a cluster of one-storey houses which surround them. Although they vary considerably in size, and no two of them are identical in plan, the two-storey houses all exhibit the same essential features. The typical Christian house plan, with front room, back room or rooms, passage, and latrine is reproduced on the upper floor, while the ground floor is devoted to vaulted storage cellars. The layout of these is often labyrinthine and seems designed to confuse anyone not intimately familiar with the house. A peculiarity of all of the two-storey houses at Kulubnarti, and of at least two of them at Dal, is the inclusion on the ground floor of a secret crypt, so cleverly concealed within the thickness of the adjoining walls that its presence is almost impossible to discover. A closely similar feature has been found also in a two-storey house at Qasr Ibrim.[14] The precise architectural details of the design and location of these intriguing crypts are not the same in any two cases: each represents a unique exercise in ingenuity.

The only external access to any of the two-storey houses at Kulubnarti and Dal was through a doorway at the level of the upper floor, which presumably was reached via a retractable ladder. The ground-floor chambers, though often as tall as those on the upper floor, could be reached only by means of overhead hatchways from the living quarters above. Sometimes all of the lower rooms were interconnected, so that a single hatchway would provide access to all of them; in other cases there might be two or three unconnected chambers or groups of chambers, each requiring its own hatchway from above. In addition to the main ground-floor cellars, small crypts occupied the interstices between their vaulted ceilings (cf. Fig. 80), and these too were reached by means of hatchways from the living quarters above.

The defensive character of Late Christian domestic architecture is obvious enough, and seems to find its fullest expression in the two-storey unit houses. Above and beyond practical considerations of security, however, it is difficult to escape the impression that these buildings represent a well-developed architectural genre which was elaborated in part for its own sake. This is suggested in particular by the houses at Kulubnarti and Dal, with their recurring and obviously deliberate variations on a set theme. Each represents a specific exercise in creative originality within rigidly formal limits. It seems probable too that the buildings in the upper *Batn el Hajar* and perhaps elsewhere were the work of a group of professional architects. They may have been Nubians or, as in so many other periods in Nubian history, they may have been immigrants from Egypt; it seems certain in either case that they drew a little of their inspiration from the complex and ingenious castle architecture of the European and Near Eastern feudal age.[15]

The two-storey houses which occur in places like Serra,[16] Kulubnarti and Dal, scattered among a much larger number of less pretentious structures, probably represent simply the 'de luxe' houses of the late medieval period – the first re-emergence of the house as a status symbol since Meroitic times. In some of the smaller villages of the cataract region, however, a somewhat different interpretation is suggested. At Meinarti,[17] Abkanarti,[18] Kasanarti,[19] and a number of places farther south[20] there was only a single two-storey structure, substantially larger than any other building in the village and occupying an especially prominent location. A conspicuous example was the 'blockhouse' which dominated the Meinarti mound in Late Christian times: it measured nearly fifty feet on a side, and its exterior walls were more than three feet thick. The plan was labyrinthine, with concealed chambers and a number of vaults which could only be entered after ascending the roof through a series of tortuous passages.[21] It seems unlikely that such buildings were intended only as private residences, although such they certainly were. Probably they served also, however, as places of refuge for the whole community and its goods in time of strife – the local grandee offering protection to his poor and perhaps dependent neighbours. Here, then, we can recognize the genesis of the Nubian castle, and perhaps also of a feudal order.

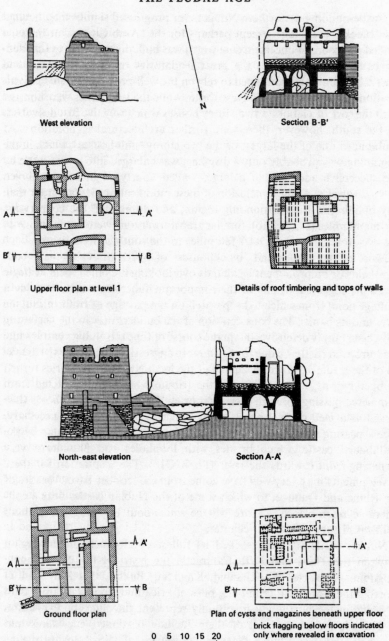

West elevation

Section B-B'

Upper floor plan at level 1

Details of roof timbering and tops of walls

North-east elevation

Section A-A'

Ground floor plan

Plan of cysts and magazines beneath upper floor
brick flagging below floors indicated
only where revealed in excavation

0 5 10 15 20
feet

Fig. 80. Plans and elevations of late medieval castle, Kulubnarti

517

Castle-building in northern Nubia never progressed significantly beyond the 'blockhouse' stage, except perhaps for the 'Arab Citadel' at Faras, a walled enclosure of uncertain date which was built directly atop the sanded-up cathedral.[22] Elsewhere the great feudatories of Late Christian and post-Christian times continued to rely on the well-preserved Meroitic fortifications at Gebel Adda and Qasr Ibrim, while the lesser ones were content with the sort of elaborate two-storey houses which we have just described. In the south, however, there were further architectural elaborations. At Kulubnarti one of the largest of the two-storey 'unit houses', which in the beginning was probably only a dwelling, was enlarged into a true castle by the successive additions of a large, walled courtyard and a loopholed bastion tower.[23] At the conclusion of these modifications it was larger than any building in the surrounding region, and dominated the countryside for many miles (Pl. XXIIb). Similar transformations were made in one of the two-storey houses at Dal, a few miles to the south of Kulubnarti.

Most of the castles and 'blockhouses' of northern Nubia were built on islands or on prominent headlands overlooking the Nile. Their strategic locations suggest that one of their important functions was to provide a vantage point from which to keep watch on the passage of traffic along the river and its banks. The consideration of the builders may in the beginning have been purely defensive, but in the course of time the Nubian castle – like the European castle – came to play a more aggressive role. After the break-up of the medieval kingdoms many of the local Nubian feudatories turned 'robber baron', living chiefly on the tribute which they extracted from commerce passing through their territories. Their island strongholds then served as armed control points from which to menace and, if necessary, attack passing boats and caravans. This is suggested in particular by the Kulubnarti castle, which bristles with loopholes and presents a very menacing front towards the river (Pl. XXIIb). The inspiration for these developments may very well have come from the 'robber baron' castles of the Rhine and Danube, to which some of the Nubian castles bear a considerable resemblance.[24] More will be said about this stage of Nubia's political history in the next chapter.

Nubian castle-building reached its fullest development in the region between the Third and Fifth Cataracts: the heart of the old Dongola kingdom. At places like Khannaj, Khandaq, Bakhit,[25] El Kab, and El Korro[26] there are vast, crumbling piles of brick and stone, far larger than anything in the north, which certainly represent the climactic expression of Nubia's feudal age. All of them include bastioned enclosures and conspicuous towers, but a detailed knowledge of their architecture as well as of their history will have to await systematic excavation. For the moment none of the Upper Nubian castles has even been carefully surveyed.

Tradition attributes the Upper Nubian castles to the Funj (post-Christian) period, when they undoubtedly achieved their maximum development and importance. It seems certain, however, that their origins go back to Christian times, for in at least two cases there are churches near by which seem to be coeval with the fortifications.[27] It is worth quoting, in this connection, the account of the Kingdom of Alwa left by the sixteenth-century missionary Francisco Alvares: 'Their churches are all in old ancient castles which there are throughout the country, and as many castles as there are, so many churches do they have.'[28]

The evidence just cited would suggest that in Upper Nubia the church continued to flourish in the earlier part of the feudal age, and presumably enjoyed the protection of the feudal nobles. This was not uniformly the case in the north. In Lower Nubia and the *Batn el Hajar* there is a conspicuous decline in ecclesiastical building concurrent with, and presumably in part because of, the growing preoccupation with military architecture. The Late Christian churches were at best small and simple in design (Fig. 72), and they became increasingly so with the passage of time.[29] Concurrently with their introduction, moreover, most of the older and more elaborate churches were abandoned and allowed to fall into ruin, as were nearly all of the known monasteries. Some of the last churches to be built in Nubia, at Diffinarti and Abd el Qadir, can only be described as minute; in their original form they measured barely more than 16 feet on a side, and cannot have held more than a dozen persons.[30] In both these churches the traditional arrangement of three eastern rooms (cf. Ch. 15) gave way to a single transverse sanctuary chamber – a feature harking all the way back to the prototype churches of the sixth or seventh century.[31]

A remarkable feature of many late Nubian churches is their physical separation from the community. As we saw in the last chapter, most Nubian churches after the seventh century were located at the edge of settlements, so as to allow space for the growth of cemeteries. Many of the churches built after the twelfth century, however, were far removed from the nearest houses. Several of the late churches at Gebel Adda[32] and Qasr Ibrim were situated well away from the settlements, whereas those of the early period had been directly in the middle of the town. The churches which served the island communities of Meinarti[33] and Kasanarti[34] at the end of the Christian period were situated on the west bank of the Nile, not on the islands with their parishioners. At Kulb and Kulubnarti[35] too, the late churches were situated at an unnecessarily far remove from the villages. On the other hand the hill towns of Diffinarti and Attiri[36] were each crowned by a tiny church built on the topmost pinnacle of the island, around and below which the ordinary houses clustered. It would appear that some of the Late Christians wished to gather as closely as possible around their church, while others tried to dissociate themselves from it. These different reactions probably have some social significance, which will be discussed further in later pages ('The twilight of Christianity', below).

As I have hinted many times before in this book, I believe that monumental architecture may often provide one of the most sensitive indicators of the self-image and the world-view of a people. This is true in the feudal age no less than in earlier times. The stoutly independent 'unit houses', the 'blockhouses' and the castles may have found their justification in immediate political conditions, but they may too have been as much the cause as the effect of a decaying central polity. At all events they must be seen, in the largest sense, as an expression of the spirit of their times. I have already suggested that the two-storey 'unit house' represents an architectural *genre* elaborated for its own sake, and the true castle marks a further step in the same direction. By the end of the Christian period it had entirely supplanted the church as the medium in which Nubia's builders and rulers sought to express their creative ingenuity. In late medieval Europe the castle always vied with the cathedral as the paramount symbol of its age; in Nubia it stood unrivalled. There is at least allegorical significance in the fact that when the magnificent cathedral of Faras became filled with sand it was overbuilt not with another church but with a fortified citadel,[37] while at Meinarti the formidable 'blockhouse' of the Terminal Christian period was similarly built upon the sanded-up remains of the monastery. The Christian faith was not officially dead, for the 'blockhouse' was adorned with a Christian invocatory text,[38] but the other-worldly spirit which had informed the lives and inspired the architecture of the earlier medieval period was certainly dead.[39]

If monumental architecture provides a measure of a people's aspirations, the development of the lesser arts more accurately reflects day-to-day social and economic conditions. Before leaving the evidence of archaeology, therefore, it is worthwhile briefly to consider the pottery and other material remains of the Late Christian and post-Christian periods. The native pottery industry, as we saw in Chapter 15, enjoyed a major revival in the twelfth century following its temporary eclipse in the later Classic Christian period. It continued to flourish for at least a century, and luxury pottery may actually have reached its peak of abundance at this time, though the forms and designs never quite recovered the elegance of the Classic period. We do not know where the pottery factories (or more probably a single factory, in view of the high standardization of the Late Christian wares) were located, but their products are abundantly distributed over the whole region from the Fourth Cataract to Aswan. This suggests the operation of a well-organized and far-flung trade network such as can only flourish in peaceful times. Imported luxuries such as glass, glazed ware and bronze were also notably common, at least at Meinarti, between about AD 1150 and 1250.[40] Evidently this opening century of the feudal age (for which historical records are entirely lacking) was one of continuing economic prosperity and social stability, even if the monarchies and the church were rapidly weakening. The incursion of Shams ed-Dawla in 1172 (Ch. 14), though it may have been the event which set Nubia on the road to feudalism, seems to have had no lasting effect on the flourishing trade with Egypt.

After 1250 the picture changes rapidly. There is an accelerating decline both in the quality and in the quantity of the Nubian wheel-made pottery. Many vessels of the Terminal Christian period (as I have elsewhere designated the last century or two of Nubian Christianity)[41] are almost grotesquely heavy and crude, lacking any of the earlier nuances of form and decoration. The extreme lack of standardization in these wares suggests too that a number of rival factories were contending for what was left of the luxury market, and there was no generally accepted stylistic canon.[42] The process of decline reached its climax either shortly before or shortly after the end of the Christian period, when the art of pottery-making on the wheel was given up altogether.[43] From then until the present day the demand for locally made pottery has been supplied by the hand-made products of the Nubian women, as it was in prehistoric times. The women potters seem at first to have made some effort to compensate for the disappearance of the wheel-made luxury wares; their products in the Terminal Christian and early post-Christian periods were more elaborately decorated than at any time before or since.[44] However, even this minor extravagance was soon given up in favour of severely utilitarian wares. For the last three or four centuries the people who once produced the elegant Meroitic and Classic Christian wares have made do with pottery which is neither technically nor artistically superior to that which their ancestors made at the dawn of history.

Equally remarkable is the disappearance of all kinds of imported goods in the later feudal age. Of the catalogued objects recovered from the late medieval site of Kulubnarti, fewer than 10 per cent were of foreign manufacture, and most of these probably date from the fairly recent past (eighteenth and nineteenth centuries). Among uncatalogued pot-sherds the percentage of imported wares is infinitesimal: a little over 600 sherds out of more than 200,000![45] It seems, then, that both manufacturing and commerce were brought virtually to a standstill by the political disturbances and economic dislocations of the feudal age. The Nubians could neither obtain manufactured goods from abroad, nor could they afford the fancier products of local artisans. Economic specialization dwindled to nothing, and Nubia reverted to something very close to the subsistence economy of much earlier days.

THE FEUDAL AGE IN EGYPT

Although archaeology furnishes a suggestive and, I believe, an accurate picture of changing social and cultural conditions in late medieval Nubia, we must of course turn to the evidence of history for a record of specific events leading up to the decline and dissolution of the medieval kingdoms. As we saw, the historical record is silent for the entire century between 1172 and 1268. Archaeology suggests that this was a time of continued peace and prosperity, and perhaps for that very reason Nubia failed to attract the notice of foreign observers. Then, between 1268 and 1323, we have an unusually detailed record of military alarums and excursions in the Dongola kingdom. Our sources are all Egyptian; the wealth of their information about events in the southern country is due to the fact that this was a half-century of almost continual Mameluke intervention in the affairs of Nubia. For the background of this development we must consider briefly the contemporary political scene in Egypt.

The Ayyubid dynasty of Egypt, founded by Salah ed-Din (Saladin) in 1171, had at first been opposed by the Nubians, as we saw in Chapter 14. Their intervention in Upper Egypt, ostensibly in support of the rival Fatimid caliph, had provoked the punitive raid of Shams ed-Dawla which culminated in the capture and sack of Qasr Ibrim.[46] Once the Ayyubids were firmly in control of Egypt, however, the Nubians seem quickly to have come to terms with them, for there is no further record of hostilities on either side during the remainder of the short-lived Ayyubid reign. The rulers who followed Salah ed-Din were in any case too weak and too pre-occupied with affairs at home to engage in military adventures in the south.

In AD 1250 the last of the Ayyubid sultans was murdered by members of his palace guard, the formidable Mamelukes. They were a corps of élite troops who served as the ruler's personal bodyguard and who were in fact legally his slaves. Their numbers were recruited by the purchase of child slaves, mostly from the Turkish and Christian populations of south-west Asia, who were then brought up as dedicated soldiers and fanatical Moslems. 'Slave armies' of this kind surrounded and theoretically protected a good many Moslem rulers in the Middle Ages; with their tight discipline and their lack of external ties they soon came to form the most cohesive and dependable military forces of their time. Not surprisingly they often became the real powers in their kingdoms and were able to make and unmake sultans at their pleasure, or even to seize the reins of power for themselves, as did the Mamelukes of Egypt in 1250.

The 'slave kings' were to govern Egypt for nearly six hundred years, first as independent rulers and then, after 1517, as vassals of the Ottoman emperor. Although many of them assumed the title of sultan, the Mamelukes never achieved a stable monarchy. They remained, as they had begun, a kind of acephalous military oligarchy in which rule went to the strongest either by informal consent or by trial of arms. Their numbers continued to be recruited primarily through the purchase of slaves rather than through inheritance, for theirs was an exclusively male society, and they were theoretically forbidden to marry outside it. In the words of a European historian:

> The only title to kingship among these nobles was personal prowess and the command of the largest number of adherents. In the absence of other influences the hereditary principle was no doubt adopted, and we even find one family . . . maintaining its succession to the throne for several generations; but as a rule the successor to the kingly power was the most powerful lord of the day, and his hold on the throne depended chiefly on the strength of his following and his conciliation of the other nobles. The annals of Mameluke dominion are full of instances of a great lord reducing the authority of the reigning sultan to a shadow, then stepping over his murdered body to the throne. Most of these sultans died violent deaths at the hands of rival emirs, and the safety of the ruler of the time depended mainly on the numbers and the courage of his guard.[47]

While the most powerful of the Mameluke nobles maintained a precarious rule in Cairo, lesser nobles were established by or in defiance of the government in provincial centres throughout the kingdom, where they kept up a virtually independent rule with the aid of slave armies of their own.[48] The period of Mameluke dominion, particularly before 1517, undoubtedly represents the climax of Egypt's own feudal age. This was the model of government which the northern country held up before the Nubians in the later Middle Ages, and its example does not seem to have been lost on them.

The Mameluke nobles typify the spirit of military feudalism. Trained as professional soldiers, and knowing no art but that of war, they had little understanding of statecraft and little appreciation for commerce. Their only lasting achievements, creditable as well as discreditable, were on the battlefield. In the north they expelled the last of the Crusaders from the Levant and also finally turned back the Mongol hordes, both during the first fifty years of their rule. During the same period, however, they made war continually upon one another and on any other convenient target for their aggression, both within and beyond their borders. Even when the sultan in Cairo was forced by considerations of prudence to adopt a conciliatory policy towards his neighbours, he was seldom able to control the military adventuring of the unruly lesser nobles.

Among the earliest victims of Mameluke intransigence were the Egyptian Christians, who were severely persecuted and saw many of their churches burned and looted. Yet the Arab nomad tribes, who themselves had once furnished Egypt's military élite, fared hardly better under Mameluke rule. They were excluded from any share in government and in the spoils of war, and in addition were saddled with heavy taxes to support the Mameluke campaigns in Syria. When the tribes which had settled in Upper Egypt revolted and refused to pay their taxes, they were attacked and harassed until many of them were forced to emigrate south, chiefly along the Red Sea Hills, into what is now the Sudan. Established within and along the fringes of the Dongola kingdom, they continued to threaten the security both of Nubia and of Upper Egypt.[49]

A particularly troublesome 'Arab' tribe during the Mameluke period were the Beni Kanz. Their origins can be traced to the migration of a part of the Rabi'a tribe from the Arabian peninsula to Upper Egypt in the early Middle Ages. Established in the Red Sea Hills, they intermarried extensively with the local Beja of the Hadariba tribe, with whom in time they completely amalgamated. As their numbers and influence grew they extended their control, at least intermittently, over Aswan and adjacent portions of the Nile Valley. In Fatimid times the leader of this combined Arab–Beja tribe was generally acknowledged as the *de facto* governor of Aswan. Much of the power of the Beni Kanz derived from their potential control of the caravan route between Upper Egypt and the Red Sea port of Aidhab, which in the Middle Ages was the main trans-shipment point for cargoes from the Indian Ocean and was also the chief port of embarkation for the pilgrimage to Mecca.[50]

In AD 1006 the ruling sheikh of the Beni Kanz assisted the Fatimid caliph in the capture of a political rival, and for this service he was rewarded with the title Kanz ed-Dawla ('treasure of the state'). The title became hereditary, and was assumed by every subsequent leader of the tribe. It was through this accident that the tribe as a whole came to be known as the Beni Kanz (more correctly Banu l-Kanz), or descendants of the Kanz ed-Dawla.[51]

By the late Fatimid period the Beni Kanz were sufficiently entrenched in Upper Egypt to challenge the authority of the central government, and an attack was launched against them in 1102 which resulted in the capture and execution of the then Kanz ed-Dawla. Hostilities broke out again in 1174 when the newly triumphant Ayyubids installed one of their own number as governor at Aswan, ignoring the traditional claim of the Kanz ed-Dawla. The Beni Kanz promptly killed the new appointee; in retaliation Salah ed-Din sent a major expedition which drove the insurgents out of Aswan and killed their leader. A good many of the refugees probably returned to their traditional habitat in the Red Sea Hills, but many who preferred a sedentary life in the river valley withdrew into the neighbouring portion of Nubia, immediately to the south of Aswan. As we saw in Chapter 14, this district had been legally open to settlement by Moslems since the ninth century.[52] The Beni Kanz soon intermarried with the local Nubian population and in time became partly Nubianized in language and culture, though they retained their Islamic faith. The result of this ethnic amalgam is the Kenzi (pl. Kanuz) Nubians who in modern times occupied the northernmost part of Nubia, between Aswan and Maharraqa.[53]

After their defeat in 1174 and their withdrawal into Nubia the Beni Kanz played no further part in Egyptian affairs for nearly two centuries. Their ambitions in the north were only temporarily dormant, for they broke out again strongly in the fourteenth century, as we shall observe later. In the meantime, however, they evidently became a force to be reckoned with in their new habitat. We have no record of events in Nubia during most of the thirteenth century, but by its end the Beni Kanz territory in the north seems to have been a quasi-independent Moslem principality,[54] and its leader, the Kanz ed-Dawla, was a figure of importance in the Nubian kingdom as a whole. He may even at times have held the traditional office of eparch ('Lord of the Mountain'[55]), though this is not clearly attested before the fourteenth century.[56] He was at all events the acknowledged leader of the growing Moslem element within the Kingdom of Makouria. Still more important, he and his family had become allied by marriage with the ruling house at Dongola itself – a sure sign that religious allegiance was no longer of paramount importance in the political sphere.[57] An alliance between the increasingly weak Christian kings and their increasingly strong Moslem vassals in the north was an obvious concession to political expediency.

Such was the chaotic political situation on the Nile at the close of the thirteenth century. The stage was set for a power struggle among three principal contenders: the ruling house at Dongola, the Mameluke sultans, and the Beni Kanz. Although their conflict was to rend and finally to destroy the Christian polity of Nubia, none of them was motivated primarily by religious considerations. The Dongola monarchs were anxious by any means to retain their weakening grip on power, and in the end were more attached to their throne than to their faith; the Mamelukes were equally anti-Christian and anti-Arab, and vacillated between a policy of wresting Nubia from the Christians and one of protecting Upper Egypt from the Beni Kanz; the Beni Kanz were on the lookout for any chance to enlarge their own interests, and were quite ready to ally themselves with either side for the purpose.[58] Once the feudal spirit was triumphant, the question of religious affiliation became almost incidental.

THE DECLINE AND FALL OF MAKOURIA

We may turn now to a consideration of the specific events which brought the Christian kingdom of Makouria to its end. Our information comes from four principal sources: Nuwairi (d. 1332), whose book of general knowledge includes an account of the Mameluke military campaigns in the south;[59] Mufaddal (c. 1340), who wrote a biography of the Mameluke Sultan Qalawun, one of the principal actors in the drama;[60] Ibn Khaldun (1332–1406), whose account of the final dissolution of the Christian kingdoms has already been quoted;[61] and Maqrizi (1364–1442), who wrote a number of important works on Egyptian history and geography.[62] The two last-named authors were among the foremost scholars of their age, but the history which they have left us seems to belong rather to the genre of medieval historical romance: an endless round of battles, massacres, and tortuous court intrigues. The profusion of character and incident – to say nothing of the frequent and precipitous coat-turnings – makes it almost impossible to distil from their pages a wholly coherent picture of personalities and events. Stripped to its essentials, and ignoring many contradictions and uncertainties, the story of the decline and fall of Makouria seems to run as follows:[63]

In 1268 a certain Nubian King Dawud (David), who had recently come to power by deposing his maternal uncle, sent a mission to Cairo seeking recognition from the Mameluke sultan, Bybars. The sultan replied somewhat inhospitably by demanding an immediate resumption of the *Baqt* payment, which had apparently been neglected for a long time. The Nubian king made no immediate response to this demand; four years later (in 1272) he expressed his resentment by attacking and plundering the Red Sea port of Aidhab, one of the mainstays of Egypt's commercial prosperity. The Mameluke governor of Upper Egypt then sent a punitive force into Lower Nubia which captured a large number of prisoners, including the Lord of the Mountain, who were later executed in Cairo.

In 1275 a Nubian Prince Shekenda, another claimant to the Dongola throne, appeared in Cairo to ask for the help of the Mamelukes in overthrowing his cousin Dawud. The sultan evidently welcomed this invitation to intervene in the political affairs of Nubia, and provided Shekenda with a sizeable force. The expedition entered Lower Nubia in January 1276, and after some opposition the fortress of Daw (? Gebel Adda) and the island of Meinarti were occupied. At this point the new Lord of the Mountain threw in his lot with the invaders, swearing an oath of fealty to the insurgent prince Shekenda and adding his own forces to those provided by the Egyptians. Presumably the Beni Kanz also joined the expeditionary force at this time, if they had not in fact done so from the beginning.

The expedition proceeded on to Upper Nubia, where the decisive engagement took place before Dongola in April 1276. The defending force was routed and King Dawud fled south to el-Abwab (presumably then, as before, the northern frontier district of the kingdom of Alwa), leaving most of his family behind as prisoners in the hands of the Mamelukes.

Shekenda was then installed as King of Makouria, but the price exacted by the Mamelukes in exchange for their support was a steep one. The new king swore an oath of fealty to the Mameluke sultan which made Nubia in effect a vassal state of Egypt. The Nubian people were offered the three choices which were traditionally held out to the inhabitants of conquered territories: to embrace Islam, to perish by the sword, or to pay an annual head tax (*jizya*) to their overlords. Choosing the third alternative, the Nubians thenceforth paid to Cairo an annual tax of one dinar for each adult citizen. The king himself agreed to send annually three giraffes, five she-leopards, a hundred swift camels, and four hundred oxen. In addition to this tribute it is presumed that the regular provisions of the *Baqt* also remained in force. Most important of all, the province of Maris (formerly Nobatia; i.e. Lower Nubia and the *Batn el Hajar*) was handed over to direct Mameluke control, its revenues to be paid to Cairo and the Lord of the Mountain becoming in effect a vassal of the sultan rather than of the Nubian king.[64] However, none of these provisions appear to have remained in force for any length of time.

After installing Shekenda on the throne the Mameluke armies withdrew to Cairo, taking with them as hostages a number of Nubian princes, some of whom were potential claimants to the throne. The fugitive King Dawud himself arrived in June 1276, having been captured and sent as a prisoner in chains by the king of el-Abwab (? Alwa), in whose domains he had sought refuge.

Shekenda evidently did not enjoy the favour of the Mamelukes for very long, for, some time after his accession, he was murdered by an assassin in the pay of the Egyptian sultan, and a king named Barak took the throne. He too proved unsatisfactory to his nominal overlords, and was deposed and killed by an expedition sent against him. The throne then passed to a certain Prince Shemamun, who may have been one of the hostages taken to Cairo in 1276.

Shemamun seems to have been a man for his times – cunning and un-scrupulous, and in the end able to beat the Mamelukes at their own game of political intrigue. For a dozen years or more he played hide-and-seek with them, defying their authority from a distance and retreating prudently out of reach whenever a force was sent to punish him. Twice he was deposed by Mameluke armies (aided by the Beni Kanz) and fled to el-Abwab, while a nephew was installed in his place. Each time he returned to Dongola as soon as the invaders were safely out of sight, and succeeded in recovering his throne. After his second return in 1290 Shemamun made an overture of peace and submission to the sultan, sending him a large present of slaves and promising the resumption of the *Baqt*. The Mameluke ruler, who was then preoccupied in Syria and who must have been weary of the costly and fruitless game of hide-and-seek in Nubia, was content to leave it at that, and Shemamun was not molested again. Nothing is known of the last years of his reign or of his ultimate fate.

In 1304 the whole convoluted story of treachery and intrigue began anew. A certain King Ammy, who by now had succeeded Shemamun, appeared at the sultan's court seeking help against a rebel. He in his turn was successfully restored to power with the aid of a Mameluke army, and he in his turn was murdered a few years later. His brother and successor, Kerenbes,[65] was the last Christian king of Makouria of whom we have definite knowledge.

Immediately after his accession Kerenbes went in person to Cairo, bringing a large gift in addition to the regular tribute and swearing his oath of allegiance to the sultan. Once back in Nubia, however, he resumed the old game of defiance and insubordination. The Mameluke ruler as usual mustered an army to depose him and to install in his place another Nubian prince, Barshambu. In this case, however, the would-be successor to the throne of Dongola was a Moslem, having been converted to Islam while living as a hostage in Cairo. When Kerenbes learned of the sultan's plan, he made a startling counter-proposal. His sister's son, who was also the Kanz ed-Dawla, was sent to Cairo with a letter suggesting that if it was really the sultan's intention to place a Moslem on the Nubian throne in place of Kerenbes, then the succession should properly go to the Kanz ed-Dawla, who was entitled to it according to the Nubian order of matri-lineal succession (cf. Ch. 15).

The Beni Kanz up to this point had generally taken the part of the Mamelukes in Nubia, and had participated in the expeditions against both Dawud and Shemamun. Nevertheless Sultan en-Nasir was shrewd enough to recognize that they represented at least as much of a threat to Mameluke interests in Nubia as did the recalcitrant Christian kings. The suggestion that the Nubian throne should go to the Kanz ed-Dawla, the hereditary leader of the Beni Kanz, was therefore an unwelcome one to the sultan, and he responded to it by committing the Kanz ed-Dawla to prison. The ex-peditionary force then set out for Dongola as originally planned, and Barshambu was duly installed as king. Kerenbes fled upriver to el-Abwab, as had two of his predecessors, and there he in his turn was captured and sent as a prisoner to Cairo.

With Kerenbes safely in custody and Barshambu installed at Dongola, the Mameluke ruler evidently felt that affairs in Nubia were sufficiently under control, and he consented to release the imprisoned Kanz ed-Dawla upon his promise to return to Aswan and mind his own business.[66] Once he was safely out of Cairo, however, the Beni Kanz leader made straight for Nubia. At Daw he was proclaimed king by the local populace (prob-ably consisting mostly of his own Beni Kanz followers), and from there he proceeded to Dongola. As a result of his intrigues Barshambu was murdered by some of his own people, and Kanz ed-Dawla took the throne.

From this point on the Nubian claimants were mere puppets in the struggle for control of their kingdom; the real contenders were the Mamelukes and the Beni Kanz. The sultan had once again seen his ambitions in the southern kingdom thwarted, and once again he felt compelled to intervene. Abraam, a brother of Kerenbes and apparently a Christian, was sent at the head of a Mameluke army to depose his nephew the Kanz ed-Dawla. Arrived at Dongola, he was, according to some accounts, readily acknowledged as the legitimate ruler by his nephew, who voluntarily stepped aside.[67] Abraam nevertheless distrusted his abdicated predecessor and had him imprisoned, with the intention of sending him back to Cairo, but the unexpected death of the new king three days later forestalled this event. Kanz ed-Dawla then apparently had no difficulty in resuming the throne.

The captive Kerenbes was now the last card in the sultan's hand. The former king was released and, in 1323, was sent back to Nubia in one last effort to recover the throne from the Kanz ed-Dawla – the same nephew whom he himself had recommended as his successor eight years earlier. This time Kanz ed-Dawla did not wait to welcome his uncle, but fled once more to el-Abwab, and Kerenbes was restored without opposition. His nephew, however, took a leaf from Shemamun's book; as soon as the invaders were gone he reappeared at Dongola, drove out Kerenbes, and immediately recovered his throne. The deposed king fell back on Aswan, where he waited in vain for Mameluke reinforcements. To quote the words of Yusuf Hasan: 'The expected help never came; indeed, only on very rare occasions did the Mamelukes ever again intervene in Nubian affairs. The reasons for this sudden change are not clear. Although the Mamelukes now left Nubia to face its own destiny under the Beni Kanz, it was they who had played a major role in weakening it beyond recovery.'[68]

The accession of Kanz ed-Dawla has conventionally been regarded as marking the end of Christian rule in northern Nubia, and the year 1323 is therefore sometimes identified as the beginning of the Islamic era.[69] This interpretation can no longer be justified either in a narrow or in a broad sense. On the one hand it is apparent, as we shall see in a moment, that parts of Lower Nubia remained under the rule of Christian princelings for another 150 years. On the other hand, in a wider sense Makouria in the feudal age had already ceased to be a Christian kingdom. The fact that a Moslem could ascend its throne with the consent of most of its subjects, and without occasioning serious internal disturbances, is the best proof of that fact. Makouria in the fourteenth century was a secular monarchy most of whose subjects were Christians, and whose rulers also happened to profess the Christian faith until 1323. But the old, close alliance between church and state was dead; Shekenda, Shemamun, and Kerenbes are nowhere portrayed on the walls of churches or identified in dedicatory texts as the patrons and protectors of religion.[70]

The history of Makouria under Moslem rule is both short and obscure. The Kanz ed-Dawla or one of his descendants was evidently still on the throne in 1349, for al-Umari, writing in that year, described Nubia as a Christian country ruled by Moslem kings of the family of Kanz ed-Dawla.[71] He also stated that the kingdom was tributary to the sultan of Egypt, which was probably true more in theory than in fact.[72] By 1365, however, the picture seems to have changed again. In that year an embassy from an unnamed Nubian king came to Cairo to seek help against certain Arab tribes which were ravaging the kingdom, including, apparently, the Beni Ja'd, the Beni Ikrima, and the Beni Kanz. The circumstances as well as the consequences of this mission, as related by Maqrizi,[73] deserve a moment's consideration, for they shed the only light we possess on a critical juncture in Nubian history.

Some time before 1365 there had apparently been another of the interminable palace revolutions at Dongola, in which – as so often in Nubian history – a reigning king had been deposed and killed by his nephew. The cause of the nephew had been supported by the Beni Ja'd, an Arab tribe who had settled in large numbers in the Dongola region. Once installed on the throne, however, the new king had turned on his erstwhile allies and had massacred most of their leaders. After this act of treachery he found his position at Dongola untenable, and he and his court withdrew northwards to Daw (? Gebel Adda), leaving his capital and the southern district at the mercy of the Beni Ja'd. The Arabs seem to have wreaked what vengeance they could by sacking and destroying the city after the king's departure. In the north, the king found himself threatened by the Beni Kanz and their allies the Beni Ikrima, so that his position was hardly more secure than it had been at Dongola. It was at this point that he decided to appeal to the sultan for help.

The Mamelukes, having apparently forgotten the lessons of a generation earlier, accepted this further invitation to intervene in Nubian affairs. According to Hasan the expedition which they sent forth had three principal objectives: to restore the Nubian king to his throne at Dongola, to punish the Beni Kanz and the Beni Ikrima, and to re-establish Mameluke influence in Nubia.[74] Only the second of these aims was to be realized. The Mameluke horsemen successfully dispersed the Beni Kanz and Beni Ikrima and captured their leaders, thereby relieving the immediate threat to Daw, but they made no further move towards the south. The Nubian king had decided to remain where he was rather than try to recover his ruined capital and the hostile surrounding district, and his decision was endorsed by the Mameluke commander, who forthwith retired to Egypt.

The southern parts of the kingdom, its capital and its traditional heartland, were thus relinquished to the unruly Arabs, and Makouria as a
political entity ceased to exist. Thenceforth it was to know no government
but that of robber barons, so that a European traveller little more than a
century later could write: ' . . . on the way beyond the Nile going to the
province of Nubi they are bad people, robbers, murderers, and most of all
in the province of Nuba.'[75]

Maqrizi's account of these events is far from explicit. Certain aspects
of the story suggest, however, that the last rulers of Makouria – who are
nowhere mentioned by name – may have reverted to the faith which was still
professed by the great majority of their subjects. That they were no longer
members of the Beni Kanz is apparent. The recurrence of a dynastic quarrel between an uncle and his nephew (a regular event in Late Christian
times because of the matrilineal rule of succession) suggests too that the
matrilineal succession may have been revived, which would hardly have
happened under a Moslem régime. Finally, the withdrawal of the rulers
to Daw, and their decision to remain there, may be linked to the fact that
this was the seat of the Christian successor state of Dotawo, about which
more will be said presently.

Relations between Nubian kings and Mameluke sultans, which had
proved so unprofitable to both, were not quite at an end. In 1397 the
old story was repeated one more time: a certain Nubian king Nasir
(whose capital is not mentioned) came to Cairo to seek assistance against
an insubordinate cousin.[76] The sultan received him with honour and ordered the governor of Aswan to help him, but this was probably recognized
by both parties as a hollow gesture. By this time the Beni Kanz had reduced Aswan and the district around it to a state of chaos, and the
governor himself had been forced to take refuge in Nubia only the year
before. With this rather futile episode the recorded history of medieval
Nubia comes to an end until the advent of Ottoman rule more than a
century later.

THE SUCCESSORS OF MAKOURIA

With the fall of Makouria the feudal age in Nubia had fully arrived. The
power which had once been wielded by a single king was now divided
among at least three groups: the Arab–Nubian Beni Kanz in the north,
the successor state of Dotawo near the Second Cataract, and the Arab
tribesmen who had taken political control of the Dongola region.

As we saw a moment ago, the leader of the Beni Kanz had assumed the
throne of Makouria in 1323, but had apparently lost it again by the time
the kingdom broke up forty years later. From that time onwards we hear no
more of the Kanz ed-Dawla by name, but it is apparent that the power of

the Beni Kanz was by no means at an end. Having surrendered (it seems) any share in responsible government, they reverted to the predatory role of earlier times. Throughout their history they were by nature and inclination a 'barbarian warband',[77] and their aim was usually to rob rather than to rule.

Whether or not the Beni Kanz played any further part in Nubian political affairs after their defeat at Daw in 1365 is uncertain, but it is evident that after that time their aggression was directed chiefly against Upper Egypt and its Mameluke rulers. Four times between 1365 and 1403 they attacked and pillaged Aswan, sometimes alone and sometimes in concert with other tribes, committing atrocities for which they were repaid with interest by the Mamelukes. By the end of the fourteenth century they had succeeded in reducing the Aswan region to a state of anarchy: effective Mameluke control was at an end, commerce over the desert road to Aidhab was completely disrupted, and the great seaport gradually fell into ruins. Thenceforth until the coming of the Turks in 1517 Upper Egypt and the adjoining part of Lower Nubia were to all intents and purposes a fief of the Beni Kanz and their allies.[78] It is difficult to describe their polity as a state or even as a principality, in view of its essentially predatory character, but it was at all events one of the successors to the power of Makouria.

South of the Beni Kanz, and hidden by them from the view of the outside world, the shadowy Christian kingdom of Dotawo, and perhaps other splinter kingdoms, persisted for a time.[79] The details of their history will probably never be known; our only knowledge of their existence comes from passing reference in a few late Nubian texts, supported to some extent by the evidence of archaeology. The known references to Dotawo and its rulers, all in the Old Nubian language, are these:

1. An undated religious text, written on parchment, contains among the protocols the phrase 'Elteeit ... being King of Dotawo'. Its place of origin is not known.[80]

2. Two documents found in the Upper Egyptian site of Edfu, dated in the year 1331, mention a certain Siti, King of Dotawo.[81]

3. A graffito of fourteen lines on the wall of the rock-cut shrine of Horemheb near Gebel Adda (which in Christian times was decorated and fitted out as a church), begins: 'In the name of the Father and of the Son and of the Spirit: I, Joel, King of Kings of Dotawo, for whom this inscription was written in the grotto of Epimaco [evidently the patron saint of the church].' The remainder of the text is obscure, but seems to be a list of religious officials and their obligations.[82]

4. Two other graffiti in the same chamber mention a King Koudlaniel, whose kingdom is not named, and who apparently commissioned the

restoration of one of the frescoes in the grotto-church, and a King Tienossi of Ilenat, who sent an embassy to the grotto-church. Since the aforementioned Joel calls himself 'King of Kings of Dotawo', it might be inferred that Tienossi was a vassal monarch. Koudlaniel might have been either a king of Dotawo or a vassal.[83]

5. A letter found at Gebel Adda in 1966 is described by the excavator as ' . . . a fine leather document of the late fifteenth century, dated in the reign of Joel, king of Dotawo, and mentioning a long list of court and sacerdotal officials in the usual way. Among them appear Bishop Merki of Qasr Ibrim and another priest, Urtigaddi, whose name turns up on an ostracon draft of a similar document found in one of the storerooms of the palace.'[84] The text of this intriguing find has not yet been published, but the date is given as AD 1484[85] – more than 150 years after the supposed disappearance of Christian rule in Nubia!

6. By far the most important repository of information about Dotawo which has thus far come to light is embodied in a group of leather scrolls uncovered at Qasr Ibrim in 1964 and 1966. In this case too the discoverer's account is worth quoting:

It can be stated that all are Christian documents, for each begins with an ascription to the Holy Trinity. All appear to contain the names of various kings of the kingdom of Dotawo together with the names of officials and their respective offices. What is of particular interest is that some of the documents are clearly dated. Further examination may reveal dates on others. Present investigations suggest that these leather scrolls cover a period of two centuries.

. . . The latest of the scrolls bears the date 1464. King Joel is mentioned as being the ruler of Dotawo, the modern Gebel Adda . . . The latest scroll from Ibrim besides mentioning King Joel also contains the name of Merkos[86] as being Bishop or Papas (Metropolitan) of Ibrim. In the Ibrim scroll the names of five other persons holding high offices are recorded.

The other certain dates which can be read on other scrolls are 1334, 1287, and 1281. The dated scroll of the year 1334 records that the king of Dotawo was Siti, whose name has been attested from Arabic sources. A second, undated, scroll is also to be assigned to his reign. In 1287 the king of Dotawo was George Simon. Another scroll also belongs to his time, but this is damaged where the date should be expected to occur. The last dated scroll, 1281, mentions a king of Dotawo whose name appears to be P(i)arl. Two more scrolls, the dates of which yet cannot be determined, belong to the reign of a king called David. In both of these scrolls the name of Ibrim in its medieval form Phrim appears together with the name of its Bishop, Chael. In three of the scrolls the title Papas, perhaps equivalent to Metropolitan, appears. Thus we have Shenoute in the reign of David, Kosmos in the reign of Simon, and Merkos in the reign of Joel.[87]

7. To the foregoing must now be added a series of paper and leather documents found at Qasr Ibrim in 1974. On the basis of very preliminary examination they appear to be legal and/or administrative records gener-

ally similar to those found in 1964 and 1966. Among the names mentioned are two or three Kings of Dotawo: Moses George, George (who may or may not be a different individual from the aforenamed), and Basil, together with eparchs, bishops, and officials. The most unexpected feature of these newly found documents is their dates, which range from AD 1144 to 1199.[88] We now know for the first time that Dotawo was already in existence – presumably as a vassal of Makouria – at a time when the Dongola kingdom was still at the height of its power (cf. Ch. 15).

8. The name of Joel (apparently the most active of the Dotawo kings, as well as the last of whom we have knowledge) has also been found recently in a dedicatory inscription in a church at Tamit,[89] and perhaps also at Faras.[90]

Although the name of Dotawo is not mentioned by any contemporary historian, there are a few indirect and admittedly ambiguous references to the continued existence of Christian kingdoms in northern Nubia after 1323. Al-Umari, writing after 1342, mentions '"Rum" [a term often used by the Arabs to designate 'Roman', i.e. Christian, principalities[91]] of Nubia beyond the cataract'.[92] An Abyssinian account of a pilgrimage to Jerusalem between 1327 and 1339 speaks of a Christian King Sab'a Nol who reigned in Nubia at that time.[93] Finally, the *Book of the Knowledge of all the Kingdoms* written by an anonymous Spanish monk some time after 1360 not only speaks of a Christian king at Dongola (!), but even reproduces his purported coat-of-arms.[94] However, this is generally acknowledged to be a very unreliable source.[95]

From these few and scattered references we can deduce only a few particulars about the history and character of Dotawo. The 'kingdom' (principality would probably be a better word) endured for nearly three and a half centuries, from some time before 1144 to some time after 1484. It counted at least eight kings: Moses George, Basil, P(i)arl, George Simon, David, Siti, Elteeit, and Joel, to whom we should perhaps also add the names of George and of Koudlaniel, and there may have been vassal kings as well. The rulers were not merely Christians but looked upon themselves as the patrons and protectors of the church, in accordance with the traditions of the pre-feudal age. In fact, the lack of differentiation between religious and civil officials in the inscriptions of Joel suggests that in the twilight years of Nubian Christianity church and state may have been reunited in one body. Dotawo may in any case be regarded, and probably regarded itself, as the only legitimate successor state to Christian Makouria.

The territorial extent of Dotawo can only be conjectured. Undoubtedly the kingdom was centred in the southern part of Lower Nubia, and perhaps had its capital or one of its capitals at Gebel Adda. That it extended as far north as Qasr Ibrim is obvious from the numerous manuscript finds there, and from the mention of Bishops of Ibrim among the king's retinue. To the north of Qasr Ibrim there are almost no known remains of the late medieval period; this was the region which was evidently laid waste by the Beni Kanz, and much of its population may have fled south, as we observed at the beginning of the chapter. In the south, the numerous evidences for a late survival of Christianity in the *Batn el Hajar*[96] suggest the possibility that this region may have formed another part of the territory of Dotawo.

Millet believes that he has discovered within the hilltop fortress of Gebel Adda the remains of a palace of the kings of Dotawo.[97] This was a complex of monumental brick buildings arranged in the shape of a U, with the open end facing the central plaza of the citadel. One end of the U was formed by a church, which was directly adjoined by the other buildings of the complex. Most of these were too ruined to permit any detailed reconstruction, and their identification as a palace is conjectural. However, the various graffiti in the nearby grotto of Horemheb as well as the leather document previously alluded to indicate that Gebel Adda was a place of importance within the kingdom.

In modern Nubian the suffix *-tawo* signifies 'beneath' or 'under', and often occurs in place names. It therefore seems reasonable to believe that Dotawo means 'the country below Do', or perhaps more figuratively 'the principality governed from Do' – which must surely be the Daw of the Arabic manuscripts.[98] In view of the numerous associations of both names with Gebel Adda it seems more than probable that Do, Daw, and Adda[99] are one and the same place,[100] though attempts have also been made to identify Daw with Derr,[101] with Sheikh Daud,[102] and even with the pharaonic fortress of Du in the Abri-Delgo Reach.[103]

Monneret de Villard[104] and Michalowski[105] have suggested that the dynasty of the kings of Dotawo was founded by the eparchs of Lower Nubia, who declared their independence of Dongola after the accession of the Kanz ed-Dawla in 1323. This theory is no longer tenable in view of the recent finds at Qasr Ibrim, which show not only that Dotawo was in existence long before the decline of Makouria, but which also mention the king and the eparch by name as different individuals. We must therefore assume that the earliest kings of Dotawo were vassals of Dongola and its eparch, though the later ones presumably declared their independence. Another find from Qasr Ibrim shows that there was still an eparch (or at least an official addressed in Arabic as 'Lord of the Mountain') in the late thirteenth or early fourteenth century.[106] Thereafter we hear no more of a separate eparchal office, perhaps because the later Kings of Dotawo had proclaimed their independence of Makouria and its viceroy. It is worth recalling however that in 1365 the ruling king from Dongola himself withdrew to Daw, where he made his residence thereafter. According to the account of Maqrizi, upon arrival at Daw he made peace with a faction which was already established there.[107] It therefore seems possible that after 1365 the dynasty of Dotawo represents a continuation not of the eparchal line but of the traditional dynasty of Makouria itself.

It is remarkable, amid the chaotic political conditions of the feudal age, that the splinter state of Dotawo should have persisted for as much as two centuries seemingly unmolested by its Moslem neighbours to the north and south. Its survival can only be attributed to the accidents of history and geography. The Beni Kanz, after their expulsion from Dongola, seem to have been fully preoccupied in the attempt to reassert their control over the Aswan district, which they continually terrorized and intermittently occupied. Beni Kanz intransigence thus formed a buffer against the southern expansion of the Egyptian Mamelukes, and it was apparently behind that screen of inadvertent protection that Dotawo survived. Meanwhile the monarchy at Dongola was rocked by wave after wave of Arab migrations, and was far too weak to assert its historic claim to Lower Nubia. The Nile corridor was now a backwater, by-passed by the main trade and migration routes and therefore of little interest to any outside power. It was in that political and cultural backwater that Nubian Christianity suffered its final, lingering death, though under what circumstances we shall probably never know. Joel is the last king of Dotawo of whom we have any knowledge; apparently all trace both of his kingdom and of an organized Christian faith had disappeared when the Ottoman Turks annexed Lower Nubia early in the sixteenth century (cf. Ch. 18).[108]

The political history of Upper Nubia after the withdrawal of the court from Dongola can only be conjectured. There was again a king at Dongola in the seventeenth century – a vassal of the Funj – who was regarded as the most powerful of the numerous warlords in the Dongola Reach (cf. Ch. 18), but whether this monarchy was a direct successor to that of Makouria or whether it was revived at a later date is not known. In the absence of other evidence we have no choice but to accept the word of Ibn Khaldun that 'no kingly government was possible by reason of the ruination which prevented any union between the princes and split them into factions . . .'[109] It would seem that Upper Nubia for a considerable time was at the mercy of predatory warbands of the same stripe as the Beni Kanz.[110]

THE END OF ALWA

The history of the southern Nubian kingdom is obscure at all times (cf. Ch. 15), and its ultimate fate is doubly so. We seldom hear its name mentioned in the historical accounts which were quoted earlier in this chapter; they speak occasionally of the King of el-Abwab, but not of the King of

Alwa. El-Abwab ('the gates') was traditionally the northern frontier district of Alwa (Ch. 15), but whether this means that 'King of el-Abwab' should be read as synonymous with 'King of Alwa', or whether the kingdom had already broken up into feudal principalities, we do not know. According to Spaulding,[111] 'Excavations at Soba reveal a serious decline in the material culture of the capital of Alwa by the thirteenth century.[112] The thirteenth-century geographer al-Harrānī was told that the southern Nubian capital had shifted from Alwa to "Waylūla",[113] while his contemporary, the Mamlūk emissary Alm al-Din Sanjar, found that he had to deal with nine individual rulers on his mission to Alwa.[114] The kingdoms of southern Nubia had thus lapsed, not into chaos, but into their constituent parts.'

Alwa, whose territory included some of the richest grazing lands in the Sudan, must have been even more heavily infiltrated and more seriously threatened by the nomad hordes who came to the Sudan between the eleventh and fifteenth centuries than was Makouria. The most powerful of the tribes which settled in the southern territories were the Juhayna and the Quraysh – both peoples of the Hejaz who had migrated to Upper Egypt in Fatimid times and then, under Mameluke pressure, had moved on southward in search of greener pastures. According to Yusuf Hasan:

The immigrants did not come in the form of invading hordes but of successive small parties . . . Although the general pattern of this infiltration was probably a peaceful one, the eventual appearance of local clashes and of tribal warfare was inevitable. In their attempts to control the pasture lands, the nomads might conceivably have driven out the original stock or raided the rich riverain lands. In any case their presence in the kingdom of Alwa must have exerted pressure on the government – a pressure about which very little is known. The state of Alwa was at first capable of defending itself and of forcing small bands of Arabs to respect its authority. However, with the increase in the numbers of Arab immigrants and with the formation of large tribal associations, the balance was drastically upset . . .[115]

The bedouin tide was not the only threat with which the rulers of Alwa had to contend. They seem also to have been on almost continual bad terms with the rulers of Makouria, possibly as a result of Makourian slave-raiding in their territory. Moslem slavers were apparently also active in the kingdom.[116] Above and beyond these problems, however, the rulers of Alwa had to face a new and previously unfamiliar menace: the rising power of the black tribes to their south and west.[117] It was at least partly from this direction that destruction finally came.

There are only two important notices of Alwa after the thirteenth century. In the early fourteenth century a writer named al-Dimashqi reported that the king of Alwa resided at a place called Kusha, far to the west of the Nile, where water was obtained from underground wells. This might suggest that the king had been driven out of his traditional homeland on the Nile by the Arab invaders; however, the account of al-Dimashqi is not based on first-hand information and is of dubious value.[118]

A persistent Sudanese tradition attributes the final downfall of Alwa and its capital city of Soba to the combined attacks of bedouin Arabs and the black Funj Sultans, with whom we will be concerned at more length in Chapter 18. The history of the Funj (the 'Funj Chronicle') was written down late in the nineteenth century from an assortment of documents and oral traditions which had been in existence much earlier;[119] an account of the overthrow of Alwa forms its opening chapter. After the usual invocation, the story begins with the following words:

It is related in the histories which I have seen that the first of the kings of the Funj who was invested with the royal power was King Umara Dunqas, who founded the city of Sennar in AH 910 [= AD 1504]. Previous to this date the Funj had overthrown the Nuba and made the city of Soba their metropolis; and in that city were beautiful buildings and gardens and a hostel occupied by the Mohammedans. [There follows a description of Soba in Christian times which is obviously taken from that of Ibn Selim, as preserved in Maqrizi.[120] The text then continues:] Let us now return to our subject. Know that the reign of Umara Dunqas began by his gathering people around him and they went on increasing and he was staying with them in Jebel Moya, situated west of Sennar. There came to him Abd Allah Jamma of the Qawasma Arabs ... The Funj decided to make war on the kings of Soba and Qerri. Therefore Umara and Abd Allah Jamma set off with their army, fought the kings of Soba and Qerri and defeated them and slew them. Thereupon they agreed together that Umara should be king in place of the King of Alwa, that is to say Soba, since he was the greater, and that Abd Allah Jamma should be in place of the King of Qerri. Umara and Abd Allah continued to be like brothers, but the rank of Umara took precedence over the rank of Abd Allah if they were together in the same place.[121]

Reading between the lines of the 'Chronicle', it looks as if the once extensive territories of Alwa had been nibbled away by bedouin encroachment until nothing remained but the riverain district near the junction of the Niles; the Arabs and Funj then decided to finish off the moribund kingdom and divide its remaining territories between themselves.

The accession of Umara Dunqas, the first of the Black Sultans of Sennar, is historically attested.[122] However, modern scholarship has cast doubt upon the tradition that his reign began with the overthrow of Alwa. It is now believed that this was the work of the Arabs alone, and that they in their turn were subjugated by the Funj at a later date. The conquerors then appropriated to their own history the exploit of their predecessors.[123] Whether or not it is authentic, however, the traditional version of the tale as told in the 'Funj Chronicle' is interesting for its overtone of state propaganda. The Black Sultans obviously sought to legitimize their rule by identifying their kingdom of Sennar as a successor state (by right of conquest) to Alwa. Since the Funj themselves never ruled at Soba, the extended description of the city's power and wealth in Christian times, with which the chronicle opens, can only be understood as an attempt to reflect some of its glory upon its conquerors. It seems, then, that the name and reputation of Alwa – whatever the actual date of its fall – could still command respect and authority in the sixteenth century, and for that matter even in the nineteenth.

A somewhat variant tradition preserved by the Abdallab Arabs (as the destroyers of Soba came to be known after the days of their eponymous leader) asserts that the last survivors of the Arab attack escaped from Soba and made a last stand in a fortress at Qerri, some forty miles to the north.[124] On the basis of this legend H. N. Chittick has identified a rather crude fortified hilltop compound at the mouth of the Shabaloka gorge, close to the modern village of Qerri, as 'the last Christian stronghold in the Sudan'.[125] Apart from the questionable authenticity of the site, however, the 'Funj Chronicle' is far from explicit about the religion of Alwa at the time of its overthrow. The only mention of Christianity is in that part of the text which is taken from the much earlier account of Ibn Selim. Since contact with Alexandria had been broken in the fourteenth century (see below), it seems quite possible that Alwa might have passed under Moslem rule, unbeknown to the outside world, long before its final downfall.

The city of Soba was last seen as an inhabited community in 1523, when an intrepid Jewish traveller named David Reubeni passed through it on his way down the Nile from Abyssinia to Cairo. He found the place in ruins and its surviving inhabitants living in 'wooden dwellings', which can hardly have been anything but *rakubas*.[126] In later centuries the name of Soba became a metaphor for total destruction among the Sudanese Arabs,[127] yet as recently as 1930 certain members of the Hamej tribe, which had once been its subjects, were known to swear oaths by the name of 'Soba the home of my grandfathers and grandmothers, which can make the stone float and the cotton boll sink'.[128]

THE TWILIGHT OF CHRISTIANITY

It has been suggested that when the throne of Makouria passed from Christian into Moslem hands in 1323, the eventual disappearance of Nubian Christianity became inevitable.[129] This may be regarded as true in the broadest sense, yet the connection between the two events was by no means direct or immediate. We have to recall that Christian communities have survived for centuries under Moslem rule in other countries, notably including Egypt, and it is now apparent that they did so for a while in

Nubia as well. At no time is there evidence of overt hostility towards Christianity on the part of the later Nubian rulers or their subjects. The late Nubian churches do not show signs of pillage and desecration; on the contrary, many of those in the Second Cataract region were so well preserved when they were first seen by Europeans in the nineteenth century that it seemed inconceivable that they should have been abandoned as much as 500 years earlier [130] – and perhaps they were not. Moreover, outside of major administrative centres like Qasr Ibrim and Dongola there is no definite evidence for the practice of Islam until the fairly recent past (cf. Ch. 17). Of the 150 known churches in Nubia [131] fewer than half a dozen were ever converted to mosques, nor are there any other mosque buildings of great antiquity in the region. In the face of such evidence it seems clear that Christianity succumbed not to the external pressure of Islam but as a result of its own organizational and spiritual weakness.

We have already observed that in the Late Christian period the Nubian church had become increasingly inward-looking and aloof from everyday affairs, and that much of its ideological force had been eroded by the secular spirit of the feudal age. The church and the monarchy were still in theory the twin pillars of the state, but their close and mutually reinforcing relationship of earlier times was at an end. The monarchs above all had been infected by the spirit of feudalism, and when in the late Middle Ages they were obliged to seek political support against their rivals they turned not to the Nubian church but to the Mameluke sultans. On the other side of the picture, the nominal support of rulers like Shekenda, Shemamun, and Kerenbes can have been of little value to the church. Over and above all these circumstances, however, the fatal weakness of the Nubian church lay in its failure to develop an effective local organization or cultural roots. [132]

By and large, the Christian communities which have fared best under Islamic rule have been the autocephalous national churches such as those of Egypt, Syria, and Armenia. The key to their survival has been organizational solidarity and discipline, which has made them independent of government support and has enabled them on occasion to exert a good deal of political weight even in their minority status. The solidarity of these churches rests not only upon organization and religious commitment, but also upon a strong strain of ethnic nationalism: each consciously preserves the local artistic and literary traditions of pre-Islamic times.

The Nubian church enjoyed none of these advantages. It had no local roots, either cultural or organizational. Its bishops and higher clergy were largely Egyptian, appointed from Alexandria, and among them there was no recognized leader who could rally the faithful in defiance of hostile governments and foreign indifference. Religious art, literature, and liturgy were equally foreign. The only thing distinctively Nubian about the 'Nubian' church was its architectural canon, but even this ceased to be true after the great basilicas fell into disuse and were replaced by the humble cupola churches of the Late Christian period. In any case these tiny and austerely plain buildings can hardly have served as an effective rallying symbol for religious fervour.

Thus constituted, the Nubian church had no organic framework of its own; it was utterly dependent either upon the parent church in Egypt or upon the Nubian monarchy. During most of its history it was actively supported by both, but when, in the late Middle Ages, both sources of support were withdrawn, it was unable to stand alone. It is important to recognize, however, that the loss of external support did not occur all at once, or at the same time in all parts of the country. The far northern region fell under the control of the anti-Christian Beni Kanz in the thirteenth century; the throne of Dongola went to a Moslem in 1323; while in the region of the Second Cataract a Christian principality survived until late in the fifteenth century.

We do not know precisely when or even why the Nubian church lost contact with Alexandria. Disturbed political conditions in Nubia and the severe persecution of the church in Egypt were probably both contributing factors. Above all, however, it must have been the chaos wrought by the Beni Kanz, particularly after 1360, which prevented effective communication between the Christian communities to the north and south of their territory.

It is recorded in a history of the Coptic Patriarchs that after 1235 no more priests were sent from Alexandria to Nubia, and the Nubian church was left to manage its own affairs.[133] This seems understandable enough in view of the chaotic political conditions in Egypt, and possibly also in Nubia, at the time. Nevertheless the breach of relations may only have been temporary, or it may have applied only to the dioceses in Upper Nubia (since Coptic historians often distinguished between the provinces of al-Maris and al-Nuba, or essentially Lower and Upper Nubia). At any rate we now have evidence of contact between Lower Nubia and Alexandria at a considerably later date. A Bishop of Faras and Qasr Ibrim was consecrated in Egypt as late as 1372; his consecration documents were found buried beside him in his tomb at Qasr Ibrim.[134] For the time being they represent our last definite evidence of communication between the Nubian church and its erstwhile patriarch.

That there was still an organized church in Lower Nubia a hundred years later is attested by the documents associated with the names of King Ioel and other kings of Dotawo (see above). Many of these are lists of religious officials, among whom the name of the Bishop of Ibrim is prominent. We cannot be sure that his appointment was recognized or even known in Alexandria; it seems at least possible that after contact with Egypt was lost the King of Dotawo absorbed the surviving religious functionaries into his own retinue and assumed the primacy of a short-lived indigenous church. At all events effective support for this last vestige of the Nubian church can only have come from the local monarchy, not from abroad. Presumably therefore the church and the monarchy perished together at the end of the fifteenth century; there is no mention of either after the year 1484.

In retrospect it is apparent that the organized practice of Christianity died out in different parts of Nubia at different times and for immediately different reasons. It must have disappeared first in the far north, under the direct oppression of the Beni Kanz. This is suggested at all events by their historically attested character and by the absence of Late Christian remains north of Qasr Ibrim. The next region to go was presumably the Dongola Reach. Here communication with Alexandria may have ceased in the thirteenth century, so that the church was left with no support but that of the weak and divided monarchy, and this passed under Moslem control in 1323. Within the territory of Dotawo, between the two aforementioned regions, organized Christianity persisted for another 150 years. Here too contact with Alexandria was eventually lost, but the traditional faith was kept alive under the patronage of native rulers who may have put themselves at its head. In the southern kingdom of Alwa we have no definite knowledge of the duration of Christianity, but there is evidence (which will be discussed presently) that here too the faith persisted until near the end of the fifteenth century

The disappearance of an organized church did not of course mean the immediate extinction of Nubia's medieval faith. Throughout the fourteenth century and even in the early fifteenth century historians continued to describe the people of the Dongola region as Christians,[135] though it seems unlikely that their ecclesiastical organization was still alive at this time. By the end of the fourteenth century, however, Leo Africanus wrote that they had 'lost the sincerity and light of the Gospel; they do embrace infinite corruptions of the Jewish and Mohammedan religions'.[136] An Arab writer of the same period found their condition equally unsatisfactory from a Mohammedan point of view; he described Dongola as 'sunk in perplexity and error'.[137] The missionary Alvares too wrote in 1540 that 'the people are neither Christians, Moors, nor Jews, but they live in the desire of being Christians'.[138] Alvares further reports that 'While we were in the country of the Prester John [i.e. the Emperor of Abyssinia] there came six men from that country [Alwa] as Ambassadors to the Prester, begging him to send them priests and monks to teach them. He did not choose to send them . . .'[139] A century later still, an Italian visitor to Upper Egypt found a colony of Nubians (or Abyssinians?) living close to the ruined monastery at Esna. They still practised the Christian rites of baptism, marriage, and burial, but had forgotten almost all of the other tenets of their ancestral faith.[140] These and other texts give us a picture of a confused and uncertain time of religious transition, during which the Nubians had apparently only the most shadowy understanding of any faith.

A letter recently discovered by a Franciscan scholar in Italy sheds additional light on the late survival of Christianity in Nubia. It was written by a missionary friar in Cairo to Cardinal Belluga in the year 1742, and contains the following passage:

A few days ago I received from a servant, a Berberine, whom I have in my house, such information that caused me great surprise. It is: that in his village, called Tangos, which is in an island of the Nile, in the Kingdom of Nubia, there are still some Christians; although they have endured many troubles, disturbances, and wars from the Turks, to force them to embrace Mohammedanism, they, even at the cost of their lives, have always persevered as Christians and still hold in their hands a monastery (but without monks), in which there is a beautiful church decorated with wall- and cloth-paintings.[141]

This is our last definite evidence of Christians in Nubia, although a generation later James Bruce described in Upper Egypt a 'Convent of religious Franciscans, for the entertainment of the converts, or persecuted Christians in Nubia, *when they can find them*'.[142]

Several of the aforementioned texts suggest a situation which is not unfamiliar in times of religious conflict: a population divided between devoted adherents of the old faith and zealous adherents of the new, with the largest element of all perhaps holding back from a strong commitment on either side to await developments.[143] Probably the division often took place along village lines, as it does today among the peasant peoples of Mediterranean and Near Eastern lands. Archaeological evidence seems to provide some confirmation for this. Those villages which clustered tightly around their churches, like Diffinarti and Attiri,[144] would perhaps represent the die-hard Christian groups. Those whose church was far away, like Meinarti and Kasanarti, may have come to be dominated by Moslem elements, or they may simply have wished to free themselves from close association with the church in case of attack by Arab tribesmen or Mameluke plunderers. Those who had no church, or who allowed their church to fall into ruin, would presumably be converts at least in name to Islam.

The condition of the surviving Nubian churches offers a few further clues to the religious situation at the close of the Middle Ages. Many of the buildings, particularly in the Second Cataract region, are (or were until recently) in a remarkable state of preservation,[145] and it is evident that by and large they had been treated with respect during the centuries since their abandonment. Probably it was hoped for a time that the priests would someday come back; even after that hope vanished some charisma must still have attached to the buildings as the tangible monuments of a half-remembered faith and civilization.

In the recent past many churches have served as animal pens, but this may have been more accidental than intentional; Nubian goats will take refuge in any open building. The only deliberate and consistent desecration in the churches has been to their wall-paintings: the eyes and sometimes the facial features have been defaced, not only in the human figures but in animal figures as well. This has been explained both as a precaution against the evil eye and as a response to the Moslem injunction against pictorial images; in either case it is found uniformly from one end of Nubia to the other. (Hence the enormous artistic importance of those churches like Abdullah Nirqi, Faras, and Sonqi which were buried in sand before they could be defaced.) It is noteworthy, however, that except for this very special and localized pattern of defacement there has been no attempt to injure the paintings or to cover them up, and no church except those at Qasr Ibrim and in the extreme south shows any signs of use as a mosque (which requires specific and easily recognized architectural modifications). Arabic graffiti are numerous on the walls of the abandoned churches, but no more so than are the Greek, Coptic, and Old Nubian graffiti which were made while they were still in use. Probably the writing of names and dates in the churches continues to be a mark of respect rather than the reverse.

A few Nubian churches show signs of use as ordinary habitations in their last years.[146] It has been suggested that the occupants were merely troglodytes, but there is evidence that some of these latter-day inhabitants made efforts to keep the buildings in repair.[147] I therefore think it possible that in the last days of Nubian Christianity the local deacons, and perhaps their descendants after them, may have taken possession of the churches for the sake of protecting them and perhaps of keeping alive some last vestiges of Christian worship.[148]

INTERPRETATIVE SUMMARY

The later Middle Ages witnessed the gradual dissolution of Nubia's medieval civilization. The stability and prosperity of the Christian kingdoms were undermined and finally destroyed by developments both within and beyond their borders. A growing spirit of military feudalism, inspired by that of contemporary Europe and the Near East, manifested itself in the appearance of castles and military architecture, in the rise of increasingly independent local feudatories, and in dynastic quarrels within the ruling houses. Meanwhile bedouin Arabs, forced out of Egypt by Mameluke harassment, settled in increasing numbers along the desert flanks of the Nubian kingdoms and even in places on the Nile itself, often ending any effective control by the monarchies. The Mameluke sultans of Egypt had political ambitions of their own in the south, and their continual intervention between 1275 and 1365 exacerbated the dynastic quarrels within the kingdom of Makouria. Under this combination of pressures and weaknesses the northern Nubian kingdom disintegrated in the later fourteenth century, and what was left of its power devolved upon splinter states and bedouin warlords.

The situation in northern Nubia after the collapse of Makouria is reminiscent of that in western Europe after the fall of the Roman Empire. Power was partly in the hands of petty successor states which tried to maintain the authority of the vanished imperium, while there were other territories which knew no rule but that of barbarian warbands. With the breakdown of internal security trade diminished almost to nothing, the mercantile class disappeared, and the country reverted to the purely agrarian economy of earlier times. Gradually there emerged a typically feudal society of peasant farmers clustered around the castles of local barons who represented their only protection and their only government. The fate of the southern kingdom of Alwa on the other hand was much more nearly akin to that of the eastern Roman Empire: its territory was nibbled away by barbarian kingdoms until nothing remained but a pathetic remnant surrounding the capital, and this was overwhelmed by a final assault at the end of the fifteenth century.

Christianity remained the official faith of the Nubian kingdoms until the fourteenth century, but it had long since given way to military feudalism as the guiding spirit of the times. The church had grown increasingly aloof from everyday affairs and at the same time had been weakened and impoverished by the political disturbances of the feudal age. The Egyptian church was similarly weakened under the harsh Mameluke régime and could no longer provide a guiding and vitalizing force from abroad. Thus as successive parts of Nubia fell under Moslem rule, either through dynastic succession or through Arab encroachment, the church was deprived of its traditional and necessary support both from the monarchies and from Alexandria. Without such support the organized practice of Christianity soon came to an end. It persisted longest in the southern part of Lower Nubia, under the aegis of a small Christian successor state which survived until the end of the fifteenth century.

Even after the disappearance of an organized church Christianity persisted for a century or two as a folk cult among certain conservative groups. Throughout the sixteenth century there were probably still pockets of nominally loyal Christians, as there were presumably also pockets of devout Moslems, among a population most of whose members had no strong religious affiliation. But the prosperous and creative civilization of Christian Nubia can have been no more than a dimly remembered legacy. Its polity, its ideology, and its art, literature, and architecture were equally extinct. Into this cultural and spiritual vacuum there entered the faith of Islam, just as Christianity itself had been drawn into the ideological vacuum left by the disintegration of pharaonic civilization a thousand years earlier.

17

THE ANVIL OF ISLAM

THE ARAB MIGRATIONS AND THE ARABIZATION
OF THE NUBIANS

In his earliest work on Nubia, Reisner had opined that ' . . . its history is
hardly more than an account of its use or neglect by Egypt, its enrichment
or impoverishment by changes of the Nile and the climate'.[1] While this
view hardly does justice to the Nubians' own contribution to their history,
it is nevertheless true that from the earliest times until the end of the
Middle Ages the story of their cultural development can be told very largely
in terms of the influence of their northern neighbours. Only once, and
briefly, did a 'third party' enter the picture, when Axumite invaders may
have dealt the *coup de grâce* to the Meroitic empire (Ch. 13). But the Abyssinians soon returned to their mountain fastness, and never again appeared
on the Nile. The scattered and primitive hinterland peoples who were the
Nubians' more immediate neighbours made no significant contribution to
their history; to the valley dwellers they represented only an intermittent
threat, and just as often an exploitable resource. The Nubians could
usually dominate and intimidate them through their superior numbers and
higher civilization, as they themselves were often dominated and intimidated by the Egyptians.

That situation ended forever in the late Middle Ages with the appearance
of a 'third party' who did not go away. Though they came primarily by
way of Egypt, the Arab tribesmen who poured southward through the
Red Sea Hills and then westward across the pasturelands of the Sudan were
neither Egyptians nor Nubians; they were in fact the hereditary enemies of
all the settled valley peoples. Yet it was chiefly these illiterate nomads who
wrought the last major transformation in the cultural development of the
Nubians. If Mameluke armies were the hammers of Islam, the Arab tribes
who came to surround the Nubians on the south, east, and west were the
anvil upon which their post-Christian society was forged.

The coming of the Arabs ended for ever the pre-eminence which the
Nubians had enjoyed among their African neighbours. The invaders
rapidly overran the Nile hinterlands, absorbing most of the scattered earlier
inhabitants, until in time their numbers considerably exceeded those of the

valley dwellers. The Arabs also possessed a martial spirit and a degree of mobility which the Nubians lacked. As a result the balance of military power was tipped, for the first time in history, away from the riverain peoples and in favour of the steppe and desert tribes who surrounded them. The Nubians have lived ever since, in one sense or another, as vassals of the more powerful hinterland peoples.

If the numerical supremacy of the Nubians was ended by the coming of the Arabs, their ideological supremacy was similarly ended by the coming of Islam. The processes of Arabization and of Islamization should not be confused, though in Nubia they went hand in hand[2] (and are usually confused in the minds of the Nubians themselves, as we shall see presently). The Arabs transformed the situation of the Nubians by their superior numbers; Islam transformed their situation in a more subtle and lasting way by its superior appeal to peoples who had long dwelt outside the pale of civilization. Thus, while large-scale bedouin migrations were confined to the eastern Sudan (the hinterland of Nubia), Islam at the end of the Middle Ages swept across sub-Saharan Africa from the Red Sea to the Atlantic.

The civilization of Islam, martial in its origins, had been re-invigorated rather than undermined by the feudal spirit. The successful expulsion of the Crusaders and Mongols from the Near East was followed by a wave of Islamic expansion second only to that of the seventh century. Not only in Nubia but all across Africa adherents of the newly revitalized faith moved south over the Saharan caravan tracks and into the rich but culturally backward steppelands beyond. Whether bedouins from Egypt or soldiers, merchants, and teachers from the Mahgreb (north-west Africa), they penetrated into regions never previously visited by the envoys of civilization. Moreover, they brought with them a special kind of civilizing tradition; a civilization made by and for desert dwellers. It demanded neither learning nor literacy, but only a profession of faith and the performance of a few simple obligations.[3] It also demanded no submission to an organized church; social cohesion was provided instead through the much more familiar mechanism of fictive kinship (see below).

Where Christianity and earlier civilizations had been, by their very nature, incapable of expansion beyond the settled populations of the Mediterranean littoral and the Nile Valley, Islam spread like a grassfire among the tribesmen of the Sudanic belt. It was the first civilizing tradition in history which succeeded in penetrating the African interior; peoples who for thousands of years had been by-passed by the main currents of history, despised and exploited by their northern neighbours, now became part of a new world *oikoumêne*.[4] Thus ended the Nubians' age-old cultural pre-eminence in inner Africa; they found themselves at last surrounded by a rival civilization which, if not more advanced than their own, was better adapted both to its environment and to its times.

The expansion of Islam into the African interior gave rise almost immediately to a series of short-lived but powerful empires where only inconsequential chiefdoms had existed a short time before. The imperial movement began in West Africa, and spread gradually east across the continent. Mali and Songhai, the successors of ancient Ghana, occupied progressively larger portions of the Niger drainage; Kanem and then Bornu made their appearance in the Chad Basin;[5] the sultanates of Darfur and the Funj fell heirs to the power of Christian Nubia; and in Abyssinia the short-lived empire of the Galla arose to challenge the longstanding supremacy of the Christian Amhara. All of these were African, not Arab, states, but all of them derived their ideological force from the newly introduced religion of Islam. It was in the beginning an élite cult through which the ruling classes established their divine right to govern their pagan subjects, both within their own tribes and in the surrounding tribes whom they conquered.[6] Later, a wave of purification movements was to result in the Islamization of subjects as well as rulers, and the suppression of acknowledged pagan practices. However, the Islam of central and west Africa to this day exhibits a strong pagan substratum.[7]

In many ways the history of the 'empires of the steppes' parallels that of Kush 2,000 years earlier. Each of them combined the ideological charisma of an imported civilizing tradition, commercial prosperity derived from the trade in gold, ivory and slaves, and military power arising from their own warlike prowess. Each was a barbarian state on the frontiers of civilization, whose existence depended on the maintenance of trade with the more powerful kingdoms of the Mediterranean basin. If the history of the medieval empires was infinitely briefer than that of Kush, it was partly because no one of them enjoyed the monopoly of civilization which the Nubians had possessed, but even more because they were soon to be overwhelmed by the far greater power of the European imperialists.

It was, then, not merely Nubia but the whole of sub-Saharan Africa that was transformed by the Islamic wave of the late Middle Ages. No longer simply an outpost of Mediterranean civilization in the darkness of inner Africa, the Nubians found themselves part of a new mosaic of Sudanic civilization which spread right across the continent. The common religion of Islam, the common fiction of Arab descent, and the concomitant of membership in a region-wide tribal system, all combined to level the age-long cultural difference between riverain farmers and desert nomads, and to produce a sense of community between them which had not existed since pre-pharaonic days. From the Middle Ages to modern times, the destiny of the Nubians has been bound up less with the Egyptians than with the sudanic peoples who surround them.

The Islamization of the Nubians may thus be seen in general terms as part of a continent-wide process; however, it differed in important respects from the Islamization of the central and west Africans. The actual process of religious and cultural conversion appears in many respects to have been closer to that which took place during the first wave of Islamic expansion into the Christian lands of the Near East. The Nubians, like the Egyptians and Syrians before them, were not pagans eager for acceptance into the civilized world but adherents of a tradition older and in some ways more advanced than that of their mentors. Moreover the first agents of their conversion were neither missionaries nor scholars but illiterate bedouin overlords, and conversion was not so much an ideological process as a social and political one. As Trimingham has said, 'The nomad Arab, who is rarely fanatical and completely devoid of missionary zeal, makes no attempt at proselytization. The spread of Islam was mainly through penetration, intermarriage, a strategic policy of winning chiefs and group leaders (which includes forcible measures), trade, and the appropriation of slaves. As in the early days of the primary Islamic conquest, conversion to Islam connected the convert to the Arab tribal system as a client.'[8]

In short the process of Islamization in Nubia, as in Egypt and the Near East at an earlier date, was inextricably bound up with that of Arabization. I. M. Lewis remarks that ' . . . the direct experience, at first hand, of Arabian Islam . . . has had a profound effect which is readily apparent in the close association of Islam with Arab identity. More than for most of the other Moslem peoples of Africa, for the [eastern] Sudanese to be a Moslem is to be an Arab. It is this deep assimilation of Islam and identification with Arab culture and society which is expressed in the universal claim of Arab ancestry and the overwhelming currency of [the] Arabic [language].'[9]

Most West African Moslems also claim Arab descent, but they are apt to do so on the basis of individual pedigrees rather than of tribal genealogies or migration legends. In this way a claim of Arab ancestry does not necessarily conflict with membership in a non-Arab tribe or with the speaking of a non-Arabic language.[10] On the other hand the eastern Sudanese, including even Nubians and Beja who do not speak Arabic, claim to be Arabs on a tribal rather than an individual basis. It may therefore be said that while the western Sudanese claims to be an Arab, *pro forma*, because he is a Moslem, the eastern Sudanese claims to be a Moslem because he is an Arab, and Islam is his tribal religion. The significance of this peculiar view of Islamic identity will be more fully discussed in later pages (see 'The genealogical tradition', below).

THE ARAB MIGRATIONS

Although, as we shall see, not many bedouins actually settled within Nubia, the Arab migrations were nevertheless one of the most important population movements in Nubian history, both because they permanently altered the ecological balance between the desert and the sown land and because they led to the last major transformation in Nubian culture. We must therefore consider, in somewhat more detail than in earlier chapters, the circumstances which brought these restless and unruly peoples to the once-empty Sudan. Unlike earlier migrations in the same area, those of the bedouins did not go unrecorded by contemporary observers. The movement of several of the tribes through Egypt was noted by such historians as Ibn Khaldun and Maqrizi, whose accounts were mentioned in the last chapter. Above and beyond the testimony of these fairly reliable witnesses, there is a wealth – even a plethora – of folk tradition relating to the Arab migrations, for migration legends are bound up with the genealogies which are faithfully preserved by most Sudanese tribes. For reasons which will be apparent later (see 'The genealogical tradition'), this mass of confusing and sometimes conflicting testimony is far from reliable, and in its raw form is almost unusable by the historian.[11] However, an exhaustive and critical analysis of Sudanese folk history was made half a century ago by the late Sir Harold MacMichael, and from his studies there has emerged a fairly coherent picture of Sudanese tribal movements. MacMichael's pioneering *History of the Arabs in the Sudan* has been the baseline for all subsequent historical studies, and will be largely followed here.[12]

Persistent Sudanese tradition asserts that certain tribes – notably the Quraysh – migrated directly across the Red Sea from the Arabian Peninsula to the Sudan.[13] However, the number of men and animals who can have made such a passage is necessarily small.[14] It is evident that the great bulk of nomad migration came to Nubia and the adjoining steppelands by way of Egypt. Our story therefore begins, like all other transforming developments in Nubian history, in the northern country.

Nomads have not, generally speaking, played an important role in Egyptian history. The lifeless deserts which stretch away from the flanks of the Nile offer no subsistence even to the hardiest of men and animals. Only the higher elevations of the Red Sea Hills, the Mediterranean coastal strip, and the oases of the western desert have provided a suitable home for pastoral nomads, but these peoples in pre-Islamic times were generally too few and too remote from the Nile to have any significant influence on the valley dwellers. From time to time bedouin groups have also attached themselves to the fringes of the cultivated valley, but in the end they have always been absorbed into the mass of *fellaheen* peasants and have lost their pastoral habits and their tribal identity.

The Arab conquest of Egypt in 640–42 was, concurrently, the first major bedouin migration to the Nile Valley. The conquering army was made up very largely of tribesmen, apparently drawn indiscriminately from most of the tribes of the Arabian Peninsula. By 642 they are said to have numbered nearly 20,000.[15] This is also the figure usually given as the size of the Moslem army which unsuccessfully invaded Nubia in 642 (Ch. 14).[16] How many of these immigrants settled down in Egypt after the conquest it is impossible to say, but probably the majority did so. During the next two centuries their numbers were continually swelled through immigration. According to MacMichael, 'The chief occasions of the immigration were the arrivals of new governors: each one came escorted by an army of anything up to 20,000 men, many of whom never returned to Syria or Arabia. A proportion of these hordes were Persian, Turkish and other tribes, but the majority were Arabs and would normally be members of the governor's own tribe.'[17] In addition to these regular increments, members of the Qays Aylan tribe were induced to settle in Lower Egypt as a counterweight to the influence of the increasingly rebellious Copts. Far from reinforcing the security of the central government, however, the tribesmen themselves became a perennial nucleus of rebellion.[18]

In the beginning most of the Arabs in Egypt did not go to join the nomad groups already resident in the Red Sea Hills and the western oases, for unlike the earlier bedouins they were not obliged to support themselves entirely or even primarily by pastoral activities. They were installed as irregular garrison forces in the provinces of Lower and Middle Egypt, as other Arab groups were similarly installed in the conquered regions of Syria and Iraq. This enabled them to graze such animals as they had along the margins and over the harvested fields of the Nile Valley, with or without the consent of the *fellaheen*. More importantly, however, it enabled them to exact tribute from the *fellaheen* themselves. The Arabs in Egypt, like many other nomad groups before and since, lived more as parasites than as pastoralists.

In order to maintain their military effectiveness and mobility, the Arabs in Egypt and the other conquered provinces were forbidden to own land or to engage in cultivation.[19] This shortsighted policy was to prove disastrous to civil order. The Arabs were not cut out by training or tradition for the military role which was assigned them once the wars of conquest were over; they were too unruly to serve as provincial garrisons and too undependable to serve as household troops. At the same time the prohibition against holding land precluded their settling down to a useful life within the conquered provinces, and practically condemned them to return to the predatory lawlessness of pre-Islamic times, even had they wished otherwise.

After the Abbasid revolution of 750[20] the Arabs found their military role increasingly pre-empted by slave armies of Persian and Turkish origin. The result was a long series of Arab revolts which further alienated the tribesmen from the government which they had helped to create. Finally, in AD 834, 'Caliph al-Mutasim inaugurated his rule by dispatching an order to his governor in Egypt to strike off the names of all Arabs from the register of pensions and to stop paying their salaries. This was indeed a turning point in the history of the Arabs in Egypt. In short, their service as fighters was no longer needed: they were replaced by Turkish military slaves . . .'[21] The displacement of the Arabs reached its culmination in 868 when one of the Turkish governors of Egypt, Ibn Tulun, renounced his allegiance to the Caliph and founded the first of Egypt's Turkish dynasties.

Not surprisingly, many of the discontented and dispossessed Egyptian Arabs began drifting away from the Nile Valley and back to the nomadic life of earlier times. Some followed the Nile to the relatively freer region of Upper Egypt; others moved west across North Africa, incidentally over-running and Arabizing many of the indigenous Berber tribes; still others joined the Beja in the eastern hills and along the Red Sea coast. 'It is a striking, but not in the least surprising, fact,' says MacMichael, 'that the tendency of each successive dynasty that ruled Egypt was increasingly to regard the Arabs, that is the nomads, not so much as forming an integral part of the state as an element of danger and unrest hovering on the borders of the country, to be made use of when convenient but never entitled to more consideration than they had the power to extort.'[22] After no more than three centuries in the sunlight of Islam, the bedouins found them-selves back where they had begun: as an external proletariat. Thereafter until modern times their energies were exerted primarily as a destructive force within and against the empire which they had helped to build.

As we saw in Chapter 14, Arab merchants and perhaps other settlers were residing in the northernmost part of Nubia even before the days of the Beni Kanz (cf. Ch. 16). So far as large-scale migration was concerned, how-ever, the way south along the Nile was blocked both by the overt hostility of the Christian kingdoms (backed up by the sanction of the *Baqt* treaty) and by the meagre pastoral resources of Lower Nubia and the *Batn el Hajar*. The real key to southern penetration was the Red Sea Hills, and it was here that the first Arab breakthrough occurred.

At the beginning of the ninth century most of the Beja tribes who dwelt in the Red Sea Hills were still pagan, although a few had adopted a nominal Christianity and others, particularly in the coastal districts, may already have embraced the faith of Islam.[23] The tribesmen continued to raid Upper Egypt when opportunity presented itself, and in 831 a punitive campaign was undertaken against them by Caliph al-Mutasim. According to Yusuf Hasan, this was the decisive event in opening up the Red Sea Hills to Arab settlement.[24] The Beja were defeated and were forced to sign a capitula-tion recognizing the caliph as their suzerain and paying an annual tribute. The agreement contained many of the same stipulations as did the *Baqt* treaty with the Nubians,[25] but it was a unilateral capitulation which guaranteed nothing to the Beja in return for their submission. The tribesmen were forbidden to enter the villages and towns of Egypt, but there was no provision, as in the case of Nubia, against the Egyptians or Arabs entering and settling in the country of the Beja. According to Hasan, 'By agreeing to pay tribute the Beja were treated as a conquered people. When Kannun [the principal Beja chief] recognized the Abbasid overlordship and became a vassal, the victorious Arabs found an opportunity to extend their own influence, at least on paper, as far south as Badi. Arab gains were thus immense and the treaty acted as a spearhead which opened up the country to Arab influence. Arabs were free to move about the area or to settle; their commercial interests, religious freedom, and personal safety were all safeguarded by this agreement.'[26] MacMichael adds that 'The chief result to Egypt was a cessation of the raids on her southern border, and to the Beja the acquisition of all tribal control by an Arab aristocracy.'[27]

While it is difficult to single out a particular historical event as the beginning of a mass population movement, there is no doubt that the era immediately following the campaign and treaty of al-Mutasim witnessed a large-scale movement of Arabs into the hill country east and south of Egypt. Again according to Hasan, one of the chief motivations of the early Arab migration was gold fever, and it was during this era that the adventurer al-Umari founded his renegade state in the mining region above Abu Hamed (Ch. 15).[28] Arab settlers and Arab influence gradually spread south over the whole of the Beja territory as far as the borders of Abyssinia; the indigenous tribes were converted to Islam through the usual processes of intermarriage and clientage, as the Nubians were later to be. The two Arab groups chiefly involved in this movement were the Rabi'a and the Juhayna – both originally tribes of the Hejaz which had been settled in Upper Egypt before their migration to the south.[29] For a time members of the two tribes ruled over the Beja as an alien aristocracy;[30] however the Rabi'a eventually coalesced with their subjects to form the Beni Kanz (cf. Ch. 16) and perhaps other hybrid Beja tribes, and their original name and identity were lost. Some members of the Juhayna may also have amalgamated with the Beja, but the greater part of this exceptionally large and cohesive tribe retained its separate identity and language, and eventually moved onward from the Beja country to the open pastures beyond the Nile (cf. Fig. 81).

From the ninth to the fourteenth century Arab settlement and Arab influence were confined to the region east of the Nile; that is essentially to the Beja country. The Christian kingdoms continued to form a barrier against the westward migration of the nomads. Pressure against them built up steadily with the continued Arab migrations, and became severe after the Mamelukes began their policy of harassment against the bedouins in Egypt. Part of the Christian barrier gave way when the northern Nubians

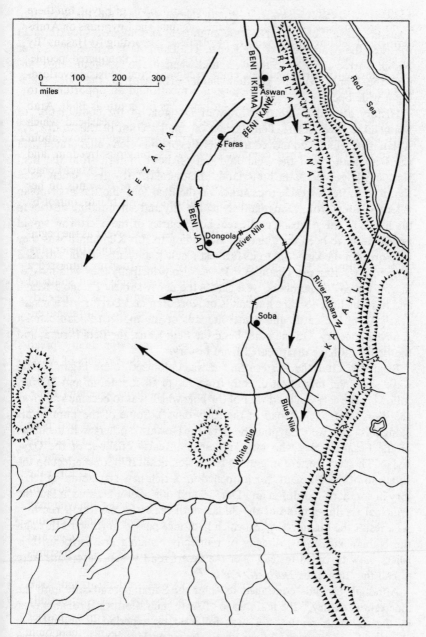

Fig. 81. Principal Arab migrations of the Middle Ages

were infiltrated and amalgamated with the Beni Kanz, but the Nile route remained unsuitable for large-scale migration, and no great breakthrough followed the Arabization of the Kenzi. The Dongola Province, not Lower Nubia, barred the way to the west, and when in the late fourteenth century the Upper Nubian kingdom finally disintegrated, the flood gates burst wide open.

History attributes the overthrow of Dongola to the combination of Mamelukes, Beni Kanz, Beni Ikrima (a small section of the Arab Qays Aylan tribe which had moved to Upper Egypt and often collaborated with the Beni Kanz) and the Beni Ja'd (an offshoot in turn from the Beni Ikrima, who settled in the hinterlands of Dongola).[31] It will be remembered that it was after a treacherous attack on the Beni Ja'd that the last Nubian ruler withdrew from Dongola, leaving the city and surrounding district in the hands of the Arabs. Yet the real beneficiaries of the overthrow would appear to have been the Juhayna. According to Ibn Khaldun it was they who overran the kingdom to its farthest reaches, and subsequently divided it up into warring principalities.[32] It was also principally they who moved, in ever increasing numbers, west across the newly subject Dongola Reach and into the little-used pasturelands of Kordofan and Darfur. As a result, nearly all of the cattle and camel nomads of the modern Sudan claim a Juhayna ancestry. On the other hand the Beni Kanz, the Beni Ikrima, and the Beni Ja'd have disappeared from history.

Belatedly, after the western Sudan was colonized, there began a final wave of nomad migration directly from Egypt to Kordofan and Darfur, following the caravan road west of the Nile which was to become known as the *Darb el-Arba'in* ('road of the forty days'). Some of the immigrants along this route were Egyptian Berbers (the Howara); others were members of the Fezara tribes who may represent an early offshoot of the Qays Aylan. This late western migration had a significant if indirect effect on the situation of the Nubians, for it opened up a rich new slave-hunting territory in southern Kordofan and Darfur, and this region became in fact the principal slaving-ground of the Sudan until the later nineteenth century. As a result the human cargoes which had once passed northward through the Nubian kingdoms, directly or indirectly bringing prosperity to their rulers, now travelled instead over the desert road which Europeans were to call the 'infamous *Darb el-Arba'in*'.[33]

Although nomads continued to enter the Sudan sporadically until the nineteenth century,[34] the main wave of Arab migration was probably over by the sixteenth century.[35] It was followed by a period of assimilation about which, unfortunately, we know almost nothing. On this subject the tribal histories are either silent or deliberately misleading, ignoring the native contribution to the present-day Sudanese cultures or else dismissing it as the incidental and accidental result of Arab intermarriage with a small number of native women.[36] Moreover, no foreign observer has left us a coherent record of events in Nubia during the sixteenth and seventeenth centuries. As a result, what little we know of the critical period of Arabization must be arrived at largely through deduction. In the pages that follow we shall have to consider three aspects of the assimilation process: first, the social and cultural rapprochement of Arabs and natives; second, the 'spiritual Arabization' of the Nubians, which is a matter not of cultural change but of redefined self-image; and thirdly the spread of the Islamic faith, which has become the genuine common denominator of all Sudanese peoples north of the tropics.

THE ARABIZATION OF THE NUBIANS

As Trimingham has pointed out, the cultural and ethnic assimilation which took place following the Arab migrations was a two-way process, involving on the one hand the Arabization of the native Sudanese and on the other the 'indigenization' of the immigrants.[37] The great majority of the newcomers were bedouins, and the cultural influence which they exerted on the Sudanese peoples was a nearly uniform one. On the other hand the indigenous peoples who had been overrun exhibited a variety of cultures and languages, and their influence upon their conquerors was correspondingly varied. There were moreover substantial environmental differences within the Arabs' new homeland which soon obliged them to adapt to a variety of local conditions. As a result, there emerged through the assimilation process a new mosaic of peoples and cultures which persists to the present day. Its one common denominator is the Islamic faith: wherever the Arabs penetrated, their religion triumphed over all competitors. The Arabic language has also become increasingly widespread, although peoples like the northern Nubians and the Beja have not only held out against it but have absorbed a number of formerly Arabic-speaking immigrants into their own dialect groups.

Although the modern inhabitants of the Arabized Sudan[38] count themselves as members of more than one hundred individual tribes,[39] five major cultural and/or linguistic divisions can be recognized among them. The Red Sea littoral and the adjacent highlands continue to be occupied by unassimilated or incompletely assimilated Beja tribes, most of whom still speak their ancestral Hamitic dialects. They were and are organized in small, scattered bands rather than in great tribal confederations like the Arab nomads.[40] Along the Nile from Aswan to Debba (at the bottom of the great bend above Dongola) there remain the unassimilated Nubians, converted to Islam but retaining their African language and the agricultural mode of life which they have followed since the days of the pharaohs. Upstream from the true Nubians as far as the junction of the Blue and

White Niles are the so-called Ja'aliyin tribes. Although claiming a purely Arab pedigree[41] they are in fact made up overwhelmingly of Arabized Nubians, with only a small admixture of genuinely Arab blood.[42] Most of the Ja'aliyin groups also continue the riverain farming life of pre-Islamic times, although a few have adopted a semi-nomadic existence in the Nile hinterlands and in southern Kordofan.

East, west, and south of the Ja'aliyin are innumerable tribes of camel nomads who follow a pastoral existence similar to that of Arabia, and who of all Sudanese peoples have the most legitimate claim to being true Arabs. Like the bedouins of the Arabian Peninsula they wander over vast territories in great, communal migrations.[43] Nearly all of the camel nomads claim a Juhayna ancestry. Finally, in the southerly grasslands of Kordofan and Darfur, west of the Nile, there has developed a special group of nomads – the Baggara tribes – who subsist on cattle rather than on camels, goats and sheep. Most of the Baggara also claim a Juhayna ancestry, but these tribes have also absorbed a good many indigenous peoples, and their particular form of pastoralism is more African than Arabian.[44]

The five aforementioned groups occupy all of the desert and steppelands of the modern Sudan, except for some tribal enclaves in the far west. The great majority of Sudanese today belong to the third, fourth, and fifth groups; that is, to the Arabic-speaking Ja'aliyin and nomads. So ubiquitous are they that the names Ja'aliyin and Juhayna have become practically generic terms for riverain farmers and bedouins respectively, and have lost any specific tribal significance.[45] To the south of all five groups there remain the purely Negro tribes of the forest and savanna, formerly pagan and now mostly Christian, who have been largely unaffected by Arab influence. These people were not drawn into effective contact with the Arabized north until the southward expansion of slave-raiding in the nineteenth century, and they are not part of our story. However, their assimilation has been a major goal and a major problem for modern Sudanese governments (cf. Ch. 19).

Since this book is properly a history of Nubia rather than of the Sudan,[46] we shall be concerned in subsequent pages only with the Arabization of the Nubians and of the ex-Nubian Ja'aliyin. Even for these peoples we cannot describe the assimilation process in any detail, for our only historical account of it is that of Ibn Khaldun: 'several clans of the Arab tribe of Juhayna dispersed throughout their country and settled there. The kings of Nubia, at first, tried to drive them out by force. They failed, so they changed their tactics and tried to win them over by offering their daughters in marriage. Thus it was that their Kingdom disintegrated, for it passed to the sons of the Juhayna from their Nubian mothers in accordance with the non-Arab practice of inheritance by the sister and her sons.'[47] As we have already noted (Ch. 16), this oft-quoted passage cannot be taken at

558

face value as an explanation for the downfall of the Christian Nubian kingdoms. On the other hand it probably does give a correct insight into the subsequent process of Arabization, suggesting that it was in the beginning a social process and only secondarily an ideological one.

In the absence of detailed historical information we can only judge the process of Arabization in terms of its end product; that is, we can observe the varying degrees of Arabization among the present-day Nubians and ex-Nubians, and try to account for them in terms of differences in environment and historical experience.

The Kenzi Nubians in the immediate vicinity of Aswan were undoubtedly the first to feel the impact of Arab migrations, as they were assuredly also the first Nubian converts to Islam. The story of their interpenetration and eventual amalgamation with the Arab–Beja Beni Kanz tribe has already been told (Ch. 16). In spite of the large historical role played by the Beni Kanz, the Arab element among them must have been relatively small, for it was ultimately swallowed up in the indigenous population. It seems, too, that active contact and intermixing between northern Nubians and Arabs was confined to the early period of the Arab migrations, between the ninth and fourteenth centuries. Once the Beja country was opened up, most of the bedouins followed the pasturelands of the Red Sea Hills in preference to the unproductive Nile Valley above Aswan. Thus isolated from later Arab movements, the Kenzi reverted more and more to a purely Nubian tribe. Today their language and way of life are essentially those of pre-Islamic times. It should be mentioned, however, that in the modern era certain alien groups – the Akelat Arabs and the Arabic-speaking Ababda – have settled among the Kenzi without being assimilated by them.[48]

The Kenzi, whose dialect is different from that of the Mahasi Nubians to the south of them, retain a strong sense of tribal identity. Most of them claim the traditional Rabi'a ancestry of the Beni Kanz,[49] which has a legitimate though exaggerated basis in historical fact. However, it appears that some Kenzi have adopted the claim of descent from Abbas, the uncle of the Prophet, which is common to all of the Ja'aliyin tribes (see below).[50]

Of all the Nubians the Mahasi speakers, whose territory extends from Maharraqa in the north nearly to Kerma in the south, have been least directly affected by the Arab migrations. Not only was their inhospitable country avoided by all of the main population movements of the Middle Ages, but, through the accidents of geography, their homeland is separated from habitable pasturelands by a much broader strip of total desert than is any other part of the Nile Valley (Fig. 9). As Hasan says, ' . . . most of the immigrants were attracted neither by the Nubian deserts nor by the narrow strip of cultivable lands along the river. They trekked on farther. The number of those who intermingled with the Nubians north of Dongola could not have been large enough to transform the inhabitants into an

Arabic-speaking population. Those who settled down had to learn about farming techniques and had to acquire the language of the sedentary farmers, which was ... Nubian, and soon they lost their identity.'[51] We have already observed that it was in the Mahasi area of Nubia that the organized practice of Christianity survived longest (Ch. 16), and it is among the Mahasi of the *Batn el Hajar* that the most obvious Christian survivals are found today.[52] In the post-Christian era, moreover, the northern Nubians were governed not by Arabs but by Turks, appointees of the Ottoman régime in Cairo.

The Mahasi Nubians do not have a strongly developed sense of tribe. They speak of themselves conventionally as belonging to three groups: the Mahas proper, the Sukkot and the Fadija, but these are in reality geographical terms referring to different parts of the Nile Valley. There has been so little historically documented Arab intermarriage that many Mahasi are obliged to claim their Moslem ancestry not from Arabs but from Turks – their former colonial overlords.[53] However, the group as a whole claims descent either from the Juhayna or from the Khazraj, according to two genealogies both of which are patently spurious.[54]

Paradoxically, although they are the least Arabized of the Nubians, the Mahasi are in some respects the best Moslems. From an early period – perhaps due to some lingering tradition carried over from Christian times – they have placed a high value on learning, and in the early modern period they produced an extraordinary number of *fekis* or religious scribes. According to MacMichael, 'At some early date, perhaps about the time of the foundation of the Funj kingdom, some of [the] Mahas with pretensions to a noble lineage and a certain amount of education left their own country and established themselves as holy-men among the more ignorant medley of Arabs, Funj and Nuba in the south. Thus arose the Mahas settlements on the lower reaches of the Blue Nile and around Khartoum . . .'[55] Some of these villages still derive a substantial income from what Trimingham calls '*feki*-mongering'.[56] These emigrant Nubians have become thoroughly Arabized, have lost their native speech, and now count themselves members of nearly a dozen 'tribes'.[57] However they retain certain traces of their northern origin, such as the practice of covering graves with white pebbles (the immemorial Nubian practice of the Kerma and Ballana cultures) and of leaving bowls of water beside the graves.[58]

The Danagla (literally, people of Dongola), extending roughly from the Third Cataract to Debba, are the most southerly of the surviving Nubian groups. They show far more Arab influence than do their northern neighbours and for that reason are classed both by MacMichael[59] and by Holt[60] among the Ja'aliyin tribes rather than as Barabra (the collective modern-day term for Nubian-speakers) even though they retain their native dialect.

We have seen that the overthrow of the medieval kingdom of Dongola was accomplished by a combination of Arab tribes and the Arab–Nubian Beni Kanz. Since that time the Danagla have lived in fairly close and continuous contact with Arabs. For a long time they were politically subject to an Arab aristocracy, although in time the Arab chiefs intermarried with the natives and, in the northern districts, reverted to the use of the Nubian language. In addition to the presence of Arab overlords, the Dongola Reach was adjoined on the south and west by marginal pasturelands which have been occupied since the Arab breakthrough by the Kababish and the Hawawir, the former a branch of the Juhayna[61] and the latter an Arabized Berber tribe.[62] As a result there has been, at least seasonally, a considerable nomad population in the Dongola region, as there has been also in all of the riverain districts farther south. Some of the Danagla have themselves taken up a nomadic or semi-nomadic life, and some have moved south-west into Kordofan, where they are both pastoralists and farmers today.[63] More recently large numbers of individual Dongolawis have penetrated into the western Sudan in pursuit of commerce and the slave trade.[64]

The Danagla as a group have no sense of ethnic solidarity, but instead consider themselves members of a number of different 'Arab' tribes, each of which until the twentieth century had its own *mek* or petty king.[65] Presumably these were the descendants of the original Arab aristocracy established in the days following the overthrow of the Christian kingdom. It was the *mek* of the Bedayria tribe who in the seventeenth and eighteenth centuries resided at Old Dongola as the erstwhile successor to the Christian monarchs (cf. Ch. 18), although he was in reality the vassal of more powerful rulers to the south.[66] Other important Danagla tribes besides the Bedayria are the Tarayfia, the Hakimab, and the Jawabra.[67] The latter, originally a branch of the Beni Ikrima,[68] are said to have been expelled from a former habitat in Lower Nubia by the Turks, and subsequently to have become the most prosperous tribe in the Dongola region.[69] All the Danagla tribes, like their Arabized cousins the Ja'aliyin, claim descent from Abbas, the uncle of the Prophet.[70]

No satisfactory explanation has yet been offered for the anomalous distribution of the modern Nubian dialects; that is, the close relationship of Kenzi and Dongolawi and their much greater distance from the intervening Mahasi language (cf. Ch. 2). The relatively minor differences between Kenzi and Dongolawi are thought to date back no more than 500 years,[71] whereas the divergence of these two from Mahasi (which is much closer to the Old Nubian of the Middle Ages) has been dated by the glottochronological method to the early part of the Christian period.[72] As a result, some movement of people around the Mahasi territory seems necessary to account for the presence of closely related dialects to the north and south of it. Given the record of such migrations by the Beni Kanz, the

Beni Ja'd, and the Jawabra, it is tempting to suggest that one or another of these Nubianized Arab groups transplanted the northern dialect into the Dongola Reach. However, Millet believes that ' . . . the historically well-attested period of Kenuz interference into the internal affairs of Dongola in the fourteenth century seems to have been too brief to have affected permanently the language of that region.'[73] Moreover, the evidence of Ibn Selim clearly indicates that there was a dialect difference between the inhabitants of Maris (Lower Nubia and the *Batn el Hajar*) and those of Makouria (Upper Nubia) as early as the tenth century.[74] At the same time the surviving Old Nubian texts do not suggest that there was a comparable dialect difference between what are today the Kenzi-speaking and Mahasi-speaking districts of Lower Nubia. Given these circumstances we should probably consider the possibility that the similarities between Kenzi and Dongolawi are due not to the southward migration of Kenzi speakers but to a northward transplantation of the Dongola dialect at the end of the Middle Ages. Without attempting to resolve the question finally, it is probably safe at least to assume that the numerous population movements between northern Nubia and the Dongola Reach which are attested in the Late Christian and post-Christian periods had something to do with the establishment and/or maintenance of a close linguistic relationship between the two areas.[75]

Upstream from Debba there are no surviving Nubian-speakers along the Nile, although most of the riverain tribes as far south as Khartoum – the so-called Ja'aliyin tribes – are known to be made up primarily of Arabized Nubians. These peoples have surrendered completely to the Arab passion for political decentralization, and they now answer to more than forty different tribal names.[76] Proceeding upriver from the true Nubian Danagla, the most important Ja'aliyin tribes are the Shaiqiya, the Rubatab, the Manasir, the Mirafab, and the Ja'aliyin proper.[77] All these groups share a common pedigree, tracing their descent from Abbas by way of a certain Ibrahim Ja'al, their eponymous ancestor.[78] According to Hasan, 'Two significant conclusions emerge from the analysis of the Ja'ali lineage: the first is the deliberate attempt to ignore the Nubian sub-stratum that the Arab immigrants had submerged. The second is the genealogists' tendency to standardize inter-relationships among these Arabized Nubians and to link them all to the genesis of the Ja'ali–Abbasi Groups. In reality the majority of the immigrants were not Abbasis but Arabs of mixed composition.'[79]

Although the Arabization of the Ja'aliyin was probably due in the broadest sense to their submission to Arab overlords and to their fairly close contacts with various bedouin peoples, it should not be supposed that the process of assimilation took place everywhere at the same rate or under the same circumstances. The Abu Hamed Reach may have been penetrated and partially Arabized even before the fall of the Christian kingdoms, since this rocky zone was not only thinly populated but lay closer to the migration route through the Red Sea Hills than did any part of the Nile further downstream (Fig. 81). Moreover the gold mines which were the scene of a good deal of Arab activity in the ninth and tenth centuries were only a short distance away.[80]

Downriver from Abu Hamed, the Arabization of the region around the Fourth Cataract was forcibly if perhaps unwittingly effected by the fierce Shaiqiya warlords, an Arab military aristocracy whose activities will be more fully recounted in the next chapter. Their harsh exactions upon the riverain farmers forced many of the Nubians to emigrate north to Dongola, while the surviving remnant was too weak to maintain a separate cultural or linguistic identity.[81] The Nubians of the Berber district, above the Fifth Cataract, were subject to the equally militant Abdallab Arabs,[82] but were themselves a good deal more numerous and more prosperous than were the Nubians of the Abu Hamed Reach. Among them pockets of Nubian speech may have survived as late as the seventeenth century.

It seems probable that the Nubian inhabitants of the Kingdom of Alwa – who were perhaps always a small ruling élite – were largely killed off or expelled by the Funj and Abdallab conquerors, as implied in the 'Funj Chronicle' (Ch. 16). At any rate in the time of the Funj kingdom the mountain of Hajar el-Asal, north of Qerri, was traditionally regarded as the southern frontier of Nubia.[83] However, there are a number of unimportant Ja'aliyin tribes in the northern Gezira which may have a partly Nubian origin.[84]

THE GENEALOGICAL TRADITION

How thoroughly the Nubians' outlook has been transformed by the coming of the Arabs may be judged from the account of their history which they gave to the Swiss explorer Burckhardt in 1813: 'According to their own traditions the present Nubians derive their origin from the Arabian bedouins who invaded the country after the promulgation of the Mohammedan creed, the greater part of the Christian inhabitants . . . having either fled before them or been killed; a few . . . embraced the religion of the invaders.'[85] This widespread folk tradition, which remains current to the present day, is symbolic of the Nubians' capitulation to the Arab invaders. Not only have they become Moslems but, in their own view, Arabs as well. Gone is any memory of the legitimate glories of the Nubian past; instead the heirs of Piankhi and the medieval kings derive their ancestry from barbarian tribes from across the Red Sea.[86] In moving from the world of Christendom to that of Islam they have embraced not only a new destiny but a new history. Even more startling is their reversion, after ages of monarchy and empire, to a tribal system of organization which harks all the way back to pre-pharaonic days.

Taken literally, the folk history of the modern Nubians is a patent absurdity. Language, culture, and physical characteristics all link them unmistakably with the medieval Christians, most of whom in fact were neither driven out nor killed off by the Arab invaders. Even the Arabized Ja'aliyin have only a small admixture of genuinely Arab blood,[87] and the Mahasi Nubians who were Burckhardt's principal informants have hardly more than a trace. Yet the Nubians' claim of Arab ancestry is not simply a capricious fabrication, for it is, properly considered, a social rather than a biological pedigree. It is the Nubians' charter of membership in the Islamic community.[88] In order to appreciate its importance, certain peculiarities of the Islamic social system must be considered.

Both medieval Christendom and medieval Islam were permeated by a sense of community; they were social and political systems as well as religious ones. For Christians, social cohesion was maintained through the institution of a highly organized church. Conversion to Christianity involved more than acknowledging a personal saviour; above all else it meant accepting the authority and discipline of the church.[89] Thus it was inevitable that when an organized church could no longer be maintained in Nubia, the Christian faith should perish along with it. In the spiritual vacuum which followed, it was also inevitable that the Nubians should turn to the rival faith of Islam. Not only was it then sweeping in full vigour across the sub-Saharan steppes, but the civilization of Islam – particularly as represented by the bedouin nomads who were its chief adherents – was ideally suited to the fragmented and culturally impoverished conditions of the feudal age.

Although Islam was and is 'not so much a creed as a social system',[90] it lacks both an organized church and an effective state. For the educated and the genuinely devout, a sufficient sense of community may be provided by a knowledge of religious tradition and by membership in a regular body of worshippers. For the illiterate bedouin and peasant masses who have always made up the bulk of the Islamic community, however, social cohesion from the beginning has been maintained through a much older organizing principle: that of kinship. A complex web of genealogies, both genuine and fictitious, links together every Moslem from Senegal to Java and makes them all descendants of the Prophet and his earliest followers.[91] The Islamic community is thus, in anthropological terms, a vast segmentary lineage system. This organizing principle, never acknowledged in orthodox political thought,[92] is nevertheless one of the enduring legacies of pre-Islamic Arabia to the civilization of Islam.[93]

The segmentary lineage system of the Arabs is first cousin to that of the Hebrews, as set down in the Book of Genesis, and serves the same function.

A carefully recorded network of kinship unites all of the tribes of the Arabian Peninsula, specifying precisely their degree of relationship to one another and therefore how they shall behave towards one another. This organizing principle has been described as a 'system of non-government'; that is, the fiction of universal kinship takes the place of formal governing institutions.[94] Whenever a tribe becomes too large to be governed on such an informal basis, it splits into smaller tribes which maintain a close relationship through their possession of a common pedigree. Tribal genealogies are thus the unacknowledged (and often unwritten) constitutions of the Arabs and similarly organized peoples. Of these traditions MacMichael has observed that ' . . . though many of the assertions of the genealogists may be incredible as literal statements of fact, yet they have considerable value if understood in a figurative sense – if, in other words, they are taken as parables.'[95]

In pre-Islamic times the lineage system of the Arabs was confined to the tribes of the Arabian Peninsula. Since many of these had indeed split off from a common ancestral stock, their genealogies probably had a certain measure of historical validity. After the wave of Islamic conquests, however, all kinds of non-Arab peoples were attached as clients to the various Arab tribes who had conquered them, and in time they appropriated the genealogies of their overlords. Moreover, the Arabs intermarried freely with all of their subject populations and since a single Arab ancestor was enough to confer an Arab pedigree, the distinction between Arab and non-Arab Moslems became impossibly blurred. This was particularly true after the use of the Arabic language became general throughout the empire, yet even the retention of a non-Arabic language was not a deterrent to a claim of Arab ancestry, as can be seen in the case of the Nubians. The story in such instances is always the same: the 'original' ancestors were Arabs, but non-Arabic speech and other customs were acquired through their intermarriage with native women.[96]

Within the *Dar el-Islam* (the Islamic *oikoumêne*) Arab identity carried both practical and spiritual advantages. Under the early caliphate the Arabs ruled over their more numerous non-Arab subjects as a genuine military aristocracy, exempt from taxation and enjoying a monopoly of the spoils of war. Even after the functions of government and war were largely taken over by Persians and Turks, in the days of the Abbasid Caliphs, Arab ancestry still conferred noble status within the highly stratified society of medieval Islam.[97] Yet it is not enough to suggest that all Moslems claim an Arab pedigree for the sake of these advantages. Bedouin and peasant peoples, in particular, also claim Arab descent because within the Islamic community there is no other recognized lineage system but that of the Arabs, and membership in such a system is, for them, the necessary basis of social interaction. The depth of Moslem feeling on this subject is eloquently expressed in the preamble to a Sudanese Arab pedigree recorded by Sir Harold MacMichael:

> This is a pedigree giving the origins of the Arabs; for the preservation and guarding of such is obligatory because of the record of blood-relationships that they contain. The object of preserving them is not to cause boastful comparisons of pedigrees; for, as was said by the Commander of the Faithful the Imam Omar ibn el Khattab . . . 'Ye know from your pedigrees how ye are connected.' Some of the learned say that Omar may have heard this from the Prophet . . . But the knowledge of the pedigrees of persons who are unrelated to yourself is of no use . . . and the following saying of the Prophet . . . about one who was learned in pedigrees bears this out: 'A knowledge of them is useless and ignorance harmless.'
>
> But if a man devote himself to the study of what does not concern him his labour is impious: that is in times of mutual love and affection; but in these present days of mutual hatred and jealousy the study of pedigrees is obligatory, for at the end of the age the use of abusive epithets will be prevalent, and the difficulty will not be resolved save by means of pedigrees. So the keeping of pedigrees has been ordained, and it is not dutiful to neglect them, and he who does so is a rebel, owing to the danger of disturbance being caused among the people, and trouble in the hearts of the various nations. Thus the study of pedigrees is obligatory because the observance of blood-relationships is obligatory by the authority of the Book of the Law and the Unanimities . . .
>
> People are reliable as to their pedigrees; and whosoever has received from his father or ancestor any charge of a pedigree is indeed whatever the pedigree in his charge shows him to be.[98]

As the foregoing passage suggests, Mohammed himself had attempted to suppress the lineage principle and to create instead a community of the faithful, without social distinctions; according to his teaching 'there are no genealogies in Islam'.[99] But he is also credited with the saying, 'Learn from your lineage enough to maintain contact with your relatives',[100] and it is this latter principle which has appealed to the illiterate mass of his followers. The Islamic social system has thus been created less by the propagation of the Prophet's creed than by the worldwide extension of the Arab lineage system which he had sought to disparage. Since to be a Moslem is, for all but the educated élite, more a matter of belonging than of believing, an Arab pedigree takes precedence even over the profession of faith,[101] just as in medieval Christendom church membership took precedence over personal conviction. It is for the sake of such Islamic membership that the Nubians, for the second time in their history, have repudiated their legitimate past in favour of a largely fictitious one.

The keepers of genealogical tradition in the Sudan are the *fekis* – men theoretically learned in jurisprudence or theology, but in reality often professional pedigree-mongers.[102] Many of the older and more widely current Sudanese tribal genealogies are said to have been compiled originally by el-Samarkandi, an immigrant *feki* (presumably from Central Asia, as his name suggests) who attached himself to the Funj court at Sennar in the sixteenth century.[103] Here he produced on demand the noble pedigrees which the newly converted Funj and other tribes so ardently craved. El-Samarkandi is credited by modern sceptics with inventing the tradition of Abbasid origin for the Ja'aliyin tribes,[104] and perhaps also the even more preposterous claim of the Funj to be descended from the lineage of the Prophet.[105] Many latter-day *fekis* claim to have had access to el-Samarkandi's manuscript, or to have memorized large parts of it, although no known copy of the work is now extant.[106]

The possession of a substantial store of genealogical knowledge, either committed to memory or in the form of a jealously guarded manuscript, may serve as the stock-in-trade of a family of *fekis* for several generations.[107] A very large part of the Sudanese population is actually in possession of *nisbas*, or fragments of written pedigrees, which have been produced for them by *fekis*. These are theoretically extracts from larger works in the possession of the *fekis*, but an attempt to trace down the parent documents is rarely successful.[108]

While the possession of an Arab pedigree is necessary for full participation in the Islamic community, its importance is social rather than strictly political. No lasting commitment to any particular tribe or faction is implied by the possession of a given pedigree. It is a paradox of the Arab tribal system (and of most other nomad tribal systems) that, although the only acknowledged principle of solidarity is that of blood relationship, the 'tribe' is in reality a loose hierarchy of voluntarily associated groups whose kinship is largely fictitious. 'Tribes' are made up of 'subtribes', 'subtribes' of 'sections', 'sections' of 'subsections', 'subsections' of 'encampments', and so on (the terminology and the number of levels of organization differs from group to group), all of which claim a common ancestry, but all of which are held together in reality by no other force than that of charismatic leadership.[109] Individuals and families continually move back and forth from section to section; sections move from tribe to tribe. Cunnison has succinctly characterized this process of restless movement among the modern Baggara Arabs of the western Sudan:

The process of splitting, migrating, and resettling which has given rise to the present distribution of Baggara groups is active also within single tribes. Sections secede, move to a new part of the tribal territory, and make brotherhood with distantly related sections; and they are at once considered close kinsmen of their new neighbors. Lineages move in dissatisfaction from one *omodiya* to another; *surras* move to join some other *omodiya* or some other lineage within their own *omodiya*. Finally, individuals occasionally go and join other *surras*.[110]

It goes without saying that the Arab tribal system has been, and is, extremely unstable. To a considerable extent this is a necessary adaptive mechanism for peoples whose survival depends on the uncertain rains. As accustomed pastures dry up in one part of the country and new ones blossom in another, old combinations are inevitably dissolved and new ones formed. While some tribes have managed to preserve a tribal name and sense of identity through hundreds of years of such vicissitudes, many others have lasted no more than a few generations. A section or even a smaller group, under the aegis of a forceful leader, may at any time break away from its ancestral tribe to form the nucleus around which a new tribe will gather, all of whose members will later claim the original leader as their eponymous ancestor. In this way new tribal names will abruptly and periodically appear in the genealogical histories. At the same time formerly independent tribes whose numbers and influence have been reduced by environmental reverses or weak leadership will inevitably have to attach themselves as sections to some larger and more powerful group, and their tribal names will disappear. This continual ebb and flow accounts for the kaleidoscopic quality of bedouin tribal history; it also accounts for the periodic waves of mass migration and conquest which have emanated from the steppelands.

Perhaps because of their instability, there is no standard terminology for the various levels of organization within the Arab tribal system. With typical Arabic hyperbole, almost any of them may be described at one time or another as 'tribes'. MacMichael's encyclopedic survey lists more than one hundred 'Arab' tribes in the Sudan alone,[111] and most of these have innumerable individually named subdivisions, each of which may also call itself a tribe, yet all of them also claim membership in or descent from no more than a dozen ancestral tribes. Thus when the historical annals speak of the movements and conquests of Arab 'tribes', we can never be sure whether mass migrations or only small redistributions of population are involved.

Unlike the true Arabs the Nubians have never been a bedouin people, and from the time when they embraced the civilization of the pharaohs until the coming of the Arabs they were not a tribal one. For them the principle of kinship had long since given way to that of subjection to centralized governments, and in their day they were the subjects as well as the rulers of some notable empires. Yet when, for the sake of an Islamic identity, they embraced the lineage system of the Arabs, they embraced also and necessarily the Arab tribal system. For a time in the early modern period they knew no more formal government than that which the tribal system provided, and even after the reappearance of more stable monarchies (cf. Ch. 18) they continued to think of themselves as tribesmen rather than as subjects or citizens, as in fact most of them do to the present day.[112] They have thus reverted in theory to a system of government, and in practice to a self-image, strikingly close to those which we attribute to the C Horizon (Ch. 6).[113]

THE PROPAGATION OF ISLAM

Trimingham has written that:

A newcomer to the Sudan, having read some standard textbook on Islam, tends to take it for granted that the religion of the people is that of the Koran and the law. The mosque is usually the most prominent object he sees and this makes him fail to understand that this is not the only, nor the most important, centre and symbol of their religion. A far more significant symbol of faith scattered about the Sudan in greater profusion than the mosque is the whitewashed domed tomb of a saint. The one may be regarded as the symbol of the system and the other of a living faith.[114]

The *gubbas* (domed tombs) of saints are not merely the centres of innumerable folk cults, however; they are also legitimate historical monuments to the men who first brought a knowledge of the Islamic faith (as distinguished from membership in the Arab community) into the spiritual wilderness of the Sudan. If these pioneer missionaries are sometimes better remembered and more genuinely venerated than the somewhat remote god and prophet whom they preached, this is in keeping with the immemorial nature of folk religion. As Hillelson says, '... the individual, in striving to know and to be saved, requires a mediator between himself and an unapproachable and inconceivable god, and it is the fact that prophets, saints, and holy men are conceived as mediators ... which gives them their peculiar virtue, and explains the irresistible power with which they sway the minds and acts of their followers.'[115]

Just as a mass of genealogical tradition records the coming of the Arabs to the Sudan, so another great body of folk literature records the propagation of the Islamic faith. It consists of innumerable biographies of the saints and holy men who first carried the teachings of the Prophet to the Sudan, and from whom all subsequent religious teachers are spiritually descended. These too are genealogical traditions of a sort, carefully recording the names of the teachers under whom the first missionaries studied as well as listing their own disciples. Among illiterate peoples noble learning, no less than noble lineage, has its pedigree,[116] and it is said that 'one who studied without a *sheikh* could never become a true *ulema*'[117] (both terms referring in this case to learned religious scholars).

Fortunately the great body of folk tradition surrounding the lives of saints has also been compiled and written down – not in this case by a European scholar but by a learned Sudanese *feki* of the early nineteenth century, Muhammad Wad Dayfallah. His book, conventionally known as the *Tabaqat*[118] of Wad Dayfallah, is a compilation of 260 biographies which were current in the Sudan in his time.[119] 'The value of the book,' says MacMichael, 'is not merely that it tells one for whom the majority of the *gubbas* that stud the Sudan were built, but that one gains some insight into the ways of living and thinking and speaking of the people of the land in the seventeenth and eighteenth centuries. Many of their beliefs and customs, their superstitions and practical ideas, are revealed ... '[120]

Hillelson adds that:

A study of these beliefs and customs is not only of historical value, but has the interest of actuality for those who strive to understand the life and ideas of the Sudan Arab at the present day. It is true that since Wad Dayfallah's day there has arisen an educated class whose religious ideas are fashioned in the moulds supplied by the modern Moslem world; ... but though the educated wage war against the 'superstitions' of their unlearned countrymen, and though a flood of new things and new ideas has poured into the country ever since the days of Muhammad Ali, it is yet a fact that the intellectual and emotional world of Wad Dayfallah's heroes still lives amongst the large majority ...[121]

The *Tabaqat* is remarkable not only for its content but because it is written in Sudanese colloquial Arabic – an unheard-of departure for a learned *feki* at the beginning of the nineteenth century.[122] The book forms the basis for nearly all of our knowledge of the spread of Islam in the Sudan, as MacMichael's compilation of the genealogical traditions forms the basis for our knowledge of the spread of the Arabs.

The biographies in the *Tabaqat* are thought to cover the period from about 1500 to 1800.[123] However, there are other and more ambiguous traditions which tell of religious teachers in the Sudan at a still earlier period. A holy man from Yemen, Ghulam Allah b. A'id, is said to have settled in Dongola in the late fourteenth century because the city was 'sunk in perplexity and error'.[124] He built a mosque and taught the Koran and religious sciences. In the next century, according to another tradition, a teacher named Hamed Abu Dunana settled in the Berber district (near the Fifth Cataract) at a time when that region may still have been subject to the Christian kingdom of Alwa.[125] There is nothing to substantiate the dates attributed to these earliest Islamic teachers, or even the fact of their existence.[126] In any case their influence does not seem to have been large, and the *Tabaqat* opens with the statement that before the time of the Funj (that is, before the sixteenth century) ' ... there flourished neither schools of learning nor reading of the Koran; it is said that a man might divorce his wife and she be married by another man the selfsame day without any period of probation, until Sheikh Mahmud al-Araki came from Egypt and taught the people to observe the laws ...'[127]

Mahmud al-Araki is the first of the historically attested sheikhs[128] whose biographies appear in the *Tabaqat* of Wad Dayfallah. After studying in Egypt, he returned to his native Sudan to found a school of religious law in the Gezira region, between the Blue and White Niles.[129] At about the same time came Ibrahim al-Buladi, who also taught law at a school in the Gezira.[130] Later in the sixteenth century Sheikh Taj al-Din al-Bahari resided for seven years at the Funj court in Sennar, and is credited with having transplanted the mystical order of the Qadiriya to the Sudan (see below).[131] In the same general era another mystic who is remembered only as al-Tilimsani (the man from Tlemcen, in North-west Africa) came to the Sudan to teach a variety of religious subjects.[132]

The Islamization of the Sudan took place at a time when the *sufi* or mystical orders were at their height in the Islamic world.[133] The *sufis*, like the early Christians and some later Protestant sects, believed in salvation through spiritual ecstasy rather than through the study of the scriptures; they often scoffed at conventional learning and even at literacy. Yet after the twelfth century the *sufis* were themselves highly tradition-bound. They were grouped into innumerable orders, each with its carefully preserved *tarikh* or 'path of enlightenment' which consisted of a combination of ritual abstentions and formulary devotions, some of which were highly complex. The *sufi* orders which are most familiar to non-Moslems are those which practise such bizarre devotions as sword-slashing, fire-walking, and ecstatic dancing ('whirling dervishes').[134]

The *sufi* orders until the nineteenth century had no very formal organization;[135] membership was a matter of undergoing a period of instruction under a recognized sheikh who had in turn been trained under a previous sheikh, in a line extending back to the founder of the order. Each sheikh would gather around him a group of disciples, one of whom (often his son) would inherit his particular mantle of sainthood after his death, while others would disperse to found new schools and further disseminate the *tarikh* of the order. The organizational structure (or lack of it) of the *sufi* movement thus closely resembled that of the Arab lineage system. In sufism, as among the Arab tribes, there has been continual splitting and recombining of sects.[136]

It was largely through the institution of local schools such as those we have just described that the knowledge and traditions of Islam were propagated in the Sudan after the first century of missionary activity.[137] However, not all of the early religious teachers were *sufis*; we have already noted that some were learned in the Koran and the law. According to Hillelson:

. . most of the currents of thought which at different times have agitated Islamic opinion have found a channel into this remote backwater of the Moslem world, and . . . the scholars and saints who fill the stage of the *Tabaqat* reflect in their different attitudes and types a variety of the spiritual and intellectual doctrines which have been the subject of theological study and controversy in Islam. In view of the isolation of the country and the backward state of learning it is not surprising that the reflection is extremely feeble, and that the subtleties of school-men and mystics . . . are reduced to the level required by scant scholarship and crude intelligence.[138]

In spite of the extent of orthodox teaching, however, the mystical strain which is so apparent in modern Sudanese Islam (see below) seems to have been predominant from the beginning, and it is noteworthy that even some of the most learned *fekis*, according to the authority of Wad Dayfallah, were motivated to teach not by the words of the Prophet but by dreams and visions. Again quoting Hillelson, ' . . . it is characteristic of the age and the country that even [the] champions of formal learning live in a world of visions and dreams and lay stress on devotions which in their essential nature do not differ from those of the [*sufis*].'[139] As a result, the long-standing and sometimes violent dispute between mystics and the ortho-dox religious establishment which disturbed other parts of the Islamic world never developed to an appreciable extent in the Islam of the Sudan. 'The most important aspect of this Islam,' says Trimingham, 'was the har-monious blending of *fiqh* and *tasawwuf*, i.e. the tempering of legalism with mysticism. We do not find that rigidity which is characteristic of Moslem leaders in Northern Nigeria. The clerics were at one and the same time *fuqaha* [scholars] and *fuqara* [ecstatics].'[140]

Most of the orthodox teachers of Islam were trained in Egypt, while the *sufi* missionaries came very largely from the Hejaz area of Arabia.[141] However the *sufi* orders, once transplanted to the Sudan, quickly became self-sustaining, whereas an advanced knowledge of the Koran and the law still required a period of study abroad, for there never developed in the Sudan any institutions of higher learning comparable to the universities of Cairo, Damascus and Baghdad. This circumstance undoubtedly helps to explain the ultimate predominance of the mystical, anti-intellectual side of Islam in the Sudan.

It will have been noted that the first century of active Islamic propaga-tion in the Sudan (the sixteenth century) corresponds to the beginnings of Funj hegemony (cf. Ch. 16 and Ch. 18), and that most of the centres of learning were established in the Funj territory, upstream from the con-fluence of the Blue and White Niles. It seems evident that the Funj rulers, in their anxiety to legitimize their Islamic identity, encouraged and sub-sidized the immigration of religious teachers, so that the initial spread of Islamic learning in the Sudan can actually be credited to these newly converted pagans.[142] As long as the sultanate lasted the main centres of religious teaching were always in the Funj territory, and particularly along the White Nile, where until the year 1684 (a disastrous year of famine and drought) there were no fewer than seventeen religious schools.[143]

The *sufi* schools present obvious parallels with the monastic establishments of the Christian world. Both were conceived in part as escapes from the corruption of everyday life, yet in the feudal age they often became the centres of extensive worldly enterprise.

There were many ways in which the world obtruded itself on those who impressed their contemporaries with their spiritual power [says Hillelson]. Wealth would be showered upon them in the form of lands granted by kings and rulers, or of pious gifts brought by the faithful. Though the sterner sort might refuse all offerings others did not disdain to make regular charges for cures and amulets. The crowds of disciples surrounding the holy man had to be maintained at the expense of their sheikh, and though visitors might bring gifts, their entertainment was apt to prove costly. In an age of feudalism the holy man's village . . . would form a small independent state, and we have already seen how El Damer in the eighteenth century was actually ruled by a dynasty of saints.[144] The kings of Sennar and Halfaya, and the numerous small dynasts of the country, fully shared the superstitious fears of the commonality, and we hear much of the respect they showed to the saints and the gifts with which they endowed them.[145]

Because of their considerable economic demands, the larger religious schools must have been confined to the more prosperous riverain districts – particularly those in which they could enjoy the patronage and protection of local *meks*. Outside of the immediate Funj domain in the Gezira we hear of such schools chiefly along the Nile from Shendi to Dongola; areas which until the seventeenth century were also under Funj hegemony. It seems very unlikely that religious instruction can have flourished on the same scale under the impoverished and chaotic conditions of Turkish rule north of the Third Cataract (Ch. 18), and in fact we have no traditions whatever relating to the propagation of Islam in this northern region. Yet diligent, if unsung, pioneers of the faith must have been at work even here, for at a surprisingly early date Mahasi Nubian *fekis* began appearing in the Funj domains.[146]

The numerous documents in the Arabic language found at Qasr Ibrim[147] bespeak a high degree of literacy in Arabic at the close of the Christian period and in the immediate post-Christian era, and we may hazard a guess that it was at this long-established urban centre in the north that the Mahasi acquired the smattering of learning which was to stand them in such good stead in the illiterate domains farther south. It is not inconceivable that members of the Nubian clerical class, recently deprived of any professional function by the disappearance of organized Christianity, may have turned to Islamic learning and to the Funj dominions as the only remaining market for their professional skills. Religious teaching has always offered an avenue of social advancement for the dispossessed in the Islamic world,[148] and it was a role which the Nubians, by virtue of their long experience of literate traditions, were ideally suited to fill. If this surmise is correct, Qasr Ibrim might represent a connecting link – the only known connecting link – between the learning and literacy of the Christian age and those of the Islamic age.

THE CHARACTER OF SUDANESE ISLAM

The folk religion of Islam as it exists in the Sudan today probably differs only in minor details from that of Wad Dayfallah's time. It continues to be dominated by the unorthodox and sometimes anti-orthodox elements of sufism. Its most important cognitive features are still the belief in saints and miracles; its main organizational structure remains that of the innumerable sheikhs and their schools.

The belief in saints – specially endowed individuals who can move back and forth between the human and divine worlds, and mediate between the two – may be regarded as the central tenet of sufism. All sheikhs and founders of schools are regarded as saints. They are endowed with *baraka*, a quality of divine blessedness some part of which can be transmitted to others by a word or a touch, and which is usually also passed on to their successors.[149] As Hillelson says:

> The most important earthly office of the saint is to confer spiritual benefit on those who come in contact with him, a result not achieved by preaching or teaching, or by the example of a holy life, but through the virtue (*baraka*) inherent in him, which acts as an influence on his surroundings. He is visited by the faithful with the object of partaking of this influence . . . and though he may give material assistance as a healer and a worker of miracles, it is the spiritual comfort of his presence which is most eagerly sought by disciples and pilgrims.[150]

The power of a saint is made manifest to his disciples through the performance of miracles. A good part of the *Tabaqat* of Wad Dayfallah is in fact taken up with a recitation of the miracles performed by the various sheikhs whose biographies are included. In this respect the book is similar to a good many Christian (as well as other Moslem) hagiographies, and the miracles recounted are in fact closely similar to those which astounded and enthralled the medieval Christian world.[151]

> It is sufficient to state that the miraculous powers of the saints have an exceedingly wide range [says Hillelson], including as they do a knowledge of the hidden thoughts of men and of future events, power over animals and inanimate objects, ability to fly in the air and walk on the surface of the waters, the art of healing by prayer and incantation, and even of restoring the dead to life. These powers are usually exercised for purposes benefiting mankind, but may be used to punish the wicked who are overtaken by sickness or sudden death . . .[152]

According to one of the more complex traditions of sufism there are three

574

orders of saints. 'The lowest degree is this: that the saint is able to fly in the air, and to walk on the water and to talk of hidden things. The middle degree is this: that God grants him the creative power whereby he says to a thing, "Be", and it is. The highest degree is that of the *Qutb* [literally "North Pole", or in other words sheikh of all the saints].'[153] The most extravagant of the hagiographies actually assert that the *Qutb* have achieved godhead.[154]

The *baraka* of a saint lives after him in the places where he lived and taught, and most particularly in the place where he is buried.[155] It is not surprising therefore that all of these places become holy shrines, and pilgrimages to them are perhaps the most important feature of folk religion in the Sudan. According to Trimingham:

> The people may not always be sure of the efficacy of the *baraka* of living *fekis*, but they have a blind faith in that of their dead saint, normally spoken of as 'our shaikh' and always as though he were living. He is in fact supposed to be slumbering and manifests himself to people in dreams and trances. His powers to bless or blight cover almost every category of human need. His power is testified by the miracles performed on behalf not only of one's dead ancestors, but also of one's living family. It is impossible to manage one's affairs properly without his help . . .[156]

The most elaborate shrines are the domed structures (*gubbas*) which cover the burial places of historically known sheikhs (Pl. XXIIIb). Although the whole of the northern Sudan is studded with these structures, they are outnumbered by the still more numerous lesser shrines which may be a simple mud building, with or without a roof, or nothing more than a ring of crudely piled stones. Some of these humbler shrines are also said to be tombs, while a greater number commemorate places where a saint is reputed to have gone into retreat or to have performed a miracle, or perhaps most often of all, a place where he has revealed himself in a dream.[157] Lesser shrines are very often situated on the tops of *jebels* or rocky promontories overlooking the Nile, where their presence is disclosed by clusters of rude banners (comprising any fragment of cloth tied to a stick) left by pious visitors. Some of these places have probably been foci of pilgrimage and worship since far back in tribal times, the character of their holiness being reinterpreted with the coming of each new religious creed.

Gubbas and other shrines are traditionally honoured as sanctuaries where fugitives from vengeance or from justice may seek asylum. According to Trimingham:

> The saint, too, protects objects deposited at his tomb for safekeeping. Ploughs will be left by cultivators whose *dura*-patches are scattered over a wide area. MacMichael mentions having seen such articles as a hair-tent, bowls, grind-

stones, left by Arabs at the tomb of Hasan Wad Hasuna until their return at the end of the season. Merchants going to Egypt still leave surplus goods at the grave of Abu Hamad, as when Cailliaud passed in 1821. Hair, nail clippings, and teeth are often left to prevent others getting them for purposes of witchcraft. Dust or stones taken from their graves also protect. They are usually attached to the cross-beam of an unused *saqiya* to prevent its being stolen. The most solemn oath that can be taken for most people is that at their saint's tomb, whereas they do not mind swearing falsely on the Koran.[158]

Worship at the shrines of saints usually takes the form of individual visits, which may be performed at any time, though some occasions are more propitious than others. Such visits may be for the purpose of doing reverence, or of asking a specific request of the sheikh. In either case various devotions are performed, their form depending chiefly on the *tarikh* of the sheikh's own order. Offerings of food, gifts, and incense are very frequently left at the tomb. In addition to these private devotions there are regular public ceremonies at some of the more famous *gubbas* in the Sudan, celebrating the birthday or the day of death of the saint. These are great village or even regional festivals, comparable to the celebration of the patron saint's day in medieval European cities.[159]

A measure of the persisting importance of sheikh cults among the present-day Nubians is suggested in the following passage from a recent study of the village of Dehmit:

In the Kenuzi district of Dahmit approximately 150 shrines of various importance were located, among a resident population of less than fifteen hundred persons. Some of these shrines, physically no more than a pile of stones, were the object of attention by a family, a single woman, or sometimes even children, who would imitate their elders by acting out cult activities as a form of play. The most important involved the entire tribe, while the lesser cults were associated with minor lineages of much more limited membership.[160]

Apart from the annual celebrations at certain sheikhs' tombs, most public worship takes place in 'mosques' belonging to the various religious orders, which are called *zawiya* mosques. They are very seldom distinguished by minarets or other features of liturgical architecture; often they are simple enclosures of mud or straw, with or without a roof. In them are performed not only the orthodox Friday prayers but the traditional devotions (*dhikr*) prescribed for the orders to which they belong.[161]

Another tenet of sufism which has played a brief but dramatic part in the history of the Sudan is the belief in the Mahdi, or expected redeemer, who will restore righteousness to the world in the days before the last judgement. Belief in the Mahdi is properly a doctrine of the heretical Shi'ite sect of Islam, which flourishes chiefly in Iran, but like a number of other Shi'a doctrines it has been incorporated, in somewhat divergent form, into the eschatology of the *sufi* orders.[162] The mahdist tenet has been particularly popular in sub-Saharan Africa; in the period of slightly more than a century between 1776 and 1898 a wave of mahdist-type states swept across the southern fringe of the Sahara from west to east.[163] In the recorded history of the Sudan there have been only two self-proclaimed Mahdis, of whom the first was notably unsuccessful;[164] yet the unanimity with which Sudanese of all sects and backgrounds rallied to the standard of the Mahdi Mohammed Ahmed in 1881 shows how deeply rooted was the latent belief in the coming redeemer. The story of the *mahdiya* of Mohammed Ahmed will be recounted in the next chapter.

In the nineteenth century, concurrently with the establishment of a centralized government under Mohammed Ali (Ch. 18), there was a strong centralizing movement among the religious orders in the Sudan. Many of the older, autochthonous orders disappeared at that time, while several new regional and even international ones were formed.[165] Today the majority of Sudanese belong to no more than a dozen orders, of which more than half originated in the nineteenth century.[166] The overwhelming majority of Nubians belong to the *Mirghaniya* or *Khatmiya* sect, founded early in the last century by Mohammed Osman al-Mirghani from Mecca. His success among the Nubians and other northern Sudanese seems to have been the result in part of his marriage to a Dongolawi woman, and it is his successors through her who have ruled the sect down to modern times.[167] According to Trimingham, 'The order is very strict in insisting on the extreme sanctity of the family and therefore refuses to allow its adherents to affiliate themselves to any other order or even to take part in their ritual.'[168]

A variety of pagan and pre-Islamic beliefs, although not formally sanctioned either by the orthodox or by the *sufi* orders, also form part of the folk religion of the Sudan. Among these are the belief in black magic, the evil eye, and an assortment of *jinns* and other spirits. There are numerous formulae – most of them highly animistic – for averting or exorcising these evil influences.[169] In the village of Dehmit there was found to be an active belief in spirits who dwell in the Nile, and whose help in everyday affairs can be invoked by specialized practitioners who become temporarily possessed by the river spirits. These beliefs and practices occurred chiefly among the women of the village.[170] Survivals of another type are the highly developed rites of passage associated in particular with circumcisions, weddings, and funerals, which constitute the chief ritual occasions in modern Nubian and Sudanese life.[171]

Side by side with the rich and diversified folk religion there exists, as in all parts of the Islamic world, the orthodox religious order whose symbol is the mosque rather than the sheikh's tomb. At its head by common consent (though not by formal investiture) are the *ulema* or doctors of theology, who may advise the government in religious and legal matters. A slightly lower, but still highly educated, class of officials are the *qadis* (judges) who preside over courts of religious law. These individuals are to be found only in the largest cities. However, nearly all cities and towns and even some villages have an orthodox mosque staffed by at least four functionaries: an *imam* to lead the regular Friday prayers, a preacher, a *muezzin* to recite the call to prayer, and a servant.[172] Conventional mosques are called *jama* ('places of assembly') in distinction to the *zawiya* mosques of the *sufi* orders. Most of those in the Sudan have been built within the present century, partly at Government expense, and, as Trimingham observes, 'The normal Sudanese does not feel at home in them as he does in the religious club atmosphere of the *zawiya*.'[173]

The lowest rung of the orthodox religious order is represented by the *fekis*, most of them barely literate, who support themselves by teaching the Koran in countless hundreds of informal village schools.

> Throughout the Sudan, in a *hosh*, in the shade of a rakuba, or under a tree in the *suq*, can be seen circles of boys around a *feki* reclining on his *angareeb* [bed]. All chant together in monotone, swaying back and forth in rhythm, droning the sections indefinitely until they are memorized. The *feki* dictates from memory and the sections are copied out on wooden slates with a pointed stick dipped in an ink solution of soot, gum, and water. For most Sudanese the Koran is a closed book; they are not taught the meaning of the language because the chanting itself is a meritorious work.[174]

Continued emphasis on the use of Classical Arabic (which is not intelligible to speakers of the modern dialects) in all religious instruction helps to explain why the orthodox aspects of Islam have had so little appeal in the Sudan.

Over most of the Sudan there was until recently no other education available but that of the village *fekis*. At a few mosques in the larger cities boys of twelve and over could advance from the Koran to the study of theology and religious law, and the mosque in Omdurman in recent years has offered advanced training modelled on that of al-Azhar University in Cairo.[175] The graduate of such training may pursue a career as an *imam* or *qadi*; he will at all events take his place among the tiny, élite and almost exclusively urban class of orthodox Moslems[176] who have some genuine knowledge of the early traditions of their faith, who attend the 'Friday mosques' in preference to the *zawiya*, and whose devotions are limited to the 'Five Pillars' (profession of faith, prayer, almsgiving, fasting and pilgrimage) prescribed by Mohammed himself. These individuals, alone among Sudanese Moslems, may make a genuine attempt to observe the requirements of orthodox religion, although seldom with absolute constancy.[177]

Among the élite group of orthodox Moslems Nubians make up an unusually high proportion, partly because of their long-standing respect for learning and partly because so many of them are engaged in commerce, in which a reputation for piety is known to be advantageous.[178] Trimingham says of them that 'They are bigoted Moslems, but their Islam lacks intensity unless stimulated by the other-than-religious traits of such a movement as the *Mahdiya* or by their passion for trading.'[179] Beyond the limits of the towns, however, the mass of Nubians, like other Sudanese, continue to prefer the more colourful and personal rituals of the *sufi* orders to the words of the Prophet and the *ulema*.

THE EVIDENCE OF ARCHAEOLOGY

Sixty years ago, Reisner justified his decision not to investigate the remains of the Christian period with the remark, 'One word only may be said: Christian Nubia appears to have differed little from modern Moslem Nubia.'[180] This judgement was largely intuitive at the time, since very few sites of either period had been adequately examined, but it was shared by two generations of Reisner's successors. The implication that ethnology (i.e. our knowledge of the modern Nubians) can tell us all that we need to know about everyday life in medieval times deterred any systematic investigation of Christian town-sites until the time of the High Dam salvage campaign, and it has continued to deter investigation of post-Christian sites down to the present day. The very few identified remains of the Islamic period which were encountered in the course of the salvage campaign of the 1960s were generally passed over as too recent and too familiar to be informative, while in Upper Nubia the much more impressive castle sites continue to await investigation as do nearly all other sites in that long-neglected region.

So scarce are recognizable sites of the post-Christian period in Lower Nubia that I once suggested that a large part of this region had been abandoned altogether after the downfall of the Christian kingdoms.[181] While I have since been forced to modify that extreme position somewhat, the evidence for a substantial decline in population remains unmistakable. It is now also apparent, however, that some of the Nubians who remained in the north reverted to a mode of life so primitive that it has left very little for the archaeologist to find.

Three sites which show definite evidence of continued occupation in the post-Christian period are Qasr Ibrim, Gebel Adda, and Faras – the great urban centres of the north since Meroitic times. Qasr Ibrim and Gebel Adda were occupied after the sixteenth century by 'Turkish' garrisons (actually made up of a mixture of Balkan and Near Eastern troops – see Ch. 18), and the clusters of brick and stone hovels which comprise the uppermost archaeological levels at the two sites are generally attributed to these intruders.[182] Yet we know from historical evidence that these Ottoman frontier garrisons were seldom relieved or rotated,[183] and as a result were soon Nubianized; and the general style of their domestic architecture (if in fact the buildings at Qasr Ibrim and Gebel Adda are theirs) is unmistakably Nubian. It is unfortunate that no detailed studies have yet been made of the post-Christian remains at Ibrim and Gebel Adda which would allow comparison with the recently investigated post-Christian sites in the *Batn el Hajar* (see below).

At Faras there is no record of a Turkish garrison, and it must therefore be assumed that the irregular, walled enclosure which was built on top of the sanded-up cathedral and bishop's palace was the work of Nubians. The excavators have attributed this structure to an undated 'Arab' period,[184] but the fact that it enclosed a crude, very late church and monastery, built on top of the former bishop's palace,[185] suggests to me that its origin belongs to the Late Christian period. The enclosure (called the 'Citadel' by Griffith[186] and Michalowski[187]) certainly continued to be occupied down to the nineteenth century, and its outer fortifications underwent many repairs and modifications.[188] Within the western part of the Citadel were about a dozen brick rooms, perhaps representing four or five houses,[189] whose tight clustering is much more reminiscent of Classic Christian domestic architecture (cf. Ch. 15) than of anything more recent, though they are surely of a later date than that.

It was dissatisfaction with the existing state of our knowledge of post-Christian Nubia which led me in 1969 to organize an expedition for the express purpose of excavating remains of this period.[190] The site chosen was that of Kulubnarti, in the *Batn el Hajar*, a settlement which had been founded in the Late Christian period and which has already been described in some detail in Chapter 16. Concurrently with the main excavation a dozen other habitation sites on the island of Kulubnarti were excavated, and extensive observations were made at another large Late Christian and post-Christian town-site at Dal, a few miles upriver. Although none of the sites could be dated with certainty, it was possible through stratigraphy and seriation to recognize a sequence of architectural and demographic changes extending from late medieval times to the present.[191] Insofar as our very limited knowledge of other sites will allow comparison, these changes seem to exemplify a region-wide and not merely a local pattern.

At Kulubnarti, the massive unit houses of the Late Christian period continued to be occupied as long as they remained in livable condition, but after the Christian period there were a number of modifications in the two-storey houses for the sake of convenience. Ground-floor entrances were hacked through the walls, eliminating the awkward necessity of descending to the lower chambers by means of hatchways from above (see Ch. 16), and apertures were also hacked through into the crypts which occupied the interstices between the ceiling vaults. (These modifications

were encountered also in the 'blockhouse' at Meinarti.[192]) As the fabric
of the buildings gradually deteriorated there was no systematic effort at
repair, and eventually (probably before the eighteenth century) they were
all abandoned except for the one two-storey house which had been progressively enlarged into a castle, as described in Chapter 16 (cf. also Pl.
XXIIb). The castle was kept in repair as the residence of a local military
governor and his household troops, and it continued to be occupied at
least intermittently until the beginning of the twentieth century.

No more of the stoutly built unit houses were constructed after the end
of the Christian period.[193] Although the conventional plan of large front
room, smaller back room, passage, and latrine (cf. Chs. 15–16) was retained
for a time, the later houses at Kulubnarti were lightly and somewhat irregularly built, often of a combination of brick and stone.[194] The walls are
thin and sometimes noticeably curving, and can only have supported a
light roof of poles and thatch (note the numerous curving and irregular
walls shown in the plan of Kulubnarti Village, Fig. 82). Presumably these

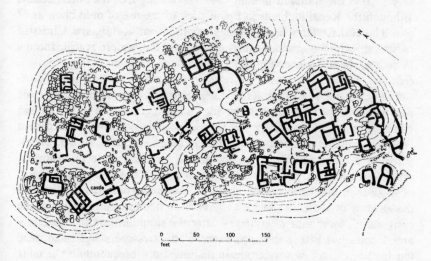

Fig. 82. Village of the late medieval period, Kulubnarti

buildings, like Nubian houses in most periods of history, were erected by
their intended occupants and not by professional builders, as the Late
Christian unit houses apparently were.

At some period before modern times there occurred a still more radical
simplification in Nubian domestic architecture. The unit house design with
its 'interior plumbing' gave way to the rudest of two-room huts, in which
one room was presumably occupied by the male members of the family
and the other by the females. It was in just such hovels that Burckhardt

found the majority of Nubians living in 1813,[195] and in the villages of the Berber and Shendi districts they remain common to the present day. At Kulubnarti and other archaeological sites in the *Batn el Hajar* there is no uniformity to these structures; some are built of brick, some of dry-piled stone, and some of a combination of the two, and the rooms may be either rectangular or rounded. There is almost never a hard-packed floor or any built-in features such as a fireplace or a mastaba.

A short-lived innovation in construction was the use of very thin, wide bricks of irregular length, which were laid lengthwise after the fashion of stone slabs. Houses constructed in this fashion have been observed at a number of sites in the upper *Batn el Hajar*, apparently all dating from a relatively brief period between the sixteenth and eighteenth centuries.[196] A much more recent innovation was the appearance of *jalus* or coursed adobe construction in place of the familiar mud brick of earlier times. Although *jalus* had been in general use in West Africa much earlier,[197] its appearance in Nubia does not seem to antedate the nineteenth century.[198] It is the standard building material throughout the Sudan today, although the Kenzi Nubians in Egypt stick to the use of mud brick as of old. The earliest *jalus* houses which we found at Kulubnarti were still two-room huts; the spacious courtyard house of the modern Nubians seems in fact to have been confined to the Nubian élite until the twentieth century.[199]

The habitation remains at Kulubnarti bespeak a very unstable pattern of occupation in the post-Christian period. While it is not uncommon to find village sites of earlier periods which were continually occupied for several centuries, none of the dozen or more habitation sites which were investigated at Kulubnarti had been continually inhabited from medieval times to the present. On the other hand, several of them showed evidence of more than one period of occupation. The main village which stood in the shadow of the castle seems to have been abandoned (except for the castle itself) some time after 1600 – after the simplification of unit house architecture but before the appearance of the two-room hut or of thin, flat mud brick. A few very crude stone huts did subsequently make their appearance among the older ruins, but they were never sufficiently numerous to form a viable community, and most of them appear to date from the fairly recent past.

After the abandonment of the main Kulubnarti village the population apparently dispersed to a number of smaller settlements which came into being at about the same time. Some of these had already been built and abandoned once before; others which were newly built were to be abandoned and then reoccupied still later in the post-Christian period. This pattern of intermittent occupation seems to be a regular feature of the sites which were investigated in the Kulubnarti area.[200] It may have been due in part to the rapid deterioration of poorly built houses and to the contamination of living sites with vermin and dung, but we need recall also Burckhardt's observation that in the nineteenth century poor villages were continually ruined, and their occupants dispersed, as a result of the rapacious exactions of the 'Turkish' governors.[201] In this connection, the nearly total abandonment of the main Kulubnarti village after the sixteenth century may perhaps reflect the desire of the inhabitants to remove themselves from the immediate proximity of the castle and its occupants.

Most of the sites of the 'dispersal period', following the abandonment of the main Kulubnarti village, were located on exceptionally high promontories or on small detached islands. It was not until around the beginning of the nineteenth century (concurrently with the introduction of *jalus* architecture) that the settlements began to move back down onto the lower and more accessible terraces close to the Nile, where most of Kulubnarti's present-day houses are located.

Among the complex of architectural and demographic changes which took place at Kulubnarti in the post-Christian period it is impossible to recognize anything which is specifically attributable to the coming of the Arabs or of Islam, unless it should be the design of the two-room houses. Among the archaeological remains there is no recognizable mosque or *zawiya* (which is hardly surprising in view of the nondescript character of these structures), and the only overt evidence for the practice of Islam consists of three ostraka inscribed in Arabic with verses from the Koran, which may date from the nineteenth century.[202] For the rest, the changes at Kulubnarti reflect neither the disappearance of Christianity nor the coming of Islam, but only a continuation and intensification of the poverty and social disruption of the feudal age.

The impression of poverty and social instability which is given by the village sites of post-Christian Nubia is reinforced by their scanty material remains. There is an almost total absence of luxury goods of any kind, in contrast to the abundant glass, bronze, decorated pottery, and coloured textiles of the Late Christian period (cf. Ch. 16). The flow of imported goods had dwindled almost to nothing, and the local production of decorated pottery had ceased. The wares of the post-Christian era are the most uninteresting of any period in Nubian history; they are confined to plain red and plain black vessels, most of which are thick, heavy, and unevenly formed.

Many opportunities to enlarge the meagre knowledge of post-Christian Nubia which was gained at Kulubnarti await the archaeologist in Upper Nubia. The picture of cultural and social conditions to be gained at some of the larger townsites, and particularly at the residences of the feudal *meks*, may not be quite so depressing as that afforded by the village remains in the *Batn el Hajar*. Old Dongola, for example, was still the most important political centre in Upper Nubia, and the residence of the Bedayria *mek*, at the end of the sixteenth century (although the French visitor Poncet described the houses as ill-built and the streets as 'half-deserted and filled with heaps of sand'[203]). Excavations here have so far not extended beyond the magnificent churches of an earlier age.[204] The really tempting post-Christian sites of Upper Nubia are however the great castles of the Dongolawi and Shaiqiya *meks*, which remain to this day among the most impressive architectural remains in the Sudan, and have been too long neglected by archaeologists.

We have already given some attention, in Chapter 16, to the castles of Upper Nubia which seem to date from the Late Christian period. In the Shaiqiya country there are still larger castles which evidently belong to a later time. Although none has been investigated in detail, Crawford gives the following general description of them:

Those that I have seen are quite distinctive and have, apart from methods of construction, one characteristic feature: the towers on the periphery of the wall are not so much towers as houses joined together by that wall. They often project slightly in front of the wall; they have more than one storey; their size is large in proportion to the wall in which they are built; and they are always rectangular. Within the wall are the remains of what would appear to have been similar houses. The resulting plan is exactly that of the modern courtyard house which may be seen in every town between Shendi and Berber. The castles are simply fortified courtyard houses, and must be genetically connected with them. But exactly how the courtyard house of the southern region evolved into a castle in Dongola we do not know.[205] One can only say that, on the present evidence, none of the castles seems to have been built until after the Christian period; a date as late as the eighteenth century is even possible for some of them.[206]

NUBIA AT THE CLOSE OF THE FEUDAL ERA

Since this chapter is concerned primarily with the culture of Nubia in the post-Christian era, it seems appropriate to conclude with an extended quotation from the journal of the explorer J. L. Burckhardt, written in 1813. This remarkably perceptive and scholarly document includes the first detailed description of Nubia and the Nubians since the time of Ibn Selim (Ch. 15). Although it is only the first of a series of distinguished travellers' accounts which appeared in the early nineteenth century,[207] Burckhardt's is the only description which antedates the considerable social and cultural upheavals wrought by the armies of Mohammed Ali (see Ch. 18).[208] It therefore affords us a unique glimpse of life in Nubia in the last years of the feudal age. Wrote Burckhardt:[209]

... Nubia is divided into two parts, called Wadi Kenuz and Wadi el Nuba ... the former extending from Aswan to Wadi Sebua, and the latter comprising the country between Sebua and the northern frontier of Dongola. The inhabitants of these two divisions are divided by their language, but in manners they appear to be the same.

Much animosity exists between the Kenuz and their southern neighbours the Nubas [i.e. the Mahas]; the latter upbraiding the former with avarice and bad faith, while the Kenuz call the Nubas filthy slaves, living like the people of the Sudan. Disputes and sanguinary quarrels often take place in consequence between the inhabitants of neighbouring villages . . .

The inhabitants of the banks of the Nile, from the First Cataract to the frontiers of Dongola, do not plough their fields after the inundation has subsided, as is done in Egypt, the waters above the cataract never rising sufficiently high to overflow the shore. In a few places where the cultivable soil is broader than usual . . . there are canals which convey the water towards the fields on the side of the mountain, but the water in them is not sufficiently high, as in Upper Egypt, to irrigate the low grounds near the hills. Irrigation in Nubia therefore is carried on entirely by means of the saqias, or waterwheels. Immediately after the river has subsided the fields are watered by them, and the first dura seed is sown, the crop from which is reaped in December and January; the ground is then again irrigated, and barley sown; and after the barley harvest the ground is sometimes sown a third time for the summer crop.[210] The barley is either sold in exchange for dura or eaten green in soups. The harvest suffers greatly from the ravages of immense flocks of sparrows, which the united efforts of all the children in the villages cannot always keep at a distance, and whole fields of dura and barley are often destroyed by a small worm which ascends the stalks of the plant. Tobacco is everywhere cultivated; it retains when dried its green colour, and exactly resembles that of the mountains on the east side of the Dead Sea. Tobacco forms the chief luxury of all the classes, who either smoke it or, mixing it with nitre, suck it by placing it between the lower gums and the lip.

The habitations of the Nubians are built either of mud or of loose stones; those of stone, as I have already observed, stand generally in the declivity of the hills, and consist of two separate round buildings, one of which is occupied by the males and the other by the females of the family. The mud dwellings are generally so low that one cannot stand upright in them; the roof is covered with dura stalks which last till they are eaten up by the cattle, when palm leaves are laid across. The houses at Derr, and those of the wealthy inhabitants of the larger villages, are well built, having a large area in the centre with apartments all around, and a separation between those of the men and of the women. The utensils of a Nubian's house consist of about half a dozen earthen jars, from one to two feet in diameter and about five feet in height, in which all the provisions of the family are kept; a few earthen plates; a hand-mill; a hatchet; and a few round sticks over which the loom is laid.

To the north of Derr the dress is usually a linen shirt only, which the wealthier classes wear of a blue colour, or the woollen cloak of the peasants of Upper Egypt; the headdress is a small white linen cap with sometimes a few rags twisted round it in the shape of a turban. Young boys and girls go naked; the women wrap themselves up in linen rags or black woollen gowns; they wear earrings and glass bracelets, and those who cannot afford to buy the latter form them of straw. Their hair falls in ringlets upon the neck, and on the back part of the head they wear short tassels of glass or stones, both as an ornament and as an amulet. The richer class wear copper or silver rings round their ankles. South of Derr, and principally at Sukkot and in Mahas, grown-up people go quite naked with the exception of the sexual parts, which the men conceal in a small sack. The hair of the people of Mahas is very thick but not woolly. All the young men wear one earring, either of silver or copper, in the right ear only, and men of all classes usually carry a rosary suspended round the neck, which they never remove; they also tie round one arm, above the elbow, a number of amulets covered with leather about three or four inches broad, consisting of mystical writing and prayers, which are sold to them by the [*fekis*].

The Nubians seldom go unarmed; as soon as a boy grows up his first endeavour is to purchase a short, crooked knife, which the men wear tied over the left elbow, under their shirt, and which they draw upon each other on the slightest quarrel. When a Nubian goes from one village to another he either carries a long heavy stick covered with iron at one of its extremities, or his lance and target [shield]. The lance is about five feet in length, including the iron point; the targets are of various sizes. Some are round with a boss in the centre; others resemble the ancient Macedonian shield, being of an oblong form, four feet in length and with curved edges, covering almost the whole body. These targets, which are sold by the Shaiqiya Arabs, are made of the skin of the hippopotamus, and are proof against the thrust of a lance or the blow of a sabre. Those who can afford it possess also a sword, resembling in shape the swords worn by the knights of the middle ages: a long straight blade about two inches in breadth with a handle in the form of a cross. The scabbard, for fashion's sake, is broader near the point than at the top. These swords are of German manufacture and are sold to the Nubians by the merchants of Egypt at from four to eight dollars apiece.[211] Firearms are not common; the richer classes possess matchlocks. Ammunition is very scarce and highly valued; travellers therefore will do well to carry with them a few dozen cartridges, which are very acceptable presents. When I left the camp of Mohammed Kashef [one of the provincial governors] at Tinareh, his nephew ran after me for at least two miles to obtain a single cartridge from me, telling me that he had shot off the only one he had during the rejoicings of the preceding day.

I have already mentioned the usual dishes of the Nubians. The dura bread is extremely coarse and is made without salt. It is prepared upon the *sadj* or thin iron plate in use among the bedouin Arabs, but as the whole operation of grinding, kneading, and baking does not occupy more than ten minutes, it may easily be supposed that it is never thoroughly baked. The dura for the day's use is ground early every morning by the women, for the Nubians never keep meal in store. In Sukkot and Mahas the bread is made in very thin round cakes, which are placed upon each other when served up at meals. Animal food [i.e. meat] is rarely tasted by the Nubians; the governors even do not eat it every day. In the larger villages palm wine is common; it is not unpleasant to the taste, although too sweet and thick to be drank in any considerable quantity. The Nubians also make a liquor called *bouza*, much resembling beer. It is extracted from dura or barley, but the best is furnished by the latter. It is of a pale muddy colour and very nutritious. At Cairo and in all the towns and villages of Upper Egypt there are shops for the sale of *bouza*, which are kept exclusively by Nubians. Great quantities both of the wine and of the spirit distilled from dates are drank at Derr, where they are sold in shops kept for the purpose, and where the upper classes are intoxicated every evening.[212] A kind of jelly or honey is also extracted from the date, which serves the rich as a sweetmeat. Except date trees and a few grapevines which I saw at Derr, there are no fruit trees in Nubia.

The men in Nubia are generally well made, strong and muscular, with fine features; in stature they are somewhat below the Egyptians. They have no mustachios and but little beard, wearing it under the chin only . . . In passing along the wadis of Nubia it often occurred to me to remark that the size and figure of the inhabitants was generally proportioned to the breadth of their cultivable soil; wherever the plain is broad and the peasants . . . are in comparatively easy circumstances, they are taller and more muscular and healthy; but in the rocky districts where the plain is not more than twenty or thirty yards in breadth they are poor meagre figures, in some places appearing almost like walking skeletons.

The women are all well made, and though not handsome have generally sweet countenances and very pleasing manners; I have even seen beauties among them . . . But they are worn down from the earliest years by continual labour, the whole business of the house being left to them while the men are occupied exclusively in the culture of the soil. Of all the women of the East those of Nubia are the most virtuous; and this is the more praiseworthy as their vicinity to Upper Egypt, where licentiousness knows no bounds, might be expected to have some influence upon them.[213]

The Nubians purchase their wives from the parents: the price usually paid by the Kenuz is twelve Mahboubs, or thirty-six piastres.[214] They frequently intermarry with the Arab Ababda, some of whom cultivate the soil like themselves; an Ababda girl is worth six camels. These are paid to her father, who gives back three to his daughter to be the common property of her and her husband. If a divorce takes place, half the value of the three camels goes to the latter. The Nubian is extremely jealous of his wife's honour, and on the slightest suspicion of infidelity towards him would carry her in the night to the side of the river, lay open her breast with a cut with his knife, and throw her into the water 'to be food for the crocodiles', as they term it. A case of this kind lately happened at Aswan.[215]

Public women, who are met with in thousands in every part of Egypt, are not tolerated in Nubia except at Derr [the provincial capital in Burckhardt's time], and these are not natives but emancipated female slaves who, being left destitute, betake themselves to this vile profession to gain a subsistence. The execrable propensities [i.e. pederasty] which the Mamelukes have rendered so common in Egypt, even amongst the lowest peasants, are held in abhorrence in Nubia except by the Kashefs [governing officials – see Ch. 18] and their relations, who endeavour to imitate the Mamelukes in everything, even in their most detestable vices.

Small looms are frequently seen in the houses of the Nubians; with these the women weave very coarse woollen mantles and cotton cloth which they make into shirts. From the leaves of the date tree they also form mats, small drinking bowls, and large plates on which the bread is served at table; and though these articles are formed entirely by the hand, they are made in so very neat a manner as to have the appearance of being wrought by instruments. The above are the only manufactures in Nubia; everything else is imported from Egypt.

The only musical instrument I saw in Nubia was a kind of Egyptian *tamboura* [lute] with five strings, and covered with the skin of a gazelle . . .[216] The girls are fond of singing, and the Nubian airs are very melodious.[217]

The game of chess is common at Derr, and that called *beyadh* is also frequently played.

I found the Nubians generally to be of a kind disposition, and without that propensity to theft so characteristic of the Egyptians – at least of those to the north of Assiut. Pilfering indeed is almost unknown amongst them, and any person convicted of such a crime would be expelled from his village by the unanimous voice of its inhabitants.[218] I did not lose the most trifling article during my journey through the country, although I always slept in the open air in front of the house when I took up my quarters for the night.[219] They are in general hospitable towards strangers, but the Kenuz and the people of Sukkot are less so than the other inhabitants. Curiosity seems to be the most prominent feature of their character, and they generally ask their guest a thousand questions about the place he comes from, and the business which brings him into Nubia.

If the government were not so extremely despotic [cf. Ch. 18] the Nubians might become dangerous neighbours to Egypt, for they are of a much bolder and more independent spirit than the Egyptians, and ardently attached to their native soil. Great numbers of them go yearly to Cairo, where they generally act as porters, and are preferred to the Egyptians on account of their honesty. After staying there six or eight years they return to their native wadi with the little property they have realized, although well knowing that the only luxuries they can there expect, in exchange for those of Cairo, are dura bread and a linen shirt. Such of them as do not travel into Egypt hardly ever go beyond the precincts of their village, for generally the Nubians have no inclination towards commercial speculations. At Ibrim I met with two old men who assured me that they had never visited Derr, though it is only five hours distant. Those Nubians who have resided in Egypt and can speak Arabic are for the most part good Moslems, and repeat their prayers daily, but in general the only prayer known to the others is the exclamation of 'Allahu Akbar' [God is most mighty]. A few make the pilgrimage to Mecca by the way of Suakin.

I estimate the whole population of Nubia, from Aswan to the southern limits of Mahas, an extent of country about five hundred miles long with an average breadth of half a mile, at one hundred thousand souls.[220]

In contrast to the poverty and oppression which were everywhere apparent in northern Nubia, Burckhardt encountered a flourishing market centre at Shendi, not far from the ruins of ancient Meroë. His colourful and perceptive description of it, which runs on for nearly a hundred pages,[221] furnishes a picture of a quite different side of medieval life in the Sudan. (The name 'Nubia' can no longer be technically applied this far south, since the Ja'aliyin tribe who were the principal inhabitants of Shendi had ceased to acknowledge any Nubian ancestry by Burckhardt's time.) Because of the length of the original description, it will be preferable to quote here the eloquent paraphrase of Alan Moorehead: [222]

The green strip on either side of the river here is not very wide . . . beyond a few hundred yards there is nothing to be seen but stark outcrops of blackish rock in a vast plain of sand and gravel, mirages quiver in the midday heat, and often great clouds of locusts and suffocating storms sweep across the country. One would have thought, therefore, that there would never have been much inducement for human beings to settle here. Yet Burckhardt found the region was fairly populous, and Shendi itself, with about six thousand inhabitants, was the largest town in the central Sudan.

Clearly there was some special reason why so many people should have chosen to live in this unattractive place, and the answer, as Burckhardt soon discovered, lay in Shendi market. It was a fabulous market for so small a place. In an open space in the centre of the town three rows of huts had been set up, and here every Friday and Saturday, a thousand miles away from any part of the world that one could call civilized, you could buy such things as spices and sandalwood from India, antimony to blacken the eyelids, medicines, German swords and razors, saddles and leather goods from Kordofan, writing paper and beads from Genoa and Venice, cloth, pottery, and basketware of every kind, soap from Egypt, cotton, salt, and Ethiopian gold. There was a lively sale in monkeys that were trained to do tricks, and Shendi's wooden dishes, battered and blackened by being held over a fire, were famous. [223] The market was also renowned for its sale of Dongola horses, and for camels and other beasts to carry these goods across the desert.

The stalls where most of the merchandise was displayed were miserable affairs, little cells measuring six feet long by four feet deep with grass matting for a roof. There was no means of locking up these stalls – in the absence of nails the doors were tied together with rope – and so each night the merchants bundled up their goods and took them to their homes in the town. Their money (mainly Spanish dollars, but any currency served) they buried in the ground, and even the richest men affected to be very poor by living in one room, sleeping on the ground and wearing little more than a loincloth. There were no fixed prices in the market (Burckhardt thought the bargaining more like downright cheating), barter often took the place of money, and quarrelling was continuous. There was little agriculture in Shendi, and the local crafts were nothing very wonderful. 'Commerce,' Burckhardt says, 'was the very life of society,' and the people never looked much further than the *bouza* shop or the swarms of prostitutes for their distractions. Yet it was an animated existence, and the traders, ranging from the fairest Arabs to the blackest Negroes, from Muhammadans in turbans and robes to naked pagans, were a wonderful hotch-potch of the tribes and races of north-eastern Africa. In the heat and the dust they squatted in front of their stalls, bargaining away from early morning until late at night, and there was always some new caravan arriving, another taking off again into the desert.

What he had discovered here, in fact, was the great crossroads of the Nile.

The river at this point made its closest approach to the southern end of the Red Sea, and thus the way was opened up to Arabia, India, and the Far East. To the west the caravan routes, keeping as far as possible within the cover of the rain belt and south of the Sahara, led on from oasis to oasis, to Lake Chad and Timbuktu. The Nile Valley itself provided a highway to Egypt in the north, and Ethiopia could be reached by the track that led up through Metemma to Gondar. In a curious but inevitable way all the themes of the river were gathered here. Invasions, slave-raiders, traders' caravans and the Mecca pilgrimage – Shendi had known them all for a thousand years, and its market-place was still a genuine capsule of the past. There were other markets upstream and down on this part of the Nile, but none was so important as this, none stretched out its contacts so far, none had such a continuous tradition or was able to reveal so much. It was, in a way, a microcosm of the river . . .

In closing we may observe that the contrast between these two passages from Burckhardt is very much the contrast which is maintained today, in the minds of the Nubians, between themselves and their 'Arab' neighbours to the north and south, on the one hand the poor but upright and self-respecting Nubians; on the other hand the effete and debauched 'Arabs'.

INTERPRETATIVE SUMMARY

From the thirteenth to the sixteenth centuries bedouin Arabs poured south from Egypt into the Sudan, first along the Red Sea Hills and then west to the Nile and beyond, destroying in the process the last remnants of the already weakened Christian kingdoms. Their coming permanently altered the ecological balance between the desert and the sown: from medieval to modern times the tribesmen of the hinterland have outnumbered the farmers along the Nile, and have generally dominated them politically. Although many of the Arab immigrants continued to pursue a nomadic existence in the Sudan, others settled down as overlords to the Nubians and other sedentary peoples, with whom they gradually amalgamated.

With their subjugation to Arab conquerors, and with the disintegration of their own medieval polity, the Nubians became affiliated by choice and necessity with the Arab tribal system. In time the Nubians upriver from Dongola, who were under direct Arab rule and who were in frequent contact with bedouins, were Arabized to the extent of losing their native language and all memory of their indigenous origins, though they persisted in the sedentary farming life of pre-Islamic times. In the eyes of themselves and of their neighbours, these people ceased to be Nubians. Yet so pervasive was the social order of the Arab lineage system that even the Nubians downriver from Dongola, who retained their native language and who had little direct experience of Arab rule, came in time to think of themselves as Arabs and as tribesmen. At times and in places the Arab tribal system provided the only government which they knew, and even after the re-emergence of more centralized governments their world-view remained essentially a tribal one, as in some ways it does to this day.

In becoming 'Arabs' the Nubians became also 'Moslems by enrolment' in a manner of speaking, but their explicit knowledge of their new religion, acquired mainly from the unschooled bedouins, hardly extended beyond the profession of faith. As the description of Burckhardt shows, this was still generally true at the beginning of the nineteenth century. For the Nubians and nearly all other Sudanese peoples being a Moslem was implicit in being an Arab; it was a matter of belonging rather than of believing.

To the extent that any real religious zeal was generated in the post-Christian Sudan, it was the work not of the bedouins but of a handful of pious religious teachers who were invited into the country by the Funj sultans. They were mostly representatives of the mystical *sufi* orders, and the form of popular worship which they implanted was that of the innumerable local cults, the belief in saints and miracles, which has always been associated with sufism, and which remains characteristic of Sudanese Islam today. The schools founded by the first missionaries were chiefly in the Funj territory in the south, but as the movements proliferated other schools were established down the Nile as far as Dongola, and also in the western Sudan. Through the agency of these schools and their presiding sheikhs many Nubians became affiliated with one or another of the mystical orders, and acquired at least a rudimentary knowledge of its special *tarikh* or 'path of enlightenment'. We know nothing of religious teaching in northern Nubia, but at a surprisingly early date Mahasi Nubian *fekis* began appearing in considerable numbers in the Funj domains.

Although the adoption of Islam and of fictitious Arab pedigrees radically altered the Nubians' view of themselves, it did not similarly affect their view of the world around them, as did their adoption of Christianity a thousand years earlier. As we have already observed, the popular cosmologies of medieval Christianity and of medieval Islam were essentially similar, with their emphasis on saints and miracles, their various pilgrimages and penances, and their expectation of a coming redeemer. Moreover the worldly circumstances of the Nubians were hardly affected by their new religion or even by the coming of the Arabs. The new overlords merely supplanted an older and almost equally fragmented feudal order, and the Nubians experienced a continuation of the poverty and political disunity which had begun long before the Arabs arrived. For all these reasons it seems legitimate, despite the lack of acknowledged continuity, to consider the Christian and Islamic periods together as making up a more broadly defined medieval horizon in Nubian cultural development[224] – a phase which did not end until the beginning of the twentieth century, and in some respects has not ended yet.

18
RETURN TO VASSALAGE

THE SUDAN UNDER FUNJ, TURKISH AND
EGYPTIAN RULE

For the Arabs the adage 'There is no history; there is only biography'[1] is almost literally true. Their culture, like those of most Near Eastern peoples, is extraordinarily people-oriented. Religious movements, political factions, schools of law, even governments and empires, develop not around geographical regions or abstract ideals but around the charismatic appeal of individual personalities. Even the historical works of such profound and critical thinkers as Ibn Khaldun and Maqrizi have a strongly biographical flavour, while the folk histories of the illiterate masses are little more than a tangle of pedigrees and biographies of saints. As we saw in the last chapter, this mass of tradition can contribute enormously, if indirectly, to our understanding of cultural history, but its worth to the conventional historiographer is slight.

From the standpoint of political history, the interval between about AD 1500 and 1800 remains to this day one of the darkest ages in Nubian history.[2] For the Nubians, both the art of writing and the appreciation of their own history disappeared along with the Christian faith, and it was not until the nineteenth century that the newly acquired language of Arabic was employed to any extent for other than religious texts. Moreover, after the fleeting visit of David Reubeni in 1522[3] (cf. Ch. 16) no foreign visitor traversed the strife-torn and impoverished country for a hundred and fifty years, and even in the eighteenth century the passage through Lower Nubia and the *Batn el Hajar* was considered so dangerous that the handful of European pioneers who ascended to Abyssinia[4] preferred the hazards of the desert caravan route to the rapaciousness of the Nubian and Ja'aliyin *meks*.[5] It was not until 1813 that the courageous and persevering Burckhardt made the direct ascent from Aswan to Dongola, and incidentally left us the first detailed description of the Nubians and their country since the time of Ibn Selim.[6] We are therefore obliged to reconstruct the political history of Nubia, particularly in the immediate post-Christian period, very largely by deduction and inference.

It seems clear that, except in the extreme south (see below), there were no direct successors to the power of the Christian Nubian kingdoms. The whole thrust of political development in the earlier part of the feudal age (between the thirteenth and sixteenth centuries) was one of increasing decentralization. The medieval monarchies were weakened even within the Christian period by the rise of local feudatories, and these in their turn were overthrown and replaced by the still more decentralized and anarchic Arab tribal system. As El Mahdi succinctly observes, 'When the Arab tribes first entered the Sudan they were unable to give the conquered territories a central government of any kind. Instead they divided up the country amongst themselves and, as a result, the only kind of government which rose in the Sudan was the traditional Arab sheikhdom based on the tribe.'[7]

We have already noted in Chapter 17 the extreme political instability of the Arab tribal system as it exists among bedouin groups. When the Arab conquerors settled down and intermarried with their Nubian subjects, however, it was inevitable that they should form somewhat more stable and lasting 'tribal' groupings which – unlike those of the bedouins – were closely and permanently tied to particular sections of the Nile Valley. Such were and are the Ja'aliyin and Nubian 'tribes' of today. The leaders, too, were able to consolidate their position and to achieve a degree of hereditary and autocratic rule which is rarely permitted to bedouin chieftains. The sheikhs of the sixteenth century became the *meks* of the seventeenth century: local dynasts who ruled over small territories with the aid of standing armies – often composed of slaves – and who lived chiefly by extracting tribute from their agrarian subjects and from passing caravans. (Their title is a corruption of *melik*, the Arabic for 'king'.) The Ja'aliyin and Nubian *meks* thus inherited, or more properly revived, the kind of power which had been wielded by the local feudatories in Late Christian times and like their predecessors they adopted the castle as the principal expression of their authority.

By the seventeenth century the Nile Valley north of Soba (i.e. the junction of the Blue and White Niles) was divided among more than a dozen *mek*ships: Qerri, Shendi, and Berber, plus the autonomous theocratic city of Damer, in the region above the Fifth Cataract; the four Shaiqiya *mek*ships of Amri, Merowe, Kajebi, and Hannek; and the districts of Dufar, Abkur, Tanqasi Island, Old Dongola, Khandaq, Khannaj, and Argo Island in the Dongola Reach. (For a complete list of the Ja'aliyin and Nubian *mek*ships and their respective 'tribes' see Fig. 83.) To the north of the Third Cataract there were no *meks* as such; the region was governed by Turkish-appointed officials called *kashefs*, whose history will be recounted in more detail later (see 'Ottoman rule in the north'). However, the allegiance of the *kashefs* to the Ottoman sultanate was no more than nominal; in practice their rule was indistinguishable from that of the *meks*.

TABLE VII

CHRONOLOGY OF FOREIGN VISITORS TO NUBIA AND THE SUDAN, 1521–1822

Year(s)	Visitor(s)	Itinerary	Purpose	Published report
1521–2	David Reubeni	Suakin to Abyssinia (?); overland to Sennar; Nile route to Egypt	Commercial? Diplomatic?	(none)
1672–3	Evliya Çelebi	Nile route to Abyssinia; returned to Egypt via Red Sea	Commercial? Diplomatic?	*Travels of Evliya Çelebi* (in Turkish),Vol. 10 (Istanbul, 1938)
1698–1700	Poncet and Brevedent	Western oasis route, Egypt to Dongola; Nile route to Sennar; overland to Abyssinia; returned to Egypt via Red Sea route	Medical, Missionary	Poncet, *A Voyage to Aethiopia* (London, 1709)
1698–1708(?)	Franciscan missionaries	Same route to Abyssinia as Poncet and Brevedent; various members returned to Egypt by different routes at different times	Missionary, Medical	Krump, *Höiher und Fruchtbärer Palm-Baum des Heiligen Evangelij* (Augsburg, 1710)
1704–5	Le Noir du Roule	Western oasis route, Egypt to Dongola; Nile route to Sennar (murdered at Sennar 1705)	Diplomatic	(none)
1737–8	Frederick Norden	Nile route, Aswan to Derr and return	Exploration	*Travels in Egypt and Nubia* (London, 1757)
1769–73	James Bruce	Red Sea route to Abyssinia; returned to Egypt via Sennar, Berber, and eastern desert route to Aswan	Exploration	*Travels to Discover the Source of the Nile* (Edinburgh, 1790)
1793–6	W. G. Browne	Western oasis route (*Darb el-Arba'in*), Egypt to Darfur and return	Exploration	*Travels in Africa, Egypt, and Syria* (London, 1799)
1813	Thomas Legh	Nile route, Aswan to Qasr Ibrim and return	Exploration	*Narrative of a Journey in Egypt* (London, 1817)

Year(s)	Visitor(s)	Itinerary	Purpose	Published report
1813	J. L. Burckhardt	Nile route, Aswan to Dongola and return	Exploration	Travels in Nubia (London, 1819)
1814	" "	Eastern desert route, Aswan to Berber; Nile route to Sennar; overland to Suakin and the Red Sea	Exploration	" "
1816, 1817	G. Belzoni	Nile route, Aswan to Second Cataract and return	Exploration	Narrative of Operations and Recent Discoveries in Egypt and Nubia (London, 1820)
1820–21	Waddington and Hanbury	Nile route, Aswan to Jebel Barkal and return (accompanied army of Ismail Pasha)	Exploration	Journal of a Visit to Some Parts of Ethiopia (London, 1822)
1820–22	Frédéric Cailliaud	Nile route, Aswan to Sennar; ascended Blue Nile to Abyssinian border (accompanied army of Ismail Pasha)	Exploration	Voyage à Méroé, et au Fleuve Blanc (Paris, 1826)
1821–2	de Bellefonds	Nile route, Aswan to Sennar and return (accompanied army of Ismail Pasha)	Exploration	Journal d'un Voyage à Méroé (Khartoum, 1958)

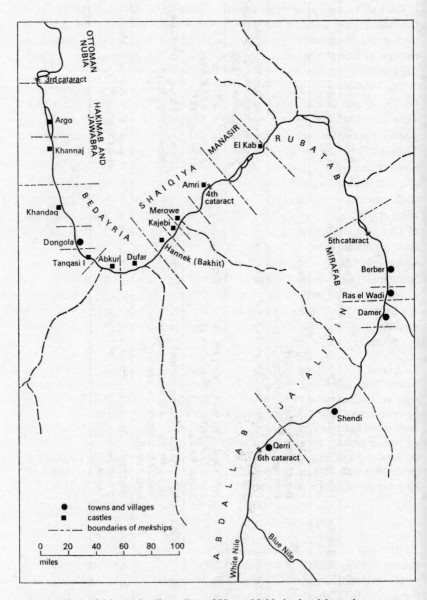

Fig. 83. *Mek*ships and ruling tribes of Upper Nubia in the eighteenth century

For three centuries these petty feudatories – *kashefs* in the north and *meks* in the south – were to provide the only stable framework of government in the Nile Valley. Some of the most powerful *meks* retained their positions even under the colonial régimes of the nineteenth and twentieth centuries; the last of them were terminated under the revolutionary governments of the 1960s.

The Ja'aliyin *meks* were first and foremost warlords. Those in the south (at Qerri and Shendi) commanded substantial bodies of slave troops, while the Shaiqiya rulers were supported by and were members of a warrior élite which held equally aloof from agriculture and from commerce. Through their continual internecine warfare there gradually emerged a hierarchical order among the various feudatories: centralized government of a sort returned to the Sudan. In the Dongola region, according to Nubian tradition, 'For several centuries Nubia was occupied by ... Arabs who were at continual war with each other, in the course of which the kings of Dongola had acquired so much influence over them as to be able at last to compel them to pay tribute.'[8] The same sort of thing evidently happened at Berber and Shendi. By the end of the sixteenth century these 'principal *meks*' were subject in their turn to a still higher authority, which was vested in the Black Sultans of Sennar (see below). Yet the kind of centralized government which they achieved was a far cry from the tight theocratic bureaucracy of the earlier Christian monarchies. As Crawford has written:

> Control was ... loose, and the subordinate riverain rulers, once they had bought their office, were left alone. We must, in studying the history of these regions, disabuse our minds of all modern European conceptions of government. The concept of trusteeship was completely unknown; political power was exercised solely for the advantage of those who had obtained it (by force or marriage) without regard for the interests of the subjects. Law and order were maintained because, without them, the bases of tribute might be endangered. The paramount ruler felt no moral responsibility for the good of his subjects. Medieval kingship in England was based upon a similar political theory ...[9]

THE SENNAR CONFEDERATION

At the top of the political pyramid in the post-Christian Sudan were the black Funj Sultans of Sennar. The domain over which they held direct sway was relatively small and it was situated far to the south of the former Nubian kingdoms and empires. Its principal territories were the Gezira region (the 'island' between the Blue and White Niles) and the upper reaches of the Blue Nile and its tributaries, on the borders of what is now Ethiopia (see Fig. 84). The city of Sennar, which they chose for their capital, was situated on the Blue Nile over 150 miles above its confluence

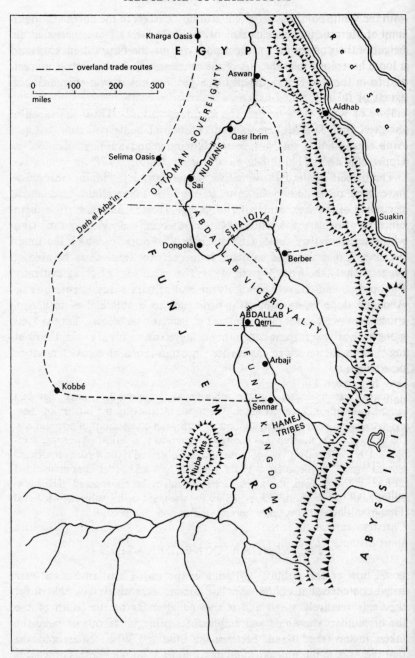

Fig. 84. Ottoman and Funj dominions in the seventeenth century

with the White Nile; it corresponded almost exactly to the known southern limit of Meroitic influence in earlier times (cf. Ch. 11). Nevertheless, at the height of their power in the seventeenth century the Funj sultans exercised a loose hegemony over the Nile Valley as far north as the Third Cataract, and from the Red Sea in the east to Kordofan in the west (Fig. 84). The extent of their domains had been exceeded in earlier times only by the empire of Kush at its height. The Funj were nominal overlords of all of the ex-Nubian Ja'aliyin tribes, of the Nubian Danagla, of many Beja and Arab nomad tribes, and of a good many indigenous black peoples on the Upper Nile and in Kordofan.

The origins of the Funj kingdom, according to the 'Funj Chronicle', have been recounted in Chapter 16. This tradition relates that at the beginning of the sixteenth century the Funj and the Abdallab Arabs combined to overthrow the last remnants of the Christian kingdom of Alwa, whose territory they divided between them, the Funj assuming primacy because of their superior military force.[10] However modern scholarship suggests that the 'Funj Chronicle' is in part a fabrication of latter-day Funj propagandists, and that the overthrow of Alwa was achieved by the Abdallab alone.[11] They were, it would appear, a confederation of Juhayna tribes who were brought together by a certain Abdallah Jamma ('the gatherer'), whose surname aptly suggests the diverse origins of his following.[12] After their victory over Alwa the Arabs formed themselves into a new tribe and adopted Abdallah Jamma as their eponymous ancestor; they have been known ever since as the Abdallab ('descendants of Abdallah'[13]). According to their own tribal tradition[14] it was they, rather than the Funj, who 'inherited the bejewelled crown of the [Nubian] kings'.[15] These words indicate that the Abdallab sheikhs regarded themselves as the legitimate successors to the rulers of Alwa, and the heirs to all the territories and tribute formerly claimed by the Christian kingdom. It was presumably for the sake of the same political pedigree that the Funj sultans later appropriated the Abdallab tradition as their own (cf. Ch. 16). The Abdallab however did not establish their headquarters at the old Christian capital of Soba; they preferred instead the village of Qerri, a short distance below the confluence of the Blue and White Niles.

It seems, then, that the beginnings of centralized government in the post-Christian Sudan must be attributed not to the Funj but to the Arab tribal confederation of the Abdallab. Their emergence (and presumably the final overthrow of Alwa) are believed to date from the latter part of the fifteenth century,[16] although accurate dating is impossible.[17] Having taken possession of the old southern Christian kingdom, it seems probable that the Abdallab began expanding their territory to the north, subjugating portions of the former kingdom of Makouria as well. We will probably never know how extensive were their conquests when, at the beginning of the sixteenth century, their kingdom was invaded from the south or west by the Funj. Apparently a brief period of hostilities between the two peoples ended in a decisive engagement at Arbaji, in 1504, in which the newcomers were victorious.[18] The Arabs and all their domains then became tributary to the Funj, who in later years still further expanded the territories which they had acquired by conquest. It is now suggested that the battle which took place in 1504, and which is recorded in the 'Funj Chronicle' as a joint attack on Soba by the Funj and the Abdallab (Ch. 16), was in reality the engagement in which the Funj wrested from the Abdallab the fruits of their earlier victory over Soba.[19]

The origin of the Funj has been, and continues to be, a source of debate. The term is not an ethnic one: there is no such thing as a Funj tribe or language.[20] They were, rather, a hereditary ruling caste whose subjects were a group of indigenous non-Arab tribes on the upper Blue Nile, who are usually designated collectively as the Hamej.[21] By the time they were first contacted by foreigners the Funj were already Moslems, speaking Arabic and claiming an Omayyad pedigree, although betraying no trace of Arab ancestry in their physical appearance. They were in fact tradition-ally known as the Black Sultans,[22] and it seems probable that their ancestry was the most purely African of all the groups which have held power in the Sudan. However, in the absence of ethnological and linguistic evidence all hope of discovering their specific tribal origin has vanished. James Bruce, who visited Sennar in 1772, reported that the Funj kings were descended from the Shilluk tribesmen of the White Nile[23] – a not unlikely suggestion in view of the warlike nature of the Shilluk and the fact that they are the most northerly and most Arab-influenced of the Sudan Negro tribes. However, later writers have derived the Funj from Darfur in the west[24] and from the Abyssinian foothills in the east,[25] while they themselves traced their ancestry directly from the family of the Prophet.[26] Whoever they were, they seem to have moved into the southern part of the territory recently subjugated by the Abdallab, and to have put themselves at the head of a confederation of indigenous tribes which then successfully overthrew the Arabs and succeeded to their power. It has been suggested that the Hamej tribes who were the principal followers of the Funj were disaffected former subjects of Alwa,[27] so that the action of the Funj in championing their cause against the Arabs might be regarded as a restora-tion rather than as a destruction of the political situation which had existed under the Christian kingdom.

It is an anomaly of history that the first Funj monarch, Umara Dunqas, is well-attested historically both because his exploits are recounted in the 'Funj Chronicle'[28] and because he happened to be on the throne when the adventurer David Reubeni passed through the Sudan in 1522[29] – the last foreign visitor to leave an account of his travels for a century and a half. After Umara, on the other hand, we know hardly more than the names of the next seven rulers, and even their sequence is uncertain.[30] Only the fifth king, Dekin, is described in any detail in the 'Chronicle': 'He was one of the greatest of the kings of the Funj. He reorganized the administration in the best possible manner, and made fixed laws that no one of all the people in his kingdom might transgress; and to every district of his kingdom he appointed a chief; and to such as were wont to be seated in his presence he gave a definite order of precedence when they were so seated in the council chamber; and he ceased not to devote himself to the organization of his realms until, after reigning fifteen years, he died in [AD 1577].'[31] This picture of tightly integrated bureaucratic administration is not supported by the knowledge we possess of the Funj empire at a later date.

A more coherent and detailed record of Funj history opens with the reign of King Adlan, at the beginning of the seventeenth century. At that time the Abdallab attempted to revolt – perhaps not for the first time[32] – under their sheikh Ajib el Manjilak.[33] The revolt was successfully put down, Ajib was killed, and members of his family were driven out of their territory and into Dongola, a region which may already have been under Abdallab control. The Funj king pursued them, but after reaching and passing Dongola he was deposed by his own troops, and a successor appointed. An agreement was then negotiated between the Funj and the Abdallab under which the son of the rebel Ajib was installed in place of his father, and he and all his successors reigned not only as sheikhs of the Abdallab but as viceroys, on behalf of the Funj, over all of the Arab, Beja, and Ja'aliyin tribes in the northern part of the empire. The Arabs were thus in effect handed back the larger part of the empire which the Funj had wrested from them a century earlier, on condition that they pass on a certain part of its tribute to the rulers at Sennar. This *modus vivendi* proved successful enough to remain in force for over 150 years, and undoubtedly gave rise to the tradition of close cooperation between Funj and Abdallab which is enshrined in the 'Funj Chronicle'. The date of the original agreement has been variously set at 1607–8,[34] 1610,[35] and 1611–12.[36]

It was during the seventeenth century, and partly as a result of Abdallab collaboration, that the Funj empire reached its widest extent. The Abdallab had been largely responsible for the subjugation of the Arab and Beja nomads to the east of the Nile. Of their condition James Bruce wrote:

The residence of [the Abdallab] prince . . . was at Qerri, a town in the very limit of the tropical rains . . . This was a very well chosen situation, it being a tollgate as it were to catch all the Arabs that had flocks, who, living within the rains in the country which was all of fat earth, were every year, about the month of May, obliged by the [tsetse] fly to pass, as it were in review, to take up their abode in the sandy desert without the tropical rains . . . The [Abdallab] chief with a large army of light unencumbered horse stood in the way of their return to their pastures till they had paid the uttermost farthing of tribute, including arrears if there were any.[37]

Until late in the seventeenth century all of the riverain districts north of the junction of the Niles, as far as the Third Cataract, also paid tribute to the Funj through the intermediary of the Abdallab. It is not certain when and by whom these northern districts were annexed to the Funj empire; they may already have formed part of the Abdallab domains at the time when the latter were defeated by the Funj, or they may have been directly subjugated by the Funj at a later date.[38] The Shaiqiya of the Middle Nile region broke free at the end of the seventeenth century (see below), but at the time of Bruce's visit in 1772 the *mek* of Dongola was still nominated by the Funj ruler.[39] The tribute from Dongola consisted chiefly of horses,[40] for which the region had been famous since the days of the first Napatan monarchs (see Ch. 10).

While the Abdallab held and administered the north, the Black Sultans turned their attention to the west. In the reign of Badi II ('The Bearded') a successful expedition to Kordofan resulted in the subjugation of a portion of the Nuba Mountains area. The expedition may have been undertaken primarily for the sake of slaves; at all events the Nuba Mountain area became, and long remained, a favourite slave-hunting ground. According to Holt, 'Badi brought back numerous prisoners whom he settled in villages around Sennar. The prisoners and their descendants, later augmented by raiding and purchase, formed a slave-army for the protection of the capital and its ruler. This shift in the military basis of the dynasty's rule, from the band of free warriors, the Funj aristocracy, to slave-troops directly dependent on the monarch, is paralleled in other Islamic states, notably in the Ottoman Empire itself.'[41]

Although there were to be later and wider conquests in the west, the first Kordofan expedition marks the high tide of Funj imperial expansion. At almost the same time the Shaiqiya successfully revolted and, in the century that followed, the Arabic-speaking and Nubian territories in the north one by one dropped away. At the end of its days (in 1821) the Funj kingdom had become a southern Sudanese confederation, extending primarily east and west of the Upper Nile, instead of an empire extending up and down the great river.

The administration of the Funj empire in its heyday has been thus described by Trimingham:

This kingdom was a loosely knit confederation rather than a state. There was no centralization of authority and no common institutions. Only the land between the two Niles was directly under Sennar, for the Funj retained regional rulers as tributary kings and allowed all indigenous institutions to continue.

The Sennar overlord exercised his authority through retaining the right of choosing his vassal's successor, and the exaction of tribute. The tie therefore was very weak and his vassal frequently refused to pay tribute. The Sennar *Makk* [*Mek*], however, maintained a large standing army of Nuba slaves (14,000 foot and 1,800 horse in Bruce's time), and during the palmy days of the kingdom was able to maintain his overlordship. In 1610, for instance, the Abdallab viceroy revolted and was defeated and killed, but the Funj king nominated his son . . . in his place.

The Funj gave these tributary kings the title of *Mānjil* (or *Mānjilak*). After the death of a *Mānjil*, candidates came to Sennar and intrigued. When one of them was chosen the king invested him with the *kakar* or chair of state,[42] the *tāqiyya umm qarnain* or headdress shaped like two horns,[43] an *'imma* (turban), a sword, and sometimes a gold chain . . .

The Abdallab, as overlord of the 'Arab' tribes north of Arbaji, appointed his own subordinate chiefs and invested them with the *tāqiyya*. Shucair writes: 'If one of these *makks* dies the whole tribe meet together, choose a *makk* to be over them, and bring him to the sheikh [of the Abdallab]. Then the sheikh shaves his head, crowns him with the *tāqiyya* having two horns stuffed with cotton, and seats him on the chair called *kakar*. He then addresses him by the title *makk'* saying 'blessing be on you,' and the *makk* kisses his hand and prays for him. Then the sheikh orders the *nahās* (tribal drum) to be beaten, thus publishing his appointment as *makk* over his people.'[44]

The Funj, however, exercised direct rule in the Jezira itself over all the tribes, including the Arabs. There was a *wazīr* [chief minister], and relatives of the *makk* also had authority . . . In the time of Bruce the law still survived that a king might 'be lawfully put to death by his subjects or slaves, upon a council being held by the great officers, if they decree that it is not for the advantage of the state that he be suffered to reign any longer.'[45] The master of the king's household, called *sīd al-qom*, had the duty of killing him.[46]

It is not certain when and by whom the Funj rulers were first converted to Islam. The account of David Reubeni clearly implies, though it does not explicitly state, that Umara Dunqas, the first Funj monarch of record, was already a Moslem at the time of Reubeni's visit (1522).[47] A century and a half later James Bruce (whose five-volume narrative of his travels to Abyssinia is the source of much of our information about the Funj) asserted that the Black Sultans had become Moslems 'for the sake of trading with Cairo'.[48] Another tradition suggests that Umara Dunqas adopted the Islamic faith in order to forestall the invasion of his kingdom by the Ottoman Sultan Selim I, who had annexed Egypt and Lower Nubia at almost the same time that the Funj hegemony was established in the south (see 'Ottoman rule in the north', below).

The story is that after Salim, Sultan of Turkey, conquered Egypt in 1517, he sent an army into Nubia . . . and also established bases at Sawākim and Masawwa, thus threatening the independence of the Beja and Abyssinia. Amāra [Umara Dunqas] took alarm at this as a threat against his own kingdom and sent a message stating that if Salim was thinking of taking the *jihād* [holy war] against him, he should know that he and his people were Arabs and true believers. As proof of this he sent genealogical tables drawn up by one As-Samarkandī who is responsible for most of the fictitious genealogies in the Sudan [cf. Ch. 17], to prove that the Funj belonged to the Banī Umayya.[49]

As we saw in Chapter 17, the Funj rulers had no sooner been converted than they opened the gates of their kingdom to Islamic religious teachers. As a result the spread of Islamic knowledge was much more rapid in the newly converted south than in the Arab-dominated districts of the Ja'aliyīn and Nubians. Unlike the early Moslem sultans of West Africa, the Funj seem to have had no desire to maintain Islam as the exclusive religion of the ruling class.[50]

Despite the extent of their nominal hegemony in the north, it is apparent that the Funj were never primarily interested in the riverain districts and their tribute. Theirs was a slave-trading empire as surely as were the sultanates further west – Mali, Songhai and Bornu – which may have been its inspiration. It is noteworthy that while the Funj were content to surrender direct control of the Islamic northern districts to their Abdallab viceroys, they were careful to keep the pagan south directly in their own hands. While the Abdallab extended their dominion over bedouins and Beja, the Funj proper concentrated their attention upon the potential slaving-ground of Kordofan. It seems probable too that the military advantage which the Funj enjoyed with respect to their Arab neighbours was due in part to their possession of slave armies, and to their closer access to the slave-hunting territories in which replenishments could be obtained.

THE SHAIQIYA REVOLT AND THE FUNJ DECLINE

Of the various tribal groupings which emerged in post-Christian Nubia none has played a more distinctive historical role than the Shaiqiya, whose territory extends from the Fourth Cataract to Debba, at the bottom of the great bend of the Nile (Fig. 9). They are the northernmost of the Arabic-speaking Ja'aliyīn tribes and the immediate neighbours of the Dongolawi Nubians. Like the other Ja'aliyīn tribes they are today a fairly homogeneous group, resulting from the amalgamation of a small number of alien conquerors with a much larger number of their Nubian subjects. It seems, however, that in the time of the Funj the amalgamation of rulers and subjects had not yet taken place: the Shaiqiya warlords were a military élite who held strictly aloof from the riverain farmers, whom they despised and intermittently terrorized.

The origins of the Shaiqiya warlords have been the subject of nearly as much speculation as have those of the Funj. MacMichael described the typical Shaiqiya as 'sallow complexioned' and 'often hard to distinguish

rom a Turk *"muwallad"* (i.e. born in the Sudan . . .)'; on this basis he
vas inclined to derive them from the garrison forces (mostly of Balkan and
Anatolian origin) stationed by the Ottomans in northern Nubia (see
pelow).[51] Yet a century earlier the traveller Waddington had described
he Shaiqiya as 'clear, glossy, jet-black'![52] Trimingham suggests a Beja
prigin for them,[53] while other writers are content to speak of them as a
mysterious people.[54] The mystery which surrounds them arises from the
act that, to a far greater extent than other peoples who settled down in the
Nile Valley, they managed to retain the discipline and traditions of a
warrior élite, as well as the predatory habits of bedouin days. Moorehead
says of them that 'There was some strain in their blood . . . that made them
ise above all the surrounding tribes, and in their prowess and appearance
hey were every bit as formidable as the Mamelukes. They lived by pillag-
ng the settled communities along the riverbank, and they were said to be
able to muster some ten thousand warriors, of whom at least two thousand
were mounted. All through this part of the Sudan their name was a byword
or piracy and destruction.'[55]

Burckhardt described the Shaiqiya in 1813 with customary vividness:

These different people are continually at war with each other, and their youth
make plundering expeditions as far as Darfur in the west and Wadi Halfa in the
north. They all fight on horseback, in coats of mail which are sold to them by the
merchants of Suakin and Sennar. Firearms are not common among them, their
only weapons being a lance, target, and sabre; they throw the lance to a great
distance with much dexterity, and always carry four or five lances in the left
hand when charging an enemy. They are all mounted on Dongola stallions and
are as famous for their horsemanship as the Mamelukes were in Egypt; they train
their horses to make violent springs with their hind legs while galloping. Their
saddles resemble the drawings I have seen of those of Abyssinia, and like the
Abyssinian horsemen they place the great toe only in the stirrup.

The Shaiqiya are a perfectly independent people and possess great wealth in
corn and cattle; like the bedouins of Arabia they pay no kind of tribute to their
chiefs, whose power is by no means so great as that of the chiefs of Dongola.
They are renowned for their hospitality, and the person of their guest or companion is sacred. If the traveller possesses a friend among them, and has been
plundered on the road, his property will be recovered, even if it has been taken
by the king.

Such of the Shaiqiya as are soldiers, and not learned men, indulge in the frequent use of wine and spirits made from dates. The manners of their women are
said to be very depraved.[56]

To this thumbnail characterization Waddington added that:

They are singularly fearless in attack, and ride up to the very faces of their
enemy with levity and gaiety of heart, as to a festival, or with joy as if to meet
friends from whom they had been long separated; they then give the 'Salam

aleikoum!' ('Peace be with you!') – the peace of death, which is to attend the lance that instantly follows the salutation: mortal thrusts are given and received with the words of love upon the lips. This contempt of life, this mockery of what is most fearful, is peculiar to themselves – the only people to whom arms are playthings and war a sport; who among their enemies seek nothing but amusement, and in death fear nothing but repose.[57]

Two more recent opinions of the Shaiqiya are also worth quoting. Late in the nineteenth century General Gordon was obliged to rely to some extent on the loyalty of the Shaiqiya in his ill-fated attempt to defend Khartoum against the Mahdi (see 'The Mahdiya', below), yet he found them a continual trial. In his posthumously published journals he complains repeatedly of their duplicity and intrigues,[58] and at one point bursts out with ' *Those Shaggyeh*! I will back them to try a man's patience more sorely than any other people in the whole world, yea, and in the Universe.'[59] Finally, in the early twentieth century MacMichael observed that 'The Sháíki stands apart from every other tribe in the Sudan in being more adventurous, more quarrelsome, and, in particular, more ready to take service as a mercenary fighter under any employer. The typical Sháíki is sallow complexioned, gaunt and alert, a hard drinker, fond of the dice, and a born liar.'[60]

Although it has been fashionable to attribute the warlike character of the Shaiqiya to some exotic strain in their blood, they seem in reality to have been docile enough in the beginning. For a century and more they submitted without undue protest to the suzerainty of the Abdallab and the Funj; we hear nothing of them prior to their successful revolt in the latter part of the seventeenth century, and their great warlike – and predatory – exploits were all achieved within a few generations thereafter. It therefore seems probable that Shaiqiya militarism was inspired by the successful example of the Funj and the Abdallab and not by the latter-day migration of some warrior group into their territory. The difference which sets the Shaiqiya apart from other Ja'aliyin tribes is the same difference that separates the Spartans from their fellow Greeks, and Ch'in from its neighbour states in ancient China. It was a product of geography and opportunity, not of heredity. The Shaiqiya warlords may in reality have been nearly pure Nubians, despite their professed disdain for their Nubian subjects; the claim of being genetically distinct from their subjects has been routinely put forward by most of the hereditary élites of earlier times. There are reports that the Shaiqiya actually spoke a Nubian dialect before the nineteenth century.[61]

The Shaiqiya region comprised the original heartland of Napata (Ch. 10): the fruitful district immediately downstream from the Fourth Cataract. Despite its agricultural wealth this region under the Funj was a cul-de-sac, by-passed by the main trade routes which linked the northern and southern parts of the empire (Fig. 84).[62] As a result the revenues of the district were probably slight, and the interest of the Abdallab and Funj overlords in securing them may have been slight in proportion. For their part the Shaiqiya *meks* must have looked with envy upon the rich tolls which the neighbouring peoples were able to extract from the caravan traffic, but which they themselves were denied as a result of their unfavourable geographical position. At any rate in the latter part of the seventeenth century the Shaiqiya *meks* united temporarily to assert their independence of Funj dominion. They may have been emboldened by a division among the Funj themselves,[63] but the actual thrust of their hostilities was directed against the Abdallab viceroys. According to their own somewhat confused tradition the Abdallab were defeated in an action at Dulga Island. The Shaiqiya then sent word of their victory to Sennar, demanding in consequence that the Abdallab *manjil* be deposed as their overlord, and one of their own sheikhs recognized in his stead – in effect demanding an affirmation of their independence.[64] This seems to have been granted *de facto* if not formally. The date of the Shaiqiya revolt has been variously fixed between 1660[65] and 1690.[66]

The newly independent Shaiqiya were unable to unite to form a stable nucleus of power on the Middle Nile. Had they done so they could certainly have displaced the Abdallab as overlords of the entire region from the Third Cataract to the junction of the Niles. However, true to the essentially bedouin tradition of political decentralization, they broke up into the four independent *mek*ships of Amri, Merowe,[67] Kajebi, and Hannek. Each of these became the base of operations for a barbarian warband similar to the Beni Kanz of old (Ch. 16). Like the Beni Kanz, the Shaiqiya preferred the predatory life to the responsibilities of keeping the peace; outside their own petty fiefs they were content to leave nominal administrative control in the hands of the Abdallab, and to extract their own form of tribute by force and terror. In the century following their independence, therefore, the military power of the Shaiqiya was expended largely in wars upon one another and in hit-and-run raids on the surrounding districts, rather than in the enlargement or consolidation of their position. 'Such were the wholly evil and disruptive results of achieving independence,' writes Crawford.[68] So frequent and severe were the Shaiqiya depredations in the Dongola region that in the eighteenth century a great many Nubians migrated westward into Kordofan,[69] yet it was not until 1782 that Funj hegemony at Dongola was finally ended.[70] In later years the Shaiqiya also turned their attention to their southern cousins: both the Ja'aliyin proper at Shendi and the Abdallab at Qerri felt the scourge of their attacks at the end of the eighteenth century.[71] However, the Shaiqiya never established a lasting rule over the neighbouring peoples; theirs was simply an ever-widening hunting ground.

It was the Shaiqiya *meks* who built the largest and most impressive of the Upper Nubian castles, already described in Chapter 17. As Cailliaud observed in 1821, they were pre-eminently a race of castle-dwellers.[72] Each of the four Shaiqiya *meks* seems to have boasted, within his minuscule domain, a principal castle and several subsidiary ones.[73] The latest and largest of these are believed to date from the eighteenth century – the Shaiqiya heyday and the climactic century of Nubia's feudal age.[74]

It was principally the Shaiqiya who made the name of Nubia a byword among travellers in the post-Christian era. Brother Thomas of Ganget had written as early as the 1520s that '. . . on the way beyond the Nile . . . they are bad people, robbers, murderers, and most of all in the province of Nuba.'[75] Two hundred and fifty years later Bruce was to learn that beyond Sennar, going north, there was 'no protection but that of heaven'.[76] Until their defeat at the hands of Ismail Pasha in 1820 (see below) the Shaiqiya warlords continued to enjoy – apparently literally – the reputation of robbers and murderers. On the eve of their defeat, according to Waddington, '"What are you but a nation of robbers?" said a Turk to them, during some negotiation. "Robbers!" was the indignant reply: "Robbers, then, were we born; and robbers will we die."'[77]

While the Shaiqiya were overrunning the erstwhile Funj domains in the north, the Abdallab themselves broke free from their longtime overlords in 1770.[78] With these two events all semblance of Funj control over the Ja'aliyin and Nubian tribes of the northern Sudan came to an end. In 1776 the Black Sultan in his turn was deposed by his Hamej vizier, and thereafter the remaining Funj monarchs were puppets of the Hamej officials. As Holt reports:

> The last forty years of . . . history are filled with the quarrels of rivals for the regency, kaleidoscopic combinations of Funj aristocrats and Abdallab chiefs, petty wars and all the symptoms of political instability. The Hamaj regents soon went the way of their Funj sovereigns. The fourth regent, Nasir . . . handed over the management of affairs to the *Arbab* Dafa'allah and gave himself up to luxury. A revolt against him was joined by his two brothers: he was captured and put to death in 1798 as an act of vengeance by his cousin . . . Although his brother and successor restored order, he held power for only five years, and after his death the disruptive tendencies of the Hamaj dynasty reasserted themselves.[79]

The final years of Funj rule seem to repeat in dreary detail the story of the decline and fall of Makouria (Ch. 16). In 1821 the last titular Funj monarch surrendered without resistance to the armies of Ismail Pasha, and independent rule in the Sudan came to an end.

OTTOMAN RULE IN THE NORTH

If the sixteenth and seventeenth centuries are a relative dark age in southern Nubia, in the north they are pitch-dark. At some time after their conquest of Egypt in 1517 the Ottoman Turks extended their dominion upriver as far as the Third Cataract, but how, when, and – for that matter – why this was undertaken remain obscure. The source of virtually all our information about Ottoman rule in the north is the folk tradition collected by Burckhardt in 1813, which may be quoted here:

The two tribes of Jawabra and el Gharbia . . . took possession of the country from Aswan to Wadi Halfa, and subsequently extended their authority over a great number of smaller tribes who had settled on the banks of the river at the period of the general invasion, among whom were the Kenuz . . . The Jawabra having nearly subdued the Gharbia, the latter sent an embassy to Constantinople in the reign of the great Sultan Selim, to seek aid against their enemies, and they succeeded in procuring from the Sultan a body of several hundred Bosnian soldiers under a commander named Hassan Coosy. By their means the Jawabra and people of Dongola were driven out of [Lower] Nubia, into the latter country, and to this day the more wealthy inhabitants of Dongola derive their origin from the tribe of Jawabra.

The Bosnian soldiers built the three castles, or rather repaired the existing fabrics, at Aswan, Ibrim, and Sai; and those who garrisoned the castles obtained certain privileges for themselves and for such of their descendants as should continue to occupy the castles and the territory attached to them. One of these privileges was an exemption from all kind of land tax, which Selim had then for the first time imposed throughout his dominions; and as the country was thought incapable of affording food sufficient for the soldiers, an annual pension was likewise assigned to them out of the Sultan's treasury at Cairo. The pay of the garrison of Ibrim was four purses, now equal only to one hundred pounds, but then probably worth four times that sum. They were also made independent of the Pashas of Egypt. While the Pashas [i.e. Ottoman deputies] had any influence in Egypt these pensions were paid, but the Mamelukes generally withheld them. Hassan Coosy with his forces, chiefly cavalry, governed Nubia while he lived, and was constantly moving from place to place. He paid an annual Miry [tribute] to the Pasha of Egypt, but in other respects was independent of him. The descendants of such of the Bosnian soldiers as intermarried with the Gharbia and Jawabra tribes still occupy the territories assigned to their ancestors, at Aswan, Ibrim, and Sai, and they continue to enjoy immunity from taxes and contributions of every kind. They call themselves Kaladshy, or the people of the castles, but are distinguished by the Nubians by the name Osmanli (Turks). They have long forgotten their native language, but their features still denote a northern origin, and their skin is of a light brown colour while that of the Nubians is almost black. They are independent of the governors of Nubia, who are extremely jealous of them, and are often at open war with them. They are governed by

609

their own Agas, who still boast of the *firmans* that render them accountable only to the Sultan.[80]

In the account of Burckhardt no date is assigned to the Ottoman conquest of Nubia. However, since the name of Sultan Selim ('Selim the Grim') is explicitly mentioned, it is assumed to have taken place at some time between his conquest of Egypt in 1517 and his death in 1520. The latter date seems to have been conventionally fixed on by historians for the beginning of Ottoman rule in Nubia.[81] Holt, however, suggests that the annexation took place a generation later, in the reign of Suleiman the Magnificent (1520–66), and that it was connected with the Ottoman penetration into the Red Sea area.[82] Even so, the question of why the Ottomans should take the trouble and expense of subjugating and garrisoning an area of so few resources and so little revenue is left unexplained. Lower Nubia in the sixteenth century did not control the main trade routes to the Red Sea or anywhere else.

Conspicuously absent from the folk history recorded by Burckhardt is any mention of Dotawo or of the Beni Kanz – the two immediate successors to the power of Makouria which, as we saw in Chapter 16, were still extant in the fifteenth century. Whether they had already succumbed to the Gharbia and Jawabra, or whether the Turks themselves delivered the *coup de grâce*, will probably never be known.

Another folk tradition asserts that the Ottoman advance into Nubia was resisted either by the Funj or by the Abdallab. A battle was fought at Hannek, a short distance north of Kerma (not to be confused with the Shaiqiya *mek*ship of Hannek, further south), in which the defenders were soundly defeated. The Turks then set up a *gubba* on the site in commemoration of their victory, and this came to mark the boundary between the Funj and Ottoman spheres of influence.[83] The name of Sultan Selim is also mentioned in one account of the Battle of Hannek, but again the date and even the historical authenticity of the battle are not certain.[84] There seems to be little doubt on the other hand that the boundary between the Funj and Ottoman territories was fixed somewhere in the vicinity of Hannek, which corresponds also to the ancient boundary between Nobatia (Maris) and Makouria, to the dialect boundary between Mahasi and Dongolawi Nubians, and to the modern administrative boundary between the districts of Dongola and Halfa.

Ottoman rule in Egypt, which lasted in theory from 1517 until 1914, was never more than nominal, and in Nubia it must have been even more so. In the northern country the unruly Mamelukes were left to pursue their anarchic administration of day-to-day affairs (cf. Ch. 16), paying only a small annual tribute to Constantinople,[85] and in Nubia the *kashefs* 'endeavoured to imitate the Mamelukes in everything, even in their most detestable vices', according to Burckhardt.[86] Just as the Mamelukes with-held tribute from the Ottoman sultan whenever they felt strong enough, so the *kashefs* in Nubia often withheld their tribute from the Mamelukes.[87]

The title *kashef* is said to be of Mameluke origin.[88] In Egypt it was given to relatively minor tax-collectors who were responsible to various higher provincial authorities.[89] In Nubia on the other hand the *kashefs* seem to have been the only civil officials ever appointed, and their nominal respon-sibility was directly to the Pasha of Egypt (i.e. the Ottoman deputy). They were the *de facto* rulers of the country; their situation differed from that of the *meks* further south only in that they had to coexist with garrison forces which were not under their direct control. The first *kashefs* were presum-ably Turks, Albanians, or Bosnians. However, the office appears to have been hereditary from the beginning (as were most provincial administra-tive offices in the Ottoman Empire), and the *kashefs*, through intermarriage, soon became indistinguishable from their subjects. They apparently had no permanent residence, nor was their number constant. In Burckhardt's time the office was held by three brothers all of whom resided nominally at Derr, but who spent most of their time travelling about their domains for the purpose of exacting taxes and tribute.

The Ottoman military garrisons, again following Burckhardt, were independent of the *kashefs* and were responsible to the Ottoman Sultan himself. Like the *kashefs*, it seems that the garrison forces were placed in the country at the beginning of the Ottoman suzerainty and then were left to perpetuate themselves through intermarriage. They too became Nubianized with the passage of time, though they retained the tradition of their northern origin. Although the original forces are conventionally identified as Bosnians, it seems that they included a good many other nationalities as well. Modern Nubian traditions speak of Bosnians, Hungarians, Albanians, Turks, and Circassians[90] – a fairly typical assort-ment for an Ottoman frontier garrison. As recently as 1952 the inhabitants of the island of Majarab, near Wadi Halfa, insisted that they were of Hungarian descent (Majar-ab signifying 'descendants of Magyars').[91] These various northern peoples were and are designated collectively as *Ghuzz* (from Turkish *oghuz*, a name originally designating the Turkic bedouin tribes of Central Asia);[92] many present-day Nubians claim to be descended from them.[93]

The military forces in northern Nubia were not confined to those at Qasr Ibrim and Sai, mentioned in Burckhardt's account, although these may have been the only ones maintained at Ottoman expense. There appears to have been some sort of force at Gebel Adda until the eighteenth century[94] and at Faras until the nineteenth[95] and there were certainly small garrisons at Kulubnarti[96] and other castle sites in the *Batn el Hajar*. However, these may have been maintained by the *kashefs* for their own purposes. In Burckhardt's time, as we shall see in a moment, the *kashefs* commanded a private force of about 100 horse.

The kind of government which the *kashefs* provided in northern Nubia was different in no significant way from that of the *meks* to the south of them or of the Mamelukes to the north. They were so treacherous to strangers and so continually at war with one another that no foreign visitor succeeded in penetrating very far into their domain until the nineteenth century. One who attempted to do so was Frederick Lewis Norden, a Danish sea-captain who in 1737 conceived the ambition of ascending from Aswan to the Second Cataract.[97] He got only as far as Derr (about 130 miles above Aswan), where for several weeks he was held virtually a prisoner while the *kashef* and his cohorts extorted nearly everything in his possession as 'gifts' or tribute. When Norden protested that he was travelling under the protection of the 'Grand Signior' (Pasha) of Egypt, the *kashef* retorted, 'I laugh at the horns of the Grand Signior; I am here Grand Signior myself and will teach you to respect me as you ought.'[98] Learning that the governor planned to have him killed as soon as the last of his possessions had been appropriated, Norden was happy to make his escape to Aswan; '. . . as they passed the various places on the river the people were everywhere surprised to find that the travellers were still alive, and that they had escaped out of the hands of the governor of Derr.'[99]

The situation was no better half a century later when another intrepid European, W. G. Browne, tried his hand in the Sudan.[100] He discovered that 'For many years Dongola, Mahas and all the borders of the Nile as far as Sennar . . . have been the scene of devastation and bloodshed, having no settled Government, but being constantly torn by internal divisions and harassed by the inroads of the Shaikie [Shaiqiya] and other tribes of Arabs.'[101] As a result Browne was obliged to avoid the Nile route altogether and to travel over the western oasis road, the *Darb el-Arba'in*, to Kordofan and Darfur, incidentally becoming the first and perhaps the only European ever to travel that famous slave-road (cf. Ch. 17).[102] Browne's description of the commercial traffic on the *Darb el-Arba'in* is astonishing: he himself travelled in a caravan of 500 camels, the value of whose cargo he estimated at £115,000.[103] The commodities which were carried for trade were much the same as those which Burckhardt was to encounter a few years later in the market at Shendi (Ch. 17). It seems probable in fact that many of the goods in Browne's caravan were destined for the markets of the Central Sudan rather than for the semi-wilderness of Kordofan and Darfur; that they should have moved by way of the roundabout and uncertain western desert road in preference to the Nile is perhaps our most telling evidence of the political and economic chaos wrought by the Nubian *kashefs* and the Shaiqiya *meks*.

Although the beginnings of Nubian emigration to Egypt may go back slightly earlier, it seems to have been in the Ottoman era that the pattern of regular annual migration – so important in the recent past – became firmly established. The fiction of a common government (the Ottoman sultanate) and the fact of a common religion (Islam) may have encouraged the Nubians to feel more at home in the northern country than at any time since the latter days of the pharaohs; at the same time the exactions of the *kashefs* and the destruction of commerce provided every inducement to leave their own country. At any rate we find, by the seventeenth century, that Nubians are described as dominating the guilds of construction workers, watchmen, and slave-dealers in Cairo. When Napoleon's *savants* arrived at the end of the eighteenth century (see below) they also found Nubians in the majority among customs guards, domestic servants, and carriage drivers.[104] A few years later Burckhardt was to write that 'Great numbers of them go yearly to Cairo, where they generally act as porters, and are preferred to the Egyptians on account of their honesty.'[105] However, the wholesale migrations of the recent past apparently did not begin until later in the nineteenth century, when Nubia and Egypt were firmly if temporarily united under the régime of Mohammed Ali (see below).[106]

It seems appropriate to conclude this section once again with a passage from Burckhardt, describing the colonial régime as he observed it in 1813. It provides incidentally our only detailed description of a system of taxation which probably endured from the days of the pharaohs until the twentieth century:

... At present the political state of the country may be said to be, nominally at least, the same as when Hassan Coosy took possession of it. The present governors, Hussein, Hassan, and Mohammed,[107] are his descendants; their father was named Suleiman, and had acquired some reputation from his vigorous system of government. The title of *Kashef*, assumed by the three brothers, is given in Egypt to the governors of districts. The brothers pay an annual tribute of about £120 into the treasury of the Pasha of Egypt, in lieu of the Miry of Nubia for which the Pasha is accountable to [Constantinople]. In the time of the Mamelukes this tribute was seldom paid, but Mohammed Ali has received it regularly for the last three years. The three *Kashefs* have about one hundred horsemen in their service, consisting chiefly of their own relations or of slaves. These troops receive no regular pay; presents are made to them occasionally, and they are considered to be on duty only when their masters are upon a journey. Derr is the chief residence of the governors, but they are almost continually moving about for the purpose of exacting the taxes from their subjects, who pay them only on the approach of superior force. During these excursions the *Kashefs* commit acts of great injustice wherever they find that there is none to resist them, which is frequently the case. The amount of the revenue is shared equally amongst the three brothers, but they are all very avaricious, extremely jealous of each other, and each robs clandestinely as much as he can. I estimate their annual income at about £3,000 each, or from 8 to £10,000 in the whole. None of them spends more than £300 a year. Their principal wealth consists in [Spanish] dollars and slaves. In their manners they affect the haughty mien and deportment of Turkish grandees, but their dress, which is worse than what a Turkish soldier would like to wear, ill accords with this assumed air of dignity.

The mode of estimating the revenue in Nubia is not from a certain extent of ground, like the Syrian and Egyptian feddan, but from every saqia or waterwheel employed by the natives. The rate of taxation is different in different places; thus at Wadi Halfa each saqia pays annually six fat sheep and six . . . measures of dura. In Mahas the melik, or king, takes from every wheel six sheep, two ardebs (26 bushels) of dura, and a linen shirt. The governors also take from every date tree two clusters of fruit, whatever may be the quantity produced, and levy a duty on all vessels that load dates at Derr. But the whole system of taxation is extremely arbitrary and irregular, and poor villages are soon ruined by it from their inability to resist the exactions made upon them, while the richer ones pay much less in proportion because the governors are afraid of driving the inhabitants to acts of open resistance. The *Kashefs* derive also a considerable income from their office of judges, the administration of justice being a mere article of merchandise.

Although the governors of Nubia extort large sums by the various means above-mentioned, yet their tyranny is exercised only upon the property of their subjects, who are never beaten or put to death except when in a state of open rebellion, which happens not infrequently. If a Nubian from whom money is to be extorted flies, his wife or his young children are imprisoned till he returns. The following is a curious method which the governors of Nubia have devised, of extorting money from their subjects. When any wealthy individual has a daughter of suitable age they demand her in marriage; the father seldom dares to refuse, and sometimes feels flattered by the honour, but he is soon ruined by his powerful son-in-law, who extorts from him every article of his property under the name of presents to his own daughter. All the governors are thus married to females in almost every considerable village; Hussein Kashef has above forty sons of whom twenty are married in the same manner.[108]

THE RETURN OF EGYPTIAN COLONIALISM

In 1798 Napoleon Bonaparte landed at Alexandria accompanied – or soon to be followed – by an army not only of soldiers but of administrators, financiers, engineers, and even of scholars and artists. Their intention was to make Egypt a French colony, to transplant the blessings of the Enlightenment and the Revolution to Oriental soil, and incidentally to menace the British position in India. This quixotic venture lasted no more than three years, and in the end it achieved nothing for France, but it did have the lasting effect of awakening Egypt from what Mohammed Ali was to call 'the sleep of ages',[109] and of setting the country on the road to modernization a century ahead of the rest of the Arab world.[110]

The most important, though unforeseen, consequence of the French occupation was the rise to power of Mohammed Ali, who was to become the
most powerful figure in Egyptian history since Salah ed-Din. He was born
in Greece, of Turkish or Albanian[111] parents, in the year 1769, and came to
Egypt in 1799 with a detachment of Albanian troops who were sent by the
Ottoman sultan in a vain effort to dislodge the French. Nothing is known
of his career for the next two or three years, but in the political chaos which
followed the departure of the French in 1801 he was able to obtain command of most of the Ottoman troops in the country and to prevent a return
to power by the Mamelukes, whom the French had expelled from Cairo
and Lower Egypt. By 1805 he commanded a force of some 10,000 men,
mostly Albanians, and was strong enough to depose the Ottoman Pasha
and take his place at the head of the state. His appointment as Pasha was
confirmed from Constantinople in the following year. In 1808 he easily
defeated a small British force which had been sent against him, and
enormously strengthened his hold on the country in the process. However,
the consolidation of his power was not complete so long as the Mamelukes
continued to hold Upper Egypt. In 1811 he invited several hundred of them,
under promises of friendship, to attend a festival in Cairo; at the conclusion of the celebration his soldiers fell upon the guests and massacred
them almost to a man. Simultaneously an attack was launched against the
remaining Mameluke nobles in Upper Egypt, of whom only about 300
men eventually escaped, together with their wives and retainers, into
Nubia.[112] They were pursued as far as Qasr Ibrim whence, after a further
defeat, the remainder fled to the Dongola region. Here they set up a walled
city which was initially known as el-Urdi (from the Turkish for 'camp'),
but which was later to replace Old Dongola as the administrative capital of
Upper Nubia.[113] It is the New Dongola of today, situated about seventy
miles downstream from its historic namesake and on the opposite (west)
bank of the Nile.

In the decade following his expulsion of the Mamelukes, Mohammed Ali
was busy with the reorganization of the state in Egypt and with a campaign against the rebel Wahhabi sect in Arabia. However he had not forgotten the presence of his enemies at Dongola; as Moorehead has said
of him, 'he never forgave an enemy on any pretext whatever'.[114] In 1820 he
launched a campaign into Nubia under the command of his youngest son,
Ismail Pasha, whose ostensible purpose was to dislodge the last of the
Mamelukes and to crush the destructive power of the Shaiqiya. However, it
is clear that from the beginning the Pasha was looking beyond these immediate objectives: he needed slave recruits for his new armies.

Mohammed Ali and his followers were Ottomans, if not specifically
Turks; like the Mamelukes they spoke Turkish rather than Arabic, and
under their administration Turkish remained the language of the governing

élites in Egypt and the Sudan until late in the nineteenth century. The force with which Ismail Pasha invaded Nubia was also comprised of the usual medley of Balkan and Near Eastern peoples who made up the Ottoman armies. For this reason the invasion and the colonial régime which followed it have always been known among Sudanese as the *Turkiya*[115] – the régime of the Turks. Yet this designation must be understood only in an ethnic and not in a political sense, for annexation of Nubia was undertaken by Mohammed Ali on his own initiative and for his own purposes, and not (as were some of his other wars) with the blessing of the Ottoman sultan. Although Mohammed Ali and his successors always professed themselves the vassals of Constantinople, the Sudan after its conquest was never considered a part of the Ottoman domains except in the very nominal sense that Egypt itself was. Its officials were appointed from Cairo, not from Constantinople, and it was an Egyptian colony as surely as in the days of the pharaohs. We are therefore justified in speaking of the invading army as an Egyptian one, and of the régime which followed it as an Egyptian administration, even though native-born Egyptians played almost no part in them.[116]

Ismail entered Nubia in 1820 with a force of about 4,000 men, commanding the first really effective firepower that had ever been seen in the southern countries.[117] Firearms among the Nubians had been so scarce as to be almost ritual weapons; the Shaiqiya and the Funj rank-and-file still fought entirely with spears and lances.[118] As a result the Egyptian invasion was hardly more than a triumphal parade. In Lower Nubia the *Kashef* Hassan, one of the three brothers mentioned in Burckhardt's account of a few years earlier, submitted without resistance to the invaders, while his brother Hussein fled to Kordofan. The commander of the 'Bosnian' garrison at Sai also submitted,[119] as did the principal *mek* of the Danagla. A few of the Mamelukes at el-Urdi (later New Dongola) also surrendered, while the major part retreated south to Shendi, to take refuge with the *mek* of the Ja'aliyin.

Next came the country of the Shaiqiya, and here, predictably, the only real resistance of the campaign was encountered. In two battles the Shaiqiya cavalry charged with all the folly and bravado which so inspired the admiration of Waddington (see above), but they were cut to pieces by the Egyptian musketry without inflicting any serious loss on their opponents. After the second battle one of the two principal Shaiqiya *meks* submitted, while the other fled south to the Ja'aliyin country. The expedition then proceeded to Berber, which surrendered without resistance, and to Shendi, where the last of the Mamelukes as well as the fugitive *mek* of the Shaiqiya were holed up under the protection of Nimr, the *mek* of the Ja'aliyin. After a period of negotiation Shendi too surrendered; the Mameluke captives were sent back to Egypt, to disappear for ever from history,[120] while the

Shaiqiya threw in their lot with the invaders. For the remainder of the campaign they accompanied the Egyptian force as irregulars, and until the end of the nineteenth century they remained an important if unreliable military adjunct of the Egyptian régime in the Sudan.

As the army proceeded south the Abdallab sheikh surrendered in his turn, and the way was open to Sennar. The Hamej viceroy Mohammed wad Adlan prepared to resist, but he was murdered by a rival faction before the arrival of the Egyptians. When the army finally appeared, the last Funj Sultan, Badi VI, came out in person to make his submission. He and his family were granted a pension, which was maintained until the overthrow of Egyptian rule in 1881. When the Egyptians entered Sennar the next day they were surprised to find it in a state of advanced decay, and the once-magnificent royal palace in ruins. Thus ended the last independent monarchy on the Nile; after 3,000 years the pharaohs had returned.[121]

Ismail's conquest had been nearly bloodless, and his policy towards the Sudanese leaders was in the beginning generally conciliatory. The reimposition of a strong hand may have been a welcome relief to many of the riverain peoples after the chaos of the preceding century.[122] However, disillusion was not long in coming. Mohammed Ali in Egypt kept pressing his son to send back more slaves – a difficult feat since very few captives had been taken – and Ismail's financial advisers sought a way out of the difficulty by imposing a nearly ruinous tax upon the owners of slaves and domesticated animals. Since there was almost no currency in circulation in the Sudan, it was expected that the tax would have to be paid largely in slaves, and this would satisfy the commander's requirements.[123] As a result of this policy, disaffection spread rapidly through the riverain districts.

Ismail returned to Shendi towards the end of 1822, where he was the guest of the Ja'aliyin *mek*, Nimr, who had previously submitted to him. The Pasha now made an enormous demand on his host for money and slaves; Nimr responded by setting fire to his quarters in the night, with the result that the Egyptian commander and most of his retinue perished. This was the signal for a general revolt against the Egyptians throughout the central Sudan. Most of the recently installed garrisons in the Gezira were driven out or forced to fall back on Wad Medani, where the invaders had established their military headquarters. However, the rebellion was a largely spontaneous and uncoordinated movement, and its leaders never succeeded in uniting. The northern districts were unaffected by the revolt, the governor at Berber held firm, and the Shaiqiya remained loyal to their new masters. In a year of skilful campaigning the Egyptian second-in-command, Mohammed Khusraw, succeeded in extinguishing the flames of rebellion in one centre after another, and peace returned to the land – the peace of death, as Moorehead puts it.[124] The campaign of pacification was accompanied by wanton atrocities and scenes of carnage which more than compensated for the bloodlessness of the original conquest; all told it is estimated that 50,000 Sudanese died to avenge the murder of Ismail.[125]

THE COLONIAL RÉGIME

In Egypt Mohammed Ali is remembered as a ruthless despot, but also as a reformer and modernizer who set the country on the road to the twentieth century. In the Sudan on the other hand his régime was no more enlightened than was that of the pharaohs, and it was motivated by the same consuming greed for gold and slaves. Yet the return of Egyptian colonial domination, after 3,000 years of independent rule, benefited the Sudan in one important respect: it put an end to the chaos of the feudal system. The unruly *meks* were deposed or left to perform a largely ceremonial function, while real power was concentrated in the hands of a rigidly centralized Turco–Egyptian bureaucracy. The presence of a large standing army, with garrisons in each of the major towns, was an effective deterrent to the resumption of tribal warfare.

At the head of the colonial government was a governor-general (*hikimdar*), who after 1825 resided at the newly founded administrative capital of Khartoum, at the junction of the Blue and White Niles. The four original provinces of Dongola, Berber, Sennar, and Kordofan were each placed under a provincial governor (*mudir*) who resided in the largest town in his district, while the undergovernor (*ma'mur*) traditionally resided in the second largest town. The provinces in turn were divided into smaller districts governed by *kashefs* (an office which was now created all over the country, instead of only in the north as in earlier times), and under the *kashefs* were the sheikhs of villages and groups of villages.[126] Needless to say none of these offices were hereditary, as was the office of *kashef* in pre-Egyptian days. The governor-general had absolute power to appoint and depose provincial governors, the provincial governors had similar power over the *kashefs*, and so on down the line.[127]

The army of occupation in the Sudan consisted in the beginning of 10,000 infantry and 9,000 cavalry.[128] Army units were stationed at Khartoum and in the provincial capitals; in addition each *kashef* was required to maintain a force of forty men at his own expense.[129] The regular forces were responsible directly to the Egyptian commander-in-chief in Cairo rather than to the civil officials in the Sudan. Almost from the beginning the bulk of the forces were made up of black slaves captured or purchased in the country, but the officers were Turks, Albanians and other Ottoman nationalities, as well as a few European soldiers of fortune. The continued use of Turkish as the language of command, as well as the requirement of literacy for the higher ranks, effectively closed the officer corps both to Sudanese and to native Egyptians.[130] In addition to the regular forces there were irregulars who were subject to almost no discipline at all, and whose chief duties were the collection of taxes and slave-raiding.[131] Among these the Shaiqiya were always prominent.

The Turco–Egyptian régime was a fairly typical colonial government, in that it was in no sense a government by or for the people. The higher officials were nearly all Turks or other Ottoman nationalities, as was required by the use of Turkish as the official language of government; after 1860 there were also a few western Europeans among them. The 23 governors-general who served between 1821 and 1885 included 8 Circassians, 5 Turks, 2 Kurds, 2 Greeks, 1 Albanian, 1 Egyptian Nubian and four of unrecorded origin,[132] and the ranks of their subordinates were probably similarly comprised. The clerical and tax officials attached to the central and provincial governments were nearly all Egyptian Copts, as were most of the financial officials in Egypt.[133] Sudanese participated in the government mainly at the lowest levels, as sheikhs of villages or tribes. In the later years of Turco–Egyptian rule there also grew up a system of local courts for the administration of *sharia* law (i.e. Moslem traditional law) in which Sudanese participated.[134] Otherwise the only laws of the land were the administrative codes governing civil officials and the army, and these were of course designed and administered by the colonial overlords.[135]

The Turco–Egyptian régime in the Sudan has been severely criticized by Europeans for its injustices and oppression. An Italian doctor or pharmacist who served in the country in the 1840s has left a pitiful account of the cupidity of the tax-collectors,[136] and the conditions encountered by Sir Samuel Baker when he became a provincial governor two decades later were even worse. According to Budge, paraphrasing the account of Baker:

Misgovernment, monopoly, extortion, and oppression were the accompaniments of the Turkish rule. The distance of Cairo from the Sudan had an evil effect on the Egyptian official character. Every official plundered; the Governor extorted from all sides, and filled his pockets by obstructing every commercial movement with the view of obtaining bribes. Dishonesty and deceit characterized officials from the highest to the lowest, and each robbed in proportion to his grade. Soldiers collected the taxes and, of course, exacted more than was due. As a result the natives produced just as much as they wanted and no more. The heaviest and most unjust tax of all was that on the waterwheels, on which the agricultural prosperity of the country depended. New settlers fled before the horde of tax-gatherers who alighted upon them, and thus whole tracts of country remained uncultivated.[137]

In his own words Baker wrote that:

The general aspect of the Sudan is that of misery, nor is there a single feature of attraction to recompense a European for the drawbacks of pestilential climate and brutal associations ... Upon existing conditions the Sudan is worthless, having neither natural capabilities nor political importance; but there is, nevertheless, a reason that first prompted its occupation by the Egyptians, and that is in force to the present day. THE SUDAN SUPPLIES SLAVES. Without the White Nile trade Khartoum would almost cease to exist; and that trade is kidnapping and murder ...[138]

With all its defects it is doubtful whether the Turco–Egyptian régime was notably more corrupt or oppressive than most of those which preceded it, or for that matter than many other colonial régimes which were established in Africa at about the same time. Europeans might have been particularly offended by the fact that the Sudan was not technically a colony at all, but an integral part of Egypt,[139] but this distinction meant nothing to Mohammed Ali. Medieval kings and emperors were accustomed to govern all of their subjects the way latter-day Europeans governed their colonies: with no regard for the consent of the governed, and very little regard for their welfare. Mohammed Ali's was not the first medieval régime in the Sudan, and it was not quite the last.

Richard Hill has given a somewhat more balanced picture of the Turco–Egyptian régime than is furnished by earlier writers:

Like all political systems under the sun the Turco-Egyptian had its strengths and weaknesses. An advantage in the condition of the time was its freedom from dependence on paper work, its mobility. Ahmad Pasha abu Adhan's entire clerical staff of the governorate-general consisted of five secretaries ... A weakness was the lack of effective communication between government and governed. There was no consultative machinery in the occupied Sudan in the way of councils of Sudanese through which the government could, if it wished, consult with the taxpayers. Nevertheless there was one means by which the government could, in a negative sense, feel the pulse of the people; that was by permitting the right of petitioning against alleged injustice. Petitioning the ruler in the Sudan was not disciplined by the rules of British Parliamentary procedure but was a spontaneous, unformalized outpouring of popular indignation. The chronicler relates how Abbas Agha, the governor of Berber, was unseated by popular petition. Here we approach a gulf which divides the Ottoman–Islamic from the western European conception of the nature of governance ... A Moslem people will band together for the purpose of righting what they may believe to be an intolerable wrong or in response to an appeal to defend the faith ... They have frequently found it more difficult to unite for more humdrum, positive ends, particularly those involving sustained collective discipline.

In the Nile Valley the Sudanese accepted the Turco-Egyptian rule after the bloody repression of the revolt of 1822–25 had shown the uselessness of resistance. All government was an exterior force, of its nature arbitrary; what could not be avoided must be borne. It was at least a Moslem government after its

620

fashion and the religious leaders and merchants learned how to profit from the new tyranny.[140]

The original Egyptian thrust into the Sudan had occupied what were essentially the old Ottoman and Funj territories: the riverain districts as far upstream as the Abyssinian foothills on the Blue Nile and a point not far south of Khartoum on the White Nile, plus the western province of Kordofan. Further expansion to the south was blocked, as it had been since time immemorial, by the fierce intractability of the Shilluk and other Nilotic tribes and by the vast expanse of the Sudd swamps. The Red Sea coast with its twin ports of Suakin and Massawa remained in theory a separate dependency of the Ottoman Empire, and in the far west Darfur was controlled by an independent sultanate. This state of affairs persisted for about two generations, although the territory around Kassala, east of the Atbara, was wrested from the Hadendowa tribe of Beja in 1840 (Fig. 85).[141]

The second major phase of imperial expansion in the Sudan began in the 1860s. Within a little more than a decade the territory under Egyptian control was nearly doubled through the addition of what were later to be the provinces of Kassala, Darfur, Upper Nile, Bahr el-Ghazal, and Equatoria.[142] Through these conquests and annexations the borders of the Egyptian Sudan reached what is essentially their present form (Fig. 85). Control of the Red Sea coast was formally ceded to Egypt by the Ottoman sultan in 1865,[143] but the other provinces were added not so much through the initiative of the government as through the bold and ruthless enterprise of private slave-dealers, who after 1860 were the unofficial rulers of the southern Sudan.

THE CLIMAX OF THE SLAVE TRADE

The provision of slaves for the Mediterranean lands had been a mainstay of Nubia's export economy since the days of the pharaohs, but the traffic reached a climax both in volume and in brutality during the last decades of the nineteenth century. With the abolition of slavery in the United States (1865) and Brazil (1871) the Ottoman Empire and other countries of the Moslem East became the last wholesale market for slaves. Thus while slave-hunting activity dwindled and finally ceased altogether on the Atlantic slope of Africa, the slavers turned their attention to new territories in the east. The headwaters of the White Nile and the lake regions of East Africa were the last great untapped reservoir of human game, and it was here that the final outburst of slave-hunting activity took place in the latter part of the nineteenth century. The organizers of this trade were merchant princes – mostly Arabs but also some Europeans – who created virtual 'empires of the bush', and who were a law unto themselves in

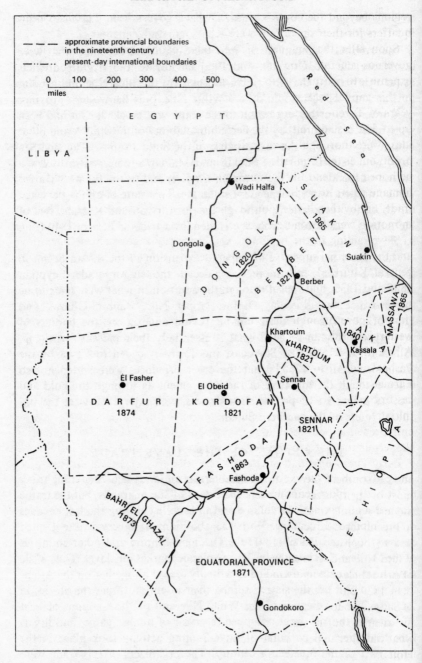

Fig. 85. Provinces of the Turco-Egyptian Sudan, with dates of acquisition

regions beyond the control of any civilized government. The main headquarters for their operations were Khartoum and Zanzibar.

Soon after the conquest of the Sudan Mohammed Ali wrote to his
governor-general, 'You are aware that the end of all our effort and this
expense is to procure Negroes. Please show zeal in carrying out our wishes
in this capital matter.'[144] This directive was to set the course for sixty
years of Turco–Egyptian rule in the Sudan. It also reveals that, however
up-to-date his administrative schemes may have been, the Pasha's military
ideas were thoroughly medieval. He wanted slaves not for commerce and
profit, but as the foundation of the New Army (*Nizam el-Jadid*) with which
he hoped to extend his power throughout the Near East. Later and more
humane rulers attempted to reverse this policy and to suppress the slave-
trade, but by then it was too late; the forces which Mohammed Ali had set
in motion were beyond control.

Slave-raiding in the beginning was primarily a government operation,
and the principal support of Mohammed Ali's régime. The first governor-
general, Khurshid, undertook slaving campaigns nearly every year between
1826 and 1833, and the practice was continued on a smaller scale by his
successors,[145] aided in many cases by the Shaiqiya. However, the continuation of governmental slave-trading became an embarrassment to the
westernized rulers who came to the throne after the death of Mohammed
Ali in 1849. (His descendants continued to rule Egypt, first as Ottoman
Pashas and later as independent kings, until the overthrow of King
Farouk in 1952.) Mohammed Sa'id, the second of Mohammed Ali's successors, ended governmental slave-trading in 1854,[146] but by this time the
initiative in slaving activity had already passed into the hands of private
entrepreneurs, both Arab and European, who flocked to the Sudan after
the termination of Mohammed Ali's state trading monopolies in 1843.[147]

Early Turco-Egyptian slave-raids had been most successful in Kordofan
and the southern Gezira, the same regions from which the Funj had drawn
most of their slaves. However, the combination of modern firearms and
modern vessels in the middle of the nineteenth century made it possible
to breach the double barrier of the Shilluk warriors and the Sudd swamps,
and to open up the previously untapped slaving ground on the upper
White Nile and its tributaries. This development resulted in a 'gold-rush'
of private slave-hunters to the southern Sudan.

In 1839 and following years flotillas of riverboats under the command
of Salim Qabudan succeeded in ascending the White Nile as far as latitude
five degrees north, where they established an outpost in the vicinity of
what was later to become the provincial capital of Equatoria. According to
Holt:

Although Salim Qabudan's expeditions failed to realize Mohammed Ali's
hopes of discovering the source of the Nile and the metals which he was con-

623

vinced must be there, they opened the way to the traders of Khartoum. At first government restrictions prevented their access to the Upper Nile, but their abolition in 1853 let in a swarm of merchants from Europe, Egypt, and the Egyptian Sudan itself. They penetrated not only the main stream of the Nile itself, where Gondokoro marked their farthest south, but also the western region of the Bahr el-Ghazal [cf. Fig. 85]. It was not a case of trade following the flag; . . . the merchants were beyond the control, as they were beyond the assistance, of settled government. Each principal had his agents and servants, his private army of armed retainers, recruited largely from the Danagla and Shaiqiya of the north. Each had his fortified stations (*zaribas*), encampments surrounded by thorn-fences, which served them as headquarters, entrepôts for their goods, and garri-son-posts in time of need. Originally they came to seek ivory, but they turned imperceptibly into slavers. Slaves were needed as concubines and porters, while slave-troops . . . usually augmented their private armies. With the local chiefs and tribes they established curious predatory alliances, and inter-tribal warfare passed into slave-raiding. At the outset the position of the 'Khartoumers' was precarious, but in the end their firearms and organization gave them the mastery over the tribal chiefs. The most powerful of them were merchant-princes, effect-ively ruling great areas. Meanwhile the ready market for slaves in the north turned them from a profitable sideline to the staple of the Khartoumers' trade.[148]

The régime of the Khedive Ismail, the third of Mohammed Ali's suc-cessors (1862–79), was marked in the Sudan by ever larger and more costly efforts to control the monster of slave-trade which his grandfather had created. Initial attempts to suppress the traffic by decree, by punitive tax-ation, and by the control of travel on the Upper White Nile all proved futile, and in the end the government could find no recourse but to extend its direct control over the regions of the slave-hunters' operations.[149] It was in this fashion that the provinces of Upper Nile (originally Fashoda), Equatoria, and Bahr el-Ghazal were somewhat reluctantly added to the Khedive's domains between 1863 and 1873. The far western province of Darfur, the seat of an ancient and long-independent sultanate, was gratui-tously conquered on behalf of the Khedive in 1874 by one of the most powerful of the merchant princes, Zubayr Rahma Mansur, because its sultan was unable to guarantee the safety of his slave caravans.[150] The effect of these annexations was nearly to double the area of the Egyptian Sudan, but there was no corresponding increase in the military forces. As a result it proved impossible to maintain order in the new territories, and the lawlessness which prevailed there affected the stability of the régime at Khartoum as well.

Despairing of bringing the 'Khartoumers' to heel through any of his own people, Ismail in the last years of his reign took to appointing Euro-pean governors to the southern Sudanese provinces, who were given almost *carte blanche* to deal with the slavers in any way they could. Two of the most famous of them were Sir Samuel Baker and General Charles Gordon

– both forceful and independent men who conceived an almost messianic mission to stop the slave-trade.[151] During their tenure (Baker from 1869 to 1874 and Gordon from 1874 to 1880) they succeeded in establishing a certain measure of order in the southern provinces, but it was at a fearful cost. The storm which broke over the Sudan a few months after Gordon's departure (see below) was at least as much a resurgence of the slave-trading elements whom he had harassed as it was an outburst against the corruption and indifference of the Turco–Egyptian régime.[152]

The Nubians, particularly the Kenzi and Mahasi, stood aloof from most of these developments in the south. Although they had been the principal victims of earlier Egyptian incursions into the Sudan, once the Egyptian base of operations was established upstream from them they and their country ceased to be of much interest to their northern neighbours. In some respects they were in fact the major beneficiaries of Mohammed Ali's régime. The rule of the latter-day *kashefs*, however oppressive, was undoubtedly preferable to that of the robber-baron *kashefs* of the Ottoman era; in addition the Nubians were freed from the menace of the Shaiqiya and from the refugee Mamelukes who had temporarily oppressed them. In the newly pacified Sudan the education and literacy to which the Nubians had long aspired were of far more practical value than in the feudal age, and they were able to move into the ranks of the growing clerical and merchant classes. Great numbers of them also flocked to Egypt, where they were much in demand as domestic servants both by the Turkish élite and by the large foreign populations which grew up in Cairo and Alexandria.[153] Finally, the Dongolawis and Ja'aliyin found special opportunities in the slave trade; the bush-empires which became the provinces of Bahr el-Ghazal and Equatoria were largely of their creation.[154]

THE MAHDIYA: EPILOGUE TO THE MEDIEVAL ERA

We have already noted (Ch. 17) that the expectation of the mahdi, or coming redeemer, is common to most of the mystical sects of Islam which have so richly proliferated in the Sudan and neighbouring countries. In the history of Moslem Africa there have been many self-proclaimed mahdis, including the founders of the Fatimid and Almohad dynasties in the north,[155] and of a whole series of more recent theocratic states in the sub-Saharan region.[156] The mahdist concept was late in arriving on the Upper Nile, yet it was the Sudanese Mahdi, Mohammed Ahmed ibn Abdallah, who made the term 'Mahdi' known around the world at the end of the nineteenth century.

Mohammed Ahmed was a Dongolawi, the son of a boat-builder, who was born somewhere in the northern part of the Dongola Province in the year 1848. The dramatic story of his career has been too eloquently – and too often – told by others[157] to be recounted in detail here; I can do no better than to quote his capsule biography by Richard Hill:

After leaving a Koranic school at Omdurman he went to Aba Island, on the White Nile, where his father was then building boats; here as a young man he began a career of study and meditation. He early attached himself to the religious brotherhood of the Ismailiya and became a pupil of Sheikh Mohammed Sharif Nur el Daim ... Disagreeing with his teacher and reproving him for worldliness he left Aba with a few disciples and lived nearby. In 1875 he transferred his religious allegiance to Shaikh el-Qurashi wad el-Zain of the Sammaniya brotherhood. About 1880 he toured Kordofan and found the state of the country irreconcilable with his religious beliefs which were now progressing towards the stage of political intervention; the nomadic tribes outside the direct influence of the Egyptian government were ravaged by internal warfare and the whole country was exasperated by the maladministration of the government, whose rule was more venal and incompetent than deliberately oppressive. The clumsy attempts of the government to suppress the slave trade had provoked resentment in a country whose economy was based on slavery; the turbulent population of the Central Sudan was ripe for the secular adventure of a concerted revolt which it had been denied since the foundation of foreign government sixty years before. [Mohammed Ahmed] represented the only apparent hope of Sudanese unity and freedom. In May 1881 he announced his divine mission and summoned the people to fight the infidel Turks as a first step towards the introduction of a purified society based on Islamic precepts. His teaching combined elements found in the Wahhabite and Sanusi movements, including the return of primitive Islam, opposition to innovations and foreign influences, prohibition of pilgrimages to tombs, of the veneration of saints, and of music and tobacco. The strong element of mysticism in his teaching appealed to a people traditionally receptive to Sufism.[158]

The deposition of the Egyptian Khedive Ismail in 1879, and the resignation of Gordon as governor-general a few months later, had left the Sudan in a state of political turmoil. Whatever impression of strength and stability the Turco–Egyptian régime had been able to convey was destroyed by these two events; the time was ripe for an independence movement. However, it was by no means foreordained that this should take the form of a millenarian religious movement; the success of the Mahdi in unifying and liberating the Sudan can be attributed in large measure to the clumsy and ineffective attempts of the Khartoum government to suppress his movement.[159]

An initial expedition against the Mahdists in 1881 resulted in their withdrawal from Aba Island to the Nuba Hills of southern Kordofan, an area which had long resisted the authority of established governments. Here the Mahdi enlisted in his cause the Baggara nomad tribes, who were to provide the principal military support of the Mahdist régime throughout its brief history. They had little interest in the religious doctrines of the

VIIa (*above*). The Meroitic 'castle' at Karanog

VIIb (*below*). Meroitic village site, Ash-Shaukan

XVIIIa (*above*). Meroitic wine press at Meinarti

XVIIIb (*below*). Fragmentary Meroitic stele, Meroë

XIXa (*top left*). Village remains of the Ballana period, Meinarti

XIXb (*top right*). The tumuli at Qustul before excavation

XIXc (*middle left*). Typical Ballana pottery vessels

XIXd (*middle right*). Contents of an offering chamber at Ballana

XIXe and XIXf. Jewelled Ballana crowns

a (*above left*). Wall painting of a Nubian king protected by the Madonna, Faras

b (*above right*). Wall painting of a Nubian bishop, Faras

c (*below*). Wall painting at Faras showing Shadrach, Meshach and Abednego in
Furnace

XXIIa. Late medieval defensive village site, Diffinarti

XXIIb. Late medieval castle at Kulubnarti

XIIIa. Tombs of the post-Christian period, Gebel Adda

XIIIb. Gubba at Mushu, near Kerma

XXIIIc. The Mahdi's tomb, Omdurman

XXIVa (*above*). The inundation of old Wadi Halfa

XXIVb (*below*). Street scene at Khashm el Girba (New Halfa) 1965

movement, but were attracted by the prospect of *jihad* (holy war) against the colonial government, which would enable them to resume the predatory life of earlier times. After the Mahdists' removal to Kordofan two expeditions which were sent against them were decisively repulsed, each success enhancing the prestige of Mohammed Ahmed and seeming to confirm the legitimacy of his divine mission.

After defeating the second punitive expedition the Mahdi for the first time took the offensive, besieging and capturing the provincial capital of El Obeid and the subsidiary garrison of Bara in 1883. As a result of this success all of Kordofan fell into his hands. The real turning point in the Mahdi's career came a few months later when an Egyptian expeditionary force of 7,000 men, under the British commander William Hicks, was annihilated in the bush country south of El Obeid. News of this triumph convinced the great majority of Sudanese that destiny lay with the Mahdi, and all semblance of Egyptian control vanished outside of the major garrison towns in the centre of the country. The provincial governors of Darfur and Bahr el-Ghazal soon found themselves besieged by Mahdist forces and cut off from support from the capital; both were compelled to surrender within a few months of Hicks' defeat. Meanwhile the Beja tribes of the Red Sea province had been rallied to the cause of the rebels by the redoubtable leader of the Hadendowa, Osman Diqna. In 1884 the Mahdist offensive, which had begun as a groundswell in the hinterlands, carried to the main Nile; Berber was besieged and captured in the middle of May, and communication between Khartoum and Egypt was temporarily cut off. The Egyptian garrisons now found themselves hopelessly isolated and besieged in a country which only two years before had seemed firmly in their control.

The vacillating policy of Great Britain contributed in large measure to the final débâcle of Turco–Egyptian rule in the Sudan. British forces had landed in Egypt in 1882, ostensibly to put down the military nationalist movement of Ahmed Arabi and to restore the authority of the Khedive Mohammed Tewfik, who had succeeded Ismail in 1879. A longer-term objective was to set the Egyptian financial house in order and to assure the continued payment of the enormous foreign debts which Ismail had incurred. The British financial overseers who were sent to Cairo became the *de facto* rulers of the country, and remained so until well into the twentieth century.[160]

The military occupation of Egypt, which continued until 1924, gave Britain a certain responsibility for protecting Egyptian interests both at home and abroad. This meant, among other things, protecting Egyptian interests in the Sudan. Yet the financial commissioners in Cairo and their superiors in London were understandably reluctant to authorize the expenditure of funds for military operations in the remote Sudan which might otherwise have gone to pay off European creditors. 'Thus,' as Holt observes, 'an illogical assemblage of political, financial, and moral considerations led the British government not only to evade involvement in the Sudanese problem, but also to check the attempts of the khedivial government to promote resolute action in the threatened provinces.'[161] It was as a result of this uncertain policy that the Egyptians were permitted to recruit the ill-fated expeditionary force of Hicks on their own responsibility, but were given no advice or support in the venture even though the commanding officer was himself a Britisher.

The culmination of British vacillation towards the Sudan was reached with the reappointment of Gordon as governor-general in 1883 – his third and last mission to the beleaguered country. His official mission was conceived, at least in London, as being that of arranging for the orderly withdrawal of the remaining Egyptian garrisons from the Sudan, in effect consigning the country to the Mahdi's rule without the embarrassment of a formal surrender. Yet he was, characteristically, equipped with two sets of orders, 'one set speaking of the restoration of good government, the other announcing the policy of evacuation'.[162] Gordon very unwisely announced the second of these objectives publicly almost as soon as he set foot in the Sudan, thus making any further appeal to the authority of the Turco–Egyptian régime impossible. Yet the governor-general was no sooner installed in Khartoum than he swung to the extreme opposite point of view, conceiving it his duty not only to hang on at all costs but, in his own words, to 'smash up the Mahdi'.[163]

In reality, the lack of support from Cairo and from London made it impossible for Gordon to carry out any of the alternatives which he had contemplated. The defeat of the Mahdi and the 'restoration of good government' were never seriously contemplated abroad, while even for the remaining loyal garrisons to fight their way out of the country alive would have required a measure of support from abroad which was not forthcoming. Gordon was left with no choice but to hang on in Khartoum with the remnant of his loyal forces, plus the ever-equivocal Shaiqiya across the river at Halfaya, while elsewhere the flames of rebellion burned throughout the country. The Mahdist forces took up a strong position at Omdurman, across the White Nile from Khartoum, in September 1884, and the Mahdi arrived in person to command them in the following month. Thenceforth Gordon and the capital were under siege.

The story of Gordon's last days in Khartoum has been poignantly told in the pages of his own journals,[164] which were miraculously posted through the Mahdi's lines to Cairo until two months before the final fall of Khartoum, and it has been retold by such distinguished authors as Sir Winston Churchill[165] and Alan Moorehead.[166] Day after day the governor-general took up his position on the roof of his palace watching the river for a sign of the relief expedition for which he had continually begged. A British relief expedition was indeed organized late in 1884, largely as a result of pressure from the press, but it proceeded sluggishly through the unfamiliar and hostile terrain. Like nearly all British military operations in Africa until the twentieth century it was overly dependent upon river transport, and the Nile cataracts continually hampered the expedition's progress. The main force never got farther south than Metemma, opposite Shendi, but from here two small steamers were sent ahead to reconnoitre. After passing the Sixth Cataract and running the gauntlet of shore batteries and rifle fire from both banks of the river they arrived in sight of Khartoum on 28 June 1885, only to find that the town had fallen two days before. The governor's palace was in ruins, and Gordon dead. The entire expedition then retraced its ponderous steps the way it had come, abandoning not only its forward positions but the territories south of Wadi Halfa which had not previously fallen to the rebels. The Mahdi was now the master of the entire Egyptian Sudan, except for one or two distant garrisons which surrendered later in the same year, and the Red Sea port of Suakin which remained in British hands. Yet this most remarkable of Sudanese leaders was granted only a brief interval to enjoy the fruits of his triumph: within six months of the fall of Khartoum he too was dead, apparently of typhus,[167] at the age of thirty-seven.[168]

The state which the Mahdi bequeathed to his successors had achieved only the most rudimentary organization. He and his adherents were imbued with the idea of recreating the primitive Islamic state, with himself as the Prophet surrounded by his traditional companions, the Four Caliphs. Hence the 'cabinet' of Mohammed Ahmed was to consist of four *khalifas* (caliphs), the successors of the Sacred Four (Abu Bakr, Omar, Osman and Ali). One of these posts was offered to the leader of the Sanusiya order in Libya, to which Mohammed Ahmed himself was a nominal adherent, but the sheikh declined the honour and the position as a result was never filled. The other three 'caliphates' were awarded, perhaps by coincidence, to representatives of the three elements which had provided the Mahdi's principal support: the genuine religious visionaries who were inspired by his mission, the Danagla and Ja'aliyin commercial entrepreneurs who were less interested in the Mahdi's doctrines than in the resumption of their slave-trading activities, and the Baggara tribesmen whose chief ambition was to resume the predatory life of feudal days.[169]

In addition to the *khalifas* there were only two important officials in the central government, a chief treasurer and a chief judge. True to his religious convictions the Mahdi abolished the onerous taxes of the Turco–Egyptian régime and reverted to the system of relatively mild taxes imposed by the Prophet. Government revenue was to be derived chiefly from the spoils of war, for the Mahdist state was in essence a warrior state, and it was the leader's announced intention to wage the *jihad* until the whole world had submitted to the true faith of early Islam. Thus the provincial governors were regarded primarily as military rather than as administrative officers, and were styled *emirs* (commanders) rather than *mudirs* (overseers). There was, needless to say, no acknowledged law but that of the Koran and the *sharia*; the Mahdi governed not through the instrument of law but through divine decrees, as had Mohammed himself.

The Mahdi's unexpected death, long before any effective machinery of state had been organized, not surprisingly caused a turmoil among his followers. Members of his family and of the Danagla–Ja'aliyin element moved to seize the positions of power as their natural right, but in the tug-of-war which ensued it became obvious that the decisive military force in the country was that of the Baggara tribes, whose representative was the Khalifa Abdallahi Mohammed Turshain. After prudently considering their best interests the other *khalifas* made their submission to him, and Abdallahi then assumed the title *Khalifat el-Mahdi* (successor to the Mahdi). He was to head the Mahdist state until its final overthrow in 1898.

During the first five years of his reign Abdallahi was almost continually at war, partly in subduing rebellious elements within his realm and partly in pursuing the policy of *jihad* which the Mahdi had proclaimed. The western province of Darfur (whose cultural and geographical orientations were towards the Chad Basin rather than towards the Nile) had been restive since its annexation in 1874, and it remained so under the *Mahdiya*. From 1885 to 1887 there were continual revolts or plotted revolts as the deposed sultans of Darfur attempted to regain their independence. There was also warfare along the Abyssinian border, following a familiar pattern of raid and counter-raid which had begun in Funj times as a result of the ill-defined nature of the frontier between highland and lowland dwellers. At one point a Sudanese army thrust into Abyssinian territory as far as Gondar, the ancient capital, but it was unable to maintain its position in the unfamiliar mountain terrain. In retribution the Abyssinians, led by the emperor himself, marched into the Sudan along the Atbara River. The defenders were routed in a first encounter, but at the end of the battle a stray bullet killed the Abyssinian ruler, and his forces immediately withdrew, anticipating (correctly) a struggle for the succession at home. The border situation was then stabilized essentially as it had been before (and remains today), with sporadic raiding from both sides but no more major engagements.

The most ambitious and also the most futile of Abdallahi's military enterprises was an invasion of Egypt in 1889 under the *Emir* Wad el-Nijumi. The rag-tag invading force proceeded along the west bank of the Nile, by-passing the Egyptian frontier post of Wadi Halfa, until it was intercepted and annihilated by an Egyptian army near Toshka in Lower

Nubia. A few survivors of the expedition settled down in the region of their defeat; their descendants were still living there at the time of the relocation in the 1960s.

The expansionist ambitions of the Mahdist state ended with the defeat at Toshka. After four years of strenuous campaigning there had been no significant increase in the domain which the *Khalifa* had inherited from his predecessor. Nevertheless the militaristic phase had considerably strengthened his hold on the country, as it often does for dictators. He had been able to dispose of a number of potentially disloyal generals, including many of the Mahdi's original appointments, and to replace them with his own men. The famine and epidemic which gripped the country in 1889 and 1890 also weakened his enemies more than himself, since their main brunt was felt by the riverain tribes who were increasingly disaffected with his régime. In 1891 the *Khalifa* felt strong enough to undertake a purge of the last remaining members of the Mahdi's family and of his earliest followers. Some of them had been plotting to overthrow him, but they were induced to surrender under a promise of amnesty and of the restoration of their titles and pensions. Nevertheless, within a year a great many of them were imprisoned or executed.

In the last years of his reign Abdallahi began to exhibit the typical symptoms of despotic paranoia. As Holt observes, 'the transformation of the theocratic state of the early Mahdiya into a secular despotism was becoming obvious'.[170] Even as his power became more secure the *Khalifa* withdrew more and more from contact with his subjects and into the walled compound which he had built in Omdurman, where he was surrounded by sycophants. Here he became increasingly suspicious of those around him, and in his last years deposed and executed a number of loyal officials, some of whom had been with him since the early days of the Mahdiya. Provincial commands were given to yes-men whose only recommendation was their blind loyalty to their chief. Like many another despot, Abdallahi in the end lived in a world of deceit and intrigue which was largely of his own making, in which he no longer knew who to believe or who to trust.

The price of Abdallahi's isolation from his subjects was to reveal itself when the British belatedly undertook to avenge the death of Gordon and to reconquer the Sudan. To achieve this purpose an Anglo–Egyptian army under the command of the redoubtable Sir Herbert Kitchener marched south from Wadi Halfa in March 1896. The northern Nubians had never been devoted adherents of the *Khalifa*, and the Danagla had long since become disenchanted with his Baggara-dominated régime; both groups openly supported the invaders. The *Khalifa*'s sycophantic commanders, paralysed by lack of specific orders from Omdurman and unable to take any initiative on their own, retreated from one position after another without offering resistance. Only at Firka was there an engagement, not because the defenders chose to make a stand but because their camp was surrounded before they could escape. The result was a loss of about a thousand men, to twenty-two for the British. The reoccupation of the whole of the Dongola Province was then completed without further resistance (cf. Fig. 86).[171]

Kitchener was determined not to repeat the mistake of his predecessors, of attempting to transport men and supplies through the hazards of the Nile cataracts. Instead he undertook the incredible feat of building a railway across the desert from Wadi Halfa to Abu Hamed – a waterless stretch of over 200 miles. Hostilities against the *Khalifa* were therefore suspended for a full year while the rails were pushed relentlessly across the desert. The invading force was to be much more depleted by this harsh task than it was by the spears of the Sudanese. Meanwhile the town of Abu Hamed, where the rail line was destined to rejoin the Nile, was captured after only the briefest resistance by a flying column which had been sent up the river from Merowe. In the wake of this reverse the Mahdist forces evacuated not only the district around Abu Hamed but the provincial capital of Berber, the key to communication with Suakin and the Red Sea. In Omdurman the *Khalifa* watched these events as if paralysed by the approach of Nemesis, giving no orders either for the resistance of the invaders or for the strengthening of his remaining forces in the north.

The railway line was completed to Abu Hamed at the end of October 1897, and communication was re-established between Berber and Suakin before the end of the year. Only then, when the enemy was deep in his territory, and his supply and communications secured, did the *Khalifa* finally bestir himself. An army was dispatched to intercept the British at the junction of the Atbara and the Nile; it was defeated in what was, for the invaders, the costliest engagement of the war. Some 560 of them were killed, while the defending army of 12,000 was scattered without a trace. About 3,000 were killed and the remainder vanished into the bush.

After the Battle of the Atbara there was another long delay while the British waited for reinforcements and cooler weather, while the *Khalifa* desperately tried to rally what was left of his empire for a last-ditch resistance. In September Kitchener's advance was resumed, and the decisive battle of the campaign took place a short distance north of Omdurman, where the *Khalifa*'s forces had massed to defend their capital. In a day's hard fighting an army of 52,000 men, armed chiefly with spears and lances, was demolished by a force about half its size in what Winston Churchill, who took part as a subaltern, was to call the death-knell of chivalry in warfare.[172] The British and Egyptians lost a little over 300 men, to about 11,000 of the defenders. The *Khalifa* himself escaped from the battlefield, to die a year later in a futile last stand on the upper White Nile,

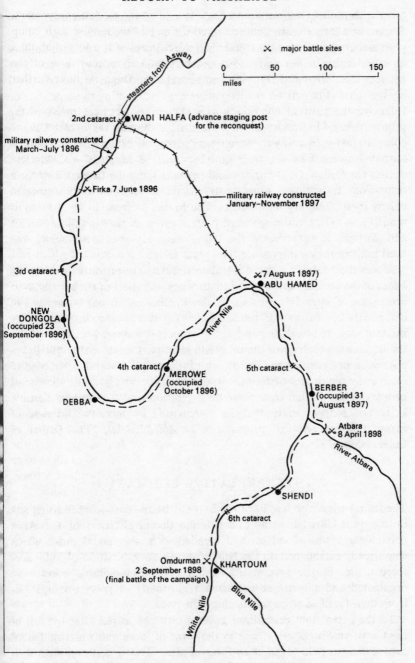

Fig. 86. The reconquest of the Sudan, 1896–8

but the Battle of Omdurman marked the end of the Mahdist state in the Sudan. In a larger sense it also marked the end of the medieval era.

In earlier chapters we have described the cultures of Kerma and Ballana as representing major transition points in Nubian history, respectively between the Tribal and Dynastic and between the Dynastic and Medieval ages. Each was in part an atavistic movement, attempting to perpetuate or to revive the cultural conditions of earlier times, yet each prepared the ground for and in important ways anticipated the new eras which were to come. In just such a way the ideological paroxysm of the Mahdiya may be regarded as marking the transition between the Medieval and Modern eras in the Sudan. (It is curious and perhaps symbolic that each of these short-lived transitional movements should have been commemorated chiefly by its funerary monuments. The Mahdi's ornate tomb in Omdurman (Pl. XXIIIc), although hardly on a par with the tumuli of Kerma and Ballana, is nevertheless the largest funerary monument which has been built in the country since the Dynastic age.)

It was the Mahdi's avowed intention to revive the primitive, communal Islam of the seventh century, and to dispense with most of the cumbersome accretions of later Islamic and secular civilization. By any standard of complexity his régime was retrogressive. Yet it was also, in a startlingly modern way, nationalistic, and in this respect it prepared the ground for the dominant ideology of the twentieth century. Far more than the Egyptians who preceded or the British who followed, the Mahdi attempted to clear away the debris of feudalism and tribalism and to unite the varied peoples of the Sudan in a common aspiration and a common destiny. It is not inappropriate that he is regarded by modern Sudanese of many different political persuasions as *Abu'l-Istiqlal*, 'The Father of Independence'.[173]

INTERPRETATIVE SUMMARY

The feudal age which had begun in Late Christian times reached its climax in the post-Christian era. The extreme decentralization of the Arab tribal system was added to, and blended with, the feudal order which was already established on the Nile. From this combination of influences there arose, in the seventeenth century, the innumerable *meks* who dominated and sometimes terrorized a multitude of petty principalities from their fortified strongholds along the river.

To the extent that centralized government reappeared after the fall of the Christian kingdoms, it was in the form of loose and unstable feudal confederations held together by force of arms. The largest and most durable of these was the Sennar confederation, originally brought together by the Abdallab Arabs but later dominated by the black Funj sultans of ennar, on the Blue Nile. In its heyday the Sennar confederation exercised n uneasy hegemony over nearly all of the Ja'aliyin and Arab tribes south f the Third Cataract, as well as over many black tribes of the southern udan. However, after the seventeenth century many of the northern eoples either broke away or were forcibly detached by the savagely ndependent Shaiqiya *meks* of the Middle Nile; in the end the authority f the Funj extended no further north than the junction of the Niles. The ar north of Nubia was nominally an Ottoman dependency, but it was in act governed by hereditary *kashefs* who were as independent, and as apacious, as the *meks* to the south of them.

The feudal age, but not the medieval age, came to an end with the re-nposition of Egyptian colonial rule in 1821. After savagely repressing an nitial revolt against their authority, the Egyptians terminated the system of ribal rule, particularly among the riverain peoples, and created in its lace a centralized bureaucratic government backed up by a strong stand-ng army. The colonial régime brought a measure of order and stability to ne war-torn Sudan, but it was not conducted for the benefit of the gover-ed or to any extent with their participation. The motives which brought ne Egyptians to the Sudan in 1821 were the same as those which prompted ne pharaohs to conquer the country 3,000 years earlier: the lust for slaves nd gold.

If the slave trade was the initial *raison d'être* for the Egyptian occupation f the Sudan, it was also its undoing. Originally a government enterprise, ne trade passed increasingly into private hands after 1843. Merchant rinces from Khartoum carried their slave-raiding activities far beyond the mits of government authority, into the wilderness of the upper White Iile, where they carved out private empires in the bush. When the colonial overnment later sought to curb their operations, it found that their ower was greater than its own. The futile campaign to control the slave ade in the 1860s and 1870s alienated a considerable part of the Sudanese opulation, whose prosperity depended on slaving, and also undermined nfidence in the power of the colonial régime. Thus, when the millenarian ovement of the Mahdi was proclaimed in 1881, it attracted a following ot only of the genuinely devout but of various elements who were nxious to be free from Egyptian harassment, or who simply doubted the oility of the Egyptians to rule the country. Within two years of its found-ng the Mahdist movement had flamed into a national rebellion; within vo more years it had expelled the last of the foreigners and had become a ational state.

The Mahdist movement was founded on principles of religious reforma-on, but after the death of its founder in 1885 it became, under the *Khalifa* bdallahi, a secular despotism dominated by the Baggara nomads. opular support among the riverain peoples was gradually lost, and when

in 1896 an Anglo–Egyptian army invaded the Sudan it met with little
resistance until it was far into the interior of the country. Two bloody and
futile battles in 1898 destroyed the last of the Mahdist forces and ended the
régime.

The Mahdist state was at the same time the last medieval régime and
the first modern national state in the Sudan. It was avowedly theocratic,
aiming at nothing less than the restoration of the primitive Islamic
community of the Prophet, yet it was also the first régime to unite the
various peoples of the Sudan in the cause of a national ideology. The
Mahdiya may therefore be identified as another of the major watersheds
in Nubian history, separating the medieval from the modern era.

EPILOGUE

19
THE LEGACY OF THE WEST
NUBIA AND THE SUDAN IN THE TWENTIETH
CENTURY

In theory, the victory at Omdurman re-established Egyptian political hegemony in the Sudan. The campaign of reconquest had been planned and financed[1] in Great Britain, and was commanded in the field by British officers, but it was undertaken in the name of Egypt. At its conclusion the authority of the Khedive was proclaimed throughout the Sudan, and the Egyptian flag flew once again over Khartoum and the provincial capitals. Nevertheless the campaign had been undertaken more in pursuit of British than of Egyptian interests, and it was clear from the beginning that the British meant to stay.

Politically, the situation of the victors was anomalous.[2] British public opinion generally blamed the rise of the Mahdi upon the corruption and indifference of the Egyptian colonial régime in the later nineteenth century,[3] yet Britain had intervened to restore the very authority whose venality was thus condemned. Under these circumstances a return to the pre-1881 *status quo* was clearly out of the question. It seemed that, having restored the Sudan to Egyptian control, Britain must now stay in the Sudan in order to protect the Sudanese from the Egyptians. This point of view was clearly expressed by Lord Cromer a decade after the reconquest: 'The cannon which swept away the Dervish hordes at Omdurman proclaimed to the world that on England – or, to be more strictly correct, on Egypt under British guidance – had devolved the solemn and responsible duty of introducing the light of Western civilization amongst the sorely tried people of the Sudan.'[4]

Nevertheless, an outright assertion of British sovereignty would have been resisted not only by Egypt but by the other major colonial powers, and would have exacerbated an already tense European situation. A somewhat specious way out of these difficulties was found in the Condominium Agreement of 1899, under which Egypt and Great Britain assumed joint sovereignty over the Sudan. Of this agreement Holt has written:

The northern boundary of the newly acquired territory, described in the Agreement as 'certain provinces in the Sudan which were in rebellion against the

639

authority of his Highness the Khedive,' was fixed at latitude 22 degrees N. The Khedive's claims were further recognized by the provisions that 'the British and Egyptian flags shall be used together, both on land and water, throughout the Sudan,' that the appointment and removal of the Governor-General should be by khedivial decree (but only on the motion of the British Government), and that proclamations of the Governor-General, having the force of law, should be notified to the President of the Egyptian Council of Ministers, as well as to the British Agent in Cairo.

These stipulations apart, the Agreement deliberately excluded both Egyptian and international authority from the Sudan. The shadowy claims of the Ottoman Sultan as suzerain were tacitly ignored. Egyptian legislation was not to apply to the Sudan unless specifically proclaimed by the Governor-General. No special privileges, such as had accrued to Europeans in Egypt under the Capitulations, were to be accorded in the Sudan. The jurisdiction of the Mixed Tribunals was excluded, and no consular representatives were to be allowed to reside in the Sudan without the previous consent of the British Government.

Within the Sudan, the supreme military and civil command was to be vested in the Governor-General, a nominee of the British Government. Although the Agreement was silent on the point of nationality, all of the Governors-General from 1899 to 1955 were British subjects from the United Kingdom. With full executive powers, the Governor-General combined . . . complete authority to legislate by proclamation. An article of the Agreement placed the Sudan under martial law for an indefinite period.[5]

The Anglo–Egyptian governor-general was thus in effect the latest in a succession of viceroys who had governed the country intermittently since the days of the pharaohs.

Holt goes on to observe that:

The Condominium Agreement was not a constitution for the Sudan: it was simply an instrument giving formal recognition to the existing situation on the morrow of the Reconquest. The name is misleading: the Agreement did not in any real sense create a true condominium, a conjoint sovereignty over the Sudan, but merely gave a nominal recognition to the historical claims of the Khedive, whilst reserving almost complete autonomy to an official nominated by the British Government. It was not seriously questioned by the European powers. It never satisfied the Egyptians, who felt, with a sullen resentment, that they had been jockeyed out of their rights. Once Egypt had passed from under British control, the artificiality of the Condominium could no longer be concealed, and from the end of the First World War onwards [it] was increasingly an embarrassment, both to successive British cabinets and to the administration in the Sudan . . .[6]

BRITISH RULE IN THE SUDAN

Under the Condominium, provincial and district administration was at first restored more or less along the lines which had been established in pre-Mahdist times. The higher administrative officials were invariably British, while the middle and lower ranks (where fluency in Arabic was necessary for effective contact with the governed) were generally filled by Egyptians or Lebanese.[7] Because of similarities in administrative structure, and the continued presence of numbers of Egyptian officials, the period of Condominium was sometimes referred to by Sudanese as 'the second *Turkiya*'. Even officials of British nationality might be included under the rubric 'Turk', thus in effect legitimizing their connection with the pre-Mahdist colonial régime.[8]

At the outset, and indeed for most of its history, the British régime in the Sudan was characterized by a benevolent if somewhat condescending paternalism. A system of public schools was created, primarily with the aim of training lower-echelon civil officials, but it was taken for granted that a long period of colonial protection would be required before the primitive Sudanese were capable of assuming control of their own affairs. In the meantime the governor-general ruled by decree, and set about developing and modernizing the country to the extent that its modest resources would allow. The various provinces were linked together, more firmly than in the past, by a network of railways and steamers, and the completion of a railway line from Atbara to the Red Sea in 1905 gave the country its first effective access to maritime trade, ending its historic dependence on the Nile and on Egypt. Other notable achievements in the material sphere were the completion of a number of dams and irrigation projects, and in particular the Gezira Scheme which brought under cultivation a very large area between the Blue and White Niles, south of Khartoum.

The first years of the Condominium were a time of relative peace and progress, though for more than a decade they were troubled by abortive Mahdist-type movements in the central Sudan. The last of these was suppressed in 1912.[9] Not long afterwards, however, political unrest began to manifest itself in a new and more typically twentieth-century form, through the ideology of nationalism. In the Sudan as elsewhere in the colonial world, the advent of public education had created hopes and expectations which the colonial rulers were in no position to fulfil. The graduates of the Gordon Memorial College in Khartoum, most of whom were employed as minor officials by the Government, became in time a dissident force demanding a greater share in the governing of their country. Because they saw no hope of standing up to the British without outside support, they tended in general to ally themselves with nationalist forces which were simultaneously challenging the British authority in Egypt. Thus the upsurge of Arab nationalism which followed the First World War, and which led eventually to the termination of British colonial rule in Egypt in 1922, had distant repercussions in the Sudan. Embryonic nationalist organizations were formed in Khartoum, and elements of the Sudanese army became disaffected.[10]

In November 1924 the Governor-General of the Sudan, Sir Lee Stack, was assassinated by an Arab nationalist on the streets of Cairo. This event provided the British authorities with an excuse to take repressive action both against the nationalists in Khartoum and against the Egyptians who were believed to be behind them. General Allenby, the commander of the British forces in Egypt, demanded the immediate withdrawal of all Egyptian army units from the Sudan, and they were soon followed by the civil officials as well. At the same time a mutinous unit of the Sudanese army was besieged and annihilated in Khartoum.[11] Thenceforward the army of the Sudan was entirely separated from that of Egypt and was made up exclusively of Sudanese troops commanded by British officers. With the events of 1924 all semblance of Egyptian participation in the Condominium government ended, although the fiction of co-rule was maintained for another thirty years.

As a countermeasure against the further growth of nationalism, the British after 1924 adopted what was called a 'devolutionary' policy in the Sudan. Its aim was to reduce the scope of bureaucratic government and to develop in its place the sort of indirect rule which seemed to be working well in other African colonies.[12] Instead of building up an educated native civil service, political power was to be returned wherever possible to tribal chiefs and elders. According to the Annual Report for 1926:

> By the judicious and progressive application of devolutionary measures in districts where conditions are suitable, and by ensuring that the native agencies which are to be responsible for administering these measures are remunerated on a scale sufficient to give them their requisite measure of status and dignity, it should be possible not only to strengthen the fabric of the native organization, but, while maintaining our supervisory staff at proper strength, gradually to reduce the number of sub-*mamurs*, clerks, accountants and similar bureaucratic adjuncts in the out-districts.[13]

At the same time some of the training courses for junior administrative officials were discontinued, and the educational establishment which had been laboriously built up in earlier years was allowed to stagnate. In 1935, a former Director of Education in the Sudan complained that 'After the troubles that culminated in Stack's murder, the British local administration took fright, and in spite of the loyalty of the educated Sudanese to the Government which had given them opportunity, the spectacle could be beheld of young administrators diligently searching for lost tribes and vanished chiefs, and trying to resurrect a social system that had vanished forever.'[14] Holt adds that:

> The exponents of this policy of 'native administration' or 'indirect administration' by the British would have been shocked to hear it compared to the Khalifa Abdallahi's calling in of the Baqqara, forty years previously, yet both

were the consequences of a failure of confidence. In both cases the ruler turned from the more advanced of his subjects, who nevertheless remained essential to the working of his bureaucratic machine, and sought to use the less sophisticated elements as the instrument and support of his authority.[15]

Under 'devolutionary' rule the Sudan remained politically quiet during the later 1920s and 1930s, but Sudanese nationalism reasserted itself with the outbreak of the Second World War. Early in the war the Sudanese army (known after 1924 as the Sudan Defence Force) had taken part in the successful campaign to expel the Italians from Abyssinia, and a sense of military power and pride probably helped to reanimate the nationalists. In 1942 a group called the Graduates' General Congress, made up of graduates of the Gordon Memorial College and the secondary schools, sent to the British civil secretary a list containing a number of political demands, the most important of which was the right to self-determination immediately after the conclusion of the war.[16]

The Graduates' letter was peremptorily rejected by the British authorities, the effect of which was to produce a deep and abiding schism in the ranks of the nationalists. Those whose main concern was to be free of British domination at an early date allied themselves with Egyptian interests, as the nationalists of the 1920s had done, and espoused the cause of ultimate union, or at least political confederation, with Egypt. Against them were ranged those who believed that, in the light of history and geography, Egypt represented a more enduring imperial threat than did Britain. Their goal was to work for eventual total independence, even if it meant continued acceptance of British rule until the institutions of independent nationhood could be developed. This latter group received tacit encouragement from the British authorities once it became apparent that nationalist aspirations in one form or another could not be ignored. Thus the two main nationalist groups in the Sudan became insensibly identified with the interests of the two rival powers who were nominally the co-rulers of their country. It was then no longer a question of whether the nationalists would ultimately win, but of which nationalist group would win.

In time the two Sudanese nationalist groups crystallized into organized political parties. The pro-Egyptian faction was originally known as the *Ashiqqa* ('brothers') and later as the National Union Party, while the more pro-British party was and is called the *Umma* ('nation') Party. They have remained the two principal political movements in the Sudan down to the present day, although they have necessarily been inactive in times of military rule. As might be expected, the National Union Party derives its strongest support from the riverain peoples of the north, including the Nubians (at least until they became disaffected over the High Dam resettlement issue), while the *Umma* draws much of its support from the same anti-Egyptian forces which supported the Mahdiya eighty years ago. It is indicative of the continuing influence of religion in Sudanese public life that the two major parties have allied themselves with two of the largest religious sects in the country, the *Khatmiya* and the *Ansar*.[17]

The principle of ultimate self-determination for the Sudan was formally espoused by the Labour Government which came to power in Britain at the end of the Second World War. However, the actual achievement of independence was delayed for a decade as a result of the continuing conflict of interest between Britain and Egypt, and between the rival political factions which they backed in the Sudan. The British, supported by the *Umma* Party, proposed to establish self-government by degrees, leading eventually to the creation of a fully independent Sudan; all such measures were opposed by the Egyptians and by the unionist faction within the country. Failing to reach any agreement with their Egyptian co-regents, the British in 1948 acted unilaterally to set up a self-governing Legislative Assembly and Governing Council for the Sudan. This measure was strongly protested by Egypt, and the ensuing elections for the Assembly were boycotted by the unionists; as a result, a legislature and executive council composed largely of *Umma* members were elected.[18]

Abortive negotiations between Britain and Egypt continued for three more years after the creation of the first Legislative Assembly. A continual stumbling block to any final settlement was the insistence of Egypt that British rule in the Sudan and British control of the Suez Canal were related questions which must be negotiated conjointly. Matters reached a head in 1951 when the Egyptians in their turn took unilateral action, repudiating the Condominium Agreement and proposing to confer upon King Farouk the title 'King of Egypt and the Sudan'.[19] The Government of the Sudan denied the validity of this action, and in April 1952 the Legislative Assembly enacted a self-governing constitution for the Sudan. It provided for a prime minister, a council of ministers, and a bicameral legislature, while various military and diplomatic powers remained in the hands of the British-appointed governor-general. It was not expected that Egyptian consent to this measure would be forthcoming, but less than three months after its enactment King Farouk was overthrown by a military junta, and one of the major obstacles to a settlement of the Sudan question was removed.

The new Egyptian Government, headed by General Mohammed Naguib, not only agreed to separate the issue of the Sudan from that of the Suez Canal, but accepted the principle of self-determination for the southern country. Thereafter the policies of Britain and of Egypt were essentially parallel, though still opposed: each nation was willing to see an independent Sudan so long as the influence of the other did not become paramount. After a good deal of further jockeying for position, therefore, an Anglo–Egyptian accord was signed in February 1953, which looked towards the formation of an interim self-government for the Sudan, to be followed at a later date by a fully independent, national régime. The form of the transitional government was essentially that which had been enacted by the legislature a year earlier, but with certain modifications aimed at curtailing the power of the governor-general. It was supposed to hold power for three years, during which time a permanent constitution and governing institutions were to be devised by the Legislative Assembly itself.[20]

Elections were held in the latter part of 1953, and the new Government of the Sudan took office on the first day of 1954. The results of the election appeared to be a setback for Britain, for the pro-Egyptian National Union Party won a clear majority, and the executive Council of Ministers was therefore made up exclusively of NUP members. The Egyptians sought to improve their advantage by an active propaganda campaign aimed towards an eventual union of the Sudan with Egypt, but their activities and growing influence led to rioting by the anti-Egyptian factions in Khartoum and elsewhere, and revealed to the Government the danger of civil war which was inherent in a too overtly pro-Egyptian policy.[21] Any lingering hope of union was dashed when, in November 1954, General Naguib was ousted from leadership of the Egyptian junta by Colonel Gamal Abdel Nasser. Naguib was half Sudanese, had been educated partly in the Sudan, and was enormously popular in the southern country; his unceremonious fall from power caused bewilderment and resentment even among the pro-Egyptian elements in the Sudan.[22]

The leader of the transitional NUP Government, who perhaps saw his political position slipping along with the unionist cause, determined to push for full independence at a date earlier than had been specified in the Anglo-Egyptian accord. In August 1955, he persuaded the legislature to call for the withdrawal of all remaining British and Egyptian army units from the country, and this was actually carried out before the end of the year. Next, the two powers who were still nominally co-rulers of the Sudan were asked to hold a plebiscite to determine once and for all the issue of full independence or federation with Egypt. When the result was heavily in favour of full independence, Parliament on 22 December passed a resolution declaring the Sudan independent then and there. A transitional constitution was adopted which in effect called for a continuation of the existing parliamentary machinery, but with the powers of the governor-general transferred to a Supreme Commission of five Sudanese members. This action was accepted without protest, and probably with relief, by the two powers whose co-rule had long been a source of discomfort and embarrassment to both. On 1 January 1956, the Union Jack and the Egyptian flag came down from the Governor's Palace in Khartoum, and the flag of the independent Republic of the Sudan went up in their place.

British rule in the Sudan had lasted no more than fifty-seven years – shorter by far than any previous episode of imperial domination in the country's history. Nevertheless the cultural transformations which took place during that half century may have been as great as any wrought by pharaohs or sultans in earlier times. Certainly there was more material and technological progress in the first half of the twentieth century than during the preceding five millennia. Although the medieval outlook still pervades many aspects of Sudanese life, it is nevertheless also true that under British rule the symbols and institutions of medieval civilization were firmly and, in all probability, finally replaced by those of modern secular nationalism.

In one form or another, and under one aegis or another, the coming of western technological civilization to the Sudan was inevitable. Essentially the same processes of modernization, secularization, and material development took place in every colonial territory in Africa, as well as in countries like Abyssinia, Iran and Turkey which were never colonies. To that extent the British in the Sudan were merely the agents of a cultural imperialism which was stronger than themselves. The specific form which westernization took in the Sudan is, however, unmistakably British. It is most perceptible not in the material but in the institutional sphere: in the educational system, the governing institutions, and above all in the system of jurisprudence which are the legacy of British rule. Whether these will prove an enduring heritage, or whether they will be superseded or transformed into more familiar and indigenous forms, it is too early to say. After a decade and a half in which British political and economic influence have been overshadowed first by those of the United States and then by those of Russia, it is still true that the British cultural legacy remains paramount among western influences in the Sudan.

THE SUDAN SINCE INDEPENDENCE

Although fifty-seven years of British rule brought enormous technical progress, it is nevertheless true that progress in the Sudan failed to keep pace with that in the rest of the world. Thus, paradoxically, at the time of independence the country found itself comparatively more underdeveloped than it had been a century earlier. It was underdeveloped not only by the standards of western industrial nations, but even in comparison with many of its African neighbours. Foreign revenues amounted to no more than 50 million pounds annually, and were derived very largely from the export of long-staple cotton, a commodity which faced a fluctuating market and an uncertain future.[23] A network of steamers and light railway lines (adapted from the original military railway of 1898, and still employing the narrow gauge favoured by Kitchener) linked the main provincial capitals, but there were no secondary lines, and motor roads were non-existent except in the southern provinces. More than one third of the country and its people lay beyond the reach of modern transportation and communication facilities. Outside the main cities and towns there were virtually no schools, and illiteracy in the rural districts approached 100 per cent. The development of a sense of national identity and national purpose had been actively discouraged by the 'devolutionary' policy of the 1920s and 1930s, and except among the educated few a tribal or local outlook still predominated.[24] All of these problems were overshadowed, however, by the continuing and seemingly insoluble problem of the unassimilated South.

The three southern provinces of Upper Nile, Bahr el-Ghazal, and Equatoria contained about one quarter of the Sudan's territory and population at the time of independence.[25] With a few exceptions the inhabitants were pagans or Christians rather than Moslems, speaking no Arabic and having little in common with their northern neighbours. As we saw in Chapter 18, the southern provinces had been annexed to the Sudan in the later nineteenth century, more through the unregulated enterprise of the slave traders than through any deliberate government policy. Under the Mahdiya they had reverted for all practical purposes to independence, but they had been reconquered along with the rest of the country in 1898.[26]

The policy of the British towards the southern Sudanese, *vis-à-vis* the northerners, exactly mirrored their policy towards the northerners *vis-à-vis* the Egyptians. Having reconquered the South in the name of a united Sudan, they stayed on to protect the southerners from the northern Sudanese. As a result, the southern provinces were ruled from the beginning as though they were a separate colony. During the first decades of the Condominium the entry of both Egyptians and Moslem Sudanese into the pagan South was prohibited; the country was ruled entirely by British district officers and native police, abetted by various Christian missionary societies which were allowed to proselytize freely in the southern provinces. Mission schools took the place of Government schools, and the language of instruction was English. The few southerners who completed the secondary school curriculum were sent for further training to Makerere College in Uganda rather than to the Gordon College, as were Moslem Sudanese from the northern provinces.[27] Thus a barrier of religion and language was erected alongside the already existing racial[28] and cultural barriers which separated the Sudanese north and south. The British policy was undoubtedly motivated by altruistic considerations, but it was never coupled with any practical programme for the development of an independently viable South. Thus its final effect was to make impossible the political integration of north and south, even while no other political solution was ever seriously contemplated.

As late as 1944, the southern provinces were excluded from representation on the advisory council of Sudanese notables which was set up in that year to assist the governor-general.[29] With the fast-rising tide of nationalism, however, the British authorities had, belatedly, to face up to the problem of what to do about the South. A conference was held at Juba in 1947, at which a number of southern tribal leaders gave their approval to the principle of national unification.[30] In the following year, when the first Legislative Assembly was called together, it included southern members for the first time. The teaching of Arabic was introduced in the elementary schools of the South in 1950, and thereafter students from the southern provinces were sent to finish their higher education in Khartoum instead of in Uganda.[31]

As it turned out, the British efforts toward integration of the Southern Sudan were too little and too late. The mass of southerners were not yet ready to accept Arab rule in place of British when, in 1955, it became apparent that full national independence was not far off. In August 1955 the Equatoria Regiment of the Sudanese army mutinied, expecting to receive British support towards the establishment of an independent Southern Sudan. The anticipated support was not forthcoming; the rebels were ordered by the governor-general to lay down their arms, and did so after a brief resistance. In the meantime, however, the revolt had spread to the bush, where it has alternately smouldered and flared ever since.[32]

Rightly or wrongly, the missionary societies were viewed by the national government as a continuing source of division and hostility in the southern Sudan. One of the first acts of the newly independent Sudanese Government was to take over from the missionaries the operation of all schools in the south, and to introduce Arabic as the universal language of instruction. This move produced further unrest, fomented (according to the Khartoum Government) by the missionaries themselves. After several years of increasing difficulties and civil disorder, the foreign missionaries in 1964 were completely expelled from the provinces of Upper Nile, Bahr el-Ghazal, and Equatoria. Open and general revolt flared almost immediately, and was particularly severe in the years 1965–8.[33]

Since 1956, each of the succeeding governments which has come to power at Khartoum (see below) has promised, among other things, a solution to the southern problem. Yet up to now none has been willing to grant either federative autonomy or complete independence on the terms demanded by the more extreme southern leaders. As a result, a period of quiescence and negotiation following the establishment of each new national régime has always been followed, sooner or later, by a resumption of hostilities in the South.[34] An agreement granting a considerable measure of political autonomy of the southern provinces was however signed in May 1972.

Not surprisingly, the host of problems which the Sudan Government inherited from its colonial predecessor has contributed to a condition of political instability in the north as well as in the south. The democratic, parliamentary government which was inaugurated in 1956 persisted for less than three years, during which there were continual realignments of factions and loyalties in the north. In November 1958 the parliamentary régime was overthrown by a military junta headed by General Ferik Ibrahim Abboud, and for the next seven years the country was governed by a Supreme Military Council. Parliamentary government was restored after a popular uprising in 1964, but the new régime proved to be as unstable as the first independent government had been, and once again there were kaleidoscopic shifts of power and position, in which for the first time the Sudanese Communist Party took an active role. In May 1969 another military junta seized power, and parliamentary institutions were suspended for a second time. The military régimes have, in general, provided more stability and direction than have the democratic régimes, but neither has been entirely free from dissension and attempted coups.

Big-power rivalries have undoubtedly played their part in the continuance of political instability in the Sudan. At the time of independence the Government had declared a policy of strict neutrality in international affairs, but it was nevertheless insensibly and inevitably drawn into the arena of Cold War politics. An offer of massive American aid created a sharp political division within the country in 1958, and was one of the factors contributing to the downfall of the first parliamentary government.[35] The aid agreement was duly ratified and, although the democratic government fell shortly afterwards, the military régime which succeeded it became one of the largest recipients of American aid in Africa. Inevitably, the Abboud régime became identified in the popular mind with American political and economic interests. Thus, the civilian government which came to power after the overthrow of Abboud in 1964 returned to a more strictly neutralist position, and American influence was sharply curtailed. The Suez War of 1967 brought a complete rupture of relations with the United States, and the Sudan, with the rest of the Arab nations, turned to the Communist bloc for its major international support. Between 1967 and 1970 diplomatic relations were established with most of the Communist nations, and Russian technicians and Russian technical assistance largely filled the gap which had been vacated by the Americans. During the same period, however, the pro-Egyptian faction within the Sudan continued to receive support and encouragement from Cairo, and this has led to additional difficulties and political divisions. When, in 1970, the military government announced a policy of national federation with Egypt, there was an attempted *coup d'état* in which the Russians were believed to have had a hand. As a result Russian influence in its turn has declined sharply in the recent past.

THE PASSING OF THE SUDANESE NUBIANS

Nubians and Sudanese of Nubian ancestry have played an active and at times a leading part in the development of the modern Sudanese nation. As we saw in Chapter 17, the gradual absorption of the Nubians into a larger, pan-Sudanic society had begun in the late Middle Ages with the introduction of Islam. By the beginning of the twentieth century perhaps half of the one-time Nubian speakers had already lost their ancestral language and all memory of their separate cultural heritage, and had come to think of themselves simply as Arabs. By and large, this process of ethnic assimilation has been accelerated by the events of the twentieth century. At least four aspects of British colonial rule have contributed to the breaking down of cultural barriers in the Sudan:

1. Improved transportation and communication have increased the scope of inter-ethnic contact, by facilitating the movement of peoples both within the Sudan and between the Sudan and Egypt. As one result, the volume of Nubian labour migration (cf. Ch. 17) has increased enormously in the twentieth century. The great majority of migrants are, as in the past, single males, most of whom ultimately return to their ancestral land and families. There has nevertheless been considerable migration of whole families to Khartoum and Omdurman; once resettled, the newcomers are sooner or later swallowed up in the pan-Sudanic urban populace.[36]

2. The development of a state educational system, begun under the Condominium and considerably enlarged since independence, has been particularly welcomed by the Nubians, with their long tradition of respect for learning and literacy. As of the 1950s there were state-operated primary schools not only in the towns of Nubia but in most of the larger villages, and it was reported that the percentage of children actually attending school was higher than in any other part of the country. For the first time the Arabic language was being taught systematically and under state auspices not only to boys but to girls also – a radical innovation in Sudanese education and one which will probably do more to break down Nubian linguistic separatism than any other development of the twentieth century.[37]

3. The creation of a national bureaucracy, again begun under colonial rule and greatly expanded since independence, has enabled Nubians to make effective use of the education which has been offered them in the state schools. In the 1950s it was estimated that 40 per cent of the civil servants in the Sudan were of Nubian ancestry.[38] They were employed not only in their native districts but in every province of the country, and in large numbers in the capital. Many were accompanied by their families. It is unlikely that most of these individuals will ever return to their an-

cestral province; for all practical purposes they have ceased to be Nubians and have joined the ranks of the Sudan's small but growing urban élite.

4. The ideology of nationalism, arising in the early twentieth century chiefly among the western-educated and the civil servant class, has affected the Nubians as much as any people in the Sudan. As a reaction against the parochialism and tribalism fostered by British 'devolutionary' policy, it aims to substitute a sense of national identity for the separate ethnic identity to which the Nubians and many other Sudanese peoples have traditionally clung. A measure of the Nubians' recent involvement in national affairs and movements may be found in the fact that most of the Sudanese cabinets since independence have included Nubian members, and the second prime minister of the independent Sudan was a Nubian.

THE NUBIANS IN EGYPT

The Condominium Agreement of 1899 fixed the boundary between Egypt and the Sudan at latitude twenty-two degrees north, a few miles downstream from the Second Cataract. Once again, as so often in the past, the Lower Nubians found themselves under direct Egyptian rule and politically separated from their kinsmen to the south. This arbitrary division, which persists to the present day, corresponds to no ethnic division within the Nubian populace: instead, it divides the Mahasi-speaking group more or less equally between Egypt and the Sudan. Close ties of culture, language, and family continue to unite the people north and south of the border, and until the time of evacuation in 1964 (see below) there was continual visiting back and forth between them. Nevertheless, the settlement of 1899 has inevitably affected differently the political and social destinies of the Egyptian and Sudanese Nubians. The northern group – comprising about one quarter of the total Nubian-speaking population in 1964 – was not subject to any of the colonial or national developments described in earlier pages of this chapter, nor has it undergone the same process of ethnic assimilation as have the Sudanese Nubians.

Although nominally Egyptian citizens, the northern Nubians during most of the twentieth century have been subject to colonialism of a special kind, emanating not from Khartoum but from Cairo. In the Egypt of Fuad and Farouk there was no local self-government above the village level; districts and provinces were ruled, much as they were in the Sudan, by appointed officials responsible only to the national government. It was not until 1960 that a measure of political autonomy was granted to the Egyptian provinces, though governors are still appointed from Cairo.[39] Throughout the twentieth century the whole of Egyptian Nubia has been included within the Governorate of Aswan, which also includes a considerable and populous area to the north of the First Cataract whose inhabitants are not Nubians.[40] As a result the Egyptian Nubians have found themselves a minority group even within their native province.[41]

Although Nubians who have migrated to Alexandria and Cairo constitute an important element in the Egyptian urban population,[42] the rural Nubians who remained within their ancestral territory have been a neglected and an exploited people during most of the present century, much as they were in earlier times. For the sake of increased agricultural productivity downstream, their country has been destroyed piecemeal by the successive dams at Aswan without any effort to gain their consent. Some attempt was made to compensate the inhabitants for the loss of their farms and date groves, and to create new sources of livelihood within Nubia, but the development of government facilities and services to the south of Aswan never kept pace with that in the rest of the country.[43] In some respects the status of Egyptian Nubia in the twentieth century could be compared with that of the 'native reserves' of southern Africa: it was left as much as possible to its own devices, and was looked on by its colonial rulers chiefly as a reservoir of migrant labour. Under these circumstances it is not surprising that tribal institutions of government have survived much more nearly intact among the Nubians than among their Egyptian neighbours.[44]

The Nubians in Egypt, unlike their kinsmen in the Sudan, are a racial as well as an ethnic minority, visibly different in appearance from the Caucasian majority. For thousands of years 'Nubian' and 'slave' were virtually synonymous in the Egyptian mind.[45] This prejudice has undoubtedly dissolved to a considerable extent in the modern era,[46] and Nubians now enjoy considerable social and economic mobility within the framework of Egyptian urban society.[47] They are not, however, being assimilated into the majority population as they are in the Sudan. Whether this circumstance results from the persistence of traditional prejudice,[48] or whether it is due to the ethnic separatism of the Nubians themselves,[49] is a matter of debate. In more general terms, however, it is noteworthy that the Sudan has been and is a melting pot, with a long history of assimilating minority peoples, while in Egypt the reverse is true: ethnic and religious differences have tended to persist over very long periods of time. For whatever reason, the Nubians have played no important part in the national life of Egypt since the time of Taharqa, nor are they being visibly assimilated into the majority population.

THE RESETTLEMENT PROGRAMMES

No aspect of twentieth-century civilization has had a more direct and immediate impact upon the Nubians than the succession of dams which have been built at Aswan. Although built under Egyptian (and latterly,

Russian) auspices, the original conception of the Aswan dams was British,[50] and their social and political effects must in the long run be included among the legacies of British rule on the Nile. Over a period of seventy years about 60 per cent of the territory of Nubia[51] has been destroyed or rendered unfit for habitation, and about half of the surviving Nubian-speaking people have been obliged to find new homes either within or outside their traditional homeland. It is doubtful if any of the numerous cataclysms visited upon the Nubians in earlier times were comparably destructive of their society and economy.

The first dam was built at Aswan in 1898, immediately following the campaign of reconquest in the Sudan. However, it was not until a decade later, when the original structure was enlarged, that the economy and society of Nubia were seriously dislocated by the impounded waters. Even more serious were the effects of the second enlargement, completed in 1934, which backed up water as far as the Sudanese frontier and inundated most of the commercial date groves as well as the most prosperous farming districts of Lower Nubia.

Notwithstanding the major population shifts which were made necessary by the first two inundations of Lower Nubia, there was no organized programme of emigration and resettlement at that time. As much as possible the Egyptian Government encouraged the Nubians to remain within their traditional habitat; new pump schemes were installed to bring under cultivation the lands along the reservoir margin. In addition the old floodplain could still be cultivated during the brief midsummer period when the Aswan Reservoir was emptied (see Ch. 2). Under these circumstances the majority of Egyptian Nubians elected to rebuild their villages along the shores of the new reservoir, either in the vicinity of their former lands or close to the new pump schemes.[52]

In spite of government attempts to ameliorate the lot of the Nubians, the inundations of 1912 and 1934 substantially reduced the productive potential of their country and resulted in considerable demographic shifts. There was some migration within Nubia, to the region immediately below the Second Cataract which was unaffected by the early inundations. In this way colonies of Kenzi Nubians found new homes among the Mahas, both in Egyptian and in Sudanese Nubia. In addition a large number of families emigrated permanently to the cities of Lower Egypt,[53] while in a few cases groups of emigré Nubian families attempted to found new agricultural villages on lands which they had purchased to the north of Aswan.[54] However, by far the most significant demographic effect of the early inundations was an enormous increase in the volume of male labour migration.[55] From about 1910 until their final destruction in the 1960s the villages of Egyptian Nubia were populated chiefly by women, children and the elderly; the great majority of able-bodied men were perforce obliged to seek a living in other parts of the country.[56] Census figures for the Kenzi-speaking portion of Nubia reveal a sex ratio of more than two women for every man throughout the period from 1920 onwards.[57]

The High Dam has finally destroyed whatever productive capacity was left by the earlier inundations of Egyptian Nubia. In this instance there was no thought of allowing the inhabitants to remain within their ancestral land; all 48,000 survivors of the earlier inundations were resettled on newly reclaimed land to the north of Aswan. Although the land which was granted to them was potentially more productive than that which they had quitted, the Nubians understandably viewed their final dispossession from their homeland with anxiety and misgivings. Fernea and Kennedy, who studied the relocation process and its social effects, wrote in 1966 that:

> Faced with the necessity of totally abandoning their homeland, the Nubians' attitudes were somewhat ambivalent. They had always stated that their native land was 'blessed'. They considered the climate, land, and water superior to that found anywhere else in the Nile Valley, and they believed their villages, which were relatively free of outside interference, to have the highest standards of peacefulness, cleanliness, honesty, and personal security in Egypt. On the other hand they were well aware of the material and social disadvantages which resulted from their isolation, and they resented their inability to participate fully in the revolutionary changes taking place elsewhere in Egypt. While most Nubians appeared to share this general ambivalence to some degree, the attitude toward resettlement varied. As might be expected, the people who enjoyed the most economic security were the least enthusiastic about moving; among these were the few prosperous farmers as well as shopkeepers, boat owners, and government employees.[58]

The resettlement of the Egyptian Nubians was carried out between October 1963 and May 1964. The evacuation has been thus described by the journalist Tom Little:

> The evacuation of Egyptian Nubia was a [relatively] orderly affair because the U.A.R. planners, who assumed from the outset that the High Dam would be built on schedule and wasted no time thinking further about it, began their work in 1961. They selected as the site for resettlement a crescent of land about forty miles long bordering the Nile in the region of Kom Ombo, which is about thirty-five miles north of Aswan. There was no nonsense over consulting the Nubians about it; only when the operation had been prepared in great detail were the representatives of the villagers called to discuss the design of the houses to be built and to see whether anything more could be done to meet their wishes within the general framework of the plan. The houses were designed on the pattern used in Nubia, each with a compound surrounded by high walls, one side of which gave access by separate doors to the rooms. One of them was built as a pattern for the Nubians to examine and only slight alterations were required to make it suit their needs.

The resettlement area was named New Nubia and each of the thirty-three villages was given the name of the old village from which its occupants would come, with the addition of the adjective 'new.' The villages were also established in the same order as they had in Nubia, so that New Debod was at the extreme north of the crescent and New Fereg far south, just as the old Fereg was near the Sudan frontier. In this way the relations between village and village as well as the family groupings of villages were preserved, and sometimes even strengthened by the proximity of each new village to its neighbors.

The houses were built of stone, without any wood in the roofs to be destroyed by the soldier ants and other insects, and so were more durable than the mud-brick structures they were replacing. They consisted of units of one to four rooms, each unit within its compound, and were built in Nubian fashion, facing north to get the cool breezes. It was not always possible to keep the houses of relatives in close proximity to each other but an effort was made to do so as far as possible. The Government even uprooted palm trees and replanted them at the new site in order to preserve some economic value from the old area and to give an air of maturity to the new. But they were essentially planners' villages, where the maximum and most careful use of the available space had from the outset been of great importance, and the final result . . . was a geometric arrangement which, despite all the efforts, bore no visual resemblance to Nubia.

The planners, starting from virgin desert, were able to provide amenities which many villages in Egypt still lack and which the Nubians almost entirely lacked at home. Each village was provided with a primary school and a public health unit, its guest house, market and bakery, and a sports field and mosque. Water was led by pipes to the villages and roads connected them to the main highways. There were, in addition, regional amenities directed from the administrative headquarters of New Nubia, known as Nasr City, including four multiple rural centers of the type provided elsewhere in Egypt (at which agricultural and craft training, medical supervision and other rural services are provided under one roof), a central hospital, secondary and teacher-training schools and police stations. The cost of constructing New Nubia was just over 13 million Egyptian Pounds . . .[59]

A problem not adequately foreseen by the Egyptian authorities was the destruction of traditional kin groupings in the resettlement process. Again quoting from Fernea and Kennedy:

In Old Nubia neighborhoods were formed largely by natural groupings of close kin. In New Nubia the assignment of houses ignored the existing social and kin groups and was based only on the size of the household unit recorded in the 1961 census. Four sizes of new houses were built, and for ease of construction, houses of the same size were grouped together. The groupings of families by size not only broke up the old neighborhoods and villages within each district but also segregated most of the older members of the community. Widows or elderly couples whose children had their own homes were assigned to the small-house section of the new community. Thus it is often difficult for their younger relatives, who live in the section of larger homes, to render the assistance customarily due elders. This is still a cause of complaint although, despite government regulations forbidding sale and transfer of houses, readjustments to bring kinsmen back together have been made in some areas.[60]

Not surprisingly, the first year in their new surroundings was a difficult one for the Egyptian Nubians. Not all of the promised facilities had been completed in the new villages when the first inhabitants moved in, and only a fraction of the land destined for Nubian use had actually been brought under irrigation. The full agricultural development of the Kom Ombo district had necessarily to wait for the completion of the High Dam itself. In the meantime many of the domestic animals which had been brought from the inundated region died for want of fodder. Both the Nubian resettlement and the enormous influx of population attending the construction of the Aswan Dam overtaxed the productive economy of southern Egypt and led to a rapid rise in prices, which threatened to consume the compensation money which had been paid to the Nubians before they could get back on their feet economically. Finally, in the anxious and angry mood which characterized the first months of their resettlement the Nubians complained about nearly everything in their new environment which differed from that to which they had been accustomed.[61]

A year later the picture appeared to be changing. With characteristic resourcefulness the Egyptian Nubians had set themselves to make the best of their new circumstances, and to recreate where appropriate the conditions of their earlier life. One of their first concerns was to convert their standardized and mass-produced new houses into something more expressive of their individualities, as the Nubian house in the past had traditionally been. As observed by Fernea and Kennedy:

Among the most obvious transformations wrought by Nubians in the new resettlement project is in the appearance and even the structure of the mass-produced dwellings. There is scarcely a neighborhood in New Nubia in which some houses have not been radically altered through the mounting of china plates over the doors, as in Old Nubia, and by plastering the exterior with mud to create a façade upon which traditional Nubian designs may be painted. Mastabas, the low clay benches running along the front of all Old Nubian houses, have also been added by many people. Frequently, one man sets a standard soon emulated by owners of other houses along the same street.

Less noticeable but more costly are interior structural alterations designed to separate human from animal quarters, to increase the enclosed area, and to organize the living area for greater efficiency and pleasure. Particularly important to the Nubians is the enlargement of space for entertaining visitors.[62]

The rich ceremonial life of Old Nubia, with its emphasis on weddings, funerals, and *mulids* (saint's day celebrations),[63] has been carried over into the new settlements, where it has occasioned unexpected social and financial problems. To quote once more from the same authorities:

... In New Nubia, with distance no longer a barrier, the cultural norm of community-wide attendance has vastly increased the size of ceremonial occasions. Social boundaries within the settlement are also still in the process of being defined, but due to the ease of transportation and increased leisure time, participation even by persons living miles from the event is no longer unusual. The attempt to fulfil the traditional hospitality requirements associated with these activities placed an almost impossible financial burden on the hosts and in addition created logistic problems. It is one thing to serve tea to 20 or 30 persons but quite another to serve refreshments to hundreds.[64]

The response of the Nubians to this problem has been to reduce the size and complexity of their ceremonies, as well as the number of ceremonial occasions. It has thus been formally decided that the celebration of *mulids* is a community-wide obligation rather than a familial one, and in addition the number of *mulids* has been restricted to one per year in each community.[65] This latter development is part of a general pattern of social change in which obligations based on residence are gradually taking precedence over those based on kinship – a common and expectable feature of the urbanization process.[66]

The resettlement of the Egyptian Nubians has occasioned other social problems which have not yet been fully resolved. For men, and even more for women, life in New Nubia involves an unexpected increase in leisure time, for which no constructive outlet has yet been found. There are no longer any number of animals and garden plots to be tended, and the simple provision of domestic water, once a major daily chore for Nubian women, is now arranged merely by turning a tap. It is these circumstances which have led to the aforementioned increase in attendance at ceremonial occasions, as well as to an increase in the frequency of drinking and disorderly behaviour among the younger men.[67]

It is the expectation of the Egyptian Government that the resettled Nubians will eventually become commercial sugar growers, devoting at least 40 per cent of their land to the production of cane for the factories at Kom Ombo.[68] However, the Nubians have no tradition of intensive cash farming, and have thus far shown little inclination to occupy the economic niche which has been assigned to them. Many have rented their new land on a share-crop basis to their Egyptian *fellaheen* neighbours and have resumed the pattern of emigré wage labour which was characteristic of earlier times.

Of the probable future of the Egyptian Nubians, Fernea and Kennedy have written:

If the Nubians are to persist in more than name they must perpetuate the basic values and norms which underlie that part of Nubian culture which is unique. These basic values and traditions are products of village life, however much they may have been modified by the urban experiences of migrants. Clearly, New

Nubia is no longer a collection of villages but is more closely akin to a large, homogeneous suburbia. Can village values be sustained under such conditions? It seems unlikely. Yet we have seen that tentative steps are already being taken to realign ceremonial and other activities on the basis of new residential arrangements rather than the old village and kinship units. Traditional rural values can perhaps be sustained only if these emerging neighborhoods become the functional equivalents of the old villages. However, the many analogies between this situation and general urbanization processes lead us to suppose that the old values and customs must give way and that some kind of compromise solution will emerge.[69]

NUBIAN RESETTLEMENT IN THE SUDAN

Unlike the earlier Aswan dam projects, the High Dam affects the Sudan as well as Egypt. One hundred miles of Sudanese territory will ultimately be destroyed, including the port town of Wadi Halfa and a dozen major villages, with an aggregate population of some 53,000.[70] The total number of Nubians dispossessed by the High Dam thus comes to just over 100,000 (48,000 in Egypt and 53,000 in the Sudan), or about half of the surviving Nubian-speaking population (cf. Ch. 2).

The resettlement of the Sudanese Nubians, which became the responsibility of the Sudan Government, was a more complex and difficult business than was the resettlement in Egypt. The Sudanese authorities had not been consulted in the early planning for the High Dam, and thus were unable to confront the Nubians with a predetermined plan for their resettlement when the imminent destruction of their homes was announced. It was clear, however, that the poverty of the Middle Nile region precluded wholesale resettlement anywhere in the immediate vicinity of Old Nubia, and that a very long move might be required. In any case the dispossession of 53,000 people was bound to have serious social and political repercussions in a country where during much of the twentieth century they had been a potent political force. Nubian resettlement was a hot political issue in the early 1960s, and one which ultimately helped to topple the military régime of General Abboud (see 'The Sudan since independence', above).[71]

The Aswan High Dam was not intended to convey any direct benefit to the Sudan, and for some years its construction was successfully opposed by the Sudan Government.[72] In 1958, however, the régime of General Abboud came to an agreement with Egypt which authorized the construction of the High Dam in exchange for an indemnity of £15,000,000 and, more importantly, a liberalization of the allocation of irrigation water between the two countries. Since 1929 Egypt had been entitled by treaty to twenty-two times as much of the Nile's water as the Sudan;[73] under the agreement of 1958 the Sudanese share was increased to one quarter.[74] This new provision obviously promised an enormous long-run benefit to the Sudanese, though not specifically to the Nubians. They, like their Egyptian kinsmen, tended to feel that their interests had been sacrificed, without their consent, for the sake of others.

Tom Little has succinctly characterized the difficulties attending the resettlement of the Sudanese Nubians:

The Sudanese would not accept the inevitability of [their] fate, stubbornly believing until very late that the dam would not be built or by some other miracle they would be reprieved. 'What now, Mohammed?' – 'All is with God;' and Mohammed would shrug and point to the sandy hill behind to suggest he would climb and build. 'But that hill will be under water, Mohammed!' – 'God is merciful.' In truth, Mohammed did not believe that his town would be left to crumble in the waters of his Nile and was inclined to say with many Halfawis, as late as 1962, that flood or no flood, he would stay beside the river.

Those Halfawis who did face up to the realities of the situation were easily recognized by their anger, and as this anger would clearly multiply as the truth was more and more recognized, the Sudan Government sought to pacify opinion in advance by forming a commission to determine where the Nubians would resettle and promising that they would not be forced to go anywhere against their will. This was a mistake, for everyone knew that they would choose to move as short a way as possible along the Nile, which meant, in terms of the potential sites, resettlement near Khartoum.

The Government had already plans to build a dam on the Atbara river, 800 miles southeast of Halfa, at a place called Khashm el-Girba, and from the Government's point of view this was a good chance to settle the land around the dam with trained farmers. Short of offering them a site away from any river, Khashm el-Girba was a place that the Nubians were least likely to choose for themselves, for it was not only far distant from the relatives who were in the towns of the Sudan and Egypt [cf. Fig. 87] but was as different as it could possibly be from their homeland. The Atbara is a seasonal river, dry for part of the year and then stormy with flood water coursing down to the Nile, and the Khashm el-Girba region is assailed by violent tropical rains. They were used to storms on the Nile and strong winds, but compared with the wild emptiness of the Atbara scrubland Halfa seemed a haven. Despite these objections, the Government decided that they would settle at Khashm el-Girba.[75]

The decision for Khashm el-Girba further exacerbated the Nubians' resentment against their government, and led for a time to political disturbances in Wadi Halfa and Khartoum.[76] These soon subsided, but they were succeeded by more stubborn forms of passive resistance which continued for several years. As Little has observed, many Nubians simply refused to accept the inevitability of their dispossession. There was continual wishful thinking to the effect that the Egyptians, even with Russian help, could never complete so ambitious a project as the High Dam; that the impounded water would soon seep out through the porous Nubian sandstone; that the high evaporation rate in Nubia would prevent the accumulation

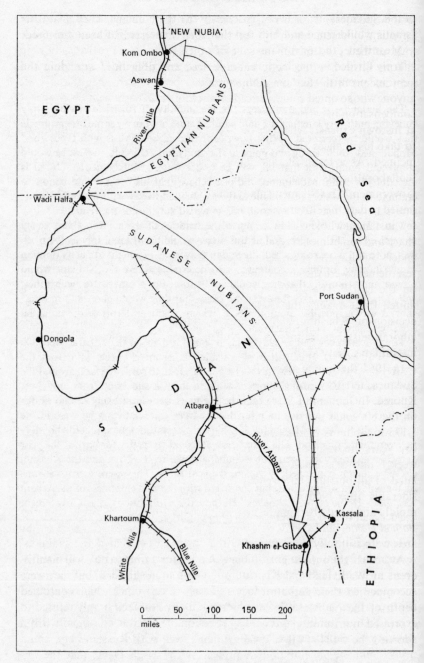

Fig. 87. Nubian resettlement in Egypt and the Sudan

660

of a large reservoir; or even, by some of the more imaginative spirits, that Israelis would come and blow up the dam as soon as it was completed.[77]

Meanwhile, those Nubians who faced the future more realistically were sharply divided in their appraisal of it. In one respect the Government had kept its promise that no Nubian should be resettled against his will: anyone who so opted could, instead of resettling at Khashm el-Girba, accept compensation in cash for his home and estate. He was then free to resettle, at his own expense, wherever he liked; even to remain within Nubia and to take his chances along the barren shores of the new lake if he were so inclined. As a result of this option a serious division arose between the 'collaborationists', who saw their best hope in going along with the Government's resettlement plan, and the 'bitter-enders' who were determined to defy the Government and to remain within Nubia at all costs. In a few instances whole villages accepted resettlement; more often there was a sharp and sometimes bitter division between 'collaborationists' and 'bitter-enders' within the same village. Two particular centres of resistance to resettlement were the large villages of Argin on the west bank and Degheim on the east.[78] The 'bitter-enders' felt that if the Nubians presented a united front against the Government they might force it to rescind the decision on Khashm el-Girba; they therefore tended to regard the 'collaborationists' as traitors to the Nubian cause. The breaches which arose in Nubian society at this time have not been fully healed even yet.

In 1964 the impounded Nile waters backed up for the first time into Sudanese territory, and the inevitability of resettlement could no longer be ignored. In January of that year the first resettlement train left Wadi Halfa on the 800 mile journey to Khashm el-Girba, carrying as passengers the 1,175 inhabitants of the frontier village of Faras.[79] Throughout the next two years the trains continued to roll, sometimes as often as three times a week,[80] until the region to the north of the Second Cataract was depopulated of all but the 'bitter-enders'. The pace of resettlement slowed considerably after 1966, partly because the Nile waters themselves rose less rapidly and partly because of the small population to be removed from the *Batn el Hajar*, but by 1970 only a few villages near the head of the reservoir area were still fully inhabited.

Although the movement of the resettlement trains became a familiar event at Wadi Halfa, the tearful lamentations and last farewells which accompanied their departure never ceased to be an affecting sight. The depth of the Nubians' feeling towards their immemorial homeland was expressed by an anonymous poet who, before leaving for Khashm el-Girba, adorned the walls of his abandoned home with this lament:

> Departed from the fatherland whose breeze I love,
> The smells of homeland are those of gardens.
> I left it with tears pouring from the eyes;

I left my heart, and I have no more than one.
I forsook it not by my own will,
But by the decision of Destiny;
And what a miserable Destiny is mine.
Fare Well.[81]

The design of the Khashm el-Girba project has many superficial resemblances to 'New Nubia', the home of the relocated Nubians in Egypt, and was probably inspired in part by it. The total area reclaimed for the use of the Nubians covers about 180,000 acres. In its centre is a market town and administrative centre named New Wadi Halfa, while at various distances from it are the relocated villages, each bearing its original name with the prefix 'new', and each bearing approximately the same geographical relation to Wadi Halfa as in Old Nubia. These new villages, as in Egypt, are planners' villages composed of symmetrical blocks of prefabricated concrete houses (cf. Pl. XXIVb).[82] Each village is designed to hold about 250 families.[83]

The initial reaction of the Sudanese Nubians to their new homes was much the same as that of their kinsmen in Egypt:

The first view of the resettlement area was drab and inhospitable to the Halfawis, used as they were to the rich green palm groves, the rocky banks and islets of the Nile and the rolling sandhills enclosing their private world and their straggling villages, which might have grown out of the ground. The flat and open landscape left them without protection and the uniform rectangular villages, with straight streets, the water tower and the central square, lacked the liveable untidiness they were used to. There was an old Khashm el-Girba village with its indigenous inhabitants, but the settlement area [for the Nubians] was uninhabited, and, like a vast new housing estate where nothing has had time to grow, was drearily inhuman in appearance.[84]

At Khashm el-Girba, as in 'New Nubia', the Nubians are expected to become commercial farmers. Each family has been allotted 15 acres on which to grow wheat, cotton, and peanuts in annual rotation, 5 acres being devoted to each crop in any given year.[85] However, during the first year after resettlement the Nubians showed a real interest only in growing wheat, which they treated not as a cash crop but as a subsistence crop.[86] Only half the intended area was planted to cotton, and the arduous work of tending and picking it was left very largely to local Arabs and migrant labourers from the Western Sudan. Only one tenth of the assigned area was planted to the unfamiliar crop of peanuts.[87] In subsequent years there has been some increase in the volume and regularity of cultivation, but there has also been a growing tendency for the Nubians to rent their allotments to local sharecroppers, and to go off in search of wage work in Khartoum and elsewhere. There is no more certainty in the Sudan than in Egypt that the resettled Nubians will be content to accept the economic niche which has been assigned to them.

So far no anthropologist has studied the adjustment of the Sudanese Nubians to their new surroundings. It seems predictable that some of the same material adaptations – particularly in the modification of houses – which were observed in 'New Nubia' will be repeated at Khashm el-Girba.[88] On the other hand the resettlement of the Sudanese Nubians has not involved a concomitant increase in urbanization, as in Egypt. Moreover, the Nubians at Khashm el-Girba now find themselves in the midst of peoples who are manifestly more primitive and traditional than themselves, rather than less so.[89] For these reasons it seems possible that the social and ritual adaptations which have taken place among Egyptian Nubians will not be repeated in the Sudan.[90]

The Sudanese Nubians, unlike their Egyptian cousins, have not necessarily seen the last of their ancestral land. Upstream from Dal the Mahas continue to occupy their native villages, as do all of the Dongolawis to the south of them. Even the reservoir area is not entirely deserted, for the continuation of commerce along the Nile is vital to the commercial interests of both Egypt and the Sudan, and as a result the port and railhead of Wadi Halfa are already being rebuilt along the shores of the new reservoir. As of 1970 the place was a bustling shantytown boasting more than 2,000 inhabitants, who were engaged partly in the construction of new port and government installations and partly in the operation of various small shops, transportation services, and an impromptu hotel. Many people, too, were simply waiting for the revival of commerce (including illicit commerce) with Egypt – long a major source of livelihood to the Halfawis. 'Bitter-enders' who refused resettlement at Khashm el-Girba have laid out whole new villages on the outskirts of the budding port town, and there is in addition a substantial number of returnees who have leased their allotments at Khashm el-Girba to other Nubians or Arabs, and have come back to their homeland. So far there has been little social mixing between 'bitter-enders' and returnees; it seems that the animosities of the resettlement period will not soon be forgotten.

One inevitable result of the High Dam and the resettlement programme has been a revival of Nubian separatism,[91] perhaps on a larger scale than has existed since the end of the Christian period. Geiser has noted that even Nubians who had emigrated a generation or two earlier now insist that 'but for the dam, no man would have left his village'.[92] The Aswan Dam has become, symbolically, the collective misfortune of the Nubian nation, the memory of which may help to unite them in the future as the memory of misfortune has similarly united Jews, Armenians and other dispossessed minorities. The Nubians both in the Sudan and in Egypt have felt them-selves betrayed by their national governments, and in both countries they have largely disavowed national causes. The Egyptian Nubians have openly, if quixotically, hoped for Israeli support, while the Nubians in the Sudan have largely abandoned their one-time pro-Egyptian political sentiments, and have spoken wistfully of a return to colonial status. At least for the time being, these sentiments are likely to retard the process of ethnic assimilation which has been going on since the end of the Middle Ages.

In a larger sense, however, no one can say whether or not the Nubians will succeed in maintaining a separate ethnic and linguistic identity under the altered circumstances of the twentieth century. Given the levelling influence of mass communication and of western technical civilization, their ultimate extinction as a separate people might seem inevitable – at least to western observers. Historical 'inevitabilities', however, are apt to be illusive. I suspect that in their time the adherents of pharaonic civiliza-tion, of Christianity, and of Islam regarded it as equally inevitable that the Nubians would fully and finally succumb to their world ideologies. In a way, and for a time, they were right, yet their triumphs did not mean the extinction of a separate and self-recognizing Nubian people.

Twentieth-century mass culture may yet succeed where earlier ideologies failed, but it is not a foregone conclusion. If the Nubians should finally succumb, however, the chronicler of these pages may be permitted to hope that their not inconsiderable achievements of the past will not be forgotten by their successors and heirs.

20
THE LESSONS OF NUBIA[1]

I have learned, in the course of writing this book, a lesson which is probably familiar to many colleagues: that the best way to study history is to write it. I began the work three years ago in the confident conviction that I understood Nubian history and knew what I wanted to say about it; I find now that I have said and thought many things which had never entered my head when I first sat down to write. Looking back, it seems as if three years of reflection and writing have enlarged my understanding at least as much as did the ten years of hard digging which preceded them. Part of this I attribute to my encounters with new and previously unfamiliar sources, part to the conscious re-thinking of old ideas, and part to the unexpected revelations which seem so often to accompany the attempt to communicate ideas to others.

My experience is hardly a unique one; I notice that many writers of comprehensive histories have concluded with a chapter – if not a whole book – of afterthoughts which express more than anything else the wisdom accumulated in the writing process itself. Two distinguished examples which come readily to mind are Grahame Clark's *Aspects of Prehistory*,[2] which is, as he says, 'the outcome of reflection following on the writing of *World Prehistory: An Outline*',[3] and Will and Ariel Durant's *The Lessons of History*,[4] which is the epilogue to their monumental, ten-volume *Story of Civilization*. Both of these are whole volumes of afterthoughts. If the lessons of Nubia do not merit quite so extended a treatment, they are at least deserving, I believe, of a final chapter in this book.

What follows is first and foremost a personal document, for history is, I realize, very much in the eye of the beholder. I can hardly hope that any two readers will contemplate the facts which I have presented and draw from them all the same conclusions which I have drawn. Yet I would not have written the book if I did not believe that at least some of the lessons which Nubia has held for me are appropriate to others as well. This is particularly true in the case of my fellow cultural anthropologists, to whom this chapter is principally addressed. Naturally enough I feel that whatever is germane to me is at least potentially germane to them also. I can speak with less confidence about what other scholars ought to learn from the study of Nubian history. Historians and Egyptologists may

665

perhaps find that some of my lessons are 'old hat' to them, and will smile at the thought that anthropologists are at last beginning to recognize some of the historical truths which they have long been aware of. I hope nevertheless that all of them, as well as interested laymen, will find some food for thought in these concluding pages of discussion.

THE DISTORTIONS OF MIGRATION THEORY

The first lesson which I learned in Nubia, and which largely impelled me to write this book, is that migration theory is no more adequate as a general explanation for the changes in Nubian history than it is for the history of most other parts of the world. By migration theory I refer to that school of historical explanation which consistently attributes major cultural and social changes, whether progressive or retrogressive, to the coming of new peoples. Such a view of history I believe to be a legacy of our pre-scientific and perhaps even of our tribal past. It embodies at all events a typically primitive view of the world, in which there is a fixed and immutable relationship between peoples and their cultures. Thus, profound cultural change can only come about when one people replaces another.

It might be argued that migration theory has never been consciously articulated as a general theory of historical explanation. Yet it fitted so neatly with the racist outlook of the later nineteenth century that migration theory became one of the unacknowledged tenets of the first archaeologists and prehistorians, and its legacy is with us still. Look where we will – to South America, to Middle America, to the American South-west, to China, to India, to Mesopotamia, to Egypt, or to Europe – we find that seemingly abrupt cultural changes have been attributed in the first instance to migrations or invasions. In areas like China, India and the Aegean the theory of successive populations is reinforced by traditional mythology; in many areas, however, it is a pure *a priori* assumption of the archaeologist or historian. Yet as more detailed and precise knowledge comes to hand, we usually find that the cultural continuities between successive periods in history begin to outweigh the discontinuities, so that in the end a hypothesis of migration or invasion creates more problems than it solves. Throughout the twentieth century we have been gradually retreating from migration theories in many parts of the world, and I suggest that it is time we did so in Nubia as well.[5]

The great Reisner, whose chronological scheme of Nubian history will probably stand for all time (cf. Ch. 3), was also the man chiefly responsible for introducing migration theory as one of its central tenets. When he first discovered the remains of the successive occupations to which he gave the designations 'A-Group', 'B-Group', 'C-Group', and so on, he identified them automatically as different peoples[6] – not on the basis of any posi-

ive criteria, but because it never occurred to him to account for cultural
differences in any other terms. Thus forearmed, his anatomist colleagues
Elliot Smith and Douglas Derry had no difficulty in discovering racial
differences between the skeletons of the various Nubian 'groups',[7] and
the theory of successive populations seemed to find independent confirmation. It has been with us ever since, and is solemnly repeated in books on
Nubian history down to and including Emery's *Egypt in Nubia*,[8] which is
one of the latest and best of them.

In spite of its continued popularity, I find migration theory no longer
tenable as a general explanation for the facts of Nubian cultural history.
Here, as surely as in other parts of the world, the accumulation of substantive evidence has gradually filled in the lacunae in the historical record,
and has given us an overall impression of cultural continuities from age to
age which far outweigh the periodic discontinuities. Changes which were
once thought to be abrupt and even revolutionary in nature can now be
seen as gradual and natural developments, more probably the result of
cultural diffusion or local evolution than of any great movement of peoples.
In addition the re-examination of earlier Nubian skeletal collections, as well
as of a great deal of new material, has shown that the supposed racial
differences between successive Nubian populations are largely mythical.[9]

There is no longer, today, any satisfactory reason for believing that the
modern Nubians are a different people from the Nubians of antiquity or
of any intervening period. On the contrary, I think everything points to their
being the same people. That their numbers have been swelled by immigration, warlike as well as peaceful, from the north and from the south, goes
without saying; that the intruders have occasionally and sometimes
drastically upset the orderly processes of social and cultural development
is likewise apparent. Yet the threads of cultural continuity from age to age
are there for all to see. They provide the underlying warp for a tapestry
of Nubian history extending from prehistoric times to the present.

THE RELEVANCE OF AN EVOLUTIONARY MODEL

This brings me to my second major lesson, which is that the main outlines
of Nubian history are best understood in the context of cultural evolution.
While there are many local aberrations, the generalized stages of prehistoric
and historic cultural development which we have recognized throughout
the Old World are faithfully reproduced on the middle Nile. Unspecialized
stone industries in the Lower and Middle Paleolithic gradually give way to
specialized, locally adaptive industries in the Upper Paleolithic, microlithic tools and food grinding appear at the end of the Paleolithic, and
finally (in Nubia very belatedly) come the appearance of food production, sedentary life, and pottery. Meanwhile metal-age civilization de-

velops in Egypt around 3200 BC, and its shadow soon falls over the Nubian scene. The next 1,500 years present a classic paradigm of political, economic and ideological encroachment, ending with the annexation of Nubia as an Egyptian colony in 1580 BC.

The process of cultural evolution does not stop with the establishment of Bronze Age civilization, although one might easily think so from reading elementary anthropology textbooks. Such books often tell the story of man in great detail from the Lower Paleolithic until the emergence of the earliest civilizations, and then skip entirely over the last 5,000 years as if to say, 'we lived happily ever after'. In my review of Nubian history, however, I have already noted that major cognitive reorientations took place after the establishment of civilization – most notably between the Dynastic and Medieval periods – and these too I believe to be part of the irreversible course of evolution. I will return to this point later, in discussing the importance of ideology.

THE LIMITATIONS OF DETERMINIST THEORY

If, as I believe, the overall pattern of Nubian history is best understood from an evolutionary perspective, it is nevertheless true that I can find no confirmation for any narrowly determinist view of evolution. Neither the challenge-and-response of Toynbee,[10] nor the irrigation hypothesis of Wittfogel,[11] nor the energy theory of Leslie White,[12] nor the currently fashionable techno-environmental determinism of the cultural ecologists[13] seems to me to provide an adequate explanation for the genesis and subsequent development of Nubian civilization.

My objections to determinist theories of evolution are of two sorts. First, I see many evolutionary developments in the cognitive sphere which seem to me to be as universal, and as irreversible, as are advances in technology and material culture, but which I am unable to attribute to any external causality. I can only account for them in terms of some immutable process of intellectual maturation, such as was long ago envisioned by some of the earliest evolutionary anthropologists.[14] I shall return to this point later. Second, I find that the concept of environment, as a determining factor in human history, is as difficult to operationalize in specific cases as is the concept of culture. In both instances anthropologists have been prone to isolate for analysis small segments of reality which are not meaningful as systems.

How shall we define the environment which determined the cultural and economic fate of the Nubians? In the beginning it was no more than a rainless desert traversed by a narrow strip of green, capable of supporting a few hundred people by an optimum combination of food production and food gathering. But from the moment, early in the Old Kingdom, when the

irst Egyptian pharaoh cast covetous eyes towards the south, the Nubian
nvironment came also to include the Egyptian people and state. With the
;radual interlinking of the ancient civilizations, the determining environ-
nent of the Nubians was further enlarged until in time it included the
vhole eastern Mediterranean world. Even before the southern peoples
urrendered their political autonomy, the demand for gold, slaves and
vory in faraway places came to have more effect on the economic and
ocial fortunes of the Nubians than had the annual rise and fall of the
Vile.

Almost at the dawn of history, in other words, the Nubians ceased to
»elong to that category of socially and economically autonomous peoples
vhom we call 'tribal', and to whom alone our theories of natural ecology
.re fully appropriate. Yet the Nubians did not become, for at least another
,500 years, genuinely civilized. In the interval they became members of
:hat very large class of mankind for whom anthropology has no proper
1ame, but who were known to the ancient world as barbarians.[15] These
vere nominally independent, unlettered peoples living beyond the frontiers
»f the ancient civilizations, but very much in their political, economic, and
deological shadow. In time they were as much influenced by the 'great
raditions'[16] of the civilized nations as were the peasants who dwelt within
:hem; when that happened they became what Arnold Toynbee has called
external proletariats'.[17] So far as Nubia is concerned it is an enormously
1seful concept. In the narrowest sense for 1,500 years, and in a broader
ense for 4,000 years, the Nubians were the 'external proletariat' of
igypt, and the northern country and its people were the most important
letermining factors in their environment. Thus, any theory which seeks
o explain the Nubians' cultural history in terms of adaptive changes
nust concern itself chiefly with their adaptation not to their own natural
nvironment but to the overshadowing colossus to the north.

THE CONSISTENCY OF DIFFUSION

`his brings me to the fourth lesson of Nubian history, which is that nearly
ll of the major cultural developments of the last 4,000 years have come to
Vubia by way of Egypt. If, as I have argued earlier, it is no longer necessary
o explain the transformations in Nubian history on the basis of invasions,
t is nevertheless impossible to do so without continual reference to foreign
nfluence.

Marvin Harris, the cultural ecologist, contemptuously dismisses diffu-
ion as a 'non-principle'.[18] One might just as legitimately call trade a
non-principle'. Both trade and diffusion in fact develop quite predictably
n circumstances of contact between complex and differentiated social and
conomic systems. Anyone who could not predict, *a priori*, a high degree

669

both of trade and of diffusion between any civilization and its barbarian neighbours must be extraordinarily ignorant of the facts of history.

I can find justification in Nubian history not only for a general principle of diffusion, but for a highly specific theory of diffusion: the *kulturkreis-lehre* or 'culture-circle theory' of the German and Austrian ethnologists.[19] The excesses which were committed in the name of this theory by its more doctrinaire proponents have led to its general repudiation in recent decades, yet I think that in the process we may have lost sight of something important.[20] *Kulturkreis* theory is not really appropriate to the pristine world of pre-civilized man which is dear to the imagination of American and British as well as German ethnologists, but it has considerable validity in explaining diffusion in a world divided between civilized peoples and their barbarian neighbours. Such a world was the ancient *oikoumênê* to which the Nubians and most other Old World peoples belonged, following the establishment of Bronze Age civilization in its earliest centres.[21]

The trouble with *kulturkreislehre* and other conventional theories of diffusion is not that they have mistakenly identified diffusion as a major source of cultural change, but that they have provided no real basis for explaining and predicting it. This is because our historical theories of diffusion have consistently ignored the social and political dimensions of cultural contact. Ethnologists have pictured ideas and cultural influences as spreading like so many contagious diseases from people to people,[22] regardless of the conscious will of donors or recipients. Yet it is a curious anomaly that our studies of diffusion as an on-going process in the modern world – i.e. what we call acculturation – have always given primary attention to the social and political nexus, and the underlying compulsions, within which cultural contact and diffusion take place.[23] 'Cultures do not meet, but people who are their carriers do',[24] as the students of acculturation have asserted, and it is widely recognized that the social and political relations between the people who do actually meet will largely determine who influences whom, and in what ways. All anthropologists who have witnessed the gradual dissolution of tribal societies in the modern world have come to recognize that when economic, political or ideological compulsions are present – and they are rarely absent when civilized man comes in contact with tribal man – certain kinds and certain directions of cultural change are absolutely predictable.

It seems to me that the same model of analysis will enable us to understand many of the regularities of cultural diffusion in the past. Today's radicals may like to think that the phenomena which they label 'ideological imperialism', 'neo-colonialism', and so on, are iniquities peculiar to western industrial civilization, but the historian knows better. The ancient *oikoumênê* was dominated for millennia by a few civilized high-pressure centres, which overshadowed and intimidated their barbarian neighbours as they in their turn imposed upon the still more primitive peoples of the farther hinterlands. Under these circumstances cultural creativity did indeed remain narrowly confined to a few places over very long periods of time, and civilizing influences tended to radiate outward in constant directions and along well-worn tracks, as is implicit in the *kulturkreis* notion. Certainly no region of the globe better illustrates this phenomenon than does Nubia, which from the time of the Egyptian New Kingdom has faithfully mirrored, sooner or later, nearly every cultural innovation which has been introduced from the civilized north, while largely rejecting impulses from other directions.

THE REALITY OF CYCLES

Another lesson which Nubia has taught me is that, notwithstanding the general evolutionary trend of history, there are cyclic recurrences which no amount of determinist theory can explain away. The fact that history does indeed repeat itself from time to time will come as no surprise to historians, though few of them have offered a satisfactory explanation for it. To anthropologists, however, with their boundless faith in linear causality, the idea of historical cycles has always been repugnant. Nevertheless the recurrences in Nubian history are too numerous and too obvious to be ignored. A gross example is represented by the cultures of Kerma and of Ballana, the former marking the transition between the Tribal and Dynastic ages and the latter the transition between the Dynastic and Medieval ages. Although separated by 2,000 years in time, they have more in common with one another than with any culture of the intervening period. Less conspicuously, there are periodic reconfigurations in art and literature; repeated introductions and subsequent disappearances of such utilitarian accomplishments as writing and pottery-making on the wheel; even the uncanny reappearance, every few hundred years, of so specific and distinctive a trait as that of bed burial. It is first attested in the Kerma period, around 1700 BC, and last found at the end of the Christian period, 3,000 years later,[25] yet there are long intervals in between for which no instances of bed burial are known.

Not all the cyclic recurrences in Nubian history are difficult to explain. From 1580 BC onwards the prosperity of the country depended as much on the export of luxury goods as it did on local food production, and the Nubians were therefore at the mercy of business cycles in the same way as we are today. When Mediterranean peoples wanted gold, ivory and slaves, and could afford to pay for them, Nubia prospered; when the foreigners were too poor or too other-worldly to care for such amenities, or when brigands disrupted the supply lines, Nubia suffered. Periods of prosperity are marked by monumental achievements in art, architecture, and literature, as well as by political stability; periods of impoverishment are represented by Nubia's recurring dark ages. The cycle repeats itself every few centuries throughout the whole of the historic period.

There are macro-cycles in the political and economic sphere also. The rising tide of Egyptian colonialism between 3000 and 1500 B C, beginning with an age of exploration under the Old Kingdom, proceeding to the establishment of an armed trade monopoly under the Middle Kingdom, and culminating in political subjugation and the establishment of a plantation economy under the New Kingdom, represents one such cycle. Step by step, it anticipates the colonial penetration of Africa by the European powers in the modern era.

Economic cycles can be most immediately explained in terms of fluctuating demand for particular commodities. Yet fluctuating demand itself is seldom understandable in wholly rational terms. Often it is a reflection of basic and deep-rooted changes in value orientation. In such cases economic cycles are merely the epiphenomena of more important ideological transformations.

Anthropologists, whose studies of the past are both selective and highly rationalistic, have generally been able to ignore ideological cycles in their interpretations of prehistory. Yet scholars in every age and in every part of the world who have attempted to understand the history of civilized man have had to find some place in their schemes for history's repetitions. Cyclic theories were commonplace among the early Greek philosophers;[26] they were revived in the Middle Ages by Moslem scholars,[27] and many of the same ideas were made popular in the West by Vico[28] and Hegel[29] in the early modern period. In our own century Spengler,[30] Sorokin,[31] and Toynbee[32] have all developed historical schemes in which recurring ideological cycles play a central part. Meanwhile Chinese and Indian philosophers have developed and continue to develop their own cyclical theories.[33]

A certain mysticism pervades all of the grand cyclic theories of history. Consciously or unconsciously their authors have adopted for civilization the metaphor of the living organism, which has a preordained life cycle independent of external causality.[34] Clearly such a conception is impossible to reconcile with the traditional anthropological view of culture as an adaptive mechanism. Yet nowhere within our own highly rationalistic science can we find a general model of explanation for cyclical, non-adaptive changes; to understand them at all we must borrow the point of view of our humanist colleagues.

Of the cyclic theories which have been propounded by twentieth-century scholars, I think that of Pitirim Sorokin comes closest to explaining the recurrences which I perceive in Nubian history. Sorokin envisions a constant fluctuation between what he calls 'ideational' and 'sensate' culture, with short-lived transitional stages which he calls 'ideological' and 'mixed'.[35] Without going into the intricacies of the scheme, and while rejecting some of its rigidity, I think what Sorokin is actually postulating is a pendulum-swing between materialist ('sensate') and anti-materialist ('ideational') values. For this I can find ample confirmation in the patterns of Nubian history. I see it in the periodic fluctuations in the size and ostentation of graves, in the fluctuating volume of luxury trade, and in the surprisingly regular alternation between simple and elaborate decoration in pottery.[36] I see it too in the periodic emergence of the house as a status symbol, which happened for the first time in the New Kingdom, for the second time in the late Meroitic, for the third time in the later Christian period, and for the fourth time in the twentieth century. In the intervals the Nubians often lived in the simplest of huts, and indeed their environment demands little else.

THE CENTRAL ROLE OF IDEOLOGY

There may have been a time when I thought, as the modern cultural materialists do, that 'we are what we eat' (*man ist was man isst*, as the Germans more cleverly put it); that is, that ways of making a living largely determine other areas of cultural behaviour and even belief. At the very least I would probably have argued, with the sociologists and British social anthropologists, that 'we are what we do'. Yet the study of Nubian history has revealed to me clearly that, so far as I personally am concerned, what is important about man is not what he eats or what he does, but what he thinks. Moreover, I am unable to see that his thought is limited to any great extent either by his diet or by the social system into which he has the good or bad fortune to be born.

Reviewing the history which is encompassed in these pages, it seems to me that what the Nubians have been eating and what they have been doing throughout their history have been largely determined by the strictures of their environment, and have remained of necessity pretty much the same from ancient to modern times. Yet in their art, architecture, graves, and other chosen forms of self-expression I see reflected profound changes in what they have been thinking; changes which have nothing to do with day-to-day subsistence or social activities. The story of those changes is to my mind the main story of Nubian cultural evolution, and the story which I have tried to tell in this book.

To take a series of illustrative examples, it seems clear to me that the changes which accompanied the introduction of Christianity in the sixth century were not simply a matter of replacing one set of symbols with another. They involved also a profound redefinition of the universe and of man's place in it. Consider a few suggestive contrasts:

From the introduction of civilization until the end of the pagan period every Nubian king built an elaborate royal tomb as the main symbol of his authority, yet we have not found the funerary monument of a single king of the Christian or post-Christian periods.

Nubian kings from Piankhi to Silko proclaimed their deeds in magniloquent inscriptions, linking themselves directly with the gods; no king of the Christian or later periods has left us such an inscription.

Throughout the Dynastic period the art, architecture, and literature of Nubia celebrated the glory of earthly kings, with the gods relegated to a subordinate position; throughout the Medieval period Nubian art and architecture celebrated a heavenly king, with scarcely a mention of temporal rulers.

As late as AD 451 the Nubians were unwilling to conclude a treaty with the Romans which should endure beyond the lifetime of the signatories,[37] since the making of permanent law was the exclusive prerogative of the gods. Two hundred years later, after the introduction of Christianity, they enacted a treaty which remained in force for 600 years.[38]

Finally, from prehistoric times until the coming of Christianity no Nubian went to the afterworld unaccompanied by the best of his earthly possessions; then within a generation the practice of interring mortuary goods with the dead disappeared forever.

It is not necessary to dwell at length upon these changes to suggest that a vast cognitive reorientation separates the Medieval from the Dynastic age. In the earlier period the human and divine realms were intimately linked through the person of the king, the priesthood and a common ideology; after the time of Christ (the last individual in whom man and god were combined) the two spheres were ideologically separated. Secular law, secular councils, transcendental religion and the separation of church and state inevitably followed. Yet none of these changes was precipitated by any significant transformation in the material circumstances of life.

The transition from Dynastic to Medieval civilization is the best-attested case of cognitive reorientation in Nubian history, but it can hardly be the only one. Presumably an equally revolutionary change took place when the complex ideology of the pharaohs supplanted the animism of prehistoric times. Still another ideological gulf separates the direct faith of the Medieval age from the rational scepticism of the modern West, but that gulf the Nubians have not yet fully crossed.

The reality of cognitive evolution has long been apparent to historians and humanists.[39] It was taken for granted also by the early evolutionists, and found its fullest expression in the theories of Lévy-Bruhl.[40] Since the time of Boas, however, it has been unfashionable to suggest that the worldview of primitive men is a child-like one in comparison to our own. Instead we have been at great pains to show that the beliefs of primitives are as rational as our own, either by their standards of logic or by ours. This dedication to cultural relativism has left us with no meaningful way of comprehending ideological change; we can see it only as a kind of stylistic drift, as Lowie apparently did.[41]

There are of course exceptions to the foregoing generalization. Marx was able to fit ideological evolution into a rationalist frame by making it the hand-maiden of economic exploitation,[42] and in this he seems to be echoed, at least *sotto voce*, by his neo-evolutionist followers. More enlightening, I think, is the explanation of cognitive evolution which is attempted by Robert Redfield in *The Primitive World and its Transformations*.[43] He sees the evolutionary changes of the historic period primarily in terms of changing world-view, arising from the increasingly technical environment created by civilizations, but he avoids the narrow determinism of the Marxists. He also recognizes that the ideologies created by civilized peoples – 'great traditions', as he calls them in another work[44] – have a charismatic appeal simply by virtue of their association with élites, which is ultimately sufficient to assure their triumph over more primitive ideologies. The main evolutionary ideas of Redfield seem close to those of Max Weber, who envisioned a progressively rational universe.[45] Similar ideas have also been expressed by Clyde Kluckhohn, in a perceptive essay on 'The Moral Order in the Expanding Society'.[46] These theories are, for the time being, far outside the conventional realm of historical anthropology, but I think that anthropology will eventually catch up with them when it applies its evolutionist approach to the study of historic societies, as it ultimately must.

THE IMPORTANCE OF STYLE

The seventh and last lesson which I have had to learn in Nubia is the determining importance of the stylistic element in culture. This is in a sense no more than a reiteration of the previous lesson, for ideology and style are intimately linked.

Insofar as I can divide the continuum of Nubian history into meaningful stages, it is chiefly on the basis of continuities and discontinuities in style rather than in the functional aspects of culture. I see continuities of style in such matters as the shapes and decoration of pottery, disposal of the dead, and the preference for certain kinds of status symbols, running through all of the later prehistoric periods from the Neolithic to the C Horizon; I see a different and much more elaborate configuration of styles introduced along with pharaonic civilization, and holding constant for 2,000 years thereafter; I see a wholesale substitution of new styles once again at the beginning of the Christian period; and finally, though less dramatically, I see important stylistic reorientations with the coming of

Islam. These 'horizon styles'[47] are, as I have already suggested, associated with distinctive ideological orientations, but they are not closely associated with social or economic developments. Nevertheless I regard the stylistic and cognitive transitions I have identified as the true turning points in Nubian history.

For anthropologists, style remains a largely unmapped area of culture. Particularists like Ruth Benedict have acknowledged its central importance in cultural systems,[48] yet they have tended to treat it as something mystical and immutable – a kind of fixed axis around which the rest of culture revolves. Only A. L. Kroeber has attempted to deal empirically and comparatively with style as a measurable variable of culture.[49]

If we have been largely able to ignore style in anthropological analyses, it is because we do not attempt to define cultural systems in cultural terms. Instead we make them dependent variables of social systems. We identify what we believe to be bounded social units – bands, tribes, and the like – and allow their social boundaries to stand as cultural boundaries also. When we speak of 'Navajo culture' we do not consider whether we are referring to beliefs or behaviour which are uniquely Navajo; we are simply designating whatever behaviour is appropriate to members of Navajo society, whether or not it is also appropriate to Hopis, Utes, or Anglo-Americans.

Among the world's complex societies it is rarely possible to identify cultural systems so tightly bounded that they are coextensive with social systems. We have attempted to do so in a few cases with our studies of 'national character',[50] but the concept has had little utility except in the study of insular societies like Japan,[51] or in those countries like France where national self-image happens to be expressed in cultural terms.[52] Much more often we find that cultural systems are widely shared in time and space among peoples of diverse origin. If the concept of culture is to have continued utility in the historic period, then, it can only be through its application to recognizable configurations of belief and behaviour which persist over time, independent of any fixed social or political matrix. In short, cultures must be defined in terms of their own constituent elements, not in terms of the people who happen to share them at any given time.

Most historians will recognize that in the historic period the configurations of belief and behaviour which most nearly agree with the anthropologist's concept of culture are those macro-configurations which we call civilizations. To the extent that our comparative natural science of man has been carried over from the primitive to the civilized world, it has been carried over in the form of comparative studies of civilizations as whole cultural systems. This field has been pioneered not by anthropologists but by historians and philosophers, yet all of them from Spengler to Toynbee have incurred a heavy programmatic debt to cultural anthropology.

Thus far about a dozen efforts have been made to enumerate and compare all the world's civilizations, past and present.[53] No two of them have employed exactly the same criteria in identifying and differentiating civilizations, yet there are large areas of agreement among them all. Apart from these systematic efforts at comparison, however, intuitive comparisons between civilizations are made and understood by nearly everyone, just as are comparisons between primitive cultures. When we encounter, in an anthropology textbook, a contrastive statement about Egyptian and Sumerian civilization, it occasions no more surprise than does a contrast between Omaha and Arapaho. Yet in the case of civilizations what we are contrasting are not socially bounded behaviour systems, but cognitive and ideological configurations whose most distinctive features are stylistic. This is why style occupies a central place in nearly every comparative scheme of civilizations.[54]

For all its determining influence, the stylistic core of civilization is not constant or immutable. Just as every synchronic functional analysis of culture must make some place for style, so also every diachronic analysis of culture change must comprehend the inevitability of stylistic change. Up to now our studies of cultural dynamics, like so much of our analytical work, have been characterized by excessive rationalism. In our models change must be related to goals – either the achievement of new goals or the better achievement of old goals. Yet stylistic change, like style itself, is unrelated to external goals. It is change for its own sake; change because the aesthetic enjoyment of any experience diminishes with repetition. No one knows why this is so, yet it is one of the best-known and most immutable features of our mentality. Teleologists will perhaps argue that it is a built-in mechanism to prevent stagnation in the human condition.

While styles can and must change, however, they are generally confined within limits of functional possibility and of ideological acceptability. This is why stylistic change seldom proceeds indefinitely in the same direction. Sooner or later a limit of tolerance is reached, the pendulum swing is halted, and movement in another direction begins. Here, it seems to me, is the explanation for many of the seemingly irrational cycles not only of behaviour but of belief, to which I have already referred. Fluctuations between materialism and anti-materialism, between worldly and other-worldly concerns, between ages of faith and ages of reason, even between order and disorder, can be seen in the largest sense as the pendulum swings of ideological fashion.[55] Old values grow tiresome, and new directions are sought.

Ideological and stylistic cycles are not to be confused with evolutionary stages. They are free fluctuations within relatively constant limits, and may recur again and again. Evolutionary change takes place when the limits of fluctuation are themselves radically altered. Evolutionary change in ideology involves what I believe to be permanent and irreversible changes in cognitive orientation: redefinitions of the universe arising from increasingly successful command of the universe. They are growth stages in the collective maturation of the human intellect.

SUMMARY AND RETROSPECT

My excursion through Nubian history must appear to many, as it does to me, as a revelation of naïveté: certainly my own, and probably also anthropology's. I went to Nubia looking for primitive man, because that is what an anthropologist always looks for in the remote corners of the world. What I found instead were the childhood and the adolescence of civilization. These are stages of human evolution for which, I find, historical anthropology provides little understanding. Bonds of empathy and rational insight link us to the aboriginal peoples of the world's marginal areas, yet they seem to exclude all of those no-longer-primitive peoples who live or have lived in the grip of what I think we still regard as ancient tyrannies.

In one way or another, all of the lessons I have learned in Nubia have served to underscore the limitations of historical theory in anthropology. Nowhere in our approach to long-range cultural dynamics can I find anything which adequately explains the transformations in the human condition since 3000 B C – that is, since culture ceased to be an adaptation primarily to nature, and became increasingly an adaptation to man himself. Ours is by origin and tradition a natural science,[56] and most of us are nature-lovers by personal inclination as well. We do not really understand man when he no longer lives in close articulation with the natural world, for this to us is an 'unnatural' condition. Instead of welcoming the chance to study civilization as the necessary and inevitable outcome of the evolutionary processes which we ourselves have charted, we more often ignore or even condemn it as a gross intrusion which comes between man and nature.

While ethnology and social anthropology have, in the twentieth century, made conscious efforts to move away from an exclusive preoccupation with the primitive, and to develop models for the study of peasant and even of urban societies, historical anthropology has remained almost defiantly confined to the study of aboriginal man. We have conjured up in our imagination (and tried to reconstruct from our archaeological evidence) a kind of pristine democracy of tribes: a world more or less equitably shared among countless scores of aboriginal groups, all living in close harmony with nature and, most of the time, with one another. If any such world ever really existed, it came to an end in 3000 B C with the appearance of the first civilizations. What emerged in its place was a series of ramifying power structures: a world divided between a few civilized 'haves' and a large number of barbarian 'have-nots'. Economic, political and ideological power became, and for millennia remained, concentrated in a few hands, while its shadow spread over half the globe. Only in the remoter corners of the Old World, beyond the limits of the *oikoumêne*, did genuinely autonomous primitive man survive.[57]

What is needed to understand the culture history of Nubia and most of the rest of the Old World, as well as of a considerable part of the New World, is an anthropology of civilizations. Unfortunately no such organized field yet exists. Courageous pioneers like Kroeber,[58] Redfield,[59] and Steward[60] have pointed the way, but few anthropologists have thus far been inclined to follow them. The challenge of examining and comparing civilizations as whole cultural systems is, it seems, beyond the capability of our traditional methodology. As a result we have confined our examination to minute and artificially delimited segments of civilizations – urban ghettos, midwestern villages, and the like – while leaving holistic comparison to less hesitant colleagues like Spengler, Sorokin, Toynbee, and a growing body of their latter-day disciples.[61] Using the very comparative method which we sometimes claim as distinctly our own,[62] they rush in where so far we have feared to tread.

It is worth reflecting that not much more than a century ago there were recognized disciplines of archaeology and ethnology, but there was no anthropology. Many excellent and detailed descriptions of primitive cultures had been written, but they lacked any theoretically distinctive point of view or organizing concepts. Instead, social historians from Herodotus to Comte had taken it for granted that primitive culture was no more than civilization writ small. It was not until a few armchair ethnologists – Bachofen and Maine, Morgan and McLennan[63] – discovered the kinship principle that anthropology was born out of ethnology. What they had discovered in fact is that primitive culture is cognitively as well as materially different from civilization, obeying laws of its own appropriate to a universe of its own.

For 110 years we have been busy discovering and exploring the parameters of primitive culture, and in the process we have added enormously to the store of human understanding. The world today turns unhesitatingly to anthropology for unique insights into the mind of primitive man. It seems, however, that we are in danger of running out of primitive man, and we are turning of necessity to the study of more complex societies. Yet we seem to have forgotten the lesson of our childhood: that there is a qualitative as well as a quantitative difference between primitive culture and civilization. If primitive culture is not simply civilization writ small, neither, assuredly, is civilization simply primitive culture writ large. Until we have relearned that lesson we will have an archaeology and an ethnology of civilizations, but we will have no anthropology of civilizations.

If we historical anthropologists are ever to have a comparative natural science of all man, and not just of primitive man, we must give serious attention to such matters as market economies, stratified societies, bureaucratic and feudal polities, military establishments, state ideologies, and all the other diversified aspects of civilization which we have too long dismissed as corrupting influences which threaten and destroy the primitive world so dear to our imagination. We must add history to prehistory, and not allow the story of cultural evolution to end at the threshold of civilization.

NOTES

INTRODUCTION

1. cf. Kees, *Ancient Egypt* (Chicago, 1961), p. 316.
2. The principal references to *Aethiopia* (Nubia) are in Book II: 29–30, 104, 137–40, 152; Book III: 17–25, 97, 114; Book VII: 69–70. For commentary on Herodotus' view of the Aethiopians see Säve-Söderbergh in *Erani*, Vol. XLIV (1946), pp. 68–80.
3. *Odyssey* I: v, 23.
4. II: 2–4.
5. *Kitab al-Ibar wa-Diwan al-Mubtada wa'l-Khabar* (the most recent printed edition is that of Beirut, 1956–61; 7 vols.).
6. *Travels in Nubia* (London, 1819).
7. *Voyage à Méroé et au Fleuve Blanc* (Paris, 1826–7; 4 vols.).
8. *Travels in Ethiopia* (London, 1835).
9. *Denkmäler aus Ägypten und Äthiopien* (Berlin, 1849–53; 12 vols.).
10. *The Egyptian Sudan* (London, 1907), Vol. I, pp. 511–12.
11. See Reisner in *Archaeological Survey of Nubia, Bulletin* No. 3 (Cairo, 1909), pp. 5–6.
12. cf. Breasted, *A History of Egypt*, 2nd ed. (New York, 1909), pp. 13–14.
13. *Archaeological Survey of Nubia, Report for 1907–1908* (Cairo, 1910), Vol. I, p. 348.
14. For a more detailed history and a comprehensive bibliography of archaeological work in Nubia see Chapter 3.
15. London, 1965.
16. A notable exception to the conventional Egyptologist's view of Nubia is represented by Torgny Säve-Söderbergh's *Ägypten und Nubien* (Lund, 1941). Unfortunately this work has never been translated into English, and has long been out of print.
17. For extended discussion of this approach to history see Adams in *Antiquity*, Vol. XLII (1968), pp. 194–215, and Trigger, *Beyond History: the Methods of Prehistory* (New York, 1968).
18. cf. Elliot Smith in *Archaeological Survey of Nubia, Bulletin* No. 3 (Cairo, 1909), pp. 21–7.
19. Yale University Publications in Anthropology, No. 69 (1965), see esp. p. 46.
20. See Editorial Foreword in *Journal of Egyptian Archaeology*, Vol. 59 (1973), p. 2 and in Vol. 60 (1974), pp. 1–2, and Plumley and Adams in *Journal of Egyptian Archaeology*, Vol. 60 (1974), pp. 212–38.

CHAPTER 1

Principal sources: this chapter is based very largely on personal observation and experience. The most important literary source which I have consulted is Barbour, *The Republic of the Sudan* (London, 1961).

1. Shelley, 'Ozymandias of Egypt'.

2. i.e. the hieroglyphic character designating Kush is regularly preceded by another which, from the context, is presumed to express contempt or execration.

3. It should be noted, however, that the sums spent for archaeology amount to only a fraction of the cost of building the High Dam.

4. The First Cataract is not actually the northern limit of Nubian settlement. Considerable numbers of Nubians also live, and have always lived, in and around the town of Aswan and in the area immediately to the north of it. However, these people during most of their history have been culturally and politically overshadowed by the Egyptians settled among them, so that it is more meaningful to speak of the Aswan district as part of Egypt than as part of Nubia.

5. Information on the Nubian climate is derived primarily from Barbour, *The Republic of the Sudan* (London, 1961), pp. 38–51; see also Republic of the Sudan, *Sudan Almanac 1959* (Khartoum, 1959), pp. 82–3.

6. Barbour, op. cit. (n. 5), p. 112.

7. In Bottéro, Cassin and Vercoutter, *The Near East: the Early Civilizations* (London, 1967), p. 279.

8. Genesis xli.

9. Lobo, *A Short Relation of the River Nile* (trans. Wyche; London, 1791), pp. 36–7.

10. Trigger, *History and Settlement in Lower Nubia*, Yale University Publications in Anthropology, No. 69 (1965), p. 20.

11. Information on flora is derived principally from Barbour, op. cit. (n. 5), pp. 62–73, and from Lebon, *Land Use in the Sudan*, World Land Use Survey, Regional Monograph No. 4 (London, 1965), pp. 19–42.

12. For detailed information on *nimittis* and their effects on man see Lewis in *Sudan Notes and Records*, Vol. XXXV (1954), Part 2, pp. 76–89.

13. See Emery, *Egypt in Nubia* (London, 1965), p. 127.

14. Lucas, *Ancient Egyptian Materials and Industries*, 3rd ed. (London, 1948), p. 236; Säve-Söderbergh, *Ägypten und Nubien* (Lund, 1941), p. 87.

15. For a map of these see Vercoutter in *Kush* VII (1959), p. 129.

16. For further discussion of Egyptian gold mining see Säve-Söderbergh, op. cit. (n. 14), pp. 210–14, and Vercoutter, op. cit. (n. 15).

17. cf. Emery, op. cit. (n. 13), p. 129.

18. For a translation of the treaty, called *baqt*, see Burckhardt, *Travels in Nubia* (London, 1819), pp. 511–12.

CHAPTER 2

Principal sources: this chapter is based in considerable part on personal observation. Important literary sources have included Barbour, *The Republic of the Sudan* (London, 1961); Tothill, Ed., *Agriculture in the Sudan* (London, 1948); Trigger, *History and Settlement in Lower Nubia*, Yale University Publications in Anthropology, No. 69 (1965); articles by the Kronenbergs in *Kush* XI (1963), pp. 302–11, *Kush* XII (1964), pp. 282–90, and *Kush* XIII (1965), pp. 205–12; and several of the contributions in Fernea, Ed., *Contemporary Egyptian Nubia* (2 vols.; New Haven, 1966).

1. cf. Chapter 1, n. 4.

2. cf. MacMichael, *A History of the Arabs in the Sudan* (London, 1922), Vol. II, pp. 324–31.

3. For an anthropometric description of the modern Nubians see Field, *Contributions to the Anthropology of the Faiyum, Sinai, Sudan, Kenya* (Berkeley and Los Angeles,

1952), pp. 194–205. Much more extensive anthropometric surveys were carried out by the Czechoslovak Expedition to Nubia in 1965–7, but only preliminary reports have thus far been published. See especially Strouhal in *Current Anthropology*, Vol. 9 (1968), pp. 540–41; in *International Biological Programme, Biology of Man in Africa* (Warsaw, 1968), pp. 179–90; and in *Anthropological Congress Dedicated to Ales Hrdlicka* (Prague, 1971), pp. 465–71.

4. For a more technical discussion of the Nubian languages and their relationship, see Trigger in *Journal of African History*, Vol. VII (1966), pp. 19–25.

5. For a detailed description of modern Nubian houses, complete with numerous floor plans, see Jaritz in Fernea and Gerster, *Nubians in Egypt* (Austin and London, 1973), pp. 49–60.

6. For Nubian house decoration see especially Wenzel, *House Decoration in Nubia* (London, 1972). According to the author this style of decoration, not found among non-Nubian peoples in the Sudan, was in general use only from 1927 until the relocation of the Nubians in the 1960s (ibid., p. 25). It seems to derive ultimately from West Africa, where carved and painted mud decoration is even more elaborately developed. See Engeström, *Notes sur les Modes de Construction au Soudan*, Statens Etnografiska Museum, Smärre Meddelanden, No. 26 (Stockholm, 1957), and Kirk-Greene, *Decorated Houses in a Northern City* (Kaduna, 1963).

7. For a detailed description of carved door locks see Merrill in *Sudan Notes and Records*, Vol. XLV (1964), pp. 29–34.

8. For more on modern Nubian and Sudanese houses see Fathi in Fernea, Ed., *Contemporary Egyptian Nubia* (New Haven, 1966), Vol. I, pp. 72–6; Rostem in *Nubie, Cahiers d'Histoire Égyptienne*, Vol. X (1967), pp. 201–8; and Lee in *Landscape*, Vol. 18 (1969), pp. 36–9.

9. Both the general plan and the method of construction found in Mahasi and Dongolawi houses seem to derive from West Africa, where they are known at a much earlier date; see Engeström, op. cit. (n. 6).

10. Wenzel, op. cit. (n. 6), pp. 20–21.

11. For more on village development see Lee in *Proceedings of the Association of American Geographers*, Vol. I (1969), pp. 80–84.

12. Yale University Publications in Anthropology, No. 69 (1965), pp. 19–21. For a more detailed description of modern Nubian farming see Dafalla in *Sudan Notes and Records*, Vol. L (1969), pp. 63–74. Additional information as of 1937, including statistics on acreage planted to various kinds of crops, will be found in Field, op. cit. (n. 3), pp. 169–80.

13. Quoted from Burckhardt, *Travels in Nubia* (London, 1819), p. 137.

14. Information from Barbour, *The Republic of the Sudan* (London, 1961), p. 141, and Tothill, Ed., *Agriculture in the Sudan* (London, 1948), pp. 627–31, 745–8.

15. Quoted from Barbour, op. cit. (n. 14), p. 142.

16. Dafalla, op. cit. (n. 12), p. 69.

17. ibid., pp. 73–4. For more technical information on date production see Field, op. cit. (n. 3), pp. 174–9.

18. cf. Barbour, op. cit. (n. 14), p. 140.

19. op. cit. (n. 12), pp. 21–2.

20. Republic of the Sudan, Wadi Halfa Social and Economic Survey, *Report on the Income and Expenditure Survey (Including Results of a Livestock Census)* (Khartoum, 1963), p. 54.

21. For a detailed description of these vessels and their construction see Hornell in *Sudan Notes and Records*, Vol. XXV (1942), pp. 1–36.

22. New Dongola or Dongola el-Urdi, usually known today simply as Dongola, is located about seventy miles downriver from the medieval city and on the opposite

bank of the Nile. It has no real historical connection with Old Dongola, which is now in ruins.

23. See Republic of the Sudan, *Population Census in Wadi Halfa Rural Area and Town* (Khartoum, 1960), pp. 36, 85.

24. For description of the assimilation of minorities in modern Nubia see Kronenberg in *Kush* XII (1964), pp. 282–5, and Riad in Fernea, op. cit. (n. 8), Vol. II, pp. 335–8.

25. cf. Säve-Söderbergh, *Ägypten und Nubien* (Lund, 1941), p. 18; Arkell, *A History of the Sudan*, 2nd ed. (London, 1961), p. 42.

26. In the inscription of the Pharaoh Mernere near Aswan; see Gardiner, *Egypt of the Pharaohs* (New York, 1961), p. 99.

27. Trimingham, *Islam in the Sudan* (London, 1949), p. 11.

28. For more on the history of the Beja see Paul, *A History of the Beja Tribes of the Sudan* (Cambridge, 1954).

29. See Riad in Fernea, op. cit. (n. 8), Vol. II, pp. 325–39.

30. ibid., pp. 326–31; Trimingham, op. cit. (n. 27), p. 15.

31. Trimingham, op. cit. (n. 27), p. 17.

32. See Riad in Fernea, op. cit. (n. 8), Vol. II, pp. 327–8.

33. See Kronenberg in *Kush* XIII (1965), p. 212.

34. See Republic of the Sudan, op. cit. (n. 23), p. 50.

35. See Abdel Rasoul in Fernea, op. cit. (n. 8), Vol. II, pp. 340–51.

36. al-Shahi in Cunnison and James, Eds., *Essays in Sudan Ethnography* (London, 1972), pp. 87–104.

37. cf. Säve-Söderbergh, op. cit. (n. 25), pp. 26–7.

38. Fernea, op. cit. (n. 8), pp. 8–9; Baer, *Egyptian Guilds in Modern Times*, Israel Oriental Society, Oriental Notes and Studies, No. 8 (1964), pp. 2–15.

39. op. cit. (n. 8), p. 2. For more on Egyptian Nubian labour migration see Scudder in Fernea, op. cit. (n. 8), pp. 100–142.

40. See Republic of the Sudan, op. cit. (n. 23), p. 85.

41. op. cit. (n. 24), pp. 287–8. For a comparable description of Nubian emigré society in Egypt see Fernea and Gerster, op. cit. (n. 5), pp. 36–44.

42. See MacMichael, op. cit. (n. 2), Vol. I, pp. 341–2.

CHAPTER 3

Principal sources: for a survey of historical sources from all periods I have relied heavily on Wallis Budge, *The Egyptian Sudan* (London, 1907). There are, however, more complete resumés for individual periods. The most exhaustive survey of ancient Egyptian hieroglyphic material on Nubia is to be found in Säve-Söderbergh, *Ägypten und Nubien* (Lund, 1941). Woolley and Randall-MacIver, *Karanog, the Romano-Nubian Cemetery*, University of Pennsylvania Museum, Eckley B. Coxe Junior Expedition to Nubia, Vol. III (1910), pp. 99–105, contains many of the most important passages from classical authors relating to Nubia. Vantini, *The Excavations at Faras, a Contribution to the History of Christian Nubia* (Bologna, 1970), pp. 49–143, contains the best survey of medieval sources, both European and Arabic. For a resumé of archaeological work I have drawn heavily on Emery's *Egypt in Nubia* (London, 1965), pp. 35–120. See also Keating, *Nubian Rescue* (London and New York, 1975).

1. London, 1907 (2 vols.).

2. For an exhaustive survey of hieroglyphic texts relating to Nubia see Breasted, *Ancient Records of Egypt* (5 vols.; New York, 1962; cf. especially Geographical

Index, Vol. V, pp. 71–104). See also Porter and Moss, *Topographical Bibliography of Ancient Egyptian Hieroglyphic Texts, Reliefs, and Paintings*, Vol. VII (Oxford, 1952).

3. For an illustration of the Jer inscription see Arkell, *A History of the Sudan*, 2nd ed. (London, 1961), p. 39; for an interpretation see Trigger, *History and Settlement in Lower Nubia*, Yale University Publications in Anthropology, No. 69 (1965), p. 73. A still older inscription from the reign of Hor-Aha, the predecessor of Jer, may relate to Nubia, but this is not certain. See Säve-Söderbergh, *Ägypten und Nubien* (Lund, 1941), p. 7.

4. But see Säve-Söderbergh, op. cit. (n. 3), pp. 42–53, and Fischer in *Kush* IX (1961), pp. 44–80.

5. cf. Säve-Söderbergh, op. cit. (n. 3), pp. 141–75. The author considers that the records of campaigns in Nubia after the time of Thutmose III cannot be taken at face value, but are merely conventional boasts which every pharaoh felt compelled to make.

6. These inscriptions are in the Carian dialect of Greek. The southernmost known example comes from a small outcrop near the Second Cataract; see Sayce in *Proceedings of the Society for Biblical Archaeology*, 40th Series, 6th Meeting (1910), pp. 262–3.

7. See especially Book II: 29–30; III: 17–25; and VII: 69–70.

8. VII: 1, 2.

9. I: 33; III: 2–8, 15–35.

10. VI: 35.

11. In Dindorfius, *Historici Graeci Minores* (Leipzig, 1870), pp. 332f.

12. Ed. Niebuhr (Bonn, 1829), p. 466.

13. I: 19–20.

14. For the original text and a translation see Budge, *The Egyptian Sudan* (London, 1907), Vol. II, pp. 308–11.

15. *Ecclesiastical History* (trans. Payne-Smith; London 1860), pp. 325f.

16. *Chronicle* (ed. Mommsen; Berlin, 1894), pp. 207–20.

17. *Annals* (Patrologiae Greco-Latina, ed. Migne, Paris, 1863, Vol. CXL), pp. 1122–3.

18. *Ecclesiastical History* (trans. Chabot; Paris, 1905), Vol. II, p. 300; Vol. III, p. 226.

19. *Kitab al-Ibar wa-Diwan al-Mubtada wa'l-Khabar*, V: 429.

20. For a translation see Burckhardt, *Travels in Nubia* (London, 1819), pp. 493–521.

21. *Prairies d'Or* (trans. Meynard and Courteille; Paris, 1863).

22. *Masalik al-Absar fi Mamalik al-Amsar* (trans. Gaudefroy–Demombynes; Paris, 1927).

23. Trans. Evetts and Butler (Oxford, 1895).

24. Fr Giovanni Vantini, of the Combonian Order in Khartoum, is currently engaged in an exhaustive search for late medieval references to Nubia. Thus far examination of the Franciscan archives in Cairo and of the Vatican archives has yielded more than a hundred letters and other documents bearing in one way or another on Nubia. Some of the first fruits of this research have been published in Vantini, *The Excavations at Faras, a Contribution to the History of Christian Nubia* (Bologna, 1970), pp. 125–43.

25. Alvares, *Narrative of the Portuguese Embassy to Abyssinia* (trans. Lord Stanley; London, 1881); Lobo, *A Voyage to Ethiopia* (trans. Johnson; London, 1735); Paez, *Historia da Etiopia* (Oporto, 1945).

26. *A Voyage to Ethiopia Made in the Years 1698, 1699, and 1700* (London, 1709).

27. *Höher und Fruchtbärer Palm-Baum des Heiligen Evangelij* (Augsburg, 1710).

28. *Travels to Discover the Source of the Nile* (Edinburgh, 1790).

29. *Travels in Nubia* (London, 1819).
30. *Journal of a Visit to some Parts of Aethiopia* (London, 1822).
31. *Voyage à Méroé et au Fleuve Blanc* (Paris, 1826).
32. *Journal d'un Voyage à Méroé*, Margaret Shinnie, Ed.; Sudan Antiquities Service Occasional Papers, No. 4 (1958).
33. *Travels in Ethiopia* (London, 1835).
34. *Denkmäler aus Ägypten und Äthiopien* (Berlin, 1849–53).
35. For a detailed account of these see Budge, op. cit. (n. 14), Vol. I, pp. 55–504.
36. See Rowe in *American Anthropologist*, Vol. 63 (1961), p. 1380.
37. cf. *Archaeological Survey of Nubia, Report for 1910–1911* (Cairo, 1927), pp. 176–7.
38. See Reisner, *Archaeological Survey of Nubia, Report for 1907–1908* (Cairo, 1910), Vol. I, pp. 96–102.
39. See ibid., pp. 14, 17–73.
40. Reisner, *Archaeological Survey of Nubia, Bulletin* No. 3 (Cairo, 1909), pp. 5–6.
41. op. cit. (n. 38), pp. 313–48.
42. The major publications of these and other Nubian expeditions will be found in the Notes to Chapters 4–19.
43. See n. 42.
44. Oxford, 1912.
45. Vols. V–VI, 1923.
46. Under the authorship of Dows Dunham; Boston, 1960 and 1967.
47. Boston, 1950, 1952, 1955, 1957, and 1963. See also the related volume by Dunham, *The Barkal Temples* (Boston, 1970).
48. For a resumé of the expedition's work in the Sudan and a complete bibliography of the published results see Dunham in *Kush* III (1955), pp. 70–74.
49. Emery, *The Royal Tombs of Ballana and Qustul* (Cairo, 1938).
50. Emery and Kirwan, *The Excavations and Survey between Wadi es-Sebua and Adindan* (Cairo, 1935).
51. *Aniba* (Cairo and Glückstadt, 1935, 1937).
52. Cairo, 1935, 1953.
53. For the major publications of these expeditions see Notes to Chapters 7–11.
54. Preliminary reports have been published in *Kush* IX (1961), pp. 17–43; X (1962), pp. 10–75; XI (1963), pp. 10–46; XII (1964), pp. 216–50; XIII (1965), pp. 145–76; XIV (1966), pp. 1–15.
55. See Notes to Chapters 9–15 for the results of these expeditions which have been published to date.
56. For fuller discussion of the implications of salvage archaeology for the study of history see Adams in Ackermann, White and Worthington, Eds., *Man-Made Lakes, Their Problems and Environmental Effects*, American Geophysical Union, Geophysical Monograph Series, Vol. 17 (1973), pp. 826–35.
57. In 1970 the Sudan Antiquities Service, aided by a team of archaeologists provided by the French Government, began systematic exploration of the area south of Dal – essentially a continuation southwards of the survey begun in connection with the High Dam salvage project. The results of this work have not yet been published.
58. A separate volume (Vol. II), with an accompanying volume of plates, was devoted to the anatomical remains.
59. Elliot Smith, *Archaeological Survey of Nubia, Bulletin* No. 3 (Cairo, 1909), p. 25.
60. For discussion of the place of racism in the nineteenth-century social and historical theory see Stocking, *Race, Culture, and Evolution* (New York, 1968), and Harris, *The Rise of Anthropological Theory* (New York, 1968), pp. 80–107.
61. Batrawi, *Report on the Human Remains* (Cairo, 1935), p. 160.
62. Vol. LXXV (1946), pp. 81–101; Vol. LXXVI (1946), pp. 131–56.

NOTES

63. *Journal of the Royal Anthropological Institute*, Vol. LXXVI (1946), p. 131.
64. Mukherjee, Rao, and Trevor, *The Ancient Inhabitants of Jebel Moya (Sudan)* (Cambridge, 1955), p. 85.
65. Greene, *Dentition of Meroitic, X-Group, and Christian Populations from Wadi Halfa, Sudan*, University of Utah Anthropological Papers, No. 85 (1967); Greene in *Journal of Human Evolution*, Vol. I (1972), pp. 315–24.
66. Vagn Nielsen, *Human Remains*, Scandinavian Joint Expedition to Sudanese Nubia Publications, Vol. 9 (1970). This study is based on the author's more detailed doctoral thesis, *The Nubian Skeleton through 4,000 Years* (Odense, 1970).
67. Vagn Nielsen, *Human Remains* (op. cit., n. 66), p. 81. Strouhal on the other hand characterizes the X-Group skeletons recently excavated by the Czechoslovak Expedition to Nubia as 'strongly Negroid', although he sees this as a continuation from Meroitic times. See *Festschrift für Professor Dr. Saller* (Stuttgart, 1968), pp. 84–92, and *Anthropological Congress Dedicated to Ales Hrdlicka* (Prague, 1971), pp. 541–7. For a general critique of the racial approach to Nubian population history see Van Gerven, Carlson and Armelagos in *Journal of African History*, Vol. XIV (1973), pp. 555–64.
68. Vagn Nielsen, *Human Remains* (op. cit., n. 66), p. 81.
69. Knips in *Koninglijke Nederlands Akademie van Wetenschappen, Proceedings* Series C, 73, No. 5 (1970), pp. 433–68.
70. op. cit. (n. 63).
71. More detailed discussion on this subject will be found in Chapter 12.
72. *The Birth of Britain* (New York, 1956), p. 47.
73. For further discussion of this important distinction see Trigger, *Beyond History: the Methods of Prehistory* (New York, 1968).

CHAPTER 4

Principal sources: in this chapter I have drawn very heavily on Fred Wendorf, Ed., *The Prehistory of Nubia* (2 vols.; Dallas, 1968), and to a lesser extent on A. J. Arkell, *Early Khartoum* (London, 1949) and *Shaheinab* (London, 1953).

1. Sandford and Arkell, *Paleolithic Man and the Nile Valley in Nubia and Upper Egypt*, Chicago Oriental Institute Publications, No. 17 (1933).
2. The principal group was the Combined Prehistoric Expedition, sponsored initially by Columbia University and later by the Museum of New Mexico and Southern Methodist University, and including scholars from many European institutions as well. Other expeditions which worked on Nubian prehistoric sites were the University of Colorado Nubia Expedition, the National Museum of Canada Expedition, the Scandinavian Joint Expedition, and the Yale Prehistoric Expedition.
3. There has been somewhat more thorough investigation of Stone-Age remains in Egypt; see Hayes, *Most Ancient Egypt* (Chicago, 1964), esp. pp. 43–146. However, Wendorf and his colleagues find little correspondence between the prehistoric industries of Egypt and those of the Sudan; see *Science*, Vol. 196 (1970), p. 1168.
4. In 1966–7 the Combined Prehistoric Expedition, which undertook the largest prehistoric survey in the Aswan Reservoir area, did further field-work in the Dongola Reach. However, very few sites were found which were comparable to those in the vicinity of Wadi Halfa. See Marks, Shiner and Hays in *Current Anthropology*, Vol. 9 (1968), pp. 319–23.
5. Edited by Fred Wendorf (Dallas, 1968). For an additional report on the work of

the Combined Prehistoric Expedition see Marks, *Preceramic Sites*, Scandinavian Joint Expedition to Sudanese Nubia Publications, Vol. 2 (1970).
6. The principal exponent of this view is Karl Butzer; see Butzer and Hansen, *Desert and River in Nubia* (Madison, 1968), pp. 436–43.
7. cf. McBurney, *The Stone Age of Northern Africa* (Harmondsworth, 1960), pp. 70–81.
8. Butzer and Hansen, op. cit. (n. 6), pp. 453–7; de Heinzelin and Paepe in Wendorf, Ed., *Contributions to the Prehistory of Nubia* (Dallas, 1965), pp. 53–5.
9. cf. Berry and Whiteman in *Geographical Journal*, Vol. 134 (1968), p. 1.
10. See McBurney, op. cit. (n. 7), pp. 94–128.
11. ibid.
12. Personal communication from Roy L. Carlson. For individual descriptions of Nubian Middle Paleolithic industries see Wendorf, Ed., *The Prehistory of Nubia* (Dallas, 1968), Vol. II, pp. 1043–4, and Irwin, Wheat and Irwin, *University of Colorado Investigations of Paleolithic and Epipaleolithic Sites in the Sudan, Africa*, University of Utah Anthropological Papers, No. 90 (1968), pp. 56–73.
13. cf. Wendorf, op. cit. (n. 12), pp. 1044–54.
14. ibid., pp. 1041–59.
15. For discussion on this point see Mellars in *World Archaeology*, Vol. II (1970), pp. 84–6.
16. cf. 'Pottery and history', in Ch. 5 of the present work.
17. Wendorf, op. cit. (n. 12), pp. 1054–7. However, Phillips has recently noted a close similarity between certain Late Paleolithic sites in Upper Egypt and in Libya. See *Current Anthropology*, Vol. 13 (1972), pp. 587–90.
18. See Sandford and Arkell, op. cit. (n. 1), pp. 37–43.
19. Wendorf, op. cit. (n. 12), pp. 940–46. Reed has recently reported grinding stones of comparable age from Kom Ombo in Upper Egypt; see Ucko and Dimbleby, *The Domestication and Exploitation of Plants and Animals* (Chicago, 1969), p. 363.
20. Wendorf, op. cit. (n. 12), pp. 1048–53.
21. See ibid., pp. 954–95; Hewes *et al.* in *Nature*, Vol. 203 (1964), pp. 341–3, and Saxe in Brown, Ed., *Approaches to the Social Dimensions of Mortuary Practices*, Memoirs of the Society for American Archaeology, No. 25 (1971), pp. 39–57.
22. cf. Wendorf, op. cit. (n. 12), pp. 991–4.
23. ibid., pp. 1028–35; see also Hewes *et al.*, op. cit. (n. 21) and Greene and Armelagos, *The Wadi Halfa Mesolithic Population*, Research Report No. 11, Department of Anthropology, University of Massachusetts, 1972.
24. Childe, *What Happened in History* (Harmondsworth, 1942).
25. cf. Reed, op. cit. (n. 19), pp. 362–4.
26. cf. ibid., p. 361.
27. See Clark in Braidwood and Willey, Eds., *Courses toward Urban Life*, Viking Fund Publications in Anthropology, No. 32 (1962), pp. 11–16.
28. cf. Trigger in McCall, Bennett, and Butler, Eds., *Eastern African History*, Boston University Papers on Africa, Vol. III (1969), pp. 84–5; Huard and Leclant in *Études Scientifiques*, September–December 1972, pp. 41–56.
29. cf. McBurney, op. cit. (n. 7), pp. 230–47.
30. cf. Clark, op. cit. (n. 27), p. 15; Huard and Leclant, op. cit. (n. 28), pp. 43–5.
31. The definitive report of these discoveries is Arkell, *Early Khartoum* (London, 1949).
32. A. J. Arkell goes even further, suggesting that pottery may have been invented for the first and only time by the Early Khartoum people, and from them spread to the rest of the world. See *Kush* V (1957), p. 11.
33. Arkell, op. cit. (n. 31), pp. 31–5.

34. McBurney, op. cit. (n. 7), p. 242.
35. cf. Arkell, *A History of the Sudan*, 2nd ed. (London, 1961), p. 28.
36. Clark, op. cit. (n. 27), p. 14.
37. ibid., pp. 11–14.
38. cf. McBurney, op. cit. (n. 7), p. 244.
39. The definitive report on the Khartoum Neolithic is Arkell, *Shaheinab* (London, 1953).
40. ibid., pp. 70–72.
41. cf. Trigger, op. cit. (n. 28), pp. 87–8.
42. Arkell, op. cit. (n. 39), pp. 20–77.
43. ibid., pp. 106–7; Otto in *Kush* XI (1963), pp. 108–15.
44. Wendorf, op. cit. (n. 12), p. 1054.
45. ibid., pp. 768–90. Additional Khartoum Neolithic sites excavated by the Scandinavian Joint Expedition are reported in Nordström, *Neolithic and A-Group Sites*, Scandinavian Joint Expedition to Sudanese Nubia Publications, Vol. 3 (1972), pp. 136–9, 212–20.
46. ibid., p. 777.
47. ibid., p. 768.
48. ibid., pp. 611–27. The original discovery and description of the Abka culture was made by O. H. Myers; see *Illustrated London News*, 13 November 1948, pp. 566–7; *Sudan Notes and Records*, Vol. XXIX (1948), p. 129; *Kush* VI (1958), pp. 131–41; and *Kush* VIII (1960), pp. 174–81. See also Vaufrey in *Kush* VI (1958), pp. 142–3 and Palma di Cesnola in *Kush* VIII (1960), pp. 182–237. For additional Abkan sites see Nordström, op. cit. (n. 45), pp. 220–22.
49. Wendorf, op. cit. (n. 12), p. 1053.
50. ibid., p. 627.
51. Nordström, op. cit. (n. 45), p. 16. Possibly related industries were found in the Dongola Reach in 1966–7, though they were not designated as Abkan by the discoverers. See Marks, Shiner and Hays, op. cit. (n. 4).
52. For a discussion of Saharan rock art and its affinities see especially McBurney, op. cit. (n. 7), pp. 258–72, and Huard and Leclant, op. cit. (n. 28), pp. 19–78.
53. This was the Epigraphic Mission of the Berlin Academy of Sciences. For preliminary accounts of its work see Hintze in *Kush* XI (1963), pp. 93–5; *Kush* XII (1964), pp. 40–42; and *Kush* XIII (1965), pp. 13–16. Nubian rock pictures have recently been the subject of an extraordinary number of other studies; cf. Bietak and Engelmayer, *Eine Frühdynastische Abri-Siedlung mit Felsbildern aus Sayala-Nubien*, Österreichische Akademie der Wissenschaften, Philosophisch-Historische Klasse Denkschriften, 82 (1963); Engelmayer, *Die Felsgravierungen im Distrikt Sayala-Nubien*, Teil I, *Die Schiffsdarstellungen*, Österreichische Akademie der Wissenschaften, Philosophisch-Historische Klasse Denkschriften, 90 (1965); Hellström and Langballe, *The Rock Drawings*, Scandinavian Joint Expedition to Sudanese Nubia Publications, Vol. 1 (1970); and Almagro and Almagro, *Estudios de Arte Rupestre Nubio*, Comite Español de Excavaciones en el Extranjero, Memorias de la Misión Arqueológica en Egipto, X (1968). All of the foregoing are based on first-hand field studies. A compilation from secondary sources is Resch, *Die Felsbilder Nubiens* (Graz, 1967). An older source is Dunbar, *The Rock-Pictures of Lower Nubia* (Cairo, 1941).
54. See Trigger, *History and Settlement in Lower Nubia*, Yale University Publications in Anthropology, No. 69 (1965), p. 63. For illustrations of many of these see Engelmayer, op. cit. (n. 53).
55. For illustrations and some description see Myers in *Illustrated London News*, 13 November 1948, pp. 556–7 and in *Kush* VI (1958), pp. 131–41.

56. cf. McBurney, op. cit. (n. 7), pp. 263–4.
57. See Myers in *Kush* VI (1958), pl. XXXIV.
58. Myers in *Kush* VIII (1960), p. 177. In view of the results obtained by Wendorf (op. cit., n. 12, p. 1053) it seems probable that the dates fall much nearer to 4000 than to 7000 BC.

CHAPTER 5

Principal sources: for cultural descriptions of the A Horizon I have drawn heavily on Arkell, *A History of the Sudan*, 2nd ed. (London, 1961), pp. 37–45; Emery, *Egypt in Nubia* (London, 1965), pp. 123–34; and Trigger, *History and Settlement in Lower Nubia*, Yale University Publications in Anthropology, No. 69 (1965), pp. 70–79. An important synthesis which has appeared since the writing of this book is Nordström, *Neolithic and A-Group Sites*, Scandinavian Joint Expedition to Sudanese Nubia Publications, Vol. 3 (1972), pp. 17–32.

1. Reisner in *Archaeological Survey of Nubia*, *Bulletin* No. 3 (Cairo, 1909), p. 5, and Reisner, *Archaeological Survey of Nubia*, *Report for 1907–1908* (Cairo, 1910), Vol. I, p. 319.
2. cf. Wendorf, Ed., *The Prehistory of Nubia* (Dallas, 1968), Vol. II, p. 1053.
3. Emery, *Egypt in Nubia* (London, 1965).
4. cf. Trigger, *History and Settlement in Lower Nubia*, Yale University Publications in Anthropology, No. 69 (1965), pp. 169–74.
5. Mills in *Kush* XIII (1965), pp. 1–10; Mills, personal communication.
6. Personal communication from J. Vercoutter.
7. See n. 1.
8. Wheeler, *Civilizations of the Indus Valley and Beyond* (London, 1966), p. 61.
9. Wendorf, loc. cit. (n. 2).
10. Arkell, *A History of the Sudan*, 2nd ed. (London, 1961), p. 35. For a description of the production of black-topped pottery in modern times see Reisner in *Journal of the American Research Center in Egypt*, Vol. V (1966), pp. 7–10.
11. See Baumgartel in *Cambridge Ancient History*, Revised Edition of Volumes I and II, Fascicle 38 (Cambridge, 1965), pp. 11–17.
12. Reisner, *Archaeological Survey of Nubia*, *Report for 1907–1908* (Cairo, 1910), Vol. I, p. 320.
13. It should be pointed out however that the earliest 'A-Group' graves often contain black-topped vessels of Egyptian type as well as those of Nubian type. The former were presumably obtained in trade, along with other objects of Egyptian manufacture which are found in the same graves.
14. Trigger, op. cit. (n. 4), p. 160.
15. ibid., pp. 71–2. Trigger believes that this may have been an unusually rich settlement; perhaps the residence of a 'chief' (personal communication). The original published description of the site is that of Reisner, op. cit. (n. 12), pp. 215–18.
16. For a partial listing of these and a bibliography of published sources see Trigger, op. cit. (n. 4), pp. 169–74. Many additional sites were discovered by the Sudan Antiquities Service and the Scandinavian Joint Expedition surveys in Sudanese Nubia; see preliminary reports by Adams and by Säve-Söderbergh in *Kush* IX (1961), pp. 7–10; *Kush* X (1962), pp. 10–18, 76–105; *Kush* XI (1963), pp. 10–69; *Kush* XII (1964), pp. 19–39; and *Kush* XV (1973), pp. 225–9. See also Bietak and Engelmayer, *Eine Fruhdynastische Abri-Siedlung mit Felsbildern aus Sayala-Nubien*, Osterreichische Akademie der Wissenschaften, Philosophisch-Historische Klasse

Denkschriften, 82 (1963), pp. 14–17, and Nordstrom, *Neolithic and A-Group Sites,* Scandinavean Joint Expedition to Sudanese Nubia Publications, Vol. 3 (1972), pp. 17–32, 134–6, 140–58, 172–80, 183–9, 190–212, 230–33, 235–9.

17. op. cit. (n. 4), p. 77. A more extended description of the site is that of Lal in *Fouilles en Nubie (1961–1963)* (Cairo, 1967), pp. 104–9.

18. cf. Griffith in *University of Liverpool Annals of Archaeology and Anthropology,* Vol. VIII (1921), p. 4. It must be added that the great majority of habitation sites of the A Horizon may have been destroyed by sheet erosion or buried under alluvium, so that we will never know whether or not the few surviving sites are typical of the period as a whole.

19. Lal, op. cit. (n. 17), p. 106.

20. Arkell, *Shaheinab* (London, 1953), pp. 15–18.

21. cf. Trigger, op. cit. (n. 4), pp. 67–8.

22. The earliest allusion to Nubian livestock is found in the famous Palermo Stone, in which it is claimed that the Pharaoh Sneferu returned from a campaign in the south with 7,000 prisoners and 200,000 'large and small cattle'. (Breasted, *Ancient Records of Egypt,* New York, 1962, Vol. I, p. 66.) However, the text refers to a time considerably later than any known remains of the A Horizon, and may possibly have to do with a different group of Nubians.

23. Piotrovsky in *Fouilles en Nubie (1961–1963)* (Cairo, 1967), p. 131.

24. ibid., p. 130.

25. Butzer's studies of the 'Saharan subpluvial' period do not indicate that there was any significant rainfall in Lower Nubia between 5000 and 2350 BC; 'the core of the Libyan desert would have been as lifeless as today'. (*Environment and Archaeology,* Chicago, 1964, p. 452; cf. also the precipitation map on p. 451.)

26. cf. Nordström, op. cit. (n. 16), pp. 23–4.

27. Carlson in *Kush* XIV (1966), p. 61. The author designates the site as Neolithic, but considers it to be contemporary with the A Horizon further north; cf. p. 62.

28. See Trigger, loc. cit. (n. 4).

29. Reported in Reisner, op. cit. (n. 12), pp. 18–52.

30. At Cemetery 79 near Gerf Hussein, reported in Firth, *Archaeological Survey of Nubia, Report for 1908–1909* (Cairo, 1912), Vol. I, pp. 127–52.

31. op. cit. (n. 3), p. 125. For a more extended discussion of burial customs in the A Horizon see Nordström, op. cit. (n. 16), pp. 27–8.

32. *Kush* XIV (1966), p. 124.

33. op. cit. (n. 4), pp. 74–5. The original description of these burials will be found in Firth, *Archaeological Survey of Nubia, Report for 1910–1911* (Cairo, 1927), pp. 204–12.

34. In *Journal of Egyptian Archaeology,* Vol. 30 (1944), p. 129.

35. cf. Evans-Pritchard, *The Nuer* (Oxford, 1940), pp. 172–6; Hambly, *Source Book for African Anthropology,* Part II, Field Museum of Natural History, Anthropological Series, Vol. XXVI (1937), pp. 552–4.

36. Trigger, op. cit. (n. 4), pp. 67–83.

37. The system was originally proposed by Petrie in *Diospolis Parva,* Egypt Exploration Fund, Excavation Memoir No. XX (1901), pp. 4ff.

38. cf. Gardiner, *Egypt of the Pharaohs* (New York, 1966), pp. 389–90. Substantial revisions in the system of sequence dating have been proposed by Kaiser in *Archaeologia Geographica,* Vol. 6 (1957), pp. 69–78.

39. cf. Nordström in *Kush* X (1962), p. 52. For an exhaustive technical and typological study of 'A-Group' pottery see Nordström, op. cit. (n. 16), pp. 33–94.

40. cf. Trigger, op. cit. (n. 4), p. 75.

41. Reference to Table II, p. 72, will reveal that in fact nearly all attribution of graves to the 'B-Group' was made during the first two seasons of the First Archaeological Survey.

42. Akademie der Wissenschaften in Wien, Philosophisch-Historische Klasse Denk-schriften, 62, Band 3 (1919).

43. cf. Säve-Söderbergh in *Kush* XII (1964), p. 29.

44. *Kush* XIV (1966), pp. 69–124.

45. ibid., pp. 95–6.

46. cf. Trigger, op. cit. (n. 4), p. 79; Kraeling and Adams, Eds., *City Invincible* (Chicago, 1960), p. 142.

47. This view is my own and is not that advanced by Smith in his reappraisal of the 'B-Group' (op. cit., n. 44). His conclusion is that there are no Nubian graves which can be dated with certainty to the period between the I and VI Dynasties, and that the so-called 'B-Group' graves probably belong to the Predynastic period (personal communication).

48. Reisner, op. cit. (n. 12), pp. 331–2.

49. For the evidence on this point see Adams in *Sudan Notes and Records*, Vol. XLVIII (1967), p. 17.

50. However, Emery found small percentages of Nubian ('B-Group') pottery in the Egyptian town-site at Buhen, which is securely dated to the IV and V Dynasties. See Emery, op. cit. (n. 3), p. 114.

51. Nordström now believes that he has found such a transitional link in pottery from the *Batn el Hajar*; see *Kush* XIV (1966), pp. 67–8. Nevertheless, Nordström endorses the traditional view that the 'A-Group' *in Lower Nubia* disappeared in the time of the Egyptian First Dynasty; see op. cit. (n. 16), p. 31.

52. This is now believed by Nordström (ibid.) and Säve-Söderbergh (personal communication).

53. This has been suggested by Trigger (personal communication); cf. also Nordström, op. cit. (n. 16), p. 32.

54. Säve-Söderbergh, *Ägypten und Nubien* (Lund, 1941), pp. 19–20.

55. Breasted, op. cit. (n. 22), Vol. I, pp. 149–50.

56. Säve-Söderbergh, op. cit. (n. 54), p. 21.

57. Trigger, personal communication.

58. See Adams in *Journal of African History* (in press).

59. cf. Trigger, op. cit. (n. 4), p. 79.

60. Winifred Needler believes that she has found still earlier Egyptian inscriptions – graffiti of the enigmatic 'Scorpion King' of late Predynastic times – at the same locality, but this is highly problematical. See *Journal of the American Research Center in Egypt*, Vol. VI (1967), pp. 87–91. For counter-comment by Inge Hofmann see *Bibliotheca Orientalis*, Vol. XXVII (1971), pp. 308–9.

61. The 'inscription' of King Jer was removed in the course of the High Dam salvage campaign and is now in the National Museum in Khartoum.

62. Trigger, op. cit. (n. 4), p. 73. For illustrations of the Jer 'inscription' see Arkell in *Journal of Egyptian Archaeology*, Vol. 36 (1950), p. 28 and pl. X, and Arkell, op. cit. (n. 10), p. 39. Attribution of the text to King Jer is not absolutely certain; see Nordström, op. cit. (n. 16), p. 32, Helck in *Mitteilungen des Deutschen Archäo-logischen Instituts, Abteilung Kairo*, Band 26 (1970), pp. 83–5, and Hofmann, op. cit. (n. 60). However, an Early Dynastic date is generally accepted.

63. Trigger (op. cit., n. 4, p. 160) estimates the maximum population of Lower Nubia in the A Horizon at 8,000.

64. See Säve-Söderbergh, op. cit. (n. 54), pp. 7–8; Smith, op. cit. (n. 44), p. 119.

65. For a synopsis of the text see Breasted, op. cit. (n. 22), Vol. I, pp. 65–6; for discus-

sion see Säve-Söderbergh, op. cit. (n. 54), pp. 9–10 and Smith, op. cit. (n. 44), p. 119.

66. Described in Emery, op. cit. (n. 3), pp. 111–14.
67. Personal communication from W. B. Emery.
68. Emery, op. cit. (n. 3), p. 111. David O'Connor, who is studying the pottery of the Old Kingdom Town for publication, informs me that 'My initial, rather superficial examination suggests to me that the material is best paralleled in the A-Group, and certainly none of the typically "early" C-Group sherds occur' (personal communication).
69. See Emery, op. cit. (n. 3), p. 129 and Trigger, op. cit. (n. 4), pp. 80–81.
70. See Simpson, *Heka-Nefer and the Dynastic Material from Toskha and Arminna*, Publications of the Pennsylvania–Yale Expedition to Egypt, No. 1 (1963), pp. 49–50. See also Engelbach in *Annales du Service des Antiquités de l'Égypte*, Vol. XXXVIII (1938), pp. 369–90 and Murray in *Geographical Journal*, Vol. 94 (1939), pp. 97–114.
71. For discussion of this very important text and its possible meanings see Budge, *The Egyptian Sudan* (London, 1907), Vol. I, pp. 519–26; Säve-Söderbergh, op. cit. (n. 54), pp. 11–30; Edel, Inschriften des Alten Reiches, V (*Ägyptologische Studien* Ed. Otto Firchow, 1955); Kadish in *Journal of Egyptian Archaeology*, Vol. 52 (1966), pp. 22–33; and Dixon in *Journal of Egyptian Archaeology*, Vol. 44 (1958), pp. 40–55.

CHAPTER 6

Principal sources: for cultural descriptions I have relied, as usual, chiefly on Arkell, *A History of the Sudan*, 2nd ed. (London, 1961), pp. 46–54; Emery, *Egypt in Nubia* (London, 1965), pp. 133–71; and Trigger, *History and Settlement in Lower Nubia*, Yale University Publications in Anthropology, No. 69 (1965), pp. 84–99. For discussion of chronological problems I am particularly indebted to Manfred Bietak, *Studien zur Chronologie der Nubischen C-Gruppe*, Österreichische Akademie der Wissenschaften, Philosophisch-Historische Klasse Denkschriften, 97 Band (1968) and to David O'Connor's unpublished doctoral thesis, *Nubian Archaeological Material of the First to the Second Intermediate Periods: an Analytical Study* (Cambridge University, 1969).

1. *Archaeological Survey of Nubia, Report for 1907–1908* (Cairo, 1910), Vol. I, p. 335.
2. cf. Arkell, *A History of the Sudan*, 2nd ed. (London, 1961), p. 46.
3. See, for example, Bates, *The Eastern Libyans* (London, 1914); Emery and Kirwan, *The Excavations and Survey between Wadi es-Sebua and Adindan* (Cairo, 1935), Vol. 1, p. 4; Arkell, op. cit. (n. 2), pp. 49–50; and Bietak, *Ausgrabungen in Sayala-Nubian 1961–1965*, Osterreichische Akademie der Wissenschaften, Philosophisch-Historische Klasse Denkschriften, 92 Band (1966), pp. 38–42.
4. Fairservis, *The Ancient Kingdoms of the Nile* (New York, 1962), pp. 100–102.
5. cf. Nordström in *Kush* XIV (1966), pp. 63–8.
6. cf. Trigger, *History and Settlement in Lower Nubia*, Yale University Publications in Anthropology, No. 69 (1965), p. 87.
7. ibid.
8. For extended discussion of the texts of Uni and Harkhuf and their implications for the study of Nubian history see especially Säve-Söderbergh, *Ägypten und Nubien* (Lund, 1941), pp. 11–30; Yoyotte in *Bulletin de l'Institut Français d'Archéologie Orientale*, Vol. LII (1953), pp. 173–8; Edel in Firchow, Ed., *Ägyptologische Studien*,

Institut für Orientforschung, Veroffentlichung No. 29 (1955), pp. 51–75; Kadish in *Journal of Egyptian Archaeology*, Vol. 52 (1966), pp. 22–33; Edel in *Orientalia*, Vol. 36 (1967), pp. 133–58; Bietak, *Studien zur Chronologie der Nubischen C-Gruppe*, Österreichische Akademie der Wissenschaften, Philosophisch-Historische Klasse Denkschriften, 97 Band (1968), pp. 144–8; and O'Connor, *Nubian Archaeological Material of the First to the Second Intermediate Periods: an Analytical Study* (unpublished doctoral dissertation, Cambridge University, 1969), pp. 207–11.

9. It seems fairly well established that most, but not necessarily all, of the lands visited by Uni and Harkhuf were in Lower Nubia. For discussion of their probable locations see Säve-Söderbergh, loc. cit. (n. 8); Edel in *Orientalia*, Vol. 36 (1967), pp. 133–58; and Dixon in *Journal of Egyptian Archaeology*, Vol. 44 (1958), pp. 40–55.

10. Trigger, op. cit. (n. 6), p. 81.

11. See n. 1.

12. Trigger, op. cit. (n. 6), p. 79.

13. cf. Emery, *Egypt in Nubia* (London, 1965), pp. 112–14, 129.

14. For studies of the internal chronology of the C Horizon see Firth, *Archaeological Survey of Nubia, Report for 1909–1910* (Cairo, 1915), pp. 13–20; Steindorff, *Aniba* I (Cairo and Glückstadt, 1935), pp. 5–10; Trigger, op. cit. (n. 6), pp. 90–106; Bietak, op. cit. (n. 8), and O'Connor, op. cit. (n. 8).

15. Trigger, op. cit. (n. 6), pp. 97–8.

16. Säve-Söderbergh in *Kush* XI (1963), p. 58.

17. Sauneron in *Bulletin de l'Institut Français d'Archéologie Orientale*, Vol. LXIII (1965), pp. 161–7.

18. Randall-MacIver and Woolley, *Areika*, University of Pennsylvania Museum, Eckley B. Coxe Junior Expedition to Nubia, Vol. I (1909), pp. 1–18.

19. Säve-Söderbergh, op. cit. (n. 8), pp. 130–32; Sauneron, op. cit. (n. 17), p. 165.

20. Säve-Söderbergh, loc. cit. (n. 16).

21. Trigger, op. cit. (n. 6), pp. 97–8.

22. cf. Steindorff, op. cit. (n. 14), pls. 56, 57, 65.

23. Trigger, op. cit. (n. 6), p. 97.

24. Emery, op. cit. (n. 13), p. 137.

25. Evans-Pritchard, *The Nuer* (Oxford, 1940), p. 16.

26. cf. McBurney, *The Stone Age of Northern Africa* (Harmondsworth, 1960), p. 243; Butzer, *Environment and Archaeology* (Chicago, 1964), pp. 449–53.

27. Personal communication from Roy L. Carlson.

28. cf. Evans-Pritchard, *Social Anthropology and Other Essays* (Glencoe, Ill., 1964), p. 193.

29. cf. Arkell, op. cit. (n. 2), pp. 48–9.

30. cf. n. 24.

31. For studies of the chronological evolution of the 'C-Group' grave see Steindorff, loc. cit. (n. 14); Emery, op. cit. (n. 13), pp. 135–68; Trigger, op. cit. (n. 6), pp. 90–106; Bietak, loc. cit. (n. 8); and O'Connor, op. cit. (n. 8), pp. 102–42.

32. Cattle skulls are found most frequently in association with 'pan-graves', which, though similar in type to the graves of the C Horizon, are apparently the work of alien intruders into Lower Nubia during the Second Intermediate Period (see Ch. 8). However, some undoubted C Horizon graves are also accompanied by cattle skulls.

33. For examples of these see especially Steindorff, op. cit. (n. 14), pls. 8–14.

34. cf. O'Connor, op. cit. (n. 8), pp. 219–20.

35. Emery, op. cit. (n. 13), p. 137.

36. For a paraphrase of the text see Budge, *The Egyptian Sudan* (London, 1907), Vol. I, pp. 518–19.

37. ibid., p. 520.
38. ibid., pp. 521–2.
39. Gardiner, *Egypt of the Pharaohs* (New York, 1966), p. 99.
40. See n. 9.
41. Trigger, op. cit. (n. 6), p. 160.
42. cf. Service, *Profiles in Ethnology* (New York, 1963), pp. xxiv–xxix.
43. For discussion of segmentary lineage systems see especially ibid., pp. xxi–xxiv; Middleton and Tait, Eds., *Tribes without Rulers* (London, 1958), pp. 1–31; and Ottenberg, *Cultures and Societies of Africa* (New York, 1960), pp. 51–2.
44. This suggestive term was coined by Meyer Fortes; cf. *The Web of Kinship among the Tallensi* (London, 1949).
45. See Middleton and Tait, op. cit. (n. 43), pp. 16–18.
46. Evans-Pritchard, op. cit. (n. 28), pp. 193–4.
47. ibid., p. 203.
48. Emery, op. cit. (n. 13), p. 139.
49. Fischer in *Kush* IX (1961), pp. 44–80.
50. For this part of the text see Budge, op. cit. (n. 36), pp. 520–22.
51. e.g. Arkell, op. cit. (n. 2), p. 60; Säve-Söderbergh, op. cit. (n. 8), pp. 83–7.
52. For detailed accounts see Säve-Söderbergh, op. cit. (n. 8), pp. 54–80.
53. cf. O'Connor, op. cit. (n. 8), pp. 216–17.

CHAPTER 7

Principal sources: for description of the archaeological remains of Egyptian activity in Nubia I have relied very heavily on Emery, *Egypt in Nubia* (London, 1965), especially pp. 101–14 and pp. 141–58. For historical texts and for interpretation of the archaeological remains my principal source has been Säve-Söderbergh, *Ägypten und Nubien* (Lund, 1941), pp. 63–116. My picture of Middle Kingdom Egypt is drawn primarily from John Wilson, *The Culture of Ancient Egypt* (Chicago, 1951), pp. 125–53. A newly published source is Trigger, *Nubia under the Pharaohs* (London, 1976), pp. 40–81.

1. For discussion of the cultures of Predynastic Egypt see especially Hayes, *Most Ancient Egypt* (Chicago, 1964), and Baumgartel, Predynastic Egypt, *Cambridge Ancient History*, Revised Edition of Volumes I and II, Fascicle 38 (1965).
2. Egyptian traditional history held that the country was first unified by a certain King Menes; see especially Emery, *Archaic Egypt* (Harmondsworth, 1961), pp. 21–37. For a discussion of what was more probably the actual course of events see especially Kaiser in *Zeitschrift für Ägyptische Sprache und Altertumskunde*, Vol. 81 (1956), pp. 87–109.
3. cf. Wilson *et al.* in Kraeling and Adams, Eds., *City Invincible* (Chicago, 1960), pp. 124–64.
4. cf. Trigger, *History and Settlement in Lower Nubia*, Yale University Publications in Anthropology, No. 69 (1965), p. 79.
5. *A Study of History*, Vol. 5 (New York, 1962), pp. 194–337.
6. Bruce Trigger (personal communication) suggests that the Old Kingdom pharaohs, beginning with Sneferu, may have pursued a deliberate policy of driving out or enslaving the native inhabitants of Lower Nubia in order to undertake their mining ventures in safety, but the evidence on this point is inconclusive. In many ways it would seem that the absence of a native population – both as a market for Egyptian goods and as a source of labour – would be more loss than gain to the Egyptians.

7. *Egypt of the Pharaohs* (New York, 1966), p. 100.

8. *Bulletin of the (Boston) Museum of Fine Arts*, Vol. XXVII (1929), p. 66.

9. See 'The textual record', Ch. 5.

10. For the appropriate texts see Breasted, *Ancient Records of Egypt* (New York, 1962), Vol. I, pp. 161–7, 204, 296; Vol. II, pp. 5, 27–35, 50, 327–9, 334–6; Vol. III, pp. 196–8; Vol. IV, pp. 80–81, 357–8. For discussion see especially Säve-Söderbergh, *Ägypten und Nubien* (Lund, 1941), pp. 7–10, 57–79, 141–75.

11. Trigger, op. cit. (n. 4), p. 160.

12. For further discussion see especially Säve-Söderbergh, op. cit. (n. 10), pp. 230–34.

13. See especially ibid., pp. 210–13, and Vercoutter in *Kush* VII (1959), pp. 133–53.

14. cf. Emery, *Egypt in Nubia* (London, 1965), p. 129; Hintze in *Kush* XIII (1965), pp. 13–14; Piotrovsky in *Fouilles en Nubie (1961–1963)* (Cairo, 1967), pp. 134–40; Simpson, *Heka-Nefer and the Dynastic Material from Toshka and Arminna*, Publications of the Pennsylvania–Yale Expedition to Egypt, No. 1 (1963), pp. 50–53.

15. cf. Wilson, *The Culture of Ancient Egypt* (Chicago, 1951), pp. 143–4, 215–18.

16. Kees, *Ancient Egypt* (Chicago, 1961), pp. 313–14. For more on the quarries see Engelbach in *Annales du Service des Antiquités de l'Égypte*, Vol. XXXIII (1933), pp. 65–74 and Vol. XXXVIII (1938), pp. 369–90; Little in *Annales du Service des Antiquités de l'Égypte*, Vol. XXXIII (1933), pp. 75–80; Murray in *Geographical Journal*, Vol. 94 (1939), pp. 97–114; and Rowe in *Annales du Service des Antiquités de l'Égypte*, Vol. XXXVIII (1938), pp. 391–6, 678–88.

17. See Simpson, op. cit. (n. 14), pp. 48–50.

18. Emery, op. cit. (n. 14), pp. 112–13.

19. Emery in *Kush* XI (1963), pp. 116–17.

20. cf. Adams in *Kush* IX (1961), pp. 33–8, and in *Kush* X (1962), pp. 62–75. It has in fact been suggested that the structures at Buhen are more probably pottery kilns than metal furnaces (Shinnie, personal communication).

21. This was evidently the excavator's impression, and is not demonstrated by actual sherd counts. According to David O'Connor (personal communication), who is studying the Buhen pottery for publication, the so-called 'B-Group' sherds from the Old Kingdom town represent a pretty typical sample of 'A-Group' types, but without the decorated 'variegated hematitic ware' (cf. Ch. 5).

22. Emery, op. cit. (n. 19), p. 120.

23. Firth, *Archaeological Survey of Nubia, Report for 1908–1909* (Cairo, 1912), Vol. I, p. 24; Lucas, *Ancient Egyptian Materials and Industries*, 3rd ed. (London, 1948), pp. 236, 239. David O'Connor believes that the original settlement at Kubban was founded during the Old Kingdom, presumably for the sake of the copper and gold deposits in the Wadi Allaqi; see *Nubian Archaeological Material of the First to the Second Intermediate Periods: an Analytical Study* (unpublished doctoral dissertation, Cambridge University, 1969), p. 207.

24. Hintze, loc. cit. (n. 14).

25. Piotrovsky, op. cit. (n. 14), pp. 134–5.

26. cf. Emery, op. cit. (n. 14), p. 114; Rowe, loc. cit. (n. 16).

27. For discussion of these see Vandier, *La Famine dans l'Égypte Ancienne* (Cairo, 1936), and Bell in *American Journal of Archaeology*, Vol. 75 (1971), pp. 1–26.

28. See Wilson, op. cit. (n. 15), p. 112.

29. See Fischer in *Kush* IX (1961), pp. 44–80.

30. cf. Wilson, op. cit. (n. 15), p. 126.

31. For discussion see Säve-Söderbergh, op. cit. (n. 10), pp. 57–61.

32. Emery, op. cit. (n. 14), pp. 141–2.

33. All but two of the Second Cataract Forts were excavated in the early part of the twentieth century by the Boston Museum of Fine Arts. For resumés of this work

see Dunham in *Kush* III (1955), pp. 70–74 and Reisner in *Kush* VIII (1960), pp. 11–24. For definitive reports see Dunham and Janssen, *Semna Kumma*, Second Cataract Forts, Vol. I (Boston, 1960) and Dunham, *Uronarti Shalfak Mirgissa*, Second Cataract Forts, Vol. II (Boston, 1967).

34. cf. Säve-Söderbergh, op. cit. (n. 10), pp. 84–5; Smith in *Kush* XIV (1966), pp. 228–9; Vercoutter, *Mirgissa* I (Paris, 1970), pp. 20–22.

35. Emery, op. cit. (n. 14), pp. 148–9.

36. ibid., p. 143.

37. For the Ramesseum list see especially Gardiner in *Journal of Egyptian Archaeology*, Vol. III (1916), pp. 184–92, and Borchardt, *Altägyptische Festungen an der Zweiten Nilschnelle*, Leipzig, Veröffentlichungen der Ernst von Sieglin-Expedition, No. 3 (1923).

38. This name, which is incomplete in the Ramesseum list, came to light in the course of recent excavations at Semna South, the southernmost of all the Egyptian forts. See Zabkar in *Journal of Egyptian Archaeology*, Vol. 58 (1972), pp. 83–91.

39. For identification by name of the various Second Cataract Forts see especially Säve-Söderbergh, op. cit. (n. 10), pp. 80–98; Vercoutter in *Kush* XIII (1965), p. 66; Knudstad in *Kush* XIV (1966), pp. 174–6; and Smith, op. cit. (n. 34), p. 230.

40. See Emery, op. cit. (n. 14), pp. 148–9.

41. See Randall-MacIver and Woolley, *Buhen*, University of Pennsylvania Museum, Eckley B. Coxe Junior Expedition to Nubia, Vols. VII–VIII (1911).

42. The definitive report on these excavations will probably be delayed by the untimely death of Prof. Emery in March 1971. Preliminary reports will be found in *Kush* VII (1959), pp. 7–14; VIII (1960), pp. 7–10; IX (1961), pp. 81–6; X (1962), pp. 106–8; XI (1963), pp. 116–20; XII (1964), pp. 43–6; and in *Journal of Egyptian Archaeology*, Vol. 44 (1958), pp. vii–viii; 45 (1959), pp. 1–2; 47 (1961), pp. 1–3; 48 (1962), pp. 1–3; 49 (1963), pp. 2–3.

43. Emery, op. cit. (n. 14), p. 149.

44. For brief popular descriptions and plans of most of the Second Cataract Forts see ibid., pp. 143–9. For a more detailed consideration of the principles of Egyptian military architecture as exemplified in the forts see Lawrence in *Journal of Egyptian Archaeology*, Vol. 51 (1965), pp. 69–94. See also Kemp in Ucko, Tringham and Dimbleby, Eds., *Man, Settlement and Urbanism* (London, 1972), pp. 651–6.

45. Emery's description of Buhen as the largest of the Second Cataract Forts (op. cit., n. 14, p. 148) was written before the full extent of the Mirgissa fortress had been revealed by excavation.

46. For preliminary accounts of the excavations at Mirgissa see Wheeler in *Kush* IX (1961), pp. 87–179, and articles by Vercoutter in *Kush* XII (1964), pp. 57–62; *Kush* XIII (1965), pp. 62–73; *Bulletin de la Société Française d'Égyptologie*, No. 37–8 (1963), pp. 23–30; No. 40 (1964), pp. 4–12; No. 43 (1965), pp. 7–13; No. 49 (1967), pp. 5–11; No. 52 (1968), pp. 7–14; *Revue d'Égyptologie*, Vol. 15 (1963), pp. 69–75; and Vol. 16 (1964), pp. 179–91. The first of several projected definitive reports is Vercoutter, op. cit. (n. 34).

47. For a report see Ruby in *Kush* XII (1964), pp. 54–6.

48. See Badawy in *Kush* XII (1964), pp. 47–53, in *Archaeology*, Vol. 18 (1965), pp. 124–31, and in *Journal of the American Research Center in Egypt*, Vol. V (1966), pp. 23–7.

49. See Dunham, *Uronarti Shalfak Mirgissa*, Second Cataract Forts, Vol. II (Boston, 1967), pp. 115–40.

50. For the definitive report on these two fortresses see Dunham and Janssen, op. cit. (n. 33).

51. For a report on trial excavations at this site see Vercoutter in *Kush* XIV (1966),

pp. 125–34. More extensive excavations by the Oriental Institute of Chicago have not yet been reported.

52. For the definitive report see Dunham, op. cit. (n. 49), pp. 3–114.

53. For brief popular descriptions and plans see Emery, op. cit. (n. 14), pp. 150–52.

54. For the excavation report on this fortress see Emery and Kirwan, *The Excavations and Survey between Wadi es-Sebua and Adindan* (Cairo, 1935), Vol. I, pp. 26–44.

55. cf. Emery op. cit. (n. 14), pp. 107–10.

56. See Vercoutter in *Bulletin de la Société Française d'Égyptologie*, No. 43 (1965), pp. 10–11 and especially Vila in *Revue d'Égyptologie*, Vol. 22 (1970), pp. 171–99.

57. op. cit. (n. 14), p. 153.

58. ibid.

59. Säve-Söderbergh, personal communication.

60. Reisner, op. cit. (n. 8), p. 68.

61. Emery, op. cit. (n. 14), p. 153.

62. For further discussion on this subject see Vila, op. cit. (n. 56), pp. 198–9.

63. Emery, op. cit. (n. 14), p. 175.

64. cf. Reisner in *Kush* III (1955), pp. 26–69.

65. See Adams and Nordström in *Kush* XI (1963), p. 23.

66. See Hintze in *Kush* XII (1964), pp. 40–41.

67. Emery, op. cit. (n. 14), p. 149.

68. As suggested by Arkell; see *A History of the Sudan*, 2nd ed. (London, 1961), p. 60.

69. Both Säve-Söderbergh (op. cit., n. 10, pp. 89–91) and Vercoutter (op. cit., n. 34, pp. 171–3) strongly disagree with this view, believing that the Second Cataract Forts played an important role in defending Egypt's southern frontier as well as in the protection of riverain commerce.

70. A suggestion already put forward by Reisner in *Sudan Notes and Records*, Vol. XII (1929), pp. 150–51, and Säve-Söderbergh, op. cit. (n. 10), p. 91.

71. Not yet fully reported in print; for preliminary reports see Vercoutter, op. cit. (n. 39), pp. 67–8 and in *Académie des Inscriptions et Belles-Lettres, Comptes Rendus des Séances de l'Année 1966*, pp. 278–9.

72. The main dock and warehouse area for Buhen seems to have been at Kor, three miles further south. For a report of excavations here see Smith, op. cit. (n. 34).

73. See Vercoutter, op. cit. (n. 39), pp. 68–9 and Vila in Vercoutter, op. cit. (n. 34) pp. 204–14.

74. It has usually been assumed from the context that Heh is another name for Semna; cf. Breasted, op. cit. (n. 10), Vol. I, p. 294; Wilson, op. cit. (n. 15), p. 137; and Emery, op. cit. (n. 14), p. 157. However this interpretation is disputed by Vercoutter, who would place Heh somewhere between Mirgissa and Buhen. See *Revue d'Égyptologie*, Vol. 16 (1964), pp. 187–8.

75. Quoted from Emery, op. cit. (n. 14), p. 157.

76. A much more truculent 'boundary stele' was erected by Senusret a few years later; for the translation see ibid., pp. 157–8.

77. cf. *Principles of Political Economy*, 5th ed. (New York, 1923), Vol. I, pp. 258–9.

78. See Smither in *Journal of Egyptian Archaeology*, Vol. XXXI (1945), pp. 3–10.

79. Trigger, op. cit. (n. 4), p. 95.

80. For discussion on this point see, among other sources, Säve-Söderbergh, op. cit. (n. 10), pp. 14–20; Dixon in *Journal of Egyptian Archaeology*, Vol. 44 (1958), pp. 40–55; and Edel in *Orientalia*, Vol. 36 (1967), pp. 133–58.

81. This has been disputed by Hintze; see *Zeitschrift für Ägyptische Sprache und Altertumskunde*, Vol. 91 (1964), pp. 79–86. Priese however has demonstrated a possible linguistic connection between the ancient name 'Yam' and the modern

name 'Kerma'; see *Altorientalische Forschungen*, Vol. I (in press). A much fuller discussion of the Kerma problem will be found in the next chapter.

32. Reisner considered that the nomads of the western desert constituted the most formidable threat to Egypt's riverain commerce; see op. cit. (n. 70), p. 146.

33. See Ch. 6.

34. For discussion see Säve-Söderbergh, op. cit. (n. 10), pp. 83–5. For the excavator's full report see Steindorff, *Aniba* II (Cairo and Glückstadt, 1937), pp. 6–16.

35. For discussion see Säve-Söderbergh, op. cit. (n. 10), pp. 85–9; for the excavator's report see Emery and Kirwan, loc. cit. (n. 54).

36. See Griffith in *University of Liverpool Annals of Archaeology and Anthropology*, Vol. VIII (1921), pp. 80–82 and pl. XVI.

37. See especially Knudstad, op. cit. (n. 39), pp. 172–8.

38. Säve-Söderbergh believes that the forts of Faras and Serra were intended for the administration of the Nubian population because he can see no other obvious reason for their existence (op. cit., n. 10, p. 85), but this is not supported by solid archaeological evidence. There is a sizeable 'C-Group' cemetery close to Faras and a much smaller one in the vicinity of Serra, but in each case much larger concentrations of population were located a few miles to the south.

39. cf. especially Lawrence, op. cit. (n. 44).

40. For this interpretation I am indebted chiefly to John Wilson; see especially op. cit. (n. 15), pp. 141–4. Many Egyptologists take a quite different view of the Middle Kingdom.

41. See Engelbach, op. cit. (n. 16), and Rowe, op. cit. (n. 16).

42. Little, op. cit. (n. 16); Murray, op. cit. (n. 16).

43. Simpson, op. cit. (n. 14), pp. 50–53. It has been suggested that the figures may represent man-hours of labour rather than numbers of men and animals (Trigger, personal communication).

44. Rowe in *Annales du Service des Antiquités de l'Égypte*, Vol. XXXIX (1939), pp. 188–91; Lucas, op. cit. (n. 23), pp. 240–41.

45. Lucas, op. cit. (n. 23), p. 239.

46. ibid., p. 236.

47. cf. Černy in *Journal of Egyptian Archaeology*, Vol. 33 (1947), p. 56; Piotrovsky, op. cit. (n. 14), p. 135.

48. See Gunn in *Annales du Service des Antiquités de l'Égypte*, Vol. XXIX (1929), p. 11.

49. cf. Säve-Söderbergh, op. cit. (n. 10), pp. 86–9.

50. See Vercoutter in *Kush* VII (1959), pp. 133–4.

51. See Chittick in *Kush* V (1957), pp. 47–8. The gold mines at Duweishat were much more fully investigated by the Sudan Antiquities Service in 1966, but no report on this work has yet appeared.

52. Quoted from Gardiner, op. cit. (n. 7), p. 166. 'Egypt' in this context must refer to all the territory which the Pharaoh considered legitimately his, presumably including Lower Nubia. There is no suggestion that Nubians ruled any part of Egypt proper during the Second Intermediate Period.

53. cf. Säve-Söderbergh, op. cit. (n. 10), pp. 128–9; Säve-Söderbergh in *Kush* IV (1956), pp. 59–60.

54. See n. 78.

55. cf. Säve-Söderbergh, op. cit. (n. 10), pp. 126–8.

56. See especially Emery, op. cit. (n. 14), pp. 102, 167.

57. See Adams in *Antiquity*, Vol. XLII (1968), pp. 207–8.

58. For the evidence of burning at Semna see Dunham and Janssen, op. cit. (n. 33), p. 6.

59. Säve-Söderbergh does not believe that the garrisons were withdrawn, but rather

that they gradually succumbed after they were cut off from support from Egypt
See op. cit. (n. 10), pp. 126–7.
110. cf. Knudstad, op. cit. (n. 39), p. 183. The excavator believes that Dorginarti fortress
was built and occupied entirely in the New Kingdom (ibid., p. 186), but I consider
that its architectural peculiarities together with the evidence just cited suggest that
it was originally built in the Middle Kingdom, and largely reconstructed (after an
interval of Nubian squatter occupation) in the New Kingdom.
111. See Badawy in *Journal of the American Research Center in Egypt*, Vol. V (1966),
pp. 23–4.
112. Säve-Söderbergh in *Journal of Egyptian Archaeology*, Vol. 35 (1949), pp. 50–58,
Barns in *Kush* II (1954), pp. 19–22.
113. Säve-Söderbergh, op. cit. (n. 112), p. 55.
114. cf. ibid., pp. 52, 56.

CHAPTER 8

Principal sources: the basic descriptive work on Kerma remains the two-volume
'Excavations at Kerma', *Harvard African Studies*, Vols. V–VI (1923), of George
A. Reisner. An important descriptive synthesis which has recently come to hand
is Mubarak al-Rayah, *The Problems of Kerma Culture of Ancient Sudan Recon
sidered in the Light of Ancient Sudan Civilization as a Continuous Process* (un
published doctoral dissertation, Humboldt-Universität zu Berlin). For considera
tion of the historical significance of Kerma I have also relied on Säve-Söderbergh
Ägypten und Nubien (Lund, 1941), pp. 103–16; Bietak, *Studien zur Chronologie
der Nubischen C-Gruppe*, Österreichische Akademie der Wissenschaften, Philoso
phisch-Historische Klasse Denkschriften, 97 (1968), pp. 117–26; and O'Connor
*Nubian Archaeological Material of the First to the Second Intermediate Periods.
an Analytical Study* (unpublished doctoral dissertation, Cambridge University,
1969).

1. Priese now believes that he has demonstrated a linguistic connection between the
modern name 'Kerma' and the ancient name 'Yam'; see *Altorientalische Forschungen*, Vol. I (in press).
2. Reisner, 'Excavations at Kerma', IV, *Harvard African Studies*, Vol. VI (1923),
pp. 323–5.
3. ibid., pp. 329–30; Vercoutter in *Mélanges offerts à Kazimierz Michalowski* (Warsaw, 1966), pp. 209–10.
4. See O'Connor, *Nubian Archaeological Material of the First to the Second Intermediate Periods: an Analytical Study* (unpublished doctoral dissertation, Cambridge University, 1969), p. 139.
5. 'Excavations at Kerma', III, *Harvard African Studies*, Vol. V (1923), p. 71.
6. cf. Junker, *Bericht über die Grabungen der Akademie der Wissenschaften in Wien
auf den Friedhöfen von El-Kubanieh-Nord, Winter 1910–1911*, Akademie der Wissenschaften in Wien, Philosophisch-Historische Klasse Denkschriften, 64, Band 3
(1920), p. 29.
7. 'Excavations at Kerma', *Harvard African Studies*, Vols. V and VI (1923).
8. cf. Säve-Söderbergh, *Ägypten und Nubien* (Lund, 1941), p. 103.
9. Reisner, op. cit. (n. 5), p. 32.
10. ibid., p. 39.
11. This is essentially the position of Säve-Söderbergh (op. cit., n. 8, pp. 103–16).
Hintze however believes that Kerma was primarily a Nubian royal residence rather

than a trade depot; see *Zeitschrift für Ägyptische Sprache und Altertumskunde*, Vol. 91 (1964), pp. 82–5.

12. cf. Reisner, op. cit. (n. 5), pp. 24–5; Säve-Söderbergh, op. cit. (n. 8), pp. 115–16; Arkell, *A History of the Sudan*, 2nd ed. (London, 1961), p. 68.

13. See Trigger, *History and Settlement in Lower Nubia*, Yale University Publications in Anthropology, No. 69 (1965), p. 95.

14. This function has already been suggested by Säve-Söderbergh, op. cit. (n. 8), p. 105.

15. Reisner, op. cit. (n. 5), pp. 61–528.

16. ibid., p. 65.

17. ibid., p. 69.

18. ibid., p. 66.

19. In Tumulus X; see ibid., p. 81.

20. ibid., p. 79.

21. This is contrary to Reisner's supposition (ibid., pp. 116–17), but appears more logical on *a priori* grounds.

22. ibid., p. 265.

23. Säve-Söderbergh points out that Reisner originally regarded the Kerma people as Nubians (see *Bulletin of the Museum of Fine Arts*, Vol. XIII, 1915, pp. 29–36, 71–83) and only later adopted the theory of their Egyptian identity. For the fullest expression of the latter view see Reisner, op. cit. (n. 2), pp. 554–9.

24. Junker, op. cit. (n. 6); Junker, *Die Nubische Ursprung der sogennanten Tell el-Jahudiye-Vasen*, Akademie der Wissenschaften in Wien, Philosophisch-Historische Klasse Sitzungsberichte, 198, Part 3 (1921); Säve-Söderbergh, op. cit. (n. 8), pp. 111–13.

25. More than one hundred whole and fragmentary statues and statuettes were found among the 'royal' tombs at Kerma; see Reisner, op. cit. (n. 2), pp. 554–9.

26. For the latest on the Kerma controversy see Hintze, op. cit. (n. 11); al-Rayah, *The Problems of Kerma Culture of Ancient Sudan Reconsidered in the Light of Ancient Sudan Civilization as a Continuous Process* (unpublished doctoral dissertation, Humboldt-Universität zu Berlin); and Adams in *Ägypten und Kusch*, Schriften zur Geschichte und Kultur des Alten Orients, Zentralinstituts für Alte Geschichte und Archaologie der Akademie der Wissenschaften der DDR, Vol. 13 (1976), pp. 38–48.

27. See n. 2.

28. See n. 24; also Hintze, loc. cit. (n. 11).

29. Extraordinarily straight walls and right-angle corners are diagnostic features of pharaonic architecture in Nubia; they are conspicuously lacking in indigenous Nubian brick construction.

30. Trigger, op. cit. (n. 13), p. 103. These ideas were originally expressed by Junker in *Studies Presented to F. Ll. Griffith* (London, 1932), pp. 297–303.

31. Hintze (loc. cit., n. 11) goes even further, denying the existence of any Egyptian commercial enterprise at Kerma. In his view the only Egyptians who might have been resident at Kerma would have been artisans in the service of the Nubian ruler.

32. Reisner, op. cit. (n. 5), p. 126.

33. This possibility was first suggested by Säve-Söderbergh, op. cit. (n. 8), p. 115, and more forcibly by Hintze, op. cit. (n. 11), p. 84. O'Connor (op. cit., n. 4, p. 79) believes that the repairs described in the Intef stele may have been carried out at the Egyptian frontier fortress of Elephantine (Aswan).

34. Reisner's very detailed reconstruction of the sequence of development of the great tumuli (op. cit., n. 5, pp. 116–21) is open to challenge on a number of grounds which cannot be elaborated here. See Adams, op. cit. (n. 26), pp. 45–7.

35. Reisner, op. cit. (n. 2), p. 86.

36. This idea has previously been advanced by Säve-Söderbergh, op. cit. (n. 8), pp. 110–16 and in *Kush* IV (1956), pp. 59–61, and by Hintze, loc. cit. (n. 11).

37. In his report he consistently referred to the southern part of the cemetery as the 'Egyptian' cemetery and to the northern part as the 'Nubian' cemetery, while acknowledging that no clearcut dividing line could be drawn. Reisner, op. cit. (n. 5), pp. 61–121.

38. cf. Posener in *Kush* VI (1958), p. 55.

39. See Mills and Nordström in *Kush* XIV (1966), pp. 8–10.

40. Discovered by the Sudan Antiquities Service between 1966 and 1969, these sites have not yet been reported in print.

41. Posener, op. cit. (n. 38), pp. 39–68; Hintze, op. cit. (n. 11), pp. 83–5.

42. See Gratien in Vercoutter *et al.*, *Études sur l'Égypte et le Soudan Anciens*, Cahier de Recherches de l'Institut de Papyrologie et d'Égyptologie de Lille (1973), pp. 143–84. For an earlier preliminary report see Vercoutter in *Kush* VI (1958), pp. 148–51.

43. I had the opportunity to examine much of the material from Ukma in the field in 1969.

44. Personal communication from André Vila.

45. Mills and Nordström, op. cit. (n. 39), pp. 10–11.

46. Säve-Söderbergh in *Kush* XV (1973), pp. 230–31.

47. Vercoutter, op. cit. (n. 3); Vila in Vercoutter, *Mirgissa* I (Paris, 1970), pp. 223–305.

48. Adams and Nordström in *Kush* XI (1963), pp. 19–21.

49. Randall-MacIver and Woolley, *Buhen*, University of Pennsylvania Museum, Eckley B. Coxe Junior Expedition to Nubia, Vols. VII–VIII (1911), pp. 133–5 and pls. 49–52.

50. Steindorff, *Aniba* I (Cairo and Glückstadt, 1935), pp. 196–201.

51. Firth, *Archaeological Survey of Nubia, Report for 1910–1911* (Cairo, 1927), pp. 50–98, 128–9.

52. See n. 47 for references.

53. See n. 48 for reference.

54. See Säve-Söderbergh in *Journal of Egyptian Archaeology*, Vol. 35 (1949), p. 55.

55. cf. especially Säve-Söderbergh in *Kush* IV (1956), pp. 54–61.

56. Gardiner, *Egypt of the Pharaohs* (New York, 1966), p. 166. See Ch. 7, n. 102.

57. For a list of the sites where pan-graves have been found in Egypt proper see Säve-Söderbergh, op. cit. (n. 8), pp. 136–7.

58. For pan-graves in Lower Nubia see Bietak, *Studien zur Chronologie der Nubischen C-Gruppe*, Österreichische Akademie der Wissenschaften, Philosophisch-Historische Klasse Denkschriften, 97 (1968), pp. 117–23, 179.

59. Junker, op. cit. (n. 6), p. 33; Emery and Kirwan, *Excavations and Survey between Wadi es-Sebua and Adindan* (Cairo, 1935), Vol. I, p. 5; Kirwan in *Journal of Egyptian Archaeology*, Vol. XXV (1939), pp. 107–9; Emery, *Egypt in Nubia* (London, 1965), p. 135.

60. See Wainwright, *Balabish*, Egypt Exploration Society, Excavation Memoir 37 (1920), pp. 42–52; Säve-Söderbergh, op. cit. (n. 8), pp. 138–40; Bietak, loc. cit. (n. 58); O'Connor, op. cit. (n. 4), pp. 37–42.

61. Säve-Söderbergh, op. cit. (n. 8), p. 139.

62. O'Connor, op. cit. (n. 4), pp. 28–9.

63. See especially Polanyi, *Dahomey and the Slave Trade* (Seattle, 1966).

CHAPTER 9

Principal sources: the most important single source for the period of New Kingdom rule in Nubia is still Säve-Söderbergh's *Ägypten und Nubien* (Lund, 1941), pp. 141–245. I have also relied, as in earlier chapters, on Arkell, *A History of the Sudan*, 2nd ed. (London, 1961), pp. 80–109; Emery, *Egypt in Nubia* (London, 1965), pp. 172–207; and Trigger, *History and Settlement in Lower Nubia*, Yale University Publications in Anthropology, No. 69 (1965), pp. 106–14. A recent publication is Trigger, *Nubia under the Pharaohs* (London, 1976).

1. Wilson, *The Culture of Ancient Egypt* (Chicago, 1951), Ch. VII. The origin of the Hyksos and the nature of their rule in Egypt has been and remains a source of controversy. For a review of the most generally accepted theory today see Säve-Söderbergh in *Journal of Egyptian Archaeology*, Vol. 37 (1951), pp. 53–71. For other views see Van Seters, *The Hyksos* (New Haven, 1966), and reviews by Uphill and Bourriau in *Journal of Near Eastern Studies*, Vol. 28 (1969), pp. 127–33.
2. Säve-Söderbergh, op. cit. (n. 1), p. 68. The author points out that this quotation is preserved not in an original text but in a folk-tale of later times which is strongly anti-Hyksos in tone. Contemporary texts do not indicate that the hostility between Egyptians and Hyksos was as great as later propaganda would suggest.
3. ibid., p. 71.
4. cf. Emery, *Egypt in Nubia* (London, 1965), p. 173.
5. See Arkell in *Journal of Egyptian Archaeology*, Vol. 36 (1950), pp. 36–9, and Arkell, *A History of the Sudan*, 2nd ed. (London, 1961), p. 89.
6. cf. Säve-Söderbergh, *Ägypten und Nubien* (Lund, 1941), pp. 155–75.
7. For discussion of the Egyptian temple-towns in Nubia see Kemp in Ucko, Tringham and Dimbleby, Eds., *Man, Settlement and Urbanism* (London, 1972), pp. 651–6, 666–7.
8. Personal communication from Ricardo Caminos.
9. Rameses was not the first Egyptian pharaoh to represent himself in this magniloquent fashion; he was anticipated (although hardly on the same scale) by Amenhotep III in the XVIII Dynasty.
10. Emery, op. cit. (n. 4), pp. 194–5.
11. Burckhardt, *Travels in Nubia* (London, 1819), pp. 90–91.
12. Emery, op. cit. (n. 4), pp. 198–9.
13. For a more detailed analysis of settlement distribution in Lower Nubia see Trigger, *History and Settlement in Lower Nubia*, Yale University Publications in Anthropology, No. 69 (1965), pp. 152–4.
14. For discussion of the relationship of temple and town in ancient Egypt and Nubia see Kemp, op. cit. (n. 7), pp. 657–76.
15. cf. Kees, *Ancient Egypt* (Chicago, 1961), p. 325. It seems probable however that Aniba was more usually the residence of the Deputy Viceroy for Lower Nubia; see Reisner in *Journal of Egyptian Archaeology*, Vol. VI (1920), pp. 84–5.
16. Reisner in *Bulletin of the (Boston) Museum of Fine Arts*, Vol. XXVII (1929), p. 74.
17. Hintze in *Kush* XIII (1965), p. 13.
18. Vercoutter in *Kush* VI (1958), p. 155. For an account of the New Kingdom remains at Sai see Vercoutter *et al.*, *Études sur l'Égypte et le Soudan Anciens*, Cahiers de Recherches de l'Institut de Papyrologie et d'Égyptologie de Lille (1973), pp. 9–38.
19. See Fairman in *Journal of Egyptian Archaeology*, Vol. XXIV (1938), p. 153; Schiff Giorgini in *Kush* IX (1961), pp. 183–5, 197.
20. cf. Fairman in *Journal of Egyptian Archaeology*, Vol. XXV (1939), p. 143.

21. These two sites have been under excavation for several years by an expedition from the University of Pisa. For preliminary reports see Schiff Giorgini in *Kush* IX (1961), pp. 182–209; *Kush* X (1962), pp. 152–69; *Kush* XII (1964), pp. 87–95; *Kush* XIII (1965), pp. 112–30; and *Kush* XIV (1966), pp. 244–61. Two definitive volumes on the Temple of Soleb have now also appeared: Schiff Giorgini, *Soleb* I (Florence, 1965), and *Soleb* II (Florence, 1972).

22. Fairman, op. cit. (n. 19), p. 153.

23. For more on the plans and features of these towns see Kemp, op. cit. (n. 7), pp. 651–6.

24. See Schiff Giorgini in *Kush* X (1962), pp. 152–61.

25. cf. Arkell, *A History of the Sudan*, 2nd ed. (London, 1961), pp. 91–3.

26. For preliminary reports see Fairman in *Journal of Egyptian Archaeology*, Vol. XXIV (1938), pp. 151–6; Vol. XXV (1939), pp. 139–44; Vol. 34 (1948), pp. 3–11; and Shinnie in *Journal of Egyptian Archaeology*, Vol. 37 (1951), pp. 5–11.

27. Fairman in *Journal of Egyptian Archaeology*, Vol. 34 (1948), p. 11.

28. Reisner in *Journal of Egyptian Archaeology*, Vol. V (1918), pp. 99–100 and in *Zeitschrift für Ägyptische Sprache und Altertumskunde*, Vol. 66 (1931), pp. 76–81.

29. Reisner in *Journal of Egyptian Archaeology*, Vol. IV (1917), pp. 215–27.

30. For definitive reports on the site of Kawa see Macadam, *The Temples of Kawa*, Vol. I (Oxford, 1949) and Vol. II (Oxford, 1955).

31. See Jacquet-Gordon *et al.* in *Journal of Egyptian Archaeology*, Vol. 55 (1969), p. 106 and pl. XXIII.

32. Thuwre may have been preceded in the viceregal office by his father Sa-tayit; see Habachi in *Kush* VII (1959), pp. 45–62.

33. For a comprehensive list and discussion of the Viceroys of Kush see Reisner in *Journal of Egyptian Archaeology*, Vol. VI (1920), pp. 28–55, 73–8.

34. Toynbee, *A Study of History*, Vol. 2 (New York, 1962), pp. 112–18.

35. Simpson interprets this passage to mean 'sandal-maker'; see *Heka-Nefer and the Dynastic Material from Toshka and Arminna*, Publications of the Pennsylvania–Yale Expedition to Egypt, No. 1 (1963), p. 5.

36. Arkell, op. cit. (n. 25), pp. 98–100. For fuller discussion of the viceregal administration see Reisner, op. cit. (n. 33), pp. 84–8 and Säve-Söderbergh, op. cit. (n. 6), pp. 177–84.

37. In the quotation from Arkell (n. 36).

38. See Davies and Gardiner, *The Tomb of Huy, Viceroy of Nubia in the Reign of Tutankhamen*, Egypt Exploration Fund, Theban Tomb Series, Memoir 4 (1926), p. 22.

39. Simpson, op. cit. (n. 35), pp. 2–18.

40. Säve-Söderbergh in *Kush* VIII (1960), pp. 25–44, and in *Kush* XI (1963), pp. 159–74.

41. Emery, op. cit. (n. 4), pp. 205–6. For the excavator's report on this tomb see Steindorff, *Aniba* II (Cairo and Glückstadt, 1937), pp. 242–7.

42. op. cit. (n. 13), pp. 111–12.

43. Säve-Söderbergh in *Kush* VIII (1960), pp. 38–44. For a fuller discussion of Nubian exports during the New Kingdom see Säve-Söderbergh, op. cit. (n. 6), pp. 206–30.

44. Säve-Söderbergh, op. cit. (n. 6), p. 200.

45. According to Säve-Söderbergh (personal communication) the introduction of the *shaduf* is not definitely attested even in Egypt before the later XVIII Dynasty.

46. Kees, op. cit. (n. 15), p. 208.

47. For more on the economic role and activities of Egyptian temples see Kemp, op. cit. (n. 7), pp. 657–76.

48. Davies and Gardiner, loc. cit. (n. 38).

49. Gardiner, *Egypt of the Pharaohs* (New York, 1966), p. 270.

50. Säve-Söderbergh, op. cit. (n. 6), p. 168.
51. Arkell, op. cit. (n. 25), p. 95.
52. cf. Säve-Söderbergh, op. cit. (n. 6), pp. 226–30.
53. Quoted from Emery, op. cit. (n. 4), p. 184. For fuller discussion see Säve-Söderbergh, op. cit. (n. 6), pp. 206–11.
54. Lucas, *Ancient Egyptian Materials and Industries*, 3rd ed. (London, 1948), p. 258.
55. See Vercoutter in *Kush* VII (1959), p. 130. For fuller discussion see Säve-Söderbergh, op. cit. (n. 6), pp. 210–66.
56. Vercoutter, loc. cit. (n. 55).
57. See ibid., pp. 147–8.
58. Quoted from Emery, op. cit. (n. 4), p. 193.
59. Piotrovsky in *Fouilles en Nubie (1961–1963)* (Cairo, 1967), pp. 136–40.
60. ibid.
61. Lucas, op. cit. (n. 54), pp. 261–2.
62. Vercoutter, op. cit. (n. 55), p. 140.
63. For a preliminary report see Mills in *Kush* XIII (1965), p. 7; see also Dunn, *Notes on the Mineral Deposits of the Anglo–Egyptian Sudan* (Khartoum, 1911), p. 17.
64. Randall-MacIver and Woolley, *Areika*, University of Pennsylvania Museum, Eckley B. Coxe Junior Expedition to Nubia, Vol. I (1909), p. 13.
65. *Kush* XII (1964), p. 31.
66. See Säve-Söderbergh, op. cit. (n. 6), pp. 187–9; Junker, *Ermenne*, Akademie der Wissenschaften in Wien, Philosophisch-Historische Klasse Denkschriften, 67, Band 1 (1925), p. 37.
67. Säve-Söderbergh, loc. cit. (n. 65).
68. See Fig. 12, p. 94; also Mukherjee, Rao and Trevor, *The Ancient Inhabitants of Jebel Moya (Sudan)* (Cambridge, 1955), p. 85.
69. I have reviewed this problem at much greater length in *Journal of Egyptian Archaeology*, Vol. 50 (1964), pp. 105–8. For rebuttals by Säve-Söderbergh, summarizing the arguments in favour of the 'acculturation hypothesis', see *Zeitschrift der Deutschen Morgenländischen Gesellschaft*, XVII, Supplementa I (1969), pp. 12–20; and in *Kush* XV (1973), pp. 237–42.
70. For documentation on this point see Adams, op. cit. (n. 69), p. 106, n. 1.
71. Emery, op. cit. (n. 4), pp. 178–9.
72. cf. especially Säve-Söderbergh in *Kush* XI (1963), pp. 59–64 and *Kush* XII (1964), pp. 31–7. By contrast Vercoutter asserts that 'The N.K. cemetery at Mirgissa numbering more than 500 graves – of which 237 were excavated – was very poor indeed. Sometimes not even one pot was placed within the grave!' (Vercoutter, personal communication.)
73. See Adams in *Antiquity*, Vol. XLII (1968), p. 203; Kroeber in *American Anthropologist*, Vol. 29 (1927), pp. 308–15.
74. See n. 65.
75. See Griffith's report on the cemetery of Sanam in *University of Liverpool Annals of Archaeology and Anthropology*, Vol. X (1923), esp. pp. 73–90.
76. Scandinavian Joint Expedition, Cemetery No. 185. For published reports see n. 72.
77. See n. 68.
78. Vagn Nielsen, *Human Remains*, Scandinavian Joint Expedition to Sudanese Nubia Publications, Vol. 9 (1970), pp. 86–7.
79. ibid., p. 86.
80. ibid., p. 87.
81. It may be noted that there is no evidence of Egyptian colonization between Kawa, near the Third Cataract, and Jebel Barkal, just below the Fourth.
82. *Archaeological Survey of Nubia, Report for 1910–1911* (Cairo, 1927), p. 28.

83. See n. 70.

84. This conspicuous hiatus in the archaeological record was first pointed out by Firth, *Archaeological Survey of Nubia, Report for 1909–1910* (Cairo, 1915), pp. 21–3, and confirmed by Griffith, *University of Liverpool Annals of Archaeology and Anthropology*, Vol. XI (1924), pp. 115–17. It might in the beginning have been supposed that the absence of archaeological remains from the last millennium BC could be attributed to unsystematic exploration, but the intensive surveys of the last decade have equally failed to find any remains from this period. For discussion see Adams in *Mélanges offerts à Kazimierz Michalowski* (Warsaw, 1966), pp. 21–2, and in *Sudan Notes and Records*, Vol. XLVIII (1967), pp. 10–11.

85. Firth, loc. cit. (n. 82).

86. See Reisner, op. cit. (n. 16), pp. 68–9; Porter and Moss, *Nubia, the Deserts, and outside Egypt, Topographical Bibliography of Ancient Egyptian Hieroglyphic Texts, Reliefs and Paintings*, VII (1962), pp. 150–51, 156. For discussion see Vercoutter in *Kush* XIV (1966), pp. 132–9.

87. Vercoutter in *Kush* XI (1963), pp. 133–4; de Heinzelin in *Kush* XII (1964), pp. 102–10; Trigger, op. cit. (n. 13), p. 31; Bell in *American Journal of Archaeology* Vol. 79 (1975), pp. 260–65.

88. For discussion on this point see Butzer in (*Mainz*) *Akademie der Wissenschaftlichen und der Literatur, Abhandlungen der Mathematisch-Naturwissenschaftlichen Klasse*, No. 2 (1959); in *Bulletin de la Société de Géographie d'Égypte*, Vol. XXXII (1959), pp. 43–87; and in *Science*, Vol. 175 (1972), pp. 1073–4. See also Trigger in Dinkler, Ed., *Kunst und Geschichte Nubiens in Christlicher Zeit* (Recklinghausen, 1970), p. 355.

89. cf. Reisner, op. cit. (n. 33), p. 53.

90. See Arkell, op. cit. (n. 25), p. 108.

91. Toynbee, loc. cit. (n. 34).

92. Reisner, op. cit. (n. 33), pp. 53–5; Emery, op. cit. (n. 4), pp. 206–7. Dixon on the other hand doubts that there were any Egyptians in Upper Nubia after the XX Dynasty; see *Journal of Egyptian Archaeology*, Vol. 50 (1964), p. 131.

93. An earlier Temple of Amon may have been built by Thutmose III or IV; see Reisner, loc. cit. (n. 28).

CHAPTER 10

Principal sources: the basic historical framework for the Napatan period is still the chronology of rulers worked out by Reisner fifty years ago, and published by him in *Harvard African Studies*, Vol. II (1918), pp. 1–64; *Sudan Notes and Records*, Vol. II (1919), pp. 237–54; *Journal of Egyptian Archaeology*, Vol. IX (1923), pp. 34–77, 157–60. Important subsequent revisions and commentary include those of Dunham and Macadam in *Journal of Egyptian Archaeology*, Vol. 35 (1949), pp. 139–49; Hintze, *Abhandlungen der Deutschen Akademie der Wissenschaften zu Berlin, Klasse für Sprachen, Literatur, und Kunst*, No. 2 (1959); and Haycock in *Sudan Notes and Records*, Vol. XLIX (1969), pp. 1–16. For popular history see especially Arkell, *A History of the Sudan*, 2nd ed. (London, 1961), pp. 110–56; Emery, *Egypt in Nubia* (London, 1965), pp. 208–21; and Shinnie, *Meroe* (New York, 1967), pp. 29–39.

1. 2 Kings xviii, 21. The translation is that of John Wilson, *The Culture of Ancient Egypt* (Chicago, 1951), p. 294.

2. According to Haycock (personal communication) the passage is actually a pun on

the word 'kush', which can be read to mean either 'reed' or the native land of the XXV Dynasty rulers.

3. cf. Gardiner, *Egypt of the Pharaohs* (New York, 1966), pp. 305–6, 317.

4. Except for a somewhat mysterious Queen Nesikhonsu several generations later. 'Only once was the title revived and then it was to satisfy the vanity of a woman ..., to give her an honorary rank which she could not claim as her birthright.' (Reisner in *Journal of Egyptian Archaeology*, Vol. VI, 1920, p. 53.)

5. ibid.

6. cf. Dixon in *Journal of Egyptian Archaeology*, Vol. 50 (1964), p. 131.

7. According to Reisner's calculation; see *Sudan Notes and Records*, Vol. II (1919), p. 246.

8. Toynbee, *A Study of History*, Vol. 8 (New York, 1963), p. 1.

9. ibid.

10. op. cit. (n. 8), Vol. 5, pp. 268–70.

11. cf. Breasted, *A History of Egypt*, 2nd ed. (London, 1909), p. 545.

12. Herodotus II: 137–40. The list of Egyptian pharaohs originally compiled by Manetho is preserved in a number of versions by later chroniclers; see Budge, *A History of Egypt* (London, 1902), Vol. I, pp. 126–46. For a resumé of hieroglyphic texts from the XXV Dynasty see Breasted, *Ancient Records of Egypt*, Vol. IV (New York, 1962), pp. 885–934.

13. 2 Kings xix, 9.

14. *Harvard African Studies*, Vol. II (1918), pp. 1–64; *Sudan Notes and Records*, Vol. II (1919), pp. 237–54; *Journal of Egyptian Archaeology*, Vol. IX (1923), pp. 34–77, 157–60.

15. cf. Dunham and Macadam in *Journal of Egyptian Archaeology*, Vol. 35 (1949), pp. 139–49; Macadam, *The Temples of Kawa*, Vol. I (Oxford, 1949), pp. 119–30; H. F. C. Smith in *Kush* III (1955), pp. 20–25; Hintze, *Studien zur Meroitischen Chronologie und zu den Opfertafeln aus den Pyramiden von Meroe*, Abhandlungen der Deutschen Akademie der Wissenschaften zu Berlin, Klasse für Sprachen, Literatur, und Kunst, No. 2 (1959); Shinnie, *Meroe* (New York, 1967), pp. 35–6, 58–61. For still more recent discussion see Hintze in *Meroitica* 1 (1973), pp. 147–74.

16. This name, although in regular use during the New Kingdom, seldom appears in native Nubian texts of the post-Egyptian period before the late (Meroitic) phase.

17. This name appears in all of Reisner's work which was published in his own lifetime.

18. See discussion by Dunham in *American Journal of Archaeology*, Vol. L (1946), p. 380, and in *Sudan Notes and Records*, Vol. XXVIII (1947), pp. 3–4.

19. See Reisner in *Sudan Notes and Records*, Vol. II (1919), pp. 35–67; Dunham in *Sudan Notes and Records*, Vol. XXVIII (1947), pp. 7–9; Wainwright in *Journal of Egyptian Archaeology*, Vol. 38 (1952), pp. 75–7; H. F. C. Smith, op. cit. (n. 15); Arkell, *A History of the Sudan*, 2nd ed. (London, 1961), pp. 145–51; Shinnie, op. cit. (n. 15), pp. 31–3. Ali goes so far as to suggest that Meroë was the royal capital of Kush from the beginning, while Napata was merely the religious capital; see 'The City of Meroe and the Myth of Napata', paper read before the 17th Annual Conference of the Philosophical Society of the Sudan, Khartoum, 2 August 1972. For the time being the evidence in support of this view does not appear very convincing.

20. Wilson, op. cit. (n. 1), p. 292.

21. Hintze (personal communication) points out, however, that the high literary quality exhibited by the great commemorative stele of Piankhi represents a

considerable cultural achievement. For further discussion see 'The Conquest of Egypt', below.

22. Haycock (personal communication) believed that the revitalization of Meroitic culture began much earlier, but the dating of most Meroitic archaeological remains is so conjectural that this must remain a moot point. For further discussion see Ch. 11.

23. See Emery, *Egypt in Nubia* (London, 1965), p. 187.

24. A stele of Amenhotep II, relating that an enemy prisoner was 'hanged on the wall of Napata', would seem to indicate that there was a specific town of Napata in the XVIII Dynasty; see Breasted, op. cit. (n. 12), Vol. II, p. 313. Presumably this was the Egyptian settlement just below Jebel Barkal. However, it seems more probable that in post-Egyptian times the name Napata was applied to the whole district within which the Nubian royal monuments are found.

25. This is a literal translation of the hieroglyphic designation for Jebel Barkal; see Dunham, *El Kurru, Royal Cemeteries of Kush*, Vol. I (1950), p. 5.

26. *Sudan Notes and Records*, Vol. II (1919), pp. 237–54.

27. ibid., p. 246.

28. Reisner's own estimate (ibid.) was thirty years per reign, but this seems unrealistically high; especially since the Kushite succession often passed from brother to brother rather than from father to son.

29. For a review and critique of these various theories see Dixon, op. cit. (n. 6).

30. *Sudan Notes and Records*, Vol. II (1919), pp. 246–8; see also *Journal of Egyptian Archaeology*, Vol. IX (1923), p. 34, in which the theory is no longer tentatively advanced but is stated as accepted fact.

31. See Dunham, op. cit. (n. 19), p. 3; Arkell, op. cit. (n. 19), pp. 114–15; Emery, op. cit. (n. 23), p. 208; Shinnie, op. cit. (n. 15), p. 30.

32. Arkell, op. cit. (n. 19), p. 114.

33. ibid., pp. 112–15; Reisner, op. cit. (n. 4), pp. 53–5; Emery, op. cit. (n. 23), pp. 206–7.

34. Drioton and Vandier, *L'Égypte* (*Les Peuples de l'Orient Mediterranéen*, 4th ed. Paris, 1962, Vol. II), p. 675. However, Parker (*Zeitschrift für Ägyptische Sprache und Altertumskunde*, Vol. 93, 1966, pp. 111–14) and Priese (*Mitteilungen des Instituts für Orientforschung*, Vol. XIV, 1968, pp. 166–75) have suggested that the name of the Nubian ruler was probably *Pi* or *Piye*, the remaining element being a determinative added by Egyptian scribes.

35. cf. references cited in n. 31.

36. *Recherches sur les Monuments Thébains de la XXVe Dynastie dite Éthiopienne*, Institut Français d'Archéologie Orientale, Bibliothèque d'Étude, Vol. XXXVI (1965), pp. 322–9.

37. See Breasted, *The Development of Religion and Thought in Ancient Egypt* (New York, 1959), p. 318.

38. *Library of History* III: 5–7.

39. See Posener, *A Dictionary of Egyptian Civilization* (London, 1962), pp. 85–6.

40. cf. Haycock in *Sudan Notes and Records*, Vol. XLIX (1968), p. 12.

41. Arkell, op. cit. (n. 19), p. 126.

42. cf. Haycock, op. cit. (n. 40), pp. 11–14.

43. See Macadam, loc. cit. (n. 15); Haycock in *Comparative Studies in Society and History*, Vol. VII (1965), pp. 466–70; Shinnie, op. cit. (n. 15), p. 153. Further discussion on this subject will be found in Priese, 'Matrilineare Erbfolge im Reich von Napata' (*Meroitica* 4, in press), and in Hintze, 'Meroitische Verwandtschaftsbezeichnungen' (MS).

44. For discussion see Macadam in *Allen Memorial Art Museum Bulletin* (Oberlin

College), Vol. XXIII (1966), pp. 46–7; Desanges in *Bulletin de l'Institut Français d'Archéologie Orientale*, Vol. XLVI (1968), pp. 89–104; and Shinnie, op. cit. (n. 15), p. 153.

45. See Macadam, op. cit. (n. 15), p. 28; Arkell, op. cit. (n. 19), p. 127.

46. Strabo, *Geography* XVII, 1: 54; Pliny, *Natural History* VI: xxv, 8; see also Acts of the Apostles viii, 28; and Desanges, op. cit. (n. 44).

47. See Griffith in *Journal of Egyptian Archaeology*, Vol. IV (1917), pp. 159–73; Reisner in *Sudan Notes and Records*, Vol. V (1922), pp. 188–94.

48. For fuller discussion of the monarchical institutions of Kush see Hofmann, *Studien zur Meroitischen Königtum*, Fondation Égyptologique Reine Élisabeth, Monographies Reine Élisabeth 2 (1971).

49. Texts found at Kawa refer to a certain Alara as the predecessor of Kashta, but nothing is known of his reign or his tomb. See Macadam, op. cit. (n. 15), pp. 121–3; and Priese in *Zeitschrift für Ägyptische Sprache und Altertumskunde*, Vol. 98 (1970), pp. 21–3.

50. For the available evidence on Kashta see Priese, op. cit. (n. 49), pp. 16–23, and Leclant in *Zeitschrift für Ägyptische Sprache und Altertumskunde*, Vol. 90 (1963), pp. 74–81.

51. Arkell, op. cit. (n. 19), p. 121.

52. This act of alliance, involving the same royal 'sister', is also attributed to several of the later XXV Dynasty pharaohs; see Breasted, op. cit. (n. 11), pp. 555–8. For further discussion see Leclant, op. cit. (n. 36), pp. 354–85.

53. cf. Haycock, op. cit. (n. 43), p. 464.

54. Arkell, op. cit. (n. 19), p. 121.

55. Priese (op. cit., n. 49, p. 21) considers that Kashta reigned from the beginning as Pharaoh at Thebes, uniting Nubia and Upper Egypt under his personal rule.

56. I will retain throughout this text the familiar form of the name, despite the recent and probably correct suggestion of Parker and Priese that it should be read as *Pi* or *Piye*. See n. 34.

57. For an early translation see Budge, *The Egyptian Sudan* (London, 1907), Vol. II, pp. 11–26; for translation with commentary see Breasted, op. cit. (n. 12), Vol. IV, pp. 406–44. For later commentary see Reisner in *Zeitschrift für Ägyptische Sprache und Altertumskunde*, Vol. 66 (1931), pp. 89–100.

58. Breasted, op. cit. (n. 11), p. 541.

59. Arkell, op. cit. (n. 19), p. 124.

60. Breasted, op. cit. (n. 11), p. 545.

61. Wilson, op. cit. (n. 1), p. 293.

62. For another example of Piankhi's exaggerated chivalry see Gardiner in *Journal of Egyptian Archaeology*, Vol. XXI (1935), pp. 219–23.

63. See for example Antar in *Aramco World Magazine*, Vol. 21 (1970), pp. 26–31.

64. Gardiner, op. cit. (n. 3), p. 342. Other authors give slightly varying dates. For further discussion of the chronology and relationships of the 'Ethiopian' pharaohs see Baer in *Journal of Near Eastern Studies*, Vol. 32 (1973), pp. 24–5.

65. Breasted, op. cit. (n. 11), p. 551.

66. 2 Kings xix, 9. Macadam (op. cit., n. 15, pp. 19–20) considers that the biblical account is 'manifestly a mistake' because of Taharqa's youth and because the passage indicates that he was already King of Egypt at this time.

67. Breasted, op. cit. (n. 11), p. 553.

68. Emery, op. cit. (n. 23), pp. 219–20. For a detailed study of XXV Dynasty building activities in Egypt see Leclant, op. cit. (n. 36).

69. See Dunham and Janssen, *Semna Kumma, Second Cataract Forts*, Vol. I (1960), esp. pp. 12–13.

70. Randall-MacIver and Woolley, *Buhen*, University of Pennsylvania Museum, Eckley B. Coxe Junior Expedition to Nubia, Vol. VII (1911), p. 17.

71. The Taharqa temple at Qasr Ibrim first came to light in the course of excavations in 1972; see Plumley and Adams in *Journal of Egyptian Archaeology*, Vol. 60 (1974), pp. 228–36, and Plumley in *Journal of Egyptian Archaeology*, Vol. 61 (1975), pp. 19–20.

72. At Gezira Dabarosa (Verwers in *Kush* X, 1962, p. 33); at Faras (Michalowski in *Kush* XIII, 1965, pp. 179–80); near Aniba (Leclant in *Académie des Inscriptions et Belles-Lettres, Comptes Rendus des Séances de l'Année 1970*, p. 253, n. 1); and at Kalabsha (Hintze in *Mitteilungen des Instituts für Orientforschung*, Vol. VII, 1960, pp. 330–33).

73. See Macadam, op. cit. (n. 15), pp. 4–43.

74. Emery, op. cit. (n. 23), p. 218. For the complete text and commentary see Breasted, op. cit. (n. 12), Vol. IV, pp. 455–7.

75. Breasted, op. cit. (n. 12), Vol. IV, pp. 458–65.

76. See Emery, *Archaic Egypt* (Harmondsworth, 1961), pp. 38–104.

77. See Reisner in *Harvard African Studies*, Vol. II (1918), pp. 45–6.

78. Schiff Giorgini in *Kush* XIII (1965), pp. 116–30; Leclant, op. cit. (n. 72), pp. 249–52. Haycock (personal communication) believed that Taharqa may have been deposed by Tenutamon and exiled to Seddenga, and thus had to content himself with the rather humble tomb which he was able to build here rather than with the much larger pyramid which he had prepared for himself at Nuri. The basis for this belief is the so-called 'dream stele' of Tenutamon; see Haycock, op. cit. (n. 40), p. 8.

79. Emery, op. cit. (n. 23), pp. 220–21.

80. Nahum iii, 8–10.

81. Except for a mysterious and so far unnamed king of the late (?) Napatan period; see Dunham, op. cit. (n. 25), p. 3.

82. For a detailed discussion of their building activities see Leclant, op. cit. (n. 36) For fuller discussion of the historical details of Nubian rule in Egypt see von Zeissl, 'Äthiopen und Assyrer in Ägypten', *Ägyptologische Forschungen*, Ed. Alexander Scharff, Vol. 14 (1944).

83. This is the traditional explanation for the semi-intelligible texts of the late Napatan period; cf. Arkell, op. cit. (n. 19), p. 153; Haycock, op. cit. (n. 40), p. 9; and Haycock, op. cit. (n. 43), p. 476. Hintze, however, believes that the Napatan scribes had succeeded in restoring the original Egyptian language to such purity that we have difficulty in understanding it, for lack of parallel examples (personal communication).

84. Haycock (personal communication) would assign him a shorter reign, beginning about 610 BC.

85. For a more detailed resumé see Arkell, op. cit. (n. 19), p. 143; for the original see Macadam, op. cit. (n. 15), pp. 44–50.

86. Reisner (op. cit., n. 77, pp. 22–3) believed that Aspalta was the son of Anlamani, but the fraternal relationship is now generally accepted. See Dunham and Macadam, op. cit. (n. 15), p. 142.

87. Or possibly the 'sister-wife' of Aspalta; see Haycock, op. cit. (n. 40), p. 12.

88. ibid.; see also Arkell, op. cit. (n. 19), p. 144.

89. II: 161. For a detailed discussion of the campaign see Sauneron and Yoyotte in *Bulletin de l'Institut Français d'Archéologie Orientale*, Vol. L (1952), pp. 157–207.

90. cf. Sayce in *Proceedings of the Society for Biblical Archaeology*, 40th Session, 6th Meeting, 14 Dec. 1910, pp. 261–3.

91. Arkell, op. cit. (n. 19), pp. 145–6; Shinnie, op. cit. (n. 15), pp. 32–3; Sauneron and Yoyotte, op. cit. (n. 89), p. 203.

92. Arkell, op. cit. (n. 19), p. 146; Shinnie, op. cit. (n. 15), p. 31; Haycock, op. cit. (n. 40), p. 8. Cartouches of Kashta, Shabataka, and Tenutamon have been found on small objects in the Meroë cemeteries, but these of course give no evidence of the actual presence of the kings. See Dunham, *The West and South Cemeteries at Meroë, Royal Cemeteries of Kush*, Vol. V (1963), pp. 304, 362, 431, 441.

93. See Griffith in *University of Liverpool Annals of Archaeology and Anthropology*, Vol. IX (1922), pp. 78–9.

94. Arkell, op. cit. (n. 19), p. 145; Emery, op. cit. (n. 23), p. 223; Shinnie, op. cit. (n. 15), p. 33.

95. Macadam, op. cit. (n. 15), pp. 50–72.

96. According to Haycock (personal communication) this is not technically correct; the text states that Aman-nete-yerike was forty-one years old when he became king, but it was not necessarily inscribed in the first year of his reign.

97. Shinnie, op. cit. (n. 15), p. 37.

98. For the texts and discussion see Budge, op. cit. (n. 57), pp. 75–103.

99. Shinnie, op. cit. (n. 15), p. 37. For a more detailed discussion of the desert route see Wainwright in *Journal of Egyptian Archaeology*, Vol. 33 (1947), pp. 58–62.

100. III: 17–25.

101. cf. Hintze, op. cit. (n. 15), pp. 17–20; Shinnie, op. cit. (n. 15), p. 39.

102. See n. 19 for references.

103. See Haycock, op. cit. (n. 40), p. 8 for further discussion on this point.

104. Reported in *Journal of Egyptian Archaeology*, Vol. IV (1917), pp. 213–27; Vol. V (1918), pp. 99–112; and Vol. VI (1920), pp. 247–64. The definitive report has only recently appeared; see Dunham, *The Barkal Temples* (Boston, 1970).

105. Directional orientations in the Napata district cause a great deal of difficulty because the Nile here flows from north-east to south-west – nearly the reverse of its normal course. Since the ancient Egyptians and Nubians generally took the river as their main point of orientation, the alignment of buildings and tombs at Napata often deviates markedly from the usual practice. Likewise what is nominally the 'west' bank of the Nile – the traditional Egyptian place of burial – is here technically the east bank.

106. The temples of Akhenaton at Thebes and Tell el-Amarna, destroyed immediately after his reign, were larger still, as was the mortuary temple of Rameses II (The Ramesseum).

107. cf. *Journal of Egyptian Archaeology*, Vol. IV (1917), pp. 215–27.

108. Reported in *Journal of Egyptian Archaeology*, Vol. V (1918), pp. 99–112 and Vol. VI (1920), pp. 247–64; see also Dunham, op. cit. (n. 104), pp. 7–13, 63–81.

109. cf. Haycock, op. cit. (n. 40), p. 10.

110. Griffith, op. cit. (n. 93), p. 75. Since the faience *ushabtis* were made exclusively for the royal dead, Haycock (personal communication) suggests that perhaps the temple of Sanam had been converted to a mortuary chapel for those who were to be interred in the nearby royal cemetery of Nuri.

111. Griffith, op. cit. (n. 93), pp. 75–6.

112. ibid., p. 115.

113. ibid., p. 117.

114. See Dunham, op. cit. (n. 25), p. 5; Shinnie, op. cit. (n. 15), p. 73.

115. Griffith, op. cit. (n. 93), pp. 78–9. Sauneron and Yoyotte argue however that this was the work of the Egyptian invaders in the reign of Psammetik II; see op. cit. (n. 89), p. 203.

116. Macadam, *The Temples of Kawa*, Vol. II (Oxford, 1955), p. 15.

117. ibid., p. 208.

118. See Macadam, op. cit. (n. 15).

119. See Jacquet-Gordon *et al.* in *Journal of Egyptian Archaeology*, Vol. 55 (1969), pp. 109–12.
120. ibid., pp. 103–12.
121. See n. 78.
122. Shinnie in *Meroitic Newsletter* No. 5 (1970), pp. 17–19.
123. See Shinnie, op. cit. (n. 15), p. 81.
124. ibid., p. 37.
125. Arkell, op. cit. (n. 19), pp. 136–7; Vercoutter in *Mélanges Mariette*, Institut Français d'Archéologie Orientale, Bibliothèque d'Étude, Vol. XXXII (1961), pp. 97–104.
126. This has been suggested by Hintze (personal communication).
127. For a resumé of the excavations see Dunham, op. cit. (n. 25), pp. 7–10; for bibliography see Dunham in *Kush* III (1955), pp. 70–74.
128. See Reisner, op. cit. (n. 77), p. 24.
129. cf. James, *The Archaeology of Ancient Egypt* (London, 1972), p. 92.
130. A succinct resumé of the chronological development of the Kushite royal pyramid is given in Dunham, op. cit. (n. 25), pp. 121–32.
131. See especially Chapman and Dunham, *Decorated Chapels of the Meroitic Pyramids at Meroë and Barkal, Royal Cemeteries of Kush*, Vol. III (1952).
132. After the time of Piankhi; in the earlier tumulus graves there seems to be no special separation of males and females.
133. For the original sources see n. 14.
134. cf. Dunham, op. cit. (n. 25), pp. 121–32 and especially Charts I–III.
135. For discussion on this point see my article in *Journal of Egyptian Archaeology*, Vol. 50 (1964), pp. 113–16, and replies by Haycock in *Journal of Egyptian Archaeology*, Vol. 53 (1967), pp. 107–20, and *Sudan Notes and Records*, Vol. XLIX (1968), pp. 1–16.
136. A *mastaba* is a solid rectangular mass of masonry with slightly in-sloping sides.
137. Arkell, op. cit. (n. 19), pp. 115–16. The definitive report on this cemetery is Dunham, op. cit. (n. 25).
138. These are illustrated in Dunham, op. cit. (n. 25), pls. IX–XX, but they seem never to have been described in print, nor the texts translated.
139. Arkell, op. cit. (n. 19), pp. 122–4.
140. Although in this region it is technically the east bank; see n. 105.
141. Arkell, op. cit. (n. 19), p. 117.
142. The definitive reports are Reisner, op. cit. (n. 77), pp. 1–64, and Dunham, *Nuri, Royal Cemeteries of Kush*, Vol. II (1955).
143. Schiff Giorgini, op. cit. (n. 78), p. 129.
144. ibid., p. 123; Leclant, op. cit. (n. 72), p. 252.
145. As suggested by Haycock; see n. 78.
146. Schiff Giorgini in *Kush* XIV (1966), p. 259.
147. Shinnie (op. cit., n. 122) has found mud-brick construction at the lowest levels at Meroë, but has also found post-holes – presumably for the supports for grass or brush structures – in the soil upon which the town was first built.
148. Reisner in *Journal of Egyptian Archaeology*, Vol. IX (1923), p. 37. The definitive report is Dunham, op. cit. (n. 92), pp. 357–449.
149. Shinnie, op. cit. (n. 15), pp. 148–50.
150. op. cit. (n. 148).
151. Griffith in *University of Liverpool Annals of Archaeology and Anthropology*, Vol. X (1923), pp. 75–6.
152. ibid., p. 87.
153. ibid., p. 88.

154. ibid., p. 89.
155. Haycock, op. cit. (n. 40), p. 13.
156. It is most clearly expressed by him in *Sudan Notes and Records*, Vol. II (1919), pp. 35–67, and by Dunham in *Sudan Notes and Records*, Vol. XXVIII (1947), pp. 1–10.
157. cf. Griffith, op. cit. (n. 151), pp. 73–90.
158. Dunham, op. cit. (n. 156), pp. 5–6, and in *American Journal of Archaeology*, Vol. L (1946), p. 385.
159. I: 29–30.
160. See n. 158.
161. Kemp has suggested that this was true for Egypt also; the temple estates were a kind of 'bank' into which the pharaoh could make 'deposits', to be withdrawn at will. See Ucko, Tringham and Dimbleby, Eds., *Man, Settlement and Urbanism* (London, 1972), pp. 657–76.

CHAPTER 11

Principal sources: the most important popular work on Meroitic sites and culture, on which I have drawn heavily throughout this chapter, is Shinnie, *Meroe* (New York, 1967). Still important for historical and chronological reconstruction are the original articles by Reisner in *Sudan Notes and Records*, Vol. V (1922), pp. 173–96, and in *Journal of Egyptian Archaeology*, Vol. IX (1923), pp. 34–77, 157–60. Recent scholarly works of importance are Hintze, *Abhandlungen der Deutschen Akademie der Wissenschaften zu Berlin, Klasse für Sprachen, Literatur, und Kunst*, 1959, No. 2, and Haycock in *Journal of Egyptian Archaeology*, Vol. 53 (1967), pp. 107–20.

1. Book II: 89.
2. III: 18.
3. I: 33; III: *passim.*
4. I: 2; XVII: 53–4.
5. VI: 35.
6. For resumés of classical sources on Meroë see Gadallah in *Kush* XI (1963), pp. 207–8, and Shinnie, *Meroe* (New York, 1967), pp. 13–22.
7. For mention of actual visits to Meroë by Greek and Roman travellers see Thompson and Ferguson, Eds., *Africa in Classical Antiquity* (Ibadan, 1969), pp. 42–4, and Haycock, *Landmarks in Cushite History* (MS), pp. 8–9.
8. 'The Greeks gave the name *Oikoumêne*, "the inhabited", to their supposed total habitable world stretching from the Pillars of Hercules to the Indians and the Seres.' Kroeber, *The Nature of Culture* (Chicago, 1952), p. 379.
9. For more on the Hellenization of Egypt see Toynbee, *A Study of History*, Vol. 8 (New York, 1963), pp. 407–8.
10. Bruce, *Travels to Discover the Source of the Nile* (Edinburgh, 1790), Vol. IV, pp. 538–9.
11. See Garstang, Sayce and Griffith, *Meroë, the City of the Ethiopians* (Oxford, 1911), p. 26.
12. For a translation of Ferlini's own account see Budge, *The Egyptian Sudan* (London, 1907), Vol. I, pp. 307–20. The original is published in Ferlini's *Cenni sugli Scavi di Nubia* (Bologna, 1837).
13. For Budge's account of his work see *The Egyptian Sudan* (London, 1907), Vol. I, pp. 337–56; for critical comment see Macadam in *Allen Memorial Art Museum Bulletin* (Oberlin College), Vol. XXIII (1966), pp. 54–5.

NOTES

14. *University of Liverpool Annals of Archaeology and Anthropology*, Vol. III (1910), pp. 53–70; Vol. IV (1911), pp. 45–71; Vol. V (1912), pp. 73–88; Vol. VI (1913), pp. 1–21; Vol. VII (1914), pp. 1–24. A somewhat longer report (cited in n. 11) was also issued at the end of the first season.

15. Shinnie, op. cit. (n. 6), p. 77.

16. See ibid., p. 28. A more recent though very brief preliminary report on the excavations at Meroë has also appeared in *Meroitic Newsletter* No. 5 (1970), pp. 17–19.

17. Chapman and Dunham, *Royal Cemeteries of Kush*, Vol. III (Boston, 1952); Dunham, *Royal Cemeteries of Kush*, Vol. IV (Boston, 1957) and Vol. V (Boston, 1963).

18. See preliminary reports by Hintze in *Kush* VII (1959), pp. 173–88; *Kush* X (1962), pp. 170–202; *Kush* XI (1963), pp. 217–26; in *Wissenschaftliche Zeitschrift der Humboldt-Universität zu Berlin, Gesellschafts- und Sprachwissenschaftliche Reihe*, Vol. XI (1962), pp. 441–88; Vol. XII (1963), pp. 63–77; Vol. XVII (1968), pp. 667–84; Vol. XX (1971), pp. 227–46; Hintze, *Die Inschriften des Löwentempels von Musawwarat es Sufra*, Abhandlungen der Deutschen Akademie der Wissenschaften zu Berlin, Klasse für Sprachen, Literatur, und Kunst, 1962, No. 1; Hintze and Hintze in Dinkler, Ed., *Kunst und Geschichte Nubiens in Christlicher Zeit* (Recklinghausen, 1970), pp. 49–70; and Priese in *Wissenschaftliche Zeitschrift der Humboldt-Universität zu Berlin, Gesellschafts- und Sprachwissenschaftliche Reihe*, Vol. XXI (1971), pp. 247–56. The first volume of a series of definitive reports has also recently appeared; see Hintze, *Der Löwentempel, Musawwarat es Sufra*, Vol. I, Part 2 (Berlin, 1971).

19. For a partial inventory of Meroitic sites in Lower Nubia see Trigger, *History and Settlement in Lower Nubia*, Yale University Publications in Anthropology, No. 69 (1965), pp. 186–97.

20. Gadallah, op. cit. (n. 6), p. 196.

21. For a popular discussion of the Meroitic language and writing see Shinnie, op. cit. (n. 6), pp. 132–40.

22. Primarily through the study of a few bilingual texts, and because of parallels to the Egyptian demotic system of writing.

23. See Greenberg, *Studies in African Linguistic Classification* (New Haven, 1955), p. 98, and Trigger in *Journal of African History*, Vol. VII (1966), pp. 19–25. For extended discussion of the history and present state of Meroitic language studies see Gadallah, loc. cit. (n. 6); Haycock, *The Problem of the Meroitic Language* (MS): and Trigger in *Meroitica* 1 (1973), pp. 243–349. A *Meroitic Newsletter* has recently been established to help keep interested scholars abreast of the latest developments in Meroitic language studies.

24. Shinnie, op. cit. (n. 6), pp. 132–3.

25. Diodorus Siculus I: 33; Strabo I: 2; Pliny VI: 36.

26. cf. Shinnie, op. cit. (n. 6), p. 16.

27. *American Journal of Archaeology*, Vol. L (1946), p. 385; cf. also Gadallah, op. cit. (n. 6), pp. 198–9.

28. XVII: I, 2.

29. For inventories and description of the Butana sites see Crowfoot and Griffith, *The Island of Meroë and Meroitic Inscriptions*, Part I, Archaeological Survey of Egypt, Memoir 19 (1911), pp. 6–29; Whitehead and Addison in *Sudan Notes and Records*, Vol. IX, No. 2 (1926), pp. 51–8; and Hintze in *Kush* VII (1959), pp. 171–96.

30. In Ucko, Tringham and Dimbleby, Eds., *Man, Settlement and Urbanism* (London, 1972), pp. 639–45.

31. Personal communication.

32. *University of Liverpool Annals of Archaeology and Anthropology*, Vol. IV (1911), p. 55.

33. cf. Trigger in *African Historical Studies*, Vol. II (1969), p. 44.

34. Dunham (loc. cit., n. 27) cites the availability of timber as a conspicuous advantage of Meroë over Napata, but in fact the growth of trees is very sparse in both areas except along the riverbank.

35. Crawford, *Castles and Churches in the Middle Nile Region*, Sudan Antiquities Service Occasional Paper No. 2 (1953), pp. 36–9.

36. cf. Chittick in *Kush* II (1954), pp. 94–5.

37. It is vividly described by Burckhardt in his *Travels in Nubia* (London, 1819), pp. 277–361; see also Moorehead, *The Blue Nile* (New York, 1962), pp. 154–66.

38. See Vercoutter in *Kush* VII (1959), p. 129, Map 2.

39. For discussion of the domestication of the camel and its introduction in caravan trade see Robinson in *Sudan Notes and Records*, Vol. XIX (1936), pp. 47–69, Zeuner, *A History of Domesticated Animals* (New York, 1963), p. 353, Huard and Leclant in *Études Scientifiques*, September–December 1972, pp. 85–9.

40. cf. Bovill, *The Golden Trade of the Moors*, 2nd ed. (London, 1970), p. 17.

41. ibid., pp. 13–27.

42. cf. Trigger in McCall, Bennett and Butler, Eds., *Eastern African History*, Boston University Papers on Africa, Vol. III (1969), pp. 92–3; and Millet, *Meroitic Nubia* (New Haven, n.d.), pp. 31–2.

43. Dunham, loc. cit. (n. 27); Arkell, *A History of the Sudan*, 2nd ed. (London, 1961), pp. 148–9; Gadallah, op. cit. (n. 6), pp. 198–9.

44. cf. Shinnie, op. cit. (n. 6), p. 31. Ali even suggests that Meroë was already the royal capital in Piankhi's time, and that it was always more important politically and commercially than Napata. See Ch. 10, n. 19.

45. ibid.

46. *Journal of Egyptian Archaeology*, Vol. IX (1923), pp. 75–6.

47. cf. ibid., p. 36.

48. ibid., p. 37.

49. ibid., p. 35.

50. Except in the most cursory fashion in preliminary excavation reports; for references see n. 14. For a more recent summary discussion of the non-royal cemeteries at Meroë see Shinnie, op. cit. (n. 6), pp. 85–6.

51. For a resumé of this development see Dunham, *Royal Cemeteries of Kush*, Vol. I (Boston, 1950), pp. 121–32.

52. Reisner in *Sudan Notes and Records*, Vol. V (1922), p. 185.

53. See Reisner, op. cit. (n. 52), pl. IV, and Dunham, *Royal Cemeteries of Kush*, Vol. IV (Boston, 1957), pls. IX, XII, XIII, XV, XXIII.

54. For a detailed resumé see Dunham, loc. cit. (n. 51).

55. Arkell, op. cit. (n. 43), p. 136.

56. Reisner, op. cit. (n. 52), p. 181.

57. Tomb W.122 in the West Cemetery; see Dunham, *Royal Cemeteries of Kush*, Vol. V (Boston, 1963), pp. 203–4.

58. See Trigger, op. cit. (n. 19), p. 117.

59. op. cit. (n. 46), p. 34.

60. The typology of the Barkal pyramids is described in ibid., pp. 56–63; the definitive report on the cemetery is Dunham, op. cit. (n. 53).

61. Or Naldamak, as she is more often called; cf. Shinnie, op. cit. (n. 6), p. 74. For discussion of this lady and her place in Meroitic history see especially Macadam op. cit. (n. 13), pp. 42–72.

62. Reisner, op. cit. (n. 46), pp. 63–7, 75–6.

63. See Macadam, *The Temples of Kawa*, Vol. I (Oxford, 1949), pp. 74–5; Vol. II (Oxford, 1955), pp. 19–20.

64. ibid., Vol. II (1955), p. 20.

65. Dunham, op. cit. (n. 53), pp. 2–8. Macadam now also rejects the second independent dynasty at Napata; see op. cit. (n. 13), pp. 61–6.

66. *Abhandlungen der Deutschen Akademie der Wissenschaften zu Berlin, Klasse für Sprachen, Literatur, und Kunst*, 1959, No. 2.

67. cf. especially Wenig in *Mitteilungen des Instituts für Orientforschung der Deutschen Akademie der Wissenschaften zu Berlin*, Vol. XIII (1967), pp. 1–44; and Hintze in *Meroitica* 1 (1973), pp. 127–44.

68. op. cit. (n. 6), p. 205.

69. For a resumé of the present state of theory and the most important remaining problems in regard to the Meroitic royal succession see Hintze, op. cit. (n. 67).

70. XVII: 53–4.

71. LIV: 5–6.

72. op. cit. (n. 42), pp. 33–42, 173a.

73. III: 6. Hintze however believes that Ergamenes is to be identified with Arkakamani, who preceded Arkamani by half a century. See *Die Inschriften des Löwentempels von Musawwarat es Sufra*, Abhandlungen der Deutschen Akademie der Wissenschaften zu Berlin, Klasse für Sprachen, Literatur, und Kunst, 1962, No. 1, pp. 14–18, and Hintze, loc. cit. (n. 67).

74. He might have been preceded by a certain King Adkeramon (Adikhalamani), whose place in the royal succession has not yet been established. See Trigger, op. cit. (n. 19), pp. 120–21.

75. See Shinnie, op. cit. (n. 6), pp. 41–2, and Haycock in *Kush* XIII (1965), pp. 264–6.

76. Arkell, op. cit. (n. 43), pp. 159–60. However, the later rulers Natakamani and Amanitere still employed Egyptian hieroglyphics in certain of their non-funerary inscriptions; cf. Crowfoot and Griffith, op. cit. (n. 29), pp. 67–8.

77. Interpreted by Phythian-Adams in *University of Liverpool Annals of Archaeology and Anthropology*, Vol. VII (1914), pp. 15–21, and by Griffith in *Journal of Egyptian Archaeology*, Vol. IV (1917), pp. 159–73.

78. See Whitehead and Addison, op. cit. (n. 29), pp. 51–2 and pls. X–XI, and Hintze in *Kush* VII (1959), pp. 189–90.

79. Shinnie op. cit. (n. 6), p. 96, observes that 'the portrayal of the sun-god shows a very marked similarity to a class of representations of a sun deity at Hatra and other west Asian sites, which are regarded as Parthian and date from the first two centuries AD'.

80. See Millet, op. cit. (n. 42), pp. vi–vii, 1–28, Haycock in *Journal of Egyptian Archaeology*, Vol. 53 (1967), pp. 107–20, and especially Griffith, *Catalogue of the Demotic Graffiti of the Dodecaschoenus* (Oxford, 1937), 2 vols.

81. Cited in n. 14.

82. Garstang in *University of Liverpool Annals of Archaeology and Anthropology*, Vol. IV (1911), p. 51.

83. Shinnie, op. cit. (n. 6), p. 80; Arkell, op. cit. (n. 43), p. 162.

84. Shinnie, op. cit. (n. 6), p. 79.

85. ibid., p. 77.

86. ibid., pp. 81–3.

87. See n. 27.

88. cf. Huard and Leclant, op. cit. (n. 39), pp. 80–83.

89. loc. cit. (n. 32).

90. However, many details of Meroitic iron-working have come to light as a result of the recent excavations of Shinnie at Meroë. See Shinnie in *Meroitic Newsletter*

NOTES

No. 5 (1970), p. 19; Tylecote in *Bulletin of the Historical Metallurgy Group* Vol. 4 (1970), pp. 67–72; and Williams in Thompson and Ferguson, op. cit. (n. 7), pp. 62–72.

91. cf. Trigger, op. cit. (n. 33), p. 45.

92. Shinnie's evidence now suggests iron-working at Meroë may date back to the fifth century BC; see op. cit. (n. 90), p. 17.

93. Trigger, op. cit. (n. 33), p. 49. See also Shinnie, *The African Iron Age* (Oxford, 1971), p. 97.

94. For description see Budge, op. cit. (n. 12), Vol. II, pp. 126–46; Whitehead in *Sudan Notes and Records*, Vol. IX, No. 2 (1926), pp. 62–4; Hintze in *Kush* VII (1959), pp. 183–7; and Shinnie, op. cit. (n. 6), pp. 88–92.

95. For extended description of this structure see Kraus in *Archäologischer Anzeiger, Jahrbuch des Deutschen Archäologischen Instituts* (1964), pp. 834–68.

96. For general description see Budge, op. cit. (n. 12), Vol. II, pp. 146–51; Whitehead, op. cit. (n. 94), pp. 64–6; Hintze in *Kush* VII (1959), pp. 183–7; and Shinnie, op. cit. (n. 6), pp. 92–5.

97. For a list of the published reports to date see n. 18. Among these the report in *Kunst und Geschichte Nubiens in Christlicher Zeit* is particularly valuable.

98. Hintze however dates the building of the central temple to the reign of Arnekhamani (c. 235–218 BC) or earlier. See Dinkler, Ed., *Kunst und Geschichte Nubiens in Christlicher Zeit* (Recklinghausen, 1970), p. 62.

99. Shinnie, op. cit. (n. 6), pp. 93–4.

100. Bevan, *The House of Ptolemy* (Chicago, 1968), p. 175. For discussion of Ptolemaic elephant-hunting in the Sudan see also Murray in *Geographical Journal*, Vol. 133 (1967), pp. 24–33; Desanges in *Actes du Quatre-Vingt-Douzième Congrès National des Sociétés Savantes, 1967, Section d'Archéologie* (Paris, 1970), pp. 31–50; and Haycock, op. cit. (n. 7), pp. 5–6.

101. cf. also Haycock in *Sudan Notes and Records*, Vol. XLIX (1968), p. 3.

102. Hintze in *Kush* VII (1959), p. 181; Shinnie, op. cit. (n. 6), p. 94.

103. For a more detailed discussion see Hintze in *Kush* XI (1963), pp. 221–4.

104. See n. 29.

105. Shinnie, op. cit. (n. 6), p. 95; for illustration see Hintze in *Kush* VII (1959), pls. XLII–XLIII. A more extended description of the site will be found in Crowfoot and Griffith, op. cit. (n. 29), pp. 13–18.

106. cf. Arkell, op. cit. (n. 43), pp. 166–8; Ali, op. cit. (n. 30).

107. cf. Hintze in *Kush* VII (1959), p. 196.

108. cf. Arkell, op. cit. (n. 43), p. 164.

109. The only report so far published is that of Vercoutter in *Syria*, Vol. XXXIX (1962), pp. 263–99. For additional description see Shinnie, op. cit. (n. 6), p. 87.

110. Vercoutter, op. cit. (n. 109), p. 295.

111. See Shinnie, op. cit. (n. 6), p. 97, and Shinnie, *Excavations at Soba*, Sudan Antiquities Service Occasional Papers, No. 3 (1955), pp. 16–17.

112. See Dixon in *Kush* XI (1963), pp. 227–34.

113. Crawford and Addison, *Abu Geili and Saqadi & Dar el Mek*, The Wellcome Excavations in the Sudan, Vol. III (1951), pp. 1–110.

114. Hintze believes however that the settlement and cemetery at Sennar belonged to the Noba tribe, which was culturally influenced by Meroë but not politically subject to it; see *Zeitschrift für Ägyptische Sprache und Altertumskunde*, Vol. 94 (1967), p. 82. For further discussion of the Noba and their relationship with Meroë see Ch. 13.

115. op. cit. (n. 109), p. 265; see also Dixon, op. cit. (n. 112), p. 234.

116. See primarily Arkell, op. cit. (n. 43), pp. 136–7 and 173–6; also Hofmann in *Meroitic Newsletter* No. 9 (1972), pp. 14–17.

117. cf. Haycock, op. cit. (n. 101), p. 4, and Trigger, op. cit. (n. 33), p. 25.
118. cf. Shinnie, op. cit. (n. 6), p. 96.
119. See ibid., p. 98. The site of Jebel Moya has been a centre of controversy almost since the moment of its excavation; for discussion see Cole, *The Prehistory of East Africa* (Harmondsworth, 1954), pp. 221–2. The definitive reports are those of Addison, *Jebel Moya*, The Wellcome Excavations in the Sudan, Vols. I–II (1949) and subsequent revisions by the same author in *Kush* IV (1956), pp. 4–18.
120. IV: 5.
121. See Shinnie, op. cit. (n. 6), p. 75, and Crowfoot and Griffith, op. cit. (n. 29), pp. 7–8, 89.
122. op. cit. (n. 101), p. 15.
123. Reported by Reisner in *Journal of Egyptian Archaeology*, Vol. V (1918), pp. 99–112 and Vol. VI (1920), pp. 247–64; see also Reisner in *Zeitschrift für Ägyptische Sprache und Altertumskunde*, Vol. 66 (1931), pp. 76–100.
124. Griffith in *University of Liverpool Annals of Archaeology and Anthropology*, Vol. IX (1922), pp. 75–6.
125. See Macadam, op. cit. (n. 63), Vol. II, pp. 114–15 and 231–7.
126. The significance of this stratigraphic separation, originally suggested by me in *Journal of Egyptian Archaeology*, Vol. 50 (1964), pp. 115–17, has been repeatedly disputed by Haycock (op. cit., n. 7, pp. 3–4; op. cit., n. 80, pp. 108–10; op. cit., n. 101, pp. 5–10).
127. For description and discussion of these figures see Dunham in *Journal of Egyptian Archaeology*, Vol. 33 (1947), pp. 63–5.
128. See Maystre in *Bulletin de la Société Française d'Égyptologie*, No. 55 (1969), p. 10; Dunham, op. cit. (n. 27), p. 388.
129. cf. Millet, op. cit. (n. 42), p. 59.
130. Reported by Schiff Giorgini in *Kush* XIII (1965), pp. 116–30 and *Kush* XIV (1966), pp. 259–60, and by Leclant in *Académie des Inscriptions et Belles-Lettres, Comptes Rendus des Séances de l'Année 1970*, pp. 246–76.
131. See Shinnie, op. cit. (n. 6), pp. 67–8. Haycock (personal communication) informs me that the temple was destroyed during the building of the military railway in 1896–7. A few denuded traces were discovered by Vila in the course of an archaeological survey in 1972; see his report in *Meroitica* 3 (in press).
132. cf. Haycock, op. cit. (n. 80), p. 111.
133. See Mills in *Kush* XIII (1965), pp. 3–12. A large Meroitic cemetery at Semna West, excavated by the Oriental Institute of Chicago, has not yet been reported. For a very brief mention see Leclant in *Orientalia*, Vol. 37 (1968), p. 120 and Figs. 34–5.
134. See Trigger, loc. cit. (n. 19), and Millet, op. cit. (n. 42), p. 190, Fig. 3.
135. Millet, op. cit. (n. 42), p. vii; Adams, *Meroitic North and South: a Study in Cultural Contrasts*, Meroitica 2 (1976).
136. Shinnie, op. cit. (n. 6), pp. 141–2.
137. ibid., p. 145.
138. Dunham, *The Egyptian Department and its Excavations* (Boston, 1958), p. 135.
139. See Budge, op. cit. (n. 12), Vol. II, p. 149.
140. For full translation see Hintze, *Die Inschriften des Löwentempels von Musawwarat es Sufra*, Abhandlungen der Deutschen Akademie der Wissenschaften zu Berlin, Klasse für Sprachen, Literatur, und Kunst, 1962, No. 1, pp. 25–32.
141. Quoted from Shinnie, op. cit. (n. 6), p. 143.
142. For more on the cult of Apedemak see Leclant in *Les Syncrétismes dans les Religions Grecque et Romaine*, Bibliothèque des Centres d'Études Supérieures Spécialisés, Travaux du Centre d'Études Supérieures Spécialisé d'Histoire des Religions de

Strasbourg (1973), pp. 139–45, and especially Zabkav, *Apedemak, Lion God of Meroe* (Warminster, 1975).

143. Shinnie, op. cit. (n. 6), p. 145.

144. ibid., p. 146.

145. Haycock, op. cit. (n. 80), p. 111.

146. cf. Dixon, op. cit. (n. 112).

147. For a discussion of Meroitic trade with Egypt see Rostovtzeff, *The Social and Economic History of the Roman Empire*, 2nd ed. (Oxford, 1957), Vol. I, esp. pp. 306–7.

148. XVII: 1; cf. also Shinnie, op. cit. (n. 6), p. 159.

149. cf. Kemp in Ucko, Tringham and Dimbleby, Eds., *Man, Settlement and Urbanism* (London, 1972), pp. 657–61.

150. XVII: 1, 2.

151. Shinnie, personal communication.

152. I cannot agree with the implication of Hintze (in Dinkler, Ed., *Kunst und Geschichte Nubiens in Christlicher Zeit*, Recklinghausen, 1970, pp. 49–65) or the more direct assertions of Haycock (in *Meroitica* 2, 1976, p. 37) and Mohammed Ali (op. cit., n. 30) that the Meriotic sites of the Butana are markedly different from those of the river littoral, and therefore must have been built by or for pastoralists. Quite apart from the ecological improbability I do not believe the meagre archaeological information available from the Butana will support this kind of generalization. For further discussion see my article and the attendant discussion in *Meroitica* 3 (in press).

153. loc. cit. (n. 148).

154. VI: 35.

155. See also, now, the reliefs from the Lion Temple at Musawwarat. Hintze, *Der Löwentempel, Musawwarat es Sufra*, Vol. I, Part 2 (1971), pls. 53–69.

156. Woolley and Randall-MacIver, *Karanog, the Romano–Nubian Cemetery*, University of Pennsylvania Museum, Eckley B. Coxe Junior Expedition to Nubia, Vols. III–IV (1910), pp. 59–60 and pls. 26–8; see also Shinnie, op. cit. (n. 6), p. 159.

157. Carter, *A Preliminary Report on the Fauna from the Excavations at Meroë in 1967, 1968 and 1969* (MS).

158. cf. Millet, op. cit. (n. 42), pp. 39–40.

159. The foregoing are all cited in Shinnie, op. cit. (n. 6), pp. 111–13, 145–6.

160. Cited by Arkell, op. cit. (n. 43), p. 166.

161. Cited by Vercoutter, op. cit. (n. 109), p. 299.

162. Shinnie, op. cit. (n. 6), p. 113. The quotation is from Vercoutter, op. cit. (n. 109), p. 293.

163. See Haycock, op. cit. (n. 101), p. 3.

CHAPTER 12

Principal sources: in this chapter I have drawn perhaps more heavily on N. B. Millet's unpublished thesis, *Meroitic Nubia* (Yale University, 1968; available from University Microfilms) than on any other single source. While I remain sceptical of some of the author's more intuitive readings of the Meroitic texts, I feel that he has made the first meaningful attempt to see Meroitic Lower Nubia in its proper perspective as a quasi-autonomous political and cultural entity rather than merely as a northward extension of the steppelands civilization. Important published sources, as in earlier chapters, have been Shinnie, *Meroe* (New York, 1967); Trigger, *History and Settlement in Lower Nubia*, Yale

University Publications in Anthropology, No. 69 (1965), pp. 120–31; and Haycock's article in *Journal of Egyptian Archaeology*, Vol. 53 (1967), pp. 107–20. Haycock also kindly sent me a number of manuscripts which have not yet been published; one of them (*Landmarks in Cushite History*) has been particularly valuable for my understanding of Ptolemaic activity in Nubia. Monneret de Villard's *La Nubia Romana* (Rome, 1941) remains the standard source on Roman Nubia. For details of Meroitic material culture and mortuary practice in the north I have drawn extensively on the published reports of the two great Meroitic cemeteries of Karanog and Faras: Woolley and Randall-MacIver, *Karanog, The Romano–Nubian Cemetery*, University of Pennsylvania Museum, Eckley B. Coxe Junior Expedition to Nubia, Vols. III–IV (1910) and Griffith in *University of Liverpool Annals of Archaeology and Anthropology*, Vol. XI (1924), pp. 141–78 and Vol. XII (1925), pp. 57–172.

1. Toynbee, *A Study of History*, Vol. 8 (New York, 1963), pp. 407–8.
2. For discussion of Ptolemaic agricultural extension see Rostovtzeff, *A Large Estate in Egypt in the Third Century BC* (Madison, 1922), pp. 3–5, and Butzer in *Bulletin de la Société de Géographie d'Égypte*, Vol. XXXIII (1960), pp. 6–17.
3. See Bevan, *The House of Ptolemy* (Chicago, 1968), pp. 186–7.
4. See especially Haycock, *Landmarks in Cushite History* (MS), pp. 4–12.
5. Desanges in *Actes du Quatre-Vingt-Douzième Congrès National des Sociétés Savantes, 1967, Section d'Archéologie* (Paris, 1970), pp. 31–50.
6. See Lucas, *Ancient Egyptian Materials and Industries*, 3rd ed. (London, 1948), pp. 261–2.
7. For discussion of the identification of Ergamenes with Arkamani see Ch. 11, n. 73.
8. Griffith, *Meroitic Inscriptions, Part II*, Archaeological Survey of Egypt, Memoir 20 (1912), p. 32; and Trigger, *History and Settlement in Lower Nubia*, Yale University Publications in Anthropology, No. 69 (1965), pp. 120–21. The king's name is also variously written as Azakheramani (Griffith) and Adikhalamani (Haycock).
9. See Arkell, *A History of the Sudan*, 2nd ed. (London, 1961), pp. 158–9; Trigger, loc. cit. (n. 8); Emery, *Egypt in Nubia* (London, 1965), p. 225; Shinnie, *Meroe* (New York, 1967), p. 41; and Millet, *Meroitic Nubia* (New Haven, n.d.), pp. 4–6.
10. See Arkell, op. cit. (n. 9), p. 159.
11. Haycock (personal communication) believed that Harsiotef ventured as far north as Aswan on one of his military campaigns (*c.* 400 BC), but this is not clear from the language of his stele. See Budge, *The Egyptian Sudan* (London, 1907), Vol. II, pp. 76–82.
12. cf. Randall-MacIver and Woolley, *Buhen*, University of Pennsylvania Museum, Eckley B. Coxe Junior Expedition to Nubia, Vol. VII (1911), pp. 125–8; and Griffith in *University of Liverpool Annals of Archaeology and Anthropology*, Vol. XI (1924) p. 118.
13. Desanges, op. cit. (n. 5), p. 50; Vercoutter, *Mirgissa I* (Paris, 1970), pp. 23, 171, 189.
14. Monneret de Villard (*La Nubia Romana*, Rome, 1941, pp. 34–5) believed that the fortifications at Gebel Adda and Qasr Ibrim were of Ptolemaic origin, but this now appears highly unlikely. See discussion under 'The Meroitic province', below. The only empirical evidence for Ptolemaic occupation which has so far come to light at Qasr Ibrim is a stone block rather crudely incised with the name PTOLEMAIOS. See Plumley in *Études et Travaux du Centre d'Archéologie Méditerranéenne de l'Académie Polonaise des Sciences*, V (1972), p. 19.
15. Griffith, loc. cit. (n. 12). Thirty *schoenoi* actually corresponds fairly closely to the distance from the First to the Second Cataract (*c.* 200 miles).
16. Haycock, op. cit. (n. 4), pp. 12–16.

17. ibid., pp. 17–18.

18. ibid., p. 17.

19. Which did not supplant Elephantine as a commercial and political centre until medieval times. In the Ptolemaic era it was a small village known as Syene ('market').

20. See especially Posener, *A Dictionary of Egyptian Civilization* (London, 1962), p. 138.

21. See Budge, *The Nile, Notes for Travellers* (London, 1902), pp. 456–65.

22. Millet, op. cit. (n. 9), p. 5.

23. ibid., p. 26.

24. ibid., pp. 26, 34.

25. See especially Monneret de Villard, *Storia della Nubia Cristiana*, Pontificio Institutum Orientalium Studiorum, Orientalia Christiana Analecta 118, (1938) pp. 19–22.

26. cf. Kirwan in *University of Liverpool Annals of Archaeology and Anthropology*, Vol. XXIV (1937), p. 97.

27. Arkell, op. cit. (n. 9), p. 159; Haycock, op. cit. (n. 4), pp. 12–15.

28. cf. Plumley, op. cit. (n. 14), pp. 8–24. The full story of Qasr Ibrim must await many years of further excavation. For discussion of the Meroitic archaeological remains as currently known see 'The Meroitic province', below.

29. See Millet, op. cit. (n. 9), pp. 12–13.

30. See especially Bowersock, *Augustus and the Greek World* (Oxford, 1965), pp. 42–61; also Desanges in *Chronique d'Égypte*, Vol. XLIV (1969), pp. 143–4.

31. See Monneret de Villard, op. cit. (n. 14), p. 2.

32. See ibid., pp. 2–4 and Kirwan in *Sudan Notes and Records*, Vol. XL (1959), p. 24.

33. Strabo XVII: 53–4.

34. Described in Chapter 11. For the original description and illustrations of the find see Bosanquet in *University of Liverpool Annals of Archaeology and Anthropology*, Vol. IV (1911), pp. 66–71 and pls. XII–XVI.

35. loc. cit. (n. 33).

36. VI: 35.

37. Kirwan, op. cit. (n. 32), pp. 24–5.

38. A different point of view is expressed by Jameson in *Journal of Roman Studies*, Vol. LVIII (1968), pp. 74–5. She considers that the expulsion of the Nubians from Pselchis constituted an adequate measure of retaliation, and that Petronius' further advance was motivated by purely economic considerations.

39. Kirwan in *Geographical Journal*, Vol. CXXIII (1957), p. 16; Emery, op. cit. (n. 9), p. 227.

40. See Millet, op. cit. (n. 9), pp. 24–6.

41. Kirwan, op. cit. (n. 39), pp. 16–17. For an attempted reconstruction of the itinerary of Nero's expedition see Priese in *Meroitica* 1 (1973), pp. 123–5.

42. VI: 8, 3.

43. VI: 35.

44. On the other hand, Hintze has attempted to resolve the discrepancies between the two accounts by suggesting that there were actually two expeditions in the reign of Nero; one in the year AD 62 (reported by Seneca) and one in AD 66 or 67 (reported by Pliny). See *Studien zur Meroitischen Chronologie und zu den Opfertafeln aus den Pyramiden von Meroe*, Abhandlungen der Deutschen Akademie der Wissenschaften zu Berlin, Klasse für Sprachen, Literatur, und Kunst, 1959, No. 2, pp. 27–9. See also Hintze and Desanges in *Meroitica* 1 (1973), pp. 140–41, 145.

45. See Bowersock, op. cit. (n. 30), p. 42.

46. See especially Monneret de Villard, op. cit. (n. 14), pp. 4–5.

47. Kirwan, op. cit. (n. 32), p. 25.
48. ibid.
49. Millet, op. cit. (n. 9), p. 26.
50. cf. ibid., p. 27, n. 2.
51. Trigger, op. cit. (n. 8), p. 124.
52. Since the foregoing was written a number of Roman houses at Taifa have been excavated by the Oriental Institute of Chicago, but have not yet been reported in detail. For the briefest of preliminary reports see Seele in *Fouilles en Nubie* (*1959–1961*) (Cairo, 1963), pp. 83–4.
53. *Antiquities of Lower Nubia in 1906–1907* (Oxford, 1907), pp. 64–7.
54. Trigger, op. cit. (n. 8), p. 126.
55. ibid., p. 124.
56. cf. ibid.; also Millet, op. cit. (n. 9), p. 27, n. 2.
57. For detailed description see Monneret de Villard, op. cit. (n. 14), pp. 5–32.
58. Trigger, op. cit. (n. 8), pp. 124–5. The original description of the site is that of Reisner in *Archaeological Survey of Nubia, Report for 1907–1908* (Cairo, 1910), Vol. I, pp. 72–3. For preliminary reports on excavations in the Roman forts at Taifa and Kertassi see Zaba in *Fouilles en Nubie* (*1959–1961*) (Cairo, 1963), pp. 46–51, and in *Fouilles en Nubie* (*1961–1963*) (Cairo, 1967), pp. 212–15.
59. Trigger, op. cit. (n. 8), p. 160.
60. ibid., pp. 123–4.
61. See Griffith, op. cit. (n. 12), p. 122, and Millet, op. cit. (n. 9), p. 31.
62. See Millet, op. cit. (n. 9), pp. 29, 40.
63. cf. Adams in *Kush* XII (1964), p. 164.
64. cf. Millet, op. cit. (n. 9), p. 29; Haycock in *Journal of Egyptian Archaeology*, Vol. 53 (1967), pp. 109–10.
65. See Plumley and Adams in *Journal of Egyptian Archaeology*, Vol. 60 (1974), pp. 228–36.
66. Millet, op. cit. (n. 9), pp. 12, 17–18.
67. cf. ibid., p. 18. For an attempted identification of the towns mentioned by Pliny see Priese, op. cit. (n. 41).
68. Millet, op. cit. (n. 9), p. 29; Haycock, loc. cit. (n. 64).
69. To my knowledge this hypothesis was first put forward by Firth in *Archaeological Survey of Nubia, Report for 1909–1910* (Cairo, 1915), p. 23. See also Trigger, op. cit. (n. 8), p. 123 and Adams in *Journal of Egyptian Archaeology*, Vol. 50 (1964), pp. 119–20.
70. Trigger, op. cit. (n. 8), p. 160.
71. Leclant, however, believes that the Meroitic occupation of Lower Nubia was 'never intense' – see *Actes du Premier Colloque International d'Archéologie Africaine*, Études et Documents Tchadiens, Mémoire I (1969), p. 250.
72. See Singer *et al.*, *A History of Technology*, Vol. II (Oxford, 1956), p. 676. Diodorus (I: 34) asserts that the *saqia* was everywhere in use in the Nile Delta in 60–59 BC but does not mention its presence in Upper Egypt.
73. See Monneret de Villard, op. cit. (n. 14), pp. 43–6.
74. See n. 68.
75. cf. Adams, loc. cit. (n. 69).
76. For a nearly complete listing of Meroitic sites in Egyptian Nubia see Trigger, op. cit. (n. 8), pp. 190–97; this list is however very incomplete for the Sudanese portion of Lower Nubia.
77. Millet, op. cit. (n. 9), pp. 30–31.
78. cf. Monneret de Villard, op. cit. (n. 14), p. 36.
79. Griffith, op. cit. (n. 12), p. 121.

NOTES

80. A description of it has been left by the classical writer Philostratus; see Kirwan, op. cit. (n. 32), p. 26.
81. Excavations are however continuing at Qasr Ibrim, which remains above the level of inundation by Lake Nasser. Up to now they have not revealed many details of the Meroitic occupation on the site.
82. For illustrations see Plumley, op. cit. (n. 14), pp. 16–17, Plumley in *Illustrated London News*, 11 July 1964, p. 52, Fig. 7, and Frend in *Journal of Egyptian Archaeology*, Vol. 60 (1974), pl. viii.
83. See n. 14.
84. Millet, op. cit. (n. 9), pp. 47–50.
85. Griffith in *University of Liverpool Annals of Archaeology and Anthropology*, Vol. XIII (1926), pp. 25–8.
86. ibid., p. 24.
87. See Michalowski, *Faras, Fouilles Polonaises 1961* (Warsaw, 1962), pp. 74–9, and *Faras, Fouilles Polonaises 1961–1962* (Warsaw, 1965), pp. 39–45.
88. Millet, op. cit. (n. 9), p. 46.
89. ibid., pp. 50–52.
90. See Plumley and Adams, op. cit. (n. 65).
91. See Plumley in *Illustrated London News*, 11 July 1964, p. 53, Fig. 8.
92. cf. Plumley, op. cit. (n. 14), pp. 18–19. A somewhat fanciful account of the Podium and its possible significance is that of Frend in *Journal of Egyptian Archaeology*, Vol. 60 (1974), pp. 30–59. For illustrations of the Podium see ibid., pls. VIII, XIII.
93. See Woolley, *Karanog, the Town*, University of Pennsylvania Museum, Eckley B. Coxe Junior Expedition to Nubia, Vol. V (1911), pp. 41–4.
94. Bearing the name of Amani-Yeshbehe (or Yesbekheamani), who is believed to have been one of the last kings of the Kushite dynasty (*c.* AD 283–300). See Plumley in *Journal of Egyptian Archaeology*, Vol. 52 (1966), p. 12 and pl. IV, no. 3.
95. Bearing the well-known names of Amanirenas and Akinidad, which occur also on a famous stele from Meroë ('Royal inscriptions', Ch. 11). The fragmentary stele at Qasr Ibrim had been re-used as a paving stone in the cathedral floor. It has not yet been fully translated, but a brief description and illustration are given in Plumley, op. cit. (n. 14), pp. 19–20.
96. Millet, op. cit. (n. 9), p. 51.
97. Two more possible Meroitic temples have been identified in Lower Nubia, at Buhen and at Meinarti. Both had been so thoroughly destroyed in post-Meroitic times that their original nature and function could not be ascertained with certainty. For descriptions see Randall-MacIver and Woolley, *Buhen*, University of Pennsylvania Museum, Eckley B. Coxe Junior Expedition to Nubia, Vol. VII (1911), pp. 125–6, and Adams in *Kush* XIII (1965), p. 162.
98. For the evidence of these see especially Griffith, *Catalogue of the Demotic Graffiti of the Dodecaschoenos*, Vol. I (Oxford, 1937), pp. 26–31, 112–22.
99. op. cit. (n. 9), p. 29.
100. cf. Trigger, *The Meroitic Funerary Inscriptions from Arminna West*, Publications of the Pennsylvania-Yale Expedition to Egypt, No. 4 (1970), pp. 50–51.
101. Millet, op. cit. (n. 9). Török has recently made an even more detailed analysis of some of the same evidence. His conclusions agree in general with those of Millet, though he identifies many offices as priestly rather than civil. See *Ägypten und Kusch*, Zentralinstituts für Alte Geschichte und Archäologie der Akademie der Wissenschaften der DDR, Schriften zur Geschichte und Kultur des Alten Orients (in press).
102. ibid., p. 37.
103. ibid., p. 52.

104. Macadam suggests that the relationship claimed may be one of clientage rather than of kinship, which would weaken Millet's argument at this point. See *Journal of Egyptian Archaeology*, Vol. 36 (1950), p. 45.

105. Millet, op. cit. (n. 9), pp. 39–40.

106. *Philology and the Use of Written Sources in Reconstructing Early Sudanese History; Reflections on the Administration of Lower Nubia in Meroitic Times* (MS), pp. 5–12.

107. Personal communication.

108. ibid.

109. See Griffith, 'Meroitic Funerary Inscriptions from Faras, Nubia', *Recueil d'Études Égyptologiques Dediées à la Mémoire de Jean-Francis Champollion* No. 21 (Paris, 1922), pp. 565–600.

110. Trigger, op. cit. (n. 100), pp. 26–30.

111. Haycock, op. cit. (n. 64), p. 117; Trigger, op. cit. (n. 100), p. 51.

112. Millet, op. cit. (n. 9), p. 46.

113. ibid., pp. 44–5.

114. For a rather similar interpretation of the origins and functions of the *pelmes* see Haycock, op. cit. (n. 106), pp. 9–12.

115. Millet, op. cit. (n. 9), pp. 57–8; Trigger, op. cit. (n. 100), p. 50.

116. Most notably Qasr Ibrim (Plumley, op. cit., n. 91), Gebel Adda (Millet in *Journal of the American Research Center in Egypt*, Vol. III, 1964, p. 12), and Meinarti (Adams, op. cit., n. 97, pp. 174–6).

117. For further discussion of this thesis see Millet in Fernea, Ed., *Contemporary Egyptian Nubia* (New Haven, 1966), Vol. I, pp. 59–77.

118. cf. Trigger in *Anthropologica*, Vol. X (1968), pp. 96–7.

119. Woolley, op. cit. (n. 93), p. 6.

120. Trigger (personal communication) believes however that large and stoutly built houses are generally characteristic of the later and larger settlements, and that the difference between these and the simple ordinary houses may reflect a rural-urban split rather than class differentiation.

121. Emery and Kirwan, *The Excavations and Survey between Wadi es-Sebua and Adindan, 1929–1931* (Cairo, 1935), Vol. I, pp. 108–22 and Vol. II, pl. 17.

122. See especially Trigger, *The Late Nubian Settlement at Arminna West*, Publications of the Pennsylvania–Yale Expedition to Egypt, No. 2 (1967), pp. 35–70 and Fig. 23.

123. See Klasens in *Fouilles en Nubie (1961–1963)* (Cairo, 1967), pp. 80–82, and Jacquet in *Beiträge zur Ägyptischen Bauforschung und Altertumskunde*, Vol. 12 (1971), pp. 121–31.

124. Excavated by the University of Colorado Nubia Expedition in 1963; not yet published.

125. See Adams, op. cit. (n. 97), pp. 151–2 and in Chang, Ed., *Settlement Archaeology* (Palo Alto, 1968), pp. 182–4, 200.

126. However, Trigger (personal communication) believes that at Arminna all of the 'de luxe' houses were later in date than were any of the ordinary houses. Elsewhere (op. cit., n. 8, p. 129 and op. cit., n. 118, p. 97) he describes the 'de luxe' houses as typical of Meroitic dwellings in general, but in fact they are less numerous than are the ordinary, flimsy houses at many Lower Nubian sites.

127. Some confirmation for this theory may be found in the fact that at esh-Shaukan a collection of ostraka was found inscribed with what are obviously the plans of 'de luxe' houses. See Jacquet, op. cit. (n. 123), pp. 130–31 and pls. 19–20.

128. For a more detailed architectural description of the Meroitic 'de luxe' houses see ibid., pp. 121–30.

129. See Adams and Nordström in *Kush* XI (1963), p. 26.

130. cf. Crawford and Addison, *Abu Geili and Saqadi & Dar el Mek*, The Wellcome

Excavations in the Sudan, Vol. III (1951), p. 10. This feature has been noted also at Meroë (personal communication from P. L. Shinnie).

131. Crawford and Addison, op. cit. (n. 130); see especially Plan of Excavations (end paper).
132. Adams and Nordström, op. cit. (n. 129), pp. 26–8.
133. ibid.
134. ibid., pp. 29, 41.
135. cf. Woolley, op. cit. (n. 93), pp. 26–40 and pls. 26–9; Adams, op. cit. (n. 97), pp. 164–5; and Trigger, op. cit. (n. 122), Fig. 23.
136. See n. 125.
137. Adams, op. cit. (n. 97), pp. 162–3.
138. Griffith, op. cit. (n. 85), pp. 21–3 and pl. XIII.
139. Trigger, op. cit. (n. 8), pp. 129–30.
140. Adams, op. cit. (n. 97), pp. 163–4 and pl. XXXIV.
141. For extended discussion see Adams in Kush XIV (1966), pp. 262–83.
142. cf. Emery and Kirwan, op. cit. (n. 121), Vol. I, pp. 108–13 and Vol. II, pls. 15–16.
143. For comparative details see Adams, op. cit. (n. 141), pp. 264–5.
144. See Vercoutter in Kush VII (1959), p. 127.
145. Much information about viticulture in Ptolemaic and Roman Egypt is provided by Pliny and Athenaeus. See Wilkinson, The Manners and Customs of the Ancient Egyptians (New York, 1878), Vol. I, pp. 382–93 and Lucas, op. cit. (n. 6), pp. 27–31.
146. cf. Adams, op. cit. (n. 141), p. 268 and Monneret de Villard, op. cit. (n. 14), pp. 40–43.
147. Adams, op. cit. (n. 141), pp. 277–8.
148. See Daremberg and Saglio, Dictionnaire des Antiquités Graeco-Romaines, Vol. III (Paris, 1900), p. 2093.
149. Emery and Kirwan, op. cit. (n. 121), Vol. I, p. 110; Adams, op. cit. (n. 97), p. 151.
150. See Burckhardt, Travels in Nubia (London, 1819), p. 512. The volume of a kanyr is not known.
151. Kromer, Römische Weinstuben in Sayala (Unternubien), Österreichische Akademie der Wissenschaften, Philosophisch-Historische Klasse Denkschriften, 95 (1967).
152. Trigger in Bibliotheca Orientalis, Vol. XXV (1968), p. 192.
153. Kromer, op. cit. (n. 151), pp. 114–17.
154. cf. Trigger, op. cit. (n. 152), pp. 192–3.
155. Adams and Nordström, op. cit. (n. 129), p. 39 and p. 37, Fig. 6, b.
156. The building was apparently begun in the Meroitic period but was not completed until the early years of the Ballana period. Thus, nearly all the deposits within it were of 'X-Group' pottery. See Plumley and Adams, op. cit. (n. 65), pp. 217–19.
157. For illustration see ibid., pl. XLIV, no. 1, and Plumley in Journal of Egyptian Archaeology, Vol. 56 (1970), pl. XXII, no. 2. Decoration of grape clusters can be seen at the lower left corner, near the bottom of the wall.
158. Plumley, op. cit. (n. 157), pl. XXIII, no. 4.
159. ibid., pp. 14–16; 'Editorial Foreword' in Journal of Egyptian Archaeology, Vol. 55 (1969), p. 1.
160. cf. Plumley and Adams, op. cit. (n. 65), pp. 218–19.
161. See Verwers in Kush X (1962), pp. 19–21.
162. In addition to the famous 'Royal Baths' described in detail in Chapter 11, two smaller baths were discovered at Meroë. From the scanty published descriptions they do not appear to have been closely similar to the structures at Faras. See Garstang in University of Liverpool Annals of Archaeology and Anthropology,

Vol. V (1912), p. 75, and Phythian-Adams in *University of Liverpool Annals of Archaeology and Anthropology*, Vol. VII (1914), p. 11.

163. Translated from Monneret de Villard, op. cit. (n. 14), p. 36.

164. Sayce in *University of Liverpool Annals of Archaeology and Anthropology*, Vol. IV (1911), p. 55; Dunham in *American Journal of Archaeology*, Vol. L (1946), p. 385; Gadallah in *Kush* XI (1963), pp. 198–9.

165. Trigger in *African Historical Studies*, Vol. II (1969), p. 45.

166. ibid., p. 46.

167. Wainwright in *Sudan Notes and Records*, Vol. XXVI (1945), p. 24.

168. Haycock believed on the basis of personal examination that the smelting remains at Kawa are those of a copper rather than of an iron industry (personal communication).

169. Trigger, op. cit. (n. 165), p. 47.

170. cf. Singer *et al.*, op. cit. (n. 72), pp. 56, 72.

171. See Arkell in *Current Anthropology*, Vol. VII (1956), p. 478; Williams in Thompson and Ferguson, Eds., *Africa in Classical Antiquity* (Ibadan, 1969), pp. 62–72; and Tylecote in *Bulletin of the Historical Metallurgy Group*, Vol. 4 (1970), pp. 67–72. Davies on the other hand suggests that the Meroitic smelter was more likely to have been a bowl-furnace; see *West Africa before the Europeans* (London, 1967), p. 239.

172. cf. Charleston, *Roman Pottery* (London, 1955), pp. 36–7 and pls. 78–80.

173. In two earlier studies (*Kush* XII, 1964, pp. 170–71 and Dinkler, Ed., *Kunst und Geschichte Nubiens in Christlicher Zeit* [Recklinghausen, 1970], p. 121) I wrote that late Napatan and early Meroitic sites in Upper Nubia are characterized almost exclusively by hand-made wares, the potter's wheel having seemingly gone out of use in late Napatan times. This was patently an error and was based on a misunderstanding of the chronological position of the 'Noba' (post-Meroitic) cemeteries at Meroë and Musawwarat, which yielded only hand-made pottery. I have since had the opportunity to examine in person a large collection of pottery from Musawwarat, as well as to see the description of the pottery published by Prof. Otto (*Zeitschrift für Archäologie*, Vol. I, 1967, pp. 1–32) and have recognized that the bulk of the material consists of undecorated wheel-made wares which essentially continue the traditions of pharaonic times. Shinnie (personal communication) reports the same characteristics in the pottery from Meroë. For fuller discussion on this subject see Adams and Otto in *Meroitica* 1 (1973), pp. 177–240.

174. For the pottery from Musawwarat see especially Otto in *Zeitschrift für Archäologie*, Vol. I (1967), pp. 1–32.

175. cf. Adams, op. cit. (n. 63), p. 171, in *Meroitica* 1 (1973), pp. 177–219, 227–40, and in *Meroitica* 2 (1976) p. 19. In the lowest levels at Qasr Ibrim, however, wares similar to those from Meroë and Musawwarat, and quite unlike other Meroitic pottery from Lower Nubia, have been found. See 'The Meroitic province', above.

176. Some very generalized resemblances may be noted between Meroitic decorated pottery and the so-called 'Hadra' vases made at Alexandria in the third century BC (cf. Guerrini, *Vasi di Hadra*, Seminario di Archeologia e Storia dell'Arte Greca e Romana dell' Università di Roma, Studi Miscellanei, 8, 1964) as well as certain Graeco–Egyptian vessels from Naukratis (Petrie, *Naukratis, Part I*, Egypt Exploration Fund, Memoir No. 3, 1888). However, the Egyptian wares exhibit only a fraction of the decorative variety found in Meroitic pottery.

177. For extended typological and historical studies of Meroitic pottery from Lower Nubia see Adams, op. cit. (n. 63); in *Kush* XV (1973), pp. 1–50; and in Dinkler, Ed., *Kunst und Geschichte Nubiens in Christlicher Zeit* (Recklinghausen, 1970), pp. 111–22. See also Shinnie, op. cit. (n. 9), pp. 114–22.

178. For coloured illustrations see especially Woolley and Randall-MacIver, *Karanog, the Romano–Nubian Cemetery*, University of Pennsylvania Museum, Eckley B. Coxe Junior Expedition to Nubia, Vols. III–IV (1910), pls. 41–52, and Almagro, *La Necropolis Meroitica de Nag Gamus (Masmas, Nubia Egipicia)*, Comité Español de la Unesco para Nubia, Memorias de la Misión Arqueológica en Nubia, VIII (1965), pls. XXIII–XXVII; many other illustrations will be found in Griffith, op. cit. (n. 12), pls. XLI–LII.

179. For the designs see especially Adams, op. cit. (n. 63), pp. 147–52 and Shinnie, op. cit. (n. 9), p. 121.

180. cf. Adams in *Kush* X (1962), p. 276, *Kush* XV (1973), p. 4, and *Kush* XVI (in press).

181. Adams and Nordström, op. cit. (n. 129), p. 26.

182. Adams in *Kush* X (1962), p. 64. Kilns were also found in the Meroitic settlement at Wadi el-Arab, but the excavators consider that they may be of Christian date. From the published illustration, however, they appear very similar to the Meroitic kiln at Argin. See Emery and Kirwan, op. cit. (n. 121), Vol. I, p. 110 and Vol. II, pl. 15. It is evident from the finding of a number of mis-fired vessels at Qasr Ibrim that Meroitic pottery was made here also (author's unpublished field notes).

183. Personal communication from P. L. Shinnie.

184. cf. Crawford and Addison, op. cit. (n. 130), pp. 50–51.

185. Dixon in *Kush* XI (1963), pp. 232–4.

186. cf. Adams in *Kush* XVI (in press).

187. Author's unpublished field notes. For description of the site see *Kush* XI (1963), p. 28. Haycock (personal communication) reported that large numbers of such weights have also been found at Meroë.

188. Singer *et al.*, *A History of Technology*, Vol. I (Oxford, 1954), pp. 426–8, 443–5.

189. Lucas, op. cit. (n. 6), p. 170.

190. Arkell, op. cit. (n. 9), p. 166.

191. XIII: 28.

192. Lucas, op. cit. (n. 6), p. 170.

193. Arkell, op. cit. (n. 9), p. 166.

194. cf. Woolley and Randall-MacIver, op. cit. (n. 178), pp. 27–8, 245; pl. 108.

195. Shinnie, op. cit. (n. 9), p. 129.

196. cf. Adams and Nordström, op. cit. (n. 129), p. 30 and pl. III.

197. Woolley and Randall-MacIver, op. cit. (n. 178), p. 28.

198. ibid., p. 109.

199. cf. ibid., p. 61 and Shinnie, op. cit. (n. 9), pp. 122–31.

200. See especially Woolley and Randall-MacIver, op. cit. (n. 178), pls. 21–40.

201. See Griffith, op. cit. (n. 12), pls. LIII–LXIV.

202. Author's unpublished field notes.

203. See especially Woolley and Randall-MacIver, op. cit. (n. 178), pp. 59–62 and pls. 26–8; Griffith, op. cit. (n. 12), pl. LIII; Dunham, *Royal Tombs at Meroë and Barkal*, Royal Cemeteries of Kush, Vol. IV (1957), pp. 136, 138, 148, 150, 168–9; Shinnie, op. cit. (n. 9), p. 126.

204. cf. Griffith, op. cit. (n. 12), p. 144 and pl. XL; Säve-Söderbergh in *Kush* XI (1963), p. 65; Pellicer and Llongueras, *Las Necropolis Meroiticas del Grupo 'X' y Cristianas de Nag-el-Arab*, Comité Español de la Unesco para Nubia, Memorias de la Misión Arqueológica en Nubia, V (1965), pl. XVIII.

205. Woolley and Randall-MacIver, op. cit. (n. 178), pl. 35.

206. Haycock (personal communication) reported that such anklets are still occasionally worn by women in the Central Sudan.

207. cf. Shinnie, op. cit. (n. 9), p. 130.

208. Woolley and Randall-MacIver, op. cit. (n. 178), p. 74. For illustrations of glass

vessels found in Meroitic sites see ibid., pls. 37–9; Griffith, op. cit. (n. 12), pl. LI; Säve-Söderbergh, op. cit. (n. 204), pl. XII; and Leclant in *Académie des Inscriptions et Belles-Lettres, Comptes Rendus des Séances de l'Année 1970*, pp. 269–74, Figs. 13–18.

209. See Leclant, op. cit. (n. 208), pp. 269–73, and in *Les Syncrétismes dans les Religions Grecque et Romaine*, Bibliothèque des Centres d'Études Supérieures Spécialisées, Travaux du Centre d'Études Supérieures Spécialisées d'Histoire des Religions de Strasbourg (1973), pp. 135–9.

210. Leclant, op. cit. (n. 208), p. 273, Fig. 17.

211. Except for small clay crucibles used in making beads, which are very common in Christian Nubian sites.

212. Woolley and Randall-MacIver, op. cit. (n. 178), pp. 74–5. For coloured illustration see ibid., pl. 40.

213. Griffith, op. cit. (n. 12), pl. LXI.

214. See Woolley and Randall-MacIver, op. cit. (n. 178), pp. 69–72 and pls. 21–5.

215. cf. Trigger, op. cit. (n. 8), pp. 186–97.

216. Woolley and Randall-MacIver, op. cit. (n. 178), p. 81.

217. ibid., p. 3.

218. See especially Millet, op. cit. (n. 9), p. 52 and in *Journal of the American Research Center in Egypt*, Vol. II (1963), pp. 154–64.

219. cf. Griffith in *University of Liverpool Annals of Archaeology and Anthropology*, Vol. XII (1925), p. 64; Millet in *Journal of the American Research Center in Egypt*, Vol. II (1963), p. 161, and Leclant, op. cit. (n. 208), pp. 247–57.

220. Millet, loc. cit., n. 219.

221. Schiff Giorgini in *Kush* XIII (1965), pp. 129–30; Leclant, op. cit. (n. 208), p. 253.

222. Woolley and Randall-MacIver, op. cit. (n. 178), p. 14.

223. cf. Leclant, op. cit. (n. 208), p. 249.

224. Woolley and Randall-MacIver, op. cit. (n. 178), p. 81.

225. Griffith, op. cit. (n. 12), pp. 144–6.

226. Adams and Nordström, op. cit. (n. 129), p. 29; Adams, loc. cit. (n. 63), and op. cit. (n. 69), p. 118.

227. Griffith in *University of Liverpool Annals of Archaeology and Anthropology*, Vol. X (1923), pp. 73–171.

228. cf. Woolley and Randall-MacIver, op. cit. (n. 178), p. 81.

229. cf. Griffith, op. cit. (n. 12), p. 146 and pl. XXXV, 2; Shinnie, op. cit. (n. 9), p. 155.

230. Trigger, op. cit. (n. 8), p. 127.

231. Woolley and Randall-MacIver, op. cit. (n. 178), p. 27; Vila, *Aksha* II (Paris, 1967), pp. 332–3.

232. cf. Emery, op. cit. (n. 9), p. 228, Fig. 42.

233. Woolley and Randall-MacIver, op. cit. (n. 178), p. 29.

234. ibid., p. 30.

235. Adams and Nordström, op. cit. (n. 129), pp. 26–8.

236. Woolley and Randall-MacIver, op. cit. (n. 178), pp. 9–11.

237. For illustrations see ibid., pls. 11–14, 19; and Griffith, op. cit. (n. 12), pl. LXV.

238. Woolley and Randall-MacIver, op. cit. (n. 178), pp. 9–10.

239. For illustrations see ibid., pls. 15–17.

240. ibid., p. 8.

241. See ibid., pl. 1.

242. For illustrations see especially ibid., pls. 1–10, and Griffith, op. cit. (n. 12), pls. LXVI–LXVII.

243. Posener, op. cit. (n. 20), p. 266.

244. Woolley and Randall-MacIver, op. cit. (n. 178), p. 46.

245. ibid., pp. 10–11.
246. The southernmost known examples are from the Meroitic cemetery at Seddenga (Leclant, op. cit., n. 208, p. 259). The author believes that the *ba* statuettes here were originally placed in a special chamber (*serdab*) within the tomb pyramid.
247. At least in their inscriptions written in Egyptian hieroglyphics. Royal inscriptions in the Meroitic language, insofar as we can decipher them, seem to employ a rather different titulary.

CHAPTER 13

Principal sources: for the archaeology of the Ballana culture I have drawn heavily on Emery's *The Royal Tombs of Ballana and Qustul* (Cairo, 1938; 2 vols.) and on his later *Egypt in Nubia* (London, 1965), pp. 57–90, 232–47. For additional interpretation of the Ballana archaeological remains I am particularly indebted to Trigger's *History and Settlement in Lower Nubia*, Yale University Publications in Anthropology, No. 69 (1965), pp. 131–40, and to two articles by the same author in *Journal of Egyptian Archaeology*, Vol. 55 (1969), pp. 117–28 and in *Journal of Near Eastern Studies*, Vol. 28 (1969), pp. 255–61. In treating the historical texts I have relied heavily on a number of articles published by L. P. Kirwan, most notably in *University of Liverpool Annals of Archaeology and Anthropology*, Vol. XXIV (1937), pp. 69–105; in *Sudan Notes and Records*, Vol. XX (1937), pp. 47–62; in *Sudan Notes and Records*, Vol. XL (1959), pp. 23–37; and in *The Geographical Journal*, Vol. 138 (1972), pp. 457–65.

1. Shinnie, *Meroe* (New York, 1967), p. 52.
2. ibid., p. 52; Millet, *Meroitic Nubia* (New Haven, n.d.), pp. 35–6.
3. *Studien zur Meroitischen Chronologie und zu den Opfertafeln aus den Pyramiden von Meroe*, Abhandlungen der Deutschen Akademie der Wissenschaften zu Berlin, Klasse für Sprachen, Literatur, und Kunst, 1959, No. 2, p. 31.
4. *The Royal Cemeteries of Kush*, Vol. IV (Boston, 1957), p. 7.
5. cf. Kirwan in *Sudan Notes and Records*, Vol. XX (1937), p. 53 and Trigger, *History and Settlement in Lower Nubia*, Yale University Publications in Anthropology, No. 69 (1965), p. 131.
6. op. cit. (n. 5).
7. Jones and Monroe, *A History of Ethiopia* (Oxford, 1955), p. 22.
8. See Kirwan in *University of Liverpool Annals of Archaeology and Anthropology*, Vol. XXIV (1937), p. 70, and in *The Geographical Journal*, Vol. 138 (1972), pp. 171–2. However, there is so far no archaeological confirmation for the existence of Adulis in pre-Axumite times.
9. For translation see Schoff, *The Periplus of the Erythraean Sea* (New York, 1912).
10. For translation see McCrindle, *Christian Topography of Cosmas, an Egyptian Monk* (London, 1897).
11. Kirwan in *University of Liverpool Annals of Archaeology and Anthropology*, Vol. XXIV (1937), p. 69, and in *The Geographical Journal*, Vol. 138 (1972), pp. 169–71; Jones and Monroe, op. cit. (n. 7), pp. 22–3.
12. Arkell, *A History of the Sudan*, 2nd ed. (London, 1961), p. 180.
13. McCrindle, op. cit. (n. 10), p. 371.
14. The inscription of Aezanas (see below) shows that during the heyday of their power the Axumites exerted considerable influence over their Beja neighbours, although in earlier and later times they were almost continually at war with one or another of the nomad tribes. See especially Kirwan in *University of Liverpool Annals of*

NOTES

Archaeology and Anthropology, Vol. XXIV (1937), pp. 70–71, and Paul, *A History of the Beja Tribes of the Sudan* (Cambridge, 1954), pp. 45–6.

15. See Jones and Monroe, op. cit. (n. 7), p. 24.

16. Taken from the translation of Budge in *A History of Ethiopia* (London, 1928), Vol. I, pp. 252–8. I have selected this version primarily for the sake of its brevity. A much fuller and more technically correct translation into English is that of Kirwan in *Kush* VIII (1960), pp. 163–5, from the German of Littmann in *Miscellanea Academica Berolinensa*, Vol. II, Part 2 (1950), pp. 97–127.

17. See Kirwan, op. cit. (n. 16), p. 163, and in *The Geographical Journal*, Vol. 138 (1972), p. 461.

18. A second stele of Aezanas with Christian protocols came to light at Axum in 1969; see Kirwan in *The Geographical Journal*, Vol. 138 (1972), pp. 460–62. It is apparently a partial account of the same campaign as that described in the more famous stele

19. XVII: 1, 2.

20. IV: 5.

21. As implied by several late classical authors. See Kirwan, op. cit. (n. 5), pp. 48–9.

22. For extended commentary on the Aezanas inscription and its topographic and historic significance see Hintze in *Zeitschrift für Ägyptische Sprache und Altertumskunde*, Vol. 94 (1967), pp. 79–86, and Kirwan, op. cit. (n. 18).

23. cf. Shinnie in *Kush* III (1955), pp. 82–3.

24. In *Kush* VII (1959), p. 190.

25. Kirwan, op. cit. (n. 16), pp. 171–2. Kirwan now believes that the author of the Adulis inscription may have been an Arabian king; see *The Geographical Journal*, Vol. 138 (1972), pp. 175–6.

26. See Ullendorff, *The Ethiopians* (London, 1960), pp. 55–7.

27. For discussion on this point see 'Ideology and religion in the post-Meroitic era', below.

28. See Kirwan in *Mélanges offerts à Kazimierz Michalowski* (Warsaw, 1966), p. 121.

29. Emery, *Egypt in Nubia* (London, 1965), pp. 232–4. For discussion of the Blemmyes based on contemporary sources see Revillout, *Mémoire sur les Blemmyes, à propos d'une Inscription Copte*, Mémoires Présentés par Divers Savants à l'Académie des Inscriptions et Belles-Lettres, Vol. VIII, Part 2, Series 1 (1874), and in *Revue Égyptologique*, Vol. V (1887), pp. 1–47.

30. This has now been definitely confirmed by a textual find from Qasr Ibrim (to be described in Ch. 14), in which the terms Beja and Blemmye are used interchangeably. See also Kirwan, op. cit. (n. 14), pp. 69–76.

31. cf. ibid., pp. 70–71 and n. 5.

32. *De Bello Persico* I: xix. For a translation of the passage describing the Roman withdrawal from the Dodekaschoenos see Emery, op. cit. (n. 29), p. 235.

33. Kirwan, op. cit. (n. 28), p. 122.

34. Haycock in *Journal of Egyptian Archaeology*, Vol. 53 (1967), p. 119; Trigger in *Journal of Egyptian Archaeology*, Vol. 55 (1969), p. 126.

35. It was initially described by Reisner in *Archaeological Survey of Nubia, Bulletin No. 3* (Cairo, 1909), p. 6.

36. *Archaeological Survey of Nubia, Report for 1907–1908* (Cairo, 1910), Vol. I, p. 345.

37. *Archaeological Survey of Nubia, Bulletin No. 5* (Cairo, 1910), p. 12.

38. Batrawi in *Journal of the Royal Anthropological Institute*, Vol. LXXV (1946), Part II, pp. 81–101 and Vol. LXXVI (1946), Part II, pp. 131–56; Mukherjee, Rao and Trevor, *The Ancient Inhabitants of Jebel Moya (Sudan)* (Cambridge, 1955), p. 85; Greene, *Dentition of Meroitic, X-Group, and Christian Populations from*

Wadi Halfa, Sudan, University of Utah Anthropological Papers, No. 85 (1967); Millet, op. cit. (n. 2), p. 193; Duane Burnor, personal communication.

39. However, the question of what 'negroid' means in terms of skeletal anatomy is still very far from clear.

40. cf. Vagn Nielsen, *Human Remains,* The Scandinavian Joint Expedition to Sudanese Nubia Publications, Vol. 9 (1970), p. 81; Strouhal in *Anthropologie und Humangenetik; Festschrift zum 65. Geburtstag von Prof. Dr K. Saller* (Stuttgart, 1968), pp. 84–92; and Strouhal in *Anthropological Congress Dedicated to Ales Hrdlicka, 30th August–5th September 1969* (Prague, 1971), pp. 541–7.

41. Batrawi in *Journal of the Royal Anthropological Institute,* Vol. LXXVI (1946), Part II, p. 145.

42. Griffith in *University of Liverpool Annals of Archaeology and Anthropology,* Vol. XII (1925), p. 70.

43. Junker, *Ermenne, Bericht über die Grabungen der Akademie der Wissenschaften in Wien auf den Friedhöfen von Ermenne (Nubien),* Akademie der Wissenschaften in Wien, Philosophisch-Historische Klasse Denkschriften, 67, Part 1 (1925), p. 85; translated in Trigger, op. cit. (n. 5), p. 133.

44. See Adams in *Kush* XII (1964), p. 172.

45. Adams in *Kush* XIII (1965), p. 176; Trigger, *The Late Nubian Settlement at Arminna West,* Publications of the Pennsylvania–Yale Expedition to Egypt, No. 2 (1967), pp. 79–83; Millet, op. cit. (n. 2), p. 193.

46. Trigger, op. cit. (n. 5), p. 132. Kirwan used the term 'Ballana Civilization' more than a decade earlier (*Bulletin de la Société de Géographie d'Égypte,* Vol. XXV, 1953, pp. 103–10) but did not formally propose it as a synonym for 'X-Group'.

47. Trigger, op. cit. (n. 5), pp. 136–7.

48. e.g. those of Kirwan cited in n. 5, n. 8, and n. 16, and those of Emery in *Egypt in Nubia* (op. cit., n. 29), pp. 232–45 and *The Royal Tombs of Ballana and Qustul* (Cairo, 1938), Vol. I, pp. 5–24.

49. See n. 32.

50. His work survives only in an abridgement by Photius. For the original text of this see Woolley and Randall-MacIver, *Karanog, the Romano–Nubian Cemetery,* University of Pennsylvania Museum, Eckley B. Coxe Junior Expedition to Nubia, Vol. III (1910), p. 103; for partial translation see Emery, op. cit. (n. 29), p. 236.

51. For the original version of the text see Woolley and Randall-MacIver, op. cit. (n. 50), pp. 103–4; for discussion see Kirwan, op. cit. (n. 5), pp. 53–4.

52. cf. Trigger, op. cit. (n. 5), p. 133.

53. For a complete list of Ballana sites in Egyptian Nubia see ibid., pp. 186–7. For summary numerical tallies of sites in Sudanese Nubia see Adams in *Kush* X (1962), p. 12, Adams and Nordström in *Kush* XI (1963), pp. 13–16, and Mills in *Kush* XIII (1965), pp. 3–12.

54. cf. Mills, op. cit. (n. 53).

55. See Pellicer and Llongueras, *Las Necrópolis Meroíticas del Grupo 'X' y Cristianas de Nag-el-Arab,* Comité Español de la Unesco para Nubia, Memorias de la Misión Arqueológica en Nubia, V (1965), p. 35.

56. e.g. the great cemeteries at Ballana and Qustul, to be described presently, and the cemetery at Sai Island (Vercoutter in *Kush* VI, 1958, pls. XLIX–L).

57. Based on unpublished archives of the Archaeological Survey of Sudanese Nubia. cf. also Adams in *Sudan Notes and Records,* Vol. XLVIII (1967), p. 17, and in *Antiquity,* Vol. XLII (1968), p. 207.

58. The full extent of Ballana settlement in the area between the Sudan–Egyptian frontier and the Second Cataract did not become apparent until the area was surveyed in 1960–65. Earlier, Emery had written that 'the greatest concentration of their

NOTES

burials is around the district of Ibrim'. See *The Royal Tombs of Ballana and Qustul* (Cairo, 1938), Vol. I, p. 18.

59. As was clearly demonstrated by the excavations of 1972 and 1974; see Plumley and Adams in *Journal of Egyptian Archaeology*, Vol. 60 (1974), pp. 212–38. Qasr Ibrim was described by Olympiodorus in the early fifth century as an important Blemmye stronghold; see Kirwan, op. cit. (n. 14), pp. 77–80.

60. See Ch. 3.

61. cf. Mills, op. cit. (n. 53).

62. As attested by the very large and rich Ballana tombs at Firka; see Kirwan in *Journal of Egyptian Archaeology*, Vol. XXI (1935), pp. 191–8, and *The Oxford University Excavations at Firka* (Oxford, 1939).

63. See Vercoutter, loc. cit. (n. 56); Bates and Dunham in *Harvard African Studies*, Vol. VIII (1927), p. 117; and Kirwan, *The Oxford University Excavations at Firka* (Oxford, 1939), pp. 28–9. There may be a small Ballana cemetery a few miles still farther south, at Wawa; see Kirwan, op. cit. (above), p. 29.

64. cf. Kirwan in *Sudan Notes and Records*, Vol. XL (1959), p. 30; Trigger, op. cit. (n. 5), p. 133.

65. Garstang *et al.*, *Meroë, the City of the Ethiopians* (Oxford, 1911), p. 30; Dunham in *Archaeology*, Vol. 6 (1953), p. 94.

66. cf. Trigger, op. cit. (n. 34), p. 120.

67. ibid.

68. For the best illustration of one of these quivers see Millet in *Journal of the American Research Center in Egypt*, Vol. II (1963), p. 155.

69. cf. Emery and Kirwan, *The Excavations and Survey between Wadi es-Sebua and Adindan* (Cairo, 1935), Vol. I, pp. 268–77.

70. Emery, op. cit. (n. 58).

71. Bates and Dunham, op. cit. (n. 63), pp. 69–96.

72. Kirwan, op. cit. (n. 63).

73. Millet, op. cit. (n. 2), pp. 193–4; Adams, op. cit. (n. 44).

74. For description and documentation see 'Town and village life', Ch. 12.

75. Emery and Kirwan, op. cit. (n. 69), pp. 108–22 and pl. 17.

76. Adams, op. cit. (n. 45), pp. 153–5.

77. Verwers in *Kush* X (1962), p. 30; Hewes in *Kush* XII (1964), pp. 180–83.

78. Site 5-S-24; see Adams and Nordström, op. cit. (n. 53), p. 30 and p. 27, Fig. 4.

79. Site 5-S-23, not reported in print.

80. See Randall-MacIver and Woolley, *Buhen*, University of Pennsylvania Museum, Eckley B. Coxe Junior Expedition to Nubia, Vols. VII–VIII (1911), p. 125 and pl. 68.

81. Millet identified similar houses at Gebel Adda as belonging to the Meroitic period, but this is debatable. See n. 84, below.

82. In post-Ballana times goods were stored not in specially constructed houses but in deep storage pits dug down into and through the accumulated deposits of earlier times. Scores of these pits were found in every part of the site; they had in fact disturbed the stratigraphy nearly everywhere. They seem to date from every period of occupation from Early Christian to late Medieval. See Plumley and Adams, op. cit. (n. 59).

83. For further discussion see 'Ideology and religion in the post-Meroitic era', below.

84. Substantial houses found by Millet at Gebel Adda were attributed by him to the Meroitic rather than to the Ballana period, but I think this may have been due to a misinterpretation of the ceramic stratigraphy. See Millet in *Journal of the American Research Center in Egypt*, Vol. VI (1967), p. 58.

85. For further discussion of Ballana pottery see Adams in *Kush* XV (1973), pp. 1–50.

86. See Adams in *Kush* X (1962), pp. 66–70.
87. For discussion of the evolution of Nubian hand-made pottery see Adams in Dinkler, Ed., *Kunst und Geschichte Nubiens in Christlicher Zeit* (Recklinghausen, 1970), pp. 114–15, and op. cit. (n. 85), pp. 35–6.
88. Trigger in *African Historical Studies*, Vol. II (1969), p. 49.
89. cf. Emery, op. cit. (n. 29), p. 69.
90. See Adams and Nordström, op. cit. (n. 53), p. 31 and pl. IV b.
91. Description based on the author's unpublished field notes. For preliminary report see Plumley and Adams, op. cit. (n. 59).
92. For documentation see n. 69–72.
93. The definitive report is Emery, op. cit. (n. 58); see also Emery, *Nubian Treasure* (London, 1948).
94. Emery, op. cit. (n. 29), pp. 58–9. The reference is to Weigall's *Antiquities of Lower Nubia in 1906–1907* (Oxford, 1907).
95. Emery, op. cit. (n. 29), pp. 63–7.
96. Emery, op. cit. (n. 58), pp. 25–6.
97. cf. ibid., pp. 182–399. See also Emery, *Nubian Treasure* (London, 1948), and Kirwan in Bacon, Ed., *Vanished Civilizations* (New York, 1963), p. 77.
98. Emery, op. cit. (n. 58), p. 180. Kirwan (personal communication) now prefers a dating between the fourth and the early sixth centuries.
99. For detailed descriptions and illustrations see Emery, op. cit. (n. 58), pp. 182–6 and pls. 32–6; for coloured illustrations see Kirwan, op. cit. (n. 63), pp. 62–3. For discussion of the iconography and cultural significance of the Ballana crowns see Trigger in *Journal of Near Eastern Studies*, Vol. 28 (1969), pp. 255–61.
100. Emery, op. cit. (n. 58), p. 182.
101. ibid., p. 26.
102. cf. Dunham, op. cit. (n. 65), pp. 93–4.
103. Tomb 3 at Ballana; see Emery, op. cit. (n. 58), p. 78.
104. Tumulus III: see Reisner in *Harvard African Studies*, Vol. V (1923), p. 81.
105. Emery, op. cit. (n. 58), p. 26.
106. See especially Trigger, op. cit. (n. 34), pp. 121–2 and pl. XXIX.
107. ibid., p. 122.
108. ibid., p. 123 and n. 1.
109. For further discussion of this problem see ibid.; also Trigger, op. cit. (n. 99).
110. op. cit. (n. 34), p. 128.
111. Emery, op. cit. (n. 58), pp. 180–81.
112. op. cit. (n. 34), p. 125.
113. Trigger, op. cit. (n. 99), pp. 258–61.
114. cf. Kirwan, op. cit. (n. 5), p. 56.
115. op. cit. (n. 34), p. 125.
16. cf. Kirwan in Bacon, Ed., *Vanished Civilizations* (New York, 1963), p. 77.
17. Millet believes however that the excavations at Gebel Adda were sufficient to establish that the royal residence was not here; see loc. cit. (n. 84).
18. See 'The archaeology of the Ballana Culture', above.
19. e.g. Kirwan, op. cit. (n. 5), pp. 59–60.
20. For documentation see n. 69, n. 71, and n. 72.
21. op. cit. (n. 34), p. 128.
22. Emery, op. cit. (n. 58), pp. 22–3; Kirwan, op. cit. (n. 5), p. 60.
23. Emery, op. cit. (n. 58), p. 25 and pl. 27, B and D.
24. ibid., pl. 27, B.
25. ibid., pp. 182–6 and pls. 32–6.
26. ibid., pls. 42, 48, 63, 67, 69, 86, 109.

127. ibid., pls. 57, 62, 65, 68, 98, 102.
128. cf. Plumley and Adams, op. cit. (n. 59), p. 226.
129. Griffith, *The Nubian Texts of the Christian Period*, Abhandlungen der Königlichen Preussischen Akademie der Wissenschaften (1913), p. 73; see also Millet in Fernea, Ed., *Contemporary Egyptian Nubia* (New Haven, 1966), Vol. 1, pp. 5–6.
130. cf. Kirwan, op. cit. (n. 14), pp. 84–5.
131. Another graffito in the temple of Kalabsha, a proclamation in the Meroitic language by a certain King Kharamadeye, is also thought by Millet to date from the immediate post-Meroitic period, but this is almost wholly conjectural. See Millet, op. cit. (n. 2), pp. 203–12, 269–304.
132. Quoted from Emery, op. cit. (n. 58), p. 239.
133. cf. Arkell, op. cit. (n. 12), pp. 170–71; Kirwan, op. cit. (n. 5), p. 60.
134. Trigger, op. cit. (n. 34), p. 120.
135. Millet, op. cit. (n. 2), pp. 193–4.
136. Adams, op. cit. (n. 45).
137. Randall-MacIver and Woolley, op. cit. (n. 80), pp. 125–6 and pl. 68, a.
138. Author's unpublished field notes.
139. cf. Toynbee, *A Study of History*, Vol. 6 (New York, 1962), pp. 49–97.
140. See n. 65.
141. cf. Kirwan, op. cit. (n. 14), p. 76.
142. Quoted from Emery, op. cit. (n. 29), p. 238.
143. Kirwan, op. cit. (n. 14), pp. 89–90.
144. Griffith in *University of Liverpool Annals of Archaeology and Anthropology*, Vol. XIII (1926), pp. 49–50 and pl. XXXVII; Emery, op. cit. (n. 58), p. 136 and pl. 27, D.
145. No full description or illustration of these objects has been published, to my knowledge. For a very brief mention see Hewes, op. cit. (n. 77), p. 181; for illustration of a rather atypical specimen see Woolley and Randall-MacIver, op. cit. (n. 50), pl. 109.
146. Adams, op. cit. (n. 45), p. 155. Mention should also be made of a primitive grave stele in Greek found at Jebel Barkal in 1916. Reisner believed that it had come from a nearby pre-Christian cemetery, although it was not actually found *in situ*. Unfortunately no formal account either of the stele or of the cemetery has ever been published. For a brief preliminary report see Reisner in *Harvard African Studies*, Vol. I (1917), pp. 197–8; for illustration see also Dunham, *The Barkal Temples* (Boston, 1970), pl. LIX, A. For still other evidence of Christianity in Ballana times see Donadoni in *Mémoires de l'Institut d'Égypte*, Vol. LIX (1969), pp. 26–7.
147. Kirwan, op. cit. (n. 28), p. 127. The charms have been described by Barb in Momigliano, Ed., *The Conflict between Paganism and Christianity in the Fourth Century* (Oxford, 1963), p. 121.
148. See Ch. 12, n. 151 and n. 160.
149. cf. Adams, op. cit. (n. 45), p. 150.
150. Author's unpublished field notes.
151. Kirwan, op. cit. (n. 5), p. 60.
152. For a resumé of classical passages relating to Nubia see Woolley and Randall-MacIver, op. cit. (n. 50), pp. 99–103. Complete citation of the original sources will be found in this work. For additional sources and commentary see especially Kirwan, op. cit. (n. 14).
153. cf. Kirwan, op. cit. (n. 14), pp. 69–76; Monneret de Villard, *Storia della Nubia Cristiana*, Pontificium Institutum Orientalium Studiorum, Orientalia Christiana Analecta 118 (1938), pp. 25–6; and Paul, op. cit. (n. 14). cf. also n. 30.
154. Emery, op. cit. (n. 58), p. 23.

NOTES

155. Zyhlarz in *Wiener Zeitschrift für die Kunde des Morgenlandes*, Vol. XXXV (1928); discussed by Hillelson in *Sudan Notes and Records*, Vol. XIII (1930), pp. 137–48 and by Kirwan, op. cit. (n. 5), pp. 55–60.

156. Monneret de Villard, op. cit. (n. 153), pp. 39, 89–91.

157. *De Bello Persico* I: xix.

158. cf. Kirwan, op. cit. (n. 5), pp. 61–2 and in *Kush* VI (1958), pp. 70–71. The same author has written further in a personal communication that 'Procopius could be a very unreliable historian. His is a compressed account. Diocletian may well have made some formal withdrawal of the frontier as elsewhere. But the introduction of barbarian tribes under their own leaders to defend the frontiers – a risky operation – probably dates from the late fourth or even fifth century ... It could only have been a central policy decision ...'

159. W. B. Emery is the primary champion of the Blemmye theory; cf. op. cit. (n. 58), pp. 5–24 and op. cit. (n. 29), pp. 244–5. Most other scholars opt for the Nobatae. The case for them is most fully developed in various articles by L. P. Kirwan (op. cit., n. 5, 8, 28, 46, 63 and 64).

160. cf. Emery, op. cit. (n. 29), p. 231; Kirwan, op. cit. (n. 5), p. 55.

161. cf. especially Kirwan, op. cit. (n. 5), pp. 56–62.

162. This hypothesis does not originate with me. It has been proposed in somewhat different form by Millet, op. cit. (n. 129), pp. 59–71.

163. cf. Hillelson, op. cit. (n. 155).

164. cf. Priese in *Études et Travaux du Centre d'Archéologie Méditerranéenne de l'Académie Polonaise des Sciences*, Vol. VII (1973), pp. 156–62.

165. cf. Kirwan, op. cit. (n. 5), p. 53.

166. cf. Millet, op. cit. (n. 2), pp. 58–61.

167. cf. Redfield, *The Primitive World and its Transformations* (Ithaca, 1953), esp. Ch. III.

168. e.g. by Reisner and Elliot Smith; see n. 36.

169. cf. Kirwan, op. cit. (n. 5), p. 60.

170. cf. Batrawi, *Report on the Human Remains* (Cairo, 1935), pp. 174–5. It is necessary to emphasize, however, that the supposed negroid characteristics of the Qustul burials were largely a subjective impression, as the poor preservation of the skeletal remains precluded accurate metrical analysis (Kirwan, personal communication).

171. Quoted from Kirwan, op. cit. (n. 14), pp. 83–4; see also Emery, op. cit. (n. 29), p. 239. For the original text see Woolley and Randall-MacIver, op. cit. (n. 50), pp. 104–5.

172. Kirwan, op. cit. (n. 14), p. 85.

173. ibid., n. 5.

174. cf. ibid., p. 96. Other writers, including Emery (op. cit., n. 29, p. 239) have assumed that Silko was a Christian. For further discussion of this question see Kraus *Die Anfänge des Christentums in Nubien* (Vienna, 1930), pp. 100–109.

175. Emery, op. cit. (n. 58), p. 17.

176. Strabo XVII: 1, 2; Ptolemy IV: 5; Pliny VI: 35.

177. See Trigger, op. cit. (n. 5), p. 136, and Shinnie in *Kush* II (1954), p. 84.

178. Chittick in *Kush* V (1957), p. 73. See also Kirwan in the same volume, pp. 37–41.

179. cf. Trigger, op. cit. (n. 5), p. 136.

180. cf. Kirwan, op. cit. (n. 63), pp. 42–3, and Trigger, op. cit. (n. 5), pp. 136–7.

181. See Garstang in *University of Liverpool Annals of Archaeology and Anthropology*, Vol. III (1910), pp. 69–70, and Garstang et al., op. cit. (n. 65), pp. 29–33.

182. cf. Kirwan, op. cit. (n. 63), pp. 42–3 and op. cit. (n. 178), p. 39; Shinnie, op. cit. (n. 23), p. 84.

183. Kirwan, op. cit. (n. 63), p. 42.

184. For a preliminary report on a small post-Meroitic cemetery at Musawwarat es-Sufra see Hintze in *Wissenschaftliche Zeitschrift der Humboldt-Universität zu Berlin, Gesellschafts- und Sprachwissenschaftliche Reihe*, Vol. XVII (1968), p. 681. For an analysis of the skeletal remains see Strouhal in the same journal, Vol. XX (1971), pp. 257–66. The skeletons are said to exhibit a 'markedly negroid' character (ibid., p. 266).
185. Shinnie, op. cit. (n. 177), p. 68.
186. ibid., p. 73.
187. See Chittick, op. cit. (n. 178), pp. 73–7.
188. Marshall and Abd el Rahman in *Kush* I (1953), pp. 40–46.
189. cf. Shinnie, op. cit. (n. 177), p. 84.
190. ibid.
191. See Kirwan, op. cit. (n. 63), p. 42; Bentley and Crowfoot in *Sudan Notes and Records*, Vol. VII (1924), No. 2, pp. 18–28.
192. cf. Dunham, op. cit. (n. 65), pp. 93–4.

CHAPTER 14

Principal sources: the primary source on the history of Christian Nubia, upon which I have drawn heavily in this and subsequent chapters, is Monneret de Villard's *Storia della Nubia Cristiana*, Pontificio Institutum Orientalium Studiorum, Orientalia Christiana Analecta 118 (1938). The evangelization of Nubia is also discussed at length in an earlier work by Kraus, *Die Anfänge des Christentums in Nubien* (Vienna, 1930), and in articles by Kirwan in *University of Liverpool Annals of Archaeology and Anthropology*, Vol. XXIV (1937), pp. 69–105, and by Donadoni in *Mémoires de l'Institut d'Égypte*, Vol. LIX (1969), pp. 25–33. For discussion of the *Baqt* treaty and its significance I am particularly indebted to an article by Forand in *Der Islam*, Vol. 48 (1971), pp. 111–21.

1. Kroeber, *The Nature of Culture* (Chicago, 1952), pp. 381–2.
2. cf. Momigliano, Ed. *The Conflict between Paganism and Christianity in the Fourth Century* (Oxford, 1963), pp. 18–19.
3. Crowfoot in *Journal of Egyptian Archaeology*, Vol. XIII (1927), p. 14.
4. cf. Olmstead, *History of the Persian Empire* (Chicago, 1948), pp. 119–28.
5. cf. Kirwan in *University of Liverpool Annals of Archaeology and Anthropology*, Vol. XXIV (1937), pp. 82–3.
6. There are a number of Arabic versions of this affair. The most complete is that of Mas'udi, *Les Prairies d'Or*, trans. Meynard and Courteille (Paris, 1863), Vol. II, pp. 22–3. For a discussion in English see Forand in *Der Islam*, Vol. 48 (1971), pp. 117–18.
7. See Adams in *Journal of the American Research Center in Egypt*, Vol. IV (1965), pp. 126–33.
8. See Bell, *Cults and Creeds in Graeco–Roman Egypt* (Liverpool, 1953), pp. 78–84, and Shore in Harris, Ed., *The Legacy of Egypt*, 2nd ed. (Oxford, 1971), pp. 396–7.
9. Momigliano, op. cit. (n. 2), p. 19.
10. Bell, *Egypt from Alexander the Great to the Arab Conquest* (Oxford, 1948), pp. 112–16.
11. ibid., p. 114.
12. ibid., p. 115.
13. Shore, op. cit. (n. 8), p. 415; cf. also Butcher, *The Story of the Church of Egypt* (London, 1897), p. 301.

NOTES

14. Bell, op. cit. (n. 10), p. 116.
15. Kirwan, op. cit. (n. 5), p. 97.
16. Procopius, *De Bello Persico* I: xix, 27–36.
17. Kirwan, op. cit. (n. 5), p. 96.
18. cf. Kirwan in *Sudan Notes and Records*, Vol. XL (1959), p. 31.
19. *Ecclesiastical History*, trans. Payne-Smith (London, 1860), Part III.
20. Gadallah in *Sudan Notes and Records*, Vol. XL (1959), pp. 39–40.
21. IV: II, 19.
22. See Mommsen in *Monumenta Germaniae Historica, Auctores Antiquissimi*, Vol. XI (Berlin, 1894), pp. 207–20.
23. cf. also Meinardus in *Nubie, Cahiers d'Histoire Égyptienne*, Vol. X (1967), pp. 137–41.
24. For a perceptive discussion of the political overtones of Nubia's evangelization see Donadoni in *Mémoires de l'Institut d'Égypte*, Vol. LIX (1969), pp. 25–33.
25. Kirwan, op. cit. (n. 5), p. 103.
26. Kirwan's characterization of the change in burial customs as gradual and evolutionary (ibid., p. 103) is not supported by the evidence from the recent archaeological surveys in Nubia.
27. For further discussion along these lines see Michalowski, *Faras, Centre Artistique de la Nubie Chrétienne* (Leiden, 1966), pp. 7–9.
28. See Kirwan, *The Oxford University Excavations at Firka* (Oxford, 1939), pp. 49–50.
29. cf. Michalowski in Dinkler, Ed., *Kunst und Geschichte Nubiens in Christlicher Zeit* (Recklinghausen, 1970), pp. 14–17, Krause in the same volume, pp. 71–86, and Jakobielski, *Faras* III (Warsaw, 1972), pp. 35–6.
30. cf. Adams, op. cit. (n. 7), p. 121.
31. Michalowski, op. cit. (n. 29), p. 14; Wessel, *Christentum am Nil* (Recklinghausen, 1964), p. 234; Jakobielski, op. cit. (n. 29), pp. 140–43.
32. Junker in *Zeitschrift für Ägyptische Sprache und Altertumskunde*, Vol. 60 (1925), pp. 124–48; Monneret de Villard in *Aegyptus*, Vol. XII (1932), pp. 309–16; Jakobielski, op. cit. (n. 29), pp. 143–5.
33. See Krause, op. cit. (n. 29); Säve-Söderbergh in the same volume, pp. 238–9; and Van Moorsel in the same volume, pp. 281–90.
34. See Gadallah, op. cit. (n. 20), p. 41.
35. cf. Shore, op. cit. (n. 8), pp. 422–33.
36. Gadallah, op. cit. (n. 20), p. 41; cf. also Kirwan, op. cit. (n. 28), p. 51.
37. Gadallah, op. cit. (n. 20), pp. 41–2; Jakobielski, op. cit. (n. 29), pp. 14–15.
38. Kirwan, op. cit. (n. 28), p. 50.
39. Michalowski, op. cit. (n. 29), pp. 14–17; Jakobielski, op. cit. (n. 29), pp. 140–68.
40. Säve-Söderbergh, op. cit. (n. 33), p. 239.
41. cf. ibid.; also Jakobielski, op. cit. (n. 29), pp. 140–68.
42. cf. Alvares, *The Prester John of the Indies*, trans. Lord Stanley (Cambridge, 1961), p. 461.
43. See Ch. 15.
44. For preliminary reports see Plumley in *Journal of Egyptian Archaeology*, Vol. 50 (1964), pp. 3–4; Vol. 52 (1966), pp. 9–11; Vol. 56 (1970), pp. 12–17; and in *Illustrated London News*, 11 July 1964, pp. 50–52; Plumley and Adams in *Journal of Egyptian Archaeology*, Vol. 60 (1974), pp. 212–38; Frend in *Byzantinoslavica*, Vol. XXXIII (1972), pp. 224–9, and in *Journal of Egyptian Archaeology*, Vol. 60 (1974), pp. 30–59.
45. Budge, *The Egyptian Sudan* (London, 1907), Vol. II, pp. 288–308.
46. When the First Archaeological Survey was beginning its work, in 1907, Reisner excavated more than 1,600 Christian graves in a cemetery near Shellal (*Archaeologi-*

cal Survey of Nubia, Report for 1907–1908, Cairo, 1910, Vol. I, p. 96). This number probably exceeds the total of Christian graves which have been excavated in all the years since.

47. For commentary on the attitude of many Egyptologists towards 'Coptic' remains see Donadoni, op. cit. (n. 24), p. 29.

48. Reported in *University of Liverpool Annals of Archaeology and Anthropology*, Vol. XIII (1926), pp. 50–93; Vol. XIV (1927), pp. 57–116; and Vol. XV (1928), pp. 63–88. The actual excavations were carried out in 1910–12.

49. In *Journal of Theological Studies*, Vol. X (1909), p. 545 ff., and *The Nubian Texts of the Christian Period*, Abhandlungen der Königlichen Preussischen Akademie der Wissenschaften, 1913.

50. *La Nubia Medioevale*, Vols. I–II (Cairo, 1935).

51. cf. Emery, *Egypt in Nubia* (London, 1965), pp. 55–6.

52. Pontificio Institutum Orientalium Studiorum, Orientalia Christiana Analecta 118 (1938).

53. cf. Michalowski, op. cit. (n. 29), pp. 17–18.

54. Monneret de Villard, op. cit. (n. 52), p. 70.

55. For a more detailed account see Lane-Poole, *A History of Egypt in the Middle Ages* (London, 1901), pp. 1–15.

56. The Nubian archers were described as 'pupil-smiters'; see Shinnie, *Medieval Nubia*, Sudan Antiquities Service Museum Pamphlet No. 2 (1954), p. 4.

57. See ibid.

58. cf. Crawford, *The Fung Kingdom of Sennar* (Gloucester, 1951), pp. 51–3.

59. A quotation from the Koran, X: 109.

60. Translated versions vary slightly. The above is quoted from Forand, op. cit. (n. 6), pp. 114–15. The earliest English translation is that of Burckhardt, *Travels in Nubia* (London, 1819), pp. 511–12.

61. Procopius, *De Bello Persico* I: xix.

62. N. B. Millet informs me that 'We found a piece of cotton marked *baqt* in Arabic at [Gebel] Adda, in one of the burials thought to be end of the thirteenth century' (personal communication).

63. Burckhardt, op. cit. (n. 60), p. 512. An *ardeb* is today equal to about six bushels; the volume of a *kanyr* of wine has never been ascertained.

64. See Forand, op. cit. (n. 6), p. 121.

65. ibid., p. 113.

66. ibid., pp. 113, 116.

67. Old Dongola, the capital of Nubia throughout the Middle Ages, was situated on the east bank of the Nile about half way between the Third and Fourth Cataracts. It should not be confused with 'New' Dongola (Dongola el-Urdi), the modern administrative centre which is located about seventy miles downstream and on the opposite side of the river. Old Dongola was abandoned in the nineteenth century, after the establishment of the newer community.

68. As stipulated in the first paragraph of the treaty, quoted earlier.

69. As argued by Kirwan in *Journal of Egyptian Archaeology*, Vol. XXI (1935), p. 61.

70. op. cit. (n. 52), pp. 81–3.

71. e.g. Michalowski in *Kush* XII (1964), p. 199 and n. 12; Jakobielski, op. cit. (n. 29), pp. 35–6.

72. Michalowski, loc. cit. (n. 71); Jakobielski, op. cit. (n. 29), pp. 35–46.

73. cf. Kirwan, op. cit. (n. 69), p. 62.

74. Kirwan, op. cit. (n. 69), p. 62. However, the toponyms Nobatia and Maris are not absolutely interchangeable; for discussion see 'The organization of the medieval states', Ch. 15.

75. It is recounted in Abu Salih, *The Churches and Monasteries of Egypt and some Neighbouring Countries*, trans. Evetts and Butler (London, 1895), pp. 267-8.
76. cf. Meinardus, op. cit. (n. 23), p. 147, n. 59.
77. cf. Hasan, *The Arabs and the Sudan* (Edinburgh, 1967), pp. 92-3.
78. For the full text and commentary see Plumley in *Journal of Egyptian Archaeology*, Vol. 61 (1975), pp. 241-5.
79. For extended discussion see Vantini in Dinkler, op. cit. (n. 29), pp. 41-8.
80. ibid., p. 47.
81. Forand, op. cit. (n. 6), p. 120.
82. ibid., p. 119.
83. cf. Vantini in Dinkler, op. cit. (n. 29), pp. 41-8.
84. For a chronicle of these events see Monneret de Villard, op. cit. (n. 52), pp. 122-9.
85. Meinardus, op. cit. (n. 23), p. 150.
86. cf. Lane-Poole, op. cit. (n. 55), p. 197.
87. The story of the invasion is told by Abu Salih, op. cit. (n. 75), pp. 266-7. For a more detailed discussion see Monneret de Villard, op. cit. (n. 52), pp. 196-8.

CHAPTER 15

Principal sources: for historical data I have drawn heavily, as before, on Monneret de Villard's *Storia della Nubia Cristiana*, Pontificio Institutum Orientalium Studiorum, Orientalia Christiana Analecta 118 (1938). The passages from Maqrizi translated and annotated in Burckhardt, *Travels in Nubia* (London, 1819), pp. 493-543, have also been of enormous value. Most of the archaeological discoveries relating to Christian Nubia are too recent to have been synthesized in any general work; consequently I have been obliged to draw upon a very large number of preliminary excavation reports which are cited in individual notes. Many of the latest preliminary reports are brought together in Dinkler, Ed., *Kunst und Geschichte Nubiens in Christlicher Zeit* (Recklinghausen, 1970). Syntheses of cultural development in Christian Nubian architecture and pottery will be found in Monneret de Villard, *La Nubia Medioevale* (Cairo, 1935 and 1953), and in several of my own articles: *Kush* X (1962), pp. 245-88; *Kush* XV (1973), pp. 1-50; *Kush* XVI (in press); *Journal of the American Research Center in Egypt*, Vol. IV (1965), pp. 87-140; and Dinkler, Ed., *Kunst und Geschichte Nubiens* (cited above), pp. 111-28. An overall cultural chronology for the Christian period is proposed in my article in *Kush* XII (1964), pp. 241-7.

1. For tabulations see Trigger, *History and Settlement in Lower Nubia*, Yale University Publications in Anthropology, Vol. 69 (1965), pp. 186-97; Adams in *Kush* X (1962), p. 12; Adams and Nordström in *Kush* XI (1963), p. 15; and Mills in *Kush* XIII (1965), pp. 3-12.
2. cf. Dinkler, Ed., *Kunst und Geschichte Nubiens in Christlicher Zeit* (Recklinghausen, 1970), pp. 7-10.
3. For a list of these see Monneret de Villard, *La Nubia Medioevale*, Vol. I (Cairo, 1935), p. 285.
4. Most of these studies have been my own. They are partially reported in *Kush* X (1962), pp. 245-88; *Kush* XV (1973), pp. 1-50; *Kush* XVI (in press); and in Dinkler, op. cit. (n. 2), pp. 111-28. A two-volume definitive work on Christian Nubian pottery is in preparation.
5. Adams in *Journal of the American Research Center in Egypt*, Vol. IV (1965), pp. 87-140. A definitive work on Nubian church architecture is in preparation.

NOTES

6. cf. Michalowski in Wessel, Ed., *Christentum am Nil* (Recklinghausen, 1964), pp. 79–92; Michalowski, *Faras, Centre Artistique de la Nubie Chrétienne* (Leiden, 1966); and Michalowski in Dinkler, op. cit. (n. 2), pp. 11–28.

7. For discussion of the characteristics of the individual periods see Adams in *Kush* XII (1964), pp. 241–7, and Säve-Söderbergh in Gardberg, *Late Nubian Sites*, The Scandinavian Joint Expedition to Sudanese Nubia Publications, Vol. 7 (1970), pp. 14–21.

8. See especially Adams in Chang, Ed., *Settlement Archaeology* (Palo Alto, 1968), pp. 174–207. See also Trigger, op. cit. (n. 1), pp. 143–50.

9. *Kitab al-Mawa'iz wa'l-Itibar fi Dhikr al-Khitat wa'l-Athar*, Ed. al-Adawi (Cairo, 1853–4). The passages excerpted from Ibn Selim are translated in Burckhardt, *Travels in Nubia* (London, 1819), pp. 493–521.

10. Translated by Evetts and Butler (Oxford, 1895). For comment on the date and reliability of the surviving MS see ibid., pp. ix–xiii.

11. See Monneret de Villard, *Storia della Nubia Cristiana*, Pontificio Institutum Orientalium Studiorum, Orientalia Christiana Analecta 118 (1938), pp. 109–15; for accounts in English see Meinardus in *Nubie, Cahiers d'Histoire Égyptienne*, Vol. X (1967), pp. 148–9, and Hasan, *The Arabs and the Sudan* (Edinburgh, 1967), pp. 52–6.

12. Quoted from Trimingham, *Islam in the Sudan* (London, 1949), p. 65.

13. Arkell, *A History of the Sudan*, 2nd ed. (London, 1961), p. 194.

14. cf. Shinnie, *Excavations at Soba*, Sudan Antiquities Service Occasional Papers, No. 3 (1955).

15. Abu Salih, op. cit. (n. 10), pp. ix–x.

16. ibid., pp. 260–77.

17. The full extent of the archaeological record is not yet known, since excavations have only recently begun at Old Dongola, the secular capital of medieval Nubia. Here royal palaces, royal inscriptions, and even royal tombs may yet come to light.

18. See Monneret de Villard, op. cit. (n. 11), p. 169.

19. Abu Salih, op. cit. (n. 10), p. 272.

20. cf. Monneret de Villard, op. cit. (n. 11), pp. 172–4.

21. ibid., pp. 177–80.

22. See especially Michalowski, *Faras, Die Kathedrale aus dem Wüstensand* (Zurich and Cologne, 1967), pls. 38, 70, 94–5.

23. Abu Salih's description of the crown of King George (op. cit., n. 10, p. 273) is also based upon such a mural portrait of the king and not upon first-hand observation.

24. Monneret de Villard, op. cit. (n. 11), pp. 175–7.

25. Abu Salih, op. cit. (n. 10), pp. 271–2.

26. For discussion see Trimingham, op. cit. (n. 12), pp. 71–2.

27. For preliminary reports see Michalowski in *Kush* XIV (1966), pp. 289–99 and in Dinkler, op. cit. (n. 2), pp. 163–70; and Jakobielski in Dinkler, op. cit. (n. 2), pp. 171–80.

28. Michalowski in Dinkler, op. cit. (n. 2), p. 165.

29. cf. Crawford, *The Fung Kingdom of Sennar* (Gloucester, 1951), p. 35; for an illustration see Arkell, op. cit. (n. 13), pl. 22, b.

30. Abu Salih, op. cit. (n. 10), p. 272.

31. Meaning of course south of Egypt; Maris was the northernmost district of Nubia.

32. The earliest mention of the eparch is in a dedication stele from the Faras Cathedral, dated AD 707. See Jakobielski in *KL10*, Vol. 51 (1969), p. 500.

33. Plumley in *Journal of Egyptian Archaeology*, Vol. 56 (1970), p. 14.

34. For illustrations see Griffith in *University of Liverpool Annals of Archaeology and Anthropology*, Vol. XV (1928), pl. XXXII, and Shinnie, *Medieval Nubia*, Sudan Antiquities Service Museum Pamphlet No. 2 (1954), p. 12.

35. Translated in Burckhardt, op. cit. (n. 9), p. 494.

36. Plumley in Michalowski, Ed., *Nubia Récentes Recherches* (Warsaw, 1975), p. 106.

37. Arkell, op. cit. (n. 13), p. 191.

38. See Griffith, loc. cit. (n. 34) and in *University of Liverpool Annals of Archaeology and Anthropology*, Vol. XIII (1926), pl. LXI; and Michalowski, op. cit. (n. 22), pls. 13, 92, 93, 95b.

39. cf. Monneret de Villard, op. cit. (n. 11), pp. 184–7, and Arkell, op. cit. (n. 13), pp. 210–11.

40. op. cit. (n. 22), p. 44.

41. ibid.

42. cf. MacMichael, *A History of the Arabs in the Sudan* (London, 1922), Vol. I, pp. 248–9, and Crawford, op. cit. (n. 29), pp. 325–7.

43. Griffith, loc. cit. (n. 34).

44. The documents were discovered in a buried jar during the writer's excavations at Qasr Ibrim in 1974; see Plumley in *Journal of Egyptian Archaeology*, Vol. 61 (1975), pp. 6–7. A preliminary translation has kindly been provided by Prof. J. M. Plumley.

45. For discussion of the etymology of the name see 'The successors of Makouria', Ch. 16.

46. cf. Monneret de Villard, op. cit. (n. 11), pp. 187–8; Millet in *Journal of the American Research Center in Egypt*, Vol. VI (1967), p. 62.

47. However, the recently discovered documents from Qasr Ibrim (cf. n. 44) mention other officials with purely Nubian titles: *ñonnen* and *papsa*.

48. For discussion see Monneret de Villard, op. cit. (n. 11), pp. 189–91.

49. Kirwan in *Sudan Notes and Records*, Vol. XX (1937), p. 60.

50. This has been suggested by Michalowski, the excavator of the 'Bishop's Palace'. See *Kush* XII (1964), p. 196 and pl. XXXVIII, a.

51. See Plumley, loc. cit. (n. 33); also Plumley, op. cit. (n. 36).

52. Michalowski, op. cit. (n. 22), p. 45.

53. Millet, op. cit. (n. 46), p. 59.

54. Monneret de Villard, op. cit. (n. 11), p. 140.

55. Abu Salih, op. cit. (n. 10), p. 262.

56. cf. Plumley in *Illustrated London News*, 11 July 1964, pp. 50–52, and op. cit. (n. 33), pp. 13–14.

57. This affair is described by Monneret de Villard, op. cit. (n. 11), pp. 169–70, and by Forand in *Der Islam*, Vol. 48 (1971), pp. 117–18.

58. See Monneret de Villard, op. cit. (n. 11), p. 118; Adams, op. cit. (n. 7), p. 236; Sherif in *Kush* XII (1964), pp. 249–50; Millet, op. cit. (n. 46), p. 59; Säve-Söderbergh in *Kush* XII (1964), p. 39; Holthoer *et al.* in *Studia Orientalia*, Vol. XXVIII, No. 15 (1964), pp. 10–13; and Hasan, op. cit. (n. 11), p. 238, n. 43.

59. cf. Hasan, op. cit. (n. 11), p. 93.

60. Quoted from Burckhardt, op. cit. (n. 9), pp. 494–5.

61. Abu Salih, op. cit. (n. 10), p. 263.

62. Monneret de Villard, op. cit. (n. 11), pp. 136–7.

63. Abu Salih, op. cit. (n. 10), pp. 262–3.

64. Burckhardt, op. cit. (n. 9), p. 494.

65. Emery, *Egypt in Nubia* (London, 1965), p. 157.

66. Ibn Selim did encounter some Moslem traders at Dongola, but their entry was strictly regulated. See Quatremère, *Mémoires sur l'Égypte* (Paris, 1811), Vol. II, pp. 81–4.

67. For discussion see Kirwan in *Journal of Egyptian Archaeology*, Vol. XXI (1935), p. 60.

NOTES

68. See Burckhardt, op. cit. (n. 9), p. 497.
69. cf. Kirwan, loc. cit. (n. 67).
70. Monneret de Villard (op. cit., n. 11, pp. 135–9) failed to perceive this distinction when he identified Upper Maqs, the political frontier of the Upper Nubian 'closed district', as the boundary between Nobatia and Makouria.
71. cf. Kirwan, op. cit. (n. 67), p. 62.
72. cf. Burckhardt, op. cit. (n. 9), pp. 497–503.
73. op. cit. (n. 10), pp. 263–5.
74. Burckhardt, op. cit. (n. 9), p. 496.
75. Kirwan, op. cit. (n. 67), p. 61.
76. Arkell, op. cit. (n. 13), p. 194.
77. The very few Old Nubian documents which have been recovered from the vicinity of Soba suggest that the dialect spoken there was different from that found in the Old Nubian texts of Lower Nubia. See Monneret de Villard, op. cit. (n. 11), pp. 156–7, and Haycock in *Sudan Notes and Records*, Vol. LIII (1972), p. 27.
78. Burckhardt, op. cit. (n. 9), p. 500.
79. cf. Monneret de Villard, op. cit. (n. 3), Vol. I, pp. 269–79; and Arkell in *Kush* VII (1959), pp. 115–19.
80. cf. Monneret de Villard, op. cit. (n. 11), pp. 152–6.
81. Burckhardt, op. cit. (n. 9), p. 500.
82. Not specifically the kings of Alwa but those of el-Abwab, which was the northern frontier district of Alwa. cf. Ch. 16.
83. The name of the town is thus recorded by Ibn Selim. Abu Salih (op. cit., n. 10, pp. 263–4) called it simply 'Town of Alwa'.
84. See Shinnie, op. cit. (n. 14), p. 10.
85. ibid., pp. 18–27.
86. op. cit. (n. 10), p. 263.
87. This is given as incidental information in a biography of the Coptic Patriarch Michael written by a certain 'Deacon John'. See Monneret de Villard, op. cit. (n. 11), pp. 96, 160.
88. ibid., pp. 160–61; Michalowski, *Faras, Centre Artistique de la Nubie Chrétienne* (Leiden, 1966), p. 6; Jakobielski, *Faras* III (Warsaw, 1972), pp. 74, 84–99.
89. cf. especially Jones and Monroe, *A History of Ethiopia* (Oxford, 1955), pp. 35–6.
90. cf. Michalowski in Dinkler, op. cit. (n. 2), p. 13.
91. cf. sources cited in n. 88; also Trimingham, op. cit. (n. 12), p. 64; Kirwan, *The Oxford University Excavations at Firka* (Oxford, 1939), pp. 49–51; and Abu Salih, op. cit. (n. 10), p. 272.
92. Jones and Monroe, loc. cit. (n. 89).
93. Vansleb, *Histoire de l'Église de l'Alexandrie* (Paris, 1677), pp. 29–30. See footnote 15 in Crawford, op. cit. (n. 29), p. 25.
94. Monneret de Villard, op. cit. (n. 11), pp. 162–5.
95. According to some texts the four most important bishoprics in Nubia were those at Qasr Ibrim, Faras, Sai, and Dongola. See Vercoutter in *Bulletin de la Société Française d'Égyptologie*, No. 58 (1970), p. 23.
96. For a comprehensive resumé of our current knowledge of the Faras bishops see Jakobielski, op. cit. (n. 88).
97. Preliminary accounts of the Faras excavations which have thus far been published include those of Michalowski in *Kush* X (1962), pp. 220–44; *Kush* XI (1963), pp. 235–56; *Kush* XII (1964), pp. 195–207; *Kush* XIII (1965), pp. 177–89; *Faras, Fouilles Polonaises 1961* (Warsaw, 1962); *Faras, Fouilles Polonaises 1961–1962* (Warsaw, 1965); op. cit. (n. 22); and additional sources cited in n. 6; and Jakobielski in *Études et Travaux du Centre d'Archéologie Mediterrànéenne de l'Académie*

Polonaise des Sciences, Vol. III (1966), pp. 151–70; in *Mélanges offerts à Kazimierz Michalowski* (Warsaw, 1966), pp. 101–8; op. cit. (n. 32); in Dinkler, op. cit. (n. 2), pp. 29–38; and Jakobielski, op. cit. (n. 88).

98. See Michalowski in *Kush* XI (1963), pp. 238–40 and pl. LVI; Plumley in *Journal of Egyptian Archaeology*, Vol. 50 (1964), pp. 3–4.

99. For more detailed discussion and illustrations of the bishops' garb see Michalowski, op. cit. (n. 22), pp. 45–6 and pls. 37, 57–9, 80–82, 86; Monneret de Villard, op. cit. (n. 11), p. 166; and Shinnie, op. cit. (n. 34), pp. 11–12.

100. Monneret de Villard, op. cit. (n. 11), pp. 166–7.

101. *Ecclesiastical History*, trans. Payne-Smith (London, 1860), Part III, p. 257.

102. See Adams, op. cit. (n. 5), pp. 101–2.

103. cf. Kirwan in *University of Liverpool Annals of Archaeology and Anthropology*, Vol. XXIV (1937), p. 101. For illustrations see Plumley in *Illustrated London News*, 11 July 1964, pp. 52–3, and Monneret de Villard, op. cit. (n. 3), Vol. II, pls. LVI–LX. Recent excavations have revealed that the cathedral at Qasr Ibrim was preceded by a church built within the partially dilapidated walls of the Napatan-Meroitic temple (cf. Ch. 12). For a preliminary report see Plumley and Adams in *Journal of Egyptian Archaeology*, Vol. 60 (1974), pp. 228–36.

104. The discussion of Nubian church architecture which follows is drawn almost entirely from my 'Architectural Evolution of the Nubian Church, 500–1400 AD' (op. cit., n. 5). A comprehensive list and a bibliography of Nubian churches will be found in this source, pp. 126–38.

105. See Finegan, *Light from the Ancient Past* (Princeton, 1946), pp. 506–8.

106. For a detailed discussion of the architectural technology of the Nubian vault see Somers Clarke, *Christian Antiquities in the Nile Valley* (Oxford, 1912), pp. 24–7.

107. cf. Monneret de Villard, op. cit. (n. 3), Vol. III, pp. 3–8.

108. cf. Klasens in *Fouilles en Nubie (1961–1963)* (Cairo, 1967), pp. 83–4; Van Moorsel in *Spiegel Historiael*, Vol. 2 (1967), pp. 387–92; and especially Schneider in Dinkler, op. cit. (n. 2), pp. 87–98.

109. See Adams in *Kush* XIII (1965), p. 167.

110. While there is good reason for dating the majority of cupola churches to the thirteenth century or later (cf. Adams, op. cit., n. 5, p. 138), it would appear that at least one example, at Sonqi Tino, may go back to the beginning of the tenth century. See Vantini and Donadoni in *Rendiconti della Pontificia Academia di Archeologia*, Vol. XL (1967–1968), pp. 256–9; Donadoni in *Cultura e Scuola*, No. 36 (1970), p. 149; and Donadoni in Dinkler, op. cit. (n. 2), p. 215.

111. See Meinardus, op. cit. (n. 11), pp. 159–64.

112. The largest number of churches in any one community was at Faras West, which at one time or another counted no fewer than ten church buildings (cf. Adams, op. cit., n. 5, p. 129). The next largest number of churches, eight, was found at the relatively insignificant community of Tamit, about 15 miles north of Faras. See Bresciani in Missione Archeologica in Egitto dell'Università di Roma, *Tamit (1964)* (Rome, 1967), pp. 27–38.

113. cf. especially Burckhardt, op. cit. (n. 9), p. 496.

114. op. cit. (n. 10). The author mentions half a dozen Nubian monasteries by name, but only one of them (at Wadi Ghazali, near the Fourth Cataract) can be specifically identified with a known archaeological site.

115. cf. Monneret de Villard, op. cit. (n. 3), Vol. III, pp. 61–2.

116. ibid., Vol. I, pp. 132–42.

117. Scanlon in *Journal of Egyptian Archaeology*, Vol. 56 (1970), pp. 29–57, and Vol. 58 (1972), pp. 7–42.

118. Shinnie and Chittick, *Ghazali – a Monastery in the Northern Sudan*, Sudan Antiquities Service Occasional Papers, No. 5 (1961).

119. cf. especially Scanlon in *Journal of Egyptian Archaeology*, Vol. 58 (1972), pp. 7–42.

120. For preliminary accounts see Mills, op. cit. (n. 1), pp. 10–11; Dinkler, op. cit. (n. 2), pp. 267–71; and Maystre in Dinkler, op. cit. (n. 2), pp. 181–8.

121. cf. Maystre, loc. cit. (n. 120). The second site which included a church was excavated by James Knudstad in 1969, but has not yet been reported in print.

122. cf. especially Meinardus, *Monks and Monasteries of the Egyptian Deserts* (Cairo, 1961).

123. cf. Shinnie and Chittick, op. cit. (n. 118), pp. 69–94.

124. Coptic tombstones occur sporadically in many other Nubian cemeteries, but they are usually outnumbered by Greek ones.

125. The well-known 'Anchorite's Grotto' at Faras; see Griffith in *University of Liverpool Annals of Archaeology and Anthropology*, Vol. XIV (1927), pp. 81–91. From traces found in them it appears also that at least one and possibly all three of the rock-tombs at Toshka West had been appropriated as dwellings by Christian anchorites; see Simpson, *Heka-Nefer and the Dynastic Material from Toshka and Arminna*, Publications of the Pennsylvania–Yale Expedition to Egypt, No. 1 (1963), pp. 13, 18–21. Still another rock-cut hermitage has been reported from ez-Zuma, near Kareima (Monneret de Villard, op. cit., n. 3, p. 251).

126. Adams, op. cit. (n. 7), pp. 228–31.

127. This is suggested by the extraordinary concentration of churches at Tamit. See Bresciani, op. cit. (n. 112), esp. Fig. 2.

128. Unpublished archives of the Archaeological Survey of Sudanese Nubia.

129. See Michalowski in *Kush* X (1962), pp. 234–5, and in *Kush* XI (1963), pp. 238–40 and pl. LVI; Plumley, loc. cit. (n. 98); and Millet, op. cit. (n. 46), p. 60.

130. See Adams in Dinkler, op. cit. (n. 2), p. 149.

131. Emery, op. cit. (n. 65), p. 203.

132. For further discussion of Christian Nubian tombs see Monneret de Villard, op. cit. (n. 3), Vol. III, pp. 63–78.

133. This happened at Meinarti; see Adams, op. cit. (n. 109), pp. 169–70.

134. The discussion of church decoration which follows is once again drawn chiefly from Adams, op. cit. (n. 5), esp. p. 100. A Dictionary of Christian Nubian Iconography is currently in preparation by a group of Polish scholars.

135. For illustrations of Nubian carved capitals and other elements see Griffith in *University of Liverpool Annals of Archaeology and Anthropology*, Vol. XIII (1926), pls. XXXVII–XXXIX, LI–LIII, LXII; Griffith, op. cit. (n. 125), pl. LXXVII; Monneret de Villard, op. cit. (n. 3), Vol. II, pls. II–V, XII, XXI, XXIV, XXXII, XLII, LX, LXXVI, LXXXIII, LXXXV–LXXXVIII, XCII, XCIV, XCVII; Michalowski, *Faras, Fouilles Polonaises 1961* (Warsaw, 1962), pls. 81–165; Michalowski, *Faras, Fouilles Polonaises 1961–1962* (Warsaw, 1965), pls. XIX–XXV; de Contenson, *Aksha* I (Paris, 1966), pls. I, IV; Trigger, *The Late Nubian Settlement at Arminna West*, Publications of the Pennsylvania–Yale Expedition to Egypt, No. 2 (1967), pls. X–XI; Gardberg, op. cit. (n. 7), pls. 38, 44, 57; Dinkler, op. cit. (n. 2), pls. 29, 36, 37, 73–112, 125–8, 130–33, 148–50, 196–7.

136. The best-known examples were those found by Griffith in the Rivergate Church at Faras (*University of Liverpool Annals of Archaeology and Anthropology*, Vol. XIII, 1926, pp. 73–93 and pls. LIV–LXI) and at Abd el Qadir (Griffith, op. cit., n. 34, pp. 63–80 and pls. XXXI–XLVI).

137. The fullest treatment and illustration of the Faras paintings which has so far been published is that of Michalowski, op. cit. (n. 22). See also sources cited in n. 97.

138. Van Moorsel, Jacquet and Schneider, *The Central Church of Abdallah Nirqi* (Leiden, 1975); see also articles by Schneider and Van Moorsel in Dinkler, op. cit. (n.2), pp. 87–107.

139. For references see n. 110.

140. For technical descriptions and illustrations of the process of fresco removal and conservation see Jedrzejewska in *Bulletin du Musée National de Varsovie*, Vol. VII (1966), pp. 81–9, and Gerster in *Unesco Courier*, December 1964, pp. 19–22.

141. e.g. Michalowski, op. cit. (n. 22), op. cit. (n. 88), and in Dinkler, op. cit. (n. 2), pp. 1–16; Gerster, *Nubien – Goldland am Nil* (Zurich and Stuttgart, 1964), pp. 129–38; Hintze, *Civilizations of the Old Sudan* (Leipzig and Amsterdam, 1968), pls. 138–45; *Das Wonder aus Faras* (Essen, 1969), pls. 1–21.

142. Michalowski, op. cit. (n. 22).

143. Daniel iii, 28.

144. Their names are given as ARNIAS and LEKOTES; see Michalowski in Dinkler, op. cit. (n. 2), p. 15 and pl. 5. The name of ARNIAS has subsequently been found also in a nativity scene at Kulubnarti (author's unpublished excavation notes).

145. cf. Weitzmann in Dinkler, op. cit. (n. 2), p. 335.

146. For examples see Griffith in *University of Liverpool Annals of Archaeology and Anthropology*, Vol. XIII (1926), pl. XXXIV, and Michalowski, op. cit. (n. 22), pls. 40–42.

147. A well preserved example was found at Sonqi, but has not yet been published (cf. Vantini and Donadoni, op. cit., n. 110, p. 254). Another example of which portions survived until recently was in a church at Debeira West (Monneret de Villard, op. cit., n. 3, Vol. I, p. 206). Unfortunately it seems never to have been photographed or copied.

148. Illustrated examples include Griffith, op. cit. (n. 34), pl. XLV; Michalowski, op. cit. (n. 22), pls. 63–9; Michalowski in Dinkler, op. cit. (n. 2), pl. 1; and Van Moorsel in Dinkler, op. cit. (n. 2), pl. 48.

149. The best illustrated example is Michalowski, op. cit. (n. 22), pl. 71.

150. Examples of this design are particularly numerous and highly varied. See Griffith, op. cit. (n. 34), pl. XXXIX; Michalowski, op. cit. (n. 22), pls. 87–9; Van Moorsel in Dinkler, op. cit. (n. 2), pl. 40; Adams in Dinkler, op. cit. (n. 2), pl. 121; Donadoni in Dinkler, op. cit. (n. 2), pl. 192.

151. See Griffith, op. cit. (n. 146), pl. LVIII; Griffith, op. cit. (n. 34), pls. XXXIV–XXXVI, XLII–XLIII; Michalowski, op. cit. (n. 22), pl. 48; Van Moorsel in Dinkler, op. cit. (n. 2), pls. 42, 46.

152. Michalowski in Dinkler, op. cit. (n. 2), p. 15.

153. Weitzmann in Dinkler, op. cit. (n. 2), p. 327.

154. cf. Griffith, op. cit. (n. 34), pls. XXXI–XLVII.

155. For extended discussion see Weitzmann in Dinkler, op. cit. (n. 2), esp. pp. 325–9.

156. See, e.g., Michalowski, op. cit. (n. 22), pls. 57, 59, 77, 79, 94, 95.

157. For general discussion see Jakobielski in Dinkler, op. cit. (n. 2), pp. 29–38, and Shinnie in Abdalla, Ed., *Studies in Ancient Languages of the Sudan*, Sudan Research Unit, Sudan Studies Library, 3 (1975), pp. 41–7.

158. cf. Adams, op. cit. (n. 130), p. 149. Note that the inscriptions in the very late church of Abd el Qadir are also entirely in Greek (Griffith, op. cit., n. 34, p. 67).

159. It includes also two letters not found in either Coptic or Greek, and possibly derived from the Meroitic alphabet. See Griffith, *The Nubian Texts of the Christian Period*, Abhandlungen der Königlichen Preussischen Akademie der Wissenschaften (1913), p. 73.

160. op. cit. (n. 157), pp. 31–2; op. cit. (n. 88), pp. 14–16.

161. For further discussion on this subject see Plumley, op. cit. (n. 36), and Oates in

Journal of Egyptian Archaeology, Vol. 49 (1963), pp. 161–71. The latter author asserts (p. 164) that ' . . . the quality of Greek in [the Nubian] stones is very high and [some] would do justice to the best periods of Greek epigraphy. Even . . . the most misspelled of [the] group compares favourably with stones of the same period found in Asia Minor, Syria, Greece, or Egypt.' In contrast, however, see Zilliacus in Holthoer *et al.*, op. cit. (n. 58), p. 14: ' . . . the Greek language of the texts is faulty and debased, influenced by Coptic and Nubian spelling . . . Evidently the stone-cutters or engravers of Nubia did not possess any real command of Greek.' Further complication is introduced by a series of graffiti found near Qasr Ibrim in 1972 (cf. Plumley and Adams, op. cit., n. 103), which seem to be in a mixture of barbarized Coptic and Old Nubian. So far as I know this combination has not previously been encountered.

162. cf. Jakobielski in *Mélanges offerts à Kazimierz Michalowski* (Warsaw, 1966), pp. 103–8, in *KL10*, Vol. 51 (1969), p. 500, and op. cit. (n. 88), pp. 37–47.

163. See Junker in *Zeitschrift für Ägyptische Sprache und Altertumskunde*, Vol. 60 (1925), pp. 124–48, and Monneret de Villard in *Aegyptus*, Vol. XII (1932), pp. 309–16.

164. Jacobielski in Dinkler, op. cit. (n. 2), pp. 31–2; Frend in *Byzantinoslavica*, Vol. XXXIII (1972), pp. 224–9.

165. Three of them are published in Griffith, op. cit. (n. 159). Two more recently discovered books from Serra East and from Qasr el-Wizz have not yet been described in detail. For notices of their discovery see Scanlon in *African Arts*, Vol. II (1968), p. 65 and Fig. 4, and Knudstad in *Kush* XIV (1966), p. 171.

166. Jakobielski in Dinkler, op. cit. (n. 2), pp. 29–30; see also sources cited in n. 162.

167. Knudstad, loc. cit. (n. 165).

168. Scanlon, loc. cit. (n. 117).

169. Plumley in *Journal of Egyptian Archaeology*, Vol. 50 (1964), pp. 4–5; Vol. 52 (1966), pp. 11–12; Vol. 61 (1975), pp. 6–7; and op. cit. (n. 36); Frend, op. cit. (n. 164).

170. For further discussion of medieval Nubian literature see Haycock, op. cit. (n. 77).

171. Griffith, op. cit. (n. 125), pp. 82–3.

172. For discussion of this formula and its Nubian variants see especially Junker, op. cit. (n. 163), and Oates, op. cit. (n. 161).

173. The Coptic Church and most other Eastern churches calculate our era from the persecutions in the reign of Diocletian, AD 280, rather than from the birth of Christ. The death of Peter the Deacon therefore occurred in the year AD 1025 according to our calendar.

174. Quoted in Mileham, *Churches in Lower Nubia*, University of Pennsylvania Museum, Eckley B. Coxe Junior Expedition to Nubia, Vol. II (1910), p. 19.

175. Qasr Ibrim has not been entirely inundated, and excavations here are continuing.

176. See n. 60.

177. Trigger, op. cit. (n. 135); Weeks, *The Classic Christian Townsite at Arminna West*, Publications of the Pennsylvania–Yale Expedition to Egypt, No. 3 (1967).

178. Missione Archeologica in Egitto dell'Università di Roma, op. cit. (n. 127).

179. Shinnie in *Kush* XI (1963), pp. 257–63; *Kush* XII (1964), pp. 208–15; and *Kush* XIII (1965), pp. 190–94.

180. Adams, op. cit. (n. 7), pp. 222–40, and op. cit. (n. 109).

181. Adams, op. cit. (n. 7), pp. 218–40.

182. See Weeks, op. cit. (n. 177), pp. 17–21. This suggestion is not endorsed by Trigger (personal communication).

183. See Adams, op. cit. (n. 8), p. 187.

184. ibid., p. 188.

185. i.e. in the Christian period. The total number of stratigraphic levels in the site was eighteen. For a chronological resumé see Adams, op. cit. (n. 109), p. 150.

186. cf. my 'Settlement Pattern in Microcosm: the Changing Aspect of a Nubian Village during Twelve Centuries' (Adams, op. cit., n. 8). The discussion which follows is largely condensed from this source.

187. This is attested by records of the annual flood levels kept at Roda, near Cairo, from the year AD 622 onwards. See Jarvis in *Journal of Cycle Research*, Vol. 2 (1953), pp. 96–100.

188. cf. Adams, op. cit. (n. 7), p. 219, Fig. 2.

189. See especially Shinnie in *Kush* XII (1964), p. 211, Fig. 3.

190. cf. Weeks, op. cit. (n. 177), Fig. 1.

191. For discussion of these sites see especially Adams and Nordström, op. cit. (n. 1), pp. 42–4; Presedo Velo, *El Poblado Cristiano de la Isla de Abkanarti*, Comité Español de la Unesco para Nubia, Memorias de la Misión Arqueológica en Nubia, VII (1965); and Gardberg, op. cit. (n. 7), pp. 47–52.

192. Adams and Nordström, op. cit. (n. 1), pp. 43–4.

193. Jarvis, loc. cit. (n. 187).

194. Curto *et al.*, *Kalabsha*, Centro per le Antichità e la Storia dell'Arte del Vicino Oriente, Orientis Antiqui Collectio, V (1965).

195. Bresciani *et al.*, *Sabagura*, Centro per le Antichità e la Storia dell'Arte del Vicino Oriente, Orientis Antiqui Collectio, I (1962).

196. Presedo Velo, *La Fortaleza Nubia de Cheikh-Daud*, Comité Español de la Unesco para Nubia, Memorias de la Misión Arqueológica en Nubia, IV (1964).

197. Stenico in *Acme*, Vol. XIII (1960), pp. 31–76.

198. ibid., Fig. 2 (following p. 32).

199. Presedo Velo, op. cit. (n. 196), Plan following p. 10.

200. The great Roman temple of Kalabsha, converted into a church in the early Christian period, also occupied a prominent place within its walled precinct. See Curto *et al.*, op. cit. (n. 194), pp. 44–5.

201. Stenico, op. cit. (n. 197), pp. 67–76; Donadoni in *Mémoires de l'Institut d'Égypte*, Vol. LIX (1969), p. 30.

202. cf. Donadoni, op. cit. (n. 201), pp. 29–30, and in *La Parola del Passato*, Vol. 69 (1959), pp. 458–69.

203. Trigger, op. cit. (n. 1), p. 146.

204. See, e.g., Reisner, *Archaeological Survey of Nubia, Report for 1907–1908* (Cairo, 1910), Vol. I, pp. 346–7; Firth, *Archaeological Survey of Nubia, Report for 1910–1911* (Cairo, 1927), p. 33.

205. See especially Adams, op. cit. (n. 7), pp. 236–8.

206. For more extended discussion of the stylistic evolution of Christian Nubian pottery see the various sources cited in n. 4.

207. cf. Weitzmann in Dinkler, op. cit. (n. 2), p. 338; and Jansma, *Ornements des Manuscrits Coptes du Monastère Blanc* (unpublished doctoral dissertation, Rijksuniversiteit te Groningen, 1973). However, Millet (personal communication) points out that the *guilloche* is much more highly developed as a decorative motif in Nubia than in Byzantium or anywhere else.

208. See Griffith, op. cit. (n. 146), pp. 63–5 and pls. XLI–XLV.

209. Adams in *Kush* IX (1961), pp. 30–43. The discussion which follows is condensed from this source.

210. For discussion see especially Lane, *Early Islamic Pottery* (London, 1947), pp. 10–24.

211. The most extensive discussion of Fostat glazed pottery is that of Bahgat and Massoul, *La Céramique Musulmane de l'Égypte* (Cairo, 1930); cf. also Scanlon in Richards, Ed., *Islam and the Trade of Asia* (Philadelphia, 1970), pp. 81–95, and in *Archaeology*, Vol. 24 (1971), pp. 220–33.

212. It is not common before the middle of the eleventh century; however, Scanlon

(op. cit., n. 117, p. 43) has shown that the earliest glazed pieces in Nubia can be assigned to the tenth century.

213. For discussion see Haynes, *Glass through the Ages* (Harmondsworth, 1948), pp. 52–4, and Smith, *Glass from the Ancient World* (Corning, N.Y., 1957), pp. 227–32.
214. Preliminary examination and identification of the Meinarti glass was made by Mr Ray Winfield Smith. Detailed study of this material is underway at the present time. For a published analysis of glass sherds from another medieval Nubian site see Harden in Shinnie, op. cit. (n. 14), pp. 60–76.
215. Burckhardt, op. cit. (n. 9), p. 512.
216. The fabric was incorrectly identified as cotton in a preliminary report; see Adams, op. cit. (n. 7), p. 238. Similar finds by the Scandinavian Joint Expedition to Sudanese Nubia have been found to be woven chiefly of camel's wool. See Bergman, *Late Nubian Textiles*, Scandinavian Joint Expedition to Sudanese Nubia Publications, Vol. 8 (1975), pp. 10–12.
217. cf. Adams in Dinkler, op. cit. (n. 2), p. 149.
218. Trigger in Dinkler, op. cit. (n. 2), p. 347.
219. See Monneret de Villard, op. cit. (n. 11), pp. 169–70, and Forand, op. cit. (n. 57), pp. 117–18.
220. See especially Trigger in Dinkler, op. cit. (n. 2), pp. 354–5.
221. ibid., p. 355; Adams and Nordström, op. cit. (n. 1), pp. 42–4.
222. cf. Trigger in Dinkler, op. cit. (n. 2), p. 355.
223. cf. Huntingford, *The Land Charters of Northern Ethiopia*, Monographs in Ethiopian Land Tenure, No. 1 (1965).
224. This is assumed by Jakobielski; see op. cit. (n. 88), p. 73.
225. For evidence of monastic wine production in Egypt see especially Winlock and Crum, *The Monastery of Epiphanius at Thebes*, Part I, Metropolitan Museum of Art Egyptian Expedition Publications, Vol. III (1926), pp. 161–2.
226. See Adams in *Kush* X (1962), pp. 72–4; and Adams and Nordström, op. cit. (n. 1), p. 42.
227. For discussion see Adams in *Kush* XIV (1966), pp. 279–82.
228. Forand, op. cit. (n. 57), p. 120.
229. Adams, loc. cit. (n. 227).
230. For discussion of the fluctuating trade in imported pottery see Adams in Dinkler, op. cit. (n. 2), pp. 118–21.
231. 'The organization of the medieval states', above.
232. cf. especially Plumley, op. cit. (n. 36).
233. See Forand, op. cit. (n. 57), p. 116.
234. Hasan, op. cit. (n. 11), pp. 45–7.
235. Fernea, *Contemporary Egyptian Nubia* (New Haven, 1966), Vol. I, p. 9.
236. Trimingham, loc. cit. (n. 12).
237. cf. Hasan, op. cit. (n. 11), pp. 42–50.

CHAPTER 16

Principal sources: there are a number of synopses of historical information about the late period of Nubian Christianity; among them Monneret de Villard, *Storia della Nubia Cristiana*, Pontificio Institutum Orientalium Studiorum, Orientalia Christiana Analecta 118 (1938), Ch. XXII, and Arkell, *A History of the Sudan*, 2nd ed. (London, 1961), Ch. IX, are noteworthy. The information given by medieval Arab writers is particularly well summarized in Hasan, *The*

Arabs and the Sudan (Edinburgh, 1967), Ch. 4 and Appendix, and in Vantini, *The Excavations at Faras, a Contribution to the History of Christian Nubia* (Bologna, 1970), pp. 59–143. Additional information will be found in Budge, *The Egyptian Sudan* (London, 1907), Vol. II, Ch. XII. For the Mameluke régime in Egypt I have relied chiefly on Lane-Poole, *A History of Egypt in the Middle Ages* (London, 1968), Ch. IX–X.

1. Ibn Khaldun, *Kitab al-Ibar wa-Diwan al-Mubtada wa'l-Khabar* (Beirut, 1956–1961), Vol. V, p. 429. The translation is from Crowfoot in *Journal of Egyptian Archaeology*, Vol. XIII (1927), p. 148.
2. cf. Crowfoot, loc. cit. (n. 1).
3. cf. Arkell, *A History of the Sudan*, 2nd ed. (London, 1961), p. 196.
4. See Griffith in *University of Liverpool Annals of Archaeology and Anthropology*, Vol. XIV (1927), pp. 102–3.
5. cf. Plumley in *Illustrated London News*, 11 July 1964, p. 51.
6. For a preliminary excavation report see Knudstad in *Kush* XIV (1966), pp. 165–78.
7. cf. Millet in *Journal of the American Research Center in Egypt*, Vol. VI (1967), pp. 60–61.
8. Only two churches are described in Monneret de Villard, *La Nubia Medioevale*, Vol. I (Cairo, 1935), pp. 108–20. The other two churches were discovered in the course of excavations in 1966 and 1972; see Plumley in *Journal of Egyptian Archaeology*, Vol. 52 (1966), pp. 10–11, and Plumley and Adams in *Journal of Egyptian Archaeology*, Vol. 60 (1974), pp. 228–36. It is entirely possible that further excavation will disclose additional churches at Qasr Ibrim.
9. cf. Adams in *Journal of the American Research Center in Egypt*, Vol. IV (1965), pp. 137–8.
10. Mills in *Kush* XIII (1965), pp. 3–10.
11. The site was excavated by the UNESCO–Sudan Antiquities Service team in 1966, but has not yet been reported in print. For the church see Monneret de Villard, *La Nubia Medioevale*, Vol. I (Cairo, 1935), pp. 230–31, and Adams, op. cit. (n. 9), pp. 119–20.
12. Shown on several maps as Susinarti. For further accounts of the site see Chittick in *Kush* V (1957), pp. 45–7; Grossmann in *Archäologischer Anzeiger, Jahrbuch des Deutschen Archäologischen Instituts* (1968), pp. 721–32; and Dinkler, Ed., *Kunst und Geschichte Nubiens in Christlicher Zeit* (Recklinghausen, 1970), pp. 265–6.
13. They were recorded in the course of my excavations at Kulubnarti in 1969, which are not yet published. For a very brief preliminary report see Adams in Dinkler, op. cit. (n. 12), p. 143. The sites are here described in the present tense because they will not be inundated by the Aswan High Dam.
14. Plumley, op. cit. (n. 8), pp. 9–10.
15. cf. Arkell, loc. cit. (n. 3).
16. Knudstad, op. cit. (n. 6), pp. 169–70.
17. Adams in *Kush* XII (1964), pp. 231–3.
18. Presedo Velo, *El Poblado Cristiano de la Isla de Abkanarti*, Comité Español de la Unesco para Nubia, Memorias de la Misión Arqueológica en Nubia, VII (1965), pp. 12–13.
19. Adams, op. cit. (n. 17), p. 222.
20. e.g. Turmuki Island; see Grossmann in *Archäologischer Anzeiger, Jahrbuch des Deutschen Archäologischen Instituts* (1971), pp. 140–43.
21. Adams, op. cit. (n. 17), p. 232, Fig. 4.
22. cf. Michalowski, *Faras, Fouilles Polonaises 1961* (Warsaw, 1962), pp. 173–81,

and in *Kush* X (1962), pp. 242–4; and Vantini, *The Excavations at Faras, a Contribution to the History of Christian Nubia* (Bologna, 1970), pp. 259–62.

23. See Adams in Dinkler, op. cit. (n. 12), pp. 144–6.

24. ibid., p. 150; Arkell, loc. cit. (n. 3).

25. For a report on these three castles and others in their vicinity see Crawford, *The Fung Kingdom of Sennar* (Gloucester, 1951), pp. 30–52.

26. For these two castles and others in the region between the Fourth and Fifth Cataracts see Crawford, *Castles and Churches in the Middle Nile Region*, Sudan Antiquities Service Occasional Papers, No. 2 (1953).

27. ibid., pp. 20–21, 31–4.

28. Alvares, *The Prester John of the Indies*, trans. Lord Stanley (Cambridge, 1961), p. 461.

29. See Adams, op. cit. (n. 9), pp. 116–20.

30. ibid., pp. 119–20. The church at Abd el Qadir was later somewhat enlarged by the addition of chapels on either side. For the enlarged plan see Griffith in *University of Liverpool Annals of Archaeology and Anthropology*, Vol. XV (1928), pl. XXV.

31. cf. Adams, op. cit. (n. 9), pp. 119–20.

32. cf. Millet in *Journal of the American Research Center in Egypt*, Vol. III (1964), p. 10, and op. cit. (n. 7), pp. 59–61.

33. The earlier church on the island of Meinarti (see Adams in *Kush* XIII, 1965, pp. 165–8) may have been abandoned before the end of the Christian period. I assume that the church at Abd el Qadir, about half a mile away on the west bank, was built primarily for the benefit of the Meinarti congregation, since there are no other settlements for several miles in any direction.

34. cf. Adams, op. cit. (n. 17), p. 222.

35. Adams in Dinkler, op. cit. (n. 12), p. 146.

36. Both these sites were excavated by the UNESCO–Sudan Antiquities Service team between 1966 and 1968, but have not yet been reported in print. For a description of Diffinarti prior to its excavation see Monneret de Villard, loc. cit. (n. 11). The church at Attiri was not recognized as such until excavation had actually been carried out.

37. See n. 22.

38. See Adams, op. cit. (n. 17), p. 232.

39. The apparent popularity of cavalier saints as a decorative motif in the later Nubian churches might be cited as further evidence of the growing feudal spirit. See Griffith, op. cit. (n. 30), pls. XXXIV–XXXVI, XLII–XLIV; and Millet, op. cit. (n. 7), p. 61.

40. Adams, op. cit. (n. 17), pp. 237–8.

41. cf. ibid., p. 247.

42. The development of Late Christian pottery is described by me in much greater detail in *Kush* XV (1973), pp. 1–50.

43. Except for the mass production of pots for use on the *saqia* (water-wheel), which has apparently continued down to modern times.

44. See Adams in Dinkler, op. cit. (n. 12), p. 115 and pls. 49–50.

45. Author's unpublished excavation notes.

46. cf. Shinnie in Hasan, Ed., *Sudan in Africa*, Sudan Research Unit, Sudan Studies Library, 2 (1971), p. 46.

47. Lane-Poole, *A History of Egypt in the Middle Ages* (London, 1968), p. 244.

48. ibid., p. 245.

49. For a discussion of this aspect of Mameluke policy see Abdin in *Sudan Notes and Records*, Vol. XL (1959), pp. 59–60; Hasan in *Arabica*, Vol. XIV (1967), pp. 27–8; and especially Hasan, *The Arabs and the Sudan* (Edinburgh, 1967), pp. 100–106.

50. For the origins and early history of the Beni Kanz see MacMichael, *A History of the Arabs in the Sudan* (London, 1922), Vol. I, pp. 149–51; Trimingham, *Islam in the Sudan* (London, 1949), p. 68; and Hasan, *The Arabs and the Sudan* (Edinburgh, 1967), pp. 58–60.

51. cf. Hasan in *Arabica*, Vol. XIV (1967), pp. 23–4.

52. That some Beni Kanz were already active in Lower Nubia before the general exodus of 1174 is attested by a number of letters dating from the late Fatimid period which have recently come to light at Qasr Ibrim. They are addressed to the eparch by various of the Beni Kanz emirs, and have to do with Beni Kanz settlement and business activities in Lower Nubia. See Plumley in Michalowski, Ed., *Nubia, Récentes Recherches* (Warsaw, 1975), p. 106.

53. cf. Trimingham, loc. cit. (n. 50), and Musad in *Nubie, Cahiers d'Histoire Égyptienne*, Vol. X (1967), p. 170.

54. MacMichael, op. cit. (n. 50), p. 150; Musad, loc. cit. (n. 53); Hasan, op. cit. (n. 51), p. 24.

55. Or 'Lord of the Horses', according to Plumley's reading of the eparch's Arabic title. See Plumley in *Journal of Egyptian Archaeology*, Vol. 56 (1970), p. 14.

56. cf. Vantini, op. cit. (n. 22), p. 261.

57. MacMichael, op. cit. (n. 50), p. 150.

58. cf. ibid.

59. *Nihayat al-Arab fi Funun al-Adab* (Cairo, 1923), Vol. I. For commentary see Hasan, op. cit. (n. 50), pp. 197–8, and Vantini, op. cit. (n. 22), p. 103.

60. *Al-Nahj al-Sadid wa'l-Durr al-Farid*, ed. E. Blochet (3 vols., Paris, 1919–1928). For commentary see Hasan, op. cit. (n. 50), pp. 198–9, and Vantini, op. cit. (n. 22), p. 104.

61. See n. 1. For commentary see Hasan, op. cit. (n. 50), p. 199, and Vantini, op. cit. (n. 22), pp. 106–10.

62. His main work on the Mameluke period is *Kitab al-Suluk fi Ma'rifat Duwal al-Muluk* (2 vols., Cairo, 1934). For commentary see Hasan, op. cit. (n. 50), p. 201, and Vantini, op. cit. (n. 22), pp. 112–19.

63. This story has been retold by a number of modern authors, including Budge, *The Egyptian Sudan* (London, 1907), Vol. II, pp. 193–9; Trimingham, op. cit. (n. 50), pp. 69–72; Arkell, op. cit. (n. 3), pp. 196–200; and Musad in *Sudan Notes and Records*, Vol. XL (1959), pp. 124–6. The most detailed and probably the most accurate version in English, upon which I have principally relied, is that of Hasan, op. cit. (n. 50), pp. 106–23.

64. The full text of the treaty signed by Shekenda is given in Nuwairi, op. cit. (n. 59), fol. 259. For a resumé of the provisions in English see Hasan, op. cit. (n. 50), pp. 109–10.

65. This is the usual transliteration of the name as it appears in Arabic texts. In Old Nubian texts it appears as Kudanbas or Kudanbes.

66. cf. Hasan, op. cit. (n. 50), p. 119.

67. ibid., p. 120.

68. ibid., p. 121.

69. e.g. Arkell, op. cit. (n. 3), p. 200; Musad, loc. cit. (n. 63); Shinnie, *Medieval Nubia*, Sudan Antiquities Service Museum Pamphlets, No. 2 (1954), p. 7.

70. However, in a very obscure 'pseudo-Greek' inscription at Aswan the name of Kerenbes seems to be linked with those of various earlier rulers as well as of saints. See Griffith, *Christian Documents from Nubia*, Proceedings of the British Academy, Vol. XIV (1928), p. 134, and Monneret de Villard, *Storia della Nubia Cristiana*, Pontificio Institutum Orientalium Studiorum, Orientalia Christiana Analecta 118 (1938), p. 164.

71. *Masalik al-Absar fi Mamalik al-Amsar*, trans. Gaudefroy-Demombynes (Paris, 1927), pp. 48–9. For commentary see Vantini, op. cit. (n. 22), pp. 104–5.
72. *Ta'rif bi'l-Mustalah ash-Sharif* (Cairo, 1894), p. 29.
73. op. cit. (n. 62). For longer synopses in English see Budge, op. cit. (n. 63), Vol. II, pp. 197–8, and Hasan, op. cit. (n. 50), pp. 121–3.
74. op. cit. (n. 50), p. 122.
75. This was reported by a certain Brother Thomas of Ganget, who served with the Portuguese mission to Ethiopia in the 1520s. See Crawford, *Ethiopian Itineraries, c. 1400–1524* (Cambridge, 1958), pp. 180–81.
76. cf. Budge, op. cit. (n. 63), Vol. II, p. 198, and Hasan, op. cit. (n. 50), p. 123.
77. cf. Toynbee, *A Study of History*, Vol. 8 (New York, 1963), esp. pp. 1–73.
78. For details of this phase of Beni Kanz history see especially Budge, op. cit. (n. 63), Vol. II, pp. 197–9; also MacMichael, op. cit. (n. 50), Vol. I, pp. 188–9.
79. Haycock believed that there is also evidence for a very late survival of Christianity in the region between the Fourth and Fifth Cataracts (presumably the old territory of el-Abwab). See *Sudan Notes and Records*, Vol. LIII (1972), p. 20.
80. Griffith, *The Nubian Texts of the Christian Period*, Abhandlungen der Königlichen Preussischen Akademie der Wissenschaften, 1913, p. 52; Monneret de Villard, op. cit. (n. 70), p. 141. A name similar to Elteeit appears in one of the texts found at Qasr Ibrim in 1974, to be described in a later paragraph. In this case it seems to be the surname of a ruler whose principal name was George.
81. Monneret de Villard, loc. cit. (n. 70).
82. Griffith, op. cit. (n. 80), pp. 64–5; Monneret de Villard, op. cit. (n. 11), Vol. I, p. 174.
83. Griffith, op. cit. (n. 80), p. 166; Monneret de Villard, op. cit. (n. 11), Vol. I, pp. 174–5.
84. Millet, op. cit. (n. 7), p. 62.
85. Personal communication from N. B. Millet.
86. This is surely the Merki of the Gebel Adda text (see n. 84).
87. Plumley, op. cit. (n. 52).
88. The documents were found in a sealed jar buried beneath a house floor, during the excavations of 1974. See Plumley in *Journal of Egyptian Archaeology*, Vol. 61 (1975), pp. 6–7. I am greatly indebted to Prof. J. M. Plumley for every effort to produce a preliminary translation in time for inclusion in this edition.
89. Donadoni in Missione Archeologica in Egitto dell'Università di Roma, *Tamit (1964)* (Rome, 1967), pp. 62–4. For other, more dubious textual references to King Joel see ibid., p. 63, n. 9.
90. Personal communication from Stefan Jakobielski. The identification seems doubtful in view of the probability that the Faras Cathedral was already sanded up in the thirteenth century (see Ch. 15).
91. cf. Holt, *Egypt and the Fertile Crescent 1516–1922* (Ithaca, 1966), p. 15, n. 1.
92. See Monneret de Villard, op. cit. (n. 70), p. 221.
93. ibid.
94. See Markham, Ed., *Book of the Knowledge of all the Kingdoms*, etc. (London, 1912), p. 32 and pl. 14.
95. cf. ibid., pp. ix–xii; Crawford, op. cit. (n. 25), p. 134.
96. cf. Kronenberg in *Kush* XI (1963), pp. 304, 311; in *Kush* XII (1964), pp. 285–6; and Adams in Dinkler, op. cit. (n. 12), p. 150.
97. Millet, op. cit. (n. 7), pp. 61–2.
98. Griffith, op. cit. (n. 4), p. 103; Monneret de Villard, op. cit. (n. 70), p. 141.
99. Very probably an Arabization of the older name by the usual practice of prefixing the definite article: ad-Daw. However, Bruce Trigger (personal communication)

points out that the Meroitic name of Adda was something like Ado, which suggests a direct antecedent of the modern name. Thus, if Adda is to be identified with Daw, the loss and subsequent reappearance of the initial A remains unexplained.

100. As suggested by Griffith, op. cit. (n. 4), pp. 103–4.

101. cf. Monneret de Villard, op. cit. (n. 70), p. 140.

102. ibid., p. 141.

103. Arkell, op. cit. (n. 3), pp. 190, 197, 200.

104. op. cit. (n. 70), p. 188.

105. *Faras, die Kathedrale aus dem Wüstensand* (Zurich and Cologne, 1967), p. 44.

106. cf. Plumley, op. cit. (n. 52).

107. cf. Budge, op. cit. (n. 63), Vol. II, p. 197.

108. However, there is a tradition that Christianity persisted until very late at Taifa in Lower Nubia; the place was still referred to as 'the village of Christians' in the recent past (personal communication from Bruce Trigger).

109. Quoted from Crowfoot, loc. cit. (n. 1).

110. cf. Musad, op. cit. (n. 63), p. 127.

111. In *Journal of African History*, Vol. XIII (1972), p. 40.

112. Shinnie, *Excavations at Soba*, Sudan Antiquities Service Occasional Papers, No. 3 (1961), p. 76.

113. Al-Harrani, *Monumenta Cartographica Africae et Aegyptii*, ed. Prince Youssouf Kamal (Leiden, 1926–53), Vol. IV, Fasc. 1.

114. Abd al-Zahir, *Tashrif al-Ayyam wa'l-'Usur fi Sirat al-Malik al-Mansur* (Cairo, 1961), pp. 144–5.

115. Hasan, op. cit. (n. 50), pp. 128–9.

116. ibid., pp. 130–31.

117. ibid.

118. cf. Monneret de Villard, op. cit. (n. 70), pp. 154–5, 200; Crawford, op. cit. (n. 25), pp. 27–8; Hasan, op. cit. (n. 50), p. 198.

119. For a critical discussion as well as a full translation see MacMichael, op. cit. (n. 50), Vol. II, pp. 354–434.

120. cf. ibid., p. 358.

121. ibid., pp. 358–9; Trimingham, op. cit. (n. 50), p. 74, n. 3.

122. See especially MacMichael, op. cit. (n. 50), Vol. II, pp. 431–3, and Crawford, op. cit. (n. 25), pp. 163–4.

123. See Holt in *Bulletin of the School of Oriental and African Studies*, Vol. XXIII (1960), pp. 1–12, and in *Journal of African History*, Vol. IV (1963), pp. 39–55; and Hasan, op. cit. (n. 50), p. 132.

124. Translated by Penn in *Sudan Notes and Records*, Vol. XVII (1934), pp. 59–83.

125. *Kush* XI (1963), pp. 264–72.

126. See Crawford, op. cit. (n. 25), p. 137.

127. ibid., p. 152.

128. ibid.; Chataway in *Sudan Notes and Records*, Vol. XIII (1930), p. 256.

129. Hasan, op. cit. (n. 50), p. 126; Trimingham, op. cit. (n. 50), p. 78; Shinnie, op. cit. (n. 69), p. 7.

130. See for example Burckhardt, *Travels in Nubia* (London, 1819), p. 78; Cailliaud, *Voyage à Méroé et au Fleuve Blanc* (Paris, 1826), Vol. III, pp. 258–61; Linant de Bellefonds, *Journal d'un Voyage à Méroé dans les Années 1821 et 1822*, Sudan Antiquities Service Occasional Papers, No. 4 (1958), pp. 3, 10–11.

131. Adams, op. cit. (n. 9), pp. 126–33.

132. The reasons for the decline and disappearance of Nubian Christianity are discussed at greater length in Trimingham, op. cit. (n. 50), pp. 75–80; Hasan, op. cit. (n. 50), pp. 124–8; and Vantini, op. cit. (n. 22), pp. 274–8.

133. Budge, op. cit. (n. 63), Vol. II, p. 306; Hasan, op. cit. (n. 50), p. 126.
134. Plumley in *Journal of Egyptian Archaeology*, Vol. 50 (1964), pp. 3–4. For full translation and commentary see Plumley, *The Scrolls of Bishop Timotheos*, Egypt Exploration Society, Texts from Excavations, Memoir 1, 1975.
135. e.g. al-Umari, op. cit. (n. 71); Ibn Battuta, *Travels in Asia and Africa*, trans. Gibb (London, 1929), p. 323; al-Bakawi, *Kitab Talkhis al-Athar wa Ajab al-Malik al-Qahhar* (see Vantini, op. cit., n. 22, pp. 110–11).
136. See Budge, op. cit. (n. 63), Vol. II, p. 307.
137. MacMichael, op. cit. (n. 50), Vol. II, p. 35; Crawford, op. cit. (n. 25), p. 27.
138. Alvares, loc. cit. (n. 28).
139. ibid.
140. cf. Monneret de Villard, op. cit. (n. 70), pp. 124–5.
141. Vantini, op. cit. (n. 22), p. 141.
142. Bruce, *Travels to Discover the Source of the Nile, in the Years 1768, 1769, 1770, 1771, 1772, and 1773* (Edinburgh, 1790), Vol. I, p. 98. Italics are in the original.
143. An Abyssinian monk who passed through Dongola in 1596 still distinguished between the 'Nubian' and 'Moslem' elements in the population. See Trimingham, *The Influence of Islam upon Africa* (London, 1968), pp. 23–4.
144. There is an abandoned mosque at Attiri, but the character of its architecture suggests that it was built much later than was the church at the same site.
145. See n. 130.
146. Among them are churches at Arminna West (Trigger, *The Late Nubian Settlement at Arminna West*, Publications of the Pennsylvania–Yale Expedition to Egypt, No. 2, 1967, pp. 15–17); Gebel Adda (Millet, op. cit., n. 7, p. 61); Meili Island (Adams and Nordström in *Kush* XI, 1963, p. 34); and Kulubnarti (Adams in Dinkler, op. cit., n. 12, p. 146).
147. cf. Trigger, op. cit. (n. 146), p. 115 and n. 26.
148. cf. Millet, op. cit. (n. 7), p. 61.

CHAPTER 17

Principal sources: the main substance of this chapter is drawn from three works of outstanding and almost equal value: MacMichael, *A History of the Arabs in the Sudan* (2 vols., London, 1922); Hasan, *The Arabs and the Sudan* (Edinburgh, 1967); and Trimingham, *Islam in the Sudan* (London, 1949). The first two are of particular value for the Arab migrations, and the third for the propagation and the nature of Sudanese Islam. In the latter area I have also made extensive use of Hillelson's eloquent commentary on the *Tabaqat* of Wad Dayfallah in *Sudan Notes and Records*, Vol. VI (1923), pp. 191–231. The extended passages of ethnographic description at the close of the chapter are quoted from Burckhardt, *Travels in Nubia* (London, 1819). Of the various Europeans who visited and subsequently wrote about Nubia at the beginning of the modern era, the sensitive and self-effacing Burckhardt stands alone as an ethnographic observer; he deserves to be ranked with the great ethnographers of all ages.

1. *Archaeological Survey of Nubia, Report for 1907–1908* (Cairo, 1910), Vol. I, p. 348.
2. For discussion on this point see Trimingham, *Islam in the Sudan* (London, 1949), pp. 81–3, and Hasan, *The Arabs and the Sudan* (Edinburgh, 1967), pp. 174–6.
3. cf. Hasan, op. cit. (n. 2), p. 177.
4. For a general review of the Islamization of the African sudanic belt see I. M. Lewis, Ed., *Islam in Tropical Africa* (Oxford, 1966), pp. 4–96.

5. For a brief popular history of these empires see Margaret Shinnie, *Ancient African Kingdoms* (London, 1965). There are more comprehensive histories of several of them individually.

6. cf. Trimingham in Lewis, op. cit. (n. 4), p. 128.

7. For more detail see ibid., pp. 127–9.

8. Trimingham, op. cit. (n. 2), p. 99.

9. Lewis, op. cit. (n. 4), p. 5.

10. cf. Adams in *Ethnohistory*, Vol. 16 (1969), pp. 280–82.

11. cf. Hasan, op. cit. (n. 2), pp. 135–6, and Cunnison in Hasan, Ed., *Sudan in Africa*, Sudan Research Unit, Sudan Studies Library, 2 (1971), pp. 186–96.

12. MacMichael, *A History of the Arabs in the Sudan* (2 vols., London, 1922). For more abbreviated treatment of the Arab migrations see Trimingham, op. cit. (n. 2), pp. 81–9; Hasan, op. cit. (n. 2), pp. 135–81; Holt, *A Modern History of the Sudan* (New York, 1961), pp. 5–25; and Abdin in *Sudan Notes and Records*, Vol. XL (1959), pp. 48–74.

13. MacMichael, op. cit. (n. 12), Vol. I, pp. 145, 162; Hasan, op. cit. (n. 2), pp. 137–8, 161; Abdin, op. cit. (n. 12), p. 58.

14. It is possible that there was no Quraysh migration at all. Since Quraysh ancestry (i.e. membership in the Prophet's own tribe) carries exceptionally high status in the Islamic world, it is often claimed by individuals and even whole tribes who have no historic connection with the Quraysh.

15. MacMichael, op. cit. (n. 12), Vol. I, p. 155.

16. ibid., p. 156.

17. ibid., p. 159.

18. cf. ibid., pp. 142–3, 160.

19. ibid., p. 157.

20. cf. Lewis, *The Arabs in History* (New York, 1960), pp. 80, 84, 92–3.

21. Hasan, op. cit. (n. 2), p. 36.

22. MacMichael, op. cit. (n. 12), Vol. I, p. 174.

23. Trimingham, op. cit. (n. 2), pp. 58–9, esp. n. 5; Hasan, op. cit. (n. 2), pp. 10, 40.

24. op. cit. (n. 2), p. 40.

25. For a summary of its provisions see Hasan, op. cit. (n. 2), pp. 39–40.

26. ibid., p. 40.

27. MacMichael, op. cit. (n. 12), Vol. I, p. 167.

28. Hasan, op. cit. (n. 2), pp. 40–41, 50–62.

29. For their respective tribal histories see MacMichael, op. cit. (n. 12), Vol. I, pp. 138–9, 148–51.

30. ibid., p. 167.

31. For the tribal histories of the latter groups see ibid., pp. 145, 187–8.

32. 'Their kingdom was torn apart and the Juhayna Arabs took possession of their country'; cf. Crowfoot in *Journal of Egyptian Archaeology*, Vol. XIII (1927), p. 148.

33. For something of its history and geography see Shaw in *Sudan Notes and Records*, Vol. XII (1929), Part I, pp. 63–72.

34. cf. Hasan, op. cit. (n. 2), p. 176.

35. ibid., p. 175.

36. cf. ibid., pp. 135–6; also Adams, loc. cit. (n. 10).

37. Trimingham, op. cit. (n. 2), p. 82.

38. That is, the northern part of the country excluding the pagan (and latterly Christian) south.

39. They are enumerated in MacMichael, op. cit. (n. 12), Vol. I; see especially Table of Contents.

40. Trimingham, op. cit. (n. 2), p. 11.
41. For their genealogical traditions see MacMichael, op. cit. (n. 12), Vol. I, pp. 197–236.
42. Trimingham, op. cit. (n. 2), p. 17.
43. For maps showing tribal migration routes in the western Sudan see Barbour, *The Republic of the Sudan* (London, 1961), p. 150, and Haaland in Barth, Ed., *Ethnic Groups and Boundaries* (London, 1969), p. 60.
44. For further discussion of Baggara ancestry see Cunnison, op. cit. (n. 11). For a modern ethnography see Cunnison, *Baggara Arabs* (Oxford, 1966).
45. cf. Hasan, op. cit. (n. 2), p. 136; Holt, op. cit. (n. 12), p. 6.
46. There are a number of general histories of the Sudan, including those of Arkell, *A History of the Sudan*, 2nd ed. (London, 1961); Holt, op. cit. (n. 12); and El Mahdi, *A Short History of the Sudan* (London, 1965).
47. Quoted from Hasan, op. cit. (n. 2), p. 127.
48. cf. Riad in Fernea, Ed., *Contemporary Egyptian Nubia* (New Haven, 1966), Vol. II, pp. 325–39.
49. See Hasan, op. cit. (n. 2), p. 249, n. 42.
50. See MacMichael, op. cit. (n. 12), Vol. I, pp. 99–100.
51. Hasan, op. cit. (n. 2), p. 143.
52. See Kronenberg in *Kush* XI (1963), pp. 304, 311, and in *Kush* XII (1964), pp. 285–6.
53. Trimingham, op. cit. (n. 2), p. 84.
54. cf. Hasan, op. cit. (n. 2), pp. 143–4.
55. MacMichael, op. cit. (n. 12), Vol. I, p. 341.
56. Trimingham, op. cit. (n. 2), p. 8.
57. MacMichael, op. cit. (n. 12), Vol. I, p. 342.
58. ibid., pp. 342–3.
59. ibid., pp. 198–200.
60. op. cit. (n. 12), p. 7.
61. For their genealogy and history see MacMichael, op. cit. (n. 12), Vol. I, pp. 307–16. For a modern ethnography see Asad, *The Kababish Arabs* (London, 1970).
62. For their genealogy and history see MacMichael, op. cit. (n. 12), Vol. I, pp. 335–7.
63. ibid., p. 199.
64. ibid., p. 203; Trimingham, op. cit. (n. 2), p. 9.
65. A Sudanese corruption of the Arabic *melik* ('king'), which is widely applied to the chiefs of the sedentary tribes. For further detail see Chapter 18.
66. MacMichael, op. cit. (n. 12), Vol. I, p. 201.
67. See ibid., pp. 201–3, 212–13.
68. According to Hasan, op. cit. (n. 2), p. 144.
69. cf. Burckhardt, *Travels in Nubia* (London, 1819), pp. 133–4.
70. MacMichael, op. cit. (n. 12), Vol. I, p. 197.
71. See Adams in *Journal of Egyptian Archaeology*, Vol. 52 (1966), p. 154.
72. Trigger in *Journal of African History*, Vol. VII (1966), p. 21.
73. Millet in Fernea, op. cit. (n. 48), Vol. I, pp. 59–60.
74. See Burckhardt, op. cit. (n. 69), p. 497.
75. For a critical review of theories in respect to the Nubian dialects see Trigger, op. cit. (n. 72).
76. cf. MacMichael, op. cit. (n. 12), Vol. I, p. 200.
77. Ja'aliyin is used both as a generic term for all of the Arabized Nubian tribes and as the specific term for the tribe which occupies the modern district of Shendi. See Hasan, op. cit. (n. 2), p. 146.
78. See ibid., pp. 146–52.
79. ibid., p. 152.

80. See ibid., pp. 145–6. Haycock on the other hand believed that the Abu Hamed Reach was one of the last refuges of Nubian Christianity; see *Sudan Notes and Records*, Vol. LIII (1952), p. 20.

81. cf. Trimingham, op. cit. (n. 2), p. 89, and MacMichael, op. cit. (n. 12), Vol. I, p. 216.

82. Trimingham, op. cit. (n. 2), p. 88; MacMichael, op. cit. (n. 12), Vol. I, p. 234.

83. cf. Holt, op. cit. (n. 12), p. 18.

84. MacMichael, op. cit. (n. 12), Vol. I, pp. 221–2.

85. Burckhardt, op. cit. (n. 69), p. 133.

86. This extreme view has been somewhat modified since the publication of various modern works pointing out the glories of the pre-Islamic past. Thus, a manuscript history of the Nubians written in 1911 by Daud Kubbara of Wadi Halfa begins with a mention of Taharqa and Shabaka, but then proceeds immediately to repeat the familiar claim of Arab ancestry. See MacMichael, op. cit. (n. 12), Vol. II, p. 325.

87. Trimingham, op. cit. (n. 2), p. 17.

88. For this usage cf. Cunnison, op. cit. (n. 11), p. 192. See also Abd al-Rahim in Hasan, op. cit. (n. 11), pp. 228–32.

89. Hastings, Ed., *Encyclopedia of Religion and Ethics* (New York, 1914), Vol. IV, p. 108.

90. Trimingham, op. cit. (n. 2), p. 105.

91. cf. Levy, *The Social Structure of Islam* (Cambridge, 1965), p. 461.

92. ibid., pp. 53–7.

93. See especially Robertson Smith, *Kinship and Marriage in Early Arabia* (London, 1903).

94. For more extended discussion see Gellner, *Saints of the Atlas* (Chicago, 1969), pp. 41–9.

95. MacMichael, op. cit. (n. 12), Vol. I, p. 131, n. 2.

96. See especially Hasan, op. cit. (n. 2), pp. 137–54.

97. For more detailed discussion see Levy, op. cit. (n. 91), pp. 57–68.

98. MacMichael, op. cit. (n. 12), Vol. II, pp. 16–18.

99. Levy, op. cit. (n. 91), p. 56.

100. See Hasan, op. cit. (n. 2), p. 205.

101. For more extended discussion see Adams, op. cit. (n. 10), pp. 277–88.

102. cf. MacMichael, op. cit. (n. 12), Vol. II, p. 273.

103. See Hasan, op. cit. (n. 2), pp. 211–12.

104. See MacMichael, op. cit. (n. 12), Vol. I, pp. 198–9.

105. Hasan, op. cit. (n. 2), pp. 211–12; see also Hasan in *Sudan Notes and Records*, Vol. XLVI (1965), pp. 27–32.

106. Hasan, op. cit. (n. 2), p. 211.

107. For a good general discussion of this type of 'tradition-mongering' among non-literate peoples see Goody, Ed., *Literacy in Traditional Societies* (Cambridge, 1968), esp. pp. 11–20.

108. See MacMichael, op. cit. (n. 12), Vol. I, p. v.

109. For a brilliantly lucid description and analysis of a nomad tribal system in day-to-day operation see Barth, *Nomads of South Persia* (Boston, 1961).

110. Cunnison, *Baggara Arabs* (Oxford, 1966), pp. 11–12. *Omodiya* and *surra* are common names for the lesser subdivisions in Sudanese tribes. See also Cunnison, op. cit. (n. 11), and Haaland, op. cit. (n. 43).

111. MacMichael, op. cit. (n. 12), Vol. I; see especially Table of Contents.

112. cf. Abd al-Rahim, op. cit. (n. 88), p. 231.

113. For accounts of the lineage system among the modern Nubians see Herzog, *Die*

Nubier (Berlin, 1957), pp. 106–7; Kronenberg in *Kush* XI (1963), pp. 306–9. Callender in Fernea, op. cit. (n. 48), pp. 181–217; and Fernea and Gerster, *Nubians in Egypt* (Austin and London, 1973), pp. 17–26.

114. Trimingham, op. cit. (n. 2), p. 105.

115. Hillelson in *Sudan Notes and Records*, Vol. VI (1923), p. 195.

116. cf. Goody, op. cit. (n. 107), pp. 13–14.

117. Hillelson, op. cit. (n. 115), p. 197.

118. Meaning literally 'book of classes', a conventional title for works of this kind because the biographies are usually classified according to the branch of learning represented by the biographees, e.g. ministers, judges, philosophers, poets, etc., although this practice is not actually followed by Wad Dayfallah. See Hillelson, op. cit. (n. 115), p. 191.

119. For a commentary and translation of considerable portions of the *Tabaqat* see MacMichael, op. cit. (n. 12), Vol. II, pp. 217–323. Even more valuable is the commentary of Hillelson, op. cit. (n. 115).

120. MacMichael, op. cit. (n. 12), Vol. II, p. 218.

121. Hillelson, op. cit. (n. 115), p. 194.

122. For discussion on this point see ibid., p. 193 and MacMichael, op. cit. (n. 12), Vol. II, p. 218.

123. MacMichael, op. cit. (n. 12), Vol. II, p. 217.

124. ibid., p. 217; Trimingham, op. cit. (n. 2), p. 100; Hasan, op. cit. (n. 2), p. 178.

125. Trimingham, op. cit. (n. 2), pp. 96, 223.

126. cf. Hasan, op. cit. (n. 2), p. 178.

127. Quoted from ibid., p. 179.

128. In the western world this word is usually thought of as signifying a tribal chief, but in fact it designates any kind of a leader, civil or religious, who is invested with formal power. In the Sudan it is more often applied to saints and leaders of religious sects than in any other context.

129. MacMichael, op. cit. (n. 12), Vol. II, p. 220; Hasan, op. cit. (n. 2), p. 179.

130. MacMichael, op. cit. (n. 12), Vol. II, p. 220; Hasan, op. cit. (n. 2), p. 180.

131. MacMichael, op. cit. (n. 12), Vol. II, p. 220; Hasan, op. cit. (n. 2), p. 180.

132. MacMichael, op. cit. (n. 12), Vol. II, p. 220; Holt, op. cit. (n. 12), p. 30.

133. cf. Gibb, *Mohammedanism* (New York, 1962), p. 162.

134. For general discussion of the *sufi* movement see ibid., pp. 127–64; Guillaume, *Islam* (Harmondsworth, 1954), pp. 143–54; and especially Trimingham, *The Sufi Orders in Islam* (Oxford, 1971).

135. cf. Hillelson, op. cit. (n. 115), p. 228.

136. cf. Trimingham, op. cit. (n. 2), pp. 191–5; Abd al-Rahim, op. cit. (n. 88), p. 232.

137. For details of the establishment of the *sufi* orders in the Sudan see Trimingham, op. cit. (n. 2), pp. 195–202, and Hasan, Ed., *Sudan in Africa*, Sudan Research Unit, Sudan Studies Library, 2 (1971), pp. 79–82.

138. Hillelson, op. cit. (n. 115), p. 195.

139. ibid., p. 199.

140. Trimingham in Lewis, op. cit. (n. 4), p. 137.

141. Trimingham, op. cit. (n. 2), pp. 100–101; Abdin, op. cit. (n. 12), p. 63.

142. cf. Hasan, op. cit. (n. 2), pp. 180–81; Holt, op. cit. (n. 12), pp. 29–30; Abdin, op. cit. (n. 12), p. 63.

143. Holt, op. cit. (n. 12), p. 29.

144. Reference here is to the description of Damer (near the mouth of the Atbara River) given by Burckhardt in 1813; see Burckhardt, op. cit. (n. 69), pp. 265–70.

145. Hillelson, op. cit. (n. 115), p. 227; cf. also Gibb, op. cit. (n. 133), pp. 151–2.

146. Trimingham, op. cit. (n. 2), p. 101.
147. See Plumley in *Journal of Egyptian Archaeology*, Vol. 50 (1964), pp. 4–5, and in Michalowski, Ed., *Nubia, Récentes Recherches* (Warsaw, 1975), pp. 106–7.
148. cf. Lewis, op. cit. (n. 4), p. 28.
149. For a general discussion of saint-worship and its various aspects see Trimingham, op. cit. (n. 2), pp. 126–41.
150. Hillelson, op. cit. (n. 115), pp. 218–19.
151. cf. ibid., p. 218.
152. ibid.
153. ibid., p. 219.
154. ibid., pp. 219–20.
155. ibid., p. 219.
156. Trimingham, op. cit. (n. 2), p. 141.
157. For a general discussion of the various types of *gubbas* and shrines see ibid., pp. 142–4.
158. ibid., pp. 143–4.
159. For more detailed discussion of the rituals of worship at saints' tombs see ibid., pp. 144–8, and Fernea and Gerster, op. cit. (n. 113), pp. 33–4.
160. Fernea and Gerster, op. cit. (n. 113), p. 33. For the original study see Nadim in Fernea, op. cit. (n. 48), Vol. II, pp. 219–37.
161. Trimingham, op. cit. (n. 2), pp. 122–3.
162. For a general discussion of mahdism in the Sudan and elsewhere see ibid., pp. 148–63.
163. cf. Trimingham in Lewis, op. cit. (n. 4), pp. 128–9, and Hodgkin in Hasan, Ed., *Sudan in Africa*, Sudan Research Unit, Sudan Studies Library, 2 (1971), pp. 109–27.
164. Trimingham, op. cit. (n. 2), p. 150.
165. Hillelson, op. cit. (n. 115), p. 228.
166. cf. Trimingham, op. cit. (n. 2), pp. 217–41.
167. ibid., pp. 232–4.
168. ibid., p. 234.
169. See ibid., pp. 166–78, and Callender and El Guindi, *Life-Crisis Rituals among the Kenuz*, Case Western Reserve University Studies in Anthropology, No. 3 (1971), pp. 11–16.
170. El Guindi in Fernea, op. cit. (n. 48), Vol. II, pp. 239–56.
171. For more extended discussion see Trimingham, op. cit. (n. 2), pp. 180–84, and more particularly Callender and El Guindi, op. cit. (n. 169).
172. For discussion of orthodox religion in the Sudan see Trimingham, op. cit. (n. 2), pp. 115–25.
173. ibid., p. 123.
174. ibid., p. 117.
175. ibid., pp. 121–2.
176. cf. ibid., pp. 111–12, 122.
177. ibid., pp. 123–4.
178. ibid., p. 123.
179. ibid., p. 9.
180. Reisner, op. cit. (n. 1), p. 347.
181. See *Journal of Egyptian Archaeology*, Vol. 52 (1966), pp. 152–5.
182. cf. Millet in *Journal of the American Research Center in Egypt*, Vol. III (1964), p. 11; Plumley in *Illustrated London News*, 11 July 1964, pp. 51 and 53, Fig. 9.
183. cf. Plumley, op. cit. (n. 182), p. 53.
184. See Michalowski, *Faras, Fouilles Polonaises 1961* (Warsaw, 1962), pp. 173–81;

Vantini, *The Excavations at Faras, a Contribution to the History of Christian Nubia* (Bologna, 1970), pp. 257–62.

185. cf. Vantini, op. cit. (n. 184), p. 257.

186. *University of Liverpool Annals of Archaeology and Anthropology*, Vol. XIII (1926), p. 57.

187. Michalowski, op. cit. (n. 184), p. 173.

188. Vantini, op. cit. (n. 184), p. 257.

189. See Michalowski in *Kush* X (1962), Fig. 1 following p. 222.

190. For a report on these excavations see Adams in Dinkler, Ed., *Kunst und Geschichte Nubiens in Christlicher Zeit* (Recklinghausen, 1970), pp. 141–54.

191. For a chronology of the occupation of these sites see ibid., p. 151.

192. See Adams in *Kush* XII (1965), p. 233.

193. This is attested by the fact that the last of the unit houses contained Christian invocatory texts, written in Greek. See Adams, op. cit. (n. 190), p. 149.

194. ibid., pp. 145–6.

195. Burckhardt, op. cit. (n. 69), p. 140.

196. Adams, op. cit. (n. 190), pp. 146–7, and n. 12.

197. cf. Engeström, *Notes sur les Modes de Construction au Soudan*, Statens Etnografiska Museum, Smärre Meddelanden No. 26 (Stockholm, 1957).

198. See ibid., p. 148.

199. Both the general plan and the style of decoration found in modern Nubian houses seem to derive from West Africa, where they are known at a much earlier date; cf. Engeström, op. cit. (n. 197). For more detail on modern Sudanese house construction and types see Lee in *The Professional Geographer*, Vol. XXI (1969), pp. 393–7 and in *Landscape*, Vol. 18 (1969), pp. 36–9; Jaritz in Fernea and Gerster, op. cit. (n. 113), pp. 49–60.

200. See Adams, op. cit. (n. 190), p. 151.

201. Burckhardt, op. cit. (n. 69), pp. 137–8.

202. Adams, op. cit. (n. 190), p. 149.

203. Poncet, *A Voyage to Aethiopia Made in the Years 1698, 1699, and 1700* (London, 1709), p. 14.

204. See Michalowski in *Kush* XIV (1966), pp. 289–99, and in Dinkler, op. cit. (n. 190), pp. 163–70; and Jakobielski in Dinkler, op. cit. (n. 190), pp. 171–80.

205. Nevertheless, we are so far unable to trace any connection between the modern Sudanese courtyard houses and the castles of the late Middle Ages.

206. Crawford, *The Fung Kingdom of Sennar* (Gloucester, 1951), p. 44. Haycock, however, believed that nearly all of the larger castles were built originally in Christian times; see *Adab, Journal of the Faculty of Arts* (Khartoum University), Vol. I (1973), pp. 1–12.

207. Others include Waddington and Hanbury, *Journal of a Visit to some Parts of Aethiopia* (London, 1822), Cailliaud, *Voyage à Méroé et au Fleuve Blanc* (Paris, 1826–7; 4 vols.), and Hoskins, *Travels in Ethiopia* (London, 1835). The journal of Linant de Bellefonds, although written in 1821 and 1822, was not published until 1958 (*Journal d'un Voyage à Méroé dans les Années 1821 et 1822*, Ed. Margaret Shinnie, Khartoum, Sudan Antiquities Service Occasional Papers, No. 4, 1958). The *Narrative of a Journey in Egypt and the Country beyond the Cataracts* of Thomas Legh (London, 1817), who ascended as far as Qasr Ibrim in 1812–13, actually precedes that of Burckhardt by a few months, but is concerned mostly with the country and the antiquities rather than with the Nubians.

208. For an account of the remarkable circumstances of Burckhardt's journey see Moorehead, *The Blue Nile* (New York, 1962), pp. 141–66.

209. The passage which follows is taken, *passim*, from Burckhardt, op. cit. (n. 69),

pp. 132–48. Considerable portions dealing with governmental administration have been omitted, but will be cited in the next chapter. The spelling and punctuation have been slightly revised.

210. The farming practices of the modern Nubians differ little from Burckhardt's description; see Chapter 2.

211. The armament here described is virtually identical to that which is still carried by members of some of the Beja tribes, although Nubians have long since given it up.

212. Burckhardt was later to find this practice common in Upper Nubia as well; see op. cit. (n. 69), pp. 217–19, 269, 280.

213. Nubians still pride themselves on the virtue of their womenfolk. Their concern on this score is usually given as the reason for leaving their wives and daughters at home when the men go abroad to work, so that they will not be corrupted by the licentious habits of Cairo and Khartoum.

214. At today's exchange rate this would be worth about one American dollar, but in Burckhardt's time its equivalent value must have been much greater. The bride-price for a peasant girl today may range up to 200 Sudanese Pounds.

215. A case of this kind occurred at Faras in the 1960s (personal communication from Andreas Kronenberg).

216. The *tamboura* is still the only common musical instrument in Nubia.

217. Most Europeans continue to find them so; particularly in contrast to the monotonous music of Egypt.

218. This characteristic remains a source of pride to the modern Nubians, and explains their popularity as servants throughout Egypt and the Sudan.

219. It should be noted too that Burckhardt travelled in no official capacity and without a military escort of any kind.

220. This is about half the estimated modern population; see Ch. 2.

221. Burckhardt, op. cit. (n. 69), pp. 277–361.

222. Moorehead, op. cit. (n. 208), pp. 157–60, *passim.*

223. Most Nubian families in the 1960s were in possession of one or more of these bowls.

224. cf. also Haycock, op. cit. (n. 80).

CHAPTER 18

Principal sources: the definitive source for the Funj sultanate is Crawford, *The Fung Kingdom of Sennar* (Gloucester, 1951) – a work of such outstanding historical value that it is difficult to realize that the author was obliged to have it privately printed, for want of general interest, only twenty years ago. A more recent source is O'Fahey and Spaulding, *Kingdoms of the Sudan* (London, 1974), Part I. There is first-hand information in James Bruce, *Travels to Discover the Source of the Nile in the Years 1768, 1769, 1770, 1771, 1772, and 1773* (Edinburgh, 1790), Vol. IV, pp. 429–561. The history of the Shaiqiya is best recounted by Crawford, op. cit., pp. 43–52 and 193–5; there is also a book about them (Nicholls, *The Shaikiya*; Dublin, 1913) which I have never had the opportunity to consult. The primary source of information about Lower Nubia under Ottoman rule is the account of Burckhardt, *Travels in Nubia* (London, 1819), pp. 132–48, from which extensive passages were quoted in the last chapter. For the period of Turco–Egyptian colonialism there are three important sources: Deherain, *Le Soudan Égyptien sous Mehmet Ali* (Paris, 1898); Hill, *Egypt in the Sudan 1820–1881* (London, 1959); and Holt, *A Modern History of the Sudan* (New York, 1961), pp. 35–108. For the Mahdiya the best modern sources are

Theobald, *The Mahdiya* (London, 1951), and Holt, *The Mahdist State in the Sudan 1881–1898* (2nd ed., Oxford, 1970).

1. Attributed in slightly varying forms to Carlyle and to Emerson. See Bartlett, *Familiar Quotations*, 14th ed. (Boston, 1968), pp. 577a, 605b.
2. cf. Crawford, *The Fung Kingdom of Sennar* (Gloucester, 1951), p. 186, and Holt, *A Modern History of the Sudan* (New York, 1961), p. 18.
3. See Crawford, op. cit. (n. 2), pp. 134–42; Hillelson in *Sudan Notes and Records*, Vol. XVI (1933), pp. 55–66.
4. For a chronology of visitors to Nubia in the early modern era see Table VII.
5. cf. Budge, *The Egyptian Sudan* (London, 1907), Vol. I, p. 22, and Shaw in *Sudan Notes and Records*, Vol. XII (1929), Part I, p. 64.
6. *Travels in Nubia* (London, 1819). For a vivid recreation of Burckhardt's travels and adventures see Moorehead, *The Blue Nile* (New York, 1962), pp. 141–66.
7. El Mahdi, *A Short History of the Sudan* (London, 1965), p. 35.
8. Burckhardt, op. cit. (n. 6), p. 133.
9. Crawford, op. cit. (n. 2), p. 65.
10. For the complete 'Funj Chronicle' see MacMichael, *A History of the Arabs in the Sudan* (London, 1922), Vol. II, pp. 354–438.
11. cf. Holt in *Bulletin of the School of Oriental and African Studies*, Vol. XXIII (1960), pp. 1–12, and in *Journal of African History*, Vol. IV (1963), pp. 39–55; also Hasan, *The Arabs and the Sudan* (Edinburgh, 1967), pp. 132–3.
12. cf. Holt, op. cit. (n. 2), p. 18; Hasan, op. cit. (n. 11), p. 132.
13. The suffix *-ab*, attached to the name of an eponymous ancestor or tribal group, signifies 'descendants of (such-and-such a person or group)'. Although of Beja origin, it is employed by most of the Arab and Ja'aliyin tribes in the Nile Valley and to the east of it. See Hasan, op. cit. (n. 11), p. 142.
14. Translated by Penn in *Sudan Notes and Records*, Vol. XVII (1934), pp. 59–83.
15. cf. Hasan, op. cit. (n. 11), p. 133.
16. cf. ibid.
17. Crawford (op. cit., n. 2, pp. 164–6, 332–4) suggests a date early in the sixteenth century for the reign of Abdallah Jamma on the basis of what is probably an incomplete tribal genealogy of the Abdallab. See n. 33, below.
18. Holt, op. cit. (n. 2), p. 19; Hasan, op. cit. (n. 11), p. 134.
19. Hasan, op. cit. (n. 11), p. 134.
20. cf. Trimingham, *Islam in the Sudan* (London, 1949), p. 85.
21. Crawford, op. cit. (n. 2), p. 154; Holt, op. cit. (n. 2), p. 22.
22. Holt, op. cit. (n. 2), p. 19; Arkell, *A History of the Sudan*, 2nd ed. (London, 1961), p. 208.
23. Bruce, *Travels to Discover the Source of the Nile in the Years 1768, 1769, 1770, 1771, 1772, and 1773*, 2nd ed. (Edinburgh, 1805), Vol. VI, p. 370. Spaulding has recently revived the theory that the Funj came originally from the upper White Nile, but believes that they were predecessors of the Shilluk in that area. See *Journal of African History*, Vol. XIII (1972), pp. 39–53.
24. Arkell in *Sudan Notes and Records*, Vol. XXVII (1946), pp. 87–98; Arkell, op. cit. (n. 22), pp. 206–9.
25. Chataway in *Sudan Notes and Records*, Vol. XIII (1930), pp. 247–58; Nalder in *Sudan Notes and Records*, Vol. XIV (1931), pp. 61–6; Crawford, op. cit. (n. 2), pp. 143–55.
26. cf. Hasan in *Sudan Notes and Records*, Vol. XLVI (1965), pp. 27–32; Hasan, op. cit. (n. 11), p. 246.
27. Crawford, op. cit. (n. 2), p. 154; Trimingham, op. cit. (n. 20), p. 75.

28. MacMichael, op. cit. (n. 10), Vol. II, pp. 358–60.
29. cf. Crawford, op. cit. (n. 2), pp. 136–7.
30. ibid., pp. 172, 174; MacMichael, op. cit. (n. 10), Vol. II, pp. 431–3.
31. MacMichael, op. cit. (n. 10), Vol. II, p. 360.
32. cf. Holt, op. cit. (n. 2), p. 19; Hasan, op. cit. (n. 11), p. 134.
33. The Abdallab tradition which makes him the son of Abdallah Jamma, the founder of the tribe, must be due to the omission of several generations from the Abdallab genealogy. See Crawford, op. cit. (n. 2), p. 174, and MacMichael, op. cit. (n. 10), Vol. I, pp. 245–6.
34. Holt, op. cit. (n. 2), pp. 19–20.
35. Trimingham, op. cit. (n. 20), p. 87.
36. Crawford, op. cit. (n. 2), p. 179.
37. Bruce, op. cit. (n. 23), Vol. VII, Ch. 9.
38. cf. Crawford, op. cit. (n. 2), p. 30.
39. Bruce, op. cit. (n. 23), Vol. VI, p. 391. This assertion has been challenged; see Nicholls, *The Shaikiya* (Dublin, 1913), pp. 17–18.
40. Bruce, op. cit. (n. 23), Vol. VI, pp. 370, 423, 428–9.
41. Holt, op. cit. (n. 2), p. 21.
42. Actually a stool, the inspiration for which is almost certainly West African. See Arkell, op. cit. (n. 22), p. 211 and Fig. 27.
43. The famous horned crown of the Funj is thought to be derived from the headdress of the Christian Nubian eparchs, though a direct connection has never been demonstrated. See Arkell, op. cit. (n. 22), p. 210 and Fig. 26, p. 211; MacMichael, op. cit. (n. 10), Vol. I, pp. 248–9; and Crawford, op. cit. (n. 2), pp. 325–7.
44. Naum Shucair, *Tarikh es-Sudan* (Cairo, 1903), Vol. II, pp. 100–101.
45. Bruce, op. cit. (n. 23), Vol. VI, pp. 372–3.
46. Trimingham, op. cit. (n. 20), pp. 86–7.
47. cf. Crawford, op. cit. (n. 2), p. 136; Hasan, op. cit. (n. 11), p. 174.
48. Bruce, op. cit. (n. 23), Vol. VI, pp. 371–2.
49. Trimingham, op. cit. (n. 20), p. 85. Holt has shown, however, that the invasion of Nubia by Selim I is a historical fiction; see *Journal of African History*, Vol. VIII (1967), pp. 19–23.
50. cf. Trimingham in Lewis, Ed., *Islam in Tropical Africa* (London, 1966), p. 128.
51. MacMichael, op. cit. (n. 10), Vol. I, pp. 213–15.
52. Waddington and Hanbury, *Journal of a Visit to Some Parts of Ethiopia* (London, 1822), p. 122.
53. Trimingham, op. cit. (n. 20), p. 88.
54. Crawford, op. cit. (n. 2), p. 44; Holt, op. cit. (n. 2), p. 7; Moorehead, op. cit. (n. 6), p. 151.
55. Moorehead, op. cit. (n. 6), p. 151.
56. Burckhardt, op. cit. (n. 6), pp. 70–71.
57. Waddington and Hanbury, op. cit. (n. 52), pp. 98–9.
58. cf. Hake, Ed., *The Journals of Major-Gen. C. G. Gordon at Kartoum* (London, 1885), pp. 30, 68, 78, 130, 166, 185, 208, 241, 259, 266–7, 314, 342, 347, 351.
59. ibid., p. 166.
60. MacMichael, op. cit. (n. 10), Vol. I, p. 213.
61. This has been asserted by Crawford (op. cit., n. 2, p. 44), following Hartmann in *Zeitschrift für Allgemeine Erdkunde*, Vol. XIV (1863), p. 167. It is denied by MacMichael (op. cit., n. 10, Vol. I, p. 213, n. 4) on the evidence of Burckhardt (op. cit., n. 6, p. 70) and Schweinfurth (*The Heart of Africa*, London, 1868, Vol. II, p. 194).
62. cf. Crawford, op. cit. (n. 2), p. 193.

63. cf. MacMichael, op. cit. (n. 10), Vol. I, p. 216.
64. See Crawford, op. cit. (n. 2), p. 194.
65. ibid., pp. 193–5.
66. Trimingham, op. cit. (n. 20), pp. 88–9.
67. This name should not be confused with that of ancient Meroë, although it is pronounced the same. Modern Merowe is a village just below the Fourth Cataract, in the district of ancient Napata. It is not certain whether the name was bestowed by early European travellers, who, seeing the conspicuous pyramid-fields in the vicinity (cf. Ch. 10), assumed that this *was* ancient Meroë, or whether it is an accidental homonym of Arabic origin. The proximity of Merowe to the ruins of Napata – rather than to those of Meroë which are 150 miles farther up the river – remains today a source of endless confusion.
68. op. cit. (n. 2), p. 195.
69. MacMichael, op. cit. (n. 10), Vol. I, p. 216; Trimingham, op. cit. (n. 20), p. 89.
70. Crawford, op. cit. (n. 2), p. 195.
71. MacMichael, op. cit. (n. 10), Vol. I, p. 217.
72. Cailliaud, *Voyage à Méroé et au Fleuve Blanc* (Paris, 1826), Vol. II, pp. 40–41.
73. For detailed descriptions of many of these see Crawford, op. cit. (n. 2), pp. 43–9.
74. ibid., p. 44. Haycock believed, however, that the largest castles had been built originally in Christian times. See *Adab: Journal of the Faculty of Arts* (Khartoum University), Vol. I (1973), p. 2.
75. Quoted from Crawford, *Ethiopian Itineraries, c. 1400–1524* (Cambridge, 1958), pp. 180–81.
76. Bruce, op. cit. (n. 23), Vol. VI, p. 418; cf. also Browne, *Travels in Africa, Egypt and Syria from the Year 1792 to 1798* (London, 1799), p. 182.
77. Waddington and Hanbury, op. cit. (n. 52), p. 103.
78. Trimingham, op. cit. (n. 20), p. 88.
79. Holt, op. cit. (n. 2), pp. 22–3.
80. Quoted, *passim*, from Burckhardt, op. cit. (n. 6), pp. 133–5. Spelling and punctuation slightly revised.
81. cf. Budge, op. cit. (n. 5), Vol. II, p. 207; Crawford, op. cit. (n. 2), p. 171, n. 16; Trimingham, op. cit. (n. 20), p. 84; Herzog, *Die Nubier* (Berlin, 1957), p. 74.
82. Holt, op. cit. (n. 2), pp. 23–4, and op. cit. (n. 49). The author suggests a date after 1550 for the Ottoman annexation; on the other hand Plumley, the excavator of Qasr Ibrim, believes that the Ottoman occupation there began in 1528 (personal communication).
83. cf. Budge, op. cit. (n. 5), Vol. I, pp. 207–8; Trimingham, op. cit. (n. 20), p. 84; Crawford, op. cit. (n. 2), pp. 168–71; Holt, op. cit. (n. 2), p. 24.
84. cf. Crawford, op. cit. (n. 2), pp. 169–70; Holt, op. cit. (n. 49).
85. For an account of Egypt under Ottoman rule see Holt, *Egypt and the Fertile Crescent 1516–1922* (Ithaca, 1966).
86. op. cit. (n. 6), p. 146.
87. ibid., p. 135.
88. See Holt, op. cit. (n. 2), p. 24.
89. For more information about *kashefs* and their duties see Vansleb, *The Present State of Egypt* (London, 1678), pp. 16–19; MacMichael, op. cit. (n. 10), Vol. II, p. 331; and Hill, *On the Frontiers of Islam* (Oxford, 1970), p. xvii.
90. Herzog, op. cit. (n. 81), p. 76.
91. ibid., pp. 76–7; Field, *Contributions to the Anthropology of the Faiyum, Sinai, Sudan, Kenya* (Berkeley and Los Angeles, 1952), p. 165.
92. cf. MacMichael, op. cit. (n. 10), Vol. I, p. 166, n. 1.
93. Trimingham, op. cit. (n. 20), p. 84.

94. Millet in *Journal of the American Research Center in Egypt*, Vol. III (1964), p. 11.
95. Vantini, *The Excavations at Faras, a Contribution to the History of Christian Nubia* (Bologna, 1970), p. 262.
96. Adams in Dinkler, Ed., *Kunst und Geschichte Nubiens in Christlicher Zeit* (Recklinghausen, 1970), pp. 144–5.
97. For Norden's own account see his *Travels in Egypt and Nubia*, trans. Tempelmann (London, 1757). For a brief paraphrase see Budge, op. cit. (n. 5), Vol. I, pp. 13–17.
98. Budge, op. cit. (n. 5), Vol. I, p. 15.
99. ibid., p. 18.
100. See Browne, op. cit. (n. 76) for his own account. For a brief resumé of his travels see Budge, op. cit. (n. 5), Vol. I, pp. 22–5.
101. cf. Shaw in *Sudan Notes and Records*, Vol. XII (1929), Part I, p. 64.
102. ibid.
103. ibid.
104. cf. Baer, *Egyptian Guilds in Modern Times*, Israel Oriental Society, Oriental Notes and Studies, No. 8 (1964), pp. 2–15; Fernea, Ed., *Contemporary Egyptian Nubia* (New Haven, 1966), Vol. I, pp. 8–9.
105. Burckhardt, op. cit. (n. 6), p. 147.
106. Baer, op. cit. (n. 104), p. 135.
107. For a biographical note on these three individuals see Jungfleisch in *Sudan Notes and Records*, Vol. XXVII (1946), pp. 239–40.
108. Burckhardt, op. cit. (n. 6), pp. 135–9, *passim*. Spelling and punctuation slightly revised.
109. See Nutting, *The Arabs* (New York, 1964), p. 212.
110. For a colourful and thoroughly readable account of the French expedition to Egypt see Moorehead, op. cit. (n. 6), pp. 47–132.
111. Mohammed Ali's traditionally alleged Albanian ancestry (cf. Holt, op. cit., n. 85, p. 13) is disputed by Richard Hill; see *A Biographical Dictionary of the Sudan*, 2nd ed. (London, 1967), p. 249 and *Egypt in the Sudan 1820–1881* (London, 1959), p. 4.
112. The foregoing account is taken principally from Moorehead, op. cit. (n. 6), pp. 133–40; see also Holt, op. cit. (n. 85), pp. 176–80.
113. See Holt, op. cit. (n. 2), p. 36.
114. Moorehead, op. cit. (n. 6), p. 135.
115. cf. Holt, op. cit. (n. 2), p. 37.
116. For further discussion of this point see Holt, op. cit. (n. 2), pp. 35–7, and Hill, *Egypt in the Sudan 1820–1881* (London, 1959), pp. 1–4.
117. Holt, op. cit. (n. 2), pp. 37, 39.
118. Arkell's assertion that the possession of firearms played an important part in the rise to power of the Funj and Darfur sultanates (op. cit., n. 22, pp. 203–16) is not supported by historical evidence.
119. cf. Holt, op. cit. (n. 2), p. 38.
120. For an account of the brief interval of Mameluke residence in the Sudan see Robinson in *Sudan Notes and Records*, Vol. V (1922), pp. 88–94.
121. The foregoing resumé of Ismail's campaign is taken chiefly from Holt, op. cit. (n. 2), pp. 38–41. For a more extended and colourful account see Moorehead, op. cit. (n. 6), pp. 166–86. Firsthand accounts of the campaign are those of Waddington and Hanbury (op. cit., n. 52) and Cailliaud (op. cit., n. 72).
122. cf. Holt, op. cit. (n. 2), p. 42.
123. ibid., pp. 43–4.
124. op. cit. (n. 6), p. 186.
125. ibid.

126. This description of the colonial administration is taken chiefly from Hill, op. cit. (n. 89), p. 43; see also Hill, op. cit. (n. 116), pp. 22–4. It should be pointed out, however, that there were numerous administrative reorganizations during the Turco–Egyptian régime. For a short time the central government was abolished altogether, and the provincial governors were made separately answerable to Cairo. See ibid., pp. 95–7.

127. Hill, op. cit. (n. 89), p. 46.

128. Hill, op. cit. (n. 116), p. 25.

129. Hill, op. cit. (n. 89), p. 43.

130. Hill, op. cit. (n. 116), pp. 46–7.

131. ibid., pp. 27–8.

132. ibid., p. 1.

133. Hill, op. cit. (n. 89), pp. xvii, 48–51.

134. Hill, op. cit. (n. 116), p. 43. For a discussion of *sharia* law and its place in the Sudanese legal system see Akolawin in Hasan, Ed., *Sudan in Africa*, Sudan Research Unit, Sudan Studies Library, 2 (1971), pp. 279–301.

135. Hill, op. cit. (n. 116), pp. 43–5.

136. Hill, op. cit. (n. 89), pp. 43–50.

137. Budge, op. cit. (n. 5), Vol. II, p. 223.

138. Baker, *The Albert N'yanza and the Great Basin of the Nile* (London, 1866), Vol. I, p. 11.

139. cf. Hill, op. cit. (n. 89), p. xv.

140. ibid., pp. xviii–xix.

141. See Hill, op. cit. (n. 116), pp. 70–72.

142. See especially ibid., pp. 134–42 and Holt, op. cit. (n. 2), pp. 62–71.

143. Holt, op. cit. (n. 2), pp. 58–69.

144. ibid., p. 33.

145. See especially Hill, op. cit. (n. 116), pp. 62–4.

146. ibid., pp. 101–2.

147. ibid., pp. 73–4, 78–9; Holt, op. cit. (n. 2), p. 61.

148. Holt, op. cit. (n. 2), pp. 63–4.

149. ibid., pp. 64–6.

150. ibid., p. 68.

151. cf. ibid., pp. 66–71.

152. cf. ibid., pp. 75–9.

153. cf. Baer, op. cit. (n. 104), p. 135.

154. Holt, op. cit. (n. 2), p. 79.

155. ibid., p. 78.

156. See Lewis, Ed., *Islam in Tropical Africa* (London, 1966), pp. 38–44, and Hodgkin in Hasan, op. cit. (n. 134), pp. 109–27.

157. There are three dramatic (and at times lurid) first-hand accounts of the Mahdiya: Wingate, *Mahdiism and the Egyptian Sudan* (London, 1891); Ohrwalder and Wingate, *Ten Years' Captivity in the Mahdi's Camp, 1882–1892* (London, 1892); and Slatin, *Fire and Sword in the Sudan* (London, 1896). More balanced and scholarly modern treatments are those of Theobald, *The Mahdiya* (London, 1951), pp. 27–122, and Holt, *The Mahdist State in the Sudan 1881–1898*, 2nd ed. (London, 1970), pp. 45–132. For popular accounts see Churchill, *The River War* (London, 1899), pp. 1–34, and Moorehead, *The White Nile* (London, 1960), pp. 207–75.

158. Hill, op. cit. (n. 111), p. 247.

159. This account of the Mahdi's rise and of the overthrow of the Turco–Egyptian régime follows that of Holt, op. cit. (n. 2), pp. 75–8 and Theobald, op. cit. (n. 157), pp. 27–122.

160. For more information about this episode and its influence on events in the Sudan see Holt, op. cit. (n. 85), pp. 211–30.

161. Holt, op. cit. (n. 2), p. 82.

162. ibid., p. 85.

163. See ibid., p. 89 and Moorehead, op. cit. (n. 157), p. 228.

164. Hake, op. cit. (n. 58).

165. op. cit. (n. 157), pp. 35–68.

166. op. cit. (n. 157), pp. 233–75.

167. Theobald, op. cit. (n. 157), p. 140.

168. For an analysis of the charismatic quality of the Mahdi's leadership see Dekmejian and Wyszomirski in *Comparative Studies in Society and History*, Vol. 14 (1972), pp. 193–214.

169. This account of the Mahdist state is taken chiefly from Holt, op. cit. (n. 2), pp. 86–9. For more detail see Theobald, op. cit. (n. 157), pp. 172–88 and Holt, op. cit. (n. 157), pp. 105–222.

170. Holt, op. cit. (n. 2), p. 100.

171. For more detailed accounts of the campaign of reconquest see Theobald, op. cit. (n. 157), pp. 189–262; Holt, op. cit. (n. 157), pp. 223–42; Moorehead, op. cit. (n. 157), pp. 332–47; and especially Churchill, op. cit. (n. 157), pp. 107–364.

172. See *Life*, 4 April 1955, p. 31. For Churchill's full description of the Battle of Omdurman see op. cit. (n. 157), pp. 257–300.

173. Holt, op. cit. (n. 2), p. 77.

CHAPTER 19

Principal sources: for twentieth-century Sudanese history I have relied heavily on Holt, *A Modern History of the Sudan* (New York, 1961), Parts III–IV. For the resettlement of the Egyptian Nubians I have drawn on an article by Fernea and Kennedy in *Current Anthropology*, Vol. 7 (1966), pp. 349–54, and on several of the contributions in Fernea, Ed., *Contemporary Egyptian Nubia* (New Haven, 1966). The resettlement of the Sudanese Nubians is described mostly on the basis of first-hand knowledge; some valuable information about resettlement both in the Sudan and in Egypt has also been obtained from Little, *High Dam at Aswan* (London, 1965), pp. 134–45.

1. Under a loan of £800,000 to the Egyptian Government, which was later commuted to an outright gift. See Theobald, *The Mahdiya* (London, 1951), pp. 195–6.

2. cf. especially Cromer, *Modern Egypt* (New York, 1909), Vol. II, pp. 112–15, and Holt, *A Modern History of the Sudan* (New York, 1961), pp. 109–10.

3. cf. Holt, op. cit. (n. 2), p. 109.

4. Cromer, op. cit. (n. 2), Vol. II, p. 110.

5. Holt, op. cit. (n. 2), p. 111.

6. ibid., pp. 111–12.

7. ibid., p. 117.

8. See Holt, *The Mahdist State in the Sudan 1881–1898*, 2nd ed. (Oxford, 1970), p. 14.

9. See especially Holt, op. cit. (n. 2), p. 113.

10. See especially ibid., pp. 127–9; also Abd al-Rahim in Hasan, Ed., *Sudan in Africa*, Sudan Research Unit, Sudan Studies Library, 2 (1971), pp. 232–3.

11. Holt, op. cit. (n. 2), p. 129.

12. For further discussion see Bakheit in Hasan, op. cit. (n. 10), pp. 256–78.

13. Quoted from Holt, op. cit. (n. 2), p. 133.

14. Currie in *Journal of the African Society*, Vol. XXXIV (1935), p. 49.
15. Holt, op. cit. (n. 2), p. 133.
16. ibid., pp. 142–3.
17. For more detail on the background and development of the Sudanese political parties see ibid., pp. 143–6, and Abd al-Rahim in Hasan, op. cit. (n. 10), pp. 232–3.
18. Holt, op. cit. (n. 2), pp. 151–2.
19. The successors of Mohammed Ali had taken the title 'King' after 1922; see ibid., p. 125.
20. ibid., p. 162.
21. ibid., pp. 165–6.
22. ibid., pp. 160, 166.
23. See Republic of the Sudan, *Sudan Almanac 1959* (Khartoum, 1959), pp. 135–7.
24. cf. Abd al-Rahim in Hasan, op. cit. (n. 10), pp. 230–31.
25. Barbour, *The Republic of the Sudan* (London, 1961), p. 108.
26. Darfur actually remained independent until its reconquest in 1916.
27. Holt, op. cit. (n. 2), pp. 147–50, 153.
28. The southern Sudanese have virtually no admixture of Caucasian blood, and hence are much darker in colour than the Moslem northerners. This visible difference makes them subject to considerable racial prejudice in the north.
29. Holt, op. cit. (n. 2), p. 146.
30. For an extended report on the Juba Conference see Said, *The Sudan, Crossroads of Africa* (London, 1965), pp. 46–71.
31. Holt, op. cit. (n. 2), pp. 152–3.
32. ibid., pp. 166–7.
33. For more detailed discussion of Sudan Government policy toward the missionaries see Said, op. cit. (n. 30), pp. 85–114.
34. For northern Sudanese views of the southern problem see ibid. and Beshir, *The Southern Sudan* (New York, 1968). For the southern point of view see Oduho and Deng, *The Problem of the Southern Sudan* (London, 1963), and Albino, *The Sudan, A Southern Viewpoint* (London, 1970).
35. See Holt, op. cit. (n. 2), p. 174.
36. A census of Omdurman in 1921 revealed that no less than 32·7 per cent of the population was made up of Nubians, of whom the great majority were Dongolawis. By 1956 the figure had shrunk to 13·7 per cent – not because of emigration but because of the assimilation of the second generation of Nubians into the purely 'Arab' populace. See Rehfisch in *Sudan Notes and Records*, Vol. XLVI (1965), esp. p. 39.
37. The persistence of the Nubian speech is attributable in large measure to the fact that until recently Nubian women have not learned to speak Arabic, and it is from them, almost exclusively, that Nubian children obtain their earliest education.
38. Personal communication from J. Vercoutter.
39. See Wilber, *The United Arab Republic, Egypt* (New Haven, 1969), pp. 189–90.
40. ibid., pp. 40–42.
41. Technically, this is true also in the Sudan. The whole of Sudanese Nubia is included within the Northern Province, which extends from the Egyptian frontier nearly to Khartoum and includes many peoples beside the Mahasi and Dongolawi Nubians.
42. cf. Fernea and Gerster, *Nubians in Egypt* (Austin and London, 1973), pp. 36–44; Geiser in *American Anthropologist*, Vol. 75 (1973), pp. 188–92.
43. cf. Fernea and Kennedy in *Current Anthropology*, Vol. 7 (1966), p. 350, n. 3.
44. cf. especially Callender in Fernea, Ed., *Contemporary Egyptian Nubia* (New Haven, 1966), Vol. II, pp. 183–217.
45. Modern Arabic dictionaries still give *abd* as the term both for 'slave' and for

NOTES

'Negro'; cf. Elias, *Practical Dictionary of the Colloquial Arabic of the Middle East*, 3rd ed. (Cairo, n.d.), pp. 137, 198. For further discussion see Lewis, *Race and Color in Islam* (New York, 1971), esp. pp. 38–64.

46. However, contrary to frequent claims, racial prejudice is as recurrent a theme in Islamic civilization as it is in the West; cf. Lewis, op. cit. (n. 45).

47. cf. Fernea and Gerster, loc. cit. (n. 42); Geiser, loc. cit. (n. 42).

48. cf. Wilber, op. cit. (n. 39), p. 50.

49. As argued by Fernea, op. cit. (n. 44), Vol. I, p. 11, and in Fernea and Gerster, loc. cit. (n. 42); cf. also Geiser, loc. cit. (n. 42).

50. See especially Peel, *The Binding of the Nile and the New Soudan* (London, 1904), pp. 68–100; also Holt, *Egypt and the Fertile Crescent 1516–1922* (Ithaca, 1966), pp. 228–9.

51. That is, the region between Aswan and Debba which has been inhabited by Nubian-speakers in modern times.

52. For discussion see Trigger, *History and Settlement in Lower Nubia*, Yale University Publications in Anthropology, No. 69 (1965), pp. 12–13, and Kennedy in Fernea, op. cit. (n. 44), Vol. II, pp. 356–7.

53. Fernea and Gerster, loc. cit. (n. 42); Geiser, loc. cit. (n. 42).

54. See Kennedy in Fernea, op. cit. (n. 44), Vol. II, pp. 356–7.

55. See especially Scudder in Fernea, op. cit. (n. 44), Vol. I, pp. 123–7.

56. cf. Trigger, op. cit. (n. 52), p. 19.

57. See especially Scudder in Fernea, op. cit. (n. 44), Vol. I, p. 125.

58. Fernea and Kennedy, op. cit. (n. 43), pp. 349–50.

59. Little, *High Dam at Aswan* (London, 1965), pp. 140–42.

60. Fernea and Kennedy, op. cit. (n. 43), p. 352.

61. For more detail see ibid., pp. 350–51, and Little, op. cit. (n. 59), pp. 142–4.

62. Fernea and Kennedy, op. cit. (n. 43), p. 351.

63. cf. Callender and El Guindi, *Life Crisis Rituals among the Kenuz*, Case Western Reserve University Studies in Anthropology, No. 3 (1971).

64. Fernea and Kennedy, op. cit. (n. 43), p. 352.

65. ibid., pp. 352–3.

66. ibid., p. 354.

67. ibid., pp. 351–2.

68. ibid., p. 353.

69. ibid., p. 354. For a note on continuing anthropological studies among the resettled Egyptian Nubians see Fahim in *Current Anthropology*, Vol. 14 (1973), pp. 483–5.

70. cf. Republic of the Sudan, *Population Census in Wadi Halfa Rural Area and Town* (Khartoum, 1960), pp. 36, 85.

71. cf. Little, op. cit. (n. 59), pp. 135–6.

72. Holt, op. cit. (n. 2), pp. 176, 187.

73. ibid., p. 130.

74. ibid., p. 187.

75. Little, op. cit. (n. 59), pp. 134–5. For a detailed resumé of the political complexities and manoeuvrings which led up to the Khashm el-Girba decision see Abdalla in *Sudan Notes and Records*, Vol. LI (1970), pp. 56–74. For a moving account of the whole resettlement programme in the Sudan see Dafalla, *The Nubian Exodus* (London, 1975).

76. Little, op. cit. (n. 59), pp. 135–6.

77. So pervasive was this naïve optimism that my wife and I, who lived continuously in Wadi Halfa from 1960 until 1964, came to share the general disbelief that we would ever really be forced to leave our comfortable home. It was not until 1964 that we finally and reluctantly accepted the inevitability of leaving.

78. cf. Little, op. cit. (n. 59), pp. 136–7.
79. ibid., p. 139.
80. ibid. p. 140.
81. Quoted from Wenzel, *House Decoration in Nubia* (London, 1972), p. 1. For a photograph of the inscription see facing page.
82. For more on the Nubian houses at Khashm el-Girba see Lee in *Landscape*, Vol. 18 (1969), pp. 38–9.
83. Little, op. cit. (n. 59), p. 137.
84. ibid.
85. See Sid Ahmed in *Sudan Notes and Records*, Vol. XLVIII (1967), p. 161.
86. ibid., p. 162.
87. ibid., p. 161.
88. cf. Little, op. cit. (n. 59), p. 137.
89. Primarily Arab tribes of the Shukriya group, and Beja of the Hadendowa tribe.
90. For a very brief report on the status of the Nubians at Khashm el-Girba after five years see Fahim, *Nubian Resettlement in the Sudan*, Field Research Projects, Miami (1972).
91. cf. Fernea and Kennedy, op. cit. (n. 43), p. 354.
92. Geiser, op. cit. (n. 42), p. 189. Geiser believes that the dams have only given impetus to a process of emigration that was already well under way. In his view the 'myth of the dam' permits the Nubians to perpetuate the myth of devotion to an ancestral homeland while relieving them of the obligation to live in it.

CHAPTER 20

1. The main substance of this chapter was read as a contributed paper at an interdisciplinary symposium on the Nile Valley sponsored by the University of Colorado Program in African and Near Eastern Studies, 29 April–1 May 1971.
2. Berkeley and Los Angeles, 1970.
3. ibid., p. xii.
4. New York, 1968.
5. For more extended discussion of this issue see Adams in *Antiquity*, Vol. XLII (1968), pp. 194–215.
6. Originally in *Archaeological Survey of Nubia*, *Bulletin* No. 3 (Cairo, 1909), pp. 5–6.
7. cf. ibid., pp. 21–52.
8. London, 1965. Other recent histories of Nubia which continue to iterate Reisner's migration theories include Arkell, *A History of the Sudan*, 2nd ed. (London, 1961), and Fairservis, *The Ancient Kingdoms of the Nile* (New York, 1962).
9. For further discussion and references see Chapter 3.
10. See especially *A Study of History* (New York, 1962), Vols. 1–2.
11. As outlined in *Oriental Despotism* (New Haven, 1957).
12. See especially *The Science of Culture* (New York, 1949), pp. 363–98.
13. See especially Harris, *The Rise of Anthropological Theory* (New York, 1968), pp. 643–87.
14. Among those who seem to me to have expressed this point of view are Henry Sumner Maine in *Ancient Law* (London, 1861), E. B. Tylor in *Primitive Culture* (London, 1871), Émile Durkheim in *Les Formes Élémentaires de la Vie Religieuse* (Paris, 1912), and Lucien Lévy-Bruhl in *Les Fonctions Mentales dans les Sociétés Inférieures* (Paris, 1910) and *La Mentalité Primitive* (Paris, 1912).
15. For discussion of the image of the barbarian in ancient and medieval times see Jones and Thapar in *Comparative Studies in Society and History*, Vol. 13 (1971), pp. 376–436.

NOTES

16. For the significance of this term see especially Redfield, *The Little Community and Peasant Society and Culture* (Chicago, 1960), pp. 40–59.
17. cf. Toynbee, op. cit. (n. 10), Vol. 8, pp. 1–72.
18. Harris, op. cit. (n. 13), pp. 377–8.
19. See especially Graebner, *Methode der Ethnologie* (Heidelberg, 1911), and Schmidt, *The Culture Historical Method of Ethnology*, trans. Sieber (New York, 1939).
20. For a balanced appraisal of the strengths and weaknesses of *kulturkreislehre* see Kluckhohn in *American Anthropologist*, Vol. 38 (1936), pp. 157–96.
21. For further development of this thesis see Kroeber, *The Nature of Culture* (Chicago, 1952), pp. 379–95.
22. For the 'contagiousness' of culture see Kluckhohn, op. cit. (n. 20), p. 165.
23. cf. especially Redfield, Linton and Herskovits in *American Anthropologist*, Vol. 38 (1936), pp. 149–52; Linton, Ed., *Acculturation in Seven American Indian Tribes* (New York, 1940), pp. 463–520; Barnett, *Innovation: The Basis of Cultural Change* (New York, 1953); and Barnett *et al.* in *American Anthropologist*, Vol. 56 (1954), pp. 973–1002.
24. Barnett *et al.*, op. cit. (n. 23), p. 980.
25. As represented by the bed burial recently found at Kulubnarti; see Adams in Dinkler, Ed., *Kunst und Geschichte Nubiens in Christlicher Zeit* (Recklinghausen, 1970), p. 149.
26. See especially Cairns, *Philosophies of History* (New York, 1962), pp. 204–30.
27. cf. ibid., pp. 256–76, 322–36, and Mahdi, *Ibn Khaldun's Philosophy of History* (Chicago, 1964), pp. 255–7.
28. In *The New Science*, trans. Bergin and Fisch (New York, 1961), esp. Books Four and Five. (First published 1725.)
29. In *The Philosophy of History*, trans. Sibree (New York, 1944). (First published 1837.)
30. *The Decline of the West*, trans. Atkinson (2 vols., New York, 1932). (First published 1918.)
31. *Social and Cultural Dynamics* (4 vols., New York, 1937); *The Crisis of our Age* (New York, 1941).
32. *A Study of History* (12 vols., New York, 1962–1963). (Vols. 1–3 first published 1934; Vols. 4–6 first published 1939; Vols. 7–11 first published 1954; Vol. 12 first published 1961.)
33. For discussion of some of these see Cairns, op. cit. (n. 26), pp. 35–195, 299–319.
34. For discussion on this topic see especially Nisbet, *Social Change and History* (New York, 1969).
35. *Social and Cultural Dynamics* (New York, 1937), esp. Vol. IV.
36. For further discussion see Adams in Dinkler, Ed., *Kunst und Geschichte Nubiens in Christlicher Zeit* (Recklinghausen, 1970), pp. 111–28.
37. i.e. the treaty signed with the Roman general Florus at Aswan; see Ch. 13.
38. The *Baqt* treaty; see Ch. 14.
39. See, for example, Cassirer, *The Philosophy of Symbolic Forms*, trans. Manheim (New Haven, 1953), Vol. II (first published 1925); Collingwood, *The Idea of History* (New York, 1956); Frankfort *et al.*, *Before Philosophy* (Harmondsworth, 1949), esp. pp. 11–38, 237–63.
40. op. cit. (n. 14).
41. e.g. in *Primitive Society* (New York, 1920), p. 441.
42. Most notably in *Zur Kritik der Politischen Ökonomie* (Berlin, 1859).
43. Ithaca, 1953.
44. See n. 16.
45. cf. Gerth and Mills, *From Max Weber: Essays in Sociology* (New York, 1946), pp. 51–5.

46. In Kraeling and Adams, Eds., *City Invincible* (Chicago, 1960), pp. 391–404.

47. For discussion of the concept of 'horizon styles' see Willey in Bennett, Ed., *A Reappraisal of Peruvian Archaeology*, Memoirs of the Society for American Archaeology, No. 4 (1948), pp. 8–19.

48. Most conspicuously in *Patterns of Culture* (New York, 1946), pp. 41–51.

49. cf. *Configurations of Culture Growth* (Berkeley and Los Angeles, 1944), and *The Nature of Culture* (Chicago, 1952), pp. 358–72.

50. cf. Mead in Lerner and Haswell, Eds., *The Policy Sciences* (Stanford, 1951), pp. 70–85, and in Kroeber, Ed., *Anthropology Today* (Chicago, 1953), pp. 358–72.

51. Benedict, *The Chrysanthemum and the Sword* (Boston, 1946).

52. cf. Métraux, *Themes in French Culture* (Stanford University Hoover Institute Studies, Series D, No. 1, 1954).

53. For reviews of these efforts see Sorokin, *Social Philosophies in an Age of Crisis* (Boston, 1950); Kroeber, *Style and Civilizations* (Berkeley and Los Angeles, 1963), pp. 83–160; Melko, *The Nature of Civilizations* (Boston, 1969); and Wescott, *The Enumeration of Civilizations* (MS).

54. For discussion cf. especially Kroeber, op. cit. (n. 53) and Melko, op. cit. (n. 53).

55. This idea has been most fully developed in Sorokin, op. cit. (n. 35). See also Kroeber in *Current Anthropology*, Vol. 3 (1962), pp. 79–97.

56. For the natural science background of anthropology see especially Penniman, *A Hundred Years of Anthropology*, 3rd ed. (London, 1965), pp. 49–180.

57. cf. especially Kroeber, op. cit. (n. 21), pp. 379–95.

58. Most notably in *Configurations of Culture Growth* (Berkeley and Los Angeles, 1944); *An Anthropologist Looks at History* (Berkeley and Los Angeles, 1963); op. cit. (n. 53); and op. cit. (n. 55).

59. op. cit. (n. 16) and *The Primitive World and its Transformations* (Ithaca, 1953).

60. Especially in the various articles collected in *Theory of Culture Change* (Urbana, 1955).

61. e.g. Herbert Muller (*The Uses of the Past*; New York, 1952, and *Freedom in the Ancient World*; New York, 1961); Rushton Coulborn (*The Origin of Civilized Societies*; Princeton, 1959); Carroll Quigley (*The Evolution of Civilizations*; New York, 1961); Phillip Bagby (*Culture and History*; Berkeley and Los Angeles, 1963); and Matthew Melko (op. cit., n. 53).

62. For discussion of the comparative method see, among many other sources, Ackerknecht in Spencer, Ed., *Method and Perspective in Anthropology* (Minneapolis, 1954), pp. 117–25; Eggan in Spiro, Ed., *Context and Meaning in Cultural Anthropology* (New York, 1965), pp. 357–72; and Harris, op. cit. (n. 13), pp. 150–62.

63. For appraisals of their work see especially Lowie, *The History of Ethnological Theory* (New York, 1937), pp. 39–67; Hays, *From Ape to Angel* (New York, 1964), pp. 32–49; and Harris, op. cit. (n. 13), pp. 180–200.

INDEX

Arabic names with prefixed definite article (al-, ar-, as-, el-, en-, esh-, etc.,) are indexed according to the first letter of the word following the article.

'A-Group', 7; cemeteries, 79; culture, 96, 118–19, 122, 130–35; graves, 5, 72, 74, 76, 127–35, 136, 137; identification, 3, 74, 90, 122; population, 118; pottery, 122; racial character, 91; remains, 77, 83–4; *see also* A Horizon, Old Kingdom

A Horizon, 7; cemeteries, 120, 127; chronology, 130–35; culture, 118–19, 140–41; Egyptian influence, 135–41, 166, 169, 174; graves, 127–35, 166, 169; houses, 124–5; identity, 118–19; material culture, 125, 129, 136–7, 140, 169; origins, 118–19; pastoralism, 125–7; pottery, 122–3, Pl. IVb; settlements, 123–5; subsistence, 125–7, 140; *see also* 'A-Group', Old Kingdom

Aba Island, 626

Ababda tribe, 58, 559, 587

abandonment, 240–43, 244, 582, 583

Abbas, uncle of the Prophet, 559, 561, 562

Abbasid, 437, 454, 455, 567

Abboud, General Ferik Ibrahim, 649, 658

Abd Allah ibn Sa'd ibn Sarh, 451

Abd el Qadir: church, 484, 519; tavern, 363; wall paintings, 464, 466, 467

Abdallab tribe: hegemony, 563, 601–2, 604, 606–7; origins, 599; rebellion, 608; subjection to Funj, 600–604; surrender to Egyptians, 617; tribal tradition, 539, 599–600

Abdallah Jamma, 538, 599

Abdallahi, Khalifa, *see* Khalifa Abdallahi Mohammed Turshain

Abdullah Nirqi, 477, 482–3, 544

Abka, 79, 116, 214, Pl. IVa

Abkan Neolithic Culture, 114–15, 116, 122

Abkanarti, 84, 516

Abkur, 593

Abraam, King of Makouria, 529

Abraham, 487

Abri-Delgo Reach, 24; A Horizon remains, 119, 123; archaeological work, 77; Ballana remains, 393; Meroitic remains, 324; pharaonic town-sites, 227–8; physiography, 28–9; reported tomb of Taharqa, 266, 277; temple of Amenhotep III, 220, Pl. Xa

Abu Geili, 323, 329, 358, 370

Abu Hamad, Sheikh, 576

Abu Hamed: bend of the Nile, 22, 32; British reconquest, 632; boundary stelae, 218; frontier of Makouria, 462; mining district, 461, 554; sheikh's tomb, Pl. XXIIIb; terminus of Korosko Road, 304

Abu Hamed Reach, 24, 31–2, 303, 562–3

Abu'l-Istiqlal, 634

Abu Salih, 70, 460, 508; on capture of Qasr Ibrim, 456; on government of medieval Nubia, 462–4, 468–71; on Nubian monasteries, 478

Abu Seyal, 188

Abu Simbel: conservation of, 81; graffiti, 68, 268; temples of Rameses II, 222–4, 241, Pls. IXa and b

Abu Sir, Rock of, 214

Abuna, 472

el-Abwab, 526, 527, 528, 529, 536–7

Abyssinia: Christianity, 446–7, 472; churches, 477; invasion of Kush, 385–8; trade routes, 303, 332; *see also* Axum

acculturation, 236–40, 670

Acheulian industry, 103–4

Adeqetali, King of Kush, 252

Adindan, 79

Adkeramon, King of Kush, 334

Adlan, Funj Sultan, 601

administration: British colonial 640–43; Christian Nubian, 462–71; ecclesiastical, 471–3; Funj, 601–3; Meroitic, 328–32, 352–6; Napatan, 288–92; pharaonic, 229–32; Roman, 338–44; Turco-Egyptian, 618–21; *see also* bureaucracy, government, political organization and activity

Adulis, 385, 386, 387

Aethiopia, 13, 101; *see also* Abyssinia, 'Ethiopia'

Aezanas, Axumite ruler, 386–8, 424, 442

Afyeh, 84, 124

Agatharchides, 234, 320

agriculture: in A Horizon, 125; in C Horizon, 152, 154, 161; Christian Nubian, 502, 503; development of, 641; Meroitic, 301, 322, 329–30, 346–8; modern Nubian, 50–54, 585, 653, 657, 662; Napatan, 291, 293; Neolithic, 115; New Kingdom, 230–31, 241–2; origins of, 110–12, 117; Ptolemaic, 334; *see also* irrigation

Ahmad Pasha abu Adhan, 620

Ahmed Arabi, 627

Ahmose, 217, 218, 227, 229

Aidhab, 466, 524, 526, 532

Ajib el Manjilak, 601

Ajuala, 342

Akasha, 86, 469, 479

Akelat tribe, 60, 559

Akhenaton, 222, 227, 228, 232, 305

Akhraten, King of Kush, 251

Akin, 354, 421

Akinidad, King of Kush, 312, 316

773

INDEX

Ibn Selim el Aswani—*contd.*
460–62; on Alwa, 461–2, 470–71, 538–9; embassy to Nubia, 456, 463; on government of Nubia, 464–6, 468–9, 508; on monasteries, 478; on Nubian languages, 562; on Nubian society, 501; quoted, 461, 464–6, 468, 470; on trade in medieval Nubia, 468, 488, 500, 504–5
Ibrahim al-Buladi, 571
Ibrahim Ja'al, 562
ideology: of Ballana period, 413–19, 423–4, 428–9; of Christian Nubia, 435–8, 445–7, 460, 462–3, 486–7, 506; dynastic, 211, 215–16, 278, 413; feudal, 509–10; importance of, 673–8; Isis cult, 336–8; Islamic, 548, 550, 563–9, 574–9; Mahdist, 626, 629–30, 634; Meroitic, 326–8; militarist, 187–8, 509–10, 523; nationalist, 641–2, 646, 651, 664; pastoralist, 152–4; *Pax Romana*, 382–3; pharaonic, 164–5, 220, 230–31, 247–8, 257–9, 288–90, 413; pre-scientific, 5; Ptolemaic, 333–4, 336–8; racist, 92; transformations, 338, 429, 435–8, 509–10, 563–4, 568–9, 634, 672; *see also* religion
Iken, 185, 469; *see also* Mirgissa
Ikhmindi, 494–5
Ikhnaton, *see* Akhenaton
ikonostasis, 476–7
independence, Sudanese, 643–7, 649, 651
inscriptions: of Aezanas, 386–8; in Ballana period, 409, 422–3; Christian Nubian, 448, 473, 483, 485–8, 532–4; First Intermediate Period, 175; in Meroitic Nubia, 334–5, 337, 345, 352–5, 377–8, 389; in Meroitic Sudan, 280, 297–8, 308, 312, 316, 320, 325, 327–8; Middle Kingdom, 176, 183, 185, 188, 210–12; Napatan, 248, 260–62, 265–6, 268–70, 277, 288, 303; New Kingdom, 218, 223, 227, 229, 230, 233; Old Kingdom, 138–40, 144, 167, 170; recording of, 86; Second Intermediate Period, 190–91, 214; *see also* graffiti, stele, texts
Intef, 210–12
intermarriage, 554, 556–7, 565, 593, 611
Inu, 180, 183
iron: in Ballana tombs, 391–2, 397, 406–7; destroyed by Aezanas, 387; grave offerings, 391–2, 397, 402, 406–7; implements, 317–18, 365–6, 391–2, 402, 406–7, 500; at Meroë, 300, 316–17, 365–6; ornaments, 500; smelting, 300–302, 316–18, 366; trade in, 468, 495; weapons, 391–2, 397, 407; working, 317–18, 366, 402, 500, 503
irrigation: basin, 51, 199, 464; at Dongola, 464; at Kerma, 199; Meroitic, 346–8, 420; modern Nubian, 50–52, 585, 641, 658; Napatan, 291; New Kingdom, 230, 242; *see also* agriculture
Irtet, 158, 186
Isis: 'Agents' of, 337, 355; priests of, 337; representations of, 408, 414, 417; temples of, 316, 327, 337, 417, 422, 440, Pl. XVIa; worship in Ballana period, 417, 422, 440, 443; worship in Meroitic Nubia,

337–8, 348, 353; worship in Meroitic Sudan, 327–8
Islam, Islamic: archaeological evidence of, 583; among Beja, 553–4; character of, 433, 548, 574–8; Islamic–Nubian relations, 450–58, 469; law, 437; propagation of, 569–74, 604; rise of, 433; scholars, 449–50; spread of, 27, 548–50; social system, 566; status of Christians under, 445–6; sufism, 571–2, 574–7; *see also* Moslems, *sufis*
Islamization, 547–50; by conquest, 527; of Funj, 603–4; through intermarriage, 463; through migration, 509–10
'Island of Meroë', 33, 298–301, 323, 325, 387; *see also* Butana Steppe
Ismail Pasha, 608, 615–17, 618
ivory: demand for, 42, 669, 671; found at Sanam, 275; goods, 372, 495, 504; inlaid, 373–4, 407; supply of, 42, 137, 166, 231–2; trade, 137, 166, 385, 471

Ja'aliyin tribes: ancestry, 60, 558, 562, 564; Arabization of, 562–3; under Funj hegemony, 599, 601, 608; under Mahdiya, 629–30; *meks*, 593–7, 616; member tribes, 562–3; Shaiqiya attacks on, 607; slave trading, 625, 629; surrender to Ismail Pasha, 616; tribal pedigree, 559, 561, 562, 567

Jacobites, *see* Monophysites
Jakobielski, Stefan, 485, 486
jalus, 48, 582, 583
Jawabra tribe, 561, 562, 609
Jebel Adda, *see* Gebel Adda
Jebel Barkal: administrative centre, 228, 243, 256–9, 270–71; Amon cult, 247, 257–8, 292; physiography, 228, 256, 271, Pl. Xb; Piankhi Stele, 261; priesthood of Amon, 257–9, 269, 270, 275, 290, 292, 305, 311; royal tombs, 247, 254–6, 278, 281–2, 308–11; Stele of Aspalta, 268; Stelae of Harsiotef and Nastasen, 269–70; temples, 222, 228, 254–6, 271–4, 324; Temple of Amon, 222, 228, 243, 256, 270, 271, 312, Pl. Xb, Pl. XIa; town-site, 274; *see also* Napata
Jebel Moya, 78, 93, 323, 538
Jebel Qeili, 312–13, 327, 331, 387
Jebel Sahaba, 109
Jebel Sheikh Suleiman, 138, 167
Jer, King of Egypt, 67, 138–9, 167
jewelry, jewels: in A Horizon, 128–9, 169; in Ballana Culture, 407–8, 419; in C Horizon, 152, 169; Christian Nubian, 463, 480; at Kerma, 201–2, 203–4; Meroitic, 365, 373, 376–7; modern Nubian, 586; in New Kingdom, 238
jihad, 604, 627, 630
jinn, 577
Joel, King of Dotawo, 532–4, 536, 541
John of Biclarum, 69, 442–4
John of Ephesus, 69, 441–4, 473
Juhayna tribes, 508, 536, 554–6, 558, 560, 599
Julian, evangelist, 441

INDEX

Mahdi Mohammed Ahmed bn Abdallah, 577, 625–30, 634, 639, Pl. XXIIIc; see also Mahdiya
mahdism, 576–7, 625, 641
Mahdiya, 625–34, 635–6, 647
Mahmud al-Araki, 570–71
Maine, Sir Henry S., 679
Majarab Nubians, 611
Makouria: Arab migrations to, 599–600; bishops, 472; capital of, 453–4, 464; Christianization, 442–3, 445–6; conquest of Nobatia, 445, 462; court language, 485; decline of, 525–31; description of Ibn Selim, 461–2; earliest mentions, 442; government, 462–70; kingdom of, 453–4, 455, 462, 525–31; kings, 453–4, 462–4, 467, 526–31, 536, 539; location of, 30; slaving activities, 505; successor states, 531–6; see also Christian Nubia, Dongola Kingdom
Makwar, 323, 370
Malakal, 342
Malenaqen, King of Kush, 251, 277
Maleqerabar, King of Kush, 252
Malewiebamani, King of Kush, 251
Mamelukes: bedouin policy, 58, 544–5, 554; at Dongola el-Urdi, 60, 615–16, 625; in Egypt, 458, 522–5, 610–11, 615; intervention in Nubia, 458, 526–31, 543, 545, 556; sultans, 471, 523, 526, 530, 540
ma'mur, 618
Manasir tribe, 562
Mandulis, 343
Manetho, 3, 248, 262
manjilak, 603, 607
Maqrizi, Ahmad ben Ali: on Arab migrations, 551; on Baqt treaty, 451–2; excerpts from Ibn Selim, 461–2, 538; al-Khitat, 70, 460, 592; on late history of Makouria, 526, 530–31, 536; on Nubian Christianity, 445; story of al-Umari, 460–61
Maris: capital of, 467; eparchs, 464; identity of, 454, 464, 541; under Mameluke hegemony, 527; territory of, 468, 469; see also Nobatia
markets, 166–7, 349, 360–61, 364, 398; see also trade
Marx, Karl, 675
Massawa, 385, 603, 621
mastaba: in Christian Nubian houses, 491; Christian tomb superstructures, 481; Meroitic tomb superstructures, 282, 328, 374, 377, 395; in modern Nubian houses, 656
Mas'udi, Ali ben al-Husayn, 70, 410
matrilineal succession, 260, 463, 528, 531
matting, see basketry
Meded, 269
Mediken, King of Kush, 268
Medjay: identified with Beja, 58, 389, 419; identified with pan-graves, 215; in Middle Kingdom, 183; 'Repelling the', 180; rulers of, 158; see also Beja, Blemmyes
Meheila Road, 219, 228, 253, 291, 303
Meili Island, 358, 365, 371

Meinarti: archaeological work, 85; associated with eparch, 467; Ballana village, 397–400, 418, Pl. XIXa; 'blockhouse', 516, 520, 581; Christian Nubian village, 480, 488–93, 511; church, 477, 519, 543; material culture, 495, 500; Meroitic temple, 360, 397, 415; Meroitic village, 357, 360–61, 365, 372; occupied by Mamelukes, 526; refectory, 480; wine press, 360–62, 363, 372, Pl. XVIIIa
meks, 561, 583, 593–7, 634; Abdallab, 596; Bedayria, 561, 584; deposition of, 618; Dongolawi, 561, 584, 593, 596, 602; Funj, 603; Ja'aliyin, 592, 593, 596–7, 616; Nubian, 592, 593, 596; Shaiqiya, 584, 593, 596–7, 607–8, 616, 635
melik, see meks
Melik en-Nasir, 86
Melkite, see Dyophysites
Menkaure, King of Egypt, 173
Mentuemhat, 266
merchants, see entrepreneurs
Mercurios, King of Makouria, 453–4
Merkos (Merki), Bishop of Qasr Ibrim, 533
Mernere, King of Egypt, 137, 140, 158
Meroë: abandonment of, 387, 419, 424; Axumite invasion of, 386–8; baths, 315; capital of Kush, 270–71, 305–6; in classical texts, 33, 294–6, 298, 330; common graves, 285–8, 290, 425; earliest remains, 269–70; environment, 300–303; excavations, 75, 78–9, 88, 285, 295–6, 313–16; iron smelting, 316–17; location of, 33, 298–300; Napatan city, 269–70, 277; origins of, 298–306; rediscovery of, 295; royal cemeteries, 278–81, 299, 306–11, 365, Pl. XIIIb, Pls. XIVa and b; Royal City, 299, 314–15; temples, 315–17
Meroitic Culture and period: 7; administration in Lower Nubia, 352–6, 380–81; art, 313, 331–2; baths, 315, 364; burial customs, 376–7; cemeteries, 323–4, 328, 374; cities, 300, 313–25, 380, Pl. XIIIa; cities in Lower Nubia, 349–52, Pl. XVIb, Pl. XVIIa; compared to Ballana Culture, 395–6, 401–3, 408–9, 413–19; compared to Christian Nubian culture, 481, 496; compared to Napatan culture, 250–54; compared to Tanqasi Culture, 425–7; conflict with Axum, 385–8, 428; continued occupation of villages, 397–400; culture, 254, 294–5, 328–32, 379–80, 390; decline and fall, 383–90, 428; deities, 325–7; economy, 329–31, 348–9, 380; excavations, 75–7, 88; graves, 374–7; houses, 356–60, 673; iron smelting, 316–18, 365–6; kings, 249–52, 310–12, 334–5, 385; material culture, 365–74; monuments, 32–3; palaces, 314–15, 322–3, 324, 326; population, 96, 345, 391–2, 420–21; pottery, 366–71; relations with Rome, 338–43; relationship to 'X-Group', 390–92; religion, 325–8, 380–81; reoccupation of Lower Nubia, 334–5, 345–7, 379; royal cemeteries, 306–11, Pl. XIIIb, Pls.

787

INDEX

DATE DUE			